Officially Licensed

# NASCAR ®

# 2005 RECORD & FACT BOOK

## SportingNews
### BOOKS

## PHOTO CREDITS

T= top   B=Bottom   L=Left   R=Right
**Cover photo credits:** Petty, Waltrip—Bob Leverone / Sporting News;
Gordon, Johnson, Earnhardt Jr.—Harold Hinson For Sporting News
Earnhardt—Sporting News Archives

## CONTRIBUTING PHOTOGRAPHERS

**Bob Leverone/Sporting News**—17, 22B, 37, 51R, 58R, 59R, 67, 93, 96-99, 122B, 140-143, 146B, 149B, 193, 276, 278, 325, 342, 346, 352, 353, 374B, 383T, 387, 394T, 396, 397L

**Harold Hinson for Sporting News**—7, 10,11,18, 34, 38, 40, 41L, 42, 43, 45-47, 49-51, 52, 54, 56-58L, 59L, 60, 62, 63, 65, 66, 68, 69L, 71L, 72, 73, 75, 76, 79-81, 83-92, 94, 95, 98, 101,119, 126-134, 135, 144, 146T-149T, 150, 152-156, 277, 280-307, 310-311, 328, 343- 345, 354, 356-358, 359B, 360T, 363, 364, 366-368, 371B, 372, 374T, 377L, 378, 380B, 381, 382, 384, 385B, 386-390, 392B, 393T, 394L, 396T, 398, 399

**Erik Perel For Sporting News**—156R

**Sporting News Archives**—358B

**Copyright NASCAR®/Sherryl Creekmore**—9, 10, 41R, 69R, 71R, 113-125, 126-134, 280-296, 307-309, 330-339, 359T, 360, 361, 366L, 369, 370, 371T, 373, 375, 377L, 380T, 383B, 385T, 389, 391, 393B, 396L, 397,

**Don Hunter**—12-14, 103-112, 231, 233, 243,247, 258-260, 358T, 363T, 364T, 366T, 369L, 377TL, 392T, 393L

**International Motorsports Hall of Fame**—199, 215T, 221, 237, 249,

**AP Wide World**—207, 215B, 223,

**Bill Gutweiler for TSN**—8, 145, 151

## NASCAR RECORD & FACT BOOK

**Editors:** SPORTING NEWS—Jim Gilstrap, Kathy Sheldon, Jessica Daues, David Bukovich, Matt Crossman, Corrie Anderson, Dan Graf, Chris Bergeron, Katie Koss, Dale Bye; NASCAR—Jennifer White, Catherine McNeill, Tracey Eberts, Scott Bowman, Buz McKim, Herb Branham
**Cover design by:** Chad Painter
**Page design by:** Chad Painter, Michael Behrens, Angie Pillman, Bill Wilson, Russ Carr
**Photo editors:** Fred Barnes, Paul Nisely, Michael McNamara
**Prepress specialists:** Steve Romer, Pamela Speh, Vern Kasal, Russ Carr

# NASCAR NEXTEL Cup Series schedule

| Date | Race | Track | TV/Radio | Time (Eastern) | 2004 Winner |
|------|------|-------|----------|----------------|-------------|
| February 12 | Budweiser Shootout* | Daytona International Speedway | FOX/MRN | 8 p.m. | Dale Jarrett |
| February 17 | Gatorade 150s* | Daytona International Speedway | FX/MRN | 1 p.m. | Dale Earnhardt Jr. |
| | | | | | Elliott Sadler |
| February 20 | Daytona 500 | Daytona International Speedway | FOX/MRN | 1 p.m. | Dale Earnhardt Jr. |
| February 27 | Auto Club 500 | California Speedway | FOX/MRN | 2 p.m. | Jeff Gordon |
| March 13 | UAW-DaimlerChrysler 400 | Las Vegas Motor Speedway | FOX/PRN | 2 p.m. | Matt Kenseth |
| March 20 | Golden Corral 500 | Atlanta Motor Speedway | FOX/PRN | 12:30 p.m. | Dale Earnhardt Jr. |
| April 3 | Food City 500 | Bristol Motor Speedway | FOX/PRN | 12:30 p.m. | Kurt Busch |
| April 10 | Advance Auto Parts 500 | Martinsville Speedway | FOX/MRN | 12:30 p.m. | Rusty Wallace |
| April 17 | Samsung/RadioShack 500 | Texas Motor Speedway | FOX/PRN | 12:30 p.m. | Elliott Sadler |
| April 23 | Arizona 500 | Phoenix International Raceway | FOX/MRN | 7:30 p.m. | Inaugural event |
| May 1 | Aaron's 499 | Talladega Superspeedway | FOX/MRN | 12:30 p.m. | Jeff Gordon |
| May 7 | Carolina Dodge Dealers 500 | Darlington Raceway | FOX/MRN | 7 p.m. | Jimmie Johnson |
| May 14 | Chevy American Revolution 400 | Richmond International Raceway | FX/MRN | 7 p.m. | Dale Earnhardt Jr. |
| May 21 | NASCAR NEXTEL All-Star Challenge* | Lowe's Motor Speedway | FX/MRN | 7 p.m. | Matt Kenseth |
| May 29 | Coca-Cola 600 | Lowe's Motor Speedway | FOX/PRN | 5 p.m. | Jimmie Johnson |
| June 5 | MBNA 400 | Dover International Speedway | FX/MRN | 12:30 p.m. | Mark Martin |
| June 12 | Pocono 500 | Pocono Raceway | FOX/MRN | 1 p.m. | Jimmie Johnson |
| June 19 | DHL 400 | Michigan International Speedway | FOX/MRN | 1:30 p.m. | Ryan Newman |
| June 26 | Dodge/Save Mart 350 | Infineon Raceway | FOX/PRN | 2:30 p.m. | Jeff Gordon |
| July 2 | Pepsi 400 | Daytona International Speedway | NBC/MRN | 7 p.m. | Jeff Gordon |
| July 10 | Tropicana 400 | Chicagoland Speedway | NBC/MRN | 2:30 p.m. | Tony Stewart |
| July 17 | Siemens 300 | New Hampshire International Speedway | TNT/MRN | 1:30 p.m. | Kurt Busch |
| July 24 | Pennsylvania 500 | Pocono Raceway | TNT/MRN | 1 p.m. | Jimmie Johnson |
| August 7 | Brickyard 400 | Indianapolis Motor Speedway | NBC/IMS | 2 p.m. | Jeff Gordon |
| August 14 | Sirius at The Glen | Watkins Glen International | NBC/MRN | 1 p.m. | Tony Stewart |
| August 21 | GFS Marketplace 400 | Michigan International Speedway | TNT/MRN | 1:30 p.m. | Greg Biffle |
| August 27 | Sharpie 500 | Bristol Motor Speedway | TNT/PRN | 7 p.m. | Dale Earnhardt Jr. |
| September 4 | Pop Secret 500 | California Speedway | NBC/MRN | TBA | Elliott Sadler |
| September 10 | Chevy Rock & Roll 400 | Richmond International Raceway | TNT/MRN | 7 p.m. | Jeremy Mayfield |
| September 18 | Sylvania 300 | New Hampshire International Speedway | TNT/MRN | 12:30 p.m. | Kurt Busch |
| September 25 | MBNA America 400 | Dover International Speedway | TNT/MRN | 12:30 p.m. | Ryan Newman |
| October 2 | EA Sports 500 | Talladega Superspeedway | NBC/MRN | TBA | Dale Earnhardt Jr. |
| October 9 | Banquet 400 | Kansas Speedway | NBC/MRN | 12:30 p.m. | Joe Nemechek |
| October 15 | UAW-GM Quality 500 | Lowe's Motor Speedway | NBC/PRN | 7 p.m. | Jimmie Johnson |
| October 23 | Subway 500 | Martinsville Speedway | NBC/MRN | 12:30 p.m. | Jimmie Johnson |
| October 30 | Bass Pro Shops MBNA 500 | Atlanta Motor Speedway | NBC/PRN | Noon | Jimmie Johnson |
| November 6 | Dickies 500 | Texas Motor Speedway | NBC/MRN | 12:30 p.m. | Inaugural event |
| November 13 | Checker Auto Parts 500 | Phoenix International Raceway | NBC/MRN | TBA | Dale Earnhardt Jr. |
| November 20 | Ford 400 | Homestead-Miami Speedway | NBC/MRN | 12:30 p.m. | Greg Biffle |

**NOTE:** Information in the schedule is subject to change. *Non-points events.

# NASCAR Busch Series schedule

| Date | Race | Track | TV/Radio | Time (Eastern) | 2004 Winner |
|------|------|-------|----------|----------------|-------------|
| February 19 | Hershey's 300 | Daytona International Speedway | FOX/MRN | 2 p.m. | Dale Earnhardt Jr. |
| February 26 | Stater Brothers 300 | California Speedway | FX/MRN | 5:30 p.m. | Greg Biffle |
| March 6 | TBA | Autodromo Hermanos Rodriguez | FOX/TBA | 3 p.m. | Inaugural event |
| March 12 | Sam's Town 300 | Las Vegas Motor Speedway | FX/PRN | 3:30 p.m. | Kevin Harvick |
| March 19 | Aaron's 312 | Atlanta Motor Speedway | FX/PRN | 2:30 p.m. | Matt Kenseth |
| March 26 | Pepsi 300 | Nashville Superspeedway | FX/MRN | 3:30 p.m. | Michael Waltrip |
| April 2 | Sharpie Professional 250 | Bristol Motor Speedway | FOX/PRN | 3 p.m. | Martin Truex Jr. |
| April 16 | O'Reilly 300 | Texas Motor Speedway | FOX/MRN | 2 p.m. | Matt Kenseth |
| April 22 | TBA | Phoenix International Raceway | FX/MRN | 8:30 p.m. | Inaugural event |
| April 30 | Aaron's 312 | Talladega Superspeedway | FOX/MRN | 2 p.m. | Martin Truex Jr. |
| May 6 | Diamond Hill Plywood 200 | Darlington Raceway | FX/MRN | 7:30 p.m. | Greg Biffle |
| May 13 | Funai 250 | Richmond International Raceway | FX/MRN | 7:30 p.m. | Kyle Busch |
| May 28 | CARQUEST Auto Parts 300 | Lowe's Motor Speedway | FX/PRN | 6:30 p.m. | Kyle Busch |
| June 4 | MBNA America 200 | Dover International Speedway | FX/MRN | 1 p.m. | Greg Biffle |
| June 11 | Federated Auto Parts 300 | Nashville Superspeedway | FX/MRN | 7:30 p.m. | Jason Leffler |
| June 18 | The Meijer 300 | Kentucky Speedway | FX/MRN | 7:30 p.m. | Kyle Busch |
| June 25 | Alan Kulwicki 250 | The Milwaukee Mile | FX/MRN | 8:30 p.m. | Ron Hornaday |
| July 1 | Winn-Dixie 250 | Daytona International Speedway | TNT/MRN | 7:30 p.m. | Mike Wallace |
| July 9 | Tropicana Twister 300 | Chicagoland Speedway | NBC/MRN | 2 p.m. | Justin Labonte |
| July 16 | Siemens 200 | New Hampshire International Speedway | TNT/MRN | 3 p.m. | Matt Kenseth |
| July 23 | Goulds Pumps/ITT Inds. 250 | Pikes Peak International Raceway | TNT/MRN | TBA | Greg Biffle |
| July 30 | Charter 250 | Gateway International Raceway | TNT/MRN | 8 p.m. | Martin Truex Jr. |
| August 6 | Kroger 200 | Indianapolis Raceway Park | TNT/MRN | 8:30 p.m. | Kyle Busch |
| August 13 | TBA | Watkins Glen International | NBC/MRN | 3 p.m. | No race in 2004 |
| August 20 | Cabela's 250 | Michigan International Speedway | TNT/MRN | 3 p.m. | Kyle Busch |
| August 26 | Food City 250 | Bristol Motor Speedway | TNT/PRN | 8 p.m. | Dale Earnhardt Jr. |
| September 3 | Target House 300 | California Speedway | NBC/MRN | 6 p.m. | Greg Biffle |
| September 9 | Emerson Radio 250 | Richmond International Raceway | TNT/MRN | 8 p.m. | Robby Gordon |
| September 24 | Stacker 200 | Dover International Speedway | TNT/MRN | 1 p.m. | Martin Truex Jr. |
| October 8 | Mr. Goodcents 300 | Kansas Speedway | NBC/MRN | 4 p.m. | Joe Nemechek |
| October 14 | Charlotte 300 | Lowe's Motor Speedway | TNT/PRN | 8 p.m. | Mike Bliss |
| October 22 | Sam's Town 250 | Memphis Motorsports Park | TNT/MRN | 3:30 p.m. | Martin Truex Jr. |
| November 5 | O'Reilly Challenge | Texas Motor Speedway | TNT/MRN | 2 p.m. | Inaugural event |
| November 12 | Bashas' Supermarkets 200 | Phoenix International Raceway | TNT/MRN | 5 p.m. | Jamie McMurray |
| November 19 | Ford 300 | Homestead-Miami Speedway | NBC/MRN | 2 p.m. | Kevin Harvick |

**NOTE:** Information in the schedule is subject to change.

# NASCAR Craftsman Truck Series schedule

| Date | Race | Track | TV/Radio | Time (Eastern) | 2004 Winner |
|------|------|-------|----------|----------------|-------------|
| February 18 | Florida Dodge Dealers 250 | Daytona International Speedway | SPEED/MRN | 8 p.m. | Carl Edwards |
| February 25 | American Racing Wheels 200 | California Speedway | SPEED/MRN | 9 p.m. | Todd Bodine |
| March 18 | EasyCare Vehicle Service 200 | Atlanta Motor Speedway | SPEED/MRN | 9 p.m. | Bobby Hamilton |
| April 9 | Truck Series 200 | Martinsville Speedway | SPEED/MRN | 1 p.m. | Rick Crawford |
| April 30 | Ram Tough 200 | Gateway International Raceway | SPEED/MRN | 8 p.m. | David Starr |
| May 15 | UAW/GM Ohio 250 | Mansfield Motorsports Speedway | SPEED/MRN | 2 p.m. | Jack Sprague |
| May 20 | Infineon 200 | Lowe's Motor Speedway | SPEED/MRN | 8:30 p.m. | Dennis Setzer |
| June 3 | MBNA America 200 | Dover International Speedway | SPEED/MRN | 4:30 p.m. | Chad Chaffin |
| June 10 | Fort Worth 400K | Texas Motor Speedway | SPEED/MRN | 8 p.m. | Dennis Setzer |
| June 18 | Line-X Spray-On Bedliner 200 | Michigan International Speedway | SPEED/MRN | 3 p.m. | Travis Kvapil |
| June 24 | Black Fireworks 200 | The Milwaukee Mile | SPEED/MRN | 9 p.m. | Ted Musgrave |
| July 2 | O'Reilly Auto Parts 250 | Kansas Speedway | SPEED/MRN | 3 p.m. | Carl Edwards |
| July 9 | Built Ford Tough 225 | Kentucky Speedway | SPEED/MRN | 8 p.m. | Bobby Hamilton |
| July 23 | O'Reilly 200K | Memphis MotorSports Park | SPEED/MRN | 8 p.m. | Bobby Hamilton |
| August 5 | Power Stroke Diesel 200 | Indianapolis Raceway Park | SPEED/MRN | 8:30 p.m. | Chad Chaffin |
| August 13 | Toyota Tundra 200 | Nashville Superspeedway | SPEED/MRN | 6 p.m. | Bobby Hamilton |
| August 24 | O'Reilly 200 | Bristol Motor Speedway | SPEED/MRN | 9 p.m. | Carl Edwards |
| September 8 | Kroger 200 | Richmond International Raceway | SPEED/MRN | 8:30 p.m. | Ted Musgrave |
| September 17 | New Hampshire 200 | New Hampshire International Speedway | SPEED/MRN | 3 p.m. | Travis Kvapil |
| September 24 | Las Vegas 350 | Las Vegas Motor Speedway | SPEED/MRN | 9 p.m. | Shane Hmiel |
| October 22 | Kroger 200 | Martinsville Speedway | SPEED/MRN | 1 p.m. | Jamie McMurray |
| October 29 | TBA | Atlanta Motor Speedway | SPEED/MRN | 3 p.m. | Inaugural event |
| November 4 | Silverado 350K | Texas Motor Speedway | SPEED/MRN | 9 p.m. | Todd Bodine |
| November 11 | Chevy Silverado 150 | Phoenix International Raceway | SPEED/MRN | 8 p.m. | David Starr |
| November 18 | Ford 200 | Homestead-Miami Speedway | SPEED/MRN | 8 p.m. | Kasey Kahne |

**NOTE:** Information in the the schedule is subject to change.

# Contents

# NASCAR NEXTEL Cup drivers

# FOREWORD • By George Pyne

I always wanted to make it into the pages of the *Sporting News*. I admit, though, that I had a slightly different appearance in mind. My grandfather, father and brother all played in the National Football League and thus got their mentions in TSN in the traditional manner. I had aspirations of following in their footsteps, but that didn't work out. So that's why you're reading my name in the front of this *NASCAR Record & Fact Book* instead of somewhere in the middle. Hey, I'll take it.

I grew up in a sports-oriented family not far from the sports-crazed city of Boston, and the *Sporting News* was a staple in our household. I've been a subscriber since I was a kid. Because of that lifelong affinity for the magazine, it's been especially pleasing for me personally to see TSN become one of the leading sources of information for NASCAR's 75 million fans throughout America.

To supplement the great coverage in the *Sporting News* magazine, the NASCAR-savvy staff at TSN has recognized the need for NASCAR to join their *Record & Fact Book* lineup. This book gives fans a comprehensive statistical history of NASCAR, with all the names and numbers that have combined to make our sport so great.

I hope you will enjoy this book as much as I will. I know I'm going to display it conspicuously around my house whenever my family is visiting.

And you can bet I'll have this foreword page bookmarked so they can't miss it.

Best Regards,

George Pyne
Chief Operating Officer, NASCAR

## About George Pyne

Pyne was named NASCAR's chief operating officer and appointed as a member of the board of directors in December 2002, after serving for two years as senior vice president. Pyne continues to have operational responsibilities for each of NASCAR's departments, including competition, corporate marketing, licensing, broadcasting, public relations, series marketing and administration.

# The France family

You need look only at the France family tree to understand NASCAR's history—and its current position at the pinnacle of American motorsports.

From founder William H.G. France to his son William C. France to third-generation leader Brian Z. France—who took over the sport's leadership in October 2003—the family's expertise is obvious, evidenced by NASCAR's steady growth.

Last fall, Brian Z. France was announced as NASCAR's Chairman of the Board and Chief Executive Officer, replacing his father, William C. France. That announcement completed a natural progression. Brian has been at the forefront of NASCAR's dramatic sponsorship growth, including the ground-breaking announcement of Nextel Communications as the new sponsor of the NASCAR NEXTEL Cup Series as of 2004.

Brian clearly respects—and represents—the vision of his grandfather "Big Bill" France, who created the National Association for Stock Car Auto Racing (NASCAR) in 1948 to organize and promote stock car racing on tracks such as the one carved out of the sand of Daytona Beach. Through dogged determination, Big Bill legitimized a sport that was, at the time, an unorganized hobby of sorts.

His two sons, Bill and Jim, were handed the reins to the company upon their father's retirement. Bill became president, and Jim took over the role of executive vice president and secretary, as well as president of ISC.

Other than the creation of the organization, Bill France's ascension to the leadership role of NASCAR is likely the most important event in the sanctioning body's history. As rule maker, promoter, ambassador and salesman, he set the standard by which all other forms of motorsports are measured.

In November of 2000, Bill France announced that he would

Brian France

Bill France

serve as chairman of a newly formed five-member board of directors for NASCAR that consisted of him, Jim France, Brian Z. France, Lesa France Kennedy and Mike Helton and was responsible for developing policy and vision for the sport. At that time, Bill stepped down as president and was replaced by Helton. Brian's move into the Chairman/CEO positions resulted in Bill becoming a NASCAR vice chairman. The board of directors was expanded when NASCAR Chief Operating Officer George Pyne was appointed in December of 2002.

"Big Bill" France passed away in 1992. His induction into the International Motorsports Hall of Fame and the National Motorsports Press Association Hall of Fame are testaments not only to his accomplishments but to the efforts of his entire family.

## Mike Helton, President

Mike Helton assumed the role of NASCAR president in November 2000, succeeding Bill France Jr., who had served in the role since 1972. Helton became the first person outside the France family to take over the day-to-day operations of NASCAR when he was promoted from his position as vice president for competition and was named senior vice president and chief operating officer in February 1999.

### NASCAR Officials
**Gary Nelson** • Managing Director of Research and Development
**John Darby** • NASCAR NEXTEL Cup Series Director
**Joe Balash** • NASCAR Busch Series Director
**Wayne Auton** • NASCAR Craftsman Truck Series Director

Inside NASCAR

# Milestones

Since its inception as the Strictly Stock division, the NASCAR NEXTEL Cup Series has seen many changes. In the beginning, the racecars were driven off the street and onto the track. But as safety technology advanced, changes were made, making the cars of today more complicated. NASCAR has grown from the small organization formed on the beaches of Daytona to a thriving sport that can be reached by anyone around the world through television and the Internet. This, along with an expanded schedule and more race-tracks throughout the nation, has made the NASCAR NEXTEL Cup Series more accessible to fans. NASCAR is America's fastest-growing sport. Important milestones for the NASCAR Cup series:

**December 14, 1947:** Bill France Sr. organizes a meeting at the Streamline Hotel in Daytona Beach, Fla., to discuss the future of stock car racing. NASCAR (the National Association for Stock Car Auto Racing) is conceived.

**February 15, 1948:** NASCAR runs its first race in Daytona Beach at the beach-road course. The race is won by Red Byron.

**February 21, 1948:** NASCAR is incorporated.

**June 19, 1949:** The first NASCAR Strictly Stock (currently known as the NASCAR NEXTEL Cup Series) race is held at Charlotte Fairgrounds Speedway. Bob Flock wins the first pole, Jim Roper wins the racem and Sara Christian, who finished 14th, is the first woman to start a NASCAR race.

**October 16, 1949:** Red Byron is the NASCAR Strictly Stock champion. Byron earned $5,800 in six starts and collected two wins.

**1950:** Bill France Sr. changes the name of NASCAR's top series from Strictly Stock to Grand National.

**September 4, 1950:** Darlington Raceway, NASCAR's first paved superspeedway, hosts the Southern 500. The first 500-mile event in NASCAR history is won by Johnny Mantz in a 1950 Plymouth. Seventy-five drivers started the event, which featured two caution periods and lasted more than 6 hours.

**April 8, 1951:** The first NASCAR Grand National race west of the Mississippi River is held at Carrell Speedway, a half-mile dirt track in Gardena, Calif.

**1952:** Sponsors step up in the NASCAR Grand National division. Pure Oil provides contingency monies and free gasoline during Daytona's SpeedWeeks, and Champion Spark Plugs contributes $5,000 to the year-end point fund.

**June 13, 1954:** The International 100 is held at Linden Airport in New Jersey, becoming the first road race in what is now the NASCAR NEXTEL Cup Series.

**1955:** Car owner Carl Kiekhaefer enters cars in 40 Grand National events and wins 22 of them. Kiekhaefer becomes the first owner to use major sponsorships when he provides drivers with financial and technical backing.

**1958:** The Florida Sports Writers Association votes Fireball Roberts as Professional Athlete of the Year. This is the first time the honor is given to a racecar driver.

**February 23, 1958:** Paul Goldsmith captures the final race on Daytona's famed Beach and Road Course.

**February 22, 1959:** The high-banked, 2.5-mile Daytona International Speedway hosts the first Daytona 500, attracting 41,000 fans. Sixty-one hours after the checkered flag flies over an extremely close finish, Lee Petty is declared the winner by 2 feet after Bill France Sr. reviews footage from a newsreel.

**January 31, 1960:** CBS Sports broadcasts its first live NASCAR Grand National events. *CBS Sports Spectacular* televises the Grand National Pole Position races from Daytona. The 2-hour program is the first devoted entirely to stock car racing.

**June 19, 1960:** Charlotte Motor Speedway plays host to its first NASCAR event. The World 600 is won by Joe Lee Johnson in a time of slightly more than $5^{1}/_{2}$ hours.

**July 4, 1960:** Bud Moore and Jack Smith communicate by two-way radio in the Firecracker 250, marking the first time two-way radio communication is used in the sport.

**July 16, 1960:** ABC Sports televises the Firecracker 250 from Daytona International Speedway as part of *Wide World of Sports*.

**September 13, 1962:** Mamie Reynolds becomes the first woman to win as an owner when Fred Lorenzen takes the checkered flag at Augusta (Ga.) Speedway.

**February 24, 1963:** Tiny Lund subs for injured Marvin Panch and wins the Daytona 500.

**December 1, 1963:** Wendell Scott becomes the first black driver to win a race at NASCAR's highest level, beating Buck Baker at Jacksonville (Fla.) Speedway.

**1964:** The Goodyear Tire & Rubber Company tests and begins use of an inner liner for all NASCAR Grand National tires.

**1964:** Richard Petty, NASCAR's all-time wins leader, captures his first championship.

**1965:** The Firestone Racesafe Fuel Cell bladder is implemented.

**1967:** Richard Petty sets three records by collecting the most wins in one season (27), most consecutive wins (10) and most victories from the pole in one season (15).

**September 14, 1969:** Alabama International Speedway opens in Talladega, Ala., as the largest oval on the NASCAR circuit.

**March 24, 1970:** Buddy Baker becomes the first driver to break the 200-mph barrier in a stock car, doing so at a test run at Talladega.

**September 30, 1970:** The final NASCAR Grand National division race is run on dirt at State Fairgrounds Speedway in Raleigh, N.C.

**1971:** R.J. Reynolds Winston brand becomes the title sponsor of NASCAR's top division, which is renamed the NASCAR Winston Cup Grand National Division.

**February 14, 1971:** Motor Racing Network (MRN) broadcasts its first Daytona 500. Ken Squier anchors the broadcast for the racing-only network.

**January 10, 1972:** The founder of NASCAR, Bill France Sr., hands over the reins of leadership to his son Bill France, Jr., who becomes the second president in NASCAR's history.

**1972:** The NASCAR Winston Cup Grand National Division schedule is trimmed from 48 races to 31, marking the beginning of the Modern Era.

**February 15, 1976:** David Pearson and Richard Petty battle at Daytona for a win on national television, as the two cars are involved in an accident near the finish line, with Pearson hobbling to the checkered flag first.

**February 20, 1977:** Janet Guthrie becomes the first woman to qualify for the Daytona 500. She qualifies 39th and finishes 12th.

**1978:** President Jimmy Carter and First Lady Rosalyn Carter invite NASCAR drivers to the White House in the same year Cale Yarborough wins his third straight NASCAR Winston Cup title.

Bill France Sr.

Bill Elliott

**February 18, 1979:** CBS Sports presents the first live flag-to-flag coverage of a NASCAR event with the Daytona 500. Richard Petty avoids a wreck between Cale Yarborough and Donnie Allison on the last lap to win the race.

**April 8, 1979:** The teaming of David Pearson and the Wood Brothers ends in Darlington.

**September 3, 1979:** David Pearson sits in for rookie Dale Earnhardt and leads the final 70 laps of the Southern 500 at Darlington to win the race.

**1979:** Richard Petty wins his record seventh series points championship.

**April 29, 1982:** Benny Parsons becomes the first driver in NASCAR history to post an official qualifying lap faster than 200 mph, accomplishing the feat at Talladega.

**May 6, 1984:** In the most competitive race in NASCAR history, the lead changes 75 times among 13 drivers at Talladega.

**July 4, 1984:** In the Firecracker 400 at Daytona International Speedway, Richard Petty earns his 200th win, setting a mark that has yet to be challenged.

**May 5, 1985:** Bill Elliott falls to 26th and two laps down at Talladega in the Winston 500 but fights back to lead the last 20 laps and win the race.

**July 4, 1985:** Greg Sacks, with a limited number of team members, takes the lead with nine laps to go in the Firecracker 400 to win his only NASCAR Winston Cup Series race.

**September 1, 1985:** Bill Elliott claims a $1 million bonus from R.J. Reynolds for winning three of the four crown jewel races on the schedule—the Daytona 500, the Winston 500 at Talladega and the Southern 500 at Darlington.

**1985:** After trailing Bill Elliott by 206 points with eight races to go, Darrell Waltrip's late-season streak leads him to win the NASCAR Winston Cup Series championship.

**1986:** NASCAR drops "Grand National" from its top division, renaming it the NASCAR Winston Cup Series.

**April 30, 1987:** Bill Elliott sets the fastest lap time in NASCAR history, turning a blazing lap of 212.809 mph at Talladega Superspeedway.

**1987:** Dale Earnhardt makes his famous "pass in the grass" in The Winston, the all-star race at Charlotte Motor Speedway, shooting through the infield and back onto the track to maintain the lead and eventually win the race.

**February 14, 1988:** Bobby Allison and Davey Allison finish first and second, respectively, in the Daytona 500.

**1989:** For the first time, every NASCAR Winston Cup Series race is televised.

**February 18, 1990:** Dale Earnhardt leads 155 of 200 laps of the Daytona 500 but loses the race with a mile to go after blowing a tire on a piece of debris.

**September 1991:** Harry Gant, at 51, is tabbed "Mr. September" after winning four consecutive races in the month.

**May 16, 1992:** For the first time, Charlotte Motor Speedway holds The Winston under the lights, which ends as Davey Allison takes the checkered flag before losing control of his car.

**November 15, 1992:** Richard Petty retires after 35 years of racing in NASCAR. He ends his career with 200 wins and 549 top five finishes in almost 1,200 races. The points championship is won by Alan Kulwicki, who leads one more lap than Bill Elliott in the final race at Atlanta Motor Speedway, clinching the title by 10 points.

**August 6, 1994:** The NASCAR championship schedule expands to include the famed 2.5-mile Indianapolis Motor Speedway. Jeff Gordon wins the first Cup race at the Brickyard.

**1994:** Dale Earnhardt joins Richard Petty as the only driver to win seven NASCAR championships.

**August 9, 1996:** Dale Earnhardt, with a broken collarbone, wheels around Watkins Glen to win the pole and sets a track record.

**November 24, 1996:** NASCAR runs a demonstration race in Suzuka, Japan.

**November 16, 1997:** Jeff Gordon clinches his second NASCAR championship, making him the youngest two-time winner.

**1997:** Two new tracks appear on the NASCAR schedule: Texas Motor Speedway and California Speedway. In front of sold-out crowds, Jeff Burton and Jeff Gordon, respectively, win the races.

**March 1, 1998:** NASCAR celebrates its 50th anniversary while adding Las Vegas Motor Speedway to the schedule. Mark Martin wins the inaugural event.

**February 1999:** NASCAR president Bill France Jr. hands over the day-to-day operations to senior vice president and chief operating officer Mike Helton, marking the first time someone from outside the France family controls the operations of the sport.

**November 11, 1999:** NASCAR announces multiyear partnerships with FOX, NBC and Turner Sports; the consolidated television package is set to begin in 2001.

**January 2000:** The NASCAR Winston Cup Point Fund increases from $5 million to $10 million; the champion's share increases to $3 million.

**November 28, 2000:** Mike Helton becomes the third president in

NASCAR history as Bill France Jr. passes the torch of leadership to a non-France family member for the first time.

**February 18, 2001:** FOX Sports telecasts the Daytona 500, its first telecast as part of an eight-year network TV agreement along with its cable network partner FX. Michael Waltrip's victory in the Daytona 500 is his first win, coming in his 463rd start.

**July 7, 2001:** NBC Sports kicks off its six-year network TV agreement by telecasting the Pepsi 400. NBC's cable partner, TNT, goes on to televise seven of the season's races.

**September 25, 2001:** NASCAR Radio, the first 24-hour radio station dedicated to a single sport, debuts on XM Satellite Radio, the first commercial satellite radio service in the United States.

**2001:** NASCAR comes to two new tracks: Chicagoland Speedway and Kansas Speedway; Kevin Harvick and Jeff Gordon are the respective winners.

**September 2002:** NASCAR announces its NASCAR Craftsman Truck Series races will be televised live on the SPEED Channel in 2003.

**February 12, 2003:** NASCAR announces that Toyota will join the Craftsman Truck Series in 2004, marking the first time a NASCAR series includes a foreign automaker.

**June 19, 2003:** NASCAR announces that the sponsorship of its top series will shift from Winston to Nextel in 2004. In 2004, drivers will contend for the NASCAR NEXTEL Cup Series championship. It is a 10-year agreement.

**August 15, 2003:** NASCAR announces a 10-year deal for Sunoco to replace Unocal 76 as the Official Fuel of NASCAR beginning in 2004.

**October, 2003:** Brian Z. France becomes the new Chairman of the Board and CEO of NASCAR, replacing his father, Bill France Jr.

**November 16, 2003:** Matt Kenseth celebrates winning the final NASCAR Winston Cup Series championship, marking the end of Winston's 33-year sponsorship of NASCAR's top series. Bobby Labonte wins the final race of the Winston era at Homestead-Miami Speedway.

**February 22, 2004:** Matt Kenseth wins the final NASCAR NEXTEL Cup race run at North Carolina Speedway in Rockingham.

**July 31, 2004:** Travis Kvapil's NASCAR Craftsman Truck Series victory in the Line-X Spray-on Truck Bedliners 200 at Michigan International Speedway gives Toyota its first fictory in a NASCAR series.

**September 11, 2004:** After the Chevy Rock & Roll 400 at Richmond, 10 drivers qualify for the inaugural Chase for the NASCAR NEXTEL Cup: Kurt Busch, Dale Earnhardt Jr., Jeff Gordon, Jimmie Johnson, Matt Kenseth, Mark Martin, Jeremy Mayfield, Ryan Newman, Selliott Sadler and Tony Stewart. Over the final 10 races of the season, Busch wins the first NASCAR NEXTEL Cup championship by eight points, the closest margin in NASCAR history, over Jimmie Johnson.

# Race procedures

NASCAR officials follow guidelines and rules, as any other sport or competition does. Race procedures include everything from the start of a race to flags, pit stops, restarts and, of course, the checkered flag. A pace or caution car leads the field before the start of a race.

## Pace laps

Normally, the pace car completes three laps before turning onto pit road, allowing the field to begin the race. The pace laps serve several purposes, the first of which is to allow each car to warm up its engine and its tires. Like most street vehicles, NASCAR racecars need to warm up their engines to perform to their potential. Drivers create better grip in their tires by warming them up through swerving back and forth during the pace laps.

The pace laps also serve another purpose. Because pit road has a speed limit and drivers do not have speedometers in the cars (they have tachometers that gauge the engine's revolutions per minute, or rpms), the pace car drives the pit road speed limit the first time by the frontstretch so drivers can locate that same speed on their tachometer.

## Flags

NASCAR officials signal messages to drivers during races by waving an assortment of colored flags.

The flagman, who is always located on a stand high above the start/finish line, plays an important role.

**Green flag:** The green flag is displayed at the start of each race and for restarts during the race. Cars must maintain position as designated by NASCAR officials until they have crossed the start/finish line, and the No. 2 qualifier must not beat the No. 1 qualifier to the start/finish line. On restarts, the race will resume immediately when the green flag is waved.

**Yellow flag:** The yellow flag signifies caution and is given to the first car passing the starter immediately following the occurrence of the cause for caution. All cars receiving the yellow flag at the start/finish line shall slow down to a cautious pace, hold their position and form a single line behind the lead car.

**Red flag:** The red flag means the race must be stopped immediately, regardless of the position of the cars on the track. The red flag shall be used if, in the opinion of NASCAR officials, the race should be stopped. Cars should be brought to a stop in an area designated by NASCAR officials. Repairs, service of any nature, or refueling, whether on pit road or in the garage, will not be permitted when the race is halted due to a red flag unless the car has withdrawn from the event.

**Black flag:** The black flag means a car must go to the pits immediately and report to the NASCAR official at the car's pit area. It does not mean automatic disqualification. At the discretion of NASCAR officials, if the driver does not obey the black-flag directive, the driver might be given the black flag with a white cross at the start/finish line to inform the driver that any additional scoring of his or her car will be discontinued until further notice.

**Blue flag with diagonal yellow stripe:** Although the blue flag with its diagonal yellow stripe is typically displayed the most during races, it is probably the least recognized. This flag is displayed when drivers who are a lap down or significantly slower are about to be passed by lead-lap cars. Drivers who are shown the blue and diagonally yellow-striped flag must yield to the faster lead-lap cars.

**White flag:** The white flag waves when the driver in the lead begins his final lap.

**Checkered flag:** The most famous of all flags, the black and white checkered flag is displayed when the winner has crossed the finish line. All cars remaining on the track will take the checkered flag once.

## Pit stops

Pit road, a road usually adjacent to the front stretch, is where drivers come in for a pit stop. Teams choose which pit stall location they will use according to how they qualify. The pole winner has the first choice, followed by the outside pole winner and so on. The pit stall is where teams store their equipment used during the pits stops: tools, tires and fuel are just a few. When a driver enters pit road, he must enter into his designated pit box area.

Drivers who come onto pit road for service are usually in need of fuel, new tires and perhaps a mechanical adjustment to improve the handling. Crews might also make minor repairs to the vehicle on pit road. However, any major repairs must be made behind pit wall or in the garage area.

**Green-flag pit stops:** During green-flag competition, drivers are allowed to make pit stops as needed. However, drivers generally will try to stretch their fuel mileage as long as possible, hoping for a caution or yellow flag to make their pit stop. Generally, if a driver makes a green-flag pit stop for fuel, the leader might lap him one or more times. However, if the race stays "green" for the entire "fuel window," the driver might earn his lap back when the rest of the field pits for fuel.

However, if a caution flag comes out after a driver has made a green-flag pit stop, it might allow those drivers who have not yet pitted to do so under the caution and could keep those drivers who did pit under the green flag a lap down.

**Yellow-flag pit stops:** During a caution period, NASCAR will make the determination to open and close pit road. A NASCAR official, in front of the entrance to pit road, will use an open/closed flag to communicate to drivers when the pits are open or closed. Once the pits are open, only the lead-lap cars are allowed to pit the first time around. Cars that are down a lap or more must wait until the second time around to make their pit stop. Once all cars exit pit road, they must rejoin the field behind the pace car.

## Restarts

In 2003, NASCAR moved to prevent the practice of racing back to the start/finish line after a yellow flag is displayed. The rule provides for the first driver running one lap behind the leader when a caution is displayed to start in the last position on the lead lap when the race is restarted. All other cars one lap behind the leader will stay one lap behind the lead lap and in their respective positions from when the caution flag was displayed.

Following caution periods, NASCAR officials communicate to the drivers of a restart when there is one lap to go before the green flag is waved. The flag man signals one lap to go at the start/finish line by holding up one finger. Generally, team spotters and crew chiefs help communicate to their drivers over the radio when there is one lap remaining before the restart.

For restarts during the race, except those during the final 25 laps, cars on the lead lap line up on the outside toward the wall while the lapped cars line up to the inside for a double-file restart.

NASCAR uses a 25-lap rule and a 10-lap rule for restarts late in the race. The 25-lap rule states that if a restart occurs with less than 25 laps remaining and more than 10 laps remaining, only lead-lap cars are permitted to restart in the outside line.

The 10-lap rule states that if there are 10 or fewer laps remaining in an event, cars restart in single file with the leader of the race first in line and remaining lead-lap cars behind. All other cars must hold their respective track positions, regardless of running order.

When the green flag waves on restarts, all passing must be done on the righthand side until drivers cross the start/finish line.

## Green-white-checkered finishes

In 2004, NASCAR worked to ensure that races would not finish under yellow-flag conditions by instituting a green-white-checkered system. The new procedure consists of a restart of two laps—green flag for the first lap of the restart and the white flag signaling the final lap leading to the checkered flag. If a caution should come out on either lap, the race will be completed under caution.

# Qualifying

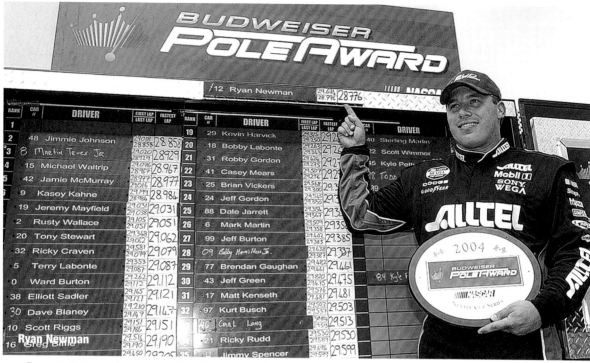

| RANK | CAR # | DRIVER | FIRST LAP LAST LAP | FASTEST LAP | RANK | CAR # | DRIVER | FIRST LAP LAST LAP | FASTEST LAP | CAR # | DRIVER |
|------|-------|--------|--------------------|-------------|------|-------|--------|--------------------|-------------|-------|--------|
| 1 | | | | | | | /12 Ryan Newman | 29.616 28.776 | 28.776 | | |
| 2 | 48 | Jimmie Johnson | 29.018 28.855 | 28.858 | 19 | 29 | Kevin Harvick | 23.815 28.150 | 29.24 | 40 | Sterling Marlin |
| 3 | 8 | Martin Truex Jr. | 29.020 28.729 | 28.929 | 20 | 18 | Bobby Labonte | 29.175 28.343 | 29.26 | 22 | Scott Wimmer |
| 4 | 15 | Michael Waltrip | 29.076 28.967 | 28.967 | 21 | 31 | Robby Gordon | 29.124 28.225 | 29.2 | 45 | Kyle Petty |
| 5 | 42 | Jamie McMurray | 28.997 29.016 | 28.977 | 22 | 41 | Casey Mears | 29.507 28.276 | 29.2 | 98 | Todd |
| 6 | 9 | Kasey Kahne | 29.199 28.984 | 28.986 | 23 | 25 | Brian Vickers | 29.568 29.300 | 29.3 | 89 | |
| 7 | 19 | Jeremy Mayfield | 29.031 29.058 | 29.031 | 24 | 24 | Jeff Gordon | 29.151 29.355 | 29.3 | | |
| 8 | 2 | Rusty Wallace | 29.105 29.051 | 29.051 | 25 | 88 | Dale Jarrett | 29.352 29.367 | 29.3 | | |
| 9 | 20 | Tony Stewart | 29.348 29.062 | 29.062 | 26 | 6 | Mark Martin | 29.509 29.358 | 29.358 | | |
| 10 | 32 | Ricky Craven | 29.581 29.079 | 29.079 | 27 | 99 | Jeff Burton | 29.402 29.385 | 29.385 | | |
| 11 | 5 | Terry Labonte | 29.353 29.087 | 29.087 | 28 | 09 | Bobby Hamilton Jr. | 29.638 29.387 | 29.387 | | |
| 12 | 0 | Ward Burton | 29.262 29.112 | 29.112 | 29 | 77 | Brendan Gaughan | 29.482 29.461 | 29.461 | | |
| 13 | 38 | Elliott Sadler | 29.165 29.121 | 29.121 | 30 | 43 | Jeff Green | 29.820 29.475 | 29.475 | 84 | Kyle |
| 14 | 30 | Dave Blaney | 29.210 29.149 | 29.147 | 31 | 17 | Matt Kenseth | 29.576 29.481 | 29.481 | | |
| 15 | 10 | Scott Riggs | 29.151 29.186 | 29.151 | 32 | 97 | Kurt Busch | 29.503 29.537 | 29.503 | | |
| 16 | | Ryan Newman | 29.514 29.190 | 29.190 | | | Carl Long | 29.802 29.513 | 29.513 | | |
| | | Greg Biffle | | | | 21 | Ricky Rudd | 29.530 29.585 | 29.530 | | |
| | | | 29.650 | 29.205 | | | Jimmy Spencer | 29.696 29.599 | 29.599 | | |

For any given NASCAR NEXTEL Cup Series event, it is unknown how many cars will enter. But one thing is certain: a maximum of 43 cars will start. NASCAR uses time trials, known as qualifying, to choose which teams make "The Show."

## Qualifying draw

NASCAR officials use a draw to determine the qualifying order. Each team sends its crew chief or a representative to draw a number at the qualifying lottery, which is usually on the morning of qualifying. If 50 cars are entered, the NASCAR official will put Nos. 1-51 (always one more than there are entries) into a spinning ball. Each team representative draws one number, starting with the crew chief whose owner is highest in the owner point standings. After each team draws, officials record the number. When every team has drawn, the qualifying order is set.

## Qualifying

To qualify for a race, drivers take one or two timed laps, depending on the track. Drivers receive one warmup lap before taking the green flag. The driver with the quickest qualifying time starts on the pole, which is the inside (left side) of the front row. The one exception to these procedures is the Daytona 500, which follows a different qualifying method (see Daytona 500 qualifying).

## Post-qualifying impound

More than half of the events on the 2005 schedule will use a new race procedure designed to help teams contain costs.

After qualifying, NASCAR will impound the cars for the starting field of 43 cars. The teams then will not be allowed to work on the cars except in special circumstances. The rule change allows teams to focus on their race setup rather than work on a special qualifying setup and then switch to a racing setup.

## Daytona 500 qualifying

The Great American Race uses a unique qualifying procedure. In the first round of qualifying, the fastest car earns the pole position for both the Daytona 500 and the first of two 150-mile qualifying races known as the Gatorade 150s. The second-fastest car earns the outside pole for the Daytona 500 and starts on the pole for the second Gatorade 150 race.

Drivers qualifying in odd-numbered positions (first, third, fifth, etc.) compete in the first Gatorade 150 race; drivers qualifying in even-numbered positions (second, fourth, sixth, etc.) compete in the second.

The top 14 finishers, not including the pole sitter, in the first 150-mile qualifying race line up behind the pole sitter for the Daytona 500, and the top 14 finishers, not including the outside pole sitter, in the second 150-mile qualifying race line up behind the outside pole sitter. Thus, the first 30 of 43 positions are filled. The rest of the positions (31-43) in the field are awarded to drivers based on qualifying times and provisionals.

# How points are awarded

The winner of each NASCAR race receives 180 points. The runner-up in each event scores 170. From there, the point total decreases in five-point increments for places two through six, points awarded drop four points per driver for positions seven through 11, and three-point increments separate drivers' points for finishers in 12th place or lower. The 43rd, or last-place driver, gets 34 points.

There are also bonus points up for grabs at each event. Drivers receive five points for leading a lap and an additional five points for leading the most laps.

In NASCAR NEXTEL Cup racing, after the 26th race of the season, all drivers in the top 10 in points and any others within 400 points of the leader earn a berth in the Chase for the NASCAR NEXTEL Cup.

All drivers in the Chase for the NASCAR NEXTEL Cup have their point totals adjusted. The first-place driver in the standings will begin with 5,050 points; the second-place driver will start with 5,045, etc. Incremental five-point decreases continue through the rest of the championship contenders.

Owners are rewarded in the points race in much the same fashion but, unlike drivers, they earn points for attempting to make a race. If an owner shows up with a pair of drivers and one fails to qualify, the owner still receives points for the non-qualifying effort.

The fastest non-qualifier on race day earns 31 points for his owner, three down from the 43rd-place points. The scale continues downward from there for all nonqualifiers, with the lowest possible point(s) awarded being one.

# NASCAR NEXTEL Cup points system

| Finish | Points | Finish | Points | Finish | Points | Finish | Points |
|--------|--------|--------|--------|--------|--------|--------|--------|
| 1. | 180 | 13. | 124 | 25. | 88 | 37. | 52 |
| 2. | 170 | 14. | 121 | 26. | 85 | 38. | 49 |
| 3. | 165 | 15. | 118 | 27. | 82 | 39. | 46 |
| 4. | 160 | 16. | 115 | 28. | 79 | 40. | 43 |
| 5. | 155 | 17. | 112 | 29. | 76 | 41. | 40 |
| 6. | 150 | 18. | 109 | 30. | 73 | 42. | 37 |
| 7. | 146 | 19. | 106 | 31. | 70 | 43. | 34 |
| 8. | 142 | 20. | 103 | 32. | 67 | Each driver who leads a lap |
| 9. | 138 | 21. | 100 | 33. | 64 | during the race is awarded 5 |
| 10. | 134 | 22. | 97 | 34. | 61 | bonus points. The driver who |
| 11. | 130 | 23. | 94 | 35. | 58 | leads the most laps is awarded |
| 12. | 127 | 24. | 91 | 36. | 55 | an additional 5 bonus points. |

# Chase for the NASCAR NEXTEL Cup

The top 10 drivers in points (or any driver within 400 points of the leader after race No. 26) qualify for the Chase for the NASCAR NEXTEL Cup and have their point totals reset after the September race at Richmond, which is the 26th race of the season.

The 10-race Chase begins at New Hampshire in 2005; the last race will be at Homestead. Races will be scored the same way they were scored the rest of the year, except drivers outside the top 10 are not eligible to win the championship. The driver within the Chase for the NASCAR NEXTEL Cup who has the most points after Homestead will be the champion.

# History of the points system

Several different point systems have been used in NASCAR's top series since its inception in 1949. Basically, five systems were used with several variations, combining for a total of 11 separate point systems used since 1949.

Now the point system is standardized, decreasing sequentially from first place to last. This form of the system was introduced in 1975, with five bonus points awarded to each driver who leads a lap and an additional five bonus points awarded to the driver who leads the most laps in a race.

In 2004, the point system was tweaked again to provide additional points to the race winner, resulting in a 10-point difference between first and second places. The Chase for the NASCAR NEXTEL Cup adjusted the point total after the 26th race, creating a large margin between the drivers who are eligible for the Chase for the NASCAR NEXTEL Cup and the rest of the field.

# Tech elements

| | NASCAR NEXTEL CUP SERIES | NASCAR BUSCH SERIES | NASCAR CRAFTSMAN TRUCK SERIES |
|---|---|---|---|
| **ELIGIBLE MODELS** | Chevrolet Monte Carlo<br>Dodge Charger, Dodge Intrepid<br>Ford Taurus<br>Pontiac Grand Prix | Chevrolet Monte Carlo<br>Dodge Charger, Dodge Intrepid<br>Ford Taurus<br>Pontiac Grand Prix | Chevrolet C1500 (Silverado)<br>Dodge Ram 1500<br>Ford F150<br>Toyota Tundra |
| **YEARS** | 2003-2005 | 2003-2005 | 2003-2005 |
| **ENGINE** | Cast Iron 5.7L V8<br>Aluminum cylinder heads | Cast Iron 5.7L V8<br>Aluminum cylinder heads | Cast Iron 5.7L V8<br>Aluminum cylinder heads |
| **HORSEPOWER\*** | 790 @ 9400 rpm | 660 @ 7900 rpm | 650 @ 8000 rpm |
| **COMPRESSION RATIO** | 12:1 | 12:1 | 12:1 |
| **TORQUE** | 550 ft/lb @ 7500 rpm | 540 ft/lb @ 6400 rpm | 535 ft/lb @ 6000 rpm |
| **DISPLACEMENT** | 358 c.i. max | 358 c.i. max | 358 c.i. max |
| **INDUCTION** | One 4V Holley carburetor | One 4V Holley carburetor | One 4V Holley carburetor |
| **TOP SPEED** | 200 mph (est.) | 195 mph (est.) | 185 mph (est.) |
| **TRANSMISSION** | 4-Speed | 4-Speed | 4-Speed |
| **FUEL\*** | 110 octane<br>22-gallon capacity | 112 octane<br>22-gallon capacity | 112 octane<br>22-gallon capacity |
| **FRONT SUSPENSION** | Independent coil springs,<br>Twin control arms | Independent coil springs,<br>Twin control arms | Independent coil springs,<br>Twin control arms |
| **REAR SUSPENSION** | Trailing arms, coil springs,<br>panhard bar | Trailing arms, coil springs,<br>panhard bar | Trailing arms, coil springs,<br>panhard bar |
| **CHASSIS** | Rectangular steel tubing<br>w/integral roll-cage | Rectangular steel tubing<br>w/integral roll-cage | Rectangular steel tubing<br>w/integral roll-cage |
| **BODY LENGTH** | 200.7 inches | 203.5 inches | 206 inches |
| **BODY WIDTH** | 72.5 inches | 74.5 inches | 75 inches |
| **HEIGHT** | 51 inches (min) | 50.5 inches (min) | 59 inches (min) |
| **WEIGHT** | 3400 lbs (w/o driver) | 3,400 lbs (w/o driver) | 3,400 lbs (w/o driver) |
| **FRONT AIR DAM\*** | 3.5 inches | 4 inches | 4 inches |
| **GEAR RATIO** | TBD | TBD | TBD |
| **SPOILER\*** | 55" wide x 5.0" high<br>for 2004-2005 makes;<br>2003 makes vary | 57" wide x 5.7" high<br>for all makes | 66.75" wide x 8" high for all makes<br>68.75" wide x 8" high at designated<br>speedways |
| **WHEEL BASE** | 110 inches | 105 inches | 112 inches |
| **WHEELS** | Steel 15" x 9.5" | Steel 15" x 9.5" | Steel 15" x 9.5" |
| **TREAD WIDTH** | 60.5 inches (max) | 60.5 inches (max) | 60.5 inches (max) |
| **FRONT BRAKES** | Disc | Disc | Disc |
| **REAR BRAKES** | Disc | Disc | Disc |

**Note:** Information subject to change. \*Specifications may vary from restrictor-plate races. Eligible model years for the Dodge Intrepid are 2003 and 2004. Eligible model year for the Pontiac Grand Prix is 2003.

# CUTAWAY CAR

Source: NASCAR

**1 Front grill openings** – These inlets allow air to pass through the radiator and ensure that the engine performs at the optimum temperature. Additional air ducts to the side help cool the brake systems.

**2 Hood pins** – There are four metal-and-wire hood pins with wire tethers that serve as a safety feature by keeping the hood closed.

**3 Shock absorbers** – These help control the compression and rebound of the suspension springs and provide a smooth and controlled ride to the driver.

**4 Cowl induction** – The housing for the air cleaner connects the air intake at the base of the windshield to the carburetor.

**5 Jack post** – This is the area where the jackman must place the jack on each side of the car during a pit stop. Some teams place a piece of fluorescent or bright-colored tape on the body of the car to indicate the specific area of the jack brace.

**6 Impact data recorder** – The impact data recorder, which records numerous measurements such as G Forces and Delta V (change in speed) from an accident, is located on the left side of the driver's seat.

**7 Roll cage** – A cage made of steel tubing inside the stock car's interior that is designed to protect the driver from impacts and rollovers. The roll cages must adhere to strict NASCAR safety guidelines and are inspected regularly.

**8 Window net** – This safety device is located on the driver's side window and is designed to keep his head and arms inside the car during an accident.

**9 Windshield clips** – The clips attach the windshield to the chassis and allow for easy removal should a driver need to be extricated from the vehicle.

**10 Television camera** – A miniature camera is mounted on the roof of the car that allows NASCAR fans a great view of their favorite drivers in race traffic.

**11 Roof strips** – The two half-inch tall aluminum strips which run length wise on the roof and help prevent the stock car from flipping when it is turned sideways during a spin or accident.

**12 Roof flaps** – The flaps, which were first used in NASCAR competition in 1994, are a safety feature that was developed to help prevent the stock car from becoming airborne when it is turned sideways or backward during a spin or accident.

**13 Jacking bolt** – This area is where the crew uses a tool to adjust the handling of the car by altering pressure on the rear springs. A wrench is inserted into a jack bolt attached to the springs and is used to adjust the preload on the springs and, in turn, the handling of the race car. Sometimes will hear the slang reference that the team is putting in a round (one turn) of wedge.

**14 Rear spoiler** – A metal blade that is attached to the deck lid of the car. The spoiler deflects the air coming off the roof and onto the rear deck lid which, in turn, creates rear downforce and more rear traction for the car.

**15 Dry break fuel cell** – The holding tank for a racecar's gasoline supply consists of a metal box containing a flexible, tear-resistant bladder and foam baffling, both of which are safety enhancements. The cell can hold 22 gallons of fuel. The Dry Break Inlet is a spring-loaded tube, allowing fast refueling without fuel spillage.

**16 Deck lid** – The term used for the trunk lid of a stock car.

**17 Firewall** – Sheet steel plate separates the engine compartment from the driver's compartment of the racecar. It's also used at the rear to separate the fuel cell compartment from the driver's compartment.

**18 Track bar** – A lateral bar that keeps the rear tires centered within the body of the car. The bar connects the frame on one side to the rear axle on the opposite side and can be adjusted in height to alter the handling of the car.

**19 Sway or anti-roll bar** – It's used to resist or counteract the rolling force of the car body through the turns.

**20 Alternate exit** – NASCAR issued a recommendation to teams in 2003 for an alternate exit, more commonly known as a roof hatch. The safety initiative provides drivers with an alternate exit through a "hatch" in the roof of the car in the event of an emergency situation.

## A

**Aerodynamics**: As applied to racing, the study of airflow and the forces of resistance and pressure that result from the flow of air over, under and around a moving car.

**A-Frame**: Either the upper or lower connecting suspension piece (in the shape of an A) locking the frame to the spindle.

**Air box**: Housing for the air cleaner that connects the air intake at the base of the windshield to the carburetor.

**Air dam**: A metal strip that hangs beneath the front grill, often just inches from the ground. The air dam helps provide aerodynamic downforce at the front of the car.

**Air filter**: Paper, gauze or synthetic fiber element used to prevent dirt particles from entering the engine. Located in the air box.

**Air Pressure**: Force exerted by air within a tire, expressed in pounds per square inch (psi).

**Alternator**: A belt-driven device mounted on the front of the engine that recharges the battery while the engine is running.

**A-post**: The post extending from the roofline to the base of the windshield on either side of the car.

**Bias-ply tires are composed of fabric woven in angles.**

**Apron**: The paved portion of a racetrack that separates the racing surface from the (usually unpaved) infield.

**Axle**: Rotating shafts connecting the rear differential gears to the rear wheels.

## B

**Ball Joint**: A ball inside a socket that can turn and pivot in any direction. Used to allow suspension to travel while the driver steers the car.

**Banking**: The sloping of a racetrack, particularly at a curve or corner, from the apron to the outside wall. Degree of banking refers to the height of a track's slope at its outside edge.

**Bell housing**: A cover, shaped like a bell, that surrounds the flywheel, clutch that connects the engine to the transmission.

**Bias-ply**: Layers of fabric within a tire that are woven in angles. Also used as a term to describe tires made in this manner.

**Bite**: (1) "Round of bite" describes the turning or adjusting of a car's jacking screws found at each wheel. "Weight jacking" distributes the car's weight at each wheel. (2) Adhesion of a tire to the track surface.

**Bleeder valve**: A valve in the wheel used to reduce air pressure in tires.

**Blend line**: Line painted on the track near the apron and extending from the pit road exit into the first turn. When leaving the pits, a driver must stay below it to safely blend back into traffic.

**Blister**: An overheating of the tread compound resulting in bubbles on the tire surface.

**Bodywork**: The fabricated sheet metal that encloses the chassis.

**Bore**: Pistons travel up and down within each cylinder, or bore, in the engine block.

**B-post**: Post extending from the roofline to the base of the window behind the driver's head.

**Brake caliper**: The part of the braking system that, when applied by the driver, clamps the brake disk/rotor to slow or stop the car.

## C

**Camber**: The amount a tire is tilted in or out from vertical. Described in degrees, either positive or negative.

**Camshaft**: A rotating shaft within the engine that opens and closes the intake and exhaust valves in the engine.

**Carburetor**: A device connected directly to the gas pedal and mounted on top of the intake manifold that controls the air/fuel mixture going to the engine.

**Chassis**: The steel structure or frame of the car.

**Chute**: A racetrack straightaway.

# STUDY OF RACE TIRE vs. STREET TIRE

On a typical race weekend, a NASCAR NEXTEL Cup Series team will use between nine and 14 sets of tires depending upon the length of the race and the type of track – short track, speedway, superspeedway or road course. By comparison, an average set of street tires gets replaced approximately every three years. NASCAR NEXTEL Cup Series racing tire specifications also differ from race to race depending upon the degree of track banking and the type of racing surface (asphalt, concrete or a mixture of both). Goodyear uses about 18 different tire codes to cover the needs of the NASCAR NEXTEL Cup Series during the course of a racing season.

## Goodyear Eagle Race Tire vs. Goodyear Eagle Street Tire

**Estimated cost** $389 each / $150-200 each
**Average life** 150 miles / 50,000 miles
**Air pressure** (cold psi) 30 psi, left and 45 psi, right / all infladed to 35 psi
**Inflated with** dry air or nitrogen / air
**Weight** 24 pounds / 30 pounds
**Tread thickness** 1/8 inch / 3/8 inch

## Race tire safety

Introduced in 1966, the Goodyear Lifeguard Inner Liner Safety Spare allows the car to return to the pits in the event of an air loss. Based on a tire-within-a-tire concept, it features a separate valve system that eliminates air equalization and prevents the tire and wheel assembly from becoming unbalanced.

## Goodyear Lifeguard inner liner safety spare

As a rule, the Goodyear Lifeguard inner liner safety spare is used on oval tracks one mile or more in length. It's also used on the right-side tires at Bristol Motor Speedway. The inner liner can be reused up to a dozen times if not damaged. It weighs 10 pounds and is generally inflated 12 to 25 pounds higher than the outer Goodyear Eagle race tire. The original version of this tire was first tested by drivers Richard Petty and Darel Dieringer and was used until 1992 before it was replaced by the current tubeless model.

**Compound**: A formula or recipe of rubber composing a particular tire. Different tracks require different tire compounds. Left-side tires are considerably softer than right-side tires, and it's against the rules to run left sides on the right. There are four basic components: rubber polymers, carbon blacks, oils and curatives.

**Compression ratio**: Amount that the air-fuel mixture is compressed as the piston reaches the top of the bore. The higher the compression, the more horsepower produced.

**Cowl**: A removable metal scoop at the base of the windshield and rear of the hood that directs air into the air box.

**C-post**: The post extending from the roofline of a race car to the base of the rear window to the top of the deck lid.

**Crankcase**: The area of the engine block that houses the crankshaft.

**Crankshaft**: The rotating shaft within the engine that delivers the power from the pistons to the flywheel, and from there to the transmission.

**Cubic-inch displacement**: The size of the engine measured in cubic inches.

**Cylinder head**: Made of aluminum, it is bolted to the top of each side of the engine block. Cylinder heads hold the valves and spark plugs. Passages through the heads make up the intake and exhaust ports.

**Deck lid**: Slang term for the trunk lid of a racecar.

**Dirty air**: Aerodynamic term for the turbulent air currents caused by fast moving cars that can cause a particular car to lose control.

**Donuts**: Slang term for black, circular, dent-line marks on the side panels of stock cars, usually caused after rubbing against other cars at high speed.

**Downforce**: A combination of aerodynamic and centrifugal forces. The more downforce, the more grip a racecar has. But more downforce also means more drag, which can rob a racecar of speed.

**Draft**: Slang term for the aerodynamic effect that allows two or more cars traveling nose-to-tail to run faster than a single car. When one car follows another closely, the one in front cuts through the air, providing a cleaner path of air (that is, less resistance) for the car in back.

**Drafting**: The practice of two or more cars, running nose-to-tail, almost touching, while racing. The lead car, by displacing the air in front of it, creates a vacuum between its rear end and the nose of the following car, actually pulling the second car along with it.

**Drag**: The resistance a car experiences when passing through air at high speeds. A resisting force exerted on a car parallel to its airstream and opposite in direction to its motion.

**Driveshaft**: A steel tube that connects the transmission of a race car to the rear end housing.

**Dyno**: Shortened term for dynamometer, a machine used to measure an engine's horsepower.

**Engine block**: An iron casting from the manufacturer that envelopes the crankshaft, connecting rods and pistons.

**Equalized**: When the inner liner of a tire loses air pressure and that pressure becomes the same as that within the outer tire, creating a vibration. The inner shield should have a higher psi than the outer tire.

**Esses**: Slang term used for a series of acute left- and right-hand turns on a road course, one turn immediately following another.

**Fabricator**: A person who specializes in creating the sheet metal body of a stock car. Most teams employ two or more.

**Factory**: A term designating the "Big Three" auto manufacturers: General Motors (GM), Ford and Daimler Chrysler. The "factory days" refer to the periods in the 1950s and '60s when the manufacturers actively and openly provided sponsorship money and technical support to some race teams.

**Fan**: An electrically or mechanically driven device that is used to pull air through the radiator or oil cooler. Heat is transferred from the hot oil or water in the radiator to the moving air.

**Firewall**: A solid metal plate that separates the engine compartment from the driver's compartment of the race car.

**Flat-out**: Slang term for racing a car as fast as possible under the given weather and track conditions.

**Flywheel**: A heavy metal rotating wheel that is part of the race car's clutch system, used to keep elements such as the crank shaft turning steadily.

# DRAFTING

Source: NASCAR

## Aerodynamics

Study of airflow in regard to a stock car, including the effects of downforce and drag.

## Drag

The resistance a car experiences when passing through air at high speeds. An example of drag occurs when holding your hand outside the car window while traveling down the highway. Drag is what pushes your hand back – minimize the shape of your hand and the drag or force is less.

## Downforce

A combination of aerodynamic and centrifugal forces at work. Downforce can be altered to improve the car's grip or traction by adjusting the spoiler as well as other aerodynamic changes to the car and its setup. As downforce is increased, the grip/traction is increased, as well as tire wear. Increasing downforce comes at the expense of creating more drag, which will reduce fuel efficiency.

Teams will tolerate any amount of drag for an increase in downforce at all tracks, with the exception of the two largest superspeedways, Daytona International Speedway and Talladega Superspeedway.

## Draft

The aerodynamic effect that allows two or more cars traveling nose to tail to run faster than a single car. When one car follows another closely, the one in front punches through the air and provides a cleaner, less resistant path for the trailing cars.

## Drafting

The practice, which is prevalent on superspeedways such as Daytona and Talladega, of two or more cars running nose to tail to create more speed for the group. The lead car displaces the air in front of it, creates a vacuum effect between its rear end and the nose of the second car and pulls the trailing cars along with it with less overall resistance. Two or more cars drafting will travel faster than a single car.

# Glossary

**Four-barrel**: A type of carburetor.

**Frame**: The metal skeleton or structure of a race car, on which the sheet metal of the car's body is formed. Also referred to as a chassis.

**Front clip**: Beginning at the firewall, the frontmost section of a racecar. Holds the engine and its associated electrical, lubricating and cooling apparatus, as well as the braking, steering, and suspension mechanisms.

**Front steer**: A racecar in which the steering components are located ahead of the front axle.

**Fuel cell**: A holding tank for a race car's supply of gasoline. Consists of a metal box that contains a flexible, tear-resistant bladder and foam baffling. A product of aerospace technology, it's designed to eliminate or minimize fuel spillage. A fuel cell holds approximately 22 gallons.

**Fuel pump**: A device that pumps fuel from the fuel cell through the fuel line into the carburetor.

**Gasket**: A thin material, made of paper, metal, silicone or other synthetic materials, used as a seal between two similar machined metal surfaces, such as cylinder heads and the engine block.

**Gauge**: An instrument, usually mounted on the dashboard, used to monitor engine conditions, such as fuel pressure, oil pressure and temperature, water pressure and temperature, and RPM (revolutions per minute).

**Gears**: Circular, wheel-shaped parts with teeth along the edges. The interlocking of these two mechanisms enables one to turn the other.

**Greenhouse**: The upper area of the racecar that extends from the base of the windshield in the front, the tops of the doors on the sides and the base of the rear window in the back. Includes all of the A, B and C pillars, the entire glass area and the car's roof.

**Groove**: Slang term for the best route around the racetrack; the most efficient or quickest way around the track for a particular driver. The "high groove" takes a car closer to the outside wall for most of a lap, while the "low groove" takes a car closer to the apron than the outside wall. Road racers use the term "line." Drivers search for a fast groove, which has been known to change, depending on track and weather conditions.

**Happy hour**: Slang term for the last official practice session held before an event. Usually takes place the day before the race.

**Harmonic balancer**: An element used to reduce vibrations in the crankshaft.

**Handling**: Generally, a racecar's performance while racing, qualifying and practicing. How a car handles is determined by its tires, suspension geometry, aerodynamics, and other factors.

**Hauler**: The 18-wheel tractor-trailer rig that teams use to transport two racecars, engines, tools and support equipment to the racetracks. Cars are stowed in the top section, while the bottom floor is used for work space.

**Horsepower**: A measurement of mechanical or engine power. Measured in the amount of power it takes to move 33,000 pounds one foot in a minute.

**Ignition**: An electrical system used to ignite the air-fuel mixture in an internal combustion engine.

**Intake manifold**: A housing that directs the air-fuel mixture through the port openings in the cylinder heads.

**Intermediate track**: Term describing a racetrack one mile or more, but less than two miles, in length.

**Interval**: The time-distance between two cars. Referred to roughly in car lengths, or precisely in seconds.

**Jet**: When air is sent at a high velocity through the carburetor, jets direct the fuel into the airstream. Jets are made slightly larger to make a richer mixture or slightly smaller to make a more lean mixture, depending on track and weather conditions.

**Line**: See Groove

**Loose**: Also known as "oversteer." When the rear tires of the car have trouble sticking in the corners. This causes the car to "fishtail" as the rear end swings outward during turns. A minor amount of this effect can be desirable on certain tracks.

# TIGHT vs. LOOSE CONDITIONS

**Tight:** Also known as understeer. This occurs when the front wheels lose traction before the rear wheels. It causes the stock car to have trouble steering sharply and smoothly through the turns as the front end pushes toward the wall.

**Loose:** Also known as oversteer. This occurs when the rear tires of the stock car have trouble sticking in the corners. This causes the car to fishtail as the rear end swings outward while turning in the corners.

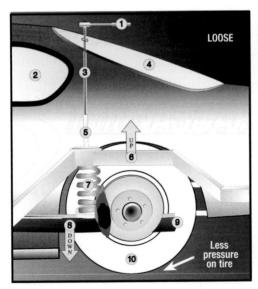

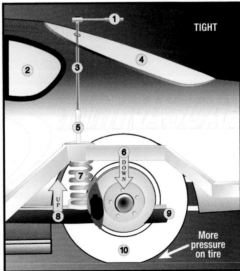

During a pit stop, one of the crewmen will sometimes add or subtract spring pressure by attaching a rachet and manually rotating it one way or the other. This tightens or loosens the spring and brings the frame and trailing arm forward or away from each other, applying more or less pressure on the tire when the car goes into a turn. This is known as adding or subtracting wedge.

1. Rachet inserted by crewman
2. Side window
3. Rachet extension
4. Rear window
5. Screw jack
6. Chassis frame
7. Coil spring
8. Trailing arm
9. Trailing arm end
10. Goodyear tire

**Lug nuts**: Large nuts applied with a high-pressure air wrench to wheel during a pit stop to secure the tires in place. All NASCAR cars use five lug nuts on each wheel, and penalties are assessed it a team fails to put all five on during a pit stop.

**Magnaflux**: Short for "magnetic particle inspection." A procedure for checking all ferrous (steel) parts (suspension pieces, connecting rods, cylinder heads, etc.) for cracks and other defects by utilizing a solution of metal particles and fluorescent dye and a black light. Surface cracks will appear as red lines.

**Marbles**: Excess rubber build-up above the upper groove on the racetrack.

**Neutral**: A term drivers use when referring to how their car is handling. When a car is neither loose nor pushing (tight).

**Oil pump**: This device pumps oil to lubricate all moving engine parts.

**P&G**: Basically, the procedure for checking the cubic-inch displacement of an engine. The term comes from the manufacturer of the particular gauge used.

**Panhard bar**: A lateral bar that keeps the rear tires centered within the body of the car. It connects the frame on one side and the rear axle on the other. Also called the track bar.

**Piston**: A circular element that moves up and down in the cylinder, compressing the air-fuel mixture in the top of the chamber, helping to produce horsepower.

**Pit road**: The area where pit crews service the cars. Generally located along the front straightaway, but because of space limitations, some race tracks sport pit roads on both the front and back straightaways.

**Pit stall**: The area along pit road that is designated for a particular team's use during pit stops. Each car stops in the team's stall before being serviced.

**Pole position**: Term for the first position on the starting grid, awarded to the fastest qualifier.

**Post-entry (PE)**: A team or driver who submits an entry blank for a race after the deadline for submission has passed. A post-entry receives no driver or owner points.

**Push**: See Tight.

**Quarter-panel**: The sheet metal on both sides of the car from the C-post to the rear bumper below the deck lid and above the wheel well.

**R**

**Rear clip**: The section of a race car that begins at the base of the rear windshield and extends to the rear bumper. Contains the car's fuel cell and rear suspension components.

**Rear-steer**: A car in which the steering components are located behind the front axle.

**Restart**: The waving of the green flag following a caution period.

**Restrictor plate**: A thin metal plate with four holes that restrict airflow from the carburetor into the engine. Used to reduce horsepower and keep speeds down. The restrictor plates are currently used at Daytona International Speedway and Talladega Superspeedway, the two biggest and fastest tracks in NASCAR.

**Ride height**: The distance between the car's frame rails and the ground.

**RPM**: Short for revolutions per minute, a measurement of the speed of the engine's crankshaft.

**Roll cage**: The steel tubing inside the racecar's interior. Designed to protect the driver from impacts or rollovers, the roll cage must meet strict NASCAR safety guidelines and is inspected regularly.

**Round**: Slang term for a way of making chassis adjustments utilizing the racecar's springs. A wrench is inserted in a jack bolt attached to the springs and is used to tighten or loosen the amount of play in the spring. This in turn can loosen or tighten up the handling of a racecar.

**S**

**Safety shield**: Also called a safety liner. A safety feature often referred to as a "tire within a tire." This inner tire is used in the NASCAR NEXTEL Cup Series and will hold a car up if the outer tire is cut down.

# RESTRICTOR PLATE

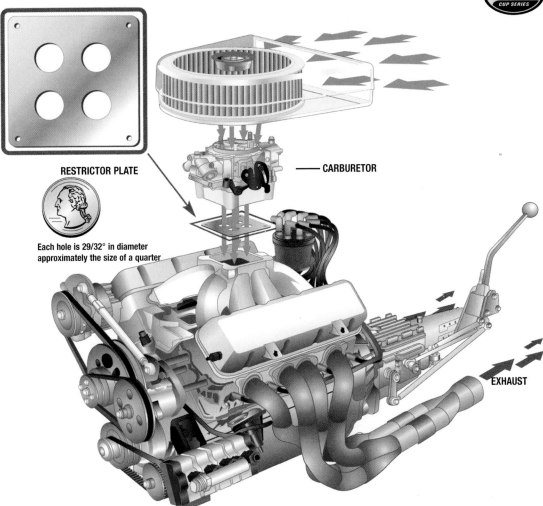

**RESTRICTOR PLATE**

Each hole is 29/32° in diameter
approximately the size of a quarter

**CARBURETOR**

**EXHAUST**

The restrictor plate is a thin, square aluminum piece with four holes that restricts airflow from the carburetor to the engine, resulting in less horsepower and a reduction in the stock car's speed. It is located between the engine's carburetor and intake manifold.

The restrictor plates, 1/8 of an inch in thickness, range in hole size from 3/4 of an inch to 1-1/2 inches. As the hole sizes decrease, it will have more of an effect on the reduction of horsepower.

From 3/4 of an inch to 1 inch, the plates increase in size by increments of 1/64 of an inch. From 1 to 1-1/2 inches the plates increase by increments of 1/16 of an inch. The restrictor plate size currently being used is 29/32 of an inch.

The restrictor plate is used at the NASCAR NEXTEL Cup Series' two largest superspeedways: the 2.5-mile Daytona International Speedway and the 2.66-mile Talladega Superspeedway. NASCAR distributes the restrictor plates to the teams during those race weekends, collects them following on-track activity each day as well as at the conclusion of the event.

The version of the restrictor plates currently in use was introduced to the NASCAR NEXTEL Cup Series in 1989, beginning with the season-opening Daytona 500 at Daytona International Speedway.

**Scuffs**: Slang term for tires that have been used at least once and saved for further racing. A lap or two is enough to "scuff" them in. Most often used in qualifying.

**Setup**: Slang term for the tuning and adjustments made to a racecar's suspension before and during a race.

**Short track**: Racetracks that are less than a mile in length.

**Silly Season**: Slang for the period that begins during the latter part of the current season, where in some teams announce driver, crew and/or sponsor changes for the following year.

**Slick**: A track condition where, for a number of reasons, it's hard for a car's tires to adhere to the surface or get a good "bite." A slick racetrack is not necessarily wet or slippery because of oil, water, etc. Temperature and the amount of rubber on a track are among factors that can create a slick track.

**Slingshot**: A maneuver in which a car following the leader in a draft suddenly steers around it, breaking the vacuum; this provides an extra burst of speed that allows the second car to take the lead. See Drafting.

**Splash and Go**: A quick pit stop that involves nothing more than refueling the race car with the amount of fuel necessary to finish the race.

**Spoiler**: A metal blade attached to the rear deck lid of the car. It helps restrict airflow over the rear of the car, providing downforce and traction.

**Stagger**: The difference in size between the tires on the left and right sides of a car. Because of a tire's makeup, slight variations in circumference result. Stagger between right-side and left-side tires may range from less than a half inch to more than an inch. Stagger applies to only bias-ply tires and not radials.

**Stick**: Slang term used for tire traction, as in "the car's sticking to the track."

**Stickers**: Slang term for new tires. The name is derived from the manufacturer's stickers that are affixed to each new tire's contact surface.

**Stop and Go**: A penalty, usually assessed for speeding on pit road or for unsafe driving. The car must be brought onto pit road at the appropriate speed and stopped for one full second in the team's pit stall before returning to the track.

**Superspeedway**: A racetrack of a mile or more in distance. Racers refer to three types of oval tracks. Short tracks are under one mile, intermediate tracks are at least a mile but under two miles, and speedways are two miles and longer.

**Sway bar**: Sometimes called an "anti-roll bar." Bar used to resist or counteract the rolling force of the car body through the turns.

# T

**Template**: A device used to check the body shape and size, to ensure compliance with the rules. The template closely resembles the shape of the factory version of the car.

**Tight**: Also known as "understeer." A car is said to be tight if the front wheels lose traction before the rear wheels do. A tight race car doesn't seem able to steer sharply enough through the turns. Instead, the front end continues toward the wall.

**Toe**: Looking at the car from the front, the amount the tires are turned in or out. If you imagine your feet to be the two front tires of a racecar, standing with your toes together would represent toe-in. Standing with your heels together would represent toe-out.

**Track bar**: See Panhard Bar.

**Trading paint**: Slang term used to describe aggressive driving involving a lot of bumping and rubbing.

**Trailing arm**: A rear suspension piece holding the rear axle firmly fore and aft yet allowing it to travel up and down.

**Trioval**: A racetrack that has a "hump" or "fifth turn" in addition to the standard four corners. Not to be confused with a triangle-shaped speedway, which has only three distinct corners.

# V

**Victory lane**: Sometimes called the "winner's circle." The spot on each racetrack's infield where the race winner parks for the celebration.

# W

**Wedge, round of**: Adjusting the handling of the car by altering pressure on the rear springs.

**Wedge**: Term that refers to the cross weight adjustment on a racecar.

**Window net**: A woven mesh that hangs across the driver's side window, to prevent the driver's head and limbs from being exposed during an accident.

# INSIDE THE COCKPIT

The cockpit of a NASCAR NEXTEL Cup Series stock car serves as the "weekend office" for NASCAR NEXTEL Cup Series drivers. Configured uniquely by each team, it features an extensive army of safety features, as well as instrument gauges that allow the driver to monitor the car's performance.

Source: NASCAR

**1 Main Switch Panel**
Contains switches for starter, ignition and cooling fans

**2 Tachometer**
Monitors revolutions per minute (RPMs) of engine, assisting driver in selecting gears and monitoring engine power

**3 Engine Gauge Cluster**
Monitors engine oil pressure, water temperature, oil temperature, voltage and fuel pressure

**4 Auxiliary Switches**
Can serve a number of purposes, including turning on the backup ignition system, ventilating fans or helmet cooling system

**5 Master Switch**
Shuts down electrical system in emergency situations

**6 Ignition Kill Switch**
Shuts off engine in emergency situation

**7 Radio Button**
Controls communication to pits and race spotter

**8 Gearshift**
Controls four-speed manual transmission

**9 Safety Seat**
Provides extra support and protection for head, shoulders, ribs and lower extremities

**10 Head and Neck Restraint**
NASCAR mandates the use of a head-and-neck restraint system, either the approved HANS Device or Hutchens Device, for all drivers competing in any of NASCAR's three national series (NASCAR NEXTEL Cup Series, NASCAR Busch Series, NASCAR Craftsman Truck Series), as well as its touring series

**11 Window Net**
Keeps a driver's head and limbs inside the car during accidents

**12 Rearview Mirror**

**13 Fresh Air Vent**
Directs outside air into the driving compartment

**14 Main Rearview Mirror**

**15 Fire Extinguisher**

**16 Seat Belt Harness**

**17 Fire Extinguisher Switch**
Discharges fire-suppressing chemicals into the driving compartment

**18 Fire Extinguisher Discharge Nozzle**

**19 Helmet Hook**

# ⫽⫽⫽NASCAR. HAND SIGNALS (A+B=C)

NASCAR introduced in 2004, hand signals for officials in its three national series—NASCAR's NEXTEL Cup Series, NASCAR Busch Series and NASCAR Craftsman Truck Series—to convey some of the basic penalties to the competitors as well as its fans both at the track and watching on television.

Much like other major sports where the officials signal violations, the officials in NASCAR's three national series use hand signals to identify the infractions. As shown here, the officials—through the use of hand signals—convey who or what is responsible for the penalty: A—the driver, team or equipment; B—what is the extent of the penalty (15 seconds, 1 lap, pass through, stop and go, or tail end of the longest line); and C—the specific violation.

The system focuses on five common penalties that occur in the pits (pitting out of the box, non-compliant refueling, too many men over the wall, removing equipment and over the wall too soon) and has the ability to expand in the future. The system debuted in 2004 during Speed Weeks at Daytona International Speedway with the Budweiser Shootout.

## A - CATEGORY SIGNALS

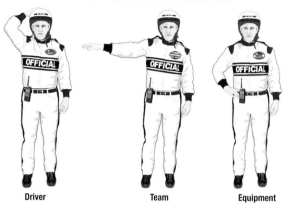

Driver     Team     Equipment

## B - CATEGORY SIGNALS

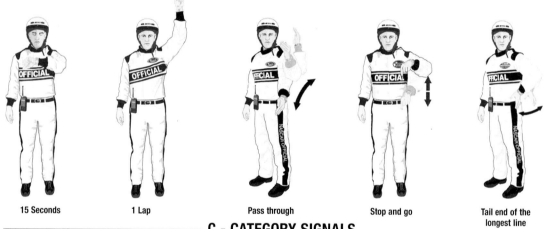

15 Seconds     1 Lap     Pass through     Stop and go     Tail end of the longest line

## C - CATEGORY SIGNALS

Non-compliant refueling     Removing equipment     Too many men over the wall     Pitting out of the box     Over the wall too soon

# ANATOMY OF A PIT STOP

The competitive balance found in the NASCAR NEXTEL Cup Series has made the execution of pit stops pivotal during each race. A miscue can be extremely costly for the team's fortunes, and a perfectly executed pit stop can aid the team's hopes of victory. Seven NASCAR NEXTEL Cup crew members are routinely allowed over the wall during pit stops per NASCAR rules. At times, NASCAR will inform teams that an eighth crew member will be allowed over the wall for a pit stop with the responsi-bility of cleaning the windshield. An average efficient pit stop that consists of the changing of all four tires and a full tank of fuel can take anywhere between 13 and 15 seconds. The number of pit stops during a race vary due to numerous factors—race length, caution flags, fuel mileage, tire wear and pit strategy to name a few. Below is a look at the pit crew and their responsibilities during a routine stop during a race.

**Catch Can Man**
Holds a can that collects over-flow from the fuel cell as it is being filled. He also signals the rest of the team that the refueling process is finished by raising his hand.

**Gas Man**
Empties two 12-gallon (81 pounds each) dump cans of fuel into the car's 22-gallon fuel cell.

**Support Crew**
Assists the "over the wall" crew by rolling them tires, handing them fuel and retrieving air hoses and wrenches. According to NASCAR rules, sup-port crew members must remain behind the pit wall during all stops.

**Rear Tire Carrier**
Assists the rear tire changer by handing him a new right-side tire that he has car-ried from behind the pit wall. He repeats the process on the left side of the car with a tire rolled to him by another crew member from behind the pit wall. May also adjust the rear jack bolt to change the car's handling.

**Extra Man**
On occasion, and at the discretion of NASCAR officials, an eighth or "extra man" is allowed over the wall to clean the windshield and assist the driver if necessary.

**Jackman**
Operates a 20-pound hydraulic jack that is used to raise the car for tire changes. After new tires are bolted onto the right side of the car, he drops the car to the ground and repeats the process on the left side.

**NASCAR Official**
Watches for rules violations and helps maintain pit lane safety.

**Rear Tire Changer**
First removes and replaces right rear tire using an air-powered impact wrench to loosen and tighten five lug nuts holding the tire rim in place. He then moves to the opposite side of the car to change the left rear tire.

**Front Tire Carrier**
Assists the front tire changer by handing him a new right-side tire that he has carried from behind the pit wall. He repeats the process on the left side of the car with a tire rolled to him by another crew member from behind the pit wall.

**Front Tire Changer**
First removes and replaces right front tire using an air-powered impact wrench to loosen and tighten five lug nuts holding the tire rim in place. He then moves to the opposite side of the car to change the left front tire.

# HANS DEVICE

As part of its continuing safety initiatives, NASCAR became the world's first major auto racing sanctioning body to mandate the use of an approved head and neck restraint by all drivers on every type of race circuit, which began with the 2002 season. This head and neck restraint—the HANS Device—helps reduce extreme head motion during accidents and sudden stops. The device is required for use in NASCAR's three national series—the NASCAR NEXTEL Cup Series, NASCAR Busch Series, and NASCAR Craftsman Truck Series—as well as its seven Touring Series. How the HANS Device works is illustrated below.

**With HANS Device**
Upon impact or sudden stop, the two tethers attached to a specially designed shoulder harness help keep the driver's head and neck in a stationary, upright position.

**Head Security**
Tethers are attached from the HANS collar to both sides of the driver's helmet.

Driver's standard safety belts overlap HANS shoulder harness, securing it in place.

Safety belt camlock.

**Without HANS Device**
Unrestrained, the head and neck of a driver moves forward and/or to the side as the rest of his body and his car decelerate during impact orsudden stop.

# NASCAR Ladder System

From the sport's "grassroots" in the NASCAR Dodge Weekly Series, to the "developmental series" in NASCAR's regional touring divisions and the sensational NASCAR Toyota All-Star Showdown, the sport's local and regional divisions include a variety of opportunities for competitors to build their racing careers.

## NASCAR Dodge Weekly Series

At more than 70 short tracks operating across the country on a weekly basis, the NASCAR Dodge Weekly Series is the true foundation of NASCAR. An early training ground for drivers, crew members and officials, this series also creates hometown heroes for the fans.

A wide variety of race cars can be found in this series—Late Model Stock Cars, Modifieds, Street Stocks, Trucks, Dirt Late Models, Sportsman and others. Drivers compete at their home tracks for local prizes, as well as a regional and national championship and a share of the $1.7 million championship point fund. Dodge, the Official Automobile of NASCAR, has sponsored the series since 2002.

Participating tracks are divided into geographic regions, offering teams and drivers at each facility a chance to compete against weekly stars from other area tracks—without leaving their home tracks. NASCAR's Competition Performance Index (CPI) rates drivers based on their on-track performance and determines the championship standings at the end of the season.

Since it was founded in 1982, the NASCAR Dodge Weekly Series has been the starting point for many of today's top drivers. Greg Biffle, Clint Bowyer, Jeff and Ward Burton, Kurt Busch, Stacy Compton, Dale Earnhardt Jr., Jeff Green, Kevin Harvick, Bobby Labonte, Jamie McMurray, Scott Riggs, Elliott Sadler and Brian Vickers began their careers in the NASCAR Dodge Weekly Series.

## NASCAR AutoZone Elite Division
### Midwest Series · Northwest Series · Southeast Series · Southwest Series

Four separate series—using identical racecars—comprise this division, which is designed to serve as a local driver's first step toward NASCAR's three national series. The four participating series compete on short tracks, superspeedways and road courses, providing opportunities for teams and drivers to sharpen their skills and work toward their career goals. AutoZone, the nation's leading auto parts retailer, joined as the title sponsor of this division beginning in 2004.

The NASCAR AutoZone Elite Division features 2,900-pound racecars using metal or fiberglass bodies, powered by 350 to 358 cubic-inch engines. The cars have a wheelbase between 101 and 105 inches and are driven on Hoosier bias-ply racing tires.

Midwest Series events are scheduled primarily throughout Illinois, Minnesota and Wisconsin, and as far west as Colorado. Stretching across Washington, Idaho and Montana, the Northwest Series was originally founded in 1985, making it one of the oldest of the four series in the NASCAR AutoZone Elite Division. 2002 NASCAR Busch Series champion Greg Biffle was a standout competitor in the Northwest Series in the late 1990s.

The Southeast Series covers Kentucky, Tennessee, Alabama, South Carolina and Virginia as its home territory. Matt Kenseth, the 2003 NASCAR NEXTEL Cup Series champion, used this series—formerly known as the All Pro Series—as a stepping stone during his rise to stardom in the late 1990s.

The Southwest Series covers Arizona and California, while also venturing into Colorado for select events. Kurt Busch, Kevin Harvick, Matt Crafton and Ron Hornaday Jr. are some of this series' famous alumni.

## NASCAR Grand National Division
### Busch North Series · West Series

When NASCAR realigned its regional touring divisions to create a two-tier driver developmental system, the Busch North Series was combined with the (formerly Winston) West Series to form the NASCAR Grand National Division. Although the name has been a part of NASCAR since the beginning—NASCAR Grand National Division was the original name of what is now the NASCAR NEXTEL Cup Series—this was a brand-new direction for the sanctioning body.

These cars are powered by 350 to 358 cubic-inch V-8 engines with a maximum compression ratio of 12:1. The cars have a 105-inch wheelbase, weigh 3,100 pounds and are equipped with Goodyear bias-ply tires.

The West Series enters its 52nd season in 2005. This series, which competes in Washington, Oregon, California, Nevada, Utah and Arizona, has been a launching pad for the careers of Brendan Gaughan, Harvick, Lance Hooper, Rick Carelli, Chad Little and many other drivers.

At race tracks in Maine, New Hampshire, Vermont, Massachusetts, Connecticut, New York, Pennsylvania, New Jersey and Delaware, the Busch North Series will stage its 18th season in 2004. New Jersey competitor Martin Truex Jr., the 2004 NASCAR Busch Series champion, is among the Busch North graduates.

## NASCAR Featherlite Modified Series

The Featherlite Modified Series will conduct its 20th season of competition in 2005. As the only open-wheeled division of NASCAR, the cars in this popular series are unique in many ways. Featherlite Modified Series cars weigh 2,610 pounds and have a wheelbase of 107 inches. Hoosier bias-ply tires are used to grip the track under the power provided by "small block" 350 to 360 cubic-inch engines.

The series competes throughout Maine, New Hampshire, Massachusetts, Connecticut, New York, Pennsylvania and New Jersey, on tracks ranging in size from a quarter-mile, to the 1.058-mile oval at New Hampshire International Speedway.

## Title sponsor: NEXTEL

In June of 2003, NASCAR and Nextel announced a 10-year series sponsorship agreement, beginging in 2004. The wireless communications leader realized the opportunities associated with the 56-year-old sanctioning body as well as the numerous ways that Nextel's technology could enhance the sport for fans, competitors, series officials, media, sponsors and tracks. Nextel's investment in the NASCAR NEXTEL Cup Series will go beyond the racetrack as it will activate several fan interactive, product, technology, community and charity initiatives. NEXTEL Communications Inc., a FORTUNE 300 company based in Reston, Va., is a leading provider of fully integrated wireless communications services. Nextel and Nextel Partners, Inc., currently serve 293 of the top 300 U.S. markets, where approximately 248 million people live or work.

**America Online**
Official Internet service provider

**AutoZone**
Official series sponsor

**Best Western**
Official hotel

**Budweiser**
Official beer

**Checkers**
Official burger

**Chevrolet (Monte Carlo)**
Official pace car

**Centrix**
Official auto finance partner

**Cintas**
Preferred uniform/uniform, first-aid supplier

**Coca-Cola**
Official soft drink

**Craftsman Tools**
Official tools

**Dasani**
Official water

**Daytona USA**
Official attraction

**Dodge Intrepid**
Official passenger car

**Domino's Pizza**
Official pizza delivery

**DuPont Automotive**
Official finish

**Duracell**
Official household battery

**Eastman Kodak**
Official film and single-use camera

**NOTE:** This list is subject to additions and changes.

**EXIDE**
Official automotive battery

**Featherlite-Vantare**
Official trailers and luxury coaches

**Ford Trucks**
Official truck

**Gillette**
Official shaving product

**Goody's**
Official pain reliever

**Goodyear**
Exclusive tire supplier

**The Home Depot**
Official home improvement warehouse

**International Truck & Engine Co.**
Official industrial tractor (semis)

**Kellogg's**
Official breakfast food/cereal

**Levis**
Official partner

**Minute Maid**
Official juice

**Mobil 1**
Official lubricant

**Nextel**
Official series sponsor

**Oral B**
Official oral care products

**POWERADE**
Official sports beverage

**Raybestos**
Official brakes/Northwest Series title sponsor

**Sunoco**
Official fuel

**Sunoco Aplus Convenience**
Official convenience store

**Sun Trust**
Official bank

**The Home Depot**
Official home improvement warehouse

**Toyota**
Official partner/manufacturer

**UPS**
Official delivery service

**U.S. Army**
Official armed service

**Visa**
Official credit card

**XM Satellite Radio**
Exclusive satellite radio service

## Promotional partners

The Compass Group; Combos; Country Crock; DuPont Tyvek; Hellmann's; Husqvarna; Masterfoods USA (M&Ms/Combos); Maxwell House; MeadWestvaco; Nabisco; Old Spice; Outback Steakhouse; Pedigree; Planter's; Ragu; Solo Cup; Tide; USG; Waste Management.

**NASCAR NEXTEL CUP SERIES**

LAP
TIME

POS

CHRONDEK

1

2

3

4

5

NEXTEL CUP SERIES

# NASCAR NEXTEL Cup Series 2005 lineup

| Car | Driver | Make | Sponsor | Team | Crew chief |
|-----|--------|------|---------|------|-----------|
| 0 | Mike Bliss | Chevrolet | NetZero HiSpeed | Haas CNC Racing | Robert Barker |
| 01 | Joe Nemechek | Chevrolet | U.S. Army | MB2 Motorsports | Ryan Pemberton |
| 2 | Rusty Wallace | Dodge | Miller Lite | Penske Racing | Larry Carter |
| 5 | Kyle Busch* | Chevrolet | Kellogg's | Hendrick Motorsports | Alan Gustafson |
| 6 | Mark Martin | Ford | Viagra | Roush Racing | Pat Tryson |
| 7 | Robby Gordon | Chevrolet | Fruit of the Loom | Robby Gordon/Jim Smith | Bob Temple |
| 07 | Dave Blaney | Chevrolet | Jack Daniels | Richard Childress Racing | Philippe Lopez |
| 8 | Dale Earnhardt Jr. | Chevrolet | Budweiser | Dale Earnhardt Inc. | Pete Rondeau |
| 9 | Kasey Kahne | Dodge | Dodge Dealers | Evernham Motorsports | Tommy Baldwin |
| 10 | Scott Riggs | Chevrolet | Valvoline | MBV Motorsports | Doug Randolph |
| 11 | Jason Leffler | Chevrolet | FedEx | Joe Gibbs Racing | Dave Rogers |
| 12 | Ryan Newman | Dodge | ALLTEL | Penske Racing | Matt Borland |
| 14 | John Andretti | Ford | APlus/Victory Brand | ppc Racing | Dave Charpentier |
| 15 | Michael Waltrip | Chevrolet | NAPA Auto Parts | Dale Earnhardt Inc. | Tony Eury Jr. |
| 16 | Greg Biffle | Ford | National Guard | Roush Racing | Doug Richert |
| 17 | Matt Kenseth | Ford | DeWalt Power Tools | Roush Racing | Robbie Reiser |
| 18 | Bobby Labonte | Chevrolet | Interstate Batteries | Joe Gibbs Racing | Steve Addington |
| 19 | Jeremy Mayfield | Dodge | Dodge Dealers | Evernham Motorsports | Richard Labbe |
| 20 | Tony Stewart | Chevrolet | Home Depot | Joe Gibbs Racing | Greg Zipadelli |
| 21 | Ricky Rudd | Ford | Motorcraft Quality Parts | Wood Brothers Racing | Michael McSwain |
| 22 | Scott Wimmer | Dodge | Caterpillar | Bill Davis Racing | Derrick Finley |
| 24 | Jeff Gordon | Chevrolet | DuPont | Hendrick Motorsports | Robbie Loomis |
| 25 | Brian Vickers | Chevrolet | GMAC | Hendrick Motorsports | Lance McGrew |
| 29 | Kevin Harvick | Chevrolet | GM Goodwrench Service | Richard Childress Racing | Todd Berrier |
| 31 | Jeff Burton | Chevrolet | Cingular Wireless | Richard Childress Racing | Kevin Hamlin |
| 32 | Bobby Hamilton Jr. | Chevrolet | Tide | PPI Motorsports | Harold Holly |
| 38 | Elliott Sadler | Ford | M&M's | Robert Yates Racing | Todd Parrott |
| 40 | Sterling Marlin | Dodge | Coors Light | Chip Ganassi Racing | Tony Glover |
| 41 | Casey Mears | Dodge | Target | Chip Ganassi Racing | Jimmy Elledge |
| 42 | Jamie McMurray | Dodge | Texaco/Havoline | Chip Ganassi Racing | Donnie Wingo |
| 43 | Jeff Green | Dodge | Cheerios/Betty Crocker | Petty Enterprises | Greg Steadman |
| 44 | Terry Labonte | Chevrolet | Kellogg's | Hendrick Motorsports | Peter Sospenzo |
| 45 | Kyle Petty | Dodge | Georgia Pacific/Brawny | Petty Enterprises | Bill Henderson |
| 48 | Jimmie Johnson | Chevrolet | Lowe's | Hendrick Motorsports | Chad Knaus |
| 49 | Ken Schrader | Dodge | Schwan's | BAM Racing | David Hyder |
| 77 | Travis Kvapil* | Dodge | Kodak | Jasper-Penske | Shane Wilson |
| 88 | Dale Jarrett | Ford | UPS | Robert Yates Racing | Mike Ford |
| 97 | Kurt Busch | Ford | Sharpie/Rubbermaid | Roush Racing | Jimmy Fennig |
| 99 | Carl Edwards | Ford | TBA | Roush Racing | Bob Osborne |

*Rookie.
NOTE: Some information subject to change.

DRIVERS

# John Andretti

**14**

**Date of birth:** March 12, 1963 **Hometown:** Indianapolis **Resides:** Mooresville, N.C. **Spouse:** Nancy **Children:** Jarrett, Olivia, Amelia **Height:** 5-5 **Weight:** 140 **Hobbies:** Playing the stock market

## NASCAR ACHIEVEMENTS

**First NASCAR Cup start:** October 3, 1993 (North Wilkesboro)
**Best points finish:** 11 (1998)
**Career victories:** 2—Daytona (97b), Martinsville (99a)
**First victory:** July 5, 1997 (Daytona)
**Last victory:** April 18, 1999 (Martinsville)
**Career poles:** 4—Atlanta (98a), Darlington (95b), Phoenix (99), Talladega (97a)
**First pole:** September 14, 1995 (Darlington)
**Best career finish:** 1  **Best career start:** 1

## FAST FACTS

- Began racing go-karts at age 11.
- Began open-wheel auto racing at age 16, attending Andre Pilette's driving school in Belgium with cousin Michael Andretti.
- USAC Midget Rookie of the Year in 1983.
- Made CART debut in 1987, finishing sixth at Elkhart Lake.
- Raced in the 24 Hours of LeMans in 1988 with uncle Mario Andretti and Michael.
- Raced in the Indianapolis 500 for the first time in 1988, finishing 21st.

### CAR FACTS

**Car:** No. 14 Ford
**Primary sponsor:** APlus/ Victory Brand
**Owner:** Greg Pollex
**Team:** ppc Racing
**Crew chief:** Dave Charpentier
**Engine builder:** Yates/Roush

- Co-drove to a Rolex 24 victory at Daytona International Speedway in 1989.
- Got first CART victory in 1991, at Gold Coast Grand Prix in Australia.
- Finished fifth in 1991 Indy 500.
- Reached the semifinals in his first NHRA Top Fuel event, in 1993.
- Andretti's father, Aldo, is Mario Andretti's twin brother.
- A.J. Foyt is his godfather.
- Younger brother Adam made his NASCAR debut in 2002, running three events in the NASCAR AutoZone Elite Division, Southwest Series.
- Graduated from Moravian College with a degree in business management.
- Thinks he would've been an investment banker or stock broker if he hadn't started racing.

## CAREER HIGHLIGHTS

- Andretti ran a limited schedule in 2004, driving some for Dale Earnhardt Inc. and some for ppc Racing, owned by Greg Pollex. Andretti replaced Dale Earnhardt Jr. at Pocono when Earnhardt had to get out of car because of painful burns. Andretti will run a full schedule in a ppc Racing Ford in 2005.
- After a disappointing 2002 and first half of 2003, he was fired by Petty Enterprises. He piloted an experimental 2004 car for Richard Childress Racing in the September Talladega race in 2003 and finished an impressive 15th place. He also ran races for Dale Earnhardt Inc. and CNC Racing in 2003.
- 2001 was marked by good qualifying performances and poor race finishes as Andretti's team, along with the other Petty Enterprises teams, switched to Dodges from Pontiacs. Highlight of the season was a second-place run in the spring race at Bristol. He lost to Elliott Sadler, who gained his first career victory, by .426 seconds.
- Slumped in 2000, with only two top 10s, his lowest total since 1994, his first full Cup season. After the season, crew chief Robbie Loomis left the team to join Jeff Gordon's team.
- Finished a career-best 11th in points in his first full season with Petty Enterprises in 1998, with three top fives and 10 top 10s. He matched those totals in 1999 and added a win (Martinsville), but he was bogged down by 10 DNFs and finished only 17th in points.
- Had 10 DNFs in his first 22 races in 1996 while driving for Kranefuss-Haas and moved to Cale Yarborough Racing. He found his first career NASCAR Cup victory with Yarborough in 1997 (fall Daytona race) and was strong in restrictor-plate races at Talladega in 1997, finishing third and fourth, and taking one pole. But his team lost its sponsorship, and Andretti moved to Petty Enterprises in 1998.
- Won his first career pole for the Southern 500 in 1995. Competed for the full season for Kranefuss-Haas Racing and finished 18th in points.
- In 1994, he became the first driver to run the Indianapolis 500 and the Coca-Cola 600 in the same day; he finished 10th at Indy and 36th in Charlotte.
- Began his career with Billy Hagan Racing in 1993, but after 18 races in 1994, the team had sponsorship problems. Andretti switched to Petty Enterprises in August 1994 and then joined Kranefuss-Hass for the 1995 and '96 seasons.

## CAREER STATISTICS

| Year | Car owner | Races | Champ. finish | Won | Top 5 | Top 10 | DNF | Poles | Money won |
|------|-----------|-------|---------------|-----|-------|--------|-----|-------|-----------|
| 1993 | Billy Hagan | 4 | 50 | 0 | 0 | 0 | 2 | 0 | $24,915 |
| 1994 | Billy Hagan | 18 | | 0 | 0 | 0 | 10 | 0 | $275,520 |
| | Petty Enterprises | 11 | 32 | 0 | 0 | 0 | 2 | 0 | $116,400 |
| 1995 | Michael Kranefuss | 31 | 18 | 0 | 1 | 5 | 7 | 1 | $593,542 |
| 1996 | Michael Kranefuss | 22 | | 0 | 1 | 1 | 10 | 0 | $571,481 |
| | Cale Yarborough | 8 | 31 | 0 | 1 | 1 | 1 | 0 | $117,030 |
| 1997 | Cale Yarborough | 32 | 23 | 1 | 3 | 4 | 3 | 1 | $1,143,725 |
| 1998 | Petty Enterpises | 33 | 11 | 0 | 3 | 10 | 5 | 1 | $1,838,379 |
| 1999 | Petty Enterprises | 34 | 17 | 1 | 3 | 10 | 10 | 1 | $2,001,832 |
| 2000 | Petty Enterprises | 34 | 23 | 0 | 0 | 2 | 7 | 0 | $2,035,902 |
| 2001 | Petty Enterprises | 35 | 31 | 0 | 1 | 2 | 4 | 0 | $2,873,184 |
| 2002 | Petty Enterprises | 36 | 28 | 0 | 0 | 1 | 7 | 0 | $2,954,229 |
| 2003 | Petty Enterprises | 14 | | 0 | 0 | 1 | 2 | 0 | $1,490,636 |
| | Gene Haas | 3 | | 0 | 0 | 0 | 0 | 0 | $142,770 |
| | Richard Childress | 1 | | 0 | 0 | 0 | 1 | 0 | $102,400 |
| | Teresa Earnhardt | 11 | 38 | 0 | 0 | 0 | 1 | 0 | $841,810 |
| 2004 | Teresa Earnhardt | 5 | | 0 | 0 | 0 | 1 | 0 | $519,261 |
| | A.J. Foyt | 4 | 45 | 0 | 0 | 0 | 0 | 0 | $233,125 |
| **TOTALS** | | **336** | | **2** | **13** | **37** | **73** | **4** | **$17,876,141** |

## 2004 RESULTS

| Race | Track | Start | Finish | Laps | Led | Status | Winnings | Rank |
|------|-------|-------|--------|------|-----|--------|----------|------|
| Daytona 500 | Daytona | 29 | 13 | 200/200 | 1 | Running | $235,287 | 12 |
| Subway 400 | N. Carolina | 39 | 29 | 388/393 | 0 | Running | $64,000 | 24 |
| Coca-Cola 600 | Lowe's | 25 | 19 | 398/400 | 0 | Running | $79,975 | 40 |
| Pepsi 400 | Daytona | 18 | 43 | 44/160 | 0 | Accident | $66,749 | 43 |
| Tropicana 400 | Chicago | 31 | 16 | 267/267 | 0 | Running | $73,250 | 41 |
| UAW-GM Quality 500 | Lowe's | 20 | 22 | 330/334 | 0 | Running | $56,675 | 47 |
| Bass Pro Shops MBNA 500 | Atlanta | 17 | 25 | 320/325 | 0 | Running | $69,000 | 46 |
| Checker Auto Parts 500 | Phoenix | 21 | 31 | 311/315 | 0 | Running | $52,300 | 45 |
| Ford 400 | Homestead | 23 | 20 | 271/271 | 0 | Running | $55,150 | 45 |

# Greg Biffle
## 16

**Date of birth:** December 23, 1969 **Hometown:** Vancouver, Wash. **Resides:** Mooresville, N.C. **Spouse:** Single **Children:** None **Height:** 5-9 **Weight:** 170 **Hobbies:** Flying, boating

**DRIVERS**

## NASCAR ACHIEVEMENTS

**First NASCAR Cup start:** April 28, 2002
**Best points finish:** 17 (2004)
**Career victories:** 3—Daytona (03b), Michigan (04b), Homestead (04)
**First victory:** July 5, 2003 (Daytona)
**Last victory:** November 21, 2004 (Homestead)
**Career poles:** 1—Daytona (04a)
**First pole:** February 15, 2004 (Daytona)
**Best career finish:** 1 **Best career start:** 1

## FAST FACTS

● A superb example of NASCAR's developmental system, he progressed through every level in NASCAR racing before making his NASCAR Cup debut in 2002.
● Was the 2002 Busch Series champion.
● Named 2001 Busch Series Rookie of the Year.
● Won 2000 NASCAR Craftsman Truck Series championship.
● Won nine NASCAR Craftsman Truck Series

## CAR FACTS

**Car:** No. 16 Ford
**Primary sponsor:** National Guard/Subway
**Owner:** Jack Roush
**Team:** Roush Racing
**Crew chief:** Doug Richert
**Engine builder:** Karl Bausman

races in 1999 and finished second in points.
● Was the 1998 NASCAR Craftsman Truck Series Rookie of the Year.
● Participated in the Raybestos Brakes Northwest Series in 1997, capturing one victory.
● Competed in the NASCAR Weekly Racing Series presented by Dodge from 1994-97, winning Late Model track championships at Tri City Raceway in West Richland, Wash., and at Portland (Ore.) Speedway.
● Is the only driver to win both the NASCAR Craftsman Truck Series and the NASCAR Busch Series championships; also is the only driver to win Raybestos Rookie of the Year awards in both series.
● Gave Roush Racing its first NASCAR championship when he won the 2000 trucks title.

## CAREER HIGHLIGHTS

● Biffle had an up-and-down sophomore year in 2004. He showed that when he has a fast car, he gets to the front and stays there. He ended the season on a positive note, leading the most laps and winning at Homestead. Biffle won the second race at Michigan by holding off a charging Mark Martin in a day dominated by Roush Racing Fords. He needs to work on restrictor-plate racing—his average finish was 21.5. He could surprise in 2005.

- His 20th-place points finish in 2003 is more impressive when you consider he missed a race, failing to qualify in Las Vegas. He got his first win, in a night race at Daytona in July, by holding off teammates Jeff Burton and Bobby Labonte in the closing laps. He finished second to Jamie McMurray for Raybestos Rookie of the Year honors.

- Qualified in the top five in three events he ran in 2002. He made four starts subbing for Bobby Hamilton, two starts for Petty Enterprises and one for Roush Racing

## CAREER STATISTICS

| Year | Car owner | Races | Champ. finish | Won | Top 5 | Top 10 | DNF | Poles | Money won |
|------|-----------|-------|---------------|-----|-------|--------|-----|-------|-----------|
| 2002 | Jack Roush | 1 | | 0 | 0 | 0 | 0 | 0 | $80,059 |
| | Andy Petree | 4 | | 0 | 0 | 0 | 1 | 0 | $218,700 |
| | Petty Enterprises | 2 | 48 | 0 | 0 | 0 | 0 | 0 | $96,014 |
| 2003 | Jack Roush | 35 | 20 | 1 | 3 | 6 | 6 | 0 | $2,805,673 |
| 2004 | Jack Roush | 36 | 17 | 2 | 4 | 8 | 5 | 1 | $4,092,877 |
| TOTALS | | 78 | | 3 | 7 | 14 | 12 | 1 | $7,293,323 |

## 2004 RESULTS

| Race | Track | Start | Finish | Laps | Led | Status | Winnings | Rank |
|------|-------|-------|--------|------|-----|--------|----------|------|
| Daytona 500 | Daytona | 1 | 12 | 200/200 | 0 | Running | $249,312 | 13 |
| Subway 400 | N. Carolina | 10 | 23 | 390/393 | 0 | Running | $69,185 | 14 |
| UAW-DaimlerChrysler 400 | Las Vegas | 9 | 40 | 23/267 | 0 | Engine | $71,750 | 27 |
| Golden Corral 500 | Atlanta | 13 | 8 | 325/325 | 2 | Running | $74,000 | 23 |
| Carolina Dodge Dealers 400 | Darlington | 3 | 12 | 293/293 | 3 | Running | $67,945 | 18 |
| Food City 500 | Bristol | 3 | 12 | 500/500 | 58 | Running | $84,890 | 16 |
| Samsung/RadioShack 500 | Texas | 4 | 31 | 318/334 | 0 | Engine | $79,775 | 19 |

| Race | Track | Start | Finish | Laps | Led | Status | Winnings | Rank |
|------|-------|-------|--------|------|-----|--------|----------|------|
| Advance Auto Parts 500 | Martinsville | 24 | 35 | 445/500 | 0 | Running | $62,650 | 21 |
| Aaron's 499 | Talladega | 18 | 15 | 188/188 | 1 | Running | $86,480 | 20 |
| Auto Club 500 | California | 18 | 33 | 223/250 | 28 | Running | $74,500 | 23 |
| Chevy Amer. Revolution 400 | Richmond | 10 | 21 | 398/400 | 0 | Running | $69,100 | 21 |
| Coca-Cola 600 | Lowe's | 30 | 21 | 397/400 | 0 | Running | $86,025 | 21 |
| MBNA 400 'A Salute to Heroes' | Dover | 40 | 26 | 370/400 | 0 | Running | $74,005 | 25 |
| Pocono 500 | Pocono | 9 | 11 | 200/200 | 2 | Running | $71,240 | 23 |
| DHL 400 | Michigan | 13 | 23 | 200/200 | 0 | Running | $72,190 | 23 |
| Dodge/Save Mart 350 | Infineon | 7 | 13 | 110/110 | 0 | Running | $76,475 | 22 |
| Pepsi 400 | Daytona | 9 | 31 | 159/160 | 0 | Running | $79,125 | 24 |
| Tropicana 400 | Chicago | 5 | 20 | 267/267 | 0 | Running | $84,400 | 23 |
| Siemens 300 | New Hamp. | 16 | 35 | 270/300 | 0 | Accident | $66,600 | 25 |
| Pennsylvania 500 | Pocono | 19 | 4 | 200/200 | 0 | Running | $98,430 | 23 |
| Brickyard 400 | Indianapolis | 35 | 6 | 161/161 | 0 | Running | $188,175 | 21 |
| Sirius at the Glen | Watkins Glen | 21 | 35 | 71/90 | 0 | Engine | $61,175 | 24 |
| GFS Marketplace 400 | Michigan | 24 | 1 | 200/200 | 73 | Running | $190,180 | 18 |
| Sharpie 500 | Bristol | 10 | 11 | 499/500 | 0 | Running | $92,165 | 18 |
| Pop Secret 500 | California | 7 | 36 | 213/250 | 0 | Accident | $84,900 | 22 |
| Chevy Rock & Roll 400 | Richmond | 8 | 8 | 400/400 | 0 | Running | $74,580 | 20 |
| Sylvania 300 | New Hamp. | 20 | 28 | 297/300 | 0 | Running | $70,675 | 21 |
| MBNA America 400 | Dover | 19 | 11 | 399/400 | 0 | Running | $75,630 | 19 |
| EA Sports 500 | Talladega | 12 | 28 | 187/188 | 0 | Running | $73,625 | 21 |
| Banquet 400 | Kansas | 6 | 3 | 267/267 | 64 | Running | $147,825 | 18 |
| UAW-GM Quality 500 | Lowe's | 18 | 33 | 265/334 | 0 | Running | $63,550 | 22 |
| Subway 500 | Martinsville | 21 | 17 | 500/500 | 0 | Running | $68,925 | 20 |
| Bass Pro Shops MBNA 500 | Atlanta | 5 | 10 | 324/325 | 0 | Running | $95,735 | 21 |
| Checker Auto Parts 500 | Phoenix | 23 | 13 | 315/315 | 0 | Running | $70,225 | 20 |
| Southern 500 | Darlington | 19 | 24 | 365/367 | 8 | Running | $69,550 | 21 |
| Ford 400 | Homestead | 2 | 1 | 271/271 | 116 | Running | $314,850 | 17 |

# Dave Blaney

07

**Date of birth:** October 24, 1962 **Hometown:** Hartford, Ohio **Resides:** Trinity, N.C. **Spouse:** Lisa **Children:** Emma, Ryan, Erin **Height:** 5-8 **Weight:** 170 **Hobbies:** Basketball, working with his World of Outlaws sprint car team

## NASCAR ACHIEVEMENTS

**First NASCAR Cup start:** October 25, 1992 (Rockingham)
**Best points finish:** 19 (2002)
**Career victories:** 0
**Career poles:** 1—Rockingham (03a)
**Best career finish:** 3 **Best career start:** 1

## FAST FACTS

- Finished seventh in the NASCAR Busch Series in 1999, posting five top fives, 12 top 10s and four poles in 31 starts.
- Made his first NASCAR Busch Series start in 1998 and won one pole while competing in 20 races.

- Won the 1995 World of Outlaws championship and was-named that year's Sprint Car Driver of the Year.
- Was the runner-up in the World of Outlaws sprint car circuit in 1993, 1994, 1996 and 1997.
- Won the Syracuse Nationals at the New York State Fairgrounds in 1987 and 1993).
- Won the Pacific Coast

## CAR FACTS

**Car:** No. 07 Chevrolet
**Primary sponsor:** Jack Daniels
**Owner:** Richard Childress
**Team:** Richard Childress Racing
**Crew chief:** Philippe Lopez
**Engine builder:** Childress Racing

Nationals at Ascot Speedway (Calif.) in 1990.
- Posted 76 top five finishes in 85 races in sprints and modifieds in 1989.
- Won the Easter World Sprint Car championship in 1988 in Hagerstown, Md.
- Won first career World of Outlaws series race at Tri-City in '85.
- Won USAC Silver Crown championship in 1984, becoming the youngest driver to win that division.
- Won Rookie of the Year honors on the All-Star Circuit of Champions sprint series in 1983.
- Began professional racing career in 1981, racing sprint cars.
- Has competed in all three major sprint car associations— World of Outlaws National Challenge Series, United Sprint Association and All-Star Circuit of Champions.
- Owns a World of Outlaws team for which his brother, Dale, is the driver.
- Owns "Outlaw Driving Experience" racing school for sprint cars, which is based in Hartford, Ohio.
- Brother, Dale, played college basketball at West Virginia, was drafted by the L.A. Lakers and played in the NBA and CBA.
- Owns Sharon Speedway in Hartford, Ohio, with his family.
- Father, Lou, also raced sprint cars.

## CAREER HIGHLIGHTS

- Four accidents aside, Blaney posted impressive results considering he drove for different teams in different situations in cars manufactured by different companies. He posted top 15s in a Dodge owned by Bill Davis and in a Chevy owned by Richard Childress. Blaney will drive full time for Childress this season.
- Had a hot start in 2003 with three top 10 finishes in the first five races, including his first-ever top five, which vaulted him to as high as seventh in points. But Blaney had only one more top 10 finish and quickly dropped to the mid-20s and never made much progress from there.
- In 2002, his first season driving for Jasper Motorsports, Blaney cracked the top 20 with a 19th finish in points, the highest rank for a driver with no top five finishes that year. After the season, crew chief Ryan Pemberton left Blaney's team to work with Jerry Nadeau and MB2 Motorsports.
- In his final season with Bill Davis Racing in 2001, he had six top 10 finishes, including career-best sixths at Texas, Michigan and Homestead. He qualified a career-best third at Atlanta in November and led 70 laps before mechanical problems ruined a strong run.
- Never finished higher than 31st in points in his first two seasons with Davis. His best race finish in 1999 was 23rd, at Homestead. Blaney's 2000 season was an improvement: He finished with two tops 10s in the final three races and third in the rookie of the year standings. He would have scored a top five at Atlanta, but a late-race incident knocked him to 18th.

## CAREER STATISTICS

| Year | Car owner | Races | Champ. finish | Won | Top 5 | Top 10 | DNF | Poles | Money won |
|------|-----------|-------|---------------|-----|-------|--------|-----|-------|-----------|
| 1992 | Stanton Hover Jr. | 1 | 80 | 0 | 0 | 0 | 1 | 0 | $4,500 |
| 1999 | Bill Davis | 5 | 51 | 0 | 0 | 0 | 2 | 0 | $212,170 |
| 2000 | Bill Davis | 33 | 31 | 0 | 0 | 2 | 7 | 0 | $1,272,689 |
| 2001 | Bill Davis | 36 | 22 | 0 | 0 | 6 | 6 | 0 | $1,827,896 |
| 2002 | Doug Bawel | 36 | 19 | 0 | 0 | 5 | 3 | 0 | $2,978,593 |
| 2003 | Doug Bawel | 36 | 28 | 0 | 1 | 4 | 4 | 1 | $2,828,692 |
| 2004 | Bill Davis | 6 | | 0 | 0 | 0 | 2 | 0 | $608,932 |
| | Jim Smith | 1 | | 0 | 0 | 0 | 1 | 0 | $55,555 |
| | Richard Childress | 8 | | 0 | 0 | 0 | 1 | 0 | $667,293 |
| | Jack Roush | 1 | 38 | 0 | 0 | 0 | 1 | 0 | $88,087 |
| **TOTALS** | | **163** | | **0** | **1** | **17** | **28** | **1** | **$10,613,812** |

## 2004 RESULTS

| Race | Track | Start | Finish | Laps | Led | Status | Winnings | Rank |
|------|-------|-------|--------|------|-----|--------|----------|------|
| Daytona 500 | Daytona | 23 | 15 | 200/200 | 0 | Running | $232,762 | 15 |
| Golden Corral 500 | Atlanta | 14 | 11 | 325/325 | 0 | Running | $64,275 | 38 |
| Samsung/RadioShack 500 | Texas | 20 | 11 | 334/334 | 0 | Running | $106,250 | 38 |
| Aaron's 499 | Talladega | 42 | 39 | 81/188 | 0 | Accident | $62,150 | 38 |
| Chevy Amer. Revolution 400 | Richmond | 24 | 40 | 123/400 | 0 | Vibration | $55,555 | 37 |
| Coca-Cola 600 | Lowe's | 11 | 17 | 398/400 | 0 | Running | $82,450 | 37 |
| MBNA 400 'A Salute to Heroes' | Dover | 27 | 33 | 344/400 | 0 | Accident | $61,045 | 38 |
| Pocono 500 | Pocono | 29 | 29 | 191/200 | 0 | Running | $63,790 | 38 |
| DHL 400 | Michigan | 39 | 15 | 200/200 | 0 | Running | $75,415 | 38 |
| Pepsi 400 | Daytona | 23 | 15 | 160/160 | 1 | Running | $118,303 | 36 |
| Tropicana 400 | Chicago | 36 | 37 | 129/267 | 1 | Accident | $72,175 | 36 |
| Siemens 300 | New Hamp. | 14 | 33 | 295/300 | 0 | Running | $67,960 | 37 |
| Pennsylvania 500 | Pocono | 31 | 27 | 187/200 | 2 | Running | $64,615 | 37 |
| Brickyard 400 | Indianapolis | 38 | 21 | 161/161 | 0 | Running | $139,250 | 37 |
| Sirius at the Glen | Watkins Glen | 27 | 24 | 90/90 | 0 | Running | $65,785 | 35 |
| UAW-GM Quality 500 | Lowe's | 10 | 37 | 218/334 | 0 | Accident | $88,087 | 36 |

# Mike Bliss

**Date of birth:** April 5, 1965 **Hometown:** Milwaukie, Ore. **Resides:** Milwaukie, Ore. **Spouse:** Sue **Children:** Brittney **Height:** 6-1 **Weight:** 190 **Hobbies:** Boating, fishing

## NASCAR ACHIEVEMENTS

**First NASCAR Cup start:** September 27, 1998 (Martinsville)
**Best points finish:** 39
**Career victories:** 0
**Career poles:** 0
**Best career finish:** 4 **Best career start:** 7

## FAST FACTS

● Finished seventh in the NASCAR Busch Series in 1999, posting five top fives, 12 top 10s and four poles in 31 starts.

### CAR FACTS

**Car:** No. 0 Chevrolet
**Primary sponsor:** NetZero
**Owner:** Gene Haas
**Team:** Haas CNC Racing
**Crew chief:** Robert Barker
**Engine builder:** Hendrick Motorsports

● Made his first NASCAR Busch Series start in 1998 and won one pole and competed in 20 races.
● Won the 1995 World of Outlaws championship and was named that year's Sprint Car Driver of the Year.
● Won the 2002 NASCAR Craftsman Truck Series championship.
● Competed in the first NASCAR Craftsman Truck Series event.
● One of three drivers with a victory in six different NASCAR Craftsman Truck Series seasons.
● Won his first NASCAR Busch Series race in 2004, at Lowe's Motor Speedway in October.

## CAREER HIGHLIGHTS

● Bliss took over the driving duties of the No. 0 for the final two races of 2004 and ran well enough to land the ride for 2005. In four starts, he had a top five and a top 10—not bad.
● Finished fourth, his first top five, in 2004 in the Chevy Rock & Roll 400 at Richmond while driving for Joe Gibbs.
● Got his first top 10 finish at Talladega in 2000, driving the No. 27 car for Jack Birmingham.
● Finished the first two NASCAR Cup races he started in 1998, driving for Buz McCall.

### CAREER STATISTICS

| Year | Car owner | Races | Champ. finish | Won | Top 5 | Top 10 | DNF | Poles | Money won |
|------|-----------|-------|--------|-----|-----|-----|-----|-------|-----------|
| 1998 | Buz McCall | 2 | 58 | 0 | 0 | 0 | 0 | 0 | $32,520 |
| 1999 | Chuck Rider | 2 | 58 | 0 | 0 | 0 | 1 | 0 | $42,475 |
| 2000 | A.J. Foyt | 1 | | 0 | 0 | 0 | 0 | 0 | $103,996 |
| | Jack Birmingham | 24 | 39 | 0 | 0 | 1 | 8 | 0 | $849,952 |
| 2002 | Chip Ganassi | 1 | 64 | 0 | 0 | 0 | 0 | 0 | $81,942 |
| 2003 | Joe Gibbs | 1 | 65 | 0 | 0 | 0 | 0 | 0 | $65,300 |
| 2004 | Joe Gibbs | 2 | | 0 | 1 | 1 | 1 | 0 | $148,555 |
| | Gene Haas | 2 | 49 | 0 | 0 | 1 | 1 | 0 | $135,850 |
| **TOTALS** | | **35** | | **0** | **1** | **3** | **11** | **0** | **$1,460,590** |

### 2004 RESULTS

| Race | Track | Start | Finish | Laps | Led | Status | Winnings | Rank |
|------|-------|-------|--------|------|-----|--------|----------|------|
| Tropicana 400 | Chicago | 7 | 31 | 205/267 | 0 | Accident | $65,900 | 66 |
| Chevy Rock & Roll 400 | Richmond | 33 | 4 | 400/400 | 0 | Running | $82,655 | 52 |
| Southern 500 | Darlington . | 30 | 10 | 367/367 | 0 | Running | $86,750 | 49 |
| Ford 400 | Homestead | 12 | 40 | 145/271 | 0 | Accident | $49,100 | 49 |

**DRIVERS**

# Todd Bodine

**Date of birth:** February 27, 1964 **Hometown:** Chemung, N.Y. **Resides:** Concord, N.C. **Spouse:** Lynn **Children:** Ashlyn **Height:** 5-7 **Weight:** 190 **Hobbies:** Art

## NASCAR ACHIEVEMENTS

**First NASCAR Cup start:** August 9, 1992 (Watkins Glen)
**Best points finish:** 20 (1994)
**Career victories:** 0
**Career poles:** 5—Chicago (01), Las Vegas (02), Martinsville (01b), Pocono (01b), Watkins Glen (97)
**First pole:** August 19, 1997 (Watkins Glen)
**Best career finish:** 3 **Best career start:** 1

## FAST FACTS

● Finished 23rd in the 2002 NASCAR Busch Series, competing in

28 races with one win, six top fives and eight top 10s.

● Finished fourth in 2000 NASCAR Busch Series for second straight year.

● Finished second in 1997 and third in the 1996 NASCAR Busch Series.

● Won first NASCAR Busch Series race (Dover, 1991) in his 22nd start.

● Made his NASCAR Busch Series debut in 1986, in a car owned by "Tiger" Tom Pistone.

● Began his racing career driving modifieds from 1983-85 at tracks such as Stafford Springs (Conn.) and Seekonk, (Mass.).

● Worked as a fabricator for Bobby Hillin's team and drove in the sportsman series before moving into NASCAR Busch Series rides.

● Considers Friday the 13th his lucky day. He married his wife, Lynn, on Friday, November 13, 1987.

● Growing up, spent Saturday nights working at family-owned Chemung Speedrome in his hometown of Chemung, N.Y.

Drove late models, worked at Buck Baker Driving School and hung bodies on cars for Billy Standridge to pay the bills.

## CAREER HIGHLIGHTS

● Bodine didn't have a full-time ride entering 2004 but drove in the NASCAR NEXTEL Cup Series, the NASCAR Busch Series and NASCAR Craftsman Truck Series, demonstrating his versatility. He won back-to-back races in the NASCAR Craftsman Truck Series. ... Drove most of his NASCAR NEXTEL Cup Series races for Don Arnold, who also owned the winning truck, but never finished better than 23rd in NASCAR NEXTEL Cup races.

● Started only six races because of funding problems in 2003. Lost primary sponsor, Hooters Restaurants, in mid-June. Started the spring races at Atlanta, Darlington and Bristol. Also started at Texas, the June race at Dover and qualified for the June race at Michigan. ... Season ended following a final-practice accident at Michigan in which he suffered a broken right clavicle. Older brother Geoffrey started in his place on Sunday. Best finish was 24th at Bristol.

● Nearly shut down the team in 2002 before securing sponsorship from Hooters Restaurants in March.

● Set fastest time for a NASCAR Cup driver in history of Indianapolis Motor Speedway, in 2000, a record that stood until 2003.

● Started all 32 races in 1998 and earned over $1 million for the first time in his career. ... Edged out Joe Nemechek by 10 points for the 25th and final paying position of the points fund.

● Purchased the once-heralded No. 11 team from legendary car owner Junior Johnson in 1996 and began first season as an owner/driver.

● Competed in his sixth and final season for car owner and famed drag racer Kenny Bernstein in 1994. ... Recorded six top 10 finishes. ... Finished second in the

first Brickyard 400 at Indianapolis Motor Speedway.

● Drove five races with a fractured left wrist in 1993 after a practice accident at Dover in the fall.

● Enjoyed career-best season in 1990 driving in his first year for owner Kenny Bernstein and paired with crew chief Larry McReynolds. Posted one win, five top fives and nine top 10 finishes. Charged from the 20th starting position to win his only career race at North Wilkesboro. Won his first pole at Charlotte.

## CAREER STATISTICS

| Year | Car owner | Races | Champ. finish | Won | Top 5 | Top 10 | DNF | Poles | Money won |
|------|-----------|-------|---------------|-----|-------|--------|-----|-------|-----------|
| 1992 | Frank Cicci | 1 | 87 | 0 | 0 | 0 | 1 | 0 | $3,485 |
| 1993 | B. Rahilly/B. Mock | 10 | 40 | 0 | 0 | 0 | 5 | 0 | $63,245 |
| 1994 | Butch Mock | 30 | 20 | 0 | 2 | 7 | 6 | 0 | $494,316 |
| 1995 | Butch Mock | 28 | 33 | 0 | 1 | 3 | 10 | 0 | $664,620 |
| 1996 | Bill Elliott | 4 | | 0 | 0 | 1 | 1 | 0 | $92,945 |
| | David Blair | 3 | 40 | 0 | 0 | 0 | 0 | 0 | $32,800 |
| | Andy Petree | 3 | | 0 | 0 | 0 | 0 | 0 | $72,780 |
| 1997 | Geoffrey Bodine | 1 | 52 | 0 | 0 | 0 | 1 | 0 | $25,400 |
| | Rick Hendrick | 1 | | 0 | 0 | 0 | 0 | 0 | $58,500 |
| | Frank Cicci | 1 | | 0 | 0 | 0 | 1 | 1 | $16,465 |
| | Bob Hancher | 1 | | 0 | 0 | 0 | 0 | 0 | $13,160 |
| | Buz McCall | 1 | | 0 | 0 | 0 | 1 | 0 | $12,270 |
| 1998 | Joe Falk | 7 | 41 | 0 | 1 | 1 | 1 | 0 | $194,865 |
| | Bob Hancher | 7 | | 0 | 0 | 1 | 1 | 0 | $183,901 |
| 1999 | Jack Birmingham | 7 | 46 | 0 | 0 | 0 | 2 | 0 | $208,382 |
| 2000 | Joe Falk | 2 | | 0 | 0 | 1 | 1 | 0 | $52,745 |
| | Rick Hendrick | 1 | 49 | 0 | 0 | 0 | 0 | 0 | $117,260 |
| | Travis Carter | 1 | | 0 | 0 | 0 | 0 | 0 | $39,300 |
| | Frank Cicci | 1 | | 0 | 0 | 0 | 1 | 0 | $24,760 |
| 2001 | Travis Carter | 35 | 29 | 0 | 2 | 2 | 12 | 3 | $1,740,315 |
| 2002 | Travis Carter | 24 | 38 | 0 | 1 | 4 | 9 | 1 | $1,879,767 |
| 2003 | Travis Carter | 35 | 31 | 0 | 0 | 1 | 9 | 0 | $2,521,724 |
| 2004 | William Edwards | 8 | | 0 | 0 | 0 | 7 | 0 | $455,749 |
| | John Carter | 2 | | 0 | 0 | 0 | 2 | 0 | $109,370 |
| | Don Arnold | 11 | 41 | 0 | 0 | 0 | 9 | 0 | $710,411 |
| **TOTALS** | | **225** | | **0** | **7** | **21** | **80** | **5** | **$9,788,585** |

## 2004 RESULTS

| Race | Track | Start | Finish | Laps | Led | Status | Winnings | Rank |
|------|-------|-------|--------|------|-----|--------|----------|------|
| Golden Corral 500 | Atlanta | 38 | 41 | 16/325 | 0 | Engine | $54,800 | 52 |
| Carolina Dodge Dealers 400 | Darlington | 35 | 40 | 33/293 | 2 | Rear end | $51,015 | 51 |
| Samsung/RadioShack 500 | Texas | 36 | 43 | 5/334 | 0 | Engine | $63,634 | 51 |
| Advance Auto Parts 500 | Martinsville | 43 | 39 | 151/500 | 0 | Brakes | $54,440 | 49 |
| Auto Club 500 | California | 41 | 34 | 209/250 | 2 | Engine | $65,375 | 48 |
| Chevy American Revolution 400 | Richmond | 36 | 33 | 373/400 | 0 | Running | $56,850 | 43 |
| Pocono 500 | Pocono | 28 | 42 | 11/200 | 0 | Overheat | $51,275 | 43 |
| DHL 400 | Michigan | 38 | 36 | 170/200 | 0 | Vibration | $58,095 | 42 |
| Siemens 300 | New Hamp. | 40 | 41 | 153/300 | 0 | Engine | $57,850 | 43 |
| Pennsylvania 500 | Pocono | 37 | 38 | 72/200 | 0 | Engine | $51,785 | 42 |
| Brickyard 400 | Indianapolis | 41 | 41 | 16/161 | 0 | Vibration | $116,320 | 41 |
| Sirius at the Glen | Watkins Glen | 36 | 41 | 7/90 | 0 | Brakes | $52,780 | 41 |
| GFS Marketplace 400 | Michigan | 36 | 43 | 11/200 | 0 | Overheat | $56,822 | 41 |
| Sharpie 500 | Bristol | 40 | 23 | 495/500 | 3 | Running | $76,785 | 40 |
| Chevy Rock & Roll 400 | Richmond | 40 | 43 | 9/400 | 0 | Accident | $56,303 | 40 |
| Sylvania 300 | New Hamp. | 36 | 23 | 298/300 | 0 | Running | $65,425 | 40 |
| Banquet 400 | Kansas | 20 | 39 | 66/267 | 0 | Steering | $63,765 | 41 |
| Subway 500 | Martinsville | 40 | 43 | 1/500 | 0 | Accident | $52,891 | 41 |
| Bass Pro Shops MBNA 500 | Atlanta | 24 | 39 | 222/325 | 0 | Handling | $65,150 | 41 |
| Checker Auto Parts 500 | Phoenix | 36 | 43 | 11/315 | 0 | Vibration | $50,447 | 41 |
| Southern 500 | Darlington | 38 | 39 | 143/367 | 0 | Accident | $53,725 | 41 |

DRIVERS

# Jeff Burton
## 31

**Date of birth:** June 26, 1967 **Hometown:** South Boston, Va.
**Resides:** Cornelius, N.C. **Spouse:** Kim **Children:** Kimberle,
Harrison **Height:** 5-7 **Weight:** 155 **Hobbies:** Golf, boating

## NASCAR ACHIEVEMENTS

**First NASCAR Cup start:** July 11, 1993 (New Hampshire)
**Best points finish:** 3 (2000)
**Career victories:** 18—Charlotte (99a, 01a), Darlington (99a, 99b, 00a), Daytona (00b), Las Vegas (99, 00), Martinsville (97b), New Hampshire (97a, 98a, 99a, 00b), Phoenix (00, 01), Richmond (98b), Rockingham (99b), Texas (97)
**First victory:** April 6, 1997 (Texas)
**Last victory:** October 28, 2001 (Phoenix)
**Career poles:** 2—Michigan (96b), Richmond (00b)
**First pole:** August 16, 1996 (Michigan)
**Best career finish:** 1 **Best career start:** 1

## FAST FACTS

● Continues to compete part time in the NASCAR Busch Series.
● Won five NASCAR Busch Series races in 2002, in 13 starts.
● Won seven of 21 late model stock races at South Boston Speedway in 1988 and was voted the track's most popular driver.
● Began racing in the pure stock class at South Boston in 1984.
● Was a two-time Virginia state go-kart champion and finished second four times; began racing go-karts at age 8.
● Was an outstanding high school athlete in several sports.

## CAREER HIGHLIGHTS

● His 2004 season proved an old racing cliche: Sometimes you just have to be in the right situation. He left his No. 99 team at Roush Racing for the No. 30 car, and results for both teams greatly improved. The switch wasn't that easy, though—in his first race in the No. 30, he mistakenly approached the No. 99's pit box. It's interesting that Burton is with Childress—the late Dale Earnhardt, who drove for Childress, named Burton as a driver to replace himself. Burton will stay with Childress in 2005 but will drive the No. 31 car.
● In 2002, finished outside of the top 10 in points and was winless for the first time since 1996. Similar disappointment followed in 2003 after a promising start to the season. He was ninth in points after four races, but engine failures and inconsistent performances left Burton with his second straight 12th-place finish in points and again without a victory in the season.
● Won the Coca-Cola 600 at Charlotte in May 2001, his second victory in three seasons in NASCAR Cup's longest event. He also won in 1999.
● Finished a personal-best third in points in 2000. Two wins that season (Las Vegas and Darlington) came ahead of his brother, Ward, who finished second.
● Swept the Darlington races in 1999.
● Won at least one New Hampshire race for four straight seasons (1997-2000).
● Joined Roush Racing in 1996 and experienced a breakthrough year in 1997, winning his first race in April at Texas, then finding victory lane at New Hampshire and Martinsville. He punctuated his emergence with a fourth-place finish in series points.
● Won Raybestos Rookie of the Year honors in 1994.

### CAR FACTS

**Car:** No. 31 Chevrolet
**Primary sponsor:** Cingular
**Owner:** Richard Childress
**Team:** Richard Childress Racing
**Crew chief:** Kevin Hamlin
**Engine builder:** Childress Racing

### CAREER STATISTICS

| Year | Car owner | Races | Champ. finish | Won | Top 5 | Top 10 | DNF | Poles | Money won |
|---|---|---|---|---|---|---|---|---|---|
| 1993 | Filbert Martocci | 1 | 83 | 0 | 0 | 0 | 1 | 0 | $9,550 |
| 1994 | William Stavola | 30 | 24 | 0 | 2 | 3 | 7 | 0 | $594,700 |
| 1995 | William Stavola | 29 | 32 | 0 | 1 | 2 | 6 | 0 | $630,770 |
| 1996 | Jack Roush | 30 | 13 | 0 | 6 | 12 | 1 | 1 | $884,303 |
| 1997 | Jack Roush | 32 | 4 | 3 | 13 | 18 | 1 | 0 | $2,296,614 |
| 1998 | Jack Roush | 33 | 5 | 2 | 18 | 23 | 4 | 0 | $2,626,987 |
| 1999 | Jack Roush | 34 | 5 | 6 | 18 | 23 | 3 | 0 | $5,725,399 |
| 2000 | Jack Roush | 34 | 3 | 4 | 15 | 22 | 2 | 1 | $5,959,439 |
| 2001 | Jack Roush | 36 | 10 | 2 | 8 | 16 | 1 | 0 | $4,230,737 |
| 2002 | Jack Roush | 36 | 12 | 0 | 5 | 14 | 5 | 0 | $4,244,856 |
| 2003 | Jack Roush | 36 | 12 | 0 | 3 | 11 | 4 | 0 | $4,384,752 |
| 2004 | Jack Roush | 21 | 0 | 0 | 1 | 3 | 5 | 0 | $2,444,513 |
|  | Richard Childress | 15 | 18 | 0 | 1 | 1 | 1 | 0 | $1,250,562 |
| **TOTALS** |  | **367** |  | **17** | **91** | **150** | **41** | **2** | **$35,283,182** |

### 2004 RESULTS

| Race | Track | Start | Finish | Laps | Led | Status | Winnings | Rank |
|---|---|---|---|---|---|---|---|---|
| Daytona 500 | Daytona | 11 | 42 | 25/200 | 0 | Engine | $239,554 | 42 |
| Subway 400 | N. Carolina | 28 | 37 | 344/393 | 0 | Engine | $88,592 | 42 |
| UAW-DaimlerChrysler 400 | Las Vegas | 28 | 13 | 267/267 | 1 | Running | $119,417 | 31 |
| Golden Corral 500 | Atlanta | 32 | 20 | 322/325 | 0 | Running | $96,182 | 30 |

## 2004 RESULTS

| Race | Track | Start | Finish | Laps | Led | Status | Winnings | Rank |
|------|-------|-------|--------|------|-----|--------|----------|------|
| Carolina Dodge Dealers 400 | Darlington | 33 | 11 | 293/293 | 0 | Running | $95,092 | 27 |
| Food City 500 | Bristol | 31 | 38 | 138/500 | 0 | Too slow | $99,977 | 30 |
| Samsung/RadioShack 500 | Texas | 23 | 27 | 330/334 | 0 | Running | $113,842 | 30 |
| Advance Auto Parts 500 | Martinsville | 27 | 25 | 497/500 | 0 | Running | $93,417 | 33 |
| Aaron's 499 | Talladega | 25 | 7 | 188/188 | 0 | Running | $126,572 | 28 |
| Auto Club 500 | California | 30 | 26 | 249/250 | 0 | Running | $104,317 | 29 |
| Chevy Amer. Revolution 400 | Richmond | 17 | 14 | 399/400 | 0 | Running | $97,342 | 29 |
| Coca-Cola 600 | Lowe's | 34 | 22 | 397/400 | 0 | Running | $110,517 | 29 |
| MBNA 400 'A Salute to Heroes' | Dover | 22 | 4 | 400/400 | 15 | Running | $149,172 | 24 |
| Pocono 500 | Pocono | 39 | 24 | 196/200 | 0 | Engine | $90,632 | 25 |
| DHL 400 | Michigan | 17 | 13 | 200/200 | 0 | Running | $101,807 | 24 |
| Dodge/Save Mart 350 | Infineon | 13 | 9 | 110/110 | 0 | Running | $108,482 | 21 |
| Pepsi 400 | Daytona | 26 | 23 | 160/160 | 0 | Running | $109,642 | 22 |
| Tropicana 400 | Chicago | 6 | 33 | 197/267 | 0 | Running | $99,342 | 24 |
| Siemens 300 | New Hamp. | 27 | 12 | 300/300 | 0 | Running | $103,917 | 23 |
| Pennsylvania 500 | Pocono | 23 | 34 | 126/200 | 0 | Accident | $86,782 | 25 |
| Brickyard 400 | Indianapolis | 19 | 12 | 161/161 | 0 | Running | $177,342 | 24 |
| Sirius at the Glen | Watkins Glen | 24 | 12 | 90/90 | 0 | Running | $94,992 | 23 |
| GFS Marketplace 400 | Michigan | 28 | 12 | 200/200 | 0 | Running | $80,640 | 22 |
| Sharpie 500 | Bristol | 15 | 4 | 500/500 | 26 | Running | $128,280 | 20 |
| Pop Secret 500 | California | 34 | 15 | 250/250 | 0 | Running | $96,200 | 18 |
| Chevy Rock & Roll 400 | Richmond | 5 | 23 | 399/400 | 8 | Running | $69,905 | 21 |
| Sylvania 300 | New Hamp. | 26 | 15 | 300/300 | 0 | Running | $77,275 | 19 |
| MBNA America 400 | Dover | 33 | 33 | 167/400 | 0 | Running | $66,730 | 21 |
| EA Sports 500 | Talladega | 13 | 13 | 188/188 | 6 | Running | $79,180 | 20 |
| Banquet 400 | Kansas | 17 | 15 | 267/267 | 0 | Running | $86,750 | 19 |
| UAW-GM Quality 500 | Lowe's | 35 | 9 | 334/334 | 0 | Running | $77,700 | 17 |
| Subway 500 | Martinsville | 12 | 11 | 500/500 | 0 | Running | $73,175 | 17 |
| Bass Pro Shops MBNA 500 | Atlanta | 21 | 6 | 325/325 | 0 | Running | $110,700 | 16 |
| Checker Auto Parts 500 | Phoenix | 20 | 11 | 315/315 | 0 | Running | $72,500 | 16 |
| Southern 500 | Darlington | 21 | 13 | 367/367 | 0 | Running | $78,600 | 16 |
| Ford 400 | Homestead | 40 | 36 | 231/271 | 0 | Running | $57,935 | 18 |

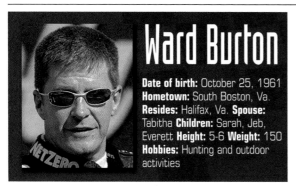

# Ward Burton

**Date of birth:** October 25, 1961
**Hometown:** South Boston, Va.
**Resides:** Halifax, Va. **Spouse:** Tabitha **Children:** Sarah, Jeb, Everett **Height:** 5-6 **Weight:** 150 **Hobbies:** Hunting and outdoor activities

## NASCAR ACHIEVEMENTS

**First NASCAR Cup start:** March 6, 1994 (Richmond)
**Best points finish:** 9 (1999)
**Career victories:** 5—Darlington (00a, 01b), Daytona (02a) New Hampshire (02a), Rockingham (95b)
**First victory:** October 25, 1995 (Rockingham)
**Last victory:** July 21, 2002 (New Hampshire)
**Career poles:** 7—Charlotte (94b), Darlington (96a), Martinsville (97b), Michigan (96a, 99b), Pocono (98b), Richmond (02a)
**First pole:** October 5, 1994 (Charlotte)
**Best career finish:** 1 **Best career start:** 1

## FAST FACTS

● Competed in the NASCAR Busch Series from 1990-93.
● Finished sixth in NASCAR Busch Series points in 1993, with three wins and four poles.
● Was second to Joe Nemechek in NASCAR Busch Series Rookie of the Year points in 1990.
● Won three races and was voted Most Popular Driver at South Boston Speedway in 1989.
● Began racing go-karts at age 8.

● Raced on Virginia Karting Association circuit until he was 16.
● Raced mini-stocks and street stocks in South Boston, Va., before moving into late model stock cars in 1986.
● Attended Hargrave Military Academy beginning in 10th grade and ranked first on the school's rifle team.
● After college, spent two years living in a cabin surviving off the land.
● Operates the Ward Burton Wildlife Foundation, which purchases land in an effort to conserve and protect wildlife habitats.

## CAREER HIGHLIGHTS

● 2004 was a lost season for the Virginia native. His Hendrick Engine-powered Chevys never contended, and he was replaced for the final two races. The Haas CNC Racing team is a single-car team, with no teammates to learn from or share information with. Burton led just one race all season and never finished in the top five. Plenty of engine problems didn't help matters. Nor did going through three crew chiefs. Burton's status for 2005 is uncertain.
● Lost his ride with Bill Davis Racing toward the end of the 2003 season and landed with Haas-CNC Racing. He finished with zero top fives and never posted back-to-back top 10s. It was a difficult time for both Davis and Burton because the two had been together for nine consecutive seasons.
● Won the Daytona 500 in 2002, scoring the biggest win of his career. He also won at New Hampshire, posting a career-high two victories in a season. But he was hampered by nine DNFs, and the Richmond race began a six-race string of finished 30th or worse that dropped him from 14th in points to 25th. In the second half of the season, his long-time crew chief, Tommy Baldwin, was replaced by Frank Stoddard.
● Struggled early in 2001 after a switch from Pontiac to Dodge, scoring only one top 10 in the first 11 races. But

**DRIVERS**

beginning with Bristol in August, he rallied to post top 15 finishes in eight of 12 races. He finished 14th in points despite nine DNFs.
- Finished 10th in points in 2000, his second straight year with a top 10 finish. He started the season very strong, with eight top 10s in the first 13 races, and reached second in points. But he stumbled in the second half, with four DNFs.
- Didn't win a race in 1999 but finished second three times, all three times behind his brother, Jeff (Rockingham, Las Vegas, Darlington). He finished ninth in points that year, a career-high.
- Won a career-high two poles (Michigan, Pocono) in 1998.
- Joined Bill Davis Racing for the final nine races in 1995 and proved it was a good move when he got his first career win at Rockingham.
- Struggled early in 1994, his first full season in Cup racing. He missed the first two races and recorded two DNFs in the third and fourth races of the season. After seven straight finishes of 29th of worse, he was second at Pocono.

## CAREER STATISTICS

| Year | Car owner | Races | Champ. finish | Won | Top 5 | Top 10 | DNF | Poles | Money won |
|------|-----------|-------|---------------|-----|-------|--------|-----|-------|-----------|
| 1994 | A. Dillard | 26 | 35 | 0 | 1 | 2 | 12 | 1 | $304,700 |
| 1995 | A. Dillard | 20 | | 0 | 0 | 2 | 4 | 0 | 334,330 |
| | Bill Davis | 9 | 22 | 1 | 3 | 4 | 2 | 0 | 300,325 |
| 1996 | Bill Davis | 27 | 33 | 0 | 0 | 4 | 10 | 1 | 873,619 |
| 1997 | Bill Davis | 31 | 24 | 0 | 0 | 7 | 7 | 1 | 1,004,944 |
| 1998 | Bill Davis | 33 | 16 | 0 | 1 | 5 | 4 | 2 | 1,516,183 |
| 1999 | Bill Davis | 34 | 9 | 0 | 6 | 16 | 3 | 1 | 2,405,913 |
| 2000 | Bill Davis | 34 | 10 | 1 | 4 | 17 | 4 | 0 | 2,699,604 |
| 2001 | Bill Davis | 36 | 14 | 1 | 6 | 10 | 9 | 0 | 3,633,692 |
| 2002 | Bill Davis | 36 | 25 | 2 | 3 | 8 | 9 | 1 | 4,899,884 |
| 2003 | Bill Davis | 32 | | 0 | 0 | 4 | 4 | 0 | 3,280,950 |
| | Gene Haas | 4 | 21 | 0 | 0 | 0 | 2 | 0 | 347,650 |
| 2004 | Gene Haas | 34 | 32 | 0 | 0 | 3 | 8 | 0 | 2,471,940 |
| **TOTALS** | | **356** | | **5** | **24** | **82** | **78** | **7** | **$24,023,734** |

## 2004 RESULTS

| Race | Track | Start | Finish | Laps | Led | Status | Winnings | Rank |
|------|-------|-------|--------|------|-----|--------|----------|------|
| Daytona 500 | Daytona | 19 | 17 | 199/200 | 0 | Running | $218,912 | 17 |
| Subway 400 | N. Carolina | 16 | 9 | 393/393 | 0 | Running | $66,035 | 9 |
| UAW-DaimlerChrysler 400 | Las Vegas | 34 | 26 | 265/267 | 0 | Running | $70,750 | 15 |
| Golden Corral 500 | Atlanta | 21 | 13 | 324/325 | 0 | Running | $63,775 | 14 |
| Carolina Dodge Dealers 400 | Darlington | 13 | 18 | 293/293 | 0 | Running | $57,720 | 15 |
| Food City 500 | Bristol | 39 | 28 | 496/500 | 0 | Running | $71,150 | 20 |
| Samsung/RadioShack 500 | Texas | 27 | 32 | 304/334 | 0 | Running | $70,675 | 22 |
| Advance Auto Parts 500 | Martinsville | 6 | 22 | 499/500 | 0 | Running | $60,425 | 19 |
| Aaron's 499 | Talladega | 10 | 40 | 66/188 | 0 | Engine | $61,900 | 25 |
| Auto Club 500 | California | 15 | 10 | 250/250 | 0 | Running | $88,350 | 24 |
| Chevy Amer. Revolution 400 | Richmond | 15 | 20 | 398/400 | 0 | Running | $63,475 | 22 |
| Coca-Cola 600 | Lowe's | 17 | 16 | 398/400 | 0 | Running | $83,650 | 20 |
| MBNA 400 'A Salute to Heroes' | Dover | 25 | 19 | 391/400 | 0 | Running | $70,285 | 22 |
| Pocono 500 | Pocono | 26 | 17 | 200/200 | 0 | Running | $59,290 | 21 |
| DHL 400 | Michigan | 14 | 30 | 191/200 | 0 | Engine | $59,190 | 25 |
| Dodge/Save Mart 350 | Infineon | 14 | 24 | 110/110 | 0 | Running | $62,630 | 25 |
| Pepsi 400 | Daytona | 8 | 40 | 84/160 | 0 | Running | $66,875 | 25 |
| Tropicana 400 | Chicago | 22 | 19 | 267/267 | 0 | Running | $75,150 | 26 |
| Siemens 300 | New Hamp. | 12 | 29 | 300/300 | 0 | Running | $62,390 | 26 |
| Pennsylvania 500 | Pocono | 27 | 31 | 162/200 | 0 | Trans. | $52,990 | 27 |
| Brickyard 400 | Indianapolis | 2 | 39 | 72/161 | 0 | Accident | $120,005 | 27 |
| Sirius at the Glen | Watkins Glen | 28 | 37 | 47/90 | 0 | Engine | $53,050 | 28 |
| GFS Marketplace 400 | Michigan | 29 | 30 | 196/200 | 0 | Running | $58,915 | 28 |
| Sharpie 500 | Bristol | 16 | 18 | 497/500 | 0 | Running | $79,075 | 28 |
| Pop Secret 500 | California | 39 | 31 | 248/250 | 0 | Running | $80,150 | 28 |
| Chevy Rock & Roll 400 | Richmond | 38 | 40 | 192/400 | 0 | Accident | $56,185 | 28 |
| Sylvania 300 | New Hamp. | 29 | 25 | 298/300 | 0 | Running | $64,285 | 28 |
| MBNA America 400 | Dover | 17 | 37 | 50/400 | 0 | Engine | $57,125 | 28 |
| EA Sports 500 | Talladega | 28 | 10 | 188/188 | 1 | Running | $76,000 | 28 |
| Banquet 400 | Kansas | 35 | 30 | 255/267 | 0 | Running | $66,100 | 29 |
| UAW-GM Quality 500 | Lowe's | 43 | 19 | 331/334 | 0 | Running | $61,350 | 28 |
| Subway 500 | Martinsville | 4 | 28 | 497/500 | 0 | Running | $58,085 | 28 |
| Bass Pro Shops MBNA 500 | Atlanta | 34 | 30 | 318/325 | 0 | Running | $69,500 | 28 |
| Checker Auto Parts 500 | Phoenix | 39 | 40 | 201/315 | 0 | Rear end | $50,600 | 29 |

# Kurt Busch
## 97

**Date of birth:** August 4, 1978 **Hometown:** Las Vegas **Resides:** Concord, N.C. **Spouse:** Single **Children:** None **Height:** 5-11 **Weight:** 150 **Hobbies:** Jet skiing, water skiing, snow skiing

## NASCAR ACHIEVEMENTS

**First NASCAR Cup start:** September 24, 2000 (Dover)
**Best points finish:** 3 (2002)
**Career victories:** 10—Atlanta (02b), Bristol (02a, 03a, 03b, 04a), California (03) Homestead (02), Martinsville (02b), Michigan (03), New Hampshire (04a, 04b)
**First victory:** March 24, 2002 (Bristol)
**Last victory:** September 19, 2004 (New Hampshire)
**Career poles:** 3—Darlington (01b), Homestead (02, 04)
**First pole:** September 2, 2001 (Darlington)
**Best career finish:** 1 **Best career start:** 1

# FAST FACTS

- Was the first champion in the NASCAR NEXTEL Cup era after winning the innaugural Chase for the NASCAR NEXTEL Cup.
- Was runner-up in the 2000 NASCAR Craftsman Truck Series and had four victories.
- In 1999, won the Featherlite Southwest Series, NASCAR Touring championship driving for Craig Keough. Was the youngest driver to win that series' championship at age 21.
- Named Featherlite Southwest Series Rookie of the Year in 1998.
- Competed in the Featherlite Southwest Series from 1997-1999, recording seven wins.
- Won the 1996 Hobby Stock track championship at the Las Vegas Speedway Park.
- Was the 1996 Legend Cars National Rookie of the Year and Legend Cars Western States champion.
- Won the Nevada Dwarf Car championship in 1995.
- Was the 1994 Nevada State Dwarf Car Rookie of the Year.
- Began racing at age 14, in Dwarf Cars at Parhump Valley Speedway near Las Vegas.
- Won the 2002 Outback Steakhouse "Bloomin' Favorite Driver" award.

# CAREER HIGHLIGHTS

- The first champion in the Nextel era, Busch won by being consistent—not his strength before the 2004 season. The aggressive Busch of his first four NASCAR Cup seasons gave way to Kensethian patience. And the Las Vegas native got hot at exactly the right time, ripping off nine top 10 finishes during the 10-race Chase for the NASCAR NEXTEL Cup. A short track ace, Busch showed improvement at restrictor-plate and intermediate tracks.
- Busch's four 2003 wins were second best on the circuit but were offset by 10 finishes outside of the top 35. Three of those poor finishes came in succession in October and cost him a top 10 points finish.
- Showed his short-track prowess by sweeping the 2003 races at Bristol.
- Had a breakthrough season in 2002, with four wins (Bristol, Martinsville, Atlanta and Homestead), three in the final five weeks of the season.
- His incredible success with Roush Racing in the 2000 Craftsman Truck Series led owner Jack Roush to move Busch straight to Cup racing in 2001, an unprecedented

## CAR FACTS

**Car:** No.97 Ford
**Primary sponsor:** Sharpie/Irwin
**Owner:** Jack Roush
**Team:** Roush Racing
**Crew chief:** Jimmy Fennig
**Engine builder:** Roush/Yates

move. Busch quieted skeptics when he finished in the top 10 six times and finished second for Raybestos Rookie of the Year honors.

## CAREER STATISTICS

| Year | Car owner | Races | Champ. finish | Won | Top 5 | Top 10 | DNF | Poles | Money won |
|------|-----------|-------|-------|-----|-----|------|-----|-------|-------|
| 2000 | Jack Roush | 7 | 48 | 0 | 0 | 0 | 0 | 0 | $311,915 |
| 2001 | Jack Roush | 35 | 27 | 0 | 3 | 6 | 7 | 1 | $2,170,629 |
| 2002 | Jack Roush | 36 | 3 | 4 | 12 | 20 | 4 | 1 | $5,105,394 |
| 2003 | Jack Roush | 36 | 11 | 4 | 9 | 14 | 8 | 0 | $5,587,384 |
| 2004 | Jack Roush | 36 | 1 | 3 | 10 | 21 | 3 | 1 | $9,677,543 |
| **TOTALS** | | **150** | | **11** | **34** | **61** | **22** | **3** | **$22,860,894** |

## 2004 RESULTS

| Race | Track | Start | Finish | Laps | Led | Status | Winnings | Rank |
|------|-------|-------|--------|------|-----|--------|----------|------|
| Daytona 500 | Daytona | 15 | 16 | 199/200 | 0 | Running | $236,887 | 16 |
| Subway 400 | N. Carolina | 27 | 8 | 393/393 | 0 | Running | $83,785 | 7 |
| UAW-DaimlerChrysler 400 | Las Vegas | 2 | 9 | 267/267 | 4 | Running | $108,500 | 5 |
| Golden Corral 500 | Atlanta | 20 | 12 | 325/325 | 0 | Running | $78,950 | 6 |
| Carolina Dodge Dealers 400 | Darlington | 4 | 6 | 293/293 | 76 | Running | $86,275 | 4 |
| Food City 500 | Bristol | 13 | 1 | 500/500 | 119 | Running | $173,465 | 2 |
| Samsung/RadioShack 500 | Texas | 12 | 6 | 334/334 | 1 | Running | $165,050 | 1 |
| Advance Auto Parts 500 | Martinsville | 7 | 11 | 500/500 | 0 | Running | $80,100 | 2 |
| Aaron's 499 | Talladega | 22 | 36 | 82/188 | 1 | Accident | $82,875 | 4 |
| Auto Club 500 | California | 21 | 23 | 249/250 | 0 | Running | $90,550 | 5 |
| Chevy Amer. Revolution 400 | Richmond | 23 | 31 | 386/400 | 6 | Running | $76,025 | 9 |
| Coca-Cola 600 | Lowe's | 32 | 11 | 400/400 | 0 | Running | $107,380 | 8 |
| MBNA 400 'A Salute to Heroes' | Dover | 11 | 12 | 398/400 | 0 | Running | $91,535 | 6 |
| Pocono 500 | Pocono | 27 | 5 | 200/200 | 0 | Running | $95,600 | 5 |
| DHL 400 | Michigan | 7 | 11 | 200/200 | 0 | Running | $85,705 | 8 |
| Dodge/Save Mart 350 | Infineon | 3 | 36 | 94/110 | 1 | Running | $78,160 | 8 |
| Pepsi 400 | Daytona | 35 | 4 | 160/160 | 0 | Running | $142,625 | 7 |
| Tropicana 400 | Chicago | 21 | 35 | 151/267 | 0 | Running | $84,600 | 9 |
| Siemens 300 | New Hamp. | 32 | 1 | 300/300 | 110 | Running | $222,225 | 6 |
| Pennsylvania 500 | Pocono | 3 | 26 | 192/200 | 0 | Trans. | $74,165 | 7 |
| Brickyard 400 | Indianapolis | 15 | 10 | 161/161 | 0 | Running | $172,900 | 7 |
| Sirius at the Glen | Watkins Glen | 7 | 10 | 90/90 | 1 | Running | $81,140 | 7 |
| GFS Marketplace 400 | Michigan | 7 | 6 | 200/200 | 4 | Running | $89,540 | 6 |
| Sharpie 500 | Bristol | 24 | 8 | 499/500 | 0 | Running | $107,515 | 6 |
| Pop Secret 500 | California | 4 | 11 | 250/250 | 7 | Running | $108,425 | 7 |
| Chevy Rock & Roll 400 | Richmond | 17 | 15 | 399/400 | 94 | Running | $80,830 | 7 |
| Sylvania 300 | New Hamp. | 7 | 1 | 300/300 | 155 | Running | $237,225 | 2 |
| MBNA America 400 | Dover | 13 | 5 | 400/400 | 12 | Running | $99,745 | 2 |
| EA Sports 500 | Talladega | 8 | 5 | 188/188 | 4 | Running | $104,290 | 1 |
| Banquet 400 | Kansas | 22 | 6 | 267/267 | 1 | Running | $111,825 | 1 |
| UAW-GM Quality 500 | Lowe's | 21 | 4 | 334/334 | 3 | Running | $110,250 | 1 |
| Subway 500 | Martinsville | 7 | 5 | 500/500 | 120 | Running | $107,175 | 1 |
| Bass Pro Shops MBNA 500 | Atlanta | 22 | 42 | 51/325 | 0 | Engine | $84,790 | 1 |
| Checker Auto Parts 500 | Phoenix | 28 | 10 | 315/315 | 14 | Running | $84,300 | 1 |
| Southern 500 | Darlington | 1 | 6 | 367/367 | 9 | Running | $103,275 | 1 |
| Ford 400 | Homestead | 1 | 5 | 271/271 | 4 | Running | $130,650 | 1 |

# Kyle Busch

## 5

**Date of birth:** May 2, 1985 **Hometown:** Las Vegas **Resides:** Las Vegas **Spouse:** Single **Children:** None **Height:** 6-1 **Weight:** 160 **Hobbies:** Playing X-Box, NASCAR Thunder

## NASCAR ACHIEVEMENTS

**First NASCAR Cup start:** March 7, 2004 (Las Vegas)
**Best points finish:** 52
**Career victories:** 0
**Career poles:** 0
**Best career finish:** 24    **Best career start:** 18

### FAST FACTS

● Finished second at Charlotte during his 2003 NASCAR Busch Series debut. Ran seven races, finishing in the top 10 three times.
● Surprised the racing world by signing with Hendrick Motorsports, rather than Roush Racing, for whom his brother, Kurt, drives full time in NASCAR NEXTEL Cup.
● Won twice in seven ARCA starts for Hendrick Motorsports before he turned 18 on May 2, 2003, making him eligible for NASCAR competition.

### CAR FACTS

**Car:** No. 5 Chevrolet
**Primary sponsor:** Kellogg's
**Owner:** Rick Hendrick
**Team:** Hendrick Motorsports
**Crew chief:** Alan Gustafson
**Engine builder:** Hendrick Motorsports

● Spent the 2002 season driving for Roush Racing in ASA, placing third in the Rookie of the Year standings.
● Ran six NASCAR Craftsman Truck Series events for Roush Racing in 2001 as a high school junior and had two top 10

finishes. But he wasn't allowed to compete in the season finale because Marlboro was a sponsor of the weekend's events, and he was only 16. Soon after, NASCAR wrote a rule that all drivers had to be at least 18 to compete.
● Began racing Legends cars at his hometown track, Las Vegas Motor Speedway, at 13 and won two championships.

## CAREER HIGHLIGHTS

● He ran a limited schedule for Hendrick Motorsports in preparation for 2005, his rookie season. Busch didn't wow anyone with results at the NASCAR NEXTEL Cup level, but in his first full season of NASCAR Busch Series competition, he finished second in points. An aggressive, hard-charger, he will drive the No. 5 car vacated by Terry Labonte.

### CAREER STATISTICS

| Year | Car owner | Races | Champ. finish | Won | Top 5 | Top 10 | DNF | Poles | Money won |
|------|-----------|-------|---------------|-----|-------|--------|-----|-------|-----------|
| 2004 | Rick Hendrick | 6 | 52 | 0 | 0 | 0 | 0 | 4 | $394,489 |
| **TOTALS** | | **6** | | **0** | **0** | **4** | **0** | | **$394,489** |

### 2004 RESULTS

| Race | Track | Start | Finish | Laps | Led | Status | Winnings | Rank |
|------|-------|-------|--------|------|-----|--------|----------|------|
| UAW-DaimlerChrysler 400 | Las Vegas | 18 | 41 | 11/267 | 0 | Accident | $63,555 | 48 |
| Coca-Cola 600 | Lowe's | 27 | 32 | 393/400 | 0 | Running | $69,025 | 52 |
| Pop Secret 500 | California | 18 | 24 | 250/250 | 0 | Running | $78,250 | 57 |
| Banquet 400 | Kansas | 34 | 37 | 136/267 | 0 | Accident | $64,175 | 54 |
| UAW-GM Quality 500 | Lowe's | 38 | 34 | 264/334 | 0 | Accident | $54,575 | 50 |
| Bass Pro Shops MBNA 500 | Atlanta | 28 | 43 | 44/325 | 0 | Time belt | $64,909 | 49 |

DRIVERS

**Dale Earnhardt Jr.**

**8**

**Date of birth:** October 10, 1974 **Hometown:** Kannapolis, N.C.
**Resides:** Mooresville, N.C. **Spouse:** Single **Children:** None.
**Height:** 6-0 **Weight:** 165. **Hobbies:** Car restoration, music,
computers, video games

## NASCAR ACHIEVEMENTS

**First NASCAR Cup start:** May 30, 2000 (Charlotte)
**Best points finish:** 3 (2003)
**Career victories:** 15—Atlanta (04a), Bristol (04b), Daytona
(01b, 04a), Dover (01b), Phoenix (03, 04), Richmond (00a,
04a), Talladega (01b, 02a, 02b, 03a, 04b), Texas (00)
**First victory:** April 2, 2000 (Texas)
**Last victory:** November 7, 2004 (Phoenix)
**Career poles:** 6—Atlanta (02b), Charlotte (00a), Kansas (02),
Michigan (00b, 02b), Texas (01)
**First pole:** May 28, 2000 (Charlotte)
**Best career finish:** 1 **Best career start:** 1

## FAST FACTS

● Won back-to-back NASCAR Busch Series Championships
in 1998 and 1999, his only two full seasons of NASCAR
Busch competition.
● Began his professional career at age 17, competing in the
street stock division at Concord Motorsport Park and later
moving up to late model stock division.
● Raced against brother Kerry and sister Kelley at the beginning of his career.
● Won three feature victories in his NASCAR late model
stock career from 1994-96.
● When he raced in the Pepsi 400 at Michigan in 2000 along
with his late father, Dale, and Kerry, it was the second time
a father and two sons ran in the same Cup event. Lee Petty
also raced against his sons, Richard and Maurice.
● Says his hero is his father, seven-time NASCAR Cup
champion, Dale Earnhardt.
● Began his racing career when he and Kerry sold a go-kart for
$500 to purchase a 1978
Chevy Monte Carlo street
stock car for $200. Later
sold the car to NASCAR
Busch Series competitor
Hank Parker Jr.
● Began his career in the
NASCAR Busch Series in
1996 but took off in

### CAR FACTS

**Car:** No.8 Chevrolet
**Primary sponsor:** Budweiser
**Owner:** Teresa Earnhardt
**Team:** Dale Earnhardt Inc.
**Crew chief:** Pete Rondeau
**Engine builder:** Richie Gilmore

1998, winning the NASCAR Busch Series title in his first
season paired with crew chief Tony Eury Sr.
● 1998 NASCAR Busch Series title made him the first third-
generation NASCAR champion. Other champion Earnhardts
are his father, Dale, and his grandfather, Ralph. His mater-
nal grandfather, Robert Gee, was a well-known NASCAR
fabricator and mechanic.

## CAREER HIGHLIGHTS

● Earnhardt was a title contender throughout the 2004 Chase
for the NASCAR NEXTEL Cup. He came back strong after
suffering burns in practice for a non-NASCAR race in
August. He won two races in the Chase for the NASCAR
NEXTEL Cup, but an accident late in the race at Atlanta hurt
his title chances.
● Resiliency was the key to Earnhardt's success in 2003; he
followed four of his five finishes outside of the top 30 with
a top 10. He finished third in points and ended a long win-
less drought on non-superspeedway tracks with a victory
at Phoenix.
● Led 1,068 laps in 2002, more than any other driver.
● Finished second in all three nonpoints events in 2002: the
Budwesier Shootout, a Twin 125 qualifying race and the
All-Star race.
● First win of the 2001 season came in the July Daytona
race, the first race held there since his father's death in the
Daytona 500 on February 18. His next victory was at Dover,
in the NASCAR Cup circuit's first race back after the
September 11 terrorist attacks. He punctuated that win
with a victory lap carrying an American flag. His third win
was at Talladega, the site of his father's final career victory
a year earlier. He went on to win four consecutive Talladega
races (the second race in 2001, both races in 2002 and the
first race in 2003).
● Made a splash as a rookie in 2000 with two wins (Texas,
Richmond) and two poles (Charlotte, Michigan) and was
only 42 points shy of winning the Raybestos Rookie of the
Year title behind Matt Kenseth. Earnhardt matched the
modern-era record (two wins in first 16 races) set by
Davey Allison in 1987. He also became the first rookie to
win the All-Star race.

## CAREER STATISTICS

| Year | Car owner | Races | Champ. finish | Won | Top 5 | Top 10 | DNF | Poles | Money won |
|---|---|---|---|---|---|---|---|---|---|
| 1999 | Dale Earnhardt | 5 | | 0 | 0 | 1 | 1 | 0 | $162,095 |
| 2000 | Dale Earnhardt | 34 | 16 | 2 | 3 | 5 | 7 | 2 | 2,801,881 |
| 2001 | Dale Earnhardt | 36 | 8 | 3 | 9 | 15 | 4 | 2 | 5,827,542 |
| 2002 | Teresa Earnhardt | 36 | 11 | 2 | 11 | 16 | 3 | 2 | 4,970,034 |
| 2003 | Teresa Earnhardt | 36 | 3 | 2 | 13 | 21 | 4 | 0 | 6,880,807 |
| 2004 | Teresa Earnhardt | 36 | 5 | 6 | 16 | 21 | 4 | 0 | $8,913,510 |
| TOTALS | | 183 | | 15 | 52 | 79 | 23 | 6 | $29,555,869 |

## 2004 RESULTS

| Race | Track | Start | Finish | Laps | Led | Status | Winnings | Rank |
|---|---|---|---|---|---|---|---|---|
| Daytona 500 | Daytona | 3 | 1 | 200/200 | 58 | Running | $1,495,070 | 1 |
| Subway 400 | N. Carolina | 7 | 5 | 393/393 | 0 | Running | $118,303 | 1 |
| UAW-DaimlerChrysler 400 | Las Vegas | 26 | 35 | 196/267 | 0 | Handling | $111,978 | 7 |
| Golden Corral 500 | Atlanta | 7 | 1 | 325/325 | 55 | Running | $180,078 | 3 |
| Carolina Dodge Dealers 400 | Darlington | 2 | 10 | 293/293 | 18 | Running | $106,983 | 2 |
| Food City 500 | Bristol | 18 | 11 | 500/500 | 91 | Running | $118,748 | 3 |
| Samsung/RadioShack 500 | Texas | 7 | 4 | 334/334 | 4 | Running | $227,653 | 3 |
| Advance Auto Parts 500 | Martinsville | 4 | 3 | 500/500 | 154 | Running | $135,103 | 1 |
| Aaron's 499 | Talladega | 3 | 2 | 188/188 | 57 | Running | $241,433 | 1 |
| Auto Club 500 | California | 10 | 19 | 249/250 | 0 | Running | $119,203 | 1 |
| Chevy Amer. Revolution 400 | Richmond | 4 | 1 | 400/400 | 115 | Running | $285,053 | 1 |
| Coca-Cola 600 | Lowe's | 10 | 6 | 400/400 | 2 | Running | $152,053 | 1 |
| MBNA 400 'A Salute to Heroes' | Dover | 26 | 3 | 400/400 | 0 | Running | $186,828 | 1 |
| Pocono 500 | Pocono | 16 | 6 | 200/200 | 0 | Running | $121,718 | 1 |
| DHL 400 | Michigan | 11 | 21 | 200/200 | 0 | Running | $107,593 | 2 |
| Dodge/Save Mart 350 | Infineon | 20 | 11 | 110/110 | 9 | Running | $114,078 | 2 |
| Pepsi 400 | Daytona | 5 | 3 | 160/160 | 23 | Running | $196,528 | 2 |
| Tropicana 400 | Chicago | 25 | 22 | 267/267 | 0 | Running | $116,828 | 2 |
| Siemens 300 | New Hamp. | 3 | 31 | 298/300 | 0 | Running | $108,628 | 2 |
| Pennsylvania 500 | Pocono | 16 | 25 | 193/200 | 0 | Running | $101,093 | 3 |
| Brickyard 400 | Indianapolis | 5 | 27 | 161/161 | 0 | Running | $169,078 | 3 |
| Sirius at the Glen | Watkins Glen | 3 | 5 | 90/90 | 1 | Running | $111,708 | 3 |
| GFS Marketplace 400 | Michigan | 3 | 21 | 199/200 | 0 | Running | $107,393 | 3 |
| Sharpie 500 | Bristol | 30 | 1 | 500/500 | 295 | Running | $322,443 | 3 |
| Pop Secret 500 | California | 12 | 34 | 231/250 | 0 | Accident | $125,103 | 3 |
| Chevy Rock & Roll 400 | Richmond | 14 | 2 | 400/400 | 42 | Running | $153,543 | 3 |
| Sylvania 300 | New Hamp. | 3 | 3 | 300/300 | 2 | Running | $155,158 | 1 |
| MBNA America 400 | Dover | 16 | 9 | 399/400 | 1 | Running | $113,293 | 3 |
| EA Sports 500 | Talladega | 10 | 1 | 188/188 | 78 | Running | $305,968 | 2 |
| Banquet 400 | Kansas | 8 | 9 | 267/267 | 0 | Running | $135,678 | 2 |
| UAW-GM Quality 500 | Lowe's | 25 | 3 | 334/334 | 8 | Running | $155,928 | 2 |
| Subway 500 | Martinsville | 3 | 33 | 449/500 | 0 | Accident | $103,173 | 3 |
| Bass Pro Shops MBNA 500 | Atlanta | 6 | 33 | 311/325 | 0 | Accident | $114,103 | 5 |
| Checker Auto Parts 500 | Phoenix | 14 | 1 | 315/315 | 118 | Running | $274,503 | 3 |
| Southern 500 | Darlington | 3 | 11 | 367/367 | 0 | Running | $114,253 | 4 |
| Ford 400 | Homestead | 16 | 23 | 271/271 | 0 | Running | $100,703 | 5 |

# Carl Edwards

**Date of birth:** August 15, 1979 **Hometown:** Columbia, Mo.
**Resides:** Mooresville, N.C. **Spouse:** Single **Children:** None
**Height:** 6-1 **Weight:** 185

## NASCAR ACHIEVEMENTS

**First NASCAR Cup start:** August 22, 2004 (Michigan)
**Best points finish:** 37
**Career victories:** 0
**Career poles:** 0
**Best career finish:** 1 **Best career start:** 1

## FAST FACTS

● Exploded onto the NASCAR Craftsman Truck Series scene in 2003, snagging three wins and Raybestos Rookie of the Year while driving for Roush Racing. He spent the final 18 weeks of the season in the top 10 in points.
● Made seven NASCAR Craftsman Truck Series starts in 2002 and finished in the top 10 at Kansas Speedway. He also won the 2002 Baby Grand national title.
● Won NASCAR Dodge Weekly Racing Series championships at Capital Speedway, near Jefferson City, Mo., in modifieds in 1999 and pro modifieds in 2000.
● Began racing at 13, driving four-cylinder mini-sprints. He won 18 races in the mini-sprint series in four years. In 1997, Edwards switched to dirt-track racing in the IMCA modified division.
● Mike Edwards, his father, won more than 200 feature races at several Midwestern tracks in modifieds and midgets.
● Was a student at the University of Missouri and a part-time substitute teacher before signing with Roush Racing before the 2003 season.

## CAR FACTS

**Car:** No.99 Ford
**Primary sponsor:** TBA
**Owner:** Jack Roush
**Team:** Roush Racing
**Crew chief:** Bob Osborne
**Engine builder:** Roush/Yates

## CAREER HIGHLIGHTS

● Edwards jumped from the NASCAR Craftsman Truck Series to NASCAR NEXTEL Cup in 2004, taking over the No. 99

Ford for Roush Racing in August after Jeff Burton left to join Richard Childress Racing. Edwards posted strong results—three top 10s in his first four races. He learned early what it's like to drive a big-time car, then learned at Kansas what it's like to hold on with a crummy car. Both experiences will prove valuable as he heads into his first full season. Because he ran more than seven NASCAR NEXTEL Cup races in 2004, he won't be classified as a rookie in 2005.

## 2004 RESULTS

| Race | Track | Start | Finish | Laps | Led | Status | Winnings | Rank |
|------|-------|-------|--------|------|-----|--------|----------|------|
| GFS Marketplace 400 | Michigan | 23 | 10 | 200/200 | 0 | Running | $105,332 | 61 |
| Sharpie 500 | Bristol | 25 | 33 | 386/500 | 0 | Accident | $103,187 | 55 |
| Pop Secret 500 | California | 19 | 6 | 250/250 | 0 | Running | $136,792 | 47 |
| Chevy Rock & Roll 400 | Richmond | 13 | 6 | 400/400 | 0 | Running | $102,997 | 44 |
| Sylvania 300 | New Hamp. | 21 | 20 | 299/300 | 0 | Running | $100,817 | 42 |
| MBNA America 400 | Dover | 15 | 18 | 397/400 | 0 | Running | $97,417 | 41 |
| EA Sports 500 | Talladega | 25 | 42 | 122/188 | 0 | Engine | $94,477 | 41 |
| Banquet 400 | Kansas | 16 | 22 | 267/267 | 0 | Running | $106,467 | 40 |
| Subway 500 | Martinsville | 22 | 24 | 500/500 | 0 | Running | $92,042 | 40 |
| Bass Pro Shops MBNA 500 | Atlanta | 4 | 3 | 325/325 | 15 | Running | $180,117 | 38 |
| Checker Auto Parts 500 | Phoenix | 29 | 37 | 272/315 | 0 | Running | $84,417 | 38 |
| Southern 500 | Darlington | 24 | 7 | 367/367 | 0 | Running | $114,642 | 38 |
| Ford 400 | Homestead | 22 | 14 | 271/271 | 0 | Running | $91,867 | 37 |

## CAREER STATISTICS

| Year | Car owner | Races | Champ. finish | Won | Top 5 | Top 10 | DNF | Poles | Money won |
|------|-----------|-------|---------------|-----|-------|--------|-----|-------|-----------|
| 2004 | Jack Roush | 13 | 37 | 0 | 1 | 5 | 2 | 0 | $1,454,380 |
| **TOTALS** | | **13** | | **0** | **1** | **5** | **2** | **0** | **$1,454,380** |

# Bill Elliott
## 91

**Date of birth:** October 8, 1955 **Hometown:** Dawsonville, Ga. **Resides:** Blairsville, Ga. **Spouse:** Cindy **Children:** Starr, Brittany, Chase **Height:** 6-1 **Weight:** 185 **Hobbies:** Skiing, snowboarding, flying

## NASCAR ACHIEVEMENTS

**First NASCAR Cup start:** February 29, 1976 (Rockingham)
**Best points finish:** 1 (1988)
**Career victories:** 44—Atlanta (85a, 85b, 87b, 92a, 92b), Bristol (88a), Charlotte (84b, 85a, 87b), Darlington (85a, 85b, 88b, 92a, 94b), Daytona (85a, 87a, 88b, 91b), Dover (85a, 88a, 88b, 91b), Homestead (01), Indianapolis (02), Michigan (84a, 85a, 85b, 86a, 86b, 87b, 89a), Phoenix (89), Pocono (85a, 85b, 88b, 89b, 02b), Richmond (92a), Riverside (83b), Rockingham (84b, 87b, 92a, 03b), Talladega (87b)
**First victory:** November 20, 1983 (Riverside)
**Last victory:** November 9, 2003 (Rockingham)
**Career poles:** 55—Atlanta (84b, 86b, 87b, 91b, 02a), Bristol (91b), Charlotte (85a, 87a, 89b, 92a), Darlington (81a, 85a, 85b, 88a, 94a), Daytona (85a, 85b, 87a, 01a), Dover ( 87a, 90b), Homestead (01), Michigan (82a, 84a, 84b, 85a, 85b, 88a, 88b), New Hampshire (02a), North Wilkesboro (87a, 87b, 88b), Phoenix (93, 95), Pocono (84b, 85a, 85b, 95b, 02b), Richmond (89b, 92a, 97b), Rockingham (88a, 88b), Talladega (85a, 85b, 86a, 86b, 87a, 87b, 90a, 93b), Texas (02)
**First pole:** April 10, 1981 (Darlington)
**Best career finish:** 1   **Best career start:** 1

## FAST FACTS

● Began his racing career on short tracks in Georgia, working with his brothers Dan and Ernie, under the guidance of his father, George.
● Got his biggest break when Harry Melling bought the family's team in 1982.

● Shares the modern-era record with a streak of four straight victories in 1992.
● Named driver of the decade for the 1980s in an ESPN fans poll.
● Won the National Motorsports Press Association's Most Popular Driver Award 16 times. Upon his retirement from NASCAR NEXTEL Cup racing, the NMPA has voted to name the trophy for that award the Bill Elliott Trophy.

## CAREER HIGHLIGHTS

● Elliott spent much of 2004 behind the scenes, tutoring Kasey Kahne and testing Dodges for Evernham Motorsports. Elliott will run a limited schedule again in 2005.
● Ranks 10th all-time in races won from the pole (15) and sixth among all-time pole winners (55). He also ranks second among all-time superspeedway pole winners with 48.
● Had one win in 2003 (Rockingham), but he could easily have had three after he dominated at Kansas but finished second because of fuel mileage, and he was way out in front on the final lap at Homestead but cut a tire and finished eighth. He announced during the offseason that he planned to run a partial schedule in 2004.
● Teamed with owner Ray Evernham in 2001 and drove a Dodge for the first time in his NASCAR Cup career. The combination didn't work out too badly: He won his 50th career pole

## CAR FACTS

**Car:** No. 91 Dodge
**Primary sponsor:** TBA
**Owner:** Ray Evernham
**Team:** Evernham Motorsports
**Crew chief:** Chris Andrews
**Engine builder:** Evernham Motorsports

**DRIVERS**

at the Daytona 500 and recorded his first victory, at Homestead, since 1994. In 2002, he scored six top fives, his most since 1994, and finished second only to Ryan Newman (six) in poles won (four).

- Made 600th career start at Talladega in 2000. He had a career-high eight DNFs in his last season as an owner/driver. He also missed two races (Bristol and Darlington) after injuring himself while doing yard work.
- Mechanical problems in 1999 resulted in his fewest top 10 finishes (two) since 1977.
- Began the 1998 season with seven straight top 15s, but accidents at Talladega and California stifled a strong run. Also in 1998, he was inducted into the Georgia Sports Hall of Fame.
- Made 500th career start at Bristol in April 1997.
- Began tenure as a driver/owner in 1995 and struggled early but managed to finish a respectable eighth in points. But he missed 10 races in the 1996 season after breaking his left thigh bone in an accident at Talladega and finished 30th in points. His 1996 season was his first without a top five finish since he began racing full time in 1983.
- Battled uphill in 1993 beginning with a blown engine at the Daytona 500 and just two top 10s in the first 10 races. But three straight top fives to end the season brought him up to eighth in points.
- Bounced back from a disappointing year in 1992 with a second-place finish in his first season driving for Junior Johnson. He won four straight races (Rockingham, Richmond, Atlanta and Darlington) He lost the championship by only 10 points to Alan Kulwicki, then the smallest margin of victory in NASCAR Cup history. He won the season's final race, but led one lap fewer than Kulwicki; the bonus for leading the most laps during the race was the decisive factor.
- Finished 11th in points in 1991, making it the first season since racing full time that Elliott finished outside of the top 10 in points. He had only one victory for the second year in a row but had half as many top 5 finishes as 1990, when he finished fourth.
- Broke his streak of six consecutive years with top five finishes by finishing sixth in series points in 1989.
- Won the NASCAR Cup championship in 1988, the first Ford driver to win the title since David Pearson in 1969. He was a model of consistency that season, finishing all 29 races 19th or better. He scored 15 top 10s in the last 16 races, 11 of which he was in the top five. He again was named Georgia Professional Athlete of the Year and American Driver of the Year.
- Finished in the top five in points for the fourth consecutive season in 1986 with a fourth-place finish. He swept the Michigan races for the second straight year and won the NASCAR All-Star race. In 1987, he continued his streak of top-five finishes by ending the year second in points.
- Won an astounding 11 races and 11 poles in 1985 to finish second in points. He swept the Michigan, Pocono, Darlington and Atlanta races. He won numerous awards that season, including the Georgia Professional Athlete of the Year, National

Motorsports Press Association Driver of the Year, American Driver of the Year and Auto Racing Digest Driver of the Year.
- Won the Winston Million in 1985, the first year it was offered, by winning three of the four "crown jewel" races: Daytona 500 (first), Coca-Cola 500 (18th), Winston 500 (first at Talladega) and Southern 500 (first at Darlington). After the Darlington victory, he made the cover of *Sports Illustrated* and earned the nickname "Million Dollar Bill."
- Finished third in points in his first full NASCAR Cup schedule in 1983. He also got his first career NASCAR Cup victory in his 117th start at Riverside. He finished third again in 1984 and was voted NASCAR's Most Popular Driver for the first time.
- Had 10 top fives and 32 top 10s before he even began racing full time in 1983. He debuted in 1976, making his first career start at Rockingham with his family-owned team, finishing 33rd and winning $640. He never won a race before racing full time, but he finished second four times.

## CAREER STATISTICS

| Year | Car owner | Races | Champ. finish | Won | Top 5 | Top 10 | DNF | Poles | Money won |
|------|-----------|-------|---------------|-----|-------|--------|-----|-------|-----------|
| 1976 | Elliott Racing | 7 | 41 | 0 | 0 | 0 | 5 | 0 | $11,635 |
| 1977 | Elliott Racing | 10 | 35 | 0 | 0 | 2 | 5 | 0 | $20,575 |
| 1978 | Elliott Racing | 10 | 33 | 0 | 0 | 5 | 3 | 0 | $42,065 |
| 1979 | Elliott Racing | 10 | 28 | 0 | 1 | 4 | 2 | 0 | $50,475 |
|      | Roger Hamby | 4 |  | 0 | 0 | 1 | 1 | 0 | $6,975 |
| 1980 | Elliott Racing | 11 | 34 | 0 | 0 | 4 | 4 | 0 | $42,545 |
| 1981 | Elliott Racing | 13 | 30 | 0 | 1 | 7 | 5 | 1 | $70,320 |
| 1982 | Harry Melling | 21 | 25 | 0 | 8 | 9 | 6 | 1 | $226,780 |
| 1983 | Harry Melling | 30 | 3 | 1 | 12 | 22 | 3 | 0 | $479,965 |
| 1984 | Harry Melling | 30 | 3 | 3 | 13 | 24 | 2 | 4 | $660,226 |
| 1985 | Harry Melling | 28 | 2 | 11 | 16 | 18 | 3 | 11 | $2,433,187 |
| 1986 | Harry Melling | 29 | 4 | 2 | 8 | 16 | 6 | 4 | $1,069,142 |
| 1987 | Harry Melling | 29 | 2 | 6 | 16 | 20 | 5 | 8 | $1,619,210 |
| 1988 | Harry Melling | 29 | 1 | 6 | 15 | 22 | 1 | 6 | $1,574,639 |
| 1989 | Harry Melling | 29 | 6 | 3 | 8 | 14 | 4 | 2 | $854,570 |
| 1990 | Harry Melling | 29 | 4 | 1 | 12 | 16 | 2 | 2 | $1,090,730 |
| 1991 | Harry Melling | 29 | 11 | 1 | 6 | 12 | 2 | 2 | $705,605 |
| 1992 | Junior Johnson | 29 | 2 | 5 | 14 | 17 | 2 | 2 | $1,692,381 |
| 1993 | Junior Johnson | 30 | 8 | 0 | 6 | 15 | 3 | 2 | $955,859 |
| 1994 | Junior Johnson | 31 | 10 | 1 | 6 | 12 | 5 | 1 | $936,779 |
| 1995 | Bill Elliott | 31 | 8 | 0 | 4 | 11 | 4 | 2 | $996,816 |
| 1996 | Bill Elliott | 24 | 30 | 0 | 0 | 6 | 3 | 0 | $716,506 |
| 1997 | Bill Elliott | 32 | 8 | 0 | 5 | 14 | 3 | 1 | $1,607,827 |
| 1998 | Bill Elliott | 32 | 18 | 0 | 0 | 5 | 7 | 0 | $1,618,421 |
| 1999 | Bill Elliott | 34 | 21 | 0 | 1 | 2 | 4 | 0 | $1,624,101 |
| 2000 | Bill Elliott | 32 | 21 | 0 | 3 | 7 | 8 | 0 | $2,580,823 |
| 2001 | Ray Evernham | 36 | 15 | 1 | 5 | 9 | 2 | 2 | $3,618,017 |
| 2002 | Ray Evernham | 36 | 13 | 2 | 6 | 13 | 4 | 4 | $4,122,699 |
| 2003 | Ray Evernham | 36 | 9 | 1 | 9 | 12 | 2 | 0 | $5,008,530 |
| 2004 | Ray Evernham | 6 | 48 | 0 | 0 | 1 | 1 | 0 | $567,900 |
| **TOTALS** | | **737** | | **44** | **175** | **320** | **106** | **55** | **$36,995,303** |

## 2004 RESULTS

| Race | Track | Start | Finish | Laps | Led | Status | Winnings | Rank |
|------|-------|-------|--------|------|-----|--------|----------|------|
| UAW-DaimlerChrysler 400 | Las Vegas | 10 | 20 | 266/267 | 0 | Running | $76,200 | 42 |
| Samsung/RadioShack 500 | Texas | 2 | 36 | 273/334 | 26 | Accident | $72,350 | 45 |
| Pepsi 400 | Daytona | 34 | 18 | 160/160 | 0 | Running | $75,425 | 44 |
| Brickyard 400 | Indianapolis | 18 | 9 | 161/161 | 0 | Running | $156,300 | 44 |
| Pop Secret 500 | California | 3 | 25 | 250/250 | 0 | Running | $77,925 | 42 |
| Bass Pro Shops MBNA 500 | Atlanta | 38 | 22 | 322/325 | 0 | Running | $70,700 | 47 |

DRIVERS

# Brendan Gaughan

**Date of birth:** July 10, 1975
**Hometown:** Las Vegas **Resides:**
Las Vegas **Spouse:** Single
**Children:** None **Height:** 5-9
**Weight:** 180 **Hobbies:** Off road-
ing, basketball, snow skiing

## CAREER STATISTICS

| Year | Car owner | Races | Chamn. finish | Won | Top 5 | Top 10 | DNF | Poles | Money won |
|------|-----------|-------|--------------|-----|-------|--------|-----|-------|-----------|
| 2004 | Douglas Bawel | 36 | 28 | 0 | 1 | 3 | 0 | 0 | $2,929,400 |
| **TOTALS** | | **36** | | **0** | **1** | **3** | **8** | **0** | **$2,929,400** |

## 2004 RESULTS

| Race | Track | Start | Finish | Laps | Led | Status | Winnings | Rank |
|------|-------|-------|--------|------|-----|--------|----------|------|
| Daytona 500 | Daytona | 17 | 19 | 199/200 | 0 | Running | $225,887 | 20 |
| Subway 400 | N. Carolina | 15 | 20 | 391/393 | 0 | Running | $70,110 | 22 |
| UAW-DaimlerChrysler 400 | Las Vegas | 8 | 22 | 266/267 | 0 | Running | $83,450 | 23 |
| Golden Corral 500 | Atlanta | 25 | 33 | 314/325 | 0 | Running | $63,120 | 25 |
| Carolina Dodge Dealers 400 | Darlington | 37 | 27 | 291/293 | 0 | Running | $63,110 | 26 |
| Food City 500 | Bristol | 7 | 20 | 500/500 | 0 | Running | $81,900 | 26 |
| Samsung/RadioShack 500 | Texas | 16 | 38 | 230/334 | 0 | Engine | $72,000 | 29 |
| Advance Auto Parts 500 | Martinsville | 11 | 17 | 500/500 | 0 | Running | $70,450 | 28 |
| Aaron's 499 | Talladega | 20 | 13 | 188/188 | 0 | Running | $89,015 | 27 |
| Auto Club 500 | California | 5 | 6 | 250/250 | 1 | Running | $106,125 | 22 |
| Chevy Amer. Revolution 400 | Richmond | 40 | 34 | 362/400 | 0 | Running | $66,375 | 26 |
| Coca-Cola 600 | Lowe's | 7 | 33 | 392/400 | 0 | Running | $77,500 | 28 |
| MBNA 400 'A Salute to Heroes' | Dover | 5 | 27 | 361/400 | 0 | Running | $73,335 | 29 |
| Pocono 500 | Pocono | 31 | 39 | 59/200 | 0 | Engine | $59,660 | 29 |
| DHL 400 | Michigan | 6 | 16 | 200/200 | 13 | Running | $74,065 | 29 |
| Dodge/Save Mart 350 | Infineon | 33 | 26 | 110/110 | 0 | Running | $69,425 | 29 |
| Pepsi 400 | Daytona | 12 | 36 | 136/160 | 0 | Running | $75,450 | 29 |
| Tropicana 400 | Chicago | 15 | 30 | 240/267 | 0 | Running | $76,100 | 29 |
| Siemens 300 | New Hamp. | 29 | 22 | 300/300 | 0 | Running | $72,800 | 29 |
| Pennsylvania 500 | Pocono | 10 | 28 | 177/200 | 0 | Accident | $63,965 | 29 |
| Brickyard 400 | Indianapolis | 30 | 35 | 95/161 | 0 | Accident | $124,925 | 29 |
| Sirius at the Glen | Watkins Glen | 30 | 34 | 74/90 | 7 | Too slow | $61,240 | 29 |
| GFS Marketplace 400 | Michigan | 30 | 33 | 157/200 | 2 | Engine | $66,140 | 30 |
| Sharpie 500 | Bristol | 17 | 35 | 313/500 | 0 | Accident | $76,615 | 29 |
| Pop Secret 500 | California | 22 | 42 | 32/250 | 0 | Accident | $84,585 | 31 |
| Chevy Rock & Roll 400 | Richmond | 37 | 27 | 398/400 | 0 | Running | $68,005 | 31 |
| Sylvania 300 | New Hamp. | 32 | 30 | 296/300 | 0 | Running | $67,650 | 32 |
| MBNA America 400 | Dover | 25 | 22 | 396/400 | 0 | Running | $72,565 | 32 |
| EA Sports 500 | Talladega | 26 | 4 | 188/188 | 7 | Running | $100,640 | 32 |
| Banquet 400 | Kansas | 13 | 10 | 267/267 | 0 | Running | $94,475 | 30 |
| UAW-GM Quality 500 | Lowe's | 16 | 23 | 329/334 | 0 | Running | $69,375 | 30 |
| Subway 500 | Martinsville | 14 | 34 | 424/500 | 0 | Running | $62,020 | 30 |
| Bass Pro Shops MBNA 500 | Atlanta | 25 | 18 | 323/325 | 0 | Running | $85,225 | 29 |
| Checker Auto Parts 500 | Phoenix | 40 | 30 | 311/315 | 0 | Running | $59,925 | 28 |
| Southern 500 | Darlington | 29 | 27 | 363/367 | 0 | Running | $67,375 | 28 |
| Ford 400 | Homestead | 17 | 6 | 271/271 | 0 | Running | $102,000 | 28 |

## NASCAR ACHIEVEMENTS

**First NASCAR Cup start:** February 15, 2004 (Daytona)
**Best points finish:** 28 (2004)
**Career victories:** 0  **Career poles:** 0
**Best career finish:** 4  **Best career start:** 5

## FAST FACTS

● Is the son of Las Vegas hotel and casino magnate Michael
Gaughan and the grandson of local gaming pioneer Jackie
Gaughan.
● A graduate of Georgetown University with a degree in busi-
ness management, he played on the basketball and football
teams.

## CAREER HIGHLIGHTS

● Gaughan didn't have the most talked about rookie season in
2004, but at least he talked the most. The gregarious driver
of the No. 77 car struggled to find the right combination
most of the year. He lost the ride at the end of the season.
● Finished fourth in the 2003 NASCAR Craftsman Truck
Series and won six races. Was first in points heading to the
season finale but finished 29th in the race after getting
caught up in an accident with 33 laps remaining.
● Won the Winston West title in 2000 and 2001 before
moving to the NASCAR Craftsman Truck Series in 2002.

# Jeff Gordon

**24**

**Date of birth:** August 4, 1971. **Hometown:** Vallejo, Calif.
**Resides:** Charlotte **Spouse:** Single **Children:** None
**Height:** 5-7 **Weight:** 150 **Hobbies:** Skiing, video games, golf,
racquetball, bowling, scuba diving

## NASCAR ACHIEVEMENTS

**First NASCAR Cup start:** November 15, 1992 (Atlanta)
**Best points finish:** 1 (1995, 1997, 1998, 2001)
**Career victories:** 69—Atlanta (95a, 98b, 99a, 03b), Bristol

(95a, 96a, 97a, 98a, 02b), California (97, 99, 04a), Charlotte
(94a, 97a, 98a, 99b), Darlington (95b, 96a, 96b, 97b, 98b,
02b), Daytona (95b, 97a, 98b, 99a, 04b), Dover (95b, 96a,
96b, 01a), Indianapolis (94, 98, 01, 04), Kansas (01, 02),

Las Vegas (01), Martinsville (96b, 97a, 99b, 03a, 03b), Michigan (98b, 01a), North Wilkesboro (96b), New Hampshire (95, 97b, 98b), Pocono (96a, 97a, 98b), Richmond (96a, 00b), Rockingham (95a, 97a, 98a, 98b), Sonoma (98, 99, 00, 04), Talladega (96b, 00a, 04a), Watkins Glen (97, 98, 99, 01, 03)

**First victory:** May 29, 1994 (Charlotte)

**Last victory:** August 5, 2004 (Indianapolis)

**Career poles:** 52—Atlanta (00b), Bristol (02a, 02b, 03b, 04b), California (98), Charlotte (93b, 94a, 95a, 96a, 97a, 98a, 00b), Chicago (04), Darlington (95a, 99a, 00a), Daytona (96b, 99a, 04b), Dover (95a, 96a), Indianapolis (95, 96, 99), Martinsville (01a, 02a, 03a, 03b, 04a), Michigan (95a, 99a, 01a, 04a), New Hampshire (98b, 99a, 01a), North Wilkesboro (95a), Pocono (96a, 98a), Richmond (95a, 98a, 99a, 01b), Rockingham (95a, 01a), Sonoma (98, 99, 01, 04), Watkins Glen (98, 03)

**First pole:** October 6, 1993 (Charlotte)

**Best career finish:** 1  **Best career start:** 1

## FAST FACTS

- Is ranked seventh in career wins with 69 and leads all-time money winnings with $66,964,439. Also leads in career wins in road races with seven.
- Set the NASCAR Busch Series record with 11 poles in 1992; also won three races that season—all from the pole.
- Named NASCAR Busch Series Rookie of the Year in 1991 following an 11th place finish in the points standings.
- Won the USAC Silver Crown Series championship in 1991.
- Was the 1990 USAC Midget champion at age 19, making him the youngest driver ever to win the title; was also the youngest driver ever awarded a USAC license at 16.
- Won three quarter-midget national championships and four karting titles.
- Won more than 600 short-track races as a youngster after beginning in the sport in his native California at age 5; the family later relocated to Pittsboro, Ind., where he honed his skills.
- Gordon is one of NASCAR's most active drivers on behalf of charitable causes. The Jeff Gordon Foundation, founded in 1999, primarily supports charities working on behalf of children in need. The Foundation supports the Leukemia & Lymphoma Society, the Make-A-Wish Foundation, the Hendrick Bone Marrow Foundation and Riley Hospital for Children in Indianapolis.
- Along with Darrell Waltrip, was named 1997 NASCAR Person of the Year by *Winston Cup Illustrated.*
- Won the True Value Man of the Year Award in 1996 for his work on behalf of leukemia research.

## CAREER HIGHLIGHTS

- Gordon was near the top of the points standings all season in 2004, showing a renewed focus and passion for winning the championship. He put together an incredible streak in the early summer, winning four straight poles and the middle two of those races. Also, he led the most laps in the first three of those four. Robbie Loomis is an elite crew chief, the guys over the wall are so good you never hear about them, and the Hendrick Motorsports engines are among the best in the sport. He led the points going into the Chase for the NASCAR NEXTEL Cup but didn't win a race during the Chase or put together a streak necessary to win the title.
- Holds the record for most consecutive years leading the circuit in wins with five (1995-1999).
- Has finished in the top 10 in points the past 10 seasons.
- A rough midseason stretch with five of six finishes outside of the top 20 left Gordon out of the championship race in 2003. But he did lead more laps than any other driver on the circuit.
- A win at Darlington in 2002 pushed him up to second in points with 11 races to go, but four finishes of 36th or lower in the following seven races ended his shot at a fifth NASCAR Cup championship.

- Became part-owner, with Rick Hendrick, of Jimmie Johnson's No. 48 team in 2002.
- Bounced back from a down season in 2000 with his fourth NASCAR Cup championship in 2001, placing him third on the list of all-time champs behind seven-time winners Richard Petty and Dale Earnhardt. Gordon led the circuit in wins and poles with six, marking the sixth time in seven years he posted more wins than any other driver.
- Won the NASCAR All-Star race for the third time in his career in 2001, tying Dale Earnhardt for the most wins at the event. He also won the inaugural event at Kansas.
- Finished ninth in points in 2000, his lowest finish since 1993. He didn't have back-to-back wins for the first time since 1995, and his three victories were his fewest since 1994.
- Won his third NASCAR Cup championship in 1998, his third in four seasons, and became the youngest three-time champ at 27. He tied Richard Petty's modern-era record for most wins in a season (13) and tied the likes of Cale Yarborough, Dale Earnhardt and Mark Martin for most consecutive wins with four (Pocono, Indianapolis, Watkins Glen, Michigan).
- Won his second NASCAR Cup championship in 1997. Also became the first driver to win more than $6 million in a season and the youngest driver, at 26, to win the Daytona 500.
- Mechanical problems in the 1996 season finale at Atlanta put him two laps down in the 10th lap and ended his

chances to catch eventual champion Terry Labonte. Gordon finished second in series points, 37 behind Labonte.

● Became the youngest champion in the modern era, at 24, when he won his first NASCAR Cup championship in 1995. He won eight poles and won back-to-back races for the first time in his career.

● Won the inaugural Brickyard 400 in his adopted home state of Indiana in 1994. He became the first driver to win there twice in his career when he finished first again in 1998, the first to win the Brickyard three times with a victory in 2001 and the first to win four times with his win in 2004

● At 23, was the youngest driver in 30 years to win a Gatorade 125 qualifying race at Daytona in 1993.

● Was the first driver to win Rookie of the Year honors in both the NASCAR Busch Series and NASCAR Cup when he was named the Raybestos Rookie of the Year in 1993.

● First career race was the last in the illustrious career of "The King," Richard Petty, the final race of the 1992 season at Atlanta.

## 2004 RESULTS

| Race | Track | Start | Finish | Laps | Led | Status | Winnings | Rank |
|---|---|---|---|---|---|---|---|---|
| Daytona 500 | Daytona | 39 | 8 | 200/200 | 8 | Running | $318,490 | 7 |
| Subway 400 | N. Carolina | 5 | 10 | 391/393 | 39 | Running | $111,363 | 5 |
| UAW-DaimlerChrysler 400 | Las Vegas | 20 | 15 | 267/267 | 0 | Running | $128,128 | 4 |
| Golden Corral 500 | Atlanta | 4 | 10 | 325/325 | 38 | Running | $114,228 | 5 |
| Carolina Dodge Dealers 400 | Darlington | 9 | 41 | 27/293 | 0 | Accident | $98,328 | 13 |
| Food City 500 | Bristol | 2 | 9 | 500/500 | 0 | Running | $120,168 | 12 |
| Samsung/RadioShack 500 | Texas | 9 | 3 | 334/334 | 47 | Running | $253,178 | 9 |
| Advance Auto Parts 500 | Martinsville | 1 | 6 | 500/500 | 180 | Running | $141,403 | 7 |
| Aaron's 499 | Talladega | 11 | 1 | 188/188 | 15 | Running | $320,258 | 3 |
| Auto Club 500 | California | 16 | 1 | 250/250 | 81 | Running | $318,628 | 3 |
| Chevy Amer. Revolution 400 | Richmond | 13 | 6 | 400/400 | 2 | Running | $113,278 | 3 |
| Coca-Cola 600 | Lowe's | 3 | 30 | 393/400 | 0 | Running | $120,678 | 4 |
| MBNA 400 'A Salute to Heroes' | Dover | 13 | 36 | 221/400 | 0 | Accident | $107,908 | 5 |
| Pocono 500 | Pocono | 6 | 4 | 200/200 | 19 | Running | $132,858 | 4 |
| DHL 400 | Michigan | 1 | 38 | 88/200 | 81 | Engine | $120,923 | 6 |
| Dodge/Save Mart 350 | Infineon | 1 | 1 | 110/110 | 92 | Running | $388,103 | 4 |
| Pepsi 400 | Daytona | 1 | 1 | 160/160 | 61 | Running | $346,703 | 3 |
| Tropicana 400 | Chicago | 1 | 4 | 267/267 | 14 | Running | $172,453 | 3 |
| Siemens 300 | New Hamp. | 24 | 2 | 300/300 | 0 | Running | $170,458 | 3 |
| Pennsylvania 500 | Pocono | 13 | 5 | 200/200 | 11 | Running | $121,728 | 2 |
| Brickyard 400 | Indianapolis | 1 | 1 | 161/161 | 124 | Running | $518,053 | 2 |
| Sirius at the Glen | Watkins Glen | 2 | 21 | 90/90 | 13 | Running | $103,413 | 2 |
| GFS Marketplace 400 | Michigan | 2 | 7 | 200/200 | 37 | Running | $119,968 | 1 |
| Sharpie 500 | Bristol | 1 | 14 | 498/500 | 60 | Running | $135,118 | 1 |
| Pop Secret 500 | California | 8 | 37 | 209/250 | 0 | Engine | $124,228 | 2 |
| Chevy Rock & Roll 400 | Richmond | 9 | 3 | 400/400 | 20 | Running | $138,333 | 1 |
| Sylvania 300 | New Hamp. | 1 | 7 | 300/300 | 21 | Running | $116,478 | 3 |
| MBNA America 400 | Dover | 21 | 3 | 400/400 | 1 | Running | $140,533 | 1 |
| EA Sports 500 | Talladega | 5 | 19 | 188/188 | 12 | Running | $112,428 | 3 |
| Banquet 400 | Kansas | 30 | 13 | 267/267 | 0 | Running | $129,078 | 3 |
| UAW-GM Quality 500 | Lowe's | 23 | 2 | 334/334 | 0 | Running | $161,678 | 3 |
| Subway 500 | Martinsville | 15 | 9 | 500/500 | 6 | Running | $107,853 | 2 |
| Bass Pro Shops MBNA 500 | Atlanta | 10 | 34 | 299/325 | 0 | Running | $113,228 | 3 |
| Checker Auto Parts 500 | Phoenix | 8 | 3 | 315/315 | 100 | Running | $170,503 | 2 |
| Southern 500 | Darlington | 2 | 3 | 367/367 | 155 | Running | $185,403 | 3 |
| Ford 400 | Homestead | 5 | 3 | 271/271 | 0 | Running | $208,708 | 3 |

## CAREER STATISTICS

| Year | Car owner | Races | Champ. finish | Won | Top 5 | Top 10 | DNF | Poles | Money won |
|---|---|---|---|---|---|---|---|---|---|
| 1992 | Rick Hendrick | 1 | 79 | 0 | 0 | 0 | 1 | 0 | $6,285 |
| 1993 | Rick Hendrick | 30 | 14 | 0 | 7 | 11 | 11 | 1 | $765,168 |
| 1994 | Rick Hendrick | 31 | 8 | 2 | 7 | 14 | 10 | 1 | $1,779,523 |
| 1995 | Rick Hendrick | 31 | 1 | 7 | 17 | 23 | 3 | 8 | $4,347,343 |
| 1996 | Rick Hendrick | 31 | 2 | 10 | 21 | 24 | 5 | 5 | $3,428,485 |
| 1997 | Rick Hendrick | 32 | 1 | 10 | 22 | 23 | 2 | 1 | $6,375,658 |
| 1998 | Rick Hendrick | 33 | 1 | 13 | 26 | 28 | 2 | 7 | $9,306,584 |
| 1999 | Rick Hendrick | 34 | 6 | 7 | 18 | 21 | 7 | 7 | $5,858,633 |
| 2000 | Rick Hendrick | 34 | 9 | 3 | 11 | 22 | 2 | 3 | $3,001,144 |
| 2001 | Rick Hendrick | 36 | 1 | 6 | 18 | 24 | 2 | 6 | $10,879,757 |
| 2002 | Rick Hendrick | 36 | 4 | 3 | 13 | 20 | 3 | 3 | $6,154,475 |
| 2003 | Rick Hendrick | 36 | 4 | 3 | 15 | 20 | 5 | 4 | $6,622,002 |
| 2004 | Rick Hendrick | 36 | 3 | 5 | 16 | 25 | 4 | 6 | $8,439,382 |
| **TOTALS** | | **401** | | **69** | **191** | **255** | **57** | **52** | **$66,964,439** |

# Robby Gordon

**Date of birth:** January 2, 1969 **Hometown:** Cerritos, Calif. **Resides:** Orange, Calif., and Parker, Ariz. **Spouse:** Single **Children:** None **Height:** 5-10 **Weight:** 180 **Hobbies:** Boating, mountain biking, water skiing

## NASCAR ACHIEVEMENTS

**First NASCAR Cup start:** February 17, 1991 (Daytona)
**Best points finish:** 16 (2003)
**Career victories:** 3—New Hampshire (01b), Sonoma (03), Watkins Glen (03)
**First victory:** November 23, 2001 (New Hampshire)
**Last victory:** August 10, 2003 (Watkins Glen)
**Career poles:** 1—Atlanta (97)
**First pole:** March 7, 1997 (Atlanta)
**Best career finish:** 1  **Best career start:** 1

## FAST FACTS

- Runs in the Indy 500 each year; finished a career-best fourth there in 1999.
- Drove for his own CART series team in 1999 and for Arciero-Wells Racing in 1998.
- Finished second in the 1996 and 1997 IROC series.
- Won the 1996 SCORE Off-Road Trophy Truck Championship with four wins.
- Won CART races at Detroit and Phoenix in 1995 and finished fifth in the point standings.
- Voted most improved driver by his peers in the 1994 PPG IndyCar World Series.
- First full IndyCar season was in 1993, driving for the legendary A.J. Foyt.
- Won GTS class in IMSA 24 Hours of Daytona in 1993, his fourth straight victory in that event, all for car owner Jack Roush.
- Won Sports Car Club of America Trans-Am race at Long Beach, Calif., in 1992, also for Roush Racing.
- In 1991, won five IMSA GTO races in a Roush Racing Ford Mustang.
- Finished second in 1990 GTO season standings.
- Overall winner of the Baja 1000 in 1987 and 1989.
- Won the Mickey Thompson Stadium Series championships in 1988 and 1989.
- Was the SCORE Off-Road champion for five straight years, beginning in 1985.
- Elected to the American Auto Racing Writers and Broadcasters Association All-American Team in 1989.
- Sometimes goes by the nickname of "Flash."
- His only pre-race ritual is eating a turkey sandwich for lunch.
- First job was working in his dad's feed yard raking chaff (strands left over from bales of hay).

- Qualified third and led 22 laps in the 2001 Indianapolis 500.
- Perhaps his most famous moment came at the 1999 Indianapolis 500. After leading 33 laps, he ran out of fuel while leading on the race's final lap.

## CAREER HIGHLIGHTS

- No less an authority than Tony Stewart considers Robby Gordon the most talented driver in NASCAR NEXTEL Cup, but Gordon's results hardly merit such lofty praise. Gordon got in Richard Childress' doghouse when he intentionally wrecked Greg Biffle at New Hampshire in the first race of the Chase for the NASCAR NEXTEL Cup, taking out Tony Stewart and Jeremy Mayfield in the process. Gordon lost his No. 31 ride and will drive for himself in 2005, elevating his NASCAR Busch Series team to NASCAR NEXTEL Cup with co-owner Jim Smith.

- Swept the road courses in 2003 (Sonoma, Watkins Glen), and his two wins and 16th-place finish in points were career bests. The best stretch of his season—a win sandwiched between two sixth-place finishes—was followed by his worst stretch: In the last 13 races, his best finish was 12th; the rest of his finishes were 20th or worse.
- Has been at his best at road courses, getting his only top five in 1997 at Watkins Glen, two top 10s in 2000 at Sears Point and Watkins Glen and his only top five in 2002 at Watkins Glen.
- Completed his first full season in NASCAR Cup in 2002.
- Returned to Cup racing in 2000 after a one-year hiatus in a car he co-owned with Mike Held and John Menard.
- Won his only career pole in 1997 in Atlanta.
- Had one start in 1993, and it was significant. He drove the No. 28 Texaco Havoline Ford at Talladega in that team's first race since the death of Davey Allison.
- Made only seven starts in NASCAR Cup from his debut in 1991 through 1996, failing to produce any top 10s. He did have five DNFs.

**DRIVERS**

## CAREER STATISTICS

| Year | Car owner | Races | Champ. finish | Won | Top 5 | Top 10 | DNF | Poles | Money won |
|------|-----------|-------|---------------|-----|-------|--------|-----|-------|-----------|
| 1991 | Junie Donlavey | 2 | 55 | 0 | 0 | 0 | 0 | 0 | $27,265 |
| 1993 | Robert Yates | 1 | 94 | 0 | 0 | 0 | 1 | 0 | $17,665 |
| 1994 | Michael Kranefuss | 1 | 76 | 0 | 0 | 0 | 1 | 0 | $7,965 |
| 1996 | Teresa Earnhardt | 1 | | 0 | 0 | 0 | 1 | 0 | $4,800 |
| | Felix Sabates | 2 | 57 | 0 | 0 | 0 | 2 | 0 | $29,115 |
| 1997 | Felix Sabates | 20 | 40 | 0 | 1 | 1 | 7 | 1 | $622,439 |
| 1998 | Buz McCall | 1 | 67 | 0 | 0 | 0 | 1 | 0 | $24,765 |
| 2000 | Robby Gordon | 17 | 43 | 0 | 1 | 2 | 7 | 0 | $620,781 |
| 2001 | Larry McClure | 5 | | 0 | 0 | 0 | 1 | 0 | $287,545 |
| | Jim Smith | 2 | | 0 | 1 | 1 | 0 | 0 | $167,335 |
| | Richard Childress | 10 | 44 | 1 | 1 | 2 | 0 | 0 | $917,020 |
| 2002 | Richard Childress | 36 | 20 | 0 | 1 | 5 | 4 | 0 | $3,342,703 |
| 2003 | Richard Childress | 36 | 16 | 2 | 4 | 10 | 2 | 0 | $4,157,064 |
| 2004 | Richard Childress | 36 | 23 | 0 | 2 | 6 | 3 | 0 | $4,225,719 |
| **TOTALS** | | **170** | | **3** | **11** | **27** | **31** | **1** | **$14,452,181** |

## 2004 RESULTS

| Race | Track | Start | Finish | Laps | Led | Status | Winnings | Rank |
|------|-------|-------|--------|------|-----|--------|----------|------|
| Daytona 500 | Daytona | 30 | 35 | 78/200 | 0 | Accident | $241,230 | 35 |
| Subway 400 | N. Carolina | 34 | 36 | 350/393 | 5 | Accident | $90,412 | 38 |
| UAW-DaimlerChrysler 400 | Las Vegas | 22 | 30 | 264/267 | 0 | Running | $101,487 | 37 |
| Golden Corral 500 | Atlanta | 23 | 17 | 323/325 | 1 | Running | $92,987 | 32 |
| Carolina Dodge Dealers 400 | Darlington | 29 | 4 | 293/293 | 0 | Running | $119,117 | 24 |
| Food City 500 | Bristol | 32 | 19 | 500/500 | 1 | Running | $104,792 | 24 |
| Samsung/RadioShack 500 | Texas | 18 | 23 | 331/334 | 0 | Running | $119,537 | 25 |
| Advance Auto Parts 500 | Martinsville | 21 | 30 | 493/500 | 0 | Running | $91,012 | 25 |
| Aaron's 499 | Talladega | 21 | 5 | 188/188 | 22 | Running | $139,927 | 22 |
| Auto Club 500 | California | 23 | 12 | 250/250 | 0 | Running | $112,437 | 19 |
| Chevy Amer. Revolution 400 | Richmond | 6 | 24 | 397/400 | 0 | Running | $93,012 | 19 |
| Coca-Cola 600 | Lowe's | 20 | 20 | 397/400 | 0 | Running | $112,487 | 19 |
| MBNA 400 'A Salute to Heroes' | Dover | 24 | 14 | 398/400 | 0 | Running | $106,022 | 19 |
| Pocono 500 | Pocono | 13 | 8 | 200/200 | 0 | Running | $98,377 | 18 |
| DHL 400 | Michigan | 5 | 33 | 188/200 | 0 | Running | $94,502 | 20 |
| Dodge/Save Mart 350 | Infineon | 24 | 34 | 100/110 | 0 | Running | $92,917 | 23 |
| Pepsi 400 | Daytona | 25 | 19 | 160/160 | 0 | Running | $109,862 | 23 |
| Tropicana 400 | Chicago | 23 | 17 | 267/267 | 2 | Running | $107,837 | 22 |
| Siemens 300 | New Hamp. | 21 | 25 | 300/300 | 0 | Running | $96,372 | 22 |
| Pennsylvania 500 | Pocono | 22 | 7 | 200/200 | 0 | Running | $105,827 | 22 |
| Brickyard 400 | Indianapolis | 20 | 22 | 161/161 | 0 | Running | $160,992 | 23 |
| Sirius at the Glen | Watkins Glen | 23 | 16 | 90/90 | 12 | Running | $91,387 | 19 |
| GFS Marketplace 400 | Michigan | 19 | 25 | 199/200 | 0 | Running | $95,827 | 21 |
| harpie 500 | Bristol | 18 | 12 | 499/500 | 0 | Running | $114,152 | 22 |
| Pop Secret 500 | California | 35 | 9 | 250/250 | 8 | Running | $128,612 | 19 |
| Chevy Rock & Roll 400 | Richmond | 28 | 32 | 396/400 | 0 | Running | $91,717 | 22 |
| Sylvania 300 | New Hamp. | 22 | 32 | 293/300 | 0 | Running | $94,417 | 22 |
| MBNA America 400 | Dover | 32 | 30 | 385/400 | 0 | Running | $93,977 | 22 |
| EA Sports 500 | Talladega | 36 | 9 | 188/188 | 0 | Running | $108,562 | 22 |
| Banquet 400 | Kansas | 23 | 28 | 265/267 | 0 | Running | $101,237 | 23 |
| UAW-GM Quality 500 | Lowe's | 19 | 18 | 332/334 | 0 | Running | $93,137 | 23 |
| Subway 500 | Martinsville | 36 | 23 | 500/500 | 0 | Running | $91,487 | 23 |
| Bass Pro Shops MBNA 500 | Atlanta | 14 | 16 | 324/325 | 0 | Running | $110,512 | 23 |
| Checker Auto Parts 500 | Phoenix | 17 | 35 | 306/315 | 0 | Engine | $86,462 | 23 |
| Southern 500 | Darlington | 23 | 15 | 367/367 | 0 | Running | $100,562 | 23 |
| Ford 400 | Homestead | 33 | 29 | 266/271 | 0 | Running | $86,552 | 23 |

# Jeff Green
## 43

**Date of birth:** September 6, 1962 **Hometown:** Owensboro, Ky. **Resides:** Davidson, N.C. **Spouse:** Michelle **Children:** None **Height:** 5-8 **Weight:** 190 **Hobbies:** Hunting, radio-controlled cars

## NASCAR ACHIEVEMENTS

**First NASCAR Cup start:** September 10, 1994 (Richmond)
**Best points finish:** 17 (2002)
**Career victories:** 0
**Career poles:** 2—Bristol (01b), Daytona (03a)
**First pole:** August 24, 2001 (Bristol)
**Best career finish:** 2  **Best career start:** 1

## FAST FACTS

● Finished second in 2001 NASCAR Busch Series' points.
● Won the 2000 NASCAR Busch Series championship by a record 616 points over second-place Jason Keller.

● First racing experience was in go-karts.
● Green and brother David, the 1994 NASCAR Busch Series champion, were the first siblings to both win a major auto racing championship.

## CAREER HIGHLIGHTS

● The No. 43 team didn't post its first top 10 in 2004 until the 32nd race of the season. Owner Kyle Petty said the team would hire someone else to build its engines for 2005, and that will be Evernham Motorsports. That doesn't guarantee better results, but it can't hurt.
● Raced for the big boys (Richard Childress Racing, Dale Earnhardt Inc. and Petty Enterprises) in 2003 but posted just

## CAR FACTS

**Car:** No. 43 Dodge
**Primary sponsor:** Cheerios/Betty Crocker
**Owner:** Petty Enterprises
**Team:** Petty Enterprises
**Crew chief:** Greg Steadman
**Engine builder:** Evernham Motorsports

one top 10 (Texas). His season started well, as he won the pole at the Daytona 500. But he was involved in an accident and finished 39th.

● Completed his first full NASCAR Cup season in 2002 and finished 17th in series points. He had a career-high four top fives, but qualifying problems hindered him—he qualified in the top 10 only twice.

● Made eight NASCAR Cup starts in 2001, all for Childress.

● Left the NASCAR Busch Series at midseason to drive for Gary Bechtel in 1997. Green qualified fourth in his first race. He finished third for Raybestos Rookie of the Year behind Mike Skinner and brother David Green.

### CAREER STATISTICS

| Year | Car owner | Races | Champ. finish | Won | Top 5 | Top 10 | DNF | Poles | Money won |
|------|-----------|-------|---------------|-----|-------|--------|-----|-------|-----------|
| 1994 | Earl Sadler | 2 | 51 | 0 | 0 | 0 | 1 | 0 | $11,455 |
| | Junior Johnson | 1 | | 0 | 0 | 0 | 0 | 0 | $8,815 |
| 1996 | Teresa Earnhardt | 2 | 49 | 0 | 0 | 0 | 2 | 0 | $16,835 |
| | Gary Bechtel | 2 | | 0 | 0 | 0 | 0 | 0 | $30,040 |
| 1997 | Gary Bechtel | 20 | 39 | 0 | 1 | 2 | 4 | 0 | $434,685 |
| 1998 | Gart Bechtel | 3 | 40 | 0 | 0 | 0 | 0 | 0 | $107,880 |
| | Chuck Rider | 1 | | 0 | 0 | 0 | 0 | 0 | $32,350 |
| | Felix Sabates | 18 | | 0 | 0 | 0 | 7 | 0 | $449,611 |
| 1999 | Felix Sabates | 0 | 60 | 0 | 0 | 0 | 0 | 0 | $62,921 |
| 2001 | Richard Childress | 8 | 48 | 0 | 0 | 1 | 3 | 0 | $441,449 |
| 2002 | Richard Childress | 36 | 17 | 0 | 4 | 6 | 2 | 0 | $2,531,339 |
| 2003 | Richard Childress | 11 | 32 | 0 | 0 | 1 | 2 | 1 | $987,249 |
| | Teresa Earnhardt | 12 | 33 | 0 | 0 | 0 | 2 | 0 | $1,020,671 |
| | Petty Enterprises | 8 | 34 | 0 | 0 | 0 | 2 | 0 | $715,044 |
| 2004 | Petty Enterprises | 36 | 30 | 0 | 0 | 1 | 11 | 0 | $3,483,436 |
| **TOTALS** | | **161** | | **0** | **5** | **11** | **36** | **2** | **$10,304,349** |

### 2004 RESULTS

| Race | Track | Start | Finish | Laps | Led | Status | Winnings | Rank |
|------|-------|-------|--------|------|-----|--------|----------|------|
| Daytona 500 | Daytona | 34 | 33 | 110/200 | 0 | Accident | $232,087 | 33 |
| Subway 400 | N. Carolina | 8 | 28 | 389/393 | 0 | Running | $82,510 | 34 |
| UAW-DaimlerChrysler 400 | Las Vegas | 24 | 34 | 200/267 | 0 | Accident | $91,250 | 35 |
| Golden Corral 500 | Atlanta | 18 | 19 | 322/325 | 0 | Running | $83,615 | 31 |
| Carolina Dodge Dealers 400 | Darlington | 30 | 24 | 292/293 | 0 | Running | $79,010 | 31 |
| Food City 500 | Bristol | 29 | 29 | 496/500 | 0 | Running | $94,285 | 33 |
| Samsung/RadioShack 500 | Texas | 33 | 35 | 290/334 | 0 | Engine | $93,625 | 35 |
| Advance Auto Parts 500 | Martinsville | 33 | 24 | 498/500 | 0 | Running | $82,775 | 35 |
| Aaron's 499 | Talladega | 15 | 19 | 188/188 | 0 | Running | $95,845 | 33 |
| Auto Club 500 | California | 3 | 37 | 147/250 | 0 | Engine | $91,050 | 34 |
| Chevy Amer. Revolution 400 | Richmond | 3 | 37 | 239/400 | 0 | Accident | $81,975 | 35 |
| Coca-Cola 600 | Lowe's | 8 | 27 | 395/400 | 0 | Running | $96,825 | 35 |
| MBNA 400 'A Salute to Heroes' | Dover | 19 | 31 | 349/400 | 0 | Accident | $87,605 | 35 |
| Pocono 500 | Pocono | 32 | 15 | 200/200 | 0 | Running | $87,740 | 34 |
| DHL 400 | Michigan | 23 | 27 | 199/200 | 0 | Running | $88,375 | 35 |
| Dodge/Save Mart 350 | Infineon | 36 | 27 | 110/110 | 0 | Running | $87,520 | 33 |
| Pepsi 400 | Daytona | 30 | 30 | 159/160 | 0 | Running | $98,050 | 34 |
| Tropicana 400 | Chicago | 38 | 28 | 248/267 | 0 | Accident | $95,300 | 34 |
| Siemens 300 | New Hamp. | 30 | 24 | 300/300 | 1 | Running | $90,450 | 34 |
| Pennsylvania 500 | Pocono | 32 | 33 | 128/200 | 0 | Engine | $78,890 | 34 |
| Brickyard 400 | Indianapolis | 14 | 14 | 161/161 | 0 | Running | $164,075 | 34 |
| Sirius at the Glen | Watkins Glen | 35 | 17 | 90/90 | 0 | Running | $86,430 | 33 |
| GFS Marketplace 400 | Michigan | 34 | 23 | 199/200 | 0 | Running | $89,140 | 32 |
| Sharpie 500 | Bristol | 27 | 29 | 462/500 | 0 | Running | $98,635 | 31 |
| Pop Secret 500 | California | 13 | 27 | 250/250 | 0 | Running | $106,935 | 30 |
| Chevy Rock & Roll 400 | Richmond | 10 | 25 | 399/400 | 0 | Running | $87,105 | 30 |
| Sylvania 300 | New Hamp. | 31 | 19 | 299/300 | 0 | Running | $92,000 | 30 |
| MBNA America 400 | Dover | 28 | 21 | 396/400 | 0 | Running | $89,565 | 30 |
| EA Sports 500 | Talladega | 18 | 39 | 142/188 | 0 | Accident | $87,495 | 32 |
| Banquet 400 | Kansas | 27 | 29 | 262/267 | 0 | Running | $94,600 | 32 |
| UAW-GM Quality 500 | Lowe's | 33 | 35 | 238/334 | 0 | Engine | $80,750 | 32 |
| Subway 500 | Martinsville | 10 | 7 | 500/500 | 0 | Running | $93,600 | 31 |
| Bass Pro Shops MBNA 500 | Atlanta | 35 | 21 | 322/325 | 0 | Running | $101,050 | 30 |
| Checker Auto Parts 500 | Phoenix | 12 | 23 | 315/315 | 0 | Running | $82,375 | 31 |
| Southern 500 | Darlington | 32 | 14 | 367/367 | 0 | Running | $95,025 | 29 |
| Ford 400 | Homestead | 31 | 37 | 223/271 | 0 | Engine | $75,975 | 30 |

**Date of birth:** January 8, 1978 **Hometown:** Nashville
**Resides:** Nashville **Spouse:** Stephanie **Children:** Haley
**Height:** 5-5 **Weight:** 170

## NASCAR ACHIEVEMENTS

**First NASCAR Cup start:** November 12, 2000 (Homestead)
**Best points finish:** 39 (2004)
**Career victories:** 0
**Career poles:** 0
**Best career finish:** 11   **Best career start:** 11

## FAST FACTS

● Continued his NASCAR Busch Series success with crew chief Harold Holly in 2004 as he entered the top 10 in points in April and remained there until leaving to race full time in NASCAR NEXTEL Cup in late August.
● Was paired with Holly halfway through the 2003 NASCAR

Busch Series season and found a new level of success. He won four races that season and was in contention for the points championship until the season finale at Homestead. He finished fourth in points.

## CAR FACTS

**Car:** No. 32 Chevrolet
**Primary sponsor:** Tide
**Owner:** Cal Wells
**Team:** PPI Motorsports
**Crew chief:** Harold Holly
**Engine builder:** Richard Childress Racing

● Finished in the top 10 in points (eighth) in the NASCAR Busch Series for the first time in 2002. He also got his first NASCAR Busch Series win, at New Hampshire in May.
● In 2000, began to race full time in the NASCAR Busch Series and finished fourth at Talladega in the spring.
● Son of 2004 NASCAR Craftsman Truck Series champion Bobby Hamilton.
● Started racing at age 15 when he came home from high school and found a 1971 Pinto in his driveway, a gift from his father. The two fixed up the Pinto and started racing in the mini-modified division at Highland Rim Speedway near Ridgetop, Tenn.

## CAREER HIGHLIGHTS

● Hamilton Jr. loves to beat and bang, and he got his first taste of full-time NASCAR NEXTEL Cup racing after taking over in the No. 32 for Ricky Craven halfway through the 2004 season. The results weren't much, but give Hamilton time to make the team his own.
● Made 14 starts at the NASCAR Cup level from 2000 to 2003; his best finishes were a 14th at Talladega in 2001 and 14th at Kansas in 2003.

## CAREER STATISTICS

| Year | Car owner | Races | Champ. finish | Won | Top 5 | Top 10 | DNF | Poles | Money won |
|------|-----------|-------|---------------|-----|-------|--------|-----|-------|-----------|
| 2000 | Bobby Hamilton | 1 | | 0 | 0 | 0 | 0 | 0 | $35,500 |
| | Chip Ganassi | 1 | 60 | 0 | 0 | 0 | 0 | 0 | $46,890 |
| 2001 | Andy Petree | 3 | | 0 | 0 | 0 | 2 | 0 | $241,142 |
| | Larry McClure | 7 | 47 | 0 | 0 | 0 | 2 | 0 | $305,705 |
| 2003 | Ed Rensi | 2 | 54 | 0 | 0 | 0 | 0 | 0 | $128,725 |
| 2004 | James Finch | 6 | | 0 | 0 | 0 | 4 | 0 | $379,665 |
| | Cal Wells | 11 | 39 | 0 | 0 | 0 | 2 | 0 | $879,548 |
| **TOTALS** | | **31** | | **0** | **0** | **0** | **10** | **0** | **$2,017,175** |

## 2004 RESULTS

| Race | Track | Start | Finish | Laps | Led | Status | Winnings | Rank |
|------|-------|-------|--------|------|-----|--------|----------|------|
| Chevy Amer. Revolution 400 | Richmond | 26 | 17 | 399/400 | 0 | Running | $58,470 | 51 |
| Coca-Cola 600 | Lowe's | 31 | 42 | 73/400 | 0 | Handling | $67,760 | 51 |
| Pepsi 400 | Daytona | 28 | 42 | 71/160 | 0 | Accident | $66,640 | 52 |
| Tropicana 400 | Chicago | 28 | 41 | 86/267 | 0 | Engine | $63,355 | 48 |
| Siemens 300 | New Hamp. | 28 | 19 | 300/300 | 0 | Running | $65,750 | 45 |
| GFS Marketplace 400 | Michigan | 41 | 38 | 105/200 | 0 | Engine | $57,690 | 46 |
| Pop Secret 500 | California | 24 | 38 | 207/250 | 0 | Running | $84,800 | 46 |
| Chevy Rock & Roll 400 | Richmond | 22 | 11 | 400/400 | 0 | Running | $89,680 | 42 |
| MBNA America 400 | Dover | 22 | 29 | 385/400 | 0 | Running | $77,829 | 43 |
| EA Sports 500 | Talladega | 39 | 43 | 120/188 | 0 | Accident | $69,261 | 43 |
| Banquet 400 | Kansas | 31 | 23 | 267/267 | 0 | Running | $94,275 | 42 |
| UAW-GM Quality 500 | Lowe's | 11 | 15 | 333/334 | 0 | Running | $88,150 | 39 |
| Subway 500 | Martinsville | 35 | 36 | 404/500 | 0 | Accident | $61,925 | 39 |
| Bass Pro Shops MBNA 500 | Atlanta | 27 | 38 | 225/325 | 0 | Running | $81,664 | 40 |
| Checker Auto Parts 500 | Phoenix | 32 | 16 | 315/315 | 0 | Running | $80,950 | 39 |
| Southern 500 | Darlington | 35 | 31 | 357/367 | 0 | Running | $71,514 | 39 |
| Ford 400 | Homestead | 29 | 21 | 271/271 | 0 | Running | $79,500 | 39 |

# Kevin Harvick 29

**Date of birth:** December 8, 1975 **Hometown:** Bakersfield, Calif. **Resides:** Winston-Salem, N.C. **Spouse:** DeLana **Children:** None **Height:** 5-10 **Weight:** 175 **Hobbies:** Radio-controlled racecars

DRIVERS

## NASCAR ACHIEVEMENTS

**First NASCAR Cup start:** February 25, 2001 (Rockingham)
**Best points finish:** 5 (2003)
**Career victories:** 4—Atlanta (01a), Chicagoland (01, 02), Indianapolis (03)
**First victory:** March 11, 2001 (Atlanta)
**Last victory:** August 3, 2003 (Indianapolis)
**Career poles:** 2—Daytona (02b), Indianapolis (03)
**First pole:** July 6, 2002 (Daytona)
**Best career finish:** 1   **Best career start:** 1

## FAST FACTS

● Won the 2002 IROC championship.
● Was the 2001 NASCAR Cup Raybestos Rookie of the Year in 2001 and also won the NASCAR Busch Series championship.
● Won NASCAR Busch Series Raybestos Rookie of the Year in 2000, winning three races and two poles on his way to a third-place finish in points.
● Had 11 top 10 finishes in the NASCAR Craftsman Truck Series in 1999.
● Won the 1998 NASCAR Winston West Series championship.

- Was Rookie of the Year in the Featherlite Southwest Series in 1995, winning at Tucson and finishing 11th in points.
- Won the 1993 late model championship at Mesa Marin Raceway in his hometown of Bakersfield, Calif.
- Began racing go-karts at age 5, winning seven national titles and two Grand National championships.
- Has a dog named Backup, whom he got just before the start of the 2001 season after another pet died.
- Kevin and his wife, DeLana, were married in Las Vegas in February 2001, two days after he made his NASCAR Cup debut at Rockingham.
- Won the 2002 IROC championship.

## CAREER HIGHLIGHTS

- Harvick was the biggest name and best driver to fail to qualify for the Chase for the NASCAR NEXTEL Cup in 2004. He missed the Chase for the NASCAR NEXTEL Cup not because of an overabundance of bad races but because he had too many mediocre finishes and not enough good ones. He struggled through the middle of the season, usually his strong point. He went from the first race at Talladega to the second without a top five finish. His usually reliable Richard Childress Racing cars broke down repeatedly, and Harvick openly questioned the quality of the engines.

### CAR FACTS

**Car:** No. 29 Chevrolet
**Primary sponsor:** GM Goodwrench
**Owner:** Richard Childress
**Team:** Richard Childress Racing
**Crew chief:** Todd Berrier
**Engine builder:** Childress Racing

- Is one of only six drivers to win races in all three of NASCAR's national series.
- Finished a career-high fifth in points in a 2003 season plagued by inconsistency and slow starts. He finished 25th or worse in five of the first 14 races but got hot early in the second half of the season. Starting with a win from the pole August 3 at the Brickyard 400, Harvick had five straight top fives.
- Became the first driver in NASCAR Cup history to be forced to sit out of a race because of his actions on the track. Already on probation for rough driving, Harvick was suspended for the April race at Martinsville after he spun out another driver in a NASCAR Craftsman Truck race.
- Was the Raybestos Rookie of the Year in 2001, while also winning the NASCAR Busch Series championship. He won in only his third career Cup start, at Atlanta, and also won the inaugural race at Chicagoland Speedway.
- Competed in 35 Cup races in 2001, taking over as the driver of the Chevrolet owned by Richard Childress after the death of Dale Earnhardt in the Daytona 500.

## CAREER STATISTICS

| Year | Car owner | Races | Champ. finish | Won | Top 5 | Top 10 | DNF | Poles | Money won |
|------|-----------|-------|-------|-----|-----|-----|-----|-------|-----|
| 2001 | Richard Childress | 35 | 9 | 2 | 6 | 16 | 1 | 0 | $4,302,202 |
| 2002 | Richard Childress | 35 | 21 | 1 | 5 | 8 | 6 | 1 | $3,849,216 |
| 2003 | Richard Childress | 36 | 5 | 1 | 11 | 18 | 0 | 1 | $6,237,119 |
| 2004 | Richard Childress | 36 | 14 | 0 | 5 | 14 | 4 | 0 | $5,321,337 |
| **TOTALS** | | **142** | | **4** | **27** | **56** | **11** | **2** | **$19,709,874** |

## 2004 RESULTS

| Race | Track | Start | Finish | Laps | Led | Status | Winnings | Rank |
|------|-------|-------|--------|------|-----|--------|----------|------|
| Daytona 500 | Daytona | 10 | 4 | 200/200 | 6 | Running | $610,792 | 4 |
| Subway 400 | N. Carolina | 32 | 13 | 391/393 | 2 | Running | $100,763 | 3 |
| UAW-DaimlerChrysler 400 | Las Vegas | 16 | 21 | 266/267 | 43 | Running | $112,328 | 6 |
| Golden Corral 500 | Atlanta | 8 | 32 | 318/325 | 0 | Running | $90,963 | 12 |
| Carolina Dodge Dealers 400 | Darlington | 23 | 8 | 293/293 | 0 | Running | $98,743 | 11 |
| Food City 500 | Bristol | 14 | 3 | 500/500 | 0 | Running | $131,978 | 7 |
| Samsung/RadioShack 500 | Texas | 22 | 13 | 333/334 | 0 | Running | $139,253 | 8 |
| Advance Auto Parts 500 | Martinsville | 5 | 19 | 500/500 | 0 | Running | $97,403 | 10 |
| Aaron's 499 | Talladega | 14 | 3 | 188/188 | 14 | Running | $185,808 | 6 |
| Auto Club 500 | California | 24 | 9 | 250/250 | 3 | Running | $123,203 | 6 |
| Chevy Amer. Revolution 400 | Richmond | 20 | 25 | 397/400 | 0 | Running | $96,328 | 8 |
| Coca-Cola 600 | Lowe's | 23 | 23 | 396/400 | 0 | Running | $112,878 | 10 |
| MBNA 400 'A Salute to Heroes' | Dover | 33 | 10 | 398/400 | 0 | Running | $116,538 | 9 |
| Pocono 500 | Pocono | 23 | 20 | 200/200 | 0 | Running | $95,593 | 9 |
| DHL 400 | Michigan | 21 | 17 | 200/200 | 0 | Running | $101,043 | 10 |
| Dodge/Save Mart 350 | Infineon | 8 | 12 | 110/110 | 0 | Running | $105,838 | 10 |
| Pepsi 400 | Daytona | 11 | 14 | 160/160 | 0 | Running | $118,303 | 10 |
| Tropicana 400 | Chicago | 17 | 10 | 267/267 | 0 | Running | $122,053 | 8 |
| Siemens 300 | New Hamp. | 19 | 13 | 300/300 | 0 | Running | $106,203 | 9 |
| Pennsylvania 500 | Pocono | 18 | 32 | 141/200 | 0 | Engine | $88,618 | 10 |
| Brickyard 400 | Indianapolis | 32 | 8 | 161/161 | 0 | Running | $205,178 | 9 |
| Sirius at the Glen | Watkins Glen | 9 | 6 | 90/90 | 1 | Running | $102,943 | 8 |
| GFS Marketplace 400 | Michigan | 8 | 16 | 200/200 | 0 | Running | $101,093 | 8 |
| Sharpie 500 | Bristol | 21 | 24 | 494/500 | 0 | Running | $110,963 | 8 |
| Pop Secret 500 | California | 27 | 28 | 250/250 | 0 | Running | $116,238 | 15 |
| Chevy Rock & Roll 400 | Richmond | 27 | 12 | 400/400 | 0 | Running | $99,843 | 14 |
| Sylvania 300 | New Hamp. | 14 | 10 | 300/300 | 1 | Running | $109,778 | 13 |
| MBNA America 400 | Dover | 30 | 19 | 397/400 | 0 | Running | $99,493 | 12 |
| EA Sports 500 | Talladega | 15 | 2 | 188/188 | 3 | Running | $165,208 | 12 |
| Banquet 400 | Kansas | 29 | 35 | 160/267 | 0 | Overheat | $100,378 | 13 |
| UAW-GM Quality 500 | Lowe's | 7 | 36 | 221/334 | 0 | Engine | $90,793 | 13 |
| Subway 500 | Martinsville | 19 | 8 | 500/500 | 104 | Running | $101,903 | 13 |
| Bass Pro Shops MBNA 500 | Atlanta | 9 | 35 | 296/325 | 0 | Engine | $101,478 | 14 |
| Checker Auto Parts 500 | Phoenix | 5 | 4 | 315/315 | 0 | Running | $134,938 | 14 |
| Southern 500 | Darlington | 14 | 32 | 354/367 | 0 | Running | $90,728 | 15 |
| Ford 400 | Homestead | 9 | 10 | 271/271 | 0 | Running | $99,728 | 14 |

# Dale Jarrett
## 88

**Date of birth:** November 26, 1956 **Hometown:** Hickory, N.C.
**Resides:** Hickory, N.C. **Spouse:** Kelley **Children:** Jason, Natalee,
Karsyn, Zachary **Height:** 6-2 **Weight:** 215 **Hobbies:** Golf

## NASCAR ACHIEVEMENTS

**First NASCAR Cup start:** April 29, 1984 (Martinsville)
**Best points finish:** 1 (1999)
**Career victories:** 31—Atlanta (97a), Bristol (97b), Charlotte
(94b, 96a, 97b), Darlington (97a, 98a, 01a), Daytona (93a,
96a, 99b, 00a), Dover (98a), Indianapolis (96, 99),
Martinsville (01a), Michigan (91b, 96b, 99a, 02b), New
Hampshire (01a), Phoenix (97), Pocono (95b, 97b, 02a)
Richmond (97b, 99a), Rockingham (00b, 03a), Talladega
(98b), Texas (01)
**First victory:** August 18, 1991 (Michigan)
**Last victory:** February 23, 2003 (Rockingham)
**Career poles:** 15—Atlanta (00a, 01a), Darlington (96b, 97a,
98b), Daytona (95a, 00a, 00b), Dover (01b), Las Vegas (98,
01), Michigan (02a), Rockingham (96b) Texas (97), Watkins
Glen (01)
**First pole:** February 11, 1995 (Daytona)
**Best career finish:** 1 **Best career start:** 1

## FAST FACTS

● Began racing in 1977 in the Limited Sportsman division
at Hickory Motor Speedway, where his father, two-time
NASCAR champion Ned Jarrett, once was a track pro-
moter.
● Is considered one of the charter drivers in the NASCAR
Busch Series, competing as a regular in 1982, the first year
of competition for the division.
● Won 11 races and 14 poles in the NASCAR Busch Series.
● Competed in IROC seven times (1994, '97, '98, '99, '00, '01
and '02).
● Has two IROC wins, Daytona ('01) and Indianapolis ('02).
● Was all-conference in football, basketball and golf at
Newton-Conover (N.C.) High School. Also played baseball
and was offered a full golf scholarship to the University of
South Carolina.
● NASCAR Cup team owner Andy Petree helped build and
was part-owner of Jarrett's first racecar.
● An excellent golfer, Jarrett has played some of America's
most famous courses. If not for racing, he would have
attempted a professional golf career.
● Won the True Value Man of the Year Award in NASCAR in
2000 for his charity work on behalf of the Susan G. Komen
Breast Cancer Foundation. Also was nominated for the

award in 1996 for his fundraising efforts for Brenner
Children's Hospital and for Carly Brayton, son of driver
Scott Brayton, who was fatally injured in an accident during
Indianapolis 500 practice that year.

## CAREER HIGHLIGHTS

● A miserable 2003 carried over to 2004 until the Pocono
500, when Jarrett turned his season around and stopped
his downward career spiral. Although he finished poorly in
that race because his engine blew five laps from the finish,
his car was good. He scored his first top five of 2004 the
next week. Jarrett climbed in the standings from there and
had a shot at qualifying for the Chase for the NASCAR
NEXTEL Cup—which seemed impossible two months earlier—but failed after a
bad performance at
Richmond. Still, he put
together several strong
finishes in the last 10
races, building
momentum for 2005.
● Had a six-year streak of
top five points finishes
from 1996 to 2001.
Jarrett finished in the
top 10 in points from 1996 to 2002.
● Won the Daytona 500 three times, in 1993, 1996 and 2000.
During his 1993 victory, his father was the commentator
for CBS' national broadcast. He also won the 1999 Daytona
summer race.
● In 2003, had his worst season (26th in points) since 1987.
For Jarrett, it was a disaster of a year filled with personnel
changes, bad luck and ill-handling cars. He struggled even
at tracks he usually thrived at; he finished 32nd and 23rd at
Michigan, where he has four career wins.
● Made his 500th start in the 2003 spring Darlington race.
● Came close to his second NASCAR Cup championship in
2001, when a July victory at New Hampshire drew him
even with Jeff Gordon in the standings. But Jarrett's hopes
for a title unraveled with four finishes of 30th or worse in
the next six races, and he finished fifth in the standings.
● Received a Driver of the Year ESPY in 1999, the same year
he won the NASCAR Cup title. With his father, he became

part of only the second father-son combination to win championships—joining Lee and Richard Petty. He also led the circuit with 24 top fives and 29 top 10s in 1999.

● Joined Robert Yates Racing in 1995 and teamed with crew chief Todd Parrott from 1996 until 2001, winning 24 races and scoring 107 top fives and a NASCAR Cup title.

● Became the first NASCAR Cup driver for Joe Gibbs Racing in 1992 and got the company's first win, in the 1993 February Daytona 500.

● Got his first NASCAR Cup win at Michigan in 1991 after 128 starts, beating Davey Allison by only a few feet.

● Finished second to Davey Allison for Raybestos Rookie of the Year in 1987.

## CAREER STATISTICS

| Year | Car owner | Races | Champ. finish | Won | Top 5 | Top 10 | DNF | Poles | Money won |
|------|-----------|-------|---------------|-----|-------|--------|-----|-------|-----------|
| 1984 | Emanuel Zervakis | 2 | | 0 | 0 | 0 | 1 | 0 | $2,350 |
| | Jimmy Means | 1 | 72 | 0 | 0 | 0 | 0 | 0 | $4,995 |
| 1986 | Mike Curb | 1 | 108 | 0 | 0 | 0 | 1 | 0 | $990 |
| 1987 | Eric Freedlander | 24 | | 0 | 0 | 2 | 11 | 0 | $143,405 |
| 1988 | Cale Yarborough | 19 | | 0 | 0 | 1 | 8 | 0 | $60,610 |
| | Hoss Ellington | 8 | | 0 | 0 | 0 | 4 | 0 | $51,655 |
| | Ralph Ball | 1 | | 0 | 0 | 0 | 1 | 0 | $2,175 |
| | Buddy Arrington | 1 | 23 | 0 | 0 | 0 | 1 | 0 | $4,200 |
| 1989 | Cale Yarborough | 29 | 24 | 0 | 2 | 5 | 11 | 0 | $232,317 |
| 1990 | Wood Brothers | 24 | 25 | 0 | 1 | 7 | 9 | 0 | $214,495 |
| 1991 | Wood Brothers | 29 | 17 | 1 | 3 | 8 | 9 | 0 | $444,256 |
| 1992 | Joe Gibbs | 29 | 19 | 0 | 2 | 8 | 5 | 0 | $418,648 |
| 1993 | Joe Gibbs | 30 | 9 | 1 | 13 | 18 | 5 | 0 | $1,242,394 |
| 1994 | Joe Gibbs | 30 | 16 | 1 | 4 | 9 | 7 | 0 | $881,754 |
| 1995 | Robert Yates | 31 | 13 | 1 | 9 | 14 | 6 | 1 | $1,363,158 |
| 1996 | Robert Yates | 31 | 3 | 4 | 17 | 21 | 3 | 2 | $2,985,418 |
| 1997 | Robert Yates | 32 | 2 | 7 | 20 | 23 | 1 | 2 | $3,240,542 |
| 1998 | Robert Yates | 33 | 3 | 3 | 19 | 22 | 3 | 2 | $4,019,657 |
| 1999 | Robert Yates | 34 | 1 | 4 | 24 | 29 | 1 | 0 | $6,649,596 |
| 2000 | Robert Yates | 34 | 4 | 2 | 15 | 24 | 2 | 3 | $5,934,475 |
| 2001 | Robert Yates | 36 | 5 | 4 | 12 | 19 | 4 | 4 | $5,377,742 |
| 2002 | Robert Yates | 36 | 9 | 2 | 10 | 18 | 5 | 1 | $4,421,951 |
| 2003 | Robert Yates | 36 | 26 | 1 | 1 | 7 | 9 | 0 | $4,121,487 |
| 2004 | Robert Yates | 36 | 15 | 0 | 6 | 14 | 3 | 0 | $5,097,396 |
| **TOTALS** | | **567** | | **31** | **158** | **249** | **109** | **15** | **$46,915,666** |

## 2004 RESULTS

| Race | Track | Start | Finish | Laps | Led | Status | Winnings | rank |
|------|-------|-------|--------|------|-----|--------|----------|------|
| Daytona 500 | Daytona | 31 | 10 | 200/200 | 0 | Running | $279,529 | 10 |
| Subway 400 | N. Carolina | 9 | 40 | 210/393 | 0 | Engine | $85,907 | 26 |
| UAW-DaimlerChrysler 400 | Las Vegas | 29 | 11 | 267/267 | 0 | Running | $120,492 | 22 |
| Golden Corral 500 | Atlanta | 6 | 9 | 325/325 | 0 | Running | $96,217 | 15 |
| Carolina Dodge Dealers 400 | Darlington | 22 | 32 | 279/293 | 0 | Running | $82,442 | 22 |
| Food City 500 | Bristol | 30 | 21 | 500/500 | 0 | Running | $104,557 | 22 |
| Samsung/RadioShack 500 | Texas | 11 | 18 | 332/334 | 0 | Running | $125,442 | 20 |
| Advance Auto Parts 500 | Martinsville | 25 | 10 | 500/500 | 0 | Running | $99,117 | 17 |
| Aaron's 499 | Talladega | 7 | 16 | 188/188 | 3 | Running | $106,957 | 17 |
| Auto Club 500 | California | 31 | 24 | 249/250 | 0 | Running | $103,217 | 18 |
| Chevy Amer. Revolution 400 | Richmond | 31 | 13 | 399/400 | 1 | Running | $96,067 | 17 |
| Coca-Cola 600 | Lowe's | 33 | 18 | 398/400 | 0 | Running | $112,067 | 17 |
| MBNA 400 'A Salute to Heroes' | Dover | 29 | 11 | 398/400 | 0 | Running | $107,967 | 16 |
| Pocono 500 | Pocono | 10 | 26 | 195/200 | 2 | Engine | $88,082 | 17 |
| DHL 400 | Michigan | 37 | 3 | 200/200 | 13 | Running | $142,817 | 14 |
| Dodge/Save Mart 350 | Infineon | 23 | 18 | 110/110 | 0 | Running | $93,742 | 14 |
| Pepsi 400 | Daytona | 4 | 16 | 160/160 | 0 | Running | $111,817 | 15 |
| Tropicana 400 | Chicago | 29 | 3 | 267/267 | 0 | Running | $183,592 | 12 |
| Siemens 300 | New Hamp. | 25 | 9 | 300/300 | 0 | Running | $103,317 | 12 |
| Pennsylvania 500 | Pocono | 24 | 24 | 194/200 | 1 | Running | $88,032 | 14 |
| Brickyard 400 | Indianapolis | 17 | 2 | 161/161 | 0 | Running | $323,367 | 13 |
| Sirius at the Glen | Watkins Glen | 13 | 27 | 89/90 | 0 | Running | $88,457 | 14 |
| GFS Marketplace 400 | Michigan | 14 | 3 | 200/200 | 0 | Running | $123,727 | 14 |
| Sharpie 500 | Bristol | 14 | 10 | 499/500 | 1 | Running | $119,232 | 14 |
| Pop Secret 500 | California | 25 | 8 | 250/250 | 0 | Running | $124,642 | 13 |
| Chevy Rock & Roll 400 | Richmond | 25 | 26 | 398/400 | 0 | Running | $91,147 | 15 |
| Sylvania 300 | New Hamp. | 15 | 27 | 297/300 | 0 | Running | $94,267 | 15 |
| MBNA America 400 | Dover | 11 | 4 | 400/400 | 0 | Running | $122,877 | 15 |
| EA Sports 500 | Talladega | 3 | 3 | 188/188 | 0 | Running | $137,922 | 13 |
| Banquet 400 | Kansas | 9 | 8 | 267/267 | 4 | Running | $119,917 | 12 |
| UAW-GM Quality 500 | Lowe's | 39 | 6 | 334/334 | 0 | Running | $113,992 | 12 |
| Subway 500 | Martinsville | 32 | 37 | 403/500 | 0 | Running | $84,792 | 12 |
| Bass Pro Shops MBNA 500 | Atlanta | 20 | 15 | 324/325 | 0 | Running | $111,742 | 12 |
| Checker Auto Parts 500 | Phoenix | 26 | 22 | 315/315 | 0 | Running | $87,767 | 12 |
| Southern 500 | Darlington | 12 | 37 | 194/367 | 0 | Accident | $84,992 | 14 |
| Ford 400 | Homestead | 27 | 24 | 270/271 | 0 | Running | $86,717 | 15 |

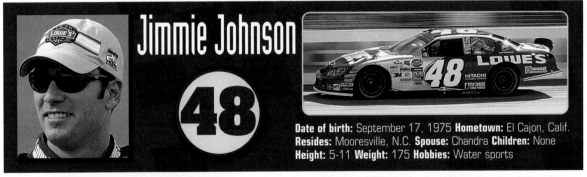

# Jimmie Johnson
## 48

**Date of birth:** September 17, 1975 **Hometown:** El Cajon, Calif.
**Resides:** Mooresville, N.C. **Spouse:** Chandra **Children:** None
**Height:** 5-11 **Weight:** 175 **Hobbies:** Water sports

## NASCAR ACHIEVEMENTS

**First NASCAR Cup start:** October 7, 2001 (Charlotte)
**Best points finish:** 2 (2004, 2003)
**Career victories:** 14—Atlanta (04b), California (02), Charlotte (03a, 04a, 04b), Darlington (04a, 04b), Dover (02a, 02b), Martinsville (04b), New Hampshire (03a, 03b), Pocono (04a, 04b)
**First victory:** April 28, 2002 (California)
**Last victory:** November 14, 2004 (Darlington)

**Career poles:** 7—Charlotte (02a, 04a), Daytona (02a), Kansas (03), Pocono (03a), Richmond (02b),Talladega (02a)

**First pole:** February 17, 2002 (Daytona)

**Best career finish:** 1    **Best career start:** 1

# FAST FACTS

● Finished eighth in NASCAR Busch Series points in 2001, driving for Herzog Motorsports.

● Got his first career NASCAR Busch Series victory in the series' inaugural race at Chicagoland Speedway.

● Won $1,556,668 in 72 NASCAR Busch Series events from 1998-2001.

● Won Rookie of the Year honors in the ASA ACDelco Challenge Series in 1998.

● Before racing stock cars, he won six off-road racing titles— the 1992, '93, and '94 Mickey Thompson Stadium Truck Series championships, the '94 SCORE Desert championship and the '96 and '97 SODA Winter Series championship.

● Competed in the 1995 SCORE Trophy Truck Series and the 1991 MTEG Series.

● Began racing in motocross events at age 4.

● Johnson and Jeff Gordon joined World Superbike champion Colin Edwards in Europe and won the 2002 Race of Champions Nations Cup, an annual event pitting the world's best rally, motorcycle and circuit racers against one another.

● During the 2000 season, Johnson was selected as one of *People*'s "Sexiest Men in the Fast Lane," along with other NASCAR Cup and NASCAR Busch Series drivers.

● Johnson was the youngest driver ever in the Mickey Thompson Stadium Truck Series.

## CAR FACTS

**Car:** No. 48 Chevrolet
**Primary sponsor:** Lowe's
**Owner:** Rick Hendrick
**Team:** Hendrick Motorsports
**Crew chief:** Chad Knaus
**Engine builder:** Hendrick Motorsports

# CAREER HIGHLIGHTS

● After it appeared a pair of DNFs would knock him out of contention in the Chase for the NASCAR NEXTEL Cup in 2004, Johnson rallied with three consecutive victories and four in the next five races. He fell short to Kurt Busch for the championship by just eight points, the slimmest margin in NASCAR history. Johnson finished with eight wins, tops among all drivers, but he had seven DNFs. He swept races at Pocono, Charlotte and Darlington, giving him a sweep at one track (Dover, 2002; New Hampshire, 2003) in each of his three seasons in NASCAR Cup. Johnson led the points standings for nine weeks in 2004..

● A late-season charge in 2003—Johnson finished in the top three in the final six races—helped him end up second in points in only his second season. He finished the year two spots above his car owner, Jeff Gordon. Johnson's finishes

revealed no weaknesses—he had at least one top 10 at a superspeedway, intermediate track, short track and road course.

● His sweep at Dover in 2002 was the first by a rookie in NASCAR Cup history.

● Finished fifth in series points in 2002, one of the best rookie performances since Tony Stewart's three-win season in 1999. His first career NASCAR Cup win came in only his 13th NASCAR Cup start, and he led the NASCAR Cup standings for one week after the Kansas race in September.

## CAREER STATISTICS

| Year | Car owner | Races | Champ. finish | Won | Top 5 | Top 10 | DNF | Poles | Money won |
|------|-----------|-------|---------------|-----|-------|--------|-----|-------|-----------|
| 2001 | Rick Hendrick | 3 | 52 | 0 | 0 | 0 | 1 | 0 | $122,320 |
| 2002 | Rick Hendrick | 36 | 5 | 3 | 6 | 21 | 3 | 4 | $3,788,268 |
| 2003 | Rick Hendrick | 36 | 2 | 3 | 14 | 20 | 3 | 2 | $7,745,530 |
| 2004 | Rick Hendrick | 36 | 2 | 8 | 20 | 23 | 7 | 1 | $8,275,721 |
| **TOTALS** | | **111** | | **14** | **40** | **64** | **14** | **7** | **$19,931,839** |

## 2004 RESULTS

| Race | Track | Start | Finish | Laps | Led | Status | Winnings | rank |
|------|-------|-------|--------|------|-----|--------|----------|------|
| Daytona 500 | Daytona | 6 | 5 | 200/200 | 16 | Running | $472,189 | 5 |
| Subway 400 | N. Carolina | 29 | 41 | 128/393 | 0 | Accident | $74,750 | 25 |
| UAW-DaimlerChrysler 400 | Las Vegas | 12 | 16 | 267/267 | 5 | Running | $98,050 | 19 |
| Golden Corral 500 | Atlanta | 3 | 4 | 325/325 | 0 | Running | $97,400 | 9 |
| Carolina Dodge Dealers 400 | Darlington | 11 | 1 | 293/293 | 69 | Running | $151,150 | 6 |
| Food City 500 | Bristol | 11 | 16 | 500/500 | 8 | Running | $90,215 | 6 |
| Samsung/RadioShack 500 | Texas | 9 | 3 | 334/334 | 0 | Running | $126,475 | 6 |
| Advance Auto Parts 500 | Martinsville | 8 | 4 | 500/500 | 104 | Running | $99,975 | 4 |
| Aaron's 499 | Talladega | 8 | 4 | 188/188 | 25 | Running | $139,655 | 2 |
| Auto Club 500 | California | 19 | 2 | 250/250 | 37 | Running | $194,675 | 2 |
| Chevy Amer. Revolution 400 | Richmond | 5 | 2 | 400/400 | 91 | Running | $135,350 | 2 |
| Coca-Cola 600 | Lowe's | 1 | 1 | 400/400 | 334 | Running | $426,350 | 2 |
| MBNA 400 'A Salute to Heroes' | Dover | 14 | 32 | 345/400 | 1 | Accident | $80,995 | 2 |
| Pocono 500 | Pocono | 5 | 1 | 200/200 | 126 | Running | $186,950 | 2 |
| DHL 400 | Michigan | 3 | 4 | 200/200 | 6 | Running | $100,600 | 1 |
| Dodge/Save Mart 350 | Infineon | 34 | 5 | 110/110 | 0 | Running | $112,915 | 1 |
| Pepsi 400 | Daytona | 19 | 2 | 160/160 | 0 | Running | $193,125 | 1 |
| Tropicana 400 | Chicago | 3 | 2 | 267/267 | 31 | Running | $208,640 | 1 |
| Siemens 300 | New Hamp. | 2 | 11 | 300/300 | 0 | Running | $89,700 | 1 |
| Pennsylvania 500 | Pocono | 14 | 1 | 200/200 | 124 | Running | $276,950 | 1 |
| Brickyard 400 | Indianapolis | 9 | 36 | 88/161 | 0 | Engine | $136,625 | 1 |
| Sirius at the Glen | Watkins Glen | 1 | 40 | 23/90 | 1 | Engine | $72,640 | 1 |
| GFS Marketplace 400 | Michigan | 1 | 40 | 81/200 | 0 | Engine | $77,385 | 2 |
| Sharpie 500 | Bristol | 11 | 3 | 500/500 | 20 | Running | $169,590 | 1 |
| Pop Secret 500 | California | 16 | 14 | 250/250 | 1 | Running | $103,800 | 1 |
| Chevy Rock & Roll 400 | Richmond | 3 | 36 | 338/400 | 32 | Running | $76,165 | 2 |
| Sylvania 300 | New Hamp. | 2 | 11 | 300/300 | 3 | Running | $86,800 | 5 |
| MBNA America 400 | Dover | 9 | 10 | 399/400 | 0 | Running | $86,415 | 4 |
| EA Sports 500 | Talladega | 16 | 37 | 157/188 | 35 | Overheat | $81,150 | 9 |
| Banquet 400 | Kansas | 4 | 32 | 239/267 | 0 | Accident | $85,000 | 9 |
| UAW-GM Quality 500 | Lowe's | 9 | 1 | 334/334 | 35 | Running | $191,450 | 8 |
| Subway 500 | Martinsville | 18 | 1 | 500/500 | 67 | Running | $157,440 | 4 |
| Bass Pro Shops MBNA 500 | Atlanta | 8 | 1 | 325/325 | 17 | Running | $298,250 | 2 |
| Checker Auto Parts 500 | Phoenix | 13 | 6 | 315/315 | 0 | Running | $96,225 | 1 |
| Southern 500 | Darlington | 4 | 1 | 367/367 | 124 | Running | $269,675 | 2 |
| Ford 400 | Homestead | 39 | 2 | 271/271 | 0 | Running | $231,705 | 2 |

DRIVERS

# Kasey Kahne

**9**

**Date of birth:** April 10, 1980 **Hometown:** Enumclaw, Wash. **Resides:** Huntersville, N.C. **Spouse:** Single **Children:** None **Height:** 5-8 **Weight:** 150 **Hobbies:** Snowmobiles

## NASCAR ACHIEVEMENTS

**First NASCAR Cup start:** February 15, 2004 (Daytona)
**Best points finish:** 13 (2004)
**Career victories:** 0
**Career poles:** 4—California (04a), Darlington (04a), Las Vegas (04), Pocono (04a)
**First pole:** March 5, 2004 (Las Vegas)
**Best career finish:** 2 **Best career start:** 1

## FAST FACTS

- Began racing Micro Midgets at age 14 in 1994.
- Won the Mini-Sprint Class Hannigan (Wash.) Speedway championship and Northwest Mini-Sprint Car championship in 1996.
- Second in the Northern Sprint Tour championship in 1997.
- Won 2000 USAC Midget championship and was named the 2000 USAC Rookie of the Year and Midget Driver of the Year.
- Finished seventh in the NASCAR Busch Series in 2003 and 33rd as a rookie in 2002.

## CAREER HIGHLIGHTS

- A veteran of the open-wheel USAC circuit, Kahne has incredible car control—he can steer through anything. The Rookie of the Year in 2004 combined incredible skill and incredible cars with incredibly bad luck. He lost sure wins with a blown tire and a wreck after slipping in spilled oil left from a blown engine. He won four poles, which is remarkable considering how little experience he has at most tracks. Inconsistency prevented him from qualifying for the Chase for the NASCAR NEXTEL Cup. He also won back-to-back races, his first starts, in the NASCAR Craftsman Truck Series.

### CAR FACTS

**Car:** No. 9 Dodge
**Primary sponsor:** Dodge Dealers
**Owner:** Ray Evernham
**Team:** Evernham Motorsports
**Crew chief:** Tommy Baldwin
**Engine builder:** Evernham Motorsports

- Pegged to take over the No. 9 Dodge for Evernham Motorsports in 2004 after driver Bill Elliott announced he would run a partial schedule.

- Won the "Night before the 500" Classic at Indianapolis in 2000 and '01.

### CAREER STATISTICS

| Year | Car owner | Races | Champ. finish | Won | Top 5 | Top 10 | DNF | Poles | Money won |
|---|---|---|---|---|---|---|---|---|---|
| 2004 | Ray Evernham | 36 | 13 | 0 | 13 | 14 | 7 | 4 | $5,415,611 |
| TOTALS | | 36 | | 0 | 13 | 14 | 7 | 4 | $5,415,611 |

### 2004 RESULTS

| Race | Track | Start | Finish | Laps | Led | Status | Winnings | rank |
|---|---|---|---|---|---|---|---|---|
| Daytona 500 | Daytona | 27 | 41 | 42/200 | 0 | Engine | $231,887 | 41 |
| Subway 400 | North Carolina | 3 | 2 | 393/393 | 0 | Running | $130,125 | 21 |
| UAW-DaimlerChrysler 400 | Las Vegas | 1 | 2 | 267/267 | 43 | Running | $260,775 | 8 |
| Golden Corral 500 | Atlanta | 12 | 3 | 325/325 | 0 | Running | $120,125 | 4 |
| Carolina Dodge Dealers 400 | Darlington | 1 | 13 | 293/293 | 24 | Running | $103,590 | 5 |
| Food City 500 | Bristol | 5 | 40 | 57/500 | 0 | Accident | $96,315 | 11 |
| Samsung/RadioShack 500 | Texas | 3 | 2 | 334/334 | 148 | Running | $341,550 | 7 |
| Advance Auto Parts 500 | Martinsville | 15 | 21 | 499/500 | 1 | Running | $91,050 | 9 |
| Aaron's 499 | Talladega | 26 | 30 | 150/188 | 0 | Running | $97,080 | 11 |
| Auto Club 500 | California | 1 | 13 | 250/250 | 77 | Running | $127,250 | 11 |
| Chevy Amer. Revolution 400 | Richmond | 39 | 28 | 394/400 | 0 | Running | $89,350 | 11 |
| Coca-Cola 600 | Lowe's | 19 | 12 | 400/400 | 5 | Running | $119,750 | 11 |
| MBNA 400 'A Salute to Heroes' | Dover | 12 | 21 | 381/400 | 36 | Accident | $103,960 | 12 |
| Pocono 500 | Pocono | 1 | 14 | 200/200 | 4 | Running | $107,990 | 13 |
| DHL 400 | Michigan | 34 | 2 | 200/200 | 0 | Running | $155,900 | 11 |
| Dodge/Save Mart 350 | Infineon | 30 | 31 | 109/110 | 0 | Running | $90,250 | 12 |
| Pepsi 400 | Daytona | 31 | 25 | 160/160 | 1 | Running | $103,700 | 11 |
| Tropicana 400 | Chicago | 2 | 36 | 136/267 | 10 | Accident | $94,275 | 14 |
| Siemens 300 | New Hamp. | 6 | 8 | 300/300 | 0 | Running | $106,075 | 14 |
| Pennsylvania 500 | Pocono | 20 | 3 | 200/200 | 0 | Running | $131,645 | 12 |
| Brickyard 400 | Indianapolis | 12 | 4 | 161/161 | 0 | Running | $263,325 | 11 |
| Sirius at the Glen | Watkins Glen | 11 | 14 | 90/90 | 0 | Running | $92,085 | 11 |
| GFS Marketplace 400 | Michigan | 11 | 5 | 200/200 | 6 | Running | $110,455 | 10 |
| Sharpie 500 | Bristol | 21 | 2 | 496/500 | 0 | Running | $107,535 | 11 |
| Pop Secret 500 | California | 5 | 2 | 250/250 | 39 | Running | $190,315 | 9 |
| Chevy Rock & Roll 400 | Richmond | 11 | 24 | 399/400 | 0 | Running | $92,080 | 12 |
| Sylvania 300 | New Hamp. | 12 | 4 | 300/300 | 31 | Running | $131,700 | 12 |
| MBNA America 400 | Dover | 20 | 42 | 13/400 | 0 | Flywheel | $86,300 | 14 |
| EA Sports 500 | Talladega | 23 | 27 | 187/188 | 0 | Running | $95,360 | 15 |
| Banquet 400 | Kansas | 2 | 12 | 267/267 | 39 | Running | $110,450 | 14 |
| UAW-GM Quality 500 | Lowe's | 2 | 32 | 267/334 | 207 | Accident | $133,050 | 15 |
| Subway 500 | Martinsville | 38 | 18 | 500/500 | 17 | Running | $99,350 | 15 |
| Bass Pro Shops MBNA 500 | Atlanta | 32 | 5 | 325/325 | 4 | Running | $137,275 | 13 |
| Checker Auto Parts 500 | Phoenix | 4 | 5 | 315/315 | 0 | Running | $126,950 | 13 |
| Southern 500 | Darlington | 13 | 5 | 367/367 | 0 | Running | $129,550 | 12 |
| Ford 400 | Homestead | 4 | 38 | 192/271 | 0 | Accident | $79,400 | 13 |

# Matt Kenseth

## 17

**Date of birth:** March 10, 1972 **Hometown:** Cambridge, Wis.
**Resides:** Terrell, N.C. **Spouse:** Katie **Children:** Ross
**Height:** 5-9 **Weight:** 150 **Hobbies:** Motorcycling, boating, golf, computer games

## NASCAR ACHIEVEMENTS

**First NASCAR Cup start:** September 20, 1998 (Dover)
**Best points finish:** 1 (2003)
**Career victories:** 9—Charlotte (00a), Las Vegas (03, 04), Michigan (02), North Carolina (02a, 04), Phoenix (02), Richmond (02), Texas (02)
**First victory:** May 28, 2000 (Charlotte)
**Last victory:** March 7, 2004 (Las Vegas)
**Career poles:** 1—Dover (02a)
**First pole:** June 2, 2002 (Dover)
**Best career finish:** 1  **Best career start:** 1

## FAST FACTS

● Finished third in 1999 NASCAR Busch Series standings with four wins and two poles.
● Was second in 1998 NASCAR Busch Series points race with three victories.
● Finished second in the 1997 NASCAR Busch Series Rookie of the Year race despite starting only 21 races.
● Was running second in the ASA standings when he left for the NASCAR Busch Series in 1997.
● Began his short-track career at age 16, winning his first feature in his third race while he was a high school junior.
● Won 10 features in his first two seasons at tracks in Wisconsin and had 46 super late-model victories over the next three seasons.
● Won the Alan Kulwicki Memorial race in 1993 and track titles at Madison International and Wisconsin International tracks the following year.
● Won another track title at Wisconsin International in 1995, with 15 wins in 60 races.
● Made his NASCAR All-Pro Series debut in 1995, finishing in the top three in three of four starts.
● Won one race and finished third in the Hooters ProCup Series in 1996.

### CAR FACTS

**Car:** No. 17 Ford
**Primary sponsor:** DeWalt Tools
**Owner:** Jack Roush
**Team:** Roush Racing
**Crew chief:** Robbie Reiser
**Engine builder:** Roush/Yates

● Worked on his father's racecar for three years before starting to drive it.
● Won ARTGO Challenge Series race at La Crosse, Wis., at age 19, becoming the youngest winner ever in that series. He broke the record held by Mark Martin, his eventual Winston Cup mentor.

## CAREER HIGHLIGHTS

● Determined to prove wrong those who criticized his 2003 championship as boring, Kenseth needed only three races to double his win total from that season. Kenseth easily qualified for the Chase for the NASCAR NEXTEL Cup but sputtered once it started. Neither his luck nor his car was consistently good.
● Although Kenseth had only one win in 2003 (Las Vegas), he built an insurmountable early-season points lead by finishing in the top 10 in 12 of the first 14 races. He finished the season as the NASCAR Cup champion, with a series-best 25 top 10s, and he never went more than three races without a top 10 finish. He set a modern-era record by assuming the points lead in the season's fourth race and holding it for 33 consecutive weeks.
● Won five races in 2002 (North Carolina, Texas, Michigan, Richmond, Phoenix), the most of any driver on the circuit.
● Won the Raybestos Rookie of the Year award in 2000 over Dale Earnhardt Jr. Kenseth's first career win was the prestigious Coca-Cola 600 at Charlotte, the circuit's longest race. He followed that victory with a second-place finish at Dover the next weekend.
● Made his NASCAR Cup debut in 1998 in the No. 94 Ford. He filled in for Bill Elliott so Elliott could attend his father's funeral. Kenseth finished sixth in the race.

## CAREER STATISTICS

| Year | Car owner | Races | Champ. finish | Won | Top 5 | Top 10 | DNF | Poles | Money won |
|------|-----------|-------|--------------|-----|-------|--------|-----|-------|-----------|
| 1998 | Bill Elliott | 1 | 57 | 0 | 0 | 1 | 0 | 0 | $42,340 |
| 1999 | Jack Roush | 5 | 49 | 0 | 1 | 1 | 3 | 0 | $143,561 |
| 2000 | Jack Roush | 34 | 14 | 1 | 4 | 11 | 5 | 0 | $2,408,138 |
| 2001 | Jack Roush | 36 | 13 | 0 | 4 | 9 | 5 | 0 | $2,565,579 |
| 2002 | Jack Roush | 36 | 8 | 5 | 11 | 19 | 3 | 1 | $4,514,203 |
| 2003 | Jack Roush | 36 | 1 | 1 | 11 | 25 | 2 | 0 | $9,422,764 |
| 2004 | Jack Roush | 36 | 8 | 2 | 8 | 16 | 6 | 0 | $7,405,309 |
| **TOTALS** | | **184** | | **9** | **39** | **82** | **24** | **1** | **$26,501,894** |

| Race | Track | Start | Finish | Laps | Led | Status | Winnings | Rank |
|---|---|---|---|---|---|---|---|---|
| Daytona 500 | Daytona | 12 | 9 | 200/200 | 2 | Running | $307,917 | 9 |
| Subway 400 | N. Carolina | 23 | 1 | 393/393 | 259 | Running | $222,303 | 2 |
| UAW-DaimlerChrysler 400 | Las Vegas | 25 | 1 | 267/267 | 123 | Running | $458,828 | 1 |
| Golden Corral 500 | Atlanta | 30 | 6 | 325/325 | 0 | Running | $120,728 | 1 |
| Carolina Dodge Dealers 400 | Darlington | 15 | 31 | 289/293 | 0 | Running | $102,358 | 1 |
| Food City 500 | Bristol | 23 | 5 | 500/500 | 0 | Running | $136,098 | 1 |
| Samsung/RadioShack 500 | Texas | 25 | 16 | 332/334 | 0 | Running | $145,103 | 2 |
| Advance Auto Parts 500 | Martinsville | 29 | 8 | 500/500 | 0 | Running | $113,728 | 3 |
| Aaron's 499 | Talladega | 31 | 42 | 59/188 | 0 | Engine | $112,298 | 5 |
| Auto Club 500 | California | 25 | 4 | 250/250 | 11 | Running | $172,578 | 4 |
| Chevy Amer. Revolution 400 | Richmond | 29 | 5 | 400/400 | 4 | Running | $122,303 | 4 |
| Coca-Cola 600 | Lowe's | 37 | 3 | 400/400 | 1 | Running | $222,478 | 3 |
| MBNA 400 'A Salute to Heroes' | Dover | 39 | 22 | 381/400 | 0 | Accident | $115,913 | 3 |
| Pocono 500 | Pocono | 15 | 21 | 200/200 | 5 | Running | $105,918 | 3 |
| DHL 400 | Michigan | 18 | 7 | 200/200 | 1 | Running | $119,093 | 3 |
| Dodge/Save Mart 350 | Infineon | 5 | 20 | 110/110 | 0 | Running | $111,603 | 3 |
| Pepsi 400 | Daytona | 36 | 39 | 110/160 | 0 | Accident | $117,803 | 5 |
| Tropicana 400 | Chicago | 26 | 12 | 267/267 | 1 | Running | $127,853 | 5 |
| Siemens 300 | New Hamp. | 31 | 4 | 300/300 | 0 | Running | $146,103 | 5 |
| Pennsylvania 500 | Pocono | 15 | 8 | 200/200 | 0 | Running | $113,968 | 4 |
| Brickyard 400 | Indianapolis | 23 | 16 | 161/161 | 0 | Running | $192,603 | 5 |
| Sirius at the Glen | Watkins Glen | 5 | 9 | 90/90 | 0 | Running | $109,808 | 5 |
| GFS Marketplace 400 | Michigan | 5 | 8 | 200/200 | 0 | Running | $117,343 | 5 |
| Sharpie 500 | Bristol | 23 | 9 | 499/500 | 0 | Running | $134,168 | 5 |
| Pop Secret 500 | California | 30 | 22 | 250/250 | 0 | Running | $129,803 | 5 |
| Chevy Rock & Roll 400 | Richmond | 16 | 28 | 397/400 | 5 | Running | $107,658 | 5 |
| Sylvania 300 | New Hamp. | 5 | 2 | 300/300 | 0 | Running | $175,108 | 4 |
| MBNA America 400 | Dover | 8 | 32 | 319/400 | 58 | Accident | $118,833 | 7 |
| EA Sports 500 | Talladega | 7 | 14 | 188/188 | 0 | Running | $116,973 | 5 |
| Banquet 400 | Kansas | 15 | 17 | 267/267 | 0 | Running | $123,428 | 7 |
| UAW-GM Quality 500 | Lowe's | 36 | 11 | 334/334 | 0 | Running | $113,803 | 7 |
| Subway 500 | Martinsville | 25 | 16 | 500/500 | 2 | Running | $108,203 | 8 |
| Bass Pro Shops MBNA 500 | Atlanta | 39 | 41 | 175/325 | 0 | Engine | $115,678 | 9 |
| Checker Auto Parts 500 | Phoenix | 16 | 36 | 280/315 | 4 | Engine | $101,903 | 9 |
| Southern 500 | Darlington | 9 | 20 | 365/367 | 1 | Running | $113,603 | 8 |
| Ford 400 | Homestead | 30 | 19 | 271/271 | 0 | Running | $104,203 | 8 |

# Travis Kvapil

**Date of birth:** March 1, 1976 **Hometown:** Janesville, Wis.
**Spouse:** Jennifer **Children:** Kelsey, Carson **Height:** 6-0
**Weight:** 190 **Hobbies:** Watching the Green Bay Packers

## NASCAR ACHIEVEMENTS

**First NASCAR Cup start:** October 24, 2004 (Martinsville)
**Best points finish:** 63 (2004)
**Career victories:** 0   **Career poles:** 0
**Best career finish:** 21   **Best career start:** 5

## FAST FACTS

● Won the 2003 NASCAR Craftsman Truck Series championship with one win and 22 top 10 finishes in 25 starts.
● Before reaching the NASCAR Craftsman Trucks Series, Kvapil starred in the Re/Max Challenge Series in 1999 and 2000, winning twice at Pikes Peak International Raceway.
● Was the 1996 Late Model champion of Madison (Wis.) International Speedway.
● Won 2001 Raybestos Rookie of the Year in the NASCAR Craftsman Truck Series. That season he won his first race and finished fourth in the points standings.

## CAR FACTS

**Car:** No. 77 Dodge
**Primary sponsor:** Kodak
**Owner:** Doug Bawel
**Team:** Penske-Jasper Racing
**Crew chief:** Shane Wilson
**Engine builder:** Penske-Jasper

## CAREER HIGHLIGHTS

● Kvapil got his feet wet in the NASCAR NEXTEL Cup Series in 2004, running three races in a developmental program with Penske Racing. He was named to drive the No. 77 Dodge, replacing Brendan Gaughan, after the end of the season. Kvapil finished eighth in the NASCAR Craftsman Truck Series standings in 2004.

### CAREER STATISTICS

| Year | Car owner | Races | Champ. finish | Won | Top 5 | Top 10 | DNF | Poles | Money won |
|---|---|---|---|---|---|---|---|---|---|
| 2004 | Roger Penske | 3 | 63 | 0 | 0 | 16 | 0 | 0 | $171,475 |
| **TOTALS** | | **3** | | **0** | **0** | **0** | **0** | **0** | **$171,475** |

### 2004 RESULTS

| Race | Track | Start | Finish | Laps | Led | Status | Winnings | rank |
|---|---|---|---|---|---|---|---|---|
| Subway 500 | Martinsville | 5 | 21 | 500/500 | 0 | Running | $55,975 | 71 |
| Bass Pro Shops MBNA 500 | Atlanta | 26 | 32 | 317/325 | 0 | Running | $66,175 | 67 |
| Ford 400 | Homestead | 26 | 39 | 162/271 | 0 | Accident | $49,325 | 63 |

**DRIVERS**

**Bobby Labonte**

**18**

**Date of birth:** May 8, 1964 **Hometown:** Corpus Christi, Texas
**Resides:** Trinity, N.C. **Spouse:** Donna **Children:** Robert, Madison
**Height:** 5-9 **Weight:** 175 **Hobbies:** Fishing

## NASCAR ACHIEVEMENTS

**First NASCAR Cup start:** June 2, 1991 (Dover)
**Best points finish:** 1 (2000)
**Career victories:** 21—Atlanta (96b, 97b, 98a, 99b, 01b, 03a), Charlotte (95a, 00b), Darlington (00b), Dover (99a), Homestead (03), Indianapolis (00), Martinsville (02a), Michigan (95a, 95b, 99b), Pocono (99a, 99b, 01b), Rockingham (00a), Talladega (98a), Texas (04a)
**First victory:** May 28, 1995 (Charlotte)
**Last victory:** November 16, 2003 (Homestead)
**Career poles:** 26—Atlanta (96b, 99a), California (01), Charlotte (96b, 99a, 99b), Darlington (97b), Daytona (98a, 98b), Dover (96b, 97a, 99a), Las Vegas (99, 03), Martinsville (95a), Michigan (94a, 00a, 03a, 03b), New Hampshire (00b), Phoenix (96), Richmond (93b), Rockingham (97b), Talladega (98a), Texas (03, 04)
**First pole:** September 9, 1993 (Richmond)
**Best career finish:** 1    **Best career start:** 1

## FAST FACTS

- Began his career in 1984 as a Hagan Racing crew member; his brother Terry was the team's driver.
- Raced late model stock cars at Caraway Speedway in Asheboro, N.C., winning the 1987 track championship with 12 victories in 23 races.
- Won the NASCAR Busch Series championship in 1991 and finished second in 1992 behind Joe Nemechek; Nemechek's winning margin of three points was closest in the history of NASCAR's three national series.
- Ran quarter-midgets in Texas as a boy.
- In 2001, Bobby and Terry had a park named in their honor, in their hometown of Corpus Christi, Texas.
- With Terry, was inducted into the Texas Sports Hall of Fame in 2001, nearly doubling the class of four inductees from the racing community. The Labontes' class included Texas football greats Troy Aikman, Dick "Night Train" Lane, Bruce Matthews and Mike Munchak, along with baseball great Norm Cash.

## CAREER HIGHLIGHTS

- A decent 2004 turned disastrous after the firing of crew chief Michael "Fatback" McSwain. After McSwain's departure on July 14 following the 18th race of the season, Labonte did not finish in the top 10 again untl the 34th race. The drop in performance left him out of the Chase for the NASCAR NEXTEL Cup. He summed it up best before the Richmond race. Asked whether he would run differently or whether it would be business as usual, he said he sure hoped it wasn't business as usual because business hadn't been good.
- Looked great early in the 2003 season with a streak of eight top 10s in nine races, but he faltered after that, with seven consecutive finishes of 14th or worse. The season ended on a high note with a victory at Homestead.
- In 2002, snapped a run of five consecutive seasons of finishing among the top seven in points. His 16th-place finish was his worst since joining Joe Gibbs Racing in 1995.
- Won the NASCAR Cup championship in 2000. Bobby and his brother, Terry, became the only brothers who each have won the title. He grabbed the points lead after the third race of the season at Las Vegas and fell out of the top spot just once the rest of the way. He had only two finishes outside of the top 20.
- Broke his shoulder in 1999 during a NASCAR Busch Series practice in March at Darlington, but he did not miss a Cup start and finished second in points to Dale Jarrett. He also swept the Pocono races.
- In 1996, got a win in the series finale at Atlanta, the same day his brother, Terry, celebrated clinching the Cup championship. He won the series finale in Atlanta again in 1997.
- Moved from Bill Davis Racing to Joe Gibbs Racing in 1995 and enjoyed a breakthrough season, replacing Dale Jarrett in the No. 18 car. Labonte's first career win came in his

**CAR FACTS**

**Car:** No. 18 Chevrolet
**Primary sponsor:** Interstate Batteries
**Owner:** Joe Gibbs
**Team:** Joe Gibbs Racing
**Crew chief:** Steve Addington
**Engine builder:** Mark Cronquist

74th career start, at the Coca-Cola 600 at Charlotte. He also swept the Michigan races.

● Landed with Bill Davis Racing in 1993 and lost out on Raybestos Rookie of the Year honors to Jeff Gordon.

● Made his NASCAR Cup debut as a driver/owner in 1991, competing in two events and also running full time in the NASCAR Busch Series and winning that championship.

## CAREER STATISTICS

| Year | Car owner | Races | Champ. finish | Won | Top 5 | Top 10 | DNF | Poles | Money won |
|------|-----------|-------|---------------|-----|-------|--------|-----|-------|-----------|
| 1991 | Bobby Labonte | 2 | 66 | 0 | 0 | 0 | 2 | 0 | $8,350 |
| 1993 | Bill Davis | 30 | 19 | 0 | 0 | 6 | 6 | 1 | $395,660 |
| 1994 | Bill Davis | 31 | 21 | 0 | 1 | 2 | 7 | 0 | $550,305 |
| 1995 | Joe Gibbs | 31 | 10 | 3 | 7 | 14 | 6 | 2 | $1,413,682 |
| 1996 | Joe Gibbs | 31 | 11 | 1 | 5 | 14 | 5 | 4 | $1,475,196 |
| 1997 | Joe Gibbs | 32 | 7 | 1 | 9 | 18 | 1 | 3 | $2,217,999 |
| 1998 | Joe Gibbs | 33 | 6 | 2 | 11 | 18 | 6 | 3 | $2,980,052 |
| 1999 | Joe Gibbs | 34 | 2 | 5 | 23 | 26 | 1 | 5 | $4,763,615 |
| 2000 | Joe Gibbs | 34 | 1 | 4 | 19 | 24 | 0 | 2 | $7,361,386 |
| 2001 | Joe Gibbs | 36 | 6 | 2 | 9 | 20 | 6 | 1 | $4,786,779 |
| 2002 | Joe Gibbs | 36 | 16 | 1 | 5 | 7 | 4 | 0 | $4,183,715 |
| 2003 | Joe Gibbs | 36 | 8 | 2 | 12 | 17 | 5 | 4 | $5,505,018 |
| 2004 | Joe Gibbs | 36 | 12 | 0 | 5 | 11 | 2 | 1 | $5,201,397 |
| **TOTALS** | | **402** | | **21** | **106** | **177** | **51** | **26** | **$40,843,154** |

## 2004 RESULTS

| Race | Track | Start | Finish | Laps | Led | Status | Winnings | Rank |
|------|-------|-------|--------|------|-----|--------|----------|------|
| Daytona 500 | Daytona | 13 | 11 | 200/200 | 0 | Running | $278,445 | 11 |
| Subway 400 | N. Carolina | 11 | 25 | 389/393 | 0 | Running | $102,318 | 17 |
| UAW-DaimlerChrysler 400 | Las Vegas | 7 | 8 | 267/267 | 0 | Running | $136,583 | 11 |
| Golden Corral 500 | Atlanta | 10 | 18 | 323/325 | 0 | Running | $102,673 | 10 |
| Carolina Dodge Dealers 400 | Darlington | 12 | 2 | 293/293 | 18 | Running | $136,183 | 8 |
| Food City 500 | Bristol | 27 | 33 | 428/500 | 0 | Running | $112,808 | 13 |
| Samsung/RadioShack 500 | Texas | 1 | 25 | 330/334 | 5 | Running | $139,908 | 15 |
| Advance Auto Parts 500 | Martinsville | 23 | 2 | 500/500 | 0 | Running | $143,198 | 12 |
| Aaron's 499 | Talladega | 19 | 10 | 188/188 | 1 | Running | $126,313 | 10 |
| Auto Club 500 | California | 27 | 5 | 250/250 | 0 | Running | $150,233 | 9 |
| Chevy Amer. Revolution 400 | Richmond | 27 | 3 | 400/400 | 0 | Running | $142,333 | 7 |
| Coca-Cola 600 | Lowe's | 9 | 13 | 400/400 | 0 | Running | $129,283 | 8 |
| MBNA 400 'A Salute to Heroes' | Dover | 18 | 25 | 370/400 | 0 | Running | $108,938 | 8 |
| Pocono 500 | Pocono | 17 | 3 | 200/200 | 1 | Running | $139,953 | 6 |
| DHL 400 | Michigan | 12 | 8 | 200/200 | 0 | Running | $111,723 | 4 |
| Dodge/Save Mart 350 | Infineon | 10 | 33 | 104/110 | 18 | Running | $103,773 | 7 |
| Pepsi 400 | Daytona | 15 | 7 | 160/160 | 0 | Running | $135,658 | 6 |
| Tropicana 400 | Chicago | 11 | 18 | 267/267 | 1 | Running | $117,133 | 6 |
| Siemens 300 | New Hamp. | 20 | 17 | 300/300 | 0 | Running | $107,933 | 7 |
| Pennsylvania 500 | Pocono | 17 | 29 | 175/200 | 0 | Accident | $98,373 | 9 |
| Brickyard 400 | Indianapolis | 39 | 15 | 161/161 | 0 | Running | $180,333 | 8 |
| Sirius at the Glen | Watkins Glen | 8 | 11 | 90/90 | 0 | Running | $102,813 | 9 |
| GFS Marketplace 400 | Michigan | 9 | 26 | 199/200 | 0 | Running | $104,098 | 9 |
| Sharpie 500 | Bristol | 19 | 16 | 498/500 | 1 | Running | $121,468 | 9 |
| Pop Secret 500 | California | 37 | 20 | 250/250 | 0 | Running | $127,033 | 12 |
| Chevy Rock & Roll 400 | Richmond | 18 | 16 | 399/400 | 0 | Running | $104,213 | 13 |
| Sylvania 300 | New Hamp. | 13 | 18 | 299/300 | 0 | Running | $107,333 | 14 |
| MBNA America 400 | Dover | 6 | 14 | 398/400 | 0 | Running | $107,123 | 13 |
| EA Sports 500 | Talladega | 27 | 35 | 177/188 | 0 | Accident | $106,533 | 14 |
| Banquet 400 | Kansas | 5 | 16 | 267/267 | 0 | Running | $73,650 | 15 |
| UAW-GM Quality 500 | Lowe's | 34 | 17 | 332/334 | 0 | Running | $103,483 | 14 |
| Subway 500 | Martinsville | 17 | 18 | 500/500 | 0 | Running | $101,813 | 14 |
| Bass Pro Shops MBNA 500 | Atlanta | 19 | 20 | 323/325 | 0 | Running | $119,233 | 15 |
| Checker Auto Parts 500 | Phoenix | 27 | 9 | 315/315 | 4 | Running | $113,083 | 15 |
| Southern 500 | Darlington | 15 | 9 | 367/367 | 0 | Running | $115,958 | 13 |
| Ford 400 | Homestead | 6 | 12 | 271/271 | 10 | Running | $100,133 | 12 |

**Terry Labonte** 44

**Date of birth:** November 16, 1956 **Hometown:** Corpus Christi, Texas **Resides:** Thomasville, N.C. **Spouse:** Kim **Children:** Justin, Kristen **Height:** 5-10 **Weight:** 165 **Hobbies:** Hunting, fishing

DRIVERS

## NASCAR ACHIEVEMENTS

**First NASCAR Cup start:** September 4, 1978 (Darlington)
**Best points finish:** 1 (1984, 1996)
**Career victories:** 22—Bristol (84b, 95b), Charlotte (96b), Darlington (80b, 03b), North Wilkesboro (87b, 88a, 94a, 96a), Phoenix (94), Pocono (89a, 95s), Richmond (94b, 95a, 98a), Riverside (84a, 85a), Rockingham (83b, 86a), Talladega (89b, 97b), Texas (99)
**First victory:** September 1, 1980 (Darlington)
**Last victory:** August 31, 2003 (Darlington
**Career poles:** 27—Atlanta (81a), Bristol (87b), Dover (83b, 85a), Martinsville (82a), North Wilkesboro (88a, 96a), Pocono (87a), Richmond (96a, 03a), Riverside (82a, 84a, 84b, 85a, 87a), Rockingham (85a, 85b, 86a, 96a), Sonoma (96), Talladega (95a), Texas (00), Texas World (81), Watkins Glen (87, 91)
**First pole:** March 13, 1981 (Atlanta)
**Best career finish:** 1   **Best career start:** 1

## FAST FACTS

● Started racing in quarter-midgets when he was 7.
● At age 16, moved into stock cars that were first owned by

his father, Bob, then by former NASCAR Cup owner Billy Hagan.

- His family moved to North Carolina in the late 1970s to get Labonte closer to the NASCAR Cup scene, where he debuted with Hagan in 1978.
- Won his first NASCAR Busch Series race in 1985 and won 11 total in that series.

## CAR FACTS

**Car:** No. 44 Chevrolet
**Primary sponsor:** Kellogg's
**Owner:** Rick Hendrick
**Team:** Hendrick Motorsports
**Crew chief:** Peter Sospenzo
**Engine builder:** Hendrick Motorsports

- Won the 1989 IROC title.
- Has competed in the NASCAR Craftsman Truck Series, winning at Richmond in 1995, which made him one of only six drivers to win a race in each of NASCAR's national series.
- Was inducted into the Texas Sports Hall of Fame in 2001. Labonte and his brother, Bobby, are among the four auto racing inductees in the Hall, which also includes Carroll Shelby and Johnny Rutherford.
- Labonte's son, Justin, has competed on the Busch and ARCA circuits.

## CAREER HIGHLIGHTS

- The Ice Man announced 2004 would be his final full-time season. He'll run a partial schedule, driving the No. 44, in 2005. Rookie Kyle Busch will take over Labonte's No. 5.
- Entered the 2004 season fifth on the all-time list for career starts with 781 and boosted that number to 817. He trails only Richard Petty (1,184), Dave Marcis (883), Darrell Waltrip (809) and Ricky Rudd (839).
- In 2003, finished 10th in points, his best standing since 1998, and the key to his resurgence was consistency. He finished 39th in the spring race at Bristol but didn't miss the top 25 again until the October race at Atlanta. He won the final Southern 500 to be run on Labor Day weekend, which was his first trip to victory lane since 1999.
- Forced to miss races at Indianapolis and Watkins Glen in 2000 because of injuries suffered in an accident in Daytona in July, which ended his NASCAR Cup record of 655 consecutive starts. He recovered in time to start his 700th race, at Dover.
- In 1998, started second at the Daytona 500 next to his brother, Bobby. It was the only time brothers have shared the front row for the prestigious event.
- Won his second NASCAR Cup title in 1996 and became the fifth driver in the modern era to win multiple titles. Labonte also broke Richard Petty's record with his 514th consecutive start on April 21, 1996, at Martinsville.

- Made his 500th start, at Watkins Glen in 1995.
- Leapfrogged from owner Richard Jackson in 1990 to Billy Hagan in 1991, then joined Hendrick Motorsports in 1994. With Hendrick, Labonte hit a streak of five straight top 10 points finishes (1994-98) and broke a four-year winless streak with three victories (North Wilkesboro, Phoenix, Richmond) during his first season with Hendrick.
- Got the first of his two NASCAR All-Star race victories on May 22, 1988. He got the second on May 22,1999, exactly 11 years later.
- Joined Junior Johnson in 1987 and jumped to third in points after finishing 12th in in 1986, his worst finish since starting racing NASCAR Cup full time.
- Won the 1984 NASCAR Cup championship and won two races in a season (Riverside, Bristol) for the first time in his career. The championship season was the last in a four-year streak of top five points finishes (1981-84). During those four years, Labonte won only one other race (Rockingham, 1983).
- His fourth-place finish at Martinsville in October 1982 made Labonte, 25, the youngest driver in history to win $1 million and the 12th driver to reach the mark.
- Finished second to Dale Earnhardt for 1979 Raybestos Rookie of the Year.
- In 1978, placed in the top 10 in his first three NASCAR Cup races, including his first ever NASCAR Cup race, the Southern 500, where he finished fourth.

## CAREER STATISTICS

| Year | Car owner | Races | Champ. finish | Won | Top 5 | Top 10 | DNF | Poles | Money won |
|------|-----------|-------|------|-----|-----|-----|-----|-----|-----|
| 1978 | Billy Hagan | 5 | 39 | 0 | 1 | 3 | 2 | 0 | $20,545 |
| 1979 | Billy Hagan | 31 | 10 | 0 | 2 | 13 | 10 | 0 | $130,057 |
| 1980 | Billy Hagan | 31 | 8 | 1 | 6 | 16 | 12 | 0 | $215,889 |
| 1981 | Billy Hagan | 31 | 4 | 0 | 8 | 17 | 8 | 2 | $334,987 |
| 1982 | Billy Hagan | 30 | 3 | 0 | 17 | 21 | 8 | 2 | $363,970 |
| 1983 | Billy Hagan | 30 | 5 | 1 | 11 | 20 | 7 | 3 | $362,790 |
| 1984 | Billy Hagan | 30 | 1 | 2 | 17 | 24 | 3 | 2 | $713,010 |
| 1985 | Billy Hagan | 28 | 7 | 1 | 8 | 17 | 8 | 4 | $694,510 |
| 1986 | Billy Hagan | 29 | 12 | 1 | 5 | 10 | 12 | 1 | $522,235 |
| 1987 | Junior Johnson | 29 | 3 | 1 | 13 | 22 | 5 | 4 | $825,369 |
| 1988 | Junior Johnson | 29 | 4 | 1 | 11 | 18 | 3 | 1 | $950,781 |
| 1989 | Junior Johnson | 29 | 10 | 2 | 9 | 11 | 6 | 0 | $704,806 |
| 1990 | Richard Jackson | 29 | 15 | 0 | 4 | 9 | 5 | 0 | $450,230 |
| 1991 | Billy Hagan | 29 | 18 | 0 | 1 | 7 | 8 | 1 | $348,898 |
| 1992 | Billy Hagan | 29 | 8 | 0 | 4 | 16 | 3 | 0 | $600,381 |
| 1993 | Billy Hagan | 30 | 18 | 0 | 0 | 10 | 6 | 0 | $531,717 |
| 1994 | Rick Hendrick | 31 | 7 | 3 | 6 | 14 | 4 | 0 | $1,125,921 |
| 1995 | Rick Hendrick | 31 | 6 | 3 | 14 | 17 | 3 | 1 | $1,558,659 |
| 1996 | Rick Hendrick | 31 | 1 | 2 | 21 | 24 | 3 | 4 | $4,030,648 |
| 1997 | Rick Hendrick | 32 | 6 | 1 | 8 | 20 | 3 | 0 | $2,270,144 |
| 1998 | Rick Hendrick | 33 | 9 | 1 | 5 | 15 | 4 | 0 | $2,054,163 |
| 1999 | Rick Hendrick | 34 | 12 | 1 | 1 | 7 | 6 | 0 | $2,475,365 |
| 2000 | Rick Hendrick | 32 | 17 | 0 | 3 | 6 | 3 | 1 | $2,239,716 |
| 2001 | Rick Hendrick | 36 | 23 | 0 | 1 | 3 | 8 | 0 | $3,011,901 |
| 2002 | Rick Hendrick | 36 | 24 | 0 | 1 | 4 | 6 | 0 | $3,244,240 |
| 2003 | Rick Hendrick | 36 | 10 | 1 | 4 | 9 | 0 | 1 | $4,283,625 |
| 2004 | Rick Hendrick | 36 | 26 | 0 | 0 | 6 | 5 | 0 | $3,745,240 |
| **TOTALS** | | 817 | | 22 | 181 | 359 | 149 | 27 | $37,809,797 |

| Race | Track | Start | Finish | Laps | Led | Status | Winnings | Rank |
|---|---|---|---|---|---|---|---|---|
| Daytona 500 | Daytona | 38 | 20 | 199/200 | 1 | Running | $245,812 | 19 |
| Subway 400 | N. Carolina | 35 | 17 | 391/393 | 0 | Running | $89,110 | 16 |
| UAW-DaimlerChrysler 400 | Las Vegas | 37 | 17 | 267/267 | 0 | Running | $107,600 | 17 |
| Golden Corral 500 | Atlanta | 36 | 24 | 321/325 | 0 | Running | $86,560 | 20 |
| Carolina Dodge Dealers 400 | Darlington | 26 | 19 | 293/293 | 0 | Running | $84,140 | 21 |
| Food City 500 | Bristol | 33 | 18 | 500/500 | 0 | Running | $100,065 | 21 |
| Samsung/RadioShack 500 | Texas | 30 | 41 | 119/334 | 0 | Engine | $90,385 | 23 |
| Advance Auto Parts 500 | Martinsville | 28 | 23 | 498/500 | 0 | Running | $87,800 | 23 |
| Aaron's 499 | Talladega | 13 | 25 | 188/188 | 1 | Running | $96,930 | 24 |
| Auto Club 500 | California | 29 | 7 | 250/250 | 0 | Running | $119,625 | 21 |
| Chevy Amer. Revolution 400 | Richmond | 19 | 18 | 398/400 | 0 | Running | $89,150 | 20 |
| Coca-Cola 600 | Lowe's | 35 | 37 | 385/400 | 0 | Running | $95,045 | 25 |
| MBNA 400 'A Salute to Heroes' | Dover | 34 | 7 | 399/400 | 0 | Running | $118,335 | 21 |
| Pocono 500 | Pocono | 19 | 7 | 200/200 | 1 | Running | $96,640 | 19 |
| DHL 400 | Michigan | 31 | 26 | 199/200 | 0 | Accident | $89,140 | 21 |
| Dodge/Save Mart 350 | Infineon | 15 | 40 | 67/110 | 0 | Engine | $84,250 | 24 |
| Pepsi 400 | Daytona | 10 | 8 | 160/160 | 0 | Running | $119,500 | 21 |
| Tropicana 400 | Chicago | 24 | 6 | 267/267 | 1 | Running | $123,075 | 21 |
| Siemens 300 | New Hamp. | 11 | 16 | 300/300 | 0 | Running | $94,625 | 20 |
| Pennsylvania 500 | Pocono | 29 | 6 | 200/200 | 0 | Running | $103,440 | 19 |
| Brickyard 400 | Indianapolis | 21 | 38 | 72/161 | 0 | Accident | $143,360 | 20 |
| Sirius at the Glen | Watkins Glen | 20 | 39 | 35/90 | 0 | Engine | $79,665 | 21 |
| GFS Marketplace 400 | Michigan | 21 | 27 | 199/200 | 1 | Running | $88,575 | 23 |
| Sharpie 500 | Bristol | 12 | 15 | 498/500 | 0 | Running | $109,335 | 23 |
| Pop Secret 500 | California | 15 | 19 | 250/250 | 0 | Running | $110,775 | 24 |
| Chevy Rock & Roll 400 | Richmond | 23 | 18 | 399/400 | 0 | Running | $89,230 | 23 |
| Sylvania 300 | New Hamp. | 23 | 24 | 298/300 | 0 | Running | $90,950 | 21 |
| MBNA America 400 | Dover | 38 | 27 | 393/400 | 0 | Running | $88,515 | 23 |
| EA Sports 500 | Talladega | 38 | 21 | 188/188 | 0 | Running | $95,285 | 23 |
| Banquet 400 | Kansas | 19 | 21 | 267/267 | 1 | Running | $100,500 | 24 |
| UAW-GM Quality 500 | Lowe's | 40 | 25 | 328/334 | 0 | Running | $86,325 | 24 |
| Subway 500 | Martinsville | 27 | 25 | 500/500 | 30 | Running | $85,500 | 24 |
| Bass Pro Shops MBNA 500 | Atlanta | 42 | 31 | 318/325 | 0 | Running | $93,100 | 24 |
| Checker Auto Parts 500 | Phoenix | 31 | 32 | 309/315 | 0 | Running | $78,400 | 24 |
| Southern 500 | Darlington | 25 | 28 | 363/367 | 0 | Running | $85,500 | 25 |
| Ford 400 | Homestead | 42 | 31 | 264/271 | 0 | Running | $81,100 | 26 |

# Jason Leffler

**11**

**Date of birth:** September 16, 1975 **Hometown:** Indianapolis
**Resides:** Long Beach, Calif. **Spouse:** Alison **Children:** None
**Height:** 5-3 **Weight:** 130

## NASCAR ACHIEVEMENTS

**First NASCAR Cup start:** February 18, 2001 (Daytona)
**Best points finish:** 37 (2001)
**Career victories:** 0
**Career poles:** 1—Kansas (01)
**First pole:** September 30, 2001 (Kansas)
**Best career finish:** 10 **Best career start:** 1

## FAST FACTS

● Starting racing quarter-midgets at age 13.
● Won the 1998 USAC Silver Crown title in his first season.
● Became the first driver in 37 years to capture three straight USAC National Midget championships in 1999.

### CAR FACTS

**Car:** No. 11 Chevrolet
**Primary sponsor:** FedEx
**Owner:** Joe Gibbs
**Team:** Joe Gibbs Racing
**Crew chief:** Dave Rogers
**Engine builder:** Gibbs Racing

● Finished fifth in his ARCA debut in 1999.
● Joined Joe Gibbs Racing in 2000 and scored three poles in his rookie season in the NASCAR Busch Series.
● Joined the NASCAR Craftsman Truck Series as a driver for owner Jim Smith in 2002 and finished runner-up six times.

● Got his first NASCAR win in the May 30, 2003, NASCAR Craftsman Truck race at Dover, but he didn't complete the season, moving to NASCAR Cup for 10 races late in the year.

## CAREER HIGHLIGHTS

● Leffler will return in 2005 for a second full-time try at NASCAR Cup racing, also his second stint with Joe Gibbs Racing. He left a Joe Gibbs Busch team to run NASCAR Cup races for Chip Ganassi in 2001. He'll drive the No. 11 Chevrolet with FedEx as his primary sponsor.
● Chip Ganassi signed Leffler to the No. 01 NASCAR Cup team for the 2001 season, but Leffler had only one top 10 finish with Ganassi.

### CAREER STATISTICS

| Year | Car owner | Races | Champ. finish | Won | Top 5 | Top 10 | DNF | Poles | Money won |
|---|---|---|---|---|---|---|---|---|---|
| 2001 | Chip Ganassi | 30 | 37 | 0 | 0 | 1 | 8 | 1 | $1,724,692 |
| 2002 | Jim Smith | 2 | 63 | 0 | 0 | 0 | 0 | 0 | $78,500 |
| 2003 | Gene Haas | 10 | 47 | 0 | 0 | 0 | 0 | 0 | $594,500 |
| 2004 | Gene Haas | 1 | 88 | 0 | 0 | 0 | 1 | 0 | $116,359 |
| **TOTALS** | | **43** | | **0** | **0** | **1** | **0** | **1** | **$2,514,051** |

### 2004 RESULTS

| Race | Track | Start | Finish | Laps | Led | Status | Winnings | Rank |
|---|---|---|---|---|---|---|---|---|
| Brickyard 400 | Indianapolis | 25 | 43 | 3/161 | 0 | Accident | $116,359 | 77 |

# Sterling Marlin

## 40

**Date of birth:** June 30, 1957 **Hometown:** Columbia, Tenn. **Resides:** Columbia, Tenn. **Spouse:** Paula **Children:** Steadman, Sutherlin **Height:** 6-0 **Weight:** 180 **Hobbies:** Civil War history, collecting artifacts, following University of Tennessee football

## NASCAR ACHIEVEMENTS

**First NASCAR Cup start:** May 8, 1976 (Nashville)
**Best points finish:** 3 (2001)
**Career victories:** 10—Charlotte (01b), Darlington (95a, 02a), Daytona (94a, 95a, 96b), Las Vegas (02), Michigan (01b), Talladega (95b, 96a)
**First victory:** February 20, 1994 (Daytona)
**Last victory:** March 17, 2002 (Darlington)
**Career poles:** 11—Darlington (92a, 92b), Daytona (91b, 92a, 92b, 01b), Phoenix (94), Pocono (99a), Talladega (95b, 96a, 96b)
**First pole:** July 4, 1991 (Daytona)
**Best career finish:** 1 **Best career start:** 1

## FAST FACTS

● Won three consecutive track championships at Nashville Raceway from 1980-82.
● Has two career victories in the NASCAR Busch Series.
● Marlin was named Professional Athlete of the Year in Tennessee in 1995 and '96.
● Was the team captain and an All Mid-State selection, playing quarterback and linebacker at Spring Hill (Tenn.) High School.
● Played basketball in high school.

## CAREER HIGHLIGHTS

● It was a quiet season in 2004 for Marlin, and that's not necessarily a good thing. He never had consecutive top 10 finishes. A major reason why is he didn't complete enough laps. He had DNFs because of accidents, engine failures, a brake failure and overheating.
● After two promising seasons, Marlin finished a disappointing 18th in points in 2003. He appeared on the verge of a strong season with eight top 10s in the first 15 races, but he never finished better than 10th the rest of the season. He made his 600th career start at the October race at Martinsville.
● Was having the most productive year of his career in 2002 when a neck injury that was a result of an accident

at Kansas on September 29 ended his season. He had led in points for 25 consecutive races, from Rockingham, the second race of the season, through Richmond in September. Jamie McMurray replaced him.
● Was part of a bizarre incident during the 2002 Daytona 500, which was red-flagged while he was leading the race. While the cars were stopped, he got out of his car and began working on some body damage. He was penalized for the infraction and ultimately finished eighth.
● 2001 was Marlin's first season driving a Dodge, and he experienced a renaissance, finishing third in points with two wins (Michigan, Charlotte) and a career-best 12 top fives. The victory at Michigan was Marlin's first in five seasons. It also was Dodge's first victory since Neil Bonnett won in 1977 in Ontario, Calif.
● Had three mediocre seasons under Felix Sabates (1998-2000) that produced only three top fives. 2000 was his final season with Chevrolet and Sabates, who sold the majority interests of the team to Chip Ganassi.
● Got his first NASCAR Cup victory at the 1994 Daytona 500 in his 279th start. It was his first start with a new team, having moved from the Stavola Brothers to Morgan-McClure. The season began Marlin's best three-year stretch (1994-96), during which he posted six victories and 19 top fives and finished in the top 15 all three seasons, including a career-high finish of third in points in 1995.
● After not winning a pole for more than 200 career NASCAR Cup starts, Marlin won two poles in three races in 1991 (Daytona and Talladega).
● Was Raybestos Rookie of the Year in 1983. He didn't race another full season of NASCAR Cup until 1998.
● Made his first NASCAR Cup start in 1976 at 18 at Nashville after his father, Coo Coo, sustained a broken shoulder and entered his son in the race in his place.

### CAR FACTS

**Car:** No. 40 Dodge
**Primary sponsor:** Coors Light
**Owner:** Chip Ganassi
**Team:** Ganassi Racing
**Crew chief:** Tony Glover
**Engine builder:** Ernie Elliott

## CAREER STATISTICS

| Year | Car owner | Races | Champ. finish | Won | Top 5 | Top 10 | DNF | Poles | Money won |
|------|-----------|-------|---------------|-----|-------|--------|-----|-------|-----------|
| 1976 | H.B. Cunningham | 1 | 101 | 0 | 0 | 0 | 1 | 0 | $565 |
| 1978 | H.B. Cunningham | 2 | 67 | 0 | 0 | 1 | 1 | 0 | $10,170 |
| 1979 | H.B. Cunningham | 1 | 85 | 0 | 0 | 0 | 1 | 0 | $505 |
| 1980 | H.B. Cunningham | 2 | | 0 | 0 | 1 | 1 | 0 | $18,750 |
| | Jim Stacy | 2 | | 0 | 0 | 0 | 0 | 0 | $6,725 |
| | D.K. Ulrich | 1 | 49 | 0 | 0 | 1 | 0 | 0 | $4,335 |
| 1981 | Coo Coo Marlin | 1 | | 0 | 0 | 0 | 1 | 0 | $1,225 |
| | D.K. Ulrich | 1 | 93 | 0 | 0 | 0 | 1 | 0 | $730 |
| 1982 | Billy Matthews | 1 | | 0 | 0 | 0 | 1 | 0 | $4,015 |
| 1983 | Roger Hamby | 30 | 19 | 0 | 0 | 1 | 11 | 0 | $143,564 |
| 1984 | Earl Sadler | 11 | | 0 | 0 | 2 | 7 | 0 | $35,320 |
| | Roger Hamby | 1 | 0 | 0 | 0 | 0 | 0 | | $15,150 |
| | Dick Bahre | 1 | | 0 | 0 | 0 | 1 | 0 | $1,085 |
| | Jimmy Means | 1 | 37 | 0 | 0 | 0 | 1 | 0 | $2,800 |
| 1985 | Earl Sadler | 7 | | 0 | 0 | 0 | 5 | 0 | $29,805 |
| | Helen Rae Smith | 1 | 37 | 0 | 0 | 0 | 1 | 0 | $1,350 |
| 1986 | Hoss Ellington | 10 | 36 | 0 | 2 | 4 | 7 | 0 | $113,070 |
| 1987 | Billy Hagan | 29 | 11 | 0 | 4 | 8 | 6 | 0 | $306,412 |
| 1988 | Billy Hagan | 29 | 10 | 0 | 6 | 13 | 6 | 0 | $521,464 |
| 1989 | Billy Hagan | 29 | 12 | 0 | 4 | 13 | 5 | 0 | $473,267 |
| 1990 | Billy Hagan | 29 | 14 | 0 | 5 | 10 | 8 | 0 | $369,167 |
| 1991 | Junior Johnson | 29 | 7 | 0 | 7 | 16 | 2 | 2 | $633,690 |
| 1992 | Junior Johnson | 29 | 10 | 0 | 6 | 13 | 4 | 5 | $649,048 |
| 1993 | William Stavola | 30 | 15 | 0 | 1 | 8 | 3 | 0 | $628,835 |
| 1994 | Larry McClure | 31 | 14 | 1 | 5 | 11 | 7 | 1 | $1,127,683 |
| 1995 | Larry McClure | 31 | 3 | 3 | 9 | 22 | 2 | 1 | $2,253,502 |
| 1996 | Larry McClure | 31 | 8 | 2 | 5 | 10 | 6 | 0 | $1,588,425 |
| 1997 | Larry McClure | 32 | 25 | 0 | 2 | 6 | 8 | 0 | $1,301,370 |
| 1998 | Felix Sabates | 32 | 13 | 0 | 0 | 6 | 1 | 0 | $1,350,161 |
| 1999 | Felix Sabates | 34 | 16 | 0 | 2 | 5 | 3 | 1 | $1,797,416 |
| 2000 | Felix Sabates | 34 | 19 | 0 | 1 | 7 | 4 | 0 | $1,992,301 |
| 2001 | Chip Ganassi | 36 | 3 | 2 | 12 | 20 | 2 | 1 | $4,517,634 |
| 2002 | Chip Ganassi | 29 | 18 | 2 | 8 | 14 | 3 | 0 | $4,228,889 |
| 2003 | Chip Ganassi | 36 | 18 | 0 | 0 | 11 | 8 | 0 | $4,384,491 |
| 2004 | Chip Ganassi | 36 | 21 | 0 | 3 | 7 | 9 | 0 | $4,457,443 |
| **TOTALS** | | **640** | | **10** | **82** | **210** | **127** | **11** | **$32,970,362** |

## 2004 RESULTS

| Race | Track | Start | Finish | Laps | Led | Status | Winnings | Rank |
|------|-------|-------|--------|------|-----|--------|----------|------|
| Daytona 500 | Daytona | 4 | 37 | 75/200 | 0 | Accident | $254,714 | 37 |
| Subway 400 | N. Carolina | 13 | 4 | 393/393 | 0 | Running | $114,900 | 20 |
| UAW-DaimlerChrysler 400 | Las Vegas | 23 | 18 | 266/267 | 0 | Running | $112,750 | 18 |
| Golden Corral 500 | Atlanta | 31 | 16 | 323/325 | 0 | Running | $94,800 | 18 |
| Carolina Dodge Dealers 400 | Darlington | 17 | 14 | 293/293 | 1 | Running | $92,110 | 16 |
| Food City 500 | Bristol | 17 | 4 | 500/500 | 72 | Running | $135,125 | 10 |
| Samsung/RadioShack 500 | Texas | 14 | 26 | 330/334 | 18 | Running | $115,025 | 14 |
| Advance Auto Parts 500 | Martinsville | 18 | 9 | 500/500 | 0 | Running | $100,300 | 13 |
| Aaron's 499 | Talladega | 9 | 31 | 146/188 | 2 | Overheat | $109,050 | 14 |
| Auto Club 500 | California | 8 | 27 | 249/250 | 0 | Running | $103,200 | 15 |
| Chevy Amer. Revolution 400 | Richmond | 32 | 15 | 399/400 | 0 | Running | $99,255 | 15 |
| Coca-Cola 600 | Lowe's | 36 | 39 | 331/400 | 0 | Rear end | $101,075 | 18 |
| MBNA 400 'A Salute to Heroes' | Dover | 16 | 29 | 352/400 | 1 | Accident | $97,155 | 18 |
| Pocono 500 | Pocono | 20 | 31 | 176/200 | 2 | Accident | $86,490 | 20 |
| DHL 400 | Michigan | 24 | 6 | 200/200 | 44 | Running | $108,665 | 18 |
| Dodge/Save Mart 350 | Infineon | 26 | 21 | 110/110 | 0 | Running | $95,275 | 19 |
| Pepsi 400 | Daytona | 22 | 20 | 160/160 | 0 | Running | $112,575 | 20 |
| Tropicana 400 | Chicago | 32 | 7 | 267/267 | 9 | Running | $126,200 | 19 |
| Siemens 300 | New Hamp. | 37 | 21 | 300/300 | 0 | Running | $98,125 | 18 |
| Pennsylvania 500 | Pocono | 4 | 15 | 200/200 | 0 | Running | $94,290 | 18 |
| Brickyard 400 | Indianapolis | 10 | 33 | 116/161 | 0 | Brakes | $151,400 | 19 |
| Sirius at the Glen | Watkins Glen | 19 | 36 | 50/90 | 0 | Engine | $86,100 | 20 |
| GFS Marketplace 400 | Michigan | 20 | 15 | 200/200 | 0 | Running | $100,390 | 20 |
| Sharpie 500 | Bristol | 3 | 6 | 500/500 | 0 | Running | $132,115 | 19 |
| Pop Secret 500 | California | 31 | 26 | 250/250 | 0 | Running | $114,325 | 21 |
| Chevy Rock & Roll 400 | Richmond | 24 | 14 | 399/400 | 0 | Running | $96,455 | 19 |
| Sylvania 300 | New Hamp. | 19 | 12 | 300/300 | 0 | Running | $103,200 | 18 |
| MBNA America 400 | Dover | 34 | 15 | 398/400 | 0 | Running | $104,415 | 18 |
| EA Sports 500 | Talladega | 32 | 34 | 177/188 | 0 | Accident | $94,555 | 19 |
| Banquet 400 | Kansas | 28 | 34 | 216/267 | 0 | Accident | $98,725 | 22 |
| UAW-GM Quality 500 | Lowe's | 31 | 12 | 334/334 | 1 | Running | $100,525 | 21 |
| Subway 500 | Martinsville | 16 | 4 | 500/500 | 50 | Running | $113,545 | 19 |
| Bass Pro Shops MBNA 500 | Atlanta | 41 | 19 | 323/325 | 0 | Running | $109,400 | 20 |
| Checker Auto Parts 500 | Phoenix | 35 | 25 | 314/315 | 0 | Running | $89,050 | 21 |
| Southern 500 | Darlington | 20 | 12 | 367/367 | 1 | Running | $103,450 | 20 |
| Ford 400 | Homestead | 38 | 16 | 271/271 | 0 | Running | $91,925 | 21 |

# Mark Martin

## 6

**Date of birth:** January 9, 1959 **Hometown:** Batesville, Ark. **Resides:** Daytona Beach, Fla. **Spouse:** Arlene **Children:** Amy, Rachel, Heather, Stacy, Matthew **Height:** 5-6 **Weight:** 135 **Hobbies:** Weight training, quarter-midget racing with his son.

## NASCAR ACHIEVEMENTS

**First NASCAR Cup start:** April 5, 1981 (North Wilkesboro)
**Best points finish:** 2 (1990, 1994, 1998, 2002)
**Career victories:** 34—Atlanta (91b, 94b), Bristol (93b, 98b), California (98), Charlotte (92b, 95b, 98b, 02a), Darlington (93b), Dover (97b, 98b, 99b, 04a), Las Vegas (98), Martinsville (92a, 00a), Michigan (90b, 93b, 97b, 98a), North Wilkesboro (90b, 95b), Phoenix (93), Richmond (90a), Rockingham (89b, 99a), Sonoma (97), Talladega (95a, 97a), Texas (98), Watkins Glen (93, 94, 95)
**First victory:** October 22, 1989 (Rockingham)
**Last victory:** June 6, 2004 (Dover)
**Career poles:** 41—Atlanta (92a), Bristol (89a, 93a, 95b, 96a,

96b, 01a), Charlotte (91a, 91b), Darlington (89a, 98a), Daytona (89b), Dover (88b, 89a, 97b, 98b), Martinsville (90b, 91a, 91b), Nashville (81b), New Hampshire (93, 95), North Wilkesboro (90a), Pocono (90b, 91a, 96b), Richmond (81b, 96b, 01a), Rockingham (93a, 93b, 97a, 98b, 99b), Sonoma (97), Talladega (89a, 89b), Watkins Glen (93, 94, 95)

**First pole:** July 9, 1981 (Nashville)
**Best career finish:** 1    **Best career start:** 1

## FAST FACTS

● Has a series-leading 45 victories in the NASCAR Busch Series.
● Grew up racing up short tracks throughout the Midwest.
● Won three consecutive ASA championships from 1978-80 before moving to NASCAR; returned to ASA and won the 1986 title before making a permanent move to NASCAR.
● Owns Mark Martin Performance, a company that sells quarter-midget racing chassis.
● Helped build the quarter-midget track at the New Smyrna (Fla.) Speedway.

## CAREER HIGHLIGHTS

● Martin had a resurgent year in 2004, driving the fastest car he's had since 1998. He stormed into the Chase for the NASCAR NEXTEL Cup, and although he didn't contend for the championship, he sure had fun along the way. Still, the strain of racing is wearing him down, and he announced 2005 will be his last full-time season.
● Is 11th in career poles, with 41. Martin is eighth in poles at superspeedways and ninth in poles in road races.
● Has won more money ($46,135,779) than all but three other drivers: Dale Earnhardt, Dale Jarrett and Jeff Gordon.
● In 2003, four engine failures and three accidents led to Martin completing only 89.4 percent of his laps on the way to a 17th-place points finish. He couldn't maintain positive momentum; he never had any consecutive top fives and never had more than two straight top 10s.
● Finished second in 2002 for the fourth time in his NASCAR Cup career, 38 points behind champion Tony Stewart. His other second-place finishes: 1998, 364 points behind Jeff Gordon; 1994, 444 points behind Dale Earnhardt, and 1990, 26 points behind Earnhardt. The 2002 season was especially heartbreaking for Martin because he held the points lead for two weeks late in the season.
● Made his 500th start in 2002, in March at Bristol.
● Had only three top fives in 2001, his fewest since 1988, his first season under Roush. That contributed to a 12th-place finish in points, his lowest since 1988.
● Won the inaugural race at Las Vegas in 1998.
● Won the Watkins Glen race from the pole three consecutive seasons (1993-95)
● Tied a record for consecutive wins with four straight (Watkins Glen, Michigan, Bristol, Darlington) in 1993.

### CAR FACTS

**Car:** No. 6 Ford
**Primary sponsor:** Viagra
**Owner:** Jack Roush
**Team:** Roush Racing
**Crew chief:** Pat Tryson
**Engine builder:** Mike Kasch

● Led the NASCAR Cup circuit with five poles in 1991 (both Charlotte races, both Martinsville races, Pocono).
● Had a breakthrough season in 1989 and finished third in points. He got his first career win in his 113th start at Rockingham and won six poles, tying Alan Kulwicki for the series' season high. That year, he began a streak of 12 seasons with a top 10 finish in points. During that span, Martin had a seven-year streak of top five points finishes from 1993 to 1999.
● A win in the 1987 NASCAR Busch Series race at Dover grabbed the attention of Jack Roush, who was starting his own team the next season. Martin became Roush's first NASCAR Cup driver in 1988.
● Put in a second season as a driver/owner in 1982 and finished runner-up to Geoff Bodine for Raybestos Rookie of the Year. But Martin couldn't keep his team afloat and auctioned off his shop. He didn't compete full time in NASCAR Cup racing again until 1988.
● Made a splash in his first NASCAR season with five races as a driver/owner and a fifth-place finish at Martinsville in 1981. He also got his first career pole at Nashville in only his third career start.

### CAREER STATISTICS

| Year | Car owner | Races | Champ. finish | Won | Top 5 | Top 10 | DNF | Poles | Money won |
|------|-----------|-------|---------------|-----|-------|--------|-----|-------|-----------|
| 1981 | Mark Martin | 5 | 42 | 0 | 1 | 2 | 2 | 2 | $13,950 |
| 1982 | Mark Martin | 29 | | 0 | 2 | 8 | 11 | 4 | $124,215 |
| | Bob Rogers | 1 | 14 | 0 | 0 | 0 | 1 | 0 | $2,440 |
| 1983 | J.D. Stacy | 7 | | 0 | 1 | 2 | 3 | 0 | $75,240 |
| | D.K. Ulrich | 2 | | 0 | 0 | 0 | 2 | 0 | $5,745 |
| | Mark Martin | 1 | | 0 | 0 | 0 | 1 | 0 | $1,640 |
| | Morgan-McClure | 6 | 30 | 0 | 0 | 1 | 2 | 0 | $17,030 |
| 1986 | Gerry Gunderman | 5 | 48 | 0 | 0 | 0 | 2 | 0 | $20,515 |
| 1987 | Roger Hamby | 1 | 101 | 0 | 0 | 0 | 1 | 0 | $3,550 |
| 1988 | Jack Roush | 29 | 15 | 0 | 3 | 10 | 10 | 1 | $223,630 |
| 1989 | Jack Roush | 29 | 3 | 1 | 14 | 18 | 4 | 6 | $1,019,250 |
| 1990 | Jack Roush | 29 | 2 | 3 | 16 | 23 | 1 | 3 | $1,302,958 |
| 1991 | Jack Roush | 29 | 6 | 1 | 14 | 17 | 5 | 5 | $1,039,991 |
| 1992 | Jack Roush | 29 | 6 | 2 | 10 | 17 | 5 | 1 | $1,000,571 |
| 1993 | Jack Roush | 30 | 3 | 5 | 12 | 19 | 5 | 5 | $1,657,662 |
| 1994 | Jack Roush | 31 | 2 | 2 | 15 | 20 | 8 | 1 | $1,628,906 |
| 1995 | Jack Roush | 31 | 4 | 4 | 13 | 22 | 1 | 4 | $1,893,519 |
| 1996 | Jack Roush | 31 | 5 | 0 | 14 | 23 | 4 | 4 | $1,887,396 |
| 1997 | Jack Roush | 32 | 3 | 4 | 16 | 24 | 3 | 3 | $2,532,484 |
| 1998 | Jack Roush | 33 | 2 | 7 | 22 | 26 | 1 | 3 | $4,309,006 |
| 1999 | Jack Roush | 34 | 3 | 2 | 19 | 26 | 3 | 1 | $3,509,744 |
| 2000 | Jack Roush | 34 | 8 | 1 | 13 | 20 | 6 | 0 | $3,098,874 |
| 2001 | Jack Roush | 36 | 12 | 0 | 3 | 15 | 4 | 2 | $3,797,006 |
| 2002 | Jack Roush | 36 | 2 | 1 | 12 | 22 | 3 | 0 | $7,004,893 |
| 2003 | Jack Roush | 36 | 17 | 0 | 5 | 10 | 7 | 0 | $4,486,560 |
| 2004 | Jack Roush | 36 | 4 | 1 | 10 | 15 | 2 | 0 | $5,479,004 |
| **TOTALS** | | **602** | | **34** | **215** | **340** | **97** | **41** | **$46,135,779** |

DRIVERS

| Race | Track | Start | Finish | Laps | Led | Status | Winnings | Rank |
|------|-------|-------|--------|------|-----|--------|----------|------|
| Daytona 500 | Daytona | 8 | 43 | 7/200 | 0 | Engine | $216,997 | 43 |
| Subway 400 | N. Carolina | 21 | 12 | 391/393 | 0 | Running | $72,960 | 28 |
| UAW-DaimlerChrysler 400 | Las Vegas | 27 | 5 | 267/267 | 0 | Running | $127,875 | 20 |
| Golden Corral 500 | Atlanta | 28 | 14 | 324/325 | 0 | Running | $70,550 | 17 |
| Carolina Dodge Dealers 400 | Darlington | 20 | 7 | 293/293 | 0 | Running | $72,345 | 12 |
| Food City 500 | Bristol | 21 | 23 | 499/500 | 0 | Running | $81,045 | 15 |
| Samsung/RadioShack 500 | Texas | 28 | 17 | 332/334 | 0 | Running | $104,125 | 16 |
| Advance Auto Parts 500 | Martinsville | 19 | 34 | 469/500 | 0 | Running | $65,200 | 18 |
| Aaron's 499 | Talladega | 6 | 6 | 188/188 | 6 | Running | $108,380 | 15 |
| Auto Club 500 | California | 26 | 11 | 250/250 | 0 | Running | $90,450 | 13 |
| Chevy Amer. Revolution 400 | Richmond | 12 | 7 | 400/400 | 0 | Running | $76,825 | 12 |
| Coca-Cola 600 | Lowe's | 18 | 36 | 387/400 | 0 | Running | $76,425 | 15 |
| MBNA 400 'A Salute to Heroes' | Dover | 7 | 1 | 400/400 | 19 | Running | $271,900 | 13 |
| Pocono 500 | Pocono | 4 | 36 | 112/200 | 2 | Engine | $60,065 | 14 |
| DHL 400 | Michigan | 15 | 34 | 182/200 | 0 | Running | $66,285 | 16 |
| Dodge/Save Mart 350 | Infineon | 4 | 8 | 110/110 | 1 | Running | $89,315 | 15 |
| Pepsi 400 | Daytona | 21 | 6 | 160/160 | 0 | Running | $108,375 | 14 |
| Tropicana 400 | Chicago | 18 | 24 | 265/267 | 10 | Running | $79,850 | 15 |
| Siemens 300 | New Hamp. | 26 | 14 | 300/300 | 0 | Running | $76,800 | 15 |
| Pennsylvania 500 | Pocono | 21 | 2 | 200/200 | 11 | Running | $132,895 | 13 |
| Brickyard 400 | Indianapolis | 16 | 25 | 161/161 | 0 | Running | $134,380 | 15 |
| Sirius at the Glen | Watkins Glen | 15 | 3 | 90/90 | 0 | Running | $98,910 | 13 |
| GFS Marketplace 400 | Michigan | 13 | 2 | 200/200 | 46 | Running | $115,680 | 12 |
| Sharpie 500 | Bristol | 7 | 13 | 499/500 | 0 | Running | $91,440 | 12 |
| Pop Secret 500 | California | 11 | 3 | 250/250 | 65 | Running | $144,450 | 10 |
| Chevy Rock & Roll 400 | Richmond | 2 | 5 | 400/400 | 0 | Running | $84,055 | 8 |
| Sylvania 300 | New Hamp. | 8 | 13 | 300/300 | 0 | Running | $78,425 | 7 |
| MBNA America 400 | Dover | 12 | 2 | 400/400 | 2 | Running | $138,560 | 5 |
| EA Sports 500 | Talladega | 17 | 15 | 188/188 | 0 | Running | $79,035 | 4 |
| Banquet 400 | Kansas | 18 | 20 | 267/267 | 0 | Running | $84,400 | 5 |
| UAW-GM Quality 500 | Lowe's | 12 | 13 | 334/334 | 32 | Running | $74,500 | 5 |
| Subway 500 | Martinsville | 23 | 12 | 500/500 | 0 | Running | $70,550 | 5 |
| Bass Pro Shops MBNA 500 | Atlanta | 7 | 2 | 325/325 | 227 | Running | $238,500 | 4 |
| Checker Auto Parts 500 | Phoenix | 22 | 15 | 315/315 | 0 | Running | $67,975 | 5 |
| Southern 500 | Darlington | 5 | 2 | 367/367 | 36 | Running | $190,825 | 5 |
| Ford 400 | Homestead | 11 | 11 | 271/271 | 8 | Running | $67,950 | 4 |

# Jeremy Mayfield

**19**

**Date of birth:** May 27, 1969 **Hometown:** Owensboro, Ky.
**Resides:** Mooresville, N.C. **Spouse:** Shana **Children:** None
**Height:** 6-0 **Weight:** 190 **Hobbies:** Four-wheel vehicles

## NASCAR ACHIEVEMENTS

**First NASCAR Cup start:** October 10, 1993 (Charlotte)
**Best points finish:** 7 (1998)
**Career victories:** 4—California (00), Pocono (98a, 00a), Richmond (04a)
**First victory:** June 1, 1998 (Pocono)
**Last victory:** September 11, 2004 (Richmond)
**Career poles:** 9—Darlington (00b), Dover (00b, 04a, 04b), Rockingham (00b), Talladega (96b, 00a, 03a), Texas (98)
**First pole:** July 6, 1998 (Talladega)
**Best career finish:** 1  **Best career start:** 1

## FAST FACTS

● Began racing go-karts in 1982 and then moved up through the weekly programs at tracks in central Tennessee.
● Raced street stocks, sportsman and late-model stocks in Tennessee.
● Was the 1987 Kentucky Motor Speedway Rookie of the Year.

● Was the ARCA Rookie of the Year in 1993, with eight top fives and 10 top 10s.
● Favorite driver is childhood hero Darrell Waltrip.

## CAREER HIGHLIGHTS

● If NASCAR had a comeback driver of the year award, Mayfield would have won it in 2004—not just for the season as a whole but for the way he qualified for the Chase for the NASCAR NEXTEL Cup. His win at Richmond was truly historic and put him into a higher class of drivers. He brought up the rear of the field when the Chase was over, finishing the season 10th.
● Was fired from Penske Racing's No. 12 Ford in October 2001, 28 races into the season. He landed with Evernham Motorsports for the 2002 season but had

### CAR FACTS

**Car:** No. 19 Dodge
**Primary sponsor:** Dodge Dealers/UAW
**Owner:** Ray Evernham
**Team:** Evernham Motorsports
**Crew chief:** Richard Labbe
**Engine builder:** Mark McArdle

disappointing finishes with Evernham in 2002 (26th) and 2003 (19th).

● Had a roller-coaster 2000 season that included a career-high two wins (Pocono, California) and four poles (Talladega, Darlington, Dover and Rockingham) but 11 DNFs. He missed two races after sustaining a head injury in a practice accident at the Brickyard 400.

● Won his first NASCAR Cup race in 1998 at Pocono, passing boyhood hero Darrell Waltrip for the lead 20 laps from the end. Led the points race four times in the first 16 races and finished the year seventh in points, a career high. Mayfield has finished out of the top 10 in points in seven of his nine full seasons.

● First full season in NASCAR Cup was underwhelming, as Mayfield registered only one top 10 and finished 31st in points in 1995.

## 2004 RESULTS

| Race | Track | Start | Finish | Laps | Led | Status | Winnings | Rank |
|---|---|---|---|---|---|---|---|---|
| Daytona 500 | Daytona | 22 | 25 | 195/200 | 0 | Running | $222,889 | 25 |
| Subway 400 | N. Carolina | 6 | 11 | 391/393 | 0 | Running | $90,210 | 18 |
| UAW-DaimlerChrysler 400 | Las Vegas | 6 | 14 | 267/267 | 0 | Running | $104,950 | 14 |
| Golden Corral 500 | Atlanta | 16 | 2 | 325/325 | 22 | Running | $137,750 | 7 |
| Carolina Dodge Dealers 400 | Darlington | 18 | 9 | 293/293 | 0 | Running | $88,635 | 7 |
| Food City 500 | Bristol | 16 | 17 | 500/500 | 0 | Running | $96,565 | 8 |
| Samsung/RadioShack 500 | Texas | 21 | 34 | 293/334 | 0 | Accident | $76,475 | 12 |
| Advance Auto Parts 500 | Martinsville | 10 | 36 | 390/500 | 0 | Running | $70,989 | 15 |
| Aaron's 499 | Talladega | 38 | 21 | 188/188 | 0 | Running | $90,095 | 16 |
| Auto Club 500 | California | 20 | 14 | 249/250 | 1 | Running | $112,025 | 16 |
| Chevy Amer. Revolution 400 | Richmond | 11 | 22 | 397/400 | 23 | Running | $85,875 | 16 |
| Coca-Cola 600 | Lowe's | 15 | 8 | 400/400 | 0 | Running | $120,700 | 14 |
| MBNA 400 'A Salute to Heroes' | Dover | 1 | 8 | 399/400 | 78 | Running | $116,065 | 15 |
| Pocono 500 | Pocono | 7 | 2 | 200/200 | 5 | Running | $149,895 | 11 |
| DHL 400 | Michigan | 8 | 19 | 200/200 | 0 | Running | $85,465 | 12 |
| Dodge/Save Mart 350 | Infineon | 21 | 30 | 109/110 | 0 | Running | $77,849 | 13 |
| Pepsi 400 | Daytona | 16 | 22 | 160/160 | 0 | Running | $97,075 | 12 |
| Tropicana 400 | Chicago | 19 | 5 | 267/267 | 26 | Running | $130,575 | 11 |
| Siemens 300 | New Hamp. | 7 | 10 | 300/300 | 0 | Running | $98,500 | 11 |
| Pennsylvania 500 | Pocono | 9 | 9 | 200/200 | 0 | Running | $92,490 | 11 |
| Brickyard 400 | Indianapolis | 13 | 11 | 161/161 | 0 | Running | $174,050 | 12 |
| Sirius at the Glen | Watkins Glen | 12 | 7 | 90/90 | 0 | Running | $89,585 | 10 |
| GFS Marketplace 400 | Michigan | 10 | 11 | 200/200 | 0 | Running | $94,480 | 11 |
| Sharpie 500 | Bristol | 9 | 22 | 496/500 | 0 | Running | $101,510 | 13 |
| Pop Secret 500 | California | 2 | 16 | 250/250 | 9 | Running | $110,900 | 14 |
| Chevy Rock & Roll 400 | Richmond | 7 | 1 | 400/400 | 151 | Running | $211,120 | 9 |
| Sylvania 300 | New Hamp. | 9 | 35 | 251/300 | 0 | Running | $74,989 | 10 |
| MBNA America 400 | Dover | 1 | 7 | 400/400 | 0 | Running | $105,015 | 10 |
| EA Sports 500 | Talladega | 9 | 38 | 147/188 | 0 | Accident | $77,689 | 10 |
| Banquet 400 | Kansas | 3 | 5 | 267/267 | 72 | Running | $138,075 | 10 |
| UAW-GM Quality 500 | Lowe's | 13 | 30 | 277/334 | 0 | Accident | $66,425 | 10 |
| Subway 500 | Martinsville | 11 | 6 | 500/500 | 0 | Running | $95,350 | 10 |
| Bass Pro Shops MBNA 500 | Atlanta | 11 | 26 | 320/325 | 0 | Running | $92,000 | 10 |
| Checker Auto Parts 500 | Phoenix | 24 | 21 | 315/315 | 0 | Running | $78,525 | 10 |
| Southern 500 | Darlington | 10 | 19 | 365/367 | 0 | Running | $88,150 | 10 |
| Ford 400 | Homestead | 20 | 35 | 231/271 | 0 | Running | $69,039 | 10 |

## CAREER STATISTICS

| Year | Car owner | Races | Champ. finish | Won | Top 5 | Top 10 | DNF | Poles | Money won |
|---|---|---|---|---|---|---|---|---|---|
| 1993 | Earl Sadler | 1 | 74 | 0 | 0 | 0 | 0 | 0 | $4,830 |
| 1994 | Earl Sadler | 4 | | 0 | 0 | 0 | 2 | 0 | $48,255 |
| | T.W. Taylor | 4 | | 0 | 0 | 0 | 0 | 0 | $40,145 |
| | Cale Yarborough | 12 | 37 | 0 | 0 | 0 | 3 | 0 | $137,865 |
| 1995 | Cale Yarborough | 27 | 31 | 0 | 0 | 1 | 2 | 0 | $436,805 |
| 1996 | Cale Yarborough | 23 | | 0 | 2 | 2 | 4 | 1 | $463,863 |
| | Michael Kranefuss | 7 | 26 | 0 | 0 | 0 | 4 | 0 | $128,990 |
| 1997 | Michael Kranefuss | 32 | 13 | 0 | 3 | 8 | 3 | 0 | $1,067,203 |
| 1998 | Penske-Kranefuss | 33 | 7 | 1 | 12 | 16 | 2 | 1 | $2,332,034 |
| 1999 | Penske-Kranefuss | 34 | 11 | 0 | 5 | 12 | 4 | 0 | $2,125,227 |
| 2000 | Penske-Kranefuss | 27 | | 2 | 4 | 10 | 9 | 3 | $1,617,951 |
| | Roger Penske | 5 | 24 | 0 | 2 | 2 | 2 | 1 | $551,300 |
| 2001 | Roger Penske | 28 | 35 | 0 | 5 | 7 | 4 | 0 | $2,682,603 |
| 2002 | Ray Evernham | 36 | 26 | 0 | 2 | 4 | 7 | 0 | $2,494,583 |
| 2003 | Ray Evernham | 36 | 19 | 0 | 4 | 12 | 6 | 1 | $3,371,879 |
| 2004 | Ray Evernham | 36 | 10 | 1 | 5 | 13 | 3 | 2 | $4,919,342 |
| **TOTALS** | | **345** | | **4** | **44** | **87** | **55** | **9** | **$22,515,017** |

# Jamie McMurray

**Date of birth:** June 3, 1976 **Hometown:** Joplin, Mo.
**Spouse:** Single **Children:** None **Height:** 5-8 **Weight:** 150
**Hobbies:** Radio-controlled cars

DRIVERS

## NASCAR ACHIEVEMENTS

**First NASCAR Cup start:** October 6, 2002 (Talladega)
**Best points finish:** 11 (2004)
**Career victories:** 1—Charlotte (02b)
**First and last victory:** October 13, 2002 (Charlotte)
**Career poles:** 1
**First pole:** November 14, 2003 (Homestead)
**Best career finish:** 1   **Best career start:** 1

## FAST FACTS

● NASCAR's version of Mr. October won his first two NASCAR Busch Series races and his first NASCAR Cup event within a four-week period in 2002.

● Ran in 69 NASCAR Busch Series races from 2000-02, winning twice and earning six top fives and 17 top 10s.

● Finished third in the NASCAR Busch Series Raybestos Rookie of the Year standings in 2001.

- Finished 22nd in the 2000 NASCAR Craftsman Truck Series standings.
- Ran five NASCAR Craftsman Truck Series races in 1999 while also racing in the NASCAR RE/MAX Challenge Series.
- Ran in the NASCAR Racing Series at several tracks in his home state of Missouri, most notably the I-44 Speedway, where he was track champion in 1997.
- Competed in the Grand American Late Model class from 1996-98 and in the Grand American Modified division from 1994-95.
- Began racing Late Models at age 16 and go-karts at age 8.
- Won four U.S. Go-Kart titles between 1986-92 and was the World Go-Kart champion in 1991.
- Selected as one of only 10 Americans to represent the U.S. in an international karting event in the former Soviet Union in 1989.
- His NASCAR Busch Series victory on October 26, 2002, gave him the distinction of becoming the 100th driver to win a NASCAR Busch Series race.
- Became associated with 2002 NASCAR Cup champion Tony Stewart during their days on the go-kart circuit while Stewart was in the junior class and McMurray was in the rookie-junior class.

## CAR FACTS

**Car:** No. 42 Dodge
**Primary sponsor:** Texaco/Havoline
**Owner:** Chip Ganassi
**Team:** Ganassi Racing
**Crew chief:** Donnie Wingo
**Engine builder:** Ernie Elliott

## CAREER HIGHLIGHTS

- McMurray easily had the best 2004 season among drivers who did not make the Chase for the NASCAR NEXTEL Cup, and he had a better season overall then several who made the big show. McMurry didn't notch a win, but his No. 42 Dodge was strong week in and week out. Although he has been a NASCAR Cup driver for only two years, he has the respect of veterans in the garage because he drives like them. He did find victory lane in 2004 but won in the NASCAR Busch Series and NASCAR Craftsman Truck Series.
- Won the Raybestos Rookie of the Year award in 2003 with a consistent second half. He finished outside of the top 20 just once in the last 13 races and grabbed his first pole in the season finale at Homestead.
- Became only the 11th driver to visit victory lane in only his second NASCAR Cup start. McMurray did it by holding off

Bobby Labonte on the last lap in the 2002 October race in Charlotte. McMurray was racing in place of Sterling Marlin for Chip Ganassi after a neck injury ended Marlin's season.

## CAREER STATISTICS

| Year | Car owner | Races | Champ. finish | Won | Top 5 | Top 10 | DNF | Poles | Money won |
|------|-----------|-------|--------------|-----|-------|--------|-----|-------|-----------|
| 2002 | Chip Ganassi | 6 | 46 | 1 | 1 | 2 | 1 | 0 | $717,942 |
| 2003 | Chip Ganassi | 36 | 13 | 0 | 5 | 13 | 4 | 1 | $3,258,806 |
| 2004 | Chip Ganassi | 36 | 11 | 0 | 9 | 23 | 6 | 0 | $4,676,311 |
| **TOTALS** | | **78** | | **1** | **15** | **38** | **11** | **1** | **$8,653,059** |

## 2004 RESULTS

| Race | Track | Start | Finish | Laps | Led | Status | Winnings | Rank |
|------|-------|-------|--------|------|-----|--------|----------|------|
| Daytona 500 | Daytona | 7 | 36 | 75/200 | 0 | Accident | $224,137 | 36 |
| Subway 400 | North Carolina | 2 | 3 | 393/393 | 76 | Running | $96,425 | 11 |
| UAW-DaimlerChrysler 400 | Las Vegas | 4 | 4 | 267/267 | 0 | Running | $150,925 | 9 |
| Golden Corral 500 | Atlanta | 22 | 37 | 245/325 | 0 | Engine | $62,970 | 16 |
| Carolina Dodge Dealers 400 | Darlington | 21 | 21 | 292/293 | 40 | Running | $74,705 | 19 |
| Food City 500 | Bristol | 6 | 8 | 500/500 | 0 | Running | $87,095 | 14 |
| Samsung/RadioShack 500 | Texas | 26 | 10 | 334/334 | 0 | Running | $118,550 | 13 |
| Advance Auto Parts 500 | Martinsville | 2 | 7 | 500/500 | 0 | Running | $80,725 | 14 |
| Aaron's 499 | Talladega | 33 | 9 | 188/188 | 4 | Running | $115,705 | 11 |
| Auto Club 500 | California | 12 | 15 | 249/250 | 0 | Running | $87,725 | 12 |
| Chevy Amer. Revolution 400 | Richmond | 37 | 38 | 202/400 | 0 | Accident | $63,675 | 13 |
| Coca-Cola 600 | Lowe's | 21 | 4 | 400/400 | 15 | Running | $145,800 | 12 |
| MBNA 400 'A Salute to Heroes' | Dover | 9 | 15 | 397/400 | 0 | Running | $82,510 | 12 |
| Pocono 500 | Pocono | 14 | 9 | 200/200 | 0 | Running | $75,390 | 12 |
| DHL 400 | Michigan | 30 | 37 | 114/200 | 0 | Engine | $66,045 | 13 |
| Dodge/Save Mart 350 | Infineon | 11 | 2 | 110/110 | 0 | Running | $176,500 | 11 |
| Pepsi 400 | Daytona | 32 | 37 | 126/160 | 0 | Oil pump | $75,300 | 12 |
| Tropicana 400 | Chicago | 14 | 13 | 267/267 | 0 | Running | $88,100 | 13 |
| Siemens 300 | New Hamp. | 5 | 7 | 300/300 | 0 | Running | $84,600 | 13 |
| Pennsylvania 500 | Pocono | 7 | 30 | 170/200 | 0 | Engine | $61,640 | 15 |
| Brickyard 400 | Indianapolis | 8 | 7 | 161/161 | 0 | Running | $179,025 | 14 |
| Sirius at the Glen | Watkins Glen | 14 | 13 | 90/90 | 0 | Running | $70,075 | 15 |
| GFS Marketplace 400 | Michigan | 15 | 4 | 200/200 | 3 | Running | $93,695 | 15 |
| Sharpie 500 | Bristol | 5 | 7 | 500/500 | 8 | Running | $101,715 | 15 |
| Pop Secret 500 | California | 23 | 4 | 250/250 | 0 | Running | $124,500 | 11 |
| Chevy Rock & Roll 400 | Richmond | 36 | 9 | 400/400 | 0 | Running | $74,180 | 11 |
| Sylvania 300 | New Hamp. | 11 | 5 | 300/300 | 1 | Running | $92,400 | 11 |
| MBNA America 400 | Dover | 10 | 8 | 400/400 | 0 | Running | $79,715 | 11 |
| EA Sports 500 | Talladega | 24 | 17 | 188/188 | 0 | Running | $76,985 | 11 |
| Banquet 400 | Kansas | 10 | 7 | 267/267 | 19 | Running | $101,100 | 11 |
| UAW-GM Quality 500 | Lowe's | 24 | 8 | 334/334 | 0 | Running | $80,625 | 11 |
| Subway 500 | Martinsville | 8 | 2 | 500/500 | 43 | Running | $104,025 | 11 |
| Bass Pro Shops MBNA 500 | Atlanta | 29 | 8 | 325/325 | 0 | Running | $99,325 | 11 |
| Checker Auto Parts 500 | Phoenix | 10 | 24 | 315/315 | 0 | Running | $64,800 | 11 |
| Southern 500 | Darlington | 11 | 4 | 367/367 | 15 | Running | $118,675 | 11 |
| Ford 400 | Homestead | 18 | 7 | 271/271 | 0 | Running | $88,950 | 11 |

DRIVERS

# Casey Mears

**Date of birth:** March 12, 1978 **Hometown:** Bakersfield, Calif.
**Resides:** Huntersville, N.C. **Spouse:** Single **Children:** None
**Height:** 5-8 **Weight:** 158 **Hobbies:** Wakeboarding, snowboarding

## NASCAR ACHIEVEMENTS

**First NASCAR Cup start:** February 16, 2003 (Daytona)
**Best points finish:** 22 (2004)
**Career victories:** 0
**Career poles:** 2—Pocono (04b), Indianapolis (04)
**First pole:** August 1, 2004 (Pocono)
**Best career finish:** 4 **Best career start:** 1

## FAST FACTS

- Finished 21st in his rookie season in the NASCAR Busch Series in 2002, scoring one top five.
- In 2001, had two top 10s in four starts in CART after replacing Alex Zanardi, who was involved in a career-ending crash.
- In 2000, finished third in the Indy Lights Series, scoring his first win at the Grand Prix of Houston.
- Made his first CART start at California Speedway in 2000, finishing a career-best fourth.
- Finished second in the Indy Lights Series in 1999, becoming only the fourth driver in series history to complete every lap.
- Won three races in off-road stadium SuperLites in 1996.
- Won the 1995 Jim Russell USAC Triple Crown championship at age 17.
- Is the nephew of four-time Indy 500 winner Rick Mears.
- Is the son of two-time Indy 500 starter and off-road legend Roger Mears.
- Was the second-youngest driver in USAC history to win a feature race (Mesa Marin, 1994) at age 16.

## CAREER HIGHLIGHTS

- Mears' 2004 was leaps and bounds better than his 2003, when he struggled to a 35th-place finish in the points race. He didn't win in 2004, but he had a strong enough car to do so several times. He qualified well, too. He clearly was more comfortable with the car and the rhythm of NASCAR NEXTEL Cup racing.
- Struggled during his 2003 rookie season, with 10 DNFs. Coming from open-wheel racing, Mears still was trying to figure out stock cars.

### CAR FACTS

**Car:** No. 41 Dodge
**Primary sponsor:** Target
**Owner:** Chip Ganassi
**Team:** Ganassi Racing
**Crew chief:** Jimmy Elledge
**Engine builder:** Ernie Elliott

## CAREER STATISTICS

| Year | Car owner | Races | Champ. finish | Won | Top 5 | Top 10 | DNF | Poles | Money won |
|------|-----------|-------|---------------|-----|-------|--------|-----|-------|-----------|
| 2003 | Chip Ganassi | 36 | 35 | 0 | 0 | 0 | 10 | 0 | $2,639,180 |
| 2004 | Chip Ganassi | 36 | 22 | 0 | 1 | 9 | 3 | 2 | $3,462,623 |
| **TOTALS** | | **72** | | **0** | **1** | **9** | **13** | **2** | **$6,101,801** |

## 2004 RESULTS

| Race | Track | Start | Finish | Laps | Led | Status | Winnings | Rank |
|------|-------|-------|--------|------|-----|--------|----------|------|
| Daytona 500 | Daytona | 25 | 14 | 200/200 | 0 | Running | $235,087 | 14 |
| Subway 400 | N. Carolina | 14 | 21 | 390/393 | 0 | Running | $74,810 | 15 |
| UAW-DaimlerChrysler 400 | Las Vegas | 13 | 7 | 267/267 | 0 | Running | $117,050 | 10 |
| Golden Corral 500 | Atlanta | 9 | 34 | 302/325 | 37 | Engine | $56,000 | 19 |
| Carolina Dodge Dealers 400 | Darlington | 19 | 15 | 293/293 | 0 | Running | $75,130 | 17 |
| Food City 500 | Bristol | 24 | 36 | 331/500 | 0 | Accident | $66,645 | 23 |
| Samsung/RadioShack 500 | Texas | 6 | 7 | 334/334 | 0 | Running | $139,375 | 18 |
| Advance Auto Parts 500 | Martinsville | 12 | 37 | 366/500 | 0 | Running | $54,550 | 20 |
| Aaron's 499 | Talladega | 16 | 8 | 188/188 | 5 | Running | $108,205 | 18 |
| Auto Club 500 | California | 13 | 8 | 250/250 | 0 | Running | $108,375 | 17 |
| Chevy Amer. Revolution 400 | Richmond | 9 | 32 | 380/400 | 2 | Running | $67,364 | 18 |
| Coca-Cola 600 | Lowe's | 14 | 7 | 400/400 | 2 | Running | $119,550 | 16 |
| MBNA 400 'A Salute to Heroes' | Dover | 17 | 28 | 356/400 | 0 | Running | $73,194 | 17 |
| Pocono 500 | Pocono | 21 | 10 | 200/200 | 0 | Running | $82,090 | 16 |
| DHL 400 | Michigan | 9 | 31 | 191/200 | 0 | Running | $58,540 | 17 |
| Dodge/Save Mart 350 | Infineon | 29 | 7 | 110/110 | 5 | Running | $100,265 | 17 |
| Pepsi 400 | Daytona | 24 | 11 | 160/160 | 1 | Running | $101,575 | 16 |
| Tropicana 400 | Chicago | 12 | 15 | 267/267 | 0 | Running | $92,150 | 16 |
| Siemens 300 | New Hamp. | 22 | 26 | 300/300 | 0 | Running | $74,175 | 17 |
| Pennsylvania 500 | Pocono | 1 | 18 | 200/200 | 17 | Running | $82,215 | 16 |
| Brickyard 400 | Indianapolis | 1 | 26 | 161/161 | 0 | Running | $139,539 | 16 |
| Sirius at the Glen | Watkins Glen | 16 | 4 | 90/90 | 8 | Running | $96,150 | 16 |
| GFS Marketplace 400 | Michigan | 16 | 20 | 199/200 | 0 | Running | $76,215 | 16 |
| Sharpie 500 | Bristol | 22 | 30 | 433/500 | 0 | Accident | $87,675 | 16 |
| Pop Secret 500 | California | 6 | 29 | 249/250 | 0 | Running | $90,750 | 16 |
| Chevy Rock & Roll 400 | Richmond | 29 | 35 | 352/400 | 0 | Running | $64,789 | 18 |
| Sylvania 300 | New Hamp. | 18 | 29 | 296/300 | 7 | Running | $70,390 | 20 |
| MBNA America 400 | Dover | 26 | 24 | 395/400 | 0 | Running | $73,065 | 20 |
| EA Sports 500 | Talladega | 34 | 8 | 188/188 | 5 | Running | $100,000 | 18 |
| Banquet 400 | Kansas | 21 | 31 | 243/267 | 14 | Running | $75,900 | 20 |
| UAW-GM Quality 500 | Lowe's | 3 | 20 | 331/334 | 0 | Running | $79,400 | 20 |
| Subway 500 | Martinsville | 28 | 29 | 496/500 | 0 | Running | $67,950 | 22 |
| Bass Pro Shops MBNA 500 | Atlanta | 16 | 13 | 324/325 | 0 | Running | $98,625 | 22 |
| Checker Auto Parts 500 | Phoenix | 7 | 34 | 306/315 | 0 | Accident | $51,400 | 22 |
| Southern 500 | Darlington | 22 | 26 | 364/367 | 0 | Running | $70,575 | 22 |
| Ford 400 | Homestead | 41 | 26 | 268/271 | 0 | Running | $68,575 | 22 |

# Joe Nemechek

**01**

**Date of birth:** September 26, 1963 **Hometown:** Lakeland, Fla.
**Resides:** Mooresville, N.C. **Spouse:** Andrea **Children:** John, Blair,
Kennedy **Height:** 5-9 **Weight:** 185 **Hobbies:** Fishing, skiing

## NASCAR ACHIEVEMENTS

**First NASCAR Cup start:** July 11, 1993 (New Hampshire)
**Best points finish:** 15 (2000)
**Career victories:** 4—Kansas (04), New Hampshire (99b),
Richmond (03a), Rockingham (01b)
**First victory:** September 19, 1999 (New Hampshire)
**Last victory:** October 10, 2004 (Kansas)
**Career poles:** 8—California (97), Daytona (99b), Kansas (04),
Martinsville (99b), Pocono (97b), Talladega (99b, 00b, 04b)
**First pole:** June 22, 1997 (California)
**Best career finish:** 1 **Best career start:** 1

## FAST FACTS

● Finished second in a NASCAR Craftsman Truck event at
Watkins Glen in 1996.

### CAR FACTS

**Car:** No. 01 Chevrolet
**Primary sponsor:** U.S. Army
**Owner:** Tom Beard
**Team:** MB2 Motorsports
**Crew chief:** Ryan Pemberton
**Engine builder:** Hendrick
Motorsports

● Won 1992 NASCAR
Busch Series champi-
onship, edging Bobby
Labonte by three points,
the closest champion's
margin in the history of
NASCAR's three national
series.
● Named the NASCAR
Busch Series Rookie of

the Year in 1990.
● Won the championship and Rookie of the Year honors in
NASCAR's All-Pro Series in 1989.
● Won the championship and Rookie of the Year honors in
the United Stock Car Alliance series in 1988.
● Named Lakeland Interstate Speedway's Rookie of the Year
in 1987.
● Began racing in 1983, in motocross; won more than 300
trophies in six years of competition.

## CAREER HIGHLIGHTS

● For Nemechek, the weekend of October 9-10 at Kansas
Speedway was the highlight of the season. He won the
NASCAR Busch Series race and the NASCAR NEXTEL Cup
race, the latter from the pole. Using Hendrick Motorsports

engines, his MB2 Chevy often was stout, but too many
DNFs doomed his season. He completed just 86.7 percent
of laps.
● Appeared to be on the way to a strong 2003 season after
winning the spring Richmond race. But he had only three
top 10s the rest of the way and eventually lost his job with
Hendrick Motorsports. He ran the last four races of the
season for MB2.
● Started his 300th career race at Pocono in June 2003.
● Began 2002 with Haas-Carter Motorsports, but the team
ceased operations after only seven starts. He started one
race as a replacement for the injured Johnny Benson, then
replaced Jerry Nadeau in the No. 25 Hendrick Motorsports
entry for the rest of the season. Despite the instability in
ownership, Nemechek tied a career high with three top fives.
● Joined Andy Petree for the 2000 and 2001 seasons and
had a career-high nine top 10s in 2000. He posted the
second victory of his career at Rockingham in 2001.
● In 1999, won a career-best three poles (Daytona,
Martinsville, Talladega) and got his first victory (New
Hampshire) while driving for Felix Sabates.
● Ran two full seasons as a driver/owner in 1995 and '96
after spending his first full NASCAR Cup season driving for
Larry Hedrick in 1994.

## CAREER STATISTICS

| Year | Car owner | Races | Champ. finish | Won | Top 5 | Top 10 | DNF | Poles | Money won |
|------|-----------|-------|--------|-----|-------|--------|-----|-------|-----------|
| 1993 | Joe Nemechek | 3 | | 0 | 0 | 0 | 2 | 0 | $24,300 |
| | Larry McClure | 2 | 44 | 0 | 0 | 0 | 0 | 0 | $32,280 |
| 1994 | Larry Hedrick | 29 | 27 | 0 | 1 | 3 | 9 | 0 | $389,565 |
| 1995 | Joe Nemechek | 29 | 28 | 0 | 1 | 4 | 5 | 0 | $428,925 |
| 1996 | Joe Nemechek | 29 | 34 | 0 | 0 | 2 | 8 | 0 | $666,247 |
| 1997 | Felix Sabates | 30 | 28 | 0 | 0 | 3 | 5 | 2 | $732,194 |
| 1998 | Felix Sabates | 32 | 26 | 0 | 1 | 4 | 5 | 0 | $1,343,991 |
| 1999 | Felix Sabates | 34 | 30 | 1 | 1 | 3 | 5 | 3 | $1,634,946 |
| 2000 | Andy Petree | 34 | 15 | 0 | 3 | 9 | 6 | 1 | $2,105,041 |
| 2001 | Andy Petree | 31 | 28 | 1 | 1 | 4 | 6 | 0 | $2,543,660 |
| 2002 | Travis Carter | 7 | | 0 | 0 | | | 0 | $612,062 |
| | Tom Beard | 1 | | 0 | 0 | | | 0 | $74,710 |
| | Rick Hendrick | 25 | 34 | 0 | 3 | 3 | | 0 | $1,766,252 |
| 2003 | Rick Hendrick | 32 | | 1 | 2 | 5 | 7 | 0 | $2,355,059 |
| | Tom Beard | 4 | 25 | 0 | 0 | 1 | 0 | 0 | $271,425 |
| 2004 | Tom Beard | 36 | 19 | 1 | 3 | 9 | 6 | 2 | $4,345,554 |
| **TOTALS** | | **358** | | **4** | **16** | **50** | **74** | **8** | **$19,327,669** |

## 2004 RESULTS

| Race | Track | Start | Finish | Laps | Led | Status | Winnings | Rank | Race | Track | Start | Finish | Laps | Led | Status | Winnings | Rank |
|------|-------|-------|--------|------|-----|--------|----------|------|------|-------|-------|--------|------|-----|--------|----------|------|
| Daytona 500 | Daytona | 14 | 6 | 200/200 | 0 | Running | $358,839 | 6 | Siemens 300 | New Hamp. | 18 | 20 | 300/300 | 0 | Running | $88,400 | 24 |
| Subway 400 | N. Carolina | 12 | 24 | 390/393 | 0 | Running | $75,949 | 10 | Pennsylvania 500 | Pocono | 2 | 16 | 200/200 | 31 | Running | $85,590 | 24 |
| UAW-DaimlerChrysler 400 | Las Vegas | 38 | 19 | 266/267 | 0 | Running | $97,150 | 13 | Brickyard 400 | Indianapolis | 4 | 17 | 161/161 | 0 | Running | $158,850 | 25 |
| Golden Corral 500 | Atlanta | 26 | 15 | 324/325 | 0 | Running | $86,750 | 13 | Sirius at the Glen | Watkins Glen | 25 | 22 | 90/90 | 0 | Running | $74,754 | 25 |
| Carolina Dodge Dealers 400 | Darlington | 34 | 20 | 292/293 | 0 | Running | $77,470 | 14 | GFS Marketplace 400 | Michigan | 25 | 13 | 200/200 | 0 | Running | $90,865 | 25 |
| Food City 500 | Bristol | 26 | 27 | 496/500 | 0 | Running | $87,694 | 19 | Sharpie 500 | Bristol | 37 | 42 | 31/500 | 0 | Accident | $75,755 | 25 |
| Samsung/RadioShack 500 | Texas | 5 | 14 | 333/334 | 33 | Running | $123,925 | 17 | Pop Secret 500 | California | 10 | 12 | 250/250 | 0 | Running | $114,700 | 25 |
| Advance Auto Parts 500 | Martinsville | 20 | 27 | 496/500 | 0 | Running | $80,035 | 16 | Chevy Rock & Roll 400 | Richmond | 4 | 22 | 399/400 | 0 | Running | $82,705 | 25 |
| Aaron's 499 | Talladega | 4 | 32 | 146/188 | 3 | Engine | $71,500 | 19 | Sylvania 300 | New Hamp. | 25 | 6 | 300/300 | 0 | Running | $105,725 | 24 |
| Auto Club 500 | California | 2 | 28 | 249/250 | 2 | Running | $88,100 | 20 | MBNA America 400 | Dover | 24 | 35 | 91/400 | 0 | Overheating | $65,380 | 24 |
| Chevy Amer. Revolution 400 | Richmond | 8 | 36 | 265/400 | 0 | Accident | $63,775 | 25 | EA Sports 500 | Talladega | 1 | 7 | 188/188 | 1 | Running | $106,075 | 24 |
| Coca-Cola 600 | Lowe's | 13 | 14 | 398/400 | 0 | Running | $107,050 | 23 | Banquet 400 | Kansas | 1 | 1 | 267/267 | 41 | Running | $310,725 | 21 |
| MBNA 400 'A Salute to Heroes' | Dover | 32 | 38 | 156/400 | 0 | Accident | $68,265 | 27 | UAW-GM Quality 500 | Lowe's | 8 | 5 | 334/334 | 4 | Running | $112,750 | 19 |
| Pocono 500 | Pocono | 3 | 18 | 200/200 | 10 | Running | $85,090 | 26 | Subway 500 | Martinsville | 29 | 30 | 488/500 | 0 | Running | $73,764 | 19 |
| DHL 400 | Michigan | 16 | 35 | 174/200 | 0 | Engine | $66,145 | 28 | Bass Pro Shops MBNA 500 | Atlanta | 2 | 4 | 325/325 | 3 | Running | $145,050 | 19 |
| Dodge/Save Mart 350 | Infineon | 9 | 29 | 109/110 | 0 | Running | $79,515 | 28 | Checker Auto Parts 500 | Phoenix | 3 | 12 | 315/315 | 0 | Running | $88,200 | 19 |
| Pepsi 400 | Daytona | 6 | 10 | 160/160 | 0 | Running | $114,625 | 26 | Southern 500 | Darlington | 18 | 8 | 367/367 | 1 | Running | $102,625 | 18 |
| Tropicana 400 | Chicago | 9 | 8 | 267/267 | 0 | Running | $112,850 | 25 | Ford 400 | Homestead | 19 | 27 | 267/271 | 0 | Running | $73,375 | 19 |

# Ryan Newman
## 12

**Date of birth:** December 8, 1977 **Hometown:** South Bend, Ind. **Resides:** Sherrills Ford, N.C. **Spouse:** Krissie **Children:** None **Height:** 5-11 **Weight:** 207 **Hobbies:** Fishing, radio-controlled cars

## NASCAR ACHIEVEMENTS

**First NASCAR Cup start:** November 5, 2000 (Phoenix)
**Best points finish:** 6 (2002, 2003)
**Career victories:** 11—Chicago (03), Dover (03a, 03b, 04b), Kansas (03), Michigan (03b, 04a), New Hampshire (02b), Pocono (03b), Richmond (03b), Texas (03)
**First victory:** September 15, 2002 (New Hampshire)
**Last victory:** September 26, 2004 (Dover)
**Career poles:** 27—Atlanta (03a, 03b, 04a, 04b), Bristol (03a, 04a), California (02), Charlotte (01a, 03a, 03b, 04b), Chicago (02), Darlington (03b), Dover (03a), Martinsville (02b, 04b), New Hampshire (02b, 03b, 04a), Phoenix (02, 03, 04), Pocono (03b), Richmond (04b), Rockingham (02b, 03b, 04)
**First pole:** May 25, 2001 (Charlotte)
**Best career finish:** 1 **Best career start:** 1

## FAST FACTS

● Ran 15 Busch Series races in 2001, winning one.
● Made his stock car debut in an ARCA race at Michigan in 2000, then won the next race he entered at Pocono; also won ARCA races that year at Kentucky and Charlotte.
● Won the 1999 USAC Coors Light Silver Bullet Series national championship with two wins and 12 top 10s.
● Won seven times in midgets and once in sprint cars.
● Named Rookie of the Year in Sprint Cars (1999), USAC Silver Crown (1996) and USAC National Midgets (1995).
● Was the 1993 All-American Midget Series champion and Rookie of the Year.
● Is a member of the Quarter-Midget Hall of Fame.
● Started racing quarter-midgets at age 4.
● Graduated from Purdue University in August 2001 with a degree in Vehicle Structural Engineering.
● Enjoys working on vintage cars.

## CAREER HIGHLIGHTS

● Newman won nine poles and two races in 2004, but his season was a bit of a disappointment. He didn't approach his 2003 win total of eight, and he didn't dominate very often. His car was often good, but the team couldn't sustain success and barely qualified for the Chase for the NASCAR NEXTEL Cup. Still, he remains the best qualifier on the circuit, and when he's good, he wins. He dominated Dover more than any driver dominated a race all season.

● Had more wins than any two drivers combined (eight) in 2003 and led the circuit in top fives (17). But Newman was inconsistent and unlucky early in the season, with five DNFs in the first half, and never could dig himself out of a points hole. In one stretch, he finished outside of the top 35 in five of seven races.

## CAR FACTS

**Car:** No. 12 Dodge
**Primary sponsor:** ALLTEL
**Owner:** Roger Penske
**Team:** Penske South
**Crew chief:** Matt Borland
**Engine builder:** Penske/Jasper

● Topped Jimmie Johnson for the 2002 Raybestos Rookie of the Year award in one of the most heated rookie battles in years. Newman also set a rookie record by tying Mark Martin's overall record for the most top 10s (22) in a season. He led the series with six poles, setting another rookie record for most poles in a season and topping Davey Allison's five poles in 1987. Newman also tied series champion Tony Stewart in races led (22) and became only the second Raybestos Rookie of the Year to win the All-Star race.

● Scored his first pole in only his third career NASCAR Cup start, at the Coca-Cola 600 in Charlotte in 2001, tying Mark Martin's record for earliest career pole.

### CAREER STATISTICS

| Year | Car owner | Races | Champ. finish | Won | Top 5 | Top 10 | DNF | Poles | Money won |
|------|-----------|-------|---------------|-----|-------|--------|-----|-------|-----------|
| 2000 | Roger Penske | 1 | | 0 | 0 | 0 | 1 | 0 | $37,825 |
| 2001 | Roger Penske | 7 | 49 | 0 | 2 | 2 | 2 | 1 | $465,276 |
| 2002 | Roger Penske | 36 | 6 | 1 | 14 | 22 | 5 | 6 | $5,346,651 |
| 2003 | Roger Penske | 36 | 6 | 8 | 17 | 22 | 7 | 11 | $6,100,877 |
| 2004 | Roger Penske | 36 | 7 | 2 | 11 | 14 | 9 | 9 | $6,354,256 |
| **TOTALS** | | **116** | | **11** | **44** | **60** | **24** | **27** | **$18,304,885** |

### 2004 RESULTS

| Race | Track | Start | Finish | Laps | Led | Status | Winnings | Rank |
|------|-------|-------|--------|------|-----|--------|----------|------|
| Daytona 500 | Daytona | 20 | 31 | 149/200 | 0 | Running | $255,056 | 31 |
| Subway 400 | N. Carolina | 1 | 6 | 393/393 | 12 | Running | $116,152 | 12 |
| UAW-DaimlerChrysler 400 | Las Vegas | 5 | 27 | 265/267 | 0 | Running | $114,117 | 21 |
| Golden Corral 500 | Atlanta | 1 | 5 | 325/325 | 43 | Running | $120,467 | 11 |
| Carolina Dodge Dealers 400 | Darlington | 6 | 3 | 293/293 | 39 | Running | $120,912 | 9 |
| Food City 500 | Bristol | 1 | 7 | 500/500 | 25 | Running | $124,862 | 5 |
| Samsung/RadioShack 500 | Texas | 15 | 39 | 194/334 | 0 | Accident | $110,742 | 10 |
| Advance Auto Parts 500 | Martinsville | 3 | 5 | 500/500 | 16 | Running | $113,242 | 11 |
| Aaron's 499 | Talladega | 17 | 11 | 188/188 | 1 | Running | $123,592 | 9 |
| Auto Club 500 | California | 7 | 3 | 250/250 | 2 | Running | $191,267 | 7 |
| Chevy Amer. Revolution 400 | Richmond | 2 | 9 | 400/400 | 9 | Running | $108,642 | 6 |
| Coca-Cola 600 | Lowe's | 2 | 35 | 390/400 | 0 | Engine | $120,417 | 9 |
| MBNA 400 'A Salute to Heroes' | Dover | 2 | 24 | 374/400 | 9 | Running | $111,297 | 10 |
| Pocono 500 | Pocono | 11 | 30 | 183/200 | 18 | Accident | $100,007 | 10 |
| DHL 400 | Michigan | 4 | 1 | 200/200 | 22 | Running | $176,367 | 9 |
| Dodge/Save Mart 350 | Infineon | 22 | 14 | 110/110 | 0 | Running | $106,742 | 9 |
| Pepsi 400 | Daytona | 13 | 12 | 160/160 | 2 | Running | $126,742 | 9 |
| Tropicana 400 | Chicago | 8 | 34 | 166/267 | 0 | Accident | $111,667 | 10 |
| Siemens 300 | New Hamp. | 1 | 3 | 300/300 | 187 | Running | $165,997 | 10 |
| Pennsylvania 500 | Pocono | 30 | 13 | 200/200 | 0 | Running | $103,457 | 8 |
| Brickyard 400 | Indianapolis | 7 | 31 | 154/161 | 0 | Accident | $165,092 | 10 |
| Sirius at the Glen | Watkins Glen | 10 | 26 | 89/90 | 0 | Running | $101,032 | 12 |
| GFS Marketplace 400 | Michigan | 12 | 14 | 200/200 | 0 | Running | $109,507 | 13 |
| Sharpie 500 | Bristol | 4 | 2 | 500/500 | 0 | Running | $213,887 | 10 |
| Pop Secret 500 | California | 14 | 5 | 250/250 | 2 | Running | $154,367 | 8 |
| Chevy Rock & Roll 400 | Richmond | 1 | 20 | 399/400 | 3 | Running | $110,572 | 10 |
| Sylvania 300 | New Hamp. | 10 | 33 | 262/300 | 4 | Engine | $105,902 | 9 |
| MBNA America 400 | Dover | 2 | 1 | 400/400 | 325 | Running | $195,477 | 8 |
| EA Sports 500 | Talladega | 19 | 16 | 188/188 | 1 | Running | $112,492 | 7 |
| Banquet 400 | Kansas | 7 | 33 | 223/267 | 8 | Accident | $121,867 | 8 |
| UAW-GM Quality 500 | Lowe's | 1 | 14 | 334/334 | 31 | Running | $136,117 | 9 |
| Subway 500 | Martinsville | 1 | 3 | 500/500 | 9 | Running | $132,517 | 9 |
| Bass Pro Shops MBNA 500 | Atlanta | 1 | 17 | 323/325 | 58 | Running | $138,092 | 7 |
| Checker Auto Parts 500 | Phoenix | 1 | 2 | 315/315 | 59 | Running | $181,167 | 7 |
| Southern 500 | Darlington | 7 | 34 | 330/367 | 0 | Engine | $101,517 | 7 |
| Ford 400 | Homestead | 3 | 30 | 264/271 | 72 | Accident | $107,917 | 7 |

# Kyle Petty
## 45

**Date of birth:** June 20, 1960 **Hometown:** Trinity, N.C. **Resides:** Trinity, N.C. **Spouse:** Pattie **Children:** Adam (deceased) Austin, Montgomery **Height:** 6-2 **Weight:** 195 **Hobbies:** Reading, riding motorcycles, collecting books, collecting Elvis memorabilia

## NASCAR ACHIEVEMENTS

**First NASCAR Cup start:** August 5, 1979 (Talladega)
**Best points finish:** 5 (1992, 1993)
**Career victories:** 8—Charlotte (87a), Dover (95a), Pocono (93a), Richmond (86a), Rockingham (90a, 91a, 92b), Watkins Glen (92)

**First victory:** February 23, 1986 (Richmond)
**Last victory:** June 4, 1995 (Dover)
**Career poles:** 8—Daytona (93a), Martinsville (92b), North Wilkesboro (90b), Rockingham (90a, 91a, 91b, 92a, 92b)
**First pole:** March 2, 1990 (Rockingham)
**Best career finish:** 1 **Best career start:** 1

# FAST FACTS

- Kyle and his wife, Pattie, were named recipients of the Myers Brothers Award, which recognizes individuals and/or groups who have provided outstanding contributions to the sport of stock car racing, in 2004. The Pettys turned a dream into reality in June of 2004, when the Victory Junction Gang Camp, a summer home for chronically ill children, officially opened its doors.
- Won the ARCA 200 at Daytona International Speedway in February 1979. It was his first race on a closed course, and the victory led to the beginning of his NASCAR Cup Series career that same season.
- Petty, his father Richard and the entire Petty family were named Persons of the Year for 2000 by *NASCAR Winston Cup Illustrated*, for their charitable work.

## CAR FACTS

**Car:** No. 45 Dodge
**Primary sponsor:** Georgia Pacific/Brawney
**Owner:** Petty Enterprises
**Team:** Petty Enterprises
**Crew chief:** Bill Henderson
**Engine builder:** Evernham Motorsports

- Kyle Petty's Charity Ride Across America was founded in 1995. Petty also works with the Make-A-Wish Foundation, the Boy Scouts of America, the NEXTEL Cup Racing Wives Auxiliary and the Victory Junction Game Camp.
- Named NASCAR True Value Man of the Year in 1998, 2002.
- Petty was recruited by several colleges as a quarterback; others talked to him about a baseball scholarship.

## CAREER HIGHLIGHTS

- Petty, who made his 700th career start in 2004, will have new engines in 2005, and maybe that will help him. Petty failed to notch a top 10 finish in 2004. Too often, he was just out there turning laps, and he didn't turn enough, completing less than 90 percent of them. He never started better than 18th, and his season-best finish was 12th, his only top 15.
- Made his 600th career NASCAR Cup start in the 2001 August Michigan race.
- Competed in 19 NASCAR Cup races in 2000 for Petty Enterprises before moving from his No. 44 NASCAR Cup car to his late son Adam's No. 45 car in the NASCAR Busch Series.
- Left owner Felix Sabates after the 1996 season after finishes of 30th and 27th the past two seasons. He ran as an owner/driver in 1997 and shot up to 15th in points but fell back down to 30th in 1998.
- Finished a career-high fifth in points in 1992 and '93. In 1992, he made a late-season bid for the championship with seven top fives in the last 10 races.
- Sat out 11 races in 1991 after an accident in Talladega left him with a broken thigh bone.
- Finished 11th in points in 1990. He found victory lane once, at Rockingham, and Sabates was so elated, he presented Petty with a Rolls Royce. Petty won twice more at Rockingham in the next two seasons.
- Joined Sabates in 1989 and fell to 30th in points that season—even with two top 10s in the final three races.

- Became the first third-generation driver to win a NASCAR Cup race, following father Richard and grandfather Lee, with a victory at Richmond in 1986.
- Joined the Wood Brothers team in 1985. He finished ninth in points and won the Comeback Driver of the Year award.
- Made his NASCAR Cup debut in 1979, running five races for Petty Enterprises.

## CAREER STATISTICS

| Year | Car owner | Races | Champ. finish | Won | Top 5 | Top 10 | DNF | Poles | Money won |
|------|-----------|-------|---------------|-----|-------|--------|-----|-------|-----------|
| 1979 | Petty Enterprises | 5 | 37 | 0 | 0 | 1 | 1 | 0 | $10,810 |
| 1980 | Petty Enterprises | 14 |  | 0 | 0 | 6 | 5 | 0 | $35,575 |
|  | B. Rahilly/B. Mock | 1 | 28 | 0 | 0 | 0 | 0 | 0 | $775 |
| 1981 | Petty Enterprises | 31 | 12 | 0 | 1 | 10 | 18 | 0 | $112,289 |
| 1982 | Petty Enterprises | 23 |  | 0 | 2 | 4 | 13 | 0 | $108,715 |
|  | Hoss Ellington | 6 | 15 | 0 | 0 | 0 | 3 | 0 | $12,015 |
| 1983 | Petty Enterprises | 30 | 13 | 0 | 0 | 2 | 10 | 0 | $157,820 |
| 1984 | Petty Enterprises | 30 | 16 | 0 | 1 | 6 | 7 | 0 | $324,555 |
| 1985 | Wood Brothers | 28 | 9 | 0 | 7 | 12 | 4 | 0 | $296,367 |
| 1986 | Wood Brothers | 29 | 10 | 1 | 4 | 14 | 6 | 0 | $403,242 |
| 1987 | Wood Brothers | 29 | 7 | 1 | 6 | 14 | 4 | 0 | $544,437 |
| 1988 | Wood Brothers | 29 | 13 | 0 | 2 | 8 | 6 | 0 | $377,092 |
| 1989 | Felix Sabates | 18 |  | 0 | 1 | 5 | 7 | 0 | $111,022 |
|  | Rick Hendrick | 1 | 30 | 0 | 0 | 0 | 0 | 0 | $6,000 |
| 1990 | Felix Sabates | 29 | 11 | 1 | 2 | 14 | 5 | 2 | $746,326 |
| 1991 | Felix Sabates | 18 | 31 | 1 | 2 | 4 | 5 | 2 | $413,727 |
| 1992 | Felix Sabates | 29 | 5 | 2 | 9 | 17 | 5 | 3 | $1,107,063 |
| 1993 | Felix Sabates | 30 | 5 | 1 | 9 | 15 | 5 | 1 | $914,662 |
| 1994 | Felix Sabates | 31 | 15 | 0 | 2 | 7 | 3 | 0 | $806,332 |
| 1995 | Felix Sabates | 31 | 30 | 1 | 1 | 5 | 10 | 0 | $698,875 |
| 1996 | Felix Sabates | 28 | 27 | 0 | 0 | 2 | 4 | 0 | $689,041 |
| 1997 | Kyle Petty | 32 | 15 | 0 | 2 | 9 | 2 | 0 | $984,314 |
| 1998 | Kyle Petty | 33 | 30 | 0 | 0 | 2 | 8 | 0 | $1,287,731 |
| 1999 | Petty Enterprises | 32 | 26 | 0 | 0 | 9 | 4 | 0 | $1,278,953 |
| 2000 | Petty Enterprises | 19 |  | 0 | 0 | 1 | 6 | 0 | $797,176 |
|  | Michael Kranefuss | 1 | 41 | 0 | 0 | 0 | 0 | 0 | $97,735 |
| 2001 | Petty Enterprises | 24 | 43 | 0 | 0 | 0 | 0 | 0 | $1,008,919 |
| 2002 | Petty Enterprises | 36 | 22 | 0 | 0 | 1 | 1 | 0 | $2,198,073 |
| 2003 | Petty Enterprises | 33 | 37 | 0 | 0 | 0 | 5 | 0 | $2,293,222 |
| 2004 | Petty Enterprises | 35 | 33 | 0 | 0 | 0 | 9 | 0 | $2,780,131 |
| TOTALS | | 713 | | 8 | 51 | 168 | 164 | 8 | $20,602,994 |

## 2004 RESULTS

| Race | Track | Start | Finish | Laps | Led | Status | Winnings | rank |
|------|-------|-------|--------|------|-----|--------|----------|------|
| Daytona 500 | Daytona | 33 | 21 | 199/200 | 5 | Running | $226,127 | 21 |
| Subway 400 | N. Carolina | 30 | 39 | 221/393 | 0 | Engine | $55,070 | 31 |
| UAW-DaimlerChrysler 400 | Las Vegas | 32 | 12 | 267/267 | 0 | Running | $101,275 | 26 |
| Golden Corral 500 | Atlanta | 27 | 28 | 321/325 | 0 | Running | $67,059 | 27 |
| Carolina Dodge Dealers 400 | Darlington | 32 | 34 | 245/293 | 0 | Engine | $51,365 | 30 |
| Food City 500 | Bristol | 36 | 25 | 498/500 | 0 | Running | $82,570 | 29 |
| Samsung/RadioShack 500 | Texas | 38 | 21 | 332/334 | 1 | Running | $103,775 | 28 |
| Advance Auto Parts 500 | Martinsville | 31 | 18 | 500/500 | 0 | Running | $76,725 | 27 |
| Aaron's 499 | Talladega | 28 | 24 | 188/188 | 0 | Running | $77,949 | 29 |
| Auto Club 500 | California | 28 | 39 | 40/250 | 0 | Engine | $64,430 | 32 |
| Chevy Amer. Revolution 400 | Richmond | 22 | 27 | 395/400 | 0 | Running | $72,700 | 32 |
| Coca-Cola 600 | Lowe's | 42 | 38 | 384/400 | 0 | Running | $68,185 | 33 |
| MBNA 400 'A Salute to Heroes' | Dover | 30 | 37 | 217/400 | 0 | Handling | $60,375 | 34 |
| Pocono 500 | Pocono | 25 | 37 | 101/200 | 0 | Engine | $51,900 | 35 |
| DHL 400 | Michigan | 33 | 18 | 200/200 | 0 | Running | $79,865 | 34 |
| Dodge/Save Mart 350 | Infineon | 27 | 32 | 109/110 | 0 | Running | $57,800 | 34 |
| Pepsi 400 | Daytona | 33 | 24 | 160/160 | 0 | Running | $85,075 | 33 |
| Tropicana 400 | Chicago | 42 | 26 | 265/267 | 0 | Running | $78,839 | 33 |

| Race | Track | Start | Finish | Laps | Led | Status | Winnings | Rank |
|------|-------|-------|--------|------|-----|--------|----------|------|
| Siemens 300 | New Hamp. | 39 | 27 | 300/300 | 0 | Running | $71,739 | 31 |
| Pennsylvania 500 | Pocono | 25 | 19 | 200/200 | 0 | Running | $67,029 | 31 |
| Brickyard 400 | Indianapolis | 26 | 23 | 161/161 | 0 | Running | $141,180 | 32 |
| Sirius at the Glen | Watkins Glen | 33 | 18 | 90/90 | 0 | Running | $72,460 | 31 |
| GFS Marketplace 400 | Michigan | 32 | 29 | 199/200 | 0 | Running | $66,879 | 31 |
| Sharpie 500 | Bristol | 31 | 37 | 150/500 | 0 | Accident | $76,759 | 33 |
| Pop Secret 500 | California | 28 | 35 | 225/250 | 0 | Engine | $85,339 | 33 |
| Chevy Rock & Roll 400 | Richmond | 31 | 34 | 392/400 | 0 | Running | $66,935 | 33 |
| Sylvania 300 | New Hamp. | 34 | 21 | 299/300 | 0 | Running | $78,125 | 33 |

| Race | Track | Start | Finish | Laps | Led | Status | Winnings | Rank |
|------|-------|-------|--------|------|-----|--------|----------|------|
| MBNA America 400 | Dover | 27 | 17 | 397/400 | 0 | Running | $79,415 | 33 |
| EA Sports 500 | Talladega | 35 | 29 | 187/188 | 0 | Running | $78,065 | 33 |
| Banquet 400 | Kansas | 39 | 38 | 88/267 | 0 | Handling | $63,975 | 33 |
| UAW-GM Quality 500 | Lowe's | 32 | 27 | 326/334 | 0 | Running | $66,934 | 33 |
| Subway 500 | Martinsville | 26 | 22 | 500/500 | 0 | Running | $72,025 | 33 |
| Bass Pro Shops MBNA 500 | Atlanta | 18 | 29 | 319/325 | 0 | Running | $80,150 | 33 |
| Checker Auto Parts 500 | Phoenix | 34 | 28 | 313/315 | 0 | Running | $63,564 | 33 |
| Southern 500 | Darlington | 34 | 35 | 300/367 | 0 | Accident | $54,425 | 33 |

# Scott Riggs

## 10

**Date of birth:** January 1, 1971 **Hometown:** Bahama, N.C.
**Resides:** Bahama, N.C. **Spouse:** Jai **Children:** Layne
**Height:** 5-6 **Weight:** 175 **Hobbies:** Horseback riding, riding dirt and road bikes and water sports

## NASCAR ACHIEVEMENTS

**First NASCAR Cup start:** February 15, 2004 (Daytona)
**Best points finish:** 29 (2004)
**Career victories:** 0
**Career poles:** 0
**Best career finish:** 5  **Best career start:** 4

## FAST FACTS

● Finished 10th in the 2002 NASCAR Busch Series, winning the Raybestos Rookie of the Year award.
● Finished fifth in the NASCAR Craftsman Truck Series in 2001, with five wins and 14 top fives; also ran on that circuit in 1999 and 2000.
● Was a two-time champion at the Southern National Speedway in Kenley, N.C., where he has 60 victories.
● Has competed on the Hills Brothers All-Pro Series of NASCAR Touring, posting eight top 10s in 13 races in 1998.
● Was voted the NASCAR Busch Series' 2003 Most Popular Driver by fans. He contended for the championship in 2003 and ultimately finished sixth in points, with two wins.
● Got his start in racing at age 14 when he began running dirt bikes in AMA Motocross competition. He finished third in the 1987 National AMA Competition but began running in NASCAR in 1988 because his family thought it was safer than dirt bikes.

### CAR FACTS

**Car:** No. 10 Chevrolet
**Primary sponsor:** Valvoline
**Owner:** James Rocco
**Team:** MBV Motorsports
**Crew chief:** Doug Randolph
**Engine builder:** Hendrick Motorsports

## CAREER HIGHLIGHTS

● In a frustrating 2004 season, Riggs never went five races without a DNF and completed just 89.9 percent of his laps. In an era in which rookies are expected to produce right away, he wasn't a factor in the Raybestos Rookie of the Year race.

### CAREER STATISTICS

| Year | Car owner | Races | Champ. finish | Won | Top 5 | Top 10 | DNF | Poles | Money won |
|------|-----------|-------|---------------|-----|-------|--------|-----|-------|-----------|
| 2004 | James Rocco | 35 | 29 | 0 | 1 | 2 | 8 | 0 | $3,443,345 |
| **TOTALS** | | **35** | | **0** | **1** | **2** | **8** | **0** | **$3,443,345** |

### 2004 RESULTS

| Race | Track | Start | Finish | Laps | Led | Status | Winnings | Rank |
|------|-------|-------|--------|------|-----|--------|----------|------|
| Daytona 500 | Daytona | 36 | 34 | 109/200 | 0 | Accident | $231,328 | 34 |
| Subway 400 | N. Carolina | 19 | 31 | 383/393 | 0 | Running | $80,937 | 35 |
| UAW-DaimlerChrysler 400 | Las Vegas | 15 | 29 | 264/267 | 1 | Running | $91,237 | 32 |
| Golden Corral 500 | Atlanta | 17 | 25 | 321/325 | 0 | Running | $85,072 | 33 |
| Carolina Dodge Dealers 400 | Darlington | 27 | 30 | 290/293 | 0 | Running | $77,372 | 34 |
| Food City 500 | Bristol | 28 | 34 | 404/500 | 0 | Accident | $91,922 | 35 |
| Samsung/RadioShack 500 | Texas | 24 | 15 | 332/334 | 0 | Running | $125,512 | 34 |
| Advance Auto Parts 500 | Martinsville | 13 | 28 | 495/500 | 0 | Running | $83,922 | 34 |
| Aaron's 499 | Talladega | 5 | 34 | 144/188 | 0 | Running | $89,322 | 35 |
| Auto Club 500 | California | 4 | 25 | 249/250 | 0 | Running | $97,187 | 35 |
| Chevy Amer. Revolution 400 | Richmond | 16 | 35 | 341/400 | 0 | Engine | $81,012 | 34 |
| Coca-Cola 600 | Lowe's | 28 | 25 | 395/400 | 0 | Running | $100,087 | 34 |
| MBNA 400 'A Salute to Heroes' | Dover | 23 | 5 | 400/400 | 0 | Running | $126,487 | 33 |
| Pocono 500 | Pocono | 40 | 16 | 200/200 | 0 | Running | $89,777 | 31 |
| DHL 400 | Michigan | 20 | 20 | 200/200 | 1 | Running | $91,202 | 30 |
| Dodge/Save Mart 350 | Infineon | 41 | 42 | 51/110 | 0 | Accident | $82,597 | 31 |
| Pepsi 400 | Daytona | 7 | 21 | 160/160 | 0 | Running | $101,987 | 30 |
| Tropicana 400 | Chicago | 16 | 29 | 245/267 | 0 | Running | $94,037 | 30 |
| Siemens 300 | New Hamp. | 15 | 28 | 300/300 | 0 | Running | $88,362 | 30 |
| Pennsylvania 500 | Pocono | 26 | 22 | 200/200 | 0 | Running | $82,877 | 30 |

| Race | Track | Start | Finish | Laps | Led | Status | Winnings | Rank |
|------|-------|-------|--------|------|-----|--------|----------|------|
| Brickyard 400 | Indianapolis | 27 | 37 | 72/161 | 0 | Accident | $141,927 | 30 |
| Sirius at the Glen | Watkins Glen | 31 | 23 | 90/90 | 0 | Running | $84,157 | 30 |
| GFS Marketplace 400 | Michigan | 31 | 19 | 199/200 | 12 | Running | $89,352 | 29 |
| Sharpie 500 | Bristol | 39 | 17 | 497/500 | 0 | Running | $111,522 | 29 |
| Pop Secret 500 | California | 9 | 7 | 250/250 | 0 | Running | $12,437 | 29 |
| Chevy Rock & Roll 400 | Richmond | 35 | 39 | 292/400 | 0 | Engine | $81,442 | 29 |
| Sylvania 300 | New Hamp. | 30 | 26 | 298/300 | 0 | Running | $88,762 | 29 |
| MBNA America 400 | Dover | 18 | 31 | 363/400 | 0 | Wheel bearing | $85,802 | 29 |

| Race | Track | Start | Finish | Laps | Led | Status | Winnings | Rank |
|------|-------|-------|--------|------|-----|--------|----------|------|
| EA Sports 500 | Talladega | 4 | 11 | 188/188 | 1 | Running | $96,952 | 29 |
| Banquet 400 | Kansas | 14 | 26 | 265/267 | 0 | Running | $95,437 | 28 |
| UAW-GM Quality 500 | Lowe's | 4 | 38 | 30/334 | 0 | Engine | $82,022 | 30 |
| Subway 500 | Martinsville | 6 | 26 | 500/500 | 0 | Running | $83,287 | 29 |
| Checker Auto Parts 500 | Phoenix | 11 | 14 | 315/315 | 0 | Running | $85,187 | 30 |
| Southern 500 | Darlington | 31 | 25 | 364/367 | 0 | Running | $86,437 | 30 |
| Ford 400 | Homestead | 25 | 15 | 271/271 | 0 | Running | $84,712 | 29 |

**Ricky Rudd**

**21**

**Date of birth:** September 12, 1956 **Hometown:** Chesapeake, Va.
**Resides:** Cornelius, N.C. **Spouse:** Linda **Children:** Landon
**Height:** 5-8 **Weight:** 160 **Hobbies:** Flying, being outdoors, boating, water sports

## NASCAR ACHIEVEMENTS

**First NASCAR Cup start:** March 2, 1975 (Rockingham)
**Best points finish:** 2 (1991)
**Career victories:** 23—Atlanta (87), Darlington (91a), Dover (86b, 87b, 92b, 97a), Indianapolis (97), Martinsville (83b, 86a, 98b), Michigan (93a), New Hampshire (94), Phoenix (95), Pocono (01a), Richmond (84b, 01b), Rockingham (96b), Sonoma (89, 02), Watkins Glen (88,90)
**First victory:** June 5, 1983
**Last victory:** June 23, 2002 (Sonoma)
**Career poles:** 29—Bristol (84b), Charlotte (96b), Daytona (83a), Dover (81b, 82b, 84a, 88a), Indianapolis (00), Las Vegas (00), Martinsville (81a, 82b, 83a, 88a), Nashville (81a, 84b), North Wilkesboro (84a), Pocono (01a), Richmond (83a, 90a), Riverside (88), Rockingham (83a, 94b, 99a), Sonoma (90, 91, 91, 95), Talladega (04a), Watkins Glen (02)
**First pole:** April 24, 1981 (Martinsville)
**Best career finish:** 1 **Best career start:** 1

## FAST FACTS

● Started racing at age 9 and raced in motorcross and go-karts as a teenager.
● Won the IROC championship in 1992.
● Father, Al Rudd Jr., owned an auto salvage business that led to Ricky's interest in cars.
● NASCAR's iron man, with 752 consecutive starts dating back to 1981.

## CAREER HIGHLIGHTS

● A gloomy 2004 season brightened when Rudd was again paired with former crew chief Michael "Fatback" McSwain. A near win at Kansas and other strong performances late in the season gave Rudd and Wood Brothers Racing reason to look forward to 2005. It always will be hard for one-car teams to keep up, but the veteran pairing of McSwain and Rudd has as good a chance to succeed as any.
● Ranks third on the list of career NASCAR Cup starts, with 839. Only Richard Petty (1,185) and Dave Marcis (883) have more. Rudd is first in consecutive starts with 752, a streak that began on January 11, 1981.

### CAR FACTS

**Car:** No. 21 Ford
**Primary sponsor:** Motorcraft Quality Parts
**Owner:** Wood Brothers
**Team:** Wood Brothers Racing
**Crew chief:** Michael McSwain
**Engine builder:** Roush/Yates

● Made his 800th career Cup start in the October 2003 Atlanta race. He finished 31st. 2003 was his first season with the Wood Brothers, and he was plagued by car problems, with nine DNFs. He completed only 92.5 percent of his laps and finished the season without a victory for the third time in five years. His problems began with qualifying; his average starting position was 27.1.
● Started his 656th consecutive race in 2002 on May 26 at Charlotte, breaking Terry Labonte's record of 655 career starts.
● Ended an 88-race winless streak with a victory from the pole at Pocono in June 2001. He also won the Richmond fall race and was in contention for the championship until August. He finished fourth in points.
● Experienced a renaissance of sorts with Robert Yates Racing in 2000; he finished fifth in points with 12 top fives, his most since 1985. His only win was in a nonpoints race, the Daytona 500 125-mile qualifier.
● Ran as an owner/driver from 1994 to '99. He had success during his first three seasons as an owner, finishing in the

top 10 in points with one win in all three seasons. But he took a nose dive in his next three seasons, finishing 17th, 22nd and 31st in points in 1997, '98 and '99. He hit bottom in 1999, finishing the season without a victory for the first time since 1982, and with only five top 10s. After the season, he sold his shop to Robert Yates Racing, and the shop became the home of the No. 28 team.

● Finished a career-high second in points in 1991, 195 points behind champion Dale Earnhardt. He extended his string of consecutive years with at least one victory to nine with a win at Darlington.

● Won at Watkins Glen in 1988, his first of four victories at road races (Watkins Glen: 1988, '90; Sonoma: 1989, 2002).

● Won the fall Dover race in 1986. It was the first of four victories there; the others were in 1987, '92 and '97.

● Had a breakthrough year in 1983, his second season with Richard Childress Racing. He got his first Cup win in his 161st start, at Riverside, and also won the September Martinsville race. He had a career-high four poles, including one at the Daytona 500.

● Had a career-high 14 top fives in 1981, his lone season racing for Bill Gardner.

● Raced for his father Al Rudd Sr.'s team from 1976 to 1978, and in 1980. He was Raybestos Rookie of the Year in 1977 and gained attention in 1980 by qualifying second and finishing fourth in the Charlotte fall race.

## CAREER STATISTICS

| Year | Car owner | Races | Champ. finish | Won | Top 5 | Top 10 | DNF | Poles | Money won |
|------|-----------|-------|---------------|-----|-------|--------|-----|-------|-----------|
| 1975 | Bill Champion | 4 | 47 | 0 | 0 | 1 | 2 | 0 | $4,345 |
| 1976 | Al Rudd Sr. | 4 | 53 | 0 | 0 | 1 | 2 | 0 | $7,525 |
| 1977 | Al Rudd Sr. | 25 | 17 | 0 | 1 | 10 | 11 | 0 | $68,448 |
| 1978 | Al Rudd Sr. | 13 | 31 | 0 | 0 | 4 | 7 | 0 | $49,610 |
| 1979 | Junie Donlavey | 28 | 17 | 0 | 4 | 17 | 6 | 0 | $146,302 |
| 1980 | Nelson Malloch | 7 | | 0 | 0 | 1 | 4 | 0 | $18,745 |
|  | D.K. Ulrich | 3 | | 0 | 0 | 0 | 1 | 0 | $8,025 |
|  | Al Rudd Sr. | 3 | 34 | 0 | 1 | 2 | 1 | 0 | $23,515 |
| 1981 | Bill Gardner | 31 | 6 | 0 | 14 | 17 | 9 | 3 | $381,968 |
| 1982 | Richard Childress | 30 | 9 | 0 | 6 | 13 | 13 | 2 | $201,130 |
| 1983 | Richard Childress | 30 | 9 | 2 | 7 | 14 | 8 | 4 | $257,585 |
| 1984 | Bud Moore | 30 | 7 | 1 | 7 | 16 | 6 | 4 | $476,602 |
| 1985 | Bud Moore | 28 | 6 | 1 | 13 | 19 | 5 | 0 | $512,441 |
| 1986 | Bud Moore | 29 | 5 | 2 | 11 | 17 | 7 | 1 | $671,548 |
| 1987 | Bud Moore | 29 | 6 | 2 | 10 | 13 | 9 | 0 | $653,508 |
| 1988 | Kenny Bernstein | 29 | 11 | 1 | 6 | 11 | 12 | 2 | $410,954 |
| 1989 | Kenny Bernstein | 29 | 8 | 1 | 7 | 15 | 5 | 0 | $534,824 |
| 1990 | Rick Hendrick | 29 | 7 | 1 | 8 | 15 | 5 | 2 | $573,650 |
| 1991 | Rick Hendrick | 29 | 2 | 1 | 9 | 17 | 1 | 1 | $1,093,765 |
| 1992 | Rick Hendrick | 29 | 7 | 1 | 9 | 18 | 4 | 1 | $793,903 |
| 1993 | Rick Hendrick | 30 | 10 | 1 | 9 | 14 | 6 | 0 | $752,562 |
| 1994 | Ricky Rudd | 31 | 5 | 1 | 6 | 15 | 2 | 1 | $1,044,441 |
| 1995 | Ricky Rudd | 31 | 9 | 1 | 10 | 16 | 6 | 2 | $1,337,703 |
| 1996 | Ricky Rudd | 31 | 6 | 1 | 5 | 16 | 1 | 0 | $1,503,025 |
| 1997 | Ricky Rudd | 32 | 17 | 2 | 6 | 11 | 7 | 0 | $1,975,981 |
| 1998 | Ricky Rudd | 33 | 22 | 1 | 1 | 5 | 7 | 0 | $1,602,895 |
| 1999 | Ricky Rudd | 34 | 31 | 0 | 3 | 5 | 7 | 1 | $1,632,011 |
| 2000 | Robert Yates | 34 | 5 | 0 | 12 | 19 | 1 | 2 | $2,914,970 |
| 2001 | Robert Yates | 36 | 4 | 2 | 14 | 22 | 4 | 1 | $4,878,027 |
| 2002 | Robert Yates | 36 | 10 | 1 | 8 | 12 | 4 | 1 | $4,444,614 |
| 2003 | Wood Brothers | 36 | 23 | 0 | 4 | 5 | 9 | 0 | $3,240,614 |
| 2004 | Wood Brothers | 36 | 24 | 0 | 1 | 3 | 6 | 1 | $3,905,141 |
| **TOTALS** | | **839** | | **23** | **192** | **364** | **179** | **29** | **$36,120,592** |

## 2004 RESULTS

| Race | Track | Start | Finish | Laps | Led | Status | Winnings | Rank |
|------|-------|-------|--------|------|-----|--------|----------|------|
| Daytona 500 | Daytona | 16 | 18 | 199/200 | 0 | Running | $246,020 | 18 |
| Subway 400 | N. Carolina | 22 | 19 | 391/393 | 0 | Running | $87,566 | 19 |
| UAW-DaimlerChrysler 400 | Las Vegas | 33 | 28 | 264/267 | 0 | Running | $92,306 | 25 |
| Golden Corral 500 | Atlanta | 33 | 31 | 320/325 | 0 | Running | $81,316 | 26 |
| Carolina Dodge Dealers 400 | Darlington | 25 | 33 | 275/293 | 0 | Running | $77,481 | 29 |
| Food City 500 | Bristol | 15 | 37 | 166/500 | 0 | Accident | $92,666 | 32 |
| Samsung/RadioShack 500 | Texas | 29 | 22 | 332/334 | 0 | Running | $114,281 | 31 |
| Advance Auto Parts 500 | Martinsville | 14 | 20 | 499/500 | 0 | Running | $88,581 | 30 |
| Aaron's 499 | Talladega | 1 | 17 | 188/188 | 0 | Running | $106,281 | 31 |
| Auto Club 500 | California | 35 | 17 | 249/250 | 0 | Running | $102,981 | 28 |
| Chevy Amer. Revolution 400 | Richmond | 30 | 11 | 400/400 | 2 | Running | $91,831 | 28 |
| Coca-Cola 600 | Lowe's | 40 | 26 | 395/400 | 0 | Running | $99,756 | 27 |
| MBNA 400 'A Salute to Heroes' | Dover | 28 | 30 | 351/400 | 0 | Accident | $88,061 | 30 |
| Pocono 500 | Pocono | 35 | 19 | 200/200 | 0 | Running | $84,696 | 28 |
| DHL 400 | Michigan | 25 | 12 | 200/200 | 0 | Running | $94,121 | 27 |
| Dodge/Save Mart 350 | Infineon | 12 | 35 | 97/110 | 0 | Running | $83,751 | 27 |
| Pepsi 400 | Daytona | 3 | 17 | 160/160 | 0 | Running | $107,356 | 28 |
| Tropicana 400 | Chicago | 30 | 32 | 204/267 | 0 | Running | $91,256 | 28 |
| Siemens 300 | New Hamp. | 34 | 39 | 208/300 | 0 | Accident | $84,091 | 28 |
| Pennsylvania 500 | Pocono | 33 | 12 | 200/200 | 1 | Running | $87,506 | 28 |
| Brickyard 400 | Indianapolis | 40 | 28 | 160/161 | 0 | Accident | $148,806 | 28 |
| Sirius at the Glen | Watkins Glen | 29 | 8 | 90/90 | 0 | Running | $94,966 | 27 |
| GFS Marketplace 400 | Michigan | 27 | 24 | 199/200 | 0 | Running | $88,646 | 27 |
| Sharpie 500 | Bristol | 32 | 40 | 64/500 | 0 | Accident | $94,056 | 27 |
| Pop Secret 500 | California | 20 | 17 | 250/250 | 0 | Running | $111,556 | 27 |
| Chevy Rock & Roll 400 | Richmond | 6 | 21 | 399/400 | 0 | Running | $88,536 | 27 |
| Sylvania 300 | New Hamp. | 28 | 37 | 192/300 | 0 | Overheat | $84,306 | 27 |
| MBNA America 400 | Dover | 14 | 12 | 399/400 | 0 | Running | $92,321 | 26 |
| EA Sports 500 | Talladega | 2 | 12 | 188/188 | 0 | Running | $97,471 | 26 |
| Banquet 400 | Kansas | 12 | 2 | 267/267 | 2 | Running | $208,896 | 26 |
| UAW-GM Quality 500 | Lowe's | 41 | 16 | 332/334 | 0 | Running | $89,006 | 25 |
| Subway 500 | Martinsville | 9 | 14 | 500/500 | 0 | Running | $87,681 | 25 |
| Bass Pro Shops MBNA 500 | Atlanta | 43 | 12 | 324/325 | 0 | Running | $108,456 | 25 |
| Checker Auto Parts 500 | Phoenix | 25 | 19 | 315/315 | 0 | Running | $83,081 | 25 |
| Southern 500 | Darlington | 26 | 16 | 367/367 | 0 | Running | $93,731 | 25 |
| Ford 400 | Homestead | 7 | 9 | 271/271 | 0 | Running | $90,806 | 24 |

# Elliott Sadler

**Date of birth:** April 30, 1975 **Hometown:** Emporia, Va. **Resides:** Emporia, Va. **Spouse:** Single **Children:** None **Height:** 6-2 **Weight:** 195 **Hobbies:** Golf, hunting, basketball, water sports

## NASCAR ACHIEVEMENTS

**First NASCAR Cup start:** May 24, 1998 (Charlotte)
**Best points finish:** 9 (2004)
**Career victories:** 3—Bristol (01a), California (04b), Texas (04a)
**First victory:** March 25, 2001 (Bristol)
**Last victory:** September 5, 2004 (California)
**Career poles:** 2—Darlington (03a), Talladega (03b)
**Best career finish:** 1  **Best career start:** 1

## FAST FACTS

- Had five races, five pole positions and 12 top fives in 76 career NASCAR Busch Series starts before moving into NASCAR NEXTEL Cup full time.
- Crowned track champion at South Boston Speedway in 1995, winning 13 races.
- Moved into the Winston Racing Series at age 18.
- Began racing at age in go-karts at age 7 and won more than 200 races; also won the 1983-84 Virginia State Karting Championship.
- Is a hunting guide and raises Walker hunting dogs in the winter months.
- His father, Herman, raced late model stocks in Virginia.
- Received a basketball scholarship to James Madison University to play for coach Lefty Driessell but suffered a knee injury that "allowed him to pursue a sit-down job."

## CAREER HIGHLIGHTS

- For Sadler, 2004 was when performance caught up with potential. Long considered a driver with abundant skill but no results to show for it, Sadler joined the top 10 for the first time in his career after the season-opening race and never left. He won twice, a career high, and qualified well. Crew chief Todd Parrott consistently built Sadler outstanding racecars powered by strong yet reliable Roush-Yates engines.
- Joined Robert Yates Racing in 2003 and shot up to 10th in points after

### CAR FACTS

**Car:** No. 38 Ford
**Primary sponsor:** M&Ms
**Owner:** Robert Yates
**Team:** Robert Yates Racing
**Crew chief:** Todd Parrott
**Engine builder:** Yates/Roush

10 races. But consecutive finishes of 37th, 36th and 33rd pushed him out of the top 10 for good.
- Took the Wood Brothers to victory lane for the first time since 1993 with a victory at Bristol in March 2001. It was Sadler's first career win in his 75th NASCAR Cup start. The team started 38th on a provisional in a backup car after Sadler wrecked his primary Ford in practice.
- Took a step back in 2000, finishing 29th. He failed to qualify at Talladega. The team used six provisionals and had five DNFs.
- Was second to Tony Stewart for 1999 Raybestos Rookie of the Year and finished 24th in points.

### CAREER STATISTICS

| Year | Car owner | Races | Champ. finish | Won | Top 5 | Top 10 | DNF | Poles | Money won |
|------|-----------|-------|---------------|-----|-------|--------|-----|-------|-----------|
| 1998 | Gary Bechtel | 2 | 59 | 0 | 0 | 0 | 1 | 0 | $45,325 |
| 1999 | Wood Brothers | 34 | 24 | 0 | 0 | 1 | 2 | 0 | $1,589,221 |
| 2000 | Wood Brothers | 33 | 29 | 0 | 0 | 1 | 5 | 0 | $1,579,656 |
| 2001 | Wood Brothers | 36 | 20 | 1 | 2 | 2 | 2 | 0 | $2,683,225 |
| 2002 | Wood Brothers | 36 | 23 | 0 | 2 | 7 | 6 | 0 | $3,491,694 |
| 2003 | Robert Yates | 36 | 22 | 0 | 2 | 9 | 9 | 2 | $3,795,174 |
| 2004 | Robert Yates | 36 | 9 | 2 | 8 | 14 | 1 | 0 | $6,244,954 |
| **TOTALS** | | **213** | | **3** | **14** | **34** | **26** | **2** | **$19,429,249** |

### 2004 RESULTS

| Race | Track | Start | Finish | Laps | Led | Status | Winnings | Rank |
|------|-------|-------|--------|------|-----|--------|----------|------|
| Daytona 500 | Daytona | 2 | 7 | 200/200 | 0 | Running | $358,772 | 8 |
| Subway 400 | N. Carolina | 25 | 18 | 391/393 | 0 | Running | $90,793 | 8 |
| UAW-DaimlerChrysler 400 | Las Vegas | 11 | 6 | 267/267 | 0 | Running | $131,808 | 3 |
| Golden Corral 500 | Atlanta | 5 | 29 | 320/325 | 0 | Running | $87,293 | 8 |
| Carolina Dodge Dealers 400 | Darlington | 10 | 5 | 293/293 | 0 | Running | $102,233 | 10 |
| Food City 500 | Bristol | 9 | 14 | 500/500 | 0 | Running | $103,273 | 9 |
| Samsung/RadioShack 500 | Texas | 19 | 1 | 334/334 | 48 | Running | $507,733 | 5 |
| Advance Auto Parts 500 | Martinsville | 9 | 12 | 500/500 | 0 | Running | $98,408 | 5 |
| Aaron's 499 | Talladega | 12 | 28 | 185/188 | 1 | Running | $102,903 | 8 |
| Auto Club 500 | California | 14 | 22 | 249/250 | 0 | Running | $109,058 | 10 |
| Chevy Amer. Revolution 400 | Richmond | 14 | 12 | 399/400 | 0 | Running | $99,393 | 10 |
| Coca-Cola 600 | Lowe's | 4 | 5 | 400/400 | 41 | Running | $178,683 | 7 |
| MBNA 400 'A Salute to Heroes' | Dover | 6 | 18 | 391/400 | 0 | Running | $106,243 | 7 |
| Pocono 500 | Pocono | 12 | 12 | 200/200 | 0 | Running | $96,183 | 8 |
| DHL 400 | Michigan | 22 | 5 | 200/200 | 12 | Running | $113,508 | 7 |
| Dodge/Save Mart 350 | Infineon | 16 | 10 | 110/110 | 0 | Running | $109,943 | 5 |
| Pepsi 400 | Daytona | 39 | 26 | 160/160 | 0 | Running | $109,208 | 8 |
| Tropicana 400 | Chicago | 13 | 21 | 267/267 | 0 | Running | $109,083 | 7 |
| Siemens 300 | New Hamp. | 13 | 15 | 300/300 | 0 | Running | $104,008 | 8 |
| Pennsylvania 500 | Pocono | 5 | 10 | 200/200 | 0 | Running | $101,823 | 6 |

| Race | Track | Start | Finish | Laps | Led | Status | Winnings | Rank |
|------|-------|-------|--------|------|-----|--------|----------|------|
| Brickyard 400 | Indianapolis | 3 | 3 | 161/161 | 32 | Running | $309,158 | 6 |
| Sirius at the Glen | Watkins Glen | 6 | 15 | 90/90 | 0 | Running | $96,353 | 6 |
| GFS Marketplace 400 | Michigan | 6 | 32 | 179/200 | 9 | Running | $97,048 | 7 |
| Sharpie 500 | Bristol | 8 | 5 | 500/500 | 0 | Running | $142,158 | 7 |
| Pop Secret 500 | California | 17 | 1 | 250/250 | 59 | Running | $279,398 | 6 |
| Chevy Rock & Roll 400 | Richmond | 20 | 17 | 399/400 | 0 | Running | $97,763 | 6 |
| Sylvania 300 | New Hamp. | 6 | 8 | 300/300 | 20 | Running | $107,333 | 6 |
| MBNA America 400 | Dover | 4 | 20 | 397/400 | 0 | Running | $100,648 | 6 |

| Race | Track | Start | Finish | Laps | Led | Status | Winnings | Rank |
|------|-------|-------|--------|------|-----|--------|----------|------|
| EA Sports 500 | Talladega | 6 | 22 | 188/188 | 1 | Running | $102,398 | 8 |
| Banquet 400 | Kansas | 11 | 4 | 267/267 | 2 | Running | $159,708 | 4 |
| UAW-GM Quality 500 | Lowe's | 5 | 7 | 334/334 | 13 | Running | $112,158 | 4 |
| Subway 500 | Martinsville | 33 | 32 | 475/500 | 0 | Accident | $93,033 | 7 |
| Bass Pro Shops MBNA 500 | Atlanta | 3 | 36 | 262/325 | 0 | Running | $104,883 | 8 |
| Checker Auto Parts 500 | Phoenix | 9 | 38 | 252/315 | 16 | Running | $89,708 | 8 |
| Southern 500 | Darlington | 8 | 23 | 365/367 | 0 | Running | $98,683 | 9 |
| Ford 400 | Homestead | 15 | 34 | 232/271 | 0 | Running | $89,183 | 9 |

# Ken Schrader

**49**

**Date of birth:** May 29, 1955 **Hometown:** Fenton, Mo. **Resides:** Concord, N.C. **Spouse:** Ann **Children:** Dorothy Lynn, Sheldon **Height:** 5-9 **Weight:** 200 **Hobbies:** Driving in a number of racing series, riding dirt bikes and motorcycles

## NASCAR ACHIEVEMENTS

**First NASCAR Cup start:** July 14, 1984 (Nashville)
**Best points finish:** 4 (1994)
**Career victories:** 4—Atlanta (91a), Charlotte (89a), Dover (91a), Talladega (88b)
**First victory:** July 31, 1988 (Talladega)
**Last victory:** June 3, 1991 (Dover)
**Career poles:** 23—Charlotte (90a, 93a), Darlington (87a, 88a, 90a), Daytona (88a, 89a, 90a), Michigan (89a, 93b), New Hampshire (97a, 97b), Phoenix (89, 98), Pocono (89b, 92a, 93a, 93b, 95a), Richmond (93a), Rockingham (90b), Talladega (98b, 99a)
**First pole:** March 27, 1987 (Darlington)
**Best career finish:** 1 **Best career start:** 1

## FAST FACTS

● Won a Sprint Car national championship in 1983.
● Named USAC's stock car Rookie of the Year in 1990.
● Won the 1982 USAC Silver Crown title and the 1983 USAC Sprint Car championship.
● Won four USAC sprint races, six in the USAC Silver Crown division and 21 in USAC Midgets; won 24 midget races in other divisions.
● Won races on in the NASCAR Busch Series, the NASCAR Craftsman Truck Series and in three NASCAR Touring divisions—Busch North, Featherlite Southwest and Winston West; is one of six drivers to win in all three of NASCAR's national series.
● Began racing on local tracks around his home in Missouri in 1971, primarily in open-wheel competition.
● Owns I-55 Raceway in Pevely, Mo.

## CAR FACTS

**Car:** No. 49 Dodge
**Primary sponsor:** Schwan's
**Owner:** Beth Ann Morgenthau
**Team:** BAM Racing
**Crew chief:** David Hyder
**Engine builder:** Joey Arrington

## CAREER HIGHLIGHTS

● It was a tough season in 2004 for one of NASCAR's strong old-school personalities. Schrader will race anything with wheels, but it's asking a lot of anyone to expect strong results with a small-budget, one-car team. Still, Schrader managed an impressive sixth-place finish at Bristol and was solid at times elsewhere.
● Finished 36th in points and put together consecutive top 15 finishes just once in 2003, with an eighth at Michigan and a 12th at Bristol. His failure to qualify for the Brickyard 400 ended a streak of 579 career starts that begin in 1985.
● Finished the 2002 season 30th in series points, his first season outside of the top 20 in points since 1984. Nine DNFs didn't help; seven of them were mechanical.
● Made his 500th career start in 2001 at Martinsville.
● Bounced back into the top 10 in points in 1997 after joining Andy Petree Racing but never cracked the top 10 again with Petree. He joined MB2 Motorsports in 2000 after the retirement of Ernie Irvan and flirted with top 10 in points early in the season but scored only one top 10 in the second half.
● Qualified in the top 10 13 times in 1995 but couldn't take advantage of the strong starting positions. He finished the season 17th in points with only two top fives and zero wins.
● Four finishes of 20th or worse in 1993 left Schrader 19th in points after just sixth races. But he battled back to fifth by midseason by scoring five top fives in six races. He ended the season with a ninth-place finish. He kept the good vibes

**DRIVERS**

coming in 1994 with a career-best fourth-place finish in points, tying a career-high with 18 top 10s.
- Finished ninth in points in 1991, but five finishes of 30th or worse in the last 14 races kept him out of the title hunt. He won a career-high two races (Atlanta, Dover).
- Joined Rick Hendrick and enjoyed a breakthrough season in 1988, finishing fifth in points with four top fives and 17 top 10s. He won the pole at the Daytona 500 in 1988 and won it again the next two seasons, 1989 and '90.
- Broke into the top 10 in points in 1987, the same year he won his first pole (Darlington) and won one of the 125-mile qualifying races at Daytona.
- Was the 1985 Raybestos Rookie of the Year.
- Broke into the series in 1984 by renting Fords from owner Elmo Langley for his first three starts; Langley rewarded Schrader with two more starts after he took good care of the equipment.

## CAREER STATISTICS

| Year | Car owner | Races | Champ. finish | Won | Top 5 | Top 10 | DNF | Poles | Money won |
|------|-----------|-------|---------------|-----|-------|--------|-----|-------|-----------|
| 1984 | Elmo Langley | 5 | 53 | 0 | 0 | 0 | 0 | 0 | $16,425 |
| 1985 | Junie Donlavey | 28 | 16 | 0 | 0 | 3 | 7 | 0 | $211,523 |
| 1986 | Junie Donlavey | 29 | 16 | 0 | 0 | 4 | 9 | 0 | $235,904 |
| 1987 | Junie Donlavey | 29 | 10 | 0 | 1 | 10 | 8 | 1 | $375,918 |
| 1988 | Rick Hendrick | 28 | | 1 | 4 | 17 | 1 | 2 | $626,934 |
| | Buddy Arrington | 1 | 5 | 0 | 0 | 0 | 0 | 0 | $4,610 |
| 1989 | Rick Hendrick | 29 | 5 | 1 | 10 | 14 | 6 | 4 | $1,039,441 |
| 1990 | Rick Hendrick | 29 | 10 | 0 | 7 | 14 | 8 | 3 | $769,934 |
| 1991 | Rick Hendrick | 29 | 9 | 2 | 10 | 18 | 6 | 0 | $772,439 |
| 1992 | Rick Hendrick | 29 | 17 | 0 | 4 | 11 | 6 | 1 | $639,679 |
| 1993 | Rick Hendrick | 30 | 9 | 0 | 9 | 15 | 4 | 6 | $952,748 |
| 1994 | Rick Hendrick | 31 | 4 | 0 | 9 | 18 | 2 | 0 | $1,171,062 |
| 1995 | Rick Hendrick | 31 | 17 | 0 | 2 | 10 | 9 | 1 | $886,566 |
| 1996 | Rick Hendrick | 31 | 12 | 0 | 3 | 10 | 2 | 0 | $1,089,603 |
| 1997 | Andy Petree | 32 | 10 | 0 | 2 | 8 | 1 | 2 | $1,355,292 |
| 1998 | Andy Petree | 33 | 12 | 0 | 3 | 11 | 5 | 2 | $1,887,399 |
| 1999 | Andy Petree | 34 | 15 | 0 | 0 | 6 | 1 | 1 | $1,939,147 |
| 2000 | Tom Beard | 34 | 18 | 0 | 0 | 2 | 2 | 0 | $1,711,476 |
| 2001 | Tom Beard | 36 | 19 | 0 | 0 | 5 | 2 | 0 | $2,418,181 |
| 2002 | Tom Beard | 36 | 30 | 0 | 0 | 0 | 8 | 0 | $2,460,140 |
| 2003 | B.A. Morgenthau | 32 | 36 | 0 | 0 | 2 | 8 | 0 | $2,007,424 |
| 2004 | B.A. Morgenthau | 36 | 31 | 0 | 0 | 1 | 5 | 0 | $2,666,592 |
| **TOTALS** | | **632** | | **4** | **64** | **179** | **95** | **23** | **$25,234,437** |

## 2004 RESULTS

| Race | Track | Start | Finish | Laps | Led | Status | Winnings | rank |
|------|-------|-------|--------|------|-----|--------|----------|------|
| Daytona 500 | Daytona | 37 | 40 | 59/200 | 0 | Accident | $203,438 | 40 |
| Subway 400 | N. Carolina | 18 | 27 | 389/393 | 0 | Running | $56,410 | 36 |
| UAW-DaimlerChrysler 400 | Las Vegas | 31 | 32 | 263/267 | 0 | Running | $65,400 | 36 |
| Golden Corral 500 | Atlanta | 24 | 26 | 321/325 | 0 | Running | $59,235 | 34 |
| Carolina Dodge Dealers 400 | Darlington | 16 | 22 | 292/293 | 0 | Running | $56,390 | 33 |
| Food City 500 | Bristol | 19 | 6 | 500/500 | 0 | Running | $77,945 | 27 |
| Samsung/RadioShack 500 | Texas | 39 | 19 | 332/334 | 0 | Running | $92,925 | 27 |
| Advance Auto Parts 500 | Martinsville | 26 | 40 | 118/500 | 0 | Brakes | $54,365 | 32 |
| Aaron's 499 | Talladega | 40 | 23 | 188/188 | 0 | Running | $70,265 | 32 |
| Auto Club 500 | California | 32 | 20 | 249/250 | 1 | Running | $74,925 | 31 |
| Chevy Amer. Revolution 400 | Richmond | 34 | 23 | 397/400 | 0 | Running | $60,575 | 31 |
| Coca-Cola 600 | Lowe's | 41 | 31 | 393/400 | 0 | Running | $71,650 | 31 |
| MBNA 400 'A Salute to Heroes' | Dover | 15 | 34 | 337/400 | 0 | Running | $60,860 | 32 |
| Pocono 500 | Pocono | 18 | 25 | 196/200 | 0 | Running | $56,915 | 32 |
| DHL 400 | Michigan | 28 | 39 | 86/200 | 0 | Engine | $57,900 | 32 |
| Dodge/Save Mart 350 | Infineon | 18 | 23 | 110/110 | 0 | Running | $61,900 | 32 |
| Pepsi 400 | Daytona | 29 | 35 | 151/160 | 0 | Running | $67,615 | 32 |
| Tropicana 400 | Chicago | 41 | 27 | 263/267 | 0 | Running | $69,750 | 32 |
| Siemens 300 | New Hamp. | 17 | 37 | 221/300 | 0 | Engine | $58,250 | 33 |
| Pennsylvania 500 | Pocono | 39 | 21 | 200/200 | 1 | Running | $57,990 | 32 |
| Brickyard 400 | Indianapolis | 31 | 18 | 161/161 | 1 | Running | $133,900 | 31 |
| Sirius at the Glen | Watkins Glen | 32 | 28 | 89/90 | 0 | Running | $56,880 | 32 |
| GFS Marketplace 400 | Michigan | 33 | 28 | 199/200 | 0 | Running | $61,175 | 33 |
| Sharpie 500 | Bristol | 26 | 32 | 418/500 | 0 | Running | $71,455 | 32 |
| Pop Secret 500 | California | 40 | 33 | 231/250 | 1 | Engine | $77,050 | 32 |
| Chevy Rock & Roll 400 | Richmond | 32 | 30 | 397/400 | 0 | Running | $59,600 | 32 |
| Sylvania 300 | New Hamp. | 33 | 16 | 300/300 | 0 | Running | $67,875 | 31 |
| MBNA America 400 | Dover | 31 | 25 | 394/400 | 1 | Running | $62,265 | 31 |
| EA Sports 500 | Talladega | 37 | 20 | 188/188 | 1 | Running | $68,140 | 31 |
| Banquet 400 | Kansas | 32 | 27 | 265/267 | 0 | Running | $69,650 | 31 |
| UAW-GM Quality 500 | Lowe's | 30 | 21 | 331/334 | 0 | Running | $60,550 | 31 |
| Subway 500 | Martinsville | 20 | 31 | 484/500 | 0 | Running | $54,275 | 31 |
| Bass Pro Shops MBNA 500 | Atlanta | 37 | 23 | 321/325 | 0 | Running | $73,200 | 31 |
| Checker Auto Parts 500 | Phoenix | 18 | 20 | 315/315 | 0 | Running | $57,300 | 31 |
| Southern 500 | Darlington | 33 | 30 | 362/367 | 0 | Running | $55,875 | 31 |
| Ford 400 | Homestead | 43 | 25 | 269/271 | 0 | Running | $55,500 | 31 |

# Tony Stewart
## 20

**Date of birth:** May 20, 1971 **Hometown:** Rushville, Ind. **Resides:** Columbus, Ind., and Cornelius, N.C. **Spouse:** Single **Children:** None **Height:** 5-9 **Weight:** 170 **Hobbies:** Pool, bowling, boating, fishing

## NASCAR ACHIEVEMENTS

**First NASCAR Cup start:** February 14, 1999 (Daytona)
**Best points finish:** 1 (2002)
**Career victories:** 19—Atlanta (02a), Bristol (01b), Chicago (04), Dover (00a, 00b), Homestead (99, 00), Martinsville (00b), Michigan (00a), New Hampshire (00a), Phoenix (99), Pocono (03a), Richmond (99b, 01a, 02a, 02b), Sonoma (01), Watkins Glen (02, 04)
**First victory:** September 11, 1999 (Richmond)
**Last victory:** August 15, 2004 (Watkins Glen)
**Career poles:** 7—Bristol (99b), Chicago (03), Indianapolis (02), Martinsville (99a, 00b), Pocono (00b), Sonoma (02)
**First pole:** October 1, 1999 (Martinsville)
**Best career finish:** 1  **Best career start:** 1

## FAST FACTS

● Was recognized for his philanthrophy in 2004 as NASCAR's USG Person of the Year. Stewart donated the $100,000 award to the Victory Junction Gang Camp, a facility for chronically ill children in Randleman, N.C.

### CAR FACTS

**Car:** No. 20 Chevrolet
**Primary sponsor:** Home Depot
**Owner:** Joe Gibbs
**Team:** Joe Gibbs Racing
**Crew chief:** Greg Zipadelli
**Engine builder:** Mark Cronquist

● Ran 22 NASCAR Busch Series races for Joe Gibbs Racing in 1998, winning two poles and posting five top fives.
● Ran a full Indy Racing League schedule in 1998.
● Won the Indy Racing League championship in 1997 and was the IRL Rookie of the Year in 1996.
● Was the Indianapolis 500 Rookie of the Year in 1996.
● Swept championships in the USAC Midget, Sprint Car and Silver Crown competition in 1995, becoming first driver to do so.
● Was the 1994 USAC Midget national champ.
● Was the 1991 USAC Sprint Car Rookie of the Year.
● Won the 1987 World Karting Association national title.
● Won the 1983 International Karting Foundation Grand National title.
● Has a World of Outlaws sprint car team.
● Stewart's favorite driver is A.J. Foyt.

## CAREER HIGHLIGHTS

● Stewart won two races in 2004 and led a ton of laps, but the season must be labeled a disappointment because he never made a real run at the championship. He qualified easily for the Chase for the NASCAR NEXTEL Cup, but he wasn't a factor in the final 10 races. He and crew chief Greg Zipadelli form one of the best duos in the sport, but they never put the No. 20 into elite status in 2004.
● Struggled early in 2003 after switching from Pontiac to Chevrolet; he finished 40th or worse in three straight races in late April and early May. He salvaged his season with six straight top fives, starting at Dover on September 21 and ending at Atlanta on October 27.
● Won the NASCAR Cup championship in 2002, bouncing back after a last-place finish in the Daytona 500. His march to the top began at New Hampshire in July with the first of nine consecutive top 15s. The championship, along with Bobby Labonte's in 2000, gave owner Joe Gibbs his second title in three years.
● Won at Richmond in May 2002, giving him three victories there (1999, 2001, 2002) in four seasons.
● Won the 2001 Budweiser Shootout in Daytona, a non-points event, his first victory in restrictor-plate racing.
● Raced in the Indianapolis 500 and the Coca-Cola 600 on May 27, 2001, finishing sixth at Indianapolis and third at Charlotte. He raced both on the same day in 1999 as well, finishing ninth at Indy and fourth at Charlotte.
● Won the 1999 Raybestos Rookie of the Year award, winning three races (Phoenix, Richmond, Homestead) in the second half of the season. He became the first NASCAR Cup series rookie to win three races.

## CAREER STATISTICS

| Year | Car owner | Races | Champ. finish | Won | Top 5 | Top 10 | DNF | Poles | Money won |
|------|-----------|-------|---------------|-----|-------|--------|-----|-------|-----------|
| 1999 | Joe Gibbs | 34 | 4 | 3 | 12 | 21 | 1 | 2 | $3,190,149 |
| 2000 | Joe Gibbs | 34 | 6 | 6 | 12 | 23 | 5 | 2 | $3,642,348 |
| 2001 | Joe Gibbs | 36 | 2 | 3 | 15 | 22 | 4 | 0 | $4,941,463 |
| 2002 | Joe Gibbs | 36 | 1 | 3 | 15 | 21 | 6 | 2 | $9,163,761 |
| 2003 | Joe Gibbs | 36 | 7 | 2 | 12 | 18 | 5 | 1 | $6,131,633 |
| 2004 | Joe Gibbs | 36 | 6 | 2 | 10 | 19 | 2 | 0 | $7,830,807 |
| **TOTALS** | | **212** | | **19** | **76** | **124** | **23** | **7** | **$34,905,161** |

# 2004 RESULTS

| Race | Track | Start | Finish | Laps | Led | Status | Winnings | Rank |
|------|-------|-------|--------|------|-----|--------|----------|------|
| Daytona 500 | Daytona | 5 | 2 | 200/200 | 98 | Running | $1,096,160 | 2 |
| Subway 400 | N. Carolina | 24 | 26 | 389/393 | 0 | Running | $103,403 | 6 |
| UAW-DaimlerChrysler 400 | Las Vegas | 19 | 3 | 267/267 | 45 | Running | $219,603 | 2 |
| Golden Corral 500 | Atlanta | 19 | 7 | 325/325 | 127 | Running | $133,778 | 2 |
| Carolina Dodge Dealers 400 | Darlington | 8 | 17 | 293/293 | 1 | Running | $101,118 | 3 |
| Food City 500 | Bristol | 12 | 24 | 498/500 | 25 | Running | $115,518 | 4 |
| Samsung/RadioShack 500 | Texas | 17 | 8 | 334/334 | 0 | Running | $156,453 | 4 |
| Advance Auto Parts 500 | Martinsville | 30 | 14 | 500/500 | 0 | Running | $105,753 | 6 |
| Aaron's 499 | Talladega | 37 | 22 | 188/188 | 6 | Running | $114,353 | 7 |
| Auto Club 500 | California | 11 | 16 | 249/250 | 0 | Running | $120,603 | 8 |
| Chevy Amer. Revolution 400 | Richmond | 28 | 4 | 400/400 | 59 | Running | $127,478 | 5 |
| Coca-Cola 600 | Lowe's | 6 | 9 | 400/400 | 0 | Running | $137,678 | 5 |
| MBNA 400 'A Salute to Heroes' | Dover | 10 | 2 | 400/400 | 234 | Running | $227,978 | 4 |
| Pocono 500 | Pocono | 8 | 27 | 194/200 | 1 | Running | $100,393 | 5 |
| DHL 400 | Michigan | 27 | 24 | 200/200 | 0 | Running | $106,543 | 5 |
| Dodge/Save Mart 350 | Infineon | 17 | 15 | 110/110 | 1 | Running | $107,653 | 6 |
| Pepsi 400 | Daytona | 17 | 5 | 160/160 | 12 | Running | $149,628 | 4 |
| Tropicana 400 | Chicago | 10 | 1 | 267/267 | 160 | Running | $336,803 | 4 |
| Siemens 300 | New Hamp. | 9 | 5 | 300/300 | 0 | Running | $126,178 | 4 |
| Pennsylvania 500 | Pocono | 8 | 35 | 107/200 | 0 | Accident | $99,043 | 5 |
| Brickyard 400 | Indianapolis | 24 | 5 | 161/161 | 0 | Running | $247,278 | 4 |
| Sirius at the Glen | Watkins Glen | 4 | 1 | 90/90 | 46 | Running | $195,288 | 4 |
| GFS Marketplace 400 | Michigan | 4 | 9 | 200/200 | 0 | Running | $112,493 | 4 |
| Sharpie 500 | Bristol | 6 | 19 | 497/500 | 0 | Running | $121,528 | 4 |
| Pop Secret 500 | California | 33 | 18 | 250/250 | 0 | Running | $127,978 | 4 |
| Chevy Rock & Roll 400 | Richmond | 15 | 19 | 399/400 | 0 | Running | $105,433 | 4 |
| Sylvania 300 | New Hamp. | 4 | 39 | 83/300 | 16 | Accident | $104,813 | 8 |
| MBNA America 400 | Dover | 23 | 6 | 400/400 | 0 | Running | $117,168 | 9 |
| EA Sports 500 | Talladega | 30 | 6 | 188/188 | 4 | Running | $120,603 | 6 |
| Banquet 400 | Kansas | 24 | 14 | 267/267 | 0 | Running | $121,228 | 6 |
| UAW-GM Quality 500 | Lowe's | 15 | 10 | 334/334 | 0 | Running | $113,903 | 6 |
| Subway 500 | Martinsville | 13 | 15 | 500/500 | 18 | Running | $105,903 | 6 |
| Bass Pro Shops MBNA 500 | Atlanta | 15 | 9 | 324/325 | 0 | Running | $130,063 | 6 |
| Checker Auto Parts 500 | Phoenix | 6 | 8 | 315/315 | 0 | Running | $112,028 | 6 |
| Southern 500 | Darlington | 6 | 17 | 366/367 | 0 | Running | $109,678 | 6 |
| Ford 400 | Homestead | 8 | 4 | 271/271 | 34 | Running | $167,003 | 6 |

# Brian Vickers · 25

**Date of birth:** October 24, 1983 **Hometown:** Thomasville, N.C.
**Resides:** Thomasville, N.C. **Spouse:** Single **Children:** None
**Height:** 5-11 **Weight:** 160 **Hobbies:** Golf and video games

## NASCAR ACHIEVEMENTS

**First NASCAR Cup start:** October 11, 2003 (Charlotte)
**Best points finish:** 25 (2004)
**Career victories:** 0
**Career poles:** 2—California (04b), Richmond (04a)
**Best career finish:** 7   **Best career start:** 1

## FAST FACTS

● Ran partial NASCAR Busch Series schedules in 2001 and 2002 before winning the series championship in his first full season in 2003.

● Was a three-time World Karting Association national champion in the mid-1990s.

● Began racing late model stocks in the NASCAR Weekly Racing Series in 1999. Was named the series Rookie of the Year and Most Popular Driver.

### CAR FACTS

**Car:** No. 25 Chevrolet
**Primary sponsor:** GMAC
**Owner:** Rick Hendrick
**Team:** Hendrick Motorsports
**Crew chief:** Lance McGrew
**Engine builder:** Hendrick Motorsports

● Was the 2000 USAR ProCup Series Rookie of the Year and finished second in that series in 2001.

## CAREER HIGHLIGHTS

● Taking into consideration what was expected of him, Vickers struggled in his rookie season in 2004. He rubbed fenders too often when he didn't intend to, and he just didn't put together enough strong performances for his season to be anything but a disappointment. Still, he's only 21, and he's abundantly talented. He'll be around for years and should make a jump in 2005.

● Ran five NASCAR Cup races in 2003 while running a full NASCAR Busch Series schedule and winning the NASCAR Busch Series championship, becoming the youngest NASCAR champion ever at age 20. In his NASCAR Cup efforts, he qualified in the top five in four of the five races he entered.

## CAREER STATISTICS

| Year | Car owner | Races | Champ. finish | Won | Top 5 | Top 10 | DNF | Poles | Money won |
|------|-----------|-------|---------------|-----|-------|--------|-----|-------|-----------|
| 2003 | Rick Hendrick | 5 | 49 | 0 | 0 | 0 | 1 | 0 | $263,484 |
| 2004 | Rick Hendrick | 36 | 25 | 0 | 0 | 4 | 6 | 2 | $3,135,886 |
| TOTALS | | 41 | | 0 | 0 | 4 | 7 | 2 | $3,399,370 |

## 2004 RESULTS

| Race | Track | Start | Finish | Laps | Led | Status | Winnings | Rank |
|---|---|---|---|---|---|---|---|---|
| Daytona 500 | Daytona | 35 | 39 | 70/200 | 0 | Accident | $211,888 | 39 |
| Subway 400 | N. Carolina | 20 | 16 | 391/393 | 0 | Running | $70,760 | 29 |
| UAW-DaimlerChrysler 400 | Las Vegas | 3 | 23 | 266/267 | 0 | Running | $83,275 | 28 |
| Golden Corral 500 | Atlanta | 2 | 21 | 322/325 | 0 | Running | $69,315 | 28 |
| Carolina Dodge Dealers 400 | Darlington | 28 | 23 | 292/293 | 0 | Running | $65,000 | 28 |
| Food City 500 | Bristol | 22 | 35 | 377/500 | 0 | Accident | $74,690 | 28 |
| Samsung/RadioShack 500 | Texas | 13 | 12 | 333/334 | 0 | Running | $112,150 | 26 |
| Advance Auto Parts 500 | Martinsville | 35 | 13 | 500/500 | 0 | Running | $78,900 | 24 |
| Aaron's 499 | Talladega | 39 | 27 | 188/188 | 2 | Running | $75,620 | 26 |
| Auto Club 500 | California | 6 | 29 | 248/250 | 1 | Running | $76,900 | 27 |
| Chevy Amer. Revolution 400 | Richmond | 1 | 8 | 400/400 | 32 | Running | $81,775 | 23 |
| Coca-Cola 600 | Lowe's | 5 | 15 | 398/400 | 0 | Running | $95,850 | 22 |
| MBNA 400 'A Salute to Heroes' | Dover | 3 | 23 | 380/400 | 7 | Accident | $76,810 | 23 |
| Pocono 500 | Pocono | 2 | 13 | 200/200 | 1 | Running | $71,215 | 22 |
| DHL 400 | Michigan | 2 | 9 | 200/200 | 0 | Running | $79,190 | 19 |
| Dodge/Save Mart 350 | Infineon | 39 | 22 | 110/110 | 0 | Running | $71,550 | 20 |
| Pepsi 400 | Daytona | 14 | 9 | 160/160 | 0 | Running | $99,050 | 19 |
| Tropicana 400 | Chicago | 4 | 14 | 267/267 | 0 | Running | $87,950 | 20 |
| Siemens 300 | New Hamp. | 23 | 34 | 293/300 | 0 | Running | $66,800 | 21 |
| Pennsylvania 500 | Pocono | 6 | 14 | 200/200 | 0 | Running | $69,215 | 21 |
| Brickyard 400 | Indianapolis | 6 | 29 | 158/161 | 0 | Accident | $136,000 | 22 |
| Sirius at the Glen | Watkins Glen | 22 | 30 | 89/90 | 0 | Running | $65,050 | 22 |
| GFS Marketplace 400 | Michigan | 22 | 22 | 199/200 | 0 | Running | $71,215 | 24 |
| Sharpie 500 | Bristol | 20 | 20 | 497/500 | 0 | Running | $87,835 | 24 |
| Pop Secret 500 | California | 1 | 13 | 250/250 | 44 | Running | $107,625 | 23 |
| Chevy Rock & Roll 400 | Richmond | 26 | 37 | 335/400 | 0 | Running | $64,330 | 24 |
| Sylvania 300 | New Hamp. | 24 | 22 | 298/300 | 0 | Running | $72,800 | 25 |
| MBNA America 400 | Dover | 3 | 38 | 46/400 | 0 | Accident | $65,100 | 25 |
| EA Sports 500 | Talladega | 21 | 36 | 164/188 | 0 | Overheating | $69,400 | 25 |
| Banquet 400 | Kansas | 25 | 19 | 267/267 | 0 | Running | $83,150 | 25 |
| UAW-GM Quality 500 | Lowe's | 17 | 40 | 22/334 | 0 | Accident | $62,255 | 26 |
| Subway 500 | Martinsville | 34 | 27 | 498/500 | 0 | Running | $65,835 | 26 |
| Bass Pro Shops MBNA 500 | Atlanta | 13 | 7 | 325/325 | 0 | Running | $100,250 | 26 |
| Checker Auto Parts 500 | Phoenix | 2 | 18 | 315/315 | 0 | Running | $65,825 | 26 |
| Southern 500 | Darlington | 27 | 21 | 365/367 | 0 | Running | $71,700 | 26 |
| Ford 400 | Homestead | 14 | 18 | 271/271 | 0 | Running | $65,225 | 25 |

# Mike Wallace

**Date of birth:** March 10, 1969
**Hometown:** St. Louis **Resides:** St. Louis **Spouse:** Carla
**Children:** Lyndsey, Christina, Matthew, Ryan **Height:** 6-0
**Weight:** 220 **Hobbies:** Flying, Working with heavy equipment

## NASCAR ACHIEVEMENTS

**First NASCAR Cup start:** November 3, 1991 (Phoenix)
**Best points finish:** 33 (1994)
**Career victories:** 0  **Career poles:** 0
**Best career finish:** 2  **Best career start:** 12

## FAST FACTS

● In 2003 became the first driver to finish races in the top 10 in all three of NASCAR's top divisions while driving for three different manufacturers.
● Was the Mid-America Region Champion for the Winston West Series after winning 21 of 29 races.

## CAREER HIGHLIGHTS

● Wallace continued his pinch-hit role in the NASCAR NEXTEL Cup Series in 2004, driving cars for three owners: Don Arnold, James Finch and Larry McClure. Wallace's best run of the season came for Finch at Richmond, where Wallace finished seventh in the Chevy Rock & Roll 400.
● Came close enough to victory to taste it while driving for Roger Penske in 2001, posting a second-place finish in the Checker Auto Parts 500 at Phoenix. He drove the final eight races for Penske that season after Jeremy Mayfield was released from the car.

## CAREER STATISTICS

| Year | Car owner | Races | Champ. finish | Won | Top 5 | Top 10 | DNF | Poles | Money won |
|---|---|---|---|---|---|---|---|---|---|
| 2003 | Rick Hendrick | 5 | 49 | 0 | 0 | 0 | 1 | 0 | $263,484 |
| 1991 | Jimmy Means | 2 | 62 | 0 | 0 | 0 | 1 | 0 | $7,000 |
| 1992 | Richard Moroso | 1 | 50 | 0 | 0 | 0 | 0 | 0 | $7,980 |
| | Pat Rissi | 2 | | 0 | 0 | 0 | 0 | 0 | $12,235 |
| 1993 | Mike Pritchard | 3 | 46 | 0 | 0 | 0 | 1 | 0 | $25,400 |
| | Jimmy Means | 1 | | 0 | 0 | 0 | 0 | 0 | $4,725 |
| 1994 | Junie Donlavey | 22 | 33 | 0 | 1 | 1 | 3 | 0 | $265,115 |
| 1995 | Junie Donlavey | 26 | 34 | 0 | 0 | 1 | 9 | 0 | $428,006 |
| 1996 | Junie Donlavey | 10 | 41 | 0 | 0 | 0 | 6 | 0 | $152,417 |
| | Mark Smith | 1 | | 0 | 0 | 0 | 0 | 0 | $16,665 |
| 1997 | Joe Falk | 7 | 46 | 0 | 0 | 0 | 1 | 0 | $159,303 |
| 1998 | Phil Barkdoll | 1 | 62 | 0 | 0 | 0 | 0 | 0 | $86,105 |
| 1999 | Junie Donlavey | 1 | 53 | 0 | 0 | 0 | 0 | 0 | $11,806 |
| | Fred Biagi | 1 | | 0 | 0 | 0 | 0 | 0 | $23,455 |
| 2001 | Roger Penske | 8 | 34 | 0 | 1 | 2 | 1 | 0 | $706,673 |
| | J. Smith/R. Evernham | 21 | | 0 | 0 | 4 | 3 | 0 | $1,394,697 |
| 2002 | A. J. Foyt | 16 | | 0 | 0 | 1 | 4 | 0 | $883,891 |
| | Andy Petree | 4 | | 0 | 0 | 0 | 2 | 0 | $390,812 |
| | Tom Beard | 1 | 41 | 0 | 0 | 0 | 1 | 0 | $80,150 |
| 2003 | Tom Beard | 8 | 42 | 0 | 0 | 0 | 2 | 0 | $384,479 |
| | James Finch | 6 | | 0 | 0 | 2 | 1 | 0 | $517,717 |
| 2004 | Don Arnold | 3 | | 0 | 0 | 0 | 2 | 0 | $187,550 |
| | James Finch | 4 | | 0 | 0 | 1 | 1 | 0 | $279,420 |
| | Larry McClure | 3 | 46 | 0 | 0 | 0 | 2 | 0 | $162,880 |
| TOTALS | | 152 | | 0 | 2 | 12 | 40 | 0 | $6,332,238 |

## 2004 RESULTS

| Race | Track | Start | Finish | Laps | Led | Status | Winnings | Rank |
|---|---|---|---|---|---|---|---|---|
| MBNA 400 'A Salute to Heroes' | Dover | 36 | 35 | 239/400 | 0 | Wheel b. | $61,570 | 58 |
| Pepsi 400 | Daytona | 41 | 41 | 77/160 | 1 | Suspens. | $66,750 | 62 |
| Siemens 300 | New Hamp. | 36 | 32 | 298/300 | 0 | Running | $59,230 | 56 |

## 2004 RESULTS

| Race | Track | Start | Finish | Laps | Led | Status | Winnings | Rank | Race | Track | Start | Finish | Laps | Led | Status | Winnings | Rank |
|---|---|---|---|---|---|---|---|---|---|---|---|---|---|---|---|---|---|
| Sharpie 500 | Bristol | 41 | 28 | 468/500 | 0 | Running | $72,595 | 50 | Checker Auto Parts 500 | Phoenix | 33 | 29 | 313/315 | 0 | Running | $54,550 | 47 |
| Chevy Rock & Roll 400 | Richmond | 41 | 7 | 400/400 | 45 | Running | $78,430 | 48 | Southern 500 | Darlington | 37 | 38 | 180/367 | 0 | Oil pump | $53,850 | 47 |
| Sylvania 300 | New Hamp. | 41 | 34 | 256/300 | 0 | Accident | $59,725 | 47 | Ford 400 | Homestead | 28 | 33 | 247/271 | 0 | Wheel b. | $54,480 | 46 |
| EA Sports 500 | Talladega | 41 | 18 | 188/188 | 4 | Running | $68,670 | 46 | | | | | | | | | |

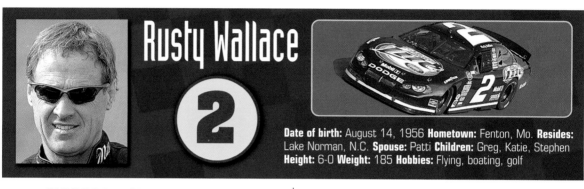

# Rusty Wallace

**(2)**

**Date of birth:** August 14, 1956 **Hometown:** Fenton, Mo. **Resides:** Lake Norman, N.C. **Spouse:** Patti **Children:** Greg, Katie, Stephen **Height:** 6-0 **Weight:** 185 **Hobbies:** Flying, boating, golf

## NASCAR ACHIEVEMENTS

**First NASCAR Cup start:** March 16, 1980 (Atlanta)
**Best points finish:** 1 (1989)
**Career victories:** 55—Atlanta (88b, 93b), Bristol (86a, 89a, 91a, 93a, 94b, 96a, 99a, 00a, 00b), California (01), Charlotte (88b, 90a), Dover (93b, 94a, 94b), Martinsville (86b, 93a, 94a, 94b, 95a, 96a, 04a), Michigan (88a, 89b, 94a, 96a, 00b), New Hampshire (90), North Wilkesboro (88b, 93a, 93b), Phoenix (98), Pocono (91b, 94a, 96b, 00b), Richmond (89a, 89b, 92b, 93b, 95b, 97a), Riverside (87b, 88), Rockingham (88b, 89a, 93a, 93b, 94a), Sonoma (90, 96), Watkins Glen (87, 89)
**First victory:** April 6, 1986 (Bristol)
**Last victory:** April 18, 2004 (Martinsville)
**Career poles:** 36—Atlanta (88b, 90b, 93a), Bristol (91a, 93a, 97a, 98a, 99a, 00b), Dover (93b, 98a, 99b, 00a, 02b), Martinsville (88b, 94a, 00a), New Hampshire (99b, 00a), North Wilkesboro (89a), Phoenix (90, 92, 000, Pocono (89a, 94a, 00a), Richmond (91b, 98b, 00a), Rockingham (89a, 00a), Sonoma (89, 00), Watkins Glen (99)
**First pole:** June 6, 1987 (Michigan)
**Best career finish:** 1 **Best career start:** 1

## FAST FACTS

- Made his driving debut at Lakehill Speedway in Valley Park, Mo., in 1973.
- Named 1973 Central Racing Association Rookie of the Year.
- Won more than 200 stock car features from 1974-78 before joining the USAC stock car circuit in 1979.
- Named USAC's Rookie of the Year in 1979, winning five races and finishing second in points.
- Won the 1983 ASA championship.
- Is a nine-time IROC participant, with four victories in the series.

- Is an avid aviator who owns his own airplanes and helicopter; is a jet-rated pilot and says he likely would be a commercial pilot if he were not a race driver.
- Father was a three-time track champion in the St. Louis area.
- Once crashed while waving to the crowd after winning a race in Springfield, Mo.

## CAREER HIGHLIGHTS

- The popular veteran broke a 105-race winless streak with a victory at Martinsville in 2004. Wallace's No. 2 car often was good, but the finishes didn't measure up. The 2005 season will be "Rusty's Last Call," his final season as a full-time NASCAR NEXTEL Cup driver.
- Is second only to Jeff Gordon among active drivers in races won with 55. He ranks ninth on the all-time list.
- Is second only to Gordon and is tied with Richard Petty, Bobby Allison and Ricky Rudd for second in career road races won (six).
- Made his 600th start in February 2003 at Rockingham.
- Did not record a victory in 2002, ending the second-longest streak in NASCAR history for most consecutive seasons with a victory (16), which trails only Petty. Wallace put up a good fight, though, finishing second three times. He didn't win a race in 2003, either, and finished 14th in points, his worst finish in 18 seasons and first finish outside of the top 10 since 1992.
- Won the pole for the 2003 NASCAR All-Star race.
- Got his 50th career victory at Bristol in 2000, winning the Food City 500. He swept the two Bristol races that season and won a career-best nine poles.

### CAR FACTS

**Car:** No. 2 Dodge
**Primary sponsor:** Miller Lite
**Owner:** Roger Penske
**Team:** Penske Racing South
**Crew chief:** Larry Carter
**Engine builder:** Penske-Jasper

**DRIVERS**

- Led the circuit in wins, with eight, for the second consecutive year in 1994. He swept the Dover and Martinsville races and won the season's second race in Rockingham, proving his switch from Pontiac to Ford was a success.
- Bounced back from a tough 1992 season by finishing runner-up in series points in 1993 behind nemesis Dale Earnhardt. He won a career-high and circuit-best 10 races, swept the North Wilkesboro and Rockingham races and led the most laps during the season (2,860 of 10,004). His team also won the Unocal Pit Crew Championship at Rockingham.
- Spent his first season as a driver/co-owner with Roger Penske in 1991. He hit a low in 1992, finishing 13th in points, his first time out of the top 10 since 1985.
- Won the 1989 NASCAR Cup title, edging out Dale Earnhardt by 12 points. Wallace also won the 1989 All-Star race.
- In 1988, won the last NASCAR event on the road course at Riverside. He ended the season second in points behind Bill Elliott.
- First career win came in his 72nd career start, at Bristol in April 1986. It was the first of nine career victories there.
- Was the Raybestos Rookie of the Year in 1984.
- Started seventh in his first NASCAR Cup race, the Atlanta 500 in March 1980, and finished second to Earnhardt.

## CAREER STATISTICS

| Year | Car owner | Races | Champ. finish | Won | Top 5 | Top 10 | DNF | Poles | Money won |
|------|-----------|-------|---------------|-----|-------|--------|-----|-------|-----------|
| 1980 | Roger Penske | 2 | 57 | 0 | 1 | 1 | 0 | 0 | $22,760 |
| 1981 | Ron Benfield | 2 | | 0 | 0 | 0 | 2 | 0 | $4,245 |
| | John Childs | 2 | 64 | 0 | 0 | 1 | 1 | 0 | $8,650 |
| 1982 | John Childs | 3 | 64 | 0 | 0 | 0 | 3 | 0 | $7,655 |
| 1984 | Cliff Stewart | 30 | 14 | 0 | 2 | 4 | 9 | 0 | $195,927 |
| 1985 | Cliff Stewart | 28 | 19 | 0 | 2 | 8 | 12 | 0 | $233,670 |
| 1986 | Raymond Beadle | 29 | 6 | 2 | 4 | 16 | 4 | 0 | $557,354 |
| 1987 | Raymond Beadle | 29 | 5 | 2 | 9 | 16 | 7 | 1 | $690,652 |
| 1988 | Raymond Beadle | 29 | 2 | 6 | 19 | 23 | 2 | 2 | $1,411,567 |
| 1989 | Raymond Beadle | 29 | 1 | 6 | 13 | 20 | 4 | 4 | $2,247,950 |
| 1990 | Raymond Beadle | 29 | 6 | 2 | 9 | 16 | 8 | 2 | $954,129 |
| 1991 | Roger Penske | 29 | 10 | 2 | 9 | 14 | 10 | 2 | $502,073 |
| 1992 | Roger Penske | 29 | 13 | 1 | 5 | 12 | 5 | 1 | $657,925 |
| 1993 | Roger Penske | 30 | 2 | 10 | 19 | 21 | 5 | 3 | $1,702,154 |
| 1994 | Roger Penske | 31 | 3 | 8 | 17 | 20 | 5 | 2 | $1,914,072 |
| 1995 | Roger Penske | 31 | 5 | 2 | 15 | 19 | 4 | 0 | $1,642,837 |
| 1996 | Roger Penske | 31 | 7 | 5 | 8 | 18 | 6 | 0 | $1,665,315 |
| 1997 | Roger Penske | 32 | 9 | 1 | 8 | 12 | 11 | 1 | $1,705,625 |
| 1998 | Roger Penske | 33 | 4 | 1 | 15 | 21 | 2 | 4 | $2,667,889 |
| 1999 | Roger Penske | 34 | 8 | 1 | 7 | 16 | 3 | 4 | $2,454,050 |
| 2000 | Roger Penske | 34 | 7 | 4 | 12 | 20 | 3 | 9 | $3,621,468 |
| 2001 | Roger Penske | 36 | 7 | 1 | 8 | 14 | 3 | 0 | $4,788,652 |
| 2002 | Roger Penske | 36 | 7 | 0 | 7 | 17 | 1 | 1 | $4,785,134 |
| 2003 | Roger Penske | 36 | 14 | 0 | 2 | 14 | 4 | 0 | $4,246,547 |
| 2004 | Roger Penske | 36 | 16 | 1 | 3 | 11 | 3 | 0 | $4,981,100 |
| TOTALS | | 670 | | 55 | 194 | 332 | 117 | 36 | $43,670,500 |

## 2004 RESULTS

| Race | Track | Start | Finish | Laps | Led | Status | Winnings | Rank |
|------|-------|-------|--------|------|-----|--------|----------|------|
| Daytona 500 | Daytona | 18 | 29 | 154/200 | 0 | Running | $245,572 | 29 |
| Subway 400 | N. Carolina | 4 | 7 | 393/393 | 0 | Running | $100,643 | 13 |
| UAW-DaimlerChrysler 400 | Las Vegas | 21 | 10 | 267/267 | 0 | Running | $129,108 | 12 |
| Golden Corral 500 | Atlanta | 11 | 35 | 291/325 | 0 | Running | $88,873 | 22 |
| Carolina Dodge Dealers 400 | Darlington | 7 | 29 | 290/293 | 0 | Running | $85,588 | 23 |
| Food City 500 | Bristol | 4 | 2 | 500/500 | 100 | Running | $141,878 | 17 |
| Samsung/RadioShack 500 | Texas | 10 | 5 | 334/334 | 2 | Running | $179,883 | 11 |
| Advance Auto Parts 500 | Martinsville | 17 | 1 | 500/500 | 45 | Running | $170,998 | 8 |
| Aaron's 499 | Talladega | 32 | 33 | 144/188 | 0 | Running | $107,108 | 13 |
| Auto Club 500 | California | 9 | 35 | 193/250 | 0 | Running | $109,008 | 14 |
| Chevy Amer. Revolution 400 | Richmond | 7 | 16 | 399/400 | 0 | Running | $102,983 | 14 |
| Coca-Cola 600 | Lowe's | 16 | 10 | 400/400 | 0 | Running | $131,658 | 14 |
| MBNA 400 'A Salute to Heroes' | Dover | 4 | 13 | 398/400 | 0 | Running | $114,578 | 14 |
| Pocono 500 | Pocono | 30 | 32 | 167/200 | 0 | Accident | $96,673 | 15 |
| DHL 400 | Michigan | 10 | 22 | 200/200 | 7 | Running | $104,048 | 15 |
| Dodge/Save Mart 350 | Infineon | 2 | 28 | 109/110 | 0 | Gas | $102,883 | 16 |
| Pepsi 400 | Daytona | 27 | 27 | 160/160 | 0 | Running | $113,158 | 17 |
| Tropicana 400 | Chicago | 20 | 11 | 267/267 | 0 | Running | $121,908 | 17 |
| Siemens 300 | New Hamp. | 8 | 30 | 299/300 | 0 | Running | $103,483 | 19 |
| Pennsylvania 500 | Pocono | 12 | 17 | 200/200 | 0 | Running | $99,423 | 20 |
| Brickyard 400 | Indianapolis | 29 | 13 | 161/161 | 0 | Running | $178,658 | 17 |
| Sirius at the Glen | Watkins Glen | 17 | 25 | 89/90 | 0 | Running | $98,158 | 18 |
| GFS Marketplace 400 | Michigan | 18 | 36 | 109/200 | 0 | Engine | $101,673 | 19 |
| Sharpie 500 | Bristol | 13 | 26 | 490/500 | 79 | Running | $114,248 | 21 |
| Pop Secret 500 | California | 26 | 10 | 250/250 | 0 | Running | $13,808 | 20 |
| Chevy Rock & Roll 400 | Richmond | 12 | 10 | 400/400 | 0 | Running | $105,863 | 17 |
| Sylvania 300 | New Hamp. | 17 | 14 | 300/300 | 0 | Running | $108,533 | 17 |
| MBNA America 400 | Dover | 7 | 13 | 398/400 | 0 | Running | $105,348 | 17 |
| EA Sports 500 | Talladega | 33 | 26 | 188/188 | 15 | Running | $106,403 | 17 |
| Banquet 400 | Kansas | 36 | 18 | 267/267 | 0 | Running | $115,883 | 17 |
| UAW-GM Quality 500 | Lowe's | 14 | 31 | 274/334 | 0 | Running | $98,633 | 18 |
| Subway 500 | Martinsville | 2 | 10 | 500/500 | 34 | Running | $106,308 | 18 |
| Bass Pro Shops MBNA 500 | Atlanta | 12 | 11 | 324/325 | 0 | Running | $128,233 | 18 |
| Checker Auto Parts 500 | Phoenix | 15 | 7 | 315/315 | 0 | Running | $111,658 | 17 |
| Southern 500 | Darlington | 16 | 18 | 365/367 | 0 | Running | $106,058 | 17 |
| Ford 400 | Homestead | 10 | 8 | 271/271 | 26 | Running | $110,983 | 16 |

# Michael Waltrip

## 15

**Date of birth:** April 30, 1963 **Hometown:** Owensboro, Ky.
**Resides:** Sherrills Ford, N.C. **Spouse:** Elizabeth "Buffy"
**Children:** Caitlin, Margaret **Height:** 6-5 **Weight:** 210
**Hobbies:** Running, golf, tennis, boating

## NASCAR ACHIEVEMENTS

**First NASCAR Cup start:** May 26, 1985 (Charlotte)
**Best points finish:** 12 (1994, 1995)
**Career victories:** 4—Daytona (01a, 02b, 03a), Talladega (03b)
**First victory:** February 18, 2001 (Daytona)
**Last victory:** September 28, 2003 (Talladega)
**Career poles:** 2—Dover (91a) Michigan (91a)
**First pole:** May 30, 1991 (Dover)
**Best career finish:** 1 **Best career start:** 1

## FAST FACTS

- Began racing in go-karts in the mid-1970s and won numerous races.
- Started in stock cars in 1981, when he was the Kentucky Motor Speedway champion in the Mini-Modified Division.
- Won the Goody's Dash Series championship in 1983 and was that series' Most Popular Driver in 1983 and '84.
- Still is a regular on the NASCAR Busch Series.
- Cites winning the All-Star race in 1996 and a NASCAR Busch Series race at Bristol in 1993 as top memories.
- After taking the first-ever backward victory lap in memory of Alan Kulwicki at Bristol, he proposed in victory lane to his wife, Buffy.
- An avid distance runner, Waltrip has competed in several marathons including the prestigious Boston Marathon. He also had the honor of being a torch bearer in the 2002 Olympic Torch Relay to Salt Lake City.
- Waltrip lived with Richard and Lynda Petty when he first moved to North Carolina from his native Kentucky in order to establish himself in NASCAR Cup racing.

## CAR FACTS

**Car:** No. 15 Chevrolet
**Primary sponsor:** NAPA Auto Parts
**Owner:** Teresa Earnhardt
**Team:** Dale Earnhardt Inc.
**Crew chief:** Tony Eury Jr.
**Engine builder:** Jeff Opal

## CAREER HIGHLIGHTS

- Waltrip dug himself a huge hole at Daytona—literally and figuratively—and never completely climbed out in 2004. He was good at restrictor-plate races but not in many other situations. Toward the end of the season, he got a new crew chief, Pete Rondeau, and they worked hard to build positive momentum for 2005, but at the end of the season, a team shakeup sent Rondeau to be crew chief for Dale Earnhardt Jr. Tony Eury Jr., who was car chief for Earnhardt, will be Waltrip's crew chief. Waltrip made his 600th start in 2004.
- Matched his career total in wins during the 2003 season, when he won two races (the Daytona 500 and Talladega). He became one of only eight drivers to win the Daytona 500 more than once. But his strong season (he was in the top 10 in points the first two-thirds of the season) fell apart starting with the 24th race at Bristol. From there, he finished out of the top 25 in 10 of 13 races. Still, he ended up 15th in points, had a career-high eight top fives and showed he is not just a restrictor-plate racer.
- Got his 500th career NASCAR Cup start in 2002 at the February Rockingham race. He finished within the top 15 in points in 2002 for the first time in six seasons. He also won a Gatorade 125 event.
- Won his first NASCAR Cup points race at the 2001 Daytona 500, his 463rd career start. He finished second to Dale Earnhardt Jr. in the second Daytona race that year.
- Has his string of 387 consecutive starts snapped in 1998 when he failed to qualify at Phoenix.
- Won the 1996 NASCAR All-Star race in his first year with Wood Brothers. He was the first to do so after transferring from the Open.
- Cracked the top 15 in points for the first time in 1991. He won his first two career NASCAR Cup poles that year in a four-race span (June 2 at Dover and June 23 at Michigan).
- Was runner-up for 1986 Raybestos Rookie of the Year to Alan Kulwicki.
- First NASCAR Cup start was in the May Charlotte race in 1985. Michael finished 28th, and brother Darrell won.

## CAREER STATISTICS

| Year | Car owner | Races | Champ. finish | Won | Top 5 | Top 10 | DNF | Poles | Money won |
|------|-----------|-------|---------------|-----|-------|--------|-----|-------|-----------|
| 1985 | Dick Bahre | 5 | 57 | 0 | 0 | 0 | 4 | 0 | $9,540 |
| 1986 | Dick Bahre | 28 | 19 | 0 | 0 | 0 | 8 | 0 | $108,767 |
| 1987 | Dick Bahre | 29 | 20 | 0 | 0 | 1 | 8 | 0 | $205,370 |
| 1988 | Chuck Rider | 29 | 18 | 0 | 1 | 3 | 8 | 0 | $240,400 |

| Year | Car owner | Races | Champ. finish | Won | Top 5 | Top 10 | DNF | Poles | Money won |
|------|-----------|-------|---------------|-----|-------|--------|-----|-------|-----------|
| 1989 | Chuck Rider | 29 | 18 | 0 | 0 | 5 | 9 | 0 | $249,233 |
| 1990 | Chuck Rider | 29 | 16 | 0 | 5 | 10 | 7 | 0 | $395,507 |
| 1991 | Chuck Rider | 29 | 15 | 0 | 4 | 12 | 6 | 2 | $440,812 |
| 1992 | Chuck Rider | 29 | 23 | 0 | 1 | 2 | 8 | 0 | $410,545 |
| 1993 | Chuck Rider | 30 | 17 | 0 | 0 | 5 | 4 | 0 | $529,923 |
| 1994 | Chuck Rider | 31 | 12 | 0 | 2 | 10 | 3 | 0 | $706,426 |
| 1995 | Chuck Rider | 31 | 12 | 0 | 2 | 8 | 2 | 0 | $898,338 |
| 1996 | Wood Brothers | 31 | 14 | 0 | 1 | 11 | 3 | 0 | $1,182,811 |
| 1997 | Wood Brothers | 32 | 18 | 0 | 0 | 6 | 4 | 0 | $1,138,599 |
| 1998 | Wood Brothers | 32 | 17 | 0 | 0 | 5 | 3 | 0 | $1,508,680 |
| 1999 | J. Mattei/J. Smith | 34 | 29 | 0 | 1 | 3 | 10 | 0 | $1,702,460 |
| 2000 | J. Mattei/J. Smith | 34 | 27 | 0 | 1 | 1 | 10 | 0 | $1,690,821 |
| 2001 | Dale Earnhardt | 36 | 24 | 1 | 3 | 3 | 6 | 0 | $3,411,644 |
| 2002 | Teresa Earnhardt | 36 | 14 | 1 | 4 | 10 | 4 | 0 | $3,185,969 |
| 2003 | Teresa Earnhardt | 36 | 15 | 2 | 8 | 11 | 6 | 0 | $4,929,620 |
| 2004 | Teresa Earnhardt | 36 | 20 | 0 | 2 | 9 | 6 | 0 | $4,694,564 |
| **TOTALS** | | **606** | | **4** | **35** | **115** | **120** | **2** | **$27,640,029** |

| Race | Track | Start | Finish | Laps | Led | Status | Winnings | Rank |
|------|-------|-------|--------|------|-----|--------|----------|------|
| Advance Auto Parts 500 | Martinsville | 39 | 15 | 500/500 | 0 | Running | $95,706 | 31 |
| Aaron's 499 | Talladega | 2 | 12 | 188/188 | 13 | Running | $112,301 | 30 |
| Auto Club 500 | California | 17 | 32 | 245/250 | 0 | Running | $101,831 | 30 |
| Chevy Amer. Revolution 400 | Richmond | 18 | 10 | 400/400 | 56 | Running | $110,581 | 30 |
| Coca-Cola 600 | Lowe's | 12 | 2 | 400/400 | 0 | Running | $254,456 | 24 |
| MBNA 400 'A Salute to Heroes' | Dover | 8 | 6 | 399/400 | 0 | Running | $123,611 | 20 |
| Pocono 500 | Pocono | 22 | 33 | 166/200 | 0 | Accident | $89,621 | 24 |
| DHL 400 | Michigan | 19 | 10 | 200/200 | 0 | Running | $103,846 | 22 |
| Dodge/Save Mart 350 | Infineon | 40 | 4 | 110/110 | 0 | Running | $147,646 | 18 |
| Pepsi 400 | Daytona | 2 | 13 | 160/160 | 57 | Running | $118,331 | 18 |
| Tropicana 400 | Chicago | 39 | 9 | 267/267 | 0 | Running | $129,556 | 18 |
| Siemens 300 | New Hamp. | 4 | 6 | 300/300 | 0 | Running | $110,481 | 16 |
| Pennsylvania 500 | Pocono | 11 | 36 | 100/200 | 0 | Engine | $88,121 | 17 |
| Brickyard 400 | Indianapolis | 28 | 20 | 161/161 | 0 | Running | $164,856 | 18 |
| Sirius at the Glen | Watkins Glen | 18 | 20 | 90/90 | 0 | Running | $92,366 | 17 |
| GFS Marketplace 400 | Michigan | 17 | 17 | 200/200 | 1 | Running | $97,421 | 17 |
| Sharpie 500 | Bristol | 36 | 27 | 481/500 | 7 | Running | $105,961 | 17 |
| Pop Secret 500 | California | 21 | 23 | 250/250 | 10 | Running | $115,606 | 17 |
| Chevy Rock & Roll 400 | Richmond | 19 | 13 | 399/400 | 0 | Running | $96,836 | 16 |
| Sylvania 300 | New Hamp. | 16 | 9 | 300/300 | 39 | Running | $103,956 | 16 |
| MBNA America 400 | Dover | 5 | 16 | 397/400 | 0 | Running | $96,671 | 16 |
| EA Sports 500 | Talladega | 14 | 25 | 188/188 | 7 | Running | $98,786 | 16 |
| Banquet 400 | Kansas | 26 | 11 | 267/267 | 0 | Running | $115,131 | 16 |
| UAW-GM Quality 500 | Lowe's | 6 | 28 | 319/334 | 0 | Accident | $91,991 | 16 |
| Subway 500 | Martinsville | 30 | 19 | 500/500 | 0 | Running | $92,131 | 16 |
| Bass Pro Shops MBNA 500 | Atlanta | 40 | 14 | 324/325 | 1 | Running | $113,081 | 17 |
| Checker Auto Parts 500 | Phoenix | 19 | 17 | 315/315 | 0 | Running | $91,006 | 18 |
| Southern 500 | Darlington | 17 | 33 | 336/367 | 0 | Running | $91,756 | 19 |
| Ford 400 | Homestead | 24 | 17 | 271/271 | 0 | Running | $89,881 | 20 |

## 2004 RESULTS

| Race | Track | Start | Finish | Laps | Led | Status | Winnings | Rank |
|------|-------|-------|--------|------|-----|--------|----------|------|
| Daytona 500 | Daytona | 9 | 38 | 70/200 | 0 | Accident | $246,193 | 38 |
| Subway 400 | N. Carolina | 33 | 33 | 379/393 | 0 | Running | $92,481 | 39 |
| UAW-DaimlerChrysler 400 | Las Vegas | 14 | 37 | 163/267 | 1 | Accident | $100,431 | 38 |
| Golden Corral 500 | Atlanta | 15 | 23 | 321/325 | 0 | Running | $93,591 | 36 |
| Carolina Dodge Dealers 400 | Darlington | 39 | 35 | 181/293 | 0 | Accident | $88,291 | 37 |
| Food City 500 | Bristol | 8 | 10 | 500/500 | 0 | Running | $110,796 | 34 |
| Samsung/RadioShack 500 | Texas | 41 | 20 | 332/334 | 0 | Running | $124,981 | 33 |

**Scott Wimmer** 22

**Date of birth:** January 26, 1976 **Hometown:** Wausau, Wis.
**Resides:** High Point, N.C. **Spouse:** Single **Children:** None
**Hobbies:** Hunting and fishing

## NASCAR ACHIEVEMENTS

**First NASCAR Cup start:** November 19, 2000 (Atlanta)
**Best points finish:** 27 (2004)
**Career victories:** 0
**Career poles:** 0
**Best career finish:** 3  **Best career start:** 14

## FAST FACTS

● Finished third in the NASCAR Busch Series in 2002 and ninth in 2003.
● Was 11th in the NASCAR Busch Series in 2001, finishing second to Greg Biffle for Raybestos Rookie of the Year honors.
● Was the 1997 Hooters Pro Cup Series Rookie of the Year.
● Finished second in the 2000 ASA rookie standings.

## CAREER HIGHLIGHTS

● A stellar third-place run at the Daytona 500 suggested good things awaited in 2004, but they never materialized. Wimmer had only one more top 10 and no more top fives He struggled to run inside the top 20.
● Replaced Ward Burton in Bill Davis' No. 22 Dodge with four races remaining in the 2003 season. Wimmer ran six races total and had impressive finishes of ninth at Phoenix and 12th at Homestead.
● Ran three races for Bill Davis Racing in 2002 but had two DNFs.

## CAR FACTS

**Car:** No. 22 Dodge
**Primary sponsor:** Caterpillar
**Owner:** Bill Davis
**Team:** Bill Davis Racing
**Crew chief:** Derrick Finley
**Engine builder:** Terry Elledge

## CAREER STATISTICS

| Year | Car owner | Races | Champ. finish | Won | Top 5 | Top 10 | DNF | Poles | Money won |
|------|-----------|-------|---------------|-----|-------|--------|-----|-------|-----------|
| 2000 | Bill Davis | 1 | 74 | 0 | 0 | 0 | 0 | 0 | $37,780 |
| 2002 | Bill Davis | 3 | 56 | 0 | 0 | 0 | 2 | 0 | $143,110 |
| 2003 | Bill Davis | 6 | 48 | 0 | 0 | 1 | 0 | 0 | $487,060 |
| 2004 | Bill Davis | 35 | 27 | 0 | 1 | 2 | 7 | 0 | $3,675,879 |
| **TOTALS** | | **45** | | **0** | **1** | **3** | **9** | **0** | **$4,343,829** |

## 2004 RESULTS

| Race | Track | Start | Finish | Laps | Led | Status | Winnings | Rank |
|------|-------|-------|--------|------|-----|--------|----------|------|
| Daytona 500 | Daytona | 26 | 3 | 200/200 | 5 | Running | $758,839 | 3 |
| Subway 400 | N. Carolina | 31 | 15 | 391/393 | 0 | Running | $87,560 | 4 |
| UAW-DaimlerChrysler 400 | Las Vegas | 39 | 39 | 37/267 | 0 | Engine | $71,975 | 16 |
| Golden Corral 500 | Atlanta | 37 | 27 | 321/325 | 0 | Running | $77,420 | 21 |
| Carolina Dodge Dealers 400 | Darlington | 14 | 16 | 293/293 | 0 | Running | $79,285 | 20 |
| Food City 500 | Bristol | 20 | 13 | 500/500 | 0 | Running | $102,440 | 18 |
| Samsung/RadioShack 500 | Texas | 32 | 33 | 294/334 | 0 | Accident | $78,500 | 21 |
| Advance Auto Parts 500 | Martinsville | 16 | 29 | 494/500 | 0 | Running | $76,950 | 22 |
| Aaron's 499 | Talladega | 30 | 18 | 188/188 | 2 | Running | $96,885 | 21 |
| Auto Club 500 | California | 39 | 30 | 248/250 | 0 | Running | $83,039 | 25 |
| Chevy Amer. Revolution 400 | Richmond | 25 | 30 | 392/400 | 0 | Running | $78,075 | 27 |
| Coca-Cola 600 | Lowe's | 29 | 28 | 394/400 | 0 | Running | $88,939 | 26 |
| MBNA 400 'A Salute to Heroes' | Dover | 21 | 9 | 398/400 | 0 | Running | $104,110 | 26 |
| Pocono 500 | Pocono | 24 | 35 | 125/200 | 0 | Accident | $60,265 | 27 |
| DHL 400 | Michigan | 29 | 14 | 200/200 | 0 | Running | $91,865 | 26 |
| Dodge/Save Mart 350 | Infineon | 25 | 25 | 110/110 | 0 | Running | $82,970 | 26 |
| Pepsi 400 | Daytona | 37 | 32 | 159/160 | 0 | Running | $86,889 | 27 |
| Tropicana 400 | Chicago | 40 | 23 | 267/267 | 0 | Running | $91,975 | 27 |
| Siemens 300 | New Hamp. | 38 | 18 | 300/300 | 0 | Running | $89,050 | 27 |
| Pennsylvania 500 | Pocono | 28 | 11 | 200/200 | 0 | Running | $87,040 | 26 |
| Brickyard 400 | Indianapolis | 34 | 32 | 148/161 | 0 | Accident | $125,730 | 26 |
| Sirius at the Glen | Watkins Glen | 26 | 19 | 90/90 | 0 | Running | $77,605 | 26 |
| GFS Marketplace 400 | Michigan | 26 | 18 | 199/200 | 3 | Running | $85,565 | 26 |
| Sharpie 500 | Bristol | 34 | 36 | 268/500 | 0 | Accident | $87,005 | 26 |
| Pop Secret 500 | California | 38 | 21 | 250/250 | 0 | Running | $103,875 | 26 |
| Chevy Rock & Roll 400 | Richmond | 21 | 38 | 297/400 | 0 | Running | $64,295 | 26 |
| Sylvania 300 | New Hamp. | 27 | 36 | 207/300 | 0 | Accident | $66,410 | 26 |
| MBNA America 400 | Dover | 29 | 23 | 395/400 | 0 | Running | $84,740 | 27 |
| EA Sports 500 | Talladega | 29 | 31 | 187/188 | 0 | Running | $82,820 | 27 |
| Banquet 400 | Kansas | 37 | 36 | 146/267 | 0 | Overheat | $80,789 | 27 |
| UAW-GM Quality 500 | Lowe's | 42 | 26 | 327/334 | 0 | Running | $77,375 | 27 |
| Subway 500 | Martinsville | 24 | 20 | 500/500 | 0 | Running | $84,425 | 27 |
| Checker Auto Parts 500 | Phoenix | 38 | 26 | 314/315 | 0 | Running | $73,925 | 27 |
| Southern 500 | Darlington | 28 | 22 | 365/367 | 0 | Running | $83,975 | 27 |
| Ford 400 | Homestead | 21 | 13 | 271/271 | 0 | Running | $86,175 | 27 |

# Johnny Benson

**Date of birth:** June 27, 1963.
**Hometown:** Grand Rapids, Mich.

## CAREER STATISTICS

| Year | Car Owner | Races | Won | Top 5 | Top 10 | DNF | Poles | Money Won |
|------|-----------|-------|-----|-------|--------|-----|-------|-----------|
| 1996 | Richard Bahre | 30 | 0 | 1 | 6 | 5 | 1 | 947,080 |
| 1997 | Richard Bahre | 32 | 0 | 0 | 8 | 2 | 1 | 1,256,457 |
| 1998 | Jack Roush | 32 | 0 | 3 | 10 | 5 | 0 | 1,360,335 |
| 1999 | Jack Roush | 34 | 0 | 0 | 2 | 5 | 0 | 1,567,668 |
| 2000 | Tim Beverley | 18 | 0 | 1 | 2 | 2 | 0 | 921,504 |
| | Tom Beard | 15 | 0 | 2 | 5 | 1 | 0 | 919,820 |
| 2001 | Tom Beard | 36 | 0 | 6 | 14 | 8 | 0 | 2,894,903 |
| 2002 | Tom Beard | 31 | 1 | 3 | 7 | 8 | 0 | 2,791,879 |
| 2003 | Tom Beard | 36 | 0 | 2 | 4 | 6 | 0 | 3,544,793 |
| 2004 | James Finch | 4 | 0 | 0 | 0 | 3 | 0 | 403,674 |
| | **TOTALS** | **268** | **1** | **18** | **58** | **45** | **2** | **$16,608,113** |

# Geoffrey Bodine

**Date of birth:** April 18, 1949.
**Hometown:** Chemung, N.Y.

| Year | Car Owner | Races | Won | Top 5 | Top 10 | DNF | Poles | Money Won |
|------|-----------|-------|-----|-------|--------|-----|-------|-----------|
| | Rick Hendrick | 29 | 1 | 9 | 11 | 7 | 3 | 620,594 |
| 1990 | Junior Johnson | 29 | 3 | 11 | 19 | 3 | 2 | 1,131,222 |
| 1991 | Junior Johnson | 27 | 1 | 6 | 12 | 7 | 2 | 625,256 |
| 1992 | Bud Moore | 29 | 2 | 7 | 11 | 7 | 0 | 716,583 |
| 1993 | Bud Moore | 23 | 1 | 2 | 8 | 5 | 1 | 613,750 |
| | Geoffrey Bodine | 7 | 0 | 0 | 1 | 4 | 0 | 170,012 |
| 1994 | Geoffrey Bodine | 31 | 3 | 7 | 10 | 15 | 5 | 1,276,126 |
| 1995 | Geoffrey Bodine | 31 | 0 | 1 | 4 | 5 | 0 | 1,011,090 |
| 1996 | Geoffrey Bodine | 31 | 1 | 2 | 6 | 5 | 0 | 1,031,762 |
| 1997 | Geoffrey Bodine | 29 | 0 | 3 | 10 | 8 | 2 | 1,092,734 |
| 1998 | James Smith | 32 | 0 | 1 | 5 | 10 | 0 | 1,247,255 |
| 1999 | Joe Bessey | 34 | 0 | 1 | 2 | 6 | 0 | 1,258,894 |
| 2000 | Joe Bessey | 12 | 0 | 0 | 0 | 4 | 0 | 626,124 |
| | Chip MacPherson | 1 | 0 | 0 | 0 | 1 | 0 | 33,875 |
| | Andy Petree | 1 | 0 | 0 | 0 | 1 | 0 | 34,982 |
| 2001 | Brett Bodine | 2 | 0 | 0 | 0 | 0 | 0 | 80,855 |
| 2002 | Bill Davis | 1 | 0 | 0 | 0 | 0 | 0 | 35,615 |
| | James Finch | 5 | 0 | 1 | 2 | 2 | 0 | 946,905 |
| | Travis Carter | 4 | 0 | 0 | 0 | 2 | 0 | 241,980 |
| 2003 | Brett Bodine | 1 | 0 | 0 | 0 | 1 | 0 | 78,150 |
| 2004 | William Edwards | 5 | 0 | 0 | 0 | 3 | 0 | 364,460 |
| | **TOTALS** | **570** | **18** | **100** | **190** | **165** | **37** | **$16,497,380** |

## CAREER STATISTICS

| Year | Car Owner | Races | Won | Top 5 | Top 10 | DNF | Poles | Money Won |
|------|-----------|-------|-----|-------|--------|-----|-------|-----------|
| 1979 | Jack Beebe | 3 | 0 | 0 | 0 | 3 | 0 | 1,224,820 |
| 1981 | Richard Bahre | 2 | 0 | 0 | 0 | 1 | 0 | 6,390 |
| | Emanuel Zervakis | 3 | 0 | 0 | 1 | 2 | 0 | 8,610 |
| 1982 | Richard Bahre | 1 | 0 | 0 | 0 | 1 | 0 | 3,450 |
| | Cliff Stewart | 24 | 0 | 4 | 10 | 8 | 2 | 255,050 |
| 1983 | Cliff Stewart | 28 | 0 | 5 | 9 | 15 | 1 | 194,476 |
| 1984 | Rick Hendrick | 30 | 3 | 7 | 14 | 8 | 3 | 393,924 |
| 1985 | Rick Hendrick | 28 | 0 | 10 | 14 | 5 | 3 | 565,865 |
| 1986 | Rick Hendrick | 29 | 2 | 10 | 15 | 12 | 8 | 795,111 |
| 1987 | Rick Hendrick | 29 | 0 | 3 | 10 | 10 | 2 | 449,816 |
| 1988 | Rick Hendrick | 29 | 1 | 10 | 16 | 4 | 3 | 570,643 |

**DRIVERS**

# Derrike Cope

**Date of birth:** November 3, 1958. **Hometown:** Spanaway, Wash.

### CAREER STATISTICS

| Year | Car Owner | Races | Won | Top 5 | Top 10 | DNF | Poles | Money Won |
|---|---|---|---|---|---|---|---|---|
| 1982 | George Jefferson | 1 | 0 | 0 | 0 | 1 | 0 | $625 |
| 1984 | George Jefferson | 3 | 0 | 0 | 0 | 1 | 0 | 6,500 |
| 1985 | George Jefferson | 2 | 0 | 0 | 0 | 0 | 0 | 7,100 |
| 1986 | Warren Razore | 5 | 0 | 0 | 1 | 2 | 0 | 8,025 |
| 1987 | Fred Stoke | 11 | 0 | 0 | 0 | 8 | 0 | 33,750 |
| 1988 | James Testa | 26 | 0 | 0 | 0 | 16 | 0 | 132,835 |
| 1989 | James Testa | 3 | 0 | 0 | 0 | 3 | 0 | 5,440 |
| | Bob Whitcomb | 20 | 0 | 0 | 4 | 9 | 0 | 120,190 |
| 1990 | Bob Whitcomb | 29 | 2 | 2 | 6 | 10 | 0 | 569,451 |
| 1991 | Bob Whitcomb | 28 | 0 | 1 | 2 | 14 | 0 | 419,380 |
| 1992 | Bob Whitcomb | 29 | 0 | 0 | 3 | 6 | 0 | 277,215 |
| 1993 | Cale Yarborough | 30 | 0 | 0 | 1 | 8 | 0 | 402,515 |
| 1994 | Cale Yarborough | 16 | 0 | 0 | 0 | 7 | 0 | 185,186 |
| | T. W. Taylor | 2 | 0 | 0 | 0 | 0 | 0 | 35,110 |
| | Bobby Allison | 12 | 0 | 0 | 2 | 3 | 0 | 178,140 |
| 1995 | Bobby Allison | 31 | 0 | 2 | 8 | 5 | 0 | 683,075 |
| 1996 | Bobby Allison | 29 | 0 | 0 | 3 | 11 | 0 | 675,781 |
| 1997 | Tom Beard | 31 | 0 | 1 | 2 | 6 | 0 | 707,404 |
| 1998 | Chuck Rider | 28 | 0 | 0 | 0 | 9 | 1 | 985,730 |
| 1999 | Chuck Rider | 11 | 0 | 0 | 0 | 3 | 0 | 507,011 |
| | Bud Moore | 1 | 0 | 0 | 0 | 0 | 0 | 19,740 |
| | Larry Hedrick | 3 | 0 | 0 | 0 | 1 | 0 | 91,225 |
| 2000 | Robert Fenley | 3 | 0 | 0 | 0 | 1 | 0 | 179,151 |
| 2001 | Edward Campbell | 1 | 0 | 0 | 0 | 0 | 0 | 47,500 |
| 2002 | Derrike Cope | 2 | 0 | 0 | 0 | 1 | 0 | 108,826 |
| | B.A. Morgenthau | 5 | 0 | 0 | 0 | 2 | 0 | 224,390 |
| 2003 | Derrike Cope | 18 | 0 | 0 | 0 | 12 | 0 | 1,030,691 |
| 2004 | Don Arnold | 12 | 0 | 0 | 0 | 3 | 0 | 185,186 |
| | Hermie Sadler | 1 | 0 | 0 | 0 | 1 | 0 | 35,110 |
| | William Edwards | 5 | 0 | 0 | 0 | 5 | 0 | 178,140 |
| | **TOTALS** | **398** | **2** | **6** | **32** | **148** | **1** | **$8,997,227** |

# Ricky Craven

**Date of birth:** May 24, 1966. **Hometown:** Newburgh, Maine

### CAREER STATISTICS

| Year | Car Owner | Races | Won | Top 5 | Top 10 | DNF | Poles | Money Won |
|---|---|---|---|---|---|---|---|---|
| 1991 | Richard Moroso | 1 | 0 | 0 | 0 | 1 | 0 | 3,750 |
| 1995 | Larry Hedrick | 31 | 0 | 0 | 4 | 4 | 0 | 597,054 |
| 1996 | Larry Hedrick | 31 | 0 | 3 | 5 | 7 | 2 | 941,959 |
| 1997 | Rick Hendrick | 30 | 0 | 4 | 7 | 7 | 0 | 1,259,550 |
| 1998 | Rick Hendrick | 8 | 0 | 0 | 1 | 0 | 1 | 422,200 |
| | Tom Beard | 3 | 0 | 0 | 0 | 0 | 0 | 84,030 |
| 1999 | Scott Barbour | 12 | 0 | 0 | 0 | 4 | 0 | 457,496 |
| | Hal Hicks | 12 | 0 | 0 | 0 | 6 | 0 | 396,339 |
| 2000 | Hal Hicks | 16 | 0 | 0 | 0 | 6 | 0 | 363,562 |
| 2001 | Cal Wells | 36 | 1 | 4 | 7 | 9 | 1 | 1,996,981 |
| 2002 | Cal Wells | 36 | 0 | 3 | 9 | 4 | 2 | 2,838,087 |
| 2003 | Cal Wells | 36 | 1 | 3 | 8 | 10 | 0 | 3,216,211 |
| 2004 | Cal Wells | 26 | 0 | 0 | 0 | 8 | 0 | 2,337,420 |
| | **TOTALS** | **278** | **2** | **17** | **41** | **66** | **6** | **$15,209,284** |

# Ron Fellows

**Date of birth:** September 28, 1959. **Hometown:** Mississaugua, Ontario

### CAREER STATISTICS

| Year | Car Owner | Races | Won | Top 5 | Top 10 | DNF | Poles | Money Won |
|---|---|---|---|---|---|---|---|---|
| 1995 | G. Bradshaw/M. Smith | 1 | 0 | 0 | 0 | 1 | 0 | 9,035 |
| 1998 | Buz McCall | 2 | 0 | 0 | 0 | 0 | 0 | 46,310 |
| 1999 | Joe Nemechek | 1 | 0 | 1 | 1 | 0 | 0 | 67,270 |
| 2000 | Joe Nemechek | 1 | 0 | 0 | 0 | 1 | 0 | 24,725 |
| 2001 | Joe Nemechek | 2 | 0 | 0 | 0 | 2 | 0 | 72,055 |
| 2002 | Joe Nemechek | 1 | 0 | 0 | 0 | 0 | 0 | 47,930 |
| 2003 | Teresa Earnhardt | 2 | 0 | 0 | 1 | 1 | 0 | 161,854 |
| 2004 | Teresa Earnhardt | 1 | 0 | 1 | 1 | 0 | 0 | 101,260 |
| | **TOTALS** | **11** | **0** | **2** | **3** | **5** | **0** | **$530,439** |

# Larry Foyt

**Date of birth:** February 22, 1977. **Hometown:** Houston

### CAREER STATISTICS

| Year | Car Owner | Races | Won | Top 5 | Top 10 | DNF | Poles | Money Won |
|---|---|---|---|---|---|---|---|---|
| 2003 | A.J. Foyt | 20 | 0 | 0 | 0 | 8 | 0 | 1,180,994 |
| 2004 | A.J. Foyt | 3 | 0 | 0 | 0 | 0 | 0 | 342,337 |
| | **TOTALS** | **23** | **0** | **0** | **0** | **8** | **0** | **$1,523,331** |

# P.J. Jones

**Date of birth:** 4/23/69. **Hometown:** Rolling Hills, Calif.

### CAREER STATISTICS

| Year | Car Owner | Races | Won | Top 5 | Top 10 | DNF | Poles | Money Won |
|---|---|---|---|---|---|---|---|---|
| 1993 | Harry Melling | 6 | 0 | 0 | 1 | 2 | 0 | 50,070 |
| 1994 | Gordon Chilson | 1 | 0 | 0 | 0 | 0 | 0 | 6,960 |
| | Doug Bawel | 1 | 0 | 0 | 0 | 1 | 0 | 6,085 |
| 2000 | M. Held/J. Menard | 1 | 0 | 0 | 0 | 0 | 0 | 33,345 |
| | Felix Sabates | 1 | 0 | 0 | 0 | 0 | 0 | 37,555 |
| 2002 | A. J. Foyt | 1 | 0 | 1 | 1 | 0 | 0 | 65,950 |
| 2003 | Larry McClure | 1 | 0 | 0 | 0 | 0 | 0 | 59,135 |
| 2004 | Don Arnold | 5 | 0 | 0 | 0 | 4 | 0 | 293,704 |
| | **TOTALS** | **17** | **0** | **1** | **2** | **7** | **0** | **$528,549** |

# Kevin Lepage

**Date of birth:** June 26, 1962. **Hometown:** Shelbourne, Vt.

### CAREER STATISTICS

| Year | Car Owner | Races | Won | Top 5 | Top 10 | DNF | Poles | Money Won |
|---|---|---|---|---|---|---|---|---|
| 1997 | Joe Falk | 3 | 0 | 0 | 0 | 1 | 0 | 1,557,720 |
| 1998 | Joe Falk | 13 | 0 | 0 | 0 | 3 | 0 | 384,591 |

DRIVERS

**Kevin Lepage continued**

| Year | Car Owner | Races | Won | Top 5 | Top 10 | DNF | Poles | Money Won |
|------|-----------|-------|-----|-------|--------|-----|-------|-----------|
| | Jack Roush | 13 | 0 | 0 | 2 | 5 | 0 | 447,745 |
| | Buz McCall | 1 | 0 | 0 | 0 | 1 | 0 | 20,385 |
| 1999 | Jack Roush | 34 | 0 | 1 | 2 | 3 | 1 | 1,587,841 |
| 2000 | Jack Roush | 32 | 0 | 1 | 3 | 5 | 0 | 1,679,186 |
| 2001 | Larry McClure | 21 | 0 | 0 | 0 | 3 | 0 | 987,976 |
| | Smith/Evernham | 8 | 0 | 0 | 1 | 0 | 0 | 436,876 |
| 2002 | Derrike Cope | 2 | 0 | 0 | 0 | 2 | 0 | 97,809 |
| | B.A. Morgenthau | 1 | 0 | 0 | 0 | 1 | 0 | 44,650 |
| 2003 | Larry McClure | 8 | 0 | 0 | 0 | 1 | 0 | 489,069 |
| | Edward Campbell | 2 | 0 | 0 | 0 | 0 | 0 | 154,345 |
| | Kevin Lepage | 1 | 0 | 0 | 0 | 0 | 0 | 69,675 |
| 2004 | Larry McClure | 6 | 0 | 0 | 0 | 1 | 0 | 531,812 |
| | Joe Auer | 5 | 0 | 0 | 0 | 5 | 0 | 299,996 |
| | John Carter | 6 | 0 | 0 | 0 | 4 | 0 | 352,092 |
| | **TOTALS** | **156** | **0** | **2** | **8** | **35** | **1** | **$7,735,704** |

# Tony Raines

**Date of birth:** April 14, 1964. **Hometown:** LaPorte, Ind.

### CAREER STATISTICS

| Year | Car Owner | Races | Won | Top 5 | Top 10 | DNF | Poles | Money Won |
|------|-----------|-------|-----|-------|--------|-----|-------|-----------|
| 2002 | Bill Baumgardner | 7 | 0 | 0 | 0 | 3 | 0 | 326,042 |
| 2003 | Bill Baumgardner | 35 | 0 | 0 | 1 | 5 | 0 | 2,122,739 |
| 2004 | James Finch | 1 | 0 | 0 | 0 | 1 | 0 | 60,025 |
| | Bill Davis | 1 | 0 | 0 | 0 | 1 | 0 | 121,730 |
| | Joe Auer | 4 | 0 | 0 | 0 | 3 | 0 | 245,239 |
| | **TOTALS** | **48** | **0** | **0** | **1** | **13** | **0** | **$2,875,775** |

# Hermie Sadler

**Date of birth:** April 24, 1969. **Hometown:** Emporia, Va.

### CAREER STATISTICS

| Year | Car Owner | Races | Won | Top 5 | Top 10 | DNF | Poles | Money Won |
|------|-----------|-------|-----|-------|--------|-----|-------|-----------|
| 1996 | William Slate Jr. | 1 | 0 | 0 | 0 | 1 | 0 | 68,657 |
| 2001 | Angela Sadler | 3 | 0 | 0 | 0 | 0 | 0 | 36,940 |
| 2002 | Junie Donlavey | 2 | 0 | 0 | 0 | 0 | 0 | 87,400 |
| | Angela Sadler | 8 | 0 | 0 | 0 | 3 | 0 | 124,340 |
| 2003 | Angela Sadler | 10 | 0 | 0 | 0 | 8 | 0 | 500,827 |
| 2004 | Angela Sadler | 16 | 0 | 0 | 0 | 11 | 0 | 945,549 |
| | **TOTALS** | **40** | **0** | **0** | **0** | **23** | **0** | **$2,106,500** |

# Boris Said

**Date of birth:** September 18, 1962. **Hometown:** Carlsbad, Calif.

### CAREER STATISTICS

| Year | Car Owner | Races | Won | Top 5 | Top 10 | DNF | Poles | Money Won |
|------|-----------|-------|-----|-------|--------|-----|-------|-----------|
| 1999 | Mark Simo | 2 | 0 | 0 | 0 | 1 | 0 | 68,657 |
| 2000 | James Spencer | 1 | 0 | 0 | 0 | 1 | 0 | 36,940 |
| 2001 | Doug Bawel | 2 | 0 | 0 | 1 | 0 | 0 | 124,340 |
| 2002 | Doug Bawel | 2 | 0 | 0 | 0 | 1 | 0 | 87,400 |
| 2003 | Tom Beard | 2 | 0 | 0 | 1 | 0 | 1 | 134,680 |
| 2004 | Nelson Bowers | 3 | 0 | 0 | 1 | 1 | 0 | 252,440 |
| | **TOTALS** | **12** | **0** | **0** | **3** | **4** | **1** | **$704,457** |

# Johnny Sauter

**Date of birth:** May 1, 1978. **Hometown:** Necedah, Wis.

### CAREER STATISTICS

| Year | Car Owner | Races | Won | Top 5 | Top 10 | DNF | Poles | Money Won |
|------|-----------|-------|-----|-------|--------|-----|-------|-----------|
| 2003 | Larry McClure | 5 | 0 | 0 | 0 | 0 | 0 | 281,335 |
| 2004 | Richard Childress | 13 | 0 | 0 | 0 | 1 | 0 | 1,164,266 |
| | James Finch | 3 | 0 | 0 | 0 | 1 | 0 | 169,254 |
| | **TOTAL** | **21** | **0** | **0** | **0** | **2** | **0** | **$1,614,855** |

# Kirk Shelmerdine

**Date of birth:** March 8, 1958. **Hometown:** Mooresville, N.C.

### CAREER STATISTICS

| Year | Car Owner | Races | Won | Top 5 | Top 10 | DNF | Poles | Money Won |
|------|-----------|-------|-----|-------|--------|-----|-------|-----------|
| 1981 | James Hylton | 1 | 0 | 0 | 1 | 1 | 0 | 950 |
| 1994 | Jimmy Means | 1 | 0 | 0 | 0 | 0 | 0 | 11,265 |
| 2002 | Kirk Shelmerdine | 2 | 0 | 0 | 0 | 2 | 0 | 97,127 |
| 2004 | Kirk Shelmerdine | 18 | 0 | 0 | 0 | 18 | 0 | 1,095,041 |
| | **TOTALS** | **22** | **0** | **0** | **0** | **21** | **0** | **$1,204,383** |

# Morgan Shepherd

**Date of birth:** October 21, 1941. **Hometown:** Conover, N.C.

### CAREER STATISTICS

| Year | Car Owner | Races | Won | Top 5 | Top 10 | DNF | Poles | Money Won |
|------|-----------|-------|-----|-------|--------|-----|-------|-----------|
| 1970 | Morgan Shepherd | 3 | 0 | 0 | 0 | 3 | 0 | $269,965 |
| 1977 | Jim Makar | 3 | 0 | 0 | 1 | 0 | 0 | 7,465 |
| 1978 | Jim Makar | 2 | 0 | 0 | 0 | 1 | 0 | 8,115 |
| 1979 | Jim Makar | 0 | 0 | 0 | 0 | 0 | 0 | 256 |
| 1981 | Cliff Stewart | 18 | 1 | 3 | 8 | 7 | 1 | 132,879 |
| | Cecil Gordon | 7 | 0 | 0 | 2 | 2 | 0 | 28,925 |
| | Ron Benfield | 3 | 0 | 0 | 0 | 3 | 0 | 2,405 |
| | Mark Martin | 1 | 0 | 0 | 0 | 1 | 0 | 1,120 |
| 1982 | Ron Benfield | 29 | 0 | 6 | 13 | 14 | 2 | 150,475 |
| 1983 | Jim Stacy | 23 | 0 | 3 | 13 | 8 | 0 | 269,001 |
| | Emanuel Zervakis | 1 | 0 | 0 | 0 | 1 | 0 | 1,000 |
| | Beare Racing | 1 | 0 | 0 | 0 | 1 | 0 | 850 |
| 1984 | R. Harrington | 1 | 0 | 0 | 0 | 1 | 0 | 1,735 |
| | Dick Bahre | 4 | 0 | 0 | 0 | 3 | 0 | 7,450 |
| | Morgan Shepherd | 3 | 0 | 0 | 0 | 1 | 0 | 3,950 |
| | D.K. Ulrich | 2 | 0 | 0 | 0 | 1 | 0 | 5,545 |
| | Jimmy Means | 1 | 0 | 0 | 0 | 1 | 0 | 4,655 |
| | Roger Hamby | 6 | 0 | 0 | 0 | 3 | 0 | 19,035 |
| | Ron Benfield | 3 | 0 | 0 | 1 | 0 | 0 | 17,300 |
| 1985 | Buddy Arrington | 1 | 0 | 0 | 0 | 1 | 0 | 15,300 |
| | Dick Bahre | 1 | 0 | 0 | 0 | 1 | 0 | 1,150 |
| | Petty Enter. | 1 | 0 | 0 | 0 | 0 | 0 | 3,415 |
| | Bobby Hawkins | 4 | 0 | 1 | 2 | 2 | 0 | 18,575 |

| Year | Car Owner | Races | Won | Top 5 | Top 10 | DNF | Poles | Money Won |
|------|-----------|-------|-----|-------|--------|-----|-------|-----------|
|      | Helen Smith | 7 | 0 | 0 | 0 | 7 | 0 | 11,130 |
|      | Morgan Shepherd | 2 | 0 | 0 | 0 | 1 | 0 | 6,415 |
| 1986 | Jack Beebe | 13 | 1 | 3 | 6 | 6 | 0 | 145,380 |
|      | Elmo Langley | 1 | 0 | 0 | 0 | 1 | 0 | 2,940 |
|      | James Hylton | 1 | 0 | 0 | 0 | 0 | 0 | 3,880 |
|      | Buster Mathis | 1 | 0 | 0 | 0 | 0 | 0 | 1,525 |
|      | Rahmoc | 11 | 0 | 1 | 2 | 8 | 0 | 90,421 |
| 1987 | Kenny Bernstein | 29 | 0 | 7 | 11 | 13 | 1 | 317,034 |
| 1988 | Tom Winkle | 3 | 0 | 0 | 1 | 1 | 1 | 37,645 |
|      | M. Shepherd | 9 | 0 | 0 | 0 | 6 | 0 | 37,755 |
|      | Mach I | 5 | 0 | 1 | 2 | 2 | 0 | 57,570 |
|      | Rahmoc | 3 | 0 | 0 | 1 | 2 | 1 | 27,685 |
|      | Baker-Schiff | 3 | 0 | 1 | 2 | 1 | 0 | 36,770 |
| 1989 | Rahmoc | 29 | 0 | 5 | 13 | 9 | 1 | 544,255 |
| 1990 | Bud Moore | 29 | 1 | 7 | 16 | 6 | 0 | 666,915 |
| 1991 | Bud Moore | 29 | 0 | 4 | 14 | 6 | 0 | 521,147 |
| 1992 | Wood Brothers | 29 | 0 | 3 | 11 | 3 | 0 | 634,222 |
| 1993 | Wood Brothers | 30 | 1 | 3 | 15 | 2 | 0 | 782,523 |
| 1994 | Wood Brothers | 31 | 0 | 9 | 16 | 2 | 0 | 1,089,038 |
| 1995 | Wood Brothers | 31 | 0 | 4 | 10 | 2 | 0 | 966,374 |
| 1996 | Butch Mock | 31 | 0 | 1 | 5 | 3 | 0 | 719,059 |
| 1997 | R. Jackson | 18 | 0 | 1 | 3 | 3 | 0 | 578,524 |
|      | Doug Bawel | 5 | 0 | 0 | 0 | 0 | 0 | 84,475 |
| 1998 | Felix Sabates | 2 | 0 | 0 | 0 | 0 | 0 | 61,611 |
|      | Richard Childress | 2 | 0 | 0 | 0 | 1 | 0 | 50,140 |
|      | William Stavola | 2 | 0 | 0 | 0 | 2 | 0 | 45,955 |
|      | Joe Falk | 6 | 0 | 0 | 0 | 3 | 0 | 206,835 |
| 1999 | M. Collins | 0 | 0 | 0 | 0 | 0 | 0 | 30,756 |
|      | Junie Donlavey | 1 | 0 | 0 | 0 | 0 | 0 | 29,400 |
|      | Morgan Shepherd | 0 | 0 | 0 | 0 | 0 | 0 | 9,147 |
| 2001 | S. Hover Jr. | 0 | 0 | 0 | 0 | 0 | 0 | 21,059 |
| 2002 | Cindy Shepherd | 5 | 0 | 0 | 0 | 5 | 0 | 214,397 |
| 2003 | Morgan Shepherd | 2 | 0 | 0 | 0 | 2 | 0 | 120,034 |
| 2004 | Morgan Shepherd | 19 | 0 | 0 | 0 | 17 | 0 | 1,133,620 |
| **TOTALS** | | **507** | **4** | **63** | **168** | **167** | **7** | **$9,987,202** |

# Mike Skinner

**Date of birth:** June 28, 1957. **Hometown:** Susanville, Calif.

## CAREER STATISTICS

| Year | Car Owner | Races | Won | Top 5 | Top 10 | DNF | Poles | Money Won |
|------|-----------|-------|-----|-------|--------|-----|-------|-----------|
| 1986 | Ozan/Wigglesworth | 3 | 0 | 0 | 0 | 1 | 0 | 4,255 |
| 1990 | Thee Dixon | 1 | 0 | 0 | 0 | 1 | 0 | 2,825 |
| 1991 | Thee Dixon | 2 | 0 | 0 | 0 | 1 | 0 | 8,505 |
| 1992 | Thee Dixon | 1 | 0 | 0 | 0 | 0 | 0 | 8,550 |
|      | Alan Aroneck | 1 | 0 | 0 | 0 | 0 | 0 | 4,900 |
| 1993 | Jimmy Means | 1 | 0 | 0 | 0 | 1 | 0 | 5,180 |
| 1994 | Jimmy Means | 1 | 0 | 0 | 0 | 0 | 0 | 9,550 |
| 1996 | Richard Childress | 5 | 0 | 0 | 0 | 1 | 0 | 65,850 |
| 1997 | Richard Childress | 31 | 0 | 0 | 3 | 7 | 2 | 900,569 |
| 1998 | Richard Childress | 30 | 0 | 4 | 9 | 3 | 0 | 1,518,901 |
| 1999 | Richard Childress | 34 | 0 | 5 | 14 | 1 | 2 | 2,499,877 |
| 2000 | Richard Childress | 34 | 0 | 1 | 11 | 2 | 1 | 2,205,320 |
| 2001 | Richard Childress | 23 | 0 | 0 | 1 | 4 | 0 | 1,921,186 |
| 2002 | Larry McClure | 36 | 0 | 0 | 1 | 6 | 0 | 2,094,232 |
| 2003 | Larry McClure | 14 | 0 | 0 | 0 | 4 | 0 | 1,025,503 |
|      | Tom Beard | 11 | 0 | 0 | 0 | 2 | 1 | 654,412 |
|      | Michael Waltrip | 1 | 0 | 0 | 0 | 1 | 0 | 102,889 |
| 2004 | Richard Childress | 1 | 0 | 0 | 0 | 0 | 0 | 251,813 |
| **TOTALS** | | **230** | **0** | **10** | **39** | **35** | **6** | **$13,284,317** |

# Jimmy Spencer

**Date of birth:** February 15, 1957. **Hometown:** Berwick, Pa.

## CAREER STATISTICS

| Year | Car Owner | Races | Won | Top 5 | Top 10 | DNF | Poles | Money Won |
|------|-----------|-------|-----|-------|--------|-----|-------|-----------|
| 1989 | B. Baker/D. Schiff | 17 | 0 | 0 | 3 | 9 | 0 | 121,065 |
| 1990 | Rod Osterlund | 26 | 0 | 0 | 2 | 5 | 0 | 219,775 |
| 1991 | Travis Carter | 29 | 0 | 1 | 6 | 14 | 0 | 283,620 |
| 1992 | Travis Carter | 7 | 0 | 0 | 0 | 4 | 0 | 76,055 |
|      | Richard Moroso | 1 | 0 | 0 | 0 | 0 | 0 | 6,125 |
|      | Bobby Allison | 4 | 0 | 3 | 3 | 0 | 0 | 103,905 |
| 1993 | Bobby Allison | 30 | 0 | 5 | 10 | 4 | 0 | 686,026 |
| 1994 | Junior Johnson | 29 | 2 | 3 | 4 | 11 | 1 | 479,235 |
| 1995 | Travis Carter | 29 | 0 | 0 | 4 | 2 | 0 | 507,210 |
| 1996 | Travis Carter | 31 | 0 | 2 | 9 | 2 | 0 | 1,090,876 |
| 1997 | Travis Carter | 32 | 0 | 1 | 4 | 6 | 0 | 1,073,779 |
| 1998 | Travis Carter | 31 | 0 | 3 | 8 | 2 | 0 | 1,741,012 |
| 1999 | Travis Carter | 34 | 0 | 2 | 4 | 6 | 0 | 1,752,299 |
| 2000 | Travis Carter | 34 | 0 | 2 | 5 | 8 | 0 | 1,936,762 |
| 2001 | Travis Carter | 36 | 0 | 3 | 8 | 7 | 2 | 2,669,638 |
| 2002 | Chip Ganassi | 34 | 0 | 2 | 6 | 7 | 0 | 2,136,792 |
| 2003 | Jim Smith | 35 | 0 | 1 | 4 | 8 | 0 | 2,565,803 |
| 2004 | Jim Smith | 1 | 0 | 0 | 0 | 0 | 0 | 223,513 |
|      | Larry McClure | 25 | 0 | 0 | 0 | 7 | 0 | 1,761,607 |
| **TOTALS** | | **465** | **2** | **28** | **80** | **102** | **3** | **$19,445,097** |

# Kenny Wallace

**Date of birth:** August 23, 1963. **Hometown:** St. Louis

## CAREER STATISTICS

| Year | Car Owner | Races | Won | Top 5 | Top 10 | DNF | Poles | Money Won |
|------|-----------|-------|-----|-------|--------|-----|-------|-----------|
| 1990 | Randy Hope | 1 | 0 | 0 | 0 | 1 | 0 | 6,050 |
| 1991 | Sam McMahon | 3 | 0 | 0 | 0 | 2 | 0 | 11,425 |
|      | Felix Sabates | 2 | 0 | 0 | 0 | 0 | 0 | 46,900 |
| 1993 | Felix Sabates | 30 | 0 | 0 | 3 | 6 | 0 | 330,325 |
| 1994 | Robert Yates | 10 | 0 | 1 | 2 | 1 | 0 | 211,810 |
|      | Filbert Martocci | 1 | 0 | 0 | 0 | 0 | 0 | 9,825 |
|      | Bill Elliott | 1 | 0 | 0 | 1 | 0 | 0 | 13,370 |
| 1995 | Filbert Martocci | 11 | 0 | 0 | 0 | 3 | 0 | 151,700 |
| 1996 | Filbert Martocci | 30 | 0 | 0 | 2 | 9 | 0 | 457,665 |
| 1997 | Filbert Martocci | 31 | 0 | 0 | 2 | 11 | 2 | 939,001 |
| 1998 | Filbert Martocci | 31 | 0 | 0 | 7 | 13 | 0 | 1,019,861 |
| 1999 | Andy Petree | 34 | 0 | 3 | 5 | 7 | 0 | 1,416,208 |
| 2000 | Andy Petree | 34 | 0 | 1 | 6 | 6 | 0 | 1,723,966 |
| 2001 | Jack Birmingham | 12 | 0 | 0 | 0 | 5 | 0 | 597,651 |
|      | Teresa Earnhardt | 12 | 0 | 1 | 2 | 1 | 1 | 965,030 |
| 2002 | Michael Waltrip | 4 | 0 | 0 | 0 | 2 | 0 | 54,570 |
|      | Richard Childress | 1 | 0 | 0 | 0 | 0 | 0 | 85,567 |
|      | Teresa Earnhardt | 4 | 0 | 0 | 1 | 0 | 0 | 454,060 |
|      | Andy Petree | 1 | 0 | 0 | 0 | 0 | 0 | 44,775 |
|      | Bill Davis | 10 | 0 | 0 | 0 | 0 | 0 | 503,085 |
|      | George Debidart | 1 | 0 | 0 | 0 | 0 | 0 | 240,635 |
| 2003 | Bill Davis | 36 | 0 | 0 | 1 | 3 | 0 | 2,480,492 |
| 2004 | Michael Waltrip | 4 | 0 | 0 | 0 | 2 | 0 | 304,420 |
|      | Teresa Earnhardt | 1 | 0 | 0 | 0 | 0 | 0 | 61,735 |
| **TOTALS** | | **305** | **0** | **6** | **27** | **72** | **3** | **$12,130,126** |

# Series champions

| Year | Car No. | Driver | Car owner | Car make | Wins | Poles | Money won |
|------|---------|--------|-----------|----------|------|-------|-----------|
| 1949 | 22 | Red Byron | Raymond Parks | Oldsmobile | 2 | 0 | $5,800 |
| 1950 | 60 | Bill Rexford | Julian Buesink | Oldsmobile | 1 | 0 | $6,175 |
| 1951 | 92 | Herb Thomas | Herb Thomas | Hudson | 7 | 4 | $18,200 |
| 1952 | 91 | Tim Flock | Ted Chester | Hudson | 8 | 4 | $20,210 |
| 1953 | 92 | Herb Thomas | Herb Thomas | Hudson | 11 | 10 | $27,300 |
| 1954 | 92 | — | Herb Thomas | Hudson | 12 | 8 | $27,540 |
| 1954 | 42 | Lee Petty | — | Chrysler | 7 | 3 | $26,706 |
| 1955 | 300 | Tim Flock | Carl Kiekhaefer | Chrysler | 18 | 19 | $33,750 |
| 1956 | 300B | Buck Baker | Carl Kiekhaefer | Chrysler | 14 | 12 | $29,790 |
| 1957 | 87 | Buck Baker | Buck Baker | Chevrolet | 10 | 5 | $24,712 |
| 1958 | 42 | Lee Petty | Petty Enterprises | Oldsmobile | 7 | 4 | $20,600 |
| 1959 | 42 | Lee Petty | Petty Enterprises | Plymouth | 10 | 2 | $45,570 |
| 1960 | 4 | Rex White | White-Clements | Chevrolet | 6 | 3 | $45,260 |
| 1961 | 11 | Ned Jarrett | W.G. Holloway Jr. | Chevrolet | 1 | 4 | $27,285 |
| 1962 | 8 | Joe Weatherly | Bud Moore | Pontiac | 9 | 6 | $56,110 |
| 1963 | 21 | — | Wood Brothers | Ford | 5 | 3 | $77,636 |
| 1963 | 8 | Joe Weatherly | — | Mercury | 3 | 6 | $58,110 |
| 1964 | 43 | Richard Petty | Petty Enterprises | Plymouth | 9 | 8 | $98,810 |
| 1965 | 11 | Ned Jarrett | Bondy Long | Ford | 13 | 9 | $77,966 |
| 1966 | 6 | David Pearson | Cotton Owens | Dodge | 14 | 7 | $59,205 |
| 1967 | 43 | Richard Petty | Petty Enterprises | Plymouth | 27 | 18 | $130,275 |
| 1968 | 17 | David Pearson | Holman-Moody | Ford | 16 | 12 | $118,842 |
| 1969 | 17 | David Pearson | Holman-Moody | Ford | 11 | 14 | $183,700 |
| 1970 | 71 | Bobby Isaac | Nord Krauskopf | Dodge | 11 | 13 | $121,470 |
| 1971 | 43 | Richard Petty | Petty Enterprises | Plymouth | 21 | 9 | $309,225 |
| 1972 | 43 | Richard Petty | Petty Enterprises | Plymouth | 8 | 3 | $227,015 |
| 1973 | 72 | Benny Parsons | L.G. DeWitt | Chevrolet | 1 | 0 | $114,345 |
| 1974 | 43 | Richard Petty | Petty Enterprises | Dodge | 10 | 7 | $299,175 |
| 1975 | 43 | Richard Petty | Petty Enterprises | Dodge | 13 | 3 | $378,865 |
| 1976 | 11 | Cale Yarborough | Junior Johnson | Chevrolet | 9 | 2 | $387,173 |
| 1977 | 11 | Cale Yarborough | Junior Johnson | Chevrolet | 9 | 3 | $477,499 |
| 1978 | 11 | Cale Yarborough | Junior Johnson | Oldsmobile | 10 | 8 | $530,751 |
| 1979 | 43 | Richard Petty | Petty Enterprises | Chevrolet | 5 | 1 | $531,292 |
| 1980 | 2 | Dale Earnhardt | Rod Osterlund | Chevrolet | 5 | 0 | $588,926 |
| 1981 | 11 | Darrell Waltrip | Junior Johnson | Buick | 12 | 11 | $693,342 |
| 1982 | 11 | Darrell Waltrip | Junior Johnson | Buick | 12 | 7 | $873,118 |
| 1983 | 22 | Bobby Allison | Bill Gardner | Buick | 6 | 0 | $828,355 |
| 1984 | 44 | Terry Labonte | Billy Hagan | Chevrolet | 2 | 2 | $713,010 |
| 1985 | 11 | Darrell Waltrip | Junior Johnson | Chevrolet | 3 | 4 | $1,318,735 |
| 1986 | 3 | Dale Earnhardt | Richard Childress | Chevrolet | 5 | 1 | $1,783,880 |
| 1987 | 3 | Dale Earnhardt | Richard Childress | Chevrolet | 11 | 1 | $2,099,243 |
| 1988 | 9 | Bill Elliott | Harry Melling | Ford | 6 | 6 | $1,574,639 |
| 1989 | 27 | Rusty Wallace | Raymond Beadle | Pontiac | 6 | 4 | $2,247,950 |
| 1990 | 3 | Dale Earnhardt | Richard Childress | Chevrolet | 9 | 4 | $3,083,056 |
| 1991 | 3 | Dale Earnhardt | Richard Childress | Chevrolet | 4 | 0 | $2,396,685 |
| 1992 | 7 | Alan Kulwicki | Alan Kulwicki | Ford | 2 | 6 | $2,322,561 |
| 1993 | 3 | Dale Earnhardt | Richard Childress | Chevrolet | 6 | 2 | $3,353,789 |
| 1994 | 3 | Dale Earnhardt | Richard Childress | Chevrolet | 4 | 2 | $3,400,733 |
| 1995 | 24 | Jeff Gordon | Rick Hendrick | Chevrolet | 7 | 8 | $4,347,343 |
| 1996 | 5 | Terry Labonte | Rick Hendrick | Chevrolet | 2 | 4 | $4,030,648 |
| 1997 | 24 | Jeff Gordon | Rick Hendrick | Chevrolet | 10 | 1 | $6,375,658 |
| 1998 | 24 | Jeff Gordon | Rick Hendrick | Chevrolet | 13 | 7 | $9,306,584 |
| 1999 | 88 | Dale Jarrett | Robert Yates | Ford | 4 | 0 | $6,649,596 |
| 2000 | 18 | Bobby Labonte | Joe Gibbs | Pontiac | 4 | 2 | $7,361,387 |
| 2001 | 24 | Jeff Gordon | Rick Hendrick | Chevrolet | 6 | 6 | $10,879,757 |
| 2002 | 20 | Tony Stewart | Joe Gibbs | Pontiac | 3 | 2 | $9,163,761 |
| 2003 | 17 | Matt Kenseth | Jack Roush | Ford | 1 | 2 | $9,422,764 |
| 2004 | 97 | Kurt Busch | Jack Roush | Ford | 3 | 1 | $9,677,543 |

**Note: In 1954 and 1963, the driver champion and car owner champion were on separate teams.**

# 97 Kurt Busch

**Car:** FORD • **Car owner:** Jack Roush
**Birth date:** 08/04/78 • **Hometown:** Las Vegas

## NASCAR NEXTEL CUP STATISTICS

**Seasons competed:** 2000-2004
**Career starts:** 150     **Career wins:** 11     **Career poles:** 3
**Championship season recap:** Homestead nearly left Busch heartbroken when a wheel fell off of the No. 97 in the season finale. But Busch entered the race 18 points ahead of Jimmie Johnson, and that proved to be enough cushion as Busch finished the 36th race of the season in fifth place. In the first Chase for the NASCAR NEXTEL Cup, consistency proved to be vital. Even though Johnson won four of the last 10 races, Busch's six top fives and nine top 10s in the final 10 races were unbeatable, and he was crowned the first champion of the NASCAR NEXTEL Cup era.

## CHAMPIONSHIP LINESCORE

| Starts | Wins | Poles | Top 5 | Top 10 | Races Led | Laps Led |
|---|---|---|---|---|---|---|
| 36 | 3 | 1 | 10 | 21 | 20 | 746 |

# Kurt Busch 2004 race by race

| No. | Race | Start | Finish | Points | Total points | Rank | Laps/ Completed | Money won | Status |
|---|---|---|---|---|---|---|---|---|---|
| 1 | Daytona 500 | 15 | 16 | 115 | 115 | 16 | 199/200 | $236,887 | Running |
| 2 | Subway 400 | 27 | 8 | 142 | 257 | 7 | 393/393 | $83,785 | Running |
| 3 | UAW-DaimlerChrysler 400 | 2 | 9 | 143 | 400 | 5 | 267/267 | $108,500 | Running |
| 4 | Golden Corral 500 | 20 | 12 | 127 | 527 | 6 | 325/325 | $78,950 | Running |
| 5 | Carolina Dodge Dealers 400 | 4 | 6 | 160 | 687 | 4 | 293/293 | $86,275 | Running |
| 6 | Food City 500 | 13 | 1 | 190 | 877 | 2 | 500/500 | $173,465 | Running |
| 7 | Samsung/RadioShack 500 | 12 | 6 | 155 | 1,032 | 1 | 334/334 | $147,050 | Running |
| 8 | Advance Auto Parts 500 | 7 | 11 | 130 | 1,162 | 2 | 500/500 | $80,100 | Running |
| 9 | Aaron's 499 | 22 | 36 | 60 | 1,222 | 4 | 82/188 | $82,875 | Accident |
| 10 | Auto Club 500 | 21 | 23 | 94 | 1,316 | 5 | 249/250 | $90,550 | Running |
| 11 | Chevy American Revolution 400 | 23 | 31 | 75 | 1,391 | 9 | 386/400 | $76,025 | Running |
| 12 | Coca-Cola 600 | 32 | 11 | 130 | 1,521 | 8 | 400/400 | $107,380 | Running |
| 13 | MBNA 400 'A Salute to Heroes' | 11 | 12 | 127 | 1,648 | 6 | 398/400 | $91,535 | Running |
| 14 | Pocono 500 | 27 | 5 | 155 | 1,803 | 7 | 200/200 | $95,600 | Running |
| 15 | DHL 400 | 7 | 11 | 130 | 1,933 | 8 | 200/200 | $85,705 | Running |
| 16 | Dodge/Save Mart 350 | 3 | 36 | 60 | 1,993 | 8 | 94/110 | $78,160 | Running |
| 17 | Pepsi 400 | 35 | 4 | 160 | 2,152 | 7 | 160/160 | $142,625 | Running |
| 18 | Tropicana 400 presented by Meijer | 21 | 35 | 58 | 2,211 | 9 | 151/267 | $84,600 | Running |
| 19 | Siemens 300 | 32 | 1 | 185 | 2,396 | 6 | 300/300 | $222,225 | Running |
| 20 | Pennsylvania 500 | 3 | 26 | 85 | 2,481 | 7 | 192/200 | $74,165 | Transmission |
| 21 | Brickyard 400 | 15 | 10 | 134 | 2,615 | 7 | 161/161 | $172,900 | Running |
| 22 | Sirius at The Glen | 7 | 10 | 139 | 2,754 | 7 | 90/90 | $81,140 | Running |
| 23 | GFS Marketplace 400 | 7 | 6 | 155 | 2,909 | 6 | 200/200 | $89,540 | Running |
| 24 | Sharpie 500 | 24 | 8 | 142 | 3,051 | 6 | 499/500 | $107,515 | Running |
| 25 | Pop Secret 500 | 4 | 11 | 135 | 3,186 | 7 | 250/250 | $108,425 | Running |
| 26 | Chevy Rock & Roll 400 | 17 | 15 | 123 | 3,309 | 7 | 399/400 | $80,830 | Running |
| 27 | Sylvania 300 | 7 | 1 | 190 | 5,210 | 2 | 300/300 | $237,225 | Running |
| 28 | MBNA America 400 | 13 | 5 | 160 | 5,370 | 2 | 400/400 | $99,745 | Running |
| 29 | EA Sports 500 | 8 | 5 | 160 | 5,530 | 1 | 188/188 | $104,290 | Running |
| 30 | Banquet 400 presented by ConAgra Foods | 22 | 6 | 155 | 5,685 | 1 | 267/267 | $91,825 | Running |
| 31 | UAW-GM Quality 500 | 21 | 4 | 165 | 5,850 | 1 | 334/334 | $110,250 | Running |
| 32 | Subway 500 | 7 | 5 | 165 | 6,015 | 1 | 500/500 | $107,175 | Running |
| 33 | Bass Pro Shops MBNA 500 | 22 | 42 | 37 | 6,052 | 1 | 51/325 | $84,790 | Engine |
| 34 | Checker Auto Parts 500 | 28 | 10 | 139 | 6,191 | 1 | 315/315 | $84,300 | Running |
| 35 | Mountain Dew Southern 500 | 1 | 6 | 155 | 6,346 | 1 | 367/367 | $103,275 | Running |
| 36 | Ford 400 | 1 | 5 | 160 | 6,506 | 1 | 271/271 | $130,650 | Running |

# Champion crew chiefs

1949: Red Vogt; 1950: Julian Buesink; 1951: Smokey Yunick; 1952: B.B. Blackburn; 1953: Smokey Yunick; 1954: Lee Petty; 1955: Carl Kiekhafer; 1956: Carl Kiekhafer; 1957: Bud Moore; 1958: Lee Petty; 1959: Lee Petty; 1960: Louis Clements; 1961: Bud Allman; 1962: Bud Moore; 1963: Bud Moore; 1964: Dale Inman; 1965: John Ervin; 1966: Cotton Owens; 1967: Dale Inman; 1968: Jake Elder; 1969: Jake Elder; 1970: Harry Hyde; 1971: Dale Inman; 1972: Dale Inman; 1973: Travis Carter; 1974: Dale Inman; 1975: Dale Inman; 1976: Herb Nab; 1977: Herb Nab; 1978: Tim Brewer/Travis Carter; 1979: Dale Inman; 1980: Doug Richert; 1981: Tim Brewer; 1982: Jeff Hammond; 1983: Gary Nelson; 1984: Dale Inman; 1985: Jeff Hammond; 1986: Kirk Shelmerdine; 1987: Kirk Shelmerdine; 1988: Ernie Elliott; 1989: Barry Dodson; 1990: Kirk Shelmerdine; 1991: Kirk Shelmerdine; 1992: Paul Andrews; 1993: Andy Petree; 1994: Andy Petree; 1995: Ray Evernham; 1996: Gary DeHart; 1997: Ray Evernham; 1998: Ray Evernham; 1999: Todd Parrott; 2000: Jimmy Makar; 2001: Robbie Loomis; 2002: Greg Zipadelli; 2003 Robbie Reiser; 2004 Jimmy Fennig.

# Champions and runners-up — Modern Era • Since 1972

| Year | Champion | Runner-up | Points Margin | Year | Champion | Runner-up | Points Margin |
|------|----------|-----------|--------------:|------|----------|-----------|--------------:|
| 1972 | Richard Petty | Bobby Allison | 127.90 | 1989 | Rusty Wallace | Dale Earnhardt | 12 |
| 1973 | Benny Parsons | Cale Yarborough | 67.15 | 1990 | Dale Earnhardt | Mark Martin | 26 |
| 1974 | Richard Petty | Cale Yarborough | 567.45 | 1991 | Dale Earnhardt | Ricky Rudd | 195 |
| *1975 | Richard Petty | Dave Marcis | 722 | 1992 | Alan Kulwicki | Bill Elliott | 10 |
| 1976 | Cale Yarborough | Richard Petty | 195 | 1993 | Dale Earnhardt | Rusty Wallace | 80 |
| 1977 | Cale Yarborough | Richard Petty | 386 | 1994 | Dale Earnhardt | Mark Martin | 444 |
| 1978 | Cale Yarborough | Bobby Allison | 474 | 1995 | Jeff Gordon | Dale Earnhardt | 34 |
| 1979 | Richard Petty | Darrell Waltrip | 11 | 1996 | Terry Labonte | Jeff Gordon | 37 |
| 1980 | Dale Earnhardt | Cale Yarborough | 19 | 1997 | Jeff Gordon | Dale Jarrett | 14 |
| 1981 | Darrell Waltrip | Bobby Allison | 53 | 1998 | Jeff Gordon | Mark Martin | 364 |
| 1982 | Darrell Waltrip | Bobby Allison | 72 | 1999 | Dale Jarrett | Bobby Labonte | 201 |
| 1983 | Bobby Allison | Darrell Waltrip | 47 | 2000 | Bobby Labonte | Dale Earnhardt | 265 |
| 1984 | Terry Labonte | Harry Gant | 65 | 2001 | Jeff Gordon | Tony Stewart | 349 |
| 1985 | Darrell Waltrip | Bill Elliott | 101 | 2002 | Tony Stewart | Mark Martin | 38 |
| 1986 | Dale Earnhardt | Darrell Waltrip | 288 | 2003 | Matt Kenseth | Jimmie Johnson | 90 |
| 1987 | Dale Earnhardt | Bill Elliott | 489 | ^2004 | Kurt Busch | Jimmie Johnson | 8 |
| 1988 | Bill Elliott | Rusty Wallace | 24 | | | | |

* Current point system instituted. ^Chase for the NASCAR NEXTEL Cup instituted.

# Top 10 closest championship points margins

| | Year | Champion | Runner-up | Points Margin | | Year | Champion | Runner-up | Points Margin |
|---|------|----------|-----------|--------------:|---|------|----------|-----------|--------------:|
| 1. | 2004 | Kurt Busch | Jimmie Johnson | 8 | 6. | 1980 | Dale Earnhardt | Cale Yarborough | 19 |
| 2. | 1992 | Alan Kulwicki | Bill Elliott | 10 | 7. | 1988 | Bill Elliott | Rusty Wallace | 24 |
| 3. | 1979 | Richard Petty | Darrell Waltrip | 11 | 8. | 1990 | Dale Earnhardt | Mark Martin | 26 |
| 4. | 1989 | Rusty Wallace | Dale Earnhardt | 12 | 9. | 1995 | Jeff Gordon | Dale Earnhardt | 34 |
| 5. | 1997 | Jeff Gordon | Dale Jarrett | 14 | 10. | 1996 | Terry Labonte | Jeff Gordon | 37 |

# Closest points battles — Modern Era • Since 1972

**Six races to go:** 1981—Darrell Waltrip leads Bobby Allison by two points.
**Five races to go:** 1985—Bill Elliott leads Darrell Waltrip by 23 points.
**Four races to go:** 1985—Darrell Waltrip leads Bill Elliott by 20 points.
**Three races to go:** 1996—Jeff Gordon leads Terry Labonte by one point.
**Two races to go:** 1979—Richard Petty leads Darrell Waltrip by eight points.
**One race to go:** 1979—Darrell Waltrip leads Richard Petty by two points.

# Bobby Allison

**Date of birth:** December 3, 1937.
**Hometown:** Hueytown, Ala.
**Years of competition:** 1961-88 (717 races).
**NASCAR Cup titles:** 1, 1983.
**Victories:** 84. **Poles:** 57. **Career earnings:** $7,102,233

**Personal:** Resides in Hueytown, Ala. ... Married (Judy). ... Career ended 13 races into the 1988 season because of injuries suffered in accident at Pocono Raceway. ... Son Davey Allison raced in NASCAR Cup division before his 1993 death in a helicopter crash. Son Clifford Allison raced in ARCA and the NASCAR Busch Series before his 1992 death in a crash at Michigan International Speedway, during Busch Series practice.

## CAREER HIGHLIGHTS

84 race victories third on all-time list (tied with Darrell Waltrip). ... Won Daytona 500 three times – 1978, '82, '88; in '88, son Davey Allison finished second. ... Brother Donnie Allison raced in NASCAR Winston Cup. ... Had best statistical season in 1972, driving for car owner Junior Johnson, winning 10 races, finishing second 12 times and taking 11 poles; finished second in series standings to Richard Petty. ... Member of NASCAR's famed "Alabama Gang." ... Inducted into International Motorsports Hall of Fame in 1993. ... Named one of NASCAR's 50 Greatest Drivers.

## CHAMPIONSHIP SEASON RECAP

Finished with six wins and 18 top fives in 30 starts. ... One of the most popular champions, who waited more than two decades to earn a series crown. ... Won $883,000 in his title campaign. ... Allison wrapped up the championship at Riverside, Calif., the season finale.

# Buck Baker

**Date of birth:** March 4, 1919.
**Hometown:** Charlotte.
**Years of competition:** 1949-76 (631 races).
**NASCAR Cup titles:** 2, 1956, 1957. **Victories:** 46. **Poles:** 44.
**Career earnings:** $325,570

**Personal:** Deceased April 14, 2002. ... Full name Elzie Wylie Baker. ... Son Buddy also was Winston Cup standout. ... Drove a bus before deciding to try auto racing, in 1939. ... Founded high-performance driving schools at Atlanta Motor Speedway, Bristol Motor Speedway, Darlington Raceway and North Carolina Speedway.

## CAREER HIGHLIGHTS

First driver to win consecutive NASCAR Cup titles. ... Finished second in NASCAR Cup point standings twice (1955, '58). ... Known for versatility.

Won races in NASCAR's Modified, Speedway, Grand American and NASCAR Cup circuits. … Career victory total of 46 is 13th-best all-time. … Inducted into International Motorsports Hall of Fame in 1990. … Named one of NASCAR's 50 Greatest Drivers.

## CHAMPIONSHIP SEASON RECAP

1956: Won first title driving for Carl Keikhaefer. … Finished with 14 wins and 39 top 10s in 48 starts. … Had $34,076 in race winnings. 1957: Won second title driving his own car. … Finished with 10 wins and 30 top fives in 40 starts. … Claimed $30,763 in race winnings.

# Red Byron

**Date of birth:** March 12, 1915.
**Hometown:** Anniston, Ala.
**Years of competition:** 1949-51 (15 races).
**NASCAR Cup titles:** 1. year, 1949. **Victories:** 2. **Poles:** 2.
**Career earnings:** $10,100

**Personal:** Deceased 11-7-60. … Real name was Robert. … Bomber tail-gunner during World War II. … Health problems led to early exit from racing.

## CAREER HIGHLIGHTS

First two-time NASCAR Cup champion. … Won first NASCAR-sanctioned race, in 1948, on the Daytona Beach road-beach course. … Was one of key early supporters of Bill France Sr.'s formation of NASCAR. … After retiring from stock car racing, became interested in sports cars; at the time of his death, was striving to develop an American car capable of winning the 24 Hours of LeMans. … Named one of NASCAR's 50 Greatest Drivers.

## CHAMPIONSHIP SEASON RECAP

1949: Season had only eight races and won the title on the strength of two wins and four top-five finishes overall in six starts. … Won $5,800 in race winnings. … Drove with a special brace fastened to the clutch to support his leg, which was wounded during World War II.

# Dale Earnhardt

**Date of birth:** April 29, 1951. **Hometown:** Kannapolis, N.C.
**Years of competition:** 1975-2001 (676 races).
**NASCAR Cup titles:** 7. years, 1980, 1986, 1987, 1990, 1991, 1993, 1994. **Victories:** 76. **Poles:** 22.
**Career earnings:** $41,742,384

**Personal:** Deceased February 18, 2001, in accident on last lap of Daytona 500. … Son Dale Jr. races in NASCAR Nextel Cup circuit. Son Kerry races in NASCAR Busch Series. … Father Ralph Earnhardt raced in Winston Cup. … Full name Ralph Dale Earnhardt. … Had two nicknames during career, "Ironhead" and "The Intimidator."

## CAREER HIGHLIGHTS

Co-holder of record for most NASCAR Cup championships with Richard Petty. … Victory total sixth-best all-time. … Second-leading all-time money winner in NASCAR Cup. … Won Daytona 500 in 1998; all-time leader in race victories at Daytona International Speedway, with 34. … Finished second in Winston Cup points three times, including 2000 season. … Named NASCAR's 2001 Most Popular Driver posthumously. … First NASCAR Cup start was in 1975 World 600 at Charlotte. Finished 22nd, one spot ahead of future car owner Richard Childress. … Named one of NASCAR's 50 Greatest Drivers.

## CHAMPIONSHIP SEASON RECAP

1980: Won first title driving for Rod Osterlund. … Won by mere 19 points over Cale Yarborough, the fifth-closest championship battle in history. … Finished with five wins and 24 top 10s in 31 starts. … Earned $671,990 in race winnings. 1986: Earned his second championship and first with owner Richard Childress. … Finished with five wins and 23 top 10s in 29 starts. … $1,768,879 in race winnings. 1987: Won back-to-back titles and third crown overall. … Clinched championship at Rockingham, three races from season's end. … Finished with 11 wins and 24 top 10s in 29 starts. … $2,069,243 in race winnings. 1990: Fourth title was controversial as runner-up Mark Martin forfeited 46 points earlier in the season because of a rules infraction. … Earnhardt's margin of victory for the title was 24 points. … Finished with nine wins and 18 top fives in 29 starts. … $3,308,056 in race winnings. 1991: Won consecutive titles for the second time in his career. … Finished with four wins and 21 top 10s in 29 starts. … $2,416,685 in race winnings. 1993: Clinched sixth title in final race of the year at Atlanta. … Finished with six wins and 21 top 10s in 30 starts. … $3,353,789 in prize money. 1994: Seventh title tied Richard Petty for most championships. … Third time in his career he posted consecutive series titles. … Won four races, including title-clincher at Rockingham.

# Tim Flock

**Date of birth:** May 11, 1924. **Hometown:** Fort Payne, Ala.
**Years of competition:** 1949-61 (189 races).
**NASCAR Cup titles:** 2, 1952, 1955. **Victories:** 40.
**Poles**: 39. **Career earnings:** $103,515

**Personal:** Deceased March 31, 1998. … Father Carl Flock was a tightrope walker. … Tim, brothers Bob and Fonty and sister Ethel all were in a race in the 1950s, the only time four siblings have been in the same Winston Cup race. Ethel finished ahead of her brothers.

## CAREER HIGHLIGHTS

Won 18 races in 1955, a single-season victory record that stood until Richard Petty won 27 in 1967. … Winning percentage of 21.2 (40 wins in 189 starts) is highest in NASCAR Cup history. … Won NASCAR's only sports car race, in 1955, driving a Mercedes-Benz 300 SL. … Occasionally drove with a monkey named Jocko Flocko as a "co-pilot." … Father was a daredevil. … Said "I always thought you could do both – win and have fun." … Inducted into International Motorsports Hall of Fame in 1991. … Named one of NASCAR's 50 Greatest Drivers.

## CHAMPIONSHIP SEASON RECAP

1952: Won first title driving Ted Chester's Hudson Hornet. … Finished with eight wins and 22 top fives in 33 starts. … $22,890 in race winnings. 1955: Won second title driving Carl Kiekhaefer's Chrysler. … Dominated with 18 wins in 38 races. … The 18 wins were a single-season victory record that stood until Richard Petty won 27 races in 1967. … $37,779 in race winnings.

# Bobby Isaac

**Date of birth:** August 1, 1932. **Hometown:** Catawba, N.C.
**Years of competition:** 1964-79 (308 races).
**NASCAR Cup titles:** 1, 1970. **Victories:** 37. **Poles:** 50.
**Career earnings:** $585,297

**Personal:** Deceased August 14, 1977. ... After parents died, quit school as teenager to work in a sawmill. ... Died after suffering a heart attack during a Late Model Sportsman race at Hickory (N.C.) Speedway.

## CAREER HIGHLIGHTS

Holds record for most poles in a season (20-1969). ... In 1964, his first full season, led every race entered. ... Won 11 races in championship season, driving futuristic-looking Dodge Daytonas. ... 50-pole total sixth-best all-time. ... Holds record for most poles in a season, with 20 in 1969. ... Set a then-record speed of 201.104 mph in a closed-course test at Talladega in 1970. ... Inducted into International Motorsports Hall of Fame in 1996. ... Named one of NASCAR's 50 Greatest Drivers.

## CHAMPIONSHIP SEASON RECAP

1970: Finished with 11 wins and 32 top-10 finishes in 47 starts. ... Won championship over Bobby Allison by only 51 points. ... Best known for his winged, orange No. 71 Dodge Daytona. ... $199,600 in race winnings.

# Ned Jarrett

**Date of birth:** March 27, 1940. **Hometown:** Newton, N.C.
**Years of competition:** 1953-66 (351 races).
**NASCAR Cup titles:** 2, 1961, 1965. **Victories:** 50. **Poles:** 35.
**Career earnings:** $289,146

**Personal:** Resides in Hickory, N.C. ... Married (Martha). ... Nicknamed "Gentleman Ned" during career. ... Since retiring, has become recognized as one of NASCAR's greatest ambassadors, and considered instrumental to NASCAR's growth via his television work. ... Son Dale competes in NEXTEL Cup, and won the series championship in 1999.

## CAREER HIGHLIGHTS

50 race victories 10th on all-time list (tied with Junior Johnson). ... 48 victories on short tracks; short-track victory total third-best all-time. ... Won total of 28 races during 1964 and '65 seasons. ... Became television commentator. ... Remembered for emotional call of son Dale Jarrett winning Daytona 500 in 1993. ... Inducted into International Motorsports Association Hall of Fame in 1991. ... Named one of NASCAR's 50 Greatest Drivers.

## CHAMPIONSHIP SEASON RECAP

1961: Won his first his championship driving a Chevrolet for B.G. Holloway. ... Finished with only one victory, but posted 34 top 10s in 46 starts. ... $41,055 in race winnings. 1965: Won second title driving for DuPont heir, Bondy Long. ... Finished with 13 wins and 42 top fives in 54 starts. ... Won the 1965 Southern 500 at Darlington by 14 laps, (17.5 miles), the largest margin of victory in NASCAR history. ... $93,624 in race winnings. ... Won title despite a back injury sustained at Greenville, S.C.

# Alan Kulwicki

**Date of birth:** December 14, 1954. **Hometown:** Greenfield, Wis.
**Years of competition:** 1985-93 (207 races).
**NASCAR Cup titles:** 1, 1992. **Victories:** 5. **Poles:** 24.
**Career earnings:** $5,059,052

**Personal:** Deceased April 1, 1993 in plane crash, en route to NASCAR Cup race at Bristol Motor Speedway. ... Held degree in mechanical engineering from the University of Wisconsin.

## CAREER HIGHLIGHTS

First Northern driver to win the NASCAR Cup title since New York's Bill Rexford in 1950. ... Won title by closest margin in series history, 10 points ahead of Bill Elliott. Was 278 points out of first place with six races remaining in season. ... Inducted into International Motorsports Hall of Fame in 2002. ... Named one of NASCAR's 50 Greatest Drivers.

## CHAMPIONSHIP SEASON RECAP

1992: Recorded just two wins during his championship season, but thrived on consistency with 17 top-10 finishes. ... $2,322,561 in race winnings. ... Although courted by top teams, always drove his own car.

# Benny Parsons

**Date of birth:** April 12, 1941. **Hometown:** Detroit.
**Years of competition:** 1970-88 (526 races).
**NASCAR Cup titles:** 1, 1973. **Victories:** 21. **Poles:** 20.
**Career earnings:** $3,926,539

**Personal:** Married (Terri). ... Resides in Concord, N.C. .... Avid golfer. ... Does television commentary for NASCAR events on NBC and TNT. ... Nicknamed the "Taxi Cab Driver from Detroit," for listing it as his occupation on race entry forms.

## CAREER HIGHLIGHTS

First driver to qualify a stock car at more than 200 mph (200.176), at 1982 Winston 500 at Talladega Superspeedway. ... Won 1975 Daytona 500. ... Finished second in Winston Cup standings twice (1955, '58). ... Finished in the top 10 in 283 of 526 events (54 percent) ... Inducted into International Motorsports Hall of Fame in 1994. ... Named one of NASCAR's 50 Greatest Drivers.

## CHAMPIONSHIP SEASON RECAP

1973: Finished with 21 top 10s in 28 starts. ... One of three drivers to win only one event during a championship season. ... Involved in one of NASCAR's most dramatic clinching scenarios. ... An early incident during the final race at Rockingham in 1973 seemed to dash his title

hopes, but several teams came to his aid and rebuilt his car for him to finish the race and clinch the championship. ... Won the title by 67 points over Cale Yarborough. ... Collected $182,321 in race winnings.

# David Pearson

**Date of birth:** December 22, 1934.
**Hometown:** Spartanburg, S.C.
**Years of competition:** 1960-86 (574 races).
**NASCAR Cup titles:** 3, 1966, 1968, 1969. **Victories:** 105.
**Poles:** 113. **Career earnings:** $2,482,596

**Personal:** Resides in Spartanburg, S.C. ... Nicknamed "The Silver Fox" during racing career. ... Son, Larry, is a former NASCAR Busch Series champion.

## CAREER HIGHLIGHTS

105 victories second-best total all-time. ... During 1968-69, had combined totals of 27 victories and 30 runner-up finishes. ... Won career-high 16 races in 1968. ... Won Daytona 500 only once, in 1976, but had six victories overall at Daytona International Speedway (tied for third all-time with Bobby Allison) via five Firecracker 400 victories. ... Drove for legendary Wood Brothers from 1972-79. ... Inducted into International Motorsports Hall of Fame in 1993. ... Named one of NASCAR's 50 Greatest Drivers.

## CHAMPIONSHIP SEASONS RECAP

1966: Won his first title driving a Cotton Owens Dodge. ... Finished with 15 victories and 33 top 10s in 42 races. ... $78,193 in race winnings. 1968: Won a career-high 16 races. ... Title came with Holman-Moody organization, his first of two in a row. ... Posted 36 top-five finishes in 47 starts. ... $133,064 in race winnings. 1969: Won his second consecutive title – and third overall – for Holman Moody. ... Finished with 11 wins and 42 top fives in 51 races. ... $229,760 in race winnings.

# Lee Petty

**Date of birth:** March 14, 1914. **Hometown:** Level Cross, N.C.
**Years of competition:** 1949-64 (429 races).
**NASCAR Cup: titles:** 3, 1954, 1958, 1959.
**Victories:** 54. **Poles:** 18. **Career earnings:** $209,780

**Personal:** Deceased April 5, 2000. ... Father of seven-time NASCAR Cup champion Richard Petty, grandfather of NEXTEL Cup driver Kyle Petty. ... Helped develop race car safety innovations such as roll bars and window webs.

## CAREER HIGHLIGHTS

First driver to win three Winston Cup titles. ... Won the first Daytona 500, edging Johnny Beauchamp in a photo finish; the result took three days to be determined. ... Upon retirement, 54 victories was best all-time total. Son Richard broke that record in 1964. Now tied for eighth all-time with Rusty Wallace. ... Inducted into International Motorsports Hall of Fame in 1990. ... Named one of NASCAR's 50 Greatest Drivers.

## CHAMPIONSHIP SEASONS RECAP

1954: Finished with seven wins and 32 top 10s in 34 starts. ... $21,101 in race winnings. 1958: Finished with seven wins and 44 top 10s in 50 starts. ... $26,565 in race winnings. Son Richard Petty began his driving career during father's second title season. 1959: Finished with 11 wins and 35 top 10s in 42 races. ... $49,219 in race winnings.

# Richard Petty

**Date of birth:** July 2, 1937. **Hometown:** Randleman, N.C. **Years of competition:** 1958-92 (1,177 races). **NASCAR Cup: titles:** 7, 1964, 1967, 1971, 1972, 1974, 1975, 1979. **Victories:** 200. **Poles:** 127. **Career earnings:** $7,755,409

**Personal:** Married (Lynda). ... Resides in Level Cross, N.C. ... Father Lee Petty won three NASCAR Winston Cup championships. ... Nicknamed "The King."

## CAREER HIGHLIGHTS

Co-holds record for most NASCAR Cup championships (7) with the late Dale Earnhardt. ... Holds records for most NASCAR Winston Cup victories (200), poles (127), victories in a season (27, 1967), consecutive victories (10, 1967) and starts (1,177). ... Last victory came in Firecracker 400 at Daytona International Speedway on July 4, 1984, with President Ronald Reagan in attendance. ... Won Daytona 500 a record seven times. ... Now heads multi-car Petty Enterprises team in NASCAR NEXTEL Cup Series, with son Kyle Petty as lead driver. ... Inducted into International Motorsports Hall of Fame in 1997. ... Named one of NASCAR's 50 Greatest Drivers.

## CHAMPIONSHIP SEASONS RECAP

1964: Finished with nine wins, 37 top fives and 43 top 10s in 61 starts. ... Won first Daytona 500, dominating with help from Chrysler's Hemi-head engine. 1967: Many consider this the greatest single-season performance in NASCAR history. ... Finished with 27 wins (including 10 in a row), and 38 top fives in 48 starts. ... Broke father Lee Petty's record for most career wins of 54 with a win at Darlington in May. 1971: Finished with 21 wins and 38 top fives in 46 starts. ... Captured third of seven Daytona 500 wins. Seven victories came on superspeedways. 1972: Finished with eight wins and 25 top fives in 31 starts. ... Won the first race – Riverside – while carrying the logo of his new sponsor, STP. Relationship between Petty and STP lasted nearly 30 seasons. 1974: Finished with 10 wins and 22 top fives in 30 races. ... Won fifth Daytona 500. 1975: Won the series title by a 722-point margin over runner-up Dave Marcis. ... Finished with 13 wins in 30 starts. ... Swept both races at Charlotte, North Wilkesboro and Bristol. 1979: Won seventh and final series title, a record that stood until the Dale Earnhardt tied it with his seventh title in 1994. ... Petty won his sixth Daytona 500 in an Oldsmobile, but drove a Chevrolet most of the season. ... Daytona 500 win was punctuated by a last-lap altercation between Cale Yarborough and Bobby Allison, an event generally regarded as a turning point in national television attention for NASCAR. ... Finished with five wins, the least amount in any of his championship seasons. ... Also had 23 top fives in 31 starts. ... Topped $500,000 in season winnings for the first time.

# Bill Rexford

**Date of birth:** March 14, 1927. **Hometown:** Conowango Valley, N.Y. **Years of competition:** 1949-53 (36 races). **NASCAR Cup: titles:** 1, 1950. **Victories:** 1. **Poles:** 1. **Career earnings:** $7,535

**Personal:** Deceased April 18, 1994. ... Stopped racing at the age of 26. ... Lived in California after retirement.

## CAREER HIGHLIGHTS

Youngest driver–23–to win the NASCAR Cup championship. ... Championship came in controversial manner; benefited from NASCAR penalizing Red Byron and Lee Petty (deducting points) for running in non-NASCAR events.

## CHAMPIONSHIP SEASON RECAP

1950: Finished with one win and 11 top 10s in 17 starts. ... Drove for New York car dealer Julian Buesink. ... $6,175 in race winnings.

# Herb Thomas

**Date of birth:** April 6, 1923. **Hometown:** Sanford, N.C. **Years of competition:** 1949-62 (230 races). **NASCAR Cup: titles:** 2, 1951, 1953. **Victories:** 48. **Poles:** 39. **Career earnings:** $126,570

**Personal:** Deceased August 8, 2000. ... Survived near-fatal racing accident in October, 1956 that curtailed career. ... After several comeback attempts, retired from racing, founded a trucking company and ran a sawmill.

## CAREER HIGHLIGHTS

First two-time NASCAR Cup champion. ... First three-time (1951, 1954, 1955) winner of the Southern 500. ... 48 career victories 12th-best total all-time. ... Series runner-up twice (1952, 1954). ... Inducted into International Motorsports Hall of Fame in 1994. ... Named one of NASCAR's 50 Greatest Drivers.

## CHAMPIONSHIP SEASON RECAP

1951: Finished with seven wins and 16 top fives in 33 races. ... $21,025 in race winnings. ... Drove a Hudson Hornet for owner Marshall Teague. 1953: Finished with 12 wins and 31 top 10s in 37 races. ... $28,909 in race winnings. ... Won second title driving a Hudson Hornet once again

# Darrell Waltrip

**Date of birth:** February 5, 1947. **Hometown:** Owensboro, Ky. **Years of competition:** 1972-2000 (809 races). **NASCAR Cup: titles:** 3, 1981, 1982, 1985. **Victories:** 84. **Poles:** 59. **Career earnings:** $19,416,618

**Personal:** Married (Stevie). ... Resides in Franklin, Tenn. ... Nicknamed "Jaws" during his career, because of outspoken demeanor. ... Younger brother Michael competes in NASCAR NEXTEL Cup.

## CAREER HIGHLIGHTS

84 career victories third all-time (tied with Bobby Allison). ... ... Won his three series titles driving for the legendary driver/owner Junior Johnson. ... Was first driver in a Tide-sponsored car. "Tide Machine" Chevrolet started one of NASCAR's longest-running and most well-known sponsorships ... Ended career-long frustration by finally winning Daytona 500 in 1989, driving Rick Hendrick-owned Chevrolet. ... Now works as television commentator on FOX Network's NASCAR NEXTEL Cup broadcasts. ... Named one of NASCAR's 50 Greatest Drivers.

## CHAMPIONSHIP SEASON RECAPS

1981: Finished with 12 wins and 21 top fives in 31 races. ... $799,134 in race winnings. ... Swept both races at Rockingham and Bristol. ... Won title by 67 points over Bobby Allison. 1982: Finished with 12 wins and 20 top 10s in 30 races. ... Swept both races at Nashville, Bristol, Talladega and North Wilkesboro. ... $923,150 in race winnings. 1985: Finished with three wins and 21 top 10s in 28 races. ... $1,318,374 in race winnings. .... Became first driver to win over $1million in a season.

# Joe Weatherly

**Date of birth:** May 29, 1922. **Hometown:** Norfolk, Va. **Years of competition:** 1960-64 (230 races). **NASCAR Cup: titles:** 2, 1962, 1963. **Victories:** 25. **Poles:** 19. **Career earnings:** $193,620

**Personal:** Deceased January 19, 1964, in racing accident at Riverside, Calif. ... One of first NASCAR "personalities" who attracted fans to the sport. ... Raced motorcycles before moving to stock cars. ... Nicknamed "Little Joe" and the "Clown Prince of Stock Car Racing" during his career.

## CAREER HIGHLIGHTS

One of six two-time Winston Cup champions. ... Accumulated 25 victories in only four seasons. ... Won 101 races in the 1952 and '53 seasons in NASCAR Modified division, winning division title in '53. ... From 1956-59 drove in NASCAR Convertible division. ... 1962 Winston Cup title was first for legendary car owner/crew chief Bud Moore. ... Inducted into International Motorsports Hall of Fame in 1994. ... Named one of NASCAR's 50 Greatest Drivers.

## CHAMPIONSHIP SEASON RECAP

1962: Finished with nine wins and 45 top 10s in 45 races. ... $70,742

in race winnings. ... Drove for owner Bud Moore. 1963: With no permanent ride, took the title by driving for a record nine different teams during the year. ... Finished with three wins in 53 starts. ... $74,623 in race winnings.

# Rex White

**Date of birth:** August 17, 1929. **Hometown:** Spartanburg, S.C. **Years of competition:** 1956-64 (233 races). **NASCAR Cup: titles:** 1, 1960. **Victories:** 28. **Poles:** 35. **Career earnings:** $190,283

**Personal:** Resides in Forest Park, Ga. ... Drove for a trucking company after leaving racing; retired in summer of 2001–at the age of 72. ... Often mistaken during his racing days for popular comedian George Gobel.

## CAREER HIGHLIGHTS

In championship season, finished 3,936 points ahead of runner-up Richard Petty. ... Career victory total of 28 is 20th-best all-time. ... Series runner-up in 1961. ... Finished in series standings top 10 in six of nine years. ... Consistency was hallmark of career. Finished in top five in 110 of 233 races; finished outside of the top 10 only 30 percent of the time. ... A short-track expert; only one victory came on a superspeedway, the 1962 Dixie 400 at Atlanta Motor Speedway. ... Named one of NASCAR's 50 Greatest Drivers.

## CHAMPIONSHIP SEASON RECAP

1960: Finished with six wins and 35 top 10s in 40 starts. ... Drove for his own team, becoming one of just five owner/drivers in history to capture the series championship. ... $57,524 in race winnings.

# Cale Yarborough

**Date of birth:** 3/27/40. **Hometown:** Sardis, S.C. **Years of competition:** 1957-88 (559 races). **NASCAR Cup titles:** 3, 1976, 1977, 1978. **Victories:** 83. **Poles:** 70. **Career earnings:** $5,003,616

**Personal:** Resides in Sardis, S.C. ... Married (Betty Jo). ... Full name William Caleb Yarborough. ... Runs car dealership in Florence, S.C.

## CAREER HIGHLIGHTS

83 race victories fifth-best total all-time. ... Only driver to win three consecutive NASCAR Cup championships. ... Finished second in series standings three times. ... Won Daytona 500 four times (1968, '77, '83, '84), second behind Richard Petty's seven victories. ... Tied with Buddy Baker and Bill Elliott for most Daytona 500 poles (four). ... Holds record for most poles overall at Daytona International Speedway (12). ... Inducted into International Motorsports Hall of Fame in 1993. ... Named one of NASCAR's 50 Greatest Drivers.

## CHAMPIONSHIP SEASONS RECAP

1976: Finished with nine wins and 22 top fives in 30 starts. ... $453,404 in race winnings. 1977: Finished with nine wins and 25 top fives in 30 starts. ... $561,641 in race winnings. 1978: Finished with 10 wins and 23 top fives in 30 races. ... $623,505 in race winnings.

# Davey Allison

**Date of birth:** February 25, 1961. **Hometown:** Hueytown, Ala. **Years of competition:** 1985-93 (191 races). **Victories:** 19. **Poles**: 14. **Career winnings:** $6,726,974

**Personal:** Deceased July 13, 1993 after a helicopter crash the day before in the Talladega Superspeedway infield. ... First job was sweeping floors at his father's auto shop, Bobby Allison Racing in Hueytown, Ala. ... Brother Clifford Allison raced in NASCAR until his death in a 1992 Busch Series practice crash at Michigan International Speedway. ... Father Bobby won the 1983 NASCAR Cup championship.

### CAREER HIGHLIGHTS

Helped popularize the No. 28 Texaco/Havoline-sponsored Ford among NASCAR fans. ... Finished second in 1988 Daytona 500 behind father Bobby. ... Won 1992 Daytona 500. ... 1987 Rookie of the Year, becoming first rookie to win two races. ... In 1987, became first rookie to qualify on front row (outside pole) for Daytona 500. ... Had 66 top-five finishes and 92 top-10 finishes. ... Inducted into International Motorsports Hall of Fame in 1998. ... Named one of NASCAR's 50 Greatest Drivers.

# Donnie Allison

**Date of birth:** September 7, 1939. **Hometown:** Hueytown, Ala. **Years of competition:** 1966-88 (241 races). **Victories:** 10. **Poles:** 17. **Career winnings:** $1,034,923

**Personal:** Resides Salisbury, N.C. ... Married (Pat). ... Original member of stock car racing's "Alabama Gang." ... Perhaps best remembered for his involvement in his and brother Bobby's nationally-televised fight with Cale Yarborough after the 1979 Daytona 500.

### CAREER HIGHLIGHTS

In 1970, won the World 600 on May 24 and six days later finished fourth in the Indianapolis 500, taking Indy Rookie of the Year honor. ... Career curtailed after accident in 1981 World 600. Competed in only 13 races from that point, with his final race at Michigan International Speedway in August, 1988. ... Had 115 top-10 finishes.

# Buddy Baker

**Date of birth:** January 25, 1941. **Hometown:** Charlotte, N.C. **Years of competition:** 1959-92 (698 races). **Victories:** 19. **Poles:** 40. **Career winnings:** $3,640,371

**Personal:** Resides in Sherrills Ford, N.C. ... At 6-6, one of tallest drivers in history. ... Nicknamed "Leadfoot" and the "Gentle Giant" during career. ... Did television race commentary after retiring from competition. ... Son of racing legend Buck Baker, who won NASCAR Cup titles in 1956 and 1957. ... Full name Elzie Wylie Baker Jr.

### CAREER HIGHLIGHTS

Won 1980 Daytona 500. ... Won consecutive (1972-73) World 600s. ... Average speed of 177.602 mph in winning Daytona 500 is still the race record, going into 2003 season. ... Finished career-high fifth in 1977 NASCAR Cup points. ... Inducted into International Motorsports Association Hall of Fame in 1997. ... Named one of NASCAR's 50 Greatest Drivers.

# Neil Bonnett

**Date of birth:** 7/30/46. **Hometown:** Bessemer, Ala. **Years of competition:** 1974-93 (363 races). **Victories:** 18. **Poles:** 20. **Career winnings:** $3,861,661

**Personal:** Deceased February 11, 1994 in accident at Daytona International Speedway, in practice for the Daytona 500. ... Original "Alabama Gang" member. ... Became television commentator in latter stages of racing career, and hosted his own race show on The Nashville Network. ... Was out of action for three years after April 1990 crash at Darlington Raceway. ... Full name Lawrence Neil Bonnett.

### CAREER HIGHLIGHTS

Won consecutive World 600s in 1982 and '83. ... Finished a career-high fourth in series points in 1985. .... Had 156 top-10 finishes. ... Won consecutive Busch Clash titles at Daytona International Speedway in 1983 and '84. ... Named one of NASCAR's 50 Greatest Drivers.

# Fonty Flock

**Date of birth:** 3/21/21. **Hometown:** Decatur, Ga. **Years of competition:** 1949-57 (154 races). **Victories:** 19. **Poles**: 33. **Career winnings:** $73,758

**Personal:** Deceased July 15, 1972. Full name Truman Fontello Flock. ... Younger brother Tim Flock won NASCAR Cup championship in 1952 and '55. ... Older brother Bob Flock made four NASCAR Cup starts between 1949-52. ... Sister Ethel also raced.

### CAREER HIGHLIGHTS

Biggest victory came in 1952 Southern 500. ... Finished a career-high second in series points in 1951. ... Had 20 runner-up finishes in career. ... Won Raleigh 300 in May 1953 after starting 43rd. ... In nine of his 19 victories, started on the pole.

# A.J. Foyt

**Date of birth:** January 16, 1935. **Hometown:** Houston.
**Years of competition:** 1963-94 (128 races). **Victories:** 7.
**Poles:** 10. **Career winnings:** $706,684

**Personal:** Resides in Hockley, Texas. ... Married (Lucy). ... Son Larry Foyt, a NASCAR Busch Series rookie in 2002, drove in the NASCAR Cup Series in 2003 and still drives part-time. ... Inducted into International Motorsports Hall of Fame in 2000.

## CAREER HIGHLIGHTS

Never raced more than seven times in a NASCAR Cup season; concentrated on legendary Indy-car career that included a record four Indianapolis 500 victories. ... Won 1971 Daytona 500; also won the Firecracker 400 at Daytona International Speedway in 1964 and 1965. ... Had six second-place finishes and four third-place finishes. ... Has fielded a NASCAR Cup car full-time or part-time since retiring from driving.

# Harry Gant

**Date of birth:** January 10, 1940. **Hometown:** Taylorsville, N.C.
**Years of competition:** 1973-94 (474 races). **Victories:** 18.
**Poles:** 17. **Career winnings:** $8,456,104

**Personal:** Resides in Taylorsville, N.C. ... Married (Peggy). ... Nicknamed "Handsome Harry" for years, then "Mr. September" after September 1991 run of four consecutive victories.

## CAREER HIGHLIGHTS

Runner-up in 1984 series championship standings. ... Won four consecutive races in September 1991 (Darlington, Richmond, Dover and Martinsville) en route to a career-best fourth-place finish in series standings. ... Three-time runner-up in NASCAR Busch Series standings (1969, '76, '77). ... Named one of NASCAR's 50 Greatest Drivers.

# Janet Guthrie

**Date of birth:** March 7, 1938. **Hometown:** Iowa City, Iowa.
**Years of competition:** 1976-78, 1980 (33 races).
**Victories:** None. **Poles:** 0. **Career winnings:** $75,309

**Personal:** Resides in Miami. ... Married (Warren Levene). ... Earned her pilot's license by age 17 and was able to fly more than 20 types of aircraft. ... Graduated from University of Michigan in 1960 with a degree in physics. ... Worked as aviation engineer and qualified for NASA astronaut program but was disqualified when a Ph.D. was subsequently made a requirement. ... Also served as a flight instructor.

## CAREER HIGHLIGHTS

In 1977, became first woman to qualify for the Daytona 500 and finished 12th; placed 11th in her only other appearance, in 1980. ... Only woman to lead a NASCAR Cup race (Ontario, 1977). ...Career-best finish was sixth at Bristol. ... Finished in the top 15 in 17 of her 33 career races with four top 10s. ... First woman to qualify for a Winston Cup race since Louise Smith in 1949 when she finished 15th at Charlotte in 1976. ... Did not succeed in her first attempt to become the first woman to qualify for the Indianapolis 500 in 1976 but did qualify in 1977 and had a career-best finish of ninth in 1978. ... Inducted into Women's Sports Hall of Fame in 1980.

# Ernie Irvan

**Date of birth:** January 13, 1959. **Hometown:** Salinas Calif.
**Years of competition:** 1987-99 (313 races). **Victories:** 15.
**Poles:** 22. **Career winnings:** $11,625,817

**Personal:** Resides in Mooresville, N.C. ... Married (Kim). ... Retired from racing in September 1999, after an August 20 accident at Michigan – five years to the day after his previous bad accident at the track. ... Fielding race team that competes in ARCA Series, with Kevin Conway driving.

## CAREER HIGHLIGHTS

Won 1991 Daytona 500 ... Finished career-best fifth in points, in 1991. ... Was polesitter in consecutive years (1997 and '98) for the Brickyard 400 at Indianapolis Motor Speedway. ... Made remarkable comeback from serious August 20, 1994 accident at Michigan International Speedway, returning to racing in October 1995 and finishing sixth at North Wilkesboro Speedway. ... Followed late Davey Allison as driver of popular No. 28 Texaco/Havoline Ford. ... Four of 15 career victories came in restrictor-plate events (two at Daytona International Speedway, two at Talladega Superspeedway). ... Named one of NASCAR's 50 Greatest Drivers.

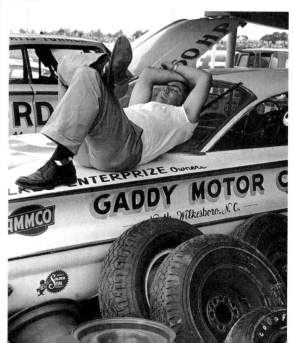

# Junior Johnson

**Date of birth:** June 28, 1931. **Hometown:** Ronda, N.C.
**Years of competition:** 1953-66 (313 races). **Victories:** 50.
**Poles:** 47. **Career winnings:** $275,910

**Personal:** Resides in Wilkesboro, N.C. ... Full name Robert Glenn Johnson. ... Married (Lisa).

**CAREER HIGHLIGHTS**

Won second annual Daytona 500 in 1960. ... Victory total ties for eighth (with Ned Jarrett) on all-time list. ... Pole total also eighth all-time. ... After retiring from driving, added to legend as car owner. His drivers won 132 races and six Winston Cup championships. ... Car owner victory total of 139, second all-time. ... Inducted into International Motorsports Hall of Fame in 1990. ... Named one of NASCAR's 50 Greatest Drivers.

# Fred Lorenzen

**Date of birth:** December 30, 1934. **Hometown:** Elmhurst, Ill.
**Years of competition:** 1956-72 (158 races). **Victories:** 26.
**Poles:** 33. **Career winnings:** $496,574

**Personal:** Resides in Oakwood, Ill. ... Immensely popular with fans. Had several nicknames, including "Golden Boy," "Fearless Freddie" and the "Elmhurst Express." ... Retired in 1967 at age of 33, became successful in real estate in his native Illinois.

**CAREER HIGHLIGHTS**

First NASCAR Cup driver to win more than $100,000 in a season, winning $113,570 in 1963. ... Won 1965 Daytona 500 in 1963. ... Won World 600 in 1965 after starting on the pole. ... Excelled especially at Martinsville Speedway, winning five of seven races there between 1963-66. ... Inducted into International Motorsports Hall of Fame in 1990. ... Named one of NASCAR's 50 Greatest Drivers.

# Tiny Lund

**Date of birth:** March 3, 1936. **Hometown:** Harlan, Iowa.
**Years of competition:** 1955-75 (303 races). **Victories:** 5.
**Poles:** 6. **Career winnings:** $185,703

**Personal:** Deceased August 17, 1975 in racing accident at Talladega Superspeedway. ... Full name DeWayne Louis Lund. ... Stature–6-5, 250 pounds–belied his nickname.

**CAREER HIGHLIGHTS**

Recorded one of the most dramatic victories in auto racing history at 1963 Daytona 500. During practice for race, rescued fellow driver Marvin

Panch from a burning car. Panch asked Lund to replace him in his Wood Brothers-owned Ford. Lund agreed and went on to win the race. Lund was awarded Carnegie Medal For Heroism, for saving Panch. ... Inducted into International Motorsports Hall of Fame in 1994. ... Named one of NASCAR's 50 Greatest Drivers.

# Dave Marcis

**Date of birth:** March 1, 1941. **Hometown:** Wausau, Wis.
**Years of competition:** 1968-2002, (882 races). **Victories:** 5.
**Poles:** 14. **Career winnings:** $7,349,818

**Personal:** Resides in Avery's Creek, N.C. ... Married (Helen). ... Retired from driving after the 2002 Daytona 500.

**CAREER HIGHLIGHTS**

An independent for most of his career, Marcis always chose to do things his way—from the shoestring budget he operated on as an owner/driver to the wing tips he preferred over state-of-the-art driving shoes. ... Had his best season driving Nord Krauskopf's No. 71 K&K Insurance Dodge in 1976, when he notched three of his five career victories and won seven poles. A victory in the Talladega 500, in which he finished 29.5 seconds ahead of Buddy Baker, was Marcis' first on a superspeedway. ... His best points finish was second, to Richard Petty, in 1975. Marcis had 16 top-five finishes that season.

# Hershel McGriff

**Date of birth:** 12/14/27. **Hometown:** Bridal Veil, Ore.
**Years of competition:** 1950-93 (86 races). **Victories:** 4.
**Poles:** 5. **Career winnings:** $130,190

**Personal:** Married (Sheri). ... Resides in Green Valley, Ariz.

**CAREER HIGHLIGHTS**

Had three stints in NASCAR Cup – 1950-54, 1971-78, 1980-93. ... Finished sixth in series standings in 1954, when he won four of the season's last nine races. ... Retired at end of 2001 season, in which he competed in NASCAR Winston West Series, at the age of 74. ... Finished 12th in his last race, at Irwindale Speedway. ... Named one of NASCAR's 50 Greatest Drivers.

# Tim Richmond

**Date of birth:** May 7, 1955. **Hometown:** Ashland, Ohio.
**Years of competition:** 1980-87 (185 races). **Victories:** 13.
**Poles:** 14. **Career winnings:** $2,310,018

**Personal:** Deceased August 13, 1989, from complications caused by Acquired Immune Deficiency Syndrome.

## CAREER HIGHLIGHTS

It's arguable that no other driver has made such an impression on NASCAR in such a short period. ... In 1986 season won a series-high seven races, finishing a career-high third in the series standings. ... Won 1986 Southern 500 after starting on the pole. ... Four victories came at Riverside International Raceway, including first career victory in 1982 and last career victory in 1987. ... Inducted into International Motorsports Hall of Fame in 2002. ... Named one of NASCAR's 50 Greatest Drivers.

# Fireball Roberts

**Date of birth:** January 20, 1929.
**Hometown:** Daytona Beach, Fla.
**Years of competition:** 1950-64 (207 races). **Victories:** 33.
**Poles:** 36. **Career winnings:** $290,309

**Personal:** Deceased July 2, 1964, 39 days after a fiery crash at Charlotte seven laps into the World 600 and is buried near Turn 3 at Daytona International Speedway in Daytona Memorial Park. ... Full name Edward Glenn Roberts; nicknamed "Fireball" from his days as a hard-throwing pitcher in high school. ... Thought of as one of NASCAR's smartest drivers, Roberts was one of the first to utilize a fitness regimen.

## CAREER HIGHLIGHTS

Perhaps the greatest driver never to win a NASCAR title and arguably stock car racing's first superstar, Roberts won some of NASCAR's most-famous events – the Daytona 500 (1962), the Southern 500 (1958, '63) and the Firecracker 400 (1963). ... Accumulated 93 top-five and 122 top-10 finishes along with 36 career poles. ... Was second in the points standings in his rookie season, and placed in the top 10 five other times. ... Despite running only 10 NASCAR races in 1958, Roberts still had six wins, one second and a third and finished 11th in points. ... Inducted into International Motorsports Hall of Fame in 1990. ... Named one of NASCAR's 50 Greatest Drivers in 1998.

# Wendell Scott

**Date of birth:** August 29, 1921. **Hometown:** Danville, Va.
**Years of competition:** 1961-1973 (495 races). **Victories:** 1.
**Poles:** 1. **Career winnings:** $180,629

**Personal:** Deceased December 22, 1990 ... Forced to end career due to a broken pelvis suffered in 1973 crash at Talladega Superspeedway. ... Former cab driver was an Army mechanic in World War II and ran his own garage upon his return from the war, fixing cars while perfecting his driving skills on Virginia tracks.

## CAREER HIGHLIGHTS

First African-American driver to compete in NASCAR Cup. ... Had 20 top-five and 147 top-10 finishes. ... Finished in the top 10 in championship

points four consecutive seasons with his best effort a sixth-place showing in 1966 ... Only victory came at Turkey Day 200 in 1964 at Jacksonville Speedway ... Inducted into the International Motorsports Hall of Fame in 1999.

# Curtis Turner

**Date of birth:** April 12, 1924. **Hometown:** Roanoke, Va.
**Years of competition:** 1949-68 (184 races). **Victories:** 17.
**Poles:** 17. **Career winnings:** $122,155

**Personal:** Deceased October 4, 1970, in airplane crash. ... *Sports Illustrated* called him the "Babe Ruth of Stock Car Racing."

## CAREER HIGHLIGHTS

Won fourth race of NASCAR's first season–1949. ... Had 73 top-10 finishes in 184 starts. ...Started on the pole in five of his victories. ... Inducted into International Motorsports Hall of Fame in 1992. ... Named one of NASCAR's 50 Greatest Drivers.

# LeeRoy Yarbrough

**Date of birth:** September 17, 1938.
**Hometown:** Jacksonville.
**Years of competition:** 1960-72 (198 races). **Victories:** 14.
**Poles:** 11. **Career winnings:** $450,329

**Personal:** Deceased December 7, 1984. ... His life away from racing was marked by personal problems; he died in a mental hospital.

## CAREER HIGHLIGHTS

Most successful season in 1969, with seven wins, all on superspeedways, also becoming first driver to win NASCAR's "Triple Crown" – the Daytona 500, the World 600 and the Southern 500 all in the same year. ... His seven superspeedway victories set the record for big track wins at the time. ... Also posted career highs with 16 top-five and 21 top-10 finishes that year. ... Accumulated 56 top-five finishes in addition to 92 top-10 efforts while averaging only 16.5 races per year. ... Also drove in three Indianapolis 500s. ... Named one of NASCAR's 50 Greatest Drivers in 1998.

# Don Arnold

**Resides:** Naples, Fla. **Years as NNCS Owner:** 1.
**Best points finish:** 37. **Career victories:** 0. **Career poles:** 0.

In his first year as a NASCAR NEXTEL Cup Series owner, Donald L. Arnold succeeded in qualifying the No. 50 car for 34 races in the 2004 season, even without the benefit of having the same sponsor or the same driver throughout the year. And Arnold Motorsports is growing in 2005, with driver Todd Bodine behind the wheel for a NASCAR Craftsman Truck Series team. Involved heavily in real estate and based in Naples, Fla., Arnold has developed, built and handled transactions involving villas in golf course communities and beachfront condominiums. The Arnold Companies include 18 corporations for which Arnold is the principal owner.

### CAREER NASCAR NEXTEL CUP SERIES STATS

| Year | Driver | Races | Won | Top 5 | Top 10 | DNF | Poles | Money Won |
|------|--------|-------|-----|-------|--------|-----|-------|-----------|
| 2004 | Todd Bodine | 11 | 0 | 0 | 0 | 9 | 0 | $710,413 |
| | Derrike Cope | 12 | 0 | 0 | 0 | 3 | 0 | $881,877 |
| | Jeff Fuller | 3 | 0 | 0 | 0 | 3 | 0 | $186,610 |
| | P.J. Jones | 5 | 0 | 0 | 0 | 4 | 0 | $293,704 |
| | Mike Wallace | 3 | 0 | 0 | 0 | 2 | 0 | $187,550 |
| **TOTALS** | | **34** | **0** | **0** | **0** | **21** | **0** | **$2,260,154** |

# Doug Bawel

**Date of birth:** 7/10/55. **Hometown:** Jasper, Ind.
**Resides:** Jasper, Ind. **Years as NNCS Owner:** 11.
**Best points finish:** 19. **Career victories:** 0. **Career poles:** 2.
**First pole:** 1994 Atlanta.

In 2004, Jasper Motorsports was acquired by Penske Racing, forming Penske-Jasper Racing. Doug Bawel remains one of seven owners; others include Roger Penske and John Erickson. Bawel is the president of Jasper Engines & Transmissions, the nation's leading remanufacturer of a diverse line of drive train components serving the automotive and truck aftermarket with remanufactured gas and diesel engines, transmissions, differentials and rear axle assemblies. Bawel has been involved with NASCAR for a decade, first fielding a NASCAR Cup Series team in 1994. In 2002, Dave Blaney was behind the wheel of the No. 77 and drove the team to its best points finish to date.

### CAREER NASCAR NEXTEL CUP SERIES STATS

| Year | Driver | Races | Won | Top 5 | Top 10 | DNF | Poles | Money Won |
|------|--------|-------|-----|-------|--------|-----|-------|-----------|
| 1994 | G. Sacks | 31 | 0 | 0 | 3 | 10 | 1 | $411,728 |
| | P.J. Jones | 1 | 0 | 0 | 0 | 1 | 0 | 6,085 |
| 1995 | B. Hillin Jr. | 18 | 0 | 0 | 1 | 4 | 0 | 241,520 |
| | D. Jones | 7 | 0 | 0 | 0 | 2 | 0 | 109,925 |
| 1996 | B. Hillin Jr. | 25 | 0 | 0 | 0 | 6 | 0 | 369,489 |
| 1997 | B. Hillin Jr. | 10 | 0 | 0 | 0 | 5 | 0 | 211,978 |
| | M. Shepherd | 5 | 0 | 0 | 0 | 0 | 0 | 84,475 |
| | R. Pressley | 7 | 0 | 0 | 0 | 3 | 0 | 103,810 |
| 1998 | R. Pressley | 30 | 0 | 1 | 1 | 7 | 0 | 996,721 |

| Year | Driver | Races | Won | Top 5 | Top 10 | DNF | Poles | Money Won |
|------|--------|-------|-----|-------|--------|-----|-------|-----------|
| | H. Stricklin | 1 | 0 | 0 | 0 | 0 | 0 | 20,265 |
| | T. Musgrave | 1 | 0 | 0 | 0 | 0 | 0 | 27,000 |
| 1999 | R. Pressley | 28 | 0 | 0 | 0 | 5 | 0 | 1,033,223 |
| 2000 | R. Pressley | 34 | 0 | 1 | 1 | 10 | 0 | 1,460,317 |
| 2001 | R. Pressley | 34 | 0 | 0 | 4 | 9 | 0 | 2,171,520 |
| | B. Said | 2 | 0 | 0 | 1 | 0 | 0 | 124,340 |
| 2002 | D. Blaney | 36 | 0 | 0 | 5 | 3 | 0 | 2,978,593 |
| | B. Said | 2 | 0 | 0 | 0 | 1 | 0 | 87,400 |
| 2003 | D. Blaney | 36 | 0 | 1 | 4 | 4 | 1 | 2,828,690 |
| 2004 | B. Gaughan | 36 | 0 | 1 | 4 | 8 | 0 | 2,884,502 |
| **TOTALS** | | **344** | **0** | **4** | **24** | **78** | **2** | **$16,151,581** |

\* Co-owner with D.K. Ulrich 1994 through Oct. 2, 1995
\*\* Co-owner with Mark Harrah and Mark Wallace since 19

# MB2/MBV Motorsports

**Owners:** Nelson Bowers, Tom Beard, Read Morton.
**Years as NNCS Ownership group:** 8. **Best points finish:** 15.
**Career victories:** 2. **First victory:** 2002 Rockingham.
**Career poles:** 18. **First pole:** 1998 Indianapolis.

MB2 Motorsports was founded in 1996 by Nelson Bowers, Tom Beard and Read Morton, all graduates of the University of Georgia. The organization's first season was 1997 and began as a one-car team with Derrike Cope as the driver. Ernie Irvan took over the ride in 1998 and provided the team with one of its first career highlights, capturing the pole position for the Brickyard 400 at Indianapolis Motor Speedway. MB2 expanded to a two-car team in the middle of 2000 with the addition of the Valvoline-sponsored No. 10 car. The architect of the team's expansion was MB2's CEO and general manager, Jay Frye, who negotiated an industry first—a sponsorship/ownership package with The Valvoline Company. Valvoline is not only the primary sponsor of the No. 10 Chevrolet but is also a 50 percent owner. The addition of the No. 10 Valvoline team created the MBV Motorsports banner. The first victory for MB2/MBV Motorsports came in November of 2002 when Johnny Benson claimed the win at North Carolina Speedway in Rockingham.

### CAREER NASCAR NEXTEL CUP SERIES STATS

| Year | Driver | Races | Won | Top 5 | Top 10 | DNF | Poles | Money Won |
|------|--------|-------|-----|-------|--------|-----|-------|-----------|
| 1997 | D. Cope | 31 | 0 | 1 | 1 | 6 | 0 | $707,404 |
| 1998 | E. Irvan | 30 | 0 | 0 | 11 | 3 | 3 | 1,600,452 |
| | R. Craven | 3 | 0 | 0 | 0 | 0 | 0 | 84,030 |
| 1999 | E. Irvan | 21 | 0 | 0 | 5 | 5 | 0 | 1,073,775 |
| | J. Nadeau | 12 | 0 | 0 | 0 | 2 | 0 | 450,775 |
| | D. Trickle | 1 | 0 | 0 | 0 | 0 | 0 | 27,620 |
| 2000 | K. Schrader | 34 | 0 | 0 | 2 | 2 | 0 | 1,711,476 |
| | J. Benson | 33 | 0 | 0 | 3 | 7 | 3 | 1,841,325 |
| 2001 | K. Schrader | 36 | 0 | 0 | 5 | 2 | 0 | 2,418,181 |
| | J. Benson | 36 | 0 | 0 | 6 | 14 | 8 | 2,894,903 |
| 2002 | K. Schrader | 36 | 0 | 0 | 0 | 9 | 0 | 2,460,140 |
| | J. Benson | 31 | 1 | 3 | 7 | 8 | 0 | 2,791,879 |
| | J. Nadeau | 3 | 0 | 0 | 0 | 0 | 0 | 275,681 |
| | J. Nemechek | 1 | 0 | 0 | 0 | 0 | 0 | 74,710 |
| | M. Wallace | 1 | 0 | 0 | 0 | 1 | 0 | 80,150 |
| 2003 | Mike Skinner | 11 | 0 | 0 | 0 | 2 | 1 | 945,373 |

## CAREER NASCAR NEXTEL CUP SERIES STATS • MB2/MBV Motorsports

| Year | Driver | Races | Won | Top 5 | Top 10 | DNF | Poles | Money Won |
|------|--------|-------|-----|-------|--------|-----|-------|-----------|
| | J. Nadeau | 10 | 0 | 1 | 1 | 3 | 0 | 861,628 |
| | Boris Said | 2 | 0 | 0 | 1 | 0 | 1 | 134,680 |
| | J. Benson | 36 | 0 | 2 | 4 | 7 | 0 | 3,411,790 |
| 2004 | J. Nemechek | 36 | 1 | 3 | 9 | 6 | 2 | 3,743,740 |
| | B. Said | 3 | 0 | 0 | 1 | 1 | 0 | 208,440 |
| **TOTALS** | | **422** | **2** | **10** | **56** | **78** | **18** | **$28,635,579** |

# Richard Childress

**Date of birth:** 9/21/45. **Hometown:** Winston-Salem, N.C.
**Resides:** Lexington, N.C. **Years as NNCS owner:** 30.
**Best points finish:** 1. **Career victories:** 76.
**First victory:** 1983 Riverside. **Career poles:** 33.
**First pole:** 1982 Martinsville.

Despite humble beginnings, Richard Childress Racing is now one of NASCAR's most formidable teams. Richard Childress was himself a driver, making his first start September 14, 1969 at Talladega. RCR was formed in 1972 when Childress competed as an owner/driver for the first time. At the start of 1976, Childress drove the famed No. 3 for the first time and drove it through the 20th race of the 1981 season. Childress, then 35 and a veteran of 285 starts, turned the wheel over to Dale Earnhardt on August 16, 1981 at Michigan. Earnhardt drove the final 11 races of the season before the pair temporarily parted. In 1982, Ricky Rudd scored RCR its first pole, and in 1983 its first win. Earnhardt and Childress paired up again in 1984, forming one of the most successful

partnerships in NASCAR history. Over the next 17 years, RCR recorded 67 wins and six NASCAR titles (Earnhardt won his first title in 1980 for Rod Osterlund). In 1995, RCR won the inaugural NASCAR Craftsman Truck Series title with driver Mike Skinner. When RCR became a two-car team in NASCAR's premier division in 1997, Skinner was the driver. In 2000, Childress began a two-car NASCAR Busch Series team with drivers Mike Dillon and Kevin Harvick. RCR was shaken dramatically on February 18, 2001, when Dale Earnhardt died in an accident on the last lap of the Daytona 500. The following week at Rockingham, RCR's famed No. 3 was changed to No. 29 with Harvick taking over and earning Raybestos Rookie of the Year honors for 2001. Harvick, working "double-duty" in NASCAR Cup and the NASCAR Busch Series, won the 2001 NASCAR Busch Series title. RCR fielded a third team for the first time in 2002. Driver Dave Blaney is the newest Cup driver in the Childress family for 2005.

## CAREER NASCAR NEXTEL CUP SERIES STATS

| Year | Driver | Races | Won | Top 5 | Top 10 | DNF | Poles | Money Won |
|------|--------|-------|-----|-------|--------|-----|-------|-----------|
| 1972 | R. Childress | 15 | 0 | 0 | 0 | 12 | 0 | $7,245 |
| 1976 | R. Childress | 30 | 0 | 0 | 11 | 9 | 0 | 85,780 |
| 1977 | R. Childress | 30 | 0 | 0 | 11 | 9 | 0 | 97,012 |
| 1978 | R. Childress | 30 | 0 | 1 | 12 | 4 | 0 | 108,106 |
| 1979 | R. Childress | 31 | 0 | 1 | 10 | 5 | 0 | 132,922 |
| 1980 | R. Childress | 31 | 0 | 0 | 10 | 4 | 0 | 157,420 |
| 1981 | R. Childress | 20 | 0 | 1 | 1 | 7 | 0 | 70,665 |
| | D. Earnhardt | 11 | 0 | 2 | 6 | 4 | 0 | 92,728 |
| 1982 | R. Rudd | 30 | 0 | 6 | 13 | 13 | 2 | 211,130 |
| 1983 | R. Rudd | 30 | 2 | 7 | 14 | 9 | 4 | 267,585 |
| 1984 | D. Earnhardt | 30 | 2 | 12 | 22 | 2 | 0 | 616,788 |
| 1985 | D. Earnhardt | 28 | 4 | 10 | 16 | 9 | 1 | 546,596 |
| 1986 | D. Earnhardt | 29 | 5 | 16 | 23 | 4 | 1 | 1,783,880 |
| 1987 | D. Earnhardt | 29 | 11 | 21 | 24 | 2 | 1 | 2,099,243 |

**Richard Childress (left) visits with Paul Newman at the opening of the Victory Junction Gang camp.**

| Year | Driver | Races | Won | Top 5 | Top 10 | DNF | Poles | Money Won |
|---|---|---|---|---|---|---|---|---|
| 1988 | D. Earnhardt | 29 | 3 | 13 | 19 | 1 | 0 | 1,214,089 |
|  | R. Combs | 1 | 0 | 0 | 0 | 1 | 0 | 1,500 |
| 1989 | D. Earnhardt | 29 | 5 | 14 | 19 | 2 | 0 | 1,435,730 |
|  | J. Hensley | 0 | 0 | 0 | 0 | 0 | 1 | 0 |
| 1990 | D. Earnhardt | 29 | 9 | 18 | 23 | 1 | 4 | 3,083,056 |
| 1991 | D. Earnhardt | 29 | 4 | 14 | 21 | 2 | 0 | 2,396,685 |
| 1992 | D. Earnhardt | 29 | 1 | 6 | 15 | 4 | 1 | 915,463 |
| 1993 | D. Earnhardt | 30 | 6 | 17 | 21 | 2 | 2 | 3,353,789 |
|  | N. Bonnett | 2 | 0 | 0 | 0 | 2 | 0 | 14,515 |
| 1994 | D. Earnhardt | 31 | 4 | 20 | 25 | 3 | 2 | 3,300,733 |
| 1995 | D. Earnhardt | 31 | 5 | 19 | 23 | 2 | 3 | 3,154,241 |
| 1996 | D. Earnhardt | 31 | 2 | 13 | 17 | 2 | 2 | 2,285,926 |
|  | M. Skinner | 5 | 0 | 0 | 0 | 1 | 0 | 65,850 |
| 1997 | D. Earnhardt | 32 | 0 | 7 | 16 | 0 | 0 | 2,151,909 |
|  | M. Skinner | 31 | 0 | 0 | 3 | 7 | 2 | 900,569 |
| 1998 | D. Earnhardt | 33 | 1 | 5 | 13 | 3 | 0 | 2,990,749 |
|  | M. Skinner | 30 | 0 | 4 | 9 | 3 | 0 | 1,518,901 |
|  | M. Shepherd | 2 | 0 | 0 | 0 | 1 | 0 | 50,140 |
|  | M. Dillon | 1 | 0 | 0 | 0 | 0 | 0 | 28,050 |
| 1999 | D. Earnhardt | 34 | 3 | 7 | 21 | 3 | 0 | 3,149,536 |
|  | M. Skinner | 34 | 0 | 0 | 9 | 1 | 2 | 2,499,877 |
| 2000 | D. Earnhardt | 34 | 2 | 13 | 24 | 0 | 0 | 4,918,886 |
|  | M. Skinner | 34 | 0 | 1 | 11 | 2 | 1 | 2,205,320 |
| 2001 | D. Earnhardt | 1 | 0 | 0 | 0 | 1 | 0 | 293,833 |
|  | M. Skinner | 23 | 0 | 0 | 1 | 4 | 0 | 1,921,186 |
|  | K. Harvick | 35 | 2 | 6 | 16 | 1 | 0 | 4,302,202 |
|  | J. Green | 8 | 0 | 0 | 1 | 3 | 1 | 441,449 |
|  | R. Gordon | 10 | 1 | 1 | 2 | 1 | 0 | 917,020 |
| 2002 | J. Green | 36 | 0 | 4 | 6 | 2 | 0 | 2,531,339 |
|  | R. Gordon | 36 | 0 | 1 | 5 | 4 | 0 | 3,342,703 |
|  | K. Harvick | 35 | 1 | 5 | 8 | 6 | 1 | 3,849,216 |
|  | K. Wallace | 1 | 0 | 0 | 0 | 0 | 0 | 85,567 |
| 2003 | K. Harvick | 36 | 1 | 11 | 18 | 0 | 1 | 4,994,250 |
|  | Robby Gordon | 36 | 2 | 4 | 10 | 2 | 0 | 3,705,320 |
|  | Steve Park | 24 | 0 | 1 | 3 | 3 | 1 | 1,653,708 |
|  | R. Hornaday | 1 | 0 | 0 | 0 | 0 | 0 | 48,950 |
| 2004 | Dave Blaney | 8 | 0 | 0 | 0 | 1 | 0 | 639,765 |
|  | Jeff Burton | 14 | 0 | 1 | 3 | 1 | 0 | 1,143,770 |
|  | Kerry Earnhardt | 3 | 0 | 0 | 0 | 0 | 0 | 194,705 |
|  | Robby Gordon | 36 | 0 | 2 | 6 | 3 | 0 | 3,844,558 |
|  | Kevin Harvick | 36 | 0 | 5 | 14 | 4 | 0 | 4,545,434 |
|  | Jim Inglebright | 1 | 0 | 0 | 0 | 0 | 0 | 70,550 |
|  | Johnny Sauter | 13 | 0 | 0 | 0 | 1 | 0 | 1,116,167 |
|  | Mike Skinner | 1 | 0 | 0 | 0 | 1 | 0 | 213,813 |
| **TOTALS** |  | **1309** | **76** | **289** | **555** | **174** | **33** | **$87,768,119** |

he fielded a part-time entry for Martin before hiring Jeff Gordon to run a full-time schedule in 1991. Davis joined NASCAR's premier series in 1993 with driver Bobby Labonte. Davis' teams have 88 top 10 finishes and have over $25 million in race winnings. Frank Stoddard joined Bill Davis Racing in 2002 with just seven races remaining. In six years as a crew chief, the New Hampshire native has 14 victories.

## CAREER NASCAR NEXTEL CUP SERIES STATS

| Year | Driver | Races | Won | Top 5 | Top 10 | DNF | Poles | Money Won |
|---|---|---|---|---|---|---|---|---|
| 1993 | B. Labonte | 30 | 0 | 0 | 6 | 6 | 1 | $395,660 |
| 1994 | B. Labonte | 31 | 0 | 1 | 1 | 7 | 0 | 550,305 |
| 1995 | R. LaJoie | 13 | 0 | 0 | 0 | 3 | 0 | 265,770 |
|  | J. Hensley | 5 | 0 | 0 | 0 | 2 | 0 | 129,595 |
|  | W. Dallenbach | 1 | 0 | 1 | 1 | 0 | 0 | 54,140 |
|  | W. Burton | 9 | 1 | 3 | 4 | 2 | 0 | 300,325 |
| 1996 | W. Burton | 27 | 0 | 0 | 4 | 10 | 1 | 873,619 |
| 1997 | W. Burton | 31 | 0 | 0 | 7 | 7 | 1 | 1,004,944 |
| 1998 | W. Burton | 33 | 0 | 1 | 5 | 4 | 2 | 1,516,183 |
| 1999 | W. Burton | 34 | 0 | 6 | 16 | 3 | 1 | 2,405,913 |
|  | D. Blaney | 5 | 0 | 0 | 0 | 2 | 0 | 212,170 |
| 2000 | W. Burton | 34 | 1 | 4 | 17 | 4 | 0 | 2,699,604 |
|  | D. Blaney | 33 | 0 | 0 | 2 | 7 | 0 | 1,272,689 |
| 2001 | W. Burton | 36 | 1 | 7 | 11 | 9 | 0 | 3,583,692 |
|  | D. Blaney | 36 | 0 | 0 | 6 | 6 | 0 | 1,827,896 |
| 2002 | W. Burton | 36 | 2 | 3 | 8 | 9 | 1 | 4,899,884 |
|  | K. Wallace | 10 | 0 | 0 | 0 | 0 | 0 | 503,085 |
|  | H. Stricklin | 22 | 0 | 0 | 0 | 5 | 0 | 1,313,548 |
|  | S. Wimmer | 3 | 0 | 0 | 0 | 2 | 0 | 143,110 |
|  | T. Hubert | 1 | 0 | 0 | 0 | 0 | 0 | 41,925 |
|  | G. Bodine | 1 | 0 | 0 | 0 | 0 | 0 | 35,615 |
| 2003 | K. Wallace | 36 | 0 | 0 | 1 | 5 | 0 | 2,480,490 |
|  | W. Burton | 32 | 0 | 0 | 4 | 4 | 0 | 3,280,950 |
|  | S. Wimmer | 6 | 0 | 0 | 1 | 0 | 0 | 479,504 |
| 2004 | D. Blaney | 6 | 0 | 0 | 0 | 0 | 0 | 604,632 |
|  | S. Hmiel | 5 | 0 | 0 | 0 | 0 | 0 | 327,785 |
|  | T. Raines | 1 | 0 | 0 | 0 | 0 | 0 | 121,730 |
|  | S. Wimmer | 35 | 0 | 1 | 2 | 0 | 0 | 3,622,391 |
| **TOTALS** |  | **552** | **5** | **27** | **96** | **97** | **7** | **$34,947,154** |

# Dale Earnhardt Inc.

**Owner:** Teresa Earnhardt. **Hometown:** Conover, N.C.
**Resides:** Mooresville, N.C. **Years as NNCS owner:** 9.
**Best points finish:** 3. **Career victories:** 21.
**First victory:** 2000 Texas. **Career poles:** 9.
**First pole:** 2000 Bristol.

# Bill Davis

**Date of birth:** 1/18/51. **Hometown:** Little Rock, Ark.
**Resides:** High Point, N.C. **Years as NNCS owner:** 11.
**Best points finish:** 9. **Career victories:** 5.
**First victory:** 1995 Rockingham. **Career poles:** 7.
**First pole:** 1993 Richmond.

Bill Davis became interested in racing through long-time friend Julian Martin, whose son, Mark, was pursuing a racing career in the sport in the 1980s. Davis built an ASA car for Mark Martin to drive in the Midwest in 1987, and the relationship continued the following year even though Martin landed a ride with owner Jack Roush in NASCAR's top series. Davis began concentrating on the NASCAR Busch Series in 1988, where

Dale Earnhardt Inc., which has captured championships in both the NASCAR Busch Series and NASCAR Craftsman Truck Series, has been making its mark in NASCAR's premier series in recent seasons. DEI, guided by Teresa Earnhardt, the widow of the late seven-time series champion Dale Earnhardt, began in 1996 with a limited three-race schedule but has grown since those early roots. DEI ran Steve Park as its first full-season entry in 1999, the same season Dale Earnhardt Jr. made his first five career starts for the team as he was locking up his second consecutive NASCAR Busch Series championship. The 2000 season marked a key time of growth for the organization as it ran Park and Earnhardt Jr. as a two-car, full-season operation, and they responded with three wins and four poles. DEI reached another milestone in 2003 as Dale Earnhardt Jr. finished third in the standings, marking the first time one of the team's drivers has finished among the top 10. DEI's 2005 NASCAR NEXTEL Cup plans include bringing NASCAR Busch Series champion Martin Truex Jr. in for up to seven races, getting him ready for a full-time Cup ride in 2006.

## CAREER NASCAR NEXTEL CUP SERIES STATS • Dale Earnhardt Inc.

| Year | Driver | Races | Won | Top 5 | Top 10 | DNF | Poles | Money Won |
|---|---|---|---|---|---|---|---|---|
| 1996 | J. Green | 2 | 0 | 0 | 0 | 2 | 0 | $16,835 |
| | R. Gordon | 1 | 0 | 0 | 0 | 1 | 0 | 4,800 |
| 1997 | S. Park | 4 | 0 | 0 | 0 | 1 | 0 | 60,405 |
| 1998 | S. Park | 17 | 0 | 0 | 0 | 5 | 0 | 487,265 |
| | D. Waltrip | 13 | 0 | 1 | 2 | 2 | 0 | 398,615 |
| 1999 | S. Park | 34 | 0 | 0 | 5 | 4 | 0 | 1,767,690 |
| | D. Earnhardt Jr. | 5 | 0 | 0 | 1 | 1 | 0 | 162,095 |
| 2000 | S. Park | 34 | 1 | 6 | 13 | 4 | 2 | 2,283,629 |
| | D. Earnhardt Jr. | 34 | 2 | 3 | 5 | 7 | 2 | 2,801,880 |
| 2001 | S. Park | 24 | 1 | 5 | 12 | 2 | 0 | 2,495,490 |
| | D. Earnhardt Jr. | 36 | 3 | 9 | 15 | 4 | 2 | 5,827,542 |
| | M. Waltrip | 36 | 1 | 3 | 3 | 6 | 0 | 3,411,644 |
| | K. Wallace | 12 | 0 | 1 | 2 | 1 | 1 | 965,030 |
| 2002 | D. Earnhardt Jr. | 36 | 2 | 11 | 16 | 3 | 2 | 4,970,034 |
| | M. Waltrip | 36 | 1 | 4 | 10 | 4 | 0 | 3,185,969 |
| | S. Park | 32 | 0 | 0 | 2 | 5 | 0 | 2,681,594 |
| | K. Wallace | 4 | 0 | 0 | 1 | 0 | 0 | 454,060 |
| 2003 | D. Earnhardt Jr. | 36 | 2 | 13 | 21 | 4 | 0 | 4,923,500 |
| | M. Waltrip | 36 | 2 | 8 | 11 | 6 | 0 | 4,463,840 |
| | J. Andretti | 11 | 0 | 0 | 0 | 1 | 0 | 886,729 |
| | R. Fellows | 2 | 0 | 0 | 1 | 1 | 0 | 161,854 |
| | J. Keller | 2 | 0 | 0 | 0 | 0 | 0 | 128,007 |
| 2004 | J. Andretti | 5 | 0 | 0 | 0 | 1 | 0 | 519,261 |
| | D. Earnhardt Jr. | 36 | 6 | 16 | 21 | 4 | 0 | 6,859,802 |
| | Ron Fellows | 1 | 0 | 1 | 1 | 0 | 0 | 101,260 |
| | Martin Truex Jr. | 2 | 0 | 0 | 0 | 2 | 0 | 116,150 |
| | Kenny Wallace | 1 | 0 | 0 | 0 | 0 | 0 | 61,735 |
| | Michael Waltrip | 36 | 0 | 2 | 9 | 6 | 0 | 4,064,232 |
| **TOTALS** | | **528** | **21** | **83** | **141** | **177** | **9** | **$50,260,947** |

## CAREER NASCAR NEXTEL CUP SERIES STATS

| Year | Driver | Races | Won | Top 5 | Top 10 | DNF | Poles | Money Won |
|---|---|---|---|---|---|---|---|---|
| 1989 | D. Johnson | 4 | 0 | 0 | 0 | 1 | 0 | $11,515 |
| 1990 | D. Johnson | 3 | 0 | 0 | 0 | 3 | 0 | 10,550 |
| | Jim Sauter | 1 | 0 | 0 | 0 | 0 | 0 | 3,925 |
| 2000 | C. Atwood | 3 | 0 | 0 | 1 | 0 | 0 | 97,030 |
| 2001 | C. Atwood | 35 | 0 | 1 | 3 | 6 | 1 | 1,797,111 |
| | B. Elliott | 36 | 1 | 5 | 9 | 2 | 2 | 3,618,017 |
| 2002 | B. Elliott | 36 | 2 | 6 | 13 | 4 | 4 | 4,122,699 |
| | J. Mayfield | 36 | 0 | 2 | 4 | 7 | 0 | 2,494,583 |
| | C. Atwood | 1 | 0 | 0 | 0 | 0 | 0 | 37,175 |
| | H. Parker Jr. | 1 | 0 | 0 | 0 | 0 | 0 | 39,325 |
| 2003 | Bill Elliott | 36 | 1 | 9 | 12 | 2 | 0 | 4,321,190 |
| | J. Mayfield | 36 | 0 | 4 | 12 | 6 | 1 | 2,962,230 |
| | C. Atwood | 2 | 0 | 0 | 0 | 1 | 0 | 149,838 |
| 2004 | B. Elliott | 5 | 0 | 0 | 1 | 1 | 0 | 453,475 |
| | K. Kahne | 36 | 0 | 13 | 14 | 7 | 4 | 4,647,947 |
| | J. Mayfield | 36 | 1 | 5 | 13 | 3 | 2 | 3,784,174 |
| **TOTALS** | | **307** | **5** | **45** | **82** | **43** | **14** | **$28,550,784** |

# James Finch

**Date of birth:** 6/16/50. **Hometown:** Lynn Haven, Fla.
**Resides:** Lynn Haven, Fla. **Years as NNCS owner:** 2.
**Best points finish:** 36. **Career victories:** 0. **Career poles:** 0.

A Florida native, one of Finch's driving goals has been to field a car in the nearby Daytona and Talladega Cup races. He achieved that goal in 2004, with the No. 50 car running in both races at Daytona and the spring race at Talladega. Finch's race shop in Lynn Haven, Fla., keeps him near home, too.

## CAREER NASCAR NEXTEL CUP SERIES STATS

| Year | Driver | Races | Won | Top 5 | Top 10 | DNF | Poles | Money Won |
|---|---|---|---|---|---|---|---|---|
| 2003 | M. Wallace | 14 | 0 | 0 | 2 | 3 | 0 | $1,031,100 |
| 2004 | J. Ruttman | 7 | 0 | 0 | 0 | 7 | 0 | $399,093 |
| | B. Hamilton Jr. | 6 | 0 | 0 | 0 | 4 | 0 | $379,665 |
| | T. Raines | 1 | 0 | 0 | 0 | 1 | 0 | $60,025 |
| | S. Pruett | 1 | 0 | 0 | 0 | 1 | 0 | $116,215 |
| | M. Wallace | 4 | 0 | 0 | 1 | 1 | 0 | $279,420 |
| | J. Sauter | 3 | 0 | 0 | 0 | 1 | 0 | $169,255 |
| **TOTALS** | | **36** | **0** | **0** | **1** | **18** | **0** | **$2,434,773** |

# Ray Evernham

**Date of birth:** 8/26/57. **Hometown:** Hazlet, N.J.
**Resides:** Cornelius, N.C. **Years as NNCS owner:** 7.
**Best points finish:** 9. **Career victories:** 5.
**First victory:** 2001 Homestead-Miami. **Career poles:** 14.
**First pole:** 2001 Daytona.

Evernham earned three series championships and 47 career wins as crew chief for Jeff Gordon, but yearned for another challenge. It came with the formation of Evernham Motorsports and a 500-day countdown to Dodge's return to the sport beginning with the 2001 Daytona 500. He would field a two-car team and coupled veteran Bill Elliott with talented youngster Casey Atwood. Evernham Motorsports and Dodge made a huge splash in its return as Elliott won the pole for the season-opening Daytona 500 in 2001. Elliott landed the organization's first victory at Homestead-Miami Speedway. The 2002 season was a year of change as Jeremy Mayfield replaced Atwood and the organization added a new 50,000 square-foot facility to its Statesville, N.C., race complex that would serve as a new base of operations for Dodge's tech center. On the track, Elliott posted two wins and four poles, which were season bests for the organization. In 2003, Elliott finished ninth in the championship, marking the first time Evernham Motorsports has cracked the top 10. At the close of the season, Elliott announced he would run a limited schedule in 2004 and serve as a mentor to rising star Kasey Kahne, who showed that he learned something from the legacy of Elliott as far as qualifying is concerned. Kahne racked up four poles in his rookie season.

# Chip Ganassi Racing
## with Felix Sabates

**Owners:** Chip Ganassi, Felix Sabates. **Years as NNCS owner:** 5.
**Best points finish:** 3. **Career victories:** 5.
**First victory:** 2001 Michigan. **Career poles:** 5.
**First pole:** 2001 Daytona.

Chip Ganassi, one of the most successful owners in open-wheel racing history, made his foray into NASCAR beginning in the middle of the 2000 season when he purchased majority ownership of the SABCO organization of Felix Sabates. Ganassi retained his ties with to the Sabates teams' special history by keeping Sabates as a minority partner. Sabates started the organization in 1988. Ganassi enjoyed immediate success in NASCAR during his first full season in 2001 as Sterling Marlin finished third in the series standings. Marlin gave Ganassi his first series win at Michigan in 2001, and Jason Leffler gave Ganassi his first pole at the inaugural race at Kansas the same year. While Jimmy Spencer joined the operation in 2002 as the replacement for Leffler, Ganassi was pursuing his first NASCAR series title with Marlin, who led the points for 25 weeks before his season was cut short by injury. Jamie McMurray took over for the injured Marlin and won at Charlotte in just his second career start, a series modern-era record. In 2003, Ganassi expanded to three teams by adding rookie Casey Mears, a former open-wheel driver and nephew of four-time Indy 500 winner Rick Mears. Ganassi enjoyed immense success on the open-wheel side prior to arriving at NASCAR and continues to thrive. A former driver himself in the CART series, Ganassi built an open-wheel dynasty at CART as his drivers captured an unprecedented four consecutive series championships from 1996-99. He also added an Indianapolis 500 crown with Juan Montoya in 2000. In 2003, he added an Indy Racing League title with driver Scott Dixon in the rival open-wheel series.

### CAREER NASCAR NEXTEL CUP SERIES STATS

| Year | Driver | Races | Won | Top 5 | Top 10 | DNF | Poles | Money Won |
|---|---|---|---|---|---|---|---|---|
| 1988 | R. Moroso | 1 | 0 | 0 | 0 | 0 | 0 | $4,500 |
| 1989 | K. Petty | 19 | 0 | 0 | 0 | 7 | 0 | 117,022 |
| 1990 | K. Petty | 29 | 1 | 2 | 14 | 5 | 2 | 746,326 |
| 1991 | K. Petty | 18 | 1 | 2 | 4 | 5 | 2 | 413,727 |
| | K. Wallace | 2 | 0 | 0 | 0 | 0 | 0 | 46,900 |
| | T. Kendall | 1 | 0 | 0 | 0 | 0 | 0 | 12,450 |
| | B. Hillin Jr. | 8 | 0 | 0 | 0 | 1 | 0 | 103,005 |
| 1992 | K. Petty | 29 | 2 | 9 | 17 | 5 | 3 | 1,107,063 |
| | T. Kendall | 1 | 0 | 0 | 0 | 0 | 0 | 6,755 |
| | S. Sharp | 1 | 0 | 0 | 0 | 0 | 0 | 7,155 |
| 1993 | K. Petty | 30 | 1 | 9 | 15 | 5 | 1 | 914,662 |
| | K. Wallace | 30 | 0 | 0 | 3 | 6 | 0 | 330,325 |
| 1994 | K. Petty | 31 | 0 | 2 | 7 | 3 | 0 | 806,332 |
| | B. Hamilton | 30 | 0 | 0 | 1 | 10 | 0 | 514,520 |
| 1995 | K. Petty | 30 | 1 | 1 | 5 | 10 | 0 | 698,875 |
| 1996 | K. Petty | 28 | 0 | 0 | 0 | 4 | 0 | 689,041 |
| | Jim Sauter | 2 | 0 | 0 | 0 | 1 | 0 | 47,700 |
| | G. Sacks | 2 | 0 | 0 | 0 | 0 | 0 | 21,190 |
| | R. Gordon | 2 | 0 | 0 | 0 | 2 | 0 | 18,565 |
| | Jay Sauter | 0 | 0 | 0 | 0 | 0 | 0 | 2,400 |
| 1997 | R. Gordon | 20 | 0 | 0 | 0 | 7 | 1 | 622,439 |
| | J. Nemechek | 29 | 0 | 0 | 3 | 4 | 2 | 679,954 |
| | W. Dallenbach Jr. | 22 | 0 | 0 | 0 | 10 | 0 | 471,479 |
| | G. Sacks | 5 | 0 | 0 | 0 | 3 | 0 | 114,035 |
| | P. Parsons | 1 | 0 | 0 | 0 | 0 | 0 | 12,854 |
| | S. Park | 1 | 0 | 0 | 0 | 1 | 0 | 14,075 |
| 1998 | J. Nemechek | 32 | 0 | 1 | 4 | 5 | 0 | 1,343,991 |
| | S. Marlin | 32 | 0 | 2 | 5 | 1 | 0 | 1,350,161 |
| | J. Green | 18 | 0 | 0 | 0 | 7 | 0 | 449,611 |
| | W. Dallenbach Jr. | 4 | 0 | 0 | 0 | 1 | 0 | 162,100 |
| | M. Shepherd | 2 | 0 | 0 | 0 | 0 | 0 | 61,611 |
| | T. Kendall | 1 | 0 | 0 | 0 | 0 | 0 | 19,405 |
| 1999 | J. Nemechek | 34 | 1 | 0 | 0 | 5 | 3 | 1,634,946 |
| | S. Marlin | 34 | 0 | 0 | 0 | 3 | 1 | 1,797,416 |
| | J. Green | 1 | 0 | 0 | 0 | 0 | 0 | 31,415 |
| | S. Grissom | 1 | 0 | 0 | 0 | 0 | 0 | 32,845 |
| | R. Hornaday Jr. | 1 | 0 | 0 | 0 | 0 | 0 | 22,810 |
| *2000 | S. Marlin | 34 | 0 | 1 | 7 | 4 | 0 | 1,992,301 |
| | K. Irwin Jr. | 17 | 0 | 1 | 1 | 2 | 0 | 949,436 |
| | T. Musgrave | 12 | 0 | 0 | 0 | 1 | 0 | 587,420 |
| | P.J. Jones | 1 | 0 | 0 | 0 | 0 | 0 | 37,555 |
| | B. Hamilton Jr. | 1 | 0 | 0 | 0 | 0 | 0 | 46,890 |

| Year | Driver | Races | Won | Top 5 | Top 10 | DNF | Poles | Money Won |
|---|---|---|---|---|---|---|---|---|
| 2001 | S. Marlin | 36 | 2 | 12 | 20 | 2 | 1 | 4,517,634 |
| | J. Leffler | 30 | 0 | 0 | 1 | 8 | 1 | 1,724,692 |
| | D. Schroeder | 1 | 0 | 0 | 0 | 0 | 0 | 52,805 |
| | S. Pruett | 1 | 0 | 0 | 0 | 0 | 0 | 57,025 |
| 2002 | S. Marlin | 29 | 2 | 8 | 14 | 3 | 0 | 4,228,889 |
| | J. Spencer | 34 | 0 | 2 | 6 | 7 | 0 | 2,136,792 |
| | J. McMurray | 6 | 1 | 1 | 2 | 1 | 0 | 717,942 |
| | M. Bliss | 1 | 0 | 0 | 0 | 0 | 0 | 90,083 |
| | S. Pruett | 1 | 0 | 0 | 1 | 0 | 0 | 66,690 |
| 2003 | S. Marlin | 36 | 0 | 0 | 11 | 8 | 0 | 3,960,810 |
| | J. McMurray | 36 | 0 | 5 | 13 | 4 | 1 | 2,699,970 |
| | C. Mears | 36 | 0 | 0 | 0 | 10 | 0 | 2,639,180 |
| | S. Pruett | 2 | 0 | 1 | 1 | 0 | 0 | 143,035 |
| 2004 | S. Marlin | 36 | 0 | 3 | 7 | 9 | 0 | 3,894,554 |
| | J. McMurray | 36 | 0 | 9 | 23 | 6 | 0 | 3,551,612 |
| | C. Mears | 36 | 0 | 1 | 9 | 4 | 2 | 3,165,343 |
| | S. Pruett | 1 | 0 | 1 | 1 | 0 | 0 | 120,100 |
| **\*TOTALS** | | **955** | **12** | **73** | **195** | **180** | **20** | **$52,810,418** |

\* Ganassi became primary owner following Race No. 18 (New Hampshire) in 2000; Felix Sabates was owner before that date.

# Joe Gibbs

**Date of birth:** 11/25/40. **Hometown:** Mocksville, N.C. **Resides:** Cornelius, N.C. **Years as NNCS owner:** 13. **Best points finish:** 1. **Career victories:** 42. **First victory:** 1993 Daytona. **Career poles:** 32. **First pole:** 1995 Martinsville.

The NFL lured Joe Gibbs back into its coaching fold in 2004, but that didn't mean that Joe Gibbs Racing was going anywhere. In fact, Gibbs Racing is expanding in 2005 to a three-car team, with Jason Leffler in the No. 11 joining Gibbs drivers Tony Stewart and Bobby Labonte. JGR ran its first season in 1992. Gibbs' son, J.D. (now president of JGR), joined full-time in July 1992. Dale Jarrett proved that JGR would be a team to be reckoned with when he scored JGR's first win in the 1993 Daytona 500 and an impressive fourth-place finish in the series championship. Beginning in 1995, JGR had a new race shop and a new driver, Bobby Labonte, who scored three wins and the team's first pole. Setting a plan for the future, Gibbs signed then open-wheel star Tony Stewart to run a limited NASCAR Busch Series schedule in 1997 and 1998—through a joint effort with Bobby Labonte's NASCAR Busch Series team—in preparation for 1999. Along with winning Raybestos Rookie of the Year honors in 1999, Stewart scored three victories. After finishing second in 1999, Labonte brought Joe Gibbs Racing its first series championship in 2000. Gibbs also began a two-car NASCAR Busch Series operation in 2000 with drivers Jason Leffler and Jeff Purvis. In 2002, Stewart brought Gibbs his second series title in three seasons. JGR also formed a Late Model Stock Car partnership with future NFL Hall of Famer Reggie White to identify and assist talented minority drivers.

### CAREER NASCAR NEXTEL CUP SERIES STATS

| Year | Driver | Races | Won | Top 5 | Top 10 | DNF | Poles | Money Won |
|---|---|---|---|---|---|---|---|---|
| 1992 | D. Jarrett | 29 | 0 | 2 | 8 | 5 | 0 | $418,648 |
| 1993 | D. Jarrett | 30 | 1 | 13 | 18 | 5 | 0 | 1,242,394 |
| 1994 | D. Jarrett | 30 | 1 | 4 | 9 | 7 | 0 | 881,754 |
| 1995 | B. Labonte | 31 | 3 | 7 | 14 | 6 | 2 | 1,413,682 |
| 1996 | B. Labonte | 31 | 1 | 5 | 14 | 5 | 4 | 1,475,196 |
| 1997 | B. Labonte | 32 | 1 | 9 | 18 | 1 | 3 | 2,217,999 |
| 1998 | B. Labonte | 33 | 2 | 11 | 18 | 6 | 3 | 2,980,052 |

117

## CAREER NASCAR NEXTEL CUP SERIES STATS • Joe Gibbs

| Year | Driver | Races | Won | Top 5 | Top 10 | DNF | Poles | Money Won |
|---|---|---|---|---|---|---|---|---|
| 1999 | B. Labonte | 34 | 5 | 23 | 26 | 1 | 5 | 4,763,615 |
| | T. Stewart | 34 | 3 | 12 | 21 | 1 | 2 | 3,190,149 |
| 2000 | B. Labonte | 34 | 4 | 19 | 24 | 0 | 2 | 7,361,386 |
| | T. Stewart | 34 | 6 | 12 | 23 | 5 | 2 | 3,642,348 |
| 2001 | T. Stewart | 36 | 3 | 15 | 22 | 4 | 0 | 4,941,463 |
| | B. Labonte | 36 | 2 | 9 | 20 | 6 | 1 | 4,786,779 |
| 2002 | T. Stewart | 36 | 3 | 15 | 21 | 6 | 2 | 9,163,761 |
| | B. Labonte | 36 | 1 | 5 | 7 | 4 | 0 | 4,183,715 |
| 2003 | T. Stewart | 36 | 2 | 12 | 18 | 5 | 1 | 5,227,500 |
| | B. Labonte | 36 | 2 | 12 | 17 | 5 | 4 | 4,745,260 |
| | M. Bliss | 1 | 0 | 0 | 0 | 0 | 0 | 65,300 |
| 2004 | M. Bliss | 2 | 0 | 1 | 1 | 1 | 0 | 148,555 |
| | R. Craven | 1 | 0 | 0 | 0 | 0 | 0 | 62,405 |
| | B. Labonte | 36 | 0 | 5 | 11 | 2 | 1 | 4,412,072 |
| | T. Stewart | 36 | 2 | 10 | 19 | 2 | 0 | 5,851,727 |
| | J.J. Yeley | 2 | 0 | 0 | 0 | 1 | 0 | 144,040 |
| **TOTALS** | | **646** | **42** | **201** | **329** | **78** | **32** | **$73,319,800** |

# Gene Haas

**Hometown:** Oxnard, Calif. **Resides:** Harrisburg, N.C.
**Years as NNCS owner:** 3. **Best points finish:** 21.
**Career victories:** 0. **Career poles:** 0.

Gene Haas has had a long-standing passion for racing. His company, Haas Automation, Inc., the largest machine tool manufacturer in the United States, was founded in 1983 and since 1995 has created technical partnerships with various racing groups, including Hendrick Motorsports. Haas CNC Racing is an associate sponsor with Hendrick and partners with the Hendrick teams for engines and technical support. In January 2002, Haas announced the formation of Haas CNC Racing and its full-time entry into NASCAR's premier series beginning in 2003. Driver Jack Sprague made the team's first start at Kansas in 2002, finishing 35th, and ran twice more in preparation for its first full-time season in the series in 2003. The team used four drivers before signing Ward Burton to drive the No. 0 Chevrolet in 2004. Not limited to only off-track ownership responsibilities, Haas teamed with co-driver Joe Custer and won the best-in-class championship in the 2001 Best of the Desert Off-Road Truck Series.

## CAREER NASCAR NEXTEL CUP SERIES STATS

| Year | Driver | Races | Won | Top 5 | Top 10 | DNF | Poles | Money Won |
|---|---|---|---|---|---|---|---|---|
| 2002 | J. Sprague | 3 | 0 | 0 | 0 | 1 | 0 | 132,000 |
| 2003 | J. Sprague | 18 | 0 | 0 | 0 | 5 | 0 | 1,187,830 |
| | J. Leffler | 10 | 0 | 0 | 0 | 0 | 0 | 594,500 |
| | J. Andretti | 3 | 0 | 0 | 0 | 0 | 0 | 2,577,620 |
| | W. Burton | 4 | 0 | 0 | 0 | 2 | 0 | 3,500,160 |
| 2004 | M. Bliss | 2 | 0 | 0 | 0 | 1 | 0 | 135,850 |
| | W. Burton | 34 | 0 | 0 | 3 | 8 | 0 | 2,436,042 |
| | J. Leffler | 1 | 0 | 0 | 0 | 1 | 0 | 116,359 |
| **TOTALS** | | **75** | **0** | **0** | **4** | **18** | **0** | **$10,680,361** |

# Rick Hendrick

**Date of birth:** 7/12/49. **Hometown:** Warrenton, N.C.
**Resides:** Charlotte, N.C. **Years as NNCS owner:** 21.
**Best points finish:** 1. **Career victories:** 130.
**First victory:** 1984 Martinsville. **Career poles:** 116.
**First pole:** 1984 Bristol.

Founded in 1984, Hendrick Motorsports fields four teams in NASCAR's premier series. It is the only organization to have won the series title in four consecutive seasons (1995-98). Hendrick Motorsports started as a one-car operation for Rick Hendrick, a racing enthusiast from South Hill, Va., who owned a championship drag racing boat team before coming to NASCAR. Hendrick founded "All-Star Racing" in 1984 with Geoffrey Bodine, driving 30 events and winning three. Later in the 1980s, Hendrick added three-time series champion Darrell Waltrip and the talented Tim Richmond to his group. In 1994, Hendrick hooked up with young Jeff Gordon, a rising open-wheel star at the time. Gordon has since won four series championships, the third-best total of all-time. Hendrick Motorsports also fields a NASCAR Busch Series team, and in 2004 Kyle Busch drove for car owner Ricky Hendrick, Rick's son. Ricky Hendrick and nine other people were killed in a plane crash just outside Martinsville, Va., in 2004, rocking the Hendrick Motorsports family. The family also lost patriarch Papa Joe Hendrick in 2004—he died at age 84. Rick Hendrick had leukemia in 1996, but the disease is now in remission. He established the Hendrick Marrow Program in 1997 to aid patients around the country who are suffering from leukemia or one of the more than 70 other life-threatening blood diseases.

## CAREER NASCAR NEXTEL CUP SERIES STATS

| Year | Driver | Races | Won | Top 5 | Top 10 | DNF | Poles | Money Won |
|---|---|---|---|---|---|---|---|---|
| 1984 | G. Bodine | 30 | 3 | 7 | 14 | 8 | 3 | $393,924 |
| 1985 | G. Bodine | 28 | 0 | 10 | 14 | 5 | 3 | 565,865 |
| | D. Brooks | 1 | 0 | 0 | 1 | 0 | 0 | 9,000 |
| 1986 | G. Bodine | 29 | 2 | 10 | 14 | 12 | 8 | 795,111 |
| | T. Richmond | 29 | 7 | 13 | 17 | 2 | 8 | 988,221 |
| | B. Bodine | 1 | 0 | 0 | 0 | 0 | 0 | 10,100 |
| 1987 | G. Bodine | 29 | 0 | 3 | 10 | 11 | 2 | 449,816 |
| | D. Waltrip | 29 | 1 | 6 | 16 | 2 | 0 | 511,768 |
| | B. Parsons | 29 | 0 | 6 | 9 | 12 | 0 | 555,584 |
| | T. Richmond | 8 | 2 | 3 | 4 | 2 | 1 | 151,850 |
| | J. Fitzgerald | 1 | 0 | 0 | 0 | 0 | 0 | 1,675 |
| | J. Means | 1 | 0 | 0 | 0 | 1 | 0 | 5,960 |
| | Rick Hendrick | 1 | 0 | 0 | 0 | 1 | 0 | 1,150 |
| 1988 | G. Bodine | 29 | 1 | 10 | 16 | 4 | 3 | 570,643 |
| | D. Waltrip | 29 | 2 | 10 | 14 | 4 | 2 | 731,659 |
| | K. Schrader | 28 | 1 | 4 | 17 | 1 | 2 | 626,934 |
| | Rick Hendrick | 1 | 0 | 0 | 0 | 0 | 0 | 2,550 |
| 1989 | G. Bodine | 29 | 1 | 9 | 11 | 6 | 3 | 620,594 |
| | D. Waltrip | 29 | 6 | 14 | 18 | 3 | 0 | 1,323,079 |
| | K. Schrader | 29 | 1 | 10 | 14 | 6 | 4 | 1,039,441 |
| | T. Kendall | 1 | 0 | 0 | 0 | 1 | 0 | 3,015 |
| 1990 | D. Waltrip | 23 | 0 | 5 | 12 | 0 | 0 | 530,420 |
| | K. Schrader | 29 | 0 | 7 | 14 | 8 | 3 | 769,934 |
| | R. Rudd | 29 | 1 | 8 | 15 | 5 | 2 | 573,650 |
| | G. Sacks | 4 | 0 | 1 | 1 | 2 | 0 | 93,315 |
| | J. Horton | 2 | 0 | 0 | 0 | 0 | 0 | 30,475 |
| | H. Stricklin | 1 | 0 | 0 | 0 | 1 | 0 | 2,765 |
| | S. Van der Merwe | 1 | 0 | 0 | 0 | 1 | 0 | 12,070 |
| 1991 | K. Schrader | 29 | 2 | 10 | 18 | 6 | 0 | 772,439 |
| | R. Rudd | 29 | 1 | 9 | 17 | 1 | 1 | 1,093,765 |
| 1992 | K. Schrader | 29 | 0 | 4 | 11 | 5 | 1 | 639,679 |
| | R. Rudd | 29 | 1 | 9 | 18 | 4 | 1 | 793,903 |
| | J. Gordon | 1 | 0 | 0 | 0 | 1 | 0 | 6,285 |
| 1993 | K. Schrader | 30 | 0 | 9 | 15 | 4 | 6 | 952,748 |
| | R. Rudd | 30 | 1 | 9 | 14 | 6 | 0 | 752,562 |
| | J. Gordon | 30 | 0 | 7 | 11 | 11 | 1 | 765,168 |
| | A. Unser Jr. | 1 | 0 | 0 | 0 | 1 | 0 | 23,005 |
| 1994 | K. Schrader | 31 | 0 | 9 | 18 | 2 | 0 | 1,171,062 |
| | J. Gordon | 31 | 2 | 7 | 14 | 10 | 1 | 1,779,523 |
| | T. Labonte | 31 | 3 | 6 | 14 | 4 | 0 | 1,125,921 |
| 1995 | K. Schrader | 31 | 0 | 2 | 10 | 9 | 1 | 886,566 |
| | J. Gordon | 31 | 7 | 17 | 23 | 3 | 8 | 4,347,343 |

| Year | Driver | Races | Won | Top 5 | Top 10 | DNF | Poles | Money Won |
|------|--------|-------|-----|-------|--------|-----|-------|-----------|
| | T. Labonte | 31 | 3 | 14 | 17 | 3 | 1 | 1,558,659 |
| | J. Purvis | 1 | 0 | 0 | 0 | 0 | 0 | 7,370 |
| 1996 | K. Schrader | 31 | 0 | 3 | 10 | 2 | 0 | 1,089,603 |
| | J. Gordon | 31 | 10 | 21 | 24 | 5 | 5 | 3,428,485 |
| | T. Labonte | 31 | 2 | 21 | 24 | 3 | 4 | 4,030,648 |
| 1997 | J. Gordon | 32 | 10 | 22 | 23 | 2 | 1 | 6,375,658 |
| | T. Labonte | 32 | 1 | 8 | 20 | 3 | 0 | 2,270,144 |
| | R. Craven | 30 | 0 | 4 | 7 | 7 | 0 | 1,259,550 |
| | T. Bodine | 1 | 0 | 0 | 0 | 0 | 0 | 58,550 |
| | J. Sprague | 1 | 0 | 0 | 0 | 1 | 0 | 18,650 |
| 1998 | J. Gordon | 33 | 13 | 26 | 28 | 2 | 7 | 9,306,584 |
| | T. Labonte | 33 | 1 | 5 | 15 | 4 | 0 | 2,054,163 |
| | W. Dallenbach Jr. | 16 | 0 | 0 | 3 | 3 | 0 | 522,996 |
| | R. LaJoie | 9 | 0 | 1 | 3 | 3 | 0 | 336,905 |
| | R. Craven | 8 | 0 | 0 | 1 | 0 | 1 | 442,200 |
| 1999 | J. Gordon | 34 | 7 | 18 | 21 | 7 | 7 | 5,858,633 |
| | T. Labonte | 34 | 1 | 1 | 6 | 6 | 0 | 2,475,365 |
| | W. Dallenbach Jr. | 34 | 0 | 1 | 6 | 5 | 0 | 1,741,176 |
| 2000 | J. Gordon | 34 | 3 | 11 | 22 | 2 | 3 | 3,001,144 |
| | T. Labonte | 32 | 0 | 3 | 6 | 3 | 1 | 2,239,716 |
| | J. Nadeau | 34 | 1 | 3 | 5 | 9 | 0 | 2,164,778 |
| | T. Bodine | 1 | 0 | 0 | 0 | 0 | 0 | 117,260 |
| | R. Hornaday Jr. | 1 | 0 | 0 | 0 | 0 | 0 | 47,020 |
| 2001 | J. Gordon | 36 | 6 | 18 | 24 | 2 | 6 | 10,879,757 |
| | T. Labonte | 36 | 0 | 1 | 3 | 8 | 0 | 3,011,901 |
| | J. Nadeau | 36 | 0 | 4 | 10 | 8 | 0 | 2,507,827 |
| | J. Johnson | 3 | 0 | 0 | 0 | 1 | 0 | 122,320 |

**Rick Hendrick (left) just missed winning a title with Jimmie Johnson in 2004.**

| Year | Driver | Races | Won | Top 5 | Top 10 | DNF | Poles | Money Won |
|------|--------|-------|-----|-------|--------|-----|-------|-----------|
| 2002 | J. Gordon | 36 | 3 | 13 | 20 | 3 | 3 | 6,154,475 |
| | J. Johnson | 36 | 3 | 6 | 21 | 3 | 4 | 3,788,268 |
| | T. Labonte | 36 | 0 | 1 | 4 | 6 | 0 | 3,244,240 |
| | J. Nadeau | 11 | 0 | 0 | 1 | 3 | 0 | 754,275 |
| | J. Nemechek | 25 | 0 | 3 | 3 | 8 | 0 | 1,766,252 |
| 2003 | J. Gordon | 36 | 3 | 15 | 20 | 5 | 4 | 5,107,760 |
| | J. Johnson | 36 | 3 | 14 | 20 | 3 | 2 | 5,517,850 |
| | T. Labonte | 36 | 1 | 4 | 9 | 0 | 1 | 3,643,690 |
| | J. Nemechek | 32 | 1 | 2 | 5 | 7 | 0 | 2,289,060 |
| | D. Green | 11 | 0 | 0 | 1 | 2 | 1 | 906,135 |
| | B. Vickers | 5 | 0 | 0 | 0 | 1 | 0 | 263,484 |
| 2004 | Ky. Busch | 6 | 0 | 0 | 0 | | 0 | 394,489 |
| | J. Gordon | 36 | 5 | 16 | 25 | | 6 | 6,256,887 |
| | J. Johnson | 36 | 8 | 20 | 23 | | 1 | 5,556,624 |
| | T. Labonte | 36 | 0 | 0 | 6 | | 0 | 3,598,892 |
| | B. Vickers | 36 | 0 | 0 | 4 | | 2 | 2,955,598 |
| **TOTALS** | | **1722** | **130** | **478** | **741** | **277** | **116** | **$145,605,578** |

# Larry McClure

**Date of birth:** 3/21/44. **Hometown:** Harmon, Va.
**Resides:** Abingdon, Va. **Years as NNCS owner:** 22.
**Best points finish:** 3. **Career victories:** 14.
**First victory:** 1990 Bristol. **Career poles:** 13.
**First pole:** 1988 Bristol.

Morgan-McClure Motorsports was formed in 1983, when Larry McClure, Ed McClure, Jerry McClure, Teddy McClure and Tim Morgan bought a car from G.C. Spencer. Larry McClure and Tim Morgan had been longtime business partners, operating a successful automobile dealership, which they continue today. One of the team's first drivers was a then 24-year-old Mark Martin. The team first broke in to the win column in 1990 with driver Ernie Irvan, marking the beginning of an eight-year run during which the team won 14 races—including eight superspeedway wins—between 1990 and '98. Among those wins were three at the Daytona 500, with Irvan in 1991 and Sterling Marlin in 1994 and '95. The 1995 season by Marlin gave the organization its best finish in the championship when he finished third.

## CAREER NASCAR NEXTEL CUP SERIES STATS

| Year | Driver | Races | Won | Top 5 | Top 10 | DNF | Poles | Money Won |
|------|--------|-------|-----|-------|--------|-----|-------|-----------|
| 1983 | L. Pond | 5 | 0 | 0 | 2 | 2 | 0 | $23,475 |
| | M. Martin | 6 | 0 | 0 | 1 | 2 | 0 | 17,030 |
| 1984 | L. Pond | 4 | 0 | 0 | 0 | 2 | 0 | 21,590 |
| | T. Ellis | 20 | 0 | 0 | 1 | 11 | 0 | 44,315 |
| | J. Ruttman | 3 | 0 | 0 | 1 | 2 | 0 | 5,525 |
| 1985 | J. Ruttman | 16 | 0 | 1 | 4 | 10 | 0 | 71,425 |
| 1986 | R. Wilson | 17 | 0 | 0 | 4 | 8 | 0 | 88,820 |
| 1987 | R. Wilson | 19 | 0 | 0 | 1 | 11 | 0 | 65,935 |
| 1988 | R. Wilson | 28 | 0 | 2 | 5 | 11 | 1 | 209,925 |
| 1989 | R. Wilson | 29 | 0 | 2 | 7 | 8 | 0 | 312,402 |
| 1990 | P. Parsons | 3 | 0 | 0 | 0 | 1 | 0 | 39,350 |
| | E. Irvan | 26 | 1 | 6 | 13 | 3 | 3 | 497,675 |
| 1991 | E. Irvan | 29 | 2 | 11 | 19 | 6 | 1 | 1,079,017 |
| 1992 | E. Irvan | 29 | 3 | 9 | 11 | 7 | 3 | 996,885 |
| 1993 | E. Irvan | 21 | 1 | 7 | 8 | 9 | 2 | 815,985 |
| | J. Purvis | 5 | 0 | 0 | 0 | 0 | 0 | 81,370 |
| | J. Nemechek | 2 | 0 | 0 | 0 | 0 | 0 | 32,280 |
| | J. Hensley | 2 | 0 | 0 | 0 | 1 | 0 | 31,895 |

## CAREER NASCAR NEXTEL CUP SERIES STATS • Larry McClure

| Year | Driver | Races | Won | Top 5 | Top 10 | DNF | Poles | Money Won |
|------|--------|-------|-----|-------|--------|-----|-------|-----------|
| 1994 | S. Marlin | 31 | 1 | 5 | 11 | 7 | 1 | 1,127,683 |
| 1995 | S. Marlin | 31 | 3 | 9 | 22 | 2 | 1 | 2,253,502 |
| 1996 | S. Marlin | 31 | 2 | 5 | 10 | 6 | 0 | 1,588,425 |
| 1997 | S. Marlin | 32 | 0 | 2 | 6 | 8 | 0 | 1,301,370 |
| 1998 | B. Hamilton | 33 | 1 | 3 | 8 | 1 | 1 | 2,089,566 |
| 1999 | B. Hamilton | 34 | 0 | 1 | 10 | 3 | 0 | 2,019,255 |
| 2000 | B. Hamilton | 34 | 0 | 0 | 2 | 11 | 0 | 1,619,775 |
| 2001 | K. Lepage | 21 | 0 | 0 | 0 | 3 | 0 | 987,976 |
|      | B. Hamilton Jr. | 7 | 0 | 0 | 0 | 0 | 0 | 305,705 |
|      | R. Gordon | 5 | 0 | 0 | 0 | 1 | 0 | 287,545 |
|      | R. Bickle Jr. | 1 | 0 | 0 | 0 | 0 | 0 | 30,300 |
| 2002 | M. Skinner | 36 | 0 | 0 | 1 | 6 | 0 | 2,094,232 |
| 2003 | K. Lepage | 11 | 0 | 0 | 0 | 1 | 0 | 742,077 |
|      | J. Sauter | 5 | 0 | 0 | 0 | 0 | 0 | 281,335 |
|      | J. Miller | 2 | 0 | 0 | 0 | 0 | 0 | 110,814 |
|      | P.J. Jones | 1 | 0 | 0 | 0 | 0 | 0 | 59,135 |
|      | S. Compton | 1 | 0 | 0 | 0 | 0 | 0 | 67,400 |
| 2004 | K. Lepage | 6 | 0 | 0 | 0 | 1 | 0 | 531,632 |
|      | E. McClure | 1 | 0 | 0 | 0 | 1 | 0 | 65,175 |
|      | J. Spencer | 25 | 0 | 0 | 0 | 7 | 0 | 1,714,310 |
|      | M. Wallace | 3 | 0 | 0 | 0 | 2 | 0 | 162,880 |
| **TOTALS** | | **615** | **14** | **63** | **147** | **154** | **13** | **$21,400,994** |

# Beth Ann Morgenthau

**Hometown:** Baltimore, Md. **Resides:** Coral Gables, Fla. **Years as NNCS owner:** 3. **Best points finish:** 31. **Career victories:** 0. **Career poles:** 0.

The Morgenthaus began their trek in ARCA, then, heeding the advice of team G.M. Eddie Jones, decided to run a limited schedule in Cup to speed their learning curve. Although the team did not qualify in eight attempts in 2001, BAM moved forward and made 17 starts in 2002 with six different drivers. BAM settled on veteran Ken Schrader to drive the team's first full-time series schedule in 2003. In 32 starts, he registered the organization's first-ever top-10 finishes and placed 36th in the championship standings. Schrader improved on that in 2004, finishing 31st in the points standings. The former Beth Ann Coulter grew up a race fan, riding her bike to local short tracks in the Miami area and getting into the speed game herself, racing go-karts and motorboats. Her family founded Coulter Electronics (now Beckman Coulter). In 1969, she married Tony Morgenthau, an investment banker who founded Morgenthau & Associates in 1972. The couple shared their passion for motorsports, venturing to dirt tracks whenever possible.
• **Active in Miami Association of Charities.**

### CAREER NASCAR NEXTEL CUP SERIES STATS

| Year | Driver | Races | Won | Top 5 | Top 10 | DNF | Poles | Money Won |
|------|--------|-------|-----|-------|--------|-----|-------|-----------|
| 2002 | S. Robinson | 7 | 0 | 0 | 0 | 4 | 0 | $428,519 |
|      | D. Cope | 5 | 0 | 0 | 0 | 0 | 0 | 224,390 |
|      | S. Compton | 2 | 0 | 0 | 0 | 1 | 0 | 90,630 |
|      | R. Hornaday | 1 | 0 | 0 | 0 | 1 | 0 | 88,476 |
|      | K. Lepage | 1 | 0 | 0 | 0 | 1 | 0 | 44,650 |
|      | S. Kirby | 1 | 0 | 0 | 0 | 0 | 0 | 53,100 |
| 2003 | K. Schrader | 32 | 0 | 0 | 2 | 8 | 0 | 2,007,420 |
| 2004 | K. Schrader | 36 | 0 | 0 | 1 | 5 | 0 | 2,666,590 |
| **TOTALS** | | **85** | **0** | **0** | **3** | **20** | **0** | **$5,603,775** |

# Roger Penske

**Hometown:** Shaker Heights, Ohio. **Resides:** Bloomfield Hills, Mich. **Years as NNCS owner:** 33. **Best points finish:** 2. **Career victories:** 53. **First victory:** 1973, Riverside. **Career poles:** 62. **First pole:** 1974, Riverside.

Roger Penske and racing have been synonymous ever since he began racing himself in 1958. Even when Penske stopped racing in 1965 and began building what is now a vast business empire, Penske Corporation, racing is, and always will be, at the core of Penske. Penske Corporation and its subsidiaries employ 34,000 people at more than 1,700 worldwide locations and generate $11 billion annually. As impressive as his business interests are, his racing successes are equally impressive. Penske has amassed 14 national championships (nine in CART, three in SCCA, two in USRRC), 139 poles and 115 wins, including 11 in the Indianapolis 500. Penske's first entry into NASCAR was in 1972 when he fielded a Matador for road-racing standout Mark Donohue at Riverside (Calif.) International Raceway. One year later, Donohue scored Penske's first NASCAR victory at Riverside. Penske had run a limited schedule each season until 1976, when Bobby Allison finished fourth for him in NASCAR's premier division. In 1977, Penske went back to running a limited schedule with driver Dave Marcis. In 1980, Penske's business partner Don Miller—now president of Penske Racing South—put together a two-race deal between Penske and driver Rusty Wallace. The team displayed a promising future from the start, scoring a second-place finish to Dale Earnhardt at Atlanta. But with most of the racing emphasis on Penske's open-wheel interests, the trio then decided against teaming up. More than a decade passed before Penske returned to NASCAR in 1991. The timing came together in late 1990, as Miller and Penske partnered with Wallace to form Penske Racing South. Many of the key players from Wallace's 1989 championship-winning Blue Max Racing team—including crew chief Jimmy Makar—joined the newly formed team after owner Raymond Beadle's Blue Max team dissolved after the 1990 season. Wallace, Miller and Penske have been a winning team ever since. The team enjoyed its most success in 1993 when Wallace won 10 races and three poles and finished as series runner-up. Penske partnered with Michael Kranefuss from 1998 to 2000, fielding a car for Jeremy Mayfield. After starting eight races for Penske between 2000-01, Ryan Newman teamed with Wallace for the 2002 season. In January of 2004, Penske Racing announced that it had acquired Jasper Motorsports to form Penske-Jasper Racing. At the same time, it was announced that Kodak—continuing their 18-year involvement in NASCAR—would sponsor the No. 77 Dodge for rookie Brendan Gaughan. Shane Wilson, who helped lead Gaughan to six wins in the 2003 NASCAR Craftsman Truck Series, served as Gaughan's crew chief.

### CAREER NASCAR NEXTEL CUP SERIES STATS

| Year | Driver | Races | Won | Top 5 | Top 10 | DNF | Poles | Money Won |
|------|--------|-------|-----|-------|--------|-----|-------|-----------|
| 1972 | D. Marcis | 7 | 0 | 0 | 3 | 4 | 0 | $9,406 |
|      | M. Donohue | 4 | 0 | 0 | 0 | 3 | 0 | 5,130 |
|      | D. Allison | 1 | 0 | 1 | 1 | 0 | 0 | 4,025 |
| 1973 | D. Marcis | 8 | 0 | 1 | 2 | 6 | 0 | 10,625 |
|      | M. Donohue | 2 | 1 | 1 | 1 | 1 | 0 | 16,120 |
| 1974 | B. Allison | 10 | 1 | 6 | 6 | 4 | 0 | 53,885 |
|      | G. Bettenhausen | 5 | 0 | 1 | 3 | 1 | 0 | 12,730 |
|      | D. Marcis | 1 | 0 | 0 | 1 | 0 | 0 | 2,025 |
|      | G. Follmer | 1 | 0 | 0 | 0 | 1 | 1 | 1,000 |
| 1975 | B. Allison | 19 | 3 | 10 | 10 | 9 | 3 | 122,435 |
| 1976 | B. Allison | 30 | 0 | 15 | 19 | 9 | 2 | 210,377 |
|      | N. Bonnett* | 0 | 0 | 0 | 0 | 0 | 1 | 0 |
| 1977 | D. Marcis | 14 | 0 | 5 | 7 | 3 | 0 | 66,545 |

## CAREER NASCAR NEXTEL CUP SERIES STATS • Roger Penske

| Year | Driver | Races | Won | Top 5 | Top 10 | DNF | Poles | Money Won |
|---|---|---|---|---|---|---|---|---|
| 1980 | R. Wallace | 2 | 0 | 1 | 1 | 0 | 0 | 22,760 |
| 1991 | R. Wallace | 29 | 2 | 9 | 14 | 10 | 2 | 502,073 |
| 1992 | R. Wallace | 29 | 1 | 5 | 12 | 5 | 1 | 657,925 |
| 1993 | R. Wallace | 30 | 10 | 19 | 21 | 5 | 3 | 1,702,154 |
| 1994 | R. Wallace | 31 | 8 | 17 | 20 | 5 | 2 | 1,914,072 |
| 1995 | R. Wallace | 31 | 2 | 15 | 19 | 4 | 0 | 1,642,837 |
| 1996 | R. Wallace | 31 | 5 | 8 | 18 | 6 | 0 | 1,665,315 |
| 1997 | R. Wallace | 32 | 1 | 8 | 12 | 11 | 1 | 1,705,625 |
| 1998 | R. Wallace | 33 | 1 | 15 | 21 | 2 | 4 | 2,667,889 |
| 1999 | R. Wallace | 34 | 1 | 7 | 16 | 3 | 4 | 2,454,050 |
| 2000 | R. Wallace | 34 | 4 | 12 | 20 | 3 | 9 | 3,621,468 |
|  | J. Mayfield | 5 | 0 | 2 | 2 | 2 | 1 | 551,300 |
|  | R. Newman | 1 | 0 | 0 | 0 | 1 | 0 | 37,825 |
| 2001 | R. Wallace | 36 | 1 | 8 | 12 | 3 | 0 | 4,788,652 |
|  | J. Mayfield | 28 | 0 | 5 | 7 | 4 | 0 | 2,682,603 |
|  | R. Newman | 7 | 0 | 2 | 2 | 2 | 1 | 465,276 |
|  | M. Wallace | 8 | 0 | 1 | 2 | 1 | 0 | 706,673 |
| 2002 | R. Newman | 36 | 1 | 14 | 22 | 5 | 6 | 5,346,651 |
|  | R. Wallace | 36 | 0 | 7 | 17 | 1 | 1 | 4,785,134 |
| 2003 | R. Newman | 36 | 8 | 17 | 22 | 7 | 11 | 4,827,380 |
|  | R. Wallace | 36 | 0 | 2 | 12 | 4 | 0 | 3,766,740 |
| 2004 | R. Newman | 36 | 2 | 11 | 14 | 9 | 9 | 4,762,399 |
|  | R. Wallace | 36 | 1 | 3 | 11 | 3 | 0 | 4,229,069 |
| **TOTALS** |  | **712** | **53** | **228** | **347** | **133** | **62** | **$56,010,767** |

\* Bonnett substituted in qualifying for Allison at Nashville and won pole; Allison started the race with Bonnett relieving him after one lap.

# Petty Enterprises

**Owner:** Richard Petty. **Date of birth:** 7/2/37.
**Hometown:** Newton, N.C. **Resides:** Level Cross, N.C.
**Years as NNCS Owner:** 17. **Years as NNCS owner:** 56.
**Best points finish:** 1. **Career victories:** 268.
**First victory:** 1949 Heidelburg Speedway, Pittsburg, Pa.
**Career poles:** 155. **First pole:** 1954 Daytona Beach roadcourse

Like NASCAR itself, Petty Enterprises traces its roots to the sands of Daytona Beach. Founded in 1949 by family patriarch Lee Petty, Petty Enterprises was there for NASCAR's inaugural NASCAR Grand National Division (now NASCAR NEXTEL Cup Series) season. Since then, Petty Enterprises has fielded cars for 45 different drivers, including four generations of the Petty family. In a 25-year span from 1954-79, the team won 10 series championships. Richard Petty, who made his No. 43 car a household icon, holds seven series titles and remains highly active in the team's operations today. The organization took on its current shape in 1999 when Kyle Petty folded his own pe2 team into Petty Enterprises, forming a two-car team. In 2001, Petty Enterprises switched to Dodge when the manufacturer made its much-anticipated return to the series.

## CAREER NASCAR NEXTEL CUP SERIES STATS

| Year | Driver | Races | Won | Top 5 | Top 10 | DNF | Poles | Money Won |
|---|---|---|---|---|---|---|---|---|
| 1949 | L. Petty | 10 | 1 | 5 | 8 | 2 | 0 | $3,875 |
| 1950 | L. Petty | 17 | 2 | 10 | 14 | 1 | 0 | 6,225 |
| 1951 | L. Petty | 33 | 1 | 11 | 19 | 10 | 0 | 7,790 |
| 1952 | L. Petty | 32 | 3 | 21 | 27 | 5 | 0 | 15,520 |
| 1953 | L. Petty | 37 | 5 | 26 | 32 | 2 | 0 | 15,550 |
| 1954 | L. Petty | 34 | 7 | 24 | 32 | 2 | 3 | 18,325 |
| 1955 | L. Petty | 42 | 6 | 20 | 30 | 9 | 1 | 16,400 |
| 1956 | L. Petty | 47 | 2 | 17 | 28 | 13 | 1 | 13,555 |
| 1957 | L. Petty | 41 | 4 | 20 | 33 | 5 | 3 | 15,620 |

| Year | Driver | Races | Won | Top 5 | Top 10 | DNF | Poles | Money Won |
|---|---|---|---|---|---|---|---|---|
|  | T. Lund | 6 | 0 | 1 | 2 | 2 | 0 | 810 |
|  | Bobby Myers | 1 | 0 | 0 | 0 | 1 | 0 | 260 |
| 1958 | L. Petty | 49 | 7 | 27 | 42 | 3 | 5 | 20,385 |
|  | R. Petty | 9 | 0 | 0 | 1 | 5 | 0 | 760 |
|  | J. Reed | 1 | 0 | 0 | 0 | 1 | 0 | 315 |
| 1959 | L. Petty | 43 | 11 | 27 | 35 | 6 | 2 | 43,765 |
|  | R. Petty | 22 | 0 | 5 | 8 | 12 | 0 | 7,630 |
|  | J. Beauchamp | 1 | 0 | 0 | 0 | 0 | 0 | 300 |
| 1960 | L. Petty | 39 | 5 | 21 | 30 | 7 | 3 | 26,650 |
|  | R. Petty | 40 | 3 | 17 | 30 | 8 | 2 | 35,180 |
|  | M. Petty | 2 | 0 | 0 | 2 | 0 | 0 | 290 |
|  | J. Paschal | 8 | 0 | 3 | 7 | 1 | 0 | 13,595 |
|  | B. Johns | 1 | 0 | 1 | 1 | 0 | 0 | 6,975 |
| 1961 | R. Petty | 42 | 2 | 16 | 20 | 18 | 2 | 22,696 |
|  | L. Petty | 3 | 1 | 2 | 2 | 1 | 1 | 1,260 |
|  | M. Petty | 9 | 0 | 2 | 4 | 3 | 0 | 1,460 |
|  | M. Porter | 2 | 0 | 1 | 1 | 1 | 0 | 450 |
|  | M. Panch | 1 | 0 | 0 | 0 | 1 | 0 | 200 |
|  | D. Dieringer | 1 | 0 | 0 | 1 | 0 | 0 | 1,375 |
|  | J. Paschal | 1 | 0 | 0 | 0 | 1 | 0 | 100 |
| 1962 | R. Petty | 52 | 8 | 32 | 38 | 11 | 4 | 52,885 |
|  | J. Paschal | 9 | 3 | 5 | 8 | 0 | 0 | 15,580 |
|  | M. Petty | 5 | 0 | 2 | 3 | 2 | 0 | 965 |
|  | B. Blackburn | 6 | 0 | 0 | 2 | 2 | 0 | 2,740 |
|  | L. Petty | 1 | 0 | 1 | 1 | 0 | 0 | 750 |
|  | S. Thompson | 1 | 0 | 0 | 1 | 0 | 0 | 900 |
| 1963 | R. Petty | 54 | 14 | 31 | 39 | 12 | 8 | 47,765 |
|  | J. Paschal | 29 | 5 | 15 | 18 | 10 | 1 | 18,515 |
|  | B. James | 4 | 0 | 0 | 0 | 3 | 0 | 1,700 |
|  | B. Welborn | 4 | 0 | 3 | 3 | 1 | 0 | 2,330 |
|  | M. Petty | 4 | 0 | 1 | 2 | 2 | 0 | 575 |
|  | L. Petty | 3 | 0 | 1 | 2 | 1 | 0 | 600 |
|  | J. Hurtubise | 3 | 0 | 0 | 0 | 3 | 0 | 975 |
|  | J. Weatherly | 1 | 0 | 1 | 1 | 0 | 0 | 500 |
|  | J. Massey | 1 | 0 | 0 | 0 | 1 | 0 | 125 |
| 1964 | R. Petty | 61 | 9 | 36 | 41 | 19 | 8 | 98,810 |
|  | J. Paschal | 13 | 1 | 7 | 8 | 5 | 0 | 47,845 |
|  | Buck Baker | 6 | 0 | 3 | 4 | 1 | 0 | 5,825 |
|  | M. Petty | 6 | 0 | 2 | 5 | 1 | 0 | 1,540 |
|  | L. Petty | 2 | 0 | 0 | 2 | 2 | 0 | 250 |
| 1965 | R. Petty | 14 | 4 | 10 | 10 | 4 | 7 | 16,450 |
|  | J. Paschal | 3 | 0 | 3 | 3 | 0 | 0 | 2,450 |
|  | L. Yarbrough | 1 | 0 | 0 | 0 | 1 | 0 | 150 |
| 1966 | R. Petty | 39 | 8 | 20 | 21 | 17 | 15 | 78,930 |
|  | M. Panch | 5 | 1 | 2 | 4 | 1 | 0 | 32,900 |
|  | J. Paschal | 1 | 0 | 0 | 0 | 1 | 0 | 325 |
|  | D. Dieringer | 1 | 0 | 0 | 1 | 0 | 0 | 570 |
|  | P. Lewis | 1 | 0 | 0 | 0 | 1 | 0 | 670 |
| 1967 | R. Petty | 48 | 27 | 38 | 39 | 8 | 18 | 130,275 |
|  | T. Lund | 4 | 0 | 3 | 3 | 1 | 0 | 11,525 |
|  | G.C. Spencer | 3 | 0 | 2 | 2 | 1 | 0 | 10,105 |
| 1968 | R. Petty | 49 | 16 | 31 | 33 | 16 | 12 | 89,103 |
| 1969 | R. Petty | 50 | 10 | 31 | 35 | 15 | 6 | 109,180 |
| 1970 | R. Petty | 40 | 18 | 25 | 29 | 10 | 9 | 138,969 |
|  | P. Hamilton | 15 | 3 | 9 | 11 | 4 | 1 | 130,806 |
|  | D. Gurney | 1 | 0 | 0 | 1 | 0 | 1 | 2,400 |
|  | J. Paschal | 1 | 0 | 0 | 0 | 0 | 0 | 1,800 |
| 1971 | R. Petty | 46 | 21 | 38 | 41 | 5 | 9 | 309,225 |
|  | Buddy Baker | 18 | 1 | 12 | 15 | 3 | 1 | 112,170 |
| 1972 | R. Petty | 31 | 8 | 25 | 27 | 4 | 3 | 227,015 |
|  | Buddy Baker | 10 | 1 | 3 | 4 | 6 | 0 | 51,875 |
| 1973 | R. Petty | 28 | 6 | 15 | 16 | 10 | 3 | 159,655 |
| 1974 | R. Petty | 30 | 10 | 22 | 23 | 7 | 7 | 299,175 |

| Year | Driver | Races | Won | Top 5 | Top 10 | DNF | Poles | Money Won |
|------|--------|-------|-----|-------|--------|-----|-------|-----------|
| | H. McGriff | 4 | 0 | 0 | 1 | 2 | 0 | 7,430 |
| 1975 | R. Petty | 30 | 13 | 21 | 24 | 6 | 3 | 378,865 |
| 1976 | R. Petty | 30 | 3 | 19 | 22 | 8 | 1 | 338,265 |
| 1977 | R. Petty | 30 | 5 | 20 | 23 | 6 | 5 | 345,886 |
| 1978 | R. Petty | 30 | 0 | 11 | 17 | 12 | 0 | 215,491 |
| 1979 | R. Petty | 31 | 5 | 23 | 27 | 3 | 1 | 531,292 |
| | K. Petty | 5 | 0 | 0 | 1 | 1 | 0 | 10,810 |
| 1980 | R. Petty | 31 | 2 | 15 | 18 | 10 | 0 | 374,092 |
| | K. Petty | 14 | 0 | 0 | 6 | 5 | 0 | 35,575 |
| 1981 | R. Petty | 31 | 3 | 11 | 15 | 14 | 0 | 389,214 |
| | K. Petty | 31 | 0 | 1 | 10 | 18 | 0 | 112,289 |
| 1982 | R. Petty | 30 | 0 | 9 | 16 | 13 | 0 | 453,832 |
| | K. Petty | 23 | 0 | 2 | 4 | 13 | 0 | 108,715 |
| 1983 | R. Petty | 30 | 3 | 9 | 21 | 5 | 0 | 491,022 |
| | K. Petty | 30 | 0 | 0 | 2 | 10 | 0 | 157,820 |
| 1984 | K. Petty | 30 | 0 | 1 | 6 | 7 | 0 | 324,555 |
| 1985 | D. Brooks | 3 | 0 | 0 | 0 | 3 | 0 | 20,340 |
| | M. Shepherd | 1 | 0 | 0 | 0 | 0 | 0 | 3,415 |
| 1986 | R. Petty | 29 | 0 | 4 | 11 | 10 | 0 | 280,657 |
| 1987 | R. Petty | 29 | 0 | 9 | 14 | 5 | 0 | 468,602 |
| 1988 | R. Petty | 29 | 0 | 1 | 5 | 15 | 0 | 190,155 |
| 1989 | R. Petty | 25 | 0 | 0 | 0 | 12 | 0 | 133,050 |
| 1990 | R. Petty | 29 | 0 | 0 | 1 | 12 | 0 | 169,465 |
| 1991 | R. Petty | 29 | 0 | 0 | 1 | 10 | 0 | 268,035 |
| 1992 | R. Petty | 29 | 0 | 0 | 0 | 5 | 0 | 348,870 |
| 1993 | R. Wilson | 29 | 0 | 0 | 1 | 6 | 0 | 299,725 |
| | J. Hensley | 1 | 0 | 0 | 0 | 1 | 0 | 5,875 |
| 1994 | W. Dallenbach Jr. | 14 | 0 | 1 | 3 | 3 | 0 | 241,492 |
| | J. Andretti | 11 | 0 | 0 | 0 | 2 | 0 | 116,400 |
| 1995 | B. Hamilton | 31 | 0 | 4 | 10 | 2 | 0 | 804,505 |
| 1996 | B. Hamilton | 31 | 1 | 3 | 11 | 4 | 2 | 1,151,235 |
| 1997 | B. Hamilton | 32 | 1 | 6 | 8 | 4 | 2 | 1,478,843 |
| 1998 | J. Andretti | 33 | 0 | 3 | 10 | 4 | 1 | 1,838,379 |
| 1999 | J. Andretti | 34 | 1 | 3 | 10 | 10 | 1 | 2,001,832 |
| | K. Petty | 32 | 0 | 0 | 9 | 4 | 0 | 1,278,953 |
| 2000 | J. Andretti | 34 | 0 | 0 | 2 | 7 | 0 | 2,035,902 |
| | K. Petty | 18 | 0 | 0 | 1 | 6 | 0 | 797,176 |
| | S. Grissom | 5 | 0 | 0 | 0 | 0 | 0 | 231,850 |
| | A. Petty | 1 | 0 | 0 | 0 | 1 | 0 | 38,675 |
| 2001 | J. Andretti | 35 | 0 | 1 | 2 | 4 | 0 | 2,873,184 |
| | K. Petty | 24 | 0 | 0 | 0 | 8 | 0 | 1,008,919 |
| | B. Jones | 30 | 0 | 0 | 0 | 10 | 0 | 1,631,488 |
| 2002 | J. Andretti | 36 | 0 | 0 | 1 | 7 | 0 | 2,954,229 |
| K. Petty | | 36 | 0 | 0 | 1 | 1 | 0 | 2,198,073 |
| | J. Nadeau | 13 | 0 | 0 | 0 | 5 | 0 | 718,202 |
| | S. Grissom | 10 | 0 | 0 | 0 | 1 | 0 | 529,781 |
| | B. Jones | 7 | 0 | 0 | 0 | 2 | 0 | 394,223 |
| | G. Biffle | 2 | 0 | 0 | 0 | 0 | 0 | 96,014 |
| | T. Musgrave | 1 | 0 | 0 | 0 | 0 | 0 | 58,450 |
| | C. Fittipaldi | 1 | 0 | 0 | 0 | 1 | 0 | 39,600 |
| 2003 | J. Green | 8 | 0 | 0 | 0 | 2 | 0 | 629,094 |
| | K. Petty | 33 | 0 | 0 | 0 | 6 | 0 | 2,293,220 |
| | C. Fittipaldi | 14 | 0 | 0 | 0 | 6 | 0 | 1,087,974 |
| 2004 | J. Green | 36 | 0 | 0 | 1 | 11 | 0 | 3,483,440 |
| | K. Petty | 35 | 0 | 0 | 0 | 9 | 0 | 2,729,682 |
| **TOTALS** | | **2,606** | **268** | **886** | **1,252** | **708** | **155** | **$43,718,371** |

# Jack Roush

**Date of birth:** 4/19/42. **Hometown:** Manchester, Ohio.
**Resides:** Northville, Mich. **Years as NNCS owner:** 17.
**Best points finish:** 1. **Career victories:** 74.
**First victory:** 1989 Rockingham. **Career poles:** 55.
**First pole:** 1988 Nashville.

As he closes in on 20 years of ownership in NASCAR's premier series, Jack Roush is basking in the glory of fielding back-to-back champions with Kurt Busch's victory in the inaugural Chase for the NASCAR NEXTEL Cup in 2004 and Matt Kenseth's Cup title in 2003. Ford teams hadn't won consecutive titles since David Pearson pulled off the double with Holman-Moody in 1968 and 1969. Roush Racing fields five NASCAR NEXTEL Cup Series teams. A former graduate-level mathematician and grass-roots racer from Michigan, Roush began competing in NASCAR's premier series in 1988 with Mark Martin's team. Since then, the stable has grown to include the teams of the No. 99 in 1996, Kenseth in 2000, Busch in 2001 and Greg Biffle in 2003. Roush Racing also fields teams in the NASCAR Craftsman Truck Series and NASCAR Busch Series and supplies engines to other NASCAR teams. An avid pilot, Roush also owns Roush Industries, a Michigan-based company that supplies parts to the automotive and transportation industries.

## CAREER NASCAR NEXTEL CUP SERIES STATS

| Year | Driver | Races | Won | Top 5 | Top 10 | DNF | Poles | Money Won |
|------|--------|-------|-----|-------|--------|-----|-------|-----------|
| 1988 | M. Martin | 29 | 0 | 3 | 10 | 10 | 1 | $223,630 |
| 1989 | M. Martin | 29 | 1 | 14 | 18 | 4 | 6 | 1,019,250 |
| 1990 | M. Martin | 29 | 3 | 17 | 24 | 1 | 3 | 1,302,958 |
| 1991 | M. Martin | 29 | 1 | 14 | 17 | 5 | 5 | 1,039,991 |
| 1992 | M. Martin | 29 | 2 | 10 | 17 | 5 | 1 | 1,000,571 |
| | W. Dallenbach Jr. | 29 | 0 | 1 | 1 | 7 | 0 | 220,245 |
| 1993 | M. Martin | 30 | 5 | 12 | 19 | 5 | 5 | 1,657,662 |
| | W. Dallenbach Jr. | 30 | 0 | 1 | 4 | 7 | 0 | 474,340 |
| 1994 | M. Martin | 31 | 2 | 15 | 20 | 8 | 1 | 1,628,906 |
| | T. Musgrave | 31 | 0 | 1 | 8 | 5 | 3 | 656,187 |
| 1995 | M. Martin | 31 | 4 | 13 | 22 | 1 | 4 | 1,893,519 |
| | T. Musgrave | 31 | 0 | 7 | 13 | 1 | 1 | 1,147,445 |
| 1996 | M. Martin | 31 | 0 | 14 | 23 | 4 | 4 | 1,887,396 |
| | T. Musgrave | 31 | 0 | 2 | 7 | 2 | 1 | 961,512 |
| | J. Burton | 30 | 0 | 6 | 12 | 1 | 1 | 884,303 |
| 1997 | M. Martin | 32 | 4 | 16 | 23 | 3 | 3 | 2,532,484 |
| | Y. Musgrave | 32 | 0 | 5 | 8 | 4 | 0 | 1,256,680 |
| | J. Burton | 32 | 3 | 13 | 18 | 1 | 0 | 2,296,614 |
| | C. Little | 11 | 0 | 0 | 0 | 1 | 0 | 212,590 |
| 1998 | M. Martin | 33 | 7 | 22 | 26 | 1 | 3 | 4,309,006 |
| | T. Musgrave | 20 | 0 | 1 | 4 | 3 | 0 | 965,076 |
| | J. Burton | 33 | 2 | 18 | 23 | 4 | 0 | 2,626,987 |
| | C. Little | 32 | 0 | 1 | 7 | 7 | 0 | 1,449,659 |
| | J. Benson | 32 | 0 | 3 | 10 | 5 | 0 | 1,360,335 |
| | K. Lepage | 13 | 0 | 0 | 2 | 5 | 0 | 447,745 |
| 1999 | M. Martin | 34 | 2 | 19 | 26 | 3 | 1 | 3,509,744 |
| | J. Burton | 34 | 6 | 18 | 23 | 3 | 0 | 5,725,399 |
| | C. Little | 34 | 0 | 0 | 5 | 4 | 0 | 1,623,976 |
| | J. Benson | 34 | 0 | 0 | 2 | 4 | 0 | 1,567,668 |
| | K. Lepage | 34 | 0 | 1 | 2 | 3 | 1 | 1,587,841 |
| | M. Kenseth | 5 | 0 | 1 | 1 | 3 | 0 | 143,561 |
| 2000 | M. Martin | 34 | 1 | 13 | 20 | 6 | 0 | 3,098,874 |
| | J. Burton | 34 | 4 | 15 | 22 | 2 | 1 | 5,959,439 |
| | C. Little | 27 | 0 | 0 | 1 | 3 | 0 | 1,418,884 |
| | K. Lepage | 32 | 0 | 1 | 3 | 5 | 0 | 1,679,186 |
| | M. Kenseth | 34 | 1 | 4 | 11 | 5 | 0 | 2,408,138 |
| 2001 | M. Martin | 36 | 0 | 3 | 15 | 4 | 2 | 3,797,006 |
| | K. Busch | 7 | 0 | 0 | 0 | 0 | 0 | 311,915 |
| | J. Burton | 36 | 2 | 8 | 16 | 1 | 0 | 4,230,737 |
| | M. Kenseth | 36 | 0 | 4 | 9 | 5 | 0 | 2,565,579 |
| | K. Busch | 35 | 0 | 3 | 6 | 7 | 1 | 2,170,629 |
| 2002 | M. Martin | 36 | 1 | 12 | 22 | 3 | 0 | 7,004,893 |
| | J. Burton | 36 | 0 | 5 | 14 | 5 | 0 | 4,244,856 |
| | K. Busch | 36 | 4 | 12 | 20 | 4 | 1 | 5,105,394 |
| | M. Kenseth | 36 | 5 | 11 | 19 | 3 | 1 | 4,514,203 |
| | G Biffle | 1 | 0 | 0 | 0 | 0 | 0 | 80,059 |

| Year | Driver | Races | Won | Top 5 | Top 10 | DNF | Poles | Money Won |
|------|--------|-------|-----|-------|--------|-----|-------|-----------|
| 2003 | M. Kenseth | 36 | 1 | 11 | 25 | 2 | 0 | 4,038,120 |
| | M. Martin | 36 | 0 | 5 | 10 | 7 | 0 | 4,048,850 |
| | K. Busch | 36 | 4 | 9 | 14 | 8 | 0 | 5,020,480 |
| | G. Biffle | 35 | 1 | 2 | 6 | 6 | 0 | 2,410,050 |
| | J. Burton | 36 | 0 | 3 | 11 | 4 | 0 | 3,846,880 |
| 2004 | K. Busch | 36 | 3 | 10 | 21 | 3 | 2 | 4,200,330 |
| | M. Martin | 36 | 1 | 10 | 15 | 2 | 0 | 3,948,500 |
| | M. Kenseth | 36 | 2 | 8 | 16 | 2 | 2 | 6,223,890 |
| | G. Biffle | 36 | 2 | 4 | 8 | 5 | 1 | 3,583,340 |
| | C. Edwards | 13 | 0 | 1 | 5 | 2 | 0 | 1,410,570 |
| | D. Blaney | 1 | 0 | 0 | 0 | 1 | 0 | 88,087 |
| **TOTALS** | | **1688** | **74** | **702** | **704** | **215** | **55** | **$135,022,169** |

| CAREER NASCAR NEXTEL CUP SERIES STATS | | | | | | | | |
|------|--------|-------|-----|-------|--------|-----|-------|-----------|
| Year | Driver | Races | Won | Top 5 | Top 10 | DNF | Poles | Money Won |
| 1985 | M. Shepherd | 1 | 0 | 0 | 0 | 0 | 0 | $55,985 |
| 1988 | M. Shepherd | 9 | 0 | 0 | 0 | 6 | 0 | 197,425 |
| 2002 | M. Shepherd | 2 | 0 | 0 | 0 | 5 | 0 | 214,397 |
| 2003 | M. Shepherd | 2 | 0 | 0 | 0 | 2 | 0 | 120,034 |
| 2004 | M. Shepherd | 19 | 0 | 0 | 0 | 17 | 0 | 1,099,319 |
| **TOTALS** | | **33** | **0** | **0** | **0** | **30** | **0** | **$1,687,160** |

# Morgan Shepherd

**Date of birth:** 10/12/41. **Hometown:** Conover, N.C.
**Resides:** Conover, N.C. **Years as NNCS owner:** 5.
**Best points finish:** 42. **Career victories:** 0. **Career poles:** 0.

Shepherd is the oldest active driver in NASCAR's Nextel Cup Series and has four career victories in the sport—including two Cup wins at Atlanta Motor Speedway. A born-again Christian, Shepherd is an independent driver who adorns the hood of the No. 89 car with "Racing With Jesus."

# Jim Smith

**Date of birth:** 3/28. **Hometown:** Altadena, Calif.
**Resides:** Orange, Calif. **Years as NNCS owner:** 7.
**Best points finish:** 27. **Career victories:** 0. **Career poles:** 0.

Jim Smith, a California-based businessman and long-time racing enthusiast, began his seventh year as a NASCAR NEXTEL Cup Series owner with Jimmy Spencer and closed it with Dave Blaney. If Ultra Motorsports needs a team-building model for its NASCAR NEXTEL Cup Series entry, it need look no further than Smith's legacy in the NASCAR Craftsman Truck Series. An original team owner in that series, Smith has enjoyed numerous victories with his NASCAR Craftsman Truck teams.

Jack Roush (left) won a championship with crew chief Robbie Reiser (right) and Matt Kenseth in 2003 and with Kurt Busch and crew chief Jimmy Fennig in 2004.

## CAREER NASCAR NEXTEL CUP SERIES STATS • Jim Smith

| Year | Driver | Races | Won | Top 5 | Top 10 | DNF | Poles | Money Won |
|------|--------|-------|-----|-------|--------|-----|-------|-----------|
| 1998 | G. Bodine | 32 | 0 | 1 | 5 | 10 | 0 | $1,247,255 |
| 1999 | M. Waltrip | 34 | 0 | 1 | 3 | 10 | 0 | 1,702,460 |
| 2000 | M. Waltrip | 34 | 0 | 1 | 1 | 10 | 0 | 1,690,821 |
| 2001 | M. Wallace | 21 | 0 | 0 | 4 | 3 | 0 | 1,394,697 |
|  | K. Lepage | 8 | 0 | 0 | 0 | 0 | 0 | 458,860 |
|  | R. Gordon | 2 | 0 | 1 | 1 | 0 | 0 | 167,335 |
|  | T. Musgrave | 1 | 0 | 0 | 0 | 0 | 0 | 43,565 |
| 2002 | C. Atwood | 34 | 0 | 0 | 0 | 5 | 0 | 1,951,079 |
|  | T. Musgrave | 4 | 0 | 0 | 0 | 0 | 0 | 225,320 |
|  | J. Leffler | 2 | 0 | 0 | 0 | 0 | 0 | 78,500 |
| 2003 | J. Spencer | 35 | 0 | 1 | 4 | 8 | 0 | 2,565,800 |
|  | T. Musgrave | 1 | 0 | 0 | 0 | 0 | 0 | 63,715 |
| 2004 | D. Blaney | 1 | 0 | 0 | 0 | 1 | 0 | 55,555 |
|  | J. Spencer | 1 | 0 | 0 | 0 | 0 | 0 | 223,513 |
| **TOTALS** |  | **210** | **0** | **5** | **18** | **47** | **0** | **$11,868,475** |

\* Co-owner with Jim Mattei 1998 through Oct. 22, 2000.

# Cal Wells

**Date of birth:** 10/12/55. **Hometown:** Pomona, Calif.
**Resides:** San Juan Capistrano, Calif. and Hickory, N.C.
**Years as NNCS owner:** 5. **Best points finish:** 15.
**Career victories:** 2. **First victory:** 2001 Martinsville.
**Career poles:** 3. **First pole:** 2001 Michigan.

With only three employees and a small garage in Westminster, Calif., in 1979, Cal Wells III founded Precision Preparation, Inc. (PPI)—a company specializing in servicing off-road racing teams. PPI eventually started fielding its own off-road competition efforts and has since evolved into a company now called PPI Motorsports. PPI Motorsports consisted of competitive stock-car, open-wheel and off-road programs. Prior to coming to NASCAR, Wells was renowned for his efforts in stadium and off-road racing. In 1994 he moved into the CART open-wheel series with drivers such as Robby Gordon and Scott Pruett. Concurrent with CART, Wells established a Toyota Atlantic program and won that series' championship in 1999. In 1999, PPI moved into the NASCAR Busch Series and a year later started competing in NASCAR's premier series with Pruett as the driver. The move to NASCAR necessitated a headquarters move from California to Hickory, N.C. Late in 2000, Wells ceased his other racing efforts to concentrate on NASCAR. Wells signed Ricky Craven as a driver prior to the 2001 season, and in October 2001 the team captured its first victory, at Martinsville Speedway. Midway through the 2004 season, Bobby Hamilton Jr. took over driving duties for PPI.

## CAREER NASCAR NEXTEL CUP SERIES STATS

| Year | Driver | Races | Won | Top 5 | Top 10 | DNF | Poles | Money Won |
|------|--------|-------|-----|-------|--------|-----|-------|-----------|
| 2000 | S. Pruett | 28 | 0 | 0 | 1 | 11 | 0 | $1,135,854 |
|  | A. Houston | 5 | 0 | 0 | 0 | 2 | 0 | 141,850 |
| 2001 | R. Craven | 36 | 1 | 4 | 7 | 9 | 1 | 1,996,981 |
|  | A. Houston | 17 | 0 | 0 | 0 | 9 | 0 | 865,263 |
| 2002 | R. Craven | 36 | 0 | 3 | 9 | 4 | 2 | 2,838,087 |
| 2003 | R. Craven | 36 | 1 | 3 | 8 | 10 | 0 | 3,116,210 |
| 2004 | R. Craven | 25 | 0 | 0 | 0 | 8 | 0 | 2,191,012 |
|  | B. Hamilton Jr. | 11 | 0 | 0 | 0 | 2 | 0 | 855,248 |
| **TOTALS** |  | **194** | **2** | **10** | **25** | **55** | **3** | **$13,140,505** |

# Wood Brothers

**Owners:** Glen Wood, Len Wood, Eddie Wood, Kim Wood Hall.
**Years as NNCS owner:** 52. **Best points finish:** 1.
**Career victories:** 97. **First victory:** 1960 Winston-Salem.
**Career poles:** 116. **First pole:** 1958 N. Wilkesboro.

Founded in 1953 by Glen Wood, Wood Brothers Racing is one of the most storied ownership organizations in the history of NASCAR. Its drivers' roll reads like a "Who's Who" of the sport, featuring some of auto racing's greatest names—David Pearson, Cale Yarborough, Marvin Panch, Tiny Lund, Fred Lorenzen, Dan Gurney, Bobby Rahal, Parnelli Jones, A.J. Foyt, Speedy Thompson, Donnie Allison, Buddy Baker, Morgan Shepherd, Dale Jarrett, Neil Bonnett, Michael Waltrip and now, Ricky Rudd. Glen Wood himself drove for his family operation from 1953-64. In 1963, the Wood Brothers took first place in the owner standings with five drivers. The Wood Brothers are credited with being the first team to truly grasp the importance of fast pit stops. They also assembled the pit crew for 1965 Indianapolis 500 winner Jim Clark.

## CAREER NASCAR NEXTEL CUP SERIES STATS

| Year | Driver | Races | Won | Top 5 | Top 10 | DNF | Poles | Money Won |
|------|--------|-------|-----|-------|--------|-----|-------|-----------|
| 1953 | G. Wood | 2 | 0 | 0 | 0 | 1 | 0 | $125 |
| 1954 | G. Wood | 1 | 0 | 0 | 0 | 1 | 0 | 0 |
| 1955 | G. Wood | 1 | 0 | 0 | 0 | 1 | 0 | 0 |
| 1956 | G. Wood | 1 | 0 | 0 | 0 | 1 | 0 | 50 |
| 1957 | G. Wood | 2 | 0 | 0 | 0 | 1 | 0 | 300 |
| 1958 | G. Wood | 5 | 0 | 1 | 5 | 0 | 1 | 1,500 |
| 1959 | G. Wood | 16 | 0 | 7 | 10 | 4 | 2 | 4,010 |
| 1960 | G. Wood | 9 | 3 | 6 | 7 | 2 | 4 | 4,910 |
|  | J. Massey | 3 | 0 | 2 | 2 | 1 | 0 | 2,085 |
|  | S. Thompson | 3 | 2 | 3 | 3 | 0 | 0 | 15,985 |
|  | F. Harb | 2 | 0 | 0 | 1 | 1 | 0 | 475 |
|  | J. Johnson | 2 | 0 | 1 | 1 | 1 | 1 | 345 |
|  | C. Turner | 1 | 0 | 0 | 0 | 1 | 0 | 50 |
|  | B. Welborn | 1 | 0 | 0 | 0 | 1 | 0 | 125 |
| 1961 | G. Wood | 6 | 0 | 3 | 3 | 3 | 1 | 2,000 |
|  | C. Turner | 7 | 0 | 1 | 1 | 6 | 0 | 5,960 |
|  | B. Matthews | 1 | 0 | 0 | 0 | 1 | 0 | 100 |
|  | S. Thompson | 1 | 0 | 0 | 0 | 1 | 0 | 825 |
| 1962 | M. Panch | 14 | 0 | 5 | 8 | 5 | 0 | 23,470 |
| 1963 | M. Panch | 12 | 1 | 9 | 12 | 0 | 3 | 37,461 |
|  | T. Lund | 7 | 1 | 5 | 6 | 1 | 0 | 33,645 |
|  | G. Wood | 3 | 1 | 2 | 2 | 1 | 2 | 1,070 |
|  | D. MacDonald | 1 | 0 | 1 | 1 | 0 | 0 | 4,655 |
|  | F. Lorenzen | 1 | 0 | 0 | 0 | 1 | 0 | 530 |
| 1964 | M. Panch | 29 | 3 | 17 | 18 | 10 | 5 | 31,785 |
|  | D. Gurney | 1 | 1 | 1 | 1 | 0 | 0 | 12,870 |

| Year | Driver | Races | Won | Top 5 | Top 10 | DNF | Poles | Money Won |
|------|--------|-------|-----|-------|--------|-----|-------|-----------|
|  | G. Wood | 2 | 0 | 1 | 1 | 1 | 1 | 530 |
| 1965 | M. Panch | 20 | 4 | 12 | 14 | 6 | 5 | 54,045 |
|  | C. Turner | 4 | 1 | 3 | 3 | 1 | 0 | 16,643 |
|  | D. Gurney | 1 | 1 | 1 | 1 | 0 | 0 | 13,625 |
|  | A.J. Foyt | 1 | 0 | 0 | 1 | 0 | 0 | 1,775 |
| 1966 | M. Panch | 6 | 0 | 1 | 1 | 5 | 0 | 3,700 |
|  | C. Turner | 6 | 0 | 2 | 2 | 3 | 0 | 6,760 |
|  | D. Gurney | 1 | 1 | 1 | 1 | 0 | 0 | 18,445 |
|  | C. Yarborough | 5 | 0 | 1 | 1 | 3 | 0 | 4,350 |
| 1967 | C. Yarborough | 15 | 2 | 7 | 7 | 8 | 4 | 56,310 |
|  | P. Jones | 1 | 1 | 1 | 1 | 0 | 0 | 18,720 |
|  | Balmer | 1 | 0 | 0 | 0 | 1 | 0 | 625 |

| Year | Driver | Races | Won | Top 5 | Top 10 | DNF | Poles | Money Won |
|---|---|---|---|---|---|---|---|---|
| 1968 | C. Yarborough | 20 | 6 | 12 | 12 | 8 | 4 | 136,536 |
| | D. Gurney | 1 | 1 | 1 | 1 | 0 | 1 | 21,250 |
| 1969 | C. Yarborough | 19 | 2 | 7 | 8 | 11 | 6 | 74,240 |
| 1970 | C. Yarborough | 18 | 3 | 11 | 12 | 6 | 5 | 114,675 |
| 1971 | D. Allison | 11 | 1 | 7 | 8 | 3 | 5 | 68,245 |
| | A.J. Foyt | 4 | 2 | 4 | 4 | 0 | 4 | 86,775 |
| 1972 | D. Pearson | 14 | 6 | 11 | 11 | 3 | 4 | 131,415 |
| | A.J. Foyt | 6 | 2 | 5 | 5 | 1 | 3 | 94,440 |
| 1973 | D. Pearson | 18 | 11 | 14 | 14 | 4 | 8 | 213,966 |
| 1974 | D. Pearson | 19 | 7 | 15 | 15 | 4 | 11 | 221,615 |
| 1975 | D. Pearson | 21 | 3 | 13 | 13 | 8 | 7 | 179,208 |
| 1976 | D. Pearson | 22 | 10 | 16 | 18 | 4 | 8 | 283,686 |
| 1977 | D. Pearson | 22 | 2 | 16 | 16 | 6 | 5 | 180,999 |
| 1978 | D. Pearson | 22 | 4 | 11 | 11 | 11 | 7 | 151,837 |
| 1979 | D. Pearson | 5 | 0 | 1 | 1 | 4 | 1 | 22,815 |
| | N. Bonnett | 17 | 3 | 4 | 6 | 11 | 4 | 131,875 |
| 1980 | N. Bonnett | 22 | 2 | 10 | 13 | 9 | 0 | 210,547 |
| 1981 | N. Bonnett | 22 | 3 | 7 | 8 | 14 | 1 | 181,670 |
| 1982 | N. Bonnett | 22 | 1 | 6 | 8 | 13 | 0 | 130,964 |
| 1983 | Buddy Baker | 21 | 1 | 5 | 12 | 8 | 1 | 206,355 |
| 1984 | Buddy Baker | 21 | 0 | 4 | 12 | 7 | 1 | 133,635 |
| | B. Rahal | 1 | 0 | 0 | 0 | 1 | 0 | 875 |
| 1985 | K. Petty | 28 | 0 | 7 | 12 | 4 | 0 | 296,367 |
| 1986 | K. Petty | 29 | 1 | 4 | 14 | 6 | 0 | 403,242 |
| 1987 | K. Petty | 29 | 1 | 6 | 14 | 4 | 0 | 544,437 |
| 1988 | K. Petty | 29 | 0 | 2 | 8 | 6 | 0 | 377,092 |
| 1989 | N. Bonnett | 26 | 0 | 0 | 11 | 5 | 0 | 271,628 |
| | T. Ellis | 3 | 0 | 0 | 0 | 1 | 0 | 15,385 |
| 1990 | D. Jarrett | 24 | 0 | 1 | 7 | 9 | 0 | 214,495 |
| | N. Bonnett | 5 | 0 | 0 | 0 | 3 | 0 | 62,600 |
| 1991 | D. Jarrett | 29 | 1 | 3 | 8 | 9 | 0 | 444,256 |
| 1992 | M. Shepherd | 29 | 0 | 3 | 11 | 3 | 0 | 634,222 |
| 1993 | M. Shepherd | 30 | 1 | 3 | 15 | 2 | 0 | 782,523 |
| 1994 | M. Shepherd | 31 | 0 | 9 | 16 | 2 | 0 | 1,089,038 |
| 1995 | M. Shepherd | 31 | 0 | 4 | 10 | 2 | 0 | 966,374 |
| 1996 | M. Waltrip | 31 | 0 | 1 | 11 | 3 | 0 | 1,182,811 |
| 1997 | M. Waltrip | 32 | 0 | 0 | 6 | 4 | 0 | 1,138,599 |
| 1998 | M. Waltrip | 32 | 0 | 0 | 5 | 3 | 0 | 1,508,680 |
| 1999 | E. Sadler | 34 | 0 | 0 | 1 | 2 | 0 | 1,589,221 |
| 2000 | E. Sadler | 33 | 0 | 0 | 1 | 5 | 0 | 1,578,356 |
| 2001 | E. Sadler | 36 | 1 | 2 | 2 | 2 | 0 | 2,683,225 |
| 2002 | E. Sadler | 36 | 0 | 2 | 7 | 6 | 0 | 3,491,694 |
| 2003 | R. Rudd | 36 | 0 | 4 | 5 | 9 | 0 | 3,106,610 |
| 2004 | R. Rudd | 36 | 0 | 1 | 3 | 6 | 1 | 3,629,869 |
| TOTALS | | 1172 | 97 | 326 | 489 | 305 | 116 | $29,368,206 |

Yarborough. From 1976-86, Yates applied his trade at DiGard Racing, helping Allison win the 1983 series title. In 1988, Yates launched his own team, Robert Yates Racing, after taking over Harry Ranier's No. 28 team. At the time, Bobby's son, Davey, was driving the No. 28 and the new team produced some memorable moments—winning the '92 Daytona 500 and being in close contention for that year's championship before Alan Kulwicki won the title by the closest margin in series history. In 1996, Yates' operation expanded to a two-car team with drivers Dale Jarrett and Ernie Irvan, a format which the team continues today. Beginning with the 2003 season, Yates' famous No. 28 car was changed to No. 38 with the addition of sponsorship from M&Ms and driver Elliot Sadler.

## CAREER NASCAR NEXTEL CUP SERIES STATS

| Year | Driver | Races | Won | Top 5 | Top 10 | DNF | Poles | Money Won |
|---|---|---|---|---|---|---|---|---|
| 1989 | Da. Allison | 29 | 2 | 7 | 13 | 6 | 1 | $640,956 |
| 1990 | Da. Allison | 29 | 2 | 5 | 10 | 2 | 0 | 640,684 |
| 1991 | Da. Allison | 29 | 5 | 12 | 16 | 4 | 3 | 1,732,924 |
| 1992 | Da. Allison | 29 | 5 | 15 | 17 | 3 | 2 | 1,955,628 |
| 1993 | Da. Allison | 16 | 1 | 6 | 8 | 1 | 0 | 513,585 |
| | E. Irvan | 9 | 2 | 5 | 6 | 1 | 2 | 584,483 |
| | L. Speed | 3 | 0 | 0 | 1 | 0 | 0 | 60,620 |
| | R. Gordon | 1 | 0 | 0 | 0 | 1 | 0 | 17,665 |
| 1994 | E. Irvan | 20 | 3 | 13 | 15 | 3 | 5 | 1,311,522 |
| | K. Wallace | 10 | 0 | 1 | 2 | 1 | 0 | 211,810 |
| 1995 | E. Irvan | 3 | 0 | 0 | 2 | 1 | 0 | 54,875 |
| | D. Jarrett | 31 | 1 | 9 | 14 | 6 | 1 | 1,363,158 |
| 1996 | E. Irvan | 31 | 2 | 12 | 16 | 5 | 1 | 1,683,313 |
| | D. Jarrett | 31 | 4 | 17 | 21 | 3 | 2 | 2,985,418 |
| 1997 | E. Irvan | 32 | 1 | 5 | 13 | 8 | 2 | 1,614,281 |
| | D. Jarrett | 32 | 7 | 20 | 23 | 1 | 2 | 3,240,542 |
| 1998 | D. Jarrett | 33 | 3 | 19 | 22 | 3 | 2 | 4,019,657 |
| | K. Irwin | 32 | 0 | 1 | 4 | 8 | 1 | 1,459,867 |
| 1999 | D. Jarrett | 34 | 4 | 24 | 29 | 1 | 0 | 6,649,596 |
| | K. Irwin | 34 | 0 | 2 | 6 | 5 | 2 | 2,125,810 |
| 2000 | D. Jarrett | 34 | 2 | 15 | 24 | 2 | 3 | 5,934,475 |
| | R. Rudd | 34 | 0 | 12 | 19 | 1 | 2 | 2,914,970 |
| 2001 | D. Jarrett | 36 | 4 | 12 | 19 | 4 | 4 | 5,377,742 |
| | R. Rudd | 36 | 2 | 14 | 22 | 4 | 1 | 4,878,027 |
| 2002 | D. Jarrett | 36 | 2 | 10 | 18 | 5 | 1 | 4,421,951 |
| | R. Rudd | 36 | 1 | 8 | 12 | 4 | 1 | 4,444,614 |
| 2003 | D. Jarrett | 36 | 1 | 1 | 7 | 9 | 0 | 4,055,490 |
| | E. Sadler | 36 | 0 | 1 | 9 | 9 | 2 | 3,660,170 |
| | J. Jarrett | 1 | 0 | 0 | 0 | 0 | 0 | 52,640 |
| 2004 | D. Jarrett | 36 | 0 | 6 | 14 | 3 | 0 | 4,208,217 |
| | E. Sadler | 36 | 2 | 8 | 14 | 1 | 0 | 4,879,129 |
| TOTALS | | 825 | 56 | 260 | 396 | 105 | 40 | $77,693,819 |

# Robert Yates

**Date of birth:** 4/19/43. **Hometown:** Charlotte, N.C.
**Resides:** Cornelius, N.C. **Years as NNCS owner:** 16.
**Best points finish:** 1. **Career victories:** 56.
**First victory:** 1989 Talladega. **Career poles:** 40.
**First pole:** 1989 Dover.

Known for his talent as an engine builder in addition to running a successful race team, Robert Yates began his career at Holman-Moody Racing in 1968. By 1971, his reputation around the shop and his skills with racing engines landed Yates a top job with Junior Johnson, where he provided power for legendary drivers Bobby Allison and Cale

# Steve Addington

**Hometown:** Spartanburg, N.C. **Team:** No. 18 Chevrolet.
**Years as crew chief with current team:** First.
**Overall seasons as crew chief:** First.

The Addington file:

The start of the 2005 season sees Addington in his first in the NASCAR NEXTEL Cup series after being promoted within Joe Gibbs Racing. Addington served as crew chief for the No. 20 car in the NASCAR Busch Series, which Mike Bliss drove and finished fifth in points. Before moving to JGR, Addington was Jason Keller's crew chief in the NASCAR Busch Series, first at KEL Racing from 1990-96 then at ppc Racing from 1999-2003.

# Tommy Baldwin

**Date of birth:** 10/27/66. **Hometown:** Bellport, N.Y.
**Resides:** Mooresville, N.C. **Team:** No. 9 Dodge.
**Years as crew chief with current team:** 1.
**Overall seasons as crew chief:** 8.

The Baldwin file:

Baldwin learned to love racing at his father's side. And Baldwin's own career has been associated with some of the legends of racing, starting in 1997 with owner Junie Donlavey. After one year, Baldwin began working for Bill Davis racing and gained the majority of his experience in that organization across more than four seasons. After two years of working with veteran driver Jimmy Spencer, in 2004 Baldwin switched gears and began working with a rookie driver, Kasey Kahne, and Evernham Motorsports. Baldwin also acts as an owner and crew chief in the NASCAR Busch Series, fielding the No. 6 Dodge in that series.

### 2004 NASCAR NEXTEL CUP SERIES STATS

| Driver | Races | Won | Top 5 | Top 10 | DNF | Poles | Money Won |
|---|---|---|---|---|---|---|---|
| Kasey Kahne | 36 | 0 | 13 | 14 | 7 | 4 | $4,647,947 |

# Robert Barker

**Date of birth:** 3/2/71. **Hometown:** Brookneal, Va.
**Resides:** Mooresville, N.C. **Team:** No. 11 Chevrolet.
**Years as crew chief with current team:** First.
**Overall seasons as crew chief:** 1.

The Barker file:

A journeyman crew chief with a mechanical engineering degree from Old Dominion, Barker cut his teeth working with Ashton Lewis on Late Models. He quickly moved on to the NASCAR Craftsman Truck Series, working for owner Kurt Roehrig. From 1998 to 1999, he worked for Bill

Davis Racing and Hendrick Motosports, earning his first shot at a crew chief job in the NASCAR Busch Series. In 2004, Barker was called upon to jump-start the No. 0 team and driver Ward Burton and to smooth Jason Leffler's transition to the NASCAR NEXTEL Cup series.

### 2004 NASCAR NEXTEL CUP SERIES STATS

| Driver | Races | Won | Top 5 | Top 10 | DNF | Poles | Money Won |
|---|---|---|---|---|---|---|---|
| Ward Burton | 2 | 0 | 0 | 0 | 1 | 0 | $120,100 |
| Jason Leffler | 1 | 0 | 0 | 0 | 1 | 0 | $116,359 |
| Mike Bliss | 2 | 0 | 0 | 1 | 1 | 0 | $135,850 |

# Todd Berrier

**Date of birth:** 5/29/70. **Hometown:** Kernersville, N.C.
**Resides:** Winston-Salem, N.C. **Team:** No. 29 Chevrolet.
**Years as crew chief with current team:** 2.
**Overall seasons as crew chief:** 2.

The Berrier file:

This driver-crew chief bond was forged in the NASCAR Busch Series, with Berrier and Kevin Harvick winning that title in 2001 in just their second year together. The pair's first year was also successful, with Harvick placing third in NASCAR Busch Series final points standings and taking home the Raybestos Rookie of the Year award. In an effort to find the match that leads to victories, Richard Childress brought Berrier to the NASCAR Cup circuit in 2003, reuniting him with Harvick. Berrier also has NASCAR Craftsman Truck Series crew chief experience, guiding the No. 3 Richard Childress Racing team from midway through 1997 to 1999. Berrier helped Jay Sauter to four victories during that time.

### 2004 NASCAR NEXTEL CUP SERIES STATS

| Driver | Races | Won | Top 5 | Top 10 | DNF | Poles | Money Won |
|---|---|---|---|---|---|---|---|
| Kevin Harvick | 36 | 0 | 5 | 14 | 4 | 0 | $4,545,434 |

# Matt Borland

**Date of birth:** 9/2/71. **Hometown:** Haslett, Mich.
**Resides:** Cornelius, N.C. **Team:** No. 12 Dodge.
**Years as crew chief with current team:** 3.
**Overall seasons as crew chief:** 3.

The Borland file:

A mechanical engineer who has CART and research experience, Borland is a perfect fit for working with the cerebral Ryan Newman. The pair worked together to build a resume of eight poles, two wins, five top fives and 11 top 10s in an ARCA-Busch-Cup whirlwind before they came into the NASCAR Cup full time in 2002. Borland guided Newman to Raybestos Rookie of the Year that season as they piled up one win, six poles and 14 top five finishes. In 2003 and 2004, they continued their pole-pounding ways, setting records for pole speeds across NASCAR nation.

### 2004 NASCAR NEXTEL CUP SERIES STATS

| Driver | Races | Won | Top 5 | Top 10 | DNF | Poles | Money Won |
|---|---|---|---|---|---|---|---|
| Ryan Newman | 36 | 2 | 11 | 14 | 9 | 9 | $4,762,399 |

# Chris Carrier

**Date of birth:** 4/6/60. **Hometown:** Bristol, Tenn.
**Resides:** Fariview, N.C. **Team:** No. 4 Chevrolet.
**Years with current team:** 3. **Years as crew chief:** 3.
**Overall seasons as crew chief:** 3.

The Carrier file:

He might have only three years of experience as a crew chief, but Carrier has been part of some impressive teams and drivers such as Morgan Shepherd, Dale Earnhardt, Bobby Allison and Harry Gant. After growing up in Bristol Motor Speedway's neck of the woods, Carrier grew up to be the head of his own racing team, becoming a crew chief for Morgan-McClure Motorsports in 2002. He guided Mike Skinner that season, and worked with Jimmy Spencer, Kevin Lepage and Mike Wallace in 2004.

### 2004 NASCAR NEXTEL CUP SERIES STATS

| Driver | Races | Won | Top 5 | Top 10 | DNF | Poles | Money Won |
|---|---|---|---|---|---|---|---|
| Kevin Lepage | 6 | 0 | 0 | 0 | 1 | 0 | $531,632 |
| Jimmy Spencer | 25 | 0 | 0 | 0 | 6 | 0 | $1,728,309 |
| Mike Wallace | 3 | 0 | 0 | 0 | 2 | 0 | $162,880 |

# Larry Carter

**Date of birth:** 9/21/62. **Hometown:** Raleigh, N.C.
**Resides:** Mooresville, N.C. **Team:** No. 2 Dodge.
**Years as crew chief with current team:** 3.
**Overall seasons as crew chief:** 3.

The Carter file:

The nephew of NASCAR team owner Travis Carter, Larry has gained a breadth of experience in just three seasons as a crew chief. His first head wrench job came at Haas Carter Motorsports. He then joined BACE Motorsports in 2003 as crew chief, working with rookie Tony Raines. Carter switched gears in 2004, working with seasoned veteran Rusty Wallace and was part of the No. 2's victory at Martinsville that broke Wallace's 105-race winless streak.

### 2004 NASCAR NEXTEL CUP SERIES STATS

| Driver | Races | Won | Top 5 | Top 10 | DNF | Poles | Money Won |
|---|---|---|---|---|---|---|---|
| Rusty Wallace | 36 | 1 | 3 | 11 | 3 | 0 | $4,229,069 |

# Dave Charpentier

**Date of birth:** 2/24/1959. **Hometown:** Havere de Grace, Md.
**Resides:** Haddenite, N.C. **Team:** No. 14 Ford.
**Years as crew chief with current team:** First.
**Overall seasons as crew chief:** 2.

The Charpentier file:

In 1997, Charpentier got his first full-time crew chief job with Rick Mast in the No. 75 car. From there, he went to Hendrick Motorsports as an engineer. His next stop was at DEI, where he worked for more than five years as manager of engineering. When the opportunity to join this new ppc Racing No. 14 team emerged in 2004, Charpentier went to work on building a program from scratch.

### 2004 NASCAR NEXTEL CUP SERIES STATS • Dave Charpentier

| Driver | Races | Won | Top 5 | Top 10 | DNF | Poles | Money Won |
|---|---|---|---|---|---|---|---|
| John Andretti | 4 | 0 | 0 | 0 | 0 | 0 | $233,125 |

# Ernie Cope

**Date of birth:** 7/17/69. **Hometown:** Tacoma, Wash. Huntersville, N.C. **Team:** No. 02 Chevrolet.
**Years as crew chief with current team:** 1.
**Overall seasons as crew chief:** 2

The Cope file:

You can't pick your family, but you can pick your crew chief, and Derrike Cope has paired with his cousin, Ernie, in NASCAR Cup racing in the past. Ernie Cope also has plenty of ARCA crew chief experience, most recently teaming up with Andy Belmont. Belmont and Cope also spent time together in 2004 on the NASCAR NEXTEL Cup circuit. As crew chief for the No. 02 car, Cope has worked with owner/driver Hermie Sadler, as well as part-time driver Carl Long. A lack of steady sponsorship has been a challenge for this team.

### 2004 NASCAR NEXTEL CUP SERIES STATS

| Driver | Races | Won | Top 5 | Top 10 | DNF | Poles | Money Won |
|---|---|---|---|---|---|---|---|
| Hermie Sadler | 16 | 0 | 0 | 0 | 11 | 0 | $945,549 |

# Jimmy Elledge

**Date of birth:** 7/14/70. **Hometown:** Redding, Calif.
**Resides:** Arden, N.C. **Team:** No. 41 Dodge.
**Years as crew chief with current team:** 1.
**Overall seasons as crew chief:** 6.

The Elledge file:

Elledge was introduced to the sport as a child, when he worked on his father's drag racing cars, but he originally intended to spend his racing career as a driver. In 1992, he decided to focus on the mechanical side of the sport and learned the trade from Robert Yates, Richard Childress and Dale Earnhardt before joining Andy Petree Racing as the crew chief for Bobby Hamilton. Elledge moved from Petree to Chip Ganassi Racing in 2003, when he became the crew chief for Casey Mears. In his rookie season, Mears was 35th in points; last season, he improved to 22nd.

### 2004 NASCAR NEXTEL CUP SERIES STATS

| Driver | Races | Won | Top 5 | Top 10 | DNF | Poles | Money Won |
|---|---|---|---|---|---|---|---|
| Casey Mears | 36 | 0 | 1 | 9 | 4 | 2 | $3,165,343 |

# Tony Eury Jr.

**Hometown:** Kannapolis, N.C.
**Resides:** Kannapolis, N.C. **Team:** No. 15 Chevrolet.
**Years as crew chief with current team:** First.
**Overall seasons as crew chief:** First.

Tony Eury Jr. takes over the position of crew chief in 2005, following almost exactly in his father's footsteps at DEI. Eury Sr. served as crew chief on the Dale Earnhardt Jr.'s No. 8 for five seasons. During that time, Eury Jr. served as car chief on Earnhardt's team. He also was instrumental in Earnhardt's two NASCAR Busch Series championships. Now Eury Jr. will work on fellow DEI driver Michael Waltrip's team.

# Jimmy Fennig

**Date of birth:** 9/15/53. **Hometown:** Milwaukee
**Resides:** Charlotte **Team:** No. 97 Ford.
**Years as crew chief with current team:** 2.
**Overall seasons as crew chief:** 18.

The Fennig file:

Fennig got his start in 1970 on the Wisconsin dirt tracks, and he spent 19 years getting experience in the Midwestern Dirt and Asphalt Series. Fennig made the move to the NASCAR Cup Series in 1984 with DiGard Racing and later spent time with Stavola Brothers Racing as Bobby Allison's crew chief. In 1990, Fennig joined with Allison at Bobby Allison Motorsports, where he remained until 1996, when he joined Roush Racing as the crew chief for Mark Martin. In 2002, Fennig moved to the No. 97 team as the crew chief for Kurt Busch.

### 2004 NASCAR NEXTEL CUP SERIES STATS

| Driver | Races | Won | Top 5 | Top 10 | DNF | Poles | Money Won |
|---|---|---|---|---|---|---|---|
| Kurt Busch | 36 | 3 | 10 | 21 | 3 | 1 | $4,026,607 |

# Mike Ford

**Date of birth:** 4/13/70. **Hometown:** Morristown, Tenn.
**Resides:** Stanley, N.C. **Team:** No. 88 Ford.
**Years as crew chief with current team:** 1.
**Overall seasons as crew chief:** 4.

The Ford File:

Ford began his racing career with Kyle Petty and then moved to Robert Yates Racing to work on the Ford Quality Care team. He then joined Evernham Motorsports, where he worked with Bill Elliott as the crew chief on the No. 9 Dodge. Ford moved to Robert Yates Racing before the 2004 season to become the crew chief for Dale Jarrett.

### 2004 NASCAR NEXTEL CUP SERIES STATS

| Driver | Races | Won | Top 5 | Top 10 | DNF | Poles | Money Won |
|---|---|---|---|---|---|---|---|
| Dale Jarrett | 36 | 0 | 6 | 14 | 3 | 0 | $4,208,217 |

# Kenny Francis

**Date of birth:** 12/1/69. **Hometown:** Jacksonville
**Team:** No. 19 Dodge. **Years as crew chief with current team:** 1 **Overall seasons as crew chief:** 1.

Francis' career began as a child, on the go kart circuits near Jacksonville. He later graduated to racing late model stock cars, but in 1996, he made the move to the mechanical side of racing when he went to work in the NASCAR Busch Series. Two years later, he jumped to the NASCAR Cup Series and in his second season worked on Dale Jarrett's championship team. In 2001, Francis joined Evernham Motorsports as the team engineer for Bill Elliott. He has been the team director for Jeremy Mayfield's No. 19 Dodge since 2003.

### 2004 NASCAR NEXTEL CUP SERIES STATS

| Driver | Races | Won | Top 5 | Top 10 | DNF | Poles | Money Won |
|---|---|---|---|---|---|---|---|
| Jeremy Mayfield | 36 | 1 | 5 | 13 | 3 | 2 | $3,784,174 |

# Tony Furr

**Date of birth:** 9/14/56. **Hometown:** Concord, N.C.
**Resides:** Concord, N.C. **Team:** No. 0 Chevrolet.
**Overall seasons as crew chief:** 9.

The Furr file:

A shop foreman in the Haas CNC Racing shop, Furr seems likely to join the ranks of NASCAR NEXTEL Cup crew chiefs again after most recently spending time as Ward Burton's crew chief in 2003. Furr has been the lead wrench in some of racing's top organizations, working with driver Casey Atwood in Evernham Motorsports and Jerry Nadeau while he was with Hendrick Motorsports. A veteran crew chief, Furr also has worked with Joe Nemechek, Jeremy Mayfield, John Andretti and Ricky Craven. Furr grew up in the sport; his father Henry was a driver, an owner and later operator of the Concord Motor Speedway in North Carolina. Furr started building NASCAR late model sportsman cars in 1974.

### 2004 NASCAR NEXTEL CUP SERIES STATS

| Driver | Races | Won | Top 5 | Top 10 | DNF | Poles | Money Won |
|---|---|---|---|---|---|---|---|
| Ward Burton | 18 | 0 | 0 | 2 | 2 | 0 | $1,370,237 |

# Tony Gibson

**Date of birth:** 11/3/64. **Hometown:** Daytona Beach, Fla.
**Resides:** Concord, N.C. **Overall seasons as crew chief:** 1.

The Gibson file:

A frequent visitor to victory lane over the years, Gibson was Jeff Gordon's car chief in 2001, the last time the No. 24 won the NASCAR Cup title. In the fall of 2002, Dale Earnhardt Inc. came calling and made Gibson the crew chief of the No. 1 team. Jeff Green was the driver at that time. Gibson isn't scheduled to work in the NASCAR NEXTEL Cup series this year but will be the full-time crew chief for Dale Earnhardt Jr.'s NASCAR Busch Series team.

### 2004 NASCAR NEXTEL CUP SERIES STATS

| Driver | Races | Won | Top 5 | Top 10 | DNF | Poles | Money Won |
|---|---|---|---|---|---|---|---|
| John Andretti | 5 | 0 | 0 | 0 | 1 | 0 | $519,261 |

# Tony Glover

**Date of birth:** 4/17/57 **Hometown:** Kingsport, Tenn.
**Resides:** Mooresville, N.C. **Team:** No. 40 Dodge.
**Years as crew chief with current team:** 1.
**Overall seasons as crew chief:** 18.

The Glover file:

When Sterling Marlin need a boost, Tony Glover is the man whom Chip Ganassi Racing called to lift the veteran driver. This pair of Tennessee natives has worked together for 10 years. And speaking of veterans, Glover's no ingenue. His first head wrench job came in 1983 working with driver Lennie Pond and owner Larry McClure in 1983. Glover stuck with Morgan-McClure Racing and guided Ernie Irvan in the early 1990s and Sterling Marlin in the latter half of the decade. Reunited for the second half of 2004, Marlin and Glover finished 21st in the point standings.

### 2004 NASCAR NEXTEL CUP SERIES STATS

| Driver | Races | Won | Top 5 | Top 10 | DNF | Poles | Money Won |
|---|---|---|---|---|---|---|---|
| Sterling Marlin | 6 | 0 | 1 | 1 | 0 | 0 | $607,895 |

# Alan Gustafson

**Hometown:** Ormond Beach, Fla.
**Team:** No. 5 Chevrolet.
**Years as crew chief with current team:** First.
**Overall seasons as crew chief:** First.

The Gustafson file:

Gustafson began his career in racing in Florida, working as a mechanic at local tracks. Meanwhile, he took courses in mechanical engineering at Embry-Riddle Aeronautical University. In 1996, he moved to North Carolina to pursue a career in motor sports, eventually joining Hendrick Motorsports' in-house chassis effort in 1999. He was named lead engineer for the No. 5 NASCAR Cup Series team in 2000 and enters his first season as crew chief in 2005 working with rookie Kyle Busch.

# Kevin Hamlin

**Date of birth:** 6/17/59. **Hometown:** Kalamazoo, Mich.
**Resides:** Winston-Salem, N.C. **Team:** No. 30 Chevrolet.
**Years as crew chief with current team:** 1.
**Overall seasons as crew chief:** 10.

The Hamlin file:

Robby Gordon won't be back as a driver for Richard Childress Racing, but Kevin Hamlin's return in a crew chief capacity is assured. Hamlin has had success with several up-and-coming Childress drivers. He guided Kevin Harvick to the 2001 Raybestos Rookie of the Year title after succeeding with Dale Earnhardt in 1998. Hamlin joined the No. 31 team midway through the 2002 season. In 2004, he switched to the No. 30 team, which was the subject of a driver merry-go-round as Gordon departed then Dave Blaney and Jeff Burton cycled through. Hamlin is described as having a low-key personality, which makes him a great complement to some of the fiery drivers in the Childress organization.

## 2004 NASCAR NEXTEL CUP SERIES STATS • Kevin Hamlin

| Driver | Races | Won | Top 5 | Top 10 | DNF | Poles | Money Won |
|---|---|---|---|---|---|---|---|
| Johnny Sauter | 13 | 0 | 0 | 0 | 1 | 0 | $1,147,550 |
| Dave Blaney | 8 | 0 | 0 | 0 | 1 | 0 | $639,765 |
| Jim Inglebright | 1 | 0 | 0 | 0 | 0 | 0 | $70,550 |
| Jeff Burton | 14 | 0 | 1 | 2 | 1 | 0 | $1,155,570 |

# Bill Henderson

**Date of birth:** 7/25/67. **Hometown:** Brookfield, Mass.
**Resides:** Mooresville, N.C. **Team:** No. 45 Dodge.
**Years as crew chief with current team:** 1.
**Overall seasons as crew chief:** 1.

The Henderson file:

A veteran mechanic with experience as a NASCAR Busch Series crew chief for Kerry Earnhardt and Tim Fedewa, Henderson made the jump to NASCAR NEXTEL Cup crew chief with Petty Enterprises after the midway point of the 2004 season. Henderson had been serving as car chief for the MBV Motorsports No. 10 car and also had served as car chief with Chip Ganassi Racing with Felix Sabates.

### 2004 NASCAR NEXTEL CUP SERIES STATS

| Driver | Races | Won | Top 5 | Top 10 | DNF | Poles | Money Won |
|---|---|---|---|---|---|---|---|
| Kyle Petty | 14 | 0 | 0 | 0 | 4 | 0 | $1,005,050 |

# Mike Hillman

**Date of birth:** 8/27/57. **Hometown:** Lockport, N.Y.
**Resides:** Mooresville, N.C. **Team:** No. 50 Dodge.
**Years as crew chief with current team:** 2.
**Overall seasons as crew chief:** 11.

The Hillman file:

Throughout his career as a NASCAR Cup Series crew chief, Hillman rarely has spent an entire season working with one driver. Early in his career, he worked with owner Dean Myers and guided drivers such as Dick Trickle and Chuck Brown. The pairing with Trickle lasted the longest for Hillman, in terms of consecutive races, as the two worked together for 25 races in 1994. Hillman also worked with drivers Bobby Hillin Jr., Joe Nemechek, Robby Gordon, Greg Sacks, Ricky Craven and many others. Hillman hooked up with Arnold Motorsports and was crew chief for Derrike Cope at the start of the 2004 season. Cope and the team parted ways, but Hillman remained, guiding Mike Wallace, Todd Bodine, Jeff Fuller and P.J. Jones in the No. 50.

### 2004 NASCAR NEXTEL CUP SERIES STATS

| Driver | Races | Won | Top 5 | Top 10 | DNF | Poles | Money Won |
|---|---|---|---|---|---|---|---|
| Derrike Cope | 12 | 0 | 0 | 0 | 4 | 0 | $881,937 |
| Mike Wallace | 3 | 0 | 0 | 0 | 2 | 0 | $187,550 |
| P.J. Jones | 5 | 0 | 0 | 0 | 4 | 0 | $293,704 |
| Jeff Fuller | 3 | 0 | 0 | 0 | 3 | 0 | $186,610 |
| Todd Bodine | 11 | 0 | 0 | 0 | 9 | 0 | $710,413 |

# Harold Holly

**Date of birth:** 3/14/67. **Hometown:** Pell City, Ala.
**Resides:** Catawba, N.C. **Team:** No. 32 Chevrolet.
**Years as crew chief with current team:** First.
**Overall seasons as crew chief:** First.

The Holly file:

Crew chief for Bobby Hamilton Jr. in the NASCAR Busch Series, Harold Holly moved to NASCAR NEXTEL Cup with Hamilton Jr. with 11 races left in the 2004 season. Mike Beam retained the title of crew chief at that time, but Holly was atop the pit box, too, building the team's foundation for a run in 2005, when Holly takes over the head wrench job. Holly was born and raised just down the road from Talladega Superspeedway and learned to love working on cars with his father and his youth football coach. At 19 he started working with Mickey Gibbs in the ARCA and ASA series and got his first taste of the NASCAR Cup series about a year later, going to work with Alan Kulwicki's team. As crew chief, he guided Jeff Green from 1999-2001, and they captured the 2000 NASCAR Busch Series title.

# David Hyder

**Date of birth:** 8/19/1967 **Hometown:** High Point, N.C.
**Resides:** Trinity, N.C. **Team:** No. 49 Dodge.
**Years as crew chief with current team:** 1.
**Overall seasons as crew chief:** 1

The Hyder file:

Hyder joined BAM Racing after the fall Talladega race in 2004 as crew chief for Ken Schrader's team, his first stint as a NASCAR Cup Series crew chief. Before that, Hyder spent more than four years with Petty Enterprises, serving as car chief for the No. 43 before his move to BAM Racing. Before taking up the wrench full-time, Hyder drove late models for 17 years and was a crew chief in the Hooters Pro Cup before moving to Petty Enterprises.

### 2004 NASCAR NEXTEL CUP SERIES STATS

| Driver | Races | Won | Top 5 | Top 10 | DNF | Poles | Money Won |
|---|---|---|---|---|---|---|---|
| Ken Schrader | 7 | 0 | 0 | 0 | 0 | 0 | $423,350 |

# Chad Knaus

**Date of birth:** 8/5/71. **Hometown:** Rockford, Ill.
**Resides:** Charlotte. **Team:** No. 48 Chevrolet.
**Years as crew chief with current team:** 3.
**Overall seasons as crew chief:** 5.

The Knaus file:

Knaus grew up racing with his father and had served as his dad's crew chief by the time he was 14, then moved on to work with Stanley Smith's stock car team. Knaus then joined Hendrick Motorsports, where he spent five years with Jeff Gordon, working his way up from general fabricator to manager of the classics and body construction. He left after the 1997 season and joined DEI as a car chief, then moved to Tyler Jet Racing and Melling Racing, where he was the crew chief for Stacy Compton. Knaus returned to Hendrick

Motorsports in December 2001 as the crew chief for Jimmie Johnson and led the No. 48 to second-place finishes in 2003 and 2004.

### 2004 NASCAR NEXTEL CUP SERIES STATS

| Driver | Races | Won | Top 5 | Top 10 | DNF | Poles | Money Won |
|---|---|---|---|---|---|---|---|
| Jimmie Johnson | 36 | 8 | 20 | 23 | 7 | 1 | $5,556,624 |

# Darin Kummrow

**Date of birth:** 9/18/78. **Team:** No. 89 Dodge.
**Years as crew chief with current team:** 1.

### 2004 NASCAR NEXTEL CUP SERIES STATS

| Driver | Races | Won | Top 5 | Top 10 | DNF | Poles | Money Won |
|---|---|---|---|---|---|---|---|
| Morgan Shepherd | 19 | 0 | 0 | 0 | 17 | 0 | $1,099,399 |

# Richard Labbe

**Date of birth:** 6/14/68. **Hometown:** Biddeford, Maine.
**Resides:** Kannapolis, N.C. **Overall seasons as crew chief:** 5.

The Labbe file:

Labbe was a tire specialist and car chief at Hendrick Motorsports and later worked with Robert Yates Racing, when he served as crew chief for Kenny Irwin during his 1998 rookie season. Labbe joined DEI as crew chief for Michael Waltrip in 2001 and won twice at Daytona. In 2004, Labbe left his crew chief position with Waltrip to assist the Chance 2 Motorsports and No. 8 Budweiser Chevrolet teams at DEI. During the offseason, Labbe joined Evernham Motorsports as Jeremy Mayfield's crew chief.

### 2004 NASCAR NEXTEL CUP SERIES STATS

| Driver | Races | Won | Top 5 | Top 10 | DNF | Poles | Money Won |
|---|---|---|---|---|---|---|---|
| Michael Waltrip | 29 | 0 | 2 | 9 | 5 | 0 | $3,410,311 |
| Martin Truex | 1 | 0 | 0 | 0 | 1 | 0 | $104,883 |

# Bobby Leslie

**Date of birth:** 6/15/53. **Hometown:** Mills, Mass.
**Resides:** Liberty, N.C. **Team:** No. 33 Chevrolet.
**Years as crew chief with current team:** 1.
**Overall seasons as crew chief:** 4.

The Leslie file:

His first NASCAR Cup crew chief job came in the Roush organization in 1999, working with Johnny Benson after serving as a NASCAR Busch Series crew chief for Roush for five years. Leslie moved on to Petty Enterprises in 2000, taking the head wrench job for Kyle Petty. Leslie later moved to Richard Childress Racing, where he has worked with Kerry Earnhardt.

### 2004 NASCAR NEXTEL CUP SERIES STATS

| Driver | Races | Won | Top 5 | Top 10 | DNF | Poles | Money Won |
|---|---|---|---|---|---|---|---|
| Mike Skinner | 1 | 0 | 0 | 0 | 0 | 0 | $213,813 |
| Kerry Earnhardt | 3 | 0 | 0 | 0 | 1 | 0 | $194,705 |

# Jim Long

**Date of birth:** 2/17/57
**Hometown:** Toledo, Ohio.
**Resides:** Denver, N.C.
**Overall seasons as crew chief:** 10.

The Long file:

Long is a racing veteran—he has worked for Melling Racing, Sabates Racing, DiGard Racing and Ultra Motorsports. Long started his NASCAR career as a volunteer for team owner J.D. Stacy and driver Morgan Shepherd in 1983. He now is in his second stint at Hendrick Motorsports and worked as Terry Labonte's crew chief on the No. 5 Chevrolet in 2004. Long was the chief mechanic at Hendrick when Geoffrey Bodine won the 1986 Daytona.

### 2004 NASCAR NEXTEL CUP SERIES STATS

| Driver | Races | Won | Top 5 | Top 10 | DNF | Poles | Money Won |
|---|---|---|---|---|---|---|---|
| Terry Labonte | 36 | 0 | 0 | 6 | 5 | 0 | $3,598,892 |

# Robbie Loomis

**Date of birth:** 6/7/64. **Hometown:** Forest City, Fla.
**Resides:** Charlotte. **Team:** No. 24 Chevrolet.
**Years as crew chief with current team:** 5.
**Overall seasons as crew chief:** 14.

The Loomis file:

Loomis got his start with Petty Enterprises on Kyle Petty's NASCAR Busch Series team and spent 11 years there, including nine as crew chief. His first crew chief position came in a pairing with Richard Petty. Loomis left Petty Enterprises and joined Hendrick Motorsports in 2000 as Jeff Gordon's crew chief. In Loomis' second year with the No. 24 team, Gordon won the NASCAR Cup championship.

### 2004 NASCAR NEXTEL CUP SERIES STATS

| Driver | Races | Won | Top 5 | Top 10 | DNF | Poles | Money Won |
|---|---|---|---|---|---|---|---|
| Jeff Gordon | 36 | 5 | 16 | 25 | 4 | 6 | $6,256,887 |

# Philippe Lopez

**Date of birth:** 1/28/63. **Hometown:** Verdun, France.
**Resides:** Mooresville, N.C. **Team:** No. 07 Chevrolet.
**Years as crew chief with current team:** First.
**Overall seasons as crew chief:** 11.

The Lopez file:

Lopez began his Cup career in 1994, working with Ward Burton for half a season. Throughout the past decade, he has worked with racing legends like driver Darrell Waltrip and owners A.J. Foyt and Travis Carter. He also worked at DEI with Steve Park's team in 1998. Now part of the changes on the Nos. 07 and 31 cars, Lopez has moved to Richard Childress Racing.

### 2004 NASCAR NEXTEL CUP SERIES STATS • Philippe Lopez

| Driver | Races | Won | Top 5 | Top 10 | DNF | Poles | Money Won |
|---|---|---|---|---|---|---|---|
| Dave Blaney | 6 | 0 | 0 | 0 | 2 | 0 | $726,362 |
| Tony Raines | 1 | 0 | 0 | 0 | 1 | 0 | $121,730 |

# Gil Martin

**Date of birth:** 1/31/66.
**Hometown:** Nashville.
**Resides:** Harrisburg, N.C.
**Overall seasons as crew chief:** 10.

The Martin file:

Taking another turn as a crew chief after serving in other capacities with Richard Childress Racing, Martin worked with Robby Gordon in 2004 until Gordon and RCR parted ways. Martin also worked with Kerry Earnhardt and will continue to work as a Busch Series crew chief as part of his role in RCR. Martin has been the team manager for RCR's No. 29 GM Goodwrench team since midway through the 2002 season. He served as that team's crew chief for the first 23 races of 2002 before handing the reins over to current crew chief Todd Berrier.

### 2004 NASCAR NEXTEL CUP SERIES STATS

| Driver | Races | Won | Top 5 | Top 10 | DNF | Poles | Money Won |
|---|---|---|---|---|---|---|---|
| Kerry Earnhardt | 1 | 0 | 0 | 0 | 0 | 0 | $63,000 |
| Robby Gordon | 6 | 0 | 0 | 0 | 1 | 0 | $568,712 |

# Michael McSwain

**Date of birth:** 1/17/67. **Hometown:** Mount Holly, N.C.
**Resides:** Huntersville, N.C. **Team:** No. 21 Ford.
**Years as crew chief with current team:** 1.
**Overall seasons as crew chief:** 9.

The McSwain file:

McSwain worked for Ricky Rudd and Rudd Performance Motorsports in 1999 and followed Rudd when he sold his team and joined Robert Yates Racing in 2000. After the 2002 season, McSwain left for Joe Gibbs Racing to crew chief Bobby Labonte in the No. 18 car, but in mid-August, 2004, McSwain joined Wood Brothers Racing and rejoined Rudd as the crew chief for the No. 21 car.

### 2004 NASCAR NEXTEL CUP SERIES STATS

| Driver | Races | Won | Top 5 | Top 10 | DNF | Poles | Money Won |
|---|---|---|---|---|---|---|---|
| Bobby Labonte | 18 | 0 | 5 | 9 | 0 | 1 | $2,417,456 |
| Ricky Rudd | 14 | 0 | 1 | 2 | 2 | 0 | $1,387,493 |

# Bob Osborne

**Date of birth:** 6/15/53. **Hometown:** Chester, Pa.
**Resides:** Harrisburg, N.C. **Team:** No. 99 Ford.
**Years as crew chief with current team:** 1.
**Overall seasons as crew chief:** 1.

The Osborne file:

A mechanical engineer with some racing experience, Osborne made his NASCAR Cup series debut working with Jeff Burton. Osborne then guided Carl Edwards in the driver's first NASCAR NEXTEL Cup race in 2004. Together, Edwards and Osborne will run a full schedule in 2005. Before being named a crew chief, Osborne was head of engineers at Roush Racing.

| 2004 NASCAR NEXTEL CUP SERIES STATS | | | | | | | |
|---|---|---|---|---|---|---|---|
| Driver | Races | Won | Top 5 | Top 10 | DNF | Poles | Money Won |
| Jeff Burton | 18 | 0 | 1 | 3 | 3 | 0 | $1,924,909 |
| Carl Edwards | 13 | 0 | 1 | 5 | 2 | 0 | $1,373,754 |

# Todd Parrott

**Date of birth:** 2/9/64. **Hometown:** Charlotte
**Resides:** Mooresville, N.C. **Team:** No. 38 Ford.
**Years as crew chief with current team:** 2.
**Overall seasons as crew chief:** 9.

The Parrott file:

Parrott didn't really have anything to prove this season; he already has a championship. He and Dale Jarrett drove to the top of the points standings in 1999, Parrott's fourth season working with Jarrett. But Parrott did prove himself again in 2004, guiding Elliott Sadler to a spot in the inaugural Chase for the NASCAR NEXTEL Cup and to Sadler's highest points finish in six years of competition. Before being pulled back into the shop, Parrott had been director of competition for Robert Yates Racing.

| 2004 NASCAR NEXTEL CUP SERIES STATS | | | | | | | |
|---|---|---|---|---|---|---|---|
| Driver | Races | Won | Top 5 | Top 10 | DNF | Poles | Money Won |
| Elliott Sadler | 36 | 2 | 8 | 14 | 1 | 0 | $4,879,129 |

# Ryan Pemberton

**Date of birth:** 6/1/69. **Hometown:** Saratoga Springs, N.Y.
**Resides:** Mooresville, N.C. **Team:** No. 01 Chevrolet.
**Years as crew chief with current team:** 2.
**Overall seasons as crew chief:** 8.

The Pemberton file:

Pemberton was offered a college basketball scholarship, but he passed it up to enter the racing world after high school. Just nine years later, Pemberton became the crew chief for Derrike Cope in the NASCAR Cup Series. He joined MB2 Motorsports in 2003 and has been the crew chief for Joe Nemechek since the beginning of the 2004 season. The pairing proved successful, with Pemberton guiding Nemechek to the pole position in back-to-back races at Talladega and Kansas—and a trip to victory lane at Kansas.

| 2004 NASCAR NEXTEL CUP SERIES STATS | | | | | | | |
|---|---|---|---|---|---|---|---|
| Driver | Races | Won | Top 5 | Top 10 | DNF | Poles | Money Won |
| Joe Nemechek | 36 | 1 | 3 | 9 | 6 | 2 | $3,743,740 |

# Billy Poindexter

**Team:** No. 37 Dodge.
**Years as crew chief with current team:** First.
**Overall seasons as crew chief:** First.

# Doug Randolph

**Date of birth:** 10/17/65. **Hometown:** Fort Bragg, N.C.
**Resides:** Mocksville, N.C. **Team:** No. 10 Chevrolet.
**Years as crew chief with current team:** 1.
**Overall seasons as crew chief:** 5.

The Randolph file:

Racing wasn't a family affair for Randolph, unlike most of his NASCAR counterparts. He began working in motorsports in college and worked for legendary team owners L.D. Ottinger, Junior Johnson and Larry Hendrick. While under Johnson in the early '90s, Randolph worked with Jimmy Spencer and Sterling Marlin. He moved to Bill Davis Racing and became crew chief for Dave Blaney in 2000. Midway through 2001, Randolph joined Chip Ganassi Racing and Felix Sabates. Randolph then moved to MBV Motorsports, serving as crew chief for Scott Riggs.

| 2004 NASCAR NEXTEL CUP SERIES STATS | | | | | | | |
|---|---|---|---|---|---|---|---|
| Driver | Races | Won | Top 5 | Top 10 | DNF | Poles | Money Won |
| Scott Riggs | 35 | 0 | 1 | 2 | 8 | 0 | $3,378,684 |

# Robbie Reiser

**Date of birth:** 6/27/63. **Hometown:** Allenton, Wis.
**Resides:** Denver, N.C. **Team:** No. 17 Ford.
**Years as crew chief with current team:** 5.
**Overall seasons as crew chief:** 5.

The Reiser file:

Reiser grew up with dreams of following in his father's footsteps as a driver, and he won a number of smaller late-model championships before running a limited NASCAR Busch Series schedule in 1994 and 1995 with his own team, Reiser Enterprises. After working briefly with Hut Stricklin's NASCAR Busch Series team, Reiser became a full-time crew chief and owner, as Tim Bender drove his Reiser Enterprises NASCAR Busch Series ride. Soon after, Reiser teamed up with Matt Kenseth, and in 2000, the pair moved to Roush Racing and the NASCAR Cup Series. They made quick progress and in 2003 ran away with the NASCAR Cup championship. Though not as strong in 2004, the No. 17 team made it into the first Chase for the NASCAR NEXTEL Cup.

| 2004 NASCAR NEXTEL CUP SERIES STATS | | | | | | | |
|---|---|---|---|---|---|---|---|
| Driver | Races | Won | Top 5 | Top 10 | DNF | Poles | Money Won |
| Matt Kenseth | 36 | 2 | 8 | 16 | 6 | 0 | $5,212,314 |

# Doug Richert

**Date of birth:** 6/14/60. **Hometown:** San Jose, Calif.
**Team:** No. 16 Ford.
**Years as crew chief with current team:** 2.
**Overall seasons as crew chief:** 16.

The Richert file:

In 2003 this veteran crew chief joined Roush Racing, working with Carl Edwards in the NASCAR Craftsman Truck Series and joined the No. 16

team late that season. Richert started out building cars for short track racing in California. He started racing in NASCAR Cup in 1976 and became Dale Earnhardt's crew chief in 1980. Together they won their first NASCAR Cup championship in 1980, and Richert was only 20. Richert also has worked with the likes of Davey Allison, Buddy Baker and Benny Parsons. He joined PPI Motorsports in 2000 and worked with Joe Gibbs Racing before moving to Roush.

### 2004 NASCAR NEXTEL CUP SERIES STATS

| Driver | Races | Won | Top 5 | Top 10 | DNF | Poles | Money Won |
|---|---|---|---|---|---|---|---|
| Greg Biffle | 36 | 2 | 4 | 8 | 5 | 1 | $3,439,842 |

# Dave Rogers

**Hometown:** Marshvield, Vt.
**Team:** No. 11 Chevrolet.
**Years as crew chief with current team:** First.
**Overall seasons as crew chief:** First.

The Rogers file:

Rogers, 30, has gained six years of experience working with a championship-caliber team: Joe Gibbs Racing's No. 20 team. Before joining JGR and learning from crew chief Greg Zipadelli, Rogers earned a degree in mechanical engineering from Clarkson University then a masters degree in science and engineering from the GMI Engineering & Management Institute in Flint, Mich. For 2005, Rogers will help launch Gibbs' third team, the No. 11, working with driver Jason Leffler.

# Pete Rondeau

**Date of birth:** 11/5/65. **Hometown:** Saco, Maine.
**Resides:** Sherrills, N.C. **Team:** No. 8 Chevrolet.
**Years as crew chief with current team:** First.
**Overall seasons as crew chief:** 1.

The Rondeau file:

Described as a true team player, Rondeau was promoted at the end of the 2004 season to crew chief for Dale Earnhardt Jr for 2005. He had served as Michael Waltrip's crew chief late in 2004 after being car chief since 2002. Rondeau guided Ron Fellows to a second-place finish at Watkins Glen in 2004 and has worked with Dale Earnhardt Jr. and Tony Stewart in various races. Before joining DEI, Rondeau worked as a car chief with Jasper motorsports on the No. 77 car.

### 2004 NASCAR NEXTEL CUP SERIES STATS

| Driver | Races | Won | Top 5 | Top 10 | DNF | Poles | Money Won |
|---|---|---|---|---|---|---|---|
| Ron Fellows | 1 | 0 | 1 | 1 | 0 | 0 | $101,260 |
| Michael Waltrip | 6 | 0 | 0 | 1 | 1 | 0 | $95,100 |

# Greg Steadman

**Date of birth:** 7/25/69. **Hometown:** Tampa.
**Resides:** Randleman, N.C. **Team:** No. 43 Dodge.
**Years as crew chief with current team:** 1.
**Overall seasons as crew chief:** 6.

The Steadman file:

A 10-year veteran at Petty Enterprises and former crew chief of the No. 45, Steadman was asked to work with Jeff Green when a midseason change was made with the No. 43 team. Steadman became crew chief

of the No. 45 in 2003, when he replaced crew chief Steve Lane. He had served as crew chief of the Nos. 43 and 44 before working as shop foreman for a time then returned to crew chiefing with the No. 45.

### 2004 NASCAR NEXTEL CUP SERIES STATS • Greg Steadman

| Driver | Races | Won | Top 5 | Top 10 | DNF | Poles | Money Won |
|---|---|---|---|---|---|---|---|
| Jeff Green | 15 | 0 | 0 | 1 | 2 | 0 | $1,360,680 |

# Mike Steurer

**Date of birth:** 9/26/52. **Hometown:** Granada Hills, Calif.
**Resides:** Mooresville, N.C. **Team:** No. 09.
**Years as crew chief with current team:** First.
**Overall seasons as crew chief:** First.

The Steurer file:

In 1964, Steurer bought a Chevy and raced it with his brother, Glen, at Saugus Speedway in California. The brothers traded off as drivers, but it got too complicated, so Mike became the permanent crew chief. The family, including the Steurers' father, Earl, became well-known in West Coast driving circles in the '70s in the Winston West circuit, and financed the entire operation by themselves. Mike eventually moved on and became crew chief for Shane Hall with Alumni Motorsports, a NASCAR Busch Series team that received technical support from Ohio State University in 1999. He became the crew chief for Brewco Motorsports' No. 37 Red Man Team in the NASCAR Craftsman Truck Series in 1998 and was the crew chief for Derrike Cope and Larry Gunselman in 2004.

### 2004 NASCAR NEXTEL CUP SERIES STATS

| Driver | Races | Won | Top 5 | Top 10 | DNF | Poles | Money Won |
|---|---|---|---|---|---|---|---|
| Derrike Cope | 5 | 0 | 0 | 0 | 5 | 0 | $375,405 |
| Larry Gunselman | 5 | 0 | 0 | 0 | 3 | 0 | $303,159 |

# Frank Stoddard

**Date of birth:** 4/20/68. **Hometown:** North Haverhill, N.H.
**Resides:** Cornelius, N.C.
**Overall seasons as crew chief:** 7.

The Stoddard file:

Stoddard grew up in North Haverhill, N.H., and raced at New Hampshire International Speedway in the Busch North Series as Dana Patten's crew chief before heading to the NASCAR Cup Series. Stoddard went on to Roush Racing, where he worked for several years as a crew chief with Jeff Burton. He was with Ward Burton in 2003.

### 2004 NASCAR NEXTEL CUP SERIES STATS

| Driver | Races | Won | Top 5 | Top 10 | DNF | Poles | Money Won |
|---|---|---|---|---|---|---|---|
| Scott Wimmer | 35 | 0 | 1 | 2 | 7 | 0 | $3,622,391 |

# Pat Tryson

**Date of birth:** 3/4/64. **Hometown:** Bryn Mawr, Pa.
**Resides:** Troutman, N.C. **Team:** No. 6 Ford.
**Years as crew chief with current team:** 2.
**Overall seasons as crew chief:** 8.

The Tryson file:

Tryson's father, Joe, built drag racing engines when Pat was growing up, and after Pat graduated from college, he went to work on Kenny Bernstein's top fuel dragster as his car chief/mechanic. Tryson has worked for several Roush Racing teams and has served as crew chief for Todd Bodine at ISM Motorsports and Geoffrey Bodine at Mattie Motorsports. He joined Wood Brothers Racing in 2000 and was paired there with Kevin Lepage, Elliott Sadler and Ricky Rudd. In 2003, Tryson rejoined Roush Racing and helped lead Mark Martin into the top 10 in the points standings through the first two-thirds of the 2004 season, qualifying for the inaugural Chase for the NASCAR NEXTEL Cup.

| 2004 NASCAR NEXTEL CUP SERIES STATS | | | | | | | |
|---|---|---|---|---|---|---|---|
| Driver | Races | Won | Top 5 | Top 10 | DNF | Poles | Money Won |
| Mark Martin | 36 | 1 | 10 | 15 | 2 | 0 | $3,792,997 |

# Shane Wilson

**Date of birth:** 11/3/68. **Hometown:** South Royalton, Vt.
**Resides:** Mooresville, N.C. **Team:** No. 77 Dodge
**Years as crew chief with current team:** 1.
**Overall seasons as crew chief:** 1.

The Wilson file:

Wilson began building racecars before he got his own driver's license and always has been interested in the mechanical side of the sport. By 1986, he owned a Street Stock team and competed in a local touring division. He moved on to Alsup Racing and the American-Canadian Tour in 1989, and in 1993, the team moved to the NASCAR All-Pro Touring Series. In 1995, Wilson left Alsup for Hendrick Motorsports, and driver Jack Sprague in the NASCAR Craftsman Truck Series. He later moved to the Winston West Series to work with Brendan Gaughan, where he became a crew chief. In 2004, he and Gaughan moved to the NASCAR NEXTEL Cup series, working for Penske-Jasper Racing as a crew chief for the No. 77.

| 2004 NASCAR NEXTEL CUP SERIES STATS | | | | | | | |
|---|---|---|---|---|---|---|---|
| Driver | Races | Won | Top 5 | Top 10 | DNF | Poles | Money Won |
| Brendan Gaughan | 36 | 0 | 1 | 4 | 8 | 0 | $2,884,502 |

# Donnie Wingo

**Date of birth:** 2/13/60. **Hometown:** Spartanburg, S.C.
**Resides:** Mooresville, N.C. **Team:** No. 42 Dodge.
**Years as crew chief with current team:** 2.
**Overall seasons as crew chief:** 13.

The Wingo file:

Wingo has been a crew chief since 1989. He spent seven years as chief for Haas Carter Motorsports, and six of those with Jimmy Spencer, before moving to Chip Ganassi Racing in 2003 to work with Jamie McMurray when Ganassi began its third NASCAR Cup team around the new Havoline sponsorship. Wingo's years of experience were crucial to the success of the team—McMurray had only six weeks of Cup experience under his belt when the two joined forces on the No. 42 Dodge.

| 2004 NEXTEL CUP SERIES STATS | | | | | | | |
|---|---|---|---|---|---|---|---|
| Driver | Races | Won | Top 5 | Top 10 | DNF | Poles | Money Won |
| Jamie McMurray | 36 | 0 | 9 | 23 | 6 | 0 | $3,551,612 |

# Jon Wolfe

**Date of birth:** 2/2/63. **Hometown:** Strasburg, Ohio.
**Resides:** Mooresville, N.C.
**Overall seasons as crew chief:** 3.

The Wolfe file:

Wolfe was one of the original members of the Joe Gibbs Racing team and was with that organization for eight years as Jimmy Makar's assistant crew chief. He worked with drivers Dale Jarrett and Bobby Labonte. In 2004, he was a consultant for MB2 Motorsports and driver Ken Schrader. He also has worked with Larry McReynolds at King Racing and with driver Brett Bodine.

| 2004 NASCAR NEXTEL CUP SERIES STATS | | | | | | | |
|---|---|---|---|---|---|---|---|
| Driver | Races | Won | Top 5 | Top 10 | DNF | Poles | Money Won |
| Joe Ruttman | 7 | 0 | 0 | 0 | 7 | 0 | $399,093 |
| Bobby Hamilton, Jr. | 6 | 0 | 0 | 0 | 4 | 0 | $379,665 |
| Tony Raines | 1 | 0 | 0 | 0 | 1 | 0 | $60,025 |
| Scott Pruett | 1 | 0 | 0 | 0 | 1 | 0 | $116,215 |
| Mike Wallace | 4 | 0 | 0 | 1 | 1 | 0 | $279,420 |
| Johnny Sauter | 3 | 0 | 0 | 0 | 1 | 0 | $169,255 |

# Greg Zipadelli

**Date of birth:** 4/21/67. **Hometown:** New Britain, Conn.
**Resides:** Huntersville, N.C. **Team:** No. 20 Chevrolet.
**Years as crew chief with current team:** 5.
**Overall seasons as crew chief:** 5.

The Zipadelli file:

Zipadelli's NASCAR ties go back to when he was a 7-year-old working on his father's NASCAR Featherlite Modified Tour car. At 14, Zipadelli had moved to working on cars for his family's Sherwood Racing team and at 20 was the crew chief for Modified Series championship winner Mike McLaughlin. He then joined Roush Racing on Jeff Burton's NASCAR Cup team before Joe Gibbs hired Zipadelli as the crew chief for Tony Stewart in the No. 20 car. The duo won the NASCAR Cup championship in 2002.

| 2004 NASCAR NEXTEL CUP SERIES STATS | | | | | | | |
|---|---|---|---|---|---|---|---|
| Driver | Races | Won | Top 5 | Top 10 | DNF | Poles | Money Won |
| Tony Stewart | 36 | 2 | 10 | 19 | 2 | 0 | $5,851,727 |

2004 Season

| Rk. | Driver | Points | Starts | Poles | Wins | Top 5 | Top 10 | Races Led | Laps Led | Miles Led | DNFs | Winnings |
|---|---|---|---|---|---|---|---|---|---|---|---|---|
| 1. | Kurt Busch | 6,506 | 36 | 1 | 3 | 10 | 21 | 20 | 746 | 684.44 | 3 | $9,677,543 |
| 2. | Jimmie Johnson | 6,498 | 36 | 1 | 8 | 20 | 23 | 24 | 1,312 | 2013.66 | 7 | $8,275,721 |
| 3. | Jeff Gordon | 6,490 | 36 | 6 | 5 | 16 | 25 | 25 | 1,237 | 1,914.12 | 4 | $8,439,382 |
| 4. | Mark Martin | 6,399 | 36 | 0 | 1 | 10 | 15 | 13 | 465 | 767.22 | 2 | $5,479,004 |
| 5. | Dale Earnhardt Jr. | 6,368 | 36 | 0 | 6 | 16 | 21 | 19 | 1,131 | 1,237.95 | 4 | $8,913,510 |
| 6. | Tony Stewart | 6,326 | 36 | 0 | 2 | 10 | 19 | 17 | 887 | 1,292.22 | 2 | $7,830,807 |
| 7. | Ryan Newman | 6,180 | 36 | 9 | 2 | 11 | 14 | 24 | 957 | 1,134.67 | 9 | $6,354,256 |
| 8. | Matt Kenseth | 6,069 | 36 | 0 | 2 | 8 | 16 | 14 | 477 | 563.57 | 6 | $7,405,309 |
| 9. | Elliott Sadler | 6,024 | 36 | 0 | 2 | 8 | 14 | 12 | 254 | 440.80 | 1 | $6,244,954 |
| 10. | Jeremy Mayfield | 6,000 | 36 | 2 | 1 | 5 | 13 | 9 | 387 | 505.40 | 3 | $4,919,342 |
| 11. | Jamie McMurray | 4,597 | 36 | 0 | 0 | 9 | 23 | 10 | 224 | 270.04 | 6 | $4,676,311 |
| 12. | Bobby Labonte | 4,277 | 36 | 1 | 0 | 5 | 11 | 8 | 41 | 58.28 | 2 | $5,201,397 |
| 13. | Kasey Kahne | 4,274 | 36 | 4 | 0 | 13 | 14 | 17 | 692 | 1,096.95 | 7 | $5,415,611 |
| 14. | Kevin Harvick | 4,228 | 36 | 0 | 0 | 5 | 14 | 9 | 177 | 190.97 | 4 | $5,321,337 |
| 15. | Dale Jarrett | 4,214 | 36 | 0 | 0 | 6 | 14 | 7 | 25 | 53.40 | 3 | $5,097,396 |
| 16. | Rusty Wallace | 3,960 | 36 | 0 | 1 | 3 | 11 | 8 | 308 | 232.86 | 3 | $4,981,100 |
| 17. | Greg Biffle | 3,902 | 36 | 1 | 2 | 4 | 8 | 10 | 356 | 604.42 | 5 | $4,092,877 |
| 18. | Jeff Burton | 3,902 | 36 | 0 | 0 | 2 | 6 | 5 | 56 | 52.32 | 6 | $4,054,310 |
| 19. | Joe Nemechek | 3,878 | 36 | 2 | 1 | 3 | 9 | 10 | 129 | 287.69 | 6 | $4,345,554 |
| 20. | Michael Waltrip | 3,878 | 36 | 0 | 0 | 2 | 9 | 10 | 192 | 307.73 | 6 | $4,694,564 |
| 21. | Sterling Marlin | 3,857 | 36 | 0 | 0 | 3 | 7 | 11 | 201 | 208.73 | 9 | $4,457,443 |
| 22. | Casey Mears | 3,690 | 36 | 2 | 0 | 1 | 9 | 11 | 103 | 210.83 | 3 | $3,462,623 |
| 23. | Robby Gordon | 3,646 | 36 | 0 | 0 | 2 | 6 | 8 | 68 | 137.30 | 3 | $4,225,719 |
| 24. | Ricky Rudd | 3,615 | 36 | 1 | 0 | 1 | 3 | 3 | 5 | 9.32 | 6 | $3,905,141 |
| 25. | Brian Vickers | 3,521 | 36 | 2 | 0 | 0 | 4 | 6 | 87 | 128.82 | 6 | $3,135,886 |
| 26. | Terry Labonte | 3,519 | 36 | 0 | 0 | 0 | 6 | 7 | 36 | 29.60 | 5 | $3,745,242 |
| 27. | Scott Wimmer | 3,198 | 35 | 0 | 0 | 1 | 2 | 3 | 10 | 23.82 | 7 | $3,675,879 |
| 28. | Brendan Gaughan | 3,165 | 36 | 0 | 0 | 1 | 4 | 5 | 30 | 67.77 | 8 | $2,929,396 |
| 29. | Scott Riggs | 3,090 | 35 | 0 | 0 | 1 | 2 | 4 | 15 | 30.16 | 8 | $3,443,345 |
| 30. | Jeff Green | 3,054 | 36 | 0 | 0 | 0 | 1 | 1 | 1 | 2.50 | 11 | $3,483,436 |
| 31. | Ken Schrader | 3,032 | 36 | 0 | 0 | 0 | 1 | 6 | 6 | 12.66 | 5 | $2,666,592 |
| 32. | Ward Burton | 2,929 | 34 | 0 | 0 | 0 | 3 | 1 | 1 | 2.66 | 8 | $2,471,941 |
| 33. | Kyle Petty | 2,811 | 35 | 0 | 0 | 0 | 0 | 2 | 6 | 14.00 | 9 | $2,780,131 |
| 34. | Ricky Craven | 2,086 | 26 | 0 | 0 | 0 | 0 | 1 | 1 | 1.50 | 8 | $2,337,417 |
| 35. | Jimmy Spencer | 1,969 | 26 | 0 | 0 | 0 | 0 | 7 | 14 | 27.65 | 7 | $1,985,121 |
| 36. | Johnny Sauter | 1,430 | 16 | 0 | 0 | 0 | 0 | 2 | 2 | 2.03 | 2 | $1,372,949 |
| 37. | Carl Edwards | 1,424 | 13 | 0 | 0 | 1 | 5 | 1 | 15 | 23.10 | 2 | $1,454,380 |
| 38. | Dave Blaney | 1,347 | 16 | 0 | 0 | 0 | 0 | 3 | 4 | 9.00 | 5 | $1,489,272 |
| 39. | Bobby Hamilton Jr. | 1,271 | 17 | 0 | 0 | 0 | 0 | 0 | 0 | 0 | 6 | $1,259,213 |
| 40. | Derrike Cope | 1,058 | 18 | 0 | 0 | 0 | 0 | 1 | 1 | 2.50 | 9 | $1,349,621 |
| 41. | Todd Bodine | 986 | 21 | 0 | 0 | 0 | 0 | 3 | 6 | 6.33 | 18 | $1,275,532 |
| 42. | Morgan Shepherd | 925 | 19 | 0 | 0 | 0 | 0 | 3 | 4 | 7.23 | 17 | $1,133,618 |
| 43. | Kevin Lepage | 915 | 17 | 0 | 0 | 0 | 0 | 1 | 1 | 1.50 | 10 | $1,217,519 |
| 44. | Hermie Sadler | 852 | 16 | 0 | 0 | 0 | 0 | 1 | 1 | 2.66 | 11 | $945,549 |
| 45. | John Andretti | 818 | 9 | 0 | 0 | 0 | 0 | 1 | 1 | 2.50 | 1 | $752,386 |
| 46. | Mike Wallace | 764 | 10 | 0 | 0 | 0 | 1 | 3 | 50 | 46.89 | 5 | $624,850 |
| 47. | Kirk Shelmerdine | 723 | 18 | 0 | 0 | 0 | 0 | 0 | 0 | 0 | 18 | $1,095,041 |
| 48. | Bill Elliott | 595 | 6 | 0 | 0 | 0 | 1 | 1 | 26 | 39.00 | 1 | $567,900 |
| 49. | Mike Bliss | 407 | 4 | 0 | 0 | 1 | 2 | 0 | 0 | 0 | 2 | $284,405 |
| 50. | Kenny Wallace | 365 | 5 | 0 | 0 | 0 | 0 | 0 | 0 | 0 | 2 | $366,155 |
| 51. | Shane Hmiel | 349 | 5 | 0 | 0 | 0 | 0 | 1 | 4 | 8.00 | 2 | $330,385 |
| 52. | Kyle Busch | 345 | 6 | 0 | 0 | 0 | 0 | 0 | 0 | 0 | 4 | $394,489 |
| 53. | Tony Raines | 318 | 6 | 0 | 0 | 0 | 0 | 1 | 0 | 0 | 5 | $426,994 |
| 54. | P.J. Jones | 316 | 5 | 0 | 0 | 0 | 0 | 1 | 1 | 2.50 | 4 | $293,704 |
| 55. | Boris Said | 302 | 3 | 0 | 0 | 0 | 1 | 0 | 0 | 0 | 1 | $252,440 |
| 56. | Geoffrey Bodine | 278 | 5 | 0 | 0 | 0 | 0 | 0 | 0 | 0 | 3 | $364,460 |
| 57. | Johnny Benson | 271 | 4 | 0 | 0 | 0 | 0 | 0 | 0 | 0 | 3 | $403,674 |
| 58. | Carl Long | 267 | 6 | 0 | 0 | 0 | 0 | 0 | 0 | 0 | 6 | $371,479 |
| 59. | Larry Gunselman | 248 | 5 | 0 | 0 | 0 | 0 | 0 | 0 | 0 | 3 | $303,159 |
| 60. | Joe Ruttman | 247 | 7 | 0 | 0 | 0 | 0 | 0 | 0 | 0 | 7 | $399,093 |
| 61. | Kerry Earnhardt | 228 | 3 | 0 | 0 | 0 | 0 | 0 | 0 | 0 | 1 | $227,779 |
| 62. | Stanton Barrett | 224 | 5 | 0 | 0 | 0 | 0 | 0 | 0 | 0 | 5 | $341,878 |

| Rk. | Driver | Points | Starts | Poles | Wins | Top 5 | Races Top 10 | Laps Led | Miles Led | Led | DNFs | Winnings |
|---|---|---|---|---|---|---|---|---|---|---|---|---|
| 63. | Travis Kvapil | 213 | 3 | 0 | 0 | 0 | 0 | 0 | 0 | 0 | 1 | $171,475 |
| 64. | Scott Pruett | 207 | 2 | 0 | 0 | 1 | 1 | 1 | 1 | 2.00 | 1 | $236,315 |
| 65. | Andy Hillenburg | 206 | 5 | 0 | 0 | 0 | 0 | 0 | 0 | 0 | 4 | $338,332 |
| 66. | Larry Foyt | 194 | 3 | 0 | 0 | 0 | 0 | 0 | 0 | 0 | 0 | $342,337 |
| 67. | Ron Fellows | 170 | 1 | 0 | 0 | 1 | 1 | 0 | 0 | 0 | 0 | $101,260 |
| 68. | Randy LaJoie | 126 | 3 | 0 | 0 | 0 | 0 | 0 | 0 | 0 | 3 | $160,261 |
| 69. | J.J. Yeley | 122 | 2 | 0 | 0 | 0 | 0 | 0 | 0 | 0 | 1 | $144,040 |
| 70. | Martin Truex Jr. | 119 | 2 | 0 | 0 | 0 | 0 | 0 | 0 | 0 | 2 | $116,150 |
| 71. | Greg Sacks | 114 | 3 | 0 | 0 | 0 | 0 | 0 | 0 | 0 | 3 | $154,100 |
| 72. | Klaus Graf | 112 | 1 | 0 | 0 | 0 | 0 | 0 | 0 | 0 | 0 | $58,925 |
| 73. | Tom Hubert | 110 | 2 | 0 | 0 | 0 | 0 | 0 | 0 | 0 | 1 | $111,250 |
| 74. | Jim Inglebright | 106 | 1 | 0 | 0 | 0 | 0 | 0 | 0 | 0 | 0 | $73,583 |
| 75. | Jeff Fuller | 105 | 3 | 0 | 0 | 0 | 0 | 0 | 0 | 0 | 3 | $186,610 |
| 76. | Andy Belmont | 98 | 2 | 0 | 0 | 0 | 0 | 0 | 0 | 0 | 2 | $139,614 |
| 77. | Mike Skinner | 97 | 1 | 0 | 0 | 0 | 0 | 1 | 1 | 2.66 | 0 | $251,813 |
| 78. | Eric McClure | 90 | 1 | 0 | 0 | 0 | 0 | 0 | 0 | 0 | 0 | $65,175 |
| 79. | Ted Christopher | 89 | 2 | 0 | 0 | 0 | 0 | 0 | 0 | 0 | 2 | $116,369 |
| 80. | Mario Gosselin | 80 | 2 | 0 | 0 | 0 | 0 | 0 | 0 | 0 | 2 | $107,090 |
| 81. | Chad Blount | 74 | 2 | 0 | 0 | 0 | 0 | 0 | 0 | 0 | 2 | $124,312 |
| 82. | Tony Ave | 70 | 1 | 0 | 0 | 0 | 0 | 0 | 0 | 0 | 0 | $53,465 |
| 83. | David Green | 70 | 1 | 0 | 0 | 0 | 0 | 0 | 0 | 0 | 0 | $56,565 |
| 84. | Austin Cameron | 49 | 1 | 0 | 0 | 0 | 0 | 0 | 0 | 0 | 0 | $57,590 |
| 85. | Chad Chaffin | 46 | 1 | 0 | 0 | 0 | 0 | 0 | 0 | 0 | 1 | $53,765 |
| 86. | Jason Jarrett | 43 | 1 | 0 | 0 | 0 | 0 | 0 | 0 | 0 | 1 | $51,505 |
| 87. | Brandon Ash | 40 | 1 | 0 | 0 | 0 | 0 | 0 | 0 | 0 | 1 | $57,450 |
| 88. | Jason Leffler | 34 | 1 | 0 | 0 | 0 | 0 | 0 | 0 | 0 | 1 | $116,359 |

*Rookie

# 2004 miles leaders standings

| | Driver | Miles Led | Times Led | Races Led | Miles Run | Possible Miles | Unfinished Miles | Laps Led | Wins | Starts |
|---|---|---|---|---|---|---|---|---|---|---|
| 1. | Jimmie Johnson | 2,013.66 | 76 | 24 | 13,660.33 | 14,773.92 | 1,113.60 | 1,312 | 8 | 36 |
| 2. | Jeff Gordon | 1,914.12 | 60 | 25 | 13,871.93 | 14,773.92 | 902.00 | 1,237 | 5 | 36 |
| 3. | Tony Stewart | 1,292.22 | 44 | 17 | 14,284.45 | 14,773.92 | 489.48 | 887 | 2 | 36 |
| 4. | Dale Earnhardt Jr. | 1,237.95 | 64 | 19 | 14,556.42 | 14,773.92 | 217.50 | 1,131 | 6 | 36 |
| 5. | Ryan Newman | 1,134.67 | 46 | 24 | 13,956.36 | 14,773.92 | 817.57 | 957 | 2 | 36 |
| 6. | Kasey Kahne | 1,096.95 | 44 | 17 | 13,207.65 | 14,773.92 | 1,566.27 | 692 | 0 | 36 |
| 7. | Mark Martin | 767.22 | 31 | 13 | 13,988.98 | 14,773.92 | 784.95 | 465 | 1 | 36 |
| 8. | Kurt Busch | 684.44 | 41 | 20 | 13,825.72 | 14,773.92 | 948.20 | 746 | 3 | 36 |
| 9. | Greg Biffle | 604.42 | 24 | 10 | 13,992.01 | 14,773.92 | 781.91 | 356 | 2 | 36 |
| 10. | Matt Kenseth | 563.57 | 25 | 14 | 13,925.80 | 14,773.92 | 848.12 | 477 | 2 | 36 |
| 11. | Jeremy Mayfield | 505.40 | 21 | 9 | 14,313.81 | 14,773.92 | 460.11 | 387 | 1 | 36 |
| 12. | Elliott Sadler | 440.80 | 25 | 12 | 14,464.31 | 14,773.92 | 309.62 | 254 | 2 | 36 |
| 13. | Michael Waltrip | 307.73 | 17 | 10 | 13,690.27 | 14,773.92 | 1,083.65 | 192 | 0 | 36 |
| 14. | Joe Nemechek | 287.69 | 14 | 10 | 13,672.72 | 14,773.92 | 1,101.20 | 129 | 1 | 36 |
| 15. | Jamie McMurray | 270.04 | 17 | 10 | 13,851.36 | 14,773.92 | 922.57 | 224 | 0 | 36 |
| 16. | Rusty Wallace | 232.86 | 16 | 8 | 13,997.06 | 14,773.92 | 776.86 | 308 | 1 | 36 |
| 17. | Casey Mears | 210.83 | 14 | 11 | 14,323.36 | 14,773.92 | 450.56 | 103 | 0 | 36 |
| 18. | Sterling Marlin | 208.73 | 16 | 11 | 13,742.62 | 14,773.92 | 1,031.30 | 201 | 0 | 36 |
| 19. | Kevin Harvick | 190.97 | 15 | 9 | 14,077.62 | 14,773.92 | 696.30 | 177 | 0 | 36 |
| 20. | Robby Gordon | 137.30 | 13 | 8 | 14,302.38 | 14,773.92 | 471.54 | 68 | 0 | 36 |
| 21. | Brian Vickers | 128.82 | 9 | 6 | 13,383.90 | 14,773.92 | 1,390.02 | 87 | 0 | 36 |
| 22. | Brendan Gaughan | 67.77 | 6 | 5 | 13,106.59 | 14,773.92 | 1,667.33 | 30 | 0 | 36 |
| 23. | Bobby Labonte | 58.28 | 8 | 8 | 14,575.68 | 14,773.92 | 198.24 | 41 | 0 | 36 |
| 24. | Dale Jarrett | 53.40 | 15 | 7 | 14,232.40 | 14,773.92 | 541.52 | 25 | 0 | 36 |
| 25. | Jeff Burton | 52.32 | 7 | 5 | 13,480.44 | 14,773.92 | 1,293.48 | 56 | 0 | 36 |
| 26. | Mike Wallace | 46.89 | 3 | 3 | 2,996.54 | 3,724.20 | 727.67 | 50 | 0 | 10 |
| 27. | Bill Elliott | 39.00 | 2 | 1 | 2,606.88 | 2,704.50 | 97.62 | 26 | 0 | 6 |
| 28. | Scott Riggs | 30.16 | 5 | 4 | 12,830.77 | 14,273.42 | 1,442.65 | 15 | 0 | 35 |
| 29. | Terry Labonte | 29.60 | 8 | 7 | 13,917.20 | 14,773.92 | 856.72 | 36 | 0 | 36 |
| 30. | Jimmy Spencer | 27.65 | 9 | 7 | 9,561.23 | 10,863.18 | 1,301.95 | 14 | 0 | 26 |
| 31. | Scott Wimmer | 23.82 | 3 | 3 | 12,968.52 | 14,273.42 | 1,304.90 | 10 | 0 | 35 |
| 32. | Carl Edwards | 23.10 | 2 | 1 | 5,097.14 | 5380.52 | 283.38 | 15 | 0 | 13 |
| 33. | Kyle Petty | 14.00 | 2 | 2 | 12,386.28 | 14,367.42 | 1,981.14 | 6 | 0 | 35 |
| 34. | Ken Schrader | 12.66 | 6 | 6 | 13,643.43 | 14,773.92 | 1,130.49 | 6 | 0 | 36 |
| 35. | Ricky Rudd | 9.32 | 3 | 3 | 13,917.27 | 14,773.92 | 856.65 | 5 | 0 | 36 |
| 36. | Dave Blaney | 9.00 | 3 | 3 | 5,950.82 | 6,943.48 | 992.66 | 4 | 0 | 16 |
| 37. | Shane Hmiel | 8.00 | 1 | 1 | 2,015.49 | 2,417.22 | 401.73 | 4 | 0 | 5 |
| 38. | Morgan Shepherd | 7.23 | 3 | 3 | 2,830.24 | 7,301.94 | 4,471.70 | 4 | 0 | 19 |
| 39. | Todd Bodine | 6.33 | 3 | 3 | 2,953.09 | 8,379.08 | 5,425.99 | 6 | 0 | 21 |
| 40. | Eric McClure | 2.66 | 1 | 1 | 500.08 | 500.08 | 0.00 | 1 | 0 | 1 |
| 40. | Hermie Sadler | 2.66 | 1 | 1 | 2,830.67 | 6,281.42 | 3,450.75 | 1 | 0 | 16 |
| 40. | Ward Burton | 2.66 | 1 | 1 | 12,158.04 | 13,866.10 | 1,708.06 | 1 | 0 | 34 |

| Date | Race | Location | Pole | Winner | Winning Owner | Time of race | Avg. Speed | Victory margin | Race ldrs. | Lead chngs. | Cau. flags | Cau. laps | Cars on ld.lap | DNFs |
|---|---|---|---|---|---|---|---|---|---|---|---|---|---|---|
| Feb. 15 | Daytona 500 | Daytona Beach, Fla. | Greg Biffle* | Dale Earnhardt Jr. | Teresa Earnhardt | 3:11:53 | 156.345 | 0.273 sec. | 10 | 28 | 4 | 23 | 15 | 12 |
| Feb. 22 | Subway 400 | Rockingham, N.C. | Ryan Newman* | Matt Kenseth | Jack Roush | 3:34:05 | 112.016 | .010 sec. | 6 | 15 | 7 | 58 | 9 | 8 |
| March 7 | UAW-DaimlerChrysler 400 | Las Vegas | Kasey Kahne* | Matt Kenseth | Jack Roush | 3:06:35 | 128.790 | 3.426 sec. | 10 | 18 | 6 | 37 | 17 | 10 |
| March 14 | Golden Corral 500 | Hampton, Ga. | Ryan Newman | Dale Earnhardt Jr. | Teresa Earnhardt | 3:09:15 | 138.679 | 4.584 sec. | 8 | 16 | 3 | 17 | 12 | 8 |
| March 21 | Carolina Dodge Dealers 400 | Darlington, S.C. | Jimmie Johnson | Jimmie Johnson | Rick Hendrick | 3:30:30 | 114.001 | 0.132 sec. | 12 | 22 | 9 | 58 | 19 | 10 |
| March 28 | Food City 500 | Bristol, Tenn. | Kasey Kahne | Kurt Busch | Jack Roush | 3:13:34 | 82.607 | 0.428 sec. | 11 | 13 | 11 | 85 | 21 | 12 |
| April 4 | Samsung/RadioShack 500 | Fort Worth, Texas | Ryan Newman | Elliott Sadler | Robert Yates | 3:36:30 | 138.845 | 0.028 sec. | 13 | 24 | 7 | 45 | 11 | 12 |
| April 18 | Advance Auto Parts 500 | Martinsville, Va. | Bobby Labonte | Rusty Wallace | Roger Penske | 3:51:29 | 68.169 | 0.538 sec. | 7 | 10 | 11 | 106 | 19 | 6 |
| April 25 | Aaron's 499 | Talladega, Ala. | Ricky Rudd | Jeff Gordon | Rick Hendrick | 3:51:53 | 129.396 | Under caution | 6 | 11 | 11 | 55 | 27 | 12 |
| May 2 | Auto Club 500 | Fontana, Calif. | Kasey Kahne | Jeff Gordon | Rick Hendrick | 3:38:33 | 137.268 | Under caution | 23 | 54 | 15 | 39 | 13 | 9 |
| May 15 | Chevy American Rev. 400 | Richmond, Va. | Brian Vickers* | Dale Earnhardt Jr. | Teresa Earnhardt | 3:03:12 | 98.253 | 12.871 sec. | 19 | 23 | 7 | 66 | 11 | 9 |
| May 30 | Coca-Cola 600 | Concord, N.C. | Jimmie Johnson | Jimmie Johnson | Rick Hendrick | 4:12:10 | 142.763 | 1.481 sec. | 16 | 19 | 9 | 37 | 13 | 9 |
| June 6 | MBNA 400 | Dover, Del. | Jeremy Mayfield | Mark Martin | Jack Roush | 4:07:19 | 97.042 | 1.702 sec. | 7 | 16 | 7 | 90 | 5 | 17 |
| June 13 | Pocono 500 | Long Pond, Pa. | Kasey Kahne | Jimmie Johnson | Rick Hendrick | 4:27:33 | 112.129 | Under caution | 16 | 30 | 11 | 57 | 22 | 16 |
| June 20 | DHL 400 | Brooklyn, Mich. | Jeff Gordon | Ryan Newman | Roger Penske | 2:52:18 | 139.292 | Under caution | 9 | 17 | 9 | 33 | 24 | 12 |
| June 27 | Dodge/Save Mart 350 | Sonoma, Calif. | Jeff Gordon | Jeff Gordon | Rick Hendrick | 2:49:34 | 77.456 | 1.032 sec. | 6 | 9 | 6 | 13 | 27 | 7 |
| July 4 | Pepsi 400 | Daytona Beach, Fla. | Jeff Gordon | Jeff Gordon | Rick Hendrick | 2:45:23 | 145.117 | 0.143 sec. | 7 | 21 | 5 | 25 | 28 | 6 |
| July 11 | Tropicana 400 | Joliet, Ill. | Jeff Gordon | Tony Stewart | Joe Gibbs | 3:05:33 | 129.507 | 2.925 sec. | 13 | 20 | 9 | 43 | 23 | 11 |
| July 25 | Siemens 300 | Loudon, N.H. | Ryan Newman | Kurt Busch | Jack Roush | 3:14:36 | 97.862 | 0.607 sec. | 3 | 4 | 12 | 62 | 29 | 9 |
| Aug. 1 | Pennsylvania 500 | Long Pond, Pa. | Casey Mears* | Jimmie Johnson | Rick Hendrick | 3:57:35 | 126.271 | 2.0138 sec. | 10 | 16 | 9 | 35 | 22 | 17 |
| Aug. 8 | Brickyard 400 | Indianapolis | Casey Mears | Jeff Gordon | Rick Hendrick | 3:29:56 | 115.037 | Under caution | 6 | 13 | 13 | 47 | 27 | 16 |
| Aug. 15 | Sirius at The Glen | Watkins Glen, N.Y. | Set by points | Tony Stewart | Joe Gibbs | 2:23:25 | 92.249 | 1.517 sec. | 9 | 13 | 9 | 11 | 24 | 12 |
| Aug. 22 | GFS Marketplace 400 | Brooklyn, Mich. | Set by points | Greg Biffle | Jack Roush | 2:52:35 | 139.063 | 8.216 sec. | 13 | 25 | 13 | 33 | 17 | 11 |
| Aug. 28 | Sharpie 500 | Bristol, Tenn. | Jeff Gordon | Jeff Gordon | Rick Hendrick | 3:00:36 | 88.538 | 4.390 sec. | 9 | 18 | 10 | 63 | 7 | 12 |
| Sept. 5 | Pop Secret 500 | Fontana, Calif. | Brian Vickers | Elliott Sadler | Robert Yates | 3:53:47 | 128.324 | 0.263 sec. | 13 | 29 | 11 | 51 | 28 | 10 |
| Sept. 11 | Chevy Rock & Roll 400 | Richmond, Va. | Ryan Newman | Jeremy Mayfield | Ray Evernham | 3:01:55 | 98.946 | 4.928 sec. | 9 | 20 | 10 | 57 | 12 | 5 |
| Sept. 19 | Sylvania 300 | Loudon, N.H. | Set by points | Kurt Busch | Jack Roush | 2:53:31 | 109.753 | 2.488 sec. | 7 | 15 | 7 | 30 | 16 | 11 |
| Sept. 26 | MBNA America 400 | Dover, Del. | Jeremy Mayfield | Ryan Newman | Roger Penske | 3:21:34 | 119.067 | 8.149 sec. | 13 | 20 | 13 | 38 | 8 | 13 |
| Oct. 3 | EA Sports 500 | Talladega, Ala. | Joe Nemechek | Dale Earnhardt Jr. | Teresa Earnhardt | 3:11:12 | 156.929 | 0.117 sec. | 20 | 47 | 5 | 22 | 26 | 10 |
| Oct. 10 | Banquet 400 | Kansas City, Kan. | Joe Nemechek | Joe Nemechek | Nelson Bowers | 3:07:39 | 128.058 | 0.081 sec. | 12 | 24 | 9 | 39 | 23 | 12 |
| Oct. 16 | UAW-GM Quality 500 | Concord, N.C. | Ryan Newman | Jimmie Johnson | Rick Hendrick | 3:50:51 | 130.214 | 1.727 sec. | 9 | 18 | 11 | 53 | 14 | 14 |
| Oct. 24 | Subway 500 | Martinsville, Va. | Ryan Newman | Jimmie Johnson | Rick Hendrick | 3:58:43 | 66.103 | 1.225 sec. | 12 | 22 | 17 | 125 | 26 | 9 |
| Oct. 31 | MBNA 500 | Hampton, Ga. | Ryan Newman | Jimmie Johnson | Rick Hendrick | 3:25:54 | 145.847 | 0.293 sec. | 7 | 16 | 6 | 33 | 8 | 8 |
| Nov. 7 | Checker Auto Parts 500 | Phoenix | Ryan Newmn | Dale Earnhardt Jr. | Teresa Earnhardt | 3:19:16 | 94.848 | 1.431 sec. | 7 | 11 | 6 | 63 | 24 | 8 |
| Nov. 14 | Southern 500 | Darlington, S.C. | Set by points | Jimmie Johnson | Rick Hendrick | 4:00:33 | 125.044 | 0.959 sec. | 10 | 27 | 8 | 47 | 16 | 10 |
| Nov. 21 | Ford 400 | Homestead, Fla. | Kurt Busch | Greg Biffle | Jack Roush | 3:50:55 | 105.623 | 0.342 sec. | 6 | 14 | 6 | 79 | 23 | 11 |

*First-time Bud Pole winner

# Kasey Kahne

**Car:** No. 9 Dodge. **Team owner:** Ray Evernham. **Birthdate:** April 10, 1980. **Hometown:** Enumclaw, Wash.

## NASCAR NEXTEL CUP SERIES STATISTICS

**Seasons competed:** 1 (2004) **Career starts:** 36
**Career wins:** 0 **Career poles:** 4
**Rookie season recap:** Kahne finished the 2004 season 13th in the points standings on the strength of four poles, 13 top five finishes and 14 top 10 finishes. He started all 36 races and was the top Raybestos Rookie in 19 of those events. Kahne's success was particularly remarkable because he began the season without any previous NASCAR Cup experience—his first NASCAR NEXTEL Cup race was the season opener at Daytona. Kahne put himself in position to contend on race day by performing well in qualifying. He tied 2002 rookie Ryan Newman for the record for most second-place finishes with five. Kahne's best points position was fourth, after race No. 4 at Atlanta, and he held a top 10 spot in the standings for seven weeks last season.

| Rk. | Driver | Rookie Points | Points behind | Starts | Wins | Top 5 | Top 10 | Winnings |
|---|---|---|---|---|---|---|---|---|
| 1. | Kasey Kahne | 376 | — | 36 | 0 | 13 | 14 | $5,415,611 |
| 2. | Brendan Gaughan | 256 | -120 | 36 | 0 | 1 | 4 | $2,929,396 |
| 3. | Brian Vickers | 255 | -121 | 36 | 0 | 0 | 4 | $3,135,886 |
| 4. | Scott Wimmer | 247 | -129 | 35 | 0 | 1 | 2 | $3,675,879 |
| 5. | Scott Riggs | 237 | -139 | 35 | 0 | 1 | 2 | $3,443,345 |
| 6. | Johnny Sauter | 155 | -221 | 16 | 0 | 0 | 0 | $1,372,949 |

# Raybestos Rookies of the Year: 1957-2004

| Year | Driver | Pts. Pos | Races | Poles | Wins | Top 5 | Top 10 | Winnings | Year | Driver | Pts. Pos | Races | Poles | Wins | Top 5 | Top 10 | Winnings |
|---|---|---|---|---|---|---|---|---|---|---|---|---|---|---|---|---|---|
| 2004 | Kasey Kahne | 13 | 36 | 4 | 0 | 13 | 14 | $5,415,611 | 1980 | Jody Ridley | 7 | 31 | 0 | 0 | 2 | 18 | $196,617 |
| 2003 | Jamie McMurray | 13 | 36 | 1 | 0 | 5 | 13 | $3,258,806 | 1979 | Dale Earnhardt | 7 | 27 | 4 | 1 | 11 | 17 | $264,086 |
| 2002 | Ryan Newman | 6 | 36 | 6 | 1 | 14 | 22 | $5,346,651 | 1978 | Ronnie Thomas | 18 | 27 | 0 | 0 | 0 | 2 | $73,037 |
| 2001 | Kevin Harvick | 9 | 35 | 0 | 2 | 6 | 16 | $4,302,202 | 1977 | Ricky Rudd | 17 | 25 | 0 | 0 | 1 | 10 | $68,448 |
| 2000 | Matt Kenseth | 14 | 34 | 0 | 1 | 4 | 11 | $2,408,138 | 1976 | Skip Manning | 18 | 27 | 0 | 0 | 0 | 4 | $55,820 |
| 1999 | Tony Stewart | 4 | 34 | 2 | 3 | 12 | 21 | $3,190,149 | 1975 | Bruce Hill | 16 | 26 | 0 | 0 | 3 | 11 | $58,138 |
| 1998 | Kenny Irwin | 28 | 32 | 1 | 0 | 1 | 4 | $1,459,967 | 1974 | Earl Ross | 8 | 21 | 0 | 1 | 5 | 10 | $64,830 |
| 1997 | Mike Skinner | 30 | 31 | 2 | 0 | 0 | 3 | $900,569 | 1973 | Lennie Pond | 23 | 23 | 0 | 0 | 1 | 9 | $25,155 |
| 1996 | Johnny Benson | 21 | 30 | 1 | 0 | 1 | 6 | $932,580 | 1972 | Larry Smith | 23 | 23 | 0 | 0 | 0 | 7 | $24,215 |
| 1995 | Ricky Craven | 24 | 31 | 0 | 0 | 0 | 4 | $597,054 | 1971 | Walter Ballard | 10 | 41 | 0 | 0 | 3 | 11 | $25,598 |
| 1994 | Jeff Burton | 24 | 30 | 0 | 0 | 2 | 3 | $594,700 | 1970 | Bill Dennis | 25 | 25 | 0 | 0 | 0 | 5 | $15,670 |
| 1993 | Jeff Gordon | 14 | 30 | 1 | 0 | 7 | 11 | $765,168 | 1969 | Dick Brooks | 21 | 28 | 0 | 0 | 3 | 12 | $27,532 |
| 1992 | Jimmy Hensley | 28 | 22 | 0 | 0 | 0 | 4 | $247,660 | 1968 | Pete Hamilton | 32 | 16 | 0 | 0 | 3 | 6 | $8,239 |
| 1991 | Bobby Hamilton | 22 | 28 | 0 | 0 | 0 | 4 | $259,105 | 1967 | Donnie Allison | 16 | 20 | 0 | 0 | 4 | 7 | $16,440 |
| 1990 | Rob Moroso | 30 | 25 | 0 | 0 | 0 | 1 | $162,002 | 1966 | James Hylton | 2 | 41 | 1 | 0 | 20 | 32 | $29,575 |
| 1989 | Dick Trickle | 15 | 28 | 0 | 0 | 6 | 9 | $343,728 | 1965 | Sam McQuagg | 24 | 15 | 0 | 0 | 2 | 5 | $10,555 |
| 1988 | Ken Bouchard | 25 | 24 | 0 | 0 | 0 | 1 | $109,410 | 1964 | Doug Cooper | 21 | 39 | 0 | 0 | 4 | 11 | $10,445 |
| 1987 | Davey Allison | 21 | 22 | 5 | 2 | 9 | 10 | $361,060 | 1963 | Billy Wade | 16 | 22 | 0 | 0 | 4 | 11 | $8,710 |
| 1986 | Alan Kulwicki | 21 | 23 | 0 | 0 | 1 | 4 | $94,450 | 1962 | Tom Cox | 18 | 40 | 0 | 0 | 12 | 20 | $8,980 |
| 1985 | Ken Schrader | 16 | 28 | 0 | 0 | 0 | 3 | $211,523 | 1961 | Woody Wilson | 41 | 5 | 0 | 0 | 0 | 1 | $2,625 |
| 1984 | Rusty Wallace | 14 | 30 | 0 | 0 | 2 | 4 | $196,617 | 1960 | David Pearson | 23 | 22 | 1 | 0 | 3 | 7 | $5,030 |
| 1983 | Sterling Marlin | 19 | 30 | 0 | 0 | 0 | 1 | $143,564 | 1959 | Richard Petty | 15 | 22 | 0 | 0 | 6 | 9 | $7,630 |
| 1982 | Geoffrey Bodine | 22 | 25 | 2 | 0 | 4 | 10 | $258,500 | 1958 | Shorty Rollins | 4 | 21 | 0 | 1 | 10 | 17 | $8,515 |
| 1981 | Ron Bouchard | 22 | 22 | 1 | 1 | 5 | 12 | $152,855 | 1957 | Ken Rush | 38 | 16 | 1 | 0 | 1 | 6 | $2,045 |

## Survival of the Fastest

The NASCAR NEXTEL All-Star Challenge, formerly known as The Winston, will continue with its 21st running of the non-points event in 2005. The annual all-star event brings together NASCAR's best under the lights at the 1.5-mile Lowe's Motor Speedway in Concord, N.C., as a prelude to the following week's Coca-Cola 600 that is annually held on Memorial Day weekend.

From the late Dale Earnhardt's famous 1987 "Pass in the Grass" to Mark Martin's improbable 1998 victory after Jeff Gordon ran out of gas on the final lap to Gordon's 2001 victory in a backup car, the all-star race has had its share of exciting moments since its inception in 1985. Since Darrell Waltrip won the inaugural event in 1985, only one driver—Davey Allison in 1991-92—has been able to win back to back.

The 2005 NASCAR NEXTEL All-Star Challenge will be run Saturday, May 21

## Drivers eligible

Drivers can become eligible for the NASCAR NEXTEL All-Star Challenge in five ways:

1) Any driver who wins one of the first 11 races of 2005 (those preceding the All-Star challenge) will be eligible. Also, drivers who won any races in the 2004 season are eligible. If a driver leaves a team with which he has won a race, he remains eligible, and the car owner's new driver also is eligible.

2) Drivers who are past NASCAR Cup champions are eligible.

3) Past winners of the All-Star race are eligible.

4) The winning driver of the NEXTEL Open qualifies.

5) If those four criteria do not produce a field of 20 drivers, then winners of races in 2003 will be added until a field of 20 drivers is achieved. For the 2005 NASCAR NEXTEL All-Star challenge, those drivers would include Ricky Craven, Robby Gordon and Kevin Harvick. If a field of 20 drivers still is not filled with 2003 winners, then otherwise not eligible drivers who won races in 2002 will be added until a roster of 20 is filled.

## Event format

The NASCAR NEXTEL All-Star Challenge consists of three segments totaling 90 laps/135 miles around the 1.5-mile Lowe's Motor Speedway track. An initial 40-lap segment advances the top 20 finishers to the second segment. From that 30-lap sprint, the top 14 advance to the final segment, which is 20 laps. There also is the X-factor to consider: A vote by fans will determine a random inversion (anywhere from three to 10 cars) of the starting order for the 20-lap finale.

# All-Star winners

| Year | Winner | Runner-up | Open Winner | Year | Winner | Runner-up | Open Winner |
|------|--------|-----------|-------------|------|--------|-----------|-------------|
| 1985 | Darrell Waltrip | Harry Gant | None | 1995 | Jeff Gordon | Sterling Marlin | Todd Bodine |
| 1986 | Bill Elliott | Dale Earnhardt | Benny Parsons* | 1996 | Michael Waltrip | Rusty Wallace | Jimmy Spencer |
| 1987 | Dale Earnhardt | Terry Labonte | Buddy Baker | 1997 | Jeff Gordon | Bobby Labonte | Ricky Craven |
| 1988 | Terry Labonte | Sterling Marlin | Sterling Marlin | 1998 | Mark Martin | Bobby Labonte | Jeremy Mayfield |
| 1989 | Rusty Wallace | Ken Schrader | Sterling Marlin | 1999 | Terry Labonte | Tony Stewart | Tony Stewart |
| 1990 | Dale Earnhardt | Ken Schrader | Dick Trickle | 2000 | Dale Earnhardt Jr. | Dale Jarrett | Steve Park |
| 1991 | Davey Allison | Ken Schrader | Michael Waltrip | 2001 | Jeff Gordon | Dale Jarrett | Johnny Benson |
| 1992 | Davey Allison | Kyle Petty | Michael Waltrip | 2002 | Ryan Newman | Dale Earnhardt Jr. | Ryan Newman |
| 1993 | Dale Earnhardt | Mark Martin | Sterling Marlin | 2003 | Jimmie Johnson | Kurt Busch | Jeff Burton |
| 1994 | Geoffrey Bodine | Sterling Marlin | Jeff Gordon | 2004 | Matt Kenseth | Ryan Newman | Sterling Marlin |

**\*Winner of the Atlanta Invitational**

# 2005 fact sheet

**Where:** Lowe's Motor Speedway
**When:** May 21, 2005
**Time:** 9 p.m. ET (approximately)

**Length:** Three segments (40, 30 and 20 laps)
**Purse:** $3,500,000 (includes NEXTEL Open)
**Winner:** $1,000,000

## THE NASCAR NEXTEL ALL-STAR CHALLENGE ELIGIBILITY LIST [as of January 1, 2005]

| Driver | Race Won | Car Owner |
|--------|----------|-----------|
| 1. Dale Earnhardt Jr. | 2004 Daytona 500, Daytona Beach, Fla. | Teresa Earnhardt |
| 2. Matt Kenseth | 2004 Subway 400, Rockingham, N.C. | Jack Roush |
| 3. Jimmie Johnson | 2004 Carolina Dodge Dealers 400, Darlington, S.C. | Rick Hendrick |
| 4. Kurt Busch | 2004 Food City 500, Bristol, Tenn. | Jack Roush |
| 5. Elliott Sadler | 2004 Samsung/RadioShack 500, Fort Worth, Texas | Robert Yates |
| 6. Rusty Wallace | 2004 Advance Auto Parts 500, Martinsville, Va. | Roger Penske |
| 7. Jeff Gordon | 2004 Aaron's 499, Talladega, Ala. | Rick Hendrick |
| 8. Mark Martin | 2004 MBNA 400 'A Salute to Heroes', Dover, Del. | Jack Roush |
| 9. Ryan Newman | 2004 DHL 400, Brooklyn, Mich. | Roger Penske |
| 10. Tony Stewart | 2004 Tropicana 400, Joliet, Ill. | Joe Gibbs |
| 11. Greg Biffle | 2004 GFS Marketplace 400, Brooklyn, Mich. | Jack Roush |
| 12. Jeremy Mayfield | 2004 Chevy Rock & Roll 400, Richmond, Va. | Ray Evernham |
| 13. Joe Nemechek | 2004 Banquet 400, Kansas City, Kan. | Nelson Bowers |

### Previous NASCAR Cup champions

(Who are not 2004/2005 winners)

| Drivers | Year(s) Won |
|---------|-------------|
| Bobby Labonte | 2000 |
| Dale Jarrett | 1999 |
| Bill Elliott | 1988 |
| Terry Labonte | 1984 |

### Previous all-star event winners

(Not otherwise eligible)

| Drivers | Year(s) Won |
|---------|-------------|
| Michael Waltrip | 1996 |
| Geoffrey Bodine | 1994 |

### Other qualified drivers

(Not otherwise eligible)
NEXTEL Open Winner

## HISTORY

The 27th edition of the Budweiser Shootout at Daytona will be run under the lights on Saturday, February 12, at Daytona International Speedway. The Budweiser Shootout traditionally kicks off Speedweeks and will be televised by FOX. The non-points event has jump-started the NASCAR NEXTEL Cup Series season since 1979. From 1979 to 1997, the event was known as the Busch Clash, and in 1998 became the Bud Shootout. The current name— Budweiser Shootout at Daytona—was adopted in 2001. The event was run under the lights for the first time in 2003, and Dale Earnhardt Jr. captured the victory. Dale Jarrett won in 2004.

## PAST WINNERS

The late Dale Earnhardt leads all drivers with six victories in Budweiser Shootout events. Dale Jarrett has three wins in the Budweiser Shootouts. The late Neil Bonnett, Jeff Gordon, Ken Schrader and Tony Stewart have two wins each.

| Year | Winner | Year | Winner |
|------|--------|------|--------|
| 2004 | Dale Jarrett | 1991 | Dale Earnhardt |
| 2003 | Dale Earnhardt Jr. | 1990 | Ken Schrader |
| 2002 | Tony Stewart | 1989 | Ken Schrader |
| 2001 | Tony Stewart | 1988 | Dale Earnhardt |
| 2000 | Dale Jarrett | 1987 | Bill Elliott |
| 1999 | Mark Martin | 1986 | Dale Earnhardt |
| 1998 | Rusty Wallace | 1985 | Terry Labonte |
| 1997 | Jeff Gordon | 1984 | Neil Bonnett |
| 1996 | Dale Jarrett | 1983 | Neil Bonnett |
| 1995 | Dale Earnhardt | 1982 | Bobby Allison |
| 1994 | Jeff Gordon | 1981 | Darrell Waltrip |
| 1993 | Dale Earnhardt | 1980 | Dale Earnhardt |
| 1992 | Geoffrey Bodine | 1979 | Buddy Baker |

Note: *From 1979-97 the race was named the Busch Clash. In 1998, the event name was changed to the Bud Shootout, and was renamed the Budweiser Shootout in 2001.*

## FORMAT

The Budweiser Shootout features drivers who earned a Bud Pole Award in the previous season and includes past champions of the Budweiser Shootout who did not earn a Bud Pole during the previous year, but finished in the top 50 in the previous season's final point standings. Past champions of the Budweiser Shootout who are eligible for 2005 include Dale Jarrett, Dale Earnhardt Jr., Mark Martin, Ken Schrader, Bill Elliott, Terry Labonte, Tony Stewart, Rusty Wallace and Geoffrey Bodine.

## 2004 Bud Pole winners

| Driver | Poles |
|--------|-------|
| Ryan Newman | 8 |
| Jeff Gordon | 6 |
| Kasey Kahne | 4 |
| Jeremy Mayfield | 2 |
| Casey Mears | 2 |
| Joe Nemechek | 2 |
| Brian Vickers | 2 |
| Greg Biffle | 1 |
| Kurt Busch | 1 |
| Jimmie Johnson | 1 |
| Bobby Labonte | 1 |
| Ricky Rudd | 1 |

Dale Jarrett

## DAYTONA 500

In NASCAR's biggest race, Dale Earnhardt Jr. learned the value of patience. He waited until the time was right. Then he slipped past Tony Stewart with 19 laps to run.

Even though Stewart was strong—he led 97 laps, more than any other driver—Earnhardt knew he could pass him because he'd been passing cars the same way all week in practice. There was no need to risk doing something foolish, something he might have done earlier in his career. This time, he kept his emotions in check and drove a steady, calm race, despite intense pressure to win.

Last year, he had the best car going into the 500 but finished 36th because of an alternator problem. His father, the late Dale Earnhardt, had won 34 races at Daytona, more than any other driver, but only one Daytona 500.

Earnhardt Jr., in his fifth 500, wanted no part of waiting so long. He admitted: "This is more important to me than any race I run all year."

Earnhardt held off Stewart at the end because he conserved his tires before making the pass. This year's softer tires will make

patient driving like Earnhardt's a key to the rest of the season. The new tires will wear out faster under an impatient driver. A driver can keep his tires fresh longer by taking corners easier, holding off on passing, occasionally lifting off the accelerator and running smooth laps.

"You can't run the fastest lap every lap that you possibly can drive," said Greg Biffle, who won the pole but started at the back because his team changed engines.

The tires will wear out eventually, no matter how a guy drives, but the more patient he is, the more fast laps he'll be able to turn. That stands in stark contrast to last season.

Stewart finished 0.273 seconds behind Earnhardt, followed by rookie Scott Wimmer, Kevin Harvick and Jimmie Johnson.

**Dale Earnhardt Jr.'s smart driving—he conserved his tires to make a final pass on Tony Stewart—won him his first Daytona 500.**

There were four cautions, the biggest coming when Michael Waltrip was caught in the middle of an 11-car melee on Lap 70 after Johnny Sauter got loose and nudged Brian Vickers. Waltrip barrel-rolled down the back stretch and planted the car 6 inches into the ground on its roof.

## SUBWAY 400

Matt Kenseth was so dominating, he almost didn't see Kasey Kahne coming. Yet there was the rookie Kahne charging to the finish in the middle groove, and Kenseth giving it everything he had on the high side. The nose of Kenseth's Ford kissed the line 0.010 seconds ahead of the nose of Kahne's Dodge, which tied for the fourth-closest finish in NASCAR's top series since the current electronic timing and scoring system was implemented in 1993.

Where did Kahne come from? Kenseth led 259 of 393 laps at North Carolina and was driving into the sunset when the race went green for the final time on Lap 364. All of a sudden, going into the final lap, Kahne was there.

"I was doing everything I could," Kenseth said. "Kasey almost got me in Turn 1 and Turn 2 one time. I didn't know whether to protect the

**Matt Kenseth barely nosed out Kasey Kahne.**

bottom or the top, so I tried to protect the middle and get a good run off the corner and not overdrive the corner.

"The last lap, I had been loose off of 4, and I got up as high as I could to get a run down off the corner as good as I could, and he got a good charge on me there."

Kahne wasn't too unhappy placing second in his second NASCAR NEXTEL Cup Series start. The previous week in the Daytona 500, he blew an engine and finished last.

Jamie McMurray finished third, though owners Chip Ganassi and Felix Sabates thought he should have won and protested to NASCAR after the race. McMurray inherited the lead when Kenseth and Kahne pitted on Lap 351, but a caution came out. Ganassi contended Kenseth and Kahne should have been scored a lap down, but because the field is frozen when the caution flag flies, the ruling was that the two drivers didn't lose a lap.

When the other lead cars made their stops during the caution, Kenseth and Kahne recycled to the front.

Sterling Marling and Dale Earnhardt Jr. rounded out the top five.

**Matt Kenseth (left) ran away with the UAW-DaimlerChrysler 400, leading almost half the laps and taking the points lead after the race. Dale Earnhardt Jr.'s (above) sub-13 second pit stop helped him find victory lane in the Golden Corral 500. Jimmie Johnson (right) outran Bobby Labonte in a four-lap run to the finish in the Carolina Dodge Dealers 400, making owner Rick Hendrick a happy man.**

# UAW-DAIMLERCHRYSLER 400

Matt Kenseth is putting a new spin on what it means to be a points racer: Win the race, lead the most laps, get the most possible points.

Kenseth led 123 of 267 laps to win at Las Vegas Motor Speedway and crossed the finish line ahead of rookie Kasey Kahne for the second consecutive race.

This time, it wasn't as close; Kenseth beat Kahne by 3.426 seconds. Kenseth led the most laps in that race, too, and scored the maximum 190 points in each event.

"It was a lot easier to run second to Matt today when he was half a straightaway ahead instead of a couple of feet," Kahne said.

Kevin Harvick was the leader and Kenseth fourth when the field took the green flag for the final time on Lap 207. But as Harvick's tires started to give, Kenseth made his move and took the lead for good on Lap 230.

Harvick appeared on his way to a second-pace finish but ran out of gas with five laps left and wound up finishing 21st. Behind Kenseth and Kahne, Tony Stewart, Jamie McMurray and Mark Martin completed the top five.

Drivers who found the right setups and conserved the new, softer tires that were being used for this race ran well throughout the day.

"When I was trying to catch (Harvick and Stewart), if I would have gotten the right-front worn out, the cars that were handling better would have passed me at the end of the run," said Kenseth.

# GOLDEN CORRAL 500

Dale Earnhardt Jr. wore his rally cap at Atlanta Motor Speedway. It was a perfect fit.

Coming off a miserable weekend in Las Vegas—the No. 8 crew missed the setup completely and finished 35th—the team rebounded with a vengeance, winning by 4.584 seconds over Jeremy Mayfield.

"They don't give up," Earnhardt said of his team's efforts. "They think you can win from 6 feet under. In our graves, they'll still be trying to crawl out."

Kasey Kahne, Jimmie Johnson and Ryan Newman completed the top five. It was Kahne's third consecutive top three finish.

When Jamie McMurray lost his engine on Lap 246, the drivers on the lead lap pitted the next time around. With a 14.1-second stop, Mayfield led everyone off pit road. But Earnhardt charged to the lead on Lap 266. With 23 laps remaining, the Earnhardt's crew performed a 12.66-second stop under green conditions—the team's second sub 13-second stop of the race. Mayfield regained the lead after the pit stops, but it didn't take long for Junior to run him down.

Earnhardt made the pass with 15 laps to go and pulled away for the victory, his second of the season.

Tony Stewart was strong early, but the car became tight, and he showed a lack of patience with Earnhardt when the No. 8 passed Stewart on Lap 177. Stewart damaged the front end of his Chevrolet after nudging

Earnhardt's, but the No. 20 team came to Stewart's rescue by working on the car the rest of the race. Stewart finished seventh and maintained second place in the standings.

# CAROLINA DODGE DEALERS 400

For Jimmie Johnson, the fast way around Darlington Raceway was down pit road. Johnson led three times in the race, including a four-lap sprint to the finish, but not once did he take the lead on the racetrack.

All three times, his crew got him out in front of the competition on pit stops. The last was during a caution that began when Kyle Petty's engine blew on Lap 275. Johnson, who was running third and more than a half straightaway behind leader Bobby Labonte, came out of the pits first and led the final 15 laps.

"When we were sitting in third, before we were able to hit pit road and get the lead, I wanted a caution to come out because I felt with the pit stops we'd been having that I could maybe have a shot at winning the race," Johnson said. "Luckily, we had a great stop."

A four-lap run to the finish was set up after Kasey Kahne spun and brought out the final caution. With two laps to go, Labonte got underneath Johnson in Turn 4 but couldn't make the pass and didn't come close again.

"I just couldn't get a run off the corner," said Labonte, whose car was better on long runs. Even though Johnson's car was loose at the end, it was a little better than Labonte's on short runs.

Ryan Newman, Robby Gordon and Elliott Sadler completed the top five.

## FOOD CITY 500

Bristol Motor Speedway might be the house that Darrell Waltrip and Rusty Wallace built, but Kurt Busch made a case for moving in after winning the Food City 500.

Busch, Waltrip, Cale Yarborough and Fred Lorenzen are the only drivers to win three consecutive races in NASCAR's top series at Bristol. Busch won both Bristol races in 2003 and has four wins at the track.

Busch, who led the final 119 laps, went against crew chief Jimmy Fennig's advice by staying on the track instead of pitting with the other leaders during a caution period that began on Lap 381. Busch assumed the lead on the next lap, and with five more cautions giving his tires opportunities to cool the rest of the way, never gave it up.

Busch survived a bump from Wallace during a green-white-checkers finish that was set up when the race was red-flagged so the track could be cleaned after Dale Jarrett's accident with eight laps remaining.

"This one by far has got to be the sweetest because of what we had to overcome," Busch said. "We had about 1,000 rpm less all day today, which provided for great forward bite. So we were able to come off the corner good, but we were junk on restarts, and I just couldn't get the car to handle the right way all day."

Wallace, who led 100 of the 500 laps, was on Busch's bumper on the final restart, but his No. 2 Dodge didn't have the momentum to pass the No. 97.

Wallace finished second, followed by Kevin Harvick, Sterling Marlin and Matt Kenseth, who retained the points lead. Busch's victory lifted him two positions to second.

## SAMSUNG/RADIOSHACK 500

Elliott Sadler spent the final laps at Texas looking in his rearview mirror. Right behind him, clear as day, was Kasey Kahne, the rookie who had dominated the race and was closing fast.

Then Sadler saw the checkered flag, and it was over. Coming off Turn 4 on the high side, Kahne had gotten the nose of his Dodge even with the door of Sadler's Ford but ran out of time and real estate. Sadler held on by .028 seconds to get his first win for Robert Yates Racing.

"Thank God they had the (start-finish) stripe where they did," Sadler said. "A few more feet toward Turn 1, and Kasey would have had me."

For Kahne, who lost by .010 seconds to Matt Kenseth at North Carolina, it hurt because his car was so good. He had led 134 of 334 laps.

"When I came off of Turn 4, knowing I was going to finish second again, I thought, 'You've got to be kidding me,' " Kahne said. "I thought we had the best car all day."

Kahne had led a stretch of 25 laps before he came in for a green flag pit stop on Lap 362. Five laps later, Ward Burton spun on the back stretch, bringing out a caution. A small group of drivers, Sadler among them, had not made green-flag stops, and Kahne found

**Two Bristol-loving drivers battled it out in the Food City 500. Kurt Busch beat out Rusty Wallace to win his third consecutive NASCAR NEXTEL Cup Series race at Bristol. Wallace has nine NASCAR Cup wins at the racetrack.**

himself a lap down, although the lucky dog pass allowed him to get back on the lead lap for the restart.

Still, Kahne lined up eighth, and Sadler started second, behind Jeff Gordon. Then, from Lap 267 to Lap 301, only nine of 35 laps were run under the green. That left Kahne back in the pack, unable to make up any ground as laps clicked off under caution.

Not long after racing resumed, Gordon had problems—he ultimately solved them by switching to his backup battery—and lost the lead to Sadler. Dale Earnhardt Jr. moved into second but didn't stay there long. Kahne swept around him on Lap 314 and began to whittle away at the 1.5-second deficit to Sadler.

On Lap 332, Kahne got a run on Sadler on the high side near the start-finish line, but Sadler moved up to block, and it slowed Kahne's momentum. Kahne was unable to muster another charge until the final lap.

## ADVANCE AUTO PARTS 500

Rusty Wallace missed the 12x12 pothole that opened up in Turn 3 of Martinsville Speedway and halted the race for nearly an hour and 20 minutes while it was repaired.

Hard to figure how Wallace dodged doom and destruction. He'd hit every pothole and suffered every pitfall during a 105-race winless streak that dated to May 2001. A loose chunk of concrete? Surely he could run over that.

But, no, Jeff Gordon did. Then Dale Earnhardt Jr.'s car went away. And Jimmie Johnson stayed out on old tires.

In the end, all Wallace had to do was drive to the front and stay there, which he did for the final 45 laps.

Wallace held off hard-charging Bobby Labonte by .538 seconds and, shortly after crossing the finish line, summed up the obvious

to his crew over the radio: "Man, that was a long streak."

A trip to victory lane in April 2001 at California gave Wallace at least one win in 16 consecutive seasons, a streak in which he took great pride. But after being shut out in 2002 and 2003, Wallace was riding a different kind of streak that was eating him up inside.

"It's great that I finally got this stupid thing behind me—105 races, that's a long time," he said. "That's too much to wait for. That last 30 laps seemed like 300."

No doubt Johnson felt the same way about the final laps. He stayed out on old tires while the rest of the field pitted during a caution with 83 laps remaining and ultimately finished fourth. Johnson led when the race resumed on Lap 423 but was passed by Wallace on Lap 456. There was one more caution and restart with 37 laps to go, but Wallace never surrendered the lead.

Labonte finished second, Earnhardt third, Johnson fourth and Ryan Newman fifth. Gordon, who finished sixth, hit the pothole that developed a little more than halfway through the race and brought out the red flag with 290 laps to go. Two other baseball-sized holes opened at the same end of the track. Gordon hit the big hole hardest, and a piece of concrete flew up into his car.

## AARON'S 499

Even though NASCAR did everything correctly, from how it determined the winner, Jeff Gordon, to how it ended the race at Talladega, there was nothing it could do to satisfy fans who starved for a green-flag ending but got yellow in one of the most exciting restrictor-plate races in years.

When Brian Vickers spun in Turn 4 to bring out a record 11th caution on Lap 184 of 188,

At Martinsville, Rusty Wallace's long-awaited victory broke a 105-race winless streak.

TURN 4

With 54 lead changes, the Aaron's 499 kept fans on edge. Jeff Gordon (below) celebrated his second win in two weeks at the Auto Club 500.

no one realized the race was over at that moment. So it didn't seem so important who had the lead—Gordon or Dale Earnhardt Jr.—when the field was frozen. But when it became clear the race would end under caution, the distinction of who was in front at the instant the yellow flag flew was the only thing that mattered.

Earnhardt thought he was in front, and at first, that's what NASCAR thought. But after officials reviewed more video, the call was made to move Gordon to the point.

Despite the controversy, Gordon simply was happy to be in victory lane for the first time in 2004. "I didn't know what was going to happen there," Gordon said. "I knew I got ahead of him going into Turn 3. I passed him, but I wasn't passing him."

Teams and drivers were told by NASCAR in the drivers meeting that the race would not be red-flagged if a caution came out with five laps or fewer to run. Because of when the caution occurred, the race could not have been restarted until the final lap, and NASCAR didn't want to put the drivers' safety at risk.

"We've had restrictor-plate races where we've tried a green-white-checkered type finish," said series director John Darby. "Today, it would have been green and white together, which is truly a recipe for disaster."

Kevin Harvick finished third, Jimmie Johnson fourth and Robby Gordon fifth.

## AUTO CLUB 500

When Jeff Gordon ran out of fuel at California, the only thing it cost him was the burnout he had planned before his crew had to push his No. 24 Chevrolet to victory lane.

For others, including Bobby Labonte, the price was much higher. Labonte, who had chopped a deficit of 3.5 seconds to less than one second, ran out of fuel in Turn 1 on the final lap. Instead of finishing second or pushing Gordon for the win, Labonte wound up fifth.

Gordon backed off to make sure he made it to the finish line, and he did, beating teammate Jimmie Johnson by 12.871 seconds and winning his second consecutive race.

After finishing 41st at Darlington in fifth race of the season, Gordon was 13th in points, 160 out of the lead. The win at California boosted him to third in the standings, just 27 points behind leader Dale Earnhardt Jr.

The pivotal point of the race came when teams decided to make final pit stops. Polesitter Kasey Kahne, who had a fast car and led 77 laps, came in for his stop on Lap 197. Gordon stayed out a lap longer. Kahne didn't make it to the end. He and teammate Jeremy Mayfield, who were running third and fourth, were among several drivers who ran out of fuel during the final two laps and had to come in. Kahne wound up 13th and Mayfield 14th.

Ryan Newman finished third, Matt Kenseth fourth, and Labonte held on for fifth. "We didn't miscalculate fuel," Labonte said. "We just ran a little faster in the last run."

## CHEVY AMERICAN REVOLUTION 400

When the call went over the radio for Dale Earnhardt Jr. to pit with 55 laps left in the race, he didn't hear it—or at least that's what he said later. Even if there was a debate, Earnhardt knew what he wanted to hear, and the decision he and his team made won him the race at Richmond.

Tony Stewart appeared headed for his first victory of the season, but when the caution flag flew on Lap 344, he decided to pit because his

car wasn't turning well, and he didn't feel like he could hold off Earnhardt and a host of others when the race restarted.

When Stewart and eight other lead lap cars dived into the pits, Earnhardt stayed out. So did Jimmie Johnson and Jeff Gordon. Earnhardt said he knew he would have been behind Stewart, Johnson and Gordon had he pitted, and that his car had been loose on new tires.

"And a lot of times in these races you get a lot of cautions at the end, when guys get racy and wrecking and stuff," he said. "Being out front was where we needed to be. My car was about as good as it was going to get."

Which, in the end, was plenty good enough. Earnhardt pulled away from Johnson after the restart, eventually winning by 1.481 seconds. Bobby Labonte finished third ahead of Stewart and Matt Kenseth. Gordon dropped back to sixth after a heated battle with Stewart.

"I had a top three night until I ran into the No. 24 car, and I know (Gordon) is mad at me," Stewart said. "I just got down into Turn 3 and got loose. We made a change, and that's probably what made it loose—not to mention all that oil dry down there."

## COCA-COLA 600

Maybe it's time Lowe's asked Jimmie Johnson to teach one of those how-to clinics at its stores. Johnson led 334 of 400 laps for his second consecutive victory in the season's longest event.

Shortened by rain last year, the 600 went the distance this time, although it finished under caution after Bobby Labonte hit the wall in Turn 2 on the final lap. The finish wouldn't have been close. Michael Waltrip was second and more concerned about keeping people behind him.

"When you watch something for 590 miles, you start to believe it," said Waltrip, who posted his best finish of the season and his best in 39 starts at Charlotte.

Johnson came close to Jim Paschal's record of 335 laps led in the 600—way back in May 1967.

Five of the seven caution flags came during the final 65 laps, and Johnson found

himself in fifth place after a pit stop under caution on Lap 369. Although Johnson and most of the lead pack pitted, Jamie McMurray stayed out and assumed the lead. Johnson took four tires. When everyone returned to the track, Johnson found himself fifth.

It didn't take him long to return to the front. He made quick work of Kasey Kahne and Jeremy Mayfield, got Waltrip on Lap 379 and passed McMurra on 384.

After Ryan Newman's engine blew on Lap 393, it set up a final dash to the finish, but Johnson pulled away easily. Behind Waltrip in second were Matt Kenseth, McMurray and Elliott Sadler.

## MBNA 400 'A SALUTE TO HEROES'

Mark Martin knows heartbreak. He has come close to winning a championship, finishing second four times. He endured a winless 2003 and wound up 17th in points—his worst finish in the 17 seasons he has run all the races. At Dover, he expected more of the same.

So when Martin held the lead late, he feared the worst. He was on old tires, and Tony

Stewart, who led 234 of the first 315 laps, was on new tires. But when the race restarted for the final time on Lap 392 of 400, Martin easily pulled away to win by 1.702 seconds. The victory ended a 72-race winless streak for Martin.

"I've dedicated my whole life to winning, and winning is why I race," he said. "It came down to whether I wanted to win or whether I wanted to lose, and I wanted to win."

**The eternal pessimist Mark Martin (above) smiled and celebrated after winning at Dover. Dale Earnhardt Jr. (left) gave his crew a victory shower after the Chevy American Revolution 400 at Richmond.**

Stewart finished second, followed by Dale Earnhardt Jr., Jeff Burton and rookie Scott Riggs. It was the best finish of the season for both Burton and Riggs, neither of whom posted a top five in the first 12 races.

Kasey Kahne appeared on his way to victory late in the race but ran into oil from Casey Mears' blown engine and hit the wall on Lap 382, prompting the second red flag of the race because the track was blocked in Turn 4.

## POCONO 500

Jimmie Johnson did the right thing in the Pocono 500 but couldn't help but wonder if everything would turn out wrong. His car was so strong, there was no need to worry.

Johnson led 126 of 200 laps, recovered from a flagman's error that cost him track position and held off Jeremy Mayfield until the 11th yellow flag of the afternoon forced the race to end under caution.

When Ricky Craven's engine blew on Lap 156 to bring out a caution, Johnson had a nine-second lead. Pit road was supposed to open for stops on the leader's second approach. But when Johnson and the rest of the leaders were coming past the first time, the flagman working the entrance of pit road waved the green flag, signaling that drivers could make stops.

All but three of the lead-lap cars pitted.

Johnson stayed out and came in on his second approach, as drivers had been instructed to do before the race.

NASCAR president Mike Helton said NASCAR could not come up with a way to correct the problem fairly for everyone involved, so drivers restarted the race on Lap 163 in the order they came off pit road. Johnson was fortunate that several cars decided to pit for fuel before the race went back to green, so he moved up to sixth for the restart.

After another caution and more pit stops, Johnson found himself second behind Mayfield. When the race restarted on Lap 173, Johnson took the lead and never gave it up the rest of the way. Bobby Labonte, Jeff Gordon and Kurt Busch completed the top five.

## DHL 400

Ryan Newman hasn't been crazy about the horsepower beneath the hood of his No. 12 Dodge this season, but he had the horses when it counted.

Newman led only 22 laps at Michigan, but when he passed Dale Jarrett with 17 laps to go, no one could catch him. Kasey Kahne mounted a late charge, but Newman was too strong in the straightaways and corners.

It was Newman's first win of the season and his first since October 2003 at Kansas.

**Jimmie Johnson almost broke the record for laps led in NASCAR's longest race, the Coca-Cola 600.**

"I don't think we're the strongest on horsepower like Penske has been in the past," Newman said. "We made it to the end today, and we had enough horsepower to be unchallenged on the straightaways."

Kahne, Jarrett, Jimmie Johnson and Elliott Sadler completed the top five. Johnson's fourth-place finish propelled him into the points lead for the first time this season.

Jeff Gordon, one of Johnson's teammates, wasn't as lucky. Gordon started from the pole and led 81 laps but lost an engine early, on Lap 88. Gordon finished 39th and fell from fourth to sixth in points.

## DODGE/SAVE MART 350

This was Jeff Gordon's race to lose, and with his recent run of bad luck, that's just what he was afraid of. He won the pole in record speed and was fastest in all of the practices, but would it add up to his fourth win at Sonoma?

Yes—and in dominating fashion. Gordon led 92 of 110 laps, beat Jamie McMurray by 1.032 seconds and at times appeared to be toying with the rest of the field.

"I was so nervous all weekend that we were going to mess it up somehow," Gordon said. "It wasn't easy. We had to fight for it. I

know it looked easy, but it wasn't a 'gimme.' "

Road-racing ace Scott Pruett, Michael Waltrip and Jimmie Johnson rounded out the top five. McMurray's second-place finish was his best on a road course and his best of the season. McMurray, Pruett and Casey Mears, who finished seventh, gave Chip Ganassi Racing three cars in the top 10.

## PEPSI 400

This time a different set of teammates stole the show at Daytona.

Jeff Gordon won the Pepsi 400 with help from Hendrick Motorsports partner Jimmie Johnson, who rode on Gordon's bumper and prevented Dale Earnhardt Jr., who finished third, from getting a shot at the victory. Gordon and Johnson swept past Tony Stewart, bringing Earnhardt with them, on Lap 154 of 160, and Gordon held the point for the final seven laps.

"Jimmie was just crucial," said Gordon, who won for the second consecutive week and moved up to third in the points standings. "He gave me a push that no one else out there would have given me. I owe this win to him, and I owe him a push."

Four Hendrick cars finished in the top 10—Gordon first, Johnson second, Terry Labonte eighth and Brian Vickers ninth. Joe Nemechek,

using a Hendrick engine, was 10th. Kurt Busch finished fourth and Stewart fifth.

Waltrip, who finished 13th, couldn't help Earnhardt because his car went away after about 10 laps into runs.

## TROPICANA 400

Tony Stewart has found himself defending his actions on and off the racetrack many times this season. At least this time, he was doing it in victory lane at Chicagoland Speedway.

There was no question Stewart had the best car. He led 160 of 267 laps and, after a restart with 11 laps to go, ran away from the competition, beating Jimmie Johnson to the finish line by 2.925 seconds for his first victory of the year. The question for Stewart was what happened during a restart on Lap 127, when he ran into the back of leader Kasey Kahne, sending Kahne's No. 9 Dodge into the wall and triggering an accident that collected eight cars.

"As far as the deal with the 9, I'm waiting for somebody to tell me what happened," Stewart said after the race. "I got a real good run on the restart, got by the 40 car and got back in line behind him and didn't even try to pass Kasey. As we came up to the wall, his car wiggled for some reason before I even got to

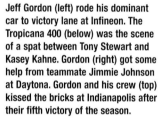

**Jeff Gordon (left) rode his dominant car to victory lane at Infineon. The Tropicana 400 (below) was the scene of a spat between Tony Stewart and Kasey Kahne. Gordon (right) got some help from teammate Jimmie Johnson at Daytona. Gordon and his crew (top) kissed the bricks at Indianapolis after their fifth victory of the season.**

him. I don't know if he missed a shift or what happened, but I already stopped my momentum of catching up, and all of a sudden, he backed up to us and we ran into the back of him."

NASCAR officials reviewed video of the accident and determined it required no penalties. Kahne, who led 10 laps, completed just 136 laps before having to park because of the accident. He finished 36th.

Jeremy Mayfield, Kahne's teammate, had a much better day, leading 26 laps and finishing fifth. He held the lead from Lap 215 through 240 until Stewart passed him and led the rest of the way.

Dale Jarrett had a solid run, finishing third, and Jeff Gordon, who started from the pole and led 14 laps, wound up fourth.

## SIEMENS 300

Call it Kurt Busch's secret weapon—the slow car that made itself fast. His Ford wasn't fast in qualifying trim—he started 32nd—but when the green flag fell, it perked up.

Ryan Newman led the first 170 laps at New Hampshire, but by the end of the race, neither Newman nor Jeff Gordon could keep up with Busch, who outlasted Gordon by .607 seconds during a three-lap sprint to the finish.

Busch took the lead on Lap 171, but his car, which was significantly stronger on long runs, couldn't get into a rhythm because there were so many caution flags. Newman got back to the front by Lap 216, but his car became looser throughout the race, and Busch capitalized. It didn't take long for Gordon to follow, but Busch was too strong through the corners for Gordon to catch him.

Newman finished third, and Matt Kenseth and Tony Stewart completed the top five.

Dale Earnhardt Jr., still recovering from burns he suffered the previous weekend in a crash during a warmup for an American Le Mans Series race at Infineon Raceway, started the race but got out of the No. 8 during a caution on Lap 61 and was replaced by Martin Truex Jr. Truex brought the car home 31st and kept Earnhardt second in the points standings.

## PENNSYLVANIA 500

Hand Jimmie Johnson another broom. For the third consecutive season, Johnson made a clean sweep of a racetrack—this time at Pocono. Just as in Johnson's win in the Pocono 500 in June, his No. 48 Chevrolet was the class of the field, again leading the most laps, 124. But Johnson said it wasn't as easy as it looked because the racetrack was so slick.

"The cool thing about the racecar was that it was forgiving enough to let me search around and find some different lines," Johnson said. "On short runs, Mark (Martin) and those guys were right there with us, and it was hard just to get a small advantage. But over the long haul, I was able to save my tires better by line selection that I just searched around and found."

Johnson's most dramatic move came on a restart on Lap 134, when he jumped from fifth to third after passing on the inside of Jeremy Mayfield and teammate Jeff Gordon. Three laps later, Johnson took the lead and held it for all but one of the final 62 laps, losing it briefly when he made his last pit stop on Lap 162.

Martin, Kasey Kahne, Greg Biffle and Gordon rounded out the top five. For the second consecutive week, Dale Earnhardt Jr. got out of his car early, this time giving way to John Andretti on Lap 53. Andretti finished 25th, but Earnhardt fell from second to third in points.

## BRICKYARD 400

Jeff Gordon was thrilled to be back home in Indiana—again. The four-time NASCAR Cup champion became the first four-time winner of the Brickyard 400 and joined A.J. Foyt, Al Unser and Rick Mears as four-time victors at Indianapolis Motor Speedway.

The race had a record-setting 13 cautions and ended with a green-white-checkered finish, the first in the NASCAR NEXTEL Cup Series, but somehow Gordon survived. He led a record-setting 124 of 161 laps but had to hold his breath after running over a big chunk of debris in Turn 4 on Lap 142.

Matt Kenseth, who was running second, wasn't as fortunate. The debris rocketed from underneath Gordon's car and hit Kenseth's Ford

Tony Stewart (far left) battled the flu and road racing ace Ron Fellows to win the Sirius at The Glen. Jeff Burton (left) made his debut in Richard Childress' No. 30 Chevrolet in the GFS Marketplace 400. Jeff Gordon finished 14th at the Sharpie 500 (below) but retained the points lead after the race.

in the right front, doing major damage. "I've never seen debris tear up a car like that," said Robbie Reiser, crew chief for Kenseth. "It knocked the sway bar tube and everything right off the car."

When Kenseth fell out of contention, Dale Jarrett and Elliott Sadler, Yates teammates who had stalked Gordon for most of the day, closed on the leader but had nothing for the No. 24 in the end. Jarrett finished second, followed by Sadler, Kasey Kahne and Tony Stewart.

## SIRIUS AT THE GLEN

Tony Stewart was bothered so much by stomach cramps early in the race that he considered getting out of his car. When Stewart finally got out of the No. 20 Chevrolet, it was in victory lane.

"These guys have never given up on me, no matter what has happened, and I'll never give up on them," he said. "I wasn't going to take a win away from them."

Stewart left victory lane immediately after getting out of his car and was driven to his motor home for rest and a change of clothes. He said his stomach first bothered him about 15 laps into the race, and the team brought road racing specialist Boris Said to its pits just in case. But Stewart, who led 46 of 90 laps, said he started feeling a little better after getting something to drink during a pit stop. Stewart took the lead for good when he passed Casey Mears on Lap 76 and beat road racing ace Ron Fellows by 1.517 seconds.

Mark Martin finished third, Mears fourth and Dale Earnhardt Jr. fifth. It was Earnhardt's first finish inside the top 20 since he ran third July 3 at Daytona—a stretch of four races. Race favorites Robby Gordon (brakes) and Jeff Gordon (brakes and transmission) fought mechanical problems and finished out of the top 10.

## GFS MARKETPLACE 400

Jack Roush could not have ordered a better homecoming. With Roush Racing head-

quartered about an hour away from Michigan International Speedway, this is Ford country, and the Roush boys were stellar.

Greg Biffle drove to a dominant 8.216-seconds victory over teammate Mark Martin during a race in which both drivers had the strongest cars. Dale Jarrett, Jamie McMurray and Kasey Kahne rounded out the top five.

It was Biffle's second career win. "My car was really, really fast when the green fell, and I started moving up real fast," said Biffle, who started 24th.

The Hendrick duo of Jimmie Johnson and Jeff Gordon started on the front row, with Gordon leading the first 30 laps. But with two

cautions in the first 30 laps, Biffle's No. 16 team made adjustments and gained positions through his pit stops. He first took the lead on Lap 42 and battled Martin throughout the race.

As the final pit stop approached, Martin was eight seconds behind Biffle, and Martin knew that making a two tire stop was the only way to salvage a win.

Fellow Roush drivers Kurt Busch and Matt Kenseth finished sixth and eighth, respectively. In his NASCAR NEXTEL Cup debut, Carl Edwards brought Roush's No. 99 home 10th. It was the first time since the 1998 Las Vegas race that all five Roush cars finished in the top 10.

# SHARPIE 500

After a dominating performance in the NASCAR Busch Series race at Bristol, Dale Earnhardt Jr. didn't make a flashy show of his victory. The bigger prize was the Sharpie 500, the NASCAR NEXTEL Cup Series race. Win that one the next night, and he'd show everybody how to celebrate.

And that he did. Earnhardt spanked the field, leading 295 of 500 laps, including the final 85, and finished 4.390 seconds ahead of Ryan Newman to win. Jimmie Johnson, Jeff Burton and Elliott Sadler rounded out the top five.

It was the first time a driver swept the NASCAR Busch Series and NASCAR NEXTEL Cup Series races at Bristol. With the trials Earnhardt has faced coming back from a crash in a non-NASCAR event six weeks earlier, he considered his 13th NASCAR Cup victory one of his biggest.

Earnhardt finished the evening third in points, 75 behind Jeff Gordon, the series leader. Gordon started from the pole and led the first 57 laps. But he was loose during the middle of the race and suffered a drive-through penalty for restarting out of position on Lap 406. He finished 14th.

Kurt Busch, who was attempting to win his fourth consecutive race at Bristol, never led a lap and finished eighth.

An unusually long green flag run of 230 laps that stretched to Lap 328 took its toll on many drivers, including Kevin Harvick, who lost the feeling in his left arm. Harvick had to give way to Kyle Petty, who was available because his car was caught up in an accident early in the race. Petty brought Harvick's No. 29 Chevrolet home 24th.

# POP SECRET 500

Elliott Sadler turned around his weekend at California Speedway much the way he has turned around his career. After a spin Saturday in Happy Hour, Sadler came back strong Sunday, leading the final 26 laps to win.

Savvy adjustments made by crew chief Todd Parrott late in the race enabled Sadler to pilot the No. 38 Ford to the front during the final green-flag run.

"When the sun went down, we just took off like a rocket," said Sadler, who led eight times for 59 laps. Sadler's second victory of the season assured him of a spot in the Chase for the NASCAR NEXTEL Cup as long as he starts the race next weekend at Richmond. Sadler, whose best points finish was 20th in 2001, has been in the top 10 all season.

Mark Martin led four times for 65 laps, but when Dale Earnhardt Jr. spun in Turn 4 with 30

laps to go, Martin's No. 6 Ford lost momentum and fell back to third, behind Kasey Kahne. With Kahne chasing Sadler, the race brought back memories of the April race at Texas, where Sadler held off Kahne by just .028 seconds.

This time it wasn't as close. Kahne settled for second for the fifth time this season. Martin finished third ahead of Jamie McMurray and Ryan Newman. Carl Edwards, in just his third NASCAR NEXTEL Cup Series race, had an excellent run and finished sixth.

# CHEVY ROCK & ROLL 400

Pick your favorite sports moment. No matter what you come up with, Jeremy Mayfield matched it at Richmond. But this wasn't just any race. It was the final race to determine which drivers would qualify for the first Chase for the NASCAR NEXTEL Cup.

Mayfield was on the outside trying to get in when the race began. Then he delivered the most dominating performance of his career, leading 151 laps, taking the checkered flag. The win was Mayfield's first since June 2000 and propelled the No. 19 team from 14th in points to ninth, a remarkable surge in one race so late in the season.

"The guys gave me a great car," Mayfield said. "You can see the motor was great. Pit stops were good. (Crew chief) Kenny (Francis) made awesome calls all night. That's what we needed. It's something we haven't had all year—everything go together perfect all night."

Anything that can happen to a racecar driver happened to Jamie McMurray at Richmond: He made an incredible maneuver to

avoid serious damage when a wreck happened in front of him. He was up, he was down, he was good, he was bad. Running on seven cylinders at the end, McMurray hung on to finish ninth, but it wasn't enough. He wound up 11th in points, one spot out of the Chase for the NASCAR NEXTEL Cup.

Kasey Kahne, who began the race ninth in points, and Dale Jarrett both struggled and missed the cut. Bobby Labonte and Kevin Harvick visited the top 10 throughout the night, but neither finished high enough to qualify for the Chase for the NASCAR Nextel Cup. Both fell out of the top 10 the previous week.

The first clue that the calm racing wouldn't last came on Lap 151, when cars went four abreast coming out of Turn 4. That proved to be the flash of lightning that announced the storm, which started on Lap 170 when several cars got together coming out of Turn 2.

In the closing laps, Busch was leading, with Mayfield hot on his tail. A shootout loomed. But Busch ran out of fuel with eight laps left, allowing Mayfield to find his way into the Chase for the NASCAR NEXTEL Cup.

# SYLVANIA 300

Kurt Busch knew the Ford he drove to victory in the Sylvania 300 would be good. It was good enough to win at New Hampshire in July—so good that Jimmy Fennig and crew decided to put the car under wraps and save it for this race, the first in the Chase for the NASCAR NEXTEL Cup. The win was Busch's third of the season and left him tied for first in points with Dale Earnhardt Jr.

Elliott Sadler left Kasey Kahne behind to win the Pop Secret 500, which gave him an all-but-certain berth in the Chase for the NASCAR NEXTEL Cup. Kahne settled for second for the fifth time of the season.

The rain that washed out qualifying and Saturday practices left many teams scrambling, but Busch's team wasn't among them. "We were able to make the right adjustments based upon our past experience here and knowing we had a good racecar, so it didn't leave many variables on what to choose for a setup," Busch said.

The day was far from perfect for three drivers—Tony Stewart, Jeremy Mayfield and Ryan Newman—who finished outside the top 30. Stewart and Mayfield were caught up in an accident triggered by Robby Gordon on Lap 64. Stewart finished 39th, and Mayfield wound up 35th. Newman also had tough luck, losing an engine on Lap 262 and finishing 33rd. He led four laps, and at times his Dodge appeared strong enough to compete with Busch.

Busch was in front for 155 of 300 laps and took the lead for good when Jimmie Johnson pitted on Lap 264. Busch beat teammate Matt Kenseth to the finish line by 2.488 seconds. Earnhardt, Kasey Kahne and Jamie McMurray rounded out the top five.

## MBNA AMERICA 400

Call Ryan Newman the Comeback Kid, and give him credit for doing everything within his power to stay alive.

Newman, coming off 33rd-place finish the week before, dominated at Dover, leading 325 of 400 laps and beating Mark Martin to the finish line by 8.149 seconds. Jeff Gordon finished third and took the points lead by a single point over Kurt Busch, who wound up fifth. Dale Jarrett had a solid run and finished fourth.

Although Newman didn't gain many positions in the standings, he demonstrated a drive

that could serve him well if he stays out of trouble during the final eight races.

"It was a big step in the right direction," Newman said. "We can't finish 33rd and then first and then 33rd again. We've got to keep those top fives going."

Jimmie Johnson and Elliott Sadler, both competing in the Chase for the NASCAR NEXTEL Cup, received penalties for speeding on pit road. Sadler, who knew he was guilty of the infraction, had tire troubles on his final stop and finished 20th. Johnson, who thought he was penalized unfairly, wound up 10th.

Eight of the 10 drivers who finished the race in the top 10 were contenders in the Chase for the NASCAR NEXTEL Cup, and that made it difficult for Newman, Tony Stewart and Jeremy Mayfield to overcome their poor finishes the week before.

## EA SPORTS 500

Although Dale Earnhardt Jr. led the most laps and had the strongest car, he didn't have track position for an easy win when the race restarted for the final time at Talladega with five laps to go.

Didn't matter. He roared from 11th to first in less than two laps, primarily using the high line to blow past drivers who elected not to make a final pit stop during the final caution or took fuel and no tires. Earnhardt took two right-side tires on his stop, the reason he was shuffled back to 11th and the reason he won the race.

"There was a big difference between my car and their cars with the tires I had," Earnhardt said. "... I don't think I would have won the race if I had not put tires on."

Kevin Harvick, who took the lead from Brendan Gaughan on Lap 185 before losing it to Earnhardt, finished second by about two car lengths.

Dale Jarrett matched his best finish in 2004, coming home third for the third time of the season. Gaughan held on for fourth, his first career top five in NASCAR NEXTEL Cup, and Kurt Busch was fifth.

Earnhardt took the points lead but lost it later in the week after NASCAR docked him 25 points and fined him $10,000 for using profanity during a television interview. Earnhardt went from 13 points ahead of Busch to 12 points behind.

Jimmie Johnson lost the most among those in the Chase for NASCAR NEXTEL Cup, dropping from fourth to ninth after losing an engine and finishing 37th. He had a strong car—he led 35 laps—but contact with Kasey Kahne on pit road damaged the front end of Johnson's car and later caused it to overheat.

## BANQUET 400

How was your weekend? Couldn't have been as exciting as Joe Nemechek's: On Saturday, Nemechek won the NASCAR Busch Series race at Kansas on the final lap. On Sunday, he started on the pole, then led the race in the final lap, only to be passed by Ricky Rudd. But Nemechek passed him back to take the checkered flag by about half a car length. It was an All-American day, with the U.S. Army car (Nemechek) finishing first, U.S. Air Force car (Rudd) second and National Guard car (Greg Biffle) third.

Biffle had the dominant car in the NASCAR NEXTEL Cup Series race, but numerous cautions near the end prevented him from moving

Jimmie Johnson didn't agree with the penalty he received for speeding on pit road in the MBNA American 400.

NASCAR NEXTEL Cup win after leading 207 of the first 267 laps. But a blown right front tire on Lap 268 ended his night.

Mark Martin and Ryan Newman also ran into bad luck. Martin and Newman were battling for second place on Lap 312 when Brendan Gaughan and Jimmy Spencer spun in front of them in Turn 4. Both Martin's and Newman's cars were damaged but did finish—Martin 13th and Newman 14th. Dale Earnhardt Jr., second in points, finished third, and Joe Nemechek finished fifth.

## SUBWAY 500

Jimmie Johnson's victory in the Subway 500 demonstrated the resilience of his Hendrick Motorsports team, but only after Johnson took the checkered flag did anyone realize how much the organization's resolve would be tested.

Johnson and the rest of the Hendrick drivers—Jeff Gordon, Terry Labonte and Brian Vickers—were told that a Hendrick Motorsports plane had crashed en route to Martinsville earlier that day. Later it was learned that all 10 passengers had died in the crash. Among the victims: Rick Hendrick's son, Ricky, who was being groomed to take over the business and his brother, John, president of the organization. Victory lane festivities were canceled.

Johnson's second consecutive victory vaulted him from eighth to fourth in the points standings. But he gained just 20 points on leader Kurt Busch, who finished fifth and led the most laps to pick up 10 bonus points.

Johnson took the lead from Sterling Marlin on Lap 440 and led the final 61 laps, although Rusty Wallace, who won in April at Martinsville, tested Johnson on the final restart with seven laps to go. Wallace tried to go around Johnson on the high side in Turns 1 and 2 but couldn't make the pass.

Perhaps the biggest surprise of the race was Jeff Green, whose seventh-place finish gave Petty Enterprises its first top 10 of the season.

## BASS PRO SHOPS MBNA 500

Mark Martin had the dominant car, but Hendrick Motorsports driver Jimmie Johnson had something that horsepower and handling couldn't overcome.

"I had 10 angels riding on this racecar," Johnson said after holding off Martin at the finish. Johnson dedicated the victory, his third consecutive, to the 10 people who died the previous Sunday when a Hendrick Motorsports plane crashed on the way to the race at Martinsville, to their families and to everyone in the Hendrick organization.

Johnson, who was in ninth place, 247 points behind Kurt Busch, after the first four races in the Chase for the NASCAR NEXTEL

**Jimmie Johnson's win in the UAW-GM Quality 500 (above) left him 227 points behind leader Kurt Busch. Johnson won again the next week in the Subway 500 (right), at Atlanta and again at Darlington, but it wasn't enough to match Busch's consistency.**

through the field quickly enough to catch Nemechek. "I don't want to act like a baby, but I'm disappointed, bad," Biffle said. "I'm pouting about it, but that's the way it is."

It was a strange race, with cars getting off their pit cycles early and several championship contenders spinning for no discernible reasons. Several competitors in the Chase for the NASCAR NEXTEL Cup struggled throughout the race, the most notable being Jimmie Johnson, who finished 32nd, and Ryan Newman, who finished 33rd. Both hinted after the race that their fading championship hopes were all but extinguished.

Points leader Kurt Busch fought an ill-handling car early in the race, but despite spinning without provocation at one point, the only damage was a slightly bruised ego. Busch recovered to finish sixth and increased his lead in the points race over Dale Earnhardt Jr.

## UAW-GM QUALITY 500

There's no place like Lowe's. There's no place like ...

Kansas wasn't the answer for Jimmie

Johnson's nightmare, so he clicked his heels and landed in victory lane at Lowe's Motor Speedway.

Johnson won in May at Lowe's, but when he returned to the site of his dominating victory, he was coming off finishes of 32nd at Kansas and 37th at Talladega. His car wasn't the class of the field like it was in May, but no other driver was better at the finish. Johnson led the final 17 laps and beat teammate Jeff Gordon by 1.727 seconds for his fifth victory of the season and his second sweep. He won both races at Pocono and Lowe's.

The victory pumped up the No. 48 team, but it meant little in the points standings because points leader Kurt Busch finished fourth.

After five second-place finishes, Kasey Kahne appeared to be on his way to his first

Busch finished 10th in the Checker Auto Parts 500, despite getting caught in an accident (left). Owner Jack Roush (right) celebrated with Ford 400 winner Greg Biffle.

Cup, ended the day in second place, just 59 points behind Busch, who blew an engine early and finished 42nd.

Martin led 227 of the 325 laps, but a couple of late cautions hurt him. When Kevin Harvick's engine failed on Lap 301, and his car stalled at the entrance to pit road to bring out a caution, Martin held the lead and was the only driver on the lead lap who didn't pit. "If we pitted, they stay out and win," Martin said. "If we stay out, they pit. So it was nobody's fault but those caution flags."

Five laps after the race resumed, Johnson passed Martin for the lead, but when Dale Earnhardt Jr. crashed after contact with Carl Edwards two laps later, Johnson and Martin both darted down pit road.

Kasey Kahne was leading with Jeff Burton and Joe Nemechek in tow when the race restarted on Lap 316, but Johnson overtook all of them before they reached Turn 3. Johnson held off Martin by about five car lengths. Edwards ran third, his best finish in a NASCAR NEXTEL Cup Series race, Nemechek was fourth and Kahne fifth.

Four drivers (Johnson, Jeff Gordon, Martin and Earnhardt) were within 100 points of leader Busch at the end of the day. Before the race, Busch held a 96-point lead over his closest competitor and was 224 points ahead of the fifth-place driver. No one figured such a swing could take place in one race, but no one figured Busch, Gordon and Earnhardt all would finish outside the top 30.

## CHECKER AUTO PARTS 500

The final laps of the Checker Auto Parts 500 provided the kind of showdown most NASCAR fans dream of: Dale Earnhardt Jr. and Jeff Gordon dueled for the victory.

At Phoenix, a green-white-checkered finish was needed before there was a winner. Earnhardt, who ran down Gordon and passed him on Lap 304, was in front of Gordon when the race, scheduled to end after 312 laps, restarted for the final time on Lap 313. Earnhardt pulled away easily for the victory, and

Gordon, unable to hold off Ryan Newman, slipped to third place.

Earnhardt led the most laps, 118, and moved from fifth to third in the standings. He trimmed his deficit behind leader Kurt Busch from 98 to 47. Gordon moved into second, trimming his deficit from 72 to 41.

Jimmie Johnson, who was going for his fourth consecutive victory, finished sixth. Even though he lost two positions in the standings, dropping to fourth, he trailed by just 48 points. He entered the race down by 59. Busch wound up 10th but maintained his points lead despite being caught up in an accident early in the race and later losing a lap because he ran out of fuel.

## MOUNTAIN DEW SOUTHERN 500

Jimmie Johnson won the final Southern 500 to complete a sweep at the historic track because his team got him out of the pits first toward the end. To win the 500, Johnson had to pass Kasey Kahne and Jamie McMurray, both of whom elected not to pit when the final caution came out on Lap 346. But on old tires, they were no match for Johnson, who took the lead with nine laps to go.

Jeff Gordon, who led the most laps (155), appeared on his way to a comfortable victory until Ryan Newman's Dodge lost an engine and put oil on the track, bringing out a caution on Lap 331. Gordon came into the pits first but left in seventh after a tire-change mishap. Gordon still managed to work his way up to third by the finish and moved to within 21 points of points leader Kurt Busch.

Mark Martin finished second and said his car was so good at the end that he wished there had been five more laps. McMurray held on for fourth place and Kahne fifth. Busch wound up sixth.

Five drivers (Busch, Jimmie Johnson, Gordon, Dale Earnhardt Jr. and Martin) left Darlington with a legitimate chance to win the championship. The difference from first to fifth: 82 points.

## FORD 400

It was a day Roush Racing won't soon forget. Kurt Busch won the NASCAR NEXTEL Cup championship, giving Jack Roush the sport's biggest prize for the second consecutive season. Teammate Greg Biffle won the race, making the decisive pass on Tony Stewart on the first lap of a green-white-checkered finish.

Busch began the race with an 18-point lead over Jimmie Johnson and beat Johnson, who finished second in the race, by eight points. Busch finished the race fifth but picked up five bonus points for leading. Johnson never led.

"To snag this first championship that NASCAR put together with this new format and to be the first NEXTEL Cup champion—it took so much from within," said Busch, who's eight-point margin of victory was the closest in history. "I was just sick to my stomach the last few laps."

Jeff Gordon finished third in the race and third in points. Mark Martin and Dale Earnhardt Jr. also were in contention for the championship when the race began, but neither finished in the top 10. Martin wound up 11th. Earnhardt battled a poor-handling car and finished 23rd.

Ryan Newman appeared on his way to victory when he took the lead on Lap 243 and held it until Lap 264, when he was passed by Stewart because the right front tire of Newman's No. 12 Dodge was losing air. Two laps later, the tire went down, and he hit the wall in Turn 2.

Because the cleanup from the accident went past the scheduled 267 laps, a green-white-checkered finish was needed. Stewart, leading when the race went green, had fuel problems and bunched up several cars, although Biffle was able to get around cleanly. Johnson passed Gordon for second, and Stewart fell to fourth, just ahead of Busch.

"I really thought we had a car to beat him," Biffle said of Stewart. "I was really good off the restarts. I thought I was going to be able to pass him, and I almost ran into him down there when his car ran out of gas on the restart. It was really close for us."

**Daytona Beach, Fla.—2.5-mile banked paved trioval • February 15, 2004—500 miles—200 laps**

| Fin. | St. | Car | Driver | Make | Sponsor | Pts./Bonus | Laps | Status | Winning |
|------|-----|-----|--------|------|---------|-----------|------|--------|---------|
| 1. | 3 | 8 | Dale Earnhardt Jr. | Chevrolet | Budweiser | 185/5 | 200 | Running | $1,495,070 |
| 2. | 5 | 20 | Tony Stewart | Chevrolet | The Home Depot | 180/10 | 200 | Running | $1,096,165 |
| 3. | 26 | 22 | Scott Wimmer* | Dodge | Caterpillar | 170/5 | 200 | Running | $758,839 |
| 4. | 10 | 29 | Kevin Harvick | Chevrolet | GM Goodwrench | 165/5 | 200 | Running | $610,792 |
| 5. | 6 | 48 | Jimmie Johnson | Chevrolet | Lowe's | 160/5 | 200 | Running | $472,189 |
| 6. | 14 | 01 | Joe Nemechek | Chevrolet | U.S. Army | 150/5 | 200 | Running | $358,839 |
| 7. | 2 | 38 | Elliott Sadler | Ford | M&M's | 146/0 | 200 | Running | $358,772 |
| 8. | 39 | 24 | Jeff Gordon | Chevrolet | DuPont | 147/5 | 200 | Running | $318,490 |
| 9. | 12 | 17 | Matt Kenseth | Ford | DeWalt Power Tools | 143/5 | 200 | Running | $307,917 |
| 10. | 31 | 88 | Dale Jarrett | Ford | UPS | 134/0 | 200 | Running | $279,529 |
| 11. | 13 | 18 | Bobby Labonte | Chevrolet | Passion of the Christ/Interstate | 130/0 | 200 | Running | $278,445 |
| 12. | 1 | 16 | Greg Biffle | Ford | National Guard | 127/0 | 200 | Running | $249,312 |
| 13. | 29 | 1 | John Andretti | Chevrolet | Post/Maxwell House Coffee | 129/5 | 200 | Running | $235,287 |
| 14. | 25 | 41 | Casey Mears | Dodge | Target | 121/0 | 200 | Running | $235,087 |
| 15. | 23 | 23 | Dave Blaney | Dodge | Whelen | 118/0 | 200 | Running | $232,762 |
| 16. | 15 | 97 | Kurt Busch | Ford | Sharpie | 115/0 | 199 | Running | $236,887 |
| 17. | 19 | 0 | Ward Burton | Chevrolet | NetZero HiSpeed | 112/0 | 199 | Running | $218,912 |
| 18. | 16 | 21 | Ricky Rudd | Ford | Motorcraft | 109/0 | 199 | Running | $246,020 |
| 19. | 17 | 77 | Brendan Gaughan* | Dodge | Kodak EasyShare/Eckerd Drugs | 106/0 | 199 | Running | $225,887 |
| 20. | 38 | 5 | Terry Labonte | Chevrolet | Kellogg's | 108/5 | 199 | Running | $245,812 |
| 21. | 33 | 45 | Kyle Petty | Dodge | Georgia-Pacific/Brawny | 105/5 | 198 | Running | $226,127 |
| 22. | 43 | 33 | Mike Skinner | Chevrolet | Bass Pro Shops/Tracker Boats | 97/0 | 198 | Running | $213,813 |
| 23. | 28 | 32 | Ricky Craven | Chevrolet | Tide/Mr. Clean AutoDry | 94/0 | 198 | Running | $225,339 |
| 24. | 40 | 7 | Jimmy Spencer | Dodge | Johnny Cat | 91/0 | 198 | Running | $223,513 |
| 25. | 22 | 19 | Jeremy Mayfield | Dodge | Dodge Dealers/UAW | 88/0 | 195 | Running | $222,889 |
| 26. | 21 | 30 | Johnny Sauter* | Chevrolet | America Online | 85/0 | 193 | Running | $213,687 |
| 27. | 24 | 09 | Johnny Benson | Dodge | Miccosukee Resort | 82/0 | 177 | Accident | $210,414 |
| 28. | 41 | 14 | Larry Foyt | Dodge | LPGA | 79/0 | 176 | Running | $212,487 |
| 29. | 18 | 2 | Rusty Wallace | Dodge | Miller Lite | 76/0 | 154 | Running | $245,572 |
| 30. | 42 | 50 | Derrike Cope | Dodge | Thrifty/Melling Engine Parts | 73/0 | 153 | Running | $207,962 |
| 31. | 20 | 12 | Ryan Newman | Dodge | ALLTEL | 70/0 | 149 | Running | $255,056 |
| 32. | 32 | 4 | Kevin Lepage | Chevrolet | YokeTV.com | 67/0 | 132 | Running | $207,488 |
| 33. | 34 | 43 | Jeff Green | Dodge | Cheerios/Betty Crocker | 64/0 | 110 | Accident | $232,087 |
| 34. | 36 | 10 | Scott Riggs* | Chevrolet | Valvoline | 61/0 | 109 | Accident | $231,328 |
| 35. | 30 | 31 | Robby Gordon | Chevrolet | Cingular Wireless | 58/0 | 78 | Accident | $241,230 |
| 36. | 7 | 42 | Jamie McMurray | Dodge | Texaco/Havoline | 55/0 | 75 | Accident | $224,137 |
| 37. | 4 | 40 | Sterling Marlin | Dodge | Coors Light | 52/0 | 75 | Accident | $254,714 |
| 38. | 9 | 15 | Michael Waltrip | Chevrolet | NAPA | 49/0 | 70 | Accident | $246,193 |
| 39. | 35 | 25 | Brian Vickers* | Chevrolet | GMAC Financial Services | 46/0 | 70 | Accident | $211,888 |
| 40. | 37 | 49 | Ken Schrader | Dodge | Schwan's Home Service | 43/0 | 59 | Accident | $203,438 |
| 41. | 27 | 9 | Kasey Kahne* | Dodge | Dodge Dealers/UAW | 40/0 | 42 | Engine | $231,887 |
| 42. | 11 | 99 | Jeff Burton | Ford | NBA All-Star Game on TNT | 37/0 | 25 | Engine | $239,554 |
| 43. | 8 | 6 | Mark Martin | Ford | Viagra | 34/0 | 7 | Engine | $216,997 |

*Rookie. Time of race: 3 hours, 11 minutes, 53 seconds. Average speed: 156.345 mph. Margin of victory: .273 seconds. Caution flags: 4 for 23 laps. 8-11(oil on track); 34-38 (Cars 50, 10—accident, Turn 4); 60-64 (Cars 43, 49, 2—accident, back stretch); 72-80 (Cars 1, 4, 5, 10, 12, 15, 25, 30, 31, 40, 42, 09—accident, back stretch). Lap leaders: 28 lead changes among 10 drivers. Greg Biffle (pole). Dale Earnhardt Jr. 1-29, Kevin Harvick 30-35, Tony Stewart 36-39, Jimmie Johnson 40-41, Jimmie Johnson 42-43, Johnson 44-52, Earnhardt 53-58, Stewart 59, Earnhardt 60, Stewart 61-71, Earnhardt 72, Kyle Petty 73-77, Jeff Gordon 78-84, Stewart 85-104, Johnson 105-107, Matt Kenseth 108, John Andretti 109, Stewart 110-136, J. Gordon 137, Kenseth 138, Johnson 139, Terry Labonte 140, Stewart 141-168, Earnhardt 169, Johnson 170, Scott Wimmer 171-175, Stewart 176-180, Earnhardt 181-200. Pole winner: Greg Biffle, 188.387 mph. Dropped to rear: Greg Biffle, Ryan Newman, Ricky Craven, Derrike Cope (engine changes), Scott Riggs (backup car). Failed to qualify: Andy Hillenburg, Kirk Shelmerdine. Estimated attendance: 200,000.

# POINTS STANDINGS

| Rk. | Driver | Behind | Rk. | Driver | Behind |
|-----|--------|--------|-----|--------|--------|
| 1. | Dale Earnhardt Jr. | — | 6. | Joe Nemechek | -35 |
| 2. | Tony Stewart | -5 | 7. | Jeff Gordon | -38 |
| 3. | Scott Wimmer | -15 | 8. | Elliott Sadler | -39 |
| 4. | Kevin Harvick | -20 | 9. | Matt Kenseth | -42 |
| 5. | Jimmie Johnson | -25 | 10. | Dale Jarrett | -51 |

# SUBWAY 400 ----------------NORTH CAROLINA SPEEDWAY

**Rockingham, N.C.—1.017-mile banked paved oval • February 22, 2004—400 miles—393 laps**

| Fin. | St. | Car | Driver | Make | Sponsor | Pts./Bonus | Laps | Status | Winnings |
|------|-----|-----|--------|------|---------|-----------|------|--------|----------|
| 1. | 23 | 17 | Matt Kenseth | Ford | DeWalt Power Tools | 190/10 | 393 | Running | $222,303 |
| 2. | 3 | 9 | Kasey Kahne* | Dodge | Dodge Dealers/UAW | 170/0 | 393 | Running | $130,125 |
| 3. | 2 | 42 | Jamie McMurray | Dodge | Texaco/Havoline | 170/5 | 393 | Running | $96,425 |
| 4. | 13 | 40 | Sterling Marlin | Dodge | Coors Light | 160/0 | 393 | Running | $114,900 |
| 5. | 7 | 8 | Dale Earnhardt Jr. | Chevrolet | Budweiser | 155/0 | 393 | Running | $118,303 |
| 6. | 1 | 12 | Ryan Newman | Dodge | ALLTEL | 155/5 | 393 | Running | $116,152 |
| 7. | 4 | 2 | Rusty Wallace | Dodge | Miller Lite | 146/0 | 393 | Running | $100,643 |
| 8. | 27 | 97 | Kurt Busch | Ford | Sharpie/IRWIN | 142/0 | 393 | Running | $83,785 |
| 9. | 16 | 0 | Ward Burton | Chevrolet | NetZero HiSpeed | 138/0 | 393 | Running | $66,035 |
| 10. | 5 | 24 | Jeff Gordon | Chevrolet | DuPont | 139/5 | 391 | Running | $111,363 |
| 11. | 6 | 19 | Jeremy Mayfield | Dodge | Dodge Dealers/UAW | 130/0 | 391 | Running | $90,210 |
| 12. | 21 | 6 | Mark Martin | Ford | Viagra | 127/0 | 391 | Running | $72,960 |
| 13. | 32 | 29 | Kevin Harvick | Chevrolet | GM Goodwrench | 129/5 | 391 | Running | $100,763 |
| 14. | 36 | 30 | Johnny Sauter* | Chevrolet | America Online | 121/0 | 391 | Running | $63,560 |
| 15. | 31 | 22 | Scott Wimmer* | Dodge | Caterpillar | 118/0 | 391 | Running | $87,560 |
| 16. | 20 | 25 | Brian Vickers* | Chevrolet | GMAC Financial Services | 115/0 | 391 | Running | $70,760 |
| 17. | 35 | 5 | Terry Labonte | Chevrolet | Kellogg's | 112/0 | 391 | Running | $89,110 |
| 18. | 25 | 38 | Elliott Sadler | Ford | M&M's | 109/0 | 391 | Running | $90,793 |
| 19. | 22 | 21 | Ricky Rudd | Ford | Motorcraft | 106/0 | 391 | Running | $87,566 |
| 20. | 15 | 77 | Brendan Gaughan* | Dodge | Kodak EasyShare | 103/0 | 391 | Running | $70,110 |
| 21. | 14 | 41 | Casey Mears | Dodge | Target | 100/0 | 390 | Running | $74,810 |
| 22. | 26 | 4 | Kevin Lepage | Chevrolet | YokeTV.com | 97/0 | 390 | Running | $71,010 |
| 23. | 10 | 16 | Greg Biffle | Ford | Subway/National Guard | 94/0 | 390 | Running | $69,185 |
| 24. | 12 | 01 | Joe Nemechek | Chevrolet | U.S. Army | 91/0 | 390 | Running | $75,949 |
| 25. | 11 | 18 | Bobby Labonte | Chevrolet | Interstate Batteries | 88/0 | 389 | Running | $102,318 |
| 26. | 24 | 20 | Tony Stewart | Chevrolet | The Home Depot | 85/0 | 389 | Running | $103,403 |
| 27. | 18 | 49 | Ken Schrader | Dodge | Schwan's Home Service | 82/0 | 389 | Running | $56,410 |
| 28. | 8 | 43 | Jeff Green | Dodge | STP/Cheerios/Betty Crocker | 79/0 | 389 | Running | $82,510 |
| 29. | 39 | 1 | John Andretti | Chevrolet | DEI/Snap-On | 76/0 | 388 | Running | $64,000 |
| 30. | 37 | 50 | Derrike Cope | Dodge | Matrix Systems | 73/0 | 386 | Running | $56,375 |
| 31. | 19 | 10 | Scott Riggs* | Chevrolet | Valvoline | 70/0 | 383 | Running | $80,937 |
| 32. | 38 | 14 | Larry Foyt | Dodge | A.J. Foyt Racing | 67/0 | 380 | Running | $55,675 |
| 33. | 33 | 15 | Michael Waltrip | Chevrolet | NAPA | 64/0 | 379 | Running | $92,481 |
| 34. | 43 | 80 | Andy Hillenburg | Ford | Commercial Truck & Trailer | 61/0 | 376 | Running | $55,425 |
| 35. | 17 | 32 | Ricky Craven | Chevrolet | Tide | 58/0 | 365 | Running | $63,275 |
| 36. | 34 | 31 | Robby Gordon | Chevrolet | Cingular Wireless | 60/5 | 350 | Accident | $90,412 |
| 37. | 28 | 99 | Jeff Burton | Ford | SKF | 52/0 | 344 | Engine | $88,592 |
| 38. | 42 | 46 | Carl Long | Dodge | Al Smith Dodge | 49/0 | 255 | Accident | $55,135 |
| 39. | 30 | 45 | Kyle Petty | Dodge | Georgia-Pacific/Brawny | 46/0 | 221 | Engine | $55,070 |
| 40. | 9 | 88 | Dale Jarrett | Ford | UPS | 43/0 | 210 | Engine | $85,907 |
| 41. | 29 | 48 | Jimmie Johnson | Chevrolet | Lowe's | 40/0 | 128 | Accident | $74,750 |
| 42. | 41 | 72 | Kirk Shelmerdine | Ford | Freddie B's/TUCSON | 37/0 | 19 | Too slow | $54,895 |
| 43. | 40 | 09 | Joe Ruttman | Dodge | Miccosukee Resort | 34/0 | 1 | Parked | $54,196 |

*Rookie. Time of race: 3 hours, 34 minutes, 5 seconds. Average speed: 112.016 mph. Margin of victory: .010 seconds. Caution flags: 7 for 58 laps. 40-45 (Car 49—accident, Turns 1-2); 53-57 (Car 45—accident, back stretch); 132-140 (Cars 48, 49—accident, Turn 4); 196-200 (Car 14—accident, Turns 1-2); 214-219 (debris); 265-279 (Cars 46, 01, 18, 77, 6—accident, back stretch); 352-363 (Cars 31, 43—accident, back stretch). Lap leaders: 15 lead changes among 6 drivers. Ryan Newman 1-2, Jamie McMurray 3-40, Jeff Gordon 41-52, McMurray 53, Robby Gordon 54-58, Newman 59-62, J. Gordon 63-89, Matt Kenseth 90-129, Newman 130-135, Kenseth 136-214, Kevin Harvick 215-216, Kenseth 217-303, McMurray 304-331, Kenseth 332-349, McMurray 350-358, Kenseth 359-393. Pole winner: Ryan Newman, 156.475 mph. Failed to qualify: Morgan Shepherd. Estimated attendance: 50,000.

## POINTS STANDINGS

| Rk. | Driver | Behind | | Rk. | Driver | Behind |
|-----|--------|--------|---|-----|--------|--------|
| 1. | Dale Earnhardt Jr. | — | | 6. | Tony Stewart | -75 |
| 2. | Matt Kenseth | -7 | | 7. | Kurt Busch | -83 |
| 3. | Kevin Harvick | -46 | | 8. | Elliott Sadler | -85 |
| 4. | Scott Wimmer | -52 | | 9. | Ward Burton | -90 |
| 5. | Jeff Gordon | -54 | | 10. | Joe Nemechek | -99 |

# UAW-DAIMLERCHRYSLER 400 - - - - LAS VEGAS MOTOR SPEEDWAY

Las Vegas—1.5-mile banked paved oval • March 7, 2004—400.5 miles—267 laps

| Fin. | St. | Car | Driver | Make | Sponsor | Pts./Bonus | Laps | Status | Winnings |
|------|-----|-----|--------|------|---------|-----------|------|--------|----------|
| 1. | 25 | 17 | Matt Kenseth | Ford | DeWalt Power Tools | 190/10 | 267 | Running | $458,828 |
| 2. | 1 | 9 | Kasey Kahne* | Dodge | Dodge Dealers/UAW | 175/5 | 267 | Running | $260,775 |
| 3. | 19 | 20 | Tony Stewart | Chevrolet | The Home Depot | 170/5 | 267 | Running | $219,603 |
| 4. | 4 | 42 | Jamie McMurray | Dodge | Texaco/Havoline | 160/0 | 267 | Running | $150,925 |
| 5. | 27 | 6 | Mark Martin | Ford | Viagra | 155/0 | 267 | Running | $127,875 |
| 6. | 11 | 38 | Elliott Sadler | Ford | M&M's | 150/0 | 267 | Running | $131,808 |
| 7. | 13 | 41 | Casey Mears | Dodge | Target | 146/0 | 267 | Running | $117,050 |
| 8. | 7 | 18 | Bobby Labonte | Chevrolet | Interstate Batteries | 142/0 | 267 | Running | $136,583 |
| 9. | 2 | 97 | Kurt Busch | Ford | IRWIN Industrial Tools | 143/5 | 267 | Running | $108,500 |
| 10. | 21 | 2 | Rusty Wallace | Dodge | Miller Lite | 134/0 | 267 | Running | $129,108 |
| 11. | 29 | 88 | Dale Jarrett | Ford | UPS | 130/0 | 267 | Running | $120,492 |
| 12. | 32 | 45 | Kyle Petty | Dodge | Georgia-Pacific/Brawny | 127/0 | 267 | Running | $101,275 |
| 13. | 28 | 99 | Jeff Burton | Ford | Pennzoil | 129/5 | 267 | Running | $119,417 |
| 14. | 6 | 19 | Jeremy Mayfield | Dodge | Dodge Dealers/UAW | 121/0 | 267 | Running | $104,950 |
| 15. | 20 | 24 | Jeff Gordon | Chevrolet | DuPont | 118/0 | 267 | Running | $128,128 |
| 16. | 12 | 48 | Jimmie Johnson | Chevrolet | Lowe's | 120/5 | 267 | Running | $98,050 |
| 17. | 37 | 5 | Terry Labonte | Chevrolet | Kellogg's | 112/0 | 267 | Running | $107,600 |
| 18. | 23 | 40 | Sterling Marlin | Dodge | Coors Light | 109/0 | 266 | Running | $112,750 |
| 19. | 38 | 01 | Joe Nemechek | Chevrolet | USG Sheetrock | 106/0 | 266 | Running | $97,150 |
| 20. | 10 | 91 | Bill Elliott | Dodge | UAW/DaimlerChrysler/NTC | 103/0 | 266 | Running | $76,200 |
| 21. | 16 | 29 | Kevin Harvick | Chevrolet | GM Goodwrench | 105/5 | 266 | Running | $112,328 |
| 22. | 8 | 77 | Brendan Gaughan* | Dodge | Kodak EasyShare | 97/0 | 266 | Running | $83,450 |
| 23. | 3 | 25 | Brian Vickers* | Chevrolet | GMAC Financial Services | 94/0 | 266 | Running | $83,275 |
| 24. | 30 | 30 | Johnny Sauter* | Chevrolet | AOL/IMAX NASCAR 3D | 91/0 | 266 | Running | $81,250 |
| 25. | 17 | 32 | Ricky Craven | Chevrolet | Tide | 93/5 | 265 | Running | $89,039 |
| 26. | 34 | 0 | Ward Burton | Chevrolet | NetZero HiSpeed | 85/0 | 265 | Running | $70,750 |
| 27. | 5 | 12 | Ryan Newman | Dodge | ALLTEL | 82/0 | 265 | Running | $114,117 |
| 28. | 33 | 21 | Ricky Rudd | Ford | Motorcraft | 79/0 | 264 | Running | $92,306 |
| 29. | 15 | 10 | Scott Riggs* | Chevrolet | Valvoline | 81/5 | 264 | Running | $91,237 |
| 30. | 22 | 31 | Robby Gordon | Chevrolet | Cingular Wireless | 73/0 | 264 | Running | $101,487 |
| 31. | 36 | 09 | Johnny Benson | Dodge | Miccosukee Resort | 70/0 | 263 | Running | $65,600 |
| 32. | 31 | 49 | Ken Schrader | Dodge | Schwan's Home Service | 67/0 | 263 | Running | $65,400 |
| 33. | 40 | 50 | Derrike Cope | Dodge | redneckjunk.com | 64/0 | 262 | Running | $66,125 |
| 34. | 24 | 43 | Jeff Green | Dodge | Lucky Charms | 61/0 | 200 | Accident | $91,250 |
| 35. | 26 | 8 | Dale Earnhardt Jr. | Chevrolet | Budweiser | 58/0 | 196 | Handling | $111,978 |
| 36. | 35 | 4 | Kevin Lepage | Chevrolet | YokeTV.com | 55/0 | 182 | Engine | $64,600 |
| 37. | 14 | 15 | Michael Waltrip | Chevrolet | NAPA | 57/5 | 163 | Accident | $100,431 |
| 38. | 41 | 02 | Carl Long | Pontiac | RacingJUNK.com | 49/0 | 145 | Oil leak | $64,175 |
| 39. | 39 | 22 | Scott Wimmer* | Dodge | Caterpillar | 46/0 | 37 | Engine | $71,975 |
| 40. | 9 | 16 | Greg Biffle | Ford | National Guard/Subway | 43/0 | 23 | Engine | $71,750 |
| 41. | 18 | 84 | Kyle Busch | Chevrolet | CARQUEST | 40/0 | 11 | Accident | $63,555 |
| 42. | 43 | 89 | Morgan Shepherd | Dodge | Voyles/Carter's Royal Dispos-all | 37/0 | 9 | Overheating | $63,375 |
| 43. | 42 | 72 | Kirk Shelmerdine | Ford | TUCSON/Freddie B's | 34/0 | 8 | Engine | $63,413 |

*Rookie. Time of race: 3 hours, 6 minutes, 35 seconds. Average speed: 128.790 mph. Margin of victory: 3.426 seconds. Caution flags: 6 for 37 laps. 40-45 (oil on track); 88-92 (Car 12—accident, Turn 4); 138-142 (Car 43—accident, Turn 2); 166-172 (Car 15—accident, Turn 4); 184-192 (oil on track); 202-206 (debris). Lap leaders: 18 lead changes among 10 drivers. Kasey Kahne-pole, Kurt Busch 1-4, Kahne 5-35, Jimmie Johnson 36-40, Scott Riggs 41, Kahne 42-53, Tony Stewart 54-88, Ricky Craven 89, Stewart 90-94, Matt Kenseth 95-138, Michael Waltrip 139, Kenseth 140-168, Stewart 169-172, Kenseth 173-184, Jeff Burton 185, Kevin Harvick 186-201, Stewart 202, Harvick 203-229, Kenseth 230-267. Pole winner: Kasey Kahne, 174.904 mph (record). Dropped to rear: Jeff Gordon, Ward Burton, Derrike Cope, Kevin Lepage (engine changes). Failed to qualify: Larry Gunselman. Estimated attendance: 148,000.

## POINTS STANDINGS

| Rk. | Driver | Behind | | Rk. | Driver | Behind |
|-----|--------|--------|---|-----|--------|--------|
| 1. | Matt Kenseth | — | | 6. | Kevin Harvick | -124 |
| 2 | Tony Stewart | -88 | | 7. | Dale Earnhardt Jr. | -125 |
| 3. | Elliott Sadler | -118 | | 8. | Kasey Kahne | -138 |
| 4. | Jeff Gordon | -119 | | 9. | Jamie McMurray | -138 |
| 5. | Kurt Busch | -123 | | 10. | Casey Mears | -156 |

# GOLDEN CORRAL 500 ---------- ATLANTA MOTOR SPEEDWAY

**Hampton, Ga.—1.54-mile banked paved oval • March 14, 2004—500.5 miles—325 laps**

| Fin. | St. | Car | Driver | Make | Sponsor | Pts./Bonus | Laps | Status | Winnings |
|------|-----|-----|--------|------|---------|-----------|------|--------|----------|
| 1. | 7 | 8 | Dale Earnhardt Jr. | Chevrolet | Budweiser | 185/5 | 325 | Running | $180,078 |
| 2. | 16 | 19 | Jeremy Mayfield | Dodge | Dodge Dealers/UAW | 175/5 | 325 | Running | $137,750 |
| 3. | 12 | 9 | Kasey Kahne* | Dodge | Dodge Dealers/UAW | 165/0 | 325 | Running | $120,125 |
| 4. | 3 | 48 | Jimmie Johnson | Chevrolet | Lowe's | 160/0 | 325 | Running | $97,400 |
| 5. | 1 | 12 | Ryan Newman | Dodge | ALLTEL | 160/5 | 325 | Running | $120,467 |
| 6. | 30 | 17 | Matt Kenseth | Ford | DeWalt Power Tools | 150/0 | 325 | Running | $120,728 |
| 7. | 19 | 20 | Tony Stewart | Chevrolet | The Home Depot | 156/10 | 325 | Running | $133,778 |
| 8. | 13 | 16 | Greg Biffle | Ford | National Guard | 147/5 | 325 | Running | $74,000 |
| 9. | 6 | 88 | Dale Jarrett | Ford | UPS/Arnold Palmer Tribute | 138/0 | 325 | Running | $96,217 |
| 10. | 4 | 24 | Jeff Gordon | Chevrolet | DuPont | 139/5 | 325 | Running | $114,228 |
| 11. | 14 | 23 | Dave Blaney | Dodge | Bill Davis Racing | 130/0 | 325 | Running | $64,275 |
| 12. | 20 | 97 | Kurt Busch | Ford | IRWIN Industrial Tools | 127/0 | 325 | Running | $78,950 |
| 13. | 21 | 0 | Ward Burton | Chevrolet | NetZero HiSpeed | 124/0 | 324 | Running | $63,775 |
| 14. | 28 | 6 | Mark Martin | Ford | Viagra | 121/0 | 324 | Running | $70,550 |
| 15. | 26 | 01 | Joe Nemechek | Chevrolet | U.S. Army | 118/0 | 324 | Running | $86,750 |
| 16. | 31 | 40 | Sterling Marlin | Dodge | Coors Light | 115/0 | 323 | Running | $94,800 |
| 17. | 23 | 31 | Robby Gordon | Chevrolet | Cingular Wireless | 117/5 | 323 | Running | $92,987 |
| 18. | 10 | 18 | Bobby Labonte | Chevrolet | Interstate Batteries | 109/0 | 323 | Running | $102,673 |
| 19. | 18 | 43 | Jeff Green | Dodge | Cheerios/Betty Crocker | 106/0 | 322 | Running | $83,615 |
| 20. | 32 | 99 | Jeff Burton | Ford | SKF | 103/0 | 322 | Running | $96,182 |
| 21. | 2 | 25 | Brian Vickers* | Chevrolet | GMAC Financial Services | 100/0 | 322 | Running | $69,315 |
| 22. | 29 | 32 | Ricky Craven | Chevrolet | Tide | 97/0 | 322 | Running | $81,310 |
| 23. | 15 | 15 | Michael Waltrip | Chevrolet | NAPA | 94/0 | 321 | Running | $93,591 |
| 24. | 36 | 5 | Terry Labonte | Chevrolet | Kellogg's | 91/0 | 321 | Running | $86,560 |
| 25. | 17 | 10 | Scott Riggs* | Chevrolet | Valvoline | 88/0 | 321 | Running | $85,072 |
| 26. | 24 | 49 | Ken Schrader | Dodge | Schwan's Home Service | 85/0 | 321 | Running | $59,235 |
| 27. | 37 | 22 | Scott Wimmer* | Dodge | Caterpillar | 82/0 | 321 | Running | $77,420 |
| 28. | 27 | 45 | Kyle Petty | Dodge | Georgia-Pacific/Brawny | 79/0 | 321 | Running | $67,059 |
| 29. | 5 | 38 | Elliott Sadler | Ford | M&M's | 76/0 | 320 | Running | $87,293 |
| 30. | 39 | 30 | Johnny Sauter* | Chevrolet | America Online | 73/0 | 320 | Running | $66,335 |
| 31. | 33 | 21 | Ricky Rudd | Ford | U.S. Air Force/Motorcraft | 70/0 | 320 | Running | $81,316 |
| 32. | 8 | 29 | Kevin Harvick | Chevrolet | GM Goodwrench | 67/0 | 318 | Running | $90,963 |
| 33. | 25 | 77 | Brendan Gaughan* | Dodge | Kodak EasyShare | 64/0 | 314 | Running | $63,120 |
| 34. | 9 | 41 | Casey Mears | Dodge | Target | 66/5 | 302 | Engine | $56,000 |
| 35. | 11 | 2 | Rusty Wallace | Dodge | Miller Lite | 58/0 | 291 | Running | $88,873 |
| 36. | 35 | 4 | Kevin Lepage | Chevrolet | Morgan-McClure | 55/0 | 287 | Running | $55,005 |
| 37. | 22 | 42 | Jamie McMurray | Dodge | Texaco/Havoline | 52/0 | 245 | Engine | $62,970 |
| 38. | 34 | 50 | Derrike Cope | Dodge | Arnold Development Co. | 49/0 | 186 | Engine | $54,935 |
| 39. | 41 | 02 | Andy Belmont | Pontiac | Intell Transportation | 46/0 | 80 | Rear end | $54,890 |
| 40. | 42 | 72 | Kirk Shelmerdine | Ford | TUCSON | 43/0 | 60 | Handling | $54,840 |
| 41. | 38 | 98 | Todd Bodine | Ford | Lucas Oil | PE | 16 | Engine | $54,800 |
| 42. | 43 | 80 | Andy Hillenburg | Ford | Commercial Truck & Trailer | 37/0 | 15 | Engine | $54,760 |
| 43. | 40 | 09 | Joe Ruttman | Dodge | Miccosukee Resort | 34/0 | 6 | Vibration | $54,071 |

*Rookie. Time of race: 3 hours, 9 minutes, 15 seconds. Average speed: 158.679 mph. Margin of victory: 4.584 seconds. Caution flags: 3 for 17 laps. 127-132 (debris); 150-155 (oil on track); 247-251 (oil on track). Lap leaders: 16 lead changes among 8 drivers. Ryan Newman 1-8, Jeff Gordon 9-46, Tony Stewart 47-58, Robby Gordon 59, Stewart 60-144, Greg Biffle 145-146, Stewart 147-172, Casey Mears 173, Stewart 174-177, Mears 178-213, Dale Earnhardt Jr. 214-216, Newman 217-248, Jeremy Mayfield 249-265, Earnhardt 266-301, Newman 302-304, Mayfield 305-309, Earnhardt 310-325. Pole winner: Ryan Newman, 193.575 mph. Failed to qualify: Morgan Shepherd. Estimated attendance: 125,000.

## POINTS STANDINGS

| Rk. | Driver | Behind | | Rk. | Driver | Behind |
|-----|--------|--------|---|-----|--------|--------|
| 1. | Matt Kenseth | — | | 6. | Kurt Busch | -146 |
| 2. | Tony Stewart | -82 | | 7. | Jeremy Mayfield | -159 |
| 3. | Dale Earnhardt Jr. | -90 | | 8. | Elliott Sadler | -192 |
| 4. | Kasey Kahne | -123 | | 9. | Jimmie Johnson | -193 |
| 5. | Jeff Gordon | -130 | | 10. | Bobby Labonte | -204 |

# CAROLINA DODGE DEALERS 400 − − − − − −DARLINGTON RACEWAY

**Darlington, S.C.—1.366-mile banked paved oval • March 21, 2004—400 miles—293 laps**

| Fin. | St. | Car | Driver | Make | Sponsor | Pts./Bonus | Laps | Status | Winnings |
|------|-----|-----|--------|------|---------|------------|------|--------|----------|
| 1. | 11 | 48 | Jimmie Johnson | Chevrolet | Lowe's | 185/5 | 293 | Running | $151,150 |
| 2. | 12 | 18 | Bobby Labonte | Chevrolet | Interstate Batteries | 175/5 | 293 | Running | $136,183 |
| 3. | 6 | 12 | Ryan Newman | Dodge | ALLTEL | 170/5 | 293 | Running | $120,912 |
| 4. | 29 | 31 | Robby Gordon | Chevrolet | Cingular Wireless | 160/0 | 293 | Running | $119,117 |
| 5. | 10 | 38 | Elliott Sadler | Ford | M&M's | 155/0 | 293 | Running | $102,233 |
| 6. | 4 | 97 | Kurt Busch | Ford | Sharpie | 160/10 | 293 | Running | $86,275 |
| 7. | 20 | 6 | Mark Martin | Ford | Viagra | 146/0 | 293 | Running | $72,345 |
| 8. | 23 | 29 | Kevin Harvick | Chevrolet | GM Goodwrench | 142/0 | 293 | Running | $98,743 |
| 9. | 18 | 19 | Jeremy Mayfield | Dodge | Dodge Dealers/UAW | 138/0 | 293 | Running | $88,635 |
| 10. | 2 | 8 | Dale Earnhardt Jr. | Chevrolet | Budweiser | 139/5 | 293 | Running | $106,983 |
| 11. | 33 | 99 | Jeff Burton | Ford | Hot Wheels | 130/0 | 293 | Running | $95,092 |
| 12. | 3 | 16 | Greg Biffle | Ford | Travelodge/National Guard | 132/5 | 293 | Running | $67,945 |
| 13. | 1 | 9 | Kasey Kahne* | Dodge | Dodge Dealers/UAW | 129/5 | 293 | Running | $103,590 |
| 14. | 17 | 40 | Sterling Marlin | Dodge | Coors Light | 126/5 | 293 | Running | $92,110 |
| 15. | 19 | 41 | Casey Mears | Dodge | Target | 118/0 | 293 | Running | $75,130 |
| 16. | 14 | 22 | Scott Wimmer* | Dodge | Caterpillar | 115/0 | 293 | Running | $79,285 |
| 17. | 8 | 20 | Tony Stewart | Chevrolet | The Home Depot | 117/5 | 293 | Running | $101,118 |
| 18. | 13 | 0 | Ward Burton | Chevrolet | NetZero HiSpeed | 109/0 | 293 | Running | $57,720 |
| 19. | 26 | 5 | Terry Labonte | Chevrolet | Kellogg's | 106/0 | 293 | Running | $84,140 |
| 20. | 34 | 01 | Joe Nemechek | Chevrolet | U.S. Army | 103/0 | 292 | Running | $77,470 |
| 21. | 21 | 42 | Jamie McMurray | Dodge | Texaco/Havoline | 105/0 | 292 | Running | $74,705 |
| 22. | 16 | 49 | Ken Schrader | Dodge | Schwan's Home Service | 97/0 | 292 | Running | $56,390 |
| 23. | 28 | 25 | Brian Vickers* | Chevrolet | GMAC Financial Services | 94/0 | 292 | Running | $65,000 |
| 24. | 30 | 43 | Jeff Green | Dodge | Cheerios/Betty Crocker | 91/0 | 292 | Running | $79,010 |
| 25. | 5 | 50 | Derrike Cope | Dodge | Arnold Development Co. | 88/0 | 292 | Running | $52,920 |
| 26. | 24 | 30 | Johnny Sauter* | Chevrolet | America Online | 85/0 | 292 | Running | $63,310 |
| 27. | 37 | 77 | Brendan Gaughan* | Dodge | Kodak EasyShare | 82/0 | 291 | Running | $63,110 |
| 28. | 31 | 4 | Kevin Lepage | Chevrolet | Morgan-McClure | 79/0 | 291 | Running | $62,844 |
| 29. | 7 | 2 | Rusty Wallace | Dodge | Miller Lite | 76/0 | 290 | Running | $85,588 |
| 30. | 27 | 10 | Scott Riggs* | Chevrolet | Valvoline | 73/0 | 290 | Running | $77,372 |
| 31. | 15 | 17 | Matt Kenseth | Ford | DeWalt Power Tools | 70/0 | 289 | Running | $102,358 |
| 32. | 22 | 88 | Dale Jarrett | Ford | UPS | 67/0 | 279 | Running | $82,442 |
| 33. | 25 | 21 | Ricky Rudd | Ford | Motorcraft | 64/0 | 275 | Running | $77,481 |
| 34. | 32 | 45 | Kyle Petty | Dodge | Georgia-Pacific/Brawny | 61/0 | 245 | Engine | $51,365 |
| 35. | 39 | 15 | Michael Waltrip | Chevrolet | NAPA | 58/0 | 181 | Accident | $88,291 |
| 36. | 36 | 32 | Ricky Craven | Chevrolet | Tide | 55/0 | 159 | Accident | $59,265 |
| 37. | 42 | 02 | Andy Belmont | Pontiac | Continental Fire & Safety | 52/0 | 69 | Brakes | $51,225 |
| 38. | 38 | 89 | Morgan Shepherd | Dodge | Voyles/Carter's Royal Dispos-all | 54/5 | 65 | Brakes | $51,175 |
| 39. | 41 | 72 | Kirk Shelmerdine | Ford | TUCSON | 46/0 | 49 | Too slow | $51,115 |
| 40. | 35 | 98 | Todd Bodine | Ford | Lucas Oil | 48/5 | 33 | Rear end | $51,015 |
| 41. | 9 | 24 | Jeff Gordon | Chevrolet | DuPont | 40/0 | 27 | Accident | $98,328 |
| 42. | 43 | 80 | Andy Hillenburg | Ford | Commercial Truck & Trailer | 37/0 | 26 | Accident | $50,890 |
| 43. | 40 | 09 | Joe Ruttman | Dodge | Miccosukee Resort | 34/0 | 21 | Vibration | $50,214 |

*Rookie. Time of race: 3 hours, 30 minutes, 39 seconds. Average speed: 114.001 mph. Margin of victory: .132 seconds. Caution flags: 9 for 58 laps. 10-14 (accident, Turn 3); 29-35 (Cars 80, 24—accident, Turn 1); 54-59 (debris); 146-151 (Car 9—spin, Turn 1); 162-169 (Cars 17, 32, 10, 25, 41, 21—accident, Turns 1 and 2); 185-190 (debris); 232-238 (debris); 276-282 (oil on track); 284-289 (Car 9—spin, Turn 3). Lap leaders: 22 lead changes among 12 drivers. Kasey Kahne 1-11, Greg Biffle 12-14, Dale Earnhardt Jr. 15-22, Kahne 23-30, Todd Bodine 31-32, Kahne 33-35, Ryan Newman 36-55, Kurt Busch 56, Morgan Shepherd 57-58, Busch 59-66, Earnhardt 67-76, Busch 77-104, Newman 105-123, Kahne 124-125, Jamie McMurray 126-165, Jimmie Johnson 166-185, Busch 186, Sterling Marlin 187, Johnson 188-221, Busch 222-259, Bobby Labonte 260-277, Tony Stewart 278, Johnson 279-293. Pole winner: Kasey Kahne, 171.716 mph. Dropped to rear: Kirk Shelmerdine (missed driver introductions). Failed to qualify: Stanton Barrett. Estimated attendance: 56,000.

## POINTS STANDINGS

| Rk. | Driver | Behind | | Rk. | Driver | Behind |
|-----|--------|--------|---|-----|--------|--------|
| 1. | Matt Kenseth | — | | 6. | Jimmie Johnson | -78 |
| 2. | Dale Earnhardt Jr. | -21 | | 7. | Jeremy Mayfield | -91 |
| 3. | Tony Stewart | -35 | | 8. | Bobby Labonte | -99 |
| 4. | Kurt Busch | -56 | | 9. | Ryan Newman | -106 |
| 5. | Kasey Kahne | -64 | | 10. | Elliott Sadler | -107 |

**Bristol, Tenn.—.533-mile high-banked concrete oval • March 28, 2004—266.5 miles—500 laps**

| Fin. | St. | Car | Driver | Make | Sponsor | Pts./Bonus | Laps | Status | Winnings |
|------|-----|-----|--------|------|---------|------------|------|--------|----------|
| 1. | 13 | 97 | Kurt Busch | Ford | Sharpie | 190/10 | 500 | Running | $173,965 |
| 2. | 4 | 2 | Rusty Wallace | Dodge | Miller Lite | 175/5 | 500 | Running | $141,878 |
| 3. | 14 | 29 | Kevin Harvick | Chevrolet | GM Goodwrench | 165/0 | 500 | Running | $131,978 |
| 4. | 17 | 40 | Sterling Marlin | Dodge | Coors Light | 165/5 | 500 | Running | $135,125 |
| 5. | 23 | 17 | Matt Kenseth | Ford | DeWalt Power Tools | 155/0 | 500 | Running | $136,098 |
| 6. | 19 | 49 | Ken Schrader | Dodge | Schwan's Home Service | 150/0 | 500 | Running | $77,945 |
| 7. | 1 | 12 | Ryan Newman | Dodge | ALLTEL | 151/5 | 500 | Running | $124,862 |
| 8. | 6 | 42 | Jamie McMurray | Dodge | Texaco/Havoline | 142/0 | 500 | Running | $87,095 |
| 9. | 2 | 24 | Jeff Gordon | Chevrolet | DuPont | 138/0 | 500 | Running | $120,168 |
| 10. | 8 | 15 | Michael Waltrip | Chevrolet | NAPA | 134/0 | 500 | Running | $110,796 |
| 11. | 18 | 8 | Dale Earnhardt Jr. | Chevrolet | Budweiser | 135/5 | 500 | Running | $118,748 |
| 12. | 3 | 16 | Greg Biffle | Ford | National Guard/Jackson Hewitt | 132/5 | 500 | Running | $84,890 |
| 13. | 20 | 22 | Scott Wimmer* | Dodge | Caterpillar | 124/0 | 500 | Running | $102,440 |
| 14. | 9 | 38 | Elliott Sadler | Ford | Pedigree/M&M's | 121/0 | 500 | Running | $103,273 |
| 15. | 10 | 30 | Johnny Sauter* | Chevrolet | America Online | 123/5 | 500 | Running | $83,090 |
| 16. | 11 | 48 | Jimmie Johnson | Chevrolet | Lowe's | 120/5 | 500 | Running | $90,215 |
| 17. | 16 | 19 | Jeremy Mayfield | Dodge | Dodge Dealers/UAW | 112/0 | 500 | Running | $96,565 |
| 18. | 33 | 5 | Terry Labonte | Chevrolet | Kellogg's | 109/0 | 500 | Running | $100,065 |
| 19. | 32 | 31 | Robby Gordon | Chevrolet | Cingular Wireless | 111/5 | 500 | Running | $104,792 |
| 20. | 7 | 77 | Brendan Gaughan* | Dodge | Kodak/Punisher | 103/0 | 500 | Running | $81,900 |
| 21. | 30 | 88 | Dale Jarrett | Ford | UPS | 100/0 | 500 | Running | $104,557 |
| 22. | 25 | 32 | Ricky Craven | Chevrolet | Tide | 97/0 | 499 | Running | $93,390 |
| 23. | 21 | 6 | Mark Martin | Ford | Viagra | 94/0 | 499 | Running | $81,045 |
| 24. | 12 | 20 | Tony Stewart | Chevrolet | The Home Depot | 96/5 | 498 | Running | $115,518 |
| 25. | 36 | 45 | Kyle Petty | Dodge | Georgia-Pacific/Brawny | 88/0 | 498 | Running | $82,570 |
| 26. | 37 | 50 | Derrike Cope | Dodge | Arnold Development Co. | 85/0 | 497 | Running | $68,440 |
| 27. | 26 | 01 | Joe Nemechek | Chevrolet | U.S. Army | 82/0 | 496 | Running | $87,694 |
| 28. | 39 | 0 | Ward Burton | Chevrolet | NetZero HiSpeed | 79/0 | 496 | Running | $71,150 |
| 29. | 29 | 43 | Jeff Green | Dodge | Cheerios/Betty Crocker | 76/0 | 496 | Running | $94,285 |
| 30. | 35 | 4 | Kevin Lepage | Chevrolet | Food City | 73/0 | 495 | Running | $70,685 |
| 31. | 42 | 02 | Hermie Sadler | Pontiac | East Tennessee Trailers | 70/0 | 490 | Running | $66,890 |
| 32. | 38 | 94 | Stanton Barrett | Chevrolet | AmericInn | 67/0 | 453 | Accident | $66,845 |
| 33. | 27 | 18 | Bobby Labonte | Chevrolet | Wellbutrin XL | 64/0 | 428 | Running | $112,808 |
| 34. | 28 | 10 | Scott Riggs* | Chevrolet | Valvoline/Harlem Globetrotters | 61/0 | 404 | Accident | $91,922 |
| 35. | 22 | 25 | Brian Vickers* | Chevrolet | GMAC Financial Services | 58/0 | 377 | Accident | $74,690 |
| 36. | 24 | 41 | Casey Mears | Dodge | Target | 55/0 | 331 | Accident | $66,645 |
| 37. | 15 | 21 | Ricky Rudd | Ford | Rent-A-Center/Motorcraft | 52/0 | 166 | Accident | $92,666 |
| 38. | 31 | 99 | Jeff Burton | Ford | Roush Racing | 49/0 | 138 | Too slow | $99,977 |
| 39. | 34 | 98 | Geoffrey Bodine | Ford | Lucas Oil | 46/0 | 59 | Brakes | $66,505 |
| 40. | 5 | 9 | Kasey Kahne* | Dodge | Dodge Dealers/UAW | 43/0 | 57 | Accident | $96,315 |
| 41. | 41 | 72 | Kirk Shelmerdine | Ford | Freddie B's | 40/0 | 7 | Handling | $66,390 |
| 42. | 40 | 09 | Joe Ruttman | Dodge | Miccosukee Resort | 37/0 | 4 | Rear end | $66,335 |
| 43. | 43 | 80 | Andy Hillenburg | Ford | Commercial Truck & Trailer | 34/0 | 4 | Brakes | $65,656 |

*Rookie. Time of race: 3 hours, 13 minutes, 34 seconds. Average speed: 82.607 mph. Margin of victory: .428 seconds. Caution flags: 11 for 85 laps. 59-65 (Cars 9, 42—accident, Turn 1); 68-73 (debris); 102-110 (Cars 29, 99, 18—accident, Turn 3); 169-178 (Cars 41, 21—accident, back stretch); 202-209 (Car 31—spin, Turn 2); 381-394 (Car 4—spin, Turn 4); 408-413 (Cars 43, 10—accident, back stretch); 432-437 (Car 8—spin, Turn 2); 464-472 (Car 94—accident, Turn 2); 483-487 (Car 77—spin, front stretch); 494-498 (Car 88—accident, Turn 1). Lap leaders: 13 lead changes among 10 drivers. Ryan Newman 1-25, Rusty Wallace 26-81, Tony Stewart 82-106, Greg Biffle 107-149, R. Wallace 150-172, Biffle 173-187, R. Wallace 188-203, Robby Gordon 204, Sterling Marlin 205-276, R. Wallace 277-281, Dale Earnhardt Jr. 282-372, Johnny Sauter 373, Jimmie Johnson 374-381, Kurt Busch 382-500. Pole winner: Ryan Newman, 128.313 mph. Dropped to rear: Robby Gordon (engine change), Derrike Cope (backup car). Estimated attendance: 160,000.

## POINTS STANDINGS

| Rk. | Driver | Behind | | Rk. | Driver | Behind |
|-----|--------|--------|---|-----|--------|--------|
| 1. | Matt Kenseth | — | | 6. | Jimmie Johnson | -113 |
| 2. | Kurt Busch | -21 | | 7. | Kevin Harvick | -125 |
| 3. | Dale Earnhardt Jr. | -41 | | 8. | Jeremy Mayfield | -134 |
| 4. | Tony Stewart | -94 | | 9. | Elliott Sadler | -141 |
| 5. | Ryan Newman | -110 | | 10. | Sterling Marlin | -171 |

**2004 SEASON**

# SAMSUNG/RADIOSHACK 500 — — — — — —TEXAS MOTOR SPEEDWAY

**Fort Worth, Texas—1.5-mile high-banked paved oval • April 4, 2004—500 miles—334 laps**

| Fin. | St. | Car | Driver | Make | Sponsor | Pts./Bonus | Laps | Status | Winnings |
|------|-----|-----|--------|------|---------|------------|------|--------|----------|
| 1. | 19 | 38 | Elliott Sadler | Ford | M&M's | 185/5 | 334 | Running | $507,733 |
| 2. | 3 | 9 | Kasey Kahne* | Dodge | Dodge Dealers/UAW | 180/10 | 334 | Running | $341,550 |
| 3. | 9 | 24 | Jeff Gordon | Chevrolet | DuPont | 170/5 | 334 | Running | $253,178 |
| 4. | 7 | 8 | Dale Earnhardt Jr. | Chevrolet | Budweiser | 165/5 | 334 | Running | $227,653 |
| 5. | 10 | 2 | Rusty Wallace | Dodge | Miller Lite | 160/5 | 334 | Running | $179,883 |
| 6. | 12 | 97 | Kurt Busch | Ford | IRWIN Industrial Tools | 155/5 | 334 | Running | $147,050 |
| 7. | 6 | 41 | Casey Mears | Dodge | Fujifilm/Target | 146/0 | 334 | Running | $139,375 |
| 8. | 17 | 20 | Tony Stewart | Chevrolet | The Home Depot | 142/0 | 334 | Running | $156,453 |
| 9. | 8 | 48 | Jimmie Johnson | Chevrolet | Lowe's | 138/0 | 334 | Running | $126,475 |
| 10. | 26 | 42 | Jamie McMurray | Dodge | Texaco/Havoline | 134/0 | 334 | Running | $118,550 |
| 11. | 20 | 23 | Dave Blaney | Dodge | Batesville Speed./Bad Boy Mowers | 130/0 | 334 | Running | $106,250 |
| 12. | 13 | 25 | Brian Vickers* | Chevrolet | GMAC Financial Services | 127/0 | 333 | Running | $112,150 |
| 13. | 22 | 29 | Kevin Harvick | Chevrolet | GM Goodwrench/Icebreakers | 124/0 | 333 | Running | $139,253 |
| 14. | 5 | 01 | Joe Nemechek | Chevrolet | U.S. Army | 126/5 | 333 | Running | $123,925 |
| 15. | 24 | 10 | Scott Riggs* | Chevrolet | Valvoline | 118/0 | 332 | Running | $125,512 |
| 16. | 25 | 17 | Matt Kenseth | Ford | DeWalt Power Tools | 115/0 | 332 | Running | $145,103 |
| 17. | 28 | 6 | Mark Martin | Ford | Viagra | 112/0 | 332 | Running | $104,125 |
| 18. | 11 | 88 | Dale Jarrett | Ford | UPS | 109/0 | 332 | Running | $125,442 |
| 19. | 39 | 49 | Ken Schrader | Dodge | Schwan's Home Service | 106/0 | 332 | Running | $92,925 |
| 20. | 41 | 15 | Michael Waltrip | Chevrolet | NAPA | 103/0 | 332 | Running | $124,981 |
| 21. | 38 | 45 | Kyle Petty | Dodge | Georgia-Pacific/Brawny | 105/5 | 332 | Running | $103,775 |
| 22. | 29 | 21 | Ricky Rudd | Ford | Keep it Genuine | 97/0 | 332 | Running | $114,251 |
| 23. | 18 | 31 | Robby Gordon | Chevrolet | Cingular Wireless | 94/0 | 331 | Running | $119,537 |
| 24. | 37 | 30 | Johnny Sauter* | Chevrolet | America Online | 96/5 | 331 | Running | $93,125 |
| 25. | 1 | 18 | Bobby Labonte | Chevrolet | Interstate Batteries | 93/5 | 330 | Running | $139,908 |
| 26. | 14 | 40 | Sterling Marlin | Dodge | Coors Light | 90/5 | 330 | Running | $115,025 |
| 27. | 23 | 99 | Jeff Burton | Ford | Roush Racing | 82/0 | 330 | Running | $113,842 |
| 28. | 40 | 32 | Ricky Craven | Chevrolet | Tide | 79/0 | 330 | Running | $97,425 |
| 29. | 42 | 4 | Jimmy Spencer | Chevrolet | Featherlite Luxury Coaches | 76/0 | 328 | Running | $85,724 |
| 30. | 35 | 14 | Larry Foyt | Dodge | Smith ChryslerDodge/Ft. Worth HD | 73/0 | 327 | Running | $74,175 |
| 31. | 4 | 16 | Greg Biffle | Ford | National Guard | 70/0 | 318 | Engine | $79,775 |
| 32. | 27 | 0 | Ward Burton | Chevrolet | NetZero HiSpeed | 67/0 | 304 | Running | $70,675 |
| 33. | 32 | 22 | Scott Wimmer* | Dodge | Caterpillar | 64/0 | 294 | Accident | $78,500 |
| 34. | 21 | 19 | Jeremy Mayfield | Dodge | Dodge Dealers/UAW | 61/0 | 293 | Accident | $76,475 |
| 35. | 33 | 43 | Jeff Green | Dodge | Cheerios/Betty Crocker | 58/0 | 290 | Engine | $93,625 |
| 36. | 2 | 91 | Bill Elliott | Dodge | Evernham Motorsports | 60/5 | 273 | Accident | $72,350 |
| 37. | 31 | 50 | Derrike Cope | Dodge | Arnold Development Co. | 52/0 | 232 | Drive shaft | $65,125 |
| 38. | 16 | 77 | Brendan Gaughan* | Dodge | Kodak EasyShare | 49/0 | 230 | Engine | $72,000 |
| 39. | 15 | 12 | Ryan Newman | Dodge | ALLTEL | 46/0 | 194 | Accident | $110,742 |
| 40. | 34 | 09 | Johnny Benson | Dodge | Miccosukee Resort | 43/0 | 151 | Rear end | $63,750 |
| 41. | 30 | 5 | Terry Labonte | Chevrolet | Kellogg's/Delphi | 40/0 | 119 | Engine | $90,385 |
| 42. | 43 | 72 | Kirk Shelmerdine | Ford | Freddie B's | 37/0 | 8 | Handling | $63,525 |
| 43. | 36 | 98 | Todd Bodine | Ford | Lucas Oil | 34/0 | 5 | Engine | $63,634 |

*Rookie. Time of race: 3 hours, 36 minutes, 30 seconds. Average speed: 138.845 mph. Margin of victory: .028 seconds. Caution flags: 7 for 45 laps. 19-23 (debris); 119-124 (debris); 197-204 (Car 12—accident, Turn 4); 267-272 (Car 0—spin, back stretch); 277-283 (Car 91—accident, Turn 3); 285-291 (Cars 22, 19, 25—accident, front stretch); 296-301 (oil on track). Lap leaders: 24 lead changes among 12 drivers. Bobby Labonte-pole, Bill Elliott 1-19, Joe Nemechek 20, Kyle Petty 21, Rusty Wallace 22-23, Sterling Marlin 24-37, Elliott 38-44, Marlin 45-48, Kasey Kahne 49-81, Elliott Sadler 82, Dale Earnhardt Jr. 83-84, Johnny Sauter 85, Kahne 86-120, Kurt Busch 121, Kahne 122-124, Sadler 125-144, Kahne 145-181, Jeff Gordon 182, Earnhardt 183-184, Kahne 185-199, B. Labonte 200-204, Nemechek 205-236, Kahne 237-261, J. Gordon 262-307, Sadler 308-334. Pole winner: Bobby Labonte, 193.903 mph. Dropped to rear: Jeremy Mayfield, Scott Wimmer, Todd Bodine, Ward Burton (engine changes). Failed to qualify: Kyle Busch, Morgan Shepherd, Andy Hillenburg, Andy Belmont. Estimated attendance: 216,000.

## POINTS STANDINGS

| Rk. | Driver | Behind | | Rk. | Driver | Behind |
|-----|--------|--------|--|-----|--------|--------|
| 1. | Kurt Busch | — | | 6. | Jimmie Johnson | -109 |
| 2. | Matt Kenseth | -19 | | 7. | Kasey Kahne | -130 |
| 3. | Dale Earnhardt Jr. | -35 | | 8. | Kevin Harvick | -135 |
| 4. | Tony Stewart | -86 | | 9. | Jeff Gordon | -141 |
| 5. | Elliott Sadler | -90 | | 10. | Ryan Newman | -198 |

**Martinsville, Va.—.526-mile paved oval • April 18, 2004—263 miles—500 laps**

| Fin. | St. | Car | Driver | Make | Sponsor | Pts./Bonus | Laps | Status | Winnings |
|------|-----|-----|--------|------|---------|-----------|------|--------|----------|
| 1. | 17 | 2 | Rusty Wallace | Dodge | Miller Lite | 185/5 | 500 | Running | $170,998 |
| 2. | 23 | 18 | Bobby Labonte | Chevrolet | Interstate Batteries | 170/0 | 500 | Running | $143,198 |
| 3. | 4 | 8 | Dale Earnhardt Jr. | Chevrolet | Budweiser | 170/5 | 500 | Running | $135,103 |
| 4. | 8 | 48 | Jimmie Johnson | Chevrolet | Lowe's | 165/5 | 500 | Running | $99,975 |
| 5. | 3 | 12 | Ryan Newman | Dodge | ALLTEL | 160/5 | 500 | Running | $113,242 |
| 6. | 1 | 24 | Jeff Gordon | Chevrolet | DuPont | 160/10 | 500 | Running | $141,403 |
| 7. | 2 | 42 | Jamie McMurray | Dodge | Texaco/Havoline | 146/0 | 500 | Running | $80,725 |
| 8. | 29 | 17 | Matt Kenseth | Ford | DeWalt Power Tools | 142/0 | 500 | Running | $113,728 |
| 9. | 18 | 40 | Sterling Marlin | Dodge | Coors Light | 138/0 | 500 | Running | $100,300 |
| 10. | 25 | 88 | Dale Jarrett | Ford | UPS | 134/0 | 500 | Running | $99,117 |
| 11. | 7 | 97 | Kurt Busch | Ford | IRWIN Industrial Tools | 130/0 | 500 | Running | $80,100 |
| 12. | 9 | 38 | Elliott Sadler | Ford | M&M's | 127/0 | 500 | Running | $98,408 |
| 13. | 35 | 25 | Brian Vickers* | Chevrolet | GMAC Financial Services | 124/0 | 500 | Running | $78,900 |
| 14. | 30 | 20 | Tony Stewart | Chevrolet | The Home Depot | 121/0 | 500 | Running | $105,753 |
| 15. | 39 | 15 | Michael Waltrip | Chevrolet | NAPA | 118/0 | 500 | Running | $95,706 |
| 16. | 32 | 32 | Ricky Craven | Chevrolet | Tide | 115/0 | 500 | Running | $88,350 |
| 17. | 11 | 77 | Brendan Gaughan* | Dodge | Kodak EasyShare | 112/0 | 500 | Running | $70,450 |
| 18. | 31 | 45 | Kyle Petty | Dodge | Georgia-Pacific/Brawny | 109/0 | 500 | Running | $76,725 |
| 19. | 5 | 29 | Kevin Harvick | Chevrolet | GM Goodwrench | 106/0 | 500 | Running | $97,403 |
| 20. | 14 | 21 | Ricky Rudd | Ford | Motorcraft | 103/0 | 499 | Running | $88,581 |
| 21. | 15 | 9 | Kasey Kahne* | Dodge | Dodge Dealers/UAW | 105/5 | 499 | Running | $91,050 |
| 22. | 6 | 0 | Ward Burton | Chevrolet | NetZero HiSpeed | 97/0 | 499 | Running | $60,425 |
| 23. | 28 | 5 | Terry Labonte | Chevrolet | Kellogg's | 94/0 | 498 | Running | $87,800 |
| 24. | 33 | 43 | Jeff Green | Dodge | Cheerios/Betty Crocker | 91/0 | 498 | Running | $82,775 |
| 25. | 27 | 99 | Jeff Burton | Ford | Team Caliber Racing | 88/0 | 497 | Running | $93,417 |
| 26. | 37 | 02 | Hermie Sadler | Chevrolet | The FanZCar | 85/0 | 497 | Running | $56,050 |
| 27. | 20 | 01 | Joe Nemechek | Chevrolet | U.S. Army | 82/0 | 496 | Running | $80,035 |
| 28. | 13 | 10 | Scott Riggs* | Chevrolet | Valvoline | 79/0 | 495 | Running | $83,922 |
| 29. | 16 | 22 | Scott Wimmer* | Dodge | Caterpillar | 76/0 | 494 | Running | $76,950 |
| 30. | 21 | 31 | Robby Gordon | Chevrolet | Cingular Wireless | 73/0 | 493 | Running | $91,012 |
| 31. | 22 | 30 | Johnny Sauter* | Chevrolet | America Online | 70/0 | 493 | Running | $66,175 |
| 32. | 42 | 89 | Morgan Shepherd | Dodge | Voyles/Carter's Royal Dispos-all | 67/0 | 492 | Running | $55,050 |
| 33. | 40 | 50 | Derrike Cope | Dodge | Arnold Development Co. | 64/0 | 491 | Running | $55,750 |
| 34. | 19 | 6 | Mark Martin | Ford | Viagra | 61/0 | 469 | Running | $65,200 |
| 35. | 24 | 16 | Greg Biffle | Ford | National Guard | 58/0 | 445 | Running | $62,650 |
| 36. | 10 | 19 | Jeremy Mayfield | Dodge | Dodge Dealers/UAW | 55/0 | 390 | Running | $70,989 |
| 37. | 12 | 41 | Casey Mears | Dodge | Target | 52/0 | 366 | Running | $54,550 |
| 38. | 34 | 4 | Jimmy Spencer | Chevrolet | Featherlite Custom Trailers | 49/0 | 272 | Engine | $54,500 |
| 39. | 43 | 98 | Todd Bodine | Ford | Lucas Oil | 46/0 | 151 | Brakes | $54,440 |
| 40. | 26 | 49 | Ken Schrader | Dodge | Schwan's Home Service | 43/0 | 118 | Accident | $54,365 |
| 41. | 36 | 94 | Stanton Barrett | Chevrolet | W.W. Motorsports | 40/0 | 65 | Brakes | $54,315 |
| 42. | 41 | 80 | Andy Hillenburg | Ford | Commercial Truck & Trailer | 37/0 | 4 | Accident | $54,265 |
| 43. | 38 | 09 | Joe Ruttman | Dodge | Miccosukee Resort | 34/0 | 2 | Brakes | $53,566 |

*Rookie. Time of race: 3 hours, 51 minutes, 29 seconds. Average speed: 68.169 mph. Margin of victory: 0.538 seconds. Caution flags: 11 for 105 laps. 7-22 (Car 80—accident, Turn 3); 27-31 (Car 31—accident, Turn 4); 120-127 (Car 49—accident, front stretch); 162-169 (Car 10—spin, front stretch); 215-223 (Car 77—accident, Turn 3); 270-277 (Car 19—accident, Turn 2); 285-301 (Cars 15, 4—accident, Turn 3); 372-380 (Cars 89, 9—accident, Turn 4); 415-422 (Car 22—accident, Turn 4); 430-439 (Car 29—accident, Turn 4); 457-463 (Cars 50, 29, 32—accident, Turn 2). Note: On Lap 290, the race was red-flagged (1 hour, 17 minutes, 28 seconds) to repair the track surface. Lap leaders: 10 lead changes among 6 drivers. Jeff Gordon 1-48, Dale Earnhardt Jr. 49-65, J. Gordon 66-117, Jimmie Johnson 118-163, Ryan Newman 164-179, Johnson 180-192, J. Gordon 193-272, Kasey Kahne 273, Earnhardt Jr. 274-410, Johnson 411-455, Rusty Wallace 456-500. Pole winner: Jeff Gordon, 93.502 mph. Dropped to rear: Jeff Burton (backup car). Failed to qualify: Kirk Shelmerdine. Estimated attendance: 91,000.

## POINTS STANDINGS

| Rk. | Driver | Behind | | Rk. | Driver | Behind |
|-----|--------|--------|---|-----|--------|--------|
| 1. | Dale Earnhardt Jr. | — | | 6. | Tony Stewart | -100 |
| 2. | Kurt Busch | -5 | | 7. | Jeff Gordon | -116 |
| 3. | Matt Kenseth | -12 | | 8. | Rusty Wallace | -157 |
| 4. | Jimmie Johnson | -79 | | 9. | Kasey Kahne | -160 |
| 5. | Elliott Sadler | -98 | | 10. | Kevin Harvick | -164 |

**Talladega, Ala.—2.66-mile high-banked paved trioval • April 25, 2004—500 miles—188 laps**

| Fin. | St. | Car | Driver | Make | Sponsor | Pts./Bonus | Laps | Status | Winnings |
|------|-----|-----|--------|------|---------|-----------|------|--------|----------|
| 1. | 11 | 24 | Jeff Gordon | Chevrolet | DuPont/Pepsi | 185/5 | 188 | Running | $320,258 |
| 2. | 3 | 8 | Dale Earnhardt Jr. | Chevrolet | Budweiser | 180/10 | 188 | Running | $241,433 |
| 3. | 14 | 29 | Kevin Harvick | Chevrolet | GM Goodwrench | 170/5 | 188 | Running | $185,808 |
| 4. | 8 | 48 | Jimmie Johnson | Chevrolet | Lowe's | 165/5 | 188 | Running | $139,655 |
| 5. | 21 | 31 | Robby Gordon | Chevrolet | Cingular Wireless | 160/5 | 188 | Running | $139,927 |
| 6. | 6 | 6 | Mark Martin | Ford | Viagra | 155/5 | 188 | Running | $108,380 |
| 7. | 25 | 99 | Jeff Burton | Ford | Roundup | 146/0 | 188 | Running | $126,572 |
| 8. | 16 | 41 | Casey Mears | Dodge | Target | 147/5 | 188 | Running | $108,205 |
| 9. | 33 | 42 | Jamie McMurray | Dodge | Texaco/Havoline | 143/5 | 188 | Running | $115,705 |
| 10. | 19 | 18 | Bobby Labonte | Chevrolet | Wellbutrin XL | 139/5 | 188 | Running | $126,313 |
| 11. | 17 | 12 | Ryan Newman | Dodge | ALLTEL | 135/5 | 188 | Running | $123,592 |
| 12. | 2 | 15 | Michael Waltrip | Chevrolet | NAPA | 132/5 | 188 | Running | $112,301 |
| 13. | 20 | 77 | Brendan Gaughan* | Dodge | Kodak EasyShare | 124/0 | 188 | Running | $89,015 |
| 14. | 29 | 30 | Johnny Sauter* | Chevrolet | America Online | 121/0 | 188 | Running | $86,935 |
| 15. | 18 | 16 | Greg Biffle | Ford | National Guard/Subway | 123/5 | 188 | Running | $86,480 |
| 16. | 7 | 88 | Dale Jarrett | Ford | UPS | 120/5 | 188 | Running | $106,957 |
| 17. | 1 | 21 | Ricky Rudd | Ford | Keep it Genuine | 112/0 | 188 | Running | $106,281 |
| 18. | 30 | 22 | Scott Wimmer* | Dodge | Caterpillar | 114/5 | 188 | Running | $96,885 |
| 19. | 15 | 43 | Jeff Green | Dodge | Cheerios/Betty Crocker | 106/0 | 188 | Running | $95,845 |
| 20. | 23 | 4 | Jimmy Spencer | Chevrolet | Morgan-McClure | 108/5 | 188 | Running | $87,335 |
| 21. | 38 | 19 | Jeremy Mayfield | Dodge | Dodge Dealers/UAW | 100/0 | 188 | Running | $90,095 |
| 22. | 37 | 20 | Tony Stewart | Chevrolet | The Home Depot | 102/5 | 188 | Running | $114,353 |
| 23. | 40 | 49 | Ken Schrader | Dodge | Schwan's Home Service | 94/0 | 188 | Running | $70,265 |
| 24. | 28 | 45 | Kyle Petty | Dodge | Georgia-Pacific/Brawny | 91/0 | 188 | Running | $77,949 |
| 25. | 13 | 5 | Terry Labonte | Chevrolet | Kellogg's | 93/5 | 188 | Running | $96,930 |
| 26. | 35 | 04 | Eric McClure | Chevrolet | 77sports.com/I CAN Learn | 90/5 | 188 | Running | $65,175 |
| 27. | 39 | 25 | Brian Vickers* | Chevrolet | GMAC Financial Services | 87/5 | 188 | Running | $75,620 |
| 28. | 12 | 38 | Elliott Sadler | Ford | M&M's | 84/5 | 185 | Running | $102,903 |
| 29. | 34 | 09 | Johnny Benson | Dodge | Miccosukee Resort | 76/0 | 151 | Suspension | $63,910 |
| 30. | 26 | 9 | Kasey Kahne* | Dodge | Dodge Dealers/UAW | 73/0 | 150 | Running | $97,080 |
| 31. | 9 | 40 | Sterling Marlin | Dodge | Coors Light | 75/5 | 146 | Overheating | $99,050 |
| 32. | 4 | 01 | Joe Nemechek | Chevrolet | U.S. Army | 72/5 | 146 | Engine | $71,500 |
| 33. | 32 | 2 | Rusty Wallace | Dodge | Miller Lite | 64/0 | 144 | Running | $107,108 |
| 34. | 5 | 10 | Scott Riggs* | Chevrolet | Valvoline | 61/0 | 144 | Running | $89,322 |
| 35. | 36 | 33 | Kerry Earnhardt | Chevrolet | Bass Pro Shops | 58/0 | 114 | Accident | $63,005 |
| 36. | 22 | 97 | Kurt Busch | Ford | Sharpie | 60/5 | 82 | Accident | $82,875 |
| 37. | 27 | 00 | Kenny Wallace | Chevrolet | Aaron's Sales & Lease | 52/0 | 82 | Accident | $62,700 |
| 38. | 41 | 50 | Derrike Cope | Dodge | Arnold Development Co. | 49/0 | 82 | Accident | $62,350 |
| 39. | 42 | 23 | Dave Blaney | Dodge | Bill Davis Racing | 46/0 | 81 | Accident | $62,150 |
| 40. | 10 | 0 | Ward Burton | Chevrolet | NetZero HiSpeed | 43/0 | 66 | Engine | $61,900 |
| 41. | 43 | 89 | Morgan Shepherd | Dodge | Voyles/Carter's Royal Dispos-all | 40/0 | 65 | Transmission | $61,705 |
| 42. | 31 | 17 | Matt Kenseth | Ford | DeWalt Power Tools | 37/0 | 59 | Engine | $112,298 |
| 43. | 24 | 32 | Ricky Craven | Chevrolet | Tide | 34/0 | 7 | Engine | $69,581 |

*Rookie. Time of race: 3 hours, 51 minutes, 53 seconds. Average speed: 129.396 mph. Margin of victory: Under caution. Caution flags: 11 for 55 laps. 4-6 (oil on track); 22-26 (Cars 17, 9—spin, front stretch); 35-39 (debris); 68-73 (oil on track); 84-88 (Cars 00, 2, 5, 9, 10, 12, 19, 23, 50—accident, Turn 4); 94-99 (debris); 115-120 (Car 33—accident, back stretch); 147-153 (debris); 167-171 (debris); 177-179 (Car 20—spin, Turn 4); 185-188 (Car 25—accident, Turn 4). Lap leaders: 54 lead changes among 23 drivers. Ricky Rudd-pole, Michael Waltrip 1-2, Joe Nemechek 3-4, Mark Martin 5-10, Dale Earnhardt Jr. 11-14, Sterling Marlin 15-16, Earnhardt 17, Kurt Busch 18, Casey Mears 19-23, Ryan Newman 24, Robby Gordon 25-30, Jeff Gordon 31-35, Dale Jarrett 36, J. Gordon 37-39, Earnhardt 40-43, Tony Stewart 44-45, Earnhardt 46, Kevin Harvick 47-49, Earnhardt 50-53, Jimmie Johnson 54-55, Earnhardt 56, Brian Vickers 57-58, Waltrip 59-68, Jarrett 69, R. Gordon 70-77, J. Gordon 78, Harvick 79-81, Earnhardt 82-84, Jarrett 85, Jimmy Spencer 86, Scott Wimmer 87-88, Harvick 89-94, Bobby Labonte 95, Eric McClure 96, Earnhardt 97-113, Jamie McMurray 114-115, Elliott Sadler 116, R. Gordon 117-120, Waltrip 121, Jamie McMurray 122-123, Jimmie Johnson 124-131, Joe Nemechek 132, Johnson 133-135, Earnhardt 136-137, Johnson 138-144, Stewart 145-148, Greg Biffle 149, Terry Labonte 150, Jimmy Spencer 151, R. Gordon 152-155, J. Johnson 156-160, Earnhardt 161-179, Harvick 180-181, Earnhardt 182, J. Gordon 183-188. Pole winner: Ricky Rudd, 191.180 mph. Dropped to rear: Elliott Sadler (engine change), Eric McClure (driver choice). Failed to qualify: Larry Foyt, Todd Bodine, Kirk Shelmerdine. Estimated attendance: 155,000.

## POINTS STANDINGS

| Rk. | Driver | Behind | | Rk. | Driver | Behind |
|-----|--------|--------|---|-----|--------|--------|
| 1. | Dale Earnhardt Jr. | — | | 6. | Kevin Harvick | -174 |
| 2. | Jimmie Johnson | -94 | | 7. | Tony Stewart | -178 |
| 3. | Jeff Gordon | -111 | | 8. | Elliott Sadler | -194 |
| 4. | Kurt Busch | -125 | | 9. | Ryan Newman | -218 |
| 5. | Matt Kenseth | -155 | | 10. | Bobby Labonte | -237 |

**Fontana, Calif.—2-mile banked paved oval • May 2, 2004—500 miles—250 laps**

| Fin. | St. | Car | Driver | Make | Sponsor | Pts./Bonus | Laps | Status | Winnings |
|------|-----|-----|--------|------|---------|-----------|------|--------|----------|
| 1. | 16 | 24 | Jeff Gordon | Chevrolet | DuPont | 190/10 | 250 | Running | $318,628 |
| 2. | 19 | 48 | Jimmie Johnson | Chevrolet | Lowe's | 175/5 | 250 | Running | $194,675 |
| 3. | 7 | 12 | Ryan Newman | Dodge | Mobil 1/ALLTEL | 170/5 | 250 | Running | $191,267 |
| 4. | 25 | 17 | Matt Kenseth | Ford | DeWalt Power Tools | 165/5 | 250 | Running | $172,578 |
| 5. | 27 | 18 | Bobby Labonte | Chevrolet | Interstate Batteries | 155/0 | 250 | Running | $150,233 |
| 6. | 5 | 77 | Brendan Gaughan* | Dodge | Kodak EasyShare | 155/5 | 250 | Running | $106,125 |
| 7. | 29 | 5 | Terry Labonte | Chevrolet | Kellogg's | 146/0 | 250 | Running | $119,625 |
| 8. | 13 | 41 | Casey Mears | Dodge | Target | 142/0 | 250 | Running | $108,375 |
| 9. | 24 | 29 | Kevin Harvick | Chevrolet | GM Goodwrench | 143/0 | 250 | Running | $123,203 |
| 10. | 15 | 0 | Ward Burton | Chevrolet | NetZero HiSpeed | 134/0 | 250 | Running | $88,350 |
| 11. | 26 | 6 | Mark Martin | Ford | Viagra | 130/0 | 250 | Running | $90,450 |
| 12. | 23 | 31 | Robby Gordon | Chevrolet | Cingular Wireless | 127/0 | 250 | Running | $112,437 |
| 13. | 1 | 9 | Kasey Kahne* | Dodge | Dodge Dealers/UAW | 129/5 | 250 | Running | $127,250 |
| 14. | 20 | 19 | Jeremy Mayfield | Dodge | Dodge Dealers/UAW | 126/5 | 249 | Running | $112,025 |
| 15. | 12 | 42 | Jamie McMurray | Dodge | Texaco/Havoline | 118/0 | 249 | Running | $87,725 |
| 16. | 11 | 20 | Tony Stewart | Chevrolet | The Home Depot | 115/0 | 249 | Running | $120,603 |
| 17. | 35 | 21 | Ricky Rudd | Ford | Keep it Genuine | 112/0 | 249 | Running | $102,981 |
| 18. | 34 | 32 | Ricky Craven | Chevrolet | Tide | 109/0 | 249 | Running | $97,225 |
| 19. | 10 | 8 | Dale Earnhardt Jr. | Chevrolet | Budweiser | 106/0 | 249 | Running | $119,203 |
| 20. | 32 | 49 | Ken Schrader | Dodge | Schwan's Home Service | 108/5 | 249 | Running | $74,925 |
| 21. | 37 | 30 | Johnny Sauter* | Chevrolet | AOL/IMAX NASCAR 3D | 100/0 | 249 | Running | $84,175 |
| 22. | 14 | 38 | Elliott Sadler | Ford | Pedigree | 97/0 | 249 | Running | $109,058 |
| 23. | 21 | 97 | Kurt Busch | Ford | IRWIN Industrial Tools | 94/0 | 249 | Running | $90,550 |
| 24. | 31 | 88 | Dale Jarrett | Ford | UPS | 91/0 | 249 | Running | $103,217 |
| 25. | 4 | 10 | Scott Riggs* | Chevrolet | Valvoline | 88/0 | 249 | Running | $97,187 |
| 26. | 30 | 99 | Jeff Burton | Ford | Roundup FastAct | 85/0 | 249 | Running | $104,317 |
| 27. | 8 | 40 | Sterling Marlin | Dodge | Coors Light | 82/0 | 249 | Running | $103,200 |
| 28. | 2 | 01 | Joe Nemechek | Chevrolet | U.S. Army | 84/5 | 249 | Running | $88,100 |
| 29. | 6 | 25 | Brian Vickers* | Chevrolet | GMAC Financial Services | 81/5 | 248 | Running | $76,900 |
| 30. | 39 | 22 | Scott Wimmer* | Dodge | Caterpillar | 73/0 | 248 | Running | $83,039 |
| 31. | 36 | 50 | Derrike Cope | Dodge | Bennett Lane Winery | 70/0 | 248 | Running | $65,975 |
| 32. | 17 | 15 | Michael Waltrip | Chevrolet | NAPA | 67/0 | 245 | Running | $101,831 |
| 33. | 18 | 16 | Greg Biffle | Ford | National Guard/Subway | 69/5 | 223 | Running | $74,500 |
| 34. | 41 | 98 | Todd Bodine | Ford | Lucas Oil | 66/5 | 209 | Rear end | $65,375 |
| 35. | 9 | 2 | Rusty Wallace | Dodge | Miller Lite | 58/0 | 193 | Running | $109,008 |
| 36. | 38 | 89 | Morgan Shepherd | Dodge | Voyles/Carter's Royal Dispos-all | 60/5 | 163 | Electrical | $65,025 |
| 37. | 3 | 43 | Jeff Green | Dodge | Cheerios/Betty Crocker | 52/0 | 147 | Engine | $91,050 |
| 38. | 22 | 4 | Jimmy Spencer | Chevrolet | Morgan-McClure | 54/5 | 127 | Engine | $64,550 |
| 39. | 28 | 45 | Kyle Petty | Dodge | Georgia-Pacific/Brawny | 46/0 | 40 | Engine | $64,430 |
| 40. | 43 | 94 | Stanton Barrett | Chevrolet | AmericInn Lodging Systems | 43/0 | 20 | Accident | $64,280 |
| 41. | 40 | 02 | Hermie Sadler | Chevrolet | The FanZCar | 40/0 | 20 | Transmission | $64,155 |
| 42. | 42 | 72 | Kirk Shelmerdine | Ford | 2nd Chance Race Parts | 37/0 | 5 | Handling | $64,050 |
| 43. | 33 | 09 | Joe Ruttman | Dodge | Miccosukee Resorts | 34/0 | 2 | Vibration | $64,161 |

*Rookie. Time of race: 3 hours, 38 minutes, 33 seconds. Average speed: 137.268 mph. Margin of victory: 12.871 seconds. Caution flags: 6 for 39 laps. 23-30 (Car 94—accident, Turn 2); 51-55 (oil on track); 58-62 (Cars 97, 2—accident, front stretch); 92-97 (debris); 141-145 (debris); 149-158 (oil on track). Lap leaders: 23 lead changes among 15 drivers. Kasey Kahne 1, Joe Nemechek 2-3, Kahne 4-24, Jimmy Spencer 25-26, Morgan Shepherd 27, Todd Bodine 28, Kahne 29-49, Jeff Gordon 50-52, Spencer 53, Matt Kenseth 54-64, J. Gordon 65, Greg Biffle 66-93, Brian Vickers 94, Kahne 95-104, Jimmie Johnson 105-141, Jeremy Mayfield 142, Ken Schrader 143, J. Gordon 144-166, Kahne 167-190, J. Gordon 191-197, Brendan Gaughan 198, Ryan Newman 199-200, Kevin Harvick 201-203, J. Gordon 204-250. Pole winner: Kasey Kahne, 186.940 mph. Dropped to rear: Casey Mears (backup car), Joe Ruttman (driver change), Scott Wimmer, Derrike Cope, Todd Bodine (engine changes). Estimated attendance: 120,000.

## POINTS STANDINGS

| Rk. | Driver | Behind | | Rk. | Driver | Behind |
|-----|--------|--------|---|-----|--------|--------|
| 1. | Dale Earnhardt Jr. | — | | 6. | Kevin Harvick | -137 |
| 2. | Jimmie Johnson | -25 | | 7. | Ryan Newman | -154 |
| 3. | Jeff Gordon | -27 | | 8. | Tony Stewart | -169 |
| 4. | Matt Kenseth | -96 | | 9. | Bobby Labonte | -188 |
| 5. | Kurt Busch | -137 | | 10. | Elliott Sadler | -203 |

# CHEVY AMERICAN REVOLUTION 400 - - RICHMOND INTERNATIONAL RACEWAY

**Richmond, Va.—.75-mile paved oval • May 15, 2004—300 miles—400 laps**

| Fin. | St. | Car | Driver | Make | Sponsor | Pts./Bonus | Laps | Status | Winnings |
|------|-----|-----|--------|------|---------|------------|------|--------|----------|
| 1. | 4 | 8 | Dale Earnhardt Jr. | Chevrolet | Budweiser | 190/10 | 400 | Running | $285,053 |
| 2. | 5 | 48 | Jimmie Johnson | Chevrolet | Lowe's | 175/5 | 400 | Running | $135,350 |
| 3. | 27 | 18 | Bobby Labonte | Chevrolet | Interstate Batteries | 165/0 | 400 | Running | $142,333 |
| 4. | 28 | 20 | Tony Stewart | Chevrolet | The Home Depot | 165/5 | 400 | Running | $127,478 |
| 5. | 29 | 17 | Matt Kenseth | Ford | DeWalt Power Tools | 160/5 | 400 | Running | $122,303 |
| 6. | 13 | 24 | Jeff Gordon | Chevrolet | DuPont | 155/5 | 400 | Running | $113,278 |
| 7. | 12 | 6 | Mark Martin | Ford | Viagra | 146/0 | 400 | Running | $76,825 |
| 8. | 1 | 25 | Brian Vickers* | Chevrolet | GMAC Financial Services | 147/5 | 400 | Running | $81,775 |
| 9. | 2 | 12 | Ryan Newman | Dodge | ALLTEL | 143/5 | 400 | Running | $108,642 |
| 10. | 18 | 15 | Michael Waltrip | Chevrolet | NAPA | 139/5 | 400 | Running | $110,581 |
| 11. | 30 | 21 | Ricky Rudd | Ford | Rent-A-Center/Motorcraft | 135/5 | 400 | Running | $91,831 |
| 12. | 14 | 38 | Elliott Sadler | Ford | Pedigree | 127/0 | 399 | Running | $99,393 |
| 13. | 31 | 88 | Dale Jarrett | Ford | UPS | 129/5 | 399 | Running | $96,067 |
| 14. | 17 | 99 | Jeff Burton | Ford | Roundup | 121/0 | 399 | Running | $97,342 |
| 15. | 32 | 40 | Sterling Marlin | Dodge | Coors Light | 118/0 | 399 | Running | $99,255 |
| 16. | 7 | 2 | Rusty Wallace | Dodge | Miller Lite | 115/0 | 399 | Running | $102,983 |
| 17. | 26 | 09 | Bobby Hamilton Jr. | Dodge | Miccosukee Resort | 112/0 | 399 | Running | $58,470 |
| 18. | 19 | 5 | Terry Labonte | Chevrolet | Kellogg's | 109/0 | 398 | Running | $89,150 |
| 19. | 35 | 30 | Johnny Sauter* | Chevrolet | America Online | 106/0 | 398 | Running | $70,175 |
| 20. | 15 | 0 | Ward Burton | Chevrolet | NetZero HiSpeed | 103/0 | 398 | Running | $63,475 |
| 21. | 10 | 16 | Greg Biffle | Ford | National Guard | 100/0 | 398 | Running | $69,100 |
| 22. | 11 | 19 | Jeremy Mayfield | Dodge | Dodge Dealers/UAW | 102/5 | 397 | Running | $85,875 |
| 23. | 34 | 49 | Ken Schrader | Dodge | Schwan's Home Service | 94/0 | 397 | Running | $60,575 |
| 24. | 6 | 31 | Robby Gordon | Chevrolet | Cingular Wireless | 91/0 | 397 | Running | $93,012 |
| 25. | 20 | 29 | Kevin Harvick | Chevrolet | GM Goodwrench | 88/0 | 397 | Running | $96,328 |
| 26. | 21 | 32 | Ricky Craven | Chevrolet | Tide | 85/0 | 396 | Running | $82,925 |
| 27. | 22 | 45 | Kyle Petty | Dodge | Georgia-Pacific/Brawny | 82/0 | 395 | Running | $72,700 |
| 28. | 39 | 9 | Kasey Kahne* | Dodge | Dodge Dealers/UAW | 79/0 | 394 | Running | $89,350 |
| 29. | 41 | 50 | Derrike Cope | Dodge | Chesapeake Mobile Home Sales | 76/0 | 392 | Running | $56,250 |
| 30. | 25 | 22 | Scott Wimmer* | Dodge | Caterpillar | 73/0 | 392 | Running | $78,075 |
| 31. | 23 | 97 | Kurt Busch | Ford | IRWIN Industrial Tools | 75/5 | 386 | Running | $76,025 |
| 32. | 9 | 41 | Casey Mears | Dodge | Target | 67/0 | 380 | Running | $67,364 |
| 33. | 36 | 98 | Todd Bodine | Ford | Lucas Oil | 64/0 | 373 | Running | $56,850 |
| 34. | 40 | 77 | Brendan Gaughan* | Dodge | Jasper Engines/Kodak | 61/0 | 362 | Running | $66,375 |
| 35. | 16 | 10 | Scott Riggs* | Chevrolet | Valvoline | 58/0 | 341 | Engine | $81,012 |
| 36. | 8 | 01 | Joe Nemechek | Chevrolet | U.S. Army | 55/0 | 265 | Accident | $63,775 |
| 37. | 3 | 43 | Jeff Green | Dodge | Cheerios/Betty Crocker | 52/0 | 239 | Accident | $81,975 |
| 38. | 37 | 42 | Jamie McMurray | Dodge | Texaco/Havoline | 49/0 | 202 | Accident | $63,675 |
| 39. | 42 | 89 | Morgan Shepherd | Dodge | Voyles/Carter's Royal Dispos-all | 46/0 | 131 | Engine | $55,620 |
| 40. | 24 | 7 | Dave Blaney | Dodge | Ultra Motorsports | 43/0 | 123 | Vibration | $55,555 |
| 41. | 38 | 4 | Jimmy Spencer | Chevrolet | Morgan-McClure | 40/0 | 118 | Accident | $55,500 |
| 42. | 33 | 02 | Hermie Sadler | Chevrolet | Jenkins & Jenkins | 37/0 | 114 | Engine | $55,450 |
| 43. | 43 | 80 | Randy LaJoie | Ford | Commercial Truck & Trailer | 34/0 | 36 | Vibration | $55,651 |

*Rookie. Time of race: 3 hours, 3 minutes, 12 seconds. Average speed: 98.253 mph. Margin of victory: 1.481 seconds. Caution flags: 9 for 66 laps. 6-12 (debris); 102-107 (Car 43—accident, Turn 2); 122-129 (Car 4—accident, Turn 2); 138-143 (Car 31—accident, Turn 4); 152-157 (Car 77—accident, Turn 3); 170-175 (Car 29—accident, Turn 2); 194-199 (Car 99—spin, front stretch); 203-211 (Cars 42, 01, 48—accident, Turn 2); 344-355 (oil on track). Lap leaders: 19 lead changes among 12 drivers. Brian Vickers 1-32, Dale Earnhardt Jr. 33-56, Jimmie Johnson 57-103, Dale Jarrett 104, Kurt Busch 105-110, Johnson 111-131, Earnhardt 132-144, Ryan Newman 145, Earnhardt 146-163, Newman 164-171, Jeremy Mayfield 172-194, Michael Waltrip 195-250, Tony Stewart 251-288, Earnhardt 289-293, Matt Kenseth 294-297, Ricky Rudd 298-299, Johnson 300-322, Jeff Gordon 323-324, Stewart 325-345, Earnhardt 346-400. Pole winner: Brian Vickers, 129.983 mph (record). Dropped to rear: Kasey Kahne, Ricky Craven (backup cars); Elliott Sadler (engine change). Estimated attendance: 115,000.

## POINTS STANDINGS

| Rk. | Driver | Behind | | Rk. | Driver | Behind |
|-----|--------|--------|---|-----|--------|--------|
| 1. | Dale Earnhardt Jr. | — | | 6. | Ryan Newman | -201 |
| 2. | Jimmie Johnson | -40 | | 7. | Bobby Labonte | -213 |
| 3. | Jeff Gordon | -62 | | 8. | Kevin Harvick | -239 |
| 4. | Matt Kenseth | -126 | | 9. | Kurt Busch | -252 |
| 5. | Tony Stewart | -194 | | 10. | Elliott Sadler | -266 |

# COCA-COLA 600 ----------- LOWE'S MOTOR SPEEDWAY

**Concord, N.C.—1.5-mile high-banked paved trioval • May 30, 2004—600 miles—400 laps**

| Fin. | St. | Car | Driver | Make | Sponsor | Pts./Bonus | Laps | Status | Winnings |
|------|-----|-----|--------|------|---------|-----------|------|--------|----------|
| 1. | 1 | 48 | Jimmie Johnson | Chevrolet | Lowe's | 190/10 | 400 | Running | $426,350 |
| 2. | 12 | 15 | Michael Waltrip | Chevrolet | NAPA | 170/0 | 400 | Running | $254,456 |
| 3. | 37 | 17 | Matt Kenseth | Ford | Smirnoff Ice/DeWalt | 170/5 | 400 | Running | $222,478 |
| 4. | 21 | 42 | Jamie McMurray | Dodge | Texaco/Havoline | 165/5 | 400 | Running | $145,800 |
| 5. | 4 | 38 | Elliott Sadler | Ford | Pedigree | 160/5 | 400 | Running | $178,683 |
| 6. | 10 | 8 | Dale Earnhardt Jr. | Chevrolet | Budweiser | 155/5 | 400 | Running | $152,053 |
| 7. | 14 | 41 | Casey Mears | Dodge | Target | 151/5 | 400 | Running | $119,550 |
| 8. | 15 | 19 | Jeremy Mayfield | Dodge | Dodge Dealers/UAW | 142/0 | 400 | Running | $120,700 |
| 9. | 6 | 20 | Tony Stewart | Chevrolet | The Home Depot | 138/0 | 400 | Running | $137,678 |
| 10. | 16 | 2 | Rusty Wallace | Dodge | Miller Lite | 134/0 | 400 | Running | $131,658 |
| 11. | 32 | 97 | Kurt Busch | Ford | IRWIN Industrial Tools | 130/0 | 400 | Running | $107,380 |
| 12. | 19 | 9 | Kasey Kahne* | Dodge | Dodge Dealers/UAW | 132/5 | 400 | Running | $119,750 |
| 13. | 9 | 18 | Bobby Labonte | Chevrolet | Interstate Batteries/Shrek 2 | 124/0 | 400 | Running | $129,283 |
| 14. | 13 | 01 | Joe Nemechek | Chevrolet | U.S. Army | 121/0 | 398 | Running | $107,050 |
| 15. | 5 | 25 | Brian Vickers* | Chevrolet | GMAC Financial Services | 118/0 | 398 | Running | $95,850 |
| 16. | 17 | 0 | Ward Burton | Chevrolet | NetZero HiSpeed | 115/0 | 398 | Running | $83,650 |
| 17. | 11 | 23 | Dave Blaney | Dodge | Whelen | 112/0 | 398 | Running | $82,450 |
| 18. | 33 | 88 | Dale Jarrett | Ford | UPS | 109/0 | 398 | Running | $112,067 |
| 19. | 25 | 1 | John Andretti | Chevrolet | Snap-On Tools | 106/0 | 398 | Running | $79,975 |
| 20. | 20 | 31 | Robby Gordon | Chevrolet | Cingular Wireless | 103/0 | 397 | Running | $112,487 |
| 21. | 30 | 16 | Greg Biffle | Ford | National Guard/Subway | 100/0 | 397 | Running | $86,025 |
| 22. | 34 | 99 | Jeff Burton | Ford | Roundup | 97/0 | 397 | Running | $110,517 |
| 23. | 23 | 29 | Kevin Harvick | Chevrolet | GM Goodwrench | 94/0 | 396 | Running | $112,878 |
| 24. | 26 | 32 | Ricky Craven | Chevrolet | Tide | 91/0 | 396 | Running | $93,800 |
| 25. | 28 | 10 | Scott Riggs* | Chevrolet | Valvoline | 88/0 | 395 | Running | $100,087 |
| 26. | 40 | 21 | Ricky Rudd | Ford | U.S. Air Force/Motorcraft | 85/0 | 395 | Running | $99,756 |
| 27. | 8 | 43 | Jeff Green | Dodge | Cheerios/Great American Bake Sale | 82/0 | 395 | Running | $96,825 |
| 28. | 29 | 22 | Scott Wimmer* | Dodge | Caterpillar | 79/0 | 394 | Running | $88,939 |
| 29. | 24 | 4 | Jimmy Spencer | Chevrolet | Morgan-McClure | 76/0 | 394 | Running | $72,425 |
| 30. | 3 | 24 | Jeff Gordon | Chevrolet | DuPont | 73/0 | 393 | Running | $120,678 |
| 31. | 41 | 49 | Ken Schrader | Dodge | Schwan's Home Service | 70/0 | 393 | Running | $71,650 |
| 32. | 27 | 84 | Kyle Busch | Chevrolet | CARQUEST | 67/0 | 393 | Running | $69,025 |
| 33. | 7 | 77 | Brendan Gaughan* | Dodge | Kodak EasyShare/Jasper | 64/0 | 392 | Running | $77,500 |
| 34. | 38 | 50 | Derrike Cope | Dodge | Bennett Lane Winery | 61/0 | 391 | Running | $69,670 |
| 35. | 2 | 12 | Ryan Newman | Dodge | ALLTEL | 58/0 | 390 | Engine | $120,417 |
| 36. | 18 | 6 | Mark Martin | Ford | Viagra | 55/0 | 387 | Running | $76,425 |
| 37. | 35 | 5 | Terry Labonte | Chevrolet | Kellogg's | 52/0 | 385 | Running | $95,045 |
| 38. | 42 | 45 | Kyle Petty | Dodge | Krazy Kritters/G.-Pacific/Brawny | 49/0 | 384 | Running | $68,185 |
| 39. | 36 | 40 | Sterling Marlin | Dodge | U.S. Marines/Coors Light | 46/0 | 331 | Rear end | $101,075 |
| 40. | 39 | 30 | Johnny Sauter* | Chevrolet | America Online | 43/0 | 203 | Accident | $75,965 |
| 41. | 43 | 02 | Hermie Sadler | Chevrolet | Zapf Creations | 40/0 | 137 | Ignition | $67,855 |
| 42. | 31 | 09 | Bobby Hamilton Jr. | Dodge | Miccosukee Resort | 37/0 | 73 | Handling | $67,760 |
| 43. | 22 | 51 | Kevin Lepage | Chevrolet | NegotiationsSeminar.com | PE | 56 | Overheating | $67,642 |

*Rookie. Time of race: 4 hours, 12 minutes, 10 seconds. Average speed: 142.763 mph. Margin of victory: Under caution. Caution flags: 7 for 37 laps. 161-166 (Car 30—accident, Turn 2); 235-243 (debris); 338-344 (Car 1—spin, trioval); 350-355 (debris); 369-373 (Cars 12, 50—accident, Turn 2); 395-397 (oil on track); 400 (Car 18—accident, Turn 2). Lap leaders: 16 lead changes among 7 drivers. Jimmie Johnson 1-53, Elliott Sadler 54-58, Johnson 59-63, Sadler 64-71, Johnson 72-130, Sadler 131-145, Johnson 146-162, Sadler 163-175, Johnson 176-229, Casey Mears 230-231, Johnson 232-295, Kasey Kahne 296-300, Matt Kenseth 301, Dale Earnhardt Jr. 302-303, Johnson 304-368, Jamie McMurray 369-383, Johnson 384-400. Pole winner: Jimmie Johnson, 187.052 mph (record). Dropped to rear: Brendan Gaughan (backup car), Robby Gordon (drivers meeting), Ward Burton, Sterling Marlin, Scott Wimmer (engine changes). Failed to qualify: Steve Park, Todd Bodine, Carl Long, Stanton Barrett, Geoffrey Bodine, Morgan Shepherd, Jeff Fultz, Kirk Shelmerdine, Andy Hillenburg. Estimated crowd: 180,000.

## POINTS STANDINGS

| Rk. | Driver | Behind | | Rk. | Driver | Behind |
|-----|--------|--------|---|-----|--------|--------|
| 1. | Dale Earnhardt Jr. | — | | 6. | Bobby Labonte | -244 |
| 2. | Jimmie Johnson | -5 | | 7. | Elliott Sadler | -261 |
| 3. | Matt Kenseth | -111 | | 8. | Kurt Busch | -277 |
| 4. | Jeff Gordon | -144 | | 9. | Ryan Newman | -298 |
| 5. | Tony Stewart | -211 | | 10. | Kevin Harvick | -300 |

# MBNA 400 'A SALUTE TO HEROES' - -DOVER INTERNATIONAL SPEEDWAY

**Dover, Del.—1-mile banked concrete oval • June 6, 2004—400 miles—400 laps**

| Fin. | St. | Car | Driver | Make | Sponsor | Pts./Bonus | Laps | Status | Winnings |
|------|-----|-----|--------|------|---------|-----------|------|--------|----------|
| 1. | 7 | 6 | Mark Martin | Ford | Viagra | 185/5 | 400 | Running | $271,900 |
| 2. | 10 | 20 | Tony Stewart | Chevrolet | The Home Depot | 180/10 | 400 | Running | $227,978 |
| 3. | 26 | 8 | Dale Earnhardt Jr. | Chevrolet | Budweiser | 165/0 | 400 | Running | $186,828 |
| 4. | 22 | 99 | Jeff Burton | Ford | Roush Racing | 165/5 | 400 | Running | $149,172 |
| 5. | 23 | 10 | Scott Riggs* | Chevrolet | Valvoline | 155/0 | 400 | Running | $126,487 |
| 6. | 8 | 15 | Michael Waltrip | Chevrolet | NAPA | 150/0 | 399 | Running | $123,611 |
| 7. | 34 | 5 | Terry Labonte | Chevrolet | Kellogg's | 146/0 | 399 | Running | $118,335 |
| 8. | 1 | 19 | Jeremy Mayfield | Dodge | Dodge Dealers/UAW | 147/5 | 399 | Running | $116,065 |
| 9. | 21 | 22 | Scott Wimmer* | Dodge | Caterpillar | 138/0 | 398 | Running | $104,110 |
| 10. | 33 | 29 | Kevin Harvick | Chevrolet | GM Goodwrench | 134/0 | 398 | Running | $116,538 |
| 11. | 29 | 88 | Dale Jarrett | Ford | UPS | 130/0 | 398 | Running | $107,967 |
| 12. | 11 | 97 | Kurt Busch | Ford | Sharpie/IRWIN Industrial Tools | 127/0 | 398 | Running | $91,535 |
| 13. | 4 | 2 | Rusty Wallace | Dodge | Miller Lite | 124/0 | 398 | Running | $114,578 |
| 14. | 24 | 31 | Robby Gordon | Chevrolet | Cingular Wireless | 121/0 | 398 | Running | $106,022 |
| 15. | 9 | 42 | Jamie McMurray | Dodge | Texaco/Havoline | 118/0 | 397 | Running | $82,510 |
| 16. | 31 | 32 | Ricky Craven | Chevrolet | Tide | 115/0 | 395 | Running | $93,310 |
| 17. | 41 | 4 | Jimmy Spencer | Chevrolet | Morgan-McClure | 112/0 | 392 | Running | $82,125 |
| 18. | 6 | 38 | Elliott Sadler | Ford | M&M's | 109/0 | 391 | Running | $106,243 |
| 19. | 25 | 0 | Ward Burton | Chevrolet | NetZero HiSpeed | 106/0 | 391 | Running | $70,285 |
| 20. | 37 | 30 | Johnny Sauter* | Chevrolet | America Online | 103/0 | 386 | Running | $79,585 |
| 21. | 12 | 9 | Kasey Kahne* | Dodge | Dodge Dealers/UAW | 105/5 | 381 | Accident | $103,960 |
| 22. | 39 | 17 | Matt Kenseth | Ford | DeWalt Power Tools | 97/0 | 381 | Accident | $115,913 |
| 23. | 3 | 25 | Brian Vickers* | Chevrolet | GMAC Financial Services | 99/5 | 380 | Accident | $76,810 |
| 24. | 2 | 12 | Ryan Newman | Dodge | ALLTEL | 96/5 | 374 | Running | $111,297 |
| 25. | 18 | 18 | Bobby Labonte | Chevrolet | MBNA/D-Day 60th Anniversary | 88/0 | 370 | Running | $108,938 |
| 26. | 40 | 16 | Greg Biffle | Ford | National Guard | 85/0 | 370 | Running | $74,005 |
| 27. | 5 | 77 | Brendan Gaughan* | Dodge | Jasper Eng. & Trans. | 82/0 | 361 | Running | $73,335 |
| 28. | 17 | 41 | Casey Mears | Dodge | Target | 79/0 | 356 | Running | $73,194 |
| 29. | 16 | 40 | Sterling Marlin | Dodge | Coors Light | 81/5 | 352 | Accident | $97,155 |
| 30. | 28 | 21 | Ricky Rudd | Ford | Keep it Genuine | 73/0 | 351 | Accident | $88,061 |
| 31. | 19 | 43 | Jeff Green | Dodge | Cheerios/Betty Crocker | 70/0 | 349 | Accident | $87,605 |
| 32. | 14 | 48 | Jimmie Johnson | Chevrolet | Lowe's | 72/5 | 345 | Accident | $80,995 |
| 33. | 27 | 23 | Dave Blaney | Dodge | Ollie's Bargain Outlet | PE | 344 | Accident | $61,045 |
| 34. | 15 | 49 | Ken Schrader | Dodge | Schwan's Home Service | 61/0 | 337 | Running | $60,860 |
| 35. | 36 | 50 | Mike Wallace | Dodge | GEICO | 58/0 | 239 | Wheel bearing | $61,570 |
| 36. | 13 | 24 | Jeff Gordon | Chevrolet | DuPont | 55/0 | 221 | Accident | $107,908 |
| 37. | 30 | 45 | Kyle Petty | Dodge | Georgia-Pacific/Brawny | 52/0 | 217 | Handling | $60,375 |
| 38. | 32 | 01 | Joe Nemechek | Chevrolet | U.S. Army | 49/0 | 156 | Accident | $68,265 |
| 39. | 43 | 72 | Kirk Shelmerdine | Ford | Freddie B's | 46/0 | 53 | Handling | $60,151 |
| 40. | 35 | 09 | Tony Raines | Dodge | Miccosukee Resort | 43/0 | 50 | Handling | $60,025 |
| 41. | 38 | 51 | Kevin Lepage | Chevrolet | NegotiationsSeminar.com | 40/0 | 38 | Transmission | $59,895 |
| 42. | 42 | 89 | Morgan Shepherd | Dodge | Red Line Oil | 37/0 | 9 | Handling | $59,800 |
| 43. | 20 | 94 | Stanton Barrett | Chevrolet | Husqvarna | 34/0 | 2 | Rear end | $59,684 |

*Rookie. Time of race: 4 hours, 7 minutes, 19 seconds. Average speed: 97.042 mph. Margin of victory: 1.702 seconds. Caution flags: 11 for 90 laps. 13-18 (Car 41—accident, front stretch); 32-37 (competition caution); 39-44 (Cars 38, 77—accident, Turn 1); 109-114 (debris); 159-164 (Car 01—accident, front stretch); 223-230 (Car 24—accident, Turn 2); 234-237 (debris); 321-345 (Car 12—accident, Turn 4); 347-354 (Cars 0, 2, 6, 10, 12, 15, 16, 19, 21, 23, 29, 40, 41, 42, 43, 48, 88, 97, 99—accident, Turn 3); 375-380 (Car 2—accident, Turn 3); 383-391 (Cars 9, 31, 25, 17—accident, Turn 4). Note: The race was red-flagged on Lap 348 for 19:23 and on Lap 383 for 19:39. Lap leaders: 13 lead changes among 9 drivers. Jeremy Mayfield 1-18, Brian Vickers 19-25, Mayfield 26-33, Jeff Burton 34-48, Tony Stewart 49-118, Mayfield 119-150, Stewart 151-160, Sterling Marlin 161, Stewart 162-315, Jimmie Johnson 316, Ryan Newman 317-325, Mayfield 326-345, Kasey Kahne 346-381, Mark Martin 382-400. Pole winner: Jeremy Mayfield, 161.522 mph (record). Dropped to rear: Michael Waltrip, Greg Biffle, Morgan Shepherd (backup cars); Stanton Barrett, Matt Kenseth (engine changes). Failed to qualify: Hermie Sadler, Todd Bodine, Larry Gunselman. Estimated attendance: 140,000.

## POINTS STANDINGS

| Rk. | Driver | Behind | | Rk. | Driver | Behind |
|-----|--------|--------|---|-----|--------|--------|
| 1. | Dale Earnhardt Jr. | — | | 6. | Kurt Busch | -315 |
| 2. | Jimmie Johnson | -98 | | 7. | Elliott Sadler | -317 |
| 3. | Matt Kenseth | -179 | | 8. | Bobby Labonte | -321 |
| 4. | Tony Stewart | -196 | | 9. | Kevin Harvick | -331 |
| 5. | Jeff Gordon | -254 | | 10. | Ryan Newman | -367 |

**Pocono, Pa.—2.5-mile banked triangular paved • June 13, 2004—500 miles—200 laps**

| Fin. | St. | Car | Driver | Make | Sponsor | Pts./Bonus | Laps | Status | Winnings |
|------|-----|-----|--------|------|---------|-----------|------|--------|----------|
| 1. | 5 | 48 | Jimmie Johnson | Chevrolet | Lowe's | 190/10 | 200 | Running | $186,950 |
| 2. | 7 | 19 | Jeremy Mayfield | Dodge | Dodge Dealers/UAW | 175/5 | 200 | Running | $149,495 |
| 3. | 17 | 18 | Bobby Labonte | Chevrolet | Interstate Batteries | 170/5 | 200 | Running | $139,953 |
| 4. | 6 | 24 | Jeff Gordon | Chevrolet | DuPont | 165/5 | 200 | Running | $132,858 |
| 5. | 27 | 97 | Kurt Busch | Ford | IRWIN Industrial Tools | 155/0 | 200 | Running | $95,600 |
| 6. | 16 | 8 | Dale Earnhardt Jr. | Chevrolet | Budweiser | 150/0 | 200 | Running | $121,718 |
| 7. | 19 | 5 | Terry Labonte | Chevrolet | Kellogg's | 151/5 | 200 | Running | $96,640 |
| 8. | 13 | 31 | Robby Gordon | Chevrolet | Cingular Wireless | 142/0 | 200 | Running | $98,377 |
| 9. | 14 | 42 | Jamie McMurray | Dodge | Texaco/Havoline | 138/0 | 200 | Running | $75,390 |
| 10. | 21 | 41 | Casey Mears | Dodge | Target | 134/0 | 200 | Running | $82,090 |
| 11. | 9 | 16 | Greg Biffle | Ford | Pennzoil/National Guard | 135/5 | 200 | Running | $71,240 |
| 12. | 12 | 38 | Elliott Sadler | Ford | M&M's | 127/0 | 200 | Running | $96,183 |
| 13. | 2 | 25 | Brian Vickers* | Chevrolet | GMAC Financial Services | 129/5 | 200 | Running | $71,215 |
| 14. | 1 | 9 | Kasey Kahne* | Dodge | Dodge Dealers/UAW | 126/5 | 200 | Running | $107,990 |
| 15. | 32 | 43 | Jeff Green | Dodge | Cheerios/Betty Crocker | 118/0 | 200 | Running | $87,740 |
| 16. | 40 | 10 | Scott Riggs* | Chevrolet | Valvoline | 115/0 | 200 | Running | $89,777 |
| 17. | 26 | 0 | Ward Burton | Chevrolet | NetZero HiSpeed | 112/0 | 200 | Running | $59,290 |
| 18. | 3 | 01 | Joe Nemechek | Chevrolet | U.S. Army | 114/5 | 200 | Running | $85,090 |
| 19. | 35 | 21 | Ricky Rudd | Ford | Keep it Genuine | 106/0 | 200 | Running | $84,696 |
| 20. | 23 | 29 | Kevin Harvick | Chevrolet | GM Goodwrench | 103/0 | 200 | Running | $95,593 |
| 21. | 15 | 17 | Matt Kenseth | Ford | DeWalt Power Tools | 105/5 | 200 | Running | $105,918 |
| 22. | 37 | 50 | P.J. Jones | Dodge | Arnold Development Co. | 102/5 | 198 | Running | $57,790 |
| 23. | 33 | 4 | Jimmy Spencer | Chevrolet | Morgan-McClure | 94/0 | 198 | Running | $68,890 |
| 24. | 39 | 99 | Jeff Burton | Ford | Duke Children's Hospital | 91/0 | 196 | Engine | $90,632 |
| 25. | 18 | 49 | Ken Schrader | Dodge | Schwan's Home Service | 88/0 | 196 | Running | $56,915 |
| 26. | 10 | 88 | Dale Jarrett | Ford | UPS | 90/5 | 195 | Engine | $88,082 |
| 27. | 8 | 20 | Tony Stewart | Chevrolet | The Home Depot | 87/5 | 194 | Running | $100,393 |
| 28. | 43 | 98 | Geoffrey Bodine | Ford | Lucas Oil | 79/0 | 194 | Running | $53,465 |
| 29. | 29 | 30 | Dave Blaney | Chevrolet | America Online | 76/0 | 191 | Running | $63,790 |
| 30. | 11 | 12 | Ryan Newman | Dodge | ALLTEL | 78/5 | 183 | Accident | $100,007 |
| 31. | 20 | 40 | Sterling Marlin | Dodge | Coors Light | 75/5 | 176 | Accident | $86,490 |
| 32. | 30 | 2 | Rusty Wallace | Dodge | Miller Lite | 67/0 | 167 | Accident | $96,673 |
| 33. | 22 | 15 | Michael Waltrip | Chevrolet | NAPA | 64/0 | 166 | Accident | $89,621 |
| 34. | 34 | 32 | Ricky Craven | Chevrolet | Tide | 61/0 | 152 | Engine | $68,829 |
| 35. | 24 | 22 | Scott Wimmer* | Dodge | Caterpillar | 58/0 | 125 | Accident | $60,265 |
| 36. | 4 | 6 | Mark Martin | Ford | Viagra | 60/5 | 112 | Engine | $60,065 |
| 37. | 25 | 45 | Kyle Petty | Dodge | Georgia-Pacific/Brawny | 52/0 | 101 | Engine | $51,900 |
| 38. | 41 | 89 | Morgan Shepherd | Dodge | Racing For Jesus/Red Line Oil | 49/0 | 71 | Handling | $51,785 |
| 39. | 31 | 77 | Brendan Gaughan* | Dodge | Kodak/Jasper | 46/0 | 59 | Engine | $59,660 |
| 40. | 42 | 72 | Kirk Shelmerdine | Ford | L.R. Lyons & Sons Transportation | 43/0 | 42 | Wheel bearing | $51,505 |
| 41. | 38 | 00 | Carl Long | Chevrolet | Buyers Choice Auto Warranty | 40/0 | 39 | Accident | $51,365 |
| 42. | 28 | 37 | Todd Bodine | Pontiac | Carter's Royal Dispos-all | 37/0 | 11 | Overheating | $51,275 |
| 43. | 36 | 51 | Kevin Lepage | Chevrolet | NegotiationsSeminar.com | 34/0 | 9 | Overheating | $51,459 |

*Rookie. Time of race: 4 hours, 27 minutes, 33 seconds. Average speed: 112.129 mph. Margin of victory: Under caution. Caution flags: 11 for 57 laps. 2-5 (oil on track); 51-54 (Car 0—spin, Turn 2); 61-66 (oil on track); 114-117 (oil on track); 121-131 (Cars 40, 22—accident, short chute); 156-162 (oil on track); 168-172 (Cars 15, 2—accident, Turn 2); 177-180 (Car 20—accident, Turn 1); 184-188 (Car 12—accident, Turn 3); 190-192 (oil on track); 197-200 (oil on track). Lap leaders: 30 lead changes among 16 drivers. Kasey Kahne-pole, Joe Nemechek 1-10, Jimmie Johnson 11-35, P.J. Jones 36, Johnson 37-50, Dale Jarrett 51, Kahne 52, Sterling Marlin 53-54, Johnson 55, Brian Vickers 56, Johnson 57-71, Jeff Gordon 72-85, Johnson 86-89, Greg Biffle 90, Ryan Newman 91, Terry Labonte 92, Tony Stewart 93, Mark Martin 94-95, Jarrett 96, Bobby Labonte 97, Matt Kenseth 98, Kahne 99, Johnson 100-113, Biffle 114, Newman 115-131, Johnson 132-156, Kenseth 157-160, Kahne 161-162, J. Gordon 163-167, Jeremy Mayfield 168-172, Johnson 173-200. Pole winner: Kasey Kahne, 172.533 mph (record). Dropped to rear: Morgan Shepherd, Geoffrey Bodine (engine changes). Failed to qualify: Stanton Barrett, Andy Hillenburg. Estimated attendance: 90,000.

## POINTS STANDINGS

| Rk. | Driver | Behind | | Rk. | Driver | Behind |
|-----|--------|--------|---|-----|--------|--------|
| 1. | Dale Earnhardt Jr. | — | | 6. | Bobby Labonte | -301 |
| 2. | Jimmie Johnson | -58 | | 7. | Kurt Busch | -310 |
| 3. | Matt Kenseth | -224 | | 8. | Elliott Sadler | -340 |
| 4. | Jeff Gordon | -239 | | 9. | Kevin Harvick | -378 |
| 5. | Tony Stewart | -259 | | 10. | Ryan Newman | -439 |

**Brooklyn, Mich.—2-mile banked paved oval • June 20, 2004—400 miles—200 laps**

| Fin. | St. | Car | Driver | Make | Sponsor | Pts./Bonus | Laps | Status | Winnings |
|------|-----|-----|--------|------|---------|-----------|------|--------|----------|
| 1. | 4 | 12 | Ryan Newman | Dodge | ALLTEL | 185/5 | 200 | Running | $176,367 |
| 2. | 34 | 9 | Kasey Kahne* | Dodge | Dodge Dealers/UAW | 170/0 | 200 | Running | $155,900 |
| 3. | 37 | 88 | Dale Jarrett | Ford | UPS | 170/5 | 200 | Running | $142,817 |
| 4. | 3 | 48 | Jimmie Johnson | Chevrolet | Lowe's | 165/5 | 200 | Running | $100,600 |
| 5. | 22 | 38 | Elliott Sadler | Ford | M&M's | 160/5 | 200 | Running | $113,508 |
| 6. | 24 | 40 | Sterling Marlin | Dodge | Coors Light | 155/5 | 200 | Running | $108,665 |
| 7. | 18 | 17 | Matt Kenseth | Ford | Carhartt/DeWalt Power Tools | 151/5 | 200 | Running | $119,093 |
| 8. | 12 | 18 | Bobby Labonte | Chevrolet | Interstate Batteries | 142/0 | 200 | Running | $111,723 |
| 9. | 2 | 25 | Brian Vickers* | Chevrolet | GMAC Financial Services | 138/0 | 200 | Running | $79,190 |
| 10. | 19 | 15 | Michael Waltrip | Chevrolet | NAPA | 134/0 | 200 | Running | $103,846 |
| 11. | 7 | 97 | Kurt Busch | Ford | Sharpie | 130/0 | 200 | Running | $85,705 |
| 12. | 25 | 21 | Ricky Rudd | Ford | Keep it Genuine | 127/0 | 200 | Running | $94,121 |
| 13. | 17 | 99 | Jeff Burton | Ford | Roush Racing | 124/0 | 200 | Running | $101,807 |
| 14. | 29 | 22 | Scott Wimmer* | Dodge | Caterpillar | 121/0 | 200 | Running | $91,865 |
| 15. | 39 | 30 | Dave Blaney | Chevrolet | America Online | 118/0 | 200 | Running | $75,415 |
| 16. | 6 | 77 | Brendan Gaughan* | Dodge | Jasper Engines/Kodak | 120/5 | 200 | Running | $74,065 |
| 17. | 21 | 29 | Kevin Harvick | Chevrolet | GM Goodwrench | 112/0 | 200 | Running | $101,043 |
| 18. | 33 | 45 | Kyle Petty | Dodge | Georgia-Pacific/Brawny | 109/0 | 200 | Running | $79,865 |
| 19. | 8 | 19 | Jeremy Mayfield | Dodge | Dodge Dealers/UAW | 106/0 | 200 | Running | $85,465 |
| 20. | 20 | 10 | Scott Riggs* | Chevrolet | Valvoline | 108/5 | 200 | Running | $91,202 |
| 21. | 11 | 8 | Dale Earnhardt Jr. | Chevrolet | Budweiser | 100/0 | 200 | Running | $107,593 |
| 22. | 10 | 2 | Rusty Wallace | Dodge | Miller Lite | 102/5 | 200 | Running | $104,048 |
| 23. | 13 | 16 | Greg Biffle | Ford | National Guard/Subway | 94/0 | 200 | Running | $72,190 |
| 24. | 27 | 20 | Tony Stewart | Chevrolet | The Home Depot | 91/0 | 200 | Running | $106,543 |
| 25. | 35 | 50 | P.J. Jones | Dodge | Arnold Development Co. | 88/0 | 199 | Accident | $63,140 |
| 26. | 31 | 5 | Terry Labonte | Chevrolet | Kellogg's | 85/0 | 199 | Accident | $89,140 |
| 27. | 23 | 43 | Jeff Green | Dodge | Cheerios/Betty Crocker | 82/0 | 199 | Running | $88,375 |
| 28. | 36 | 4 | Jimmy Spencer | Chevrolet | Morgan-McClure | 79/0 | 198 | Running | $72,475 |
| 29. | 26 | 32 | Ricky Craven | Chevrolet | Tide | 76/0 | 194 | Running | $77,654 |
| 30. | 14 | 0 | Ward Burton | Chevrolet | NetZero HiSpeed | 73/0 | 191 | Engine | $59,190 |
| 31. | 9 | 41 | Casey Mears | Dodge | Target | 70/0 | 191 | Running | $58,540 |
| 32. | 42 | 98 | Geoffrey Bodine | Ford | Lucas Oil | 67/0 | 190 | Running | $58,465 |
| 33. | 5 | 31 | Robby Gordon | Chevrolet | Cingular Wireless | 64/0 | 188 | Running | $94,502 |
| 34. | 15 | 6 | Mark Martin | Ford | Viagra | 61/0 | 182 | Running | $66,285 |
| 35. | 16 | 01 | Joe Nemechek | Chevrolet | U.S. Army | 58/0 | 174 | Engine | $66,145 |
| 36. | 38 | 37 | Todd Bodine | Dodge | Carter's Royal Dispos-all | 55/0 | 170 | Vibration | $58,095 |
| 37. | 30 | 42 | Jamie McMurray | Dodge | Texaco/Havoline | 52/0 | 114 | Engine | $66,045 |
| 38. | 1 | 24 | Jeff Gordon | Chevrolet | DuPont | 59/10 | 88 | Engine | $120,923 |
| 39. | 28 | 49 | Ken Schrader | Dodge | Schwan's Home Service | 46/0 | 86 | Engine | $57,900 |
| 40. | 40 | 89 | Morgan Shepherd | Dodge | Red Line Oil/Racing with Jesus | 43/0 | 76 | Handling | $57,865 |
| 41. | 32 | 51 | Kevin Lepage | Chevrolet | NegotiationsSeminar.com | 40/0 | 71 | Overheating | $57,830 |
| 42. | 43 | 02 | Derrike Cope | Chevrolet | The FanZCar/ETT | 37/0 | 37 | Ignition | $57,790 |
| 43. | 41 | 72 | Kirk Shelmerdine | Ford | Freddie B's | 34/0 | 13 | Handling | $57,108 |

*Rookie. Time of race: 2 hours, 52 minutes, 18 seconds. Average speed: 139.292 mph. Margin of victory: Under caution. Caution flags: 9 for 33 laps. 2-4 (Car 31—spin, back stretch); 34-38 (debris); 90-93 (oil on track); 116-120 (oil on track); 151-155 (debris); 160-163 (Car 32—spin, back stretch); 175-177 (oil on track); 194-196 (Cars 16, 20—accident, Turn 4); 200 (Car 50—accident, Turn 3). Lap leaders: 17 lead changes among 10 drivers. Jeff Gordon 1-78, Jimmie Johnson 79-82, Matt Kenseth 83, Scott Riggs 84, J. Gordon 85-87, Johnson 88-89, Rusty Wallace 90-96, Dale Jarrett 97-103, Brendan Gaughan 104-116, Jarrett 117, Elliott Sadler 118-129, Sterling Marlin 130-151, Jarrett 152, Marlin 153-174, Jarrett 175-177, Ryan Newman 178-182, Jarrett 183, Newman 184-200. Pole winner: Jeff Gordon, 190.865 mph (record). Dropped to rear: Tony Stewart (drivers meeting), Dave Blaney (backup car), Terry Labonte, Geoffrey Bodine (engine changes). Failed to qualify: Kerry Earnhardt, Carl Long. Estimated attendance: 140,000.

## POINTS STANDINGS

| Rk. | Driver | Behind | | Rk. | Driver | Behind |
|-----|--------|--------|---|-----|--------|--------|
| 1. | Jimmie Johnson | — | | 6. | Jeff Gordon | -287 |
| 2. | Dale Earnhardt Jr. | -7 | | 7. | Elliott Sadler | -287 |
| 3. | Matt Kenseth | -180 | | 8. | Kurt Busch | -287 |
| 4. | Bobby Labonte | -266 | | 9. | Ryan Newman | -361 |
| 5. | Tony Stewart | -275 | | 10. | Kevin Harvick | -373 |

Sonoma, Calif.—1.99-mile paved road course • June 27, 2004—219 miles—110 laps

**2004 SEASON**

| Fin. | St. | Car | Driver | Make | Sponsor | Pts./Bonus | Laps | Status | Winnings |
|------|-----|-----|--------|------|---------|-----------|------|--------|----------|
| 1. | 1 | 24 | Jeff Gordon | Chevrolet | DuPont | 190/10 | 110 | Running | $388,103 |
| 2. | 11 | 42 | Jamie McMurray | Dodge | Texaco/Havoline | 170/0 | 110 | Running | $176,500 |
| 3. | 6 | 39 | Scott Pruett | Dodge | Target | 170/5 | 110 | Running | $120,100 |
| 4. | 40 | 15 | Michael Waltrip | Chevrolet | NAPA | 160/0 | 110 | Running | $147,646 |
| 5. | 34 | 48 | Jimmie Johnson | Chevrolet | Lowe's | 155/0 | 110 | Running | $112,915 |
| 6. | 19 | 36 | Boris Said | Chevrolet | Centrix | 150/0 | 110 | Running | $79,165 |
| 7. | 29 | 41 | Casey Mears | Dodge | Target | 151/5 | 110 | Running | $100,265 |
| 8. | 4 | 6 | Mark Martin | Ford | Viagra | 147/5 | 110 | Running | $89,315 |
| 9. | 13 | 99 | Jeff Burton | Ford | Roush Racing | 138/0 | 110 | Running | $108,482 |
| 10. | 16 | 38 | Elliott Sadler | Ford | M&M's | 134/0 | 110 | Running | $109,943 |
| 11. | 20 | 8 | Dale Earnhardt Jr. | Chevrolet | Budweiser | 135/5 | 110 | Running | $114,078 |
| 12. | 8 | 29 | Kevin Harvick | Chevrolet | GM Goodwrench | 127/0 | 110 | Running | $105,838 |
| 13. | 7 | 16 | Greg Biffle | Ford | National Guard/Travelodge | 124/0 | 110 | Running | $76,475 |
| 14. | 22 | 12 | Ryan Newman | Dodge | ALLTEL | 121/0 | 110 | Running | $106,742 |
| 15. | 17 | 20 | Tony Stewart | Chevrolet | The Home Depot | 123/5 | 110 | Running | $107,653 |
| 16. | 42 | 32 | Ricky Craven | Chevrolet | Tide | 115/0 | 110 | Running | $86,150 |
| 17. | 38 | 59 | Klaus Graf | Dodge | SEM/Color Horizons | 112/0 | 110 | Running | $58,925 |
| 18. | 23 | 88 | Dale Jarrett | Ford | UPS | 109/0 | 110 | Running | $93,742 |
| 19. | 28 | 30 | Jim Inglebright | Chevrolet | America Online | 106/0 | 110 | Running | $70,550 |
| 20. | 5 | 17 | Matt Kenseth | Ford | DeWalt Power Tools | 103/0 | 110 | Running | $111,603 |
| 21. | 26 | 40 | Sterling Marlin | Dodge | Coors Light | 100/0 | 110 | Running | $95,275 |
| 22. | 39 | 25 | Brian Vickers* | Chevrolet | GMAC Financial Services | 97/0 | 110 | Running | $71,550 |
| 23. | 18 | 49 | Ken Schrader | Dodge | Schwan's Home Service | 94/0 | 110 | Running | $61,900 |
| 24. | 14 | 0 | Ward Burton | Chevrolet | NetZero HiSpeed | 91/0 | 110 | Running | $62,630 |
| 25. | 25 | 22 | Scott Wimmer* | Dodge | Caterpillar | 88/0 | 110 | Running | $82,970 |
| 26. | 33 | 77 | Brendan Gaughan* | Dodge | Kodak/Jasper | 85/0 | 110 | Running | $69,425 |
| 27. | 36 | 43 | Jeff Green | Dodge | Cheerios/Spoonfuls of Stories | 82/0 | 110 | Running | $87,520 |
| 28. | 2 | 2 | Rusty Wallace | Dodge | Miller Lite | 79/0 | 109 | Gas | $102,883 |
| 29. | 9 | 01 | Joe Nemechek | Chevrolet | U.S. Army | 76/0 | 109 | Running | $79,515 |
| 30. | 21 | 19 | Jeremy Mayfield | Dodge | Dodge Dealers/UAW | 73/0 | 109 | Running | $77,849 |
| 31. | 30 | 9 | Kasey Kahne* | Dodge | Dodge Dealers/UAW | 70/0 | 109 | Running | $90,250 |
| 32. | 27 | 45 | Kyle Petty | Dodge | Georgia-Pacific/Brawny | 67/0 | 109 | Running | $57,800 |
| 33. | 10 | 18 | Bobby Labonte | Chevrolet | Interstate Batteries | 64/0 | 104 | Running | $103,773 |
| 34. | 24 | 31 | Robby Gordon | Chevrolet | Cingular Wireless | 61/0 | 100 | Running | $92,917 |
| 35. | 12 | 21 | Ricky Rudd | Ford | Motorcraft | 58/0 | 97 | Running | $83,751 |
| 36. | 3 | 97 | Kurt Busch | Ford | IRWIN Industrial Tools | 60/5 | 94 | Running | $78,160 |
| 37. | 43 | 98 | Larry Gunselman | Ford | Lucas Oil/Gibson Products | 52/0 | 87 | Gas | $57,625 |
| 38. | 32 | 61 | Austin Cameron | Chevrolet | McMillin Homes/NAPA Auto Care | 49/0 | 78 | Running | $57,590 |
| 39. | 31 | 50 | P.J. Jones | Dodge | Bennett Lane Winery | 46/0 | 71 | Rear gear | $57,550 |
| 40. | 15 | 5 | Terry Labonte | Chevrolet | Kellogg's | 43/0 | 67 | Engine | $84,250 |
| 41. | 37 | 02 | Brandon Ash | Ford | Fuerza-Ash Mtsps/Health Ed. Coun. | 40/0 | 63 | Rear gear | $57,450 |
| 42. | 41 | 10 | Scott Riggs* | Chevrolet | Valvoline | 37/0 | 51 | Accident | $82,597 |
| 43. | 35 | 72 | Tom Hubert | Ford | Freddie B's | 34/0 | 5 | Too slow | $57,615 |

*Rookie. Time of race: 2 hours, 49 minutes, 34 seconds. Average speed: 77.456 mph. Margin of victory: 1.032 seconds. Caution flags: 6 for 13 laps. 4-5 (Cars 0, 20—spin, Turn 1); 17-18 (Car 31—accident, Turn 10); 46-48 (oil on track); 68-69 (Car 61—accident, Turn 7); 72-73 (Car 10—accident, Turn 10); 81-82 (debris). Lap leaders: 9 lead changes among 7 drivers. Jeff Gordon-pole, Kurt Busch 1, J. Gordon 2-34, Mark Martin 35, Tony Stewart 36, Dale Earnhardt Jr. 37-45, J. Gordon 46-67, Scott Pruett 68, Casey Mears 69-73, J. Gordon 74-110. Pole winner: Jeff Gordon, 94.303 mph (record). Dropped to rear: Matt Kenseth (backup car), Scott Riggs (missed driver introductions), Jeremy Mayfield, Michael Waltrip (engine changes). Failed to qualify: Morgan Shepherd. Estimated attendance: 100,000.

## POINTS STANDINGS

| Rk. | Driver | Behind | | Rk. | Driver | Behind |
|-----|--------|--------|---|-----|--------|--------|
| 1. | Jimmie Johnson | — | | 6. | Elliott Sadler | -308 |
| 2. | Dale Earnhardt Jr. | -27 | | 7. | Bobby Labonte | -357 |
| 3. | Matt Kenseth | -232 | | 8. | Kurt Busch | -382 |
| 4. | Jeff Gordon | -252 | | 9. | Ryan Newman | -395 |
| 5. | Tony Stewart | -307 | | 10. | Kevin Harvick | -401 |

**Daytona Beach, Fla.—2.5-mile high-banked paved trioval • July 3, 2004—400 miles—160 laps**

| Fin. | St. | Car | Driver | Make | Sponsor | Pts./Bonus | Laps | Status | Winnings |
|---|---|---|---|---|---|---|---|---|---|
| 1. | 1 | 24 | Jeff Gordon | Chevrolet | DuPont/Pepsi | 190/10 | 160 | Running | $346,703 |
| 2. | 19 | 48 | Jimmie Johnson | Chevrolet | Lowe's | 170/0 | 160 | Running | $193,125 |
| 3. | 5 | 8 | Dale Earnhardt Jr. | Chevrolet | Budweiser | 170/5 | 160 | Running | $196,528 |
| 4. | 35 | 97 | Kurt Busch | Ford | Coca-Cola C2/Sharpie | 160/0 | 160 | Running | $142,625 |
| 5. | 17 | 20 | Tony Stewart | Chevrolet | The Home Depot/Coca-Cola C2 | 160/5 | 160 | Running | $149,628 |
| 6. | 21 | 6 | Mark Martin | Ford | Viagra | 150/0 | 160 | Running | $108,375 |
| 7. | 15 | 18 | Bobby Labonte | Chevrolet | Wellbutrin XL | 146/0 | 160 | Running | $135,658 |
| 8. | 10 | 5 | Terry Labonte | Chevrolet | Cheez-It/Spider-Man 2 | 142/0 | 160 | Running | $119,500 |
| 9. | 14 | 25 | Brian Vickers* | Chevrolet | GMAC Financial Services | 138/0 | 160 | Running | $99,050 |
| 10. | 6 | 01 | Joe Nemechek | Chevrolet | U.S. Army | 134/0 | 160 | Running | $114,625 |
| 11. | 24 | 41 | Casey Mears | Dodge | Target | 135/5 | 160 | Running | $101,575 |
| 12. | 13 | 12 | Ryan Newman | Dodge | ALLTEL | 132/5 | 160 | Running | $126,742 |
| 13. | 2 | 15 | Michael Waltrip | Chevrolet | NAPA | 129/5 | 160 | Running | $118,331 |
| 14. | 11 | 29 | Kevin Harvick | Chevrolet | Coca-Cola C2/GM Goodwrench | 121/0 | 160 | Running | $118,303 |
| 15. | 23 | 30 | Dave Blaney | Chevrolet | AOL Broadband | 123/5 | 160 | Running | $90,775 |
| 16. | 4 | 88 | Dale Jarrett | Ford | UPS | 115/0 | 160 | Running | $111,817 |
| 17. | 3 | 21 | Ricky Rudd | Ford | Coca-Cola C2/Motorcraft | 112/0 | 160 | Running | $107,356 |
| 18. | 34 | 98 | Bill Elliott | Dodge | Coca-Cola C2 | 109/0 | 160 | Running | $75,425 |
| 19. | 25 | 31 | Robby Gordon | Chevrolet | Cingular Wireless | 106/0 | 160 | Running | $109,862 |
| 20. | 22 | 40 | Sterling Marlin | Dodge | Coors Light | 103/0 | 160 | Running | $112,575 |
| 21. | 7 | 10 | Scott Riggs* | Chevrolet | Valvoline | 100/0 | 160 | Running | $101,987 |
| 22. | 16 | 19 | Jeremy Mayfield | Dodge | Dodge Dealers/UAW | 97/0 | 160 | Running | $97,075 |
| 23. | 26 | 99 | Jeff Burton | Ford | Coca-Cola C2 | 94/0 | 160 | Running | $109,642 |
| 24. | 33 | 45 | Kyle Petty | Dodge | Georgia-Pacific/Brawny | 91/0 | 160 | Running | $85,075 |
| 25. | 31 | 9 | Kasey Kahne* | Dodge | Dodge Dealers/UAW | 93/5 | 160 | Running | $103,700 |
| 26. | 39 | 38 | Elliott Sadler | Ford | M&M's | 85/0 | 160 | Running | $109,208 |
| 27. | 27 | 2 | Rusty Wallace | Dodge | Miller Lite | 82/0 | 160 | Running | $113,158 |
| 28. | 20 | 33 | Kerry Earnhardt | Chevrolet | Bass Pro Shops/TRACKER | 79/0 | 160 | Running | $68,700 |
| 29. | 40 | 4 | Jimmy Spencer | Chevrolet | Morgan-McClure | 76/0 | 159 | Running | $71,575 |
| 30. | 30 | 43 | Jeff Green | Dodge | Cheerios/Betty Crocker | 73/0 | 159 | Running | $98,050 |
| 31. | 9 | 16 | Greg Biffle | Ford | Coca-Cola C2/National Guard | 70/0 | 159 | Running | $79,125 |
| 32. | 37 | 22 | Scott Wimmer* | Dodge | Caterpillar | 67/0 | 159 | Running | $86,889 |
| 33. | 43 | 89 | Morgan Shepherd | Dodge | Racing With Jesus/Red Line Oil | 69/5 | 157 | Running | $68,800 |
| 34. | 42 | 96 | Larry Gunselman | Ford | Lucas Oil | 61/0 | 156 | Running | $67,750 |
| 35. | 29 | 49 | Ken Schrader | Dodge | Schwan's Home Service | 58/0 | 151 | Running | $67,615 |
| 36. | 12 | 77 | Brendan Gaughan* | Dodge | Kodak/Jasper Eng. & Trans. | 55/0 | 136 | Running | $75,450 |
| 37. | 32 | 42 | Jamie McMurray | Dodge | Texaco/Havoline | 52/0 | 126 | Oil pump | $75,300 |
| 38. | 38 | 32 | Ricky Craven | Chevrolet | Tide | 49/0 | 121 | Running | $75,150 |
| 39. | 36 | 17 | Matt Kenseth | Ford | Smirnoff Ice/DeWalt | 46/0 | 110 | Accident | $117,803 |
| 40. | 8 | 0 | Ward Burton | Chevrolet | NetZero HiSpeed | 43/0 | 84 | Running | $66,875 |
| 41. | 41 | 50 | Mike Wallace | Dodge | SportClips | 45/5 | 77 | Suspension | $66,750 |
| 42. | 28 | 09 | Bobby Hamilton Jr. | Dodge | Miccosukee Resort | 37/0 | 71 | Accident | $66,640 |
| 43. | 18 | 1 | John Andretti | Chevrolet | Coca-Cola C2 | 34/0 | 44 | Accident | $66,749 |

*Rookie. Time of race: 2 hours, 45 minutes, 23 seconds. Average speed: 145.117 mph. Margin of victory: .143 seconds. Caution flags: 5 for 25 laps. 1-9 (competition caution); 19-22 (Cars 0, 17, 32, 49—accident, Turn 2); 46-49 (Car 1—accident, Turn 4); 72-76 (debris); 78-80 (Cars 50, 77—accident, Turn 4). Lap leaders: 21 lead changes among 10 drivers. Jeff Gordon 1-9, Michael Waltrip 10-19, Kasey Kahne 20, Waltrip 21-45, Dale Earnhardt Jr. 46, Ryan Newman 47, Waltrip 48-54, Earnhardt 55-72, Mike Wallace 73, Morgan Shepherd 74, J. Gordon 75-85, Waltrip 86-98, J. Gordon 99-107, Waltrip 108-109, Earnhardt 110-112, J. Gordon 113-137, Earnhardt 138, Casey Mears 139, Dave Blaney 140, Newman 141, Tony Stewart 142-153, J. Gordon 154-160. Pole winner: Jeff Gordon, 188.659 mph. Dropped to rear: Ward Burton, Kasey Kahne (backup cars), Jeff Burton (engine change). Failed to qualify: Chad Blount, Tony Raines, Derrike Cope, Eric McClure, Kenny Wallace, Kirk Shelmerdine. Estimated attendance: 175,000.

## POINTS STANDINGS

| Rk. | Driver | Behind | Rk. | Driver | Behind |
|---|---|---|---|---|---|
| 1. | Jimmie Johnson | — | 6. | Bobby Labonte | -381 |
| 2. | Dale Earnhardt Jr. | -27 | 7. | Kurt Busch | -392 |
| 3. | Jeff Gordon | -232 | 8. | Elliott Sadler | -393 |
| 4. | Tony Stewart | -317 | 9. | Ryan Newman | -433 |
| 5. | Matt Kenseth | -356 | 10. | Kevin Harvick | -450 |

2004 SEASON

**Joliet, Ill.—1.5-mile banked paved oval • July 11, 2004—400.5 miles—267 laps**

| Fin. | St. | Car | Driver | Make | Sponsor | Pts./Bonus | Laps | Status | Winnings |
|---|---|---|---|---|---|---|---|---|---|
| 1. | 10 | 20 | Tony Stewart | Chevrolet | The Home Depot | 190/10 | 267 | Running | $336,803 |
| 2. | 3 | 48 | Jimmie Johnson | Chevrolet | Lowe's | 175/5 | 267 | Running | $208,640 |
| 3. | 29 | 88 | Dale Jarrett | Ford | UPS | 165/0 | 267 | Running | $188,592 |
| 4. | 1 | 24 | Jeff Gordon | Chevrolet | DuPont | 165/5 | 267 | Running | $172,453 |
| 5. | 19 | 19 | Jeremy Mayfield | Dodge | Dodge Dealers/UAW | 160/5 | 267 | Running | $130,575 |
| 6. | 24 | 5 | Terry Labonte | Chevrolet | Kellogg's | 155/5 | 267 | Running | $123,075 |
| 7. | 32 | 40 | Sterling Marlin | Dodge | Coors Light | 151/5 | 267 | Running | $126,200 |
| 8. | 9 | 01 | Joe Nemechek | Chevrolet | USG Sheetrock | 142/0 | 267 | Running | $112,850 |
| 9. | 39 | 15 | Michael Waltrip | Chevrolet | NAPA | 138/0 | 267 | Running | $124,556 |
| 10. | 17 | 29 | Kevin Harvick | Chevrolet | GM Goodwrench | 134/0 | 267 | Running | $122,053 |
| 11. | 20 | 2 | Rusty Wallace | Dodge | Miller Lite | 130/0 | 267 | Running | $121,908 |
| 12. | 26 | 17 | Matt Kenseth | Ford | DeWalt Power Tools | 132/5 | 267 | Running | $127,853 |
| 13. | 14 | 42 | Jamie McMurray | Dodge | Texaco/Havoline | 124/0 | 267 | Running | $88,100 |
| 14. | 4 | 25 | Brian Vickers* | Chevrolet | GMAC Financial Services | 121/0 | 267 | Running | $87,950 |
| 15. | 12 | 41 | Casey Mears | Dodge | Target | 118/0 | 267 | Running | $92,150 |
| 16. | 31 | 1 | John Andretti | Chevrolet | Kraft Foods | 115/0 | 267 | Running | $73,250 |
| 17. | 23 | 31 | Robby Gordon | Chevrolet | Cingular Wireless | 117/5 | 267 | Running | $107,837 |
| 18. | 11 | 18 | Bobby Labonte | Chevrolet | Wellbutrin XL | 114/5 | 267 | Running | $117,133 |
| 19. | 22 | 0 | Ward Burton | Chevrolet | NetZero HiSpeed | 106/0 | 267 | Running | $75,150 |
| 20. | 5 | 16 | Greg Biffle | Ford | National Guard | 103/0 | 267 | Running | $84,400 |
| 21. | 13 | 38 | Elliott Sadler | Ford | M&M's | 100/0 | 267 | Running | $109,083 |
| 22. | 25 | 8 | Dale Earnhardt Jr. | Chevrolet | Budweiser | 97/0 | 267 | Running | $116,828 |
| 23. | 40 | 22 | Scott Wimmer* | Dodge | Caterpillar | 94/0 | 267 | Running | $91,975 |
| 24. | 18 | 6 | Mark Martin | Ford | Viagra | 96/5 | 265 | Running | $79,850 |
| 25. | 34 | 4 | Jimmy Spencer | Chevrolet | Wide Open Energy Drink | 88/0 | 265 | Running | $71,550 |
| 26. | 42 | 45 | Kyle Petty | Dodge | Georgia-Pacific/Brawny | 85/0 | 265 | Running | $78,839 |
| 27. | 41 | 49 | Ken Schrader | Dodge | Red Baron | 82/0 | 263 | Running | $69,750 |
| 28. | 38 | 43 | Jeff Green | Dodge | Cheerios/Betty Crocker | 79/0 | 248 | Accident | $95,300 |
| 29. | 16 | 10 | Scott Riggs* | Chevrolet | Valvoline | 76/0 | 245 | Running | $94,037 |
| 30. | 15 | 77 | Brendan Gaughan* | Dodge | Jasper Eng. & Trans./Kodak | 73/0 | 240 | Running | $76,100 |
| 31. | 7 | 80 | Mike Bliss | Chevrolet | Slim Jim/Act II | 70/0 | 205 | Accident | $65,900 |
| 32. | 30 | 21 | Ricky Rudd | Ford | Keep it Genuine | 67/0 | 204 | Running | $91,256 |
| 33. | 6 | 99 | Jeff Burton | Ford | Comcast High-Speed Internet | 64/0 | 197 | Running | $99,342 |
| 34. | 8 | 12 | Ryan Newman | Dodge | Mobil 1/ALLTEL | 61/0 | 166 | Accident | $111,667 |
| 35. | 21 | 97 | Kurt Busch | Ford | Sharpie | 58/0 | 151 | Running | $84,600 |
| 36. | 2 | 9 | Kasey Kahne* | Dodge | Dodge Dealers/UAW | 60/5 | 136 | Accident | $94,275 |
| 37. | 36 | 30 | Dave Blaney | Chevrolet | America Online | 57/5 | 129 | Accident | $72,175 |
| 38. | 35 | 32 | Ricky Craven | Chevrolet | Tide | 49/0 | 116 | Engine | $71,975 |
| 39. | 43 | 50 | P.J. Jones | Dodge | Arnold Development Co. | 46/0 | 108 | Too slow | $63,765 |
| 40. | 33 | 02 | Hermie Sadler | Chevrolet | The FanZCar | 43/0 | 103 | Transmission | $63,555 |
| 41. | 28 | 09 | Bobby Hamilton Jr. | Dodge | Miccosukee Resort | 40/0 | 86 | Engine | $63,355 |
| 42. | 27 | 51 | Kevin Lepage | Chevrolet | NegotiationsSeminar.com | 42/5 | 34 | Fuel pump | $63,170 |
| 43. | 37 | 37 | Chad Blount | Dodge | Carter's Royal Dispos-all | 34/0 | 3 | Electrical | $63,207 |

*Rookie. Time of race: 3 hours, 5 minutes, 33 seconds. Average speed: 129.507 mph. Margin of victory: 2.925 seconds. Caution flags: 9 for 43 laps. 19-23 (Cars 12, 97—accident, Turn 2); 25-29 (oil on track); 40-42 (debris); 121-126 (oil on track); 128-134 (Cars 1, 8, 9, 10, 20, 24, 30, 99—accident, Turn 1); 173-177 (debris); 210-214 (Car 80—accident, Turn 2); 246-249 (debris); 254-256 (Car 43—accident, Turn 3). Lap leaders: 20 lead changes among 13 drivers. Jeff Gordon 1-14, Kasey Kahne 15-19, Terry Labonte 20, Kevin Lepage 21, Tony Stewart 22-83, Jimmie Johnson 84, Mark Martin 85-94, Sterling Marlin 95-99, Matt Kenseth 100, Dave Blaney 101, Robby Gordon 102-103, Stewart 104-121, Kahne 122-126, Stewart 127-173, Marlin 174, Stewart 175-180, Johnson 181-210, Bobby Labonte 211, Marlin 212-214, Jeremy Mayfield 215-240, Stewart 241-267. Pole winner: Jeff Gordon, 186.942 mph (record). Dropped to rear: Hermie Sadler, Chad Blount, Jeff Green (engine changes). Failed to qualify: Todd Bodine, Greg Sacks, Kirk Shelmerdine. Estimated attendance: 80,000.

## POINTS STANDINGS

| Rk. | Driver | Behind | | Rk. | Driver | Behind |
|---|---|---|---|---|---|---|
| 1. | Jimmie Johnson | — | | 6. | Bobby Labonte | -442 |
| 2. | Dale Earnhardt Jr. | -105 | | 7. | Elliott Sadler | -468 |
| 3. | Jeff Gordon | -242 | | 8. | Kevin Harvick | -491 |
| 4. | Tony Stewart | -302 | | 9. | Kurt Busch | -509 |
| 5. | Matt Kenseth | -399 | | 10. | Ryan Newman | -547 |

**Loudon, N.H.—1.058-mile flat paved oval • July 25, 2004—317.4 miles—300 laps**

| Fin. | St. | Car | Driver | Make | Sponsor | Pts./Bonus | Laps | Status | Winnings |
|------|-----|-----|--------|------|---------|------------|------|--------|----------|
| 1. | 32 | 97 | Kurt Busch | Ford | IRWIN Industrial Tools | 185/5 | 300 | Running | $227,225 |
| 2. | 24 | 24 | Jeff Gordon | Chevrolet | DuPont | 170/0 | 300 | Running | $170,458 |
| 3. | 1 | 12 | Ryan Newman | Dodge | ALLTEL | 175/10 | 300 | Running | $160,997 |
| 4. | 31 | 17 | Matt Kenseth | Ford | Smirnoff Ice/DeWalt | 160/0 | 300 | Running | $146,103 |
| 5. | 9 | 20 | Tony Stewart | Chevrolet | The Home Depot | 155/0 | 300 | Running | $126,178 |
| 6. | 4 | 15 | Michael Waltrip | Chevrolet | NAPA | 150/0 | 300 | Running | $110,481 |
| 7. | 5 | 42 | Jamie McMurray | Dodge | Texaco/Havoline | 146/0 | 300 | Running | $84,600 |
| 8. | 6 | 9 | Kasey Kahne* | Dodge | Dodge Dealers/UAW | 142/0 | 300 | Running | $106,075 |
| 9. | 25 | 88 | Dale Jarrett | Ford | UPS | 138/0 | 300 | Running | $103,317 |
| 10. | 7 | 19 | Jeremy Mayfield | Dodge | Dodge Dealers/UAW | 134/0 | 300 | Running | $98,500 |
| 11. | 2 | 48 | Jimmie Johnson | Chevrolet | Lowe's | 130/0 | 300 | Running | $89,700 |
| 12. | 27 | 99 | Jeff Burton | Ford | Roush Racing | 127/0 | 300 | Running | $103,917 |
| 13. | 19 | 29 | Kevin Harvick | Chevrolet | GM Goodwrench | 124/0 | 300 | Running | $106,203 |
| 14. | 26 | 6 | Mark Martin | Ford | Viagra | 121/0 | 300 | Running | $76,800 |
| 15. | 13 | 38 | Elliott Sadler | Ford | M&M's | 118/0 | 300 | Running | $104,008 |
| 16. | 11 | 5 | Terry Labonte | Chevrolet | Kellogg's | 115/0 | 300 | Running | $94,625 |
| 17. | 20 | 18 | Bobby Labonte | Chevrolet | Interstate Batteries | 112/0 | 300 | Running | $107,933 |
| 18. | 38 | 22 | Scott Wimmer* | Dodge | Caterpillar | 109/0 | 300 | Running | $89,050 |
| 19. | 28 | 09 | Bobby Hamilton Jr. | Dodge | Miccosukee Resort | 106/0 | 300 | Running | $65,750 |
| 20. | 18 | 01 | Joe Nemechek | Chevrolet | U.S. Army | 103/0 | 300 | Running | $88,400 |
| 21. | 37 | 40 | Sterling Marlin | Dodge | Coors Light | 100/0 | 300 | Running | $98,125 |
| 22. | 29 | 77 | Brendan Gaughan* | Dodge | Kodak/Jasper Eng. & Trans. | 97/0 | 300 | Running | $72,800 |
| 23. | 35 | 4 | Jimmy Spencer | Chevrolet | Morgan-McClure | 99/5 | 300 | Running | $65,425 |
| 24. | 30 | 43 | Jeff Green | Dodge | Cheerios/Betty Crocker | 91/0 | 300 | Running | $90,450 |
| 25. | 21 | 31 | Robby Gordon | Chevrolet | Cingular Wireless | 88/0 | 300 | Running | $96,372 |
| 26. | 22 | 41 | Casey Mears | Dodge | Target | 85/0 | 300 | Running | $74,175 |
| 27. | 39 | 45 | Kyle Petty | Dodge | Georgia-Pacific/Brawny | 82/0 | 300 | Running | $71,739 |
| 28. | 15 | 10 | Scott Riggs* | Chevrolet | Valvoline | 79/0 | 300 | Running | $88,362 |
| 29. | 12 | 0 | Ward Burton | Chevrolet | NetZero HiSpeed | 76/0 | 300 | Running | $62,390 |
| 30. | 8 | 2 | Rusty Wallace | Dodge | Miller Lite | 73/0 | 299 | Running | $103,483 |
| 31. | 3 | 8 | Dale Earnhardt Jr. | Chevrolet | Budweiser | 70/0 | 298 | Running | $108,628 |
| 32. | 36 | 50 | Mike Wallace | Dodge | LesCare Kitchens | 67/0 | 298 | Running | $59,230 |
| 33. | 14 | 30 | Dave Blaney | Chevrolet | America Online | 64/0 | 295 | Running | $67,960 |
| 34. | 23 | 25 | Brian Vickers* | Chevrolet | GMAC Financial Services | 61/0 | 293 | Running | $66,800 |
| 35. | 16 | 16 | Greg Biffle | Ford | National Guard/Subway | 58/0 | 270 | Accident | $66,600 |
| 36. | 42 | 72 | Ted Christopher | Ford | Freddie B's | 55/0 | 260 | Engine | $58,410 |
| 37. | 17 | 49 | Ken Schrader | Dodge | Schwan's Home Service | 52/0 | 221 | Engine | $58,250 |
| 38. | 10 | 32 | Ricky Craven | Chevrolet | Tide | 49/0 | 213 | Accident | $66,100 |
| 39. | 34 | 21 | Ricky Rudd | Ford | Motorcraft | 46/0 | 208 | Accident | $84,091 |
| 40. | 41 | 89 | Morgan Shepherd | Dodge | Racing With Jesus/Red Line Oil | 43/0 | 192 | Ignition | $57,950 |
| 41. | 40 | 98 | Todd Bodine | Ford | Lucas Oil | 40/0 | 153 | Engine | $57,850 |
| 42. | 33 | 46 | Carl Long | Dodge | Howes Lubricator | 37/0 | 100 | Transmission | $57,800 |
| 43. | 43 | 02 | Hermie Sadler | Chevrolet | The FanZCar | 34/0 | 87 | Overheating | $57,959 |

*Rookie. Time of race: 3 hours, 14 minutes, 36 seconds. Average speed: 97.862 mph. Margin of victory: .607 seconds. Caution flags: 12 for 62 laps. 60-65 (Car 32—accident, back stretch); 91-100 (debris); 103-105 (Car 30—stalled, Turn 1); 142-145 (Car 8—accident, Turn 1); 175-179 (Car 98—stalled, Turn 1); 181-183 (Car 25—accident, Turn 4); 212-217 (Car 21—accident, Turn 3); 223-229 (Car 49—accident, Turn 4); 234-236 (Car 77—accident, Turn 2); 256-263 (Car 32—accident, Turn 3); 273-276 (Car 16—accident, Turn 3); 295-297 (Car 2—accident, Turn 4). Lap leaders: 4 lead changes among 3 drivers. Ryan Newman 1-170, Kurt Busch 171-212, Jimmy Spencer 213-215, Newman 216-232, Busch 233-300. Pole winner: Ryan Newman, 132.360 mph. Note: Martin Truex Jr. relieved Dale Earnhardt Jr. during the first caution period. Earnhardt completed 61 laps. Dropped to rear: Dale Earnhardt Jr. (driver change), Ted Christopher (engine change). Failed to qualify: Kevin Lepage, Kyle Busch. Estimated attendance: 99,000.

## POINTS STANDINGS

| Rk. | Driver | Behind |
|-----|--------|--------|
| 1. | Jimmie Johnson | — |
| 2. | Dale Earnhardt Jr. | -165 |
| 3. | Jeff Gordon | -202 |
| 4. | Tony Stewart | -302 |
| 5. | Matt Kenseth | -369 |
| 6. | Kurt Busch | -454 |
| 7. | Bobby Labonte | -460 |
| 8. | Elliott Sadler | -480 |
| 9. | Kevin Harvick | -497 |
| 10. | Ryan Newman | -502 |

**Pocono, Pa.——2.5-mile banked triangular paved • August 1, 2004—500 miles—200 laps**

| Fin. | St. | Car | Driver | Make | Sponsor | Pts./Bonus | Laps | Status | Winnings |
|------|-----|-----|--------|------|---------|-----------|------|--------|----------|
| 1. | 14 | 48 | Jimmie Johnson | Chevrolet | Lowe's | 190/10 | 200 | Running | $276,950 |
| 2. | 21 | 6 | Mark Martin | Ford | Viagra | 175/5 | 200 | Running | $132,895 |
| 3. | 20 | 9 | Kasey Kahne* | Dodge | Dodge Dealers/UAW | 165/0 | 200 | Running | $131,645 |
| 4. | 19 | 16 | Greg Biffle | Ford | National Guard | 160/0 | 200 | Running | $98,430 |
| 5. | 13 | 24 | Jeff Gordon | Chevrolet | DuPont | 160/5 | 200 | Running | $121,728 |
| 6. | 29 | 5 | Terry Labonte | Chevrolet | Kellogg's/Team USA | 150/0 | 200 | Running | $103,440 |
| 7. | 22 | 31 | Robby Gordon | Chevrolet | Cingular Wireless | 146/0 | 200 | Running | $105,827 |
| 8. | 15 | 17 | Matt Kenseth | Ford | DeWalt Power Tools | 142/0 | 200 | Running | $113,968 |
| 9. | 9 | 19 | Jeremy Mayfield | Dodge | Dodge Dealers/UAW | 138/0 | 200 | Running | $92,490 |
| 10. | 5 | 38 | Elliott Sadler | Ford | M&M's | 134/0 | 200 | Running | $101,823 |
| 11. | 28 | 22 | Scott Wimmer* | Dodge | Caterpillar | 130/0 | 200 | Running | $87,040 |
| 12. | 33 | 21 | Ricky Rudd | Ford | Keep it Genuine | 132/5 | 200 | Running | $87,506 |
| 13. | 30 | 12 | Ryan Newman | Dodge | ALLTEL | 124/0 | 200 | Running | $103,457 |
| 14. | 6 | 25 | Brian Vickers* | Chevrolet | GMAC Financial Services | 121/0 | 200 | Running | $69,215 |
| 15. | 4 | 40 | Sterling Marlin | Dodge | Aspen Edge | 118/0 | 200 | Running | $94,290 |
| 16. | 2 | 01 | Joe Nemechek | Chevrolet | U.S. Army | 120/5 | 200 | Running | $85,590 |
| 17. | 12 | 2 | Rusty Wallace | Dodge | Miller Lite | 112/0 | 200 | Running | $99,423 |
| 18. | 1 | 41 | Casey Mears | Dodge | Target | 114/5 | 200 | Running | $82,215 |
| 19. | 25 | 45 | Kyle Petty | Dodge | Georgia-Pacific/Brawny | 106/0 | 200 | Running | $67,029 |
| 20. | 35 | 32 | Ricky Craven | Chevrolet | Tide | 103/0 | 200 | Running | $68,265 |
| 21. | 39 | 49 | Ken Schrader | Dodge | Schwan's Home Service | 105/5 | 200 | Running | $57,990 |
| 22. | 26 | 10 | Scott Riggs* | Chevrolet | Valvoline | 97/0 | 200 | Running | $82,877 |
| 23. | 36 | 4 | Jimmy Spencer | Chevrolet | Morgan-McClure | 94/0 | 199 | Running | $58,290 |
| 24. | 24 | 88 | Dale Jarrett | Ford | UPS | 96/5 | 194 | Running | $88,032 |
| 25. | 16 | 8 | Dale Earnhardt Jr. | Chevrolet | Budweiser | 88/0 | 193 | Running | $101,093 |
| 26. | 3 | 97 | Kurt Busch | Ford | IRWIN Industrial Tools | 85/0 | 192 | Transmission | $74,165 |
| 27. | 31 | 30 | Dave Blaney | Chevrolet | America Online | 87/5 | 187 | Running | $64,615 |
| 28. | 10 | 77 | Brendan Gaughan* | Dodge | Kodak/Jasper Eng. & Trans. | 79/0 | 177 | Accident | $63,965 |
| 29. | 17 | 18 | Bobby Labonte | Chevrolet | Interstate Batteries | 76/0 | 175 | Accident | $98,373 |
| 30. | 7 | 42 | Jamie McMurray | Dodge | Texaco/Havoline | 73/0 | 170 | Engine | $61,640 |
| 31. | 27 | 0 | Ward Burton | Chevrolet | NetZero HiSpeed | 70/0 | 162 | Transmission | $52,990 |
| 32. | 18 | 29 | Kevin Harvick | Chevrolet | GM Goodwrench | 67/0 | 141 | Engine | $88,618 |
| 33. | 32 | 43 | Jeff Green | Dodge | Cheerios/Betty Crocker | 69/5 | 128 | Engine | $78,890 |
| 34. | 23 | 99 | Jeff Burton | Ford | Roush Racing | 61/0 | 126 | Accident | $86,782 |
| 35. | 8 | 20 | Tony Stewart | Chevrolet | The Home Depot | 58/0 | 107 | Accident | $99,043 |
| 36. | 11 | 15 | Michael Waltrip | Chevrolet | NAPA | 55/0 | 100 | Engine | $88,121 |
| 37. | 40 | 89 | Morgan Shepherd | Dodge | Racing With Jesus/Red Line Oil | 52/0 | 79 | Engine | $51,900 |
| 38. | 37 | 98 | Todd Bodine | Ford | Lucas Oil | 49/0 | 72 | Engine | $51,785 |
| 39. | 43 | 80 | Carl Long | Ford | Commercial Truck & Trailer | 46/0 | 44 | Too slow | $51,660 |
| 40. | 42 | 02 | Jason Jarrett | Chevrolet | The FanZCar | 43/0 | 40 | Handling | $51,505 |
| 41. | 41 | 72 | Kirk Shelmerdine | Ford | Freddie B's | 40/0 | 40 | Too slow | $51,365 |
| 42. | 38 | 13 | Greg Sacks | Dodge | ARC Dehooker/Vita Coco | 37/0 | 19 | Vibration | $51,275 |
| 43. | 34 | 50 | P.J. Jones | Dodge | Arnold Development Co. | 34/0 | 8 | Brakes | $51,459 |

*Rookie. Time of race: 3 hours, 57 minutes, 35 seconds. Average speed: 126.271 mph. Margin of victory: 2.138 seconds. Caution flags: 9 for 35 laps. 52-55 (Car 22—spin, Turn 2); 84-87 (oil on track); 100-103 (debris); 109-112 (Cars 20, 9—accident, Long Pond straight); 121-123 (debris); 128-133 (Cars 99, 77—accident, Turn 3); 161-164 (Car 0—accident, Turn 1); 177-180 (Cars 18, 25—accident, Turn 1); 194-195 (oil on track). Lap leaders: 16 lead changes among 10 drivers. Casey Mears-pole, Joe Nemechek 1-31, Jimmie Johnson 32-33, Ricky Rudd 34, Jeff Gordon 35-41, Johnson 42-84, Jeff Green 85, Johnson 86-100, Dale Jarrett 101, Mears 102-118, Johnson 119-121, Dave Blaney 122-123, J. Gordon 124-127, Mark Martin 128-138, Johnson 139-161, Ken Schrader 162, Johnson 163-200. Pole winner: Casey Mears, 171.720 mph. Dropped to rear: Jimmy Spencer (missed driver introductions). Failed to qualify: Kevin Lepage, Andy Hillenburg, A.J. Hendriksen. Estimated attendance: 90,000.

## POINTS STANDINGS

| Rk. | Driver | Behind | | Rk. | Driver | Behind | | Rk. | Driver | Behind |
|-----|--------|--------|---|-----|--------|--------|---|-----|--------|--------|
| 1. | Jimmie Johnson | — | | 6. | Elliott Sadler | -536 | | 11. | Jeremy Mayfield | -660 |
| 2. | Jeff Gordon | -232 | | 7. | Kurt Busch | -559 | | 12. | Kasey Kahne | -689 |
| 3. | Dale Earnhardt Jr. | -267 | | 8. | Ryan Newman | -568 | | 13. | Mark Martin | -709 |
| 4. | Matt Kenseth | -417 | | 9. | Bobby Labonte | -574 | | 14. | Dale Jarrett | -723 |
| 5. | Tony Stewart | -434 | | 10. | Kevin Harvick | -620 | | 15. | Jamie McMurray | -753 |

2004 SEASON

**Indianapolis—2.5-mile semi-banked paved oval • August 8, 2004—400 miles—160 laps**

| Fin. | St. | Car | Driver | Make | Sponsor | Pts./Bonus | Laps | Status | Winnings |
|---|---|---|---|---|---|---|---|---|---|
| 1. | 11 | 24 | Jeff Gordon | Chevrolet | DuPont | 190/10 | 161 | Running | $518,053 |
| 2. | 17 | 88 | Dale Jarrett | Ford | UPS | 170/0 | 161 | Running | $323,367 |
| 3. | 3 | 38 | Elliott Sadler | Ford | M&M's | 170/5 | 161 | Running | $309,158 |
| 4. | 12 | 9 | Kasey Kahne* | Dodge | Dodge Dealers/UAW | 160/0 | 161 | Running | $263,325 |
| 5. | 24 | 20 | Tony Stewart | Chevrolet | The Home Depot | 155/0 | 161 | Running | $247,278 |
| 6. | 35 | 16 | Greg Biffle | Ford | National Guard | 150/0 | 161 | Running | $188,175 |
| 7. | 8 | 42 | Jamie McMurray | Dodge | Texaco/Havoline | 146/0 | 161 | Running | $179,025 |
| 8. | 32 | 29 | Kevin Harvick | Chevrolet | GM Goodwrench | 142/0 | 161 | Running | $205,178 |
| 9. | 18 | 91 | Bill Elliott | Dodge | Visteon | 138/0 | 161 | Running | $156,300 |
| 10. | 15 | 97 | Kurt Busch | Ford | Sharpie | 134/0 | 161 | Running | $172,900 |
| 11. | 13 | 19 | Jeremy Mayfield | Dodge | Dodge Dealers/UAW | 130/0 | 161 | Running | $174,050 |
| 12. | 19 | 99 | Jeff Burton | Ford | Roush Racing | 127/0 | 161 | Running | $177,342 |
| 13. | 29 | 2 | Rusty Wallace | Dodge | Miller Lite | 124/0 | 161 | Running | $178,658 |
| 14. | 14 | 43 | Jeff Green | Dodge | General Mills/Boxtops for Edu. | 121/0 | 161 | Running | $164,075 |
| 15. | 39 | 18 | Bobby Labonte | Chevrolet | Interstate Batteries | 118/0 | 161 | Running | $180,333 |
| 16. | 23 | 17 | Matt Kenseth | Ford | Smirnoff Ice/DeWalt | 115/0 | 161 | Running | $192,603 |
| 17. | 4 | 01 | Joe Nemechek | Chevrolet | U.S. Army | 112/0 | 161 | Running | $158,850 |
| 18. | 31 | 49 | Ken Schrader | Dodge | Schwan's Home Service | 114/5 | 161 | Running | $133,900 |
| 19. | 33 | 4 | Jimmy Spencer | Chevrolet | Featherlite Trailers | 111/5 | 161 | Running | $132,800 |
| 20. | 28 | 15 | Michael Waltrip | Chevrolet | NAPA | 103/0 | 161 | Running | $164,856 |
| 21. | 38 | 30 | Dave Blaney | Chevrolet | America Online | 100/0 | 161 | Running | $139,250 |
| 22. | 20 | 31 | Robby Gordon | Chevrolet | Cingular Wireless | 97/0 | 161 | Running | $160,992 |
| 23. | 26 | 45 | Kyle Petty | Dodge | Georgia-Pacific/Brawny | 94/0 | 161 | Running | $141,180 |
| 24. | 37 | 32 | Ricky Craven | Chevrolet | Tide | 91/0 | 161 | Running | $146,505 |
| 25. | 16 | 6 | Mark Martin | Ford | Viagra | 88/0 | 161 | Running | $134,380 |
| 26. | 1 | 41 | Casey Mears | Dodge | Target | 90/5 | 161 | Running | $139,539 |
| 27. | 5 | 8 | Dale Earnhardt Jr. | Chevrolet | Budweiser | 82/0 | 161 | Running | $169,078 |
| 28. | 40 | 21 | Ricky Rudd | Ford | Keep it Genuine | 79/0 | 160 | Accident | $148,806 |
| 29. | 6 | 25 | Brian Vickers* | Chevrolet | GMAC Financial Services | 76/0 | 158 | Accident | $136,000 |
| 30. | 36 | 23 | Tony Raines | Dodge | Bill Davis Racing | 73/0 | 155 | Accident | $121,730 |
| 31. | 7 | 12 | Ryan Newman | Dodge | ALLTEL | 70/0 | 154 | Accident | $165,092 |
| 32. | 34 | 22 | Scott Wimmer* | Dodge | Caterpillar | 67/0 | 148 | Accident | $125,730 |
| 33. | 10 | 40 | Sterling Marlin | Dodge | Coors Light | 64/0 | 116 | Brakes | $151,400 |
| 34. | 22 | 00 | Kenny Wallace | Chevrolet | Aaron's | 61/0 | 99 | Engine | $117,180 |
| 35. | 30 | 77 | Brendan Gaughan* | Dodge | Jasper Eng. & Trans./Kodak | 58/0 | 95 | Accident | $124,925 |
| 36. | 9 | 48 | Jimmie Johnson | Chevrolet | Lowe's | 55/0 | 88 | Engine | $136,625 |
| 37. | 27 | 10 | Scott Riggs* | Chevrolet | Valvoline | 52/0 | 72 | Accident | $141,927 |
| 38. | 21 | 5 | Terry Labonte | Chevrolet | Kellogg's/Delphi | 49/0 | 72 | Accident | $143,360 |
| 39. | 2 | 0 | Ward Burton | Chevrolet | NetZero HiSpeed | 46/0 | 72 | Accident | $120,005 |
| 40. | 43 | 98 | Derrike Cope | Ford | America's Most Wanted | 48/5 | 55 | Vibration | $116,825 |
| 41. | 41 | 50 | Todd Bodine | Dodge | Arnold Development Co. | 40/0 | 16 | Vibration | $116,320 |
| 42. | 42 | 09 | Scott Pruett | Dodge | Miccosukee Resort | 37/0 | 9 | Engine | $116,215 |
| 43. | 25 | 60 | Jason Leffler | Chevrolet | Haas Automation | 34/0 | 3 | Accident | $116,359 |

*Rookie. Time of race: 3 hours, 29 minutes, 56 seconds. Average speed: 115.037 mph. Margin of victory: Under caution. Caution flags: 13 for 47 laps. 5-8 (Car 60—accident, Turn 3); 24-26 (Car 20—spin, back stretch); 31-32 (Car 48—spin, Turn 3); 44-48 (debris); 69-72 (debris); 74-78 (Cars 0, 2, 5, 10, 21, 22, 45, 99—accident, front stretch); 89-92 (oil on track); 97-101 (Car 77—accident, Turn 2); 125-128 (debris); 144-146 (debris); 150-152 (Car 22—accident, Turn 3); 156-159 (Cars 12, 25, 5—accident, Turn 2); 161 (Cars 21, 8—accident, back stretch). Lap leaders: 9 lead changes among 6 drivers. Casey Mears 1-2, Elliott Sadler 3-26, Jeff Gordon 27-46, Derrike Cope 47, J. Gordon 48-69, Jimmy Spencer 70, Sadler 71-78, J. Gordon 79-125, Ken Schrader 126, J. Gordon 127-161. Pole winner: Casey Mears, 186.293 mph (record). Dropped to rear: Bobby Labonte (engine change). Failed to qualify: Kevin Lepage, Hermie Sadler, Morgan Shepherd, Greg Sacks, Andy Hillenburg, Geoffrey Bodine, Kirk Shelmerdine. Estimated attendance: 250,000.

# POINTS STANDINGS

| Rk. | Driver | Behind | | Rk. | Driver | Behind | | Rk. | Driver | Behind |
|---|---|---|---|---|---|---|---|---|---|---|
| 1. | Jimmie Johnson | — | | 6. | Elliott Sadler | -421 | | 11. | Kasey Kahne | -584 |
| 2. | Jeff Gordon | -97 | | 7. | Kurt Busch | -480 | | 12. | Jeremy Mayfield | -585 |
| 3. | Dale Earnhardt Jr. | -240 | | 8. | Bobby Labonte | -511 | | 13. | Dale Jarrett | -608 |
| 4. | Tony Stewart | -334 | | 9. | Kevin Harvick | -533 | | 14. | Jamie McMurray | -662 |
| 5. | Matt Kenseth | -357 | | 10. | Ryan Newman | -553 | | 15. | Mark Martin | -676 |

2004 SEASON

**Watkins Glen, N.Y.—2.45-mile paved road course • August 15, 2004—220.5 miles—90 laps**

| Fin. | St. | Car | Driver | Make | Sponsor | Pts./Bonus | Laps | Status | Winnings |
|---|---|---|---|---|---|---|---|---|---|
| 1. | 4 | 20 | Tony Stewart | Chevrolet | The Home Depot | 190/10 | 90 | Running | $195,288 |
| 2. | 43 | 1 | Ron Fellows | Chevrolet | Nutter Butter/Nilla Wafers | 170/0 | 90 | Running | $101,260 |
| 3. | 15 | 6 | Mark Martin | Ford | Viagra | 165/0 | 90 | Running | $98,910 |
| 4. | 16 | 41 | Casey Mears | Dodge | Target | 165/5 | 90 | Running | $96,150 |
| 5. | 3 | 8 | Dale Earnhardt Jr. | Chevrolet | Budweiser | 160/5 | 90 | Running | $111,708 |
| 6. | 9 | 29 | Kevin Harvick | Chevrolet | GM Goodwrench | 155/5 | 90 | Running | $102,943 |
| 7. | 12 | 19 | Jeremy Mayfield | Dodge | Dodge Dealers/UAW | 146/0 | 90 | Running | $89,585 |
| 8. | 29 | 21 | Ricky Rudd | Ford | Keep it Genuine | 142/0 | 90 | Running | $94,966 |
| 9. | 5 | 17 | Matt Kenseth | Ford | DeWalt Power Tools | 138/0 | 90 | Running | $109,808 |
| 10. | 7 | 97 | Kurt Busch | Ford | IRWIN Industrial Tools | 139/5 | 90 | Running | $81,140 |
| 11. | 8 | 18 | Bobby Labonte | Chevrolet | Interstate Batteries | 130/0 | 90 | Running | $102,813 |
| 12. | 24 | 99 | Jeff Burton | Ford | Roush Racing | 127/0 | 90 | Running | $94,992 |
| 13. | 14 | 42 | Jamie McMurray | Dodge | Texaco/Havoline | 124/0 | 90 | Running | $70,075 |
| 14. | 11 | 9 | Kasey Kahne* | Dodge | Dodge Dealers/UAW | 121/0 | 90 | Running | $92,085 |
| 15. | 6 | 38 | Elliott Sadler | Ford | M&M's | 118/0 | 90 | Running | $96,353 |
| 16. | 23 | 31 | Robby Gordon | Chevrolet | Cingular Wireless | 120/5 | 90 | Running | $91,387 |
| 17. | 35 | 43 | Jeff Green | Dodge | Cheerios/Betty Crocker | 112/0 | 90 | Running | $86,430 |
| 18. | 33 | 45 | Kyle Petty | Dodge | Georgia-Pacific/Brawny | 109/0 | 90 | Running | $72,460 |
| 19. | 26 | 22 | Scott Wimmer* | Dodge | Caterpillar | 106/0 | 90 | Running | $77,605 |
| 20. | 18 | 15 | Michael Waltrip | Chevrolet | NAPA | 103/0 | 90 | Running | $92,366 |
| 21. | 2 | 24 | Jeff Gordon | Chevrolet | DuPont | 105/5 | 90 | Running | $103,413 |
| 22. | 25 | 01 | Joe Nemechek | Chevrolet | U.S. Army | 97/0 | 90 | Running | $74,754 |
| 23. | 31 | 10 | Scott Riggs* | Chevrolet | Valvoline | 94/0 | 90 | Running | $84,157 |
| 24. | 27 | 30 | Dave Blaney | Chevrolet | America Online | 91/0 | 90 | Running | $65,785 |
| 25. | 17 | 2 | Rusty Wallace | Dodge | Kodak/Miller Lite | 88/0 | 89 | Running | $98,158 |
| 26. | 10 | 12 | Ryan Newman | Dodge | ALLTEL | 85/0 | 89 | Running | $101,032 |
| 27. | 13 | 88 | Dale Jarrett | Ford | UPS | 82/0 | 89 | Running | $88,457 |
| 28. | 32 | 49 | Ken Schrader | Dodge | Schwan's Home Service | 79/0 | 89 | Running | $56,880 |
| 29. | 37 | 72 | Tom Hubert | Ford | Freddie B's | 76/0 | 89 | Running | $53,635 |
| 30. | 22 | 25 | Brian Vickers* | Chevrolet | GMAC Financial Services | 73/0 | 89 | Running | $65,050 |
| 31. | 42 | 80 | Tony Ave | Chevrolet | Lamers Motor Racing | 70/0 | 84 | Running | $53,465 |
| 32. | 34 | 32 | Ricky Craven | Chevrolet | Tide | 67/0 | 83 | Transmission | $64,375 |
| 33. | 41 | 02 | Hermie Sadler | Chevrolet | SCORE Motorsports | 64/0 | 79 | Too slow | $56,725 |
| 34. | 30 | 77 | Brendan Gaughan* | Dodge | Kodak/Jasper Eng. & Trans. | 66/5 | 74 | Transmission | $61,240 |
| 35. | 21 | 16 | Greg Biffle | Ford | Subway/National Guard | 58/0 | 71 | Engine | $61,175 |
| 36. | 19 | 40 | Sterling Marlin | Dodge | Coors Light | 55/0 | 50 | Accident | $86,100 |
| 37. | 28 | 0 | Ward Burton | Chevrolet | NetZero HiSpeed | 52/0 | 47 | Engine | $53,050 |
| 38. | 40 | 89 | Morgan Shepherd | Dodge | Racing With Jesus/Red Line Oil | 49/0 | 42 | Rear end | $52,975 |
| 39. | 20 | 5 | Terry Labonte | Chevrolet | Kellogg's | 46/0 | 36 | Engine | $79,665 |
| 40. | 1 | 48 | Jimmie Johnson | Chevrolet | Lowe's | 48/5 | 23 | Engine | $72,640 |
| 41. | 36 | 50 | Todd Bodine | Dodge | Arnold Development Co. | 40/0 | 7 | Brakes | $52,780 |
| 42. | 38 | 4 | Jimmy Spencer | Chevrolet | Lucas Oil/77sports.com | 37/0 | 2 | Engine | $52,720 |
| 43. | 39 | 98 | Larry Gunselman | Ford | Mach 1 Racing | 34/0 | 2 | Transmission | $52,039 |

*Rookie. Time of race: 2 hours, 23 minutes, 25 seconds. Average speed: 92.249 mph. Margin of victory: 1.517 seconds. Caution flags: 5 for 11 laps. 7-8 (Cars 88, 25—spin, inner loop); 17-19 (Car 40—accident, Turn 1); 33-34 (Car 02—spin, inner loop); 50-51 (oil on track); 74-75 (Car 77—spin, Turn 1). Lap leaders: 13 lead changes among 9 drivers. Jimmie Johnson 1, Tony Stewart 2-13, Jeff Gordon 14-24, Stewart 25-29, Robby Gordon 30-35, Kevin Harvick 36, R. Gordon 37-42, Stewart 43-56, J. Gordon 57-58, Kurt Busch 59, Dale Earnhardt Jr. 60, Brendan Gaughan 61-67, Casey Mears 68-75, Stewart 76-90. Pole winner: None, qualifying rained out. Dropped to rear: Jimmy Spencer, Hermie Sadler (engine changes). Failed to qualify: Scott Pruett, Boris Said, Klaus Graf, Stanton Barrett. Estimated attendance: 100,000.

## POINTS STANDINGS

| Rk. | Driver | Behind | | Rk. | Driver | Behind | | Rk. | Driver | Behind |
|---|---|---|---|---|---|---|---|---|---|---|
| 1. | Jimmie Johnson | — | | 6. | Elliott Sadler | -351 | | 11. | Kasey Kahne | -511 |
| 2. | Jeff Gordon | -40 | | 7. | Kurt Busch | -389 | | 12. | Ryan Newman | -516 |
| 3. | Dale Earnhardt Jr. | -128 | | 8. | Kevin Harvick | -426 | | 13. | Mark Martin | -559 |
| 4. | Tony Stewart | -192 | | 9. | Bobby Labonte | -429 | | 14. | Dale Jarrett | -574 |
| 5. | Matt Kenseth | -267 | | 10. | Jeremy Mayfield | -487 | | 15. | Jamie McMurray | -586 |

# GFS MARKETPLACE - - -400 MICHIGAN INTERNATIONAL SPEEDWAY

**Brooklyn, Mich.—2-mile banked paved oval • August 22, 2004—400 miles—200 laps**

| Fin. | St. | Car | Driver | Make | Sponsor | Pts./Bonus | Laps | Status | Winnings |
|------|-----|-----|--------|------|---------|------------|------|--------|----------|
| 1. | 24 | 16 | Greg Biffle | Ford | National Guard/The Flash | 190/10 | 200 | Running | $190,180 |
| 2. | 13 | 6 | Mark Martin | Ford | Viagra/Batman | 175/5 | 200 | Running | $115,680 |
| 3. | 14 | 88 | Dale Jarrett | Ford | UPS | 165/0 | 200 | Running | $123,727 |
| 4. | 15 | 42 | Jamie McMurray | Dodge | Texaco/Havoline | 165/5 | 200 | Running | $93,695 |
| 5. | 11 | 9 | Kasey Kahne* | Dodge | Dodge Dealers/UAW | 160/5 | 200 | Running | $110,455 |
| 6. | 7 | 97 | Kurt Busch | Ford | Sharpie/Superman | 155/5 | 200 | Running | $89,540 |
| 7. | 2 | 24 | Jeff Gordon | Chevrolet | DuPont | 151/5 | 200 | Running | $119,968 |
| 8. | 5 | 17 | Matt Kenseth | Ford | DeWalt Power Tools | 142/0 | 200 | Running | $117,343 |
| 9. | 4 | 20 | Tony Stewart | Chevrolet | The Home Depot/USA Olympics | 138/0 | 200 | Running | $112,493 |
| 10. | 23 | 99 | Carl Edwards | Ford | Green Lantern | 134/0 | 200 | Running | $105,332 |
| 11. | 10 | 19 | Jeremy Mayfield | Dodge | Dodge Dealers/UAW | 130/0 | 200 | Running | $94,480 |
| 12. | 28 | 30 | Jeff Burton | Chevrolet | America Online | 127/0 | 200 | Running | $80,640 |
| 13. | 25 | 01 | Joe Nemechek | Chevrolet | U.S. Army | 124/0 | 200 | Running | $90,865 |
| 14. | 12 | 12 | Ryan Newman | Dodge | ALLTEL/Justice League | 121/0 | 200 | Running | $109,507 |
| 15. | 20 | 40 | Sterling Marlin | Dodge | Coors Light | 118/0 | 200 | Running | $100,390 |
| 16. | 8 | 29 | Kevin Harvick | Chevrolet | GM Goodwrench | 115/0 | 200 | Running | $101,093 |
| 17. | 17 | 15 | Michael Waltrip | Chevrolet | NAPA | 117/5 | 200 | Running | $97,421 |
| 18. | 26 | 22 | Scott Wimmer* | Dodge | Caterpillar | 114/5 | 199 | Running | $85,565 |
| 19. | 31 | 10 | Scott Riggs* | Chevrolet | Valvoline | 111/5 | 199 | Running | $89,352 |
| 20. | 16 | 41 | Casey Mears | Dodge | Target | 103/0 | 199 | Running | $76,215 |
| 21. | 3 | 8 | Dale Earnhardt Jr. | Chevrolet | Budweiser | 100/0 | 199 | Running | $107,393 |
| 22. | 22 | 25 | Brian Vickers* | Chevrolet | GMAC Financial Services | 97/0 | 199 | Running | $71,215 |
| 23. | 34 | 43 | Jeff Green | Dodge | Cheerios/Betty Crocker | 94/0 | 199 | Running | $89,140 |
| 24. | 27 | 21 | Ricky Rudd | Ford | Motorcraft/Wonder Woman | 91/0 | 199 | Running | $88,646 |
| 25. | 19 | 31 | Robby Gordon | Chevrolet | Cingular Wireless | 88/0 | 199 | Running | $95,827 |
| 26. | 9 | 18 | Bobby Labonte | Chevrolet | Wellbutrin XL | 85/0 | 199 | Running | $104,098 |
| 27. | 21 | 5 | Terry Labonte | Chevrolet | Kellogg's/Delphi | 87/5 | 199 | Running | $88,575 |
| 28. | 33 | 49 | Ken Schrader | Dodge | Schwan's Home Service | 79/0 | 199 | Running | $61,175 |
| 29. | 32 | 45 | Kyle Petty | Dodge | Georgia-Pacific/Brawny | 76/0 | 199 | Running | $66,879 |
| 30. | 29 | 0 | Ward Burton | Chevrolet | NetZero HiSpeed | 73/0 | 196 | Running | $58,915 |
| 31. | 38 | 4 | Jimmy Spencer | Chevrolet | Lucas Oil | 75/5 | 195 | Running | $58,290 |
| 32. | 6 | 38 | Elliott Sadler | Ford | M&M's | 72/5 | 179 | Running | $97,048 |
| 33. | 30 | 77 | Brendan Gaughan* | Dodge | Kodak/Jasper Eng. & Trans. | 69/5 | 157 | Engine | $66,140 |
| 34. | 40 | 89 | Morgan Shepherd | Dodge | Racing With Jesus/Red Line Oil | 61/0 | 113 | Handling | $58,960 |
| 35. | 35 | 32 | Ricky Craven | Chevrolet | Tide | 58/0 | 111 | Clutch | $65,890 |
| 36. | 18 | 2 | Rusty Wallace | Dodge | Miller Lite | 55/0 | 109 | Engine | $101,673 |
| 37. | 37 | 72 | Kirk Shelmerdine | Ford | Freddie B's | 52/0 | 109 | Ignition | $57,790 |
| 38. | 41 | 09 | Bobby Hamilton Jr. | Dodge | Miccosukee Resort | 49/0 | 105 | Engine | $57,690 |
| 39. | 43 | 80 | Carl Long | Ford | Commercial Truck & Trailer | 46/0 | 98 | Rear end | $57,645 |
| 40. | 1 | 48 | Jimmie Johnson | Chevrolet | Lowe's | 43/0 | 81 | Engine | $77,385 |
| 41. | 39 | 98 | Derrike Cope | Ford | America's Most Wanted | 40/0 | 49 | Power steering | $57,550 |
| 42. | 42 | 02 | Hermie Sadler | Chevrolet | Zapf Creation | 37/0 | 27 | Engine | $57,510 |
| 43. | 36 | 50 | Todd Bodine | Dodge | Arnold Development Co. | 34/0 | 11 | Overheating | $56,822 |

*Rookie. Time of race: 2 hours, 52 minutes, 35 seconds. Average speed: 139.063 mph. Margin of victory: 8.216 seconds. Caution flags: 9 for 33 laps. 4-6 (Car 9—spin, Turn 2); 30-34 (fluid on back stretch); 46-49 (debris); 52-54 (debris); 58-60 (debris); 72-74 (Car 80—spin, Turn 2); 92-94 (Car 22—spin, back stretch); 99-101 (Car 97—spin, Turn 2); 130-135 (debris). Lap leaders: 25 lead changes among 13 drivers. Jimmie Johnson-pole, Jeff Gordon 1-30, Terry Labonte 31, J. Gordon 32-38, Kurt Busch 39-42, Greg Biffle 43-46, Scott Wimmer 47-49, Mark Martin 50, Biffle 51-55, Martin 56-72, Jimmy Spencer 73-75, Scott Riggs 76-80, Martin 81-82, Jamie McMurray 83-85, Martin 86-92, Brendan Gaughan 93-94, Elliott Sadler 95-103, Biffle 104-111, Martin 112-130, Michael Waltrip 131, Biffle 132-138, Kasey Kahne 139-143, Biffle 144-174, Kahne 175, Riggs 176-182, Biffle 183-200. Pole winner: None, qualifying rained out. Dropped to rear: Terry Labonte, Kyle Petty (engine changes), Ryan Newman (pre-green pit stop). Failed to qualify: Kevin Lepage, Kerry Earnhardt, Kyle Busch, Kenny Wallace, J.J. Yeley, Mike Wallace, Stan Boyd, Stanton Barrett. Estimated attendance: 160,000.

## POINTS STANDINGS

| Rk. | Driver | Behind | | Rk. | Driver | Behind | | Rk. | Driver | Behind |
|-----|--------|--------|---|-----|--------|--------|---|-----|--------|--------|
| 1. | Jeff Gordon | — | | 6. | Kurt Busch | -345 | | 11. | Jeremy Mayfield | -468 |
| 2. | Jimmie Johnson | -68 | | 7. | Elliott Sadler | -390 | | 12. | Mark Martin | -495 |
| 3. | Dale Earnhardt Jr. | -139 | | 8. | Kevin Harvick | -422 | | 13. | Ryan Newman | -506 |
| 4. | Tony Stewart | -165 | | 9. | Bobby Labonte | -455 | | 14. | Dale Jarrett | -520 |
| 5. | Matt Kenseth | -236 | | 10. | Kasey Kahne | -462 | | 15. | Jamie McMurray | -532 |

# SHARPIE 500 ------------- BRISTOL MOTOR SPEEDWAY

**Bristol, Tenn.—.533-mile high-banked concrete oval • August 28, 2004—266.5 miles—500 laps**

| Fin. | St. | Car | Driver | Make | Sponsor | Pts./Bonus | Laps | Status | Winnings |
|------|-----|-----|--------|------|---------|-----------|------|--------|----------|
| 1. | 30 | 8 | Dale Earnhardt Jr. | Chevrolet | Budweiser | 190/10 | 500 | Running | $322,443 |
| 2. | 4 | 12 | Ryan Newman | Dodge | ALLTEL | 170/0 | 500 | Running | $213,887 |
| 3. | 11 | 48 | Jimmie Johnson | Chevrolet | Lowe's | 170/5 | 500 | Running | $169,590 |
| 4. | 15 | 30 | Jeff Burton | Chevrolet | America Online | 165/5 | 500 | Running | $128,280 |
| 5. | 8 | 38 | Elliott Sadler | Ford | M&M's | 155/0 | 500 | Running | $142,158 |
| 6. | 3 | 40 | Sterling Marlin | Dodge | Coors Light | 150/0 | 500 | Running | $132,115 |
| 7. | 5 | 42 | Jamie McMurray | Dodge | Texaco/Havoline | 151/5 | 500 | Running | $101,715 |
| 8. | 24 | 97 | Kurt Busch | Ford | Sharpie Retractable | 142/0 | 499 | Running | $107,515 |
| 9. | 23 | 17 | Matt Kenseth | Ford | DeWalt Power Tools | 138/0 | 499 | Running | $134,168 |
| 10. | 14 | 88 | Dale Jarrett | Ford | UPS | 139/5 | 499 | Running | $119,232 |
| 11. | 10 | 16 | Greg Biffle | Ford | National Guard | 130/0 | 499 | Running | $92,165 |
| 12. | 18 | 31 | Robby Gordon | Chevrolet | Cingular Wireless | 127/0 | 499 | Running | $114,152 |
| 13. | 7 | 6 | Mark Martin | Ford | Viagra | 124/0 | 499 | Running | $91,440 |
| 14. | 1 | 24 | Jeff Gordon | Chevrolet | DuPont | 126/5 | 498 | Running | $135,118 |
| 15. | 12 | 5 | Terry Labonte | Chevrolet | Kellogg's | 118/0 | 498 | Running | $109,335 |
| 16. | 19 | 18 | Bobby Labonte | Chevrolet | Interstate Batteries | 120/5 | 498 | Running | $121,468 |
| 17. | 39 | 10 | Scott Riggs* | Chevrolet | Valvoline | 112/0 | 497 | Running | $111,522 |
| 18. | 16 | 0 | Ward Burton | Chevrolet | NetZero HiSpeed | 109/0 | 497 | Running | $79,075 |
| 19. | 6 | 20 | Tony Stewart | Chevrolet | The Home Depot | 106/0 | 497 | Running | $121,528 |
| 20. | 20 | 25 | Brian Vickers* | Chevrolet | GMAC Financial Services | 103/0 | 497 | Running | $87,835 |
| 21. | 2 | 9 | Kasey Kahne* | Dodge | Dodge Dealers/UAW | 100/0 | 496 | Running | $107,535 |
| 22. | 9 | 19 | Jeremy Mayfield | Dodge | Dodge Dealers/UAW | 97/0 | 496 | Running | $101,510 |
| 23. | 40 | 50 | Todd Bodine | Dodge | Arnold Development Co. | 99/5 | 495 | Running | $76,785 |
| 24. | 21 | 29 | Kevin Harvick | Chevrolet | RealTree/GM Goodwrench | 91/0 | 494 | Running | $110,963 |
| 25. | 28 | 00 | Kenny Wallace | Chevrolet | Aaron's | 88/0 | 493 | Running | $71,740 |
| 26. | 13 | 2 | Rusty Wallace | Dodge | Miller Lite | 90/5 | 490 | Running | $114,248 |
| 27. | 36 | 15 | Michael Waltrip | Chevrolet | NAPA | 87/5 | 481 | Running | $105,961 |
| 28. | 41 | 09 | Mike Wallace | Dodge | Miccosukee Resort | 79/0 | 468 | Running | $72,595 |
| 29. | 27 | 43 | Jeff Green | Dodge | Cheerios/Betty Crocker | 76/0 | 462 | Running | $98,635 |
| 30. | 22 | 41 | Casey Mears | Dodge | Energizer | 73/0 | 433 | Accident | $87,675 |
| 31. | 38 | 4 | Jimmy Spencer | Chevrolet | Food City/Supreme Clean | 70/0 | 430 | Running | $72,065 |
| 32. | 26 | 49 | Ken Schrader | Dodge | Schwan's Home Service | 67/0 | 418 | Running | $71,455 |
| 33. | 25 | 99 | Carl Edwards | Ford | Roundup | 64/0 | 386 | Accident | $103,187 |
| 34. | 35 | 32 | Ricky Craven | Chevrolet | Tide | 61/0 | 373 | Accident | $89,735 |
| 35. | 17 | 77 | Brendan Gaughan* | Dodge | Kodak/Jasper Eng. & Trans. | 58/0 | 313 | Accident | $76,615 |
| 36. | 34 | 22 | Scott Wimmer* | Dodge | Caterpillar | 55/0 | 268 | Accident | $87,005 |
| 37. | 31 | 45 | Kyle Petty | Dodge | Georgia-Pacific/Brawny | 52/0 | 150 | Accident | $76,759 |
| 38. | 42 | 98 | Derrike Cope | Ford | America's Most Wanted | 49/0 | 121 | Brakes | $68,250 |
| 39. | 33 | 51 | Tony Raines | Chevrolet | Marathon Oil/Chase | 46/0 | 88 | Accident | $68,125 |
| 40. | 32 | 21 | Ricky Rudd | Ford | Keep it Genuine | 43/0 | 64 | Accident | $94,056 |
| 41. | 43 | 89 | Morgan Shepherd | Dodge | Racing With Jesus/Red Line Oil | 40/0 | 49 | Handling | $67,875 |
| 42. | 37 | 01 | Joe Nemechek | Chevrolet | U.S. Army | 37/0 | 31 | Accident | $75,755 |
| 43. | 29 | 37 | Kevin Lepage | Dodge | Carter's Royal Dispos-all | 34/0 | 11 | Vibration | $67,862 |

*Rookie. Time of race: 3 hours, 0 minutes, 36 seconds. Average speed: 88.538 mph. Margin of victory: 4.390 seconds. Caution flags: 9 for 63 laps. 21-24 (Car 4—accident, back stretch); 34-40 (Cars 22, 01—accident, Turn 1); 58-61 (Cars 21, 09—accident, back stretch); 84-88 (Car 32—spin, Turn 4); 90-98 (Cars 17, 45, 49, 51, 77—accident, front stretch); 328-337 (debris); 359-363 (debris); 366-373 (Cars 31, 88, 43, 20, 32, 40—accident, Turn 2); 389-399 (Cars 2, 18, 9, 99, 20—accident, Turn 2). Lap leaders: 18 lead changes among 10 drivers. Jeff Gordon 1-57, Rusty Wallace 58-63, Dale Earnhardt Jr. 64-104, R. Wallace 105-118, Earnhardt 119-131, R. Wallace 132-190, Earnhardt 191-215, Jamie McMurray 216-223, J. Gordon 224-226, Dale Jarrett 227, Jeff Burton 228, Michael Waltrip 229-235, Bobby Labonte 236, Todd Bodine 237-239, Earnhardt 240-355, Jimmie Johnson 356-375, Earnhardt 376-390, J. Burton 391-415, Earnhardt 416-500. Pole winner: Jeff Gordon, 128.520 mph. Dropped to rear: Jimmie Johnson, Michael Waltrip (backup cars), Kevin Lepage (on his own). Failed to qualify: Hermie Sadler, Stanton Barrett, Brad Teague, Tony Ave, Ryan McGlynn. Estimated attendance: 160,000.

## POINTS STANDINGS

| Rk. | Driver | Behind | Rk. | Driver | Behind | Rk. | Driver | Behind |
|-----|--------|--------|-----|--------|--------|-----|--------|--------|
| 1. | Jeff Gordon | — | 6. | Kurt Busch | -329 | 11. | Kasey Kahne | -488 |
| 2. | Jimmie Johnson | -24 | 7. | Elliott Sadler | -361 | 12. | Mark Martin | -497 |
| 3. | Dale Earnhardt Jr. | -75 | 8. | Kevin Harvick | -457 | 13. | Jeremy Mayfield | -497 |
| 4. | Tony Stewart | -185 | 9. | Bobby Labonte | -461 | 14. | Dale Jarrett | -507 |
| 5. | Matt Kenseth | -224 | 10. | Ryan Newman | -462 | 15. | Jamie McMurray | -507 |

# POP SECRET 500 ------MICHIGAN INTERNATIONAL SPEEDWAY

**Brooklyn, Mich.—2-mile banked paved oval • August 22, 2004—400 miles—200 laps**

| Fin. | St. | Car | Driver | Make | Sponsor | Pts./Bonus | Laps | Status | Winnings |
|------|-----|-----|--------|------|---------|-----------|------|--------|----------|
| 1. | 17 | 38 | Elliott Sadler | Ford | M&M's | 185/5 | 250 | Running | $279,398 |
| 2. | 5 | 9 | Kasey Kahne* | Dodge | Dodge Dealers/UAW | 175/5 | 250 | Running | $190,315 |
| 3. | 11 | 6 | Mark Martin | Ford | Viagra | 175/10 | 250 | Running | $144,450 |
| 4. | 23 | 42 | Jamie McMurray | Dodge | Texaco/Havoline | 160/0 | 250 | Running | $124,500 |
| 5. | 14 | 12 | Ryan Newman | Dodge | Sony/ALLTEL | 160/5 | 250 | Running | $154,367 |
| 6. | 19 | 99 | Carl Edwards | Ford | Shop Rat | 150/0 | 250 | Running | $136,792 |
| 7. | 9 | 10 | Scott Riggs* | Chevrolet | Valvoline | 146/0 | 250 | Running | $121,437 |
| 8. | 25 | 88 | Dale Jarrett | Ford | UPS | 142/0 | 250 | Running | $124,642 |
| 9. | 35 | 31 | Robby Gordon | Chevrolet | Cingular Wireless | 143/5 | 250 | Running | $128,612 |
| 10. | 26 | 2 | Rusty Wallace | Dodge | Miller Lite | 134/0 | 250 | Running | $131,808 |
| 11. | 4 | 97 | Kurt Busch | Ford | IRWIN Industrial Tools | 135/5 | 250 | Running | $108,425 |
| 12. | 10 | 01 | Joe Nemechek | Chevrolet | U.S. Army | 127/0 | 250 | Running | $114,700 |
| 13. | 1 | 25 | Brian Vickers* | Chevrolet | GMAC Financial Services | 129/5 | 250 | Running | $107,625 |
| 14. | 16 | 48 | Jimmie Johnson | Chevrolet | Lowe's | 126/5 | 250 | Running | $103,800 |
| 15. | 34 | 30 | Jeff Burton | Chevrolet | America Online | 118/0 | 250 | Running | $96,200 |
| 16. | 2 | 19 | Jeremy Mayfield | Dodge | Dodge Dealers/UAW | 120/5 | 250 | Running | $110,900 |
| 17. | 20 | 21 | Ricky Rudd | Ford | Keep it Genuine | 112/0 | 250 | Running | $111,556 |
| 18. | 33 | 20 | Tony Stewart | Chevrolet | The Home Depot | 109/0 | 250 | Running | $127,978 |
| 19. | 15 | 5 | Terry Labonte | Chevrolet | Kellogg's | 106/0 | 250 | Running | $110,775 |
| 20. | 37 | 18 | Bobby Labonte | Chevrolet | Wellbutrin XL | 103/0 | 250 | Running | $127,033 |
| 21. | 38 | 22 | Scott Wimmer* | Dodge | Caterpillar | 100/0 | 250 | Running | $103,875 |
| 22. | 30 | 17 | Matt Kenseth | Ford | Smirnoff Ice/DeWalt | 97/0 | 250 | Running | $129,803 |
| 23. | 21 | 15 | Michael Waltrip | Chevrolet | NAPA | 99/5 | 250 | Running | $115,606 |
| 24. | 18 | 84 | Kyle Busch | Chevrolet | CARQUEST | 91/0 | 250 | Running | $78,250 |
| 25. | 3 | 98 | Bill Elliott | Dodge | McDonald's | 88/0 | 250 | Running | $77,925 |
| 26. | 31 | 40 | Sterling Marlin | Dodge | Coors Light | 85/0 | 250 | Running | $114,325 |
| 27. | 13 | 43 | Jeff Green | Dodge | Pop Secret | 82/0 | 250 | Running | $106,935 |
| 28. | 27 | 29 | Kevin Harvick | Chevrolet | GM Goodwrench | 79/0 | 250 | Running | $116,238 |
| 29. | 6 | 41 | Casey Mears | Dodge | Target House | 76/0 | 249 | Running | $90,750 |
| 30. | 36 | 36 | Boris Said | Chevrolet | Centrix | 73/0 | 249 | Running | $77,700 |
| 31. | 39 | 0 | Ward Burton | Chevrolet | NetZero/Fear Factor | 70/0 | 248 | Running | $80,150 |
| 32. | 41 | 4 | Jimmy Spencer | Chevrolet | Lucas Oil | 72/5 | 247 | Running | $79,600 |
| 33. | 40 | 49 | Ken Schrader | Dodge | Schwan's Home Service | 69/5 | 231 | Engine | $77,050 |
| 34. | 12 | 8 | Dale Earnhardt Jr. | Chevrolet | Budweiser | 61/0 | 231 | Accident | $125,103 |
| 35. | 28 | 45 | Kyle Petty | Dodge | Georgia-Pacific/Brawny | 58/0 | 225 | Engine | $85,339 |
| 36. | 7 | 16 | Greg Biffle | Ford | National Guard | 55/0 | 213 | Accident | $84,900 |
| 37. | 8 | 24 | Jeff Gordon | Chevrolet | DuPont | 52/0 | 209 | Engine | $124,228 |
| 38. | 24 | 32 | Bobby Hamilton Jr. | Chevrolet | Tide | 49/0 | 207 | Running | $84,800 |
| 39. | 29 | 23 | Shane Hmiel | Dodge | Bill Davis Racing | 51/5 | 173 | Transmission | $76,740 |
| 40. | 43 | 96 | Derrike Cope | Ford | Mach 1 Inc. | 43/0 | 154 | Accident | $76,690 |
| 41. | 32 | 11 | J.J. Yeley | Chevrolet | Vigoro/The Home Depot | 40/0 | 32 | Accident | $76,640 |
| 42. | 22 | 77 | Brendan Gaughan* | Dodge | Kodak/Jasper Eng. & Trans. | 37/0 | 32 | Accident | $84,585 |
| 43. | 42 | 50 | Jeff Fuller | Dodge | Arnold Development Co. | 34/0 | 5 | Overheating | $75,875 |

*Rookie. Time of race: 3 hours, 53 minutes, 47 seconds. Average speed: 128.324 mph. Margin of victory: .263 seconds. Caution flags: 11 for 51 laps. 27-30 (debris); 34-38 (Cars 11, 77—accident, Turn 2); 45-47 (debris); 73-77 (Car 16—accident, front stretch); 106-113 (debris); 117-119 (Cars 4, 16, 23—accident, Turn 4); 171-176 (Car 96—accident, Turn 1); 179-181 (Car 97—accident, back stretch); 220-223 (Car 8—spin, Turn 4); 226-229 (oil on track); 235-240 (Cars 49, 8—accident, Turn 4). Lap leaders: 29 lead changes among 13 drivers. Brian Vickers 1-9, Jeremy Mayfield 10-18, Vickers 19-44, Kurt Busch 45-51, Michael Waltrip 52-61, Mark Martin 62-73, Vickers 74-79, Martin 80-105, Elliott Sadler 106, Ken Schrader 107, Jimmy Spencer 108, Sadler 109-121, Kasey Kahne 122-124, Sadler 125-128, Kahne 129-133, Martin 134-157, Jimmie Johnson 158, Ryan Newman 159-160, Shane Hmiel 161-164, Kahne 165-172, Sadler 173, Robby Gordon 174-176, Sadler 177-184, R. Gordon 185-189, Sadler 190-193, Kahne 194-216, Martin 217-219, Sadler 220, Vickers 221-223, Sadler 224-250. Pole winner: Brian Vickers, 187.417 mph. Dropped to rear: Shane Hmiel (backup car). Failed to qualify: Kevin Lepage, Hermie Sadler, Mike Wallace, Morgan Shepherd, Kirk Shelmerdine. Estimated attendance: 90,000.

## POINTS STANDINGS

| Rk. | Driver | Behind | Rk. | Driver | Behind | Rk. | Driver | Behind |
|-----|--------|--------|-----|--------|--------|-----|--------|--------|
| 1. | Jimmie Johnson | — | 6. | Elliott Sadler | -278 | 11. | Jamie McMurray | -449 |
| 2. | Jeff Gordon | -50 | 7. | Kurt Busch | -296 | 12. | Bobby Labonte | -460 |
| 3. | Dale Earnhardt Jr. | -116 | 8. | Ryan Newman | -404 | 13. | Dale Jarrett | -467 |
| 4. | Tony Stewart | -178 | 9. | Kasey Kahne | -415 | 14. | Jeremy Mayfield | -479 |
| 5. | Matt Kenseth | -229 | 10. | Mark Martin | -424 | 15. | Kevin Harvick | -480 |

| Fin. | St. | Car | Driver | Make | Sponsor | Pts./Bonus | Laps | Status | Winnings |
|------|-----|-----|--------|------|---------|-----------|------|--------|----------|
| 1. | 7 | 19 | Jeremy Mayfield | Dodge | Dodge Dealers/UAW | 190/10 | 400 | Running | $211,120 |
| 2. | 14 | 8 | Dale Earnhardt Jr. | Chevrolet | Budweiser | 175/5 | 400 | Running | $158,543 |
| 3. | 9 | 24 | Jeff Gordon | Chevrolet | DuPont | 170/5 | 400 | Running | $138,333 |
| 4. | 33 | 80 | Mike Bliss | Chevrolet | ConAgra/Hunt's Ketchup | 160/0 | 400 | Running | $82,655 |
| 5. | 2 | 6 | Mark Martin | Ford | Viagra | 155/0 | 400 | Running | $84,055 |
| 6. | 13 | 99 | Carl Edwards | Ford | Roush Racing | 150/0 | 400 | Running | $102,997 |
| 7. | 41 | 09 | Mike Wallace | Dodge | Miccosukee Resort | 151/5 | 400 | Running | $73,430 |
| 8. | 8 | 16 | Greg Biffle | Ford | National Guard/Subway | 142/0 | 400 | Running | $74,580 |
| 9. | 36 | 42 | Jamie McMurray | Dodge | Texaco/Havoline | 138/0 | 400 | Running | $74,180 |
| 10. | 12 | 2 | Rusty Wallace | Dodge | Miller Lite | 134/0 | 400 | Running | $105,863 |
| 11. | 22 | 32 | Bobby Hamilton Jr. | Chevrolet | Tide | 130/0 | 400 | Running | $89,680 |
| 12. | 27 | 29 | Kevin Harvick | Chevrolet | GM Goodwrench | 127/0 | 400 | Running | $99,843 |
| 13. | 19 | 15 | Michael Waltrip | Chevrolet | NAPA | 124/0 | 399 | Running | $96,836 |
| 14. | 24 | 40 | Sterling Marlin | Dodge | Coors Light | 121/0 | 399 | Running | $96,455 |
| 15. | 17 | 97 | Kurt Busch | Ford | IRWIN Industrial Tools | 123/5 | 399 | Running | $80,830 |
| 16. | 18 | 18 | Bobby Labonte | Chevrolet | Wellbutrin XL | 115/0 | 399 | Running | $104,213 |
| 17. | 20 | 38 | Elliott Sadler | Ford | M&M's | 112/0 | 399 | Running | $97,763 |
| 18. | 23 | 5 | Terry Labonte | Chevrolet | Kellogg's | 109/0 | 399 | Running | $89,230 |
| 19. | 15 | 20 | Tony Stewart | Chevrolet | The Home Depot | 106/0 | 399 | Running | $105,433 |
| 20. | 1 | 12 | Ryan Newman | Dodge | ALLTEL | 108/5 | 399 | Running | $110,572 |
| 21. | 6 | 21 | Ricky Rudd | Ford | U.S. Air Force/Motorcraft | 100/0 | 399 | Running | $88,536 |
| 22. | 4 | 01 | Joe Nemechek | Chevrolet | U.S. Army | 97/0 | 399 | Running | $82,705 |
| 23. | 5 | 30 | Jeff Burton | Chevrolet | America Online | 99/5 | 399 | Running | $69,905 |
| 24. | 11 | 9 | Kasey Kahne* | Dodge | Dodge Dealers/UAW | 91/0 | 399 | Running | $92,080 |
| 25. | 10 | 43 | Jeff Green | Dodge | Grands Biscuits | 88/0 | 399 | Running | $87,105 |
| 26. | 25 | 88 | Dale Jarrett | Ford | UPS | 85/0 | 398 | Running | $91,147 |
| 27. | 37 | 77 | Brendan Gaughan* | Dodge | Kodak/Jasper Eng. & Trans. | 82/0 | 398 | Running | $68,005 |
| 28. | 16 | 17 | Matt Kenseth | Ford | DeWalt Power Tools | 84/5 | 397 | Running | $107,658 |
| 29. | 30 | 23 | Shane Hmiel | Dodge | Bill Davis Racing | 76/0 | 397 | Running | $59,760 |
| 30. | 32 | 49 | Ken Schrader | Dodge | Schwan's Home Service | 73/0 | 397 | Running | $59,600 |
| 31. | 34 | 27 | David Green | Chevrolet | Timber Wolf | 70/0 | 397 | Running | $56,565 |
| 32. | 28 | 31 | Robby Gordon | Chevrolet | Cingular Wireless | 67/0 | 396 | Running | $91,717 |
| 33. | 39 | 4 | Jimmy Spencer | Chevrolet | Lucas Oil | 64/0 | 392 | Running | $57,425 |
| 34. | 31 | 45 | Kyle Petty | Dodge | Georgia-Pacific/Brawny | 61/0 | 392 | Running | $66,935 |
| 35. | 29 | 41 | Casey Mears | Dodge | Target | 58/0 | 352 | Running | $64,789 |
| 36. | 3 | 48 | Jimmie Johnson | Chevrolet | Lowe's | 60/5 | 338 | Running | $76,165 |
| 37. | 26 | 25 | Brian Vickers* | Chevrolet | GMAC Financial Services | 52/0 | 335 | Running | $64,330 |
| 38. | 21 | 22 | Scott Wimmer* | Dodge | Caterpillar | 49/0 | 297 | Running | $64,295 |
| 39. | 35 | 10 | Scott Riggs* | Chevrolet | Valvoline | 46/0 | 292 | Ignition | $81,442 |
| 40. | 38 | 0 | Ward Burton | Chevrolet | NetZero HiSpeed | 43/0 | 192 | Accident | $56,185 |
| 41. | 43 | 72 | Kirk Shelmerdine | Ford | Freddie B's | 40/0 | 87 | Brakes | $56,130 |
| 42. | 42 | 98 | Derrike Cope | Ford | Mach 1 Inc. | 37/0 | 30 | Ignition | $56,090 |
| 43. | 40 | 50 | Todd Bodine | Dodge | Arnold Development Co. | 34/0 | 9 | Accident | $56,303 |

*Rookie. Time of race: 3 hours, 1 minute, 55 seconds. Average speed: 98.946 mph. Margin of victory: 4.928 seconds. Caution flags: 10 for 57 laps. 9-11 (Car 50—accident, Turn 3); 14-17 (Car 45—spin, Turn 3); 53-58 (Car 99—spin, Turn 2); 143-146 (Car 99—accident, Turn 2); 158-163 (debris); 171-174 (Cars 16, 21, 22, 27, 42, 77—accident, Turn 3); 180-191 (Cars 4, 6, 8, 21, 25, 40, 41, 48, 88, 09—accident, Turn 4); 195-201 (Car 0—accident, Turn 3); 207-210 (Car 9—accident, Turn 2); 293-299 (Car 4—accident, Turn 2). Lap leaders: 20 lead changes among 9 drivers. Ryan Newman 1, Jimmie Johnson 2-33, Jeff Gordon 34-53, Mike Wallace 54-98, Jeremy Mayfield 99-114, Kurt Busch 115-143, Mayfield 144-233, Busch 234-236, Mayfield 237-263, Matt Kenseth 264-268, Busch 269-271, Newman 272-273, Jeff Burton 274-281, Dale Earnhardt Jr. 282-294, Busch 295-306, Earnhardt 307-327, Busch 328-330, Earnhardt 331-338, Mayfield 339-348, Busch 349-392, Mayfield 393-400. Pole winner: Ryan Newman, 128.700 mph. Dropped to rear: Jimmy Spencer, Scott Riggs (engine changes). Failed to qualify: Johnny Sauter, Tony Raines, Kevin Lepage, Greg Sacks, Hermie Sadler, Brad Teague, Ryan McGlynn, Morgan Shepherd, Carl Long. Estimated attendance: 110,000.

## POINTS STANDINGS

| Rk. | Driver | Behind | Rk. | Driver | Behind | Rk. | Driver | Behind |
|-----|--------|--------|-----|--------|--------|-----|--------|--------|
| 1. | Jeff Gordon | — | 6. | Elliott Sadler | -286 | 11. | Jamie McMurray | -431 |
| 2. | Jimmie Johnson | -60 | 7. | Kurt Busch | -293 | 12. | Kasey Kahne | -444 |
| 3. | Dale Earnhardt Jr. | -61 | 8. | Mark Martin | -389 | 13. | Bobby Labonte | -465 |
| 4. | Tony Stewart | -192 | 9. | Jeremy Mayfield | -409 | 14. | Kevin Harvick | -473 |
| 5. | Matt Kenseth | -265 | 10. | Ryan Newman | -416 | 15. | Dale Jarrett | -502 |

**2004 SEASON**

# SYLVANIA 300 - - - - NEW HAMPSHIRE INTERNATIONAL SPEEDWAY

Loudon, N.H.—1.058-mile flat paved oval • September 19, 2004—317.4 miles—300 laps

| Fin. | St. | Car | Driver | Make | Sponsor | Pts./Bonus | Laps | Status | Winnings |
|------|-----|-----|--------|------|---------|------------|------|--------|----------|
| 1. | 7 | 97 | Kurt Busch | Ford | IRWIN Industrial Tools | 190/10 | 300 | Running | $237,225 |
| 2. | 5 | 17 | Matt Kenseth | Ford | DeWalt Power Tools | 170/0 | 300 | Running | $175,108 |
| 3. | 3 | 8 | Dale Earnhardt Jr. | Chevrolet | Budweiser | 170/5 | 300 | Running | $155,158 |
| 4. | 12 | 9 | Kasey Kahne* | Dodge | Dodge Dealers/UAW | 165/5 | 300 | Running | $131,700 |
| 5. | 11 | 42 | Jamie McMurray | Dodge | Texaco/Havoline | 160/5 | 300 | Running | $92,400 |
| 6. | 25 | 01 | Joe Nemechek | Chevrolet | U.S.G. Sheetrock | 150/0 | 300 | Running | $105,725 |
| 7. | 1 | 24 | Jeff Gordon | Chevrolet | DuPont | 151/5 | 300 | Running | $116,478 |
| 8. | 6 | 38 | Elliott Sadler | Ford | M&M's | 147/5 | 300 | Running | $107,333 |
| 9. | 16 | 15 | Michael Waltrip | Chevrolet | NAPA | 143/5 | 300 | Running | $103,956 |
| 10. | 14 | 29 | Kevin Harvick | Chevrolet | GM Goodwrench | 139/5 | 300 | Running | $109,778 |
| 11. | 2 | 48 | Jimmie Johnson | Chevrolet | Lowe's | 135/5 | 300 | Running | $86,800 |
| 12. | 19 | 40 | Sterling Marlin | Dodge | Coors Light | 127/0 | 300 | Running | $103,200 |
| 13. | 8 | 6 | Mark Martin | Ford | Viagra | 124/0 | 300 | Running | $78,425 |
| 14. | 17 | 2 | Rusty Wallace | Dodge | Miller Lite | 121/0 | 300 | Running | $108,533 |
| 15. | 26 | 30 | Jeff Burton | Chevrolet | America Online | 118/0 | 300 | Running | $77,275 |
| 16. | 33 | 49 | Ken Schrader | Dodge | Schwan's Home Service | 115/0 | 300 | Running | $67,875 |
| 17. | 35 | 32 | Ricky Craven | Chevrolet | Tide | 112/0 | 299 | Running | $89,650 |
| 18. | 13 | 18 | Bobby Labonte | Chevrolet | Interstate Batteries | 109/0 | 299 | Running | $107,333 |
| 19. | 31 | 43 | Jeff Green | Dodge | Cheerios/Betty Crocker | 106/0 | 299 | Running | $92,000 |
| 20. | 21 | 99 | Carl Edwards | Ford | Roush Racing | 103/0 | 299 | Running | $100,817 |
| 21. | 34 | 45 | Kyle Petty | Dodge | Georgia-Pacific/Brawny | 100/0 | 299 | Running | $78,125 |
| 22. | 24 | 25 | Brian Vickers* | Chevrolet | GMAC Financial Services | 97/0 | 298 | Running | $72,800 |
| 23. | 36 | 50 | Todd Bodine | Dodge | Arnold Development Co. | 94/0 | 298 | Running | $65,425 |
| 24. | 23 | 5 | Terry Labonte | Chevrolet | Kellogg's | 91/0 | 298 | Running | $90,950 |
| 25. | 29 | 0 | Ward Burton | Chevrolet | NetZero HiSpeed | 88/0 | 298 | Running | $64,285 |
| 26. | 30 | 10 | Scott Riggs* | Chevrolet | Valvoline | 85/0 | 298 | Running | $88,762 |
| 27. | 15 | 88 | Dale Jarrett | Ford | UPS | 82/0 | 297 | Running | $94,267 |
| 28. | 20 | 16 | Greg Biffle | Ford | National Guard | 79/0 | 297 | Running | $70,675 |
| 29. | 18 | 41 | Casey Mears | Dodge | Target | 81/5 | 296 | Running | $70,390 |
| 30. | 32 | 77 | Brendan Gaughan* | Dodge | Kodak/Jasper Eng.& Trans. | 73/0 | 296 | Running | $67,650 |
| 31. | 42 | 02 | Hermie Sadler | Chevrolet | SCORE Motorsports | 70/0 | 295 | Running | $59,950 |
| 32. | 22 | 31 | Robby Gordon | Chevrolet | Cingular Wireless | 67/0 | 293 | Running | $94,417 |
| 33. | 10 | 12 | Ryan Newman | Dodge | Mobil 1/ALLTEL | 69/5 | 262 | Engine | $105,902 |
| 34. | 41 | 09 | Mike Wallace | Dodge | Miccosukee Resort | 61/0 | 256 | Accident | $59,725 |
| 35. | 9 | 19 | Jeremy Mayfield | Dodge | Dodge Dealers/UAW | 58/0 | 251 | Running | $74,989 |
| 36. | 27 | 22 | Scott Wimmer* | Dodge | Caterpillar | 55/0 | 207 | Accident | $66,410 |
| 37. | 28 | 21 | Ricky Rudd | Ford | Motorcraft | 52/0 | 192 | Overheating | $84,306 |
| 38. | 38 | 4 | Jimmy Spencer | Chevrolet | Lucas Oil | 49/0 | 121 | Suspension | $58,100 |
| 39. | 4 | 20 | Tony Stewart | Chevrolet | The Home Depot | 51/5 | 83 | Accident | $104,813 |
| 40. | 40 | 89 | Morgan Shepherd | Dodge | Racing With Jesus/Red Line Oil | 43/0 | 81 | Too slow | $57,950 |
| 41. | 39 | 98 | Geoffrey Bodine | Ford | Mach 1 Inc. | 40/0 | 50 | Ignition | $57,850 |
| 42. | 37 | 72 | Kirk Shelmerdine | Ford | Vote for Bush | 37/0 | 30 | Too slow | $57,800 |
| 43. | 43 | 80 | Ted Christopher | Ford | Commercial Truck & Trailer | 34/0 | 17 | Engine | $57,959 |

*Rookie. Time of race: 2 hours, 53 minutes, 31 seconds. Average speed: 109.753 mph. Margin of victory: 2.488 seconds. Caution flags: 7 for 30 laps. 18-21 (Car 31—accident, Turn 1); 37-40 (competition caution); 65-70 (Cars 16, 19, 20, 31—accident, Turn 2); 104-107 (Car 22—accident, Turn 4); 114-116 (Car 31—spin, back stretch); 177-181 (debris); 277-280 (debris). Lap leaders: 15 lead changes among 12 drivers. Jeff Gordon 1-11, Tony Stewart 12-27, J. Gordon 28-37, Kasey Kahne 38-65, Michael Waltrip 66-104, Casey Mears 105-111, Elliott Sadler 112-131, Kahne 132-134, Kurt Busch 135-183, Dale Earnhardt Jr. 184-185, Busch 186-255, Ryan Newman 256-259, Jamie McMurray 260, Kevin Harvick 261, Jimmie Johnson 262-264, Busch 265-300. Pole winner: None, qualifying rained out. Failed to qualify: Kevin Lepage, Martin Truex, Johnny Sauter, Greg Sacks, Ryan McGlynn, Carl Long, Tony Raines, Stan Boyd. Estimated attendance: 101,000.

## POINTS STANDINGS

| Rk. | Driver | Behind | | Rk. | Driver | Behind |
|-----|--------|--------|---|-----|--------|--------|
| 1. | Dale Earnhardt Jr. | — | | 6. | Elliott Sadler | -38 |
| 2. | Kurt Busch | — | | 7. | Mark Martin | -71 |
| 3. | Jeff Gordon | -9 | | 8. | Tony Stewart | -124 |
| 4. | Matt Kenseth | -10 | | 9. | Ryan Newman | -136 |
| 5. | Jimmie Johnson | -30 | | 10. | Jeremy Mayfield | -142 |

Dover, Del.—1-mile banked concrete oval • September 26, 2004—400 miles—400 laps

| Fin. | St. | Car | Driver | Make | Sponsor | Pts./Bonus | Laps | Status | Winnings |
|---|---|---|---|---|---|---|---|---|---|
| 1. | 2 | 12 | Ryan Newman | Dodge | ALLTEL | 190/10 | 400 | Running | $195,477 |
| 2. | 12 | 6 | Mark Martin | Ford | Viagra | 175/5 | 400 | Running | $138,560 |
| 3. | 21 | 24 | Jeff Gordon | Chevrolet | DuPont | 170/5 | 400 | Running | $140,533 |
| 4. | 11 | 88 | Dale Jarrett | Ford | UPS | 160/0 | 400 | Running | $122,877 |
| 5. | 13 | 97 | Kurt Busch | Ford | Sharpie | 160/5 | 400 | Running | $99,745 |
| 6. | 23 | 20 | Tony Stewart | Chevrolet | The Home Depot | 150/0 | 400 | Running | $117,168 |
| 7. | 1 | 19 | Jeremy Mayfield | Dodge | Dodge Dealers/UAW | 146/0 | 400 | Running | $105,015 |
| 8. | 10 | 42 | Jamie McMurray | Dodge | Texaco/Havoline | 142/0 | 400 | Running | $79,715 |
| 9. | 16 | 8 | Dale Earnhardt Jr. | Chevrolet | Budweiser | 143/5 | 399 | Running | $113,293 |
| 10. | 9 | 48 | Jimmie Johnson | Chevrolet | Lowe's | 134/0 | 399 | Running | $86,415 |
| 11. | 19 | 16 | Greg Biffle | Ford | National Guard/Subway | 130/0 | 399 | Running | $75,630 |
| 12. | 14 | 21 | Ricky Rudd | Ford | Keep it Genuine | 127/0 | 399 | Running | $92,321 |
| 13. | 7 | 2 | Rusty Wallace | Dodge | Miller Lite | 124/0 | 398 | Running | $105,348 |
| 14. | 6 | 18 | Bobby Labonte | Chevrolet | MBNA | 121/0 | 398 | Running | $107,123 |
| 15. | 34 | 40 | Sterling Marlin | Dodge | Coors Light | 118/0 | 398 | Running | $104,415 |
| 16. | 5 | 15 | Michael Waltrip | Chevrolet | NAPA | 115/0 | 397 | Running | $96,671 |
| 17. | 27 | 45 | Kyle Petty | Dodge | Georgia-Pacific/Brawny | 112/0 | 397 | Running | $79,415 |
| 18. | 15 | 99 | Carl Edwards | Ford | Roush Racing | 109/0 | 397 | Running | $97,417 |
| 19. | 30 | 29 | Kevin Harvick | Chevrolet | GM Goodwrench | 106/0 | 397 | Running | $99,493 |
| 20. | 4 | 38 | Elliott Sadler | Ford | M&M's | 103/0 | 397 | Running | $100,648 |
| 21. | 28 | 43 | Jeff Green | Dodge | Cheerios/Betty Crocker | 100/0 | 396 | Running | $89,565 |
| 22. | 25 | 77 | Brendan Gaughan* | Dodge | Kodak/Jasper Eng. & Trans. | 97/0 | 396 | Running | $72,565 |
| 23. | 29 | 22 | Scott Wimmer* | Dodge | Caterpillar | 94/0 | 395 | Running | $84,740 |
| 24. | 26 | 41 | Casey Mears | Dodge | Target | 91/0 | 395 | Running | $73,065 |
| 25. | 31 | 49 | Ken Schrader | Dodge | Schwan's Home Service | 93/5 | 394 | Running | $62,265 |
| 26. | 36 | 4 | Jimmy Spencer | Chevrolet | Lucas Oil | 85/0 | 393 | Running | $62,415 |
| 27. | 38 | 5 | Terry Labonte | Chevrolet | Kellogg's | 82/0 | 393 | Running | $88,515 |
| 28. | 37 | 51 | Tony Raines | Chevrolet | Buddy Lee Dungarees | 79/0 | 391 | Running | $58,590 |
| 29. | 22 | 32 | Bobby Hamilton Jr. | Chevrolet | Tide | 76/0 | 385 | Running | $77,829 |
| 30. | 32 | 31 | Robby Gordon | Chevrolet | Cingular Wireless | 73/0 | 385 | Running | $93,977 |
| 31. | 18 | 10 | Scott Riggs* | Chevrolet | Valvoline | 70/0 | 363 | Wheel bearing | $85,802 |
| 32. | 8 | 17 | Matt Kenseth | Ford | DeWalt Power Tools | 72/5 | 319 | Accident | $118,833 |
| 33. | 33 | 30 | Jeff Burton | Chevrolet | America Online | 64/0 | 167 | Accident | $66,730 |
| 34. | 42 | 89 | Morgan Shepherd | Dodge | Racing With Jesus/Red Line Oil | 61/0 | 105 | Handling | $57,595 |
| 35. | 24 | 01 | Joe Nemechek | Chevrolet | U.S. Army | 58/0 | 91 | Overheating | $65,380 |
| 36. | 35 | 37 | Kevin Lepage | Dodge | Carter's Royal Dispos-all | 55/0 | 86 | Vibration | $57,250 |
| 37. | 17 | 0 | Ward Burton | Chevrolet | NetZero HiSpeed | 52/0 | 50 | Engine | $57,125 |
| 38. | 3 | 25 | Brian Vickers* | Chevrolet | GMAC Financial Services | 49/0 | 46 | Accident | $65,100 |
| 39. | 41 | 98 | Geoffrey Bodine | Ford | Mach 1 Inc. | 46/0 | 40 | Oil pressure | $56,875 |
| 40. | 43 | 72 | Kirk Shelmerdine | Ford | Vote for Bush | 43/0 | 37 | Engine | $56,705 |
| 41. | 40 | 09 | Joe Ruttman | Dodge | Miccosukee Resort | 40/0 | 27 | Rear end | $56,550 |
| 42. | 20 | 9 | Kasey Kahne* | Dodge | Dodge Dealers/UAW | 37/0 | 13 | Fly wheel | $86,300 |
| 43. | 39 | 50 | Jeff Fuller | Dodge | Arnold Development Co. | 34/0 | 7 | Overheating | $56,555 |

*Rookie. Time of race: 3 hours, 21 minutes, 34 seconds. Average speed: 119.067 mph. Margin of victory: 8.149 seconds. Caution flags: 5 for 38 laps. 15-22 (oil on track); 49-55 (Car 25—accident, Turn 2); 121-127 (Car 17—accident, Turn 4); 171-177 (Car 30—accident, Turn 3); 327-335 (debris). Note: On Lap 122, the race was red-flagged for 12 minutes, 35 seconds to repair the tire barrier alongside the entrance to pit road. Lap leaders: 13 lead changes among 7 drivers. Jeremy Mayfield-pole, Ryan Newman 1-32, Matt Kenseth 33-48, Newman 49, Ken Schrader 50, Kenseth 51-92, Newman 93-184, Kurt Busch 185-195, Newman 196-260, Mark Martin 261-262, Dale Earnhardt Jr. 263, Jeff Gordon 264, Busch 265, Newman 266-400. Pole winner: Jeremy Mayfield, 159.405 mph. Dropped to rear: Terry Labonte (backup car); Geoffrey Bodine (engine change). Failed to qualify: Hermie Sadler, Carl Long, Stanton Barrett, Greg Sacks, Kenny Hendrick, Derrike Cope, Mike Garvey. Estimated attendance: 140,000.

## POINTS STANDINGS

| Rk. | Driver | Behind |
|---|---|---|
| 1. | Jeff Gordon | — |
| 2. | Kurt Busch | -1 |
| 3. | Dale Earnhardt Jr. | -18 |
| 4. | Jimmie Johnson | -57 |
| 5. | Mark Martin | -57 |

| Rk. | Driver | Behind |
|---|---|---|
| 6. | Elliott Sadler | -96 |
| 7. | Matt Kenseth | -99 |
| 8. | Ryan Newman | -107 |
| 9. | Tony Stewart | -135 |
| 10. | Jeremy Mayfield | -157 |

**Talladega, Ala.—2.66-mile banked paved trioval • October 3, 2004—500 miles—188 laps**

| Fin. | St. | Car | Driver | Make | Sponsor | Pts./Bonus | Laps | Status | Winnings |
|------|-----|-----|--------|------|---------|------------|------|--------|----------|
| 1. | 10 | 8 | Dale Earnhardt Jr. | Chevrolet | Budweiser | 190/10 | 188 | Running | $305,968 |
| 2. | 15 | 29 | Kevin Harvick | Chevrolet | GM Goodwrench | 175/5 | 188 | Running | $165,208 |
| 3. | 3 | 88 | Dale Jarrett | Ford | UPS | 165/0 | 188 | Running | $137,922 |
| 4. | 26 | 77 | Brendan Gaughan* | Dodge | Kodak/Jasper Eng. & Trans. | 165/5 | 188 | Running | $100,640 |
| 5. | 8 | 97 | Kurt Busch | Ford | Sharpie | 160/5 | 188 | Running | $104,290 |
| 6. | 30 | 20 | Tony Stewart | Chevrolet | The Home Depot | 155/5 | 188 | Running | $120,603 |
| 7. | 1 | 01 | Joe Nemechek | Chevrolet | U.S. Army | 151/5 | 188 | Running | $106,075 |
| 8. | 34 | 41 | Casey Mears | Dodge | Target | 147/5 | 188 | Running | $100,000 |
| 9. | 36 | 31 | Robby Gordon | Chevrolet | Cingular Wireless | 138/0 | 188 | Running | $108,562 |
| 10. | 28 | 0 | Ward Burton | Chevrolet | NetZero/Shark Tale | 139/5 | 188 | Running | $76,000 |
| 11. | 4 | 10 | Scott Riggs* | Chevrolet | Zerex/Valvoline | 135/5 | 188 | Running | $96,952 |
| 12. | 2 | 21 | Ricky Rudd | Ford | Rent-A-Center/Motorcraft | 127/0 | 188 | Running | $97,471 |
| 13. | 13 | 30 | Jeff Burton | Chevrolet | America Online | 129/5 | 188 | Running | $79,180 |
| 14. | 7 | 17 | Matt Kenseth | Ford | Smirnoff Ice/DeWalt | 121/5 | 188 | Running | $116,973 |
| 15. | 17 | 6 | Mark Martin | Ford | Viagra | 118/0 | 188 | Running | $79,035 |
| 16. | 19 | 12 | Ryan Newman | Dodge | ALLTEL | 120/5 | 188 | Running | $112,492 |
| 17. | 24 | 42 | Jamie McMurray | Dodge | Texaco/Havoline | 112/0 | 188 | Running | $76,985 |
| 18. | 41 | 09 | Mike Wallace | Dodge | Miccosukee Resort | 114/5 | 188 | Running | $68,670 |
| 19. | 5 | 24 | Jeff Gordon | Chevrolet | DuPont | 111/5 | 188 | Running | $112,428 |
| 20. | 37 | 49 | Ken Schrader | Dodge | Schwan's Home Service | 108/5 | 188 | Running | $68,140 |
| 21. | 38 | 5 | Terry Labonte | Chevrolet | Kellogg's/Delphi | 100/0 | 188 | Running | $95,285 |
| 22. | 6 | 38 | Elliott Sadler | Ford | M&M's | 102/5 | 188 | Running | $102,398 |
| 23. | 11 | 02 | Hermie Sadler | Ford | East Tennessee Trailers | 99/5 | 188 | Running | $67,420 |
| 24. | 22 | 33 | Kerry Earnhardt | Chevrolet | Bass Pro Shops/Tracker | 91/0 | 188 | Running | $63,000 |
| 25. | 14 | 15 | Michael Waltrip | Chevrolet | NAPA | 93/5 | 188 | Running | $98,786 |
| 26. | 33 | 2 | Rusty Wallace | Dodge | Miller Lite | 90/5 | 188 | Running | $106,403 |
| 27. | 23 | 9 | Kasey Kahne* | Dodge | Dodge Dealers/UAW | 82/0 | 187 | Running | $95,360 |
| 28. | 12 | 16 | Greg Biffle | Ford | National Guard/Subway | 79/0 | 187 | Running | $73,625 |
| 29. | 35 | 45 | Kyle Petty | Dodge | Georgia-Pacific/Brawny | 76/0 | 187 | Running | $78,065 |
| 30. | 20 | 11 | Ricky Craven | Chevrolet | Old Spice | 73/0 | 187 | Running | $62,405 |
| 31. | 29 | 22 | Scott Wimmer* | Dodge | Caterpillar | 70/0 | 187 | Running | $82,820 |
| 32. | 43 | 1 | Kenny Wallace | Chevrolet | Aaron's | 67/0 | 185 | Running | $61,735 |
| 33. | 42 | 98 | Larry Gunselman | Ford | Mach 1 Inc. | 64/0 | 183 | Running | $62,555 |
| 34. | 32 | 40 | Sterling Marlin | Dodge | Coors Light | 61/0 | 177 | Accident | $94,555 |
| 35. | 27 | 18 | Bobby Labonte | Chevrolet | Interstate Batteries | 58/0 | 177 | Accident | $106,533 |
| 36. | 21 | 25 | Brian Vickers* | Chevrolet | GMAC Financial Services | 55/0 | 164 | Overheating | $69,400 |
| 37. | 16 | 48 | Jimmie Johnson | Chevrolet | Lowe's | 57/5 | 157 | Overheating | $81,150 |
| 38. | 9 | 19 | Jeremy Mayfield | Dodge | Dodge Dealers/UAW | 49/0 | 147 | Accident | $77,689 |
| 39. | 18 | 43 | Jeff Green | Dodge | Cheerios/Betty Crocker | 46/0 | 142 | Accident | $87,495 |
| 40. | 40 | 4 | Jimmy Spencer | Chevrolet | Lucas Oil | 48/5 | 142 | Accident | $61,155 |
| 41. | 31 | 06 | Chad Blount | Dodge | Mobil 1 | 40/0 | 131 | Engine | $61,105 |
| 42. | 25 | 99 | Carl Edwards | Ford | Roush Racing | 37/0 | 122 | Engine | $94,477 |
| 43. | 39 | 32 | Bobby Hamilton Jr. | Chevrolet | Tide | 34/0 | 120 | Accident | $69,261 |

*Rookie. Time of race: 3 hours, 11 minutes, 12 seconds. Average speed: 156.929 mph. Margin of victory: .117 seconds. Caution flags: 5 for 22 laps. 30-34 (Car 09—accident, Turn 3); 60-63 (fluid on track); 124-128 (oil on track); 144-147 (Cars 4, 19, 32, 43—accident, Turn 3); 180-183 (Cars 40, 18—accident, Turn 4). Lap leaders: 47 lead changes among 20 drivers. Joe Nemechek 1, Scott Riggs 2, Kurt Busch 3, Dale Earnhardt Jr. 4-22, Jimmie Johnson 23-28, Busch 29, Jimmy Spencer 30, Tony Stewart 31, Casey Mears 32-34, Johnson 35, Mears 36, Johnson 37-39, Rusty Wallace 40-47, Johnson 48-54, R. Wallace 55-56, Jeff Gordon 57-59, Hermie Sadler 60, Ryan Newman 61, Michael Waltrip 62-63, J. Gordon 64-65, R. Wallace 66-70, Johnson 71-75, Waltrip 76-80, Johnson 81-93, Mears 94, Brendan Gaughan 95-97, Earnhardt 98-108, Busch 109, Earnhardt 110, Busch 111, Ward Burton 112, J. Gordon 113, Earnhardt 114-117, J. Gordon 118-123, Elliott Sadler 124, Ken Schrader 125, Mike Wallace 126-129, Earnhardt 130, Jeff Burton 131, Earnhardt 132-138, J. Burton 139-143, Earnhardt 144-173, Kevin Harvick 174-175, Earnhardt 176-177, Stewart 178-180, Gaughan 181-184, Harvick 185, Earnhardt 186-188. Pole winner: Joe Nemechek, 190.749 mph. Dropped to rear: Carl Edwards (driver change). Failed to qualify: Kevin Lepage, Kirk Shelmerdine; Carl Long. Estimated attendance: 150,000.

## POINTS STANDINGS

| Rk. | Driver | Behind | | Rk. | Driver | Behind |
|-----|--------|--------|---|-----|--------|--------|
| 1. | Kurt Busch | — | | 6. | Tony Stewart | -139 |
| 2. | Dale Earnhardt Jr. | -12 | | 7. | Ryan Newman | -146 |
| 3. | Jeff Gordon | -48 | | 8. | Elliott Sadler | -153 |
| 4. | Mark Martin | -98 | | 9. | Jimmie Johnson | -159 |
| 5. | Matt Kenseth | -137 | | 10. | Jeremy Mayfield | -267 |

**Kansas City, Kan.—1.5-mile paved trioval • October 10, 2004—400.5 miles—267 laps**

| Fin. | St. | Car | Driver | Make | Sponsor | Pts./Bonus | Laps | Status | Winnings |
|------|-----|-----|--------|------|---------|------------|------|--------|----------|
| 1. | 1 | 01 | Joe Nemechek | Chevrolet | U.S. Army | 185/5 | 267 | Running | $310,725 |
| 2. | 12 | 21 | Ricky Rudd | Ford | Keep it Genuine | 175/5 | 267 | Running | $208,896 |
| 3. | 6 | 16 | Greg Biffle | Ford | National Guard/Subway | 170/5 | 267 | Running | $160,325 |
| 4. | 11 | 38 | Elliott Sadler | Ford | Pedigree/Wizard of Oz | 165/5 | 267 | Running | $159,708 |
| 5. | 3 | 19 | Jeremy Mayfield | Dodge | Dodge Dealers/UAW | 165/10 | 267 | Running | $138,075 |
| 6. | 22 | 97 | Kurt Busch | Ford | Sharpie | 155/5 | 267 | Running | $111,825 |
| 7. | 10 | 42 | Jamie McMurray | Dodge | Texaco/Havoline | 151/5 | 267 | Running | $101,100 |
| 8. | 9 | 88 | Dale Jarrett | Ford | UPS | 147/5 | 267 | Running | $119,917 |
| 9. | 8 | 8 | Dale Earnhardt Jr. | Chevrolet | Budweiser | 138/0 | 267 | Running | $135,678 |
| 10. | 13 | 77 | Brendan Gaughan* | Dodge | Kodak/Jasper/Wizard of Oz | 134/0 | 267 | Running | $94,475 |
| 11. | 26 | 15 | Michael Waltrip | Chevrolet | NAPA | 130/0 | 267 | Running | $115,131 |
| 12. | 2 | 9 | Kasey Kahne* | Dodge | Dodge Dealers/UAW | 132/5 | 267 | Running | $110,450 |
| 13. | 30 | 24 | Jeff Gordon | Chevrolet | DuPont | 124/0 | 267 | Running | $129,078 |
| 14. | 24 | 20 | Tony Stewart | Chevrolet | The Home Depot | 121/0 | 267 | Running | $121,228 |
| 15. | 17 | 30 | Jeff Burton | Chevrolet | America Online | 118/0 | 267 | Running | $86,750 |
| 16. | 5 | 18 | Bobby Labonte | Chevrolet | Interstate Batteries | 115/0 | 267 | Running | $118,733 |
| 17. | 15 | 17 | Matt Kenseth | Ford | DeWalt Power Tools | 112/0 | 267 | Running | $123,428 |
| 18. | 36 | 2 | Rusty Wallace | Dodge | Miller Lite | 109/0 | 267 | Running | $115,883 |
| 19. | 25 | 25 | Brian Vickers* | Chevrolet | GMAC Financial Services | 106/0 | 267 | Running | $83,150 |
| 20. | 18 | 6 | Mark Martin | Ford | Viagra | 103/0 | 267 | Running | $84,400 |
| 21. | 19 | 5 | Terry Labonte | Chevrolet | Kellogg's | 105/5 | 267 | Running | $100,500 |
| 22. | 16 | 99 | Carl Edwards | Ford | Roush Racing | 97/0 | 267 | Running | $106,467 |
| 23. | 31 | 32 | Bobby Hamilton Jr. | Chevrolet | Tide | 94/0 | 267 | Running | $94,275 |
| 24. | 38 | 23 | Shane Hmiel | Dodge | Bill Davis Racing | 91/0 | 265 | Running | $71,650 |
| 25. | 33 | 4 | Jimmy Spencer | Chevrolet | Lucas Oil | 88/0 | 265 | Running | $71,350 |
| 26. | 14 | 10 | Scott Riggs* | Chevrolet | Valvoline/Wizard of Oz | 85/0 | 265 | Running | $95,437 |
| 27. | 32 | 49 | Ken Schrader | Dodge | Schwan's Home Service | 82/0 | 265 | Running | $69,650 |
| 28. | 23 | 31 | Robby Gordon | Chevrolet | Cingular Wireless | 79/0 | 265 | Running | $101,237 |
| 29. | 27 | 43 | Jeff Green | Dodge | Cheerios/Betty Crocker | 76/0 | 262 | Running | $94,600 |
| 30. | 35 | 0 | Ward Burton | Chevrolet | NetZero HiSpeed | 73/0 | 255 | Running | $66,100 |
| 31. | 21 | 41 | Casey Mears | Dodge | Target/Energizer | 75/5 | 243 | Running | $75,900 |
| 32. | 4 | 48 | Jimmie Johnson | Chevrolet | Lowe's | 67/0 | 239 | Accident | $85,000 |
| 33. | 7 | 12 | Ryan Newman | Dodge | ALLTEL | 69/5 | 223 | Accident | $121,867 |
| 34. | 28 | 40 | Sterling Marlin | Dodge | Coors Light | 61/0 | 216 | Accident | $98,725 |
| 35. | 29 | 29 | Kevin Harvick | Chevrolet | GM Goodwrench | 58/0 | 160 | Overheating | $100,378 |
| 36. | 37 | 22 | Scott Wimmer* | Dodge | Caterpillar | 55/0 | 146 | Overheating | $80,789 |
| 37. | 34 | 84 | Kyle Busch | Chevrolet | CARQUEST | 52/0 | 136 | Accident | $64,175 |
| 38. | 39 | 45 | Kyle Petty | Dodge | Georgia-Pacific/Brawny | 49/0 | 88 | Handling | $63,975 |
| 39. | 20 | 50 | Todd Bodine | Dodge | Arnold Development Co. | 46/0 | 66 | Steering | $63,765 |
| 40. | 41 | 02 | Hermie Sadler | Chevrolet | SCORE Motorsports | 43/0 | 38 | Rear end | $63,550 |
| 41. | 43 | 94 | Stanton Barrett | Ford | AmericInn/Racer's Edge | 40/0 | 30 | Vibration | $63,355 |
| 42. | 40 | 98 | Larry Gunselman | Ford | Mach 1 Inc. | 37/0 | 26 | Suspension | $63,170 |
| 43. | 42 | 72 | Kirk Shelmerdine | Ford | Vote for Bush | 34/0 | 3 | Clutch | $63,212 |

*Rookie. Time of race: 3 hours, 7 minutes, 39 seconds. Average speed: 128.058 mph. Margin of victory: .081 seconds. Caution flags: 9 for 39 laps. 2-4 (debris); 17-19 (Car 99—spin, front stretch); 142-150 (debris); 153-156 (Cars 97, 48—accident, back stretch); 198-203 (Car 41—accident, Turn 2); 210-213 (Car 12—spin, front stretch); 215-217 (Car 48—accident, back stretch); 242-245 (Car 9—spin, back stretch); 252-254 (Car 31—spin, Turn 4). Lap leaders: 24 lead changes among 12 drivers. Joe Nemechek 1-4, Jeremy Mayfield 5-16, Kasey Kahne 17-19, Mayfield 20-62, Greg Biffle 63-73, Mayfield 74, Ryan Newman 75-76, Ricky Rudd 77-78, Kurt Busch 79, Kahne 80-110, Biffle 111-130, Newman 132-137, Dale Jarrett 138-139, Kahne 140-143, Mayfield 144-158, Casey Mears 159-172, Biffle 173-195, Jarrett 196-197, Kahne 198, Terry Labonte 199, Biffle 200-209, Jamie McMurray 210-228, Elliott Sadler 229-230, Nemechek 231-267. Pole winner: Joe Nemechek, 180.156 mph. Dropped to rear: Hermie Sadler, Kirk Shelmerdine, Stanton Barrett (engine changes). Failed to qualify: Mike Garvey, Mike Wallace, Carl Long, Morgan Shepherd. Estimated attendance: 90,000.

## POINTS STANDINGS

| Rk. | Driver | Behind | | Rk. | Driver | Behind |
|-----|--------|--------|---|-----|--------|--------|
| 1. | Kurt Busch | — | | 6. | Tony Stewart | -173 |
| 2. | Dale Earnhardt Jr. | -29 | | 7. | Matt Kenseth | -180 |
| 3. | Jeff Gordon | -79 | | 8. | Ryan Newman | -232 |
| 4. | Elliott Sadler | -143 | | 9. | Jimmie Johnson | -247 |
| 5. | Mark Martin | -150 | | 10. | Jeremy Mayfield | -257 |

# UAW-GM QUALITY 500 ----------LOWE'S MOTOR SPEEDWAY

**Concord, N.C.—1.5-mile high-banked paved trioval • October 16, 2004—500 miles—334 laps**

| Fin. | St. | Car | Driver | Make | Sponsor | Pts./Bonus | Laps | Status | Winnings |
|---|---|---|---|---|---|---|---|---|---|
| 1. | 9 | 48 | Jimmie Johnson | Chevrolet | Lowe's | 185/5 | 334 | Running | $191,450 |
| 2. | 23 | 24 | Jeff Gordon | Chevrolet | DuPont | 170/0 | 334 | Running | $161,678 |
| 3. | 25 | 8 | Dale Earnhardt Jr. | Chevrolet | Budweiser | 170/5 | 334 | Running | $155,928 |
| 4. | 21 | 97 | Kurt Busch | Ford | IRWIN Industrial Tools | 165/5 | 334 | Running | $110,250 |
| 5. | 8 | 01 | Joe Nemechek | Chevrolet | G.I Joe/U.S. Army | 160/5 | 334 | Running | $112,750 |
| 6. | 39 | 88 | Dale Jarrett | Ford | UPS | 150/0 | 334 | Running | $113,992 |
| 7. | 5 | 38 | Elliott Sadler | Ford | Combos | 151/5 | 334 | Running | $112,158 |
| 8. | 24 | 42 | Jamie McMurray | Dodge | Texaco/Havoline | 142/0 | 334 | Running | $80,625 |
| 9. | 35 | 30 | Jeff Burton | Chevrolet | America Online | 138/0 | 334 | Running | $77,700 |
| 10. | 15 | 20 | Tony Stewart | Chevrolet | The Home Depot | 134/0 | 334 | Running | $113,903 |
| 11. | 36 | 17 | Matt Kenseth | Ford | DeWalt Power Tools | 130/0 | 334 | Running | $113,803 |
| 12. | 31 | 40 | Sterling Marlin | Dodge | Prilosec OTC | 132/5 | 334 | Running | $100,525 |
| 13. | 12 | 6 | Mark Martin | Ford | Viagra | 129/5 | 334 | Running | $74,500 |
| 14. | 1 | 12 | Ryan Newman | Dodge | ALLTEL | 126/5 | 334 | Running | $136,117 |
| 15. | 11 | 32 | Bobby Hamilton Jr. | Chevrolet | Tide | 118/0 | 333 | Running | $88,150 |
| 16. | 41 | 21 | Ricky Rudd | Ford | Keep it Genuine | 115/0 | 332 | Running | $89,006 |
| 17. | 34 | 18 | Bobby Labonte | Chevrolet | Interstate Batteries | 112/0 | 332 | Running | $103,483 |
| 18. | 19 | 31 | Robby Gordon | Chevrolet | Cingular Wireless | 109/0 | 332 | Running | $93,137 |
| 19. | 43 | 0 | Ward Burton | Chevrolet | NetZero | 106/0 | 331 | Running | $61,350 |
| 20. | 3 | 41 | Casey Mears | Dodge | Target | 103/0 | 331 | Running | $79,400 |
| 21. | 30 | 49 | Ken Schrader | Dodge | Schwan's Home Service | 100/0 | 331 | Running | $60,550 |
| 22. | 20 | 14 | John Andretti | Ford | VB/A Plus at Sunoco | 97/0 | 330 | Running | $56,675 |
| 23. | 16 | 77 | Brendan Gaughan* | Dodge | Jasper Eng. & Trans./Kodak | 94/0 | 329 | Running | $69,375 |
| 24. | 29 | 09 | Johnny Sauter* | Dodge | Miccosukee Resort | 91/0 | 329 | Running | $60,455 |
| 25. | 40 | 5 | Terry Labonte | Chevrolet | Kellogg's | 88/0 | 328 | Running | $86,325 |
| 26. | 42 | 22 | Scott Wimmer* | Dodge | Caterpillar | 85/0 | 327 | Running | $77,375 |
| 27. | 32 | 45 | Kyle Petty | Dodge | Georgia-Pacific/Brawny | 82/0 | 326 | Running | $66,934 |
| 28. | 6 | 15 | Michael Waltrip | Chevrolet | NAPA | 79/0 | 319 | Accident | $91,991 |
| 29. | 22 | 4 | Jimmy Spencer | Chevrolet | Lucas Oil | 76/0 | 310 | Accident | $58,050 |
| 30. | 13 | 19 | Jeremy Mayfield | Dodge | Dodge Dealers/UAW | 73/0 | 277 | Accident | $66,425 |
| 31. | 14 | 2 | Rusty Wallace | Dodge | Miller Lite | 70/0 | 274 | Running | $98,633 |
| 32. | 2 | 9 | Kasey Kahne* | Dodge | Dodge Dealers/UAW | 77/10 | 267 | Accident | $133,050 |
| 33. | 18 | 16 | Greg Biffle | Ford | National Guard | 64/0 | 265 | Running | $63,550 |
| 34. | 38 | 84 | Kyle Busch | Chevrolet | CARQUEST | 61/0 | 264 | Accident | $54,575 |
| 35. | 33 | 43 | Jeff Green | Dodge | Cheerios/Betty Crocker | 58/0 | 238 | Engine | $80,750 |
| 36. | 7 | 29 | Kevin Harvick | Chevrolet | GM Goodwrench | 55/0 | 221 | Engine | $90,793 |
| 37. | 10 | 99 | Dave Blaney | Ford | Canteen Vending/Kraft Foods | 52/0 | 218 | Accident | $88,087 |
| 38. | 4 | 10 | Scott Riggs* | Chevrolet | Valvoline | 49/0 | 30 | Engine | $82,022 |
| 39. | 27 | 37 | Kevin Lepage | Dodge | Carter's Royal Dispos-all | 46/0 | 25 | Ignition | $54,290 |
| 40. | 17 | 25 | Brian Vickers* | Chevrolet | GMAC Financial Services | 43/0 | 22 | Accident | $62,255 |
| 41. | 37 | 13 | Greg Sacks | Dodge | ARC Dehooker/Vita Coco | 40/0 | 10 | Radiator | $54,220 |
| 42. | 26 | 50 | Jeff Fuller | Dodge | Arnold Development Co. | 37/0 | 7 | Accident | $54,180 |
| 43. | 28 | 51 | Tony Raines | Chevrolet | Marathon/Chase | 34/0 | 1 | Accident | $53,499 |

*Rookie. Time of race: 3 hours, 50 minutes, 51 seconds. Average speed: 130.214 mph. Margin of victory: 1.727 seconds. Caution flags: 11 for 53 laps. 2-7 (Cars 16, 97, 14, 24, 51, 49—accident, Turn 1); 9-12 (Car 50—accident, Turn 1); 24-30 (Car 25—accident, front stretch); 77-80 (Cars 24, 2—accident, front stretch); 121-124 (debris); 173-176 (Car 17—accident, Turn 3); 211-214 (debris); 224-231 (oil on track); 269-272 (Car 9—accident, Turn 1); 313-317 (Cars 4, 77, 6, 12—accident, front stretch); 320-322 (Car 15—accident, Turn 2). Note: On Lap 24, the race was red-flagged (12 minutes, 12 seconds) to repair the SAFER barrier on the front stretch. Lap leaders: 18 lead changes among 9 drivers. Ryan Newman 1-28, Elliott Sadler 29-41, Kasey Kahne 42-124, Dale Earnhardt Jr. 125-129, Kahne 130-176, Earnhardt 177-179, Jimmie Johnson 180-186, Kahne 187-215, Mark Martin 216-219, Kahne 220-267, Newman 268-269, Sterling Marlin 270, Martin 271-277, Kurt Busch 278-280, Martin 281-301, Johnson 302-312, Newman 313, Joe Nemechek 314-317, Johnson 318-334. Pole winner: Ryan Newman, 188.877 mph (record). Dropped to rear: Dave Blaney (driver change, Carl Edwards replaced Blaney on Lap 23), Jamie McMurray (backup car). Failed to qualify: Kenny Wallace, Derrike Cope, Mike Wallace, Carl Long, Kirk Shelmerdine, Larry Foyt, Hermie Sadler, Morgan Shepherd, Geoffrey Bodine. Estimated attendance: 140,000.

## POINTS STANDINGS

| Rk. | Driver | Behind | | Rk. | Driver | Behind |
|---|---|---|---|---|---|---|
| 1. | Kurt Busch | — | | 6. | Tony Stewart | -204 |
| 2. | Dale Earnhardt Jr. | -24 | | 7. | Matt Kenseth | -215 |
| 3. | Jeff Gordon | -74 | | 8. | Jimmie Johnson | -227 |
| 4. | Elliott Sadler | -157 | | 9. | Ryan Newman | -271 |
| 5. | Mark Martin | -186 | | 10. | Jeremy Mayfield | -349 |

# SUBWAY 500 ------------- MARTINSVILLE SPEEDWAY

**Martinsville, Va.—.526-mile paved oval • October 24, 2004—263 miles—500 laps**

| Fin. | St. | Car | Driver | Make | Sponsor | Pts./Bonus | Laps | Status | Winnings |
|------|-----|-----|--------|------|---------|------------|------|--------|----------|
| 1. | 18 | 48 | Jimmie Johnson | Chevrolet | Lowe's | 185/5 | 500 | Running | $157,440 |
| 2. | 8 | 42 | Jamie McMurray | Dodge | Texaco/Havoline | 175/5 | 500 | Running | $104,025 |
| 3. | 1 | 12 | Ryan Newman | Dodge | ALLTEL | 170/5 | 500 | Running | $132,517 |
| 4. | 16 | 40 | Sterling Marlin | Dodge | Coors Light | 165/5 | 500 | Running | $113,545 |
| 5. | 7 | 97 | Kurt Busch | Ford | IRWIN Industrial Tools | 165/10 | 500 | Running | $107,175 |
| 6. | 11 | 19 | Jeremy Mayfield | Dodge | Dodge Dealers/UAW | 150/5 | 500 | Running | $95,350 |
| 7. | 10 | 43 | Jeff Green | Dodge | Cheerios/Betty Crocker | 146/0 | 500 | Running | $93,600 |
| 8. | 19 | 29 | Kevin Harvick | Chevrolet | GM Goodwrench | 147/5 | 500 | Running | $101,903 |
| 9. | 15 | 24 | Jeff Gordon | Chevrolet | DuPont | 143/5 | 500 | Running | $107,853 |
| 10. | 2 | 2 | Rusty Wallace | Dodge | Miller Lite | 139/5 | 500 | Running | $106,308 |
| 11. | 12 | 30 | Jeff Burton | Chevrolet | America Online | 130/0 | 500 | Running | $73,175 |
| 12. | 23 | 6 | Mark Martin | Ford | Viagra | 127/0 | 500 | Running | $70,550 |
| 13. | 38 | 9 | Kasey Kahne* | Dodge | Dodge Dealers/UAW | 129/5 | 500 | Running | $99,350 |
| 14. | 9 | 21 | Ricky Rudd | Ford | Motorcraft | 121/0 | 500 | Running | $87,681 |
| 15. | 13 | 20 | Tony Stewart | Chevrolet | The Home Depot | 123/5 | 500 | Running | $105,903 |
| 16. | 25 | 17 | Matt Kenseth | Ford | DeWalt Power Tools | 120/5 | 500 | Running | $108,203 |
| 17. | 21 | 16 | Greg Biffle | Ford | Subway/National Guard | 112/0 | 500 | Running | $68,925 |
| 18. | 17 | 18 | Bobby Labonte | Chevrolet | Interstate Batteries | 109/0 | 500 | Running | $101,813 |
| 19. | 30 | 15 | Michael Waltrip | Chevrolet | NAPA | 106/0 | 500 | Running | $92,131 |
| 20. | 24 | 22 | Scott Wimmer* | Dodge | Caterpillar | 103/0 | 500 | Running | $84,425 |
| 21. | 5 | 06 | Travis Kvapil | Dodge | Mobil 1/Jasper Engines | 100/0 | 500 | Running | $55,975 |
| 22. | 26 | 45 | Kyle Petty | Dodge | Georgia-Pacific/Brawny | 97/0 | 500 | Running | $72,025 |
| 23. | 36 | 31 | Robby Gordon | Chevrolet | Cingular Wireless | 94/0 | 500 | Running | $91,487 |
| 24. | 22 | 99 | Carl Edwards | Ford | Roush Racing | 91/0 | 500 | Running | $92,042 |
| 25. | 27 | 5 | Terry Labonte | Chevrolet | Kellogg's | 93/5 | 500 | Running | $85,500 |
| 26. | 6 | 10 | Scott Riggs* | Chevrolet | Valvoline | 85/0 | 500 | Running | $83,287 |
| 27. | 34 | 25 | Brian Vickers* | Chevrolet | GMAC Financial Services | 82/0 | 498 | Running | $65,835 |
| 28. | 4 | 0 | Ward Burton | Chevrolet | NetZero | 79/0 | 497 | Running | $58,085 |
| 29. | 28 | 41 | Casey Mears | Dodge | Target | 76/0 | 496 | Running | $67,950 |
| 30. | 29 | 01 | Joe Nemechek | Chevrolet | U.S. Army | 73/0 | 488 | Running | $73,764 |
| 31. | 20 | 49 | Ken Schrader | Dodge | Schwan's Home Service | 70/0 | 484 | Running | $54,275 |
| 32. | 33 | 38 | Elliott Sadler | Ford | M&M's | 67/0 | 475 | Accident | $93,033 |
| 33. | 3 | 8 | Dale Earnhardt Jr. | Chevrolet | Budweiser | 64/0 | 449 | Accident | $103,173 |
| 34. | 14 | 77 | Brendan Gaughan* | Dodge | Kodak/Jasper Eng. & Trans. | 61/0 | 424 | Running | $62,020 |
| 35. | 39 | 4 | Jimmy Spencer | Chevrolet | Lucas Oil | 58/0 | 421 | Running | $53,975 |
| 36. | 35 | 32 | Bobby Hamilton Jr. | Chevrolet | Tide | 55/0 | 404 | Accident | $61,925 |
| 37. | 32 | 88 | Dale Jarrett | Ford | UPS | 52/0 | 403 | Running | $84,792 |
| 38. | 31 | 02 | Hermie Sadler | Chevrolet | SCORE Motorsports | 49/0 | 159 | Electrical | $53,825 |
| 39. | 37 | 98 | Chad Chaffin | Ford | Mach 1 Inc. | 46/0 | 100 | Rear end | $53,765 |
| 40. | 41 | 72 | Kirk Shelmerdine | Ford | Vote for Bush | 43/0 | 86 | Engine | $53,690 |
| 41. | 42 | 80 | Mario Gosselin | Ford | Hover Racing | 40/0 | 74 | Suspension | $53,640 |
| 42. | 43 | 37 | Kevin Lepage | Dodge | Carter's Royal Dispos-all | 37/0 | 11 | Vibration | $53,590 |
| 43. | 40 | 50 | Todd Bodine | Dodge | Arnold Development Co. | 34/0 | 1 | Accident | $52,891 |

*Rookie. Time of race: 3 hours, 58 minutes, 43 seconds. Average speed: 66.103 mph. Margin of victory: 1.225 seconds. Caution flags: 17 for 125 laps. 4-7 (Cars 01, 50—accident, Turn 2); 17-22 (Cars 77, 40, 19—accident, Turn 4); 41-47 (Car 21—spin, Turn 2); 66-71 (Car 31—accident, Turn 4); 77-83 (Cars 21, 31—accident, Turn 4); 107-113 (Cars 88, 41, 32, 4—accident, Turn 3); 184-201 (Car 45—spin, Turn 2); 292-297 (Car 99—spin, Turn 2); 322-335 (debris); 355-360 (Cars 18, 43, 49—accident, Turn 4); 372-376 (Car 22—spin, Turn 2); 410-416 (Car 88—spin, Turn 3); 418-427 (debris); 451-455 (Car 38—spin, Turn 4); 468-472 (Cars 8, 45—accident, Turn 2); 477-484 (Cars 01, 38—accident, Turn 2); 490-493 (Cars 99, 31—spin, Turn 3). Lap leaders: 22 lead changes among 12 drivers. Ryan Newman 1-9, Rusty Wallace 10-42, Terry Labonte 43-50, Kasey Kahne 51-67, T. Labonte 68-89, Tony Stewart 90-107, Kurt Busch 108, Sterling Marlin 109-130, Busch 131-184, Matt Kenseth 185, Busch 186-249, Kevin Harvick 250-292, Wallace 293, Kenseth 294, Harvick 295-355, Busch 356, Jamie McMurray 357-376, Jeff Gordon 377-382, McMurray 383-404, Jimmie Johnson 405-410, McMurray 411, Marlin 412-439, Johnson 440-500. Pole winner: Ryan Newman, 97.043 mph (record). Dropped to rear: Kevin Lepage, Kirk Shelmerdine (engine changes). Failed to qualify: Klaus Graf, Mike Garvey, Morgan Shepherd, Ryan McGlynn, Greg Sacks, Brad Teague, Carl Long. Estimated attendance: 91,000.

## POINTS STANDINGS

| Rk. | Driver | Behind | | Rk. | Driver | Behind |
|-----|--------|--------|---|-----|--------|--------|
| 1. | Kurt Busch | — | | 6. | Tony Stewart | -246 |
| 2. | Jeff Gordon | -96 | | 7. | Elliott Sadler | -255 |
| 3. | Dale Earnhardt Jr. | -125 | | 8. | Matt Kenseth | -260 |
| 4. | Jimmie Johnson | -207 | | 9. | Ryan Newman | -266 |
| 5. | Mark Martin | -224 | | 10. | Jeremy Mayfield | -364 |

**Hampton, Ga.—1.54-mile banked paved oval • October 31, 2004—500.5 miles—325 laps**

| Fin. | St. | Car | Driver | Make | Sponsor | Pts./Bonus | Laps | Status | Winnings |
|------|-----|-----|--------|------|---------|-----------|------|--------|----------|
| 1. | 8 | 48 | Jimmie Johnson | Chevrolet | Lowe's | 185/5 | 325 | Running | $298,250 |
| 2. | 7 | 6 | Mark Martin | Ford | Viagra | 180/10 | 325 | Running | $238,500 |
| 3. | 4 | 99 | Carl Edwards | Ford | World Financial Group | 170/5 | 325 | Running | $180,117 |
| 4. | 2 | 01 | Joe Nemechek | Chevrolet | U.S. Army | 165/5 | 325 | Running | $145,050 |
| 5. | 32 | 9 | Kasey Kahne* | Dodge | Dodge Dealers/UAW | 160/5 | 325 | Running | $137,275 |
| 6. | 21 | 30 | Jeff Burton | Chevrolet | America Online | 150/0 | 325 | Running | $110,700 |
| 7. | 13 | 25 | Brian Vickers* | Chevrolet | GMAC Financial Services | 146/0 | 325 | Running | $100,250 |
| 8. | 29 | 42 | Jamie McMurray | Dodge | Texaco/Havoline | 142/0 | 325 | Running | $99,325 |
| 9. | 15 | 20 | Tony Stewart | Chevrolet | The Home Depot | 138/0 | 324 | Running | $130,063 |
| 10. | 5 | 16 | Greg Biffle | Ford | National Guard/Subway | 134/0 | 324 | Running | $95,735 |
| 11. | 12 | 2 | Rusty Wallace | Dodge | Miller Lite | 130/0 | 324 | Running | $128,233 |
| 12. | 43 | 21 | Ricky Rudd | Ford | Rent-A-Center/Motorcraft | 127/0 | 324 | Running | $108,456 |
| 13. | 16 | 41 | Casey Mears | Dodge | Target | 124/0 | 324 | Running | $98,625 |
| 14. | 40 | 15 | Michael Waltrip | Chevrolet | NAPA | 126/5 | 324 | Running | $113,081 |
| 15. | 20 | 88 | Dale Jarrett | Ford | UPS | 118/0 | 324 | Running | $111,742 |
| 16. | 14 | 31 | Robby Gordon | Chevrolet | Cingular Wireless | 115/0 | 324 | Running | $110,512 |
| 17. | 1 | 12 | Ryan Newman | Dodge | Mobil 1/ALLTEL | 117/5 | 323 | Running | $138,092 |
| 18. | 25 | 77 | Brendan Gaughan* | Dodge | Jasper Eng. & Trans./Kodak | 109/0 | 323 | Running | $85,225 |
| 19. | 41 | 40 | Sterling Marlin | Dodge | Coors Light | 106/0 | 323 | Running | $109,400 |
| 20. | 19 | 18 | Bobby Labonte | Chevrolet | Wellbutrin XL | 103/0 | 323 | Running | $119,233 |
| 21. | 35 | 43 | Jeff Green | Dodge | Bugles | 100/0 | 322 | Running | $101,050 |
| 22. | 38 | 98 | Bill Elliott | Dodge | McDonald's | 97/0 | 322 | Running | $70,700 |
| 23. | 37 | 49 | Ken Schrader | Dodge | Red Baron Frozen Pizza | 94/0 | 321 | Running | $73,200 |
| 24. | 31 | 23 | Shane Hmiel | Dodge | Bill Davis Racing | 91/0 | 321 | Running | $73,325 |
| 25. | 17 | 14 | John Andretti | Ford | VB/APlus at Sunoco | 88/0 | 320 | Running | $69,000 |
| 26. | 11 | 19 | Jeremy Mayfield | Dodge | Dodge Dealers/UAW | 85/0 | 320 | Running | $92,000 |
| 27. | 36 | 11 | J.J. Yeley | Chevrolet | MBNA | 82/0 | 319 | Running | $67,400 |
| 28. | 23 | 37 | Kevin Lepage | Dodge | Carter Racing | 79/0 | 319 | Running | $66,800 |
| 29. | 18 | 45 | Kyle Petty | Dodge | Georgia-Pacific/Brawny | 76/0 | 319 | Running | $80,150 |
| 30. | 34 | 0 | Ward Burton | Chevrolet | NetZero | 73/0 | 318 | Running | $69,500 |
| 31. | 42 | 5 | Terry Labonte | Chevrolet | Kellogg's | 70/0 | 318 | Running | $93,100 |
| 32. | 26 | 06 | Travis Kvapil | Dodge | Mobil 1 | 67/0 | 317 | Running | $66,175 |
| 33. | 6 | 8 | Dale Earnhardt Jr. | Chevrolet | Budweiser | 64/0 | 311 | Accident | $114,103 |
| 34. | 10 | 24 | Jeff Gordon | Chevrolet | DuPont | 61/0 | 299 | Engine | $113,278 |
| 35. | 9 | 29 | Kevin Harvick | Chevrolet | GM Goodwrench | 58/0 | 296 | Engine | $101,478 |
| 36. | 3 | 38 | Elliott Sadler | Ford | M&M's | 55/0 | 262 | Running | $104,883 |
| 37. | 33 | 1 | Martin Truex Jr. | Chevrolet | Bass Pro Shops | 52/0 | 259 | Engine | $65,400 |
| 38. | 27 | 32 | Bobby Hamilton Jr. | Chevrolet | Tide | 49/0 | 225 | Running | $81,664 |
| 39. | 24 | 50 | Todd Bodine | Dodge | U.S. Micro | 46/0 | 222 | Handling | $65,150 |
| 40. | 30 | 51 | Tony Raines | Chevrolet | Universal Chevrolet/Marathon Oil | 43/0 | 220 | Oil leak | $65,025 |
| 41. | 39 | 17 | Matt Kenseth | Ford | DeWalt Power Tools | 40/0 | 175 | Engine | $115,678 |
| 42. | 22 | 97 | Kurt Busch | Ford | Sharpie | 37/0 | 51 | Engine | $84,790 |
| 43. | 28 | 84 | Kyle Busch | Chevrolet | CARQUEST | 34/0 | 44 | Timing belt | $64,909 |

*Rookie. Time of race: 3 hours, 25 minutes, 54 seconds. Average speed: 145.847 mph. Margin of victory: .293 seconds. Caution flags: 6 for 33 laps. 54-61 (oil on track); 138-142 (Car 18—spin, Turn 2); 178-181 (oil on track); 287-293 (oil on track); 301-305 (Car 29—stalled, pit road); 312-315 (Car 8—accident, back stretch). Lap leaders: 16 lead changes among 7 drivers. Ryan Newman-pole, Joe Nemechek 1, Newman 2-49, Carl Edwards 50-53, Newman 54-63, Edwards 64-74, Mark Martin 75-115, Jimmie Johnson 116-119, Martin 120-178, Michael Waltrip 179, Martin 180-236, Johnson 237, Nemechek 238-239, Martin 240-309, Johnson 310-311, Kasey Kahne 312-315, Johnson 316-325. Pole winner: Ryan Newman, 191.575 mph. Dropped to rear: Jeff Burton, Ricky Rudd (engine changes). Failed to qualify: Scott Riggs, Scott Wimmer, Kerry Earnhardt, Johnny Sauter, Hermie Sadler, Mike Wallace, Derrike Cope, Randy LaJoie, Greg Sacks, Larry Foyt, Kirk Shelmerdine, Morgan Shepherd, Andy Belmont, Larry Hollenbeck, Kenny Wallace. Estimated attendance: 104,000.

## POINTS STANDINGS

| Rk. | Driver | Behind |
|-----|--------|--------|
| 1. | Kurt Busch | — |
| 2. | Jimmie Johnson | -59 |
| 3. | Jeff Gordon | -72 |
| 4. | Mark Martin | -81 |
| 5. | Dale Earnhardt Jr. | -98 |
| 6. | Tony Stewart | -145 |
| 7. | Ryan Newman | -186 |
| 8. | Elliott Sadler | -237 |
| 9. | Matt Kenseth | -257 |
| 10. | Jeremy Mayfield | -316 |

**2004 SEASON**

**Avondale, Ariz.—1-mile paved oval • November 7, 2004—312 miles—312 laps**

| Fin. | St. | Car | Driver | Make | Sponsor | Pts./Bonus | Laps | Status | Winnings |
|---|---|---|---|---|---|---|---|---|---|
| 1. | 14 | 8 | Dale Earnhardt Jr. | Chevrolet | Budweiser | 190/10 | 315 | Running | $274,503 |
| 2. | 1 | 12 | Ryan Newman | Dodge | ALLTEL/TXT2Win MVP Sweeps. | 175/5 | 315 | Running | $181,167 |
| 3. | 8 | 24 | Jeff Gordon | Chevrolet | DuPont | 170/5 | 315 | Running | $170,503 |
| 4. | 5 | 29 | Kevin Harvick | Chevrolet | GM Goodwrench | 160/0 | 315 | Running | $134,938 |
| 5. | 4 | 9 | Kasey Kahne* | Dodge | Dodge Dealers/UAW | 155/0 | 315 | Running | $126,950 |
| 6. | 13 | 48 | Jimmie Johnson | Chevrolet | Lowe's | 150/0 | 315 | Running | $96,225 |
| 7. | 15 | 2 | Rusty Wallace | Dodge | Miller Lite | 146/0 | 315 | Running | $111,658 |
| 8. | 6 | 20 | Tony Stewart | Chevrolet | The Home Depot | 142/0 | 315 | Running | $112,028 |
| 9. | 27 | 18 | Bobby Labonte | Chevrolet | Interstate Batteries | 143/5 | 315 | Running | $113,083 |
| 10. | 28 | 97 | Kurt Busch | Ford | IRWIN Industrial Tools | 139/5 | 315 | Running | $84,300 |
| 11. | 20 | 30 | Jeff Burton | Chevrolet | America Online | 130/0 | 315 | Running | $72,500 |
| 12. | 3 | 01 | Joe Nemechek | Chevrolet | U.S. Army | 127/0 | 315 | Running | $88,200 |
| 13. | 23 | 16 | Greg Biffle | Ford | National Guard | 124/0 | 315 | Running | $70,225 |
| 14. | 11 | 10 | Scott Riggs* | Chevrolet | Valvoline | 121/0 | 315 | Running | $85,187 |
| 15. | 22 | 6 | Mark Martin | Ford | Viagra | 118/0 | 315 | Running | $67,975 |
| 16. | 32 | 32 | Bobby Hamilton Jr. | Chevrolet | Tide | 115/0 | 315 | Running | $80,950 |
| 17. | 19 | 15 | Michael Waltrip | Chevrolet | NAPA | 112/0 | 315 | Running | $91,006 |
| 18. | 2 | 25 | Brian Vickers* | Chevrolet | GMAC Financial Services | 109/0 | 315 | Running | $65,825 |
| 19. | 25 | 21 | Ricky Rudd | Ford | Motorcraft | 106/0 | 315 | Running | $83,081 |
| 20. | 18 | 49 | Ken Schrader | Dodge | Schwan's Home Service | 103/0 | 315 | Running | $57,300 |
| 21. | 24 | 19 | Jeremy Mayfield | Dodge | Dodge Dealers/UAW | 100/0 | 315 | Running | $78,525 |
| 22. | 26 | 88 | Dale Jarrett | Ford | UPS | 97/0 | 315 | Running | $87,767 |
| 23. | 12 | 43 | Jeff Green | Dodge | Cheerios/Betty Crocker | 94/0 | 315 | Running | $82,375 |
| 24. | 10 | 42 | Jamie McMurray | Dodge | Texaco/Havoline | 91/0 | 315 | Running | $64,800 |
| 25. | 35 | 40 | Sterling Marlin | Dodge | Coors Light | 88/0 | 314 | Running | $89,050 |
| 26. | 38 | 22 | Scott Wimmer* | Dodge | Caterpillar | 85/0 | 314 | Running | $73,925 |
| 27. | 37 | 37 | Kevin Lepage | Dodge | Carter Racing | 82/0 | 314 | Running | $52,300 |
| 28. | 34 | 45 | Kyle Petty | Dodge | Georgia-Pacific/Brawny | 79/0 | 313 | Running | $63,564 |
| 29. | 33 | 4 | Mike Wallace | Chevrolet | Lucas Oil | 76/0 | 313 | Running | $54,550 |
| 30. | 40 | 77 | Brendan Gaughan* | Dodge | Kodak/Jasper Eng. & Trans. | 73/0 | 311 | Running | $59,925 |
| 31. | 21 | 14 | John Andretti | Ford | VB/APlus at Sunoco | 70/0 | 311 | Running | $52,300 |
| 32. | 31 | 5 | Terry Labonte | Chevrolet | "The Incredibles"/Kellogg's | 67/0 | 309 | Running | $78,400 |
| 33. | 42 | 02 | Hermie Sadler | Chevrolet | Treasure Island-Las Vegas | 64/0 | 307 | Running | $52,450 |
| 34. | 7 | 41 | Casey Mears | Dodge | Target | 61/0 | 306 | Accident | $51,400 |
| 35. | 17 | 31 | Robby Gordon | Chevrolet | Cingular Wireless | 58/0 | 306 | Engine | $86,462 |
| 36. | 16 | 17 | Matt Kenseth | Ford | DeWalt Power Tools | 60/5 | 280 | Engine | $101,903 |
| 37. | 29 | 99 | Carl Edwards | Ford | Roush Racing | 52/0 | 272 | Running | $84,417 |
| 38. | 9 | 38 | Elliott Sadler | Ford | Pedigree | 54/5 | 252 | Running | $89,708 |
| 39. | 30 | 09 | Johnny Sauter* | Dodge | Miccosukee Resort | 46/0 | 236 | Accident | $50,750 |
| 40. | 39 | 0 | Ward Burton | Chevrolet | NetZero | 43/0 | 201 | Rear end | $50,600 |
| 41. | 43 | 89 | Morgan Shepherd | Dodge | Racing With Jesus/Red Line Oil | 40/0 | 181 | Handling | $50,460 |
| 42. | 41 | 98 | Randy LaJoie | Ford | Airaid Premium Filters | 37/0 | 105 | Transmission | $50,335 |
| 43. | 36 | 50 | Todd Bodine | Dodge | Arnold Development Co. | 34/0 | 11 | Vibration | $50,447 |

*Rookie. Time of race: 3 hours, 19 minutes, 16 seconds. Average speed: 94.848 mph. Margin of victory: 1.431 seconds. Caution flags: 11 for 63 laps. 77-80 (Car 02—stalled, Turn 3); 106-114 (debris); 120-123 (Car 14—accident, Turn 4); 129-132 (Cars 0, 01, 6, 12, 29, 42, 97—accident, Turn 4); 144-149 (Cars 10, 99—accident, Turn 4); 155-159 (Car 38—accident, Turn 1); 226-231 (Car 5—accident, front stretch); 240-243 (Car 09—accident, back stretch); 283-293 (oil on track); 299-302 (Car 42—accident, Turn 2); 308-313 (debris; Car 41—accident, Turn 2). Notes: On Lap 110, the race was red-flagged (21 minutes, 27 seconds) for rain. On Lap 309, the race was red-flagged (10 minutes, 34 seconds) to clean up oil on the track. Lap leaders: 10 lead changes among 7 drivers. Ryan Newman 1-59, Dale Earnhardt Jr. 60-107, Elliott Sadler 108-123, Jeff Gordon 124-144, Earnhardt 145-202, Matt Kenseth 203-206, Kurt Busch 207-220, Gordon 221-223, Bobby Labonte 224-227, Gordon 228-303, Earnhardt 304-315. Pole winner: Ryan Newman, 135.854 mph (record). Dropped to rear: Michael Waltrip (backup car); Sterling Marlin, Kevin Lepage (engine changes). Failed to qualify: Mike Garvey, Tony Raines, Stanton Barrett, Mario Gosselin, Ryan McGlynn, Kirk Shelmerdine, Geoffrey Bodine. Estimated attendance: 105,000.

## POINTS STANDINGS

| Rk. | Driver | Behind | | Rk. | Driver | Behind |
|---|---|---|---|---|---|---|
| 1. | Kurt Busch | — | | 6. | Tony Stewart | -142 |
| 2. | Jeff Gordon | -41 | | 7. | Ryan Newman | -150 |
| 3. | Dale Earnhardt Jr. | -47 | | 8. | Elliott Sadler | -322 |
| 4. | Jimmie Johnson | -48 | | 9. | Matt Kenseth | -336 |
| 5. | Mark Martin | -102 | | 10. | Jeremy Mayfield | -355 |

# MOUNTAIN DEW SOUTHERN 500 ------ DARLINGTON RACEWAY

**Darlington, S.C.—1.366-mile banked paved oval • November 14, 2004—500 miles—367 laps**

| Fin. | St. | Car | Driver | Make | Sponsor | Pts./Bonus | Laps | Status | Winnings |
|------|-----|-----|--------|------|---------|-----------|------|--------|----------|
| 1. | 4 | 48 | Jimmie Johnson | Chevrolet | Lowe's | 185/5 | 367 | Running | $269,675 |
| 2. | 5 | 6 | Mark Martin | Ford | Viagra | 175/5 | 367 | Running | $190,825 |
| 3. | 2 | 24 | Jeff Gordon | Chevrolet | DuPont | 175/10 | 367 | Running | $185,403 |
| 4. | 11 | 42 | Jamie McMurray | Dodge | Texaco/Havoline | 165/5 | 367 | Running | $118,675 |
| 5. | 13 | 9 | Kasey Kahne* | Dodge | Dodge Dealers/UAW | 155/0 | 367 | Running | $129,550 |
| 6. | 1 | 97 | Kurt Busch | Ford | Smirnoff Ice/Sharpie | 155/5 | 367 | Running | $103,275 |
| 7. | 24 | 99 | Carl Edwards | Ford | World Financial Group | 146/0 | 367 | Running | $114,642 |
| 8. | 18 | 01 | Joe Nemechek | Chevrolet | USG Sheetrock | 147/5 | 367 | Running | $102,625 |
| 9. | 15 | 18 | Bobby Labonte | Chevrolet | Interstate Batteries | 138/0 | 367 | Running | $115,958 |
| 10. | 30 | 0 | Mike Bliss | Chevrolet | NetZero | 134/0 | 367 | Running | $86,750 |
| 11. | 3 | 8 | Dale Earnhardt Jr. | Chevrolet | Budweiser | 130/0 | 367 | Running | $114,253 |
| 12. | 20 | 40 | Sterling Marlin | Dodge | Coors Light | 132/5 | 367 | Running | $103,450 |
| 13. | 21 | 30 | Jeff Burton | Chevrolet | America Online | 124/0 | 367 | Running | $78,600 |
| 14. | 32 | 43 | Jeff Green | Dodge | Cheerios/Betty Crocker | 121/0 | 367 | Running | $95,025 |
| 15. | 23 | 31 | Robby Gordon | Chevrolet | Cingular Wireless | 123/5 | 367 | Running | $100,562 |
| 16. | 26 | 21 | Ricky Rudd | Ford | Motorcraft | 115/0 | 367 | Running | $93,731 |
| 17. | 6 | 20 | Tony Stewart | Chevrolet | The Home Depot | 112/0 | 366 | Running | $109,678 |
| 18. | 16 | 2 | Rusty Wallace | Dodge | Miller Lite | 109/0 | 365 | Running | $106,058 |
| 19. | 10 | 19 | Jeremy Mayfield | Dodge | Dodge Dealers/UAW | 106/0 | 365 | Running | $88,150 |
| 20. | 9 | 17 | Matt Kenseth | Ford | DeWalt Power Tools | 108/5 | 365 | Running | $113,603 |
| 21. | 27 | 25 | Brian Vickers* | Chevrolet | GMAC Financial Services | 100/0 | 365 | Running | $71,700 |
| 22. | 28 | 22 | Scott Wimmer* | Dodge | Caterpillar | 97/0 | 365 | Running | $83,975 |
| 23. | 8 | 38 | Elliott Sadler | Ford | M&M's | 94/0 | 365 | Running | $98,683 |
| 24. | 19 | 16 | Greg Biffle | Ford | National Guard/Subway | 96/5 | 365 | Running | $69,550 |
| 25. | 31 | 10 | Scott Riggs* | Chevrolet | Valvoline | 88/0 | 364 | Running | $86,437 |
| 26. | 22 | 41 | Casey Mears | Dodge | Target | 85/0 | 364 | Running | $70,575 |
| 27. | 29 | 77 | Brendan Gaughan* | Dodge | Kodak/Jasper Eng. & Trans. | 82/0 | 363 | Running | $67,375 |
| 28. | 25 | 5 | Terry Labonte | Chevrolet | Kellogg's | 79/0 | 363 | Running | $85,500 |
| 29. | 42 | 09 | Johnny Sauter* | Dodge | Miccosukee Resort | 76/0 | 363 | Running | $58,050 |
| 30. | 33 | 49 | Ken Schrader | Dodge | Schwan's Home Service | 73/0 | 362 | Running | $55,875 |
| 31. | 35 | 32 | Bobby Hamilton Jr. | Chevrolet | Tide | 70/0 | 357 | Running | $71,514 |
| 32. | 14 | 29 | Kevin Harvick | Chevrolet | GM Goodwrench | 67/0 | 354 | Running | $90,728 |
| 33. | 17 | 15 | Michael Waltrip | Chevrolet | NAPA | 64/0 | 336 | Running | $91,756 |
| 34. | 7 | 12 | Ryan Newman | Dodge | ALLTEL/Mobil 1 | 61/0 | 330 | Engine | $101,517 |
| 35. | 34 | 45 | Kyle Petty | Dodge | Georgia-Pacific/Brawny | 58/0 | 300 | Accident | $54,425 |
| 36. | 39 | 98 | Randy LaJoie | Ford | Mach 1 Inc. | 55/0 | 262 | Engine | $54,275 |
| 37. | 12 | 88 | Dale Jarrett | Ford | UPS | 52/0 | 194 | Accident | $84,992 |
| 38. | 37 | 4 | Mike Wallace | Chevrolet | Lucas Oil | 49/0 | 180 | Oil pump | $53,850 |
| 39. | 38 | 50 | Todd Bodine | Dodge | Mesco Building Solutions | 46/0 | 143 | Accident | $53,725 |
| 40. | 41 | 02 | Hermie Sadler | Chevrolet | East Tennessee Trailers | 43/0 | 130 | Handling | $53,575 |
| 41. | 43 | 80 | Mario Gosselin | Ford | ADESA Impact | 40/0 | 14 | Too slow | $53,450 |
| 42. | 36 | 72 | Kirk Shelmerdine | Ford | Freddie B's | 37/0 | 14 | Too slow | $53,340 |
| 43. | 40 | 89 | Morgan Shepherd | Dodge | Racing With Jesus/Red Line Oil | 34/0 | 10 | Too slow | $53,454 |

*Rookie. Time of race: 4 hours, 0 minutes, 33 seconds. Average speed: 125.044 mph. Margin of victory: .959 seconds. Caution flags: 8 for 47 laps. 83-87 (Car 32—accident, Turn 2); 121-124 (Car 18—spin, Turn 4); 145-150 (Cars 50, 15—accident, Turn 4); 195-201 (Car 88—accident, Turn 4); 250-253 (debris); 303-309 (Cars 21, 40—accident, Turn 4); 331-340 (oil on track); 346-349 (Car 29—stalled, Turn 3). Lap leaders: 27 lead changes among 10 drivers. Kurt Busch 1, Jeff Gordon 2-19, Busch 20-26, Jimmie Johnson 27-61, Sterling Marlin 62, Joe Nemechek 63, Greg Biffle 64-65, Mark Martin 66-77, Johnson 78-82, Biffle 96-101, Johnson 102-112, Martin 113-117, Jamie McMurray 118-120, Martin 121, Robby Gordon 122-138, Johnson 139-145, Martin 146, Johnson 147-195, Martin 196, Matt Kenseth 197, J. Gordon 198-250, Martin 251-253, J. Gordon 254-337, Johnson 338-345, Busch 346, McMurray 347-358, Johnson 359-367. Pole winner: None, qualifying rained out. Dropped to rear: Elliott Sadler, Kasey Kahne, Ricky Rudd (backup cars), Kirk Shelmerdine, Hermie Sadler (engine changes). Failed to qualify: Kevin Lepage, Derrike Cope, Carl Long, John Andretti, Travis Kvapil. Estimated attendance: 70,000.

## POINTS STANDINGS

| Rk. | Driver | Behind | | Rk. | Driver | Behind |
|-----|--------|--------|---|-----|--------|--------|
| 1. | Kurt Busch | — | | 6. | Tony Stewart | -185 |
| 2. | Jimmie Johnson | -18 | | 7. | Ryan Newman | -244 |
| 3. | Jeff Gordon | -21 | | 8. | Matt Kenseth | -383 |
| 4. | Dale Earnhardt Jr. | -72 | | 9. | Elliott Sadler | -383 |
| 5. | Mark Martin | -82 | | 10. | Jeremy Mayfield | -404 |

# FORD 400 ---------- HOMESTEAD-MIAMI SPEEDWAY

**Homestead, Fla.—1.5-mile paved oval • November 21, 2004—400.5 miles—267 laps**

| Fin. | St. | Car | Driver | Make | Sponsor | Pts./Bonus | Laps | Status | Winnings |
|------|-----|-----|--------|------|---------|------------|------|--------|----------|
| 1. | 2 | 16 | Greg Biffle | Ford | National Guard | 190/10 | 271 | Running | $314,850 |
| 2. | 39 | 48 | Jimmie Johnson | Chevrolet | Lowe's | 170/0 | 271 | Running | $231,705 |
| 3. | 5 | 24 | Jeff Gordon | Chevrolet | DuPont | 165/0 | 271 | Running | $208,708 |
| 4. | 8 | 20 | Tony Stewart | Chevrolet | The Home Depot | 165/5 | 271 | Running | $167,003 |
| 5. | 1 | 97 | Kurt Busch | Ford | Sharpie | 160/5 | 271 | Running | $130,650 |
| 6. | 17 | 77 | Brendan Gaughan* | Dodge | Kodak/Jasper Eng. & Trans. | 150/0 | 271 | Running | $102,000 |
| 7. | 18 | 42 | Jamie McMurray | Dodge | Texaco/Havoline | 146/0 | 271 | Running | $88,950 |
| 8. | 10 | 2 | Rusty Wallace | Dodge | Miller Lite | 147/5 | 271 | Running | $110,983 |
| 9. | 7 | 21 | Ricky Rudd | Ford | Motorcraft | 138/0 | 271 | Running | $90,806 |
| 10. | 9 | 29 | Kevin Harvick | Chevrolet | GM Goodwrench | 134/0 | 271 | Running | $99,728 |
| 11. | 11 | 6 | Mark Martin | Ford | Viagra | 135/5 | 271 | Running | $67,950 |
| 12. | 6 | 18 | Bobby Labonte | Chevrolet | Interstate Batteries | 132/5 | 271 | Running | $100,133 |
| 13. | 21 | 22 | Scott Wimmer* | Dodge | Caterpillar | 124/0 | 271 | Running | $86,175 |
| 14. | 22 | 99 | Carl Edwards | Ford | Roush Racing | 121/0 | 271 | Running | $91,867 |
| 15. | 25 | 10 | Scott Riggs* | Chevrolet | Valvoline | 118/0 | 271 | Running | $84,712 |
| 16. | 38 | 40 | Sterling Marlin | Dodge | Coors Light/Lone Star Steakhouse | 115/0 | 271 | Running | $91,925 |
| 17. | 24 | 15 | Michael Waltrip | Chevrolet | NAPA | 112/0 | 271 | Running | $89,881 |
| 18. | 14 | 25 | Brian Vickers* | Chevrolet | GMAC Financial Services | 109/0 | 271 | Running | $65,225 |
| 19. | 30 | 17 | Matt Kenseth | Ford | DeWalt Power Tools | 106/0 | 271 | Running | $104,203 |
| 20. | 23 | 14 | John Andretti | Ford | VB/APlus at Sunoco | 103/0 | 271 | Running | $55,150 |
| 21. | 29 | 32 | Bobby Hamilton Jr. | Chevrolet | Tide | 100/0 | 271 | Running | $79,500 |
| 22. | 37 | 00 | Kenny Wallace | Chevrolet | Aaron's | 97/0 | 271 | Running | $52,800 |
| 23. | 16 | 8 | Dale Earnhardt Jr. | Chevrolet | Budweiser | 94/0 | 271 | Running | $100,703 |
| 24. | 27 | 88 | Dale Jarrett | Ford | UPS | 91/0 | 270 | Running | $86,717 |
| 25. | 43 | 49 | Ken Schrader | Dodge | Schwan's Home Service | 88/0 | 269 | Running | $55,500 |
| 26. | 41 | 41 | Casey Mears | Dodge | Target | 85/0 | 268 | Running | $68,575 |
| 27. | 19 | 01 | Joe Nemechek | Chevrolet | U.S. Army | 82/0 | 267 | Running | $73,375 |
| 28. | 32 | 36 | Boris Said | Chevrolet | USG Durock | 79/0 | 266 | Transmission | $51,575 |
| 29. | 33 | 31 | Robby Gordon | Chevrolet | Cingular Wireless | 76/0 | 266 | Running | $86,552 |
| 30. | 3 | 12 | Ryan Newman | Dodge | ALLTEL | 78/5 | 264 | Accident | $107,917 |
| 31. | 42 | 5 | Terry Labonte | Chevrolet | Kellogg's | 70/0 | 264 | Running | $81,100 |
| 32. | 35 | 1 | Martin Truex Jr. | Chevrolet | Enterprise Rent-A-Car | 67/0 | 251 | Rear tire | $50,750 |
| 33. | 28 | 4 | Mike Wallace | Chevrolet | Lucas Oil | 64/0 | 247 | Wheel bearing | $54,480 |
| 34. | 15 | 38 | Elliott Sadler | Ford | M&M's | 61/0 | 232 | Running | $89,183 |
| 35. | 20 | 19 | Jeremy Mayfield | Dodge | Dodge Dealers/UAW | 58/0 | 231 | Running | $69,039 |
| 36. | 40 | 30 | Jeff Burton | Chevrolet | America Online | 55/0 | 231 | Running | $57,935 |
| 37. | 31 | 43 | Jeff Green | Dodge | Chex Party Mix | 52/0 | 223 | Engine | $75,975 |
| 38. | 4 | 9 | Kasey Kahne* | Dodge | Dodge Dealers/UAW | 49/0 | 192 | Overheating | $79,400 |
| 39. | 26 | 06 | Travis Kvapil | Dodge | Mobil 1 | 46/0 | 162 | Accident | $49,325 |
| 40. | 12 | 0 | Mike Bliss | Chevrolet | NetZero | 43/0 | 145 | Accident | $49,100 |
| 41. | 13 | 23 | Shane Hmiel | Dodge | Miccosukee Resort | 40/0 | 115 | Accident | $48,910 |
| 42. | 34 | 13 | Greg Sacks | Dodge | ARCDehooker/Vita Coco | 37/0 | 3 | Overheating | $48,605 |
| 43. | 36 | 02 | Hermie Sadler | Chevrolet | Drive for Diversity/Sam Bass | 34/0 | 0 | Accident | $48,630 |

*Rookie. Time of race: 3 hours, 50 minutes, 55 seconds. Average speed: 105.623 mph. Margin of victory: 0.342 seconds. Caution flags: 14 for 79 laps: Laps 2-4 (Cars 0, 02—accident, Turn 1); 7-9 (Cars 30, 31, 36, 41—accident, Turn 2); 49-52 (debris); 94-97 (debris); 114-131 (Car 19—accident, Turn 2); 148-151 (Car 0—accident, Turn 2); 157-160 (Car 38—accident, front stretch); 164-170 (Cars 9, 06, 8—accident, front stretch); 174-177 (debris); 192-195 (debris); 200-207 (debris); 225-231 (oil on track); 253-257 (Car 1—accident, Turn 4); 266-269 (Car 12—accident, Turn 2). Lap leaders: 14 lead changes among 7 drivers: Kurt Busch 1-4, Greg Biffle 5-114, Ryan Newman 115-146, Biffle 147-148, Tony Stewart 149-170, Biffle 171-173, Bobby Labonte 174-183, Newman 184-191, Mark Martin 192-199, Rusty Wallace 200-225, Newman 226-235, Stewart 236-242, Newman 243-264, Stewart 265-269, Biffle 270-271. Pole winner: Kurt Busch, 179.319 mph. Dropped to rear: Casey Mears (backup car), Mike Bliss, Jeff Burton (engine changes). Failed to qualify: Kyle Petty, Johnny Sauter, Mike Garvey, Tony Raines, Kevin Lepage, Todd Bodine, J.J. Yeley, Larry Foyt, Randy LaJoie, Morgan Shepherd, Kirk Shelmerdine, Carl Long, Geoffrey Bodine. Estimated attendance: 105,000.

## POINTS STANDINGS

| Rk. | Driver | Behind | Rk. | Driver | Behind |
|-----|--------|--------|-----|--------|--------|
| 1. | Kurt Busch | — | 6. | Tony Stewart | -180 |
| 2. | Jimmie Johnson | -8 | 7. | Ryan Newman | -326 |
| 3. | Jeff Gordon | -16 | 8. | Matt Kenseth | -437 |
| 4. | Mark Martin | -107 | 9. | Elliott Sadler | -482 |
| 5. | Dale Earnhardt Jr. | -138 | 10. | Jeremy Mayfield | -506 |

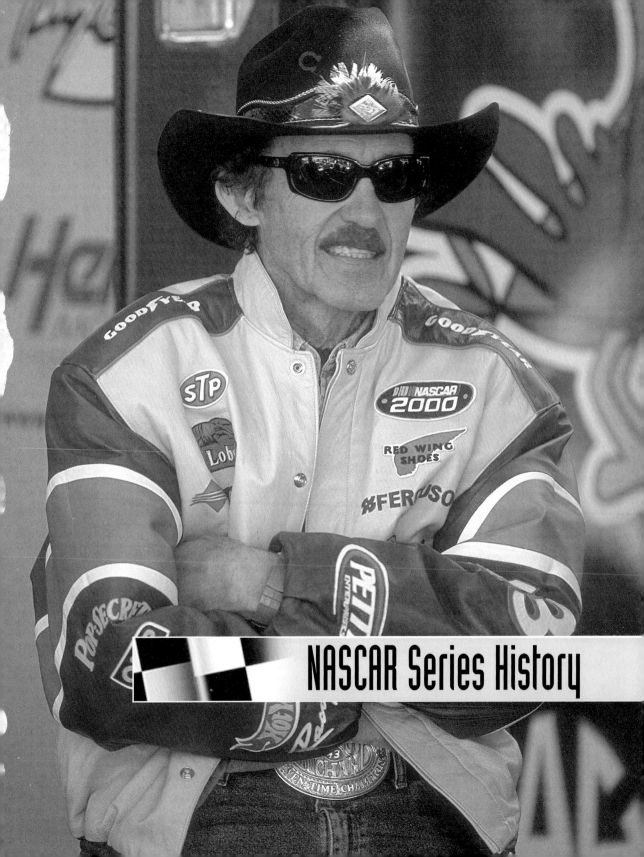

NASCAR Series History

# 2003 SEASON

| Race No. | Location | Date | Winner | Car owner |
|---|---|---|---|---|
| 1. | Daytona Beach, Fla. | Feb. 16 | Michael Waltrip | Teresa Earnhardt |
| 2. | Rockingham, N.C. | Feb. 23 | Dale Jarrett | Robert Yates |
| 3. | Las Vegas, Nev. | March 2 | Matt Kenseth | Jack Roush |
| 4. | Hampton, Ga. | March 9 | Bobby Labonte | Joe Gibbs |
| 5. | Darlington, S.C. | March 16 | Ricky Craven | Cal Wells III |
| 6. | Bristol, Tenn. | March 23 | Kurt Busch | Jack Roush |
| 7. | Justin, Texas | March 30 | Ryan Newman | Roger Penske |
| 8. | Talladega, Ala. | April 6 | Dale Earnhardt Jr. | Teresa Earnhardt |
| 9. | Martinsville, Va. | April 13 | Jeff Gordon | Rick Hendrick |
| 10. | Fontana, Calif. | April 27 | Kurt Busch | Jack Roush |
| 11. | Richmond, Va. | May 3 | Joe Nemechek | Rick Hendrick |
| 12. | Concord, N.C. | May 25 | Jimmie Johnson | Rick Hendrick |
| 13. | Dover, Del. | June 1 | Ryan Newman | Roger Penske |
| 14. | Long Pond, Pa. | June 8 | Tony Stewart | Joe Gibbs |
| 15. | Brooklyn, Mich. | June 15 | Kurt Busch | Jack Roush |
| 16. | Sonoma, Calif. | June 22 | Robby Gordon | Richard Childress |
| 17. | Daytona Beach, Fla. | July 5 | Greg Biffle | Jack Roush |
| 18. | Joliet, Ill. | July 13 | Ryan Newman | Roger Penske |
| 19. | Loudon, N.H. | July 20 | Jimmie Johnson | Rick Hendrick |
| 20. | Long Pond, Pa. | July 27 | Ryan Newman | Roger Penske |
| 21. | Indianapolis | Aug. 3 | Kevin Harvick | Richard Childress |
| 22. | Watkins Glen, N.Y. | Aug. 10 | Robby Gordon | Richard Childress |
| 23. | Brooklyn, Mich. | Aug. 17 | Ryan Newman | Roger Penske |
| 24. | Bristol, Tenn. | Aug. 23 | Kurt Busch | Jack Roush |
| 25. | Darlington, S.C. | Aug. 31 | Terry Labonte | Rick Hendrick |
| 26. | Richmond, Va. | Sept. 6 | Ryan Newman | Roger Penske |
| 27. | Loudon, N.H. | Sept. 14 | Jimmie Johnson | Rick Hendrick |
| 28. | Dover, Del. | Sept. 21 | Ryan Newman | Roger Penske |
| 29. | Talladega, Ala. | Sept. 28 | Michael Waltrip | Teresa Earnhardt |
| 30. | Kansas City, Kan. | Oct. 5 | Ryan Newman | Roger Penske |
| 31. | Concord, N.C. | Oct. 11 | Tony Stewart | Joe Gibbs |
| 32. | Martinsville, Va. | Oct. 19 | Jeff Gordon | Rick Hendrick |
| 33. | Hampton, Ga. | Oct. 27 | Jeff Gordon | Rick Hendrick |
| 34. | Phoenix | Nov. 2 | Dale Earnhardt Jr. | Teresa Earnhardt |
| 35. | Rockingham, N.C. | Nov. 9 | Bill Elliott | Ray Evernham |
| 36. | Homestead, Fla. | Nov. 16 | Bobby Labonte | Joe Gibbs |

## Points standings

1. Matt Kenseth .................5,022
2. Jimmie Johnson..............4,932
3. Dale Earnhardt Jr. ..........4,815
4. Jeff Gordon .....................4,785
5. Kevin Harvick ..................4,770
6. Ryan Newman.................4,711
7. Tony Stewart...................4,549
8. Bobby Labonte ...............4,377
9. Bill Elliott.........................4,303
10. Terry Labonte.................4,162

## Race winners  17

1. Ryan Newman ......................8
2. Kurt Busch...........................4
3. Jimmie Johnson ...................3
   Jeff Gordon ...........................3
5. Bobby Labonte .....................2
   Michael Waltrip......................2
   Robby Gordon........................2
   Dale Earnhardt Jr....................2
   Tony Stewart ..........................2
10. Joe Nemechek .....................1
    Terry Labonte .......................1
    Bill Elliott ..............................1
    Ricky Craven .........................1
    Greg Biffle ............................1
    Matt Kenseth.........................1
    Dale Jarrett ...........................1
    Kevin Harvick ........................1

## Money won leaders

1. Matt Kenseth ...........$9,422,764
2. Jimmie Johnson ........$7,745,530
3. Dale Earnhardt Jr. ......$6,880,807
4. Jeff Gordon..............$6,622,002
5. Kevin Harvick ..........$6,237,119
6. Tony Stewart ...........$6,131,633
7. Ryan Newman .........$6,100,877
8. Bobby Labonte ........$5,505,018
9. Bill Elliott ................$5,008,530
10. Terry Labonte .........$4,283,625

## Pole winners  15

1. Ryan Newman....................11
2. Bobby Labonte .....................4
   Jeff Gordon ...........................4
4. Elliott Sadler.........................2
   Steve Park ............................2
   Jimmie Johnson ....................2
7. Tony Stewart .........................1
   Mike Skinner .........................1
   Boris Said..............................1
   Kevin Harvick ........................1
   Jeff Green .............................1
   Dave Blaney ..........................1
   Jamie McMurray ....................1
   Jeremy Mayfield....................1
   Terry Labonte ........................1

HISTORY

# 2002 SEASON

| Race No. | Location | Date | Winner | Car owner |
|---|---|---|---|---|
| 1. | Daytona Beach, Fla. | Feb. 17 | Ward Burton | Bill Davis |
| 2. | Rockingham, N.C. | Feb. 24 | Matt Kenseth | Jack Roush |
| 3. | Las Vegas | March 3 | Sterling Marlin | Chip Ganassi |
| 4. | Hampton, Ga. | March 10 | Tony Stewart | Joe Gibbs |
| 5. | Darlington, S.C. | March 17 | Sterling Marlin | Chip Ganassi |
| 6. | Bristol, Tenn. | March 24 | Kurt Busch | Jack Roush |
| 7. | Justin, Texas | April 7 | Matt Kenseth | Jack Roush |
| 8. | Martinsville, Va. | April 14 | Bobby Labonte | Joe Gibbs |
| 9. | Talladega, Ala. | April 21 | Dale Earnhardt Jr. | Teresa Earnhardt |
| 10. | Fontana, Calif. | April 28 | Jimmie Johnson | Rick Hendrick |
| 11. | Richmond, Va. | May 4 | Tony Stewart | Joe Gibbs |
| 12. | Concord, N.C. | May 26 | Mark Martin | Jack Roush |
| 13. | Dover, Del. | June 2 | Jimmie Johnson | Rick Hendrick |
| 14. | Long Pond, Pa. | June 9 | Dale Jarrett | Robert Yates |
| 15. | Brooklyn, Mich. | June 16 | Matt Kenseth | Jack Roush |
| 16. | Sonoma, Calif. | June 23 | Ricky Rudd | Robert Yates |
| 17. | Daytona Beach, Fla. | July 6 | Michael Waltrip | Teresa Earnhardt |
| 18. | Joliet, Ill. | July 14 | Kevin Harvick | Richard Childress |
| 19. | Loudon, N.H. | July 21 | Ward Burton | Bill Davis |
| 20. | Long Pond, Pa. | July 28 | Bill Elliott | Ray Evernham |
| 21. | Indianapolis | Aug. 4 | Bill Elliott | Ray Evernham |
| 22. | Watkins Glen, N.Y. | Aug. 11 | Tony Stewart | Joe Gibbs |
| 23. | Brooklyn, Mich. | Aug. 18 | Dale Jarrett | Robert Yates |
| 24. | Bristol, Tenn. | Aug. 24 | Jeff Gordon | Rick Hendrick |
| 25. | Darlington, S.C. | Sept. 1 | Jeff Gordon | Rick Hendrick |
| 26. | Richmond, Va. | Sept. 7 | Matt Kenseth | Jack Roush |
| 27. | Loudon, N.H. | Sept. 15 | Ryan Newman | Roger Penske |
| 28. | Dover, Del. | Sept. 22 | Jimmie Johnson | Rick Hendrick |
| 29. | Kansas City, Kan. | Sept. 29 | Jeff Gordon | Rick Hendrick |
| 30. | Talladega, Ala. | Oct. 6 | Dale Earnhardt Jr. | Teresa Earnhardt |
| 31. | Concord, N.C. | Oct. 13 | Jamie McMurray | Chip Ganassi |
| 32. | Martinsville, Va. | Oct. 20 | Kurt Busch | Jack Roush |
| 33. | Hampton, Ga. | Oct. 27 | Kurt Busch | Jack Roush |
| 34. | Rockingham, N.C. | Nov. 3 | Johnny Benson | Nelson Bowers |
| 35. | Phoenix | Nov. 10 | Matt Kenseth | Jack Roush |
| 36. | Homestead, Fla. | Nov. 17 | Kurt Busch | Jack Roush |

## Points standings

1. Tony Stewart ...............4,800
2. Mark Martin...................4,762
3. Kurt Busch.....................4,641
4. Jeff Gordon ..................4,607
5. Jimmie Johnson ...........4,600
6. Ryan Newman...............4,593
7. Rusty Wallace ..............4,574
8. Matt Kenseth.................4,432
9. Dale Jarrett ...................4,415
10. Ricky Rudd ..................4,323

## Race winners 18

1. Matt Kenseth .......................5
2. Kurt Busch ...........................4
3. Tony Stewart .......................3
   Jeff Gordon .........................3
   Jimmie Johnson...................3
6. Dale Jarrett .........................2
   Dale Earnhardt Jr. ...............2
   Bill Elliott .............................2
   Sterling Marlin .....................2
   Ward Burton.........................2
11. Mark Martin ........................1
   Ryan Newman .....................1
   Ricky Rudd...........................1
   Michael Waltrip ...................1
   Bobby Labonte ....................1
   Kevin Harvick.......................1
   Johnny Benson.....................1
   Jamie McMurray ..................1

## Money won leaders

1. Tony Stewart ........$9,163,761
2. Mark Martin..........$7,004,893
3. Jeff Gordon ..........$6,154,475
4. Ryan Newman .....$5,346,651
5. Kurt Busch...........$5,105,394
6. Dale Earnhardt Jr. $4,970,034
7. Ward Burton .........$4,899,884
8. Rusty Wallace .....$4,785,134
9. Matt Kenseth .......$4,514,203
10. Ricky Rudd .........$4,444,614

## Pole winners 15

1. Ryan Newman .......................6
2. Bill Elliott .............................4
   Jimmie Johnson....................4
4. Jeff Gordon .........................3
5. Ricky Craven .......................2
   Dale Earnhardt Jr....... ..........2
   Tony Stewart ........................2
8. Todd Bodine .........................1
   Ward Burton ..........................1
   Kurt Busch ............................1
   Kevin Harvick ........................1
   Dale Jarrett ...........................1
   Matt Kenseth .........................1
   Ricky Rudd.............................1
   Rusty Wallace........................1

HISTORY

# 2001 SEASON

| Race No. | Location | Date | Winner | Car owner |
|---|---|---|---|---|
| 1. | Daytona Beach, Fla. | Feb. 18 | Michael Waltrip | Teresa Earnhardt |
| 2. | Rockingham, N.C. | Feb. 25 | Steve Park | Teresa Earnhardt |
| 3. | Las Vegas | March 4 | Jeff Gordon | Rick Hendrick. |
| 4. | Atlanta | March 11 | Kevin Harvick | Richard Childress |
| 5. | Darlington, S.C. | March 18 | Dale Jarrett | Robert Yates |
| 6. | Bristol, Tenn. | March 25 | Elliott Sadler | Glen Wood |
| 7. | Justin, Texas | April 1 | Dale Jarrett | Robert Yates |
| 8. | Martinsville, Va. | April 8 | Dale Jarrett | Robert Yates |
| 9. | Talladega, Ala. | April 22 | Bobby Hamilton | Andy Petree |
| 10. | Los Angeles | April 29 | Rusty Wallace | Roger Penske |
| 11. | Richmond, Va. | May 5 | Tony Stewart | Joe Gibbs |
| 12. | Concord, N.C. | May 27 | Jeff Burton | Jack Roush |
| 13. | Dover, Del. | June 3 | Jeff Gordon | Rick Hendrick |
| 14. | Brooklyn, Mich. | June 10 | Jeff Gordon | Rick Hendrick |
| 15. | Long Pond, Pa. | June 17 | Ricky Rudd | Robert Yates |
| 16. | Sonoma, Calif. | June 24 | Tony Stewart | Joe Gibbs |
| 17. | Daytona Beach, Fla. | July 7 | Dale Earnhardt Jr. | Teresa Earnhardt |
| 18. | Joliet, Ill. | July 15 | Kevin Harvick | Richard Childress |
| 19. | Loudon, N.H. | July 22 | Dale Jarrett | Robert Yates |
| 20. | Long Pond, Pa. | July 29 | Bobby Labonte | Joe Gibbs |
| 21. | Indianapolis | Aug. 5 | Jeff Gordon | Rick Hendrick |
| 22. | Watkins Glen, N.Y. | Aug. 12 | Jeff Gordon | Rick Hendrick |
| 23. | Brooklyn, Mich. | Aug. 19 | Sterling Marlin | Chip Ganassi |
| 24. | Bristol, Tenn. | Aug. 25 | Tony Stewart | Joe Gibbs |
| 25. | Darlington, S.C. | Sept. 2 | Ward Burton | Bill Davis |
| 26. | Richmond, Va. | Sept. 8 | Ricky Rudd | Robert Yates |
| 27. | Dover, Del. | Sept. 23 | Dale Earnhardt Jr. | Teresa Earnhardt |
| 28. | Kansas City, Kan. | Sept. 30 | Jeff Gordon | Rick Hendrick |
| 29. | Concord, N.C. | Oct. 7 | Sterling Marlin | Chip Ganassi |
| 30. | Martinsville, Va. | Oct. 14 | Ricky Craven | Cal Wells III |
| 31. | Talladega, Ala. | Oct. 21 | Dale Earnhardt Jr. | Teresa Earnhardt |
| 32. | Phoenix | Oct. 28 | Jeff Burton | Jack Roush |
| 33. | Rockingham, N.C. | Nov. 4 | Joe Nemechek | Andy Petree |
| 34. | Miami | Nov. 11 | Bill Elliott | Ray Evernham |
| 35. | Atlanta | Nov. 18 | Bobby Labonte | Joe Gibbs |
| 36. | Loudon, N.H. | Nov. 23 | Robby Gordon | Richard Childress |

## Points standings

1. Jeff Gordon .........................5,112
2. Tony Stewart......................4,763
3. Sterling Marlin .................4,741
4. Ricky Rudd .......................4,706
5. Dale Jarrett ......................4,612
6. Bobby Labonte .................4,561
7. Rusty Wallace ...................4,481
8. Dale Earnhardt Jr..............4,460
9. Kevin Harvick ...................4,406
10. Jeff Burton .....................4,394

## Race winners  19

1. Jeff Gordon ..........................6
2. Dale Jarrett .........................4
3. Tony Stewart .......................3
   Dale Earnhardt Jr. ...............3
5. Jeff Burton ..........................2
   Kevin Harvick .....................2
   Bobby Labonte ....................2
   Sterling Marlin ....................2
   Ricky Rudd..........................2
10. Ward Burton.......................1
    Ricky Craven ......................1
    Bill Elliott ............................1
    Robby Gordon ....................1
    Bobby Hamilton ..................1
    Joe Nemechek ....................1
    Steve Park ..........................1
    Elliott Sadler........................1
    Rusty Wallace......................1
    Michael Waltrip ...................1

## Money won leaders

1. Jeff Gordon ........$10,879,757
2. Dale Earnhardt Jr. ..5,827,542
3. Dale Jarrett ...........5,377,742
4. Tony Stewart .........4,941,463
5. Ricky Rudd ...........4,828,027
6. Rusty Wallace .......4,788,652
7. Bobby Labonte.......4,786,779
8. Sterling Marlin........4,517,634
9. Kevin Harvick .......4,302,202
10. Jeff Burton ...........4,230,737

## Pole winners  18

1. Jeff Gordon ..........................6
2. Dale Jarrett ..........................4
3. Todd Bodine.........................3
4. Stacy Compton.....................2
   Dale Earnhardt Jr. ...............2
   Bill Elliott .............................2
   Mark Martin ..........................2
   Jimmy Spencer .....................2
9. Casey Atwood ......................1
   Kurt Busch ...........................1
   Ricky Craven ........................1
   Jeff Green .............................1
   Bobby Labonte ......................1
   Jason Leffler .........................1
   Sterling Marlin .......................1
   Ryan Newman .......................1
   Ricky Rudd.............................1
   Kenny Wallace ......................1

# 2000 SEASON

| Race No. | Location | Date | Winner | Car owner |
|---|---|---|---|---|
| 1. | Daytona Beach, Fla, | Feb. 20 | Dale Jarrett | Robert Yates |
| 2. | Rockingham, N.C. | Feb. 27 | Bobby Labonte | Joe Gibbs |
| 3. | Las Vegas | March 5 | Jeff Burton | Jack Roush |
| 4. | Hampton, Ga. | March 12 | Dale Earnhardt | Richard Childress |
| 5. | Darlington, S.C. | March 19 | Ward Burton | Bill Davis |
| 6. | Bristol, Tenn. | March 26 | Rusty Wallace | Roger Penske |
| 7. | Justin, Texas | April 2 | Dale Earnhardt Jr. | Dale Earnhardt |
| 8. | Martinsville, Va. | April 9 | Mark Martin | Jack Roush |
| 9. | Talladega, Ala. | April 16 | Jeff Gordon | Rick Hendrick |
| 10. | Fontana, Calif. | April 30 | Jeremy Mayfield | Michael Kranefuss |
| 11. | Richmond, Va. | May 6 | Dale Earnhardt Jr. | Dale Earnhardt |
| 12. | Concord, N.C. | May 28 | Matt Kenseth | Mark Martin |
| 13. | Dover, Del. | June 4 | Tony Stewart | Joe Gibbs |
| 14. | Brooklyn, Mich. | June 11 | Tony Stewart | Joe Gibbs |
| 15. | Long Pond, Pa. | June 19 | Jeremy Mayfield | Michael Kranefuss |
| 16. | Sonoma, Calif. | June 25 | Jeff Gordon | Rick Hendrick |
| 17. | Daytona Beach, Fla. | July 1 | Jeff Burton | Jack Roush |
| 18. | Loudon, N.H. | July 9 | Tony Stewart | Joe Gibbs |
| 19. | Long Pond, Pa. | July 23 | Rusty Wallace | Roger Penske |
| 20. | Indianapolis | Aug. 5 | Bobby Labonte | Joe Gibbs |
| 21. | Watkins Glen, N.Y. | Aug. 13 | Steve Park | Dale Earnhardt |
| 22. | Brooklyn, Mich. | Aug. 20 | Rusty Wallace | Roger Penske |
| 23. | Bristol, Tenn. | Aug. 26 | Rusty Wallace | Roger Penske |
| 24. | Darlington, S.C. | Sept. 3 | Bobby Labonte | Joe Gibbs |
| 25. | Richmond, Va. | Sept. 9 | Jeff Gordon | Rick Hendrick |
| 26. | Loudon, N.H. | Sept. 17 | Jeff Burton | Robert Corn |
| 27. | Dover, Del. | Sept. 24 | Tony Stewart | Joe Gibbs |
| 28. | Martinsville, Va. | Oct. 1 | Tony Stewart | Joe Gibbs |
| 29. | Concord, N.C. | Oct. 8 | Bobby Labonte | Joe Gibbs |
| 30. | Talladega, Ala. | Oct. 15 | Dale Earnhardt | Richard Childress |
| 31. | Rockingham, N.C. | Oct. 22 | Dale Jarrett | Robert Yates |
| 32. | Phoenix | Nov. 5 | Jeff Burton | Jack Roush |
| 33. | Homestead, Fla. | Nov. 12 | Tony Stewart | Joe Gibbs |
| 34. | Hampton, Ga. | Nov. 20 | Jerry Nadeau | Rick Hendrick. |

## Points standings

1. Bobby Labonte ...............5,130
2. Dale Earnhardt ...............4,865
3. Jeff Burton ......................4,836
4. Dale Jarrett .....................4,684
5. Ricky Rudd .....................4,575
6. Tony Stewart ..................4,570
7. Rusty Wallace .................4,544
8. Mark Martin ....................4,410
9. Jeff Gordon ....................4,361
10. Ward Burton ..................4,152

## Race winners 14

1. Tony Stewart .......................6
2. Bobby Labonte ....................4
   Jeff Burton ...........................4
   Rusty Wallace .....................4
5. Jeff Gordon ..........................3
6. Dale Earnhardt .....................2
   Dale Earnhardt Jr. ...............2
   Dale Jarrett .........................2
   Jeremy Mayfield...................2
10. Mark Martin ........................1
    Ward Burton ......................1
    Steve Park ........................1
    Matt Kenseth .....................1
    Jerry Nadeau .....................1

## Money won leaders

1. Bobby Labonte ....$7,361,386
2. Jeff Burton ...........5,959,439
3. Dale Jarrett ......... 5,934,475
4. Dale Earnhardt .... 4,918,886
5. Tony Stewart........ 3,642,348
6. Rusty Wallace ......3,621,468
7. Mark Martin ......... 3,098,874
8. Jeff Gordon ......... 3,001,144
9. Rick Rudd ............2,914,970
10. Dale Earnhardt Jr. .. 2,801,880

## Pole winners 13

1. Rusty Wallace......................9
2. Jeremy Mayfield .................4
3. Jeff Gordon .........................3
   Dale Jarrett..........................3
5. Bobby Labonte ....................2
   Dale Earnhardt.....................2
   Steve Park ...........................2
   Dale Earnhardt Jr. ...............2
   Ricky Rudd...........................2
10. Jeff Burton ..........................1
    Terry Labonte.....................1
    Joe Nemechek....................1
    Mike Skinner ......................1

HISTORY

# 1999 SEASON

| Race No. | Location | Date | Winner | Car owner |
|----------|----------|------|--------|-----------|
| 1. | Daytona Beach, Fla. | Feb. 14 | Jeff Gordon | Rick Hendrick |
| 2. | Rockingham, N.C. | Feb. 21 | Mark Martin | Jack Roush |
| 3. | Las Vegas | Mar. 7 | Jeff Burton | Jack Roush |
| 4. | Hampton, Ga. | March 14 | Jeff Gordon | Rick Hendrick |
| 5. | Darlington, S.C. | March 21 | Jeff Burton | Jack Roush |
| 6. | Justin, Texas | March 28 | Terry Labonte | Rick Hendrick |
| 7. | Bristol, Tenn. | April 11 | Rusty Wallace | Roger Penske |
| 8. | Martinsville, Va. | April 18 | John Andretti | Richard Petty |
| 9. | Talladega, Ala. | April 25 | Dale Earnhardt | Richard Childress |
| 10. | Fontana, Calif. | May 2 | Jeff Gordon | Rick Hendrick |
| 11. | Richmond, Va. | May 15 | Dale Jarrett | Robert Yates |
| 12. | Concord, N.C. | May 30 | Jeff Burton | Rick Hendrick |
| 13. | Dover, Del. | June 6 | Bobby Labonte | Joe Gibbs |
| 14. | Brooklyn, Mich. | June 13 | Dale Jarrett | Robert Yates |
| 15. | Long Pond, Pa. | June 20 | Bobby Labonte | Joe Gibbs |
| 16. | Sonoma, Calif. | June 27 | Jeff Gordon | Rick Hendrick |
| 17. | Daytona Beach, Fla. | July 3 | Dale Jarrett | Robert Yates |
| 18. | Loudon, N.H. | July 11 | Jeff Burton | Jack Roush |
| 19. | Long Pond, Pa. | July 25 | Bobby Labonte | Joe Gibbs |
| 20. | Indianapolis | Aug. 8 | Dale Jarrett | Robert Yates |
| 21. | Watkins Glen, N.Y. | Aug. 15 | Jeff Gordon | Rick Hendrick |
| 22. | Brooklyn, Mich. | Aug. 22 | Bobby Labonte | Joe Gibbs |
| 23. | Bristol, Tenn. | Aug. 28 | Dale Earnhardt | Richard Childress |
| 24. | Darlington, S.C. | Sept. 5 | Jeff Burton | Jack Roush |
| 25. | Richmond, Va. | Sept. 11 | Tony Stewart | Joe Gibbs |
| 26. | Loudon, N.H. | Sept. 19 | Joe Nemechek | Felix Sabates |
| 27. | Dover, Del. | Sept. 26 | Mark Martin | Jack Roush |
| 28. | Martinsville, Va. | Oct. 3 | Jeff Gordon | Rick Hendrick |
| 29. | Concord, N.C. | Oct. 11 | Jeff Gordon | Rick Hendrick |
| 30. | Talladega, Ala. | Oct. 17 | Dale Earnhardt | Richard Childress |
| 31. | Rockingham, N.C. | Oct. 24 | Jeff Burton | Jack Roush |
| 32. | Phoenix | Nov. 7 | Tony Stewart | Joe Gibbs |
| 33. | Homestead, Fla. | Nov. 14 | Tony Stewart | Joe Gibbs |
| 34. | Hampton, Ga. | Nov. 21 | Bobby Labonte | Joe Gibbs |

## Points standings

1. Bobby Labonte ................5,130
2. Dale Earnhardt ................4,865
3. Jeff Burton ......................4,836
4. Dale Jarrett ......................4,684
5. Ricky Rudd ......................4,575
6. Tony Stewart ....................4,570
7. Rusty Wallace ..................4,544
8. Mark Martin ....................4,410
9. Jeff Gordon ....................4,361
10. Ward Burton ..................4,152

## Race winners 11

1. Jeff Gordon .........................7
2. Jeff Burton .........................6
3. Bobby Labonte ....................5
4. Dale Jarrett .........................4
5. Dale Earnhardt ....................3
   Tony Stewart .......................3
7. Mark Martin ........................2
8. Rusty Wallace......................1
   Terry Labonte ......................1
   John Andretti ......................1
   Joe Nemechek ....................1

## Money won leaders

1. Dale Jarrett .........$6,649.596
2. Jeff Gordon ............5,858,633
3. Jeff Burton..............5,725,399
4. Bobby Labonte........4,763,615
5. Mark Martin............3,509,744
6. Tony Stewart .........3,190,149
7. Dale Earnhardt.......3,048,236
8. Mike Skinner ..........2,499,877
9. Terry Labonte ........2,475,365
10. Rusty Wallace ........2,454,050

## Pole winners 15

1. Jeff Gordon .........................7
2. Bobby Labonte ....................5
3. Rusty Wallace......................4
4. Joe Nemechek ....................3
5. Tony Stewart .......................2
   Mike Skinner .......................2
   Kenny Irwin ........................2
8. Ward Burton........................1
   Ken Schrader .......................1
   Sterling Marlin ....................1
   Mark Martin........................1
   John Andretti ......................1
   Kevin Lepage ......................1
   Ricky Rudd..........................1
   David Green ........................1

# RECEPTION LINE: THE NO. 3 WINS THE 500

As the Daytona 500 approached, Dale Earnhardt had a look in his eye. He compared it to the look John Elway had in his eye weeks earlier, as the super quarterback finally won his elusive Super Bowl. This look, Earnhardt said, means, "I'm finally going to win my first Daytona 500." A win at the sport's biggest race had eluded the sport's biggest star for two decades. He had won at Daytona International Speedway 30 times—more than anybody, ever. He had won in NASCAR Busch Series cars and NASCAR Cup cars but never when it mattered most, never in the 500. And his near misses had been spectacular, from last-lap passes to errant birds to cut tires.

Finally, in 1998, he got it. He led five times for 107 of 200 laps. He led the final 61, the last of which was under caution, meaning there would be no last lap disaster this time. When the race ended, the world's longest reception line was there to greet him. Drivers and crew members from across the sport lined up to congratulate a legend. Three years later, at that same track, those same people would be mourning the death of a legend.

# 1998 SEASON

| Race No. | Location | Date | Winner | Car owner |
|---|---|---|---|---|
| 1. | Daytona Beach, Fla. | Feb. 15 | Dale Earnhardt | Richard Childress |
| 2. | Rockingham, N.C. | Feb. 22 | Jeff Gordon | Rick Hendrick |
| 3. | Las Vegas | March 1 | Mark Martin | Jack Roush |
| 4. | Hampton, Ga. | March 9 | Bobby Labonte | Joe Gibbs |
| 5. | Darlington, S.C. | March 22 | Dale Jarrett | Robert Yates |
| 6. | Bristol, Tenn. | March 29 | Jeff Gordon | Rick Hendrick |
| 7. | Justin, Texas | April 5 | Mark Martin | Jack Roush |
| 8. | Martinsville, Va. | April 20 | Bobby Hamilton | Larry McClure |
| 9. | Talladega, Ala. | April 26 | Bobby Labonte | Joe Gibbs |
| 10. | Fontana, Calif. | May 3 | Mark Martin | Jack Roush |
| 11. | Concord, N.C. | May 24 | Jeff Gordon | Rick Hendrick |
| 12. | Dover, Del. | May 31 | Dale Jarrett | Robert Yates |
| 13. | Richmond, Va. | June 6 | Terry Labonte | Rick Hendrick |
| 14. | Brooklyn, Mich. | June 14 | Mark Martin | Jack Roush |
| 15. | Long Pond, Pa. | June 21 | Jeremy Mayfield | Michael Kranefuss |
| 16. | Sonoma, Calif. | June 28 | Jeff Gordon | Rick Hendrick |
| 17. | Loudon, N.H. | July 12 | Jeff Burton | Jack Roush |
| 18. | Long Pond, Pa. | July 26 | Jeff Gordon | Rick Hendrick |
| 19. | Indianapolis | Aug. 1 | Jeff Gordon | Rick Hendrick |
| 20. | Watkins Glen, N.Y. | Aug. 9 | Jeff Gordon | Rick Hendrick |
| 21. | Brooklyn, Mich. | Aug. 16 | Jeff Gordon | Rick Hendrick |
| 22. | Bristol, Tenn. | Aug. 22 | Mark Martin | Jack Roush |
| 23. | Loudon, N.H. | Aug. 30 | Jeff Gordon | Rick Hendrick |
| 24. | Darlington, S.C. | Sept. 6 | Jeff Gordon | Rick Hendrick |
| 25. | Richmond, Va. | Sept. 12 | Jeff Burton | Jack Roush |
| 26. | Dover, Del. | Sept. 20 | Mark Martin | Jack Roush |
| 27. | Martinsville, Va. | Sept. 27 | Ricky Rudd | Ricky Rudd |
| 28. | Concord, N.C. | Oct. 4 | Mark Martin | Jack Roush |
| 29. | Talladega, Ala. | Oct. 11 | Dale Jarrett | Robert Yates |
| 30. | Daytona Beach, Fla. | Oct. 17 | Jeff Gordon | Rick Hendrick |
| 31. | Phoenix | Oct. 25 | Rusty Wallace | Roger Penske |
| 32. | Rockingham, N.C. | Nov. 1 | Jeff Gordon | Rick Hendrick |
| 33. | Hampton, Ga. | Nov. 8 | Jeff Gordon | Rick Hendrick |

## Points standings

1. Jeff Gordon ......................5,328
2. Mark Martin ....................4,964
3. Dale Jarrett .....................4,619
4. Rusty Wallace..................4,501
5. Jeff Burton ......................4,415
6. Bobby Labonte ................3,180
7. Jeremy Mayfield...............3,157
8. Dale Earnhardt ................3,928
9. Terry Labonte ...................3,901
10. Bobby Hamilton .............3,786

## Race winners 11

1. Jeff Gordon .......................13
2. Mark Martin ...................... 7
3. Dale Jarrett ...................... 3
4. Jeff Burton........................ 2
   Bobby Labonte .................. 2
6. Dale Earnhardt.................. 1
   Bobby Hamilton ............... 1
   Terry Labonte ................... 1
   Jeremy Mayfield ............... 1
   Ricky Rudd....................... 1
   Rusty Wallace.................... 1

## Money won leaders

1. Jeff Gordon .........$9,306,584
2. Mark Martin.......... 4,309,006
3. Dale Jarrett ......... 4,019,657
4. Dale Earnhardt .... 2,990,749
5. Bobby Labonte .... 2,980,052
6. Rusty Wallace ...... 2,667,889
7. Jeff Burton .......... 2,626,987
8. Jeremy Mayfield .. 2,332,034
9. Bobby Hamilton .. 2,089,566
10. Terry Labonte ...... 2,054,163

## Pole winners 15

1. Jeff Gordon .......................7
2. Rusty Wallace....................4
3. Ernie Irvan .......................3
   Bobby Labonte ..................3
   Mark Martin ......................3
6. Ward Burton.......................2
   Dale Jarrett .......................2
   Ken Schrader .....................2
9. John Andretti ....................1
   Derrike Cope .....................1
   Ricky Craven .....................1
   Bobby Hamilton ................1
   Kenny Irwin ......................1
   Rick Mast...........................1
   Jeremy Mayfield ................1

HISTORY

| Race No. | Location | Date | Winner | Car owner |
|---|---|---|---|---|
| 1. | Daytona Beach, Fla. | Feb. 16 | Jeff Gordon | Rick Hendrick |
| 2. | Rockingham, N.C. | Feb. 23 | Jeff Gordon | Rick Hendrick |
| 3. | Richmond, Va. | March 2 | Rusty Wallace | Roger Penske |
| 4. | Hampton, Ga. | March 9 | Dale Jarrett | Robert Yates |
| 5. | Darlington, S.C. | March 23 | Dale Jarrett | Robert Yates |
| 6. | Justin, Texas | April 6 | Jeff Burton | Jack Roush |
| 7. | Bristol, Tenn. | April 13 | Jeff Gordon | Rick Hendrick |
| 8. | Martinsville, Va. | April 20 | Jeff Gordon | Rick Hendrick |
| 9. | Sonoma, Calif. | May 5 | Mark Martin | Jack Roush |
| 10. | Talladega, Ala. | May 10 | Mark Martin | Jack Roush |
| 11. | Concord, N.C. | May 25 | Jeff Gordon | Rick Hendrick |
| 12. | Dover, Del. | June 1 | Ricky Rudd | Ricky Rudd |
| 13. | Long Pond, Pa. | June 8 | Jeff Gordon | Rick Hendrick |
| 14. | Brooklyn, Mich. | June 15 | Ernie Irvan | Robert Yates |
| 15. | Fontana, Calif. | June 22 | Jeff Gordon | Rick Hendrick |
| 16. | Daytona Beach, Fla. | July 5 | John Andretti | Cale Yarborough |
| 17. | Loudon, N.H. | July 13 | Jeff Burton | Jack Roush |
| 18. | Long Pond, Pa. | July 20 | Dale Jarrett | Robert Yates |
| 19. | Indianapolis | Aug. 2 | Ricky Rudd | Ricky Rudd |
| 20. | Watkins Glen, N.Y. | Aug. 10 | Jeff Gordon | Rick Hendrick |
| 21. | Brooklyn, Mich. | Aug. 17 | Mark Martin | Jack Roush |
| 22. | Bristol, Tenn. | Aug. 23 | Dale Jarrett | Robert Yates |
| 23. | Darlington, S.C. | Aug. 31 | Jeff Gordon | Rick Hendrick |
| 24. | Richmond, Va. | Sept. 6 | Dale Jarrett | Robert Yates |
| 25. | Loudon, N.H. | Sept. 14 | Jeff Gordon | Rick Hendrick |
| 26. | Dover, Del. | Sept. 21 | Mark Martin | Jack Roush |
| 27. | Martinsville, Va. | Sept. 29 | Jeff Burton | Jack Roush |
| 28. | Concord, N.C. | Oct. 5 | Dale Jarrett | Robert Yates |
| 29. | Talladega, Ala. | Oct. 12 | Terry Labonte | Rick Hendrick |
| 30. | Rockingham, N.C. | Oct. 27 | Bobby Hamilton | Richard Petty |
| 31. | Phoenix | Nov. 2 | Dale Jarrett | Robert Yates |
| 32. | Hampton, Ga. | Nov. 16 | Bobby Labonte | Joe Gibbs |

## Points standings

1. Jeff Gordon ...................4,710
2. Dale Jarrett ...................4,696
3. Mark Martin ...................4,681
4. Jeff Burton......................4,285
5. Dale Earnhardt................4,216
6. Terry Labonte..................4,177
7. Bobby Labonte................4,101
8. Bill Elliott .........................3,836
9. Rusty Wallace ................3,598
10. Ken Schrader.................3,576

## Race winners

1. Jeff Gordon ...................10
2. Dale Jarrett ...................7
3. Mark Martin ...................4
4. Jeff Burton.....................3
5. Ricky Rudd.....................2
6. Terry Labonte ................1
    Bobby Labonte ...............1
    Rusty Wallace .................1
    Erine Irvan .....................1
    Bobby Hamilton ..............1
    John Andretti ..................1

## Money won leaders

1. Jeff Gordon .........$6,375,658
2. Dale Jarrett .........3,240,542
3. Mark Martin..........2,532,484
4. Jeff Burton ...........2,296,614
5. Terry Labonte .......2,270,144
6. Bobby Labonte ......2,217,999
7. Dale Earnhardt ......2,151,909
8. Ricky Rudd ............1,975,981
9. Rusty Wallace .......1,705,625
10. Erine Irvan............1,614,281
11. Bill Elliott ..............1,607,827
12. Bobby Hamilton ......1,478,843
13. Ken Schrader..........1,355,292
14. Sterling Marlin........1,301,370
15. Ricky Craven ..........1,259,550
16. Ted Musgrave ........1,256,680
17. Johnny Benson ......1,256,457
18. John Andretti..........1,143,725
19. Michael Waltrip ......1,138,599
20. Geoffrey Bodine......1,092,734

## Pole winners

1. Mark Martin ....................3
    Bobby Labonte ...............3
3. Mike Skinner..................2
    Dale Jarrett.....................2
    Geoffrey Bodine..............2
    Bobby Hamilton...............2
    Ernie Irvan.....................2
    Joe Nemechek..................2
    Ken Schrader ..................2
    Kenny Wallace.................2
11. Robby Gordon ....................1
    Rusty Wallace ....................1
    John Andretti......................1
    Jeff Gordon .......................1
    Todd Bodine.......................1
    Johnny Benson ...................1
    Bill Elliott............................1
    Ward Burton .......................1

HISTORY

# 1996 SEASON

| Race No. | Location | Date | Winner | Car owner |
|---|---|---|---|---|
| 1. | Daytona Beach, Fla. | Feb. 18 | Dale Jarrett | Robert Yates |
| 2. | Rockingham, N.C. | Feb. 25 | Dale Earnhardt | Richard Childress |
| 3. | Richmond, Va. | March 3 | Jeff Gordon | Rick Hendrick |
| 4. | Hampton, Ga. | March 10 | Dale Earnhardt | Richard Childress |
| 5. | Darlington, S.C. | March 24 | Jeff Gordon | Rick Hendrick |
| 6. | Bristol, Tenn. | March 31 | Jeff Gordon | Rick Hendrick |
| 7. | N. Wilkesboro, N.C. | April 14 | Terry Labonte | Rick Hendrick |
| 8. | Martinsville, Va. | April 21 | Rusty Wallace | Roger Penske |
| 9. | Talladega, Ala. | April 28 | Sterling Marlin | Morgan-McClure |
| 10. | Sonoma, Calif. | May 5 | Rusty Wallace | Roger Penske |
| 11. | Concord, N.C. | May 26 | Dale Jarrett | Robert Yates |
| 12. | Dover, Del. | June 2 | Jeff Gordon | Rick Hendrick |
| 13. | Long Pond, Pa. | June 16 | Jeff Gordon | Rick Hendrick |
| 14. | Brooklyn, Mich. | June 23 | Rusty Wallace | Roger Penske |
| 15. | Daytona Beach, Fla. | July 6 | Sterling Marlin | Morgan-McClure |
| 16. | Loudon, N.H. | July 14 | Ernie Irvan | Robert Yates |
| 17. | Long Pond, Pa. | July 21 | Rusty Wallace | Roger Penske |
| 18. | Talladega, Ala. | July 28 | Jeff Gordon | Rick Hendrick |
| 19. | Indianapolis | Aug. 3 | Dale Jarrett | Robert Yates |
| 20. | Watkins Glen, N.Y. | Aug. 11 | Geoff Bodine | Geoff Bodine |
| 21. | Brooklyn, Mich. | Aug. 18 | Dale Jarrett | Robert Yates |
| 22. | Bristol, Tenn. | Aug. 24 | Rusty Wallace | Roger Penske |
| 23. | Darlington, S.C. | Sept. 1 | Jeff Gordon | Rick Hendrick |
| 24. | Richmond, Va. | Sept. 7 | Ernie Irvan | Robert Yates |
| 25. | Dover, Del. | Sept. 15 | Jeff Gordon | Rick Hendrick |
| 26. | Martinsville, Va. | Sept. 22 | Jeff Gordon | Rick Hendrick |
| 27. | N. Wilkesboro, N.C. | Sept. 29 | Jeff Gordon | Rick Hendrick |
| 28. | Concord, N.C. | Oct. 6 | Terry Labonte | Rick Hendrick |
| 29. | Rockingham, N.C. | Oct. 20 | Ricky Rudd | Ricky Rudd |
| 30. | Phoenix | Oct. 27 | Bobby Hamilton | Richard Petty |
| 31. | Hampton, Ga. | Nov. 10 | Bobby Labonte | Joe Gibbs |

## Points standings

1. Terry Labonte ...................4,657
2. Jeff Gordon ......................4,620
3. Dale Jarrett ......................4,568
4. Dale Earnhardt .................4,327
5. Mark Martin ....................4,278
6. Ricky Rudd.......................3,845
7. Rusty Wallace...................3,717
8. Sterling Marlin .................3,682
9. Bobby Hamilton ...............3,639
10. Ernie Irvan ......................3,632

## Race winners 11

1. Jeff Gordon ........................10
2. Rusty Wallace......................5
3. Dale Jarrett .........................4
4. Dale Earnhardt ....................2
   Sterling Marlin .....................2
   Ernie Irvan ...........................2
   Terry Labonte .......................2
8. Geoffrey Bodine ..................1
   Ricky Rudd............................1
   Bobby Hamilton ...................1
   Bobby Labonte .....................1

## Money won leaders

1. Terry Labonte ........$4,030,648
2. Jeff Gordon ............3,428,485
3. Dale Jarrett ............2,985,418
4. Dale Earnhardt .......2,285,926
5. Mark Martin ..........1,887,396
6. Ernie Irvan ............1,683,313
7. Rusty Wallace ........1,665,315
8. Sterling Marlin .......1,588,425
9. Ricky Rudd.............1,503,025
10. Bobby Hamilton ...1,151,235
11. Bobby Labonte .......1,475,196
12. Michael Waltrip ......1,182,811
13. Jimmy Spencer .......1,090,876
14. Ken Schrader ..........1,089,603
15. Geoffrey Bodine ......1,031,762
16. Ted Musgrave ...........961,512
17. Ricky Craven.............941,959
18. Rick Mast ................924,559
19. Jeff Burton ..............884,303
20. Morgan Shepherd ......719,059

## Pole winners 14

1. Jeff Gordon ............................5
2. Terry Labonte..........................4
   Bobby Labonte ........................4
   Mark Martin ............................4
5. Dale Earnhardt ........................2
   Bobby Hamilton ......................2
   Dale Jarrett ..............................2
   Ricky Craven............................2
9. Johnny Benson .......................1
   Jeremy Mayfield ....................1
   Jeff Burton...............................1
   Ward Burton.............................1
   Ted Musgrave .........................1
   Ernie Irvan ..............................1

HISTORY

# 1995 SEASON

| Race No. | Location | Date | Winner | Car owner |
|---|---|---|---|---|
| 1. | Daytona Beach, Fla. | Feb. 19 | Sterling Marlin | Morgan-McClure |
| 2. | Rockingham, N.C. | Feb. 26 | Jeff Gordon | Rick Hendrick |
| 3. | Richmond, Va. | March 5 | Terry Labonte | Rick Hendrick |
| 4. | Hampton, Ga. | March 12 | Jeff Gordon | Rick Hendrick |
| 5. | Darlington, S.C. | March 26 | Sterling Marlin | Morgan-McClure |
| 6. | Bristol, Tenn. | April 2 | Jeff Gordon | Rick Hendrick |
| 7. | N. Wilkesboro, N.C. | April 9 | Dale Earnhardt | Richard Childress |
| 8. | Martinsville, Va. | April 23 | Rusty Wallace | Roger Penske |
| 9. | Talladega, Ala. | April 30 | Mark Martin | Jack Roush |
| 10. | Sonoma, Calif. | May 7 | Dale Earnhardt | Richard Childress |
| 11. | Concord, N.C. | May 28 | Bobby Labonte | Joe Gibbs |
| 12. | Dover, Del. | June 4 | Kyle Petty | Felix Sabates |
| 13. | Long Pond, Pa. | June 11 | Terry Labonte | Rick Hendrick |
| 14. | Brooklyn, Mich. | June 18 | Bobby Labonte | Joe Gibbs |
| 15. | Daytona Beach, Fla. | July 1 | Jeff Gordon | Rick Hendrick |
| 16. | Loudon, N.H. | July 9 | Jeff Gordon | Rick Hendrick |
| 17. | Long Pond, Pa. | July 16 | Dale Jarrett | Robert Yates |
| 18. | Talladega, Ala. | July 23 | Sterling Marlin | Morgan-McClure |
| 19. | Indianapolis | Aug. 5 | Dale Earnhardt | Richard Childress |
| 20. | Watkins Glen, N.Y. | Aug. 13 | Mark Martin | Jack Roush |
| 21. | Brooklyn, Mich. | Aug. 20 | Bobby Labonte | Joe Gibbs |
| 22. | Bristol, Tenn. | Aug. 26 | Terry Labonte | Rick Hendrick |
| 23. | Darlington, S.C. | Sept. 3 | Jeff Gordon | Rick Hendrick |
| 24. | Richmond, Va. | Sept. 9 | Rusty Wallace | Roger Penske |
| 25. | Dover, Del. | Sept. 17 | Jeff Gordon | Rick Hendrick |
| 26. | Martinsville, Va. | Sept. 24 | Dale Earnhardt | Richard Childress |
| 27. | N. Wilkesboro, N.C. | Oct. 1 | Mark Martin | Jack Roush |
| 28. | Concord, N.C. | Oct. 8 | Mark Martin | Jack Roush |
| 29. | Rockingham, N.C. | Oct. 22 | Ward Burton | Bill Davis |
| 30. | Phoenix | Oct. 29 | Ricky Rudd | Ricky Rudd |
| 31. | Hampton, Ga. | Nov. 12 | Dale Earnhardt | Richard Childress |

## Points standings

1. Jeff Gordon .....................4,614
2. Dale Earnhardt................4,580
3. Sterling Marlin ................4,361
4. Mark Martin.....................4,320
5. Rusty Wallace .................4,240
6. Terry Labonte..................4,146
7. Ted Musgrave .................3,949
8. Bill Elliott .........................3,746
9. Ricky Rudd .....................3,734
10. Bobby Labonte..............3,718

## Race winners 11

1. Jeff Gordon ...........................7
2. Dale Earnhardt ...................5
3. Mark Martin .........................4
4. Sterling Marlin .....................3
   Terry Labonte ......................3
   Bobby Labonte .....................3
7. Rusty Wallace ......................2
8. Ricky Rudd...........................1
   Ward Burton ..........................1
   Kyle Petty..............................1
   Dale Jarrett ...........................1

## Money won leaders

1. Jeff Gordon .........$4,347,343
2. Dale Earnhardt ......3,154,241
3. Sterling Marlin........2,253,502
4. Mark Martin............1,893,519
5. Rusty Wallace ........1,642,837
6. Terry Labonte ........1,558,659
7. Bobby Labonte ......1,413,682
8. Dale Jarrett ...........1,363,158
9. Ricky Rudd ...........1,337,703
10. Ted Musgrave .......1,147,445
11. Geoffrey Bodine......1,011,090
12. Bill Elliott ...............996,816
13. Morgan Shepherd......966,374
14. Michael Waltrip..........898,338
15. Brett Bodine .............893,029
16. Ken Schrader ...........886,566
17. Darrell Waltrip............850,632
18. Bobby Hamilton ........804,505
19. Rick Mast .................749,550
20. Kyle Petty .................698,875

## Pole winners 15

1. Jeff Gordon ...........................8
2. Mark Martin ..........................4
3. Dale Earnhardt......................3
4. Bill Elliott .............................2
   Ricky Rudd ...........................2
   Bobby Labonte ......................2
7. Terry Labonte........................1
   Sterling Marlin .......................1
   Ted Musgrave ........................1
   Dale Jarrett ...........................1
   Ken Schrader .........................1
   John Andretti ..........................1
   Darrell Waltrip .........................1
   Rick Mast ...............................1
   Hut Stricklin ............................1

HISTORY

# 1994 SEASON

| Race No. | Location | Date | Winner | Car owner |
|---|---|---|---|---|
| 1. | Daytona Beach, Fla. | Feb. 20 | Sterling Marlin | Larry McClure |
| 2. | Rockingham, N.C. | Feb. 27 | Rusty Wallace | Roger Penske |
| 3. | Richmond, Va. | March 6 | Ernie Irvan | Robert Yates |
| 4. | Hampton, Ga. | March 13 | Ernie Irvan | Robert Yates |
| 5. | Darlington, S.C. | March 27 | Dale Earnhardt | Richard Childress |
| 6. | Bristol, Tenn. | April 10 | Dale Earnhardt | Richard Childress |
| 7. | N. Wilkesboro, N.C. | April 17 | Terry Labonte | Rick Hendrick |
| 8. | Martinsville, Va. | April 24 | Rusty Wallace | Roger Penske |
| 9. | Talladega, Ala. | May 1 | Dale Earnhardt | Richard Childress |
| 10. | Sonoma, Calif. | May 15 | Ernie Irvan | Robert Yates |
| 11. | Concord, N.C. | May 29 | Jeff Gordon | Rick Hendrick |
| 12. | Dover, Del. | June 5 | Rusty Wallace | Roger Penske |
| 13. | Long Pond, Pa. | June 12 | Rusty Wallace | Roger Penske |
| 14. | Brooklyn, Mich. | June 19 | Rusty Wallace | Roger Penske |
| 15. | Daytona Beach, Fla. | July 2 | Jimmy Spencer | Junior Johnson |
| 16. | Loudon, N.H. | July 10 | Ricky Rudd | Ricky Rudd |
| 17. | Long Pond, Pa. | July 17 | Geoff Bodine | Geoff Bodine |
| 18. | Talladega, Ala. | July 24 | Jimmy Spencer | Junior Johnson |
| 19. | Indianapolis | Aug. 6 | Jeff Gordon | Rick Hendrick |
| 20. | Watkins Glen, N.Y. | Aug. 14 | Mark Martin | Jack Roush |
| 21. | Brooklyn, Mich. | Aug. 21 | Geoff Bodine | Geoff Bodine |
| 22. | Bristol, Tenn. | Aug. 27 | Rusty Wallace | Roger Penske |
| 23. | Darlington, S.C. | Sept. 4 | Bill Elliott | Junior Johnson |
| 24. | Richmond, Va. | Sept. 10 | Terry Labonte | Rick Hendrick |
| 25. | Dover, Del. | Sept. 18 | Rusty Wallace | Roger Penske |
| 26. | Martinsville, Va. | Sept. 25 | Rusty Wallace | Roger Penske |
| 27. | N. Wilkesboro, N.C. | Oct. 2 | Geoff Bodine | Geoff Bodine |
| 28. | Concord, N.C. | Oct. 9 | Dale Jarrett | Joe Gibbs |
| 29. | Rockingham, N.C. | Oct. 23 | Dale Earnhardt | Richard Childress |
| 30. | Phoenix | Oct. 30 | Terry Labonte | Rick Hendrick |
| 31. | Hampton, Ga. | Nov. 13 | Mark Martin | Jack Roush |

## Points standings

1. Dale Earnhardt ................4,694
2. Mark Martin .....................4,250
3. Rusty Wallace .................4,207
4. Ken Schrader ...................4,060
5. Ricky Rudd ......................4,050
6. Morgan Shepherd ...........4,029
7. Terry Labonte...................3,876
8. Jeff Gordon .....................3,776
9. Darrell Waltrip .................3,688
10. Bill Elliott ......................3,617

## Race winners 12

1. Rusty Wallace ........................8
2. Dale Earnhardt .....................4
3. Ernie Irvan ...........................3
   Terry Labonte .......................3
   Geoff Bodine .........................3
6. Jeff Gordon ..........................2
   Jimmy Spencer ....................2
   Mark Martin ..........................2
9. Sterling Marlin .....................1
   Ricky Rudd............................1
   Bill Elliott .............................1
   Dale Jarrett ..........................1

## Money won leaders

1. Dale Earnhardt ......$3,300,733
2. Rusty Wallace ........1,914,072
3. Jeff Gordon ............1,779,523
4. Mark Martin ...........1,628,906
5. Geoff Bodine ..........1,276,126
6. Ken Schrader .........1,171,062
7. Sterling Marlin ........1,127,683
8. Terry Labonte..........1,125,921
9. Morgan Shepherd ...1,089,038
10. Ricky Rudd ............1,044,441
11. Bill Elliott...............936,779
12. Dale Jarrett.............881,754
13. Darrell Waltrip .........835,680
14. Lake Speed.............832,463
15. Kyle Petty .................806,332
16. Brett Bodine .............791,444
17. Rick Mast .................722,361
18. Michael Waltrip .........706,426
19. Ted Musgrave ...........656,187
20. Todd Bodine .............494,316

## Pole winners 17

1. Geoff Bodine ...........................5
   Ernie Irvan .............................5
3. Loy Allen ................................3
   Ted Musgrave .......................3
5. Rusty Wallace .......................2
   Dale Earnhardt ......................2
7. Bill Elliott ..............................1
   Chuck Bown...........................1
   Jeff Gordon ...........................1
   Rick Mast...............................1
   Mark Martin ...........................1
   Harry Gant .............................1
   Jimmy Spencer ......................1
   Ward Burton...........................1
   Ricky Rudd..............................1
   Sterling Marlin .......................1
   Greg Sacks ...........................1

HISTORY

204

# 1993 SEASON

| Race No. | Location | Date | Winner | Car owner |
|---|---|---|---|---|
| 1. | Daytona Beach, Fla. | Feb. 14 | Dale Jarrett | Joe Gibbs |
| 2. | Rockingham, N.C. | Feb. 28 | Rusty Wallace | Roger Penske |
| 3. | Richmond, Va. | March 7 | Davey Allison | Robert Yates |
| 4. | Hampton, Ga. | March 20 | Morgan Shepherd | Wood Brothers |
| 5. | Darlington, S.C. | March 28 | Dale Earnhardt | Richard Childress |
| 6. | Bristol, Tenn. | April 4 | Rusty Wallace | Roger Penske |
| 7. | N. Wilkesboro, N.C. | April 18 | Rusty Wallace | Roger Penske |
| 8. | Martinsville, Va. | April 25 | Rusty Wallace | Roger Penske |
| 9. | Talladega, Ala. | May 2 | Ernie Irvan | Larry McClure |
| 10. | Sonoma, Calif. | May 16 | Geoff Bodine | Bud Moore |
| 11. | Concord, N.C. | May 30 | Dale Earnhardt | Richard Childress |
| 12. | Dover, Del. | June 6 | Dale Earnhardt | Richard Childress |
| 13. | Long Pond, Pa. | June 13 | Kyle Petty | Felix Sabates |
| 14. | Brooklyn, Mich. | June 20 | Ricky Rudd | Rick Hendrick |
| 15. | Daytona Beach, Fla. | July 3 | Dale Earnhardt | Richard Childress |
| 16. | Loudon, N.H. | July 11 | Rusty Wallace | Roger Penske |
| 17. | Long Pond, Pa. | July 18 | Dale Earnhardt | Richard Childress |
| 18. | Talladega, Ala. | July 25 | Dale Earnhardt | Richard Childress |
| 19. | Watkins Glen, N.Y. | Aug. 8 | Mark Martin | Jack Roush |
| 20. | Brooklyn, Mich. | Aug. 15 | Mark Martin | Jack Roush |
| 21. | Bristol, Tenn. | Aug. 28 | Mark Martin | Jack Roush |
| 22. | Darlington, S.C. | Sept. 5 | Mark Martin | Jack Roush |
| 23. | Richmond, Va. | Sept. 11 | Rusty Wallace | Roger Penske |
| 24. | Dover, Del. | Sept. 19 | Rusty Wallace | Roger Penske |
| 25. | Martinsville, Va. | Sept. 26 | Ernie Irvan | Robert Yates |
| 26. | N. Wilkesboro, N.C. | Oct. 3 | Rusty Wallace | Roger Penske |
| 27. | Concord, N.C. | Oct. 10 | Ernie Irvan | Robert Yates |
| 28. | Rockingham, N.C. | Oct. 24 | Rusty Wallace | Roger Penske |
| 29. | Phoenix | Oct. 31 | Mark Martin | Jack Roush |
| 30. | Hampton, Ga. | Nov. 14 | Rusty Wallace | Roger Penske |

## Points standings

1. Dale Earnhardt ..................4,526
2. Rusty Wallace ..................4,446
3. Mark Martin .....................4,150
4. Dale Jarrett .....................4,000
5. Kyle Petty.........................3,860
6. Ernie Irvan .......................3,834
7. Morgan Shepherd ............3,807
8. Bill Elliott ..........................3,774
9. Ken Schrader ...................3,715
10. Ricky Rudd ....................3,644

## Race winners

1. Rusty Wallace......................10
2. Dale Earnhardt .....................6
3. Mark Martin ..........................5
4. Ernie Irvan ............................3
5. Davey Allison ........................1
   Geoff Bodine ........................1
   Dale Jarrett ...........................1
   Kyle Petty ..............................1
   Ricky Rudd.............................1
   Morgan Shepherd..................1

## Money won leaders

1. Dale Earnhardt .....3,353,789
2. Rusty Wallace ........1,702,154
3. Mark Martin ...........1,657,662
4. Ernie Irvan .............1,400,468
5. Dale Jarrett ...........1,242,394
6. Bill Elliott ................955,859
7. Ken Schrader ...........952,748
8. Kyle Petty.................914,662
9. Geoff Bodine ............783,762
10. Morgan Shepherd......782,523
11. Harry Gant ..............772,832
12. Jeff Gordon .............765,168
13. Ricky Rudd...............752,562
14. Darrell Waltrip ..........746,646
15. Jimmy Spencer ........686,026
16. Sterling Marlin ..........628,835
17. Brett Bodine .............582,014
18. Rick Mast..................568,095
19. Terry Labonte............531,717
20. Michael Waltrip ........529,923

## Pole winners

1. Ken Schrader ..........................6
2. Mark Martin ............................5
3. Ernie Irvan ..............................4
4. Rusty Wallace.........................3
5. Brett Bodine ...........................2
   Dale Earnhardt .......................2
   Bill Elliott ...............................2
8. Geoff Bodine ..........................1
   Jeff Gordon ............................1
   Bobby Labonte.......................1
   Kyle Petty...............................1
   Harry Gant ............................ 1

# 1992 SEASON

| Race No. | Location | Date | Winner | Car owner |
|---|---|---|---|---|
| 1. | Daytona Beach, Fla. | Feb. 16 | Davey Allison | Robert Yates |
| 2. | Rockingham, N.C. | March 1 | Bill Elliott | Junior Johnson |
| 3. | Richmond, Va. | March 8 | Bill Elliott | Junior Johnson |
| 4. | Hampton, Ga. | March 15 | Bill Elliott | Junior Johnson |
| 5. | Darlington, S.C. | March 29 | Bill Elliott | Junior Johnson |
| 6. | Bristol, Tenn. | April 5 | Alan Kulwicki | Alan Kulwicki |
| 7. | N. Wilkesboro, N.C. | April 12 | Davey Allison | Robert Yates |
| 8. | Martinsville, Va. | April 26 | Mark Martin | Jack Roush |
| 9. | Talladega, Ala. | May 3 | Davey Allison | Robert Yates |
| 10. | Concord, N.C. | May 24 | Dale Earnhardt | Richard Childress |
| 11. | Dover, Del. | May 31 | Harry Gant | Leo Jackson |
| 12. | Sonoma, Calif. | June 7 | Ernie Irvan | Larry McClure |
| 13. | Long Pond, Pa. | June 14 | Alan Kulwicki | Alan Kulwicki |
| 14. | Brooklyn, Mich. | June 21 | Davey Allison | Robert Yates |
| 15. | Daytona Beach, Fla. | July 4 | Ernie Irvan | Larry McClure |
| 16. | Long Pond, Pa. | July 19 | Darrell Waltrip | Darrell Waltrip |
| 17. | Talladega, Ala. | July 26 | Ernie Irvan | Morgan-McClure |
| 18. | Watkins Glen, N.Y. | Aug. 9 | Kyle Petty | Felix Sabates |
| 19. | Brooklyn, Mich. | Aug. 16 | Harry Gant | Leo Jackson |
| 20. | Bristol, Tenn. | Aug. 29 | Darrell Waltrip | Darrell Waltrip |
| 21. | Darlington, S.C. | Sept. 6 | Darrell Waltrip | Darrell Waltrip |
| 22. | Richmond, Va. | Sept. 12 | Rusty Wallace | Roger Penske |
| 23. | Dover, Del. | Sept. 20 | Ricky Rudd | Rick Hendrick |
| 24. | Martinsville, Va. | Sept. 28 | Geoff Bodine | Bud Moore |
| 25. | N. Wilkesboro, N.C. | Oct. 5 | Geoff Bodine | Bud Moore |
| 26. | Concord, N.C. | Oct. 11 | Mark Martin | Jack Roush |
| 27. | Rockingham, N.C. | Oct. 25 | Kyle Petty | Felix Sabates |
| 28. | Phoenix | Nov. 1 | Davey Allison | Robert Yates |
| 29. | Hampton, Ga. | Nov. 15 | Bill Elliott | Junior Johnson |

## Points standings

1. Alan Kulwicki .................4,078
2. Bill Elliott ..........................4,068
3. Davey Allison ..................4,015
4. Harry Gant .......................3,955
5. Kyle Petty ........................3,945
6. Mark Martin .....................3,887
7. Ricky Rudd ......................3,735
8. Terry Labonte ..................3,674
9. Darrell Waltrip .................3,659
10. Sterling Marlin ...............3,063

## Race winners 12

1. Davey Allison ........................5
   Bill Elliott ...............................5
3. Ernie Irvan ...........................3
   Darrell Waltrip ......................3
   Geoff Bodine ........................2
6. Harry Gant ............................2
   Alan Kulwicki ........................2
   Mark Martin ..........................2
   Kyle Petty ..............................2
10. Dale Earnhardt .....................1
   Ricky Rudd.............................1
   Rusty Wallace........................1

## Money won leaders

1. Alan Kulwicki........$2,322,561
2. Davey Allison ..........1,955,628
3. Bill Elliott ................1,692,381
4. Harry Gant..............1,122,776
5. Kyle Petty ...............1,107,063
6. Mark Martin...........1,000,571
7. Ernie Irvan ..............996,885
8. Dale Earnhardt .........915,463
9. Darrell Waltrip...........876,492
10. Ricky Rudd...............793,903
11. Geoff Bodine.............716,583
12. Rusty Wallace ...........657,925
13. Sterling Marlin ..........649,048
14. Ken Schrader ...........639,679
15. Morgan Shepherd......634,222
16. Terry Labonte ...........600,381
17. Brett Bodine ..............495,224
18. Ted Musgrave...........449,121
19. Dick Trickle...............429,521
20. Dale Jarrett ..............418,648
21. Michael Waltrip.........410,545
22. Bobby Hamilton ........367,065
23. Rick Mast .................350,740
24. Richard Petty ............348,870
25. Hut Stricklin ..............336,965

## Pole winners 14

1. Alan Kulwicki ..........................6
2. Sterling Marlin ........................5
3. Ernie Irvan .............................3
   Kyle Petty ...............................3
5. Davey Allison .........................2
   Bill Elliott ...............................2
7. Brett Bodine ...........................1
   Dale Earnhardt .......................1
   Mark Martin ...........................1
   Rick Mast................................1
   Ricky Rudd...............................1
   Ken Schrader ..........................1
   Rusty Wallace..........................1
   Darrell Waltrip ........................1

# 1992 SEASON

## PASSING THE TORCH: THE KING AND THE KID

Imagine if Babe Ruth and Barry Bonds had once played in the same game—the Bambino's last and Bonds' first. Would anybody have caught the significance then? Would anybody have grasped what Ruth had done and what Bonds would do? In NASCAR, that scenario happened in the last race of 1992, at Atlanta. It was Richard Petty's final NASCAR Cup race and Jeff Gordon's first.

At that time, Gordon was a driver worth keeping an eye on, a young hotshoe from the open-wheel circuits. But rookie debuts in the final race of the season are hardly newsworthy. Gordon wasn't a nobody, but he wasn't exactly seen as destined for greatness, either. Regardless of whether anybody was aware of it, the torch started to be passed that November 15 in Atlanta in a race won by another legend, Bill Elliott.

Neither Gordon nor Petty had a finish worth talking about. Petty jokes that he hoped to go out in a blaze of glory but got only half of that when his car caught fire. Although Petty's end and Gordon's beginning were inglorious, both have left—and continue to leave—lasting legacies on the sport. The King carried the sport when it ruled the South. Gordon was The Kid who carried the sport out of the South and into corporate boardrooms.

# 1991 SEASON

| Race No. | Location | Date | Winner | Car owner |
|---|---|---|---|---|
| 1. | Daytona Beach, Fla. | Feb. 17 | Ernie Irvan | Larry McClure |
| 2. | Richmond, Va. | Feb. 24 | Dale Earnhardt | Richard Childress |
| 3. | Rockingham, N.C. | March 3 | Kyle Petty | Felix Sabates |
| 4. | Hampton, Ga. | March 17 | Ken Schrader | Rick Hendrick |
| 5. | Darlington, S.C. | April 7 | Ricky Rudd | Rick Hendrick |
| 6. | Bristol, Tenn. | April 14 | Rusty Wallace | Roger Penske |
| 7. | N. Wilkesboro, N.C. | April 21 | Darrell Waltrip | Darrell Waltrip |
| 8. | Martinsville, Va. | April 28 | Dale Earnhardt | Richard Childress |
| 9. | Talladega, Ala. | May 6 | Harry Gant | Leo Jackson |
| 10. | Concord, N.C. | May 26 | Davey Allison | Robert Yates |
| 11. | Dover, Del. | June 2 | Ken Schrader | Rick Hendrick |
| 12. | Sonoma, Calif. | June 9 | Davey Allison | Robert Yates |
| 13. | Long Pond, Pa. | June 16 | Darrell Waltrip | Darrell Waltrip |
| 14. | Brooklyn, Mich. | June 23 | Davey Allison | Robert Yates |
| 15. | Daytona Beach, Fla. | July 6 | Bill Elliott | Harry Melling |
| 16. | Long Pond, Pa. | July 21 | Rusty Wallace | Roger Penske |
| 17. | Talladega, Ala. | July 28 | Dale Earnhardt | Richard Childress |
| 18. | Watkins Glen, N.Y. | Aug. 11 | Ernie Irvan | Larry McClure |
| 19. | Brooklyn, Mich. | Aug. 18 | Dale Jarrett | Wood Brothers |
| 20. | Bristol, Tenn. | Aug. 24 | Alan Kulwicki | Alan Kulwicki |
| 21. | Darlington, S.C. | Sept. 1 | Harry Gant | Leo Jackson |
| 22. | Richmond, Va. | Sept. 7 | Harry Gant | Leo Jackson |
| 23. | Dover, Del. | Sept. 15 | Harry Gant | Leo Jackson |
| 24. | Martinsville, Va. | Sept. 22 | Harry Gant | Leo Jackson |
| 25. | N. Wilkesboro, N.C. | Sept. 29 | Dale Earnhardt | Richard Childress |
| 26. | Concord, N.C. | Oct. 6 | Geoff Bodine | Junior Johnson |
| 27. | Rockingham, N.C. | Oct. 20 | Davey Allison | Robert Yates |
| 28. | Phoenix | Nov. 3 | Davey Allison | Robert Yates |
| 29. | Hampton, Ga. | Nov. 17 | Mark Martin | Jack Roush |

## Points standings

1. Dale Earnhardt ..................4,287
2. Ricky Rudd......................4,092
3. Davey Allison ...................4,088
4. Harry Gant ......................3,985
5. Ernie Irvan ......................3,925
6. Mark Martin .....................3,914
7. Sterling Marlin ..................3,839
8. Darrell Waltrip ..................3,711
9. Ken Schrader ...................3,690
10. Rusty Wallace ...............3,582

## Race winners 14

1. Davey Allison .........................5
   Harry Gant ............................5
3. Dale Earnhardt .....................4
4. Ernie Irvan ...........................2
   Ken Schrader .......................2
   Rusty Wallace.......................2
   Darrell Waltrip.......................2
8. Geoff Bodine ........................1
   Bill Elliott ..............................1
   Alan Kulwicki .......................1
   Dale Jarrett ..........................1
   Mark Martin ..........................1
   Ricky Rudd...........................1
   Kyle Petty .............................1

## Money won leaders

1. Dale Earnhardt ....$2,396,685
2. Davey Allison..........1,732,924
3. Harry Gant.............1,194,033
4. Ricky Rudd ...........1,093,765
5. Ernie Irvan.............1,079,017
6. Mark Martin ...........1,039,991
7. Ken Schrader ...........722,434
8. Bill Elliott ................705,605
9. Sterling Marlin ..........633,690
10. Geoff Bodine ...........625,256
11. Darrell Waltrip ..........604,854
12. Alan Kulwicki ...........595,614
13. Morgan Shepherd......521,147
14. Rusty Wallace...........502,073
15. Dale Jarrett .............444,256
16. Michael Waltrip ........440,812
17. Hut Stricklin .............426,524
18. Derrike Cope ...........419,380
19. Kyle Petty ................413,727
20. Brett Bodine............376,220
21. Joe Ruttman ...........361,661
22. Terry Labonte ..........348,898
23. Rick Mast.................344,020
24. Jimmy Spencer ........283,620
25. Richard Petty ...........268,035

## Pole winners 14

1. Mark Martin ..........................5
2. Alan Kulwicki .......................4
3. Davey Allison .......................3
4. Geoff Bodine ........................2
   Bill Elliott ..............................2
   Sterling Marlin ......................2
   Kyle Petty .............................2
   Rusty Wallace .......................2
   Michael Waltrip .....................2
10. Brett Bodine.........................1
    Harry Gant ...........................1
    Ernie Irvan ...........................1
    Terry Labonte.......................1
    Ricky Rudd ...........................1

# 1990 SEASON

| Race No. | Location | Date | Winner | Car owner |
|---|---|---|---|---|
| 1. | Daytona Beach, Fla. | Feb. 18 | Derrike Cope | Bob Whitcomb |
| 2. | Richmond, Va. | Feb. 25 | Mark Martin | Jack Roush |
| 3. | Rockingham, N.C. | March 4 | Kyle Petty | Felix Sabates |
| 4. | Hampton, Ga. | March 18 | Dale Earnhardt | Richard Childress |
| 5. | Darlington, S.C. | April 1 | Dale Earnhardt | Richard Childress |
| 6. | Bristol, Tenn. | April 8 | Davey Allison | Robert Yates |
| 7. | N. Wilkesboro, N.C. | April 22 | Brett Bodine | Kenny Bernstein |
| 8. | Martinsville, Va. | April 29 | Geoff Bodine | Junior Johnson |
| 9. | Talladega, Ala. | May 6 | Dale Earnhardt | Richard Childress |
| 10. | Concord, N.C. | May 27 | Rusty Wallace | Raymond Beadle |
| 11. | Dover, Del. | June 3 | Derrike Cope | Bob Whitcomb |
| 12. | Sonoma, Calif. | June 10 | Rusty Wallace | Raymond Beadle |
| 13. | Long Pond, Pa. | June 17 | Harry Gant | Leo Jackson |
| 14. | Brooklyn, Mich. | June 24 | Dale Earnhardt | Richard Childress |
| 15. | Daytona Beach, Fla. | July 7 | Dale Earnhardt | Richard Childress |
| 16. | Long Pond, Pa. | July 22 | Geoff Bodine | Junior Johnson |
| 17. | Talladega, Ala. | July 29 | Dale Earnhardt | Richard Childress |
| 18. | Watkins Glen, N.Y. | Aug. 12 | Ricky Rudd | Rick Hendrick |
| 19. | Brooklyn, Mich. | Aug. 19 | Mark Martin | Jack Roush |
| 20. | Bristol, Tenn. | Aug. 25 | Ernie Irvan | Larry McClure |
| 21. | Darlington, S.C. | Sept. 2 | Dale Earnhardt | Richard Childress |
| 22. | Richmond, Va. | Sept. 9 | Dale Earnhardt | Richard Childress |
| 23. | Dover, Del. | Sept. 16 | Bill Elliott | Harry Melling |
| 24. | Martinsville, Va. | Sept. 23 | Geoff Bodine | Junior Johnson |
| 25. | N. Wilkesboro, N.C. | Sept. 30 | Mark Martin | Jack Roush |
| 26. | Concord N.C. | Oct. 7 | Davey Allison | Robert Yates |
| 27. | Rockingham, N.C. | Oct. 21 | Alan Kulwicki | Alan Kulwicki |
| 28. | Phoenix | Nov. 4 | Dale Earnhardt | Richard Childress |
| 29. | Hampton, Ga. | Nov. 18 | Morgan Shepherd | Bud Moore |

## Points standings

1. Dale Earnhardt ..................4,430
2. Mark Martin ......................4,404
3. Geoff Bodine ....................4,017
4. Bill Elliott ..........................3,999
5. Morgan Shepherd .............3,689
6. Rusty Wallace...................3,676
7. Ricky Rudd.......................3,601
8. Alan Kulwicki ...................3,599
9. Ernie Irvan .......................3,593
10. Ken Schrader .................3,572

## Race winners 14

1. Dale Earnhardt ......................9
2. Geoff Bodine ........................3
   Mark Martin ..........................3
4. Derrike Cope ........................2
   Rusty Wallace .......................2
   Davey Allison ........................2
7. Kyle Petty..............................1
   Brett Bodine ..........................1
   Harry Gant ............................1
   Ricky Rudd.............................1
   Ernie Irvan ............................1
   Bill Elliott ...............................1
   Alan Kulwicki .........................1
   Morgan Shepherd..................1

## Money won leaders

1. Dale Earnhardt ....$3,083,056
2. Mark Martin ..........1,302,958
3. Geoff Bodine .........1,131,222
4. Bill Elliott..............1,090,730
5. Rusty Wallace...........954,129
6. Ken Schrader ...........769,934
7. Kyle Petty................746,326
8. Morgan Shepherd......666,915
9. Davey Allison ...........640,684
10. Ricky Rudd...............573,650
11. Derrike Cope ...........569,451
12. Alan Kulwicki ...........550,936
13. Ernie Irvan............ 535,280
14. Darrell Waltrip .........530,420
15. Harry Gant ..............522,519
16. Terry Labonte ...........450,230
17. Brett Bodine .............442,681
18. Michael Waltrip ........395,507
19. Sterling Marlin .........369,167
20. Dick Trickle .............350,990
21. Bobby Hillin .............339,366
22. Dave Marcis.............242,724
23. Rick Wilson .............242,067
24. Jimmy Spencer ........219,775
25. Greg Sacks...............216,148

## Pole winners 13

1. Dale Earnhardt ......................4
2. Ernie Irvan ...........................3
   Mark Martin ..........................3
   Ken Schrader ........................3
5. Geoff Bodine.........................2
   Ricky Rudd.............................2
   Bill Elliott ..............................2
   Kyle Petty..............................2
   Rusty Wallace ........................2
10. Dick Trickle...........................1
    Greg Sacks............................1
    Alan Kulwicki .........................1
    Brett Bodine ..........................1

HISTORY

# 1989 SEASON

| Race No. | Location | Date | Winner | Car owner |
|---|---|---|---|---|
| 1. | Daytona Beach, Fla. | Feb. 19 | Darrell Waltrip | Rick Hendrick |
| 2. | Rockingham, N.C. | Mar. 5 | Rusty Wallace | Raymond Beadle |
| 3. | Hampton, Ga. | March 19 | Darrell Waltrip | Rick Hendrick |
| 4. | Richmond, Va. | March 26 | Rusty Wallace | Raymond Beadle |
| 5. | Darlington, S.C. | April 2 | Harry Gant | Leo Jackson |
| 6. | Bristol, Tenn. | April 9 | Rusty Wallace | Raymond Beadle |
| 7. | N. Wilkesboro, N.C. | April 16 | Dale Earnhardt | Richard Childress |
| 8. | Martinsville, Va. | April 23 | Darrell Waltrip | Rick Hendrick |
| 9. | Talladega, Ala. | May 7 | Davey Allison | Robert Yates |
| 10. | Concord, N.C. | May 28 | Darrell Waltrip | Rick Hendrick |
| 11. | Dover, Del. | June 4 | Dale Earnhardt | Richard Childress |
| 12. | Sonoma, Calif. | June 11 | Ricky Rudd | Kenny Bernstein |
| 13. | Long Pond, Pa. | June 18 | Terry Labonte | Junior Johnson |
| 14. | Brooklyn, Mich. | June 25 | Bill Elliott | Harry Melling |
| 15. | Daytona Beach, Fla. | July 1 | Davey Allison | Robert Yates |
| 16. | Long Pond, Pa. | July 23 | Bill Elliott | Harry Melling |
| 17. | Talladega, Ala. | July 30 | Terry Labonte | Junior Johnson |
| 18. | Watkins Glen, N.Y. | Aug. 13 | Rusty Wallace | Raymond Beadle |
| 19. | Brooklyn, Mich. | Aug. 20 | Rusty Wallace | Raymond Beadle |
| 20. | Bristol, Tenn. | Aug. 26 | Darrell Waltrip | Rick Hendrick |
| 21. | Darlington, S.C. | Sept. 3 | Dale Earnhardt | Richard Childress |
| 22. | Richmond, Va. | Sept. 10 | Rusty Wallace | Raymond Beadle |
| 23. | Dover, Del. | Sept. 17 | Dale Earnhardt | Richard Childress |
| 24. | Martinsville, Va. | Sept. 24 | Darrell Waltrip | Rick Hendrick |
| 25. | Concord, N.C. | Oct. 8 | Ken Schrader | Rick Hendrick |
| 26. | N. Wilkesboro, N.C. | Oct. 15 | Geoff Bodine | Rick Hendrick |
| 27. | Rockingham, N.C. | Oct. 22 | Mark Martin | Jack Roush |
| 28. | Phoenix | Nov. 5 | Bill Elliott | Harry Melling |
| 29. | Hampton, Ga. | Nov. 19 | Dale Earnhardt | Richard Childress |

## Points standings

1. Rusty Wallace ..................4,176
2. Dale Earnhardt..................4,164
3. Mark Martin......................4,053
4. Darrell Waltrip .................3,971
5. Ken Schrader....................3,786
6. Bill Elliott ........................3,774
7. Harry Gant .......................3,610
8. Ricky Rudd ......................3,608
9. Geoff Bodine ...................3,600
10. Terry Labonte.................3,569

## Race winners  11

1. Rusty Wallace.......................6
   Darrell Waltrip ....................6
3. Dale Earnhardt ....................5
4. Bill Elliott ............................3
5. Davey Allison .......................2
   Terry Labonte .......................2
7. Ricky Rudd............................1
   Harry Gant ............................1
   Ken Schrader ........................1
   Geoff Bodine ........................1
   Mark Martin ..........................1

## Money won leaders

1. Rusty Wallace ......$2,247,950
2. Dale Earnhardt ......1,435,730
3. Darrell Waltrip .......1,323,079
4. Ken Schrader ........1,039,441
5. Mark Martin ..........1,019,250
6. Bill Elliott ................854,570
7. Terry Labonte ...........704,806
8. Harry Gant ...............641,092
9. Davey Allison ...........640,956
10. Geoff Bodine ...........620,594
11. Morgan Shepherd......544,255
12. Ricky Rudd................534,824
13. Alan Kulwicki ...........501,295
14. Sterling Marlin ..........473,267
15. Dick Trickle .............343,728
16. Rick Wilson .............312,402
17. Phil Parsons .............285,012
18. Bobby Hillin .............283,181
19. Brett Bodine.............281,274
20. Neil Bonnett .............271,628
21. Michael Waltrip ........249,233
22. Dale Jarrett .............232,317
23. Lake Speed .............201,227

## Pole winners  9

1. Mark Martin *.........................6
   Alan Kulwicki ..........................6
3. Rusty Wallace..........................4
   Ken Schrader ..........................4
   Geoff Bodine ..........................3
   Bill Elliott ...............................2
   Morgan Shepherd .................1
   Davey Allison .........................1
   Jimmy Hensley ......................1

# 1988 SEASON

| Race No. | Location | Date | Winner | Car owner |
|---|---|---|---|---|
| 1. | Daytona Beach, Fla. | Feb. 14 | Bobby Allison | Stavola Brothers |
| 2. | Richmond, Va. | Feb. 21 | Neil Bonnett | Rahilly-Mock |
| 3. | Rockingham, N.C. | March 6 | Neil Bonnett | Rahilly-Mock |
| 4. | Hampton, Ga. | March 20 | Dale Earnhardt | Richard Childress |
| 5. | Darlington, S.C. | March 27 | Lake Speed | Lake Speed |
| 6. | Bristol, Tenn. | April 10 | Bill Elliott | Harry Melling |
| 7. | N. Wilkesboro, N.C. | April 17 | Terry Labonte | Junior Johnson |
| 8. | Martinsville, Va. | April 24 | Dale Earnhardt | Richard Childress |
| 9. | Talladega, Ala. | May 1 | Phil Parsons | Jackson Brothers |
| 10. | Concord, N.C. | May 29 | Darrell Waltrip | Rick Hendrick |
| 11. | Dover, Del. | June 5 | Bill Elliott | Harry Melling |
| 12. | Riverside, Calif. | June 12 | Rusty Wallace | Raymond Beadle |
| 13. | Long Pond, Pa. | June 19 | Geoff Bodine | Rick Hendrick |
| 14. | Brooklyn, Mich. | June 26 | Rusty Wallace | Raymond Beadle |
| 15. | Daytona Beach, Fla. | July 2 | Bill Elliott | Harry Melling |
| 16. | Long Pond, Pa. | July 24 | Bill Elliott | Harry Melling |
| 17. | Talladega, Ala. | July 31 | Ken Schrader | Rick Hendrick |
| 18. | Watkins Glen, N.Y. | Aug. 14 | Ricky Rudd | Kenny Bernstein |
| 19. | Brooklyn, Mich. | Aug. 21 | Davey Allison | Harry Ranier |
| 20. | Bristol, Tenn. | Aug. 27 | Dale Earnhardt | Richard Childress |
| 21. | Darlington, S.C. | Sept. 4 | Bill Elliott | Harry Melling |
| 22. | Richmond, Va. | Sept. 11 | Davey Allison | Harry Ranier |
| 23. | Dover, Del. | Sept. 18 | Bill Elliott | Harry Melling |
| 24. | Martinsville, Va. | Sept. 25 | Darrell Waltrip | Rick Hendrick |
| 25. | Concord, N.C. | Oct. 9 | Rusty Wallace | Raymond Beadle |
| 26. | N. Wilkesboro, N.C. | Oct. 16 | Rusty Wallace | Raymond Beadle |
| 27. | Rockingham, N.C. | Oct. 23 | Rusty Wallace | Raymond Beadle |
| 28. | Phoenix | Nov. 6 | Alan Kulwicki | Alan Kulwicki |
| 29. | Hampton, Ga. | Nov. 20 | Rusty Wallace | Raymond Beadle |

## Points standings

1. Bill Elliott ......................4,488
2. Rusty Wallace .................4,464
3. Dale Earnhardt ...............4,256
4. Terry Labonte .................4,007
5. Ken Schrader .................3,858
6. Geoff Bodine .................3,799
7. Darrell Waltrip................3,764
8. Davey Allison ................3,631
9. Phil Parsons ..................3,630
10. Sterling Marlin .............3,621

## Race winners  14

1. Bill Elliott ..............................6
   Rusty Wallace.......................6
3. Dale Earnhardt ....................3
4. Neil Bonnett .......................2
   Davey Allison ......................2
   Darrell Waltrip .....................2
7. Bobby Allison ......................1
   Terry Labonte ......................1
   Phil Parsons ........................1
   Lake Speed .........................1
   Geoff Bodine ........................1
   Ken Schrader .......................1
   Ricky Rudd...........................1
   Alan Kulwicki .......................1

## Money won leaders

1. Bill Elliott ...........$1,574,639
2. Rusty Wallace ......1,411,567
3. Dale Earnhardt......1,214,089
4. Terry Labonte .......950,781
5. Davey Allison .......844,532
6. Darrell Waltrip.........731,659
7. Ken Schrader .........631,544
8. Geoff Bodine ...........570,643
9. Phil Parsons .........532,043
10. Sterling Marlin ........521,464
11. Alan Kulwicki .......448,547
12. Neil Bonnett .........440,139
13. Brett Bodine ..........433,658
14. Ricky Rudd .............410,954
15. Kyle Petty ...............377,092
16. Bobby Hillin, Jr. ........330,217
17. Lake Speed.............260,500
18. Michael Waltrip ........240,400
19. Mark Martin ...........223,630
20. Dave Marcis ...........212,485

## Pole winners  12

1. Bill Elliott ..............................6
2. Alan Kulwicki .......................4
3. Davey Allison .......................3
   Geoff Bodine ........................3
5. Ken Schrader .......................2
   Ricky Rudd............................2
   Morgan Shepherd...................2
   Darrell Waltrip .......................2
   Rusty Wallace.......................2
10. Rick Wilson ..........................1
    Terry Labonte.......................1
    Mark Martin .......................1

# 1987 SEASON

| Race No. | Location | Date | Winner | Car owner |
|---|---|---|---|---|
| 1. | Daytona Beach, Fla. | Feb. 15 | Bill Elliott | Harry Melling |
| 2. | Rockingham, N.C. | March 1 | Dale Earnhardt | Richard Childress |
| 3. | Richmond, Va. | March 8 | Dale Earnhardt | Richard Childress |
| 4. | Hampton, Ga. | March 15 | Ricky Rudd | Bud Moore |
| 5. | Darlington, S.C. | March 29 | Dale Earnhardt | Richard Childress |
| 6. | N. Wilkesboro, N.C. | April 5 | Dale Earnhardt | Richard Childress |
| 7. | Bristol, Tenn. | April 12 | Dale Earnhardt | Richard Childress |
| 8. | Martinsville, Va. | April 26 | Dale Earnhardt | Richard Childress |
| 9. | Talladega, Ala. | May 3 | Davey Allison | Harry Ranier |
| 10. | Concord, N.C. | May 24 | Kyle Petty | Wood Brothers |
| 11. | Dover, Del. | May 31 | Davey Allison | Harry Ranier |
| 12. | Long Pond, Pa. | June 14 | Tim Richmond | Rick Hendrick |
| 13. | Riverside, Calif. | June 21 | Tim Richmond | Rick Hendrick |
| 14. | Brooklyn, Mich. | June 28 | Dale Earnhardt | Richard Childress |
| 15. | Daytona Beach, Fla. | July 4 | Bobby Allison | Stavola Brothers |
| 16. | Long Pond, Pa. | July 19 | Dale Earnhardt | Richard Childress |
| 17. | Talladega, Ala. | July 26 | Bill Elliott | Harry Melling |
| 18. | Watkins Glen, N.Y. | Aug. 10 | Rusty Wallace | Raymond Beadle |
| 19. | Brooklyn, Mich. | Aug. 16 | Bill Elliott | Harry Melling |
| 20. | Bristol, Tenn. | Aug. 22 | Dale Earnhardt | Richard Childress |
| 21. | Darlington, S.C. | Sept. 6 | Dale Earnhardt | Richard Childress |
| 22. | Richmond, Va. | Sept. 13 | Dale Earnhardt | Richard Childress |
| 23. | Dover, Del. | Sept. 20 | Ricky Rudd | Bud Moore |
| 24. | Martinsville, Va. | Sept. 27 | Darrell Waltrip | Rick Hendrick |
| 25. | N. Wilkesboro, N.C. | Oct. 4 | Terry Labonte | Junior Johnson |
| 26. | Concord, N.C. | Oct. 11 | Bill Elliott | Harry Melling |
| 27. | Rockingham, N.C. | Oct. 25 | Bill Elliott | Harry Melling |
| 28. | Riverside, Calif. | Nov. 8 | Rusty Wallace | Raymond Beadle |
| 29. | Hampton, Ga. | Nov. 22 | Bill Elliott | Harry Melling |

## Points standings

1. Dale Earnhardt..............4,696
2. Bill Elliott ........................4,207
3. Terry Labonte..................4,007
4. Darrell Waltrip ...............3,911
5. Rusty Wallace ................3,818
6. Ricky Rudd .....................3,742
7. Kyle Petty ......................3,737
8. Richard Petty ................3,708
9. Bobby Allison ..................3,530
10. Ken Schrader................3,405

## Race winners 10

1. Dale Earnhardt ..................11
2. Bill Elliott ............................6
3. Davey Allison ......................2
   Tim Richmond ......................2
   Ricky Rudd...........................2
   Rusty Wallace......................2
7. Kyle Petty ...........................1
   Bobby Allison .......................1
   Darrell Waltrip .....................1
   Terry Labonte ......................1

## Money won leaders

1. Dale Earnhardt ....$2,099,243
2. Bill Elliott .............1,619,210
3. Terry Labonte...........825,369
4. Rusty Wallace .........690,652
5. Ricky Rudd ..............653,508
6. Benny Parsons..........566,484
7. Kyle Petty.................544,437
8. Bobby Allison ...........515,894
9. Darrell Waltrip .........511,768
10. Richard Petty ..........468,702
11. Geoff Bodine ...........449,816
12. Neil Bonnett..............401,541
13. Ken Schrader............375,918
14. Alan Kulwicki............369,889
15. Davey Allison ...........361,060
16. Bobby Hillin, Jr. ........346,735
17. Morgan Shepherd ....317,034
18. Sterling Marlin ..........306,412
19. Dave Marcis..............256,354
20. Buddy Baker ............255,320
21. Michael Waltrip ........205,370
22. Harry Gant ...............197,645
23. Phil Parsons..............180,261
24. Jimmy Means ..........154,055
25. Tim Richmond ..........151,850

## Pole winners 12

1. Bill Elliott..............................8
2. Davey Allison .......................5
3. Terry Labonte ......................4
4. Alan Kulwicki ........................3
5. Geoff Bodine .........................2
6. Dale Earnhardt .....................1
   Ken Schrader ........................1
   Harry Gant.............................1
   Morgan Shepherd ..................1
   Rusty Wallace ........................1
   Tim Richmond ........................1
   Bobby Allison..........................1

# 1986 SEASON

| Race No. | Location | Date | Winner | Car owner |
|---|---|---|---|---|
| 1. | Daytona Beach, Fla. | Feb. 16 | Geoff Bodine | Rick Hendrick |
| 2. | Richmond, Va. | Feb. 23 | Kyle Petty | Wood Brothers |
| 3. | Rockingham, N.C. | March 2 | Terry Labonte | Billy Hagan |
| 4. | Hampton, Ga. | March 16 | Morgan Shepherd | Jack Beebe |
| 5. | Bristol, Tenn. | April 6 | Rusty Wallace | Raymond Beadle |
| 6. | Darlington, S.C. | April 13 | Dale Earnhardt | Richard Childress |
| 7. | N. Wilkesboro, N.C. | April 20 | Dale Earnhardt | Richard Childress |
| 8. | Martinsville, Va. | April 27 | Ricky Rudd | Bud Moore |
| 9. | Talladega, Ala. | May 4 | Bobby Allison | Stavola Brothers |
| 10. | Dover, Del. | May 18 | Geoff Bodine | Rick Hendrick |
| 11. | Concord, N.C. | May 25 | Dale Earnhardt | Richard Childress |
| 12. | Riverside, Calif. | June 1 | Darrell Waltrip | Junior Johnson |
| 13. | Long Pond, Pa. | June 8 | Tim Richmond | Rick Hendrick |
| 14. | Brooklyn, Mich. | June 15 | Bill Elliott | Harry Melling |
| 15. | Daytona Beach, Fla. | July 4 | Tim Richmond | Rick Hendrick |
| 16. | Long Pond, Pa. | July 20 | Tim Richmond | Rick Hendrick |
| 17. | Talladega, Ala. | July 27 | Bobby Hillin, Jr. | Stavola Brothers |
| 18. | Watkins Glen, N.Y. | Aug. 10 | Tim Richmond | Rick Hendrick |
| 19. | Brooklyn, Mich. | Aug. 17 | Bill Elliott | Harry Melling |
| 20. | Bristol, Tenn. | Aug. 23 | Darrell Waltrip | Junior Johnson |
| 21. | Darlington, S.C. | Aug. 31 | Tim Richmond | Rick Hendrick |
| 22. | Richmond, Va. | Sept. 7 | Tim Richmond | Rick Hendrick |
| 23. | Dover, Del. | Sept. 14 | Ricky Rudd | Bud Moore |
| 24. | Martinsville, Va. | Sept. 21 | Rusty Wallace | Raymond Beadle |
| 25. | N. Wilkesboro, N.C. | Sept. 28 | Darrell Waltrip | Junior Johnson |
| 26. | Concord, N.C. | Oct. 5 | Dale Earnhardt | Richard Childress |
| 27. | Rockingham, N.C. | Oct. 19 | Neil Bonnett | Junior Johnson |
| 28. | Hampton, Ga. | Nov. 2 | Dale Earnhardt | Richard Childress |
| 29. | Riverside, Calif. | Nov.16 | Tim Richmond | Rick Hendrick |

## Points standings

1. Dale Earnhardt..................4,468
2. Darrell Waltrip ..................4,180
3. Tim Richmond ..................4,174
4. Bill Elliott ..........................3,844
5. Ricky Rudd ......................3,823
6. Rusty Wallace ..................3,762
7. Bobby Allison ..................3,698
8. Geoff Bodine ..................3,678
9. Bobby Hillin Jr. ..............3,546
10. Kyle Petty ......................3,537

## Race winners 13

1. Tim Richmond ......................7
2. Dale Earnhardt ....................5
3. Darrell Waltrip ....................3
4. Rusty Wallace ....................2
   Geoff Bodine ......................2
   Bill Elliott ............................2
   Ricky Rudd..........................2
8. Terry Labonte ....................1
   Morgan Shepherd................1
   Bobby Allison ....................1
   Kyle Petty ..........................1
   Bobby Hillin, Jr. ..................1
   Neil Bonnett ......................1

## Money won leaders

1. Dale Earnhardt....$1,768,880
2. Darrell Waltrip ......1,099,735
3. Bill Elliott ............1,049,142
4. Tim Richmond ........973,221
5. Geoff Bodine............795,111
6. Ricky Rudd ............671,548
7. Harry Gant ............583,024
8. Rusty Wallace ..........557,354
9. Terry Labonte ..........522,235
10. Bobby Allison ..........503,095
11. Neil Bonnett ............485,930
12. Bobby Hillin, Jr..........448,452
13. Kyle Petty ..............403,242
14. Richard Petty ..........280,657
15. Joe Ruttman............259,263
16. Morgan Shepherd....244,146
17. Kenny Schrader ......235,905
18. Dave Marcis ..........220,461
19. Buddy Arrington ......186,588
20. Benny Parsons ........176,985
21. Jimmy Means..........157,940
22. Buddy Baker............138,600
23. Cale Yarborough ......137,010
24. Sterling Marlin ........113,070
25. Mike Waltrip ............108,767
26. Ron Bouchard..........106,835
27. J.D. McDuffie ..........106,115

## Pole winners 10

1. Tim Richmond*......................8
   Geoff Bodine........................8
3. Bill Elliott ............................4
4. Harry Gant ..........................2
5. Ricky Rudd ..........................1
   Terry Labonte ......................1
   Dale Earnhardt ....................1
   Darrell Waltrip......................1
   Cale Yarborough ..................1
   Benny Parsons ....................1

# 1985 SEASON

| Race No. | Location | Date | Winner | Car owner |
|---|---|---|---|---|
| 1. | Daytona Beach, Fla. | Feb. 17 | Bill Elliott | Harry Melling |
| 2. | Richmond, Va. | Feb. 24 | Dale Earnhardt | Richard Childress |
| 3. | Rockingham, N.C. | March 3 | Neil Bonnett | Junior Johnson |
| 4. | Hampton, Ga. | March 17 | Bill Elliott | Harry Melling |
| 5. | Bristol, Tenn. | April 6 | Dale Earnhardt | Richard Childress |
| 6. | Darlington, S.C. | April 14 | Bill Elliott | Harry Melling |
| 7. | N. Wilkesboro, N.C. | April 21 | Neil Bonnett | Junior Johnson |
| 8. | Martinsville, Va. | April 28 | Harry Gant | Needham-Reynolds |
| 9. | Talladega, Ala. | May 5 | Bill Elliott | Harry Melling |
| 10. | Dover, Del. | May 19 | Bill Elliott | Harry Melling |
| 11. | Concord, N.C. | May 26 | Darrell Waltrip | Junior Johnson |
| 12. | Riverside, Calif. | June 2 | Terry Labonte | Billy Hagan |
| 13. | Long Pond, Pa. | June 9 | Bill Elliott | Harry Melling |
| 14. | Brooklyn, Mich. | June 16 | Bill Elliott | Harry Melling |
| 15. | Daytona Beach, Fla. | July 4 | Greg Sacks | Bill Gardner |
| 16. | Long Pond, Pa. | July 21 | Bill Elliott | Harry Melling |
| 17. | Talladega, Ala. | July 28 | Cale Yarborough | Harry Ranier |
| 18. | Brooklyn, Mich. | Aug. 11 | Bill Elliott | Harry Melling |
| 19. | Bristol, Tenn. | Aug. 24 | Dale Earnhardt | Richard Childress |
| 20. | Darlington, S.C. | Sept. 1 | Bill Elliott | Harry Melling |
| 21. | Richmond, Va. | Sept. 8 | Darrell Waltrip | Junior Johnson |
| 22. | Dover, Del. | Sept. 15 | Harry Gant | Needham-Reynolds |
| 23. | Martinsville, Va. | Sept. 22 | Dale Earnhardt | Richard Childress |
| 24. | N. Wilkesboro, N.C. | Sept. 29 | Harry Gant | Needham-Reynolds |
| 25. | Concord, N.C. | Oct. 6 | Cale Yarborough | Harry Ranier |
| 26. | Rockingham, N.C. | Oct. 20 | Darrell Waltrip | Junior Johnson |
| 27. | Hampton, Ga. | Nov. 3 | Bill Elliott | Harry Melling |
| 28. | Riverside, Calif. | Nov. 17 | Ricky Rudd | Bud Moore |

## Points standings

1. Darrell Waltrip ...................4,292
2. Bill Elliott ..........................4,191
3. Harry Gant .......................4,033
4. Neil Bonnett.....................3,902
5. Geoff Bodine ...................3,862
6. Ricky Rudd ......................3,857
7. Terry Labonte ..................3,683
8. Dale Earnhardt.................3,561
9. Kyle Petty .......................3,528
10. Lake Speed ...................3,507

## Race winners 9

1. Bill Elliott ............................11
2. Dale Earnhardt .....................4
3. Harry Gant ...........................3
   Darrell Waltrip .....................3
5. Neil Bonnett .........................2
   Cale Yarborough ...................2
7. Terry Labonte .......................1
   Ricky Rudd ............................1
   Greg Sacks............................1

## Money won leaders

1. Bill Elliott.............$2,383,187
2. Darrell Waltrip ........1,318,735
3. Harry Gant ...............804,287
4. Terry Labonte ...........694,510
5. Geoff Bodine ...........565,865
6. Dale Earnhardt..........546,596
7. Neil Bonnett ............530,145
8. Ricky Rudd...............512,441
9. Cale Yarborough ........310,465
10. Richard Petty ...........306,142
11. Lake Speed ..............300,326
12. Kyle Petty ................296,367
13. Tim Richmond ...........290,284
14. Bobby Allison...........272,536
15. Ron Bouchard...........240,304
16. Buddy Baker ...........235,479
17. Greg Sacks...............234,141
18. Rusty Wallace...........233,670
19. Ken Schrader ...........211,523
20. Dave Marcis.............173,467
21. Buddy Arrington ........153,222
22. Bobby Hillin, Jr. ........145,070
23. Jimmy Means............132,130
24. Clark Dwyer .............128,710
25. Phil Parsons .............104,840
26. E. Bierschwale .........102,650

## Pole winners 7

1. Bill Elliott............................11
2. Terry Labonte .......................4
   Darrell Waltrip......................4
4. Geoff Bodine .........................3
   Harry Gant ...........................3
6. Neil Bonnett ..........................1
   Dale Earnhardt .....................1

## RECORD TIMING: THAT'S 200, MR. PRESIDENT

It was Morning in America in 1984, as President Ronald Reagan prepared to crush Walter Mondale in the November election. Reagan didn't hurt his efforts by becoming the first sitting president to attend a NASCAR race. From aboard Air Force One, the commander in chief ordered the gentlemen to start their engines.

The ending of the race was every bit as historic as the beginning. It was when royalty ascended to new heights.

The King, Richard Petty, had been stuck on 199 wins since May. His total was and is far and away the most ever, but he wanted to crest that 200 mark.

There was an accident with three laps left, which meant a mad dash to the finish line of that lap would determine the winner. Petty narrowly edged Cale Yarborough, then crawled the last two laps. The 80,000 fans in attendance got to their feet, knowing they were witnessing history.

Not only had Petty hit the 200 mark, but that win also would prove to be his last. He drove until 1992 but never again visited victory lane.

# 1984 SEASON

| Race No. | Location | Date | Winner | Car owner |
|---|---|---|---|---|
| 1. | Daytona Beach, Fla. | Feb. 19 | Cale Yarborough | Harry Ranier |
| 2. | Richmond, Va. | Feb. 26 | Ricky Rudd | Bud Moore |
| 3. | Rockingham, N.C. | March 4 | Bobby Allison | Bill Gardner |
| 4. | Hampton, Ga. | March 18 | Benny Parsons | Johnny Hayes |
| 5. | Bristol, Tenn. | April 1 | Darrell Waltrip | Junior Johnson |
| 6. | N. Wilkesboro, N.C. | April 8 | Tim Richmond | Raymond Beadle |
| 7. | Darlington, S.C. | April 15 | Darrell Waltrip | Junior Johnson |
| 8. | Martinsville, Va. | April 29 | Geoff Bodine | Rick Hendrick |
| 9. | Talladega, Ala. | May 6 | Cale Yarborough | Harry Ranier |
| 10. | Nashville | May 12 | Darrell Waltrip | Junior Johnson |
| 11. | Dover, Del. | May 20 | Richard Petty | Mike Curb |
| 12. | Concord, N.C. | May 27 | Bobby Allison | Bill Gardner |
| 13. | Riverside, Calif. | June 3 | Terry Labonte | Billy Hagan |
| 14. | Long Pond, Pa. | June 10 | Cale Yarborough | Harry Ranier |
| 15. | Brooklyn, Mich. | June 17 | Bill Elliott | Harry Melling |
| 16. | Daytona Beach, Fla. | July 4 | Richard Petty | Mike Curb |
| 17. | Nashville | July 14 | Geoff Bodine | Rick Hendrick |
| 18. | Long Pond, Pa. | July 22 | Harry Gant | Needham-Reynolds |
| 19. | Talladega, Ala. | July 29 | Dale Earnhardt | Richard Childress |
| 20. | Brooklyn, Mich. | Aug. 12 | Darrell Waltrip | Junior Johnson |
| 21. | Bristol, Tenn. | Aug. 25 | Terry Labonte | Billy Hagan |
| 22. | Darlington, S.C. | Sept. 2 | Harry Gant | Needham-Reynolds |
| 23. | Richmond, Va. | Sept. 9 | Darrell Waltrip | Junior Johnson |
| 24. | Dover, Del. | Sept. 16 | Harry Gant | Needham-Reynolds |
| 25. | Martinsville, Va. | Sept. 23 | Darrell Waltrip | Junior Johnson |
| 26. | Concord, N.C. | Oct. 7 | Bill Elliott | Harry Melling |
| 27. | N. Wilkesboro, N.C.. | Oct. 14 | Darrell Waltrip | Junior Johnson |
| 28. | Rockingham, N.C. | Oct. 21 | Bill Elliott | Harry Melling |
| 29. | Hampton, Ga. | Nov. 11 | Dale Earnhardt | Richard Childress |
| 30. | Riverside, Calif. | Nov. 18 | Geoff Bodine | Rick Hendrick |

## Points standings

1. Terry Labonte ...................4,508
2. Harry Gant ........................4,443
3. Bill Elliott ...........................4,377
4. Dale Earnhardt..................4,265
5. Darrell Waltrip .................4,230
6. Bobby Allison ...................4,094
7. Ricky Rudd ......................3,918
8. Neil Bonnett.....................3,802
9. Geoff Bodine ...................3,734
10. Richard Petty .................3,643

## Race winners 12

1. Darrell Waltrip ......................7
2. Geoff Bodine ........................3
   Bill Elliott ..............................3
   Harry Gant ...........................3
   Cale Yarborough ...................3
6. Bobby Allison ........................2
   Dale Earnhardt .....................2
   Terry Labonte ........................2
   Richard Petty .........................2
10. Benny Parsons .....................1
    Tim Richmond .....................1
    Ricky Rudd...........................1

## Money won leaders

1. Terry Labonte .......$713,010
2. Darrell Waltrip ..........703,876
3. Bill Elliott ...............660,226
4. Harry Gant ..............650,707
5. Bobby Allison ...........627,637
6. Dale Earnhardt..........616,788
7. Ricky Rudd .............476,602
8. Geoff Bodine ...........393,924
9. Cale Yarborough.......385,853
10. Dave Marcis ...........330,766
11. Tim Richmond .........329,589
12. Kyle Petty ...............324,555
13. Richard Petty ...........251,226
14. Benny Parsons..........241,665
15. Ron Bouchard .........229,528
16. Neil Bonnett.............223,592
17. Rusty Wallace ..........195,927
18. Dick Brooks ............186,819
19. Trevor Boys ............160,235
20. Joe Ruttman ............150,068
21. Buddy Baker ...........133,635
22. Buddy Arrington........128,802
23. Clark Dwyer.............114,335
24. Jimmy Means ..........100,885

## Pole winners 11

1. Bill Elliott................................4
   Darrell Waltrip ......................4
   Ricky Rudd............................4
   Cale Yarborough ...................4
5. Geoff Bodine .........................3
   Harry Gant ...........................3
7. Terry Labonte .......................2
   Benny Parsons ......................2
9. Buddy Baker ..........................1
   David Pearson........................1
   Joe Ruttman .........................1

# 1983 SEASON

| Race No. | Location | Date | Winner | Car owner |
|---|---|---|---|---|
| 1. | Daytona Beach, Fla. | Feb. 20 | Cale Yarborough | Harry Ranier |
| 2. | Richmond, Va. | Feb. 27 | Bobby Allison | Bill Gardner |
| 3. | Rockingham, N.C. | March 13 | Richard Petty | Petty Enterprises |
| 4. | Hampton, Ga. | March 27 | Cale Yarborough | Harry Ranier |
| 5. | Darlington, S.C. | April 10 | Harry Gant | Needham-Reynolds |
| 6. | N. Wilkesboro, N.C. | April 17 | Darrell Waltrip | Junior Johnson |
| 7. | Martinsville, Va. | April 24 | Darrell Waltrip | Junior Johnson |
| 8. | Talladega, Ala. | May 1 | Richard Petty | Petty Enterprises |
| 9. | Nashville | May 7 | Darrell Waltrip | Junior Johnson |
| 10. | Dover, Del. | May 15 | Bobby Allison | Bill Gardner |
| 11. | Bristol, Tenn. | May 21 | Darrell Waltrip | Junior Johnson |
| 12. | Concord, N.C. | May 29 | Neil Bonnett | Rahilly-Mock |
| 13. | Riverside, Calif. | June 5 | Ricky Rudd | Richard Childress |
| 14. | Long Pond, Pa. | June 12 | Bobby Allison | Bill Gardner |
| 15. | Brooklyn, Mich. | June 19 | Cale Yarborough | Harry Ranier |
| 16. | Daytona Beach, Fla. | July 4 | Buddy Baker | Wood Brothers |
| 17. | Nashville | July 16 | Dale Earnhardt | Bud Moore |
| 18. | Long Pond, Pa. | July 24 | Tim Richmond | Raymond Beadle |
| 19. | Talladega, Ala. | July 31 | Dale Earnhardt | Bud Moore |
| 20. | Brooklyn, Mich. | Aug. 21 | Cale Yarborough | Harry Ranier |
| 21. | Bristol, Tenn. | Aug. 27 | Darrell Waltrip | Junior Johnson |
| 22. | Darlington, S.C. | Sept. 5 | Bobby Allison | Bill Gardner |
| 23. | Richmond, Va. | Sept. 11 | Bobby Allison | Bill Gardner |
| 24. | Dover, Del. | Sept. 18 | Bobby Allison | Bill Gardner |
| 25. | Martinsville, Va. | Sept. 25 | Ricky Rudd | Richard Childress |
| 26. | N. Wilkesboro, N.C. | Oct. 2 | Darrell Waltrip | Junior Johnson |
| 27. | Concord, N.C. | Oct. 9 | Richard Petty | Petty Enterprises |
| 28. | Rockingham, N.C. | Oct. 30 | Terry Labonte | Billy Hagan |
| 29. | Hampton, Ga. | Nov. 6 | Neil Bonnett | Rahilly-Mock |
| 30. | Riverside, Calif. | Nov. 20 | Bill Elliott | Harry Melling |

## Points standings

1. Bobby Allison ................... 4,667
2. Darrell Waltrip ................. 4,620
3. Bill Elliott ......................... 4,279
4. Richard Petty .................... 4,042
5. Terry Labonte ................... 4,004
6. Neil Bonnett ..................... 3,842
7. Harry Gant ........................ 3,790
8. Dale Earnhardt ................. 3,732
9. Ricky Rudd ........................ 3,693
10. Tim Richmond ................. 3,612

## Race winners 12

1. Bobby Allison ......................... 6
   Darrell Waltrip ...................... 6
3. Cale Yarborough ................... 4
4. Richard Petty ........................ 3
5. Neil Bonnett ......................... 2
   Dale Earnhardt ...................... 2
   Ricky Rudd .............................. 2
8. Buddy Baker .......................... 1
   Bill Elliott ............................... 1
   Harry Gant .............................. 1
   Terry Labonte ........................ 1
   Tim Richmond ....................... 1

## Money won leaders

1. Bobby Allison ......... $828,355
2. Darrell Waltrip ......... 824,858
3. Richard Petty ........... 491,022
4. Bill Elliott ............... 479,965
5. Neil Bonnett ............. 455,662
6. Dale Earnhardt ......... 446,272
7. Harry Gant ............... 390,189
8. Terry Labonte ........... 362,790
9. Dave Marcis ............. 306,355
10. Morgan Shepherd .... 270,851
11. Ricky Rudd ............. 257,585
12. Cale Yarborough ........ 245,535
13. Tim Richmond ......... 245,664
14. Joe Ruttman ........... 217,557
15. Buddy Baker ........... 206,355
16. Geoff Bodine ........... 194,476
17. Dick Brooks ............. 176,471
18. Kyle Petty............... 157,820
19. Sterling Marlin ......... 143,564
20. Ron Bouchard ......... 142,314
21. Buddy Arrington ....... 138,429
22. Jimmy Means ......... 132,915
23. Benny Parsons......... 119,760

## Pole winners 10

1. Darrell Waltrip ....................... 7
2. Tim Richmond....................... 4
   Ricky Rudd .............................. 4
   Neil Bonnett ......................... 4
5. Terry Labonte ........................ 3
   Cale Yarborough ................... 3
7. Joe Ruttman .......................... 2
8. Buddy Baker .......................... 1
   Geoff Bodine .......................... 1
   Ron Bouchard ........................ 1

# 1982 SEASON

| Race No. | Location | Date | Winner | Car owner |
|----------|----------|------|--------|-----------|
| 1. | Daytona Beach, Fla. | Feb. 14 | Bobby Allison | Bill Gardner |
| 2. | Richmond, Va. | Feb. 21 | Dave Marcis | Dave Marcis |
| 3. | Bristol, Tenn. | March 14 | Darrell Waltrip | Junior Johnson |
| 4. | Hampton, Ga. | March 21 | Darrell Waltrip | Junior Johnson |
| 5. | Rockingham, N.C. | March 28 | Cale Yarborough | M.C. Anderson |
| 6. | Darlington, S.C. | April 4 | Dale Earnhardt | Bud Moore |
| 7. | N. Wilkesboro, N.C. | April 18 | Darrell Waltrip | Junior Johnson |
| 8. | Martinsville, Va. | April 25 | Harry Gant | Needham-Reynolds |
| 9. | Talladega, Ala. | May 2 | Darrell Waltrip | Junior Johnson |
| 10. | Nashville | May 8 | Darrell Waltrip | Junior Johnson |
| 11. | Dover, Del. | May 16 | Bobby Allison | Bill Gardner |
| 12. | Concord, N.C. | May 30 | Neil Bonnett | Wood Brothers |
| 13. | Long Pond, Pa. | June 6 | Bobby Allison | Bill Gardner |
| 14. | Riverside, Calif. | June 13 | Tim Richmond | Jim Stacy |
| 15. | Brooklyn, Mich. | June 20 | Cale Yarborough | M.C. Anderson |
| 16. | Daytona Beach, Fla. | July 4 | Bobby Allison | Bill Gardner |
| 17. | Nashville | July 10 | Darrell Waltrip | Junior Johnson |
| 18. | Long Pond, Pa. | July 25 | Bobby Allison | Bill Gardner |
| 19. | Talladega, Ala. | Aug. 1 | Darrell Waltrip | Junior Johnson |
| 20. | Brooklyn, Mich. | Aug. 22 | Bobby Allison | Bill Gardner |
| 21. | Bristol, Tenn. | Aug. 28 | Darrell Waltrip | Junior Johnson |
| 22. | Darlington, S.C. | Sept. 6 | Cale Yarborough | M.C. Anderson |
| 23. | Richmond, Va. | Sept. 12 | Bobby Allison | Bill Gardner |
| 24. | Dover, Del. | Sept. 19 | Darrell Waltrip | Junior Johnson |
| 25. | N. Wilkesboro, N.C. | Oct. 3 | Darrell Waltrip | Junior Johnson |
| 26. | Concord, N.C. | Oct. 10 | Harry Gant | Needham-Reynolds |
| 27. | Martinsville, Va. | Oct. 17 | Darrell Waltrip | Junior Johnson |
| 28. | Rockingham, N.C. | Oct. 31 | Darrell Waltrip | Junior Johnson |
| 29. | Hampton, Ga. | Nov. 7 | Bobby Allison | Bill Gardner |
| 30. | Riverside, Calif. | Nov. 21 | Tim Richmond | Jim Stacy |

## Points standings

1. Darrell Waltrip ..................4,489
2. Bobby Allison ....................4,417
3. Terry Labonte....................4,211
4. Harry Gant ........................3,877
5. Richard Petty ....................3,817
6. Dave Marcis......................3,666
7. Buddy Arrington ................3,642
8. Ron Bouchard ..................3,545
9. Ricky Rudd ......................3,537
10. Morgan Shepherd ..........3,451

## Race winners 8

1. Darrell Waltrip ....................12
2. Bobby Allison ........................8
3. Cale Yarborough ....................3
4. Harry Gant ............................2
   Tim Richmond ......................2
6. Dave Marcis..........................1
   Dale Earnhardt ......................1
   Neil Bonnett ..........................1

## Money won leaders

1. Darrell Waltrip ........$873,118
2. Bobby Allison ............726,562
3. Richard Petty ............453,832
4. Dale Earnhardt..........375,325
5. Terry Labonte............363,970
6. Ron Bouchard ..........356,582
7. Harry Gant ................311,769
8. Jody Ridley ..............304,960
9. Geoff Bodine ............258,500
10. Buddy Baker ............253,675
11. Benny Parsons ..........248,564
12. Dave Marcis..............239,027
13. Bill Elliott ..................226,780
14. Cale Yarborough........219,090
15. Ricky Rudd ..............206,130
16. Joe Ruttman ............191,634
17. Buddy Arrington ........178,159
18. Tim Richmond ..........176,730
19. Morgan Shepherd ....150,475
20. Jimmy Means ..........148,905
21. Neil Bonnett..............140,494
22. Mark Martin..............126,655
23. Kyle Petty..................120,730
24. Lake Speed ..............114,754
25. J.D. McDuffie............112,744
26. Tommy Gale..............102,235

## Pole winners 15

1. Darrell Waltrip ........................7
2. Benny Parsons ......................3
3. Cale Yarborough ....................2
   Terry Labonte..........................2
   Ricky Rudd ............................2
   Geoff Bodine ..........................2
   Morgan Shepherd ..................2
   David Pearson ........................2
9. Dale Earnhardt ......................1
   Buddy Baker ..........................1
   Ron Bouchard ........................1
   Bill Elliott................................1
   Tim Richmond........................1
   Bobby Allison..........................1
   Harry Gant..............................1

# 1981 SEASON

| Race No. | Location | Date | Winner | Car owner |
|---|---|---|---|---|
| 1. | Riverside, Calif. | Jan. 11 | Bobby Allison | Harry Ranier |
| 2. | Daytona Beach, Fla. | Feb. 15 | Richard Petty | Petty Enterprises |
| 3. | Richmond, Va. | Feb. 22 | Darrell Waltrip | Junior Johnson |
| 4. | Rockingham, N.C. | March 1 | Darrell Waltrip | Junior Johnson |
| 5. | Hampton, Ga. | March 15 | Cale Yarborough | M.C. Anderson |
| 6. | Bristol, Tenn. | March 29 | Darrell Waltrip | Junior Johnson |
| 7. | N. Wilkesboro, N.C. | April 5 | Richard Petty | Petty Enterprises |
| 8. | Darlington, S.C. | April 12 | Darrell Waltrip | Junior Johnson |
| 9. | Martinsville, Va. | April 26 | Morgan Shepherd | Cliff Stewart |
| 10. | Talladega, Ala. | May 3 | Bobby Allison | Harry Ranier |
| 11. | Nashville | May 9 | Benny Parsons | Bud Moore |
| 12. | Dover, Del. | May 17 | Jody Ridley | Junie Donlavey |
| 13. | Concord, N.C. | May 24 | Bobby Allison | Harry Ranier |
| 14. | Bryan, Texas | June 7 | Benny Parsons | Bud Moore |
| 15. | Riverside, Calif. | June 14 | Darrell Waltrip | Junior Johnson |
| 16. | Brooklyn, Mich. | June 21 | Bobby Allison | Harry Ranier |
| 17. | Daytona Beach, Fla. | July 4 | Cale Yarborough | M.C. Anderson |
| 18. | Nashville | July 11 | Darrell Waltrip | Junior Johnson |
| 19. | Long Pond, Pa. | July 26 | Darrell Waltrip | Junior Johnson |
| 20. | Talladega, Ala. | Aug. 2 | Ron Bouchard | Jack Beebe |
| 21. | Brooklyn, Mich. | Aug. 16 | Richard Petty | Petty Enterprises |
| 22. | Bristol, Tenn. | Aug. 22 | Darrell Waltrip | Junior Johnson |
| 23. | Darlington, S.C. | Sept. 7 | Neil Bonnett | Wood Brothers |
| 24. | Richmond, Va. | Sept. 13 | Benny Parsons | Bud Moore |
| 25. | Dover, Del. | Sept. 20 | Neil Bonnett | Wood Brothers |
| 26. | Martinsville, Va. | Sept. 27 | Darrell Waltrip | Junior Johnson |
| 27. | N. Wilkesboro, N.C. | Oct. 4 | Darrell Waltrip | Junior Johnson |
| 28. | Concord, N.C. | Oct. 11 | Darrell Waltrip | Junior Johnson |
| 29. | Rockingham, N.C. | Nov. 1 | Darrell Waltrip | Junior Johnson |
| 30. | Hampton, Ga. | Nov. 8 | Neil Bonnett | Wood Brothers |
| 31. | Riverside, Calif. | Nov. 22 | Bobby Allison | Harry Ranier |

## Points standings

1. Darrell Waltrip ...............4,880
2. Bobby Allison ...................4,827
3. Harry Gant ......................4,210
4. Terry Labonte ..................4,052
5. Jody Ridley .....................4,002
6. Ricky Rudd.......................3,988
7. Dale Earnhardt ................3,975
8. Richard Petty ..................3,880
9. Dave Marcis.....................3,507
10. Benny Parsons ...............3,449

## Race winners 9

1. Darrell Waltrip ...................12
2. Bobby Allison ......................5
3. Richard Petty .......................3
   Benny Parsons .....................3
   Neil Bonnett ........................3
6. Cale Yarborough ..................2
7. Jody Ridley .........................1
   Morgan Shepherd.................1
   Ron Bouchard .....................1

## Money won leaders

1. Darrell Waltrip.......$693,352
2. Bobby Allison .........644,311
3. Richard Petty .........389,214
4. Ricky Rudd .............381,968
5. Dale Earnhardt .......347,113
6. Terry Labonte .........334,987
7. Benny Parsons .......287,949
8. Harry Gant .............280,047
9. Jody Ridley .............257,318
10. Neil Bonnett ...........181,670
11. Morgan Shepherd ....165,329
12. Dave Marcis ...........162,213
13. Ron Bouchard .........152,855
14. Cale Yarborough ......150,840
15. Joe Millikan ...........148,400
16. Joe Ruttman ...........137,275
17. Buddy Arrington ......133,928
18. Buddy Baker...........115,095
19. Kyle Petty ...............112,289
20. J.D. McDuffie ..........105,499
21. Tommy Gale ...........105,474
22. Jimmy Means ..........100,484

## Pole winners 13

1. Darrell Waltrip ...................11
2. Ricky Rudd............................3
   Harry Gant ............................3
4. Bobby Allison ........................2
   Terry Labonte........................2
   Cale Yarborough ....................2
   Mark Martin ...........................2
8. Morgan Shepherd.................1
   Dave Marcis...........................1
   Bill Elliott ..............................1
   David Pearson ......................1
   Neil Bonnett ..........................1
   Ron Bouchard ......................1

# 1980 SEASON

| Race No. | Location | Date | Winner | Car owner |
|---|---|---|---|---|
| 1. | Riverside, Calif. | Jan. 19 | Darrell Waltrip | Bill Gardner |
| 2. | Daytona Beach, Fla. | Feb. 17 | Buddy Baker | Harry Ranier |
| 3. | Richmond, Va. | Feb. 24 | Darrell Waltrip | Bill Gardner |
| 4. | Rockingham, N.C. | March 9 | Cale Yarborough | Junior Johnson |
| 5. | Hampton, Ga. | March 16 | Dale Earnhardt | Rod Osterlund |
| 6. | Bristol, Tenn. | March 30 | Dale Earnhardt | Rod Osterlund |
| 7. | Darlington, S.C. | April 13 | David Pearson | Hoss Ellington |
| 8. | N. Wilkesboro, N.C. | April 20 | Richard Petty | Petty Enterprises |
| 9. | Martinsville, Va. | April 27 | Darrell Waltrip | Bill Gardner |
| 10. | Talladega, Ala. | May 4 | Buddy Baker | Harry Ranier |
| 11. | Nashville | May 10 | Richard Petty | Petty Enterprises |
| 12. | Dover, Del. | May 18 | Bobby Allison | Bud Moore |
| 13. | Concord, N.C. | May 25 | Benny Parsons | M.C. Anderson |
| 14. | Bryan, Texas | June 1 | Cale Yarborough | Junior Johnson |
| 15. | Riverside, Calif. | June 8 | Darrell Waltrip | Bill Gardner |
| 16. | Brooklyn, Mich. | June 15 | Benny Parsons | M.C. Anderson |
| 17. | Daytona Beach, Fla. | July 4 | Bobby Allison | Bud Moore |
| 18. | Nashville | July 12 | Dale Earnhardt | Rod Osterlund |
| 19. | Long Pond, Pa. | July 27 | Neil Bonnett | Wood Brothers |
| 20. | Talladega, Ala. | Aug. 3 | Neil Bonnett | Wood Brothers |
| 21. | Brooklyn, Mich. | Aug. 17 | Cale Yarborough | Junior Johnson |
| 22. | Bristol, Tenn. | Aug. 23 | Cale Yarborough | Junior Johnson |
| 23. | Darlington, S.C. | Sept. 1 | Terry Labonte | Billy Hagan |
| 24. | Richmond, Va. | Sept. 7 | Bobby Allison | Bud Moore |
| 25. | Dover, Del. | Sept. 14 | Darrell Waltrip | Bill Gardner |
| 26. | N. Wilkesboro, N.C. | Sept. 21 | Bobby Allison | Bud Moore |
| 27. | Martinsville, Va. | Sept. 28 | Dale Earnhardt | Rod Osterlund |
| 28. | Concord, N.C. | Oct. 5 | Dale Earnhardt | Rod Osterlund |
| 29. | Rockingham, N.C. | Oct. 19 | Cale Yarborough | Junior Johnson |
| 30. | Hampton, Ga. | Nov. 2 | Cale Yarborough | Junior Johnson |
| 31. | Fontana, Calif. | Nov. 15 | Benny Parsons | M.C. Anderson |

## Points standings

1. Dale Earnhardt ..................4,661
2. Cale Yarborough ...............4,642
3. Benny Parsons ..................4,278
4. Richard Petty ....................4,255
5. Darrell Waltrip .................4,239
6. Bobby Allison ...................4,019
7. Jody Ridley ......................3,972
8. Terry Labonte ...................3,766
9. Dave Marcis ......................3,745
10. Richard Childress ............3,742

## Race winners 10

1. Cale Yarborough ...................6
2. Dale Earnhardt .....................5
   Darrell Waltrip ......................5
4. Bobby Allison .......................4
5. Benny Parsons .....................3
6. Richard Petty .......................2
   Neil Bonnett .........................2
   Buddy Baker ........................2
9. Terry Labonte .......................1
   David Pearson ......................1

## Money won leaders

1. Dale Earnhardt ......$588,926
2. Cale Yarborough ......537,358
3. Benny Parsons ........385,140
4. Darrell Waltrip..........382,138
5. Richard Petty ..........374,092
6. Bobby Allison ..........356,050
7. Buddy Baker............264,200
8. Terry Labonte ..........215,889
9. Neil Bonnett ............210,547
10. Jody Ridley..............196,617
11. Harry Gant .............162,190
12. Richard Childress ....157,420
13. Dave Marcis ...........150,165
14. Buddy Arrington ......120,355
15. James Hylton ..........109,230

## Pole winners 7

1. Cale Yarborough .................14
2. Buddy Baker ..........................6
3. Darrell Waltrip ......................5
4. Benny Parsons .....................2
   Bobby Allison ........................2
6. David Pearson.......................1
   Donnie Allison .......................1

HISTORY

220

## THE INTIMIDATOR: HE WAS GOOD BEFORE THE NICKNAME

It's not like Dale Earnhardt was unknown in 1980; he had won Rookie of the Year the season before. But Earnhardt was not yet The Intimidator. He was not yet The Man in Black. He wasn't even driving a black car yet. And he was driving the No. 2 car, not the No. 3.

But he already was a heck of a driver.

In 1980, Earnhardt won the first of his seven championships, becoming the first—and thus far, the only—driver to follow his Rookie of the Year season with a championship. He had five wins and 24 top 10s in 31 races, winning the championship by 19 points over Cale Yarborough, the fifth-closest championship in NASCAR Cup history. More important, he laid the foundation for his legend.

Ask any driver, and they'll tell you the scariest thing they've ever seen in their rearview mirror is the black No. 3 Monte Carlo, emblazoned with Goodwrench. And that's no hyperbole. The Intimidator was a fierce competitor who would do almost anything for a win. And win he did, 76 times. His seven championships leave him in a tie with Richard Petty for the most ever.

# 1979 SEASON

| Race No. | Location | Date | Winner | Car owner |
|---|---|---|---|---|
| 1. | Riverside, Calif. | Jan. 14 | Darrell Waltrip | Bill Gardner |
| 2. | Daytona Beach, Fla. | Feb. 18 | Richard Petty | Petty Enterprises |
| 3. | Rockingham, N.C. | March 4 | Bobby Allison | Bud Moore |
| 4. | Richmond, Va. | March 11 | Cale Yarborough | Junior Johnson |
| 5. | Hampton, Ga. | March 18 | Buddy Baker | Harry Ranier |
| 6. | N. Wilkesboro, N.C. | March 25 | Bobby Allison | Bud Moore |
| 7. | Bristol, Tenn. | April 1 | Dale Earnhardt | Rod Osterlund |
| 8. | Darlington, S.C. | April 8 | Darrell Waltrip | Bill Gardner |
| 9. | Martinsville, Va. | April 22 | Richard Petty | Petty Enterprises |
| 10. | Talladega, Ala. | May 6 | Bobby Allison | Bud Moore |
| 11. | Nashville | May 12 | Cale Yarborough | Junior Johnson |
| 12. | Dover, Del. | May 20 | Neil Bonnett | Wood Brothers |
| 13. | Concord, N.C. | May 27 | Darrell Waltrip | Bill Gardner |
| 14. | Bryan, Texas | June 3 | Darrell Waltrip | Bill Gardner |
| 15. | Riverside, Calif. | June 10 | Bobby Allison | Bud Moore |
| 16. | Brooklyn, Mich. | June 17 | Buddy Baker | Harry Ranier |
| 17. | Daytona Beach, Fla. | July 4 | Neil Bonnett | Wood Brothers |
| 18. | Nashville | July 14 | Darrell Waltrip | Bill Gardner |
| 19. | Long Pond, Pa. | July 30 | Cale Yarborough | Junior Johnson |
| 20. | Talladega, Ala. | Aug. 5 | Darrell Waltrip | Bill Gardner |
| 21. | Brooklyn, Mich. | Aug. 19 | Richard Petty | Petty Enterprises |
| 22. | Bristol, Tenn. | Aug. 25 | Darrell Waltrip | Bill Gardner |
| 23. | Darlington, S.C. | Sept. 3 | David Pearson | Rod Osterlund |
| 24. | Richmond, Va. | Sept. 9 | Bobby Allison | Bud Moore |
| 25. | Dover, Del. | Sept. 16 | Richard Petty | Petty Enterprises |
| 26. | Martinsville, Va. | Sept. 23 | Buddy Baker | Harry Ranier |
| 27. | Concord, N.C. | Oct. 7 | Cale Yarborough | Junior Johnson |
| 28. | N. Wilkesboro, N.C. | Oct. 14 | Benny Parsons | M.C. Anderson |
| 29. | Rockingham, N.C. | Oct. 21 | Richard Petty | Petty Enterprises |
| 30. | Hampton, Ga. | Nov. 4 | Neil Bonnett | Wood Brothers |
| 31. | Fontana, Calif. | Nov. 18 | Benny Parsons | M.C. Anderson |

HISTORY

## Points standings

1. Richard Petty ..................4,830
2. Darrell Waltrip .................4,819
3. Bobby Allison ...................4,633
4. Cale Yarborough...............4,604
5. Benny Parsons.................4,256
6. Joe Millikan ......................4,014
7. Dale Earnhardt.................3,749
8. Richard Childress.............3,735
9. Ricky Rudd ......................3,642
10. Terry Labonte.................3,615

## Race winners 9

1. Darrell Waltrip .....................7
2. Richard Petty ......................5
   Bobby Allison .......................5
4. Cale Yarborough ..................4
5. Buddy Baker .......................3
   Neil Bonnett .........................3
7. Benny Parsons ....................2
8. Dale Earnhardt .....................1
   David Pearson .....................1

## Money won leaders

1. Richard Petty ..........$531,292
2. Darrell Waltrip ..........523,691
3. Cale Yarborough........413,872
4. Bobby Allison ...........403,014
5. Buddy Baker ...........287,552
6. Dale Earnhardt ........264,086
7. Benny Parsons .........241,205
8. Joe Millikan .............222,053
9. Ricky Rudd ..............146,302
10. Donnie Allison .........144,770
11. Neil Bonnett .............140,735
12. Richard Childress......132,922
13. Buddy Arrington ........131,833
14. Terry Labonte...........130,057
15. D.K. Ulrich ...............108,862
16. J.D. McDuffie ...........103,478

## Pole winners 12

1. Buddy Baker..........................7
2. Darrell Waltrip ......................5
3. Neil Bonnett .........................4
   Dale Earnhardt .....................4
5. Bobby Allison .......................3
6. David Pearson......................2
7. Donnie Allison.......................1
   Harry Gant ...........................1
   Joe Millikan ..........................1
   Benny Parsons ......................1
   Richard Petty .......................1
   Cale Yarborough ...................1

# 1979 SEASON

## FIRST IMPRESSION: A GREAT RACE AND EVEN BETTER TELEVISION

Everybody's got their story of meeting the in-laws for the first time. You're on display for them to poke and prod and evaluate. For NASCAR, that moment was the 1979 Daytona 500, the first stock car race ever shown from the drop of the green flag on the first lap to the drop of the checkered flag at the end of the last lap.

And what an impression the burgeoning sport made.

First, it was a thrilling race, with the lead flip-flopping as drivers battled furiously for position. In particular, Donnie Allison and Cale Yarborough were all over each other throughout the race … and after it.

They wrecked, then got in a fistfight. Bobby Allison joined in, defending his brother, Donnie. It wasn't much of a fight, but it was great television.

# 1978 SEASON

| Race No. | Location | Date | Winner | Car owner |
|---|---|---|---|---|
| 1. | Riverside, Calif. | Jan. 22 | Cale Yarborough | Junior Johnson |
| 2. | Daytona Beach, Fla. | Feb. 19 | Bobby Allison | Bud Moore |
| 3. | Richmond, Va. | Feb. 26 | Benny Parsons | L.G. DeWitt |
| 4. | Rockingham, N.C. | March 5 | David Pearson | Wood Brothers |
| 5. | Hampton, Ga. | March 19 | Bobby Allison | Bud Moore |
| 6. | Bristol, Tenn. | April 2 | Darrell Waltrip | Bill Gardner |
| 7. | Darlington, S.C. | April 9 | Benny Parsons | L.G. DeWitt |
| 8. | N. Wilkesboro, N.C. | April 16 | Darrell Waltrip | Bill Gardner |
| 9. | Martinsville, Va. | April 23 | Darrell Waltrip | Bill Gardner |
| 10. | Talladega, Ala. | May 14 | Cale Yarborough | Junior Johnson |
| 11. | Dover, Del. | May 21 | David Pearson | Wood Brothers |
| 12. | Concord, N.C. | May 28 | Darrell Waltrip | Bill Gardner |
| 13. | Nashville | June 3 | Cale Yarborough | Junior Johnson |
| 14. | Riverside, Calif. | June 11 | Benny Parsons | L.G. DeWitt |
| 15. | Brooklyn, Mich. | June 18 | Cale Yarborough | Junior Johnson |
| 16. | Daytona Beach, Fla. | July 4 | David Pearson | Wood Brothers |
| 17. | Nashville | July 15 | Cale Yarborough | Junior Johnson |
| 18. | Long Pond, Pa. | July 30 | Darrell Waltrip | Bill Gardner |
| 19. | Talladega, Ala. | Aug. 6 | Lennie Pond | Harry Ranier |
| 20. | Brooklyn, Mich. | Aug. 20 | David Pearson | Wood Brothers |
| 21. | Bristol, Tenn. | Aug. 26 | Cale Yarborough | Junior Johnson |
| 22. | Darlington, S.C. | Sept. 4 | Cale Yarborough | Junior Johnson |
| 23. | Richmond, Va. | Sept. 10 | Darrell Waltrip | Bill Gardner |
| 24. | Dover, Del. | Sept. 17 | Bobby Allison | Bud Moore |
| 25. | Martinsville, Va. | Sept. 24 | Cale Yarborough | Junior Johnson |
| 26. | N. Wilkesboro, N.C. | Oct. 1 | Cale Yarborough | Junior Johnson |
| 27. | Concord, N.C. | Oct. 8 | Bobby Allison | Bud Moore |
| 28. | Rockingham, N.C. | Oct. 22 | Cale Yarborough | Junior Johnson |
| 29. | Hampton, Ga. | Nov. 5 | Donnie Allison | Hoss Ellington |
| 30. | Fontana, Calif. | Nov. 19 | Bobby Allison | Bud Moore |

## Points standings

1. Cale Yarborough ..............4,841
2. Bobby Allison ...................4,367
3. Darrell Waltrip .................4,362
4. Benny Parsons ................4,350
5. Dave Marcis.....................4,335
6. Richard Petty ...................3,949
7. Lennie Pond .....................3,794
8. Richard Brooks.................3,769
9. Buddy Arrington ...............3,626
10. Richard Childress ...........3,566

## Race winners 7

1. Cale Yarborough ..................10
2. Darrell Waltrip ......................6
3. Bobby Allison ........................5
4. David Pearson .....................4
5. Benny Parsons .....................3
6. Lennie Pond ..........................1
    Donnie Allison ......................1

## Money won leaders

1. Cale Yarborough ......$530,751
2. Darrell Waltrip...........343,367
3. Bobby Allison ...........335,635
4. Benny Parsons ..........288,458
5. Richard Petty ............215,491
6. Dave Marcis .............178,725
7. Lennie Pond .............160,627
8. Neil Bonnett .............155,875
9. David Pearson .........151,837
10. Richard Brooks ..........131,474
11. Buddy Arrington ........112,959
12. Richard Childress ......108,106
13. Buddy Baker..............104,265

## Pole winners 9

1. Cale Yarborough ...................8
2. David Pearson.....................7
3. Lennie Pond ........................5
4. Neil Bonnett .........................3
5. Benny Parsons .....................2
    Darrell Waltrip ......................2
7. Bobby Allison .......................1
    Buddy Baker .........................1
    J.D. McDuffie .......................1

HISTORY

# 1977 SEASON

| Race No. | Location | Date | Winner | Car owner |
|---|---|---|---|---|
| 1. | Riverside, Calif. | Jan. 16 | David Pearson | Wood Brothers |
| 2. | Daytona Beach, Fla. | Feb. 20 | Cale Yarborough | Junior Johnson |
| 3. | Richmond, Va. | Feb. 27 | Cale Yarborough | Junior Johnson |
| 4. | Rockingham, N.C. | March 13 | Richard Petty | Petty Enterprises |
| 5. | Hampton, Ga. | March 20 | Richard Petty | Petty Enterprises |
| 6. | N. Wilkesboro, N.C | March 27 | Cale Yarborough | Junior Johnson |
| 7. | Darlington, S.C. | April 3 | Darrell Waltrip | Bill Gardner |
| 8. | Bristol, Tenn. | April 17 | Cale Yarborough | Junior Johnson |
| 9. | Martinsville, Va. | April 24 | Cale Yarborough | Junior Johnson |
| 10. | Talladega, Ala. | May 1 | Darrell Waltrip | Bill Gardner |
| 11. | Nashville | May 7 | Benny Parsons | L.G. DeWitt |
| 12. | Dover, Del. | May 15 | Cale Yarborough | Junior Johnson |
| 13. | Concord, N.C. | May 29 | Richard Petty | Petty Enterprises |
| 14. | Riverside, Calif. | June 12 | Richard Petty | Petty Enterprises |
| 15. | Brooklyn, Mich. | June 19 | Cale Yarborough | Junior Johnson |
| 16. | Daytona Beach, Fla. | July 4 | Richard Petty | Petty Enterprises |
| 17. | Nashville | July 16 | Darrell Waltrip | Bill Gardner |
| 18. | Long Pond, Pa. | July 31 | Benny Parsons | L.G. DeWitt |
| 19. | Talladega, Ala. | Aug. 7 | Donnie Allison | Hoss Ellington |
| 20. | Brooklyn, Mich. | Aug. 22 | Darrell Waltrip | Bill Gardner |
| 21. | Bristol, Tenn. | Aug. 28 | Cale Yarborough | Junior Johnson |
| 22. | Darlington, S.C. | Sept. 5 | David Pearson | Wood Brothers |
| 23. | Richmond, Va. | Sept. 11 | Neil Bonnett | Jim Stacy |
| 24. | Dover, Del. | Sept. 18 | Benny Parsons | L.G. DeWitt |
| 25. | Martinsville, Va. | Sept. 25 | Cale Yarborough | Junior Johnson |
| 26. | N. Wilkesboro, N.C | Oct. 2 | Darrell Waltrip | Bill Gardner |
| 27. | Concord, N.C. | Oct. 9 | Benny Parsons | L.G. DeWitt |
| 28. | Rockingham, N.C. | Oct. 23 | Donnie Allison | Hoss Ellington |
| 29. | Hampton, Ga. | Nov. 6 | Darrell Waltrip | Bill Gardner |
| 30. | Fontana, Calif. | Nov. 20 | Neil Bonnett | Jim Stacy |

## Points standings

1. Cale Yarborough..............5,000
2. Richard Petty...................4,614
3. Benny Parsons.................4,570
4. Darrell Waltrip .................4,498
5. Buddy Baker ...................3,961
6. Richard Brooks ...............3,742
7. James Hylton...................3,476
8. Bobby Allison...................3,467
9. Richard Childress..............3,463
10. Cecil Gordon .................3,294

## Race winners

1. Cale Yarborough ....................9
2. Darrell Waltrip .......................6
3. Richard Petty ........................5
4. Benny Parsons .....................4
5. David Pearson ......................2
   Neil Bonnett ..........................2
   Donnie Allison .......................2

## Money won leaders

1. Cale Yarborough......$477,498
2. Richard Petty ...........345,886
3. Benny Parsons..........297,421
4. Darrell Waltrip ..........276,312
5. Buddy Baker ............205,803
6. David Pearson ..........180,999
7. Richard Brooks ........141,421
8. Donnie Allison ..........124,785
9. Neil Bonnett..............110,672
10. James Hylton............108,398

## Pole winners

1. Neil Bonnett ............................6
2. Richard Petty..........................5
   David Pearson ........................5
4. Cale Yarborough ....................3
   Donnie Allison .......................3
   Benny Parsons ......................3
   Darrell Waltrip .......................3
8. A.J. Foyt ...............................1
   Sam Sommers.......................1

# 1976 SEASON

| Race No. | Location | Date | Winner | Car owner |
|---|---|---|---|---|
| 1. | Riverside, Calif. | Jan. 18 | David Pearson | Wood Brothers |
| 2. | Daytona Beach, Fla. | Feb. 15 | David Pearson | Wood Brothers |
| 3. | Rockingham, N.C. | Feb. 29 | Richard Petty | Petty Enterprises |
| 4. | Richmond, Va. | March 7 | Dave Marcis | Nord Krauskopf |
| 5. | Bristol, Tenn. | March 14 | Cale Yarborough | Junior Johnson |
| 6. | Hampton, Ga. | March 21 | David Pearson | Wood Brothers |
| 7. | N. Wilkesboro, N.C. | April 4 | Cale Yarborough | Junior Johnson |
| 8. | Darlington, S.C. | April 11 | David Pearson | Wood Brothers |
| 9. | Martinsville, Va. | April 25 | Darrell Waltrip | Bill Gardner |
| 10. | Talladega, Ala. | May 2 | Buddy Baker | Bud Moore |
| 11. | Nashville | May 8 | Cale Yarborough | Junior Johnson |
| 12. | Dover, Del. | May 16 | Benny Parsons | L.G. DeWitt |
| 13. | Concord, N.C. | May 30 | David Pearson | Wood Brothers |
| 14. | Riverside, Calif. | June 13 | David Pearson | Wood Brothers |
| 15. | Brooklyn, Mich. | June 20 | David Pearson | Wood Brothers |
| 16. | Daytona Beach, Fla. | July 4 | Cale Yarborough | Junior Johnson |
| 17. | Nashville | July 17 | Benny Parsons | L.G. DeWitt |
| 18. | Long Pond, Pa. | Aug. 1 | Richard Petty | Petty Enterprises |
| 19. | Talladega, Ala. | Aug. 8 | Dave Marcis | Nord Krauskopf |
| 20. | Brooklyn, Mich. | Aug. 22 | David Pearson | Wood Brothers |
| 21. | Bristol, Tenn. | Aug. 29 | Cale Yarborough | Junior Johnson |
| 22. | Darlington, S.C. | Sept. 6 | David Pearson | Wood Brothers |
| 23. | Richmond, Va. | Sept. 12 | Cale Yarborough | Junior Johnson |
| 24. | Dover, Del. | Sept. 19 | Cale Yarborough | Junior Johnson |
| 25. | Martinsville, Va. | Sept. 26 | Cale Yarborough | Junior Johnson |
| 26. | N. Wilkesboro, N.C. | Oct. 3 | Cale Yarborough | Junior Johnson |
| 27. | Concord, N.C. | Oct. 10 | Donnie Allison | Hoss Ellington |
| 28. | Rockingham, N.C. | Oct. 24 | Richard Petty | Petty Enterprises |
| 29. | Hampton, Ga. | Nov. 7 | Dave Marcis | Nord Krauskopf |
| 30. | Fontana, Calif. | Nov. 21 | David Pearson | Wood Brothers |

## Points standings

1. Cale Yarborough ...........4,644
2. Richard Petty ...............4,449
3. Benny Parsons .............4,304
4. Bobby Allison ..............4,097
5. Lennie Pond ................3,930
6. Dave Marcis ................3,875
7. Buddy Baker ................3,745
8. Darrell Waltrip .............3,505
9. David Pearson .............3,483
10. Richard Brooks...........3,447

## Race winners 8

1. David Pearson ...................10
2. Cale Yarborough ..................9
3. Richard Petty .......................3
   Dave Marcis .........................3
5. Benny Parsons ....................2
6. Buddy Baker .......................1
   Darrell Waltrip ....................1
   Donnie Allison .....................1

## Money won leaders

1. Cale Yarborough .........387,173
2. Richard Petty .............338,265
3. David Pearson .............283,686
4. Benny Parsons ...........242,970
5. Buddy Baker .............214,439
6. Bobby Allison .............210,376
7. Dave Marcis...............198,199
8. Darrell Waltrip ...........191,501
9. Richard Brooks .........105,917

## Pole winners 11

1. David Pearson ........................8
2. Dave Marcis...........................7
3. Darrell Waltrip .......................3
4. Bobby Allison ........................2
   Buddy Baker .........................2
   Benny Parsons.......................2
   Cale Yarborough.....................2
8. Richard Petty ........................1
   Neil Bonnett ..........................1
   A.J. Foyt.................................1
   Ramo Stott..............................1

# 1975 SEASON

| Race No. | Location | Date | Winner | Car owner |
|---|---|---|---|---|
| 1. | Riverside, Calif. | Jan. 19 | Bobby Allison | Roger Penske |
| 2. | Daytona Beach, Fla. | Feb. 16 | Benny Parsons | L.G. DeWitt |
| 3. | Richmond, Va. | Feb. 23 | Richard Petty | Petty Enterprises |
| 4. | Rockingham, N.C. | March 2 | Cale Yarborough | Junior Johnson |
| 5. | Bristol, Tenn. | March 16 | Richard Petty | Petty Enterprises |
| 6. | Hampton, Ga. | March 23 | Richard Petty | Petty Enterprises |
| 7. | N. Wilkesboro, N.C. | April 6 | Richard Petty | Petty Enterprises |
| 8. | Darlington, S.C. | April 13 | Bobby Allison | Roger Penske |
| 9. | Martinsville, Va. | April 27 | Richard Petty | Petty Enterprises |
| 10. | Talladega, Ala. | May 4 | Buddy Baker | Bud Moore |
| 11. | Nashville | May 10 | Darrell Waltrip | Darrell Waltrip |
| 12. | Dover, Del. | May 19 | David Pearson | Wood Brothers |
| 13. | Concord, N.C. | May 25 | Richard Petty | Petty Enterprises |
| 14. | Riverside, Calif. | June 8 | Richard Petty | Petty Enterprises |
| 15. | Brooklyn, Mich. | June 15 | David Pearson | Wood Brothers |
| 16. | Daytona Beach, Fla. | July 4 | Richard Petty | Petty Enterprises |
| 17. | Nashville | July 20 | Cale Yarborough | Junior Johnson |
| 18. | Long Pond, Pa. | Aug. 3 | David Pearson | Wood Brothers |
| 19. | Talladega, Ala. | Aug. 17 | Buddy Baker | Bud Moore |
| 20. | Brooklyn, Mich. | Aug. 24 | Richard Petty | Petty Enterprises |
| 21. | Darlington, S.C. | Sept. 1 | Bobby Allison | Roger Penske |
| 22. | Dover, Del. | Sept. 14 | Richard Petty | Petty Enterprises |
| 23. | N. Wilkesboro, N.C. | Sept. 21 | Richard Petty | Petty Enterprises |
| 24. | Martinsville, Va. | Sept. 28 | Dave Marcis | Nord Krauskopf |
| 25. | Concord, N.C. | Oct. 5 | Richard Petty | Petty Enterprises |
| 26. | Richmond, Va. | Oct. 12 | Darrell Waltrip | Bill Gardner |
| 27. | Rockingham, N.C. | Oct. 19 | Cale Yarborough | Junior Johnson |
| 28. | Bristol, Tenn. | Nov. 2 | Richard Petty | Petty Enterprises |
| 29. | Hampton, Ga. | Nov. 9 | Buddy Baker | Bud Moore |
| 30. | Fontana, Calif. | Nov. 23 | Buddy Baker | Bud Moore |

## Points standings

1. Richard Petty .................4,783
2. Dave Marcis...................4,061
3. James Hylton ..................3,914
4. Benny Parsons ................3,820
5. Richard Childress.............3,818
6. Cecil Gordon ..................3,702
7. Darrell Waltrip .................3,462
8. Elmo Langley ..................3,399
9. Cale Yarborough ..............3,295
10. Richard Brooks .............3,182

## Race winners 8

1. Richard Petty .....................13
2. Buddy Baker .......................4
3. David Pearson .....................3
   Cale Yarborough ..................3
   Bobby Allison ......................3
6. Darrell Waltrip ....................2
7. Benny Parsons ....................1
   Dave Marcis........................1

## Money won leaders

1. Richard Petty ..........$378,865
2. David Pearson ...........179,207
3. Buddy Baker .............169,917
4. Dave Marcis...............149,202
5. Benny Parsons ...........140,199
6. Cale Yarborough.........139,257
7. Bobby Allison ............122,435
8. James Hylton ............101,141
9. Darrell Waltrip ...........100,191

## Pole winners 9

1. David Pearson ......................7
2. Dave Marcis.........................4
3. Bobby Allison ......................3
   Richard Petty .......................3
   Buddy Baker ........................3
   Benny Parsons .....................3
   Cale Yarborough ...................3
8. Donnie Allison .....................2
   Darrell Waltrip .................... 2

# 1974 SEASON

| Race No. | Location | Date | Winner | Car owner |
|---|---|---|---|---|
| 1. | Riverside, Calif. | Jan. 26 | Cale Yarborough | Junior Johnson |
| 2. | Daytona Beach, Fla. | Feb. 17 | Richard Petty | Petty Enterprises |
| 3. | Richmond, Va. | Feb. 24 | Bobby Allison | Bobby Allison |
| 4. | Rockingham, N.C. | March 3 | Richard Petty | Petty Enterprises |
| 5. | Bristol, Tenn. | March 17 | Cale Yarborough | Junior Johnson |
| 6. | Hampton, Ga. | March 24 | Cale Yarborough | Junior Johnson |
| 7. | Darlington, S.C. | April 7 | David Pearson | Wood Brothers |
| 8. | N. Wilkesboro, N.C. | April 21 | Richard Petty | Petty Enterprises |
| 9. | Martinsville, Va. | April 28 | Cale Yarborough | Junior Johnson |
| 10. | Talladega, Ala. | May 5 | David Pearson | Wood Brothers |
| 11. | Nashville | May 11 | Richard Petty | Petty Enterprises |
| 12. | Dover, Del. | May 19 | Cale Yarborough | Junior Johnson |
| 13. | Concord, N.C. | May 26 | David Pearson | Wood Brothers |
| 14. | Riverside, Calif. | June 9 | Cale Yarborough | Junior Johnson |
| 15. | Brooklyn, Mich. | June 16 | Richard Petty | Petty Enterprises |
| 16. | Daytona Beach, Fla. | July 4 | David Pearson | Wood Brothers |
| 17. | Bristol, Tenn. | July 14 | Cale Yarborough | Junior Johnson |
| 18. | Nashville | July 20 | Cale Yarborough | Junior Johnson |
| 19. | Hampton, Ga. | July 28 | Richard Petty | Petty Enterprises |
| 20. | Long Pond, Pa. | Aug. 4 | Richard Petty | Petty Enterprises |
| 21. | Talladega, Ala. | Aug. 11 | Richard Petty | Petty Enterprises |
| 22. | Brooklyn, Mich. | Aug. 25 | David Pearson | Wood Brothers |
| 23. | Darlington, S.C. | Sept. 2 | Cale Yarborough | Junior Johnson |
| 24. | Richmond, Va. | Sept. 8 | Richard Petty | Petty Enterprises |
| 25. | Dover, Del. | Sept. 15 | Richard Petty | Petty Enterprises |
| 26. | N. Wilkesboro, N.C. | Sept. 22 | Cale Yarborough | Junior Johnson |
| 27. | Martinsville, Va. | Sept. 29 | Earl Ross | Allan Brooke |
| 28. | Concord, N.C. | Oct. 6 | David Pearson | Wood Brothers |
| 29. | Rockingham, N.C. | Oct. 20 | David Pearson | Wood Brothers |
| 30. | Fontana, Calif. | Nov. 24 | Bobby Allison | Roger Penske |

## Points standings

1. Richard Petty.............5,037.750
2. Cale Yarborough ........4,470.300
3. David Pearson ...........2,389.250
4. Bobby Allison.............2,019.195
5. Benny Parsons .........1,591.500
6. Dave Marcis .............1,378.200
7. Buddy Baker .............1,016.880
8. Earl Ross...................1,009.470
9. Cecil Gordon .............1,000.650
10. David Sisco ...............956.200

## Race winners 5

1. Richard Petty .....................10
   Cale Yarborough .................10
3. David Pearson .....................7
4. Bobby Allison .......................2
5. Earl Ross .............................1

## Money won leaders

1. Richard Petty ...........$330,347
2. Cale Yarborough .........272,946
3. David Pearson ...........233,567
4. Bobby Allison .............129,768

## Pole winners 8

1. David Pearson .....................11
2. Richard Petty .........................7
3. Bobby Allison .........................3
   Cale Yarborough .....................3
5. Donnie Allison .......................2
   Buddy Baker ..........................2
7. Darrell Waltrip .......................1
   George Follmer.......................1

HISTORY

# 1973 SEASON

| Race No. | Location | Date | Winner | Car owner |
|---|---|---|---|---|
| 1. | Riverside, Calif. | Jan. 21 | Mark Donohue | Roger Penske |
| 2. | Daytona Beach, Fla. | Feb. 18 | Richard Petty | Petty Enterprises |
| 3. | Richmond, Va. | Feb. 25 | Richard Petty | Petty Enterprises |
| 4. | Rockingham, N.C. | March 18 | David Pearson | Wood Brothers |
| 5. | Bristol, Tenn. | March 25 | Cale Yarborough | Junior Johnson |
| 6. | Hampton, Ga. | April 1 | David Pearson | Wood Brothers |
| 7. | N. Wilkesboro, N.C. | April 8 | Richard Petty | Petty Enterprises |
| 8. | Darlington, S.C. | April 15 | David Pearson | Wood Brothers |
| 9. | Martinsville, Va. | April 29 | David Pearson | Wood Brothers |
| 10. | Talladega, Ala. | May 6 | David Pearson | Wood Brothers |
| 11. | Nashville | May 12 | Cale Yarborough | Junior Johnson |
| 12. | Concord, N.C. | May 27 | Buddy Baker | Nord Krauskopf |
| 13. | Dover, Del. | June 3 | David Pearson | Wood Brothers |
| 14. | Bryan, Texas | June 10 | Richard Petty | Petty Enterprises |
| 15. | Riverside, Calif. | June 17 | Bobby Allison | Bobby Allison |
| 16. | Brooklyn, Mich. | June 24 | David Pearson | Wood Brothers |
| 17. | Daytona Beach, Fla. | July 4 | David Pearson | Wood Brothers |
| 18. | Bristol, Tenn. | July 8 | Benny Parsons | L.G. DeWitt |
| 19. | Hampton, Ga. | July 22 | David Pearson | Wood Brothers |
| 20. | Talladega, Ala. | Aug. 12 | Dick Brooks | Crawford Brothers |
| 21. | Nashville | Aug. 25 | Buddy Baker | Nord Krauskopf |
| 22. | Darlington, S.C. | Sept. 3 | Cale Yarborough | Junior Johnson |
| 23. | Richmond, Va. | Sept. 9 | Richard Petty | Petty Enterprises |
| 24. | Dover, Del. | Sept. 16 | David Pearson | Wood Brothers |
| 25. | N. Wilkesboro, N.C. | Sept. 23 | Bobby Allison | Bobby Allison |
| 26. | Martinsville, Va. | Sept. 30 | Richard Petty | Petty Enterprises |
| 27. | Concord, N.C. | Oct. 7 | Cale Yarborough | Junior Johnson |
| 28. | Rockingham, N.C. | Oct. 21 | David Pearson | Wood Brothers |

## Points standings

1. Benny Parsons ............7,173.80
2. Cale Yarborough .........7,106.65
3. Cecil Gordon ...............7,046.80
4. James Hylton ..............6,972.75
5. Richard Petty .............6,877.955
6. Buddy Baker................6,327.60
7. Bobby Allison ..............6,272.30
8. Walter Ballard ..............5,955.70
9. Elmo Langley ..............5,826.85
10. J.D. McDuffie ............5,743.90

## Race winners 8

1. David Pearson ..................11
2. Richard Petty ......................6
3. Cale Yarborough ..................4
4. Buddy Baker .......................2
   Bobby Allison ........................2
6. Benny Parsons .....................1
   Richard Brooks......................1
   Mark Donohue .....................1

## Money won leaders

1. David Pearson .........$216,737
2. Cale Yarborough..........181,574
3. Richard Petty .............171,122
4. Benny Parsons...........114,345
5. Buddy Baker .............132,988
6. Bobby Allison .............107,299

## Pole winners 5

1. David Pearson .......................8
2. Bobby Allison .........................6
3. Buddy Baker ........................5
   Cale Yarborough.....................5
5. Richard Petty ...................... 3

# 1972 SEASON

| Race No. | Location | Date | Winner | Car owner |
|---|---|---|---|---|
| 1. | Riverside, Calif. | Jan. 23 | Richard Petty | Petty Enterprises |
| 2. | Daytona Beach, Fla. | Feb. 20 | A.J. Foyt | Wood Brothers |
| 3. | Richmond, Va. | Feb. 27 | Richard Petty | Petty Enterprises |
| 4. | Fontana, Calif. | March 5 | A.J. Foyt | Wood Brothers |
| 5. | Rockingham, N.C. | March 12 | Bobby Isaac | Nord Krauskopf |
| 6. | Hampton, Ga. | March 26 | Bobby Allison | Junior Johnson |
| 7. | Bristol, Tenn. | April 9 | Bobby Allison | Junior Johnson |
| 8. | Darlington, S.C. | April 16 | David Pearson | Wood Brothers |
| 9. | N. Wilkesboro, N.C. | April 23 | Richard Petty | Petty Enterprises |
| 10. | Martinsville, Va. | April 30 | Richard Petty | Petty Enterprises |
| 11. | Talladega, Ala. | May 7 | David Pearson | Wood Brothers |
| 12. | Concord, N.C. | May 28 | Buddy Baker | Petty Enterprises |
| 13. | Dover, Del. | June 4 | Bobby Allison | Junior Johnson |
| 14. | Brooklyn, Mich. | June 11 | David Pearson | Wood Brothers |
| 15. | Riverside, Calif. | June 18 | Ray Elder | Fred Elder |
| 16. | Bryan, Texas | June 25 | Richard Petty | Petty Enterprises |
| 17. | Daytona Beach, Fla. | July 4 | David Pearson | Wood Brothers |
| 18. | Bristol, Tenn. | July 9 | Bobby Allison | Junior Johnson |
| 19. | Trenton, N.J. | July 16 | Bobby Allison | Junior Johnson |
| 20. | Hampton, Ga. | July 23 | Bobby Allison | Junior Johnson |
| 21. | Talladega, Ala. | Aug. 6 | James Hylton | James Hylton |
| 22. | Brooklyn, Mich. | Aug. 20 | David Pearson | Wood Brothers |
| 23. | Nashville | Aug. 26 | Bobby Allison | Junior Johnson |
| 24. | Darlington, S.C. | Sept. 4 | Bobby Allison | Junior Johnson |
| 25. | Richmond, Va. | Sept. 10 | Richard Petty | Petty Enterprises |
| 26. | Dover, Del. | Sept. 17 | David Pearson | Wood Brothers |
| 27. | Martinsville, Va. | Sept. 24 | Richard Petty | Petty Enterprises |
| 28. | N. Wilkesboro, N.C. | Oct. 1 | Richard Petty | Petty Enterprises |
| 29. | Concord, N.C. | Oct. 8 | Bobby Allison | Junior Johnson |
| 30. | Rockingham, N.C. | Oct. 22 | Bobby Allison | Junior Johnson |
| 31. | Bryan, Texas | Nov. 12 | Buddy Baker | Nord Krauskopf |

## Points standings

1. Richard Petty.............8,701.40
2. Bobby Allison ............8,573.50
3. James Hylton .............8,158.70
4. Cecil Gordon ..............7,326.05
5. Benny Parsons ...........6,844.15
6. Walter Ballard .............6,781.45
7. Elmo Langley .............6,656.25
8. John Sears ................6,298.50
9. Dean Dalton ...............6,295.05
10. Ben Arnold ...............6,179.00

## Race winners 8

1. Bobby Allison ......................10
2. Richard Petty ......................8
3. David Pearson .....................6
4. Buddy Baker .......................2
   A.J. Foyt.............................2
6. James Hylton ......................1
   Bobby Isaac .......................1
   Ray Elder ...........................1

## Money won leaders

1. Bobby Allison ............$284,467
2. Richard Petty .............265,460
3. David Pearson ............139,599
4. James Hylton .............113,705

## Pole winners 6

1. Bobby Allison ........................11
2. Bobby Isaac ..........................9
3. David Pearson .......................4
4. Richard Petty ........................3
   A.J. Foyt...............................3
6. Buddy Baker .........................1

HISTORY

# 1972 SEASON

## THE WINSTON CUP: THAT'S GOT A NICE RING TO IT

You can tell what a huge impact Winston had on the sport by how hard it was for those involved with NASCAR to stop referring to the elite series as Winston Cup when it became the Nextel Cup in 2004. It took most of the first season before Nextel Cup became a natural for those who often found themselves behind microphones.

Indeed, the sport would not be where it is today had Winston not signed on as a title sponsor in 1972. Since then, Winston Cup has been synonymous with the best stock car racing on the planet. With Winston's ever-present help, NASCAR grew from a sidebar of the South into a nationwide phenomenon. In 1976, the sport took over the lead in attendance in motorsports series and never has relinquished the top spot. It's a safe bet it never will.

Although the sport wouldn't be where it is today without Winston, it can't get where it's going without Nextel. Bans on tobacco advertising limited the exposure Winston Cup could call upon itself. With that ban no longer applicable, the Nextel Cup can better market itself and thus take the sport as far beyond where it is today as Winston took it from where it was in 1972.

# 1971 SEASON

| Race No. | Location | Date | Winner | Car owner |
|---|---|---|---|---|
| 1. | Riverside, Calif. | Jan. 10 | Ray Elder | Fred Elder |
| 2. | Daytona Beach, Fla. | Feb. 11 | Pete Hamilton | Cotton Owens |
| 3. | Daytona Beach, Fla. | Feb. 11 | David Pearson | Holman-Moody |
| 4. | Daytona Beach, Fla. | Feb. 14 | Richard Petty | Petty Enterprises |
| 5. | Ontario, Calif. | Feb. 28 | A.J. Foyt | Wood Brothers |
| 6. | Richmond, Va. | March 7 | Richard Petty | Petty Enterprises |
| 7. | Rockingham, N.C. | March 14 | Richard Petty | Petty Enterprises |
| 8. | Hickory, N.C. | March 21 | Richard Petty | Petty Enterprises |
| 9. | Bristol, Tenn. | March 28 | David Pearson | Holman-Moody |
| 10. | Hampton, Ga. | April 4 | A.J. Foyt | Wood Brothers |
| 11. | Columbia, S.C. | April 8 | Richard Petty | Petty Enterprises |
| 12. | Greenville, S.C. | April 10 | Bobby Isaac | Nord Krauskopf |
| 13. | Maryville, Tenn. | April 15 | Richard Petty | Petty Enterprises |
| 14. | North Wilkesboro, N.C. | April 18 | Richard Petty | Petty Enterprises |
| 15. | Martinsville, Va. | April 25 | Richard Petty | Petty Enterprises |
| 16. | Darlington, S.C. | May 2 | Buddy Baker | Petty Enterprises |
| 17. | South Boston, Va. | May 9 | Benny Parsons | L.G. DeWitt |
| 18. | Talladega, Ala. | May 16 | Donnie Allison | Wood Brothers |
| 19. | Asheville, N.C. | May 21 | Richard Petty | Petty Enterprises |
| 20. | Kingsport, Tenn. | May 23 | Bobby Isaac | Nord Krauskopf |
| 21. | Concord, N.C. | May 30 | Bobby Allison | Holman-Moody |
| 22. | Dover, Del. | Jun. 6 | Bobby Allison | Holman-Moody |
| 23. | Brooklyn, Mich. | June 13 | Bobby Allison | Holman-Moody |
| 24. | Riverside, Calif. | June 20 | Bobby Allison | Bobby Allison |
| 25. | Houston | June 23 | Bobby Allison | Bobby Allison |
| 26. | Greenville, S.C. | June 26 | Richard Petty | Petty Enterprises |
| 27. | Daytona Beach, Fla. | July 4 | Bobby Isaac | Nord Krauskopf |
| 28. | Bristol, Tenn. | July 11 | Charlie Glotzbach | Jr. Johnson/R. Howard |
| 29. | Malta, N.Y. | July 14 | Richard Petty | Petty Enterprises |
| 30. | Islip, N.Y. | July 15 | Richard Petty | Petty Enterprises |
| 31. | Trenton, N.J. | July 18 | Richard Petty | Petty Enterprises |
| 32. | Nashville, Tenn. | July 24 | Richard Petty | Petty Enterprises |
| 33. | Hampton, Ga. | Aug. 1 | Richard Petty | Petty Enterprises |
| 34. | Winston-Salem, N.C. | Aug. 6 | Bobby Allison | Melvin Joseph |
| 35. | Ona, W.Va. | Aug. 8 | Richard Petty | Petty Enterprises |
| 36. | Brooklyn, Mich. | Aug. 15 | Bobby Allison | Holman-Moody |
| 37. | Talladega, Ala. | Aug. 22 | Bobby Allison | Holman-Moody |
| 38. | Columbia, S.C. | Aug. 27 | Richard Petty | Petty Enterprises |
| 39. | Hickory, N.C. | Aug. 28 | Tiny Lund | Ronnie Hopkins |
| 40. | Darlington, S.C. | Sep. 6 | Bobby Allison | Holman-Moody |
| 41. | Martinsville, Va. | Sep. 26 | Bobby Isaac | Nord Krauskopf |
| 42. | Concord, N.C. | Oct. 10 | Bobby Allison | Holman-Moody |
| 43. | Dover, Del. | Oct. 17 | Richard Petty | Petty Enterprises |
| 44. | Rockingham, N.C. | Oct. 24 | Richard Petty | Petty Enterprises |
| 45. | Macon, Ga. | Nov. 7 | Bobby Allison | Holman-Moody |
| 46. | Richmond, Va. | Nov. 14 | Richard Petty | Petty Enterprises |
| 47. | North Wilkesboro, N.C. | Nov. 22 | Tiny Lund | Ronnie Hopkins |
| 48. | College Station, Texas | Dec. 12 | Richard Petty | Petty Enterprises |

## Points standings

1. Richard Petty ...........4,435.00
2. James Hylton ........4,071.00
3. Cecil Gordon ..........3,677.00
4. Bobby Allison...........3,636.00
5. Elmo Langley ..........3,356.00
6. Jabe Thomas..........3,200.00
7. Bill Champion .........3,058.00
8. Frank Warren...........2,886.00
9. J.D. McDuffie...........2,862.00
10. Walter Ballard .........2,633.00

## Race winners

1. Richard Petty .........................21
2. Bobby Allison .........................11
3. Bobby Isaac ...........................4
4. Tiny Lund ................................2
   A.J. Foyt.................................2
   David Pearson .....................2
7. Benny Parsons .......................1
   Buddy Baker .....................1
   Donnie Allison ...................1
   Ray Elder .........................1
   Pete Hamilton.....................1
   Charlie Glotzbach ................1

## Money won leaders

1. Richard Petty .........$269,225
2. Bobby Allison ............235,795
3. Buddy Baker.............115,150
4. Bobby Isaac ............106,426
5. Donnie Allison ...........69,995
6. Pete Hamilton ............60,440
7. James Hylton ............55,860
8. Benny Parsons ...........48,517
9. Fred Lorenzen............45,100
10. Cecil Gordon ..............42,949

## Pole winners

1. Richard Petty .........................9
   Bobby Allison .........................9
3. Bobby Isaac ...........................5
   Donnie Allison .......................5
5. Charlie Glotzbach ...................4
   A.J. Foyt.................................4
7. Dave Marcis............................2
   David Pearson .......................2
   Pete Hamilton ........................2
   Friday Hassler .......................2
   Buddy Baker ..........................1
   Bill Dennis .............................1
   James Hylton ..........................1
   Fred Lorenzen .......................1

# 1970 SEASON

## THE GREAT DEBATE: FORD, CHEVY OR SUPERBIRD?

One fading ritual of the sport is the debate among fans of manufacturers. These days, Chevrolet rules the roost, and a small cadre of fans resents it. It's just not the big deal it used to be, for whatever reason. In the old days, fans were much more in tune with which driver drove which kind of car, and it was not uncommon for a fan to like a driver solely based on what he drove.

The allegiance went beyond rooting on Sundays. Any car dealership in the South knew the saying, "Win on Sunday, sell on Monday." Whether any empirical data backs up that assertion is irrelevant. The point is, fans stood by their manufacturers and bristled when others gained unfair advantages.

That explains the "Aero Wars" of 1969 and 1970. This was in the days before common templates, before each car was virtually the same. In 1970, the sport was awash in debate about the winged cars of Dodge and Plymouth and the sloped noses of Ford and Mercury. So did any one car have an advantage? Nice try. You're not dragging us into that one.

# 1970 SEASON

| Race No. | Location | Date | Winner | Car owner |
|---|---|---|---|---|
| 1. | Riverside, Calif. | Jan. 18 | A.J. Foyt | Jack Bowsher |
| 2. | Daytona Beach, Fla. | Feb. 19 | Cale Yarborough | Wood Brothers |
| 3. | Daytona Beach, Fla. | Feb. 19 | Charlie Glotzbach | Ray Nichels |
| 4. | Daytona Beach, Fla. | Feb. 22 | Pete Hamilton | Petty Enterprises |
| 5. | Richmond, Va. | March 1 | James Hylton | James Hylton |
| 6. | Rockingham, N.C. | March 8 | Richard Petty | Petty Enterprises |
| 7. | Savannah, Ga. | March 15 | Richard Petty | Petty Enterprises |
| 8. | Hampton, Ga. | March 29 | Bobby Allison | Mario Rossi |
| 9. | Bristol, Tenn. | April 5 | Donnie Allison | Banjo Matthews |
| 10. | Talladega, Ala. | April 12 | Pete Hamilton | Petty Enterprises |
| 11. | North Wilkesboro, N.C. | April 18 | Richard Petty | Petty Enterprises |
| 12. | Columbia, S.C. | April 30 | Richard Petty | Donald Robertson |
| 13. | Darlington, S.C. | May 9 | David Pearson | Holman-Moody |
| 14. | Beltsville, Md. | May 15 | Bobby Isaac | Nord Krauskopf |
| 15. | Hampton, Va. | May 18 | Bobby Isaac | Nord Krauskopf |
| 16. | Concord, N.C. | May 24 | Donnie Allison | Banjo Matthews |
| 17. | Maryville, Tenn. | May 28 | Bobby Isaac | Nord Krauskopf |
| 18. | Martinsville, Va. | May 31 | Bobby Isaac | Nord Krauskopf |
| 19. | Brooklyn, Mich. | June 7 | Cale Yarborough | Wood Brothers |
| 20. | Riverside, Calif. | June 14 | Richard Petty | Petty Enterprises |
| 21. | Hickory, N.C. | June 20 | Bobby Isaac | Nord Krauskopf |
| 22. | Kingsport, Tenn. | June 26 | Richard Petty | Petty Enterprises |
| 23. | Greenville, S.C. | June 27 | Bobby Isaac | Nord Krauskopf |
| 24. | Daytona Beach, Fla. | July 4 | Donnie Allison | Banjo Matthews |
| 25. | Malta, N.Y. | July 7 | Richard Petty | Petty Enterprises |
| 26. | Thompson, Conn. | July 9 | Bobby Isaac | Nord Krauskopf |
| 27. | Trenton, N.J. | July 12 | Richard Petty | Petty Enterprises |
| 28. | Bristol, Tenn. | July 19 | Bobby Allison | Bobby Allison |
| 29. | Maryville, Tenn. | July 24 | Richard Petty | Petty Enterprises |
| 30. | Nashville | July 25 | Bobby Isaac | Nord Krauskopf |
| 31. | Hampton, Ga. | Aug. 2 | Richard Petty | Petty Enterprises |
| 32. | Columbia, S.C. | Aug. 6 | Bobby Isaac | Nord Krauskopf |
| 33. | Ona, W.Va. | Aug. 11 | Richard Petty | Petty Enterprises |
| 34. | Brooklyn, Mich. | Aug. 16 | Charlie Glotzbach | Ray Nichels |
| 35. | Talladega, Ala. | Aug. 23 | Pete Hamilton | Petty Enterprises |
| 36. | Winston-Salem, N.C. | Aug. 28 | Richard Petty | Petty Enterprises |
| 37. | South Boston, Va. | Aug. 29 | Richard Petty | Petty Enterprises |
| 38. | Darlington, S.C. | Sep. 7 | Buddy Baker | Cotton Owens |
| 39. | Hickory, N.C. | Sep. 11 | Bobby Isaac | Nord Krauskopf |
| 40. | Richmond, Va. | Sep. 13 | Richard Petty | Petty Enterprises |
| 41. | Dover, Del. | Sep. 20 | Richard Petty | Petty Enterprises |
| 42. | Raleigh, N.C. | Sep. 30 | Richard Petty | Donald Robertson |
| 43. | North Wilkesboro, N.C. | Oct. 4 | Bobby Isaac | Nord Krauskopf |
| 44. | Concord, N.C. | Oct. 11 | LeeRoy Yarbrough | Junior Johnson |
| 45. | Martinsville, Va. | Oct. 18 | Richard Petty | Petty Enterprises |
| 46. | Macon, Ga. | Nov. 8 | Richard Petty | Petty Enterprises |
| 47. | Rockingham, N.C. | Nov. 15 | Cale Yarborough | Wood Brothers |
| 48. | Hampton, Va. | Nov. 22 | Bobby Allison | Bobby Allison |

## Points standings

1. Bobby Isaac ..............3,911.00
2. Bobby Allison ..........3,860.00
3. James Hylton ...........3,788.00
4. Richard Petty ...........3,447.00
5. Neil Castles ...........3,158.00
6. Elmo Langley ..........3,154.00
7. Jabe Thomas ...........3,120.00
8. Benny Parsons ........2,993.00
9. Dave Marcis ............2,820.00
10. Frank Warren ..........2,697.00

## Race winners 12

1. Richard Petty .........................18
2. Bobby Isaac ...........................11
3. Pete Hamilton ..........................3
   Cale Yarborough ...................3
   Bobby Allison .......................3
   Donnie Allison .....................3
7. Charlie Glotzbach ....................2
8. LeeRoy Yarbrough ...................1
   David Pearson ....................1
   A.J. Foyt...............................1
   James Hylton ......................1
   Buddy Baker ......................1

## Money won leaders

1. Richard Petty .........$138,969
2. Bobby Allison ..........131,965
3. Pete Hamilton .........131,406
4. Bobby Isaac .............121,470
5. Cale Yarborough .......115,875
6. Donnie Allison ...........92,606
7. David Pearson ...........87,118
8. Buddy Baker .............62,928
9. LeeRoy Yarbrough .....61,930
10. James Hylton.............59,705

## Pole winners 16

1. Bobby Isaac .........................13
2. Richard Petty .........................9
3. Cale Yarborough ....................5
   Bobby Allison ......................5
5. Charlie Glotzbach ..................4
6. David Pearson .......................2
7. LeeRoy Yarbrough ................1
   Benny Parsons.....................1
   John Sears...........................1
   Fred Lorenzen ......................1
   Larry Baumel .......................1
   Buddy Baker .......................1
   Donnie Allison .....................1
   James Hylton.......................1
   Pete Hamilton......................1
   Dan Gurney .........................1

# 1969 SEASON

| Race No. | Location | Date | Winner | Car owner |
|---|---|---|---|---|
| 1. | Macon, Ga. | Nov. 17 | Richard Petty | Petty Enterprises |
| 2. | Montgomery, Ala. | Dec. 8 | Bobby Allison | Mario Rossi |
| 3. | Riverside, Calif. | Feb. 1 | Richard Petty | Petty Enterprises |
| 4. | Daytona Beach, Fla. | Feb. 20 | David Pearson | Holman-Moody |
| 5. | Daytona Beach, Fla. | Feb. 20 | Bobby Isaac | Nord Krauskopf |
| 6. | Daytona Beach, Fla. | Feb. 23 | LeeRoy Yarbrough | Junior Johnson |
| 7. | Rockingham, N.C. | March 9 | David Pearson | Holman-Moody |
| 8. | Augusta, Ga. | March 16 | David Pearson | Holman-Moody |
| 9. | Bristol, Tenn. | March 23 | Bobby Allison | Mario Rossi |
| 10. | Hampton, Ga. | March 30 | Cale Yarborough | Wood Brothers |
| 11. | Columbia, S.C. | April 3 | Bobby Isaac | Nord Krauskopf |
| 12. | Hickory, N.C. | April 6 | Bobby Isaac | Nord Krauskopf |
| 13. | Greenville, S.C. | April 8 | Bobby Isaac | Nord Krauskopf |
| 14. | Richmond, Va. | April 13 | David Pearson | Holman-Moody |
| 15. | North Wilkesboro, N.C. | April 20 | Bobby Allison | Mario Rossi |
| 16. | Martinsville, Va. | April 27 | Richard Petty | Petty Enterprises |
| 17. | Weaverville, N.C. | May 4 | Bobby Isaac | Nord Krauskopf |
| 18. | Darlington, S.C. | May 10 | LeeRoy Yarbrough | Junior Johnson |
| 19. | Beltsville, Md. | May 16 | Bobby Isaac | Nord Krauskopf |
| 20. | Hampton, Va. | May 17 | David Pearson | Holman-Moody |
| 21. | Concord, N.C. | May 25 | LeeRoy Yarbrough | Junior Johnson |
| 22. | Macon, Ga. | June 1 | Bobby Isaac | Nord Krauskopf |
| 23. | Maryville, Tenn. | June 5 | Bobby Isaac | Nord Krauskopf |
| 24. | Brooklyn, Mich. | June 15 | Cale Yarborough | Wood Brothers |
| 25. | Kingsport, Tenn. | June 19 | Richard Petty | Petty Enterprises |
| 26. | Greenville, S.C. | June 21 | Bobby Isaac | Nord Krauskopf |
| 27. | Raleigh, N.C. | June 26 | David Pearson | Holman-Moody |
| 28. | Daytona Beach, Fla. | July 4 | LeeRoy Yarbrough | Junior Johnson |
| 29. | Dover, Del. | July 6 | Richard Petty | Petty Enterprises |
| 30. | Thompson, Conn. | July 10 | David Pearson | Holman-Moody |
| 31. | Trenton, N.J. | July 13 | David Pearson | Holman-Moody |
| 32. | Beltsville, Md. | July 15 | Richard Petty | Petty Enterprises |
| 33. | Bristol, Tenn. | July 20 | David Pearson | Holman-Moody |
| 34. | Nashville | July 26 | Richard Petty | Petty Enterprises |
| 35. | Maryville, Tenn. | July 27 | Richard Petty | Petty Enterprises |
| 36. | Hampton, Ga. | Aug. 10 | LeeRoy Yarbrough | Junior Johnson |
| 37. | Brooklyn, Mich. | Aug. 17 | David Pearson | Holman-Moody |
| 38. | South Boston, Va. | Aug. 21 | Bobby Isaac | Nord Krauskopf |
| 39. | Winston-Salem, N.C. | Aug. 22 | Richard Petty | Petty Enterprises |
| 40. | Weaverville, N.C. | Aug. 24 | Bobby Isaac | Nord Krauskopf |
| 41. | Darlington, S.C. | Sep. 1 | LeeRoy Yarbrough | Junior Johnson |
| 42. | Hickory, N.C. | Sep. 5 | Bobby Isaac | Nord Krauskopf |
| 43. | Richmond, Va. | Sep. 7 | Bobby Allison | Mario Rossi |
| 44. | Talladega, Ala. | Sep. 14 | Richard Brickhouse | Ray Nichels |
| 45. | Columbia, S.C. | Sep. 18 | Bobby Isaac | Nord Krauskopf |
| 46. | Martinsville, Va. | Sep. 28 | Richard Petty | Petty Enterprises |
| 47. | North Wilkesboro, N.C. | Oct. 5 | David Pearson | Holman-Moody |
| 48. | Concord, N.C. | Oct. 12 | Donnie Allison | Banjo Matthews |
| 49. | Savannah, Ga. | Oct. 17 | Bobby Isaac | Nord Krauskopf |
| 50. | Augusta, Ga. | Oct. 19 | Bobby Isaac | Nord Krauskopf |
| 51. | Rockingham, N.C. | Oct. 26 | LeeRoy Yarbrough | Junior Johnson |
| 52. | Jefferson, Ga. | Nov. 2 | Bobby Isaac | Nord Krauskopf |
| 53. | Macon, Ga. | Nov. 9 | Bobby Allison | Mario Rossi |
| 54. | College Station, Texas | Dec. 7 | Bobby Isaac | Nord Krauskopf |

## Points standings

1. David Pearson ............4,170.00
2. Richard Petty ............3,813.00
3. James Hylton ............3,750.00
4. Neil Castles...............3,530.00
5. Elmo Langley ............3,383.00
6. Bobby Isaac ..............3,301.00
7. John Sears ................3,166.00
8. Jabe Thomas ............3,103.00
9. Wendell Scott ............3,015.00
10. Cecil Gordon ............3,002.00

## Race winners

1. Bobby Isaac .........................17
2. David Pearson ......................11
3. Richard Petty........................10
4. LeeRoy Yarbrough ..................7
5. Bobby Allison .........................5
6. Cale Yarborough .....................2
7. Richard Brickhouse .................1
   Donnie Allison .......................1

## Money won leaders

1. LeeRoy Yarbrough ....$188,105
2. David Pearson ............183,700
3. Richard Petty..............109,180
4. Bobby Isaac ................80,560
5. Donnie Allison .............74,255
6. Cale Yarborough .........73,540
7. Bobby Allison .............66,775
8. Buddy Baker ..............57,910
9. James Hylton .............55,992
10. Richard Brickhouse ......45,312

## Pole winners

1. Bobby Isaac ........................20
2. David Pearson .....................13
3. Cale Yarborough ...................6
   Richard Petty ........................6
5. Buddy Baker .........................3
6. Donnie Allison .......................2
   Charlie Glotzbach ...................2
8. Bobby Allison ........................1
   A.J. Foyt...............................1

# 1968 SEASON

| Race No. | Location | Date | Winner | Car owner |
|---|---|---|---|---|
| 1. | Macon, Ga. | Nov. 12 | Bobby Allison | Holman-Moody |
| 2. | Montgomery, Ala. | Nov. 26 | Richard Petty | Petty Enterprises |
| 3. | Riverside, Calif. | Jan. 21 | Dan Gurney | Wood Brothers |
| 4. | Daytona Beach, Fla. | Feb. 25 | Cale Yarborough | Wood Brothers |
| 5. | Bristol, Tenn. | March 17 | David Pearson | Holman-Moody |
| 6. | Richmond, Va. | March 24 | David Pearson | Holman-Moody |
| 7. | Hampton, Ga. | March 31 | Cale Yarborough | Wood Brothers |
| 8. | Hickory, N.C. | April 7 | Richard Petty | Petty Enterprises |
| 9. | Greenville, S.C. | April 13 | Richard Petty | Petty Enterprises |
| 10. | Columbia, S.C. | April 18 | Bobby Isaac | Nord Krauskopf |
| 11. | North Wilkesboro, N.C. | April 21 | David Pearson | Holman-Moody |
| 12. | Martinsville, Va. | April 28 | Cale Yarborough | Wood Brothers |
| 13. | Augusta, Ga. | May 3 | Bobby Isaac | Nord Krauskopf |
| 14. | Weaverville, N.C. | May 5 | David Pearson | Holman-Moody |
| 15. | Darlington, S.C. | May 11 | David Pearson | Holman-Moody |
| 16. | Beltsville, Md. | May 17 | David Pearson | Holman-Moody |
| 17. | Hampton, Va. | May 18 | David Pearson | Holman-Moody |
| 18. | Concord, N.C. | May 26 | Buddy Baker | Raymond Fox |
| 19. | Asheville, N.C. | May 31 | Richard Petty | Petty Enterprises |
| 20. | Macon, Ga. | June 2 | David Pearson | Holman-Moody |
| 21. | Maryville, Tenn. | June 6 | Richard Petty | Petty Enterprises |
| 22. | Birmingham, Ala. | June 8 | Richard Petty | Petty Enterprises |
| 23. | Rockingham, N.C. | June 16 | Donnie Allison | Banjo Matthews |
| 24. | Greenville, S.C. | June 22 | Richard Petty | Petty Enterprises |
| 25. | Daytona Beach, Fla. | July 4 | Cale Yarborough | Wood Brothers |
| 26. | Islip, N.Y. | July 7 | Bobby Allison | Bobby Allison |
| 27. | Oxford, Maine | July 9 | Richard Petty | Petty Enterprises |
| 28. | Fonda, N.Y. | July 11 | Richard Petty | Petty Enterprises |
| 29. | Trenton, N.J. | July 14 | LeeRoy Yarbrough | Junior Johnson |
| 30. | Bristol, Tenn. | July 21 | David Pearson | Holman-Moody |
| 31. | Maryville, Tenn. | July 25 | Richard Petty | Petty Enterprises |
| 32. | Nashville | July 27 | David Pearson | Holman-Moody |
| 33. | Hampton, Ga. | Aug. 4 | LeeRoy Yarbrough | Junior Johnson |
| 34. | Columbia, S.C. | Aug. 8 | David Pearson | Holman-Moody |
| 35. | Winston-Salem, N.C. | Aug. 10 | David Pearson | Holman-Moody |
| 36. | Weaverville, N.C. | Aug. 18 | David Pearson | Holman-Moody |
| 37. | South Boston, Va. | Aug. 23 | Richard Petty | Petty Enterprises |
| 38. | Hampton, Va. | Aug. 24 | David Pearson | Holman-Moody |
| 39. | Darlington, S.C. | Sept. 2 | Cale Yarborough | Wood Brothers |
| 40. | Hickory, N.C. | Sept. 6 | David Pearson | Holman-Moody |
| 41. | Richmond, Va. | Sept. 8 | Richard Petty | Petty Enterprises |
| 42. | Beltsville, Md. | Sept. 13 | Bobby Isaac | Nord Krauskopf |
| 43. | Hillsboro, N.C. | Sept. 15 | Richard Petty | Petty Enterprises |
| 44. | Martinsville, Va. | Sept. 22 | Richard Petty | Petty Enterprises |
| 45. | North Wilkesboro, N.C. | Sep. 29 | Richard Petty | Petty Enterprises |
| 46. | Augusta, Ga. | Oct. 5 | David Pearson | Holman-Moody |
| 47. | Concord, N.C. | Oct. 20 | Charlie Glotzbach | Cotton Owens |
| 48. | Rockingham, N.C. | Oct. 27 | Richard Petty | Petty Enterprises |
| 49. | Jefferson, Ga. | Nov. 3 | Cale Yarborough | Wood Brothers |

## Points standings

1. David Pearson ........3,499.00
2. Bobby Isaac ..........3,373.00
3. Richard Petty .........3,123.00
4. Clyde Lynn .............3,041.00
5. John Sears .............3,017.00
6. Elmo Langley ........2,823.00
7. James Hylton .........2,719.00
8. Jabe Thomas ........2,687.00
9. Wendell Scott .........2,685.00
10. Roy Tyner ..............2,504.00

## Race winners

1. Richard Petty ...........................16
   David Pearson ...................16
3. Cale Yarborough ......................6
4. Bobby Isaac .............................3
5. Bobby Allison ............................2
   LeeRoy Yarbrough ...............2
7. Buddy Baker ..............................1
   Donnie Allison .......................1
   Dan Gurney ...........................1
   Charlie Glotzbach ..................1

## Money won leaders

1. Cale Yarborough ......$134,136
2. David Pearson............118,487
3. Richard Petty .............89,103
4. LeeRoy Yarbrough .......86,604
5. Buddy Baker ...............54,125
6. Donnie Allison ............50,815
7. Bobby Allison .............50,391
8. Bobby Isaac ...............44,530
9. Charlie Glotzbach ........41,835
10. James Hylton ............27,865

## Pole winners

1. Richard Petty ........................12
   David Pearson .....................12
3. LeeRoy Yarbrough .................6
4. Cale Yarborough .....................4
   Buddy Baker ..........................4
6. Bobby Isaac ............................3
   Charlie Glotzbach ..................3
8. Bobby Allison ..........................2
9. Donnie Allison ........................1
   Darel Dieringer......................1
   Dan Gurney ...........................1

HISTORY

# 1967 SEASON

## TWENTY-SEVEN WINS: YOU BETTER CALL HIM THE KING

You see The King every Sunday, all blazing white teeth and dark shades, blue jeans and cowboy hats. You know he's a legend. You know he drove No. 43. But just how good was he? Statistically, he's the best ever, holding virtually every relevant record. Nobody else comes close.

Let's look at just one season for an answer. In 1967, Richard Petty won 27 races—27!—including 10 in a row. For context, the sport was in a tizzy in 2004 when Jimmie Johnson won three in a row. Petty's 27 wins over 49 races is the equivalent of 20 wins in today's 36-race schedule. To put it mildly, nobody has, or ever will, approach 20 wins again. Heck, Ryan Newman won eight in 2003, and everybody thought he was cheating. (He says he wasn't.) Petty also had 19 poles and 40 top 10 finishes in winning one of his seven championships.

The only stat Petty is not on top in is career earnings. He won "just" $8,541,218 on NASCAR's top circuit. Jeff Gordon topped that by more than $2.3 million in 2001 alone.

# 1967 SEASON

| Race No. | Location | Date | Winner | Car owner |
|---|---|---|---|---|
| 1. | Augusta, Ga. | Nov. 13 | Richard Petty | Petty Enterprises |
| 2. | Riverside, Calif. | Jan. 29 | Parnelli Jones | William Stroppe |
| 3. | Daytona Beach, Fla. | Feb. 24 | LeeRoy Yarbrough | Jon Thorne |
| 4. | Daytona Beach, Fla. | Feb. 24 | Fred Lorenzen | Holman-Moody |
| 5. | Daytona Beach, Fla. | Feb. 26 | Mario Andretti | Holman-Moody |
| 6. | Weaverville, N.C. | March 5 | Richard Petty | Petty Enterprises |
| 7. | Bristol, Tenn. | March 19 | David Pearson | Cotton Owens |
| 8. | Greenville, S.C. | March 25 | David Pearson | Cotton Owens |
| 9. | Winston-Salem, N.C. | March 27 | Bobby Allison | Bobby Allison |
| 10. | Hampton, Ga. | April 2 | Cale Yarborough | Wood Brothers |
| 11. | Columbia, S.C. | April 6 | Richard Petty | Petty Enterprises |
| 12. | Hickory, N.C. | April 9 | Richard Petty | Petty Enterprises |
| 13. | North Wilkesboro, N.C. | April 16 | Darel Dieringer | Junior Johnson |
| 14. | Martinsville, Va. | April 23 | Richard Petty | Petty Enterprises |
| 15. | Savannah, Ga. | April 28 | Bobby Allison | Bobby Allison |
| 16. | Richmond, Va. | April 30 | Richard Petty | Petty Enterprises |
| 17. | Darlington, S.C. | May 13 | Richard Petty | Petty Enterprises |
| 18. | Beltsville, Md. | May 19 | Jim Paschal | Thomas Friedkin |
| 19. | Hampton, Va. | May 20 | Richard Petty | Petty Enterprises |
| 20. | Concord, N.C. | May 28 | Jim Paschal | Thomas Friedkin |
| 21. | Asheville, N.C. | June 2 | Jim Paschal | Thomas Friedkin |
| 22. | Macon, Ga. | June 6 | Richard Petty | Petty Enterprises |
| 23. | Maryville, Tenn. | June 8 | Richard Petty | Petty Enterprises |
| 24. | Birmingham, Ala. | June 10 | Bobby Allison | Cotton Owens |
| 25. | Rockingham, N.C. | June 18 | Richard Petty | Petty Enterprises |
| 26. | Greenville, S.C. | June 24 | Richard Petty | Petty Enterprises |
| 27. | Montgomery, Ala. | June 27 | Jim Paschal | Thomas Friedkin |
| 28. | Daytona Beach, Fla. | July 4 | Cale Yarborough | Wood Brothers |
| 29. | Trenton, N.J. | July 9 | Richard Petty | Petty Enterprises |
| 30. | Oxford, Maine | July 11 | Bobby Allison | Bobby Allison |
| 31. | Fonda, N.Y. | July 13 | Richard Petty | Petty Enterprises |
| 32. | Islip, N.Y. | July 15 | Richard Petty | Petty Enterprises |
| 33. | Bristol, Tenn. | July 23 | Richard Petty | Petty Enterprises |
| 34. | Maryville, Tenn. | July 27 | Dick Hutcherson | Bondy Long |
| 35. | Nashville | July 29 | Richard Petty | Petty Enterprises |
| 36. | Hampton, Ga. | Aug. 6 | Dick Hutcherson | Bondy Long |
| 37. | Winston-Salem, N.C. | Aug. 12 | Richard Petty | Petty Enterprises |
| 38. | Columbia, S.C. | Aug. 17 | Richard Petty | Petty Enterprises |
| 39. | Savannah, Ga. | Aug. 25 | Richard Petty | Petty Enterprises |
| 40. | Darlington, S.C. | Sept. 4 | Richard Petty | Petty Enterprises |
| 41. | Hickory, N.C. | Sept. 8 | Richard Petty | Petty Enterprises |
| 42. | Richmond, Va. | Sept. 10 | Richard Petty | Petty Enterprises |
| 43. | Beltsville, Md. | Sept. 15 | Richard Petty | Petty Enterprises |
| 44. | Hillsboro, N.C. | Sept. 17 | Richard Petty | Petty Enterprises |
| 45. | Martinsville, Va. | Sept. 24 | Richard Petty | Petty Enterprises |
| 46. | North Wilkesboro, N.C. | Oct. 1 | Richard Petty | Petty Enterprises |
| 47. | Concord, N.C. | Oct. 15 | Buddy Baker | Raymond Fox |
| 48. | Rockingham, N.C. | Oct. 29 | Bobby Allison | Holman-Moody |
| 49. | Weaverville, N.C. | Nov. 5 | Bobby Allison | Holman-Moody |

## Points standings

1. Richard Petty .........42,472.00
2. James Hylton ..........36,444.00
3. Dick Hutcherson......33,658.00
4. Bobby Allison ..........30,812.00
5. John Sears...............29,078.00
6. Jim Paschal .............27,624.00
7. David Pearson .......26,302.00
8. Neil Castles ............23,218.00
9. Elmo Langley ..........22,286.00
10. Wendell Scott ..........20,700.00

## Race winners 12

1. Richard Petty.........................27
2. Bobby Allison ..........................6
3. Jim Paschal ............................4
4. David Pearson ........................2
   Dick Hutcherson ....................2
   Cale Yarborough ....................2
7. LeeRoy Yarbrough ..................1
   Buddy Baker ...........................1
   Mario Andretti ........................1
   Darel Dieringer ......................1
   Fred Lorenzen.........................1
   Parnelli Jones ........................1

## Money won leaders

1. Richard Petty.........$130,275
2. Dick Hutcherson ........75,965
3. David Pearson ...........69,585
4. Cale Yarborough .......56,685
5. Bobby Allison............53,415
6. Jim Paschal...............53,380
7. Buddy Baker .............45,110
8. James Hylton ...........39,005
9. Paul Goldsmith .........35,360
10. Darel Dieringer .........32,870

## Pole winners 11

1. Richard Petty .......................19
2. Dick Hutcherson.....................9
3. Darel Dieringer......................6
4. Cale Yarborough ....................4
5. David Pearson .......................2
   Bobby Allison ........................2
   Curtis Turner ........................2
8. John Sears.............................1
   James Hunter .......................1
   James Hylton ........................1
   Jim Paschal ..........................1

# 1966 SEASON

| Race No. | Location | Date | Winner | Car owner |
|----------|----------|------|--------|-----------|
| 1. | Augusta, Ga. | Nov. 14 | Richard Petty | Petty Enterprises |
| 2. | Riverside, Calif. | Jan. 23 | Dan Gurney | Wood Brothers |
| 3. | Daytona Beach, Fla. | Feb. 25 | Paul Goldsmith | Ray Nichels |
| 4. | Daytona Beach, Fla. | Feb. 25 | Earl Balmer | Raymond Fox |
| 5. | Daytona Beach, Fla. | Feb. 27 | Richard Petty | Petty Enterprises |
| 6. | Rockingham, N.C. | March 13 | Paul Goldsmith | Ray Nichels |
| 7. | Bristol, Tenn. | March 20 | Dick Hutcherson | Holman-Moody |
| 8. | Hampton, Ga. | March 27 | Jim Hurtubise | Norm Nelson |
| 9. | Hickory, N.C. | April 3 | David Pearson | Cotton Owens |
| 10. | Columbia, S.C. | April 7 | David Pearson | Cotton Owens |
| 11. | Greenville, S.C. | April 9 | David Pearson | Cotton Owens |
| 12. | Winston-Salem, N.C. | April 11 | David Pearson | Cotton Owens |
| 13. | North Wilkesboro, N.C. | April 17 | Jim Paschal | Thomas Friedkin |
| 14. | Martinsville, Va. | April 24 | Jim Paschal | Thomas Friedkin |
| 15. | Darlington, S.C. | April 30 | Richard Petty | Petty Enterprises |
| 16. | Hampton, Va. | May 7 | Richard Petty | Petty Enterprises |
| 17. | Macon, Ga. | May 10 | Richard Petty | Petty Enterprises |
| 18. | Monroe, N.C. | May 13 | Darel Dieringer | Reid Shaw |
| 19. | Richmond, Va. | May 15 | David Pearson | Cotton Owens |
| 20. | Concord, N.C. | May 22 | Marvin Panch | Petty Enterprises |
| 21. | Moyock, N.C. | May 29 | David Pearson | Cotton Owens |
| 22. | Asheville, N.C. | June 3 | David Pearson | Cotton Owens |
| 23. | Spartanburg, S.C. | June 4 | Elmo Langley | E. Langley/H. Woodfield |
| 24. | Maryville, Tenn. | June 9 | David Pearson | Cotton Owens |
| 25. | Weaverville, N.C. | June 12 | Richard Petty | Petty Enterprises |
| 26. | Beltsville, Md. | June 15 | Tiny Lund | Lyle Stelter |
| 27. | Greenville, S.C. | June 25 | David Pearson | Cotton Owens |
| 28. | Daytona Beach, Fla. | July 4 | Sam McQuagg | Ray Nichels |
| 29. | Manassas, Va. | July 7 | Elmo Langley | E. Langley/H. Woodfield |
| 30. | Bridgehampton, N.Y. | July 10 | David Pearson | Cotton Owens |
| 31. | Oxford, Maine | July 12 | Bobby Allison | Bobby Allison |
| 32. | Fonda, N.Y. | July 14 | David Pearson | Cotton Owens |
| 33. | Islip, N.Y. | July 16 | Bobby Allison | Bobby Allison |
| 34. | Bristol, Tenn. | July 24 | Paul Goldsmith | Ray Nichels |
| 35. | Maryville, Tenn. | July 28 | Paul Lewis | Paul Lewis |
| 36. | Nashville | July 30 | Richard Petty | Petty Enterprises |
| 37. | Hampton, Ga. | Aug. 7 | Richard Petty | Petty Enterprises |
| 38. | Columbia, S.C. | Aug. 18 | David Pearson | Cotton Owens |
| 39. | Weaverville, N.C. | Aug. 21 | Darel Dieringer | Walter "Bud" Moore |
| 40. | Beltsville, Md. | Aug. 24 | Bobby Allison | Bobby Allison |
| 41. | Winston-Salem, N.C. | Aug. 27 | David Pearson | Cotton Owens |
| 42. | Darlington, S.C. | Sept. 5 | Darel Dieringer | Walter "Bud" Moore |
| 43. | Hickory, N.C. | Sept. 9 | David Pearson | Cotton Owens |
| 44. | Richmond, Va. | Sept. 11 | David Pearson | Cotton Owens |
| 45. | Hillsboro, N.C. | Sept. 18 | Dick Hutcherson | Bondy Long |
| 46. | Martinsville, Va. | Sept. 25 | Fred Lorenzen | Holman-Moody |
| 47. | North Wilkesboro, N.C. | Oct. 2 | Dick Hutcherson | Bondy Long |
| 48. | Concord, N.C. | Oct. 16 | LeeRoy Yarbrough | Jon Thorne |
| 49. | Rockingham, N.C. | Oct. 30 | Fred Lorenzen | Holman-Moody |

## Points standings

1. David Pearson .......35,638.00
2. James Hylton .........33,688.00
3. Richard Petty .........22,952.00
4. Henley Gray ...........22,468.00
5. Paul Goldsmith .......22,078.00
6. Wendell Scott .........21,702.00
7. John Sears ............21,432.00
8. J.T. Putney ...........21,208.00
9. Neil Castles ...........20,446.00
10. Bobby Allison .........19,910.00

## Race winners 17

1. David Pearson ......................15
2. Richard Petty ...........................8
3. Bobby Allison ..........................3
   Dick Hutcherson ....................3
   Darel Dieringer ......................3
   Paul Goldsmith ......................3
7. Jim Paschal ..............................2
   Fred Lorenzen .........................2
   Elmo Langley ..........................2
10. Marvin Panch ..........................1
   LeeRoy Yarbrough ..................1
   Sam McQuagg .......................1
   Dan Gurney ............................1
   Earl Balmer ............................1
   Jim Hurtubise .........................1
   Tiny Lund ................................1
   Paul Lewis ..............................1

## Money won leaders

1. Richard Petty ...........$78,840
2. David Pearson.............59,205
3. Darel Dieringer ...........50,960
4. Paul Goldsmith ...........48,075
5. Marvin Panch .............37,385
6. Fred Lorenzen.............36,310
7. James Hylton ..............29,575
8. Jim Paschal ................29,415
9. Sam McQuagg ...........27,960
10. G.C. Spencer...............25,675

## Pole winners 15

1. Richard Petty .....................16
2. David Pearson .....................7
3. Tom Pistone .........................4
   Bobby Allison ......................4
5. Junior Johnson.....................3
6. Jim Paschal ..........................2
   Curtis Turner.........................2
   LeeRoy Yarbrough................2
   Dick Hutcherson...................2
   Fred Lorenzen ......................2
11. Buddy Baker .......................1
   Paul Goldsmith ....................1
   Tiny Lund ..............................1
   Elmo Langley ........................1
   James Hylton ........................1

# 1965 SEASON

| Race No. | Location | Date | Winner | Car owner |
|---|---|---|---|---|
| 1. | Riverside, Calif. | Jan. 17 | Dan Gurney | Wood Brothers |
| 2. | Daytona Beach, Fla. | Feb. 12 | Darel Dieringer | Walter "Bud" Moore |
| 3. | Daytona Beach, Fla. | Feb. 12 | Junior Johnson | Rex Lovette |
| 4. | Daytona Beach, Fla. | Feb. 14 | Fred Lorenzen | Holman-Moody |
| 5. | Spartanburg, S.C. | Feb. 27 | Ned Jarrett | Bondy Long |
| 6. | Weaverville, N.C. | Feb. 28 | Ned Jarrett | Bondy Long |
| 7. | Richmond, Va. | March 7 | Junior Johnson | Rex Lovette |
| 8. | Hillsboro, N.C. | March 14 | Ned Jarrett | Bondy Long |
| 9. | Hampton, Ga. | April 11 | Marvin Panch | Wood Brothers |
| 10. | Greenville, S.C. | April 17 | Dick Hutcherson | Holman-Moody |
| 11. | North Wilkesboro, N.C. | April 18 | Junior Johnson | Rex Lovette |
| 12. | Martinsville, Va. | April 25 | Fred Lorenzen | Holman-Moody |
| 13. | Columbia, S.C. | April 28 | Tiny Lund | Lyle Stelter |
| 14. | Bristol, Tenn. | May 2 | Junior Johnson | Rex Lovette |
| 15. | Darlington, S.C. | May 8 | Junior Johnson | Rex Lovette |
| 16. | Hampton, Va. | May 14 | Ned Jarrett | Bondy Long |
| 17. | Winston-Salem, N.C. | May 15 | Junior Johnson | Rex Lovette |
| 18. | Hickory, N.C. | May 16 | Junior Johnson | Rex Lovette |
| 19. | Concord, N.C. | May 23 | Fred Lorenzen | Holman-Moody |
| 20. | Shelby, N.C. | May 27 | Ned Jarrett | Bondy Long |
| 21. | Asheville, N.C. | May 29 | Junior Johnson | Rex Lovette |
| 22. | Harris, N.C. | May 30 | Ned Jarrett | Bondy Long |
| 23. | Nashville | June 3 | Dick Hutcherson | Holman-Moody |
| 24. | Birmingham, Ala. | June 6 | Ned Jarrett | Bondy Long |
| 25. | Hampton, Ga. | June 13 | Marvin Panch | Wood Brothers |
| 26. | Greenville, S.C. | June 19 | Dick Hutcherson | Holman-Moody |
| 27. | Myrtle Beach, S.C. | June 24 | Dick Hutcherson | Holman-Moody |
| 28. | Valdosta, Ga. | June 27 | Cale Yarborough | Kenny Myler |
| 29. | Daytona Beach, Fla. | July. 4 | A.J. Foyt | Wood Brothers |
| 30. | Manassas, Va. | July 8 | Junior Johnson | Rex Lovette |
| 31. | Old Bridge, N.J. | July 9 | Junior Johnson | Rex Lovette |
| 32. | Islip, N.Y. | July 14 | Marvin Panch | Wood Brothers |
| 33. | Watkins Glen, N.Y. | July 18 | Marvin Panch | Wood Brothers |
| 34. | Bristol, Tenn. | July 25 | Ned Jarrett | Bondy Long |
| 35. | Nashville, Tenn. | July 31 | Richard Petty | Petty Enterprises |
| 36. | Shelby, N.C. | Aug. 5 | Ned Jarrett | Bondy Long |
| 37. | Weaverville, N.C. | Aug. 8 | Richard Petty | Petty Enterprises |
| 38. | Maryville, Tenn. | Aug. 13 | Dick Hutcherson | Holman-Moody |
| 39. | Spartanburg, S.C. | Aug. 14 | Ned Jarrett | Bondy Long |
| 40. | Augusta, Ga. | Aug. 15 | Dick Hutcherson | Holman-Moody |
| 41. | Columbus, Ga. | Aug. 19 | David Pearson | Cotton Owens |
| 42. | Moyock, N.C. | Aug. 24 | Dick Hutcherson | Holman-Moody |
| 43. | Beltsville, Md. | Aug. 25 | Ned Jarrett | Bondy Long |
| 44. | Winston-Salem, N.C. | Aug. 28 | Junior Johnson | Rex Lovette |
| 45. | Darlington, S.C. | Sept. 6 | Ned Jarrett | Bondy Long |
| 46. | Hickory, N.C. | Sept. 10 | Richard Petty | Petty Enterprises |
| 47. | New Oxford, Pa. | Sept. 14 | Dick Hutcherson | Holman-Moody |
| 48. | Manassas, Va. | Sept. 17 | Richard Petty | Petty Enterprises |
| 49. | Richmond, Va. | Sept. 18 | David Pearson | Cotton Owens |
| 50. | Martinsville, Va. | Sept. 26 | Junior Johnson | Rex Lovette |
| 51. | North Wilkesboro, N.C. | Oct. 3 | Junior Johnson | Rex Lovette |
| 52. | Concord, N.C. | Oct. 17 | Fred Lorenzen | Holman-Moody |
| 53. | Hillsboro, N.C. | Oct. 24 | Dick Hutcherson | Holman-Moody |
| 54. | Rockingham, N.C. | Oct. 31 | Curtis Turner | Wood Brothers |
| 55. | Moyock, N.C. | Nov. 7 | Ned Jarrett | Bondy Long |

## Points standings

1. Ned Jarrett ...........38,824.00
2. Dick Hutcherson....35,790.00
3. Darel Dieringer ......24,696.00
4. G.C. Spencer ........24,314.00
5. Marvin Panch .......22,798.00
6. Bob Derrington ......21,394.00
7. J.T. Putney ...........20,928.00
8. Neil Castles .........20,848.00
9. Buddy Baker.........20,672.00
10. Cale Yarborough....20,192.00

## Race winners 13

1. Ned Jarrett ........................13
   Junior Johnson ...................13
3. Dick Hutcherson ..................9
4. Richard Petty ......................4
   Marvin Panch .......................4
   Fred Lorenzen ......................4
7. David Pearson......................2
8. Darel Dieringer ....................1
   Curtis Turner ........................1
   Cale Yarborough ...................1
   Tiny Lund .............................1
   A.J. Foyt ...............................1
   Dan Gurney...........................1

## Money won leaders

1. Ned Jarrett ..............$77,966
2. Fred Lorenzen .........77,115
3. Junior Johnson ..........57,925
4. Marvin Panch ...........54,045
5. Dick Hutcherson ........49,420
6. Darel Dieringer ..........47,775
7. Buddy Baker ..............25,390
8. Cale Yarborough .........24,040
9. Bobby Johns .............23,695
10. G.C. Spencer ..............23,030

## Pole winners 13

1. Junior Johnson....................10
2. Ned Jarrett ..........................9
   Dick Hutcherson ..................9
4. Richard Petty ......................7
5. Fred Lorenzen......................6
6. Marvin Panch ......................5
7. Darel Dieringer ....................2
8. Tom Pistone ........................1
   G.C. Spencer........................1
   David Pearson .....................1
   Bobby Isaac ........................1
   Bud Moore ..........................1
   Paul Lewis ..........................1

# 1964 SEASON

| Race No. | Location | Date | Winner | Car owner |
|---|---|---|---|---|
| 1. | Concord, N.C. | Nov. 10 | Ned Jarrett | Charles Robinson |
| 2. | Augusta, Ga. | Nov. 17 | Fireball Roberts | Holman-Moody |
| 3. | Jacksonville, Fla. | Dec. 1 | Wendell Scott | Wendell Scott |
| 4. | Savannah, Ga. | Dec. 29 | Richard Petty | Petty Enterprises |
| 5. | Riverside, Calif. | Jan. 19 | Dan Gurney | Wood Brothers |
| 6. | Daytona Beach, Fla. | Feb. 21 | Junior Johnson | Raymond Fox |
| 7. | Daytona Beach, Fla. | Feb. 21 | Bobby Isaac | Ray Nichels |
| 8. | Daytona Beach, Fla. | Feb. 23 | Richard Petty | Petty Enterprises |
| 9. | Richmond, Va. | March 10 | David Pearson | Cotton Owens |
| 10. | Bristol, Tenn. | March 22 | Fred Lorenzen | Holman-Moody |
| 11. | Greenville, S.C. | March 28 | David Pearson | Cotton Owens |
| 12. | Winston-Salem, N.C. | March 30 | Marvin Panch | Wood Brothers |
| 13. | Hampton, Ga. | April 5 | Fred Lorenzen | Holman-Moody |
| 14. | Weaverville, N.C. | April 11 | Marvin Panch | Wood Brothers |
| 15. | Hillsboro, N.C. | April 12 | David Pearson | Cotton Owens |
| 16. | Spartanburg, S.C. | April 14 | Ned Jarrett | Bondy Long |
| 17. | Columbia, S.C. | April 16 | Ned Jarrett | Bondy Long |
| 18. | North Wilkesboro, N.C. | April 19 | Fred Lorenzen | Holman-Moody |
| 19. | Martinsville, Va. | April 26 | Fred Lorenzen | Holman-Moody |
| 20. | Savannah, Ga. | May 1 | LeeRoy Yarbrough | Louie Weathersby |
| 21. | Darlington, S.C. | May 9 | Fred Lorenzen | Holman-Moody |
| 22. | Hampton, Va. | May 15 | Ned Jarrett | Bondy Long |
| 23. | Hickory, N.C. | May 16 | Ned Jarrett | Bondy Long |
| 24. | South Boston, Va. | May 17 | Richard Petty | Petty Enterprises |
| 25. | Concord, N.C. | May 24 | Jim Paschal | Petty Enterprises |
| 26. | Greenville, S.C. | May 30 | LeeRoy Yarbrough | Louie Weathersby |
| 27. | Asheville, N.C. | May 31 | Ned Jarrett | Bondy Long |
| 28. | Hampton, Ga. | June 7 | Ned Jarrett | Bondy Long |
| 29. | Concord, N.C. | June 11 | Richard Petty | Petty Enterprises |
| 30. | Nashville, Tenn. | June 14 | Richard Petty | Petty Enterprises |
| 31. | Chattanooga | June 19 | David Pearson | Cotton Owens |
| 32. | Birmingham, Ala. | June 21 | Ned Jarrett | Bondy Long |
| 33. | Valdosta, Ga. | June 23 | Buck Baker | Raymond Fox |
| 34. | Spartanburg, S.C. | June 26 | Richard Petty | Petty Enterprises |
| 35. | Daytona Beach, Fla. | July 4 | A.J. Foyt | Ray Nichels |
| 36. | Manassas, Va. | July 8 | Ned Jarrett | Bondy Long |
| 37. | Old Bridge, N.J. | July 10 | Billy Wade | Walter "Bud" Moore |
| 38. | Bridgehampton, N.Y. | July 12 | Billy Wade | Walter "Bud" Moore |
| 39. | Islip, N.Y. | July 15 | Billy Wade | Walter "Bud" Moore |
| 40. | Watkins Glen, N.Y. | July 19 | Billy Wade | Walter "Bud" Moore |
| 41. | New Oxford, Pa. | July 21 | David Pearson | Cotton Owens |
| 42. | Bristol, Tenn. | July 26 | Fred Lorenzen | Holman-Moody |
| 43. | Nashville, Tenn. | Aug. 2 | Richard Petty | Petty Enterprises |
| 44. | Myrtle Beach, S.C. | Aug. 7 | David Pearson | Cotton Owens |
| 45. | Weaverville, N.C. | Aug. 9 | Ned Jarrett | Bondy Long |
| 46. | Moyock, N.C. | Aug. 13 | Ned Jarrett | Bondy Long |
| 47. | Huntington, W.Va. | Aug. 16 | Richard Petty | Petty Enterprises |
| 48. | Columbia, S.C. | Aug. 21 | David Pearson | Cotton Owens |
| 49. | Winston-Salem, N.C. | Aug. 22 | Junior Johnson | Banjo Matthews |
| 50. | Roanoke, Va. | Aug. 23 | Junior Johnson | Banjo Matthews |
| 51. | Darlington, S.C. | Sept. 7 | Buck Baker | Raymond Fox |
| 52. | Hickory, N.C. | Sept. 11 | David Pearson | Cotton Owens |
| 53. | Richmond, Va. | Sept. 14 | Cotton Owens | Cotton Owens |
| 54. | Manassas, Va. | Sept. 18 | Ned Jarrett | Bondy Long |
| 55. | Hillsboro, N.C. | Sept. 20 | Ned Jarrett | Bondy Long |
| 56. | Martinsville, Va. | Sept. 27 | Fred Lorenzen | Holman-Moody |
| 57. | Savannah, Ga. | Oct. 9 | Ned Jarrett | Bondy Long |
| 58. | North Wilkesboro, N.C. | Oct. 11 | Marvin Panch | Wood Brothers |
| 59. | Concord, N.C. | Oct. 18 | Fred Lorenzen | Holman-Moody |
| 60. | Harris, N.C. | Oct. 25 | Richard Petty | Petty Enterprises |
| 61. | Augusta, Ga. | Nov. 1 | Darel Dieringer | Walter "Bud" Moore |
| 62. | Jacksonville, N.C. | Nov. 8 | Ned Jarrett | Bondy Long |

HISTORY

## Points standings

1. Richard Petty .........40,252.00
2. Ned Jarrett ............34,950.00
3. David Pearson.........32,146.00
4. Billy Wade..............28,474.00
5. Jimmy Pardue .......26,570.00
6. Curtis Crider ..........25,606.00
7. Jim Paschal ...........25,450.00
8. Larry Thomas .........22,950.00
9. Buck Baker.............22,366.00
10. Marvin Panch .........21,480.00

## Race winners 17

1. Ned Jarrett ....................15
2. Richard Petty....................9
3. Fred Lorenzen ..................8
   David Pearson..................8
5. Billy Wade .......................4
6. Junior Johnson .................3
   Marvin Panch ...................3
8. LeeRoy Yarbrough .............2
   Buck Baker ......................2
10. Wendell Scott ...................1
    Fireball Roberts .................1
    Dan Gurney .......................1
    A.J. Foyt ...........................1
    Darel Dieringer ..................1
    Jim Paschal .......................1
    Cotton Owens .....................1
    Bobby Isaac ......................1

## Money won leaders

1. Richard Petty ..................$98,810
2. Fred Lorenzen ...................72,385
3. Ned Jarrett........................63,330
4. Jim Paschal ......................54,960
5. Buck Baker .......................41,080
6. David Pearson ...................38,175
7. Jimmy Pardue ...................36,440
8. Marvin Panch ....................32,135
9. Billy Wade ........................29,710
10. Fireball Roberts ................28,345

## Pole winners 14

1. David Pearson ...........................12
2. Ned Jarrett .................................9
   Richard Petty .............................9
4. Fred Lorenzen .............................7
5. Marvin Panch...............................5
   Billy Wade ...................................5
   Junior Johnson .............................5
8. Paul Goldsmith .............................2
   Dick Hutcherson ...........................2
   Jimmy Pardue ..............................2
11. Glen Wood ..................................1
    Doug Yates..................................1
    Jack Smith ..................................1
    Darel Dieringer ...........................1

# 1963 SEASON

| Race No. | Location | Date | Winner | Car owner |
|---|---|---|---|---|
| 1. | Birmingham, Ala. | Nov. 4 | Jim Paschal | Petty Enterprises |
| 2. | Tampa, Fla. | Nov. 11 | Richard Petty | Petty Enterprises |
| 3. | Randleman, N.C. | Nov. 22 | Jim Paschal | Petty Enterprises |
| 4. | Riverside, Calif. | Jan. 20 | Dan Gurney | Holman-Moody |
| 5. | Daytona Beach, Fla. | Feb. 22 | Junior Johnson | Raymond Fox |
| 6. | Daytona Beach, Fla. | Feb. 22 | Johnny Rutherford | Smokey Yunick |
| 7. | Daytona Beach, Fla. | Feb. 24 | Tiny Lund | Wood Brothers |
| 8. | Spartanburg, S.C. | March 2 | Richard Petty | Petty Enterprises |
| 9. | Weaverville, N.C. | March 3 | Richard Petty | Petty Enterprises |
| 10. | Hillsboro, N.C. | March 10 | Junior Johnson | Raymond Fox |
| 11. | Hampton, Ga. | March 17 | Fred Lorenzen | Holman-Moody |
| 12. | Hickory, N.C. | March 24 | Junior Johnson | Raymond Fox |
| 13. | Bristol, Tenn. | Marcg 31 | Fireball Roberts | Holman-Moody |
| 14. | Augusta, Ga. | April 4 | Ned Jarrett | Charles Robinson |
| 15. | Richmond, Va. | April 7 | Joe Weatherly | Walter "Bud" Moore |
| 16. | Greenville, S.C. | April 13 | Buck Baker | Buck Baker |
| 17. | South Boston, Va. | April 14 | Richard Petty | Petty Enterprises |
| 18. | Winston-Salem, N.C. | April 15 | Jim Paschal | Petty Enterprises |
| 19. | Martinsville, Va. | April 21 | Richard Petty | Petty Enterprises |
| 20. | North Wilkesboro, N.C. | April 28 | Richard Petty | Petty Enterprises |
| 21. | Columbia, S.C. | May 2 | Richard Petty | Petty Enterprises |
| 22. | Randleman, N.C. | May 5 | Jim Paschal | Petty Enterprises |
| 23. | Darlington, S.C. | May 11 | Joe Weatherly | Walter "Bud" Moore |
| 24. | Manassas, Va. | May 18 | Richard Petty | Petty Enterprises |
| 25. | Richmond, Va. | May 19 | Ned Jarrett | Charles Robinson |
| 26. | Concord, N.C. | June 2 | Fred Lorenzen | Holman-Moody |
| 27. | Birmingham, Ala. | June 9 | Richard Petty | Petty Enterprises |
| 28. | Hampton, Ga. | June 30 | Junior Johnson | Raymond Fox |
| 29. | Daytona Beach, Fla. | Jule 4 | Fireball Roberts | Holman-Moody |
| 30. | Myrtle Beach, S.C. | July 7 | Ned Jarrett | Charles Robinson |
| 31. | Savannah, Ga. | July 10 | Ned Jarrett | Charles Robinson |
| 32. | Moyock, N.C. | July 11 | Jimmy Pardue | Peter Stewart |
| 33. | Winston-Salem, N.C. | July 13 | Glen Wood | Wood Brothers |
| 34. | Asheville, N.C. | July 14 | Ned Jarrett | Charles Robinson |
| 35. | Old Bridge, N.J. | July 19 | Fireball Roberts | Holman-Moody |
| 36. | Bridgehampton, N.Y. | July 21 | Richard Petty | Petty Enterprises |
| 37. | Bristol, Tenn. | July 28 | Fred Lorenzen | Holman-Moody |
| 38. | Greenville, S.C. | July 30 | Richard Petty | Petty Enterprises |
| 39. | Nashville | Aug. 4 | Jim Paschal | Petty Enterprises |
| 40. | Columbia, S.C. | Aug. 8 | Richard Petty | Petty Enterprises |
| 41. | Weaverville, N.C. | Aug. 11 | Fred Lorenzen | Holman-Moody |
| 42. | Spartanburg, S.C. | Aug. 14 | Ned Jarrett | Charles Robinson |
| 43. | Winston-Salem, N.C. | Aug. 16 | Junior Johnson | Raymond Fox |
| 44. | Huntington, W.Va. | Aug. 18 | Fred Lorenzen | Holman-Moody |
| 45. | Darlington, S.C. | Sept. 2 | Fireball Roberts | Holman-Moody |
| 46. | Hickory, N.C. | Sept. 6 | Junior Johnson | Raymond Fox |
| 47. | Richmond, Va. | Sept. 8 | Ned Jarrett | Charles Robinson |
| 48. | Martinsville, Va. | Sept. 22 | Fred Lorenzen | Holman-Moody |
| 49. | Moyock, N.C. | Sept. 24 | Ned Jarrett | Charles Robinson |
| 50. | North Wilkesboro, N.C. | Sept. 29 | Marvin Panch | Wood Brothers |
| 51. | Randleman, N.C. | Oct. 5 | Richard Petty | Petty Enterprises |
| 52. | Concord, N.C. | Oct. 13 | Junior Johnson | Raymond Fox |
| 53. | South Boston, Va. | Oct. 20 | Richard Petty | Petty Enterprises |
| 54. | Hillsboro, N.C. | Oct. 27 | Joe Weatherly | Walter "Bud" Moore |
| 55. | Riverside, Calif. | Nov. 3 | Darel Dieringer | William Stroppe |

## Points standings

1. Joe Weatherly ..........33,398.00
2. Richard Petty ..........31,170.00
3. Fred Lorenzen ..........29,684.00
4. Ned Jarrett ..............27,214.00
5. Fireball Roberts........22,642.00
6. Jimmy Pardue..........22,228.00
7. Darel Dieringer .......21,418.00
8. David Pearson..........21,156.00
9. Rex White ..............20,976.00
10. Tiny Lund ..............19,624.00

## Race winners 15

1. Richard Petty ..........................14
2. Ned Jarrett ................................8
3. Junior Johnson ..........................7
4. Fred Lorenzen ............................6
5. Jim Paschal ...............................5
6. Fireball Roberts ..........................4
7. Joe Weatherly ............................3
8. Glen Wood ................................1
   Johnny Rutherford ....................1
   Dan Gurney ...............................1
   Darel Dieringer ..........................1
   Buck Baker .................................1
   Jimmy Pardue ............................1
   Marvin Panch ............................1
   Tiny Lund ..................................1

## Money won leaders

1. Fred Lorenzen ............$113,570
2. Fireball Roberts................67,320
3. Junior Johnson................65,710
4. Joe Weatherly ..................57,710
5. Richard Petty ..................47,765
6. Tiny Lund ......................40,930
7. Ned Jarrett ....................38,740
8. Marvin Panch ................37,461
9. Darel Dieringer ..............25,575
10. Rex White ......................24,235

## Pole winners 15

1. Junior Johnson........................9
   Fred Lorenzen .........................9
3. Richard Petty ..........................8
4. Joe Weatherly ..........................6
5. Ned Jarrett ..............................4
6. Rex White ................................3
   Marvin Panch ...........................3
8. Glen Wood ...............................2
   Jack Smith ................................2
   Fireball Roberts.........................2
   David Pearson...........................2
12. Paul Goldsmith .......................1
    LeeRoy Yarbrough ..................1
    Jim Paschal..............................1
    Jimmy Pardue..........................1

HISTORY

# FAST FREDDY: SHORT BUT SWEET

Fred Lorenzen became the first driver to win $100,000 in a season when he won $113,570 in 1963. He won six races in 29 starts that season, finishing third in the points race. Lorenzen won 26 races in his short, illustrious career—he made just 158 starts driving in 12 different seasons. He retired after the 1967 season and made a brief return, running 29 races combined in 1970, 1971 and 1972.

He later said he quit too soon, and his statistics suggest he could have been one of the all-time greats. Even with his limited experience, he's considered among the top 25 drivers of all time. Extrapolate his starts-to-wins ratio to Richard Petty's start total, and Lorenzen was on pace for 194 wins. Petty had 200.

# 1962 SEASON

| Race No. | Location | Date | Winner | Car owner |
|---|---|---|---|---|
| 1. | Concord, N.C. | Nov. 5 | Jack Smith | Jack Smith |
| 2. | Weaverville, N.C. | Nov. 12 | Rex White | Rex White |
| 3. | Daytona Beach, Fla. | Feb. 16 | Fireball Roberts | Jim Stephens |
| 4. | Daytona Beach, Fla. | Feb. 16 | Joe Weatherly | Bud Moore |
| 5. | Daytona Beach, Fla. | Feb. 18 | Fireball Roberts | Jim Stephens |
| 6. | Concord, N.C. | Feb. 25 | Joe Weatherly | Bud Moore |
| 7. | Weaverville, N.C. | March 4 | Joe Weatherly | Bud Moore |
| 8. | Savannah, Ga. | March 17 | Jack Smith | Jack Smith |
| 9. | Hillsboro, N.C. | March 18 | Rex White | Rex White |
| 10. | Richmond, Va. | April 1 | Rex White | Rex White |
| 11. | Columbia, S.C. | April 13 | Ned Jarrett | Bee Gee Holloway |
| 12. | North Wilkesboro, N.C. | April 15 | Richard Petty | Petty Enterprises |
| 13. | Greenville, S.C. | April 19 | Ned Jarrett | Bee Gee Holloway |
| 14. | Myrtle Beach, S.C. | April 21 | Jack Smith | Jack Smith |
| 15. | Martinsville, Va. | April 22 | Richard Petty | Petty Enterprises |
| 16. | Winston-Salem, N.C. | April 23 | Rex White | Rex White |
| 17. | Bristol, Tenn. | April 29 | Bobby Johns | Shorty Johns |
| 18. | Richmond, Va. | May 4 | Jimmy Pardue | Jimmy Pardue |
| 19. | Hickory, N.C. | May 5 | Jack Smith | Jack Smith |
| 20. | Concord, N.C. | May 6 | Joe Weatherly | Bud Moore |
| 21. | Darlington, S.C. | May 12 | Nelson Stacy | Holman-Moody |
| 22. | Spartanburg, S.C. | May 19 | Ned Jarrett | Bee Gee Holloway |
| 23. | Concord, N.C. | May 27 | Nelson Stacy | Holman-Moody |
| 24. | Hampton, Ga. | June 10 | Fred Lorenzen | Holman-Moody |
| 25. | Winston-Salem, N.C. | June 16 | Johnny Allen | Fred Lovette |
| 26. | Augusta, Ga. | June 19 | Joe Weatherly | Bud Moore |
| 27. | Richmond, Va. | June 22 | Jim Paschal | Cliff Stewart |
| 28. | South Boston, Va. | June 23 | Rex White | Rex White |
| 29. | Daytona Beach, Fla. | July 4 | Fireball Roberts | Banjo Matthews |
| 30. | Columbia, S.C. | July 7 | Rex White | Rex White |
| 31. | Asheville, N.C. | July 13 | Jack Smith | Jack Smith |
| 32. | Greenville, S.C. | July 14 | Richard Petty | Petty Enterprises |
| 33. | Augusta, Ga. | July 17 | Joe Weatherly | Bud Moore |
| 34. | Savannah, Ga. | July 20 | Joe Weatherly | Bud Moore |
| 35. | Myrtle Beach, S.C. | July 21 | Ned Jarrett | Bee Gee Holloway |
| 36. | Bristol, Tenn. | July 29 | Jim Paschal | Petty Enterprises |
| 37. | Chattanooga, Tenn. | Aug. 3 | Joe Weatherly | Bud Moore |
| 38. | Nashville | Aug. 5 | Jim Paschal | Petty Enterprises |
| 39. | Huntsville, Ala. | Aug. 8 | Richard Petty | Petty Enterprises |
| 40. | Weaverville, N.C. | Aug. 12 | Jim Paschal | Petty Enterprises |
| 41. | Roanoke, Va. | Aug. 15 | Richard Petty | Petty Enterprises |
| 42. | Winston-Salem, N.C. | Aug. 18 | Richard Petty | Petty Enterprises |
| 43. | Spartanburg, S.C. | Aug. 21 | Richard Petty | Petty Enterprises |
| 44. | Valdosta, Ga. | Aug. 25 | Ned Jarrett | Bee Gee Holloway |
| 45. | Darlington, S.C. | Sept. 3 | Larry Frank | Ratus Walters |
| 46. | Hickory, N.C. | Sept. 7 | Rex White | Rex White |
| 47. | Richmond, Va. | Sept. 9 | Joe Weatherly | Bud Moore |
| 48. | Moyock, N.C. | Sept. 11 | Ned Jarrett | Bee Gee Holloway |
| 49. | Augusta, Ga. | Sept. 13 | Fred Lorenzen | Mamie Reynolds |
| 50. | Martinsville, Va. | Sept. 23 | Nelson Stacy | Holman-Moody |
| 51. | North Wilkesboro, N.C. | Sept. 30 | Richard Petty | Petty Enterprises |
| 52. | Concord, N.C. | Oct. 14 | Junior Johnson | Raymond Fox |
| 53. | Hampton, Ga. | Oct. 28 | Rex White | Rex White |

## Points standings

1. Joe Weatherly ..........30,836.00
2. Richard Petty............28,440.00
3. Ned Jarrett ..............25,336.00
4. Jack Smith ..............22,870.00
5. Rex White ...............19,424.00
6. Jim Paschal..............18,128.00
7. Fred Lorenzen ..........17,554.00
8. Fireball Roberts ........16,380.00
9. Marvin Panch ..........15,138.00
10. David Pearson ..........14,404.00

## Race winners 14

1. Joe Weatherly ......................9
2. Richard Petty ......................8
   Rex White............................8
4. Ned Jarrett..........................6
5. Jack Smith..........................5
6. Jim Paschal ........................4
7. Nelson Stacy ......................3
   Fireball Roberts ..................3
9. Fred Lorenzen .....................2
10. Larry Frank.........................1
    Johnny Allen .......................1
    Bobby Johns .......................1
    Jimmy Pardue .....................1
    Junior Johnson.....................1

## Money won leaders

1. Joe Weatherly ...........$55,055
2. Richard Petty .............52,885
3. Fireball Roberts...........51,970
4. Fred Lorenzen ............42,948
5. Nelson Stacy ..............42,515
6. Ned Jarrett ................35,320
7. Junior Johnson ...........33,940
8. Larry Frank ................31,410
9. Rex White ..................30,643
10. Jack Smith ................28,485

## Pole winners 13

1. Fireball Roberts ...................9
   Rex White............................9
3. Jack Smith ..........................7
   Joe Weatherly......................7
5. Richard Petty ......................4
   Ned Jarrett...........................4
7. Fred Lorenzen......................3
8. Junior Johnson.....................2
   Banjo Matthews ...................2
10. Wendell Scott ......................1
    Johnny Allen.........................1
    Darel Dieringer .....................1
    Cotton Owens.......................1

HISTORY

# 1961 SEASON

| Race No. | Location | Date | Winner | Car owner |
|---|---|---|---|---|
| 1. | Charlotte | Nov. 6 | Joe Weatherly | Dr. Bradford White |
| 2. | Jacksonville, Fla. | Nov. 20 | Lee Petty | Petty Enterprises |
| 3. | Daytona Beach, Fla. | Feb. 24 | Fireball Roberts | Jim Stephens |
| 4. | Daytona Beach, Fla. | Feb. 24 | Joe Weatherly | Bud Moore |
| 5. | Daytona Beach, Fla. | Feb. 26 | Marvin Panch | Smokey Yunick |
| 6. | Spartanburg, S.C. | March 4 | Cotton Owens | Cotton Owens |
| 7. | Weaverville, N.C. | March 5 | Rex White | Rex White |
| 8. | Hanford, Calif. | March 12 | Fireball Roberts | J.D. Braswell |
| 9. | Hampton, Ga. | March 26 | Bob Burdick | Roy Burdick |
| 10. | Greenville, S.C. | April 1 | Emanuel Zervakis | Monroe Shook |
| 11. | Hillsboro, N.C. | April 2 | Cotton Owens | Cotton Owens |
| 12. | Winston-Salem, N.C. | April 3 | Rex White | Rex White |
| 13. | Martinsville, Va. | April 9 | Fred Lorenzen | Holman-Moody |
| 14. | North Wilkesboro, N.C. | April 16 | Rex White | Rex White |
| 15. | Columbia, S.C. | April 20 | Cotton Owens | Cotton Owens |
| 16. | Hickory, N.C. | April 22 | Junior Johnson | Rex Lovette |
| 17. | Richmond, Va. | April 23 | Richard Petty | Petty Enterprises |
| 18. | Martinsville, Va. | April 30 | Junior Johnson | Rex Lovette |
| 19. | Darlington, S.C. | May 6 | Fred Lorenzen | Holman-Moody |
| 20. | Concord, N.C. | May 21 | Richard Petty | Petty Enterprises |
| 21. | Concord, N.C. | May 21 | Joe Weatherly | Bud Moore |
| 22. | Riverside, Calif. | May 21 | Lloyd Dane | Lloyd Dane |
| 23. | Los Angles, Calif. | May 27 | Eddie Gray | Eddie Gray |
| 24. | Concord, N.C. | May 28 | David Pearson | John Masoni |
| 25. | Spartanburg, S.C. | June 2 | Jim Paschal | J.H. Petty |
| 26. | Birmingham, Ala. | June 4 | Ned Jarrett | Bee Gee Holloway |
| 27. | Greenville, S.C. | June 8 | Jack Smith | Jack Smith |
| 28. | Winston-Salem, N.C. | June 10 | Rex White | Rex White |
| 29. | Norwood, Mass. | June 17 | Emanuel Zervakis | Monroe Shook |
| 30. | Hartsville, S.C. | June 23 | Buck Baker | Buck Baker |
| 31. | Roanoke, Va. | June 24 | Junior Johnson | Rex Lovette |
| 32. | Daytona Beach, Fla. | July 4 | David Pearson | John Masoni |
| 33. | Hampton, Ga. | July 9 | Fred Lorenzen | Holman-Moody |
| 34. | Columbia, S.C. | July 20 | Cotton Owens | Cotton Owens |
| 35. | Myrtle Beach, S.C. | July 22 | Joe Weatherly | Bud Moore |
| 36. | Bristol, Tenn. | July 30 | Jack Smith | Jack Smith |
| 37. | Nashville | Aug. 6 | Jim Paschal | J.H. Petty |
| 38. | Winston-Salem, N.C. | Aug. 9 | Rex White | Rex White |
| 39. | Weaverville, N.C. | Aug. 13 | Junior Johnson | Rex Lovette |
| 40. | Richmond, Va. | Aug. 18 | Junior Johnson | Rex Lovette |
| 41. | South Boston, Va. | Aug. 27 | Junior Johnson | Rex Lovette |
| 42. | Darlington, S.C. | Sept. 4 | Nelson Stacy | Dudley Farrell |
| 43. | Hickory, N.C. | Sept. 8 | Rex White | Rex White |
| 44. | Richmond, Va. | Sept. 10 | Joe Weatherly | Bud Moore |
| 45. | Sacramento, Calif. | Sept. 10 | Eddie Gray | Eddie Gray |
| 46. | Hampton, Ga. | Sept. 17 | David Pearson | John Masoni |
| 47. | Martinsville, Va. | Sept. 24 | Joe Weatherly | Bud Moore |
| 48. | North Wilkesboro, N.C. | Oct. 1 | Rex White | Rex White |
| 49. | Concord, N.C. | Oct. 15 | Joe Weatherly | Bud Moore |
| 50. | Bristol, Tenn. | Oct. 22 | Joe Weatherly | Bud Moore |
| 51. | Greenville, S.C. | Oct. 28 | Junior Johnson | Rex Lovette |
| 52. | Hillsboro, N.C. | Oct. 29 | Joe Weatherly | Bud Moore |

## Points standings

1. Ned Jarrett ............27,272.00
2. Rex White ............26,442.00
3. Emanuel Zervakis ..22,312.00
4. Joe Weatherly ........17,894.00
5. Fireball Roberts ......17,600.00
6. Junior Johnson ......17,178.00
7. Jack Smith ............15,186.00
8. Richard Petty..........14,984.00
9. Jim Paschal............13,922.00
10. Buck Baker ............13,746.00

## Race winners

1. Joe Weatherly ..........................9
2. Junior Johnson ........................7
   Rex White ................................7
4. Cotton Owens ..........................4
5. David Pearson ........................3
   Fred Lorenzen ........................3
7. Richard Petty............................2
   Emanuel Zervakis ....................2
   Jack Smith ................................2
   Fireball Roberts ........................2
   Eddie Gray................................2
   Jim Paschal..............................2
13. Lloyd Dane ..............................1
   Bob Burdick..............................1
   Buck Baker ..............................1
   Nelson Stacy ............................1
   Marvin Panch ..........................1
   Ned Jarrett ..............................1
   Lee Petty ..................................1

## Money won leaders

1. David Pearson ............$49,580
2. Rex White ..................48,830
3. Joe Weatherly ..............39,965
4. Fireball Roberts ..........38,300
5. Fred Lorenzen ............29,655
6. Marvin Panch ............28,865
7. Ned Jarrett ..................27,235
8. Nelson Stacy ..............26,760
9. Junior Johnson ............25,310
10. Richard Petty ..............22,671

## Pole winners

1. Junior Johnson ........................10
2. Rex White ................................7
3. Fireball Roberts ........................6
4. Joe Weatherly ..........................4
   Fred Lorenzen ..........................4
   Ned Jarrett ..............................4
7. Cotton Owens ..........................2
   Richard Petty............................2
9. Emanuel Zervakis ....................1
   Danny Weinberg ......................1
   Glen Wood................................1
   Bob Ross..................................1
   Lee Petty ..................................1
   Buck Baker ..............................1
   Eddie Gray................................1
   Johnny Allen ............................1
   Bill Amick ................................1
   Jim Paschal..............................1
   David Pearson ..........................1
   Bobby Johns ............................1
   Marvin Panch ..........................1

# 1960 SEASON

| Race No. | Location | Date | Winner | Car owner |
|---|---|---|---|---|
| 1. | Charlotte | Nov. 8 | Jack Smith | Jack Smith |
| 2. | Columbia, S.C. | Nov. 26 | Ned Jarrett | Ned Jarrett |
| 3. | Daytona Beach, Fla. | Feb. 12 | Fireball Roberts | John Hines |
| 4. | Daytona Beach, Fla. | Feb. 12 | Jack Smith | Jack Smith |
| 5. | Daytona Beach, Fla. | Feb. 14 | Junior Johnson | John Masoni |
| 6. | Charlotte, N.C. | Feb. 28 | Richard Petty | Petty Enterprises |
| 7. | North Wilkesboro, N.C. | March 27 | Lee Petty | Petty Enterprises |
| 8. | Phoenix | April 3 | John Rostek | John Rostek |
| 9. | Columbia, S.C. | April 5 | Rex White | Rex White |
| 10. | Martinsville, Va. | April 10 | Richard Petty | Petty Enterprises |
| 11. | Hickory, N.C. | April 16 | Joe Weatherly | Holman-Moody |
| 12. | Wilson, N.C. | April 17 | Joe Weatherly | Holman-Moody |
| 13. | Winston-Salem, N.C. | April 18 | Glen Wood | Wood Brothers |
| 14. | Greenville, S.C. | April 23 | Ned Jarrett | Ned Jarrett |
| 15. | Weaverville, N.C. | April 24 | Lee Petty | Petty Enterprises |
| 16. | Darlington, S.C. | May 14 | Joe Weatherly | Holman-Moody |
| 17. | Spartanburg, S.C. | May 28 | Ned Jarrett | Ned Jarrett |
| 18. | Hillsboro, N.C. | May 29 | Lee Petty | Petty Enterprises |
| 19. | Richmond, Va. | June 5 | Lee Petty | Petty Enterprises |
| 20. | Hanford, Calif. | June 12 | Marvin Porter | Vel Miletich |
| 21. | Concord, N.C. | June 19 | Joe Lee Johnson | Paul McDuffie |
| 22. | Winston-Salem, N.C. | June 26 | Glen Wood | Wood Brothers |
| 23. | Daytona Beach, Fla. | July 4 | Jack Smith | Jack Smith |
| 24. | Heidelburg, Pa. | July 10 | Lee Petty | Petty Enterprises |
| 25. | Montgomery, N.Y. | July 17 | Rex White | Rex White |
| 26. | Myrtle Beach, S.C. | July 23 | Buck Baker | Buck Baker |
| 27. | Hampton, Ga. | July 31 | Fireball Roberts | John Hines |
| 28. | Birmingham, Ala. | Aug. 3 | Ned Jarrett | Ned Jarrett |
| 29. | Nashville | Aug. 7 | Johnny Beauchamp | Dale Swanson |
| 30. | Weaverville, N.C. | Aug. 14 | Rex White | Rex White |
| 31. | Spartanburg, S.C. | Aug. 16 | Cotton Owens | Cotton Owens |
| 32. | Columbia, S.C. | Aug. 18 | Rex White | Rex White |
| 33. | South Boston, Va. | Aug. 20 | Junior Johnson | John Masoni |
| 34. | Winston-Salem, N.C. | Aug. 23 | Glen Wood | Wood Brothers |
| 35. | Darlington, S.C. | Sept. 5 | Buck Baker | Jack Smith |
| 36. | Hickory, N.C. | Sept. 9 | Junior Johnson | John Masoni |
| 37. | Sacramento | Sept. 11 | Jim Cook | Floyd Johnson |
| 38. | Sumter, S.C. | Sept. 15 | Ned Jarrett | Ned Jarrett |
| 39. | Hillsboro, N.C. | Sept. 18 | Richard Petty | Petty Enterprises |
| 40. | Martinsville, Va. | Sept. 25 | Rex White | Rex White |
| 41. | North Wilkesboro, N.C. | Oct. 2 | Rex White | Rex White |
| 42. | Concord, N.C. | Oct. 16 | Speedy Thompson | Wood Brothers |
| 43. | Richmond, Va. | Oct. 23 | Speedy Thompson | Wood Brothers |
| 44. | Hampton, Ga. | Oct. 30 | Bobby Johns | Cotton Owens |

## Points standings

1. Rex White .............21,164.00
2. Richard Petty .........17,228.00
3. Bobby Johns .........14,964.00
4. Buck Baker ...........14,674.00
5. Ned Jarrett............14,660.00
6. Lee Petty ..............14,510.00
7. Junior Johnson..........9,932.00
8. Emanuel Zervakis......9,720.00
9. Jim Paschal .............8,968.00
10. Banjo Matthews .......8,458.00

## Race winners

1. Rex White ..............................6
2. Ned Jarrett.............................5
   Lee Petty .............................5
4. Junior Johnson .....................3
   Richard Petty .......................3
   Jack Smith ............................3
   Glen Wood ...........................3
   Joe Weatherly .....................3
9. Fireball Roberts ...................2
   Buck Baker ...........................2
   Speedy Thompson ...............2
12. John Rostek .........................1
   Bobby Johns .......................1
   Joe Lee Johnson ................1
   Jim Cook ..............................1
   Marvin Porter ......................1
   Johnny Beauchamp ............1
   Cotton Owens.....................1

## Money won leaders

1. Rex White...............$45,280
2. Bobby Johns .............40,840
3. Richard Petty .............35,180
4. Buck Baker ................33,915
5. Joe Lee Johnson ........33,388
6. Junior Johnson............30,775
7. Lee Petty ....................26,650
8. Jack Smith..................23,590
9. Ned Jarrett.................20,540
10. Fireball Roberts ..........19,895

## Pole winners

1. Fireball Roberts....................6
2. Ned Jarrett ...........................5
3. Jack Smith ...........................4
   Glen Wood ..........................4
5. Cotton Owens .....................3
   Lee Petty..............................3
   Rex White.............................3
   Junior Johnson .....................3
9. Richard Petty .......................2
   Buck Baker ...........................2
11. Jim Cook .............................1
   Curtis Turner .......................1
   Doug Yates ..........................1
   Emanuel Zervakis ................1
   Mel Larson ...........................1
   David Pearson.......................1
   John Rostek .........................1
   Tommy Irwin........................1
   Frank Secrist ........................1

# 1960 SEASON

## Grand openings: The superspeedway era officially begins

Today, NASCAR is dominated by big, wide-open tracks that allow cars to reach high speeds. But that wasn't always the case. In fact, the superspeedway era didn't officially begin until 1960, when Atlanta Motor Speedway (July 31, Dixie 300) and Charlotte Motor Speedway (June 19, World 600) opened.

Fireball Roberts won the Dixie 300 from the pole, piloting his Pontiac at an average speed of 112.653 mph. Joe Lee Johnson drove a Chevrolet to victory lane in the World 600 after starting 20th. His average speed of 107.735 mph is by far the lowest of any Cup race held there.

Both tracks have grown into popular and historic destinations, each seeing its share of monumental events.

From 1987 to 2000, Atlanta hosted the last race of the season, with all the attendant drama. Charlotte—now known as Lowe's Motor Speedway—hosts the yearly All-Star race, a popular nonpoints event that allows drivers to race all-out and not worry about the implications for the season.

Atlanta stands out as the circuit's fastest track, especially in the restrictor-plate era. Charlotte is well-known for hosting many of promoter H.A. "Humpy" Wheeler's zany ideas to promote the sport, whether it's paying heartfelt tribute to soldiers overseas or cajoling Elizabeth Taylor into being the grand marshal.

# 1959 SEASON

| Race No. | Location | Date | Winner | Car owner |
|---|---|---|---|---|
| 1. | Fayetteville, N.C. | Nov. 9 | Bob Welborn | J.H. Petty |
| 2. | Daytona Beach, Fla. | Feb. 20 | Bob Welborn | W.J. Ridgeway |
| 3. | Daytona Beach, Fla. | Feb. 22 | Lee Petty | Petty Enterprises |
| 4. | Hillsboro, N.C. | March 1 | Curtis Turner | Dr. Bradford White |
| 5. | Concord, N.C. | March 8 | Curtis Turner | Dr. Bradford White |
| 6. | Atlanta | March 22 | Johnny Beauchamp | Roy Burdick |
| 7. | Wilson, N.C. | March 29 | Junior Johnson | Paul Spaulding |
| 8. | Winston-Salem, N.C. | March 30 | Jim Reed | Jim Reed |
| 9. | Columbia, S.C. | April 4 | Jack Smith | Jack Smith |
| 10. | North Wilkesboro, N.C. | April 5 | Lee Petty | Petty Enterprises |
| 11. | Reading, Pa. | April 26 | Junior Johnson | Paul Spaulding |
| 12. | Hickory, N.C. | May 2 | Junior Johnson | Paul Spaulding |
| 13. | Martinsville, Va. | May 3 | Lee Petty | Petty Enterprises |
| 14. | Trenton, N.J. | May 17 | Tom Pistone | Carl Rupert |
| 15. | Charlotte, N.C. | May 22 | Lee Petty | Petty Enterprises |
| 16. | Nashville | May 24 | Rex White | Rex White |
| 17. | Los Angles | May 30 | Parnelli Jones | Vel Miletich |
| 18. | Spartanburg, S.C. | June 5 | Jack Smith | Jack Smith |
| 19. | Greenville, S.C. | June 13 | Junior Johnson | Paul Spaulding |
| 20. | Atlanta | June 14 | Lee Petty | Petty Enterprises |
| 21. | Columbia, S.C. | June 18 | Lee Petty | Petty Enterprises |
| 22. | Wilson, N.C. | June 20 | Junior Johnson | Paul Spaulding |
| 23. | Richmond, Va. | June 21 | Tom Pistone | Carl Rupert |
| 24. | Winston-Salem, N.C. | June 27 | Rex White | Rex White |
| 25. | Weaverville, N.C. | June 28 | Rex White | Rex White |
| 26. | Daytona Beach, Fla. | July 4 | Fireball Roberts | Jim Stephens |
| 27. | Pittsburgh | July 21 | Jim Reed | Jim Reed |
| 28. | Charlotte | July 26 | Jack Smith | Jack Smith |
| 29. | Myrtle Beach, S.C. | Aug. 1 | Ned Jarrett | Ned Jarrett |
| 30. | Charlotte | Aug. 2 | Ned Jarrett | Ned Jarrett |
| 31. | Nashville | Aug. 9 | Joe Lee Johnson | Joe Lee Johnson |
| 32. | Weaverville, N.C. | Aug. 16 | Bob Welborn | Bob Welborn |
| 33. | Winston-Salem, N.C. | Aug. 21 | Rex White | Rex White |
| 34. | Greenville, S.C. | Aug. 22 | Buck Baker | Lynton Tyson |
| 35. | Columbia, S.C. | Aug. 29 | Lee Petty | Petty Enterprises |
| 36. | Darlington, S.C. | Sept. 7 | Jim Reed | Jim Reed |
| 37. | Hickory, N.C. | Sept. 11 | Lee Petty | Petty Enterprises |
| 38. | Richmond, Va. | Sept. 13 | Cotton Owens | Cotton Owens |
| 39. | Sacramento | Sept. 13 | Eddie Gray | Vel Miletich |
| 40. | Hillsboro, N.C. | Sept. 20 | Lee Petty | Petty Enterprises |
| 41. | Martinsville, Va. | Sept. 27 | Rex White | White-Clements |
| 42. | Weaverville, N.C. | Oct. 11 | Lee Petty | Petty Enterprises |
| 43. | North Wilkesboro, N.C. | Oct. 18 | Lee Petty | Petty Enterprises |
| 44. | Concord, N.C. | Oct. 25 | Jack Smith | Jack Smith |

## Points standings

1. Lee Petty ...............11,792.00
2. Cotton Owens ...........9,962.00
3. Speedy Thompson ....7,684.00
4. Herman Beam...........7,396.00
5. Buck Baker ..............7,170.00
6. Tom Pistone .............7,050.00
7. L.D. Austin ...............6,519.00
8. Jack Smith ..............6,150.00
9. Jim Reed .................5,744.00
10. Rex White ...............5,526.00

## Race winners 16

1. Lee Petty ...........................11
2. Junior Johnson ......................5
    Rex White ..........................5
4. Jack Smith ..........................4
5. Jim Reed ............................3
    Bob Welborn .........................3
7. Tom Pistone .........................2
    Ned Jarrett..........................2
    Curtis Turner .......................2
10. Fireball Roberts ...................1
    Eddie Gray ..........................1
    Johnny Beauchamp ..............1
    Buck Baker ..........................1
    Cotton Owens........................1
    Parnelli Jones......................1
    Joe Lee Johnson .................1

## Money won leaders

1. Lee Petty .................$43,590
2. Jim Reed ...................22,784
3. Cotton Owens ...........11,925
4. Jack Smith................11,850
5. Rex White................11,560
6. Tom Pistone .............10,885
7. Fireball Roberts .........10,865
8. Bob Burdick ..............10,050
9. Buck Baker ................9,540
10. Joe Weatherly ............9,495

## Pole winners 16

1. Rex White..................................5
    Bob Welborn.........................5
3. Buck Baker ..........................4
4. Fireball Roberts .................3
    Jack Smith...........................3
    Glen Wood ..........................3
7. Lee Petty ...........................2
    Bob Burdick .........................2
    Cotton Owens.......................2
10. Curtis Turner .....................1
    Tommy Irwin .......................1
    Dick Bailey .........................1
    Junior Johnson ...................1
    Jim Reed .............................1
    Speedy Thompson .............1
    Bobby Johns .......................1

# 1959 SEASON

## THE DAYTONA 500: A PICTURE'S WORTH A THOUSAND WORDS

Daytona long has been considered the home of NASCAR, but the first race at what is now known as Daytona International Speedway didn't come until 1959, a dozen years after the sport was founded. Before 1959, races in Daytona were run on the beach, with the Atlantic Ocean blasting away and the coming and going of the tide having a strong say in the scheduling of races. But as the sport grew, the France family knew its fast cars and expanding crowds were too big for the beach.

So they set about constructing a 2.5-mile trioval, with sweeping, high-banked turns that would guarantee high speeds and plenty of excitement. With the opening of the massive speedway in 1959, the sport had a sparkling new home to show off—and a signature race that quickly would fill the sport with lore, starting with the very first race, which was so close Johnny Beauchamp initially was declared the winner but had his trophy taken away three days later, when photos and motion picture footage showed Lee Petty had won.

| Race No. | Location | Date | Winner | Car owner |
|---|---|---|---|---|
| 1. | Fayetteville, N.C. | Nov. 3 | Rex White | J.H. Petty |
| 2. | Daytona Beach, Fla. | Feb. 23 | Paul Goldsmith | Smokey Yunick |
| 3. | Concord, N.C. | Mar. 2 | Lee Petty | Petty Enterprises |
| 4. | Fayetteville, N.C. | March 15 | Curtis Turner | Holman-Moody |
| 5. | Wilson, N.C. | March 16 | Lee Petty | Petty Enterprises |
| 6. | Hillsboro, N.C. | March 23 | Buck Baker | Buck Baker |
| 7. | Fayetteville, N.C. | April 5 | Bob Welborn | J.H. Petty |
| 8. | Columbia, S.C. | April 10 | Speedy Thompson | Alfred "Speedy" Thompson |
| 9. | Spartanburg, S.C. | April 12 | Speedy Thompson | Alfred "Speedy" Thompson |
| 10. | Atlanta | April 13 | Curtis Turner | Holman-Moody |
| 11. | Charlotte | April 18 | Curtis Turner | Holman-Moody |
| 12. | Martinsville, Va. | April 20 | Bob Welborn | J.H. Petty |
| 13. | Manassas, Va. | April 25 | Frankie Schneider | Frankie Schneider |
| 14. | Old Bridge, N.J. | April 27 | Jim Reed | Jim Reed |
| 15. | Greenville, S.C. | May 3 | Jack Smith | Jack Smith |
| 16. | Greensboro, N.C. | May 11 | Bob Welborn | J.H. Petty |
| 17. | Roanoke, Va. | May 15 | Jim Reed | Jim Reed |
| 18. | North Wilkesboro, N.C. | May 18 | Junior Johnson | Paul Spaulding |
| 19. | Winston-Salem, N.C. | May 24 | Bob Welborn | J.H. Petty |
| 20. | Trenton, N.J. | May 30 | Fireball Roberts | Frank Strickland |
| 21. | Riverside, Calif. | June 1 | Eddie Gray | Eddie Gray |
| 22. | Columbia, S.C. | June 5 | Junior Johnson | Paul Spaulding |
| 23. | Bradford, Pa. | June 12 | Junior Johnson | Paul Spaulding |
| 24. | Reading, Pa. | June 15 | Junior Johnson | Paul Spaulding |
| 25. | New Oxford, Pa. | June 25 | Lee Petty | Petty Enterprises |
| 26. | Hickory, N.C. | June 28 | Lee Petty | Petty Enterprises |
| 27. | Weaverville, N.C. | June 29 | Rex White | J.H. Petty |
| 28. | Raleigh, N.C. | July 4 | Fireball Roberts | Frank Strickland |
| 29. | Asheville, N.C. | July 12 | Jim Paschal | J.H. Petty |
| 30. | Busti, N.Y. | July 16 | Shorty Rollins | Shorty Rollins |
| 31. | Toronto | July 18 | Lee Petty | Petty Enterprises |
| 32. | Buffalo, N.Y. | July 19 | Jim Reed | Jim Reed |
| 33. | Rochester, N.Y. | July 25 | Cotton Owens | Jim Stephens |
| 34. | Belmar, N.J. | July 26 | Jim Reed | Jim Reed |
| 35. | Bridgehampton, N.Y. | Aug. 2 | Jack Smith | Jack Smith |
| 36. | Columbia, S.C. | Aug. 7 | Speedy Thompson | Alfred "Speedy" Thompson |
| 37. | Nashville | Aug. 10 | Joe Weatherly | Holman-Moody |
| 38. | Weaverville, N.C. | Aug. 17 | Fireball Roberts | Frank Strickland |
| 39. | Winston-Salem, N.C. | Aug. 22 | Lee Petty | Petty Enterprises |
| 40. | Myrtle Beach, S.C. | Aug. 23 | Bob Welborn | J.H. Petty |
| 41. | Darlington, S.C. | Sept. 1 | Fireball Roberts | Frank Strickland |
| 42. | Charlotte | Sept. 5 | Buck Baker | Buck Baker |
| 43. | Birmingham, Ala. | Sept. 7 | Fireball Roberts | Frank Strickland |
| 44. | Sacramento | Sept. 7 | Parnelli Jones | Vel Miletich |
| 45. | Gastonia, N.C. | Sept. 12 | Buck Baker | Buck Baker |
| 46. | Richmond, Va. | Sept. 14 | Speedy Thompson | Alfred "Speedy" Thompson |
| 47. | Hillsboro, N.C. | Sept. 28 | Joe Eubanks | Jim Stephens |
| 48. | Salisbury, N.C. | Oct. 5 | Lee Petty | Petty Enterprises |
| 49. | Martinsville, Va. | Oct. 12 | Fireball Roberts | Frank Strickland |
| 50. | North Wilkesboro, N.C. | Oct. 19 | Junior Johnson | Paul Spaulding |
| 51. | Atlanta | Oct. 26 | Junior Johnson | Paul Spaulding |

HISTORY

## Points standings

1. Lee Petty ...............11,792.00
2. Cotton Owens ...........9,962.00
3. Speedy Thompson ....7,684.00
4. Herman Beam...........7,396.00
5. Buck Baker...............7,170.00
6. Tom Pistone .............7,050.00
7. L.D. Austin ...............6,519.00
8. Jack Smith ...............6,150.00
9. Jim Reed .................5,744.00
10. Rex White .................5,526.00

## Race winners 16

1. Lee Petty ...........................11
2. Junior Johnson ....................5
   Rex White ...........................5
4. Jack Smith ...........................4
5. Jim Reed .............................3
   Bob Welborn.........................3
7. Tom Pistone .........................2
   Ned Jarrett...........................2
   Curtis Turner ........................2
10. Fireball Roberts ...................1
    Eddie Gray ...........................1
    Johnny Beauchamp ..............1
    Buck Baker ..........................1
    Cotton Owens.......................1
    Parnelli Jones.......................1
    Joe Lee Johnson .................1

## Money won leaders

1. Lee Petty ..................$43,590
2. Jim Reed ..................22,784
3. Cotton Owens ..........11,925
4. Jack Smith................11,850
5. Rex White..................11,560
6. Tom Pistone ..............10,885
7. Fireball Roberts .........10,865
8. Bob Burdick.............10,050
9. Buck Baker .................9,540
10. Joe Weatherly ...........9,495

## Pole winners 16

1. Rex White...........................5
   Bob Welborn........................5
3. Buck Baker ..........................4
4. Fireball Roberts ...................3
   Jack Smith............................3
   Glen Wood ...........................3
7. Lee Petty .............................2
   Bob Burdick .........................2
   Cotton Owens.......................2
10. Curtis Turner .......................1
    Tommy Irwin .......................1
    Dick Bailey..........................1
    Junior Johnson ....................1
    Jim Reed .............................1
    Speedy Thompson ...............1
    Bobby Johns .......................1

# 1957 SEASON

| Race No. | Location | Date | Winner | Car owner |
|---|---|---|---|---|
| 1. | Lancaster, Calif. | Nov. 11 | Marvin Panch | Pete DePaolo |
| 2. | Concord, N.C. | Dec. 2 | Marvin Panch | Pete DePaolo |
| 3. | Titusville, Fla. | Dec. 30 | Fireball Roberts | Pete DePaolo |
| 4. | Daytona Beach, Fla. | Feb. 17 | Cotton Owens | Ray Nichels |
| 5. | Concord, N.C. | March 3 | Jack Smith | Hugh Babb |
| 6. | Wilson, N.C. | March 17 | Ralph Moody | Pete DePaolo |
| 7. | Hillsboro, N.C. | March 24 | Buck Baker | Hugh Babb |
| 8. | Weaverville, N.C. | March 31 | Buck Baker | Hugh Babb |
| 9. | North Wilkesboro, N.C. | April 7 | Fireball Roberts | Pete DePaolo |
| 10. | Langhorne, Pa. | April 14 | Fireball Roberts | Pete DePaolo |
| 11. | Charlotte | April 19 | Fireball Roberts | Pete DePaolo |
| 12. | Spartanburg, S.C. | April 27 | Marvin Panch | Pete DePaolo |
| 13. | Greensboro, N.C. | April 28 | Paul Goldsmith | Smokey Yunick |
| 14. | Portland | April 28 | Art Watts | Al Schmidhamer |
| 15. | Shelby, N.C. | May 4 | Fireball Roberts | Pete DePaolo |
| 16. | Richmond, Va. | May 5 | Paul Goldsmith | Pete DePaolo |
| 17. | Martinsville, Va. | May 19 | Buck Baker | Hugh Babb |
| 18. | Portland | May 26 | Eddie Pagan | Eddie Pagan |
| 19. | Eureka, Calif. | May 30 | Lloyd Dane | Lloyd Dane |
| 20. | New Oxford, Pa. | May 30 | Buck Baker | Hugh Babb |
| 21. | Lancaster, S.C. | June 1 | Paul Goldsmith | Smokey Yunick |
| 22. | Los Angeles | June 8 | Eddie Pagan | Eddie Pagan |
| 23. | Newport, Tenn. | June 15 | Fireball Roberts | Edward "Fireball" Robert |
| 24. | Columbia, S.C. | June 20 | Jack Smith | Jack Smith |
| 25. | Sacramento | June 22 | Bill Amick | William Amick |
| 26. | Spartanburg, S.C. | June 29 | Lee Petty | Petty Enterprises |
| 27. | Jacksonville, N.C. | June 30 | Buck Baker | Buck Baker |
| 28. | Raleigh, N.C. | July 4 | Paul Goldsmith | Smokey Yunick |
| 29. | Charlotte | July 12 | Marvin Panch | Marvin Panch |
| 30. | LeHi, Ark. | July 14 | Marvin Panch | Herb Thomas |
| 31. | Portland | July 14 | Eddie Pagan | Eddie Pagan |
| 32. | Hickory, N.C. | July 20 | Jack Smith | Jack Smith |
| 33. | Norfolk, Va. | July 24 | Buck Baker | Buck Baker |
| 34. | Lancaster, S.C. | July 30 | Speedy Thompson | Alfred "Speedy" Thompson |
| 35. | Watkins Glen, N.Y. | Aug. 4 | Buck Baker | Buck Baker |
| 36. | Bremerton, Wash. | Aug. 4 | Parnelli Jones | Oscar Maples |
| 37. | New Oxford, Pa. | Aug. 10 | Marvin Panch | Marvin Panch |
| 38. | Old Bridge, N.J. | Aug. 16 | Lee Petty | Petty Enterprises |
| 39. | Myrtle Beach, S.C. | Aug. 26 | Gwyn Staley | J.H. Petty |
| 40. | Darlington, S.C. | Sept. 2 | Speedy Thompson | Alfred "Speedy" Thompson |
| 41. | Syracuse, N.Y. | Sept. 5 | Gwyn Staley | J.H. Petty |
| 42. | Weaverville, N.C. | Sept. 8 | Lee Petty | Petty Enterprises |
| 43. | Sacramento | Sept. 8 | Danny Graves | Danny Graves |
| 44. | San Jose, Calif. | Sept. 15 | Marvin Porter | Marvin Porter |
| 45. | Langhorne, Pa. | Sept. 15 | Gwyn Staley | J.H. Petty |
| 46. | Columbia, S.C. | Sept. 19 | Buck Baker | Buck Baker |
| 47. | Shelby, N.C. | Sept. 21 | Buck Baker | Buck Baker |
| 48. | Charlotte | Oct. 5 | Lee Petty | Petty Enterprises |
| 49. | Martinsville, Va. | Oct. 6 | Bob Welborn | Bob Welborn |
| 50. | Newberry, S.C. | Oct. 12 | Fireball Roberts | Edward "Fireball" Robert |
| 51. | Concord, N.C. | Oct. 13 | Fireball Roberts | Edward "Fireball" Robert |
| 52. | North Wilkesboro, N.C. | Oct. 20 | Jack Smith | Jack Smith |
| 53. | Greensboro, N.C. | Oct. 27 | Buck Baker | Buck Baker |

## Points standings

1. Buck Baker ............10,716.00
2. Marvin Panch ..........9,956.00
3. Speedy Thompson....8,580.00
4. Lee Petty.................8,528.00
5. Jack Smith ..............8,464.00
6. Fireball Roberts.........8,268.00
7. Johnny Allen ............7,068.00
8. L.D. Austin ..............6,532.00
9. Brownie King ...........5,740.00
10. Jim Paschal ............5,136.00

## Race winners 18

1. Buck Baker ............................10
2. Fireball Roberts ........................8
3. Marvin Panch .................6
4. Lee Petty ................................4
   Jack Smith ..............................4
   Paul Goldsmith........................4
7. Eddie Pagan ............................3
   Gwyn Staley ............................3
9. Speedy Thompson ...................2
10. Bill Amick ..............................1
    Lloyd Dane ..............................1
    Art Watts ................................1
    Bob Welborn ...........................1
    Ralph Moody ...........................1
    Cotton Owens...........................1
    Parnelli Jones...........................1
    Danny Graves...........................1
    Marvin Porter...........................1

## Money won leaders

1. Buck Baker ..................$25,665
2. Speedy Thompson ..........24,710
3. Marvin Panch ................19,980
4. Fireball Roberts..............17,425
5. Lee Petty........................15,945
6. Cotton Owens ................12,325
7. Paul Goldsmith ..............11,950
8. Jack Smith ....................11,335
9. Johnny Allen ....................8,075
10. Bill Amick .....................8,030

## Pole winners 24

1. Buck Baker ...............................6
2. Art Watts ..................................5
3. Speedy Thompson ....................4
   Marvin Panch ............................4
   Paul Goldsmith ..........................4
   Fireball Roberts..........................4
7. Tiny Lund ..................................3
   Lee Petty ..................................3
9. Eddie Pagan ..............................2
   Gwyn Staley ..............................2
   Bill Amick ..................................2
   Jack Smith ................................2
13. Rex White ................................1
    Curtis Turner .............................1
    Ken Rush ..................................1
    Frankie Schneider ......................1
    Danny Graves ............................1
    Russ Hepler ..............................1
    Johnny Allen ..............................1
    Lloyd Dane ................................1
    Banjo Matthews .........................1
    Cotton Owens ............................1
    Parnelli Jones ............................1
    Mel Larson ................................1

# 1956 SEASON

| Race No. | Location | Date | Winner | Car owner |
|---|---|---|---|---|
| 1. | Hickory, N.C. | Nov. 13 | Tim Flock | Carl Kiekhafer |
| 2. | Charlotte | Nov. 20 | Fonty Flock | Carl Kiekhafer |
| 3. | Lancaster, Calif. | Nov. 20 | Chuck Stevenson | Carl Dane |
| 4. | West Palm Beach, Fla. | Dec. 11 | Herb Thomas | Herb Thomas |
| 5. | Phoenix | Jan. 22 | Buck Baker | Carl Kiekhafer |
| 6. | Daytona Beach, Fla. | Feb. 26 | Tim Flock | Carl Kiekhafer |
| 7. | West Palm Beach, Fla. | March 4 | Billy Myers | William Stroppe |
| 8. | Wilson, N.C. | March 18 | Herb Thomas | Smokey Yunick |
| 9. | Atlanta | March 25 | Buck Baker | Carl Kiekhafer |
| 10. | North Wilkesboro, N.C. | April 8 | Tim Flock | Carl Kiekhafer |
| 11. | Langhorne, Pa. | April 22 | Buck Baker | Carl Kiekhafer |
| 12. | Richmond, Va. | April 29 | Buck Baker | Carl Kiekhafer |
| 13. | Columbia, S.C. | May 5 | Speedy Thompson | Carl Kiekhafer |
| 14. | Concord, N.C. | May 6 | Speedy Thompson | Carl Kiekhafer |
| 15. | Greenville, S.C. | May 10 | Buck Baker | Carl Kiekhafer |
| 16. | Hickory, N.C. | May 12 | Speedy Thompson | Carl Kiekhafer |
| 17. | Hillsboro, N.C. | May 13 | Buck Baker | Carl Kiekhafer |
| 18. | Martinsville, Va. | May 20 | Buck Baker | Carl Kiekhafer |
| 19. | New Oxford, Pa. | May 25 | Buck Baker | Carl Kiekhafer |
| 20. | Charlotte, N.C. | May 27 | Speedy Thompson | Carl Kiekhafer |
| 21. | Portland | May 27 | Herb Thomas | Carl Kiekhafer |
| 22. | Eureka, Calif. | May 30 | Herb Thomas | Carl Kiekhafer |
| 23. | Syracuse, N.Y. | May 30 | Buck Baker | Carl Kiekhafer |
| 24. | Merced, Calif. | June 3 | Herb Thomas | Carl Kiekhafer |
| 25. | LeHi, Ark. | June 10 | Ralph Moody | Pete DePaolo |
| 26. | Charlotte | June 15 | Speedy Thompson | Carl Kiekhafer |
| 27. | Rochester, N.Y. | June 22 | Speedy Thompson | Carl Kiekhafer |
| 28. | Portland, Ore. | June 24 | John Kieper | John Kieper |
| 29. | Weaverville, N.C. | June 1 | Lee Petty | Petty Enterprises |
| 30. | Raleigh, N.C. | July 4 | Fireball Roberts | Pete DePaolo |
| 31. | Spartanburg, S.C. | July 7 | Lee Petty | Petty Enterprises |
| 32. | Sacramento | July 8 | Lloyd Dane | Lloyd Dane |
| 33. | Chicago | July 21 | Fireball Roberts | Pete DePaolo |
| 34. | Shelby, N.C. | July 27 | Speedy Thompson | Carl Kiekhafer |
| 35. | Montgomery, Ala. | July 29 | Marvin Panch | Tom Harbison |
| 36. | Oklahoma City, Okla. | Aug. 3 | Jim Paschal | Frank Hayworth |
| 37. | Elkhart Lakes, Wis. | Aug. 12 | Tim Flock | William Stroppe |
| 38. | Old Bridge, N.J. | Aug. 17 | Ralph Moody | Pete DePaolo |
| 39. | San Mateo, Calif. | Aug. 19 | Eddie Pagan | Eddie Pagan |
| 40. | Norfolk, Va. | Aug. 22 | Billy Myers | William Stroppe |
| 41. | Spartanburg, S.C. | Aug. 23 | Ralph Moody | Pete DePaolo |
| 42. | Myrtle Beach, S.C. | Aug. 25 | Fireball Roberts | Pete DePaolo |
| 43. | Portland | Aug. 26 | Royce Haggerty | Curly Weida |
| 44. | Darlington, S.C. | Sept. 3 | Curtis Turner | Charles Schwam |
| 45. | Montgomery, Ala. | Sept. 9 | Buck Baker | Carl Kiekhafer |
| 46. | Charlotte | Sept. 12 | Ralph Moody | Pete DePaolo |
| 47. | Langhorne, Pa. | Sept. 23 | Paul Goldsmith | Smokey Yunick |
| 48. | Portland | Sept. 23 | Lloyd Dane | Lloyd Dane |
| 49. | Columbia, S.C. | Sept. 29 | Buck Baker | Carl Kiekhafer |
| 50. | Hillsboro, N.C. | Sept. 30 | Fireball Roberts | Pete DePaolo |
| 51. | Newport, Tenn. | Oct. 7 | Fireball Roberts | Pete DePaolo |
| 52. | Charlotte | Oct. 17 | Buck Baker | Carl Kiekhafer |
| 53. | Shelby, N.C. | Oct. 23 | Buck Baker | Carl Kiekhafer |
| 54. | Martinsville, Va. | Oct. 28 | Jack Smith | Carl Kiekhafer |
| 55. | Hickory, N.C. | Nov. 11 | Speedy Thompson | Carl Kiekhafer |
| 56. | Wilson, N.C. | Nov. 18 | Buck Baker | Carl Kiekhafer |

## Points standings

1. Buck Baker ..............9,272.00
2. Herb Thomas............8,568.00
3. Speedy Thompson....8,328.00
4. Lee Petty .................8,324.00
5. Jim Paschal.............7,878.00
6. Billy Myers ..............6,920.00
7. Fireball Roberts .......5,794.00
8. Ralph Moody ...........5,548.00
9. Tim Flock ................5,062.00
10. Marvin Panch ..........4,680.00

## Race winners 19

1. Buck Baker ..........................14
2. Speedy Thompson ...................8
3. Herb Thomas ..........................5
   Fireball Roberts ......................5
5. Tim Flock .................................4
   Ralph Moody ...........................4
7. Billy Myers ..............................2
   Lee Petty .................................2
   Lloyd Dane ..............................2
10. Jack Smith ..............................1
    Curtis Turner ...........................1
    Chuck Stevenson .....................1
    Royce Haggerty .......................1
    Paul Goldsmith.........................1
    Fonty Flock ..............................1
    John Kieper ..............................1
    Jim Paschal .............................1
    Marvin Panch ...........................1
    Eddie Pagan ............................1

## Money won leaders

1. Buck Baker ................$29,140
2. Speedy Thompson ........24,670
3. Herb Thomas ................17,695
4. Jim Paschal ..................16,540
5. Tim Flock .......................15,409
6. Billy Myers ....................15,320
7. Ralph Moody .................14,545
8. Fireball Roberts .............14,395
9. Curtis Turner .................14,295
10. Lee Petty.......................13,455

## Pole winners 22

1. Buck Baker .............................11
2. Speedy Thompson .....................7
3. Tim Flock ..................................5
   Ralph Moody .............................5
5. Fireball Roberts ........................3
   John Kieper ...............................3
   Herb Thomas .............................3
8. Jim Reed ...................................2
   Eddie Pagan ..............................2
   Fonty Flock ................................2
   Joe Eubanks ..............................2
12. Lee Petty...................................1
    Joe Weatherly ...........................1
    Rex White ..................................1
    Jim Paschal ...............................1
    Royce Haggerty .........................1
    Ralph Earnhardt .........................1
    Doug Cox ...................................1
    Junior Johnson...........................1
    Marvin Panch .............................1
    Billy Myers .................................1
    Frank Mundy...............................1

# 1955 SEASON

| Race No. | Location | Date | Winner | Car owner |
|----------|----------|------|--------|-----------|
| 1. | High Point, N.C. | Nov. 7 | Lee Petty | Petty Enterprises |
| 2. | West Palm Beach, Fla. | Feb. 6 | Herb Thomas | Herb Thomas |
| 3. | Jacksonville, Fla. | Feb. 13 | Lee Petty | Petty Enterprises |
| 4. | Daytona Beach, Fla. | Feb. 27 | Tim Flock | Carl Kiekhafer |
| 5. | Savannah, Ga. | March 6 | Lee Petty | Petty Enterprises |
| 6. | Columbia, S.C. | March 26 | Fonty Flock | Frank Christian |
| 7. | Hillsboro, N.C. | March 27 | Jim Paschal | Ernest Woods |
| 8. | North Wilkesboro, N.C. | April 3 | Buck Baker | Bobby Griffin |
| 9. | Montgomery, Ala. | April 17 | Tim Flock | Carl Kiekhafer |
| 10. | Langhorne, Pa. | April 24 | Tim Flock | Carl Kiekhafer |
| 11. | Charlotte | May 1 | Buck Baker | Buck Baker |
| 12. | Hickory, N.C. | May 7 | Junior Johnson | Carl Beckham/Jim Lowe |
| 13. | Phoenix | May 8 | Tim Flock | Carl Kiekhafer |
| 14. | Tucson, Ariz. | May 15 | Danny Letner | Cos Concilla |
| 15. | Martinsville, Va. | May 15 | Tim Flock | Carl Kiekhafer |
| 16. | Richmond, Va. | May 22 | Tim Flock | Carl Kiekhafer |
| 17. | Raleigh, N.C. | May 28 | Junior Johnson | Carl Beckham/Jim Lowe |
| 18. | Winston-Salem, N.C. | May 29 | Lee Petty | Petty Enterprises |
| 19. | New Oxford, Pa. | June 10 | Junior Johnson | Carl Beckham/Jim Lowe |
| 20. | Rochester, N.Y. | June 17 | Tim Flock | Carl Kiekhafer |
| 21. | Fonda, N.Y. | June 18 | Junior Johnson | Carl Beckham/Jim Lowe |
| 22. | Plattsburg, N.Y. | June 19 | Lee Petty | Petty Enterprises |
| 23. | Charlotte | June 24 | Tim Flock | Carl Kiekhafer |
| 24. | Spartanburg, S.C. | July 6 | Tim Flock | Carl Kiekhafer |
| 25. | Columbia, S.C. | July 9 | Jim Paschal | Ernest Woods |
| 26. | Weaverville, N.C. | July 10 | Tim Flock | Carl Kiekhafer |
| 27. | Morristown, N.J. | July 15 | Tim Flock | Carl Kiekhafer |
| 28. | Altamont, N.Y. | July 29 | Junior Johnson | Carl Beckham/Jim Lowe |
| 29. | Syracuse, N.Y. | July 30 | Tim Flock | Carl Kiekhafer |
| 30. | San Mateo, Calif. | July 31 | Tim Flock | Carl Kiekhafer |
| 31. | Charlotte | Aug. 5 | Jim Paschal | Ernest Woods |
| 32. | Winston-Salem, N.C. | Aug. 7 | Lee Petty | Petty Enterprises |
| 33. | LeHi, Ark. | Aug. 14 | Fonty Flock | Carl Kiekhafer |
| 34. | Raleigh, N.C. | Aug. 20 | Herb Thomas | Herb Thomas |
| 35. | Darlington, S.C. | Sept. 5 | Herb Thomas | Herb Thomas |
| 36. | Montgomery, Ala. | Sept. 11 | Tim Flock | Carl Kiekhafer |
| 37. | Langhorne, Pa. | Sept. 18 | Tim Flock | Carl Kiekhafer |
| 38. | Raleigh, N.C. | Sept. 30 | Fonty Flock | Carl Kiekhafer |
| 39. | Greenville, S.C. | Oct. 6 | Tim Flock | Carl Kiekhafer |
| 40. | LeHi, Ark. | Oct. 9 | Speedy Thompson | Pete DePaolo |
| 41. | Columbia, S.C. | Oct. 15 | Tim Flock | Carl Kiekhafer |
| 42. | Martinsville, Va. | Oct. 16 | Speedy Thompson | Carl Kiekhafer |
| 43. | Las Vegas, Nev. | Oct. 16 | Norm Nelson | Carl Kiekhafer |
| 44. | North Wilkesboro, N.C. | Oct. 23 | Buck Baker | Pete DePaolo |
| 45. | Hillsboro, N.C. | Oct. 30 | Tim Flock | Carl Kiekhafer |

## Points standings

1. Tim Flock ..................9,596.00
2. Buck Baker ...........8,088.00
3. Lee Petty ..................7,194.00
4. Bob Welborn..............5,460.00
5. Herb Thomas ...........5,186.00
6. Junior Johnson...........4,810.00
7. Eddie Skinner............4,652.00
8. Jim Paschal ..............4,572.00
9. Jimmy Lewallen........4,526.00
10. Gwyn Staley ..............4,360.00

## Race winners 10

1. Tim Flock ..............................18
2. Lee Petty ...............................6
3. Junior Johnson ....................5
4. Buck Baker .........................3
   Jim Paschal ........................3
   Fonty Flock .........................3
   Herb Thomas ......................3
8. Speedy Thompson...................2
9. Danny Letner ......................1
   Norm Nelson..........................1

## Money won leaders

1. Tim Flock ...............$33,275
2. Buck Baker..............17,590
3. Lee Petty.................16,775
4. Herb Thomas .........16,320
5. Fonty Flock ............12,690
6. Junior Johnson .........10,055
7. Jim Paschal .............9,700
8. Bob Welborn .............8,275
9. Speedy Thompson ......6,680
10. Gwyn Staley .............5,815

## Pole winners 14

1. Tim Flock ............................17
2. Fonty Flock.........................6
3. Dick Rathmann ...................3
4. Jim Paschal .........................2
   Herb Thomas .......................2
   Buck Baker...........................2
   Bill Amick ............................2
   Junior Johnson.....................2
9. Dink Widenhouse .................1
   Bob Welborn .........................1
   Fireball Roberts .....................1
   Jimmy Lewallen ....................1
   Norm Nelson ........................1
   Lee Petty ..............................1

# 1954 SEASON

| Race No. | Location | Date | Winner | Car owner |
|---|---|---|---|---|
| 1. | West Palm Beach, Fla. | Feb. 7 | Herb Thomas | Herb Thomas |
| 2. | Daytona Beach, Fla. | Feb. 21 | Lee Petty | Petty Enterprises |
| 3. | Jacksonville, Fla. | March 7 | Herb Thomas | Herb Thomas |
| 4. | Atlanta | March 21 | Herb Thomas | Herb Thomas |
| 5. | Savannah, Ga. | March 28 | Al Keller | George Miller |
| 6. | Oakland, Calif. | March 28 | Dick Rathmann | Ray Erickson |
| 7. | North Wilkesboro, N.C. | April 4 | Dick Rathmann | John Ditz |
| 8. | Hillsboro, N.C. | April 18 | Herb Thomas | Herb Thomas |
| 9. | Macon, Ga. | April 25 | Gober Sosebee | Gober Sosebee |
| 10. | Langhorne, Pa. | May 2 | Herb Thomas | Herb Thomas |
| 11. | Wilson, N.C. | May 9 | Buck Baker | Ernest Woods |
| 12. | Martinsville, Va. | May 16 | Jim Paschal | Bobby Griffin |
| 13. | Sharon, Pa. | May 23 | Lee Petty | Petty Enterprises |
| 14. | Raleigh, N.C. | May 29 | Herb Thomas | Herb Thomas |
| 15. | Charlotte | May 30 | Buck Baker | Bobby Griffin |
| 16. | Gardena, Calif. | May 30 | John Soares | Charles Vance |
| 17. | Columbia, S.C. | June 6 | Curtis Turner | Elmer Brooks |
| 18. | Linden, N.J. | June 13 | Al Keller | Paul Whiteman |
| 19. | Mechanicsburg, Pa. | June 17 | Herb Thomas | Herb Thomas |
| 20. | Hickory, N.C. | June 19 | Herb Thomas | Herb Thomas |
| 21. | Rochester, N.Y. | June 25 | Lee Petty | Petty Enterprises |
| 22. | Spartanburg, S.C. | July 3 | Herb Thomas | Herb Thomas |
| 23. | Weaverville, N.C. | July 4 | Herb Thomas | Herb Thomas |
| 24. | Willow Springs, Ill. | July 10 | Dick Rathmann | John Ditz |
| 25. | Grand Rapids, Mich. | July 11 | Lee Petty | Petty Enterprises |
| 26. | Morristown, N.J. | July 30 | Buck Baker | Ernest Woods |
| 27. | Oakland | Aug. 1 | Danny Letner | Joseph Bearscheck |
| 28. | Charlotte | Aug. 13 | Lee Petty | Petty Enterprises |
| 29. | San Mateo, Calif. | Aug. 22 | Hershel McGriff | Frank Christian |
| 30. | Corbin, Ky. | Aug. 29 | Lee Petty | Petty Enterprises |
| 31. | Darlington, S.C. | Sept. 6 | Herb Thomas | Herb Thomas |
| 32. | Macon, Ga. | Sept. 12 | Hershel McGriff | Frank Christian |
| 33. | Charlotte, N.C. | Sept. 24 | Hershel McGriff | Frank Christian |
| 34. | Langhorne, Pa. | Sept. 26 | Herb Thomas | Herb Thomas |
| 35. | LeHi, Ark. | Oct. 10 | Buck Baker | Bobby Griffin |
| 36. | Martinsville, Va. | Oct. 17 | Lee Petty | Petty Enterprises |
| 37. | North Wilkesboro, N.C. | Oct. 24 | Hershel McGriff | Frank Christian |

## Points standings

1. Lee Petty ...............8,649.00
2. Herb Thomas ...........8,366.00
3. Buck Baker..............6,893.00
4. Dick Rathmann.........6,760.00
5. Joe Eubanks.............5,467.00
6. Hershel McGriff.........5,137.00
7. Jim Paschal .............3,903.00
8. Jimmy Lewallen ........3,233.00
9. Curtis Turner.............2,994.00
10. Ralph Liguori ...........2,905.00

## Race winners 11

1. Herb Thomas .......................12
2. Lee Petty ..............................7
3. Hershel McGriff ......................4
   Buck Baker ............................4
5. Dick Rathmann .....................3
6. Al Keller ................................2
7. Danny Letner .........................1
   Curtis Turner...........................1
   Gober Sosebee .......................1
   Jim Paschal ............................1
   John Soares ...........................1

## Money won leaders

1. Herb Thomas ............$27,540
2. Lee Petty ...................19,125
3. Buck Baker.................18,015
4. Dick Rathmann ...........14,910
5. Hershel McGriff............11,625
6. Curtis Turner .................9,820
7. Joe Eubanks.................7,160
8. Jim Paschal .................4,585
9. Marvin Panch ..............4,530
10. Jimmy Lewallen ...........3,965

## Pole winners 13

1. Herb Thomas ........................8
2. Buck Baker............................7
3. Hershel McGriff ......................5
4. Dick Rathmann .....................4
5. Lee Petty ..............................3
6. Jim Paschal ...........................2
7. Curtis Turner .........................1
   Gober Sosebee.......................1
   Junior Johnson ......................1
   Tim Flock ...............................1
   Al Keller .................................1
   Marvin Panch..........................1
   Danny Letner .........................1

# 1953 SEASON

| Race No. | Location | Date | Winner | Car owner |
|----------|----------|------|--------|-----------|
| 1. | West Palm Beach, Fla. | Feb. 1 | Lee Petty | Petty Enterprises |
| 2. | Daytona Beach, Fla. | Feb. 15 | Bill Blair | Bill Blair |
| 3. | Spring Lake, N.C. | March 8 | Herb Thomas | Herb Thomas |
| 4. | North Wilkesboro, N.C. | March 29 | Herb Thomas | Herb Thomas |
| 5. | Charlotte | April 5 | Dick Passwater | Frank Arford |
| 6. | Richmond, Va. | April 19 | Lee Petty | Petty Enterprises |
| 7. | Macon, Ga. | April 26 | Dick Rathmann | Walt Chapman |
| 8. | Langhorne, Pa. | May 3 | Buck Baker | Bobby Griffin |
| 9. | Columbia, S.C. | May 9 | Buck Baker | Bobby Griffin |
| 10. | Hickory, N.C. | May 16 | Tim Flock | Ted Chester |
| 11. | Martinsville, Va. | May 17 | Lee Petty | Petty Enterprises |
| 12. | Columbus, Ohio | May 24 | Herb Thomas | Herb Thomas |
| 13. | Raleigh, N.C. | May 30 | Fonty Flock | Frank Christian |
| 14. | Shreveport, La. | June 7 | Lee Petty | Petty Enterprises |
| 15. | Pensacola, Fla. | June 14 | Herb Thomas | Herb Thomas |
| 16. | Langhorne, Pa. | June 21 | Dick Rathmann | Walt Chapman |
| 17. | High Point, N.C. | June 26 | Herb Thomas | Herb Thomas |
| 18. | Wilson, N.C. | June 28 | Fonty Flock | Frank Christian |
| 19. | Rochester, N.Y. | July 3 | Herb Thomas | Herb Thomas |
| 20. | Spartanburg, S.C. | July 4 | Lee Petty | Petty Enterprises |
| 21. | Morristown, N.J. | July 10 | Dick Rathmann | Walt Chapman |
| 22. | Atlanta | July 12 | Herb Thomas | Herb Thomas |
| 23. | Rapid City, S.D. | July 22 | Herb Thomas | Herb Thomas |
| 24. | North Platte, Neb. | July 26 | Dick Rathmann | Walt Chapman |
| 25. | Davenport, Iowa | Aug. 2 | Herb Thomas | Herb Thomas |
| 26. | Hillsboro, N.C. | Aug. 9 | Curtis Turner | Frank Christian |
| 27. | Weaverville, N.C. | Aug. 16 | Fonty Flock | Frank Christian |
| 28. | Norfolk, Va. | Aug. 23 | Herb Thomas | Herb Thomas |
| 29. | Hickory, N.C. | Aug. 29 | Fonty Flock | Frank Christian |
| 30. | Darlington, S.C. | Sept. 7 | Buck Baker | Bobby Griffin |
| 31. | Macon, Ga. | Sept. 13 | Speedy Thompson | Buckshot Morris |
| 32. | Langhorne, Pa. | Sept. 20 | Dick Rathmann | Walt Chapman |
| 33. | Bloomsburg, Pa. | Oct. 3 | Herb Thomas | Herb Thomas |
| 34. | Wilson, N.C. | Oct. 4 | Herb Thomas | Herb Thomas |
| 35. | North Wilkesboro, N.C. | Oct. 11 | Speedy Thompson | Buckshot Morris |
| 36. | Martinsville, Va. | Oct. 13 | Jim Paschal | George Hutchens |
| 37. | Atlanta | Nov. 1 | Buck Baker | Bobby Griffin |

## Points standings

1. Herb Thomas ...........8,460.00
2. Lee Petty ................7,814.00
3. Dick Rathmann..........7,362.00
4. Buck Baker ..............6,713.00
5. Fonty Flock...............6,174.00
6. Tim Flock .................5,011.00
7. Jim Paschal ..............4,211.00
8. Joe Eubanks.............3,603.00
9. Jimmy Lewallen ........3,508.00
10. Curtis Turner.............3,373.00

## Race winners

1. Herb Thomas........................12
2. Dick Rathmann .......................5
   Lee Petty...............................5
4. Fonty Flock .............................4
   Buck Baker .............................4
6. Speedy Thompson....................2
7. Curtis Turner ...........................1
   Tim Flock ................................1
   Bill Blair ..................................1
   Dick Passwater .......................1
   Jim Paschal ...........................1

## Money won leaders

1. Herb Thomas ...........$24,300
2. Dick Rathmann ..........19,205
3. Lee Petty ..................17,225
4. Fonty Flock ...............16,440
5. Buck Baker ...............16,220
6. Tim Flock....................7,365
7. Speedy Thompson ........6,150
8. Jim Paschal .................4,935
9. Joe Eubanks ...............4,725
10. Bill Blair......................3,970

## Pole winners

1. Herb Thomas ...............11
2. Buck Baker .....................4
3. Fonty Flock .....................3
   Curtis Turner ....................3
   Tim Flock..........................3
6. Dick Rathmann ................2
7. Slick Smith.......................1
   Lloyd Shaw .......................1
   Joe Eubanks .....................1
   Jim Paschal ......................1
   Bob Pronger......................1

# 1952 SEASON

| Race No. | Location | Date | Winner | Car owner |
|---|---|---|---|---|
| 1. | West Palm Beach, Fla. | Jan. 20 | Tim Flock | Ted Chester |
| 2. | Daytona Beach, Fla. | Feb. 10 | Marshall Teague | Marshall Teague |
| 3. | Jacksonville, Fla. | March 6 | Marshall Teague | Marshall Teague |
| 4. | North Wilkesboro, N.C. | March 30 | Herb Thomas | Herb Thomas |
| 5. | Martinsville, Va. | April 6 | Dick Rathmann | Walt Chapman |
| 6. | Columbia, S.C. | April 12 | Buck Baker | B.A. Pless |
| 7. | Atlanta | April 20 | Bill Blair | George Hutchens |
| 8. | Macon, Ga. | April 27 | Herb Thomas | Herb Thomas |
| 9. | Langhorne, Pa. | May 4 | Dick Rathmann | Walt Chapman |
| 10. | Darlington, S.C. | May 10 | Dick Rathmann | Walt Chapman |
| 11. | Dayton, Ohio | May 18 | Dick Rathmann | Walt Chapman |
| 12. | Canfield, Ohio | May 30 | Herb Thomas | Herb Thomas |
| 13. | Augusta, Ga. | June 1 | Gober Sosebee | Sam Knox |
| 14. | Toledo, Ohio | June 1 | Tim Flock | Ted Chester |
| 15. | Hillsboro, N.C. | June 8 | Tim Flock | Ted Chester |
| 16. | Charlotte | June 15 | Herb Thomas | Herb Thomas |
| 17. | Detroit | June 29 | Tim Flock | Ted Chester |
| 18. | Niagara Falls, Ontario | July 1 | Buddy Shuman | B.A. Pless |
| 19. | Oswego, N.Y. | July 4 | Tim Flock | Ted Chester |
| 20. | Monroe, Mich. | July 6 | Tim Flock | Ted Chester |
| 21. | Morristown, N.J. | July 11 | Lee Petty | Petty Enterprises |
| 22. | South Bend, Ind. | July 20 | Tim Flock | Ted Chester |
| 23. | Rochester, N.Y. | Aug. 15 | Tim Flock | Ted Chester |
| 24. | Weaverville, N.C. | Aug. 17 | Bob Flock | Ted Chester |
| 25. | Darlington, S.C. | Sept. 1 | Fonty Flock | Frank Christian |
| 26. | Macon, Ga. | Sept. 7 | Lee Petty | Petty Enterprises |
| 27. | Langhorne, Pa. | Sept. 14 | Lee Petty | Petty Enterprises |
| 28. | Dayton, Ohio | Sept. 21 | Dick Rathmann | Walt Chapman |
| 29. | Wilson, N.C. | Sept. 28 | Herb Thomas | Herb Thomas |
| 30. | Hillsboro, N.C. | Oct. 12 | Fonty Flock | Frank Christian |
| 31. | Martinsville, Va. | Oct. 19 | Herb Thomas | Herb Thomas |
| 32. | North Wilkesboro, N.C. | Oct. 26 | Herb Thomas | Herb Thomas |
| 33. | Atlanta | Nov. 16 | Donald Thomas | Herb Thomas |
| 34. | West Palm Beach, Fla. | Nov. 30 | Herb Thomas | Herb Thomas |

## Points standings

1. Tim Flock ..................6,858.50
2. Herb Thomas ...........6,752.50
3. Lee Petty....................6,498.50
4. Fonty Flock ...............5,183.50
5. Dick Rathmann ..........3,952.50
6. Bill Blair ....................3,499.00
7. Joe Eubanks ..............3,090.50
8. Ray Duhigg ................2,986.50
9. Donald Thomas..........2,574.00
10. Buddy Shuman ..........2,483.00

## Race winners 12

1. Tim Flock ....................................8
  Herb Thomas .........................8
3. Dick Rathmann .........................5
4. Lee Petty ....................................3
5. Marshall Teague .......................2
  Fonty Flock ..............................2
7. Donald Thomas .........................1
  Buck Baker ..............................1
  Gober Sosebee ........................1
  Bob Flock .................................1
  Bill Blair ...................................1
  Buddy Shuman ........................1

## Money won leaders

1. Tim Flock..................$20,210
2. Fonty Flock ...............18,040
3. Herb Thomas .............17,625
4. Lee Petty ...................15,670
5. Dick Rathmann ..........10,309
6. Bill Blair .....................7,095
7. Buddy Shuman ...........4,210
8. Donald Thomas ..........4,075
9. Johnny Patterson .........3,350
10. Ray Duhigg .................3,275

## Pole winners 12

1. Herb Thomas .......................10
2. Fonty Flock ...........................7
3. Tim Flock...............................4
4. Buck Baker ............................2
  Dick Rathmann .....................2
6. Jack Smith .............................1
  Donald Thomas .....................1
  Marshall Teague.....................1
  Perk Brown ...........................1
  Bill Blair .................................1
  Tommy Moon .........................1
  Pat Kirkwood .........................1

# 1951 SEASON

| Race No. | Location | Date | Winner | Car owner |
|---|---|---|---|---|
| 1. | Daytona Beach, Fla. | Feb. 11 | Marshall Teague | Marshall Teague |
| 2. | Charlotte | April 1 | Curtis Turner | Nash Motor Company |
| 3. | Mobile, Ala. | April 8 | Tim Flock | Ted Chester |
| 4. | Gardena, Calif. | April 8 | Marshall Teague | Marshall Teague |
| 5. | Hillsboro, N.C. | April 15 | Fonty Flock | Frank Christian |
| 6. | Phoenix | April 22 | Marshall Teague | Marshall Teague |
| 7. | North Wilkesboro, N.C. | April 29 | Fonty Flock | Frank Christian |
| 8. | Martinsville, Va. | May 6 | Curtis Turner | John Eanes |
| 9. | Canfield, Ohio | May 30 | Marshall Teague | Marshall Teague |
| 10. | Columbus, Ga. | June 10 | Tim Flock | Ted Chester |
| 11. | Columbia, S.C. | June 16 | Frank Mundy | Perry Smith |
| 12. | Dayton, Ohio | June 24 | Curtis Turner | John Eanes |
| 13. | Gardena, Calif. | June 30 | Lou Figaro | Jack Gaynor |
| 14. | Grand Rapids, Mich. | July 1 | Marshall Teague | Marshall Teague |
| 15. | Bainbridge, Ohio | July 8 | Fonty Flock | Frank Christian |
| 16. | Carnegie, Pa. | July 15 | Herb Thomas | Hubert Westmoreland |
| 17. | Weaverville, N.C. | July 29 | Fonty Flock | Frank Christian |
| 18. | Rochester, N.Y. | July 31 | Lee Petty | Petty Enterprises |
| 19. | Altamont, N.Y. | Aug. 1 | Fonty Flock | Frank Christian |
| 20. | Detroit | Aug. 12 | Tommy Thompson | Tommy Thompson |
| 21. | Toledo, Ohio | Aug. 19 | Tim Flock | Ted Chester |
| 22. | Morristown, N.J. | Aug. 24 | Tim Flock | Ted Chester |
| 23. | Greenville, S.C. | Aug. 25 | Bob Flock | Ted Chester |
| 24. | Darlington, S.C. | Sept. 3 | Herb Thomas | Herb Thomas |
| 25. | Columbia, S.C. | Sept. 7 | Tim Flock | Ted Chester |
| 26. | Macon, Ga. | Sept. 8 | Herb Thomas | Herb Thomas |
| 27. | Langhorne, Pa. | Sept. 15 | Herb Thomas | Herb Thomas |
| 28. | Charlotte | Sept. 23 | Herb Thomas | Herb Thomas |
| 29. | Dayton, Ohio | Sept. 23 | Fonty Flock | Frank Christian |
| 30. | Wilson, N.C. | Sept. 30 | Fonty Flock | Frank Christian |
| 31. | Hillsboro, N.C. | Oct. 7 | Herb Thomas | Herb Thomas |
| 32. | Thompson, Conn. | Oct. 12 | Neil Cole | John Golabek |
| 33. | Shippenville, Pa. | Oct. 14 | Tim Flock | Ted Chester |
| 34. | Martinsville, Va. | Oct. 14 | Frank Mundy | Ted Chester |
| 35. | Oakland | Oct. 14 | Marvin Burke | Bob Phillippi |
| 36. | North Wilkesboro, N.C. | Oct. 21 | Fonty Flock | Ted Chester |
| 37. | Hanford, Calif. | Oct. 28 | Danny Weinberg | Tony Sampo |
| 38. | Jacksonville, Fla. | Nov. 4 | Herb Thomas | Marshall Teague |
| 39. | Atlanta | Nov. 11 | Tim Flock | Ted Chester |
| 40. | Gardena, Calif. | Nov. 11 | Bill Norton | Larry Bettinger |
| 41. | Mobile, Ala. | Nov. 25 | Frank Mundy | Perry Smith |

## Points standings

1. Herb Thomas ............4,208.45
2. Fonty Flock..............4,062.25
3. Tim Flock .................3,722.50
4. Lee Petty .................2,392.25
5. Frank Mundy ...........1,963.50
6. Buddy Shuman ..........1,368.75
7. Jesse James Taylor ..1,214.00
8. Dick Rathmann..........1,040.00
9. Bill Snowden ...........1,009.25
10. Joe Eubanks.............1,005.50

## Race winners 14

1. Fonty Flock ....................8
2. Tim Flock ......................7
   Herb Thomas .................7
4. Marshall Teague ...........5
5. Curtis Turner ................3
   Frank Mundy .................3
7. Tommy Thompson ........1
   Neil Cole .......................1
   Danny Weinberg ............1
   Marvin Burke .................1
   Bill Norton.....................1
   Bob Flock ......................1
   Lou Figaro.....................1
   Lee Petty.......................1

## Money won leaders

1. Herb Thomas ...........$19,425
2. Fonty Flock.................14,770
3. Tim Flock ...................14,670
4. Lee Petty ....................7,250
5. Frank Mundy ..............6,470
6. Tommy Thompson .......5,225
7. Bob Flock ...................3,375
8. Jesse James Taylor .....3,175
9. Dick Rathmann............3,105
10. Joe Eubanks................3,085

## Pole winners 12

1. Fonty Flock ........................12
2. Tim Flock ...........................6
3. Frank Mundy ......................4
   Herb Thomas ....................4
5. Billy Carden ......................2
6. Gober Sosebee....................1
   Marshall Teague.................1
   Neil Cole ...........................1
   Bill Rexford .......................1
   Bob Flock...........................1
   Lou Figaro ........................1
   Andy Pierce .......................1

# 1950 SEASON

| Race No. | Location | Date | Winner | Car owner |
|---|---|---|---|---|
| 1. | Daytona Beach, Fla. | Feb. 5 | Harold Kite | Harold Kite |
| 2. | Charlotte | April 2 | Tim Flock | Harold Kite |
| 3. | Langhorne, Pa. | April 16 | Curtis Turner | John Eanes |
| 4. | Martinsville, Va. | May 21 | Curtis Turner | John Eanes |
| 5. | Canfield, Ohio | May 30 | Bill Rexford | Julian Buesink |
| 6. | Vernon, N.Y. | June 18 | Bill Blair | Sam Rice |
| 7. | Dayton, Ohio | June 25 | Jimmy Florian | Jimmy Florian |
| 8. | Rochester, N.Y. | July 2 | Curtis Turner | John Eanes |
| 9. | Charlotte | July 23 | Curtis Turner | John Eanes |
| 10. | Hillsboro, N.C. | Aug. 13 | Fireball Roberts | Sam Rice |
| 11. | Dayton, Ohio | Aug. 20 | Dick Linder | Don Rogalla |
| 12. | Hamburg, N.Y. | Aug. 27 | Dick Linder | Don Rogalla |
| 13. | Darlington, S.C. | Sept. 4 | Johnny Mantz | Westmoreland/France Sr. |
| 14. | Langhorne, Pa. | Sept. 17 | Fonty Flock | Frank Christian |
| 15. | North Wilkesboro, N.C. | Sept. 24 | Leon Sales | Hubert Westmoreland |
| 16. | Vernon, N.Y. | Oct. 1 | Dick Linder | Don Rogalla |
| 17. | Martinsville, Va. | Oct. 15 | Herb Thomas | Herb Thomas |
| 18. | Winchester, Ind. | Oct. 15 | Lloyd Moore | Julian Buesink |
| 19. | Hillsboro, N.C. | Oct. 29 | Lee Petty | Petty Enterprises |

## Points standings

1. Bill Rexford .............1,959.00
2. Fireball Roberts.........1,848.50
3. Lee Petty.................1,590.00
4. Lloyd Moore .............1,398.00
5. Curtis Turner .............1,375.50
6. Johnny Mantz ...........1,282.00
7. Chuck Mahoney ........1,217.50
8. Dick Linder ...............1,121.00
9. Jimmy Florian .............801.00
10. Bill Blair ........................766.00

## Race winners 14

1. Curtis Turner ............................4
2. Dick Linder ...............................3
3. Bill Rexford ..............................1
   Lee Petty..................................1
   Herb Thomas ...........................1
   Leon Sales ...............................1
   Fireball Roberts.........................1
   Lloyd Moore ..............................1
   Fonty Flock ...............................1
   Tim Flock ..................................1
   Bill Blair ....................................1
   Johnny Mantz ...........................1
   Harold Kite ...............................1
   Jimmy Florian ...........................1

## Money won leaders

1. Johnny Mantz .........$10,560
2. Curtis Turner ................7,195
3. Fireball Roberts ...........6,475
4. Lee Petty .....................6,375
5. Dick Linder .................5,450
6. Lloyd Moore .................5,300
7. Bill Rexford .................5,175
8. Bill Blair ......................4,200
9. Tim Flock .....................3,975
10. Herb Thomas ..............2,825

## Pole winners 11

1. Dick Linder ................................5
2. Curtis Turner .............................4
3. Fonty Flock ................................2
4. Joe Littlejohn ............................1
   Fireball Roberts .......................1
   Chuck Mahoney ......................1
   Red Byron ...............................1
   Buck Baker ..............................1
   Wally Campbell .......................1
   Jimmy Florian .........................1
   Tim Flock .................................1

**Fireball Roberts, Red Byron and Johnny Mantz**

# THE SOUTHERN 500: A TRADITION IS BORN

Darlington Raceway is such a unique track it has two nicknames: The Lady in Black and The Track Too Tough To Tame. Drivers have such a soft spot in their hearts for the track that they refer to it as "her." The track opened in 1950 as NASCAR's first superspeedway. At 1.366 miles, it seemed huge at the time. By today's standards, it's average.

Darlington also played host to the circuit's first-ever race on asphalt. The first race—the Southern 500—was won by Johnny Mantz, who started 43rd—a remarkable feat considering that since 1955, only Bobby Labonte (37th in 2000) and Ward Burton (37th in 2001) have won after starting lower than 15th. For decades, the Southern 500, held Labor Day weekend, was a highly anticipated and closely fought battle.

Today, Darlington's asphalt drives racers crazy. Its harsh composition eats up tires, and the slippery surface means drivers frequently run into the walls, leaving "Darlington stripes" along the passenger side door area of every car worth its weight in 10W-40. But that stripe is a badge of honor, and any driver will tell you that winning a trophy from Darlington is a special treat.

# 1949 SEASON

| Race No. | Location | Date | Winner | Car owner |
|---|---|---|---|---|
| 1. | Charlotte | June 19 | Jim Roper | R.B. McIntosh |
| 2. | Daytona Beach, Fla. | July 10 | Red Byron | Raymond Parks |
| 3. | Hillsboro, N.C. | Aug. 7 | Bob Flock | Frank Christian |
| 4. | Langhorne, Pa. | Sep. 11 | Curtis Turner | Hubert Westmoreland |
| 5. | Hamburg, N.Y. | Sept. 18 | Jack White | Dailey Moyer |
| 6. | Martinsville, Va. | Sept. 25 | Red Byron | Raymond Parks |
| 7. | Carnegie, Pa. | Oct. 2 | Lee Petty | Petty Enterprises |
| 8. | North Wilkesboro, N.C. | Oct. 16 | Bob Flock | Frank Christian |

## Points standings

1. Red Byron .....................842.50
2. Lee Petty .....................725.00
3. Bob Flock......................704.00
4. Bill Blair .....................567.50
5. Fonty Flock....................554.50
6. Curtis Turner ................430.00
7. Ray Erickson ................422.00
8. Tim Flock .....................421.00
9. Glenn Dunnaway ..........384.00
10. Frank Mundy ................370.00

## Race winners  6

1. Bob Flock ...............................2
   Red Byron................................2
3. Curtis Turner ..........................1
   Jack White ..............................1
   Lee Petty ................................1
   Jim Roper ................................1

## Money won leaders

1. Red Byron....................$4,800
2. Bob Flock .....................4,550
3. Lee Petty .....................3,375
4. Curtis Turner ...............2,475
5. Jim Roper.....................2,050
6. Fonty Flock ..................1,775
7. Jack White ..................1,500
8. Tim Flock .....................1,350
9. Gober Sosebee .............1,225
10. Frank Mundy ...............1,000

## Pole winners  6

1. Red Byron ...............................2
2. Curtis Turner .........................1
   Ken Wagner ............................1
   Gober Sosebee........................1
   Al Bonnell...............................1
   Bob Flock................................1

**Lee Petty**

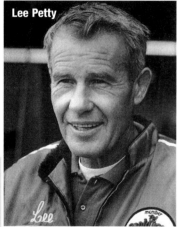

**Bill Rexford**

**Red Byron**

# 1948 SEASON

| Location | Date | Winner | Car owner |
|---|---|---|---|
| Daytona Beach, Fla. | Feb.15 | Red Byron | Raymond Parks |
| Jacksonville, Fla. | Feb. 24 | Fonty Flock | H.B .Babb & Elmer Fields |
| Atlanta | March 27 | Fonty Flock | H.B .Babb & Elmer Fields |
| Macon, Ga. | April 4 | Fonty Flock | H.B. Babb & Elmer Fields |
| Augusta, Ga. | April 11 | Bob Flock | Raymond Parks |
| Jacksonville, Fla. | April 18 | Skimp Hersey | Mac Richardson |
| Greensboro, N.C. | April 18 | Fonty Flock | H.B. Babb & Elmer Fields |
| N. Wilkesboro, N.C. | April 25 | Red Byron | Raymond Parks |
| Lexington, N.C. | May 2 | Red Byron | Raymond Parks |
| Wadesboro, N.C. | May 9 | Red Byron | Raymond Parks |
| Richmond, Va. | May 16 | Red Byron | Raymond Parks |
| Macon, Ga. | May 23 | Gober Sosebee | Gober Sosebee |
| Danville, Va. | May 23 | Bill Blair | Bill Blair |
| Dover, N.J. | May 23 | Johnny Rogers | N/A |
| Greensboro, N.C. | May 29 | Bob Flock | Raymond Parks |
| N. Wilkesboro, N.C. | May 30 | Marshall Teague | Marshall Teague |
| Jacksonville, Fla. | May 30 | Paul Pappy | N/A |
| Danville, Va. | June 4 | Bob Flock | Raymond Parks |
| Greensboro, N.C. | June 5 | Red Byron | Raymond Parks |
| Lexington, N.C. | June 6 | Bob Flock | Raymond Parks |
| Wadesboro, N.C. | June 13 | Fonty Flock | H.B. Babb & Elmer Fields |
| Birmingham, Ala. | June 20 | Fonty Flock | H.B. Babb & Elmer Fields |
| Columbus, Ga. | June 20 | Bob Flock | Raymond Parks |
| Greensboro, N.C. | June 20 | Tim Flock | Charlie Mobley |
| Occoneechee, N.C. | June 27 | Fonty Flock | H. B. Babb & Elmer Fields |
| Martinsville, Va. | July 4 | Fonty Flock | H B. Babb & Elmer Fields |
| Charlotte | July 11 | Red Byron | Raymond Parks |
| N. Wilkesboro, N.C. | July 18 | Curtis Turner | Bob Smith |
| Greensboro, N.C. | July 25 | Curtis Turner | Bob Smith |
| Columbus, Ga. | July 25 | Billy Carden | N/A |
| Lexington, N.C. | Aug. 1 | Curtis Turner | Bob Smith |
| Daytona Beach, Fla. | Aug. 8 | Fonty Flock | H.B. Babb & Elmer Fields |
| Langhorne, Pa. | Aug. 15 | Al Keller | N/A |
| Columbus, Ga. | Sept. 5 | Gober Sosebee | Gober Sosebee |
| N. Wilkesboro, N.C. (1) | Sept. 5 | Curtis Turner | Bob Smith |
| N. Wilkesboro, N.C. (2) | Sept. 5 | Curtis Turner | Bob Smith |
| Charlotte (1) | Sept. 12 | Curtis Turner | Bob Smith |
| Charlotte (2) | Sept. 12 | Buddy Shuman | Shuman-Thompson |
| Occoneechee, N.C. (1) | Sept. 19 | Fonty Flock | H.B. Babb & Elmer Fields |
| Occoneechee, N.C. (2) | Sept. 19 | Fonty Flock | H.B. Babb & Elmer Fields |
| Lexington, N.C. (1) | Sept. 26 | Fonty Flock | H.B. Babb & Elmer Fields |
| Lexington, N.C. (2) | Sept. 26 | Gober Sosebee | Gober Sosebee |
| Elkin, N.C. (1) | Oct.3 | Buddy Shuman | Shuman-Thompson |
| Elkin, N.C. (2) | Oct. 3 | Curtis Turner | Bob Smith |
| Macon, Ga, (1) | Oct. 3 | Billy Carden | N/A |
| Macon, Ga. (2) | Oct. 3 | Red Byron | Raymond Parks |
| Greensboro, N.C. | Oct. 10 | Fonty Flock | Joe Wolf |
| Greensboro, N.C. | Oct. 16 | Fonty Flock | Joe Wolf |
| N. Wilkesboro, N.C. | Oct. 17 | Red Byron | Raymond Parks |
| Charlotte | Oct. 24 | Red Byron | Raymond Parks |
| Winston-Salem, N.C. | Oct. 31 | Fonty Flock | Joe Wolf |
| Columbus, Ga. | Nov.14 | Red Byron | Raymond Parks |

## Points standings

1. Red Byron ................2996.5
2. Fonty Flock ............. 2963.75
3. Tim Flock ................... 1759.5
4. Curtis Turner ............ 1540.5
5. Buddy Shuman ............... 1350
6. Bill Blair ..................... 1188.5
7. Bob Flock ................... 1181.5
8. Marshall Teague ........ 1134.25
9. Bill Snowden ............... 1092.5
10. Buck Baker ................952.5
11. Billy Carden ..............866.5
12. Johnny Grubb ..................733
13. Speedy Thompson ...........623
13. Speedy Thompson .............623
15. Jimmy Lewallen ..............437
16. Al Keller.........................415
17. Jimmy Thompson ...........386
18. Jack Smith ..............384.75
19. Pee Wee Martin .................354
20. Fred Mahon .....................353

## Race winners 14

1. Fonty Flock ...................15
2. Red Byron ...................11
3. Curtis Turner ...............7
4. Bob Flock ....................5
5. Gober Sosebee ...........3
6. Billy Carden.................2
   Buddy Shuman ............2
8. Bill Blair.......................1
   Tim Flock ....................1
   Skimp Hersey ..............1
   Al Keller.......................1
   Paul Pappy ..................1
   Johnny Rogers ............1
   Marshall Teague ..........1

## Money won leaders

1. Red Byron...................$1,250
2. Fonty Flock.................... 600
3. Tim Flock ..................... 400
4. Curtis Turner.................. 350
5. Buddy Shuman ............. 300
6. Bill Blair ...................... 250
7. Bob Flock .................... 200
8. Marshall Teague ............ 150
   Bill Snowden ................ 150
   Buck Baker .................150
   Billy Carden .................150
   Johnny Grubb ...............150
   Speedy Thompson .........150
   Speedy Thompson .........150
15. Jimmy Lewallen .............100
    Al Keller............................100
    Jimmy Thompson ...........100
    Jack Smith .....................100
    Pee Wee Martin ...............100
    Fred Mahon .....................100

| | | | Wins |
|---|---|---|---|
| 1. | * | Richard Petty | 200 |
| 2. | * | David Pearson | 105 |
| 3. | * | Bobby Allison | 84 |
| | * | Darrell Waltrip | 84 |
| 5. | * | Cale Yarborough | 83 |
| 6. | # | Dale Earnhardt | 76 |
| 7. | | Jeff Gordon | 69 |
| 8. | # | Lee Petty | 55 |
| | | Rusty Wallace | 55 |
| 10. | * | Ned Jarrett | 50 |
| | * | Junior Johnson | 50 |
| 12. | * | Herb Thomas | 48 |
| 13. | # | Buck Baker | 46 |
| 14. | | Bill Elliott | 44 |
| 15. | # | Tim Flock | 40 |
| 16. | # | Bobby Isaac | 37 |
| 17. | | Mark Martin | 34 |
| 18. | #† | Fireball Roberts | 32 |
| 19. | | Dale Jarrett | 31 |
| 20. | *† | Rex White | 26 |
| | * | Fred Lorenzen | 26 |
| 22. | * | Jim Paschal | 25 |
| 23. | # | Joe Weatherly | 24 |
| 24. | | Ricky Rudd | 23 |
| 25. | | Terry Labonte | 22 |
| 26. | | Bobby Labonte | 21 |
| | * | Benny Parsons | 21 |
| | # | Jack Smith | 21 |
| 29. | # | Speedy Thompson | 20 |
| 30. | * | Buddy Baker | 19 |
| | # | Fonty Flock | 19 |
| | # | Davey Allison | 19 |
| | | Tony Stewart | 19 |
| 34. | | Geoffrey Bodine | 18 |
| | * | Harry Gant | 18 |
| | # | Neil Bonnett | 18 |
| 37. | | Jeff Burton | 17 |
| | * | Marvin Panch | 17 |
| | # | Curtis Turner | 17 |
| 40. | * | Ernie Irvan | 15 |
| | | Dale Earnhardt Jr. | 15 |
| 42. | * | Dick Hutcherson | 14 |

| | | | Wins |
|---|---|---|---|
| 43. | # | Lee Roy Yarbrough | 14 |
| | | Jimmie Johnson | 14 |
| 45. | # | Dick Rathmann | 13 |
| | # | Tim Richmond | 13 |
| 47. | | Kurt Busch | 11 |
| | | Ryan Newman | 11 |
| 49. | | Sterling Marlin | 10 |
| | * | Donnie Allison | 10 |
| 51. | * | Paul Goldsmith | 9 |
| | * | Cotton Owens | 9 |
| | | Matt Kenseth | 9 |
| 54. | | Kyle Petty | 8 |
| 55. | * | A.J. Foyt | 7 |
| | * | Jim Reed | 7 |
| | # | Marshall Teague | 7 |
| | # | Bob Welborn | 7 |
| | # | Darel Dieringer | 7 |
| 60. | | Ward Burton | 5 |
| | * | Dave Marcis | 5 |
| | * | Ralph Moody | 5 |
| | * | Dan Gurney | 5 |
| | # | Alan Kulwicki | 5 |
| 65. | | Ken Schrader | 4 |
| | | Bobby Hamilton | 4 |
| | | Morgan Shepherd | 4 |
| | | Kevin Harvick | 4 |
| | | Michael Waltrip | 4 |
| | * | Parnelli Jones | 4 |
| | * | Glen Wood | 4 |
| | * | Lloyd Dane | 4 |
| | * | Charlie Glotzbach | 4 |
| | * | Pete Hamilton | 4 |
| | | Hershel McGriff | 4 |
| | # | Bob Flock | 4 |
| | # | Eddie Gray | 4 |
| | # | Billy Wade | 4 |
| | # | Eddie Pagan | 4 |
| | # | Nelson Stacy | 4 |
| | | Jeremy Mayfield | 4 |
| | | Joe Nemechek III | 4 |
| 83. | | Robby Gordon | 3 |
| | * | Frank Mundy | 3 |

| | | Wins |
|---|---|---|
| # | Dick Linder | 3 |
| # | Tiny Lund | 3 |
| # | Bill Blair | 3 |
| | Elliott Sadler | 3 |
| | Greg Biffle | 3 |
| 89. | Jimmy Spencer | 2 |
| | Steve Park | 2 |
| | John Andretti | 2 |
| | Derrike Cope | 2 |
| | Ricky Craven | 2 |
| * | Tom Pistone | 2 |
| * | Danny Letner | 2 |
| * | Emanuel Zervakis | 2 |
| * | Ray Elder | 2 |
| * | James Hylton | 2 |
| * | Bobby Johns | 2 |
| # | Marvin Porter | 2 |
| # | Jimmy Pardue | 2 |
| # | Gober Sosebee | 2 |
| # | Gwyn Staley | 2 |
| # | Red Byron | 2 |
| # | Johnny Beauchamp | 2 |
| # | Al Keller | 2 |
| # | Billy Myers | 2 |
| # | Elmo Langley | 2 |
| 110. | Greg Sacks | 1 |
| | Brett Bodine | 1 |
| | Jerry Nadeau | 1 |
| | Johnny Benson | 1 |
| | Jamie McMurray | 1 |
| * | Phil Parsons | 1 |
| * | Bobby Hillin Jr. | 1 |
| * | Lake Speed | 1 |
| * | Dick Brooks | 1 |
| * | Jim Cook | 1 |
| * | Larry Frank | 1 |
| * | Danny Graves | 1 |
| * | Royce Hagerty | 1 |
| * | Joe Lee Johnson | 1 |
| * | John Kieper | 1 |
| * | Paul Lewis | 1 |
| * | Sam McQuagg | 1 |

| | | Wins |
|---|---|---|
| * | Lloyd Moore | 1 |
| * | Norm Nelson | 1 |
| * | Bill Norton | 1 |
| * | Dick Passwater | 1 |
| * | Lennie Pond | 1 |
| * | Jody Ridley | 1 |
| * | Earl Ross | 1 |
| * | John Rostek | 1 |
| * | Johnny Rutherford | 1 |
| * | Leon Sales | 1 |
| * | Frankie Schneider | 1 |
| * | John Soares Jr. | 1 |
| * | Chuck Stevenson | 1 |
| * | Tommy Thompson | 1 |
| * | Art Watts | 1 |
| * | Danny Weinberg | 1 |
| * | Jack White | 1 |
| * | Mario Andretti | 1 |
| * | Earl Balmer | 1 |
| * | Ron Bouchard | 1 |
| * | Johnny Allen | 1 |
| * | Neil Cole | 1 |
| * | Bob Burdick | 1 |
| * | Richard Brickhouse | 1 |
| * | Marvin Burke | 1 |
| * | June Cleveland | 1 |
| # | Bobby Courtwright | 1 |
| # | Mark Donohue | 1 |
| # | Joe Eubanks | 1 |
| # | Lou Figaro | 1 |
| # | Jimmy Florian | 1 |
| # | Jim Hurtubise | 1 |
| # | Harold Kite | 1 |
| # | Johnny Mantz | 1 |
| # | Bill Rexford | 1 |
| # | Shorty Rollins | 1 |
| # | Jim Roper | 1 |
| # | Wendell Scott | 1 |
| # | Buddy Shuman | 1 |
| # | Donald Thomas | 1 |
| # | Bill Amick | 1 |
| | **167 drivers,  2,023 wins** | |

KEY

* Retired
# Deceased
** 1,998 races; six wins by convertible division, three by Grand American division, three by short track division in combined races.
† Rex White and Fireball Roberts had two convertible wins not included in totals above.

HISTORY

## NMPA Driver of the Year

| Year | Drivers | Year | Drivers | Year | Drivers | Year | Drivers |
|---|---|---|---|---|---|---|---|
| 1969 | Lee Roy Yarbrough | 1978 | Cale Yarborough | 1987 | Dale Earnhardt | 1996 | Terry Labonte |
| 1970 | Bobby Isaac | 1979 | Richard Petty | 1988 | Rusty Wallace | 1997 | Dale Jarrett |
| 1971 | Bobby Allison | 1980 | Dale Earnhardt | 1989 | Mark Martin | 1998 | Jeff Gordon |
| 1972 | Bobby Allison | 1981 | Darrell Waltrip | 1990 | Dale Earnhardt | 1999 | Dale Jarrett |
| 1973 | David Pearson | 1982 | Darrell Waltrip | 1991 | Harry Gant | 2000 | Bobby Labonte |
| 1974 | Richard Petty | 1983 | Bobby Allison | 1992 | Davey Allison | 2001 | Kevin Harvick |
| 1975 | Richard Petty | 1984 | Terry Labonte | 1993 | Rusty Wallace | 2002 | Tony Stewart |
| 1976 | Cale Yarborough | 1985 | Bill Elliott | 1994 | Dale Earnhardt | 2003 | Ryan Newman |
| 1977 | Darrell Waltrip | 1986 | Dale Earnhardt | 1995 | Jeff Gordon | 2004 | To be determined |
| | | | Tim Richmond | | | | |

# Speedway race winners

| Driver | Wins | Driver | Wins | Driver | Wins | Driver | Wins | Driver | Wins | Driver | Wins |
|---|---|---|---|---|---|---|---|---|---|---|---|
| 1. Richard Petty | 55 | 19. Ricky Rudd | 12 | 37. Junior Johnson | 5 | Morgan Shepherd | 3 | Dick Brooks | 1 | Jim Reed | 1 |
| 2. David Pearson | 49 | Fred Lorenzen | 12 | Herb Thomas | 5 | Bobby Isaac | 3 | Bobby Hillin Jr. | 1 | Jody Ridley | 1 |
| 3. Dale Earnhardt | 48 | Benny Parsons | 12 | Ward Burton | 5 | Joe Nemechek | 3 | Darel Dieringer | 1 | Jack Smith | 1 |
| Jeff Gordon | 48 | D. Earnhardt Jr. | 12 | 40. Ken Schrader | 4 | Greg Biffle | 3 | Larry Frank | 1 | Mario Andretti | 1 |
| 5. C. Yarborough | 47 | 23. L. Yarbrough | 11 | Buck Baker | 4 | 58. Derrike Cope | 2 | Jim Hurtubise | 1 | T. Thompson | 1 |
| Bobby Allison | 47 | Fireball Roberts | 11 | Marvin Panch | 4 | Jimmy Spencer | 2 | Dick Hutcherson | 1 | Rex White | 1 |
| 7. Bill Elliott | 40 | Terry Labonte | 11 | Michael Waltrip | 4 | Dave Marcis | 2 | James Hylton | 1 | Bob Burdick | 1 |
| 8. Darrell Waltrip | 32 | Tony Stewart | 11 | Kevin Harvick | 4 | Charlie Glotzbach | 2 | Bobby Johns | 1 | R. Brickhouse | 1 |
| 9. Dale Jarrett | 27 | 27. Sterling Marlin | 10 | 45. Bobby Hamilton | 3 | Ned Jarrett | 2 | Joe Lee Johnson | 1 | Lake Speed | 1 |
| 10. Rusty Wallace | 24 | Ryan Newman | 10 | Jeremy Mayfield | 3 | Jim Paschal | 2 | Tiny Lund | 1 | Ron Bouchard | 1 |
| 11. Mark Martin | 23 | 29. Donnie Allison | 9 | Alan Kulwicki | 3 | Lee Petty | 2 | Johnny Mantz | 1 | Greg Sacks | 1 |
| 12. Bobby Labonte | 20 | 30. Ernie Irvan | 8 | Nelson Stacy | 3 | Curtis Turner | 2 | Hershel McGriff | 1 | Johnny Benson | 1 |
| 13. Buddy Baker | 17 | Matt Kenseth | 8 | S. Thompson | 3 | Elliott Sadler | 2 | Sam McQuagg | 1 | Jamie McMurray | 1 |
| 14. Jeff Burton | 15 | 32. Geoff Bodine | 7 | Joe Weatherly | 3 | 68. John Andretti | 1 | Ralph Moody | 1 | Ricky Craven | 1 |
| Neil Bonnett | 15 | 33. Kyle Petty | 6 | Paul Goldsmith | 3 | Phil Parsons | 1 | Eddie Pagan | 1 | **104 drivers **847 wins |  |
| 16. Davey Allison | 14 | Tim Richmond | 6 | Fonty Flock | 3 | Steve Park | 1 | Lennie Pond | 1 | **1 win by convertible |  |
| 17. Harry Gant | 13 | A.J. Foyt | 6 | Tim Flock | 3 | Jerry Nadeau | 1 | Marvin Porter | 1 | division in a combined |  |
| Jimmie Johnson | 13 | Kurt Busch | 6 | Pete Hamilton | 3 | Robby Gordon | 1 | Dick Rathmann | 1 | race. Total Races: 820 |  |

# Short track winners

| Driver | Wins | Driver | Wins | Driver | Wins | Driver | Wins | Driver | Wins | Driver | Wins |
|---|---|---|---|---|---|---|---|---|---|---|---|
| 1. Richard Petty | 139 | 23. Fred Lorenzen | 14 | Glen Wood | 4 | Billy Myers | 2 | Jimmy Florian | 1 | Frankie Schneider | 1 |
| 2. David Pearson | 52 | 24. Dick Hutcherson | 13 | Ernie Irvan | 4 | Jimmy Pardue | 2 | Danny Graves | 1 | Wendell Scott | 1 |
| Lee Petty | 52 | Jeff Gordon | 13 | Ralph Moody | 4 | Tim Richmond | 2 | Royce Hagerty | 1 | Buddy Shuman | 1 |
| 4. Ned Jarrett | 48 | 26. Dick Rathmann | 12 | 48. Lloyd Dane | 3 | Gober Sosebee | 2 | Pete Hamilton | 1 | John Soares Jr. | 1 |
| 5. Darrell Waltrip | 47 | 27. Marvin Panch | 11 | Neil Bonnett | 3 | Gwyn Staley | 2 | James Hylton | 1 | Nelson Stacy | 1 |
| 6. Junior Johnson | 45 | 28. Terry Labonte | 9 | Eddie Gray | 3 | Billy Wade | 2 | Bobby Johns | 1 | Donald Thomas | 1 |
| 7. Herb Thomas | 43 | 29. Geoff Bodine | 8 | Dick Linder | 3 | Emanuel Zervakis | 2 | Parnelli Jones | 1 | Art Watts | 1 |
| 8. Buck Baker | 41 | Cotton Owens | 8 | Hershel McGriff | 3 | Buddy Baker | 2 | Al Keller | 1 | Danny Weinberg | 1 |
| 9. Bobby Isaac | 34 | Benny Parsons | 8 | Eddie Pagan | 3 | J. Beauchamp | 2 | John Kieper | 1 | Jack White | 1 |
| Tim Flock | 34 | 32. Mark Martin | 7 | L. Yarbrough | 3 | 76. Brett Bodine | 1 | Paul Lewis | 1 | Bill Amick | 1 |
| 11. C. Yarborough | 33 | Bob Welborn | 7 | Dave Marcis | 3 | Bobby Hamilton | 1 | Lloyd Moore | 1 | John Rostek | 1 |
| 12. Bobby Allison | 31 | 34. Jim Reed | 6 | Frank Mundy | 3 | Kyle Petty | 1 | Norm Nelson | 1 | Leon Sales | 1 |
| 13. Dale Earnhardt | 27 | 35. Ricky Rudd | 5 | Dale Earnhardt Jr. | 3 | Donnie Allison | 1 | Bill Norton | 1 | Marvin Burke | 1 |
| 14. Rex White | 25 | Darel Dieringer | 5 | 58. Jeff Burton | 2 | Morgan Shepherd | 1 | Dick Passwater | 1 | Earl Balmer | 1 |
| Rusty Wallace | 25 | Paul Goldsmith | 5 | Bill Elliott | 2 | Johnny Allen | 1 | Marvin Porter | 1 | J. Rutherford | 1 |
| 16. Jim Paschal | 23 | Marshall Teague | 5 | Bill Blair | 2 | Red Byron | 1 | Bill Rexford | 1 | Matt Kenseth | 1 |
| 17. Joe Weatherly | 21 | Harry Gant | 5 | Charlie Glotzbach | 2 | June Cleveland | 1 | Shorty Rollins | 1 | Bobby Labonte | 1 |
| 18. Jack Smith | 19 | Tony Stewart | 5 | Tom Pistone | 2 | Neil Cole | 1 | Jim Roper | 1 | Joe Nemechek | 1 |
| Fireball Roberts | 19 | Kurt Busch | 5 | Alan Kulwicki | 2 | Jim Cook | 1 | Earl Ross | 1 | Ryan Newman | 1 |
| 20. S. Thompson | 17 | 42. Dale Jarrett | 4 | Elmo Langley | 2 | B. Courtwright | 1 | Elliot Sadler | 1 | Jeremy Mayfield | 1 |
| 21. Fonty Flock | 16 | Davey Allison | 4 | Danny Letner | 2 | Joe Eubanks | 1 | John Andretti | 1 | Jimmie Johnson | 1 |
| 22. Curtis Turner | 15 | Bob Flock | 4 | Tiny Lund | 2 | Lou Figaro | 1 | Ricky Craven | 1 | 129 drivers 1,097 |  |
|  |  |  |  |  |  |  |  |  |  | Total races 2,008 |  |

# Road race winners

| Driver | Wins | Driver | Wins | Driver | Wins | Driver | Wins | Driver | Wins | Driver | Wins |
|---|---|---|---|---|---|---|---|---|---|---|---|
| 1. Jeff Gordon | 8 | 9. Mark Martin | 4 | Marvin Panch | 2 | Buck Baker | 1 | A.J. Foyt | 1 | Kyle Petty | 1 |
| 2. Rusty Wallace | 6 | David Pearson | 4 | Fireball Roberts | 2 | Dale Earnhardt | 1 | Paul Goldsmith | 1 | Jack Smith | 1 |
| Richard Petty | 6 | 11. Geoff Bodine | 3 | Marshall Teague | 2 | Davey Allison | 1 | Eddie Gray | 1 | Chuck Stevenson | 1 |
| Bobby Allison | 6 | Ernie Irvan | 3 | Billy Wade | 2 | Red Byron | 1 | Al Keller | 1 | Bill Blair | 1 |
| Ricky Rudd | 6 | Cale Yarborough | 3 | Ray Elder | 2 | Lloyd Dane | 1 | Harold Kite | 1 |  |  |
| 6. Darrell Waltrip | 5 | Tim Flock | 3 | Parnelli Jones | 2 | Darel Dieringer | 1 | Cotton Owens | 1 | 44 drivers, 105 wins |  |
| Dan Gurney | 5 | Tony Stewart | 3 | Robby Gordon | 2 | Mark Donohue | 1 | Benny Parsons | 1 |  |  |
| Tim Richmond | 5 | 16. Terry Labonte | 2 | 24. Steve Park | 1 | Bill Elliott | 1 | Lee Petty | 1 |  |  |

| | Driver | Poles |
|---|---|---|
| 1. | Richard Petty | 126 |
| 2. | David Pearson | 113 |
| 3. | Cale Yarborough | 70 |
| 4. | Darrell Waltrip | 59 |
| 5. | Bobby Allison | 57 |
| 6. | Bill Elliott | 55 |
| 7. | Jeff Gordon | 52 |
| 8. | Bobby Isaac | 51 |
| 9. | Junior Johnson | 47 |
| 10. | Buck Baker | 44 |
| 11. | Mark Martin | 41 |
| 12. | Buddy Baker | 40 |
| 13. | Tim Flock | 39 |
| | Herb Thomas | 39 |
| 15. | Geoff Bodine | 37 |
| 16. | Rusty Wallace | 36 |
| 17. | Fireball Roberts | 35 |
| | Ned Jarrett | 35 |
| | Rex White | 35 |
| 20. | Fonty Flock | 34 |
| 21. | Fred Lorenzen | 33 |
| 22. | Ricky Rudd | 29 |
| 23. | Terry Labonte | 27 |
| | Ryan Newman | 27 |
| 24. | Bobby Labonte | 26 |
| 25. | Jack Smith | 24 |
| | Alan Kulwicki | 24 |
| 27. | Ken Schrader | 23 |
| 28. | Dale Earnhardt | 22 |
| | Ernie Irvan | 22 |
| | Dick Hutcherson | 22 |
| 31. | Marvin Panch | 21 |
| 32. | Neil Bonnett | 20 |
| | Benny Parsons | 20 |
| 34. | Joe Weatherly | 19 |
| | Speedy Thompson | 19 |
| 36. | Lee Petty | 18 |
| 38. | Harry Gant | 17 |
| | Curtis Turner | 17 |
| | Donnie Allison | 17 |
| 41. | Dale Jarrett | 15 |
| 42. | Tim Richmond | 14 |
| | Davey Allison | 14 |
| | Dave Marcis | 14 |
| 45. | Dick Rathmann | 13 |
| 46. | Charlie Glotzbach | 12 |
| | Jim Paschal | 12 |
| 48. | Sterling Marlin | 11 |
| | Darel Dieringer | 11 |
| | Lee Roy Yarbrough | 11 |
| | Cotton Owens | 11 |
| | Glen Wood | 11 |
| 53. | A.J. Foyt | 10 |
| 54. | Jeremy Mayfield | 9 |
| 55. | Kyle Petty | 8 |
| | Paul Goldsmith | 8 |
| | Joe Nemechek | 8 |
| 58. | Morgan Shepherd | 7 |
| | Bob Welborn | 7 |
| | Ward Burton | 7 |
| | Tony Stewart | 7 |
| | Jimmie Johnson | 7 |
| 63. | Tiny Lund | 6 |
| | Eddie Pagan | 6 |
| | Dale Earnhardt Jr. | 6 |
| | Ricky Craven | 6 |
| | Bobby Hamilton | 6 |

| | Driver | Poles |
|---|---|---|
| 68. | Ted Musgrave | 5 |
| | Mike Skinner | 5 |
| | Brett Bodine | 5 |
| | Dick Linder | 5 |
| | Hershel McGriff | 5 |
| | Ralph Moody | 5 |
| | Tom Pistone | 5 |
| | Lennie Pond | 5 |
| | Billy Wade | 5 |
| | Art Watts | 5 |
| | Bill Amick | 5 |
| | Joe Eubanks | 5 |
| | Todd Bodine | 5 |
| 81. | John Andretti | 4 |
| | Rick Mast | 4 |
| | James Hylton | 4 |
| | Gober Sosebee | 4 |
| | Jim Reed | 4 |
| | Steve Park | 4 |
| | Kasey Kahne | 4 |
| 88. | Loy Allen Jr | 3 |
| | Joe Ruttman | 3 |
| | Ron Bouchard | 3 |
| | Frank Mundy | 3 |
| | Jimmy Pardue | 3 |
| | Marshall Teague | 3 |
| | Bob Flock | 3 |
| | Johnny Allen | 3 |
| | Pete Hamilton | 3 |
| | Parnelli Jones | 3 |
| | Banjo Matthews | 3 |
| | Kenny Irwin Jr | 3 |
| | Kenny Wallace | 3 |
| | Matt Kenseth | 3 |
| 102. | Johnny Benson | 2 |
| | Michael Waltrip | 2 |
| | Jeff Burton | 2 |
| | Dan Gurney | 2 |
| | Friday Hassler | 2 |
| | Tommy Irwin | 2 |
| | Bobby Johns | 2 |
| | John Kieper | 2 |
| | Mel Larson | 2 |
| | Ken Rush | 2 |
| | John Sears | 2 |
| | Billy Carden | 2 |
| | Stacy Compton | 2 |
| | Greg Sacks | 2 |
| | Danny Graves | 2 |
| | Doug Yates | 2 |
| | Emanuel Zervakis | 2 |
| | Gwyn Staley | 2 |
| | Bob Burdick | 2 |
| | Red Byron | 2 |
| | Kurt Busch | 2 |
| | Jeff Green | 2 |
| | Kevin Harvick | 2 |
| | Elliott Sadler | 2 |
| | Casey Mears | 2 |
| | Brian Vickers | 2 |
| 128. | Jimmy Spencer | 1 |
| | Robby Gordon | 1 |
| | Jimmy Hensley | 1 |
| | Hut Stricklin | 1 |
| | Dick Trickle | 1 |
| | Derrike Cope | 1 |
| | Rick Wilson | 1 |

| Driver | Poles |
|---|---|
| David Green | 1 |
| Kevin Lepage | 1 |
| Wally Campbell | 1 |
| Neil Cole | 1 |
| Jim Cook | 1 |
| Bobby Courtwright | 1 |
| Doug Cox | 1 |
| Bill Dennis | 1 |
| Bob Duell | 1 |
| Glenn Dunaway | 1 |
| Ralph Earnhardt | 1 |
| Lou Figaro | 1 |
| Jimmy Florian | 1 |
| George Follmer | 1 |
| Eddie Gray | 1 |
| Royce Hagerty | 1 |
| Russ Hepler | 1 |
| Jim Hunter | 1 |
| Possum Jones | 1 |
| Al Keller | 1 |
| Pat Kirkwood | 1 |
| Elmo Langley | 1 |
| Danny Letner | 1 |
| Jimmie Lewallen | 1 |
| Paul Lewis | 1 |
| Joe Littlejohn | 1 |
| Chuck Mahoney | 1 |
| Jim Massey | 1 |
| J.D McDuffie | 1 |
| Joe Millikan | 1 |
| Tommy Moon | 1 |
| Paul "Bud" Moore | 1 |
| Billy Myers | 1 |
| Norm Nelson | 1 |
| Andy Pierce | 1 |
| Don Porter | 1 |
| Bob Pronger | 1 |
| Chuck Bown | 1 |
| Jason Leffler | 1 |
| Al Bonnell | 1 |
| Bob Ross | 1 |
| Slick Smith | 1 |
| Donald Thomas | 1 |
| John Rostek | 1 |
| Sam Sommers | 1 |
| Larry Baumel | 1 |
| Frankie Schneider | 1 |
| G.C. Spencer | 1 |
| Ken Wagner | 1 |
| Wendell Scott | 1 |
| Ramo Stott | 1 |
| Danny Weinberg | 1 |
| Frank Secrist | 1 |
| Dick Bailey | 1 |
| Bill Rexford | 1 |
| Lloyd Shaw | 1 |
| Lyle Tadlock | 1 |
| Perk Brown | 1 |
| Bill Benson | 1 |
| Dink Widenhouse | 1 |
| Bill Blair | 1 |
| Dave Blaney | 1 |
| Greg Biffle | 1 |
| Boris Said | 1 |
| Jamie McMurray | 1 |

**195 drivers, *1,980 poles**

*1,998 races; no qualifying for 46 races; five poles by convertible division, one by Grand American division, two by short track division in combined races.

HISTORY

# Speedway pole winners

| Driver | Poles | Driver | Poles | Driver | Poles | Driver | Poles | Driver | Poles | Driver | Poles |
|---|---|---|---|---|---|---|---|---|---|---|---|
| 1. David Pearson | 58 | Dale Jarrett | 14 | Junior Johnson | 6 | Pete Hamilton | 3 | Hut Stricklin | 1 | S. Thompson | 1 |
| 2. Bill Elliott | 48 | 21. Terry Labonte | 13 | L. Yarborough | 6 | Todd Bodine | 3 | Dick Trickle | 1 | Bob Welborn | 1 |
| 3. C. Yarborough | 46 | Ernie Irvan | 13 | Dale Earnhardt Jr. | 6 | Tony Stewart | 3 | Joe Ruttman | 1 | Frankie Schneider | 1 |
| 4. Jeff Gordon | 33 | Ricky Rudd | 13 | 42. Ward Burton | 5 | Steve Park | 3 | Robby Gordon | 1 | Friday Hassler | 1 |
| 5. Buddy Baker | 29 | 24. Dale Earnhardt | 12 | Fonty Flock | 5 | 62. J. Benson | 2 | Derrike Cope | 1 | J.D. McDuffie | 1 |
| 6. Bobby Labonte | 24 | Harry Gant | 12 | Jimmie Johnson | 5 | Morgan Shepherd | 2 | Dick Hutcherson | 1 | Kevin Lepage | 1 |
| 7. Richard Petty | 23 | Davey Allison | 12 | 45. John Andretti | 4 | Michael Waltrip | 2 | Hershel McGriff | 1 | David Green | 1 |
| 8. Mark Martin | 22 | 27. Sterling Marlin | 11 | Mike Skinner | 4 | Greg Sacks | 2 | Frank Mundy | 1 | Kenny Wallace | 1 |
| Ken Schrader | 22 | C. Glotzbach | 11 | Rick Mast | 4 | Ron Bouchard | 2 | Jimmy Pardue | 1 | Jason Leffler | 1 |
| Ryan Newman | 22 | Neil Bonnett | 11 | Darel Dieringer | 4 | Paul Goldsmith | 2 | Lee Petty | 1 | Casey Atwood | 1 |
| 11. Geoff Bodine | 21 | 30. Benny Parsons | 10 | Herb Thomas | 4 | Eddie Pagan | 2 | Dick Rathmann | 1 | Matt Kenseth | 1 |
| 12. Fireball Roberts | 20 | 31. Dave Marcis | 9 | Kasey Kahne | 4 | Banjo Matthews | 2 | Bob Ross | 1 | Jamie McMurray | 1 |
| 13. Rusty Wallace | 19 | Tim Richmond | 9 | 51. Bobby Hamilton | 3 | Jimmy Spencer | 2 | Tim Flock | 1 | Jeff Green | 1 |
| 14. Bobby Allison | 18 | Jeremy Mayfield | 9 | John Andretti | 3 | Stacy Compton | 2 | Frank Secrist | 1 | Dave Blaney | 1 |
| 15. Alan Kulwicki | 17 | 34. A.J. Foyt | 7 | Cotton Owens | 3 | Kurt Busch | 2 | Jack Smith | 1 | Greg Biffle | 1 |
| 16. Donnie Allison | 15 | Joe Nemechek | 7 | Curtis Turner | 3 | Kevin Harvick | 2 | Slick Smith | 1 | Brian Vickers | 1 |
| Darrell Waltrip | 15 | Rick Craven | 7 | Buck Baker | 3 | Elliott Sadler | 2 | Sam Sommers | 1 | **111 drivers, 827 poles** | |
| Bobby Isaac | 15 | 37. Kyle Petty | 6 | Loy Allen Jr. | 3 | Casey Mears | 2 | Ramo Stott | 1 | | |
| 19. Fred Lorenzen | 14 | Marvin Panch | 6 | Kenny Irwin Jr. | 3 | 76. Jeff Burton | 1 | Marshall Teague | 1 | | |

# Short track pole winners

| Driver | Wins | Driver | Wins | Driver | Wins | Driver | Wins | Driver | Wins | Driver | Wins |
|---|---|---|---|---|---|---|---|---|---|---|---|
| 1. Richard Petty | 97 | Dick Rathmann | 12 | Hershel McGriff | 4 | Gwyn Staley | 2 | B. Courtwright | 1 | Don Porter | 1 |
| 2. David Pearson | 47 | 29. Buddy Baker | 11 | Eddie Pagan | 4 | Marshall Teague | 2 | Doug Cox | 1 | Bill Rexford | 1 |
| 3. Junior Johnson | 40 | Glenn Wood | 11 | Billy Wade | 4 | John Kieper | 2 | Bill Dennis | 1 | John Rostek | 1 |
| 4. Buck Baker | 38 | 31. Ricky Rudd | 10 | Art Watts | 4 | Jimmy Pardue | 2 | Bob Duell | 1 | Wendell Scott | 1 |
| 5. Bobby Isaac | 36 | Benny Parsons | 10 | M. Shepherd | 4 | Billy Carden | 2 | Joe Nemechek | 1 | Lloyd Shaw | 1 |
| 6. Darrell Waltrip | 35 | 33. Neil Bonnett | 9 | 60. Tony Stewart | 3 | Doug Yates | 2 | Jeff Green | 1 | G.C. Spencer | 1 |
| Ned Jarrett | 35 | 34. Ernie Irvan | 8 | Jim Reed | 3 | E. Zervakis | 2 | Todd Bodine | 1 | Lyle Tadlock | 1 |
| Herb Thomas | 35 | Cotton Owens | 8 | Tim Richmond | 3 | Ken Rush | 2 | A.J. Foyt | 1 | Donald Thomas | 1 |
| Rex White | 35 | 36. Bill Elliott | 7 | Bob Flock | 3 | Parnelli Jones | 2 | Charlie Glotzbach | 1 | Ken Wagner | 1 |
| Tim Flock | 35 | Darrell Dieringer | 7 | Gober Sosebee | 3 | Ward Burton | 2 | Danny Graves | 1 | Danny Weinberg | 1 |
| 11. Bobby Allison | 34 | Alan Kulwicki | 7 | Paul Goldsmith | 3 | Mike Skinner | 2 | Royce Hagerty | 1 | Dink Widenhouse | 1 |
| 12. Fonty Flock | 29 | Bob Welborn | 6 | Johnny Allen | 3 | 93. Ricky Craven | 1 | Friday Hassler | 1 | Glenn Dunaway | 1 |
| 13. C. Yarborough | 22 | Tiny Lund | 6 | 67. Bobby Labonte | 2 | Ken Schrader | 1 | Russ Hepler | 1 | Ralph Earnhardt | 1 |
| Jack Smith | 22 | Terry Labonte | 6 | Kyle Petty | 2 | Jimmy Spencer | 1 | Jim Hunter | 1 | Joe Millikan | 1 |
| 15. D. Hutcherson | 20 | 42. Ted Musgrave | 5 | Kenny Wallace | 2 | Rick Wilson | 1 | Possum Jones | 1 | Dick Bailey | 1 |
| 16. Joe Weatherly | 19 | Dave Marcis | 5 | Bobby Hamilton | 2 | Chuck Bown | 1 | Al Keller | 1 | Larry Baumel | 1 |
| 17. S. Thompson | 18 | Harry Gant | 5 | Joe Ruttman | 2 | Jimmy Hensley | 1 | Elmo Langley | 1 | Lou Figaro | 1 |
| 18. Fred Lorenzen | 17 | Ralph Moody | 5 | Brett Bodine | 2 | Ron Bouchard | 1 | Danny Letner | 1 | Jimmy Florian | 1 |
| 19. Lee Petty | 16 | Tom Pistone | 5 | Davey Allison | 2 | Jeff Burton | 1 | Jimmie Lewallen | 1 | Jimmie Johnson | 1 |
| 20. Mark Martin | 15 | Lennie Pond | 5 | Donnie Allison | 2 | Steve Park | 1 | Paul Lewis | 1 | Brian Vickers | 1 |
| Fireball Roberts | 15 | Bill Amick | 5 | Tommy Irwin | 2 | Bill Benson | 1 | Chuck Mahoney | 1 | **154 drivers, 1,080 poles** | |
| 22. Rusty Wallace | 14 | Joe Eubanks | 5 | Bobby Johns | 2 | Bill Blair | 1 | Jim Massey | 1 | **Total races 2,008** | |
| Marvin Panch | 14 | Dick Linder | 5 | John Sears | 2 | Al Bonnell | 1 | Tommy Moon | 1 | | |
| Curtis Turner | 14 | L. Yarborough | 5 | Frank Mundy | 2 | Perk Brown | 1 | Paul "Bud" Moore | 1 | | |
| Geoff Bodine | 14 | Dale Earnhardt | 5 | Bob Burdick | 2 | Wally Campbell | 1 | Billy Myers | 1 | | |
| Jeff Gordon | 14 | Ryan Newman | 5 | Mel Larson | 2 | Neil Cole | 1 | Norm Nelson | 1 | | |
| 27. Jim Paschal | 12 | 54. James Hylton | 4 | Red Byron | 2 | Jim Cook | 1 | Andy Pierce | 1 | | |

# Road race pole winners

| Driver | Wins | Driver | Wins | Driver | Wins | Driver | Wins | Driver | Wins | Driver | Wins |
|---|---|---|---|---|---|---|---|---|---|---|---|
| 1. Darrell Waltrip | 9 | 9. Mark Martin | 4 | Cale Yarborough | 2 | Junior Johnson | 1 | Bob Pronger | 1 | Danny Graves | 1 |
| 2. Terry Labonte | 8 | 10. Rusty Wallace | 3 | Dan Gurney | 2 | Parnelli Jones | 1 | Jim Reed | 1 | Boris Said | 1 |
| David Pearson | 8 | Tim Flock | 3 | A.J. Foyt | 2 | Pat Kirkwood | 1 | Morgan Shepherd | 1 | Jimmie Johnson | 1 |
| 4. Richard Petty | 6 | Paul Goldsmith | 3 | 20. Todd Bodine | 1 | Tony Stewart | 1 | Jack Smith | 1 | **43 drivers, 103 poles** | |
| Ricky Rudd | 6 | Buck Baker | 3 | Dale Jarrett | 1 | Joe Littlejohn | 1 | Gober Sosebee | 1 | | |
| Jeff Gordon | 6 | 14. Geoff Bodine | 2 | Eddie Gray | 1 | Banjo Matthews | 1 | Billy Wade | 1 | | |
| 7. Dale Earnhardt | 5 | Fred Lorenzen | 2 | Dick Hutcherson | 1 | Marvin Panch | 1 | Art Watts | 1 | | |
| Bobby Allison | 5 | Tim Richmond | 2 | Ernie Irvan | 1 | Lee Petty | 1 | George Follmer | 1 | | |

# Races won from the pole

| | | | | | | | | | |
|---|---|---|---|---|---|---|---|---|---|
| 1. | Richard Petty | 61 | | Marvin Panch | 6 | Jim Reed | 2 | Lee Roy Yarbrough | 1 |
| 2. | David Pearson | 37 | | Joe Weatherly | 6 | Paul Goldsmith | 2 | Dan Gurney | 1 |
| 3. | Darrell Waltrip | 24 | | Fireball Roberts | 6 | Eddie Pagan | 2 | Dave Marcis | 1 |
| 4. | Bobby Isaac | 21 | 25. | Terry Labonte | 4 | Dick Linder | 2 | Neil Cole | 1 |
| 5. | Bobby Allison | 20 | | Bobby Labonte | 4 | Donnie Allison | 2 | Alan Kulwicki | 1 |
| 6. | Herb Thomas | 19 | | Tim Richmond | 4 | Charlie Glotzbach | 2 | Lou Figaro | 1 |
| 7. | Jeff Gordon | 17 | | Curtis Turner | 4 | Bob Welborn | 2 | Marshall Teague | 1 |
| 8. | Cale Yarborough | 16 | | Buddy Baker | 4 | Davey Allison | 2 | Gwyn Staley | 1 |
| | Tim Flock | 16 | | Dick Hutcherson | 4 | Darel Dieringer | 2 | Donald Thomas | 1 |
| 10. | Bill Elliott | 15 | | Jim Paschal | 4 | Ernie Irvan | 2 | Frank Mundy | 1 |
| 11. | Buck Baker | 12 | 32. | Dale Earnhardt | 3 | 53. | Bobby Hamilton | 1 | Kurt Busch | 1 |
| | Junior Johnson | 12 | | Kyle Petty | 3 | Tony Stewart | 1 | Kevin Harvick | 1 |
| 13. | Ned Jarrett | 11 | | Glen Wood | 3 | Sterling Marlin | 1 | Jimmie Johnson | 1 |
| | Fred Lorenzen | 11 | | Billy Wade | 3 | Ricky Rudd | 1 | Joe Nemecheck | 1 |
| 15. | Rusty Wallace | 9 | | Hershel McGriff | 3 | Benny Parsons | 1 | | |
| | Fonty Flock | 9 | | Geoff Bodine | 3 | Art Watts | 1 | **77 drivers, 464 races** | |
| 17. | Mark Martin | 7 | | A.J. Foyt | 3 | Ralph Moody | 1 | | |
| | Rex White | 7 | | Cotton Owens | 3 | Norm Nelson | 1 | | |
| | Lee Petty | 7 | | Ryan Newman | 3 | Danny Graves | 1 | | |
| | Speedy Thompson | 7 | 41. | Dale Jarrett | 2 | Parnelli Jones | 1 | | |
| 21. | Jack Smith | 6 | | Harry Gant | 2 | Jim Cook | 1 | | |

# All-time money leaders

| Rank | | Driver | Career Starts | Career Winnings | Average Per Start |
|---|---|---|---|---|---|
| 1 | | Jeff Gordon | 401 | $ 66,964,439 | $166,994 |
| 2 | | Dale Jarrett | 567 | 46,915,666 | 82,743 |
| 3 | | Mark Martin | 602 | 46,135,779 | 76,637 |
| 4 | | Rusty Wallace | 670 | 43,670,500 | 65,180 |
| 5 | # | Dale Earnhardt | 676 | 41,742,384 | 61,749 |
| 6 | | Bobby Labonte | 402 | 40,843,154 | 101,599 |
| 7 | | Terry Labonte | 817 | 37,809,799 | 46,279 |
| 8 | | Bill Elliott | 737 | 36,995,303 | 50,197 |
| 9 | | Ricky Rudd | 839 | 36,120,592 | 43,051 |
| 10 | | Jeff Burton | 367 | 35,642,417 | 97,118 |
| 11 | | Tony Stewart | 212 | 34,905,161 | 164,646 |
| 12 | | Sterling Marlin | 640 | 32,970,362 | 51,516 |
| 13 | | Dale Earnhardt Jr. | 183 | 29,555,869 | 161,507 |
| 14 | | Michael Waltrip | 606 | 27,640,029 | 45,610 |
| 15 | | Matt Kenseth | 184 | 26,501,894 | 144,032 |
| 16 | | Ken Schrader | 632 | 25,234,437 | 39,934 |
| 17 | | Ward Burton | 356 | 24,023,735 | 67,482 |
| 18 | | Kurt Busch | 150 | 22,860,894 | 152,405 |
| 19 | | Jeremy Mayfield | 345 | 22,515,017 | 65,260 |
| 20 | | Kyle Petty | 713 | 20,602,992 | 28,896 |
| 21 | | Jimmie Johnson | 111 | 19,931,839 | 179,566 |
| 22 | | Kevin Harvick | 142 | 19,709,874 | 138,801 |
| 23 | | Jimmy Spencer | 465 | 19,435,098 | 41,795 |
| 24 | | Elliott Sadler | 213 | 19,429,249 | 91,217 |
| 25 | * | Darrell Waltrip | 809 | 19,416,618 | 24,001 |
| 26 | | Joe Nemechek | 358 | 19,327,669 | 53,988 |
| 27 | | Ryan Newman | 116 | 18,304,885 | 157,800 |
| 28 | | John Andretti | 336 | 17,876,141 | 53,203 |
| 29 | | Johnny Benson | 268 | 16,608,113 | 61,971 |
| 30 | | Geoffrey Bodine | 570 | 16,497,380 | 28,942 |
| 31 | | Ricky Craven | 278 | 15,209,281 | 54,710 |
| 32 | | Bobby Hamilton | 368 | 15,187,015 | 41,269 |
| 33 | | Robby Gordon | 170 | 14,452,181 | 85,013 |
| 34 | | Brett Bodine | 480 | 13,575,991 | 28,283 |
| 35 | | Mike Skinner | 230 | 13,284,317 | 57,758 |
| 36 | | Steve Park | 181 | 12,477,063 | 68,934 |
| 37 | | Kenny Wallace | 305 | 12,130,126 | 39,771 |
| 38 | * | Ernie Irvan | 313 | 11,625,817 | 37,143 |
| 39 | | Dave Blaney | 163 | 10,613,812 | 65,115 |
| 40 | | Jeff Green | 161 | 10,304,349 | 64,002 |

Career winnings include race winnings, postseason awards, non-points race winnings and special bonuses.
**\*Retired**
**#Deceased**

# Driver records

## ALL RACES

**Most wins, career**—200, Richard Petty (1958-92).
**Most wins, season**—27, Richard Petty (1967).
**Most consecutive wins**—10, Richard Petty (1967).
**Most wins from pole, career** – 61, Richard Petty (1958-92).
**Most wins from pole, season**—15, Richard Petty (1967).
**Oldest driver to win a race**—Harry Gant, 52 years, 219 days (August 16, 1992).
**Youngest driver to win a race**—Donald Thomas, 20 years, 129 days (November 16, 1952).
**Most consecutive races won from pole**—4, Richard Petty (1967) and Darrell Waltrip (1981).
**Most years won at least one race from pole**—16, Richard Petty (1958-92).
**Most consecutive wins at one track**—7, Richard Petty, Richmond International Raceway (1970-73) and Darrell Waltrip, Bristol Motor Speedway (1981-84).

### MODERN RECORDS ALL RACES • 1972-2004

**Most wins**—84, Darrell Waltrip (1972-2000).
**Most wins, season**—13, Richard Petty (1975), Jeff Gordon (1998).

**Most consecutive wins**—4, Cale Yarborough (1976), Darrell Waltrip (1981), Dale Earnhardt (1987), Harry Gant (1991), Bill Elliott (1992), Mark Martin (1993), Jeff Gordon (1998).
**Most wins from pole, career**—24, Darrell Waltrip (1972-2000).
**Most wins from pole, season**—8, Darrell Waltrip (1981).
**Most consecutive races won from pole**—4, Darrell Waltrip (1981).
**Most years won at least one race from pole**—9, Darrell Waltrip (1972-2000).
**Most consecutive years won at least one race from pole**—7, Darrell Waltrip (1978-84).
**Most consecutive wins at one track**—7, Darrell Waltrip, Bristol Raceway (1981-84).
**Most races, career**—1,177, Richard Petty, 1958-92.
**Most years leading circuit in wins**—7, Richard Petty, 1958-92.
**Most consecutive years leading circuit in wins**—5, Jeff Gordon, 1995-99
**Best winning percentage, career**—21.2, Tim Flock (40 wins, 189 starts), 1949-1961.
**Best winning percentage, season**—61.1, David Pearson (11 wins, 18 starts), 1973.
**Most races started without a win**—653, J.D. McDuffie, 1963-91.

# All-time driver records Qualifying

## ALL RACES

**Most poles, career**—126, Richard Petty (1958-92).
**Most poles, season**—20, Bobby Isaac (1969).
**Most consecutive poles**—5, Bobby Allison (1972); Cale Yarborough (1980); Bill Elliott (1985).
**Most years won at least one pole**—23, David Pearson (1960-86).
**Most consecutive years won at least one pole**—20, David Pearson (1963-82).
**Most consecutive poles won at one track**—11, David Pearson (1973-78), Charlotte Motor Speedway.
**Most poles at one track**—14, David Pearson, Charlotte Motor Speedway.

## MODERN QUALIFYING RECORDS ALL RACES • 1972-2004

**Most poles, career**—59, Darrell Waltrip (1972-00).
**Most poles, season**—14, Cale Yarborough (1980).
**Most consecutive poles**—5, Bobby Allison (1972); Cale Yarborough (1980); Bill Elliott (1985).
**Most years won at least one pole**—16, Darrell Waltrip (1972-00).
**Most consecutive years won at least one pole**—13, Darrell Waltrip (1974-86).
**Most consecutive poles won at one track**—11, David Pearson

# First-time wins by season

| | | | |
|---|---|---|---|
| 1972 | None | 1990 | Derrike Cope, Brett Bodine, Ernie Irvan |
| 1973 | Dick Brooks, Mark Donohue | 1991 | Dale Jarrett |
| 1974 | Earl Ross | 1992 | None |
| 1975 | Dave Marcis, Darrell Waltrip | 1993 | None |
| 1976 | None | 1994 | Sterling Marlin, Jeff Gordon, Jimmy Spencer |
| 1977 | Neil Bonnett | 1995 | Bobby Labonte, Ward Burton |
| 1978 | Lennie Pond | 1996 | Bobby Hamilton |
| 1979 | Dale Earnhardt | 1997 | Jeff Burton, John Andretti |
| 1980 | Terry Labonte | 1998 | Jeremy Mayfield |
| 1981 | Morgan Shepherd, Jody Ridley, Ron Bouchard | 1999 | Tony Stewart, Joe Nemechek |
| 1982 | Harry Gant, Tim Richmond | 2000 | Dale Earnhardt Jr.; Matt Kenseth; Steve Park; Jerry Nadeau |
| 1983 | Ricky Rudd, Bill Elliott | 2001 | Michael Waltrip, Kevin Harvick, Elliott Sadler, Ricky Craven, Robby Gordon |
| 1984 | Geoff Bodine | | |
| 1985 | Greg Sacks | 2002 | Kurt Busch, Jimmie Johnson, Ryan Newman, Jamie McMurray, Johnny Benson |
| 1986 | Kyle Petty, Rusty Wallace, Bobby Hillin, Jr. | | |
| 1987 | Davey Allison | 2003 | Greg Biffle |
| 1988 | Lake Speed, Phil Parsons, Ken Schrader, Alan Kulwicki | 2004 | None |
| 1989 | Mark Martin | | |

| | Driver | 500th start | Total starts | | Driver | 500th start | Total starts |
|---|---|---|---|---|---|---|---|
| 1. | * Richard Petty | †1970 | 1,184 | 16. | Michael Waltrip | 2002 | 606 |
| 2. | * Dave Marcis | 1985 | 882 | 17. | * James Hylton | 1979 | 602 |
| 3. | Ricky Rudd | 1994 | 839 | | Mark Martin | 2002 | 602 |
| 4. | Terry Labonte | 1995 | 817 | 19. | * David Pearson | 1978 | 574 |
| 5. | * Darrell Waltrip | 1990 | 809 | 20. | Dale Jarrett | 2003 | 567 |
| 6. | Bill Elliott | 1997 | 731 | 21. | Geoffrey Bodine | 1998 | 565 |
| 7. | * Bobby Allison | 1981 | 717 | 22. | * Buddy Arrington | 1985 | 560 |
| 8. | Kyle Petty | 1997 | 713 | 23. | * Cale Yarborough | 1984 | 559 |
| 9. | * Buddy Baker | 1980 | 698 | 24. | # Elmo Langley | 1975 | 533 |
| 10. | # Dale Earnhardt | 1995 | 676 | 25. | * Benny Parsons | 1988 | 526 |
| 11. | Rusty Wallace | 2000 | 670 | 26. | Morgan Shepherd | 2004 | 507 |
| 12. | # J.D. McDuffie | 1981 | 653 | | | | |
| 13. | Sterling Marlin | 2000 | 640 | * Retired | | | |
| 14. | Ken Schrader | 2001 | 632 | † Entered 1,000th race in 1986 | | | |
| 15. | # Buck Baker | 1964 | 631 | # Deceased | | | |

| Rank | Driver | Start | End | Races |
|---|---|---|---|---|
| 1. | Ricky Rudd | Jan. 11, 1981 | — | 752 |
| 2. | Terry Labonte | Jan. 14, 1979 | Aug. 5, 2000 | 655 |
| 3. | # Dale Earnhardt | Sept. 9, 1979 | Feb. 25, 2001 | 648 |
| 4. | Rusty Wallace | Feb. 19, 1984 | — | 661 |
| 5. | Ken Schrader | Feb. 17, 1985 | August 3, 2003 | 579 |
| 6. | * Richard Petty | Nov. 14, 1971 | March 19, 1989 | 513 |
| 7. | Mark Martin | Feb. 14, 1988 | — | 545 |
| 8. | * Darrell Waltrip | Jan. 18, 1976 | June 24, 1990 | 431 |
| 9. | Michael Waltrip | Feb. 23, 1986 | Oct. 17, 1998 | 421 |
| 10. | Bill Elliott | Oct. 31, 1982 | April 28, 1996 | 395 |
| 11. | * Bobby Allison | Nov. 9, 1975 | June 19, 1988 | 374 |
| 12. | Jeff Gordon | Nov. 12, 1992 | — | 401 |
| 13. | Sterling Marlin | Feb. 15, 1987 | March 1, 1998 | 332 |
| 14. | * Benny Parsons | Nov. 14, 1971 | July 4, 1982 | 321 |

* Retired
# Deceased

HISTORY

| Year | Driver | Year | Driver | Year | Driver | Year | Driver |
|---|---|---|---|---|---|---|---|
| 1953 | Lee Petty | 1966 | Darel Dieringer | 1980 | David Pearson | 1993 | Bill Elliott |
| 1954 | Lee Petty | 1967 | Cale Yarborough | 1981 | Bobby Allison | 1994 | Bill Elliott |
| 1955 | Tim Flock | 1969 | Bobby Isaac | 1982 | Bobby Allison | 1995 | Bill Elliott |
| 1956 | Curtis Turner | 1970 | Richard Petty | 1983 | Bobby Allison | 1996 | Bill Elliott |
| 1957 | Fireball Roberts | 1971 | Bobby Allison | 1984 | Bill Elliott | 1997 | Bill Elliott |
| 1958 | Glen Wood | 1972 | Bobby Allison | 1985 | Bill Elliott | 1998 | Bill Elliott |
| 1959 | Jack Smith | 1973 | Bobby Allison | 1986 | Bill Elliott | 1999 | Bill Elliott |
| 1960 | Rex White | 1974 | Richard Petty | 1987 | Bill Elliott | 2000 | Bill Elliott |
| 1961 | Joe Weatherly | 1975 | Richard Petty | 1988 | Bill Elliott | 2001 | Dale Earnhardt |
| 1962 | Richard Petty | 1976 | Richard Petty | 1989 | Darrell Waltrip | 2002 | Bill Elliott |
| 1963 | Fred Lorenzen | 1977 | Richard Petty | 1990 | Darrell Waltrip | 2003 | Dale Earnhardt Jr. |
| 1964 | Richard Petty | 1978 | Richard Petty | 1991 | Bill Elliott | 2004 | Dale Earnhardt Jr. |
| 1965 | Fred Lorenzen | 1979 | David Pearson | 1992 | Bill Elliott | | |

## MOST CONSECUTIVE WINS 1972–2004: Four

| Year | Driver | Sites |
|------|--------|-------|
| 1976 | Cale Yarborough | Richmond, Va., Dover, Del., Martinsville, Va., N. Wilkesboro, N.C. in fall |
| 1981 | Darrell Waltrip | Martinsville, Va., N. Wilkesboro, N.C., Charlotte, Rockingham, N.C. in fall |
| 1987 | Dale Earnhardt | Darlington, S.C., N.Wilkesboro, N.C., Bristol, Tenn., Martinsville, Va. in spring |
| 1991 | Harry Gant | Darlington, S.C., Richmond, Va., Dover, Del., Martinsville, Va, in summer/fall |
| 1992 | Bill Elliott | Rockingham, N.C., Richmond, Va., Atlanta, Darlington, S.C. in spring |
| 1993 | Mark Martin | Watkins Glen, N.Y., Michigan, Bristol, Tenn., Darlington, S.C. |
| 1998 | Jeff Gordon | Pocono, Pa., Indianapolis, Watkins Glen, N.Y., Michigan |

**Note:** In 1971, both Bobby Allison and Richard Petty won five straight races in 48-race season.

## WINNING STREAKS 1972–2004

| Year | Drivers |
|------|---------|
| 1972 | Bobby Allison—3; Bobby Allison—2 (three times); Richard Petty—2 (twice). |
| 1973 | David Pearson—3; David Pearson—2; Richard Petty—2. |
| 1974 | Richard Petty—3; Richard Petty—2; David Pearson—2; Cale Yarborough—2 (twice). |
| 1975 | Richard Petty—3; Richard Petty—2 (twice); Buddy Baker—2. |
| 1976 | Cale Yarborough—4; David Pearson—3. |
| 1977 | Cale Yarborough—2 (twice); Richard Petty—2 (twice). |
| 1978 | Cale Yarborough—2 (twice); Darrell Waltrip—2. |
| 1979 | Darrell Waltrip—2. |
| 1980 | Dale Earnhardt—2 (twice); Cale Yarborough—2 (twice); Neil Bonnett—2. |
| 1981 | Darrell Waltrip—4; Darrell Waltrip—2 (twice). |
| 1982 | Darrell Waltrip—2 (four times). |
| 1983 | Bobby Allison—3; Darrell Waltrip—2. |
| 1984 | No one won two races in a row. |
| 1985 | Bill Elliott—2 (twice). |
| 1986 | Tim Richmond—2 (twice); Dale Earnhardt—2. |
| 1987 | Dale Earnhardt—4, Dale Earnhardt—3, Dale Earnhardt—2; Tim Richmond—2; Bill Elliott—2. |
| 1988 | Neil Bonnett—2; Bill Elliott—2. |
| 1989 | Rusty Wallace—2. |
| 1990 | Dale Earnhardt—2 (three times). |
| 1991 | Harry Gant—4; Davey Allison—2. |
| 1992 | Bill Elliott—4; Darrell Waltrip—2; Geoff Bodine—2. |
| 1993 | Mark Martin—4; Rusty Wallace—3; Dale Earnhardt—2 (twice). |
| 1994 | Rusty Wallace—3; Wallace—2; Ernie Irvan—2; Dale Earnhardt—2. |
| 1995 | Jeff Gordon—2; Mark Martin—2. |
| 1996 | Jeff Gordon—3; Jeff Gordon—2 (twice). |
| 1997 | Jeff Gordon—2 (twice); Dale Jarrett—2; Mark Martin—2. |
| 1998 | Jeff Gordon—4; Jeff Gordon—2; Jeff Gordon—2. |
| 1999 | Jeff Gordon—2; Tony Stewart—2. |
| 2000 | Tony Stewart—2 (twice); Rusty Wallace—2. |
| 2001 | Jeff Gordon—2 (twice); Dale Jarrett—2. |
| 2002 | Bill Elliott—2; Kurt Busch—2. |
| 2003 | Jeff Gordon—2. |
| 2004 | Jimmie Jonhson—3; Jeff Gordon—2; Matt Kenseth—2 |

## LONGEST STREAKS OF DIFFERENT RACE WINNERS IN NASCAR CUP HISTORY Before 1972

| Races | First Race in Streak | Last Race in Streak |
|-------|----------------------|---------------------|
| 13 | April 30, 1961—Martinsville, Va. | June 23, 1961—Hartsville, S.C. |
| 13 | May 6, 1961—Darlington, S.C. | June 24, 1961—Roanoke, Va. |
| 11 | June 2, 1961—Spartanburg, S.C. | July 22, 1961—Myrtle Beach, S.C. |
| 10 | July 7, 1956—Spartanburg, S.C. | Aug. 22, 1956—Norfolk, Va. |
| 10 | June 11, 1960—Hanford, Calif. | Aug. 7, 1960 — Nashville |
| 10 | June 17, 1960—Norwood, Mass. | Aug. 9, 1961—Winston-Salem, N.C. |
| 9 | Oct. 27, 1963—Hillsboro, N.C. | Feb. 21, 1964—Daytona Beach, Fla. |
| 9 | Oct. 3, 196 —N. Wilkesboro, N.C. | Feb. 25, 1966—Daytona Beach, Fla. |

## LONGEST STREAKS OF DIFFERENT RACE WINNERS IN NASCAR CUP HISTORY 1972–2004

| Races | First Race in Streak | Last Race in Streak |
|-------|----------------------|---------------------|
| 11 | Sept. 22, 1985—Martinsville, Va. | April 13, 1986—Darlington, S.C. |
| 11 | Sept. 29, 1985—N. Wilkesboro, N.C. | April 20, 1986—N. Wilkesboro, N.C. |
| 10 | May 5, 2002—Richmond, Va. | July 28, 2002—Long Pond, Pa. |
| 10 | Feb. 20, 2000—Daytona Beach, Fla. | April 30, 2000—Los Angeles |
| 10 | Oct. 2, 1983—N. Wilkesboro, N.C. | April 8, 1984—N. Wilkesboro, N.C. |
| 9 | June 16, 1981—Pocono, Pa. | Sept. 1, 1991—Darlington, S.C. |
| 9 | May 27, 1984—Charlotte | Aug. 12, 1984—Brooklyn, Mich. |
| 9 | February 6, 2003—Daytona Beach, Fla. | April 13, 2003—Martinsville, Va. |

# Inactive drivers with 50-plus victories

## Bobby Allison 1961 through 1988

ALL NASCAR CUP RACES

| Year | Car Owner | Races | Won | 2nd | 3rd | 4th | 5th | 6-10th | 11-31st | DNF | Poles | Outside Poles | Money Won |
|------|-----------|-------|-----|-----|-----|-----|-----|--------|---------|-----|-------|---------------|-----------|
| 1961 | Bobby Allison | 4 | 0 | 0 | 0 | 0 | 0 | 0 | 2 | 2 | 0 | 0 | $650 |
| 1965 | Bobby Allison | 8 | 0 | 0 | 0 | 0 | 0 | 3 | 1 | 4 | 0 | 0 | 4,780 |
| 1966 | Bobby Allison | 34 | 3 | 0 | 3 | 1 | 2 | 5 | 3 | 17 | 4 | 1 | 21,850 |
| 1967 | Bobby Allison | 28 | 3 | 2 | 2 | 3 | 2 | 4 | 1 | 11 | 1 | 2 | 12,840 |
|      | Cotton Owens | 9 | 1 | 2 | 3 | 1 | 0 | 1 | 0 | 1 | 0 | 2 | 16,130 |
|      | Bud Moore | 4 | 0 | 0 | 0 | 0 | 0 | 1 | 1 | 2 | 0 | 0 | 2,520 |
|      | Nord Krauskopf | 2 | 0 | 0 | 0 | 0 | 0 | 0 | 0 | 2 | 0 | 0 | 2,375 |
|      | Holman-Moody | 2 | 2 | 0 | 0 | 0 | 0 | 0 | 0 | 0 | 1 | 0 | 19,550 |
| 1968 | Bobby Allison | 22 | 1 | 2 | 3 | 3 | 1 | 2 | 0 | 10 | 0 | 1 | 21,263 |
|      | Bondy Long | 8 | 0 | 0 | 1 | 1 | 0 | 0 | 0 | 6 | 0 | 0 | 17,433 |
|      | Bill Ellis | 5 | 0 | 1 | 0 | 2 | 1 | 0 | 0 | 1 | 2 | 0 | 7,795 |
|      | Holman-Moody | 2 | 1 | 1 | 0 | 0 | 0 | 0 | 0 | 0 | 0 | 2 | 3,900 |
| 1969 | Mario Rossi | 23 | 4 | 3 | 1 | 1 | 2 | 1 | 0 | 11 | 1 | 2 | 64,710 |
|      | Bill Ellis | 2 | 1 | 0 | 0 | 0 | 0 | 0 | 0 | 1 | 0 | 0 | 1,275 |
|      | Bobby Allison | 2 | 0 | 0 | 0 | 0 | 0 | 1 | 0 | 1 | 0 | 0 | 790 |
| 1970 | Mario Rossi | 20 | 1 | 6 | 4 | 1 | 0 | 2 | 2 | 4 | 2 | 3 | 95,495 |
|      | Bobby Allison | 26 | 2 | 9 | 4 | 3 | 0 | 3 | 2 | 3 | 3 | 2 | 36,470 |
| 1971 | Holman-Moody | 22 | 8 | 5 | 3 | 2 | 0 | 1 | 0 | 3 | 5 | 5 | 194,665 |
|      | Bobby Allison | 18 | 2 | 1 | 0 | 3 | 1 | 3 | 2 | 6 | 3 | 2 | 44,630 |
| 1972 | Junior Johnson | 31 | 10 | 12 | 2 | 1 | 0 | 2 | 1 | 3 | 11 | 8 | 271,395 |
| 1973 | Bobby Allison | 27 | 2 | 2 | 6 | 4 | 1 | 1 | 1 | 10 | 6 | 6 | 101,380 |
| 1974 | Bobby Allison | 17 | 1 | 3 | 4 | 1 | 2 | 0 | 0 | 6 | 3 | 2 | 74,915 |
|      | Roger Penske | 10 | 1 | 0 | 1 | 1 | 3 | 0 | 0 | 4 | 0 | 3 | 42,485 |
| 1975 | Roger Penske | 19 | 3 | 3 | 1 | 2 | 1 | 0 | 0 | 9 | 3 | 2 | 122,435 |
| 1976 | Roger Penske | 30 | 0 | 2 | 6 | 5 | 2 | 4 | 2 | 9 | 2 | 4 | 210,377 |
| 1977 | Bobby Allison | 30 | 0 | 1 | 0 | 2 | 2 | 10 | 3 | 12 | 0 | 2 | 87,740 |
| 1978 | Bud Moore | 30 | 5 | 3 | 4 | 0 | 2 | 8 | 1 | 7 | 1 | 5 | 335,636 |
| 1979 | Bud Moore | 31 | 5 | 7 | 2 | 3 | 0 | 4 | 3 | 7 | 3 | 6 | 403,014 |
| 1980 | Bud Moore | 31 | 4 | 2 | 4 | 1 | 1 | 6 | 0 | 13 | 2 | 2 | 356,050 |
| 1981 | Ranier Racing | 31 | 5 | 7 | 4 | 3 | 2 | 5 | 2 | 3 | 2 | 5 | 644,311 |
| 1982 | DiGard Racing | 30 | 8 | 2 | 1 | 2 | 1 | 5 | 3 | 8 | 1 | 3 | 726,562 |
| 1983 | DiGard Racing | 30 | 6 | 5 | 6 | 1 | 0 | 7 | 3 | 2 | 0 | 0 | 828,355 |
| 1984 | DiGard Racing | 30 | 2 | 1 | 2 | 4 | 4 | 6 | 7 | 4 | 0 | 0 | 627,637 |
| 1985 | DiGard Racing | 15 | 0 | 0 | 3 | 2 | 1 | 3 | 4 | 2 | 0 | 1 | 217,690 |
|      | Bobby Allison | 13 | 0 | 0 | 0 | 1 | 0 | 1 | 5 | 6 | 0 | 0 | 54,846 |
| 1986 | Stavola Bros. | 29 | 1 | 2 | 1 | 1 | 1 | 8 | 9 | 6 | 0 | 1 | 503,095 |
| 1987 | Stavola Bros. | 29 | 1 | 1 | 0 | 1 | 1 | 9 | 7 | 9 | 1 | 2 | 515,894 |
| 1988 | Stavola Bros. | 13 | 1 | 1 | 0 | 0 | 1 | 3 | 6 | 1 | 0 | 0 | 409,295 |
| **TOTALS** | | 717 | 84 | 86 | 71 | 56 | 34 | 109 | 71 | 206 | 57 | 74 | $7,102,233 |

## Dale Earnhardt 1975 through 2001

ALL NASCAR CUP RACES

| Year | Car Owner | Races | Won | 2nd | 3rd | 4th | 5th | 6-10th | 11-31st | DNF | Poles | Outside Poles | Money Won |
|------|-----------|-------|-----|-----|-----|-----|-----|--------|---------|-----|-------|---------------|-----------|
| 1975 | Ed Negre | 1 | 0 | 0 | 0 | 0 | 0 | 0 | 1 | 1 | 0 | 0 | $1,925 |
| 1976 | W. Ballard | 1 | 0 | 0 | 0 | 0 | 0 | 0 | 0 | 1 | 0 | 0 | 1,725 |
|      | Johnny Ray | 1 | 0 | 0 | 0 | 0 | 0 | 0 | 0 | 1 | 0 | 0 | 1,360 |
| 1977 | Henley Gray | 1 | 0 | 0 | 0 | 0 | 0 | 0 | 0 | 1 | 0 | 0 | 1,375 |
| 1978 | W. Cronkrite | 4 | 0 | 0 | 0 | 0 | 0 | 1 | 3 | 0 | 0 | 0 | 13,245 |
|      | R. Osterlund | 1 | 0 | 0 | 0 | 1 | 0 | 0 | 0 | 0 | 0 | 0 | 6,900 |
| 1979 | R. Osterlund | 27 | 1 | 1 | 3 | 4 | 2 | 6 | 6 | 4 | 4 | 0 | 264,000 |
| 1980 | R. Osterlund | 31 | 5 | 3 | 4 | 3 | 4 | 4 | 4 | 4 | 0 | 1 | 588,926 |
| 1981 | R. Osterlund | 16 | 0 | 2 | 3 | 0 | 2 | 3 | 2 | 4 | 0 | 1 | 220,085 |

| Year | Car Owner | Races | Won | 2nd | 3rd | 4th | 5th | 6-10th | 11-31st | DNF | Poles | Outside Poles | Money Won |
|---|---|---|---|---|---|---|---|---|---|---|---|---|---|
| | Jim Stacy | 4 | 0 | 0 | 0 | 0 | 0 | 1 | 1 | 2 | 0 | 0 | 34,300 |
| | R. Childress | 11 | 0 | 0 | 0 | 2 | 0 | 4 | 1 | 4 | 0 | 2 | 92,728 |
| 1982 | Bud Moore | 30 | 1 | 1 | 3 | 2 | 0 | 5 | 0 | 18 | 1 | 0 | 375,325 |
| 1983 | Bud Moore | 30 | 2 | 3 | 0 | 3 | 1 | 5 | 3 | 13 | 0 | 1 | 446,272 |
| 1984 | R. Childress | 30 | 2 | 4 | 2 | 0 | 4 | 10 | 6 | 2 | 0 | 1 | 616,788 |
| 1985 | R. Childress | 28 | 4 | 0 | 0 | 4 | 2 | 6 | 3 | 9 | 1 | 0 | 546,596 |
| 1986 | R. Childress | 29 | 5 | 5 | 3 | 1 | 2 | 7 | 2 | 4 | 1 | 3 | 1,783,880 |
| 1987 | R. Childress | 29 | 11 | 5 | 1 | 2 | 2 | 3 | 3 | 2 | 1 | 4 | 2,099,243 |
| 1988 | R. Childress | 29 | 3 | 2 | 3 | 3 | 2 | 6 | 9 | 1 | 0 | 5 | 1,214,089 |
| 1989 | R. Childress | 29 | 5 | 3 | 5 | 1 | 0 | 5 | 8 | 2 | 0 | 1 | 1,435,730 |
| 1990 | R. Childress | 29 | 9 | 3 | 3 | 1 | 2 | 5 | 5 | 1 | 4 | 2 | 3,083,056 |
| 1991 | R. Childress | 29 | 4 | 3 | 4 | 1 | 2 | 7 | 6 | 2 | 0 | 1 | 2,396,685 |
| 1992 | R. Childress | 29 | 1 | 2 | 2 | 1 | 0 | 9 | 10 | 4 | 1 | 1 | 915,463 |
| 1993 | R. Childress | 30 | 6 | 5 | 3 | 3 | 0 | 4 | 7 | 2 | 2 | 1 | 3,353,789 |
| 1994 | R. Childress | 31 | 4 | 7 | 6 | 1 | 2 | 5 | 3 | 3 | 2 | 2 | 3,300,733 |
| 1995 | R. Childress | 31 | 5 | 6 | 5 | 1 | 2 | 4 | 6 | 2 | 3 | 2 | 3,154,241 |
| 1996 | R. Childress | 31 | 2 | 3 | 3 | 4 | 1 | 4 | 12 | 2 | 2 | 0 | 2,285,926 |
| 1997 | R. Childress | 32 | 0 | 4 | 1 | 1 | 1 | 9 | 16 | 0 | 0 | 1 | 2,151,909 |
| 1998 | R. Childress | 33 | 1 | 0 | 1 | 2 | 1 | 8 | 17 | 3 | 0 | 1 | 2,990,749 |
| 1999 | R. Childress | 34 | 3 | 3 | 0 | 0 | 1 | 14 | 10 | 3 | 0 | 0 | 3,149,536 |
| 2000 | R. Childress | 34 | 2 | 5 | 4 | 2 | 0 | 11 | 10 | 0 | 0 | 0 | 4,918,886 |
| 2001 | R. Childress | 1 | 0 | 0 | 0 | 0 | 0 | 0 | 0 | 1 | 0 | 0 | $ 296,833 |
| TOTALS | | 676 | 76 | 70 | 59 | 43 | 33 | 146 | 154 | 95 | 22 | 30 | $41,708,384 |

# Ned Jarrett 1953 through 1966

| Year | Car Owner | Races | Won | 2nd | 3rd | 4th | 5th | 6-10th | 11-31st | DNF | Poles | Outside Poles | Money Won |
|---|---|---|---|---|---|---|---|---|---|---|---|---|---|
| 1953 | Ned Jarrett | 2 | 0 | 0 | 0 | 0 | 0 | 0 | 0 | 2 | 0 | 0 | $125 |
| 1954 | Ned Jarrett | 2 | 0 | 0 | 0 | 0 | 0 | 0 | 1 | 1 | 0 | 0 | 25 |
| 1955 | Mellie Bernard | 3 | 0 | 0 | 0 | 0 | 0 | 0 | 1 | 2 | 0 | 0 | 260 |
| 1956 | Ned Jarrett | 2 | 0 | 0 | 0 | 0 | 0 | 0 | 1 | 1 | 0 | 0 | 60 |
| 1957 | Ned Jarrett | 1 | 0 | 0 | 0 | 0 | 0 | 0 | 0 | 1 | 0 | 0 | 50 |
| 1959 | Paul Spaulding | 1 | 0 | 1 | 0 | 0 | 0 | 0 | 0 | 0 | 0 | 0 | 525 |
| | Ned Jarrett | 15 | 2 | 0 | 1 | 0 | 0 | 2 | 3 | 7 | 0 | 0 | 3,285 |
| 1960 | Ned Jarrett | 40 | 5 | 3 | 4 | 4 | 4 | 6 | 2 | 12 | 5 | 2 | 20,540 |
| 1961 | Ned Jarrett | 2 | 0 | 0 | 0 | 0 | 0 | 0 | 0 | 2 | 0 | 0 | 110 |
| | W.G. Holloway | 44 | 1 | 4 | 8 | 4 | 6 | 10 | 2 | 9 | 4 | 3 | 27,125 |
| 1962 | W.G. Holloway | 51 | 6 | 2 | 3 | 3 | 5 | 13 | 5 | 14 | 4 | 4 | $ 34,890 |
| | J.C. Parker | 1 | 0 | 0 | 0 | 0 | 0 | 1 | 0 | 0 | 0 | 0 | 430 |
| 1963 | W.G. Holloway | 2 | 0 | 0 | 0 | 0 | 0 | 0 | 0 | 2 | 0 | 0 | 200 |
| | Burton-Robinson | 50 | 8 | 7 | 5 | 7 | 4 | 7 | 3 | 9 | 4 | 6 | 38,265 |
| | Herman Beam | 1 | 0 | 0 | 0 | 0 | 1 | 0 | 0 | 0 | 0 | 0 | 275 |
| 1964 | Burton-Robinson | 4 | 1 | 0 | 0 | 0 | 1 | 0 | 0 | 2 | 1 | 0 | 3,275 |
| | Bondy Long | 55 | 14 | 7 | 4 | 5 | 3 | 2 | 0 | 20 | 8 | 9 | 60,055 |
| 1965 | Bondy Long | 54 | 13 | 13 | 10 | 4 | 2 | 2 | 1 | 9 | 9 | 6 | 77,966 |
| 1966 | Bondy Long | 8 | 0 | 0 | 1 | 1 | 1 | 2 | 0 | 3 | 0 | 0 | 8,685 |
| | Henley Gray | 2 | 0 | 0 | 0 | 0 | 0 | 0 | 0 | 2 | 0 | 0 | 2,375 |
| | Larry Hess | 10 | 0 | 0 | 2 | 0 | 0 | 0 | 1 | 7 | 0 | 0 | 9,720 |
| | Bernard Alvarez | 1 | 0 | 0 | 0 | 0 | 0 | 0 | 0 | 1 | 0 | 0 | 905 |
| TOTALS | | 351 | 50 | 37 | 38 | 28 | 27 | 45 | 20 | 106 | 35 | 30 | $289,146 |

# Junior Johnson 1953 through 1966

| Year | Car Owner | Races | Won | 2nd | 3rd | 4th | 5th | 6-10th | 11-31st | DNF | Poles | Outside Poles | Money Won |
|---|---|---|---|---|---|---|---|---|---|---|---|---|---|
| 1953 | Gwyn Staley | 1 | 0 | 0 | 0 | 0 | 0 | 0 | 0 | 1 | 0 | 0 | $110 |
| 1954 | George Miller | 1 | 0 | 0 | 0 | 0 | 1 | 0 | 0 | 0 | 0 | 0 | 300 |
| | Paul Whiteman | 3 | 0 | 0 | 0 | 0 | 0 | 0 | 1 | 2 | 1 | 0 | 250 |
| 1955 | Junior Johnson | 1 | 0 | 0 | 0 | 0 | 0 | 0 | 0 | 1 | 0 | 0 | 25 |
| | Buchan-Lowe | 33 | 5 | 0 | 2 | 1 | 3 | 5 | 1 | 16 | 2 | 3 | 9,280 |

| Year | Car Owner | Races | Won | 2nd | 3rd | 4th | 5th | 6-10th | 11-31st | DNF | Poles | Outside Poles | Money Won |
|------|-----------|-------|-----|-----|-----|-----|-----|--------|---------|-----|-------|--------------|-----------|
| | Henry Ford | 1 | 0 | 0 | 0 | 0 | 0 | 0 | 0 | 1 | 0 | 0 | 50 |
| | Bob Welborn | 1 | 0 | 1 | 0 | 0 | 0 | 0 | 0 | 0 | 0 | 0 | 700 |
| 1956 | A.L. Bumgarner | 8 | 0 | 0 | 0 | 0 | 0 | 0 | 0 | 8 | 1 | 0 | 200 |
| | Jim Stephens | 1 | 0 | 0 | 0 | 0 | 0 | 0 | 0 | 1 | 0 | 0 | 50 |
| | Carl Kiekhaefer | 1 | 0 | 1 | 0 | 0 | 0 | 0 | 0 | 0 | 0 | 1 | 700 |
| | Pete DePaolo | 2 | 0 | 0 | 0 | 0 | 0 | 0 | 0 | 2 | 0 | 0 | 200 |
| | Smokey Yunick | 1 | 0 | 0 | 0 | 0 | 0 | 0 | 1 | 0 | 0 | 0 | 200 |
| 1957 | A.L. Bumgarner | 1 | 0 | 0 | 0 | 0 | 0 | 0 | 0 | 1 | 0 | 0 | 50 |
| 1958 | Paul Spaulding | 26 | 6 | 2 | 3 | 1 | 0 | 3 | 1 | 10 | 0 | 2 | 12,205 |
| | Dick Beaty | 1 | 0 | 0 | 0 | 0 | 0 | 1 | 0 | 0 | 0 | 0 | 215 |
| 1959 | Paul Spaulding | 26 | 5 | 1 | 3 | 2 | 2 | 1 | 3 | 9 | 1 | 0 | 8,330 |
| | Wood Brothers | 2 | 0 | 0 | 0 | 1 | 0 | 0 | 0 | 1 | 0 | 0 | 275 |
| 1960 | Paul Spaulding | 2 | 0 | 0 | 0 | 0 | 0 | 0 | 0 | 2 | 1 | 0 | 50 |
| | John Masoni | 2 | 1 | 0 | 0 | 0 | 1 | 0 | 0 | 0 | 0 | 0 | 19,875 |
| | Wood Brothers | 2 | 0 | 0 | 0 | 1 | 0 | 0 | 0 | 1 | 1 | 0 | 345 |
| | Rex Lovette | 26 | 2 | 2 | 4 | 1 | 2 | 4 | 1 | 10 | 1 | 4 | 10,320 |
| | Bob Welborn | 1 | 0 | 0 | 0 | 0 | 0 | 0 | 0 | 1 | 0 | 0 | 75 |
| | Tom Pistone | 1 | 0 | 0 | 0 | 0 | 0 | 0 | 0 | 1 | 0 | 0 | 110 |
| 1961 | Rex Lovette | 40 | 7 | 2 | 2 | 3 | 1 | 3 | 2 | 20 | 9 | 9 | 24,785 |
| | John Masoni | 1 | 0 | 1 | 0 | 0 | 0 | 0 | 0 | 0 | 1 | 0 | 525 |
| 1962 | Rex Lovette | 11 | 0 | 0 | 2 | 1 | 1 | 0 | 0 | 7 | 1 | 3 | 3,960 |
| | Buck Baker | 1 | 0 | 0 | 0 | 0 | 0 | 0 | 0 | 1 | 0 | 0 | 50 |
| | Ray Nichels | 1 | 0 | 0 | 0 | 0 | 0 | 0 | 0 | 1 | 0 | 0 | 200 |
| | Cotton Owens | 4 | 0 | 1 | 0 | 0 | 0 | 1 | 0 | 2 | 0 | 1 | 7,345 |
| | Ray Fox | 6 | 1 | 1 | 0 | 0 | 0 | 0 | 0 | 4 | 1 | 1 | 22,385 |
| 1963 | Ray Fox | 2 | 1 | 0 | 0 | 0 | 0 | 0 | 0 | 1 | 0 | 1 | 3,200 |
| | Rex Lovette | 30 | 6 | 2 | 2 | 0 | 0 | 0 | 0 | 20 | 9 | 6 | 61,210 |
| | Bill Stroppe | 1 | 0 | 0 | 0 | 0 | 1 | 0 | 0 | 0 | 0 | 0 | 1,300 |
| 1964 | Rex Lovette | 2 | 0 | 0 | 0 | 0 | 0 | 0 | 0 | 2 | 0 | 1 | 675 |
| | Ray Fox | 9 | 1 | 1 | 0 | 3 | 0 | 1 | 0 | 3 | 0 | 1 | 8,265 |
| | Banjo Matthews | 17 | 2 | 1 | 4 | 0 | 0 | 0 | 0 | 10 | 4 | 1 | 16,460 |
| | Holman-Moody | 1 | 0 | 0 | 0 | 0 | 0 | 0 | 0 | 1 | 1 | 0 | 100 |
| 1965 | Rex Lovette | 36 | 13 | 2 | 1 | 1 | 0 | 0 | 0 | 19 | 10 | 9 | 57,925 |
| 1966 | Junior Johnson | 7 | 0 | 0 | 0 | 0 | 1 | 0 | 0 | 6 | 3 | 2 | 3,610 |
| **TOTALS** | | **313** | **50** | **18** | **23** | **15** | **13** | **19** | **10** | **165** | **47** | **45** | **$275,910** |

# David Pearson 1960 through 1986

ALL NASCAR CUP RACES

| Year | Car Owner | Races | Won | 2nd | 3rd | 4th | 5th | 6-10th | 11-31st | DNF | Poles | Outside Poles | Money Won |
|------|-----------|-------|-----|-----|-----|-----|-----|--------|---------|-----|-------|--------------|-----------|
| 1960 | David Pearson | 22 | 0 | 1 | 0 | 1 | 1 | 2 | 6 | 11 | 1 | 0 | $ 5,030 |
| 1961 | Ray Fox Sr. | 7 | 3 | 0 | 1 | 0 | 0 | 0 | 0 | 3 | 1 | 2 | 47,790 |
| | David Pearson | 12 | 0 | 0 | 1 | 1 | 1 | 0 | 3 | 6 | 0 | 0 | 1,790 |
| 1962 | Ray Fox Sr. | 6 | 0 | 0 | 0 | 0 | 0 | 3 | 0 | 3 | 0 | 1 | 8,315 |
| | Cotton Owens | 4 | 0 | 0 | 0 | 1 | 0 | 0 | 1 | 2 | 0 | 1 | 5,185 |
| | David Pearson | 2 | 0 | 0 | 0 | 0 | 0 | 1 | 0 | 1 | 0 | 1 | 2,075 |
| 1963 | Cotton Owens | 41 | 0 | 3 | 2 | 5 | 3 | 6 | 6 | 16 | 2 | 1 | 21,160 |
| 1964 | Cotton Owens | 61 | 9 | 8 | 3 | 7 | 2 | 9 | 1 | 22 | 12 | 10 | 38,175 |
| 1965 | Cotton Owens | 14 | 2 | 2 | 1 | 1 | 0 | 1 | 0 | 7 | 1 | 2 | 8,925 |
| 1966 | Cotton Owens | 42 | 14 | 5 | 4 | 1 | 0 | 8 | 2 | 8 | 7 | 10 | 59,205 |
| 1967 | Holman-Moody | 12 | 0 | 5 | 1 | 1 | 0 | 0 | 0 | 5 | 2 | 0 | 53,650 |
| | Cotton Owens | 10 | 2 | 0 | 1 | 1 | 0 | 2 | 0 | 4 | 0 | 4 | 16,260 |
| 1968 | Holman-Moody | 48 | 16 | 12 | 4 | 2 | 2 | 2 | 1 | 9 | 12 | 17 | 118,842 |
| 1969 | Holman-Moody | 51 | 11 | 18 | 7 | 2 | 2 | 2 | 0 | 9 | 14 | 11 | 183,700 |
| 1970 | Holman-Moody | 19 | 1 | 2 | 2 | 3 | 1 | 1 | 0 | 9 | 2 | 4 | 87,118 |
| 1971 | Holman-Moody | 10 | 2 | 3 | 1 | 2 | 0 | 0 | 0 | 2 | 2 | 2 | 25,950 |
| | Chris Vallo | 7 | 0 | 0 | 0 | 0 | 0 | 1 | 0 | 6 | 0 | 0 | 6,085 |
| 1972 | Wood Brothers | 14 | 6 | 1 | 3 | 1 | 0 | 0 | 0 | 3 | 4 | 6 | 131,415 |
| | Bud Moore | 2 | 0 | 0 | 0 | 1 | 0 | 0 | 0 | 1 | 0 | 0 | 5,860 |
| | Junie Donlavey | 1 | 0 | 0 | 0 | 0 | 0 | 0 | 0 | 1 | 0 | 0 | 430 |
| 1973 | Wood Brothers | 18 | 11 | 2 | 1 | 0 | 0 | 0 | 0 | 4 | 8 | 5 | 213,966 |
| 1974 | Wood Brothers | 19 | 7 | 5 | 2 | 1 | 0 | 0 | 0 | 4 | 11 | 1 | 221,615 |

| Year | Car Owner | Races | Won | 2nd | 3rd | 4th | 5th | 6-10th | 11-31st | DNF | Poles | Outside Poles | Money Won |
|------|-----------|-------|-----|-----|-----|-----|-----|--------|---------|-----|-------|---------------|-----------|
| 1975 | Wood Brothers | 21 | 3 | 6 | 2 | 2 | 0 | 0 | 0 | 8 | 7 | 5 | 179,208 |
| 1976 | Wood Brothers | 22 | 10 | 3 | 2 | 1 | 0 | 2 | 0 | 4 | 8 | 5 | 283,686 |
| 1977 | Wood Brothers | 22 | 2 | 7 | 2 | 2 | 3 | 0 | 0 | 6 | 5 | 1 | 180,999 |
| 1978 | Wood Brothers | 22 | 4 | 2 | 1 | 1 | 3 | 0 | 0 | 11 | 7 | 1 | 151,837 |
| 1979 | Wood Brothers | 5 | 0 | 1 | 0 | 0 | 0 | 0 | 0 | 4 | 1 | 0 | 22,815 |
|  | Rod Osterlund | 4 | 1 | 1 | 0 | 1 | 0 | 1 | 0 | 0 | 1 | 1 | 64,865 |
| 1980 | Hoss Ellington | 9 | 1 | 2 | 1 | 0 | 0 | 1 | 0 | 4 | 1 | 3 | 94,330 |
| 1981 | Joel Halpern | 4 | 0 | 0 | 0 | 0 | 0 | 1 | 0 | 3 | 0 | 0 | 9,625 |
|  | Kennie Childers | 1 | 0 | 0 | 0 | 0 | 0 | 0 | 0 | 1 | 1 | 0 | 2,675 |
|  | Hoss Ellington | 1 | 0 | 0 | 0 | 0 | 0 | 1 | 0 | 0 | 0 | 0 | 4,850 |
| 1982 | Bobby Hawkins | 6 | 0 | 0 | 1 | 0 | 1 | 0 | 0 | 4 | 2 | 0 | 47,945 |
| 1983 | Bobby Hawkins | 10 | 0 | 0 | 1 | 0 | 0 | 3 | 0 | 6 | 0 | 0 | 59,720 |
| 1984 | Bobby Hawkins | 11 | 0 | 0 | 0 | 0 | 0 | 3 | 1 | 7 | 1 | 0 | 54,125 |
| 1985 | Hoss Ellington | 8 | 0 | 0 | 0 | 0 | 0 | 1 | 1 | 6 | 0 | 1 | 48,090 |
|  | David Pearson | 4 | 0 | 0 | 0 | 0 | 0 | 0 | 0 | 4 | 0 | 1 | 7,535 |
| 1986 | David Pearson | 2 | 0 | 0 | 0 | 0 | 0 | 1 | 0 | 1 | 0 | 0 | 8,405 |
| **TOTALS** |  | **574** | **105** | **89** | **44** | **38** | **19** | **52** | **22** | **205** | **113** | **96** | **$2,482,596** |

# Lee Petty 1949 through 1964

ALL NASCAR CUP RACES

| Year | Car Owner | Races | Won | 2nd | 3rd | 4th | 5th | 6-10th | 11-31st | DNF | Poles | Outside Poles | Money Won |
|------|-----------|-------|-----|-----|-----|-----|-----|--------|---------|-----|-------|---------------|-----------|
| 1949 | Petty Enter. | 8 | 1 | 2 | 0 | 0 | 0 | 4 | 0 | 1 | 0 | 0 | $3,475 |
| 1950 | Petty Enter. | 18 | 2 | 1 | 2 | 3 | 1 | 4 | 1 | 4 | 0 | 1 | 7,375 |
| 1951 | Petty Enter. | 32 | 1 | 4 | 2 | 1 | 3 | 8 | 7 | 6 | 0 | 0 | 7,225 |
| 1952 | Petty Enter. | 32 | 3 | 6 | 5 | 5 | 2 | 5 | 0 | 6 | 0 | 0 | 15,620 |
| 1953 | Petty Enter. | 36 | 5 | 4 | 10 | 4 | 3 | 5 | 2 | 3 | 0 | 2 | 17,225 |
| 1954 | Petty Enter. | 33 | 7 | 5 | 4 | 3 | 3 | 8 | 0 | 3 | 3 | 3 | 18,775 |
|  | Gary Drake | 1 | 0 | 0 | 0 | 1 | 0 | 0 | 0 | 0 | 0 | 0 | 350 |
| 1955 | Petty Enter. | 41 | 6 | 4 | 5 | 4 | 1 | 9 | 3 | 9 | 1 | 4 | 16,760 |
|  | Henry Ford | 1 | 0 | 0 | 0 | 0 | 0 | 0 | 0 | 1 | 0 | 0 | 50 |
| 1956 | Petty Enter. | 46 | 2 | 1 | 6 | 2 | 5 | 10 | 5 | 15 | 1 | 3 | 13,380 |
|  | Fred Frazier | 1 | 0 | 0 | 0 | 0 | 0 | 0 | 1 | 0 | 0 | 0 | 175 |
| 1957 | Petty Enter. | 41 | 4 | 4 | 3 | 3 | 6 | 12 | 3 | 6 | 3 | 3 | 15,670 |
| 1958 | Petty Enter. | 49 | 7 | 5 | 3 | 9 | 3 | 13 | 4 | 5 | 4 | 6 | 20,600 |
| 1959 | Petty Enter. | 42 | 11 | 5 | 7 | 4 | 0 | 6 | 1 | 8 | 2 | 5 | 43,590 |
| 1960 | Petty Enter. | 39 | 5 | 7 | 2 | 6 | 1 | 8 | 1 | 9 | 3 | 3 | 26,650 |
| 1961 | Petty Enter. | 3 | 1 | 0 | 1 | 0 | 0 | 0 | 0 | 1 | 1 | 0 | 1,260 |
| 1962 | Petty Enter. | 1 | 0 | 0 | 0 | 0 | 1 | 0 | 0 | 0 | 0 | 0 | 750 |
| 1963 | Petty Enter. | 3 | 0 | 0 | 0 | 1 | 0 | 1 | 0 | 1 | 0 | 0 | 600 |
| 1964 | Petty Enter. | 2 | 0 | 0 | 0 | 0 | 0 | 0 | 0 | 2 | 0 | 0 | 250 |
| **TOTALS** |  | **429** | **55** | **48** | **50** | **46** | **29** | **93** | **28** | **80** | **18** | **30** | **$209,780** |

# Richard Petty 1958 through 1992

ALL NASCAR CUP RACES

| Year | Car Owner | Races | Won | 2nd | 3rd | 4th | 5th | 6-10th | 11-31st | DNF | Poles | Outside Poles | Money Won |
|------|-----------|-------|-----|-----|-----|-----|-----|--------|---------|-----|-------|---------------|-----------|
| 1958 | Petty Enter. | 8 | 0 | 0 | 0 | 0 | 0 | 1 | 2 | 5 | 0 | 0 | $645 |
| 1959 | Petty Enter. | 16 | 0 | 0 | 2 | 1 | 1 | 3 | 1 | 8 | 0 | 1 | 5,605 |
| 1960 | Petty Enter. | 40 | 3 | 7 | 3 | 3 | 1 | 13 | 2 | 8 | 2 | 3 | 35,180 |
| 1961 | Petty Enter. | 42 | 2 | 4 | 4 | 5 | 3 | 4 | 2 | 18 | 2 | 2 | 22,671 |
| 1962 | Petty Enter. | 52 | 8 | 9 | 8 | 5 | 2 | 6 | 3 | 11 | 5 | 7 | 52,885 |
| 1963 | Petty Enter. | 54 | 14 | 10 | 2 | 4 | 1 | 8 | 4 | 12 | 8 | 7 | 47,765 |
| 1964 | Petty Enter. | 61 | 9 | 14 | 11 | 0 | 2 | 5 | 1 | 19 | 9 | 17 | 98,810 |
| 1965 | Petty Enter. | 14 | 4 | 4 | 2 | 0 | 0 | 0 | 0 | 4 | 7 | 4 | 16,450 |
| 1966 | Petty Enter. | 39 | 8 | 9 | 3 | 0 | 0 | 1 | 1 | 17 | 16 | 6 | 78,840 |
| 1967 | Petty Enter. | 48 | 27 | 7 | 2 | 1 | 1 | 1 | 1 | 8 | 19 | 15 | 130,275 |
| 1968 | Petty Enter. | 49 | 16 | 6 | 5 | 2 | 2 | 2 | 0 | 16 | 12 | 12 | 89,003 |
| 1969 | Petty Enter. | 50 | 10 | 9 | 9 | 0 | 3 | 4 | 0 | 15 | 6 | 10 | 109,180 |
| 1970 | Petty Enter. | 40 | 18 | 5 | 0 | 0 | 2 | 4 | 1 | 10 | 9 | 8 | 138,969 |

| Year | Car Owner | Races | Won | 2nd | 3rd | 4th | 5th | 6-10th | 11-31st | DNF | Poles | Outside Poles | Money Won |
|------|-----------|-------|-----|-----|-----|-----|-----|--------|---------|-----|-------|---------------|-----------|
| 1971 | Petty Enter. | 46 | 21 | 8 | 7 | 2 | 0 | 3 | 0 | 5 | 9 | 11 | 309,225 |
| 1972 | Petty Enter. | 31 | 8 | 9 | 5 | 2 | 1 | 2 | 0 | 4 | 3 | 6 | 227,015 |
| 1973 | Petty Enter. | 28 | 6 | 6 | 1 | 2 | 0 | 1 | 2 | 10 | 3 | 3 | 159,655 |
| 1974 | Petty Enter. | 30 | 10 | 8 | 4 | 0 | 0 | 1 | 0 | 7 | 7 | 8 | 299,175 |
| 1975 | Petty Enter. | 30 | 13 | 5 | 3 | 0 | 0 | 3 | 0 | 6 | 3 | 5 | 378,865 |
| 1976 | Petty Enter. | 30 | 3 | 9 | 3 | 4 | 0 | 3 | 0 | 8 | 1 | 5 | 338,265 |
| 1977 | Petty Enter. | 30 | 5 | 6 | 6 | 2 | 1 | 3 | 1 | 6 | 5 | 5 | 345,886 |
| 1978 | Petty Enter. | 30 | 0 | 3 | 3 | 3 | 2 | 6 | 1 | 12 | 0 | 1 | 215,491 |
| 1979 | Petty Enter. | 31 | 5 | 7 | 2 | 4 | 5 | 4 | 1 | 3 | 1 | 2 | 531,292 |
| 1980 | Petty Enter. | 31 | 2 | 4 | 3 | 2 | 4 | 3 | 3 | 10 | 0 | 0 | 374,092 |
| 1981 | Petty Enter. | 31 | 3 | 1 | 4 | 3 | 1 | 4 | 1 | 14 | 0 | 0 | 389,214 |
| 1982 | Petty Enter. | 30 | 0 | 5 | 2 | 1 | 1 | 7 | 1 | 13 | 0 | 0 | 453,832 |
| 1983 | Petty Enter. | 30 | 3 | 1 | 1 | 1 | 3 | 12 | 4 | 5 | 0 | 0 | 491,022 |
| 1984 | Mike Curb | 30 | 2 | 0 | 0 | 2 | 1 | 8 | 10 | 7 | 0 | 0 | 251,226 |
| 1985 | Mike Curb | 28 | 0 | 0 | 1 | 0 | 0 | 12 | 3 | 12 | 0 | 0 | 306,142 |
| 1986 | Petty Enter. | 29 | 0 | 1 | 2 | 1 | 0 | 7 | 8 | 10 | 0 | 1 | 280,657 |
| 1987 | Petty Enter. | 28 | 0 | 1 | 3 | 2 | 3 | 5 | 10 | 5 | 0 | 0 | 468,602 |
| 1988 | Petty Enter. | 29 | 0 | 0 | 1 | 0 | 0 | 4 | 9 | 15 | 0 | 0 | 190,155 |
| 1989 | Petty Enter. | 25 | 0 | 0 | 0 | 0 | 0 | 0 | 13 | 12 | 0 | 0 | 133,050 |
| 1990 | Petty Enter. | 29 | 0 | 0 | 0 | 0 | 0 | 1 | 16 | 12 | 0 | 0 | 169,465 |
| 1991 | Petty Enter. | 29 | 0 | 0 | 0 | 0 | 0 | 1 | 18 | 10 | 0 | 0 | 268,035 |
| 1992 | Petty Enter. | 29 | 0 | 0 | 0 | 0 | 0 | 0 | 24 | 5 | 0 | 1 | 348,870 |
| **TOTALS** | | 1,177 | 200 | 155 | 102 | 52 | 40 | 144 | 141 | 343 | 127 | 140 | $7,755,409 |

# Darrell Waltrip 1972 through 1999

ALL NASCAR CUP RACES

| Year | Car Owner | Races | Won | 2nd | 3rd | 4th | 5th | 6-10th | 11-31st | DNF | Poles | Outside Poles | Money Won |
|------|-----------|-------|-----|-----|-----|-----|-----|--------|---------|-----|-------|---------------|-----------|
| 1972 | D. Waltrip | 5 | 0 | 0 | 1 | 0 | 0 | 2 | 0 | 2 | 0 | 0 | $ 8,615 |
| 1973 | D. Waltrip | 14 | 0 | 1 | 0 | 0 | 0 | 3 | 3 | 7 | 0 | 0 | 27,775 |
|      | Bud Moore | 5 | 0 | 0 | 0 | 0 | 0 | 1 | 0 | 4 | 0 | 1 | 5,691 |
| 1974 | D. Waltrip | 16 | 0 | 1 | 3 | 2 | 1 | 4 | 0 | 5 | 1 | 0 | 57,690 |
| 1975 | D. Waltrip | 17 | 1 | 2 | 0 | 3 | 2 | 2 | 0 | 7 | 2 | 1 | 79,762 |
|      | Bill Gardner | 11 | 1 | 0 | 2 | 0 | 0 | 1 | 0 | 7 | 0 | 3 | 20,430 |
| 1976 | Bill Gardner | 30 | 1 | 3 | 4 | 1 | 1 | 2 | 2 | 16 | 3 | 1 | 191,501 |
| 1977 | Bill Gardner | 30 | 6 | 4 | 3 | 1 | 2 | 6 | 1 | 7 | 3 | 3 | 276,312 |
| 1978 | Bill Gardner | 30 | 6 | 6 | 4 | 1 | 1 | 1 | 2 | 9 | 2 | 7 | 343,367 |
| 1979 | Bill Gardner | 31 | 7 | 4 | 6 | 2 | 1 | 3 | 7 | 1 | 5 | 3 | 523,691 |
| 1980 | Bill Gardner | 31 | 5 | 3 | 2 | 6 | 0 | 1 | 2 | 12 | 5 | 5 | 382,138 |
| 1981 | Junior Johnson | 31 | 12 | 6 | 3 | 0 | 0 | 4 | 2 | 4 | 11 | 4 | 693,342 |
| 1982 | Junior Johnson | 30 | 12 | 1 | 3 | 0 | 1 | 2 | 3 | 8 | 7 | 6 | 873,118 |
| 1983 | Junior Johnson | 30 | 6 | 8 | 4 | 2 | 2 | 3 | 1 | 4 | 7 | 3 | 824,858 |
| 1984 | Junior Johnson | 30 | 7 | 2 | 3 | 1 | 0 | 7 | 7 | 3 | 4 | 2 | 703,876 |
| 1985 | Junior Johnson | 28 | 3 | 6 | 6 | 2 | 1 | 3 | 2 | 5 | 4 | 1 | 1,318,735 |
| 1986 | Junior Johnson | 29 | 3 | 2 | 4 | 6 | 6 | 1 | 1 | 6 | 1 | 4 | 1,099,735 |
| 1987 | Rick Hendrick | 29 | 1 | 1 | 1 | 2 | 1 | 10 | 11 | 2 | 0 | 2 | 511,768 |
| 1988 | Rick Hendrick | 29 | 2 | 1 | 1 | 2 | 4 | 4 | 11 | 4 | 2 | 1 | 731,659 |
| 1989 | Rick Hendrick | 29 | 6 | 2 | 2 | 2 | 2 | 4 | 8 | 3 | 0 | 6 | 1,323,079 |
| 1990 | Rick Hendrick | 23 | 0 | 1 | 1 | 2 | 1 | 7 | 11 | 0 | 0 | 0 | 530,420 |
| 1991 | Darrell Waltrip | 29 | 2 | 2 | 1 | 0 | 0 | 12 | 6 | 6 | 0 | 0 | 604,854 |
| 1992 | Darrell Waltrip | 29 | 3 | 2 | 3 | 0 | 2 | 3 | 12 | 4 | 1 | 0 | 876,492 |
| 1993 | Darrell Waltrip | 30 | 0 | 0 | 2 | 1 | 1 | 6 | 15 | 5 | 0 | 0 | 746,646 |
| 1994 | Darrell Waltrip | 31 | 0 | 0 | 2 | 2 | 0 | 9 | 17 | 1 | 0 | 0 | 835,680 |
| 1995 | Darrell Waltrip | 31 | 0 | 0 | 1 | 3 | 0 | 4 | 12 | 11 | 1 | 0 | 850,632 |
| 1996 | Darrell Waltrip | 31 | 0 | 0 | 0 | 0 | 0 | 2 | 18 | 11 | 0 | 0 | 740,185 |
| 1997 | Darrell Waltrip | 31 | 0 | 0 | 0 | 0 | 1 | 3 | 22 | 5 | 0 | 0 | 958,679 |
| 1998 | Darrell Waltrip | 5 | 0 | 0 | 0 | 0 | 0 | 0 | 3 | 2 | 0 | 0 | 222,865 |
|      | Dale Earnhardt | 13 | 0 | 0 | 0 | 0 | 1 | 1 | 9 | 2 | 0 | 0 | 398,615 |
|      | T. Beverly | 15 | 0 | 0 | 0 | 0 | 0 | 0 | 14 | 1 | 0 | 0 | 434,995 |
| 1999 | Travis Carter | 27 | 0 | 0 | 0 | 0 | 0 | 0 | 23 | 4 | 0 | 0 | 973,133 |
| 2000 | Travis Carter | 29 | 0 | 0 | 0 | 0 | 0 | 0 | 11 | 7 | 0 | 1 | 1,246,280 |
| **TOTALS** | | 809 | 84 | 58 | 62 | 41 | 31 | 111 | 236 | 177 | 59 | 54 | $19,416,618 |

# Cale Yarborough 1957 through 1988

| Year | Car Owner | Races | Won | 2nd | 3rd | 4th | 5th | 6-10th | 11-31st | DNF | Poles | Outside Poles | Money Won |
|------|-----------|-------|-----|-----|-----|-----|-----|--------|---------|-----|-------|--------------|-----------|
| 1957 | B. Weatherly | 1 | 0 | 0 | 0 | 0 | 0 | 0 | 0 | 1 | 0 | 0 | $100 |
| 1959 | C. Yarborough | 1 | 0 | 0 | 0 | 0 | 0 | 0 | 0 | 1 | 0 | 0 | 150 |
| 1960 | C. Yarborough | 1 | 0 | 0 | 0 | 0 | 0 | 0 | 0 | 1 | 0 | 0 | 85 |
| 1961 | C. Yarborough | 1 | 0 | 0 | 0 | 0 | 0 | 0 | 0 | 1 | 0 | 0 | 200 |
| 1962 | C. Yarborough | 8 | 0 | 0 | 0 | 0 | 0 | 1 | 1 | 6 | 0 | 0 | 2,725 |
| 1963 | Herman Beam | 14 | 0 | 0 | 0 | 0 | 3 | 4 | 7 | 0 | 0 | 0 | 4,100 |
|  | C. Yarborough | 4 | 0 | 0 | 0 | 0 | 0 | 0 | 2 | 2 | 0 | 0 | 1,450 |
| 1964 | Herman Beam | 20 | 0 | 0 | 0 | 0 | 1 | 4 | 5 | 10 | 0 | 0 | 7,680 |
|  | C. Yarborough | 4 | 0 | 0 | 0 | 0 | 0 | 2 | 0 | 2 | 0 | 0 | 1,615 |
| 1965 | C. Yarborough | 21 | 0 | 0 | 1 | 0 | 0 | 5 | 1 | 14 | 0 | 0 | 6,540 |
|  | Ken Myler | 18 | 1 | 1 | 0 | 5 | 3 | 2 | 2 | 4 | 0 | 0 | 6,305 |
|  | B. Matthews | 7 | 0 | 2 | 0 | 0 | 0 | 0 | 0 | 5 | 0 | 1 | 12,295 |
| 1966 | B. Matthews | 8 | 0 | 2 | 0 | 0 | 0 | 3 | 0 | 3 | 0 | 0 | 18,290 |
|  | Ken Myler | 1 | 0 | 0 | 0 | 0 | 0 | 1 | 0 | 0 | 0 | 0 | 390 |
|  | Wood Brothers | 5 | 0 | 0 | 0 | 1 | 0 | 0 | 1 | 3 | 0 | 0 | 4,350 |
| 1967 | Wood Brothers | 16 | 2 | 3 | 1 | 1 | 0 | 0 | 0 | 9 | 4 | 2 | 56,685 |
| 1968 | Wood Brothers | 21 | 6 | 2 | 1 | 0 | 3 | 0 | 0 | 9 | 4 | 2 | 136,786 |
| 1969 | Wood Brothers | 19 | 2 | 2 | 1 | 2 | 0 | 1 | 0 | 11 | 6 | 2 | 74,240 |
| 1970 | Wood Brothers | 18 | 3 | 4 | 2 | 0 | 1 | 1 | 0 | 7 | 5 | 1 | 114,675 |
|  | Banjo Matthews | 1 | 0 | 0 | 0 | 0 | 0 | 0 | 0 | 1 | 0 | 0 | 1,200 |
| 1971 | C. Yarborough | 4 | 0 | 0 | 0 | 0 | 0 | 1 | 0 | 3 | 0 | 0 | 3,869 |
| 1972 | C. Yarborough | 5 | 0 | 0 | 0 | 0 | 1 | 3 | 0 | 1 | 0 | 0 | 11,332 |
| 1973 | Junior Johnson | 28 | 4 | 6 | 4 | 1 | 1 | 3 | 1 | 8 | 5 | 4 | 162,235 |
| 1974 | Junior Johnson | 30 | 10 | 4 | 5 | 1 | 1 | 1 | 1 | 7 | 3 | 6 | 255,525 |
| 1975 | Junior Johnson | 27 | 3 | 3 | 3 | 3 | 1 | 0 | 0 | 14 | 3 | 0 | 139,258 |
| 1976 | Junior Johnson | 30 | 9 | 6 | 3 | 1 | 2 | 1 | 3 | 5 | 2 | 3 | 387,173 |
| 1977 | Junior Johnson | 30 | 9 | 6 | 4 | 3 | 3 | 2 | 3 | 0 | 3 | 7 | 477,499 |
| 1978 | Junior Johnson | 30 | 10 | 6 | 1 | 5 | 1 | 1 | 4 | 2 | 8 | 7 | 530,751 |
| 1979 | Junior Johnson | 31 | 4 | 2 | 6 | 4 | 2 | 3 | 4 | 6 | 1 | 4 | 413,872 |
| 1980 | Junior Johnson | 31 | 6 | 4 | 4 | 4 | 1 | 3 | 4 | 5 | 14 | 6 | 537,358 |
| 1981 | M.C. Anderson | 18 | 2 | 1 | 2 | 0 | 1 | 3 | 2 | 7 | 2 | 3 | 150,840 |
| 1982 | M.C. Anderson | 16 | 3 | 2 | 1 | 2 | 0 | 0 | 0 | 8 | 2 | 0 | 219,090 |
| 1983 | Harry Ranier | 16 | 4 | 0 | 0 | 0 | 0 | 4 | 0 | 8 | 3 | 1 | 254,535 |
| 1984 | Harry Ranier | 16 | 3 | 1 | 3 | 1 | 2 | 0 | 4 | 2 | 4 | 0 | 385,853 |
| 1985 | Harry Ranier | 16 | 2 | 2 | 2 | 0 | 0 | 1 | 0 | 9 | 0 | 4 | 310,465 |
| 1986 | Harry Ranier | 16 | 0 | 0 | 2 | 0 | 0 | 3 | 1 | 10 | 1 | 0 | 137,010 |
| 1987 | C. Yarborough | 16 | 0 | 0 | 0 | 1 | 1 | 2 | 3 | 9 | 0 | 0 | 111,025 |
| 1988 | C. Yarborough | 10 | 0 | 0 | 0 | 0 | 0 | 3 | 3 | 4 | 0 | 0 | 66,065 |
| **TOTALS** |  | **559** | **83** | **59** | **46** | **35** | **28** | **58** | **52** | **198** | **70** | **53** | **$5,003,616** |

# Owner wins 1949-2004

1. Petty Enterprises 271
2. * Junior Johnson 139
3. Rick Hendrick 126
4. Wood Brothers 97
5. * Holman-#Moody 92
6. Richard Childress 76
7. * Bud Moore 63
8. Jack Roush 69
9. Robert Yates 56
10. # Carl Kiekhaefer 54
11. Roger Penske 53
12. * Bill Gardner 43
    # Nord Krauskopf 43
14. * Cotton Owens 40
15. # Herb Thomas 39

16. Joe Gibbs 38
17. # Harry Melling 34
18. * Bondy Long 31
19. # Rex Lovette 29
20. * White-Clements #24
    # Harry Ranier 24
22. D. Earnhardt, Inc. 21
23. * Raymond Beadle 20
    * Jack Smith 20
25. # Frank Christian 19
26. # Pete DePaolo 18
27. * Ted Chester 17
28. Morgan-McClure 14
    # Buck Baker 14
30. # Marshall Teague 12

# L.G. DeWitt 12
32. # Paul Spaulding 11
33. * Ray Nichels 10
    # M.C. Anderson 10
    # T.W. Chapman 10
    # Smokey Yunick 10
37. * Needham-Reynolds 9
    * J.H. Petty 9
    * Leo Jackson 9
    # Burton-Robinson 9
    # Banjo Matthews 9
42. * John Eanes 8
    * Ray Fox 8
    * Johnny Griffin 8
45. Felix Sabates 7

* Ned Jarrett 7
* Rod Osterlund 7
* Jim Reed 7
* Bobby Allison 7
* J.D. Bracken 7
# W.G. Holloway Jr. 7
52. * Darrell Waltrip 6
    * Billy Hagan 6
    * Ricky Rudd 6
    * Tom Friedkin 6
    # Speedy Thompson 6
    # Frank Strickland 6
58. Bill Davis 5
    Chip Ganassi 5
    * Hoss Ellington 5

| | | |
|---|---|---|
| * Hugh Babb | 5 | |
| * Buchan-Lowe | 5 | |
| # Mario Rossi | 5 | |
| Ernest Woods | 5 | |
| # Alan Kulwicki | 5 | |
| # Bob Flock | 5 | |
| Jeff Gordon | 5 | |
| Ray Evernham | 5 | |
| 69. Geoff Bodine | 4 | |
| Georgetta Roush | 4 | |
| * Lloyd Dane | 4 | |
| * Stavola Brothers | 4 | |
| * Rahilly-Mock | 4 | |
| * Jim Stacy | 4 | |
| * Eddie Pagan | 4 | |
| # John Masoni | 4 | |
| Ray Evernham | 4 | |
| 78. * Penske-Kranefuss | 3 | |
| * Don Rogala | 3 | |
| * Hubert Westmoreland | 3 | |
| * Kenny Bernstein | 3 | |
| # Jim Stephens | 3 | |
| # Bradford White | 3 | |
| # Vel Miletich | 3 | |
| # Fireball Roberts | 3 | |
| 86. Andy Petree | 2 | |
| * Roy Burdick | 2 | |
| * Jack Beebe | 2 | |
| * Mike Curb | 2 | |
| * John Hines | 2 | |
| * George Hutchens | 2 | |
| * Marvin Panch | 2 | |
| * Raymond Parks | 2 | |
| * B.A. Pless | 2 | |
| * Marvin Porter | 2 | |

| | |
|---|---|
| * Monroe Shook | 2 |
| * Lyle Stelter | 2 |
| * Cliff Stewart | 2 |
| * Louie Weathersby | 2 |
| * Bob Whitcomb | 2 |
| * Rex White | 2 |
| * Guy Wilson | 2 |
| * James Hylton | 2 |
| # Fred Elder | 2 |
| # Eddie Gray | 2 |
| # Elmo Langley | 2 |
| # Buckshot Morris | 2 |
| # Sam Rice | 2 |
| # Carl Rupert | 2 |
| # Perry Smith | 2 |
| # Bill Stroppe | 2 |
| # Jon Thorne | 2 |
| # Bob Welborn | 2 |
| # John Dietz | 2 |
| # Julian Buesink | 2 |
| Nelson Bowers | 2 |
| Cal Wells, III | 2 |
| 118. Dave Marcis | 1 |
| Mark Martin | 1 |
| Geoff Smith | 1 |
| Joe Hendrick | 1 |
| * Junie Donlavey | 1 |
| * Pete Stewart | 1 |
| * Tommy Thompson | 1 |
| * Charles Vance | 1 |
| * David Vaughn | 1 |
| * Ratus Walters | 1 |
| * Cale Yarborough | 1 |
| * Lake Speed | 1 |
| * Richard Jackson | 1 |

| | |
|---|---|
| * Max Welborn | 1 |
| * Larry Bettinger | 1 |
| * Jack Bowsher | 1 |
| * J.D. Braswell | 1 |
| * Allan Brooke | 1 |
| * Elmer Brooks | 1 |
| * Marvin Burke | 1 |
| * Cos Cancilla | 1 |
| * June Cleveland | 1 |
| * Crawford Brothers | 1 |
| * John Edmunds | 1 |
| * Buddy Elliott | 1 |
| * Bill Ellis | 1 |
| * Ray Erickson | 1 |
| * Jack Gaynor | 1 |
| * John Golabek | 1 |
| * Danny Graves | 1 |
| * Tom Harbison | 1 |
| * Johnny Hayes | 1 |
| * Frank Hayworth | 1 |
| * Floyd Johnson | 1 |
| * John Kieper | 1 |
| * Sam Knox | 1 |
| * Paul Lewis | 1 |
| * Oscar Maples | 1 |
| * George Miller | 1 |
| * Lee Moyer | 1 |
| * Norm Nelson | 1 |
| * W.M. Packer | 1 |
| * Jim Paschal | 1 |
| * Mamie Reynolds | 1 |
| * John Rostek | 1 |
| * Tony Sampo | 1 |
| * Al Schmidhamer | 1 |
| * Joe Bearscheck | 1 |

| | |
|---|---|
| * W.H. Watson | 1 |
| * Reid Shaw | 1 |
| # Westmoreland France | 1 |
| # Gober Sosebee | 1 |
| # Nelson Stacy | 1 |
| # Dale Swanson | 1 |
| # Bill Blair | 1 |
| # Millard Clothier | 1 |
| # Bobby Courtwright | 1 |
| # Carl Dane | 1 |
| # Shorty Johns | 1 |
| # Harold Kite | 1 |
| # James Mulgrew | 1 |
| # Ken Myler | 1 |
| # Jimmy Pardue | 1 |
| # Shorty Rollins | 1 |
| # Charlie Schwam | 1 |
| # Frank Arford | 1 |
| # Wendell Scott | 1 |
| # Bill Amick | 1 |
| # Paul Whiteman | 1 |

**183 OWNERS    2,022**

* Team/owner(s) quit or retired
# Deceased
a 1,998 races from 1949-2002.
b 6 wins by Convertible Division, 3 by Grand American Division, 3 by Short Track Division in combined races.

**Johnny Sauter is one of eight drivers who competed in races for Richard Childress (left) in 2004. Childress didn't get a victory for the first time since 1997.**

NASCAR Busch Series

# Milestones

The NASCAR Busch Series, Grand National Division, which enters its 24th season in 2005, has established itself as the No. 2 motorsports series in the United States, second only to the NASCAR NEXTEL Cup Series.

The NASCAR Busch Series represents the middle rung in NASCAR's national series, situated between the top NASCAR NEXTEL Cup Series and NASCAR Craftsman Truck Series. The NASCAR Busch Series has proven to be an outstanding series for competitors who aspire to become NASCAR NEXTEL Cup Series drivers, with many of today's premier drivers having competed in the series over the years. Many drivers also have chosen to spend their entire careers in this division due to the competitive nature and popularity of the series.

The series was formed in 1982 when NASCAR consolidated the old Late Model Sportsman division into a touring series of nearly 30 races per year. The series, however, has roots dating back more than five decades. It debuted in 1950 as the NASCAR Sportsman Division and remained so until 1968 before being renamed the NASCAR Late Model Sportsman Division. In 1982, Anheuser-Busch, Inc. joined with NASCAR to create the evolving touring circuit now commonly known as the NASCAR Busch Series, Grand National Division.

Brian Vickers, at 20, became NASCAR's youngest champion ever when he won the NASCAR Busch Series title in 2003.

**Below are some of the milestones in the history of the series:**

**1950** The origin of the NASCAR Busch Series, Grand National Division traces back to this year when the series was known as the NASCAR Sportsman Division. Drivers would frequently compete in three to four races per week approximately 60 races per year throughout the East Coast region of the United States. Some of the notable names that claimed championships in this division during these early years were: Ralph Earnhardt (1956) and Ned Jarrett (1957-58), fathers of future NASCAR Cup Series champions Dale Earnhardt and Dale Jarrett.

**1968** The NASCAR Sportsman Division undergoes its first name change, now known as the NASCAR Late Model Sportsman Division.

**1982** NASCAR Late Model Sportsman Division is consolidated into a national touring series. The inaugural season consisted of 29 races in the first season and was renamed the NASCAR Budweiser Late Model Sportsman Series.

**February 13, 1982** First race of the new touring series was held at Daytona International Speedway the Goody's 300. Mike Porter took the pole position and Dale Earnhardt won the inaugural race in a Pontiac. This race also marked the first superspeedway event in the history of the series.

**February 20, 1982** Series has its first short track race, the Eastern 150 at Richmond (Va.) International Raceway. Tommy Houston won the event.

**March 28, 1982** Diane Teel becomes the first female driver to start a NASCAR Busch Series race, competing at Martinsville (Va.) Speedway and finishing 26th.

**October 31, 1982** The series championship comes down to the final race of the season at Martinsville Speedway between Jack Ingram and Sam Ard. Ingram, despite a 26th-place finish, holds off Ard, who finished sixth, to claim the first series title by 49 points.

**October 8, 1983** Sam Ard establishes a series record with four consecutive wins during the season. Ard won at South Boston (Va.) Speedway (9/17); Martinsville Speedway (9/24); Orange County (N.C.) Speedway (10/1); and Charlotte Motor Speedway (10/8). The series record still stands.

**1984** One of the most important milestones in series history as Anheuser-Busch switches its series sponsorship from its Budweiser brand to Busch. The NASCAR Budweiser Late Model Sportsman Series is renamed the NASCAR Busch Grand National Series.

**May 26-27, 1984** Bobby Allison becomes the first driver to sweep a race weekend, winning the NASCAR Busch Series and NASCAR Cup Series races at Charlotte Motor Speedway. He won the NASCAR Busch race the Mello Yello 300 on Saturday and came back the next day to win the NASCAR Cup event, the World 600.

**October 20, 1984** Sam Ard clinches his second consecutive NASCAR Busch Series title, becoming the first driver in history to win back-to-back championships. He also becomes the first multiple champion in the series.

**1985** Jack Ingram captures his second NASCAR Busch Series Grand National title, joining two-time champ Ard as the only champions in the four-year-old series.

**July 6, 1986** The series' first road course race is held at Road Atlanta in Braselton, Ga. The race was won by Darrell Waltrip.

**1987** Larry Pearson, son of the legendary David Pearson, wins his second consecutive series championship, joining Sam Ard (1983-84) as the only drivers at this stage to win back-to-back titles.

**1989** The Raybestos Rookie of the Year award is established, with Kenny Wallace claiming the inaugural honor. Wallace edged Bobby Hamilton for the award, posting 16 top-10 finishes in 29 starts en route to a sixth-place finish in the championship. ... Jack Ingram earns the achievement of first driver in the NASCAR Busch Series to earn $1 million in his career.

**1992** Joe Nemechek earns the NASCAR Busch Series championship in the closest battle in series history. Nemechek defeated runner-up Bobby Labonte by just three points for the crown. The margin remains the closest in series history. ... Jeff Gordon becomes the first driver to win $100,000 in a NASCAR Busch Series race at Charlotte Motor Speedway.

**1995** The series name is altered slightly, changing to the present NASCAR Busch Series, Grand National Division.

**Oct. 19, 1996** Tommy Houston, a 15-year series veteran, makes his final NASCAR Busch Series start at the season finale at North Carolina Speedway in Rockingham, N.C. Houston, who finished 39th that day, concludes his career with a series-record 417 starts.

**1997** Randy LaJoie becomes the third driver in history to win back-to-back NASCAR Busch Series championships, joining Sam Ard (1983-84) and Larry Pearson (1986-87). LaJoie also enjoyed another piece of history, becoming the first driver to earn $1 million in a single season.

**March 15, 1997** The NASCAR Busch Series travels to the West Coast for the Las Vegas 300 at Las Vegas Motor Speedway, marking the first race west of the Mississippi River in history. California Speedway, Texas Motor Speedway and Gateway International Raceway near St. Louis also were added to the series schedule that season.

**September 5, 1998** Dick Trickle, at 56 years, 11 months, becomes the oldest driver to win a NASCAR Busch Series race, at Darlington (S.C.) Raceway.

**October 17, 1998** The Petty racing legacy is extended to a fourth generation as Adam Petty, son of Kyle, makes his NASCAR Busch Series debut at Gateway International Raceway in Madison, Ill. Petty finished 27th.

**November 13, 1998** NASCAR and Anheuser-Busch announce a multi-year renewal of the Busch beer title sponsorship. With this announcement came an increase in the series' point fund ($650,000 to $1.5 million); a Busch beer marketing campaign and an integrated, media-driven marketing plan which includes: new series logo; aggressive national and market-specific public relations efforts; comprehensive coverage on NASCAR Online; and additional inclusion on licensed TV, radio and print media.

**January 1999** Final attendance figures are announced for the 1998 season and the numbers reveal that more than 2 million attended races that year.

**June 27, 1999** At Watkins Glen (N.Y.) International, Bill Lester makes history as the first African-American driver to start a NASCAR Busch Series race. Lester finished 21st after starting 24th.

**July 4, 1999** Casey Atwood, at 18 years, 11 months, wins at The Milwaukee (Wis.) Mile, becoming the youngest winner of a NASCAR Busch Series race in history. Atwood easily eclipses the mark set by Rob Moroso, who was 19 years, nine months old when he won previously at Myrtle Beach (S.C.) Speedway on July 2, 1988.

**November 11, 1999** NASCAR announces a six-year television contract with NBC Sports and Turner Sports (a joint venture) and an eight-year agreement with FOX and its FX cable network, beginning with the 2001 NASCAR Cup Series and NASCAR Busch Series seasons.

**November 13, 1999** Dale Earnhardt Jr. is crowned the 1999 series champion, becoming the fourth driver to win consecutive titles and second in a row. Earnhardt Jr. joins Sam Ard (1983-84), Larry Pearson (1986-87) and Randy LaJoie (1996-97).

**November 2000** Jeff Green earns his first NASCAR Busch Series championship and enhances the family racing legacy. Coupled with his brother David's series title in 1994, the Greens become the first brothers to win NASCAR Busch Series titles. ... For the first time in NASCAR Busch Series history, three rookies (Kevin Harvick, Ron Hornaday and Jimmie Johnson) finish in the top 10 in the final driver point standings.

**2001** As a result of increased broadcast and cable coverage on NBC/TNT and FOX/FX, the NASCAR Busch Series enjoys tremendous increases in television ratings and viewership. The number of households tuning in to watch NASCAR Busch Series races increases 33 percent compared to the previous year. The NASCAR Busch Series is establishing itself as the No. 2 motorsports series in the United States.

**November 3, 2001** Kevin Harvick becomes the 15th different NASCAR Busch Series champion since 1982 in what becomes an incredible season. While chasing the title, team owner Richard Childress asks Harvick to take over the team's NASCAR Winston Cup ride of Dale Earnhardt, who was involved in a fatal accident in the season opener. Harvick responded by finishing ninth in the NASCAR Cup championship and capturing the NASCAR Winston Cup Raybestos Rookie-of-the-Year award. ... Childress becomes the only car owner ever to win championships in all three of NASCAR's national series: NASCAR Winston Cup (1986-87, '90-91, '93-94 with Dale Earnhardt); NASCAR Craftsman Truck Series (1995 with Mike Skinner); and NASCAR Busch Series with Harvick.

**2002** Greg Biffle of Roush Racing captures the NASCAR Busch Series crown, becoming the first driver in history to win titles in the NASCAR Craftsman Series and this series. Biffle becomes the first driver in NASCAR Busch Series history to top $2 million in single-season earnings.

**2003** Brian Vickers is NASCAR's youngest champion ever at 20 years old. He edges runner-up David Green by 14 points. The No. 5 Chevrolet that Vickers drives is fielded by Hendrick Motorsports, which joins Roush Racing and Richard Childress Racing as the only teams to have won championships in each of NASCAR's top three series—Craftsman Trucks, Busch and what becomes NEXTEL Cup.

**2004** 19-year-old Kyle Busch challenged Vickers' record, but finished second in the points standings. However, Busch did become the series' youngest Raybestos Rookie of the Year. Busch also was the first rookie to lead the most miles in the series (1,390.89).

# Justin Ashburn

**Birth date:** 12/23/81
**Hometown:** Joelton, Tenn.

### CAREER STATISTICS

| Year | Rank | Starts | Wins | Poles | Top 5 | Top 10 | Races Led | Laps Led |
|------|------|--------|------|-------|-------|--------|-----------|----------|
| 2003 | 58 | 14 | 0 | 0 | 0 | 0 | 0 | 0 |
| 2004 | 69 | 8 | 0 | 0 | 0 | 0 | 1 | 1 |
| **TOTALS** | | 22 | 0 | 0 | 0 | 0 | 1 | 1 |

# Casey Atwood

**Birth date:** 08/25/80
**Hometown:** Antioch, Tenn.

### CAREER STATISTICS

| Year | Rank | Starts | Wins | Poles | Top 5 | Top 10 | Races Led | Laps Led |
|------|------|--------|------|-------|-------|--------|-----------|----------|
| 1998 | 38 | 13 | 0 | 2 | 1 | 1 | 2 | 129 |
| 1999 | 13 | 31 | 2 | 2 | 5 | 9 | 5 | 244 |
| 2000 | 8 | 32 | 0 | 2 | 0 | 8 | 3 | 108 |
| 2003 | 37 | 14 | 0 | 0 | 0 | 4 | 0 | 0 |
| 2004 | 19 | 29 | 0 | 0 | 1 | 7 | 4 | 97 |
| **TOTALS** | | 119 | 2 | 6 | 7 | 29 | 14 | 578 |

# Stanton Barrett Jr.

**Birth date:** 12/01/72 • **Hometown:** Bishop, Calif.
**Car:** CHEVROLET • **Car owner:** Carl Natale

### CAREER STATISTICS

| Year | Rank | Starts | Wins | Poles | Top 5 | Top 10 | Races Led | Laps Led |
|------|------|--------|------|-------|-------|--------|-----------|----------|
| 1992 | 99 | 1 | 0 | 0 | 0 | 0 | 0 | 0 |
| 1993 | 121 | 1 | 0 | 0 | 0 | 0 | 0 | 0 |
| 1994 | 77 | 3 | 0 | 0 | 0 | 0 | 0 | 0 |
| 1995 | 119 | 1 | 0 | 0 | 0 | 0 | 0 | 0 |
| 1996 | 64 | 2 | 0 | 0 | 1 | 1 | 0 | 0 |
| 1997 | 60 | 6 | 0 | 0 | 0 | 0 | 0 | 0 |
| 1998 | 49 | 10 | 0 | 0 | 0 | 1 | 0 | 0 |
| 1999 | 48 | 12 | 0 | 0 | 0 | 0 | 0 | 0 |
| 2001 | 74 | 6 | 0 | 0 | 0 | 0 | 0 | 0 |
| 2002 | 46 | 12 | 0 | 0 | 0 | 0 | 0 | 0 |
| 2003 | 25 | 22 | 0 | 0 | 0 | 4 | 1 | 15 |
| 2004 | 36 | 19 | 0 | 0 | 0 | 0 | 0 | 0 |
| **TOTALS** | | 95 | 0 | 0 | 1 | 6 | 1 | 15 |

# Johnny Benson

**Birth date:** 06/27/63
**Hometown:** Grand Rapids, Mich.

### CAREER STATISTICS

| Year | Rank | Starts | Wins | Poles | Top 5 | Top 10 | Races Led | Laps Led |
|------|------|--------|------|-------|-------|--------|-----------|----------|
| 1993 | 60 | 4 | 0 | 0 | 0 | 0 | 0 | 0 |
| 1994 | 6 | 28 | 1 | 0 | 6 | 9 | 5 | 154 |
| 1995 | 1 | 26 | 2 | 0 | 12 | 19 | 13 | 564 |
| 1996 | 114 | 1 | 0 | 0 | 0 | 0 | 0 | 0 |
| 1998 | 90 | 2 | 0 | 0 | 0 | 1 | 0 | 0 |
| 1999 | 46 | 13 | 0 | 0 | 0 | 1 | 0 | 0 |
| 2002 | 124 | 1 | 0 | 0 | 0 | 0 | 0 | 0 |
| 2004 | 39 | 11 | 0 | 1 | 1 | 4 | 2 | 13 |
| **TOTALS** | | 86 | 3 | 1 | 19 | 34 | 20 | 731 |

# Greg Biffle

**Birth date:** 12/23/69 • **Hometown:** Vancouver, Wash.
**Car:** FORD • **Car owner:** Clarence Brewer

### CAREER STATISTICS

| Year | Rank | Starts | Wins | Poles | Top 5 | Top 10 | Races Led | Laps Led |
|------|------|--------|------|-------|-------|--------|-----------|----------|
| 1996 | 77 | 2 | 0 | 0 | 0 | 0 | 0 | 0 |
| 2001 | 4 | 33 | 5 | 2 | 16 | 21 | 19 | 948 |
| 2002 | 1 | 34 | 4 | 5 | 20 | 25 | 22 | 1061 |
| 2003 | 35 | 14 | 2 | 2 | 3 | 4 | 4 | 222 |
| 2004 | 3 | 34 | 5 | 2 | 15 | 21 | 18 | 553 |
| **TOTALS** | | 117 | 16 | 11 | 54 | 71 | 63 | 2784 |

# Dave Blaney

**Birth date:** 10/24/62
**Hometown:** Hartford, Ohio

### CAREER STATISTICS

| Year | Rank | Starts | Wins | Poles | Top 5 | Top 10 | Races Led | Laps Led |
|------|------|--------|------|-------|-------|--------|-----------|----------|
| 1998 | 29 | 20 | 0 | 1 | 0 | 3 | 1 | 5 |
| 1999 | 7 | 31 | 0 | 4 | 5 | 12 | 6 | 139 |
| 2000 | 46 | 8 | 0 | 1 | 2 | 4 | 1 | 24 |
| 2001 | 155 | 1 | 0 | 0 | 0 | 0 | 0 | 0 |
| 2002 | 114 | 1 | 0 | 0 | 0 | 0 | 1 | 3 |
| 2003 | 43 | 10 | 0 | 0 | 0 | 3 | 0 | 0 |
| 2004 | 60 | 6 | 0 | 0 | 0 | 0 | 1 | 42 |
| **TOTALS** | | 77 | 0 | 6 | 7 | 22 | 10 | 213 |

# Mike Bliss

**Birth date:** 04/05/65
**Hometown:** Milwaukie, Ore.

### CAREER STATISTICS

| Year | Rank | Starts | Wins | Poles | Top 5 | Top 10 | Races Led | Laps Led |
|------|------|--------|------|-------|-------|--------|-----------|----------|
| 1998 | 71 | 2 | 0 | 0 | 0 | 1 | 0 | 0 |
| 1999 | 84 | 3 | 0 | 0 | 0 | 0 | 0 | 0 |
| 2000 | 100 | 1 | 0 | 0 | 0 | 0 | 0 | 0 |
| 2001 | 143 | 1 | 0 | 0 | 0 | 0 | 0 | 0 |
| 2003 | 10 | 34 | 0 | 0 | 8 | 14 | 3 | 136 |
| 2004 | 5 | 34 | 1 | 3 | 6 | 14 | 7 | 109 |
| TOTALS | | 75 | 1 | 3 | 14 | 29 | 10 | 245 |

# Todd Bodine

**Birth date:** 02/27/64 • **Hometown:** Chemung, N.Y.
**Car:** FORD • **Car owner:** Linda Marsh

### CAREER STATISTICS

| Year | Rank | Starts | Wins | Poles | Top 5 | Top 10 | Races Led | Laps Led |
|------|------|--------|------|-------|-------|--------|-----------|----------|
| 1986 | 114 | 1 | 0 | 0 | 0 | 0 | 0 | 0 |
| 1990 | 40 | 8 | 0 | 0 | 1 | 3 | 1 | 3 |
| 1991 | 7 | 31 | 1 | 2 | 7 | 15 | 7 | 214 |
| 1992 | 3 | 31 | 3 | 2 | 11 | 19 | 9 | 277 |
| 1993 | 9 | 28 | 3 | 1 | 9 | 13 | 12 | 502 |
| 1994 | 118 | 1 | 0 | 0 | 0 | 0 | 0 | 0 |
| 1995 | 59 | 3 | 1 | 0 | 1 | 1 | 1 | 1 |
| 1996 | 3 | 26 | 1 | 0 | 3 | 9 | 7 | 290 |
| 1997 | 2 | 30 | 1 | 0 | 9 | 22 | 10 | 186 |
| 1998 | 33 | 13 | 0 | 0 | 5 | 7 | 1 | 2 |
| 1999 | 4 | 32 | 0 | 0 | 10 | 21 | 7 | 178 |
| 2000 | 4 | 32 | 1 | 1 | 14 | 19 | 7 | 185 |
| 2001 | 29 | 16 | 2 | 0 | 6 | 7 | 5 | 283 |
| 2002 | 23 | 28 | 1 | 1 | 6 | 8 | 5 | 98 |
| 2003 | 17 | 22 | 1 | 0 | 6 | 11 | 6 | 102 |
| 2004 | 53 | 6 | 0 | 0 | 1 | 1 | 0 | 0 |
| TOTALS | | 308 | 15 | 7 | 89 | 156 | 78 | 2321 |

# Clint Bowyer

**Birth date:** 05/30/79 • **Hometown:** Emporia, Kan.
**Car:** CHEVROLET • **Car owner:** Richard Childress

### CAREER STATISTICS

| Year | Rank | Starts | Wins | Poles | Top 5 | Top 10 | Races Led | Laps Led |
|------|------|--------|------|-------|-------|--------|-----------|----------|
| 2004 | 29 | 17 | 0 | 1 | 4 | 7 | 2 | 108 |
| TOTALS | | 17 | 0 | 1 | 4 | 7 | 2 | 108 |

# Stan Boyd

**Birth date:** 09/16/70 • **Hometown:** Holly, Mich.
**Car:** DODGE • **Car owner:** Ware Racing

### CAREER STATISTICS

| Year | Rank | Starts | Wins | Poles | Top 5 | Top 10 | Races Led | Laps Led |
|------|------|--------|------|-------|-------|--------|-----------|----------|
| 2003 | 124 | 1 | 0 | 0 | 0 | 0 | 0 | 0 |
| 2004 | 48 | 12 | 0 | 0 | 0 | 0 | 0 | 0 |
| TOTALS | | 13 | 0 | 0 | 0 | 0 | 0 | 0 |

# Jeff Burton

**Birth date:** 06/29/67
**Hometown:** South Boston, Va.

### CAREER STATISTICS

| Year | Rank | Starts | Wins | Poles | Top 5 | Top 10 | Races Led | Laps Led |
|------|------|--------|------|-------|-------|--------|-----------|----------|
| 1988 | 44 | 5 | 0 | 0 | 0 | 0 | 0 | 0 |
| 1989 | 13 | 27 | 0 | 0 | 2 | 6 | 1 | 14 |
| 1990 | 15 | 31 | 1 | 1 | 3 | 5 | 4 | 154 |
| 1991 | 12 | 31 | 1 | 2 | 3 | 10 | 4 | 210 |
| 1992 | 9 | 31 | 1 | 0 | 4 | 10 | 7 | 101 |
| 1993 | 14 | 28 | 1 | 0 | 3 | 10 | 6 | 330 |
| 1996 | 113 | 1 | 0 | 0 | 0 | 0 | 0 | 0 |
| 1997 | 26 | 13 | 2 | 1 | 9 | 10 | 9 | 714 |
| 1998 | 30 | 13 | 3 | 2 | 7 | 9 | 7 | 441 |
| 1999 | 25 | 14 | 1 | 1 | 7 | 12 | 4 | 116 |
| 2000 | 29 | 14 | 4 | 0 | 11 | 13 | 9 | 833 |
| 2001 | 33 | 11 | 1 | 1 | 4 | 9 | 4 | 163 |
| 2002 | 31 | 13 | 5 | 2 | 8 | 9 | 7 | 586 |
| 2003 | 76 | 4 | 0 | 0 | 0 | 0 | 1 | 24 |
| 2004 | 57 | 4 | 0 | 0 | 2 | 3 | 2 | 28 |
| TOTALS | | 240 | 20 | 10 | 63 | 106 | 65 | 3714 |

# Kyle Busch

**Birth date:** 05/02/85
**Hometown:** Las Vegas

### CAREER STATISTICS

| Year | Rank | Starts | Wins | Poles | Top 5 | Top 10 | Races Led | Laps Led |
|------|------|--------|------|-------|-------|--------|-----------|----------|
| 2003 | 48 | 7 | 0 | 0 | 2 | 3 | 2 | 39 |
| 2004 | 2 | 34 | 5 | 5 | 16 | 22 | 21 | 1108 |
| TOTALS | | 41 | 5 | 5 | 18 | 25 | 23 | 1147 |

# Stacy Compton

**Birth date:** 05/26/67 • **Hometown:** Grit, Va.
**Car:** FORD • **Car owner:** ST Motorsports

## CAREER STATISTICS

| Year | Rank | Starts | Wins | Poles | Top 5 | Top 10 | Races Led | Laps Led |
|------|------|--------|------|-------|-------|--------|-----------|----------|
| 2001 | 96 | 1 | 0 | 0 | 0 | 1 | 0 | 0 |
| 2002 | 9 | 34 | 0 | 0 | 5 | 11 | 6 | 82 |
| 2003 | 11 | 34 | 0 | 1 | 3 | 11 | 6 | 49 |
| 2004 | 14 | 34 | 0 | 0 | 2 | 5 | 2 | 14 |
| **TOTALS** | | 103 | 0 | 1 | 10 | 28 | 14 | 145 |

# Derrike Cope

**Birth date:** 11/03/58 • **Hometown:** Spanaway, Wash.
**Car:** FORD • **Car owner:** Jay Robinson

## CAREER STATISTICS

| Year | Rank | Starts | Wins | Poles | Top 5 | Top 10 | Races Led | Laps Led |
|------|------|--------|------|-------|-------|--------|-----------|----------|
| 1990 | 109 | 1 | 0 | 0 | 0 | 0 | 0 | 0 |
| 1994 | 32 | 11 | 1 | 1 | 2 | 3 | 3 | 56 |
| 1995 | 52 | 5 | 0 | 0 | 0 | 2 | 0 | 0 |
| 1996 | 40 | 12 | 0 | 0 | 0 | 3 | 1 | 9 |
| 1998 | 91 | 2 | 0 | 0 | 0 | 0 | 0 | 0 |
| 1999 | 70 | 5 | 0 | 0 | 0 | 0 | 0 | 0 |
| 2001 | 71 | 4 | 0 | 0 | 0 | 0 | 0 | 0 |
| 2002 | 54 | 8 | 0 | 0 | 0 | 0 | 0 | 0 |
| 2003 | 62 | 7 | 0 | 0 | 0 | 0 | 0 | 0 |
| 2004 | 27 | 30 | 0 | 0 | 0 | 0 | 2 | 4 |
| **TOTALS** | | 85 | 1 | 1 | 2 | 8 | 6 | 69 |

# Kim Crosby

**Birth date:** 12/08/64 • **Hometown:** Tallahassee, Fla.
**Car:** DODGE • **Car owner:** Ware Racing

## CAREER STATISTICS

| Year | Rank | Starts | Wins | Poles | Top 5 | Top 10 | Races Led | Laps Led |
|------|------|--------|------|-------|-------|--------|-----------|----------|
| 2004 | 72 | 5 | 0 | 0 | 0 | 0 | 0 | 0 |
| **TOTALS** | | 5 | 0 | 0 | 0 | 0 | 0 | 0 |

# Wally Dallenbach Jr.

**Birth date:** 05/23/63 • **Hometown:** Basalt, Colo.
**Car:** FORD • **Car owner:** Sam Rensi

## CAREER STATISTICS (Wally Dallenbach Jr.)

| Year | Rank | Starts | Wins | Poles | Top 5 | Top 10 | Races Led | Laps Led |
|------|------|--------|------|-------|-------|--------|-----------|----------|
| 2002 | 62 | 3 | 0 | 0 | 0 | 2 | 0 | 0 |
| 2003 | 73 | 5 | 0 | 0 | 0 | 0 | 0 | 0 |
| 2004 | 61 | 6 | 0 | 0 | 0 | 1 | 0 | 0 |
| **TOTALS** | | 14 | 0 | 0 | 0 | 3 | 0 | 0 |

# Kertus Davis

**Birth date:** 02/26/81 • **Hometown:** Gaffney, S.C.
**Car:** CHEVROLET • **Car owner:** Johnny Davis

## CAREER STATISTICS

| Year | Rank | Starts | Wins | Poles | Top 5 | Top 10 | Races Led | Laps Led |
|------|------|--------|------|-------|-------|--------|-----------|----------|
| 2001 | 80 | 4 | 0 | 0 | 0 | 0 | 0 | 0 |
| 2002 | 67 | 5 | 0 | 0 | 0 | 0 | 0 | 0 |
| 2004 | 93 | 3 | 0 | 0 | 0 | 0 | 0 | 0 |
| **TOTALS** | | 12 | 0 | 0 | 0 | 0 | 0 | 0 |

# Dale Earnhardt Jr.

**Birth date:** 10/10/74 • **Hometown:** Kannapolis, N.C.
**Car:** CHEVROLET • **Car owner:** Teresa Earnhardt

## CAREER STATISTICS

| Year | Rank | Starts | Wins | Poles | Top 5 | Top 10 | Races Led | Laps Led |
|------|------|--------|------|-------|-------|--------|-----------|----------|
| 1996 | 79 | 1 | 0 | 0 | 0 | 0 | 0 | 0 |
| 1997 | 47 | 8 | 0 | 0 | 0 | 1 | 1 | 22 |
| 1998 | 1 | 31 | 7 | 3 | 16 | 22 | 19 | 1615 |
| 1999 | 1 | 32 | 6 | 3 | 18 | 22 | 23 | 725 |
| 2001 | 118 | 1 | 0 | 0 | 0 | 0 | 0 | 0 |
| 2002 | 60 | 3 | 2 | 1 | 2 | 2 | 2 | 249 |
| 2003 | 66 | 3 | 3 | 1 | 3 | 3 | 3 | 227 |
| 2004 | 49 | 4 | 2 | 1 | 3 | 3 | 4 | 203 |
| **TOTALS** | | 83 | 20 | 9 | 42 | 53 | 52 | 3041 |

# Carl Edwards

**Birth date:** 08/15/79 • **Hometown:** Columbia, Mo.
**Car:** FORD • **Car owner:** Jack Roush

## CAREER STATISTICS

| Year | Rank | Starts | Wins | Poles | Top 5 | Top 10 | Races Led | Laps Led |
|------|------|--------|------|-------|-------|--------|-----------|----------|
| 2002 | 117 | 1 | 0 | 0 | 0 | 0 | 0 | 0 |
| 2004 | 116 | 1 | 0 | 0 | 0 | 0 | 0 | 0 |
| **TOTALS** | | 2 | 0 | 0 | 0 | 0 | 0 | 0 |

# Tim Fedewa

**Birth date:** 05/09/67 • **Hometown:** Holt, Mich.
**Car:** CHEVROLET • **Car owner:** Armando Fitz

### CAREER STATISTICS

| Year | Rank | Starts | Wins | Poles | Top 5 | Top 10 | Races Led | Laps Led |
|------|------|--------|------|-------|-------|--------|-----------|----------|
| 1992 | 60 | 4 | 0 | 0 | 0 | 0 | 1 | 5 |
| 1993 | 18 | 25 | 0 | 0 | 1 | 4 | 1 | 8 |
| 1994 | 10 | 28 | 0 | 0 | 1 | 8 | 3 | 13 |
| 1995 | 7 | 26 | 1 | 1 | 4 | 4 | 6 | 145 |
| 1996 | 20 | 25 | 0 | 0 | 1 | 2 | 1 | 14 |
| 1997 | 9 | 30 | 0 | 1 | 4 | 11 | 4 | 88 |
| 1998 | 7 | 31 | 2 | 1 | 4 | 10 | 4 | 231 |
| 1999 | 14 | 30 | 0 | 0 | 3 | 9 | 5 | 73 |
| 2000 | 18 | 30 | 1 | 1 | 3 | 6 | 1 | 118 |
| 2001 | 25 | 25 | 0 | 0 | 2 | 6 | 1 | 1 |
| 2002 | 51 | 9 | 0 | 0 | 1 | 1 | 1 | 2 |
| 2003 | 36 | 15 | 0 | 0 | 0 | 0 | 0 | 0 |
| 2004 | 16 | 34 | 0 | 0 | 1 | 5 | 2 | 13 |
| **TOTALS** | | 312 | 4 | 4 | 25 | 66 | 30 | 711 |

# Blake Feese

**Birth date:** 02/08/82 • **Hometown:** Saybrook, Ill.

### CAREER STATISTICS

| Year | Rank | Starts | Wins | Poles | Top 5 | Top 10 | Races Led | Laps Led |
|------|------|--------|------|-------|-------|--------|-----------|----------|
| 2004 | 62 | 7 | 0 | 0 | 0 | 0 | 0 | 0 |
| **TOTALS** | | 7 | 0 | 0 | 0 | 0 | 0 | 0 |

# Aaron Fike

**Birth date:** 11/24/82 • **Hometown:** Galesburg, Ill.
**Car:** DODGE • **Car owner:** Mike Curb

### CAREER STATISTICS

| Year | Rank | Starts | Wins | Poles | Top 5 | Top 10 | Races Led | Laps Led |
|------|------|--------|------|-------|-------|--------|-----------|----------|
| 2004 | 46 | 13 | 0 | 0 | 0 | 0 | 0 | 0 |
| **TOTALS** | | 13 | 0 | 0 | 0 | 0 | 0 | 0 |

# Jeff Fuller

**Birth date:** 03/27/57 •
**Hometown:** Auburn, Mass.

### CAREER STATISTICS

| Year | Rank | Starts | Wins | Poles | Top 5 | Top 10 | Races Led | Laps Led |
|------|------|--------|------|-------|-------|--------|-----------|----------|
| 1992 | 96 | 1 | 0 | 0 | 0 | 0 | 0 | 0 |
| 1995 | 10 | 26 | 0 | 0 | 1 | 6 | 1 | 6 |

### CAREER STATISTICS (Jeff Fuller)

| Year | Rank | Starts | Wins | Poles | Top 5 | Top 10 | Races Led | Laps Led |
|------|------|--------|------|-------|-------|--------|-----------|----------|
| 1996 | 17 | 24 | 1 | 1 | 1 | 4 | 1 | 145 |
| 1997 | 21 | 28 | 0 | 0 | 1 | 4 | 1 | 66 |
| 1998 | 48 | 11 | 0 | 0 | 0 | 0 | 0 | 0 |
| 1999 | 22 | 27 | 0 | 0 | 0 | 0 | 0 | 0 |
| 2000 | 98 | 1 | 0 | 0 | 0 | 0 | 0 | 0 |
| 2001 | 147 | 1 | 0 | 0 | 0 | 0 | 0 | 0 |
| 2002 | 105 | 2 | 0 | 0 | 0 | 0 | 0 | 0 |
| 2003 | 54 | 13 | 0 | 0 | 0 | 0 | 0 | 0 |
| 2004 | 37 | 30 | 0 | 0 | 0 | 0 | 0 | 0 |
| **TOTALS** | | 164 | 1 | 1 | 3 | 14 | 3 | 217 |

# Travis Geisler

**Birth date:** 11/08/80 • **Hometown:** Pittsburgh
**Car:** CHEVROLET • **Car owner:** Carl Natale

### CAREER STATISTICS

| Year | Rank | Starts | Wins | Poles | Top 5 | Top 10 | Races Led | Laps Led |
|------|------|--------|------|-------|-------|--------|-----------|----------|
| 2004 | 41 | 12 | 0 | 0 | 0 | 0 | 0 | 0 |
| **TOTALS** | | 12 | 0 | 0 | 0 | 0 | 0 | 0 |

# Robby Gordon

**Birth date:** 01/02/69 • **Hometown:** Cerritos, Calif.
**Car:** TBA • **Car owner:** Robby Gordon

### CAREER STATISTICS

| Year | Rank | Starts | Wins | Poles | Top 5 | Top 10 | Races Led | Laps Led |
|------|------|--------|------|-------|-------|--------|-----------|----------|
| 2001 | 60 | 3 | 0 | 0 | 1 | 1 | 2 | 31 |
| 2004 | 21 | 25 | 1 | 0 | 6 | 10 | 9 | 152 |
| **TOTALS** | | 28 | 1 | 0 | 7 | 11 | 11 | 183 |

# Tina Gordon

**Birth date:** 03/14/69 • **Hometown:** Cedar Bluff, Ala.
**Car:** FORD • **Car owner:** Jay Robinson

### CAREER STATISTICS

| Year | Rank | Starts | Wins | Poles | Top 5 | Top 10 | Races Led | Laps Led |
|------|------|--------|------|-------|-------|--------|-----------|----------|
| 2001 | 154 | 1 | 0 | 0 | 0 | 0 | 0 | 0 |
| 2003 | 110 | 1 | 0 | 0 | 0 | 1 | 0 | 0 |
| 2004 | 51 | 12 | 0 | 0 | 0 | 0 | 0 | 0 |
| **TOTALS** | | 14 | 0 | 0 | 0 | 1 | 0 | 0 |

# John Graham

**Birth date:** 10/22/55
**Hometown:** Belfast, Northern Ireland

### CAREER STATISTICS

| Year | Rank | Starts | Wins | Poles | Top 5 | Top 10 | Races Led | Laps Led |
|---|---|---|---|---|---|---|---|---|
| 2004 | 81 | 4 | 0 | 0 | 0 | 0 | 0 | 0 |
| TOTALS | | 4 | 0 | 0 | 0 | 0 | 0 | 0 |

# David Green

**Birth date:** 01/28/58 • **Hometown:** Owensboro, Ky.
**Car:** FORD • **Car owner:** Clarence Brewer

### CAREER STATISTICS

| Year | Rank | Starts | Wins | Poles | Top 5 | Top 10 | Races Led | Laps Led |
|---|---|---|---|---|---|---|---|---|
| 1989 | 96 | 1 | 0 | 0 | 0 | 0 | 0 | 0 |
| 1990 | 85 | 2 | 0 | 0 | 0 | 0 | 0 | 0 |
| 1991 | 13 | 29 | 1 | 1 | 6 | 9 | 5 | 210 |
| 1993 | 3 | 28 | 0 | 0 | 6 | 16 | 5 | 94 |
| 1994 | 1 | 28 | 1 | 9 | 10 | 14 | 11 | 380 |
| 1995 | 12 | 26 | 1 | 4 | 4 | 6 | 7 | 271 |
| 1996 | 2 | 26 | 2 | 4 | 13 | 18 | 10 | 501 |
| 1998 | 26 | 19 | 0 | 0 | 7 | 8 | 1 | 32 |
| 1999 | 27 | 17 | 0 | 1 | 1 | 7 | 0 | 0 |
| 2000 | 9 | 32 | 0 | 0 | 2 | 11 | 6 | 88 |
| 2001 | 13 | 33 | 0 | 0 | 0 | 6 | 1 | 1 |
| 2002 | 40 | 12 | 0 | 0 | 3 | 4 | 1 | 9 |
| 2003 | 2 | 34 | 3 | 2 | 11 | 21 | 10 | 122 |
| 2004 | 7 | 34 | 0 | 1 | 6 | 16 | 4 | 81 |
| TOTALS | | 321 | 8 | 22 | 69 | 136 | 61 | 1789 |

# Mark Green

**Birth date:** 04/08/59 • **Hometown:** Owensboro, Ky.
**Car:** CHEVROLET • **Car owner:** Keith Coleman

### CAREER STATISTICS

| Year | Rank | Starts | Wins | Poles | Top 5 | Top 10 | Races Led | Laps Led |
|---|---|---|---|---|---|---|---|---|
| 1995 | 78 | 2 | 0 | 0 | 0 | 0 | 0 | 0 |
| 1996 | 46 | 10 | 0 | 0 | 0 | 1 | 0 | 0 |
| 1997 | 11 | 30 | 0 | 0 | 1 | 5 | 1 | 6 |
| 1998 | 13 | 31 | 0 | 0 | 0 | 4 | 1 | 66 |
| 1999 | 21 | 30 | 0 | 0 | 0 | 1 | 0 | 0 |
| 2000 | 26 | 30 | 0 | 0 | 0 | 1 | 0 | 0 |
| 2001 | 40 | 14 | 0 | 0 | 0 | 1 | 0 | 0 |
| 2002 | 32 | 21 | 0 | 0 | 0 | 0 | 0 | 0 |
| 2003 | 70 | 5 | 0 | 0 | 0 | 0 | 0 | 0 |
| 2004 | 40 | 18 | 0 | 0 | 0 | 0 | 0 | 0 |
| TOTALS | | 191 | 0 | 0 | 1 | 13 | 2 | 72 |

# Steve Grissom

**Birth date:** 06/26/63 • **Hometown:** Gadsden, Ala.
**Car:** CHEVROLET • **Car owner:** Greg Mixon

### CAREER STATISTICS

| Year | Rank | Starts | Wins | Poles | Top 5 | Top 10 | Races Led | Laps Led |
|---|---|---|---|---|---|---|---|---|
| 1986 | 78 | 2 | 0 | 0 | 0 | 0 | 0 | 0 |
| 1987 | 51 | 2 | 0 | 0 | 0 | 0 | 0 | 0 |
| 1988 | 13 | 29 | 0 | 0 | 1 | 4 | 0 | 0 |
| 1989 | 12 | 29 | 0 | 0 | 2 | 5 | 1 | 1 |
| 1990 | 3 | 31 | 4 | 1 | 11 | 15 | 9 | 486 |
| 1991 | 10 | 31 | 1 | 1 | 7 | 13 | 3 | 147 |
| 1992 | 12 | 31 | 1 | 1 | 2 | 7 | 5 | 199 |
| 1993 | 1 | 28 | 2 | 0 | 11 | 18 | 7 | 120 |
| 1994 | 43 | 11 | 0 | 0 | 1 | 1 | 0 | 0 |
| 1995 | 26 | 15 | 2 | 0 | 4 | 7 | 4 | 105 |
| 1996 | 45 | 8 | 1 | 0 | 3 | 4 | 2 | 57 |
| 1997 | 116 | 1 | 0 | 0 | 0 | 0 | 0 | 0 |
| 1998 | 78 | 2 | 0 | 1 | 0 | 0 | 1 | 88 |
| 1999 | 52 | 12 | 0 | 0 | 0 | 0 | 0 | 0 |
| 2000 | 113 | 1 | 0 | 0 | 0 | 0 | 0 | 0 |
| 2001 | 151 | 1 | 0 | 0 | 0 | 0 | 0 | 0 |
| 2002 | 56 | 7 | 0 | 0 | 0 | 0 | 0 | 0 |
| 2003 | 67 | 6 | 0 | 0 | 0 | 0 | 1 | 1 |
| 2004 | 28 | 26 | 0 | 0 | 0 | 0 | 1 | 1 |
| TOTALS | | 273 | 11 | 4 | 42 | 74 | 34 | 1205 |

# Larry Gunselman

**Birth date:** 12/01/64
**Hometown:** Sierra Village, Calif.

### CAREER STATISTICS

| Year | Rank | Starts | Wins | Poles | Top 5 | Top 10 | Races Led | Laps Led |
|---|---|---|---|---|---|---|---|---|
| 2002 | 41 | 17 | 0 | 0 | 0 | 0 | 2 | 2 |
| 2003 | 21 | 34 | 0 | 0 | 0 | 0 | 0 | 0 |
| 2004 | 99 | 2 | 0 | 0 | 0 | 0 | 0 | 0 |
| TOTALS | | 53 | 0 | 0 | 0 | 0 | 2 | 2 |

# Shane Hall

**Birth date:** 08/25/69
**Hometown:** Greenville, S.C.

### CAREER STATISTICS

| Year | Rank | Starts | Wins | Poles | Top 5 | Top 10 | Races Led | Laps Led |
|---|---|---|---|---|---|---|---|---|
| 1995 | 80 | 2 | 0 | 0 | 0 | 0 | 0 | 0 |
| 1996 | 42 | 14 | 0 | 0 | 0 | 0 | 0 | 0 |

## CAREER STATISTICS (Shane Hall)

| Year | Rank | Starts | Wins | Poles | Top 5 | Top 10 | Races Led | Laps Led |
|------|------|--------|------|-------|-------|--------|-----------|----------|
| 1997 | 23 | 28 | 0 | 1 | 0 | 1 | 1 | 12 |
| 1998 | 19 | 31 | 0 | 1 | 0 | 3 | 3 | 31 |
| 1999 | 24 | 25 | 0 | 0 | 1 | 1 | 1 | 1 |
| 2000 | 92 | 2 | 0 | 0 | 0 | 0 | 0 | 0 |
| 2001 | 23 | 33 | 0 | 0 | 0 | 0 | 1 | 4 |
| 2002 | 29 | 24 | 0 | 0 | 0 | 1 | 1 | 1 |
| 2003 | 85 | 5 | 0 | 0 | 0 | 0 | 2 | 4 |
| 2004 | 54 | 9 | 0 | 0 | 0 | 0 | 0 | 0 |
| **TOTALS** | | 173 | 0 | 2 | 1 | 6 | 9 | 53 |

# Denny Hamlin

**Birth date:** 11/18/80 • **Hometown:** Chesterfield, Va.
**Car:** CHEVROLET • **Car owner:** Joe Gibbs

## CAREER STATISTICS

| Year | Rank | Starts | Wins | Poles | Top 5 | Top 10 | Races Led | Laps Led |
|------|------|--------|------|-------|-------|--------|-----------|----------|
| 2004 | 103 | 1 | 0 | 0 | 0 | 1 | 0 | 0 |
| **TOTALS** | | 1 | 0 | 0 | 0 | 1 | 0 | 0 |

# Mike Harmon

**Birth date:** 01/24/58
**Hometown:** Birmingport, Ala.

## CAREER STATISTICS

| Year | Rank | Starts | Wins | Poles | Top 5 | Top 10 | Races Led | Laps Led |
|------|------|--------|------|-------|-------|--------|-----------|----------|
| 1996 | 56 | 7 | 0 | 0 | 0 | 0 | 0 | 0 |
| 2001 | 51 | 15 | 0 | 0 | 0 | 0 | 1 | 1 |
| 2002 | 38 | 25 | 0 | 0 | 0 | 0 | 0 | 0 |
| 2003 | 23 | 32 | 0 | 0 | 0 | 0 | 0 | 0 |
| 2004 | 67 | 7 | 0 | 0 | 0 | 0 | 0 | 0 |
| **TOTALS** | | 86 | 0 | 0 | 0 | 0 | 1 | 1 |

# Kevin Harvick

**Birth date:** 12/08/75 • **Hometown:** Bakersfield, Calif.
**Car:** CHEVROLET • **Car owner:** Richard Childress Racing

## CAREER STATISTICS (Kevin Harvick)

| Year | Rank | Starts | Wins | Poles | Top 5 | Top 10 | Races Led | Laps Led |
|------|------|--------|------|-------|-------|--------|-----------|----------|
| 1999 | 138 | 1 | 0 | 0 | 0 | 0 | 0 | 0 |
| 2000 | 3 | 31 | 3 | 2 | 8 | 16 | 11 | 665 |
| 2001 | 1 | 33 | 5 | 4 | 20 | 24 | 18 | 1265 |
| 2002 | 64 | 4 | 0 | 0 | 0 | 1 | 2 | 54 |
| 2003 | 16 | 19 | 3 | 5 | 12 | 18 | 15 | 971 |
| 2004 | 20 | 22 | 2 | 0 | 10 | 15 | 10 | 311 |
| **TOTALS** | | 110 | 13 | 11 | 50 | 74 | 56 | 3266 |

# John Hayden

**Birth date:** 12/02/68 • **Hometown:** Owensboro, Ky.
**Car:** CHEVROLET • **Car owner:** Wayne Day

## CAREER STATISTICS

| Year | Rank | Starts | Wins | Poles | Top 5 | Top 10 | Races Led | Laps Led |
|------|------|--------|------|-------|-------|--------|-----------|----------|
| 2002 | 113 | 1 | 0 | 0 | 0 | 0 | 0 | 0 |
| 2003 | 57 | 10 | 0 | 0 | 0 | 0 | 0 | 0 |
| 2004 | 89 | 3 | 0 | 0 | 0 | 0 | 0 | 0 |
| **TOTALS** | | 14 | 0 | 0 | 0 | 0 | 0 | 0 |

# Kenny Hendrick

**Birth date:** 09/10/69
**Hometown:** Chino, Calif.

## CAREER STATISTICS

| Year | Rank | Starts | Wins | Poles | Top 5 | Top 10 | Races Led | Laps Led |
|------|------|--------|------|-------|-------|--------|-----------|----------|
| 2003 | 83 | 5 | 0 | 0 | 0 | 0 | 0 | 0 |
| 2004 | 71 | 7 | 0 | 0 | 0 | 0 | 0 | 0 |
| **TOTALS** | | 12 | 0 | 0 | 0 | 0 | 0 | 0 |

# Tracy Hines

**Birth date:** 05/01/72
**Hometown:** New Castle, Ind.

## CAREER STATISTICS

| Year | Rank | Starts | Wins | Poles | Top 5 | Top 10 | Races Led | Laps Led |
|------|------|--------|------|-------|-------|--------|-----------|----------|
| 2004 | 74 | 3 | 0 | 0 | 0 | 0 | 0 | 0 |
| **TOTALS** | | 3 | 0 | 0 | 0 | 0 | 0 | 0 |

# Shane Hmiel

**Birth date:** 05/15/80 • **Hometown:** Conover, N.C.
**Car:** CHEVROLET • **Car owner:** Todd Braun

## CAREER STATISTICS

| Year | Rank | Starts | Wins | Poles | Top 5 | Top 10 | Races Led | Laps Led |
|------|------|--------|------|-------|-------|--------|-----------|----------|
| 2002 | 16 | 34 | 0 | 2 | 2 | 8 | 4 | 80 |
| 2003 | 15 | 26 | 0 | 1 | 4 | 10 | 3 | 164 |
| 2004 | 44 | 10 | 0 | 0 | 1 | 1 | 2 | 96 |
| **TOTALS** | | 70 | 0 | 3 | 7 | 19 | 9 | 340 |

# Larry Hollenbeck

**Birth date:** 04/09/49 • **Hometown:** Kalamazoo, Mich.
**Car:** CHEVROLET • **Car owner:** Larry Hollenbeck

### CAREER STATISTICS

| Year | Rank | Starts | Wins | Poles | Top 5 | Top 10 | Races Led | Laps Led |
|------|------|--------|------|-------|-------|--------|-----------|----------|
| 2003 | 101 | 2 | 0 | 0 | 0 | 0 | 0 | 0 |
| 2004 | 88 | 3 | 0 | 0 | 0 | 0 | 0 | 0 |
| **TOTALS** | | 5 | 0 | 0 | 0 | 0 | 0 | 0 |

# Ron Hornaday Jr.

**Birth date:** 06/20/58 • **Hometown:** Palmdale, Calif.
**Car:** CHEVROLET • **Car owner:** Kevin Harvick

### CAREER STATISTICS

| Year | Rank | Starts | Wins | Poles | Top 5 | Top 10 | Races Led | Laps Led |
|------|------|--------|------|-------|-------|--------|-----------|----------|
| 1998 | 61 | 4 | 0 | 0 | 0 | 1 | 0 | 0 |
| 1999 | 68 | 4 | 0 | 0 | 0 | 1 | 1 | 98 |
| 2000 | 5 | 32 | 2 | 0 | 6 | 13 | 8 | 246 |
| 2001 | 36 | 12 | 0 | 0 | 1 | 3 | 2 | 26 |
| 2002 | 18 | 30 | 0 | 1 | 5 | 8 | 6 | 231 |
| 2003 | 3 | 34 | 1 | 0 | 8 | 17 | 12 | 403 |
| 2004 | 4 | 34 | 1 | 0 | 7 | 16 | 10 | 153 |
| **TOTALS** | | 150 | 4 | 1 | 27 | 59 | 39 | 1157 |

# Shelby Howard

**Birth date:** 07/25/85 • **Hometown:** Greenwood, Ind.
**Car:** FORD • **Car owner:** Sam Rensi

### CAREER STATISTICS

| Year | Rank | Starts | Wins | Poles | Top 5 | Top 10 | Races Led | Laps Led |
|------|------|--------|------|-------|-------|--------|-----------|----------|
| 2003 | 120 | 1 | 0 | 0 | 0 | 0 | 0 | 0 |
| 2004 | 66 | 5 | 0 | 0 | 0 | 0 | 0 | 0 |
| **TOTALS** | | 6 | 0 | 0 | 0 | 0 | 0 | 0 |

# Buckshot Jones

**Birth date:** 07/23/70
**Hometown:** Monticello, Ga.

### CAREER STATISTICS

| Year | Rank | Starts | Wins | Poles | Top 5 | Top 10 | Races Led | Laps Led |
|------|------|--------|------|-------|-------|--------|-----------|----------|
| 1995 | 42 | 9 | 0 | 0 | 0 | 1 | 0 | 0 |

### CAREER STATISTICS (Buckshot Jones)

| Year | Rank | Starts | Wins | Poles | Top 5 | Top 10 | Races Led | Laps Led |
|------|------|--------|------|-------|-------|--------|-----------|----------|
| 1996 | 25 | 18 | 1 | 1 | 1 | 2 | 1 | 28 |
| 1997 | 7 | 30 | 0 | 0 | 5 | 14 | 3 | 55 |
| 1998 | 9 | 31 | 1 | 1 | 6 | 9 | 8 | 391 |
| 1999 | 28 | 19 | 0 | 0 | 0 | 2 | 1 | 4 |
| 2000 | 21 | 32 | 0 | 1 | 1 | 3 | 5 | 110 |
| 2001 | 48 | 6 | 0 | 0 | 0 | 2 | 0 | 0 |
| 2004 | 107 | 2 | 0 | 0 | 0 | 0 | 0 | 0 |
| **TOTALS** | | 147 | 2 | 3 | 13 | 33 | 18 | 588 |

# Kasey Kahne

**Birth date:** 04/10/80 • **Hometown:** Enumclaw, Wash.
**Car:** DODGE • **Car owner:** Evernham Motorsports

### CAREER STATISTICS

| Year | Rank | Starts | Wins | Poles | Top 5 | Top 10 | Races Led | Laps Led |
|------|------|--------|------|-------|-------|--------|-----------|----------|
| 2002 | 33 | 20 | 0 | 0 | 0 | 1 | 0 | 0 |
| 2003 | 7 | 34 | 1 | 1 | 4 | 14 | 6 | 47 |
| 2004 | 11 | 30 | 0 | 2 | 9 | 14 | 8 | 320 |
| **TOTALS** | | 84 | 1 | 3 | 13 | 29 | 14 | 367 |

# Jason Keller

**Birth date:** 04/23/70
**Hometown:** Greenville, S.C.

### CAREER STATISTICS

| Year | Rank | Starts | Wins | Poles | Top 5 | Top 10 | Races Led | Laps Led |
|------|------|--------|------|-------|-------|--------|-----------|----------|
| 1991 | 105 | 1 | 0 | 0 | 0 | 0 | 0 | 0 |
| 1992 | 53 | 5 | 0 | 0 | 0 | 0 | 0 | 0 |
| 1993 | 33 | 12 | 0 | 0 | 0 | 1 | 0 | 0 |
| 1994 | 17 | 27 | 0 | 3 | 1 | 7 | 3 | 99 |
| 1995 | 4 | 26 | 1 | 1 | 6 | 12 | 4 | 176 |
| 1996 | 6 | 26 | 0 | 0 | 3 | 10 | 1 | 1 |
| 1997 | 13 | 29 | 0 | 0 | 2 | 9 | 1 | 26 |
| 1998 | 16 | 31 | 0 | 0 | 2 | 8 | 1 | 1 |
| 1999 | 8 | 32 | 2 | 3 | 5 | 12 | 8 | 503 |
| 2000 | 2 | 32 | 1 | 0 | 13 | 19 | 6 | 104 |
| 2001 | 3 | 33 | 1 | 0 | 14 | 22 | 6 | 106 |
| 2002 | 2 | 34 | 4 | 2 | 17 | 22 | 15 | 785 |
| 2003 | 5 | 34 | 1 | 2 | 10 | 17 | 8 | 145 |
| 2004 | 6 | 34 | 0 | 0 | 6 | 12 | 2 | 60 |
| **TOTALS** | | 356 | 10 | 11 | 79 | 151 | 55 | 2006 |

# Matt Kenseth

**Birth date:** 03/10/72 • **Hometown:** Cambridge, Wis.
**Car:** FORD • **Car owner:** Roush Racing

### CAREER STATISTICS

| Year | Rank | Starts | Wins | Poles | Top 5 | Top 10 | Races Led | Laps Led |
|------|------|--------|------|-------|-------|--------|-----------|----------|
| 1996 | 101 | 1 | 0 | 0 | 0 | 0 | 0 | 0 |
| 1997 | 22 | 21 | 0 | 0 | 2 | 7 | 2 | 29 |
| 1998 | 2 | 31 | 3 | 1 | 17 | 23 | 10 | 437 |
| 1999 | 3 | 32 | 4 | 2 | 14 | 20 | 15 | 874 |
| 2000 | 17 | 20 | 4 | 2 | 10 | 17 | 12 | 331 |
| 2001 | 18 | 23 | 1 | 3 | 12 | 14 | 13 | 413 |
| 2002 | 77 | 4 | 0 | 0 | 1 | 2 | 0 | 0 |
| 2003 | 24 | 14 | 2 | 0 | 7 | 9 | 8 | 515 |
| 2004 | 25 | 16 | 3 | 0 | 8 | 11 | 9 | 443 |
| **TOTALS** | | 162 | 17 | 8 | 71 | 103 | 69 | 3042 |

# Jimmy Kitchens

**Birth date:** 04/26/62
**Hometown:** Hueytown, Ala.

### CAREER STATISTICS

| Year | Rank | Starts | Wins | Poles | Top 5 | Top 10 | Races Led | Laps Led |
|------|------|--------|------|-------|-------|--------|-----------|----------|
| 1994 | 101 | 1 | 0 | 0 | 0 | 0 | 0 | 0 |
| 1996 | 112 | 1 | 0 | 0 | 0 | 0 | 0 | 0 |
| 1998 | 116 | 1 | 0 | 0 | 0 | 0 | 0 | 0 |
| 1999 | 72 | 6 | 0 | 0 | 0 | 0 | 0 | 0 |
| 2002 | 43 | 14 | 0 | 0 | 0 | 1 | 0 | 0 |
| 2003 | 78 | 7 | 0 | 0 | 0 | 0 | 0 | 0 |
| 2004 | 43 | 16 | 0 | 0 | 0 | 0 | 0 | 0 |
| **TOTALS** | | 46 | 0 | 0 | 0 | 1 | 0 | 0 |

# Travis Kvapil

**Birth date:** 03/01/76 • **Hometown:** Janesville, Wis.
**Car:** DODGE • **Car owner:** Alex Meshkin

### CAREER STATISTICS

| Year | Rank | Starts | Wins | Poles | Top 5 | Top 10 | Races Led | Laps Led |
|------|------|--------|------|-------|-------|--------|-----------|----------|
| 2001 | 115 | 1 | 0 | 0 | 0 | 0 | 0 | 0 |
| **TOTALS** | | 1 | 0 | 0 | 0 | 0 | 0 | 0 |

# Bobby Labonte

**Birth date:** 05/08/64 • **Hometown:** Corpus Christi, Texas
**Car:** CHEVROLET • **Car owner:** Joe Gibbs

### CAREER STATISTICS (Bobby Labonte)

| Year | Rank | Starts | Wins | Poles | Top 5 | Top 10 | Races Led | Laps Led |
|------|------|--------|------|-------|-------|--------|-----------|----------|
| 1982 | 163 | 1 | 0 | 0 | 0 | 0 | 0 | 0 |
| 1985 | 68 | 2 | 0 | 0 | 0 | 0 | 0 | 0 |
| 1988 | 55 | 6 | 0 | 0 | 0 | 0 | 0 | 0 |
| 1989 | 41 | 7 | 0 | 0 | 1 | 3 | 0 | 0 |
| 1990 | 4 | 31 | 0 | 2 | 6 | 17 | 6 | 206 |
| 1991 | 1 | 31 | 2 | 2 | 10 | 21 | 10 | 299 |
| 1992 | 2 | 31 | 3 | 0 | 13 | 19 | 8 | 393 |
| 1993 | 62 | 2 | 0 | 1 | 1 | 1 | 1 | 153 |
| 1994 | 35 | 12 | 1 | 1 | 2 | 3 | 3 | 10 |
| 1996 | 19 | 16 | 1 | 3 | 9 | 13 | 7 | 208 |
| 1997 | 27 | 16 | 1 | 0 | 4 | 8 | 6 | 275 |
| 1998 | 54 | 5 | 1 | 1 | 2 | 3 | 3 | 40 |
| 1999 | 103 | 1 | 0 | 0 | 0 | 0 | 0 | 0 |
| 2004 | 68 | 3 | 0 | 0 | 0 | 1 | 1 | 13 |
| **TOTALS** | | 164 | 9 | 10 | 48 | 89 | 45 | 1597 |

# Justin Labonte

**Birth date:** 02/05/81 • **Hometown:** Thomasville, N.C.
**Car:** CHEVROLET • **Car owner:** Terry Labonte

### CAREER STATISTICS

| Year | Rank | Starts | Wins | Poles | Top 5 | Top 10 | Races Led | Laps Led |
|------|------|--------|------|-------|-------|--------|-----------|----------|
| 1999 | 58 | 9 | 0 | 0 | 0 | 0 | 0 | 0 |
| 2000 | 48 | 13 | 0 | 0 | 0 | 0 | 0 | 0 |
| 2003 | 135 | 1 | 0 | 0 | 0 | 0 | 0 | 0 |
| 2004 | 35 | 17 | 1 | 0 | 1 | 1 | 1 | 12 |
| **TOTALS** | | 40 | 1 | 0 | 1 | 1 | 1 | 12 |

# Randy LaJoie

**Birth date:** 08/28/61
**Hometown:** Norwalk, Conn.

### CAREER STATISTICS

| Year | Rank | Starts | Wins | Poles | Top 5 | Top 10 | Races Led | Laps Led |
|------|------|--------|------|-------|-------|--------|-----------|----------|
| 1986 | 49 | 4 | 0 | 0 | 0 | 1 | 0 | 0 |
| 1987 | 86 | 1 | 0 | 0 | 0 | 1 | 0 | 0 |
| 1988 | 72 | 2 | 0 | 0 | 1 | 1 | 1 | 1 |
| 1989 | 25 | 15 | 0 | 0 | 1 | 3 | 0 | 0 |
| 1990 | 57 | 6 | 0 | 0 | 0 | 0 | 0 | 0 |
| 1993 | 36 | 8 | 0 | 0 | 3 | 4 | 1 | 8 |
| 1994 | 16 | 27 | 0 | 1 | 4 | 7 | 8 | 156 |
| 1995 | 37 | 9 | 0 | 1 | 1 | 3 | 1 | 20 |
| 1996 | 1 | 26 | 5 | 2 | 11 | 20 | 12 | 784 |
| 1997 | 1 | 30 | 5 | 2 | 15 | 21 | 13 | 1037 |
| 1998 | 4 | 31 | 1 | 0 | 7 | 12 | 3 | 153 |
| 1999 | 10 | 32 | 1 | 0 | 6 | 7 | 6 | 313 |
| 2000 | 7 | 32 | 1 | 0 | 4 | 9 | 6 | 140 |
| 2001 | 12 | 33 | 2 | 0 | 4 | 8 | 5 | 93 |
| 2002 | 11 | 34 | 0 | 1 | 3 | 14 | 3 | 43 |
| 2003 | 26 | 19 | 0 | 2 | 2 | 4 | 2 | 63 |
| 2004 | 50 | 7 | 0 | 0 | 0 | 0 | 0 | 0 |
| **TOTALS** | | 316 | 15 | 9 | 62 | 115 | 61 | 2811 |

# Jason Leffler

**Birth date:** 09/16/75
**Hometown:** Long Beach, Calif.

### CAREER STATISTICS

| Year | Rank | Starts | Wins | Poles | Top 5 | Top 10 | Races Led | Laps Led |
|------|------|--------|------|-------|-------|--------|-----------|----------|
| 1999 | 74 | 4 | 0 | 0 | 0 | 0 | 0 | 0 |
| 2000 | 20 | 31 | 0 | 3 | 2 | 4 | 3 | 47 |
| 2003 | 52 | 6 | 0 | 0 | 1 | 1 | 2 | 6 |
| 2004 | 12 | 27 | 1 | 1 | 8 | 17 | 6 | 115 |
| **TOTALS** | | 68 | 1 | 4 | 11 | 22 | 11 | 168 |

# Kevin Lepage

**Birth date:** 06/26/62
**Hometown:** Shelburne, Vt.

### CAREER STATISTICS

| Year | Rank | Starts | Wins | Poles | Top 5 | Top 10 | Races Led | Laps Led |
|------|------|--------|------|-------|-------|--------|-----------|----------|
| 1986 | 88 | 1 | 0 | 0 | 0 | 0 | 0 | 0 |
| 1994 | 24 | 21 | 0 | 0 | 0 | 1 | 1 | 7 |
| 1995 | 18 | 22 | 0 | 0 | 0 | 5 | 1 | 4 |
| 1996 | 8 | 26 | 1 | 0 | 3 | 10 | 5 | 141 |
| 1997 | 12 | 30 | 0 | 0 | 3 | 6 | 3 | 102 |
| 1998 | 14 | 24 | 1 | 1 | 6 | 10 | 7 | 75 |
| 1999 | 35 | 14 | 0 | 0 | 2 | 6 | 1 | 24 |
| 2000 | 42 | 10 | 0 | 0 | 1 | 2 | 0 | 0 |
| 2001 | 31 | 16 | 0 | 1 | 1 | 4 | 3 | 105 |
| 2002 | 25 | 24 | 0 | 2 | 3 | 6 | 3 | 89 |
| 2004 | 42 | 11 | 0 | 0 | 0 | 0 | 0 | 0 |
| **TOTALS** | | 199 | 2 | 4 | 19 | 50 | 24 | 547 |

# Ashton Lewis Jr.

**Birth date:** 01/22/72 • **Hometown:** Chesapeake, Va.
**Car:** FORD • **Car owner:** Team Rensi

### CAREER STATISTICS

| Year | Rank | Starts | Wins | Poles | Top 5 | Top 10 | Races Led | Laps Led |
|------|------|--------|------|-------|-------|--------|-----------|----------|
| 1993 | 107 | 1 | 0 | 0 | 0 | 0 | 0 | 0 |
| 1994 | 93 | 1 | 0 | 0 | 0 | 0 | 0 | 0 |
| 1995 | 92 | 1 | 0 | 0 | 0 | 0 | 0 | 0 |
| 1998 | 53 | 8 | 0 | 0 | 1 | 1 | 1 | 3 |
| 2000 | 51 | 11 | 0 | 0 | 0 | 0 | 0 | 0 |
| 2001 | 20 | 32 | 0 | 0 | 2 | 3 | 0 | 0 |
| 2002 | 17 | 34 | 0 | 0 | 1 | 7 | 2 | 12 |
| 2003 | 12 | 34 | 0 | 1 | 2 | 10 | 2 | 45 |
| 2004 | 8 | 34 | 0 | 0 | 3 | 8 | 3 | 43 |
| **TOTALS** | | 156 | 0 | 1 | 9 | 29 | 8 | 103 |

# Damon Lusk

**Birth date:** 09/18/77
**Hometown:** Kennewick, Wash.

### CAREER STATISTICS

| Year | Rank | Starts | Wins | Poles | Top 5 | Top 10 | Races Led | Laps Led |
|------|------|--------|------|-------|-------|--------|-----------|----------|
| 1999 | 127 | 1 | 0 | 0 | 0 | 0 | 0 | 0 |
| 2002 | 92 | 2 | 0 | 0 | 0 | 0 | 0 | 0 |
| 2003 | 47 | 11 | 0 | 0 | 0 | 0 | 0 | 0 |
| 2004 | 78 | 3 | 0 | 0 | 0 | 0 | 1 | 4 |
| **TOTALS** | | 17 | 0 | 0 | 0 | 0 | 1 | 4 |

# Randy MacDonald

**Birth date:** 07/26/62 • **Hometown:** Oshawa, Ontario
**Car:** CHEVROLET • **Car owner:** Pat MacDonald

### CAREER STATISTICS

| Year | Rank | Starts | Wins | Poles | Top 5 | Top 10 | Races Led | Laps Led |
|------|------|--------|------|-------|-------|--------|-----------|----------|
| 1986 | 112 | 1 | 0 | 0 | 0 | 0 | 0 | 0 |
| 1987 | 91 | 1 | 0 | 0 | 0 | 0 | 0 | 0 |
| 1990 | 105 | 1 | 0 | 0 | 0 | 0 | 0 | 0 |
| 1991 | 84 | 1 | 0 | 0 | 0 | 1 | 0 | 0 |
| 1992 | 77 | 2 | 0 | 0 | 0 | 0 | 0 | 0 |
| 1993 | 69 | 2 | 0 | 0 | 0 | 0 | 0 | 0 |
| 1994 | 61 | 4 | 0 | 0 | 0 | 0 | 0 | 0 |
| 1995 | 102 | 1 | 0 | 0 | 0 | 0 | 0 | 0 |
| 2003 | 81 | 5 | 0 | 0 | 0 | 0 | 0 | 0 |
| 2004 | 64 | 6 | 0 | 0 | 0 | 0 | 0 | 0 |
| **TOTALS** | | 24 | 0 | 0 | 0 | 1 | 0 | 0 |

# Rick Markle

**Birth date:** 02/03/72
**Hometown:** Fowlerville, Mich.

### CAREER STATISTICS

| Year | Rank | Starts | Wins | Poles | Top 5 | Top 10 | Races Led | Laps Led |
|------|------|--------|------|-------|-------|--------|-----------|----------|
| 2001 | 110 | 2 | 0 | 0 | 0 | 0 | 0 | 0 |
| 2002 | 99 | 3 | 0 | 0 | 0 | 0 | 0 | 0 |
| 2003 | 75 | 5 | 0 | 0 | 0 | 0 | 0 | 0 |
| 2004 | 91 | 3 | 0 | 0 | 0 | 0 | 0 | 0 |
| **TOTALS** | | 13 | 0 | 0 | 0 | 0 | 0 | 0 |

# Mark Martin

**Birth date:** 01/09/59 • **Hometown:** Batesville, Ark.
**Car:** FORD • **Car owner:** Jack Roush

## CAREER STATISTICS (Mark Martin)

| Year | Rank | Starts | Wins | Poles | Top 5 | Top 10 | Races Led | Laps Led |
|------|------|--------|------|-------|-------|--------|-----------|----------|
| 1982 | 162 | 1 | 0 | 0 | 0 | 0 | 0 | 0 |
| 1987 | 8 | 27 | 3 | 6 | 5 | 13 | 8 | 257 |
| 1988 | 29 | 13 | 1 | 0 | 2 | 6 | 1 | 5 |
| 1989 | 20 | 17 | 1 | 1 | 6 | 8 | 8 | 353 |
| 1990 | 32 | 12 | 1 | 0 | 3 | 5 | 3 | 216 |
| 1991 | 102 | 1 | 0 | 0 | 0 | 0 | 0 | 0 |
| 1992 | 21 | 14 | 1 | 2 | 5 | 9 | 9 | 429 |
| 1993 | 24 | 14 | 7 | 1 | 7 | 7 | 11 | 990 |
| 1994 | 20 | 15 | 3 | 3 | 8 | 11 | 14 | 1120 |
| 1995 | 22 | 15 | 3 | 1 | 9 | 11 | 11 | 851 |
| 1996 | 21 | 14 | 6 | 2 | 11 | 12 | 14 | 991 |
| 1997 | 24 | 15 | 6 | 3 | 10 | 12 | 11 | 598 |
| 1998 | 27 | 15 | 2 | 1 | 6 | 9 | 8 | 211 |
| 1999 | 26 | 14 | 6 | 3 | 9 | 10 | 12 | 746 |
| 2000 | 27 | 13 | 5 | 4 | 12 | 13 | 12 | 969 |
| 2004 | 56 | 5 | 0 | 0 | 1 | 4 | 1 | 4 |
| **TOTALS** | | 205 | 45 | 27 | 94 | 130 | 123 | 7740 |

# Sterling Marlin

**Birth date:** 06/30/57
**Hometown:** Franklin, Tenn.

### CAREER STATISTICS

| Year | Rank | Starts | Wins | Poles | Top 5 | Top 10 | Races Led | Laps Led |
|------|------|--------|------|-------|-------|--------|-----------|----------|
| 1986 | 119 | 1 | 0 | 0 | 0 | 0 | 1 | 6 |
| 1988 | 51 | 4 | 0 | 0 | 0 | 0 | 0 | 0 |
| 1989 | 82 | 2 | 0 | 0 | 0 | 0 | 1 | 34 |
| 1990 | 48 | 5 | 1 | 0 | 2 | 2 | 5 | 114 |
| 1992 | 67 | 2 | 0 | 0 | 1 | 1 | 1 | 2 |
| 1993 | 41 | 8 | 0 | 0 | 1 | 2 | 0 | 0 |
| 1994 | 44 | 9 | 0 | 0 | 1 | 3 | 2 | 60 |
| 1995 | 121 | 1 | 0 | 0 | 0 | 0 | 0 | 0 |
| 1996 | 60 | 2 | 0 | 1 | 1 | 1 | 1 | 21 |
| 1997 | 71 | 3 | 0 | 0 | 0 | 0 | 0 | 0 |
| 1998 | 59 | 5 | 0 | 0 | 0 | 2 | 0 | 0 |
| 1999 | 54 | 7 | 0 | 0 | 1 | 3 | 3 | 163 |
| 2000 | 62 | 4 | 1 | 0 | 2 | 3 | 2 | 101 |
| 2004 | 102 | 2 | 0 | 0 | 0 | 0 | 0 | 0 |
| **TOTALS** | | 55 | 2 | 1 | 9 | 17 | 16 | 501 |

# Eric McClure

**Birth date:** 12/11/78 • **Hometown:** Chilhowie, Va.
**Car:** CHEVROLET • Morgan McClure Motorsports

### CAREER STATISTICS

| Year | Rank | Starts | Wins | Poles | Top 5 | Top 10 | Races Led | Laps Led |
|------|------|--------|------|-------|-------|--------|-----------|----------|
| 2003 | 130 | 1 | 0 | 0 | 0 | 0 | 0 | 0 |
| 2004 | 82 | 4 | 0 | 0 | 0 | 0 | 0 | 0 |
| **TOTALS** | | 5 | 0 | 0 | 0 | 0 | 0 | 0 |

# Mark McFarland

**Birth date:** 02/01/78
**Hometown:** Winchester, Va.

### CAREER STATISTICS

| Year | Rank | Starts | Wins | Poles | Top 5 | Top 10 | Races Led | Laps Led |
|------|------|--------|------|-------|-------|--------|-----------|----------|
| 1998 | 69 | 4 | 0 | 0 | 0 | 0 | 0 | 0 |
| 2000 | 114 | 1 | 0 | 0 | 0 | 0 | 0 | 0 |
| 2001 | 103 | 1 | 0 | 0 | 0 | 0 | 0 | 0 |
| 2004 | 73 | 3 | 0 | 0 | 0 | 0 | 0 | 0 |
| **TOTALS** | | 9 | 0 | 0 | 0 | 0 | 0 | 0 |

# Mike McLaughlin

**Birth date:** 10/06/56
**Hometown:** Waterloo, N.Y.

### CAREER STATISTICS

| Year | Rank | Starts | Wins | Poles | Top 5 | Top 10 | Races Led | Laps Led |
|------|------|--------|------|-------|-------|--------|-----------|----------|
| 1984 | 72 | 2 | 0 | 0 | 0 | 0 | 0 | 0 |
| 1985 | 66 | 2 | 0 | 0 | 0 | 0 | 1 | 1 |
| 1990 | 45 | 6 | 0 | 0 | 2 | 3 | 1 | 18 |
| 1991 | 45 | 8 | 0 | 0 | 0 | 0 | 0 | 0 |
| 1992 | 49 | 5 | 0 | 0 | 0 | 0 | 0 | 0 |
| 1993 | 58 | 3 | 0 | 0 | 0 | 1 | 0 | 0 |
| 1994 | 13 | 26 | 0 | 0 | 3 | 8 | 3 | 9 |
| 1995 | 3 | 26 | 1 | 1 | 9 | 14 | 5 | 82 |
| 1996 | 10 | 26 | 0 | 0 | 7 | 10 | 6 | 99 |
| 1997 | 4 | 30 | 2 | 2 | 7 | 14 | 8 | 206 |
| 1998 | 3 | 31 | 2 | 2 | 11 | 16 | 9 | 165 |
| 1999 | 9 | 32 | 0 | 0 | 3 | 8 | 4 | 53 |
| 2000 | 24 | 31 | 0 | 0 | 3 | 5 | 0 | 0 |
| 2001 | 7 | 33 | 1 | 0 | 5 | 12 | 5 | 38 |
| 2002 | 4 | 34 | 0 | 0 | 7 | 17 | 5 | 128 |
| 2003 | 61 | 7 | 0 | 0 | 0 | 1 | 0 | 0 |
| 2004 | 38 | 11 | 0 | 0 | 1 | 1 | 0 | 0 |
| **TOTALS** | | 313 | 6 | 5 | 58 | 110 | 47 | 799 |

# Jamie McMurray

**Birth date:** 06/03/76 • **Hometown:** Joplin, Mo.
**Car:** DODGE • **Car owner:** Rusty Wallace

### CAREER STATISTICS

| Year | Rank | Starts | Wins | Poles | Top 5 | Top 10 | Races Led | Laps Led |
|------|------|--------|------|-------|-------|--------|-----------|----------|
| 2000 | 93 | 2 | 0 | 0 | 0 | 0 | 0 | 0 |
| 2001 | 16 | 33 | 0 | 0 | 0 | 3 | 1 | 1 |
| 2002 | 6 | 34 | 2 | 0 | 6 | 14 | 9 | 87 |
| 2003 | 20 | 19 | 2 | 0 | 6 | 10 | 4 | 400 |
| 2004 | 32 | 14 | 3 | 1 | 6 | 8 | 6 | 170 |
| **TOTALS** | | 102 | 7 | 1 | 18 | 35 | 20 | 658 |

# Casey Mears

**Birth date:** 03/12/78
**Hometown:** Bakersfield, Calif.

## CAREER STATISTICS

| Year | Rank | Starts | Wins | Poles | Top 5 | Top 10 | Races Led | Laps Led |
|---|---|---|---|---|---|---|---|---|
| 2001 | 114 | 1 | 0 | 0 | 0 | 0 | 0 | 0 |
| 2002 | 21 | 34 | 0 | 0 | 1 | 2 | 2 | 5 |
| 2003 | 34 | 14 | 0 | 1 | 1 | 4 | 1 | 2 |
| 2004 | 34 | 13 | 0 | 3 | 2 | 6 | 6 | 133 |
| **TOTALS** | | 62 | 0 | 4 | 4 | 12 | 9 | 140 |

# Paul Menard

**Birth date:** 08/21/80 • **Hometown:** EauClaire, Wis.
**Car:** CHEVROLET • **Car owner:** Dale Earnhardt Inc.

## CAREER STATISTICS

| Year | Rank | Starts | Wins | Poles | Top 5 | Top 10 | Races Led | Laps Led |
|---|---|---|---|---|---|---|---|---|
| 2003 | 60 | 6 | 0 | 0 | 0 | 1 | 0 | 0 |
| 2004 | 23 | 27 | 0 | 1 | 0 | 0 | 0 | 0 |
| **TOTALS** | | 33 | 0 | 1 | 0 | 1 | 0 | 0 |

# Ted Musgrave

**Birth date:** 12/18/55
**Hometown:** Franklin, Wis.

## CAREER STATISTICS

| Year | Rank | Starts | Wins | Poles | Top 5 | Top 10 | Races Led | Laps Led |
|---|---|---|---|---|---|---|---|---|
| 1989 | 70 | 2 | 0 | 0 | 0 | 0 | 0 | 0 |
| 1995 | 93 | 1 | 0 | 0 | 0 | 0 | 0 | 0 |
| 1997 | 79 | 2 | 0 | 0 | 0 | 0 | 0 | 0 |
| 1999 | 105 | 1 | 0 | 0 | 0 | 0 | 0 | 0 |
| 2000 | 53 | 9 | 0 | 0 | 0 | 1 | 0 | 0 |
| 2003 | 98 | 1 | 0 | 0 | 1 | 1 | 0 | 0 |
| 2004 | 133 | 1 | 0 | 0 | 0 | 0 | 0 | 0 |
| **TOTALS** | | 17 | 0 | 0 | 1 | 2 | 0 | 0 |

# Joe Nemechek

**Birth date:** 09/26/63 • **Hometown:** Lakeland, Fla.
**Car:** CHEVROLET • **Car owner:** Andrea Nemechek

## CAREER STATISTICS (Joe Nemechek)

| Year | Rank | Starts | Wins | Poles | Top 5 | Top 10 | Races Led | Laps Led |
|---|---|---|---|---|---|---|---|---|
| 1989 | 98 | 1 | 0 | 0 | 0 | 0 | 0 | 0 |
| 1990 | 17 | 28 | 0 | 0 | 2 | 5 | 1 | 20 |
| 1991 | 6 | 31 | 0 | 0 | 5 | 16 | 4 | 34 |
| 1992 | 1 | 31 | 2 | 1 | 13 | 18 | 8 | 241 |
| 1993 | 5 | 28 | 0 | 3 | 8 | 11 | 14 | 627 |
| 1994 | 38 | 12 | 1 | 0 | 1 | 2 | 4 | 190 |
| 1995 | 43 | 6 | 0 | 1 | 2 | 4 | 2 | 71 |
| 1996 | 38 | 11 | 0 | 1 | 3 | 6 | 5 | 115 |
| 1997 | 40 | 9 | 2 | 3 | 5 | 6 | 6 | 430 |
| 1998 | 39 | 9 | 2 | 1 | 5 | 7 | 4 | 308 |
| 1999 | 33 | 12 | 1 | 0 | 6 | 7 | 5 | 82 |
| 2000 | 32 | 14 | 1 | 0 | 6 | 8 | 4 | 215 |
| 2001 | 35 | 13 | 2 | 2 | 4 | 6 | 7 | 181 |
| 2002 | 34 | 14 | 1 | 2 | 6 | 7 | 5 | 122 |
| 2003 | 31 | 16 | 3 | 2 | 5 | 6 | 4 | 133 |
| 2004 | 31 | 18 | 1 | 0 | 1 | 6 | 8 | 91 |
| **TOTALS** | | 253 | 16 | 16 | 72 | 115 | 81 | 2860 |

# Donnie Neuenberger

**Birth date:** 08/10/62
**Hometown:** Brandywine, Md.

## CAREER STATISTICS

| Year | Rank | Starts | Wins | Poles | Top 5 | Top 10 | Races Led | Laps Led |
|---|---|---|---|---|---|---|---|---|
| 2002 | 103 | 1 | 0 | 0 | 0 | 0 | 0 | 0 |
| 2003 | 74 | 6 | 0 | 0 | 0 | 0 | 0 | 0 |
| 2004 | 75 | 6 | 0 | 0 | 0 | 0 | 0 | 0 |
| **TOTALS** | | 13 | 0 | 0 | 0 | 0 | 0 | 0 |

# Billy Parker

**Birth date:** 01/09/77
**Hometown:** Denver, N.C.

## CAREER STATISTICS

| Year | Rank | Starts | Wins | Poles | Top 5 | Top 10 | Races Led | Laps Led |
|---|---|---|---|---|---|---|---|---|
| 2000 | 109 | 1 | 0 | 0 | 0 | 0 | 0 | 0 |
| 2001 | 109 | 2 | 0 | 0 | 0 | 0 | 0 | 0 |
| 2004 | 59 | 8 | 0 | 0 | 0 | 0 | 1 | 5 |
| TOTALS | | 11 | 0 | 0 | 0 | 0 | 1 | 5 |

# Andy Ponstein

**Birth date:** 05/02/76
**Hometown:** Hudsonville, Mich.

## CAREER STATISTICS (Andy Ponstein)

| Year | Rank | Starts | Wins | Poles | Top 5 | Top 10 | Races Led | Laps Led |
|---|---|---|---|---|---|---|---|---|
| 2004 | 55 | 9 | 0 | 0 | 0 | 0 | 0 | 0 |
| TOTALS | | 9 | 0 | 0 | 0 | 0 | 0 | 0 |

# Mike Potter

**Birth date:** 07/04/49 • **Hometown:** Johnson City, Tenn.

### CAREER STATISTICS

| Year | Rank | Starts | Wins | Poles | Top 5 | Top 10 | Races Led | Laps Led |
|---|---|---|---|---|---|---|---|---|
| 1982 | 173 | 1 | 0 | 0 | 0 | 0 | 0 | 0 |
| 1985 | 106 | 1 | 0 | 0 | 0 | 0 | 0 | 0 |
| 2001 | 144 | 1 | 0 | 0 | 0 | 0 | 0 | 0 |
| 2003 | 68 | 11 | 0 | 0 | 0 | 0 | 0 | 0 |
| 2004 | 126 | 2 | 0 | 0 | 0 | 0 | 0 | 0 |
| TOTALS | | 16 | 0 | 0 | 0 | 0 | 0 | 0 |

# Robert Pressley

**Birth date:** 04/08/59 • **Hometown:** Asheville, N.C.
**Car:** FORD • **Car owner:** Jodi Geschickter

### CAREER STATISTICS

| Year | Rank | Starts | Wins | Poles | Top 5 | Top 10 | Races Led | Laps Led |
|---|---|---|---|---|---|---|---|---|
| 1984 | 109 | 1 | 0 | 0 | 0 | 0 | 0 | 0 |
| 1989 | 18 | 19 | 1 | 0 | 1 | 3 | 1 | 108 |
| 1990 | 12 | 31 | 0 | 0 | 5 | 9 | 4 | 183 |
| 1991 | 3 | 31 | 1 | 1 | 8 | 15 | 7 | 441 |
| 1992 | 5 | 31 | 5 | 2 | 11 | 16 | 10 | 736 |
| 1993 | 8 | 28 | 3 | 0 | 8 | 13 | 9 | 382 |
| 1994 | 12 | 28 | 0 | 1 | 2 | 9 | 3 | 74 |
| 1997 | 33 | 15 | 0 | 0 | 2 | 3 | 2 | 39 |
| 1998 | 31 | 18 | 0 | 2 | 0 | 6 | 3 | 169 |
| 1999 | 77 | 3 | 0 | 0 | 0 | 0 | 0 | 0 |
| 2004 | 15 | 34 | 0 | 0 | 1 | 2 | 2 | 14 |
| TOTALS | | 239 | 10 | 6 | 38 | 76 | 41 | 2146 |

# Jeff Purvis

**Birth date:** 02/19/59 • **Hometown:** Clarksville, Tenn.

### CAREER STATISTICS

| Year | Rank | Starts | Wins | Poles | Top 5 | Top 10 | Races Led | Laps Led |
|---|---|---|---|---|---|---|---|---|
| 1989 | 103 | 1 | 0 | 0 | 0 | 0 | 0 | 0 |
| 1990 | 65 | 4 | 0 | 0 | 0 | 0 | 0 | 0 |
| 1991 | 65 | 4 | 0 | 0 | 0 | 0 | 0 | 0 |

## CAREER STATISTICS (Jeff Purvis)

| Year | Rank | Starts | Wins | Poles | Top 5 | Top 10 | Races Led | Laps Led |
|---|---|---|---|---|---|---|---|---|
| 1992 | 48 | 4 | 0 | 0 | 0 | 1 | 0 | 0 |
| 1993 | 80 | 2 | 0 | 0 | 0 | 0 | 0 | 0 |
| 1994 | 59 | 4 | 0 | 1 | 1 | 1 | 1 | 1 |
| 1995 | 38 | 9 | 0 | 1 | 1 | 3 | 4 | 40 |
| 1996 | 7 | 26 | 2 | 2 | 4 | 7 | 5 | 72 |
| 1997 | 44 | 10 | 0 | 0 | 1 | 3 | 1 | 15 |
| 1998 | 15 | 26 | 0 | 1 | 6 | 10 | 5 | 146 |
| 1999 | 6 | 32 | 0 | 0 | 4 | 12 | 4 | 63 |
| 2000 | 11 | 29 | 0 | 1 | 4 | 11 | 4 | 57 |
| 2001 | 21 | 23 | 1 | 0 | 3 | 8 | 5 | 196 |
| 2002 | 39 | 12 | 1 | 0 | 1 | 1 | 2 | 7 |
| 2004 | 113 | 1 | 0 | 0 | 0 | 0 | 0 | 0 |
| TOTALS | | 187 | 4 | 6 | 25 | 57 | 31 | 597 |

# Tony Raines

**Birth date:** 04/14/64 • **Hometown:** LaPorte, Ind.
**Car:** CHEVROLET • **Car owner:** Kevin Harvick

### CAREER STATISTICS

| Year | Rank | Starts | Wins | Poles | Top 5 | Top 10 | Races Led | Laps Led |
|---|---|---|---|---|---|---|---|---|
| 1999 | 12 | 31 | 0 | 0 | 1 | 3 | 0 | 0 |
| 2000 | 15 | 32 | 0 | 0 | 1 | 1 | 5 | 154 |
| 2001 | 6 | 33 | 0 | 1 | 4 | 13 | 4 | 26 |
| 2002 | 12 | 34 | 0 | 0 | 5 | 11 | 5 | 28 |
| 2003 | 39 | 12 | 0 | 0 | 2 | 5 | 0 | 0 |
| 2004 | 33 | 18 | 0 | 0 | 0 | 2 | 1 | 3 |
| TOTALS | | 160 | 0 | 1 | 13 | 35 | 15 | 211 |

# Boston Reid

**Birth date:** 12/29/82 • **Hometown:** Logansport, Ind.

### CAREER STATISTICS

| Year | Rank | Starts | Wins | Poles | Top 5 | Top 10 | Races Led | Laps Led |
|---|---|---|---|---|---|---|---|---|
| 2004 | 97 | 3 | 0 | 0 | 0 | 0 | 0 | 0 |
| TOTALS | | 3 | 0 | 0 | 0 | 0 | 0 | 0 |

# David Reutimann

**Birth date:** 03/02/70
**Hometown:** Zephyrhills, Fla.

### CAREER STATISTICS

| Year | Rank | Starts | Wins | Poles | Top 5 | Top 10 | Races Led | Laps Led |
|---|---|---|---|---|---|---|---|---|
| 2002 | 63 | 4 | 0 | 0 | 0 | 0 | 1 | 12 |
| 2003 | 50 | 7 | 0 | 0 | 2 | 3 | 1 | 22 |
| 2004 | 70 | 4 | 0 | 0 | 0 | 0 | 0 | 0 |
| TOTALS | | 15 | 0 | 0 | 2 | 3 | 2 | 34 |

# Josh Richeson

**Birth date:** 09/04/81
**Hometown:** Davidson, N.C.

## CAREER STATISTICS

| Year | Rank | Starts | Wins | Poles | Top 5 | Top 10 | Races Led | Laps Led |
|------|------|--------|------|-------|-------|--------|-----------|----------|
| 2001 | 105 | 2 | 0 | 0 | 0 | 0 | 0 | 0 |
| 2002 | 57 | 9 | 0 | 0 | 0 | 0 | 0 | 0 |
| 2003 | 79 | 8 | 0 | 0 | 0 | 0 | 0 | 0 |
| 2004 | 84 | 4 | 0 | 0 | 0 | 0 | 0 | 0 |
| **TOTALS** | | 23 | 0 | 0 | 0 | 0 | 0 | 0 |

# Jason Rudd

**Birth date:** 04/15/79
**Hometown:** Norfolk, Va.

## CAREER STATISTICS

| Year | Rank | Starts | Wins | Poles | Top 5 | Top 10 | Races Led | Laps Led |
|------|------|--------|------|-------|-------|--------|-----------|----------|
| 2001 | 64 | 6 | 0 | 0 | 0 | 0 | 0 | 0 |
| 2003 | 107 | 2 | 0 | 0 | 0 | 0 | 0 | 0 |
| 2004 | 150 | 1 | 0 | 0 | 0 | 0 | 0 | 0 |
| **TOTALS** | | 9 | 0 | 0 | 0 | 0 | 0 | 0 |

# Hermie Sadler

**Birth date:** 04/24/69 • **Hometown:** Emporia, Va.
**Car:** CHEVROLET • **Car owner:** Bryant Stith

## CAREER STATISTICS

| Year | Rank | Starts | Wins | Poles | Top 5 | Top 10 | Races Led | Laps Led |
|------|------|--------|------|-------|-------|--------|-----------|----------|
| 1992 | 51 | 5 | 0 | 0 | 0 | 0 | 0 | 0 |
| 1993 | 10 | 28 | 1 | 0 | 4 | 8 | 1 | 8 |
| 1994 | 5 | 28 | 1 | 0 | 6 | 11 | 7 | 291 |
| 1995 | 13 | 26 | 0 | 0 | 3 | 6 | 2 | 114 |
| 1996 | 15 | 26 | 0 | 1 | 1 | 5 | 4 | 184 |
| 1997 | 10 | 30 | 0 | 2 | 2 | 7 | 5 | 54 |
| 1998 | 10 | 31 | 0 | 0 | 2 | 5 | 3 | 18 |
| 1999 | 37 | 17 | 0 | 0 | 0 | 1 | 0 | 0 |
| 2000 | 35 | 16 | 0 | 0 | 0 | 1 | 2 | 4 |
| 2002 | 66 | 6 | 0 | 0 | 0 | 0 | 0 | 0 |
| 2003 | 44 | 13 | 0 | 0 | 0 | 0 | 0 | 0 |
| 2004 | 24 | 30 | 0 | 0 | 0 | 0 | 1 | 1 |
| **TOTALS** | | 256 | 2 | 3 | 18 | 44 | 25 | 674 |

# Jay Sauter

**Birth date:** 06/22/62 • **Hometown:** West Salem, Wis.
**Car:** CHEVROLET • **Car owner:** Charlie Henderson

## CAREER STATISTICS

| Year | Rank | Starts | Wins | Poles | Top 5 | Top 10 | Races Led | Laps Led |
|------|------|--------|------|-------|-------|--------|-----------|----------|
| 1997 | 86 | 1 | 0 | 0 | 0 | 0 | 0 | 0 |
| 2000 | 16 | 31 | 0 | 0 | 1 | 8 | 3 | 25 |
| 2001 | 19 | 31 | 0 | 1 | 2 | 7 | 2 | 13 |
| 2002 | 36 | 14 | 0 | 0 | 1 | 4 | 4 | 47 |
| 2003 | 49 | 10 | 0 | 0 | 0 | 1 | 1 | 2 |
| 2004 | 63 | 6 | 0 | 0 | 0 | 0 | 0 | 0 |
| **TOTALS** | | 93 | 0 | 1 | 4 | 20 | 10 | 87 |

# Johnny Sauter

**Birth date:** 05/01/78 • **Hometown:** Necedah, Wis.
**Car:** DODGE • **Car owner:** James Finch

## CAREER STATISTICS

| Year | Rank | Starts | Wins | Poles | Top 5 | Top 10 | Races Led | Laps Led |
|------|------|--------|------|-------|-------|--------|-----------|----------|
| 2001 | 55 | 5 | 0 | 0 | 1 | 1 | 1 | 13 |
| 2002 | 15 | 33 | 1 | 1 | 3 | 6 | 5 | 86 |
| 2003 | 8 | 34 | 1 | 0 | 6 | 14 | 10 | 231 |
| 2004 | 18 | 34 | 0 | 1 | 4 | 8 | 7 | 193 |
| **TOTALS** | | 106 | 2 | 2 | 14 | 29 | 23 | 523 |

# Tim Sauter

**Birth date:** 10/13/64
**Hometown:** Necedah, Wis.

## CAREER STATISTICS

| Year | Rank | Starts | Wins | Poles | Top 5 | Top 10 | Races Led | Laps Led |
|------|------|--------|------|-------|-------|--------|-----------|----------|
| 2000 | 73 | 3 | 0 | 0 | 0 | 0 | 0 | 0 |
| 2001 | 32 | 18 | 0 | 0 | 0 | 2 | 0 | 0 |
| 2002 | 13 | 34 | 0 | 0 | 0 | 7 | 4 | 12 |
| 2003 | 46 | 12 | 0 | 0 | 0 | 0 | 1 | 4 |
| 2004 | 79 | 4 | 0 | 0 | 0 | 0 | 0 | 0 |
| **TOTALS** | | 71 | 0 | 0 | 0 | 9 | 5 | 16 |

# Jason Schuler

**Birth date:** 02/24/72
**Hometown:** Cambridge, Wis.

## CAREER STATISTICS (Jason Schuler)

| Year | Rank | Starts | Wins | Poles | Top 5 | Top 10 | Races Led | Laps Led |
|------|------|--------|------|-------|-------|--------|-----------|----------|
| 2000 | 44 | 11 | 0 | 0 | 0 | 0 | 1 | 2 |
| 2001 | 104 | 2 | 0 | 0 | 0 | 0 | 0 | 0 |
| 2002 | 78 | 5 | 0 | 0 | 0 | 0 | 0 | 0 |
| 2003 | 28 | 27 | 0 | 0 | 0 | 0 | 2 | 12 |
| 2004 | 65 | 7 | 0 | 0 | 0 | 0 | 0 | 0 |
| TOTALS | | 52 | 0 | 0 | 0 | 0 | 3 | 14 |

# C.W. Smith

**Birth date:** 10/28/47 • **Hometown:** Williamsport, Pa.
**Car:** CHEVROLET • **Car owner:** Michael Smith

### CAREER STATISTICS

| Year | Rank | Starts | Wins | Poles | Top 5 | Top 10 | Races Led | Laps Led |
|------|------|--------|------|-------|-------|--------|-----------|----------|
| 2002 | 86 | 2 | 0 | 0 | 0 | 0 | 0 | 0 |
| 2004 | 94 | 3 | 0 | 0 | 0 | 0 | 0 | 0 |
| TOTALS | | 5 | 0 | 0 | 0 | 0 | 0 | 0 |

# Regan Smith

**Birth date:** 09/23/83
**Hometown:** Cato, N.Y.

### CAREER STATISTICS

| Year | Rank | Starts | Wins | Poles | Top 5 | Top 10 | Races Led | Laps Led |
|------|------|--------|------|-------|-------|--------|-----------|----------|
| 2002 | 118 | 1 | 0 | 0 | 0 | 0 | 0 | 0 |
| 2003 | 38 | 18 | 0 | 0 | 0 | 0 | 0 | 0 |
| 2004 | 45 | 10 | 0 | 0 | 0 | 0 | 0 | 0 |
| TOTALS | | 29 | 0 | 0 | 0 | 0 | 0 | 0 |

# Brian Sockwell

**Birth date:** 06/07/68
**Hometown:** Brown Summit, N.C.

### CAREER STATISTICS

| Year | Rank | Starts | Wins | Poles | Top 5 | Top 10 | Races Led | Laps Led |
|------|------|--------|------|-------|-------|--------|-----------|----------|
| 2004 | 100 | 3 | 0 | 0 | 0 | 0 | 0 | 0 |
| TOTALS | | 3 | 0 | 0 | 0 | 0 | 0 | 0 |

# Reed Sorenson

**Birth date:** 02/05/86 • **Hometown:** Forest Park, Ga.
**Car:** DODGE • **Car owner:** Ganassi Racing

## CAREER STATISTICS (Reed Sorenson)

| Year | Rank | Starts | Wins | Poles | Top 5 | Top 10 | Races Led | Laps Led |
|------|------|--------|------|-------|-------|--------|-----------|----------|
| 2004 | 52 | 5 | 0 | 0 | 1 | 3 | 1 | 47 |
| TOTALS | | 5 | 0 | 0 | 1 | 3 | 1 | 47 |

# Jimmy Spencer

**Birth date:** 02/15/57
**Hometown:** Berwick, Pa.

### CAREER STATISTICS

| Year | Rank | Starts | Wins | Poles | Top 5 | Top 10 | Races Led | Laps Led |
|------|------|--------|------|-------|-------|--------|-----------|----------|
| 1985 | 84 | 1 | 0 | 0 | 0 | 0 | 0 | 0 |
| 1987 | 75 | 2 | 0 | 0 | 0 | 0 | 0 | 0 |
| 1988 | 7 | 30 | 0 | 0 | 5 | 13 | 5 | 102 |
| 1989 | 15 | 22 | 3 | 1 | 4 | 11 | 3 | 377 |
| 1990 | 44 | 6 | 0 | 0 | 1 | 2 | 2 | 9 |
| 1991 | 43 | 6 | 0 | 0 | 1 | 2 | 0 | 0 |
| 1992 | 17 | 25 | 2 | 0 | 6 | 10 | 9 | 456 |
| 1993 | 42 | 9 | 0 | 0 | 0 | 2 | 0 | 0 |
| 1994 | 64 | 3 | 0 | 0 | 1 | 1 | 1 | 20 |
| 1995 | 34 | 12 | 0 | 0 | 1 | 5 | 2 | 30 |
| 1996 | 32 | 13 | 0 | 0 | 1 | 6 | 4 | 118 |
| 1997 | 30 | 12 | 2 | 0 | 7 | 7 | 5 | 327 |
| 1998 | 43 | 8 | 1 | 0 | 5 | 6 | 5 | 195 |
| 1999 | 43 | 9 | 0 | 0 | 5 | 6 | 4 | 131 |
| 2000 | 65 | 6 | 0 | 0 | 0 | 1 | 1 | 19 |
| 2001 | 26 | 18 | 3 | 2 | 5 | 10 | 9 | 493 |
| 2002 | 26 | 23 | 1 | 0 | 2 | 10 | 6 | 181 |
| 2003 | 86 | 2 | 0 | 0 | 0 | 1 | 0 | 0 |
| 2004 | 92 | 3 | 0 | 0 | 0 | 0 | 0 | 0 |
| TOTALS | | 210 | 12 | 3 | 44 | 93 | 56 | 2458 |

# David Starr

**Birth date:** 10/11/67
**Hometown:** Houston

### CAREER STATISTICS

| Year | Rank | Starts | Wins | Poles | Top 5 | Top 10 | Races Led | Laps Led |
|------|------|--------|------|-------|-------|--------|-----------|----------|
| 2000 | 120 | 1 | 0 | 0 | 0 | 0 | 0 | 0 |
| 2001 | 68 | 4 | 0 | 0 | 0 | 0 | 0 | 0 |
| 2002 | 112 | 1 | 0 | 0 | 0 | 0 | 0 | 0 |
| 2004 | 86 | 3 | 0 | 0 | 0 | 0 | 0 | 0 |
| TOTALS | | 9 | 0 | 0 | 0 | 0 | 0 | 0 |

# Tony Stewart

**Birth date:** 05/20/71 • **Hometown:** Rushville, Ind.
**Car:** CHEVROLET • **Car owner:** Kevin Harvick Inc.

### CAREER STATISTICS (Tony Stewart)

| Year | Rank | Starts | Wins | Poles | Top 5 | Top 10 | Races Led | Laps Led |
|---|---|---|---|---|---|---|---|---|
| 1996 | 49 | 9 | 0 | 0 | 0 | 0 | 0 | 0 |
| 1997 | 58 | 5 | 0 | 0 | 1 | 2 | 0 | 0 |
| 1998 | 21 | 22 | 0 | 2 | 5 | 5 | 6 | 157 |
| 2003 | 109 | 1 | 0 | 0 | 0 | 0 | 1 | 86 |
| 2004 | 58 | 4 | 0 | 0 | 2 | 2 | 3 | 129 |
| TOTALS | | 41 | 0 | 2 | 8 | 9 | 10 | 372 |

# David Stremme

**Birth date:** 06/19/77 • **Hometown:** South Bend, Ind.
**Car:** DODGE • **Car owner:** Terry Bradshaw

### CAREER STATISTICS

| Year | Rank | Starts | Wins | Poles | Top 5 | Top 10 | Races Led | Laps Led |
|---|---|---|---|---|---|---|---|---|
| 2003 | 22 | 18 | 0 | 0 | 3 | 7 | 6 | 86 |
| 2004 | 10 | 34 | 0 | 1 | 5 | 14 | 1 | 75 |
| TOTALS | | 52 | 0 | 1 | 8 | 21 | 7 | 161 |

# Todd Szegedy

**Birth date:** 05/06/76
**Hometown:** Ridgefield, Conn.

### CAREER STATISTICS (Todd Szegedy)

| Year | Rank | Starts | Wins | Poles | Top 5 | Top 10 | Races Led | Laps Led |
|---|---|---|---|---|---|---|---|---|
| 2004 | 83 | 3 | 0 | 0 | 0 | 0 | 0 | 0 |
| TOTALS | | 3 | 0 | 0 | 0 | 0 | 0 | 0 |

# Brad Teague

**Birth date:** 12/09/47 • **Hometown:** Johnson City, Tenn.
**Car:** FORD • **Car owner:** Butch Jarvis

### CAREER STATISTICS

| Year | Rank | Starts | Wins | Poles | Top 5 | Top 10 | Races Led | Laps Led |
|---|---|---|---|---|---|---|---|---|
| 1982 | 107 | 1 | 0 | 0 | 1 | 1 | 0 | 0 |
| 1983 | 136 | 1 | 0 | 0 | 0 | 0 | 0 | 0 |
| 1984 | 27 | 10 | 0 | 0 | 4 | 8 | 1 | 34 |
| 1985 | 13 | 24 | 0 | 2 | 2 | 7 | 8 | 129 |
| 1986 | 19 | 20 | 0 | 0 | 1 | 10 | 3 | 52 |
| 1987 | 7 | 27 | 1 | 0 | 1 | 10 | 2 | 97 |
| 1988 | 23 | 17 | 0 | 0 | 1 | 5 | 4 | 101 |
| 1989 | 52 | 6 | 0 | 0 | 1 | 1 | 0 | 0 |
| 1990 | 49 | 6 | 0 | 0 | 0 | 0 | 1 | 4 |
| 1991 | 98 | 1 | 0 | 0 | 0 | 0 | 0 | 0 |
| 1995 | 66 | 2 | 0 | 0 | 0 | 1 | 0 | 0 |
| 1996 | 62 | 3 | 0 | 0 | 0 | 0 | 0 | 0 |
| 1997 | 56 | 5 | 0 | 0 | 0 | 0 | 0 | 0 |

Martin Truex Jr. won the most races (six) and poles (seven) and had the most top 10s ( 26) in 2004.

## CAREER STATISTICS (Brad Teague)

| Year | Rank | Starts | Wins | Poles | Top 5 | Top 10 | Races Led | Laps Led |
|------|------|--------|------|-------|-------|--------|-----------|----------|
| 1999 | 110  | 1      | 0    | 0     | 0     | 0      | 0         | 0        |
| 2001 | 47   | 16     | 0    | 0     | 0     | 0      | 0         | 0        |
| 2002 | 42   | 19     | 0    | 0     | 0     | 0      | 0         | 0        |
| 2003 | 32   | 26     | 0    | 0     | 0     | 0      | 1         | 1        |
| 2004 | 47   | 15     | 0    | 0     | 0     | 0      | 0         | 0        |
| TOTALS |    | 200    | 1    | 2     | 11    | 43     | 20        | 418      |

# Martin Truex Jr.

**Birth date:** 06/29/80 • **Hometown:** Mayetta, N.J.
**Car:** CHEVROLET • **Car owner:** Teresa Earnhardt

## CAREER STATISTICS

| Year | Rank | Starts | Wins | Poles | Top 5 | Top 10 | Races Led | Laps Led |
|------|------|--------|------|-------|-------|--------|-----------|----------|
| 2001 | 133  | 1      | 0    | 0     | 0     | 0      | 0         | 0        |
| 2002 | 65   | 4      | 0    | 0     | 0     | 0      | 0         | 0        |
| 2003 | 40   | 10     | 0    | 0     | 2     | 3      | 1         | 11       |
| 2004 | 1    | 34     | 6    | 7     | 17    | 26     | 21        | 954      |
| TOTALS |    | 49     | 6    | 7     | 19    | 29     | 22        | 965      |

# Kenny Wallace

**Birth date:** 08/23/63
**Hometown:** St. Louis

## CAREER STATISTICS

| Year | Rank | Starts | Wins | Poles | Top 5 | Top 10 | Races Led | Laps Led |
|------|------|--------|------|-------|-------|--------|-----------|----------|
| 1988 | 81   | 1      | 0    | 0     | 0     | 0      | 0         | 0        |
| 1989 | 6    | 29     | 0    | 3     | 4     | 16     | 4         | 259      |
| 1990 | 7    | 31     | 0    | 1     | 4     | 14     | 4         | 131      |
| 1991 | 2    | 31     | 2    | 1     | 11    | 17     | 10        | 745      |
| 1992 | 6    | 31     | 1    | 2     | 7     | 15     | 7         | 238      |
| 1994 | 4    | 28     | 3    | 1     | 11    | 15     | 12        | 865      |
| 1995 | 27   | 15     | 1    | 0     | 5     | 7      | 3         | 205      |
| 1996 | 41   | 10     | 1    | 0     | 3     | 4      | 2         | 380      |
| 1997 | 101  | 1      | 0    | 0     | 0     | 0      | 0         | 0        |
| 1999 | 23   | 18     | 0    | 0     | 2     | 8      | 1         | 4        |
| 2000 | 30   | 15     | 0    | 0     | 2     | 8      | 1         | 3        |
| 2001 | 10   | 33     | 1    | 2     | 7     | 13     | 4         | 20       |
| 2002 | 7    | 34     | 0    | 0     | 2     | 13     | 1         | 8        |
| 2003 | 155  | 1      | 0    | 0     | 0     | 1      | 0         | 0        |
| 2004 | 9    | 34     | 0    | 0     | 0     | 10     | 6         | 158      |
| TOTALS |    | 312    | 9    | 10    | 58    | 141    | 55        | 3016     |

# Mike Wallace

**Birth date:** 03/10/59
**Hometown:** St. Louis

## CAREER STATISTICS (Mike Wallace)

| Year | Rank | Starts | Wins | Poles | Top 5 | Top 10 | Races Led | Laps Led |
|------|------|--------|------|-------|-------|--------|-----------|----------|
| 1990 | 82   | 1      | 0    | 0     | 0     | 1      | 0         | 0        |
| 1991 | 39   | 9      | 0    | 0     | 1     | 2      | 1         | 4        |
| 1992 | 22   | 17     | 0    | 0     | 1     | 3      | 1         | 110      |
| 1993 | 12   | 28     | 0    | 0     | 1     | 9      | 1         | 4        |
| 1994 | 19   | 22     | 3    | 0     | 6     | 9      | 7         | 338      |
| 1995 | 20   | 19     | 0    | 0     | 4     | 9      | 8         | 148      |
| 1996 | 26   | 17     | 0    | 0     | 2     | 5      | 0         | 0        |
| 1997 | 59   | 6      | 0    | 0     | 0     | 0      | 0         | 0        |
| 1998 | 57   | 6      | 0    | 0     | 0     | 1      | 0         | 0        |
| 1999 | 136  | 1      | 0    | 0     | 0     | 0      | 0         | 0        |
| 2000 | 59   | 8      | 0    | 0     | 0     | 0      | 0         | 0        |
| 2001 | 50   | 8      | 0    | 0     | 0     | 1      | 0         | 0        |
| 2002 | 37   | 17     | 0    | 0     | 0     | 0      | 2         | 10       |
| 2003 | 13   | 32     | 0    | 0     | 1     | 3      | 0         | 0        |
| 2004 | 17   | 34     | 1    | 0     | 1     | 4      | 8         | 33       |
| TOTALS |    | 225    | 4    | 0     | 17    | 47     | 28        | 647      |

# Tyler Walker

**Birth date:** 07/16/79 • **Hometown:** North Hills, Calif.
**Car:** DODGE • **Car owner:** Brad Akins

## CAREER STATISTICS

| Year | Rank | Starts | Wins | Poles | Top 5 | Top 10 | Races Led | Laps Led |
|------|------|--------|------|-------|-------|--------|-----------|----------|
| 2004 | 80   | 3      | 0    | 0     | 0     | 0      | 0         | 0        |
| TOTALS |    | 3      | 0    | 0     | 0     | 0      | 0         | 0        |

# Michael Waltrip

**Birth date:** 04/30/63 • **Hometown:** Owensboro, Ky.
**Car:** CHEVROLET • **Car owner:** Michael Waltrip

## CAREER STATISTICS

| Year | Rank | Starts | Wins | Poles | Top 5 | Top 10 | Races Led | Laps Led |
|------|------|--------|------|-------|-------|--------|-----------|----------|
| 1988 | 41   | 5      | 1    | 0     | 2     | 2      | 2         | 8        |
| 1989 | 22   | 14     | 1    | 4     | 5     | 8      | 6         | 201      |
| 1990 | 30   | 13     | 2    | 2     | 4     | 4      | 5         | 306      |
| 1991 | 34   | 10     | 0    | 0     | 5     | 5      | 5         | 75       |
| 1992 | 26   | 11     | 1    | 1     | 3     | 6      | 4         | 83       |
| 1993 | 30   | 10     | 2    | 0     | 4     | 5      | 8         | 194      |
| 1994 | 41   | 9      | 0    | 1     | 2     | 4      | 5         | 47       |
| 1995 | 48   | 6      | 0    | 1     | 2     | 2      | 3         | 56       |
| 1996 | 34   | 13     | 0    | 1     | 3     | 3      | 5         | 66       |
| 1997 | 29   | 16     | 0    | 1     | 4     | 5      | 5         | 36       |
| 1998 | 34   | 15     | 0    | 0     | 1     | 6      | 2         | 29       |
| 1999 | 29   | 15     | 1    | 0     | 3     | 7      | 2         | 27       |
| 2000 | 37   | 12     | 0    | 0     | 2     | 4      | 2         | 19       |
| 2001 | 41   | 12     | 0    | 0     | 1     | 3      | 1         | 55       |
| 2002 | 27   | 19     | 1    | 2     | 6     | 11     | 9         | 389      |
| 2003 | 18   | 20     | 1    | 2     | 8     | 13     | 9         | 419      |
| 2004 | 13   | 31     | 1    | 0     | 3     | 9      | 9         | 79       |
| TOTALS |    | 231    | 11   | 15    | 58    | 97     | 82        | 2089     |

# Gus Wasson

**Birth date:** 03/20/74 • **Hometown:** Bloomdale, Ohio
**Car:** CHEVROLET • **Car owner:** Johnny Davis

## CAREER STATISTICS

| Year | Rank | Starts | Wins | Poles | Top 5 | Top 10 | Races Led | Laps Led |
|------|------|--------|------|-------|-------|--------|-----------|----------|
| 1998 | 102 | 1 | 0 | 0 | 0 | 0 | 0 | 0 |
| 1999 | 73 | 5 | 0 | 0 | 0 | 0 | 1 | 7 |
| 2000 | 84 | 3 | 0 | 0 | 0 | 0 | 0 | 0 |
| 2001 | 123 | 1 | 0 | 0 | 0 | 0 | 0 | 0 |
| 2002 | 127 | 1 | 0 | 0 | 0 | 0 | 0 | 0 |
| 2003 | 56 | 9 | 0 | 0 | 0 | 0 | 0 | 0 |
| 2004 | 26 | 31 | 0 | 0 | 0 | 0 | 0 | 0 |
| **TOTALS** | | 51 | 0 | 0 | 0 | 0 | 1 | 7 |

# Jason White

**Birth date:** 06/05/79
**Hometown:** Powhatan, Va.

**Jon Wood moves to the NASCAR Busch Series after four seasons in the NASCAR Craftsman Truck Series.**

## CAREER STATISTICS (Jason White)

| Year | Rank | Starts | Wins | Poles | Top 5 | Top 10 | Races Led | Laps Led |
|------|------|--------|------|-------|-------|--------|-----------|----------|
| 1999 | 102 | 2 | 0 | 0 | 0 | 0 | 0 | 0 |
| 2000 | 86 | 2 | 0 | 0 | 0 | 0 | 0 | 0 |
| 2002 | 75 | 4 | 0 | 0 | 0 | 0 | 0 | 0 |
| 2003 | 29 | 23 | 0 | 0 | 0 | 0 | 0 | 0 |
| 2004 | 85 | 4 | 0 | 0 | 0 | 0 | 0 | 0 |
| **TOTALS** | | 35 | 0 | 0 | 0 | 0 | 0 | 0 |

# Paul Wolfe

**Birth date:** 04/24/77 • **Hometown:** Milford, N.Y.
**Car:** DODGE • **Car owner:** Ray Evernham

## CAREER STATISTICS

| Year | Rank | Starts | Wins | Poles | Top 5 | Top 10 | Races Led | Laps Led |
|------|------|--------|------|-------|-------|--------|-----------|----------|
| 2003 | 89 | 2 | 0 | 0 | 0 | 0 | 0 | 0 |
| 2004 | 77 | 3 | 0 | 0 | 0 | 0 | 0 | 0 |
| **TOTALS** | | 5 | 0 | 0 | 0 | 0 | 0 | 0 |

# Jon Wood

**Birth date:** 10/25/81 • **Hometown:** Stuart, Va.
**Car:** FORD • **Car owner:** ST Motorsports

## CAREER STATISTICS

| Year | Rank | Starts | Wins | Poles | Top 5 | Top 10 | Races Led | Laps Led |
|------|------|--------|------|-------|-------|--------|-----------|----------|
| 2002 | 88 | 1 | 0 | 0 | 0 | 1 | 0 | 0 |
| 2003 | 123 | 1 | 0 | 0 | 0 | 0 | 0 | 0 |
| **TOTALS** | | 2 | 0 | 0 | 0 | 1 | 0 | 0 |

# J.J. Yeley

**Birth date:** 10/05/76 • **Hometown:** Phoenix
**Car:** CHEVROLET • **Car owner:** Joe Gibbs

## CAREER STATISTICS

| Year | Rank | Starts | Wins | Poles | Top 5 | Top 10 | Races Led | Laps Led |
|------|------|--------|------|-------|-------|--------|-----------|----------|
| 2004 | 30 | 17 | 0 | 0 | 0 | 4 | 2 | 42 |
| **TOTALS** | | 17 | 0 | 0 | 0 | 4 | 2 | 42 |

# 2004 race results

| No. | Date | Race | Track | Pole winner | Race winner |
|-----|------|------|-------|-------------|-------------|
| 1 | February 16 | Hershey's Kisses 300 | Daytona International Speedway | Martin Truex Jr. | Dale Earnhardt Jr. |
| 2 | February 21 | Goody's Headache Powder 200 | North Carolina Speedway | Johnny Benson | Jamie McMurray |
| 3 | March 6 | Sam's Town 300 | Las Vegas Motor Speedway | Mike Bliss | Kevin Harvick |
| 4 | March 20 | Diamond Hill Plywood Co. 200 | Darlington Raceway | Kyle Busch | Greg Biffle |
| 5 | March 27 | Sharpie Pofessional 250 | Bristol Motor Speedway | Greg Biffle | Martin Truex Jr. |
| 6 | April 3 | O'Reilly 300 | Texas Motor Speedway | Kyle Busch | Matt Kenseth |
| 7 | April 10 | Pepsi 300 | Nashville Superspeedway | Martin Truex Jr. | Michael Waltrip |
| 8 | April 24 | Aaron's 312 | Talladega Superspeedway | Clint Bowyer | Martin Truex Jr. |
| 9 | May 1 | Starter Bros. 300/Gatorade | California Speedway | Jason Leffler | Greg Biffle |
| 10 | May 8 | Charter 250 | Gateway International Raceway | Martin Truex Jr. | Martin Truex Jr. |
| 11 | May 14 | Funai 250 | Richmond International Raceway | Kyle Busch | Kyle Busch |
| 12 | May 23 | Goulds Pumps ITT Indus. 200 | Nazareth Speedway | Kyle Busch | Martin Truex Jr. |
| 13 | May 29 | CARQUEST Auto Parts 300 | Lowe's Motor Speedway | Greg Biffle | Kyle Busch |
| 14 | June 7 | MBNA America 200 | Dover International Speedway | David Green | Greg Biffle |
| 15 | June 12 | Federated Auto Parts 300 | Nashville Superspeedway | Martin Truex Jr. | Kyle Busch |
| 16 | June 19 | Meijer 300 presented by Oreo | Kentucky Speedway | Martin Truex Jr. | Jason Leffler |
| 17 | June 26 | Alan Kulwicki 250 presented by Forest Co. Potawatomi Racing | The Milwaukee Mile | David Stremme | Ron Hornaday |
| 18 | July 2 | Winn-Dixie 250 by PepsiCo | Daytona International Speedway | Mike Bliss | Mike Wallace |
| 19 | July 10 | Tropicana Twister 300 | Chicagoland Speedway | Bobby Hamilton Jr. | Justin Labonte |
| 20 | July 24 | Siemens 200 | N. Hampshire International Speedway | Jamie McMurray | Matt Kenseth |
| 21 | July 31 | Goulds Pumps/ITT Indus. Salute to Troops 250 by Dodge | Pikes Peak International Raceway | Martin Truex Jr. | Greg Biffle |
| 22 | August 7 | Kroger 200 by Tom Raper RVs | Indianapolis Raceway Park | Johnny Sauter | Kyle Busch |
| 23 | August 21 | Cabela's 250 | Michigan International Speedway | Martin Truex Jr. | Kyle Busch |
| 24 | August 27 | Food City 250 | Bristol Motor Speedway | Dale Earnhardt Jr. | Dale Earnhardt Jr. |
| 25 | September 4 | Target House 300 | California Speedway | Casey Mears | Greg Biffle |
| 26 | September 10 | Emerson Radio 250 | Richmond International Raceway | Kasey Kahne | Robby Gordon |
| 27 | September 25 | Stacker 200 by YJ Stinger | Dover International Speedway | Kasey Kahne | Martin Truex Jr. |
| 28 | October 9 | Mr. Goodcents 300 | Kansas Speedway | Paul Menard | Joe Nemechek |
| 29 | October 15 | SpongeBob SquarePants 300 | Lowe's Motor Speedway | Casey Mears | Mike Bliss |
| 30 | October 23 | Sam's Town 250 benefitting St. Jude | Memphis Motorsports Park | Martin Truex Jr. | Martin Truex Jr. |
| 31 | October 30 | Aaron's 312 | Atlanta Motor Speedway | Mike Bliss | Matt Kenseth |
| 32 | November 6 | Bashas' Supermarkets 200 | Phoenix International Raceway | Kyle Busch | Jamie McMurray |
| 33 | November 13 | Bi-Lo 200 | Darlington Raceway | Martin Truex Jr. | Jamie McMurray |
| 34 | November 20 | Ford 300 | Homestead-Miami Speedway | Casey Mears | Kevin Harvick |

Martin Truex Jr. (center) celebrates his 2004 NASCAR Busch Series championship with car owners Teresa Earnhardt (left) and Dale Earnhardt Jr. (right).

# 2004 points standings

| Pos. | Driver | Points | Behind | Starts | Wins | Top 5 | Top 10 | Money won |
|------|--------|--------|--------|--------|------|-------|--------|-----------|
| 1. | Martin Truex Jr. | 5,173 | Leader | 34 | 6 | 17 | 26 | $2,537,171 |
| 2. | Kyle Busch* | 4,943 | -230 | 34 | 5 | 16 | 22 | $2,027,050 |
| 3. | Greg Biffle | 4,568 | -605 | 34 | 5 | 15 | 21 | $1,568,712 |
| 4. | Ron Hornaday | 4,258 | -915 | 34 | 1 | 7 | 16 | $1,539,519 |
| 5. | Mike Bliss | 4,115 | -1,058 | 34 | 1 | 6 | 14 | $1,298,784 |
| 6. | Jason Keller | 4,088 | -1,085 | 34 | 0 | 6 | 12 | $1,345,009 |
| 7. | David Green | 4,082 | -1,091 | 34 | 0 | 6 | 16 | $1,318,024 |
| 8. | Ashton Lewis | 3,892 | -1,281 | 34 | 0 | 3 | 8 | $1,013,987 |
| 9. | Kenny Wallace | 3,851 | -1,322 | 34 | 0 | 0 | 10 | $952,076 |
| 10. | David Stremme | 3,738 | -1,435 | 34 | 0 | 5 | 14 | $1,017,952 |
| 11. | Kasey Kahne | 3,713 | -1,460 | 30 | 0 | 9 | 14 | $910,661 |
| 12. | Jason Leffler | 3,661 | -1,512 | 27 | 1 | 8 | 17 | $1,168,779 |
| 13. | Michael Waltrip | 3,649 | -1,524 | 31 | 1 | 3 | 9 | $752,429 |
| 14. | Stacy Compton | 3,614 | -1,559 | 34 | 0 | 2 | 5 | $958,176 |
| 15. | Robert Pressley | 3,604 | -1,569 | 34 | 0 | 1 | 2 | $873,445 |
| 16. | Tim Fedewa | 3,480 | -1,693 | 34 | 0 | 1 | 5 | $871,147 |
| 17. | Mike Wallace | 3,461 | -1,712 | 34 | 1 | 1 | 4 | $960,326 |
| 18. | Johnny Sauter | 3,411 | -1,762 | 34 | 0 | 4 | 8 | $820,751 |
| 19. | Casey Atwood | 3,130 | -2,043 | 29 | 0 | 1 | 7 | $763,441 |
| 20. | Kevin Harvick | 3,129 | -2,044 | 22 | 2 | 10 | 15 | $812,232 |
| 21. | Robby Gordon | 3,105 | -2,068 | 25 | 1 | 6 | 10 | $542,530 |
| 22. | Bobby Hamilton Jr. | 2,896 | -2,277 | 23 | 0 | 7 | 12 | $809,534 |
| 23. | Paul Menard* | 2,742 | -2,431 | 27 | 0 | 0 | 0 | $535,900 |
| 24. | Hermie Sadler | 2,414 | -2,759 | 30 | 0 | 0 | 0 | $586,274 |
| 25. | Matt Kenseth | 2,253 | -2,920 | 16 | 3 | 8 | 11 | $497,765 |
| 26. | Gus Wasson | 2,239 | -2,934 | 31 | 0 | 0 | 0 | $723,225 |
| 27. | Derrike Cope | 2,050 | -3,123 | 30 | 0 | 0 | 0 | $589,731 |
| 28. | Steve Grissom | 2,011 | -3,162 | 26 | 0 | 0 | 0 | $482,604 |
| 29. | Clint Bowyer* | 1,933 | -3,240 | 17 | 0 | 4 | 7 | $496,079 |
| 30. | J.J. Yeley* | 1,859 | -3,314 | 17 | 0 | 0 | 4 | $355,145 |
| 31. | Joe Nemechek | 1,777 | -3,396 | 18 | 1 | 1 | 6 | $389,124 |
| 32. | Jamie McMurray | 1,765 | -3,408 | 14 | 3 | 6 | 8 | $386,166 |
| 33. | Tony Raines | 1,553 | -3,620 | 18 | 0 | 0 | 2 | $363,651 |
| 34. | Casey Mears | 1,511 | -3,662 | 13 | 0 | 2 | 6 | $305,835 |
| 35. | Justin Labonte | 1,415 | -3,758 | 17 | 1 | 1 | 1 | $345,787 |
| 36. | Stanton Barrett | 1,330 | -3,843 | 19 | 0 | 0 | 0 | $301,460 |
| 37. | Jeff Fuller | 1,221 | -3,952 | 30 | 0 | 0 | 0 | $596,496 |
| 38. | Mike McLaughlin | 1,140 | -4,033 | 11 | 0 | 1 | 1 | $316,082 |
| 39. | Johnny Benson | 1,136 | -4,037 | 11 | 0 | 1 | 4 | $334,841 |
| 40. | Mark Green | 1,097 | -4,076 | 18 | 0 | 0 | 0 | $275,921 |
| 41. | Travis Geisler* | 1,002 | -4,171 | 12 | 0 | 0 | 0 | $213,965 |
| 42. | Kevin Lepage | 956 | -4,217 | 11 | 0 | 0 | 0 | $193,270 |
| 43. | Jimmy Kitchens | 901 | -4,272 | 16 | 0 | 0 | 0 | $273,305 |
| 44. | Shane Hmiel | 868 | -4,305 | 10 | 0 | 1 | 1 | $191,456 |
| 45. | Regan Smith | 802 | -4,371 | 10 | 0 | 0 | 0 | $158,819 |
| 46. | Aaron Fike | 802 | -4,371 | 13 | 0 | 0 | 0 | $179,736 |
| 47. | Brad Teague | 780 | -4,393 | 15 | 0 | 0 | 0 | $207,731 |
| 48. | Stan Boyd* | 699 | -4,474 | 12 | 0 | 0 | 0 | $191,956 |
| 49. | Dale Earnhardt Jr. | 677 | -4,496 | 4 | 2 | 3 | 3 | $188,925 |
| 50. | Randy LaJoie | 673 | -4,500 | 7 | 0 | 0 | 0 | $117,790 |
| 51. | Tina Gordon | 666 | -4,507 | 12 | 0 | 0 | 0 | $214,725 |
| 52. | Reed Sorenson | 637 | -4,536 | 5 | 0 | 1 | 3 | $107,359 |
| 53. | Todd Bodine | 628 | -4,545 | 6 | 0 | 1 | 1 | $109,875 |
| 54. | Shane Hall | 618 | -4,555 | 9 | 0 | 0 | 0 | $139,685 |
| 55. | Andy Ponstein | 618 | -4,555 | 9 | 0 | 0 | 0 | $137,650 |
| 56. | Mark Martin | 617 | -4,556 | 5 | 0 | 1 | 4 | $101,055 |
| 57. | Jeff Burton | 598 | -4,575 | 4 | 0 | 2 | 3 | $115,220 |
| 58. | Tony Stewart | 563 | -4,610 | 4 | 0 | 2 | 2 | $109,255 |
| 59. | Billy Parker* | 514 | -4,659 | 8 | 0 | 0 | 0 | $139,593 |
| 60. | Dave Blaney | 497 | -4,676 | 6 | 0 | 0 | 0 | $104,031 |
| 61. | Wally Dallenbach | 484 | -4,689 | 6 | 0 | 0 | 1 | $135,035 |
| 62. | Blake Feese | 469 | -4,704 | 7 | 0 | 0 | 0 | $160,043 |
| 63. | Jay Sauter | 453 | -4,720 | 6 | 0 | 0 | 0 | $90,170 |
| 64. | Randy MacDonald | 426 | -4,747 | 6 | 0 | 0 | 0 | $99,340 |
| 65. | Jason Schuler | 421 | -4,752 | 7 | 0 | 0 | 0 | $177,630 |
| 66. | Shelby Howard | 413 | -4,760 | 5 | 0 | 0 | 0 | $66,880 |
| 67. | Mike Harmon | 406 | -4,767 | 7 | 0 | 0 | 0 | $114,760 |
| 68. | Bobby Labonte | 402 | -4,771 | 3 | 0 | 0 | 1 | $69,550 |
| 69. | Justin Ashburn | 394 | -4,779 | 8 | 0 | 0 | 0 | $151,970 |
| 70. | David Reutimann | 379 | -4,794 | 4 | 0 | 0 | 0 | $71,735 |
| 71. | Kenny Hendrick | 348 | -4,825 | 7 | 0 | 0 | 0 | $113,550 |
| 72. | Kim Crosby | 314 | -4,859 | 5 | 0 | 0 | 0 | $79,560 |

| Pos. | Driver | Points | Behind | Starts | Wins | Top 5 | Top 10 | Money won |
|------|--------|--------|--------|--------|------|-------|--------|-----------|
| 73. | Mark McFarland | 306 | -4,867 | 3 | 0 | 0 | 0 | $40,885 |
| 74. | Tracy Hines | 303 | -4,870 | 3 | 0 | 0 | 0 | $51,960 |
| 75. | Donnie Neuenberger* | 300 | -4,873 | 6 | 0 | 0 | 0 | $118,132 |
| 76. | Rusty Wallace | 296 | -4,877 | 2 | 0 | 0 | 2 | $38,600 |
| 77. | Paul Wolfe | 291 | -4,882 | 3 | 0 | 0 | 0 | $72,860 |
| 78. | Damon Lusk | 284 | -4,889 | 3 | 0 | 0 | 0 | $68,555 |
| 79. | Tim Sauter | 283 | -4,890 | 4 | 0 | 0 | 0 | $52,760 |
| 80. | Tyler Walker | 282 | -4,891 | 3 | 0 | 0 | 0 | $49,310 |
| 81. | John Graham | 274 | -4,899 | 4 | 0 | 0 | 0 | $65,155 |
| 82. | Eric McClure | 268 | -4,905 | 4 | 0 | 0 | 0 | $68,090 |
| 83. | Todd Szegedy | 264 | -4,909 | 3 | 0 | 0 | 0 | $52,210 |
| 84. | Josh Richeson | 244 | -4,929 | 4 | 0 | 0 | 0 | $85,300 |
| 85. | Jason White | 241 | -4,932 | 4 | 0 | 0 | 0 | $59,540 |
| 86. | David Starr | 240 | -4,933 | 3 | 0 | 0 | 0 | $50,780 |
| 87. | David Keith | 228 | -4,945 | 3 | 0 | 0 | 0 | $48,181 |
| 88. | Larry Hollenbeck | 228 | -4,945 | 3 | 0 | 0 | 0 | $71,180 |
| 89. | John Hayden | 228 | -4,945 | 3 | 0 | 0 | 0 | $46,330 |
| 90. | Clint Vahsholtz | 225 | -4,948 | 3 | 0 | 0 | 0 | $48,165 |
| 91. | Rick Markle* | 222 | -4,951 | 3 | 0 | 0 | 0 | $72,050 |
| 92. | Jimmy Spencer | 222 | -4,951 | 3 | 0 | 0 | 0 | $54,035 |
| 93. | Kertus Davis | 219 | -4,954 | 3 | 0 | 0 | 0 | $36,495 |
| 94. | C.W. Smith | 210 | -4,963 | 3 | 0 | 0 | 0 | $71,355 |
| 95. | Jerry Hill | 182 | -4,991 | 2 | 0 | 0 | 0 | $43,445 |
| 96. | Brent Sherman | 177 | -4,996 | 3 | 0 | 0 | 0 | $49,295 |
| 97. | Boston Reid | 174 | -4,999 | 3 | 0 | 0 | 0 | $42,765 |
| 98. | Jimmie Johnson | 170 | -5,003 | 1 | 0 | 1 | 1 | $35,800 |
| 99. | Larry Gunselman | 167 | -5,006 | 2 | 0 | 0 | 0 | $54,745 |
| 100. | Brian Sockwell | 161 | -5,012 | 3 | 0 | 0 | 0 | $37,680 |
| 101. | Shane Wallace | 152 | -5,021 | 2 | 0 | 0 | 0 | $25,825 |
| 102. | Sterling Marlin | 152 | -5,021 | 2 | 0 | 0 | 0 | $32,530 |
| 103. | Denny Hamlin | 142 | -5,031 | 1 | 0 | 0 | 1 | $15,540 |
| 104. | Mike Garvey | 137 | -5,036 | 2 | 0 | 0 | 0 | $24,610 |
| 105. | Eric Jones | 134 | -5,039 | 2 | 0 | 0 | 0 | $35,070 |
| 106. | Ricky Craven | 130 | -5,043 | 1 | 0 | 0 | 0 | $21,975 |
| 107. | Buckshot Jones | 125 | -5,048 | 2 | 0 | 0 | 0 | $33,570 |
| 108. | Bruce Bechtel | 125 | -5,048 | 2 | 0 | 0 | 0 | $36,890 |
| 109. | Carl Long | 119 | -5,054 | 2 | 0 | 0 | 0 | $25,845 |
| 110. | Eddie Beahr | 119 | -5,054 | 2 | 0 | 0 | 0 | $23,025 |
| 111. | Bobby Hamilton | 115 | -5,058 | 1 | 0 | 0 | 0 | $13,480 |
| 112. | Brandon Miller | 115 | -5,058 | 1 | 0 | 0 | 0 | $19,720 |
| 113. | Jeff Purvis | 112 | -5,061 | 1 | 0 | 0 | 0 | $13,570 |
| 114. | Bill Hoff | 110 | -5,063 | 2 | 0 | 0 | 0 | $22,780 |
| 115. | Jeremy Mayfield | 109 | -5,064 | 1 | 0 | 0 | 0 | $22,000 |
| 116. | Carl Edwards | 106 | -5,067 | 1 | 0 | 0 | 0 | $18,710 |
| 117. | Morgan Shepherd | 104 | -5,069 | 2 | 0 | 0 | 0 | $28,435 |
| 118. | Lowell Bennett | 104 | -5,069 | 2 | 0 | 0 | 0 | $23,350 |
| 119. | Bill Elliott | 103 | -5,070 | 1 | 0 | 0 | 0 | $18,260 |
| 120. | Kerry Earnhardt | 94 | -5,079 | 1 | 0 | 0 | 0 | $13,695 |
| 121. | Shane Sieg | 89 | -5,084 | 2 | 0 | 0 | 0 | $30,770 |
| 122. | Butch Jarvis | 89 | -5,084 | 2 | 0 | 0 | 0 | $22,415 |
| 123. | Travis Kittleson | 88 | -5,085 | 1 | 0 | 0 | 0 | $15,985 |
| 124. | Jamie Mosley | 85 | -5,088 | 1 | 0 | 0 | 0 | $18,700 |
| 125. | Bobby Dotter | 85 | -5,088 | 1 | 0 | 0 | 0 | $13,220 |
| 126. | Mike Potter | 80 | -5,093 | 2 | 0 | 0 | 0 | $22,262 |
| 127. | Caleb Holman | 79 | -5,094 | 1 | 0 | 0 | 0 | $14,125 |
| 128. | Dion Ciccarelli | 76 | -5,097 | 1 | 0 | 0 | 0 | $10,860 |
| 129. | John Borneman III | 73 | -5,100 | 1 | 0 | 0 | 0 | $14,025 |
| 130. | Garrett Liberty | 70 | -5,103 | 1 | 0 | 0 | 0 | $17,585 |
| 131. | David Ragan | 70 | -5,103 | 1 | 0 | 0 | 0 | $16,855 |
| 132. | Matthew Kobyluck | 61 | -5,112 | 1 | 0 | 0 | 0 | $13,285 |
| 133. | Ted Musgrave | 61 | -5,112 | 1 | 0 | 0 | 0 | $12,830 |
| 134. | Lance Hooper | 58 | -5,115 | 1 | 0 | 0 | 0 | $19,660 |
| 135. | Jeff Spraker | 55 | -5,118 | 1 | 0 | 0 | 0 | $19,640 |
| 136. | Dana White | 55 | -5,118 | 1 | 0 | 0 | 0 | $12,265 |
| 137. | Chad Beahr | 52 | -5,121 | 1 | 0 | 0 | 0 | $11,920 |
| 138. | Roland Isaacs | 52 | -5,121 | 1 | 0 | 0 | 0 | $15,765 |
| 139. | Bill Eversole | 52 | -5,121 | 1 | 0 | 0 | 0 | $16,365 |
| 140. | Scott Lynch | 51 | -5,122 | 1 | 0 | 0 | 0 | $12,315 |
| 141. | Norm Benning | 49 | -5,124 | 1 | 0 | 0 | 0 | $10,620 |
| 142. | Keith Murt | 49 | -5,124 | 1 | 0 | 0 | 0 | $17,545 |
| 143. | Jamey Caudill | 49 | -5,124 | 1 | 0 | 0 | 0 | $15,350 |
| 144. | Greg Sacks | 43 | -5,130 | 1 | 0 | 0 | 0 | $12,745 |
| 145. | David Eshleman | 43 | -5,130 | 1 | 0 | 0 | 0 | $13,700 |
| 146. | Travis Powell | 40 | -5,133 | 1 | 0 | 0 | 0 | $10,560 |
| 147. | Jason Jefferson | 40 | -5,133 | 1 | 0 | 0 | 0 | $19,285 |
| 148. | Brian Tyler | 37 | -5,136 | 1 | 0 | 0 | 0 | $10,640 |
| 149. | Jennifer Cobb | 34 | -5,139 | 1 | 0 | 0 | 0 | $16,224 |
| 150. | Jason Rudd | 12 | -5,161 | 1 | 0 | 0 | 0 | $10,540 |
| 151. | Chad Blount | 0 | -5,173 | 1 | 0 | 0 | 0 | $13,295 |
| 152. | Randy Briggs | 0 | -5,173 | 1 | 0 | 0 | 0 | $16,015 |

**\*Rookie**

# 2004 miles leaders

| Rank | Driver | Miles Led | Times Led | Races Led | Miles Run | Possible Miles | Unfinished Miles | Laps Led | Wins | Starts |
|---|---|---|---|---|---|---|---|---|---|---|
| 1. | Kyle Busch | 1,387.49 | 42 | 21 | 8,123.17 | 8,250.09 | 126.92 | 1,108 | 5 | 34 |
| 2. | Martin Truex | 1,005.84 | 40 | 21 | 8,111.59 | 8,250.09 | 138.50 | 954 | 6 | 34 |
| 3. | Greg Biffle | 634.84 | 40 | 18 | 7,565.43 | 8,250.09 | 684.66 | 553 | 5 | 34 |
| 4. | Matt Kenseth | 632.30 | 20 | 9 | 3,352.17 | 3,874.17 | 522.00 | 443 | 3 | 15 |
| 5. | Bobby Hamilton Jr. | 542.73 | 15 | 9 | 5,401.89 | 5,747.17 | 345.28 | 425 | 0 | 23 |
| 6. | Kevin Harvick | 437.19 | 14 | 10 | 4,982.49 | 5,254.57 | 272.08 | 311 | 2 | 22 |
| 7. | Robby Gordon | 284.61 | 18 | 9 | 5,974.57 | 6,256.94 | 282.37 | 152 | 1 | 25 |
| 8. | Kasey Kahne | 269.95 | 15 | 7 | 6,908.01 | 7,421.64 | 513.63 | 257 | 0 | 30 |
| 9. | Dale Earnhardt Jr. | 262.27 | 15 | 4 | 997.67 | 997.67 | 0.00 | 203 | 2 | 4 |
| 10. | Ron Hornaday | 194.93 | 12 | 10 | 8,009.55 | 8,113.64 | 104.09 | 153 | 1 | 33 |
| 11. | Tony Stewart | 194.00 | 5 | 3 | 1,217.32 | 1,226.32 | 9.00 | 129 | 0 | 4 |
| 12. | Kenny Wallace | 187.54 | 6 | 6 | 7,626.32 | 8,250.09 | 623.77 | 157 | 0 | 34 |
| 13. | Casey Mears | 179.22 | 12 | 5 | 2,669.08 | 3,061.67 | 392.59 | 122 | 0 | 13 |
| 14. | Jamie McMurray | 172.99 | 11 | 6 | 2,937.73 | 3,383.02 | 445.29 | 170 | 3 | 14 |
| 15. | Mike Bliss | 171.66 | 9 | 7 | 7,897.05 | 8,250.09 | 353.04 | 109 | 1 | 34 |
| 16. | Johnny Sauter | 163.09 | 11 | 7 | 7,167.25 | 8,250.09 | 1,082.84 | 193 | 0 | 34 |
| 17. | Jason Leffler | 155.71 | 9 | 6 | 6,375.56 | 6,476.02 | 100.46 | 115 | 1 | 27 |
| 18. | Clint Bowyer | 144.63 | 5 | 2 | 3,667.97 | 4,367.34 | 699.37 | 108 | 0 | 17 |
| 19. | Joe Nemechek | 138.60 | 8 | 8 | 3,498.86 | 4,430.17 | 931.31 | 91 | 1 | 17 |
| 20. | Michael Waltrip | 136.75 | 13 | 9 | 7,225.15 | 7,500.09 | 274.94 | 79 | 1 | 31 |
| 21. | Shane Hmiel | 96.54 | 5 | 2 | 1,883.10 | 2,314.02 | 430.92 | 96 | 0 | 10 |
| 22. | Casey Atwood | 79.75 | 4 | 4 | 6,668.25 | 7,082.02 | 413.77 | 97 | 0 | 29 |
| 23. | David Green | 76.72 | 6 | 4 | 7,699.54 | 8,250.09 | 550.55 | 81 | 0 | 34 |
| 24. | David Stremme | 75.00 | 5 | 1 | 7,409.12 | 8,250.09 | 840.97 | 75 | 0 | 34 |
| 25. | Reed Sorenson | 72.38 | 3 | 1 | 1,089.49 | 1,100.27 | 10.78 | 47 | 0 | 5 |
| 26. | Mark Martin | 69.16 | 4 | 2 | 1,162.82 | 1,162.82 | 0.00 | 67 | 0 | 5 |
| 27. | Jason Keller | 60.00 | 2 | 2 | 7,812.61 | 8,250.09 | 437.48 | 60 | 0 | 34 |
| 28. | Aaron Fike | 55.74 | 3 | 3 | 8,057.78 | 8,250.09 | 192.31 | 43 | 0 | 34 |
| 28. | Ashton Lewis | 55.74 | 3 | 3 | 8,057.78 | 8,250.09 | 192.31 | 43 | 0 | 34 |
| 30. | Mike Wallace | 50.32 | 8 | 8 | 7,381.18 | 8,250.09 | 868.91 | 33 | 1 | 34 |
| 31. | J.J. Yeley | 46.56 | 3 | 2 | 3,958.25 | 4,369.62 | 411.37 | 42 | 0 | 17 |
| 32. | Jimmie Johnson | 45.00 | 2 | 1 | 300.00 | 300.00 | 0.00 | 30 | 0 | 1 |
| 33. | Jeff Burton | 39.52 | 4 | 2 | 1,100.80 | 1,100.80 | 0.00 | 28 | 0 | 4 |
| 34. | Dave Blaney | 31.50 | 1 | 1 | 1,367.63 | 1,560.75 | 193.12 | 42 | 0 | 6 |
| 35 | Tim Fedewa | 18.16 | 3 | 2 | 7,407.02 | 8,250.09 | 843.07 | 13 | 0 | 34 |
| 36. | Justin Labonte | 18.00 | 2 | 1 | 3,822.45 | 4,396.22 | 573.77 | 12 | 1 | 17 |
| 37. | Bobby Labonte | 17.76 | 1 | 1 | 804.90 | 804.90 | 0.00 | 13 | 0 | 3 |
| 38. | Johnny Benson | 17.46 | 2 | 2 | 2,270.99 | 2,495.55 | 224.56 | 13 | 0 | 10 |
| 39. | David Reutimann | 16.50 | 3 | 1 | 859.14 | 950.27 | 91.13 | 11 | 0 | 4 |
| 40. | Stacy Compton | 15.00 | 2 | 2 | 7,853.80 | 8,247.09 | 393.29 | 14 | 0 | 34 |
| 41. | Robert Pressley | 14.50 | 2 | 2 | 7,989.09 | 8,250.09 | 261.00 | 14 | 0 | 34 |
| 42. | Billy Parker | 10.00 | 1 | 1 | 1,311.75 | 2,150.00 | 838.25 | 5 | 0 | 8 |
| 43. | Derrike Cope | 9.00 | 2 | 2 | 5,735.80 | 7,462.89 | 1,727.09 | 4 | 0 | 30 |
| 44. | Damond Lusk | 5.46 | 1 | 1 | 693.22 | 701.15 | 7.93 | 4 | 0 | 3 |
| 45. | Tony Raines | 4.50 | 1 | 1 | 3,467.82 | 4,509.67 | 1,041.85 | 3 | 0 | 18 |
| 46. | Justin Ashburn | 2.50 | 1 | 1 | 862.23 | 1,662.37 | 800.15 | 1 | 0 | 7 |
| 47. | Hermie Sadler | 1.50 | 1 | 1 | 5,815.45 | 7,333.62 | 1,518.17 | 1 | 0 | 30 |
| 48. | Steve Grissom | 1.50 | 1 | 1 | 4,446.69 | 6,185.74 | 1,489.05 | 1 | 0 | 25 |
| 49. | Scott Lynch | 1.06 | 1 | 1 | 122.73 | 264.50 | 141.77 | 1 | 0 | 1 |

# 8 Martin Truex Jr.

**Car:** CHEVROLET • **Car owner:** Teresa Earnhardt
**Birth date:** 06/05/79 • **Hometown:** Mayetta, N.J.

## NASCAR BUSCH SERIES STATISTICS

**Seasons competed:** 2001-2004
**Career starts:** 49      **Career wins:** 6      **Career poles:** 7
**Championship season recap:** With a fourth place finish at Darlington, Truex sealed the 2004 championship in just his first full season in the NASCAR Busch Series. With only one finish outside the top 10 in August, September and October, Truex held off Kyle Busch. Truex had finished 2003 strong, with second-place finishes in the final two races of that season, building momentum for 2004. In 2005, Truex is scheduled to run several NASCAR NEXTEL Cup Series events for Dale Earnhardt Inc. and run a full NASCAR Busch Series schedule.

## CHAMPIONSHIP LINESCORE

| Starts | Wins | Poles | Top 5 | Top 10 | Races Led | Laps Led |
|---|---|---|---|---|---|---|
| 34 | 6 | 7 | 17 | 26 | 21 | 954 |

# Martin Truex Jr. 2004 race by race

| No. | Race | Start | Finish | Points | Rank | Laps/completed | Money won | Status |
|---|---|---|---|---|---|---|---|---|
| 1. | Hershey's Kisses 300 | 1 | 28 | 84 | 27 | 93/120 | $38,875 | Running |
| 2. | Goody's Headache Powder 200 | 11 | 2 | 180 | 9 | 197/197 | $26,820 | Running |
| 3. | Sam's Town 300 | 4 | 14 | 126 | 8 | 200/200 | $21,770 | Running |
| 4. | Diamond Hill Plywood Co. 200 | 10 | 4 | 160 | 4 | 147/147 | $18,845 | Running |
| 5. | Sharpie Professional 250 | 2 | 1 | 190 | 3 | 250/250 | $53,865 | Running |
| 6. | O'Reilly 300 | 5 | 10 | 134 | 2 | 200/200 | $27,400 | Running |
| 7. | Pepsi 300 | 1 | 23 | 94 | 4 | 219/225 | $18,855 | Running |
| 8. | Aaron's 312 | 3 | 1 | 185 | 3 | 117/117 | $53,135 | Running |
| 9. | Stater Bros. 300 presented by Gatorade | 2 | 13 | 129 | 3 | 150/150 | $30,780 | Running |
| 10. | Charter 250 | 1 | 1 | 190 | 1 | 200/200 | $66,955 | Running |
| 11. | Funai 250 | 17 | 7 | 146 | 2 | 250/250 | $19,680 | Running |
| 12. | Goulds Pumps ITT Industries 200 | 20 | 1 | 185 | 1 | 200/200 | $42,455 | Running |
| 13. | CARQUEST Auto Parts 300 | 7 | 14 | 121 | 2 | 200/200 | $20,260 | Running |
| 14. | MBNA America 200 | 9 | 2 | 180 | 2 | 200/200 | $42,610 | Running |
| 15. | Federated Auto Parts 300 | 1 | 2 | 175 | 1 | 225/225 | $42,000 | Running |
| 16. | Meijer 300 presented by Oreo | 1 | 6 | 155 | 1 | 200/200 | $32,650 | Running |
| 17. | Alan Kulwicki 250 | 17 | 9 | 138 | 1 | 250/250 | $20,585 | Running |
| 18. | Winn-Dixie 250 presented by PepsiCo | 6 | 3 | 170 | 1 | 100/100 | $53,340 | Running |
| 19. | Tropicana Twister 300 | 16 | 14 | 121 | 1 | 200/200 | $25,565 | Running |
| 20. | Siemens 200 | 13 | 11 | 130 | 1 | 200/200 | $20,010 | Running |
| 21. | Goulds Pumps/ITT Inds. Salute to Troops 250 | 1 | 5 | 165 | 1 | 250/250 | $40,815 | Running |
| 22. | Kroger 200 presented by Tom Raper RVs | 2 | 4 | 160 | 1 | 200/200 | $23,375 | Running |
| 23. | Cabela's 250 | 1 | 3 | 170 | 1 | 125/125 | $30,280 | Running |
| 24. | Food City 250 | 12 | 7 | 146 | 1 | 256/256 | $27,715 | Running |
| 25. | Target House 300 | 2 | 6 | 155 | 1 | 150/150 | $38,720 | Running |
| 26. | Emerson Radio 250 | 7 | 3 | 165 | 1 | 250/250 | $27,755 | Running |
| 27. | Stacker 2 Hundred presented by YJ Stinger | 2 | 1 | 185 | 1 | 200/200 | $45,630 | Running |
| 28. | Mr. Goodcents 300 | 5 | 30 | 73 | 1 | 162/204 | $22,075 | Running |
| 29. | Lowe's/SpongeBob SquarePants Movie 300 | 9 | 6 | 155 | 1 | 200/200 | $29,700 | Running |
| 30. | Sam's Town 'He Dared To Rock' 250 | 1 | 1 | 190 | 1 | 255/255 | $62,505 | Running |
| 31. | Aaron's 312 | 2 | 9 | 143 | 1 | 208/208 | $22,200 | Running |
| 32. | Bashas' Supermarkets 200 | 9 | 3 | 165 | 1 | 205/205 | $37,205 | Running |
| 33. | BI-LO 200 | 1 | 4 | 165 | 1 | 147/147 | $24,120 | Running |
| 34. | Ford 300 | 2 | 9 | 143 | 1 | 203/203 | $32,050 | Running |

# Series champions

The NASCAR Busch Series, Grand National Division started in 1982, but the circuit's roots date back more than five decades. Originally formed as the NASCAR Sportsman Division in 1950, the series competed until 1968 under that name before becoming the NASCAR Late Model Sportsman Division. Fourteen years later, Anheuser-Busch, Inc. joined with NASCAR to create the NASCAR Busch Series.

## All-time title winners

| | | | | |
|---|---|---|---|---|
| **1950:** Mike Klapak * | **1961:** Dick Nephew | **1972:** Jack Ingram | **1983:** Sam Ard | **1994:** David Green |
| **1951:** Mike Klapak | **1962:** Rene Charland | **1973:** Jack Ingram | **1984:** Sam Ard ∞ | **1995:** Johnny Benson § |
| **1952:** Mike Klapak | **1963:** Rene Charland | **1974:** Jack Ingram | **1985:** Jack Ingram | **1996:** Randy LaJoie |
| **1953:** Johnny Roberts | **1964:** Rene Charland | **1975:** L.D. Ottinger | **1986:** Larry Pearson | **1997:** Randy LaJoie |
| **1954:** Danny Graves | **1965:** Rene Charland | **1976:** L.D. Ottinger | **1987:** Larry Pearson | **1998:** Dale Earnhardt Jr. |
| **1955:** Billy Myers | **1966:** Don MacTavish | **1977:** Butch Lindley | **1988:** Tommy Ellis | **1999:** Dale Earnhardt Jr. |
| **1956:** Ralph Earnhardt | **1967:** Pete Hamilton | **1978:** Butch Lindley | **1989:** Rob Moroso | **2000:** Jeff Green |
| **1957:** Ned Jarrett | **1968:** Joe Thurman † | **1979:** Gene Glover | **1990:** Chuck Bown | **2001:** Kevin Harvick |
| **1958:** Ned Jarrett | **1969:** Red Farmer | **1980:** Morgan Shepherd | **1991:** Bobby Labonte | **2002:** Greg Biffle |
| **1959:** Rick Henderson | **1970:** Red Farmer | **1981:** Tommy Ellis | **1992:** Joe Nemechek | **2003:** Brian Vickers |
| **1960:** Bill Wimble | **1971:** Red Farmer | **1982:** Jack Ingram ‡ | **1993:** Steve Grissom | **2004:** Martin Truex Jr. |

**KEY**
* NASCAR Sportsman Division was formed in 1950
† Series changed name to NASCAR Late Model Sportsman Division in 1968
‡ Series changed name to NASCAR Budweiser Late Model Sportsman Series in 1982
∞ Series changed name to NASCAR Busch Grand National Series in 1984
§ Series changed name to NASCAR Busch Series, Grand National Division in 1995

# Season by season champions

| Year | Car No. | Driver | Car Owner | Car Make | Wins | Poles | Winnings | Runner-up | Margin of Victory |
|---|---|---|---|---|---|---|---|---|---|
| 1982 | 11 | Jack Ingram | Aline Ingram | Olds/Pont. | 7 | 1 | $122,100 | Sam Ard | 49 |
| 1983 | 00 | Sam Ard | Howard Thomas | Oldsmobile | 10 | 10 | $192,362 | Jack Ingram | 87 |
| 1984 | 00 | Sam Ard | Howard Thomas | Oldsmobile | 8 | 7 | $217,531 | Jack Ingram | 426 |
| 1985 | 11 | Jack Ingram | Aline Ingram | Pontiac | 5 | 2 | $164,710 | Jimmy Hensley | 29 |
| 1986 | 21 | Larry Pearson | David Pearson | Pontiac | 1 | 1 | $184,344 | Brett Bodine | 20 |
| 1987 | 21 | Larry Pearson | David Pearson | Chevrolet | 6 | 3 | $256,372 | Jimmy Hensley | 382 |
| 1988 | 99 | Tommy Ellis | John Jackson | Buick | 3 | 5 | $200,003 | Rob Moroso | 239 |
| 1989 | 25 | Rob Moroso | Dick Moroso | Oldsmobile | 4 | 6 | $346,739 | Tommy Houston | 55 |
| 1990 | 63 | Chuck Bown | Hubert Hensley | Pontiac | 6 | 4 | $323,399 | Jimmy Hensley | 200 |
| 1991 | 44 | Bobby Labonte | Bobby Labonte | Oldsmobile | 2 | 2 | $246,368 | Kenny Wallace | 74 |
| 1992 | 87 | Joe Nemechek | Joe Nemechek | Chevrolet | 2 | 1 | $285,008 | Bobby Labonte | 3 |
| 1993 | 31 | Steve Grissom | Wayne Grissom | Chevrolet | 2 | 0 | $336,432 | Ricky Craven | 253 |
| 1994 | 44 | David Green | Bobby Labonte | Chevrolet | 1 | 9 | $391,670 | Ricky Craven | 46 |
| 1995 | 74 | Johnny Benson | William Baumgardner | Chevrolet | 2 | 0 | $469,129 | Chad Little | 404 |
| 1996 | 74 | Randy LaJoie | William Baumgardner | Chevrolet | 5 | 2 | $532,823 | David Green | 29 |
| 1997 | 74 | Randy LaJoie | William Baumgardner | Chevrolet | 5 | 2 | $1,105,201 | Todd Bodine | 266 |
| 1998 | 3 | Dale Earnhardt Jr. | Dale Earnhardt | Chevrolet | 5 | 3 | $1,332,701 | Matt Kenseth | 48 |
| 1999 | 3 | Dale Earnhardt Jr. | Dale Earnhardt | Chevrolet | 6 | 3 | $1,680,549 | Jeff Green | 280 |
| 2000 | 10 | Jeff Green | Greg Pollex | Chevrolet | 6 | 7 | $1,929,937 | Jason Keller | 616 |
| 2001 | 2 | Kevin Harvick | Richard Childress | Chevrolet | 5 | 5 | $1,833,570 | Jeff Green | 124 |
| 2002 | 60 | Greg Biffle | Jack Roush | Ford | 4 | 5 | $2,337,255 | Jason Keller | 264 |
| 2003 | 5 | Brian Vickers | Rick Hendrick | Chevrolet | 3 | 1 | $1,987,255 | David Green | 14 |
| 2004 | 8 | Martin Truex Jr. | Teresa Earnhardt | Chevrolet | 6 | 7 | $2,537,171 | Kyle Busch | 230 |

## 5 Brian Vickers

**Car:** CHEVROLET • **Car owner:** Ricky Hendrick
**Birth date:** 10/24/83 • **Hometown:** Thomasville, N.C.

### NASCAR BUSCH SERIES STATISTICS

**Seasons Competed:** 2001-2003
**Career starts:** 59     **Career wins:** 3     **Career poles:** 1
**Championship season recap:** Vickers became the youngest winner ever of a NASCAR series title, capturing the NASCAR Busch Series crown at 20 years old. In a close battle for the points championship, Vickers finished 11th in the last race of the season at Homestead-Miami Speedway after gaining back a lost lap. That kept Vickers just 14 points ahead of 1995 series champion David Green, who finished ninth at Homestead. It was the second-closest title race in series history.

#### CHAMPIONSHIP LINESCORE

| Starts | Wins | Poles | Top 5 | Top 10 | Races Led | Laps Led |
|---|---|---|---|---|---|---|
| 34 | 3 | 1 | 13 | 21 | 14 | 623 |

## 60 Greg Biffle

**Car:** FORD • **Car owner:** Jack Roush
**Birth date:** 12/23/69 • **Hometown:** Vancouver, Wash.

### NASCAR BUSCH SERIES STATISTICS

**Seasons competed:** 5 (1996, 2001-2004)
**Career starts:** 117     **Career wins:** 16     **Career poles:** 11
**Championship season recap:** Biffle became the first driver to win the crown in the NASCAR Busch Series and the NASCAR Craftsman Truck Series (2000), both with Roush Racing. He was a model of consistency en route to the title, posting a series-leading 25 top 10 finishes in 34 starts, including four wins. He also led the series in top five efforts (20) and laps led (1,058). He was among the top eight in the championship for all but one race during the 34-race season—the season opener at Daytona—and took the lead for good following a runnerup finish at the July event at Daytona. He held the top spot for the remaining 16 races of the season en route to a 264-point advantage over runner-up Jason Keller.

#### CHAMPIONSHIP LINESCORE

| Starts | Wins | Poles | Top 5 | Top 10 | Races Led | Laps Led |
|---|---|---|---|---|---|---|
| 34 | 4 | 5 | 20 | 25 | 22 | 1,061 |

## 2 Kevin Harvick

**Car:** CHEVROLET • **Car owner:** Richard Childress
**Birth date:** 12/08/75 • **Hometown:** Bakersfield, Calif.

### NASCAR BUSCH SERIES STATISTICS

**Seasons competed:** 5 (1999-2004)
**Career starts:** 117     **Career wins:** 16     **Career poles:** 11
**Championship season recap:** Harvick followed up his rookie-of-the-year campaign with a championship. He was powered by five wins, four poles and 20 top five finishes for a 124-point margin over runnerup and defending series champion Jeff Green. Harvick never fell outside the top three in the championship race and regained the lead after the 15th race and did not relinquish it the remainder of the season. His performance was even more impressive considering that team owner Richard Childress called upon him to replace the late Dale Earnhardt in the NASCAR Cup Series and responded with an Rookie-of-the-Year performance, finishing ninth in the NASCAR Cup points standings.

#### CHAMPIONSHIP LINESCORE

| Starts | Wins | Poles | Top 5 | Top 10 | Races Led | Laps Led |
|---|---|---|---|---|---|---|
| 33 | 5 | 4 | 20 | 24 | 18 | 1,265 |

# 10 Jeff Green

**Car:** CHEVROLET • **Car owner:** Greg Pollex
**Birth date:** 09/06/62 • **Hometown:** Owensboro, Ky.

## NASCAR BUSCH SERIES STATISTICS

**Seasons competed:** 14 (1990-2003)
**Career starts:** 240    **Career wins:** 16    **Career poles:** 23

**Championship season recap:** Green, who finished runner-up in the championship the previous year, would not be denied this season as he constructed the most dominant performance in NASCAR Busch Series history. He led in wins (6), poles (7), top 5s (25) and top 10s (27) en route to the largest points differential ever, 616 over runner-up Jason Keller. Matt Kenseth led the championship for the first seven races; Todd Bodine took over after the eighth, with Green in third. Green finished fifth in the following race at Talladega to claim the championship lead and he held the top spot for the final 23 races.

### CHAMPIONSHIP LINESCORE

| Starts | Wins | Poles | Top 5 | Top 10 | Races Led | Laps Led |
|--------|------|-------|-------|--------|-----------|----------|
| 32 | 6 | 7 | 25 | 27 | 19 | 1,480 |

# 3 Dale Earnhardt Jr.

**Car:** CHEVROLET • **Car Owner:** Dale Earnhardt
**Birth date:** 10/10/74 •
**Hometown:** Kannapolis, N.C.

## NASCAR BUSCH SERIES STATISTICS

**Seasons competed:** 8 (1996-99, 2001-2004)
**Career starts:** 83    **Career wins:** 20    **Career poles:** 9

**1999 championship season recap:** Earnhardt Jr. became the fourth driver—and second in a row—in NASCAR Busch Series history to win consecutive championships. He followed up Randy LaJoie's feat in 1996-97 and joined the company of Sam Ard (1982-83) and Larry Pearson (1986-87) as a two-time champion. Earnhardt enjoyed a strong campaign as he led the series in wins (6), top 5s (18) and top 10s (22) and rolled to a 280-point advantage over runner-up Jeff Green. Earnhardt's fourth win of the season—Gateway—allowed him to overtake Matt Kenseth for the championship lead, one he would not surrender.

### 1999 CHAMPIONSHIP LINESCORE

| Starts | Wins | Poles | Top 5 | Top 10 | Races Led | Laps Led |
|--------|------|-------|-------|--------|-----------|----------|
| 32 | 6 | 3 | 18 | 22 | 23 | 725 |

**1998 Championship season recap:** Earnhardt Jr., after just nine career starts in the previous two seasons, stormed into title contention. Earnhardt led the series in wins (7) and poles (3), and ranked second in top-five (16) and top-10 (22) finishes. Earnhardt's win at California Speedway handed him the championship lead and kept Matt Kenseth at bay the rest of the way. His second-place finish at Atlanta gave him a 166-point lead heading into the season finale, and he needed it. He finished 42nd because of an engine failure while Kenseth finished fourth, but Earnhardt had enough cushion to secure the title.

### 1998 CHAMPIONSHIP LINESCORE

| Starts | Wins | Poles | Top 5 | Top 10 | Races Led | Laps Led |
|--------|------|-------|-------|--------|-----------|----------|
| 31 | 7 | 3 | 16 | 22 | 19 | 1,615 |

## 97-96 Champion

# 74 Randy LaJoie

**Car:** CHEVROLET • **Car owner:** William Baumgardner
**Birth date:** 08/28/61 • **Hometown:** South Norwalk, Conn.

## NASCAR BUSCH SERIES STATISTICS

**Seasons competed:** 16 (1986-90, 1993-2004)
**Career starts:** 316    **Career wins:** 15    **Career poles:** 9

**1997 Championship season recap:** LaJoie was the third driver to win consecutive NASCAR Busch Series titles and fourth multiple champion. LaJoie led the series with 15 top five finishes and was second in wins (5) and top 10 efforts (21), coasting by runner-up Todd Bodine by 266 points. LaJoie's win at Milwaukee in the 18th race gave him the championship lead, which he held the rest of the season. He earned $1,105,201, becoming the first NASCAR Busch Series champion to top the $1 million mark in single-season earnings. Owner William Baumgardner also made history as the only owner to win three consecutive NASCAR Busch series crowns.

### 1997 CHAMPIONSHIP LINESCORE

| Starts | Wins | Poles | Top 5 | Top 10 | Races Led | Laps Led |
|---|---|---|---|---|---|---|
| 30 | 5 | 2 | 15 | 21 | 13 | 1,037 |

**1996 Championship season recap:** In the third-closest championship race in history, LaJoie nipped 1994 NASCAR Busch Series champion David Green by 29 points. LaJoie was paced by five wins, which ranked second in the series, and a series-leading 20 top 10 efforts. LaJoie overtook Green for the points lead by virtue of a sixth-place finish at Charlotte with two races left. LaJoie held a 33-point lead going into the season-ending race at Miami, and used a 10th-place finish to offset a ninth-place performance by Green to secure the title.

### 1996 CHAMPIONSHIP LINESCORE

| Starts | Wins | Poles | Top 5 | Top 10 | Races Led | Laps Led |
|---|---|---|---|---|---|---|
| 26 | 5 | 2 | 11 | 20 | 12 | 784 |

## 1995 Champion

# 74 Johnny Benson

**Car:** CHEVROLET • **Car Owner:** William Baumgardner
**Birth date:** 06/27/63 •
**Hometown:** Grand Rapids, Mich.

## NASCAR BUSCH SERIES STATISTICS

**Seasons competed:** 14 (1990-2004)
**Career starts:** 86    **Career wins:** 3    **Career poles:** 1

**Championship season recap:** Benson posted just a pair or wins, but his consistency in placing among the top 10 let him roll to his first NASCAR Busch Series crown. He recorded 19 top 10 finishes—12 among the top five—to outdistance runner-up Chad Little by 404 points, the third-largest margin in series history. Benson won the fourth race of the season, Atlanta, to grab the points lead from Terry Labonte and relinquished the top spot just once the rest of the season.

### CHAMPIONSHIP LINESCORE

| Starts | Wins | Poles | Top 5 | Top 10 | Races Led | Laps Led |
|---|---|---|---|---|---|---|
| 26 | 2 | 0 | 12 | 19 | 13 | 564 |

# 44 David Green

**Car:** CHEVROLET • **Car owner:** Bobby Labonte
**Birth date:** 01/28/58 • **Hometown:** Owensboro, Ky.

## NASCAR BUSCH SERIES STATISTICS

**Seasons competed:** 13 (1989-91,1993-96, 1998-2004)
**Career starts:** 321 **Career wins:** 8 **Career poles:** 22
**Championship season recap:** Green became only the second driver to register one victory yet win the championship. Green edged Ricky Craven by 46 points. Green's fourth-place finish at South Boston in the 17th race pushed him past Craven as the leader, and he maintained the lead. Green was boosted by 10 top five finishes and just one DNF. He had a series-leading nine poles.

### CHAMPIONSHIP LINESCORE

| Starts | Wins | Poles | Top 5 | Top 10 | Races Led | Laps Led |
|--------|------|-------|-------|--------|-----------|----------|
| 28 | 1 | 9 | 10 | 14 | 11 | 380 |

# 31 Steve Grissom

**Car:** CHEVROLET • **Car owner:** Wayne Grissom
**Birth date:** 06/26/63 • **Hometown:** Gadsden, Ala.

## NASCAR BUSCH SERIES STATISTICS

**Seasons competed:** 17 (1986-2003)
**Career starts:** 273 **Career wins:** 11 **Career poles:** 4
**Championship season recap:** Grissom's consistency among the top five paved the way to his first championship. His series-leading 11 top five finishes boosted him to a 253-point spread over runner-up Ricky Craven. Grissom took the lead from David Green with a fourth-place finish at Michigan, the 18th race of the season, and held the top spot for the rest of the year.

### CHAMPIONSHIP LINESCORE

| Starts | Wins | Poles | Top 5 | Top 10 | Races Led | Laps Led |
|--------|------|-------|-------|--------|-----------|----------|
| 28 | 2 | 0 | 11 | 18 | 7 | 120 |

# 87 Joe Nemechek

**Car:** CHEVROLET • **Car owner:** Joe Nemechek
**Birth date:** 09/26/63 • **Hometown:** Lakeland, Fla.

## NASCAR BUSCH SERIES STATISTICS

**Seasons competed:** 15 (1989-2004)
**Career starts:** 253 **Career wins:** 16 **Career poles:** 16
**Championship season recap:** Nemechek took on defending series champion, Bobby Labonte, and outlasted him in the closest championship battle in NASCAR Busch Series history. Nemechek wrestled the lead from Todd Bodine with three races remaining. Labonte won two of the final three races, including the season finale at Hickory, but Nemechek finished sixth at Hickory to edge him by three points.

### CHAMPIONSHIP LINESCORE

| Starts | Wins | Poles | Top 5 | Top 10 | Races Led | Laps Led |
|--------|------|-------|-------|--------|-----------|----------|
| 31 | 2 | 1 | 13 | 18 | 8 | 241 |

## 1991 Champion

# 44 Bobby Labonte

**Car:** OLDSMOBILE • **Car owner:** Bobby Labonte
**Birth date:** 05/08/64 •
**Hometown:** Corpus Christi, Texas

### NASCAR BUSCH SERIES STATISTICS

**Seasons competed:** 13 (1982, 1985, 1988-94, 1996-1999, 2004)
**Career starts:** 164 **Career wins:** 9 **Career poles:** 10
**Championship season recap:** Kenny Wallace took the lead from Labonte with three races to go, but Labonte overcame the 33-point deficit. Labonte had a pair of top five finishes coupled with an eighth-place effort while Wallace cracked the top 20 just once in that span. With two to go, Labonte held a 42-point lead and clinched finishing fifth in the finale at Martinsville.

#### CHAMPIONSHIP LINESCORE

| Starts | Wins | Poles | Top 5 | Top 10 | Races Led | Laps Led |
|--------|------|-------|-------|--------|-----------|----------|
| 31 | 2 | 2 | 10 | 21 | 10 | 299 |

## 1990 Champion

# 63 Chuck Bown

**Car:** PONTIAC • **Car owner:** Hubert Hensley
**Birth date:** 02/22/54 • **Hometown:** Portland

### NASCAR BUSCH SERIES STATISTICS

**Seasons competed:** 11 (1986-93, 1995-96, 1999)
**Career starts:** 187 **Career wins:** 11 **Career poles:** 13
**Championship season recap:** Bown, buoyed by a series-high six wins, earned his first NASCAR Busch Series title by a 200-point margin over Jimmy Hensley. Bown took the lead after a win at Hickory in the 11th race of the season and never relinquished the top spot.

#### CHAMPIONSHIP LINESCORE

| Starts | Wins | Poles | Top 5 | Top 10 | Races Led | Laps Led |
|--------|------|-------|-------|--------|-----------|----------|
| 31 | 6 | 4 | 13 | 18 | 14 | 1,224 |

## 1989 Champion

# 25 Rob Moroso

**Car:** OLDSMOBILE • **Car owner:** Dick Moroso
**Birth date:** 09/28/68 • **Hometown:** Madison, Conn.

### NASCAR BUSCH SERIES STATISTICS

**Seasons competed:** 4 (1986-1989)
**Career starts:** 86 **Career wins:** 6 **Career poles:** 8
**Championship season recap:** Moroso overcame Tommy Houston to capture his first NASCAR Busch Series crown. Moroso topped Houston by 55 points, but was trailing him down the stretch. Moroso grabbed the lead from Houston with a win at Charlotte, but lost it the following race at Rockingham after finishing 12th. Houston came into the season finale at Martinsville with a 19-point lead, but lost the title when he finished 24th due to engine failure as Moroso finished third. Moroso had a series-leading four wins and series-high six poles.

#### CHAMPIONSHIP LINESCORE

| Starts | Wins | Poles | Top 5 | Top 10 | Races Led | Laps Led |
|--------|------|-------|-------|--------|-----------|----------|
| 29 | 4 | 6 | 12 | 16 | 11 | 566 |

 **Tommy Ellis**

**Car:** BUICK • **Car Owner:** John Jackson
**Birth date:** 08/08/47 • **Hometown:** Richmond, Va.

## NASCAR BUSCH SERIES STATISTICS

**Seasons competed:** 14 (1982-1995)
**Career starts:** 235 **Career wins:** 22 **Career poles:** 28
**Championship season recap:** Ellis, after a stint in the NASCAR Cup Series, returned to the NASCAR Busch Series and promptly captured his first championship. He posted a 239-point spread over runnerup Rob Moroso. Ellis was tied for second in the series in wins with three–trailing only Harry Gant (5)—and notched 20 top 10 finishes in 30 starts. He also had a series-leading five poles.

### CHAMPIONSHIP LINESCORE

| Starts | Wins | Poles | Top 5 | Top 10 | Races Led | Laps Led |
|---|---|---|---|---|---|---|
| 30 | 3 | 5 | 12 | 20 | 13 | 740 |

## **Larry Pearson**

**Car:** CHEVROLET • **Car owner:** David Pearson
**Birth date:** 11/02/53 • **Hometown:** Spartanburg, S.C.

## NASCAR BUSCH SERIES STATISTICS

**Seasons competed:** 16 (1982-90, 1993-99)
**Career starts:** 259 **Career wins:** 15 **Career poles:** 11
**1987 Championship season recap:** Pearson became the second driver to win consecutive NASCAR Busch Series crowns and the third multiple champion in the series. While his first title run was one of the closest in history, he rolled to his second as he outdistanced runner-up Jimmy Hensley by 382 points. Pearson led the series with six wins and registered 20 top 10 finishes. He joined Sam Ard as the only back-to-back champions.

### 1987 CHAMPIONSHIP LINESCORE

| Starts | Wins | Poles | Top 5 | Top 10 | Races Led | Laps Led |
|---|---|---|---|---|---|---|
| 27 | 6 | 3 | 16 | 20 | 13 | 720 |

**1986 Championship season recap:** Pearson rallied late to claim his first NASCAR Busch Series title, edging Brett Bodine by 20 points. The points battle would be the second closest in series history. Bodine led Pearson by 19 points with five races to go, but two races later Pearson grabbed the lead by six points. Pearson extended the lead to 30 heading into the season finale at Martinsville and clinched with a runnerup showing while Bodine made a final gasp with a victory.

### 1986 CHAMPIONSHIP LINESCORE

| Starts | Wins | Poles | Top 5 | Top 10 | Races Led | Laps Led |
|---|---|---|---|---|---|---|
| 31 | 1 | 1 | 17 | 24 | 7 | 200 |

# 11 Jack Ingram

**Car:** PONTIAC • **Car owner:** Aline Ingram
**Birth date:** 12/28/36 • **Hometown:** Asheville, N.C.

## NASCAR BUSCH SERIES STATISTICS

**Seasons competed:** 10 (1982-1991)
**Career starts:** 274     **Career wins:** 31     **Career poles:** 5
**1985 Championship season recap:** Ingram joined Sam Ard as a multiple champion in the NASCAR Busch Series, adding this crown to the one he captured in the inaugural 1982 season. Ingram had another tough battle en route to this title as well, edging Jimmy Hensley by 29 points. Ard owned a 39-point lead with one to go, and iced it with a fifth-place finish in the season finale at Martinsville. The points margin is tied for the third-closest in NASCAR Busch Series history. Ingram was boosted by five wins—which tied for the series lead with Tommy Ellis—and 22 top 10 finishes in 27 starts.

| | | | | | | |
|---|---|---|---|---|---|---|
| **1985 CHAMPIONSHIP LINESCORE** | | | | | | |
| Starts | Wins | Poles | Top 5 | Top 10 | Races Led | DNFs |
| 27 | 5 | 2 | 17 | 22 | 15 | 4 |

**1982 Championship season recap:** Ingram became the inaugural NASCAR Busch Series, Grand National Division champion, edging Sam Ard by 49 points. Ingram had an incredible run of consistency as he posted 23 top five finishes, including a series leading seven victories. Ard, with four wins, was trailing by 58 points with three races remaining, but never was able to get closer to Ingram than 43 points over that span.

| | | | | | | |
|---|---|---|---|---|---|---|
| **1982 CHAMPIONSHIP LINESCORE** | | | | | | |
| Starts | Wins | Poles | Top 5 | Top 10 | Races Led | DNFs |
| 29 | 7 | 1 | 23 | 24 | NA | 4 |

# 00 Sam Ard

**Car:** OLDSMOBILE • **Car owner:** Howard Thomas
**Birth date:** 02/14/39 • **Hometown:** Asheboro, N.C.

## NASCAR BUSCH SERIES STATISTICS

**Seasons competed:** 3 (1982-84)
**Career starts:** 92     **Career wins:** 22     **Career poles:** 25
**1984 Championship season recap:** Ard and Jack Ingram had squared off for the championship the first two seasons, with each earning a title, but the third battle between the two was no contest. Ard became the series' first multiple and back-to-back champion by rolling to a 426-point spread over Ingram, the second-largest points difference in history. Ard and Ingram tied for the series lead in wins with eight each, but it was Ard's consistency that allowed him to coast to the crown. He recorded 24 top-five finishes in 28 starts and finished outside the top 10 just twice.

| | | | | | | |
|---|---|---|---|---|---|---|
| **1984 CHAMPIONSHIP LINESCORE** | | | | | | |
| Starts | Wins | Poles | Top 5 | Top 10 | Races Led | DNFs |
| 32 | 6 | 3 | 18 | 22 | 23 | 4 |

**1983 Championship season recap:** It was a battle between the top two contenders—Ard and defending champion Jack Ingram—from the inaugural 1982 season, but this time Ard prevailed. He needed a NASCAR Busch Series history record 10 victories to fend off Ingram and claim the title by 87 points. He also led the series with 10 poles. Ingram stayed in the hunt though behind five wins and 29 top-10 efforts, but could not run down the dominating Ard in the end.

| | | | | | | |
|---|---|---|---|---|---|---|
| **1983 CHAMPIONSHIP LINESCORE** | | | | | | |
| Starts | Wins | Poles | Top 5 | Top 10 | Races Led | DNFs |
| 31 | 7 | 3 | 16 | 22 | 19 | 3 |

## 5 Kyle Busch

**Car:** CHEVROLET • **Car owner:** Rick Hendrick
**Birth date:** 5/2/85 • **Hometown:** Las Vegas

### NASCAR BUSCH SERIES STATISTICS

**Seasons competed:** 1 (2003, 2004)
**Career starts:** 41  **Career wins:** 5  **Career poles:** 5

**Rookie of the Year season recap:** Busch gave NASCAR Busch Series 2004 champion Martin Truex Jr. a run for his money, even leading the points standings for three weeks. Busch finished just 230 points behind the leader—375 points ahead of third-place finisher Greg Biffle—achieving the highest points finish for a rookie in series history. Consistency was a hallmark of Busch's season as he accumulated five victories, five poles, 16 top fives and 10 top-10 finishes. At 19, Busch became the series' youngest Raybestos Rookie of the Year.

### CHAMPIONSHIP LINESCORE

| Starts | Wins | Poles | Top 5 | Top 10 | Races Led | Laps Led |
|---|---|---|---|---|---|---|
| 34 | 5 | 5 | 16 | 22 | 21 | 1,108 |

# Rookie of the Year winners

| Year | Driver | Points | Finish | Races | Poles | Wins | Top 5 | Top 10 | Winnings | Hometown |
|---|---|---|---|---|---|---|---|---|---|---|
| 2004 | Kyle Busch | 4,943 | 2 | 34 | 5 | 5 | 16 | 22 | $2,027,050 | Las Vegas |
| 2003 | David Stremme | 2,354 | 22 | 18 | 0 | 0 | 3 | 7 | $443,537 | South Bend, Ind. |
| 2002 | Scott Riggs | 4,023 | 10 | 34 | 2 | 2 | 8 | 13 | $1,170,846 | Bahama, N.C. |
| 2001 | Greg Biffle | 4,509 | 4 | 33 | 2 | 5 | 16 | 21 | $1,623,546 | Vancouver, Wash. |
| 2000 | Kevin Harvick | 4,113 | 3 | 31 | 2 | 3 | 8 | 16 | $995,274 | Bakersfield, Calif. |
| 1999 | Tony Raines | 3,142 | 12 | 31 | 0 | 0 | 1 | 3 | $657,220 | LaPorte, Ind. |
| 1998 | Andy Santerre | 2,598 | 20 | 29 | 1 | 0 | 1 | 2 | $307,835 | Cherryfield, Maine |
| 1997 | Steve Park | 4,080 | 3 | 30 | 1 | 3 | 12 | 20 | $677,921 | East Northport, N.Y. |
| 1996 | Glenn Allen | 2,593 | 14 | 26 | 0 | 0 | 0 | 2 | $176,372 | Cincinnati |
| 1995 | Jeff Fuller | 2,845 | 10 | 26 | 1 | 0 | 1 | 6 | $174,950 | Auburn, Mass. |
| 1994 | Johnny Benson | 3,303 | 6 | 28 | 0 | 1 | 6 | 9 | $190,011 | Grand Rapids, Mich. |
| 1993 | Hermie Sadler | 3,362 | 10 | 28 | 0 | 1 | 4 | 8 | $149,596 | Emporia, Va. |
| 1992 | Ricky Craven | 3,456 | 14 | 31 | 1 | 0 | 0 | 5 | $167,618 | Newburgh, Maine |
| 1991 | Jeff Gordon | 3,582 | 11 | 30 | 1 | 0 | 5 | 10 | $111,608 | Pittsboro, Ind. |
| 1990 | Joe Nemechek | 3,022 | 17 | 28 | 0 | 0 | 2 | 5 | $70,279 | Lakeland, Fla. |
| 1989 | Kenny Wallace | 3,750 | 6 | 29 | 3 | 0 | 4 | 16 | $88,423 | St. Louis |

# Miscellaneous records

**Most races started:** 417, Tommy Houston (1982-1996)
**Most wins, season:** 10,Sam Ard (1983)
**Most wins, career:** 45, Mark Martin (1982-2000)
**Most superspeedway wins, season:** 5, Dale Earnhardt Jr. (1998)
   Mark Martin (1993, '96, '97, '00)
   Chad Little (1995)
   Greg Biffle (2001, 2004)
   Truex Jr. (2004)
**Most superspeedway wins, career:** 36, Mark Martin (1982-2000)
**Most short track wins, season:** 9, Sam Ard (1983)
**Most short track wins, career:** 29, Jack Ingram (1982-1991)
**Most years winning at least one race:** 13, Dale Earnhardt, Mark Martin
**Most different race winners, season:** 18 (1988, 89)
**Most wins at one track:** 11, Mark Martin, Rockingham
**Most races won from pole, career:** 9, Sam Ard (1982-84),
   Mark Martin (1987-2000)
**Most races won from pole, season:** 4, Sam Ard (1983)
**Oldest driver to win:** Dick Trickle (56 years, 11 months) Darlington, Sept. 5, 1998
**Youngest driver To win:** Casey Atwood (18 years, 10 months),
   Milwaukee, July 4, 1999
**Most races started without winning:** Ed Berrier, 208 (1984-1997)
**Most top-five finishes, season:** 25, Jeff Green (2000)
**Most top-five finishes, career:** 123, Tommy Houston (1982-1996)
**Most top-10 finishes, season:** 30, Sam Ard (1983)
**Most top-10 finishes, career:** 198, Tommy Houston (1982-1996)
**Most poles, season:** 11, Jeff Gordon (1992)
**Most poles, career:** 28, Tommy Ellis (1982-1995)
**Most years winning at least one pole:** 11, Mark Martin
**Most different pole winners, season:** 24 (1998)
**Most poles at one track:** 7, Tommy Ellis, Hickory
   Mark Martin, Darlington
**Most money won, season:** $2,537,171, Martin Truex Jr. (2004)
**Most money won, career:** $9,395,624, Jason Keller (1991-current)
**Most money won, race:** $113,844, Jeff Gordon, Charlotte, May 23, 1982
**Largest purse, superspeedway:** $1,924,431, Daytona (2004)
**Largest purse, short track:** $1,054,532, Memphis (2002)
**Largest margin of victory by series champion:** 616 points, Jeff Green over
   Jason Keller (2000)
**Smallest margin of victory by series champion:** 3 points, Joe Nemechek
   over Bobby Labonte (1992)

# Series race records

**Longest race, distance:** 400 miles, Charlotte, Oct. 5, 1985
**Longest race, time:** 3 hrs., 41 min., 58 sec. , New Hampshire, July 15, 1990
**Shortest race, distance:** 56.25 miles, Orange County, 1985-1988
**Shortest race, time:** 38 min., 4 sec., Orange County, June 14, 1986
**Fastest average speed:** 169.571 mph, Michigan, Aug. 19, 1995
**Slowest average speed:** 48.842 mph, Orange County, Aug. 13, 1982
**Most caution flags, race:** 26, Hickory, April 18, 1992
**Most caution laps, race:** 132, Hickory, April 18, 1992
**Fewest caution flags, race:** 0, Five times—most recent, Michigan, Aug. 15, 1998
**Fewest caution laps, race:** 0, Five times—most recent, Michigan, Aug. 15, 1998
**Most lead changes, race:** 35, Three times—most recent, Rockingham,
   Feb. 22, 1997
**Most cars finishing on lead lap, race:** 31, Michigan, 2004
**Fewest cars finishing on lead lap:** 1, 12 times—most recent, Orange County,
   Aug. 10, 1991
**Largest starting field:** 47, Oxford, Maine, July 10, 1988
**Smallest starting field:** 17, Hampton, Va., May 8, 1982
**Most cars running at finish:** 43, Michigan, Aug. 15, 1998
**Fewest DNFs, race:** 0, Michigan, Aug. 15, 1998
**Fewest cars running at finish:** 10, North Wilkesboro, April 8, 1983
**Most DNFs, race:** 26, Charlotte, Nov., 10, 1987

# Records set in consecutive years

**Most consecutive starts:** 360, Tommy Houston (Feb. 13, 1982—Feb. 26, 1994)
**Most consecutive races won:** 4, Sam Ard (1983)
**Most consecutive years winning at least one race:** 10, Dale Earnhardt
   (1985-1994)
**Most consecutive different race winners, season:** 13 (1988)
**Most consecutive wins at one track:** 5, Dale Earnhardt, Daytona (1990-94);
   Jack Ingram, South Boston (1986)
**Most consecutive wins by a car manufacturer:** 11, Chevrolet (2000)
**Most consecutive races running at finish:** 60, Kevin Harvick
   (Mar. 18, 2000—Nov. 3, 2001)
**Most consecutive poles:** 3 , Four drivers (most recent, Jeff Gordon, 1992)
**Most consecutive different pole winners, season:** 15 (1995)
**Most consecutive poles at one track:** 4, David Green, Hickory (1994-1996)
**Most consecutive years winning at least one pole:** 9, Mark Martin (1992-2000)

# Series firsts

**First race:** Daytona International Speedway; Feb. 13, 1982
**First winner:** Dale Earnhardt
**First pole winner:** Mike Porter; Daytona, Feb. 9, 1982
**First superspeedway race:** Daytona; Feb. 13, 1982
**First superspeedway winner:** Dale Earnhardt Daytona; Feb. 13, 1982
**First short track race:** Richmond; Feb. 20, 1982
**First short track winner:** Tommy Houston; Richmond, Feb. 20, 1982
**First road course race:** Road Atlanta, July 6, 1986
**First road course winner:** Darrell Waltrip, Road Atlanta, July 6, 1986
**First Chevrolet win:** Tommy Houston, Hickory, Aug. 1, 1982
**First Dodge win:** Hank Parker Jr., Pikes Peak, July 27, 2002
**First Ford win:** Mark Martin, Dover, May 30, 1987
**First champion:** Jack Ingram, 1982
**First rookie of the year:** Kenny Wallace, 1989
**First driver to win $1 million in career:** Jack Ingram 1989
**First driver to win $1 million in a season:** Randy LaJoie 1997
**First driver to win $100,000 in a race:** Jeff Gordon 1992
**First race west of Mississippi River:** Las Vegas 300, March 15, 1997
**First brothers to win championships:** David Green (1994),
   Jeff Green (2000)

# All-time race winners

| DRIVER | Tot. | DRIVER | Tot. | DRIVER | Tot. | DRIVER | Tot. | DRIVER | Tot. |
|---|---|---|---|---|---|---|---|---|---|
| Mark Martin | 45 | Dale Jarrett | 11 | Kyle Busch | 5 | Butch Miller | 2 | Bobby Hamilton | 1 |
| Jack Ingram | 31 | Terry Labonte | 11 | Ward Burton | 4 | Hank Parker Jr. | 2 | Tracy Leslie | 1 |
| Tommy Houston | 24 | Michael Waltrip | 11 | Ricky Craven | 4 | Phil Parsons | 2 | Dick McCabe | *1 |
| Sam Ard | 22 | Robert Pressley | 10 | Tim Fedewa | 4 | Tim Richmond | 2 | David Pearson | 1 |
| Tommy Ellis | 22 | Jason Keller | 10 | Jeff Purvis | 4 | Johnny Rumley | 2 | Larry Pollard | 1 |
| Dale Earnhardt | 21 | Jimmy Hensley | 9 | Scott Riggs | 4 | Hermie Sadler | 2 | Ricky Rudd | 1 |
| Harry Gant | 21 | Bobby Labonte | 9 | Ron Hornaday | 4 | Elton Sawyer | 2 | Joe Ruttman | 1 |
| Jeff Burton | 20 | Rick Mast | 9 | Mike Wallace | 4 | Ken Schrader | 2 | Greg Sacks | 1 |
| Dale Earnhardt Jr. | 20 | Kenny Wallace | 9 | Johnny Benson | 3 | Dennis Setzer | 2 | Andy Santerre | 1 |
| Matt Kenseth | 17 | David Green | 8 | Ron Fellows | 3 | Ronnie Silver | 2 | John Settlemyre | 1 |
| Jeff Green | 16 | Jamie McMurray | 7 | Ernie Irvan | 3 | Dick Trickle | 2 | Mike Skinner | 1 |
| Greg Biffle | 16 | Geoffrey Bodine | 6 | L.D. Ottinger | 3 | Rick Wilson | 2 | Jack Sprague | 1 |
| Joe Nemechek | 16 | Butch Lindley | 6 | Steve Park | 3 | Johnny Sauter | 2 | Brad Teague | 1 |
| Larry Pearson | 15 | Chad Little | 6 | Brian Vickers | 3 | Jamie Aube | *1 | Ryan Newman | 1 |
| Morgan Shepherd | 15 | Mike McLaughlin | 6 | Mike Alexander | 2 | Ed Berrier | 1 | Jimmy Johnson | 1 |
| Randy LaJoie | 15 | Martin Truex Jr. | 6 | Bobby Allison | 2 | Joe Bessey | 1 | Kasey Kahne | 1 |
| Todd Bodine | 15 | Rob Moroso | 6 | Casey Atwood | 2 | Neil Bonnett | 1 | Jason Leffler | 1 |
| Darrell Waltrip | 13 | Brett Bodine | 5 | Ron Bouchard | 2 | Ronald Cooper | 1 | Justin Labonte | 1 |
| Kevin Harvick | 13 | Jeff Gordon | 5 | Bobby Hillin | 2 | Derrike Cope | 1 | Robby Gordon | 1 |
| Jimmy Spencer | 12 | Elliott Sadler | 5 | Buckshot Jones | 2 | Bobby Dotter | 1 | Mike Bliss | 1 |
| Chuck Bown | 11 | Scott Wimmer | 5 | Kevin Lepage | 2 | Bill Elliott | 1 | | |
| Steve Grissom | 11 | Bobby Hamilton Jr. | 5 | Sterling Marlin | 2 | Jeff Fuller | 1 | | |

**\* Busch North Series, NASCAR Touring wins in "combination" races**

# All-time pole winners

| DRIVER | Totals | DRIVER | Totals | DRIVER | Totals | DRIVER | Totals | DRIVER | Totals |
|---|---|---|---|---|---|---|---|---|---|
| Tommy Ellis | 28 | Dale Earnhardt Jr | 8 | Shane Hmiel | 3 | Scott Riggs | 2 | Steve Park | 1 |
| Mark Martin | 27 | Todd Bodine | 7 | Terry Labonte | 4 | Greg Sacks | 2 | Hank Parker Jr. | 1 |
| Sam Ard | 24 | Ward Burton | 7 | Kevin Lepage | 4 | Elton Sawyer | 2 | Randy Porter | 1 |
| Jeff Green | 23 | Dale Earnhardt | 7 | Butch Miller | 4 | Tony Stewart | 2 | Scott Pruett | 1 |
| David Green | 22 | Dick Trickle | 7 | L.D. Ottinger | 4 | Hut Stricklin | 2 | Tony Raines | 1 |
| Tommy Houston | 18 | Martin Truex Jr. | 6 | Darrell Waltrip | 4 | Brad Teague | 2 | Stevie Reeves | 1 |
| Joe Nemechek | 17 | Casey Atwood | 6 | Kyle Busch | 4 | Rusty Wallace | 2 | David Reutimann | 1 |
| Brett Bodine | 16 | Dave Blaney | 6 | Jason Leffler | 4 | Stanton Barrett | 2 | Shawna Robinson | 1 |
| Jimmy Hensley | 15 | Ryan Newman | 6 | Casey Mears | 4 | Tim Bender | 1 | Johnny Rumley | 1 |
| Michael Waltrip | 15 | Phil Parsons | 6 | Mike Alexander | 3 | Ed Berrier | 1 | Boris Said | 1 |
| Harry Gant | 14 | Robert Pressley | 6 | Buckshot Jones | 3 | Rich Bickle | 1 | Andy Santerre | 1 |
| Dale Jarrett | 14 | Jeff Purvis | 6 | David Pearson | 3 | Jim Bown | 1 | Jay Sauter | 1 |
| Geoffrey Bodine | 13 | Tim Richmond | 6 | Hermie Sadler | 3 | Stacy Compton | 1 | Dennis Setzer | 1 |
| Chuck Bown | 12 | Morgan Shepherd | 6 | Mike Skinner | 3 | Derrike Cope | 1 | Bob Shreeves | 1 |
| Jeff Gordon | 12 | Jack Ingram | 5 | Jimmy Spencer | 3 | Dave Dion | 1 | Jack Sprague | 1 |
| Kevin Harvick | 11 | Ernie Irvan | 5 | Johnny Sauter | 3 | Eddie Falk | ^1 | Mike Swaim | 1 |
| Jason Keller | 11 | Butch Lindley | 5 | Kasey Kahne | 3 | Jeff Fuller | 1 | Brian Vickers | 1 |
| Larry Pearson | 11 | Rick Mast | 5 | Mike Bliss | 3 | Wayne Grubb | 1 | Rick Wilson | 1 |
| Greg Biffle | 11 | Mike McLaughlin | 5 | Davey Allison | 2 | Kevin Grubb | 1 | Johnny Benson | 1 |
| Jeff Burton | 10 | Elliott Sadler | 5 | Joe Bessey | 2 | Ron Hornaday | 1 | Mike Bliss | 1 |
| Bobby Labonte | 10 | Ken Schrader | 5 | Bill Elliott | 2 | Robert Ingram | 1 | Clint Bowyer | 1 |
| Kenny Wallace | 10 | Kyle Busch | 5 | Ron Fellows | 2 | Alan Kulwicki | 1 | Jamie McMurray | 1 |
| Randy LaJoie | 9 | Ron Bouchard | 4 | Shane Hall | 2 | Ashton Lewis | 1 | Johnny Benson | 1 |
| Martin Truex Jr. | 9 | Bobby Dotter | 4 | Tracy Leslie | 2 | Chad Little | 1 | David Stremme | 1 |
| Ricky Craven | 8 | Tim Fedewa | 4 | Dave Mader III | 2 | Curtis Markham | 1 | Jamie McMurray | 1 |
| Matt Kenseth | 8 | Steve Grissom | 4 | Kelly Moore | ^2 | Sterling Marlin | 1 | Clint Bowyer | 1 |
| Rob Moroso | 8 | Bobby Hamilton Jr. | 4 | Mike Porter | 2 | Gary Niece | 1 | Paul Menard | 1 |

**\* Includes races where qualifying rained out; 27 races started by points.**
**^ Busch North Series, NASCAR Touring Poles in "combination" races.**

# 200 or more career starts

| Driver | Starts | 200th Start at | Date | Driver | Starts | 200th Start at | Date |
|---|---|---|---|---|---|---|---|
| Tommy Houston | 417 | Rougemont | 8/18/88 | Joe Nemechek | 253 | Richmond | 9/07/01 |
| Elton Sawyer | 392 | Nashville | 3/19/95 | Ed Berrier | 250 | Rockingham | 10/25/97 |
| Jason Keller | 356 | Richmond | 5/5/00 | Rick Mast | 243 | Hickory | 3/25/90 |
| Dale Jarrett | 324 | Charlotte | 10/07/89 | Jeff Green | 240 | Pikes Peak | 7/28/01 |
| David Green | 321 | Bristol | 8/25/00 | Jeff Burton | 240 | California | 4/29/00 |
| Randy LaJoie | 316 | Talladega | 4/15/00 | Robert Pressley | 239 | Rockingham | 10/31/98 |
| Mike McLaughlin | 313 | Atlanta | 3/11/00 | Tommy Ellis | 235 | Daytona Beach | 2/17/91 |
| Tim Fedewa | 312 | Daytona Beach | 2/19/00 | Michael Waltrip | 231 | Homestead | 11/15/03 |
| Kenny Wallace | 312 | Bristol | 3/25/00 | Mike Wallace | 225 | Fontana | 5/01/04 |
| Todd Bodine | 308 | Dover | 9/25/99 | Bobby Dotter | 209 | Indianapolis | 8/02/96 |
| Phil Parsons | 285 | New Hampshire | 5/09/98 | Jimmy Spencer | 210 | Dover | 9/21/02 |
| Jack Ingram | 274 | Darlington | 9/03/88 | Tracy Leslie | 206 | Bristol | 8/21/98 |
| Steve Grissom | 273 | Talladega | 7/22/95 | L.D. Ottinger | 206 | Dover | 9/15/90 |
| Larry Pearson | 259 | Myrtle Beach | 6/10/95 | Mark Martin | 205 | Homestead | 11/11/00 |
| Jimmy Hensley | 255 | Rougemont | 8/11/90 | Brad Teague | 200 | Darlington | 11/13/04 |
| Hermie Sadler | 256 | Michigan | 8/19/00 | | | | |

**Notes:** Houston's 300th start was 2/15/92 at Daytona Beach
Jarrett's 300th start was 2/22/97 at Rockingham
Sawyer's 300th start was 4/10/99 at Bristol
LaJoie's 300th start was 5/2/03 at Richmond
Bodine's 300th start was 10/4/03 at Kansas
McLaughlin's 300th start was 07/19/03
Fedewa's 300th start was 8/27/04 at Indianapolis Raceway
Green's 300th start was 5/29/04 at Charlotte
Houston's 400th start was 3/9/96 at Atlanta
Kenny Wallace's 300th start was 8/21/04 at Michigan

# Career money leaders

| Rk. | Driver | Starts | Poles | Wins | Top 5 | Top 10 | Money |
|---|---|---|---|---|---|---|---|
| 1. | Jason Keller | 356 | 11 | 10 | 79 | 151 | $9,395,624 |
| 2. | Randy LaJoie | 316 | 9 | 15 | 62 | 115 | $6,869,830 |
| 3. | David Green | 321 | 22 | 8 | 69 | 136 | $6,734,016 |
| 4. | Jeff Green | 240 | 23 | 16 | 87 | 126 | $6,663,313 |
| 5. | Mike McLaughlin | 313 | 5 | 6 | 58 | 110 | $6,257,873 |
| 6. | Greg Biffle | 117 | 11 | 16 | 54 | 71 | $5,902,726 |
| 7. | Todd Bodine | 308 | 7 | 15 | 89 | 156 | $5,457,475 |
| 8. | Ron Hornaday Jr. | 150 | 1 | 4 | 27 | 59 | $4,903,700 |
| 9. | Matt Kenseth | 162 | 8 | 17 | 71 | 103 | $4,901,182 |
| 10. | Bobby Hamilton Jr. | 176 | 4 | 5 | 29 | 58 | $4,800,824 |
| 11. | Elton Sawyer | 392 | 2 | 2 | 51 | 131 | $4,704,263 |
| 12. | Kevin Harvick | 110 | 11 | 13 | 50 | 74 | $4,674,040 |
| 13. | Tim Fedewa | 312 | 4 | 4 | 25 | 66 | $4,464,730 |
| 14. | Kenny Wallace | 312 | 10 | 9 | 58 | 141 | $4,304,627 |
| 15. | Dale Earnhardt Jr. | 83 | 9 | 20 | 42 | 53 | $3,577,104 |
| 16. | Joe Nemechek | 253 | 17 | 16 | 72 | 115 | $3,562,591 |
| 17. | Tony Raines | 160 | 1 | 0 | 13 | 35 | $3,528,153 |
| 18. | Jeff Purvis | 187 | 6 | 4 | 25 | 57 | $3,323,266 |
| 19. | Ashton Lewis Jr. | 156 | 1 | 0 | 9 | 29 | $3,273,822 |
| 20. | Michael Waltrip | 231 | 15 | 11 | 58 | 97 | $3,268,998 |
| 21. | Scott Wimmer | 104 | 0 | 5 | 17 | 37 | $3,228,783 |
| 22. | Johnny Sauter | 106 | 2 | 2 | 14 | 29 | $3,050,682 |
| 23. | Mark Martin | 205 | 27 | 45 | 94 | 130 | $2,983,835 |
| 24. | Jeff Burton | 240 | 10 | 20 | 63 | 106 | $2,948,139 |
| 25. | Kevin Grubb | 169 | 1 | 0 | 10 | 31 | $2,931,371 |

# 2004 season

| Pos. | Driver | Points | Starts | Poles | Wins | Top 5 | Top 10 | Winnings |
|------|--------|--------|--------|-------|------|-------|--------|----------|
| 1. | Martin Truex Jr. | 5,173 | 34 | 7 | 6 | 17 | 26 | $2,537,171 |
| 2. | # Kyle Busch | 4,943 | 34 | 5 | 5 | 16 | 22 | $2,027,050 |
| 3. | Greg Biffle | 4,568 | 34 | 2 | 5 | 15 | 21 | $1,568,712 |
| 4. | Ron Hornaday | 4,258 | 34 | 0 | 1 | 7 | 16 | $1,539,519 |
| 5. | Mike Bliss | 4,115 | 34 | 3 | 1 | 6 | 14 | $1,298,784 |
| 6. | Jason Keller | 4,088 | 34 | 0 | 0 | 6 | 12 | $1,345,009 |
| 7. | David Green | 4,082 | 34 | 1 | 0 | 6 | 16 | $1,318,024 |
| 8. | Ashton Lewis | 3,892 | 34 | 0 | 0 | 3 | 8 | $1,013,987 |
| 9. | Kenny Wallace | 3,851 | 34 | 0 | 0 | 0 | 10 | $952,076 |
| 10. | David Stremme | 3,738 | 34 | 1 | 0 | 5 | 14 | $1,017,952 |

#Raybestos Rookie of the Year candidate

## Race winners • 15

| | |
|---|---|
| Martin Truex Jr. | 6 |
| Kyle Busch | 5 |
| Greg Biffle | 5 |
| Matt Kenseth | 3 |
| Jamie McMurray | 3 |
| Kevin Harvick | 2 |
| Dale Earnhardt Jr. | 2 |
| Ron Hornaday | 1 |
| Mike Bliss | 1 |
| Jason Leffler | 1 |
| Michael Waltrip | 1 |
| Mike Wallace | 1 |
| Robby Gordon | 1 |
| Joe Nemechek | 1 |
| Justin Labonte | 1 |

## Money won

| | |
|---|---|
| Martin Truex Jr. | $2,537,171 |
| Kyle Busch | 2,027,050 |
| Greg Biffle | 1,568,712 |
| Ron Hornaday | 1,539,519 |
| Jason Keller | 1,345,009 |
| David Green | 1,318,024 |
| Mike Bliss | 1,298,784 |
| Jason Leffler | 1,168,779 |
| David Stremme | 1,017,952 |
| Ashton Lewis | 1,013,987 |

## Pole winners • 16

| | |
|---|---|
| Martin Truex Jr. | 7 |
| Kyle Busch | 5 |
| Mike Bliss | 3 |
| Casey Mears | 3 |
| Greg Biffle | 2 |
| Kasey Kahne | 2 |
| David Green | 1 |
| David Stremme | 1 |
| Jason Leffler | 1 |
| Johnny Sauter | 1 |
| Bobby Hamilton Jr. | 1 |
| Paul Menard | 1 |
| Clint Bowyer | 1 |
| Jamie McMurray | 1 |
| Johnny Benson | 1 |
| Dale Earnhardt Jr. | 1 |

# 2003 season

| Pos. | Driver | Points | Starts | Poles | Wins | Top 5 | Top 10 | Winnings |
|------|--------|--------|--------|-------|------|-------|--------|----------|
| 1. | Brian Vickers | 4,637 | 34 | 1 | 3 | 13 | 21 | $1,987,255 |
| 2. | David Green | 4,623 | 34 | 2 | 3 | 11 | 21 | $1,721,860 |
| 3. | Ron Hornaday | 4,591 | 34 | 0 | 1 | 8 | 17 | $1,441,770 |
| 4. | Bobby Hamilton Jr. | 4,588 | 34 | 1 | 4 | 13 | 22 | $1,619,965 |
| 5. | Jason Keller | 4,528 | 34 | 1 | 1 | 10 | 17 | $1,488,340 |
| 6. | Scott Riggs | 4,462 | 34 | 0 | 2 | 11 | 17 | $1,435,530 |
| 7. | Kasey Kahne | 4,104 | 34 | 1 | 1 | 4 | 14 | $1,073,665 |
| 8. | Johnny Sauter | 4,098 | 34 | 0 | 1 | 6 | 14 | $1,143,460 |
| 9. | Scott Wimmer | 4,059 | 34 | 0 | 1 | 4 | 12 | $1,159,160 |
| 10. | Mike Bliss | 3,932 | 34 | 0 | 0 | 8 | 14 | $935,035 |

## Race winners • 17

| | |
|---|---|
| Bobby Hamilton Jr. | 4 |
| Brian Vickers | 3 |
| David Green | 3 |
| Kevin Harvick | 3 |
| Dale Earnhardt Jr. | 3 |
| Joe Nemechek | 3 |
| Scott Riggs | 2 |
| Jamie Mc Murray | 2 |
| Matt Kenseth | 2 |
| Greg Biffle | 2 |
| Ron Hornaday | 1 |
| Jason Keller | 1 |
| Kasey Kahne | 1 |
| Johnny Sauter | 1 |
| Scott Wimmer | 1 |
| Todd Bodine | 1 |
| Michael Waltrip | 1 |

## Money won

| | |
|---|---|
| Brian Vickers | $1,987,255 |
| David Green | 1,721,860 |
| Bobby Hamilton Jr. | 1,619,965 |
| Jason Keller | 1,488,340 |
| Ron Hornaday | 1,441,770 |
| Scott Riggs | 1,435,530 |
| Scott Wimmer | 1,159,160 |
| Johnny Sauter | 1,143,460 |
| Kasey Kahne | 1,073,665 |
| Mike Bliss | 935,035 |

## Pole winners • 16

| | |
|---|---|
| Kevin Harvick | 5 |
| Joe Nemechek | 3 |
| David Green | 2 |
| Randy LaJoie | 2 |
| Michael Waltrip | 2 |
| Greg Biffle | 2 |
| Stacy Compton | 1 |
| Dale Earnhardt Jr. | 1 |
| Bobby Hamilton Jr. | 1 |
| Shane Hmiel | 1 |
| Kasey Kahne | 1 |
| Jason Keller | 1 |
| Ashton Lewis Jr. | 1 |
| Casey Mears | 1 |
| David Reutimann | 1 |
| Brian Vickers | 1 |

# 2002 season

| Pos. | Driver | Points | Starts | Poles | Wins | Top 5 | Top 10 | Winnings |
|------|--------|--------|--------|-------|------|-------|--------|----------|
| 1. | Greg Biffle | 4919 | 34 | 5 | 4 | 20 | 25 | $2,337,254 |
| 2. | Jason Keller | 4655 | 34 | 2 | 4 | 17 | 22 | 1,669,642 |
| 3. | Scott Wimmer | 4488 | 34 | 0 | 4 | 11 | 17 | 1,332,409 |
| 4. | Mike McLaughlin | 4253 | 34 | 0 | 0 | 7 | 17 | 1,281,356 |
| 5. | Jack Sprague | 4206 | 34 | 0 | 1 | 9 | 15 | 1,103,989 |
| 6. | Jamie McMurray | 4147 | 34 | 0 | 2 | 6 | 14 | 1,044,282 |
| 7. | Kenny Wallace | 4078 | 34 | 0 | 0 | 2 | 13 | 882,800 |
| 8. | Bobby Hamilton Jr. | 4058 | 34 | 0 | 1 | 6 | 15 | 1,072,280 |
| 9. | Stacy Compton | 4042 | 34 | 0 | 0 | 5 | 11 | 861,924 |
| 10. # | Scott Riggs | 4023 | 34 | 2 | 2 | 8 | 13 | 1,170,846 |

**# Raybestos Rookie of the Year candidate**

## Race winners • 17

| | |
|---|---|
| Jeff Burton | 5 |
| Scott Wimmer | 4 |
| Greg Biffle | 4 |
| Jason Keller | 4 |
| Dale Earnhardt Jr. | 2 |
| Jeff Green | 2 |
| Jamie McMurray | 2 |
| Scott Riggs | 2 |
| Bobby Hamilton Jr. | 1 |
| Joe Nemechek | 1 |
| Todd Bodine | 1 |
| Hank Parker Jr. | 1 |
| Jeff Purvis | 1 |
| Johnny Sauter | 1 |
| Jimmy Spencer | 1 |
| Jack Sprague | 1 |
| Michael Waltrip | 1 |

## Money won

| | |
|---|---|
| Greg Biffle | $2,337,254 |
| Jason Keller | 1,669,642 |
| Scott Wimmer | 1,332,409 |
| Mike McLaughlin | 1,281,356 |
| Scott Riggs | 1,170,846 |
| Bobby Hamilton Jr. | 1,072,280 |
| Jamie McMurray | 1,044,282 |
| Randy LaJoie | 1,018,629 |
| Johnny Sauter | 991,534 |
| Kenny Wallace | 882,800 |

## Pole winners • 14

| | |
|---|---|
| Greg Biffle | 5 |
| Jeff Green | 5 |
| Jeff Burton | 2 |
| Shane Hmiel | 2 |
| Jason Keller | 2 |
| Kevin Lepage | 2 |
| Joe Nemechek | 2 |
| Scott Riggs | 2 |
| Michael Waltrip | 2 |
| Dale Earnhardt Jr. | 1 |
| Todd Bodine | 1 |
| Ron Hornaday | 1 |
| Randy LaJoie | 1 |
| Johnny Sauter | 1 |

**Note:**
No qualifying was held at California, Richmond (May), Nazareth, Darlington (Aug. 31), and Atlanta due to rain.

# 2001 season

| Pos. | Driver | Points | Starts | Poles | Wins | Top 5 | Top 10 | Winnings |
|------|--------|--------|--------|-------|------|-------|--------|----------|
| 1. | Kevin Harvick | 4813 | 33 | 5 | 5 | 20 | 24 | $1,833,570 |
| 2. | Jeff Green | 4689 | 33 | 2 | 4 | 16 | 26 | 1,797,836 |
| 3. | Jason Keller | 4637 | 33 | 0 | 1 | 14 | 22 | 1,519,811 |
| 4. # | Greg Biffle | 4509 | 33 | 2 | 5 | 16 | 21 | 1,623,546 |
| 5. | Elton Sawyer | 4100 | 33 | 0 | 0 | 6 | 19 | 1,079,093 |
| 6. | Tony Raines | 3975 | 33 | 1 | 0 | 4 | 13 | 921,777 |
| 7. | Mike McLaughlin | 3962 | 33 | 0 | 1 | 5 | 12 | 951,682 |
| 8. | Jimmie Johnson | 3871 | 33 | 0 | 1 | 4 | 9 | 920,192 |
| 9. | Chad Little | 3846 | 33 | 0 | 0 | 2 | 6 | 690,321 |
| 10. | Kenny Wallace | 3799 | 33 | 2 | 1 | 7 | 13 | 821,665 |

**# Raybestos Rookie of the Year candidate**

## Race winners • 17

| | |
|---|---|
| Greg Biffle | 5 |
| Kevin Harvick | 5 |
| Jeff Green | 4 |
| Jimmy Spencer | 3 |
| Todd Bodine | 2 |
| Randy LaJoie | 2 |
| Joe Nemechek | 2 |
| Jeff Burton | 1 |
| Ron Fellows | 1 |
| Jimmie Johnson | 1 |
| Jason Keller | 1 |
| Matt Kenseth | 1 |
| Mike McLaughlin | 1 |
| Rayn Newman | 1 |
| Hank Parker Jr. | 1 |
| Jeff Purvis | 1 |
| Kenny Wallace | 1 |

## Money won

| | |
|---|---|
| Kevin Harvick | $1,833,570 |
| Jeff Green | 1,797,836 |
| Greg Biffle | 1,623,546 |
| Jason Keller | 1,519,811 |
| Elton Sawyer | 1,079,093 |
| Mike McLaughlin | 951,682 |
| Hank Parker Jr. | 936,819 |
| Tony Raines | 921,777 |
| Jimmie Johnson | 920,192 |
| Randy LaJoie | 917,791 |

## Pole winners • 15

| | |
|---|---|
| Ryan Newman | 6 |
| Kevin Harvick | 5 |
| Matt Kenseth | 3 |
| Greg Biffle | 2 |
| Jeff Green | 2 |
| Joe Nemechek | 2 |
| Kenny Wallace | 2 |
| Jeff Burton | 1 |
| Bobby Hamilton Jr. | 1 |
| Kevin Lepage | 1 |
| Scott Pruett | 1 |
| Tony Raines | 1 |
| Jay Sauter | 1 |
| Mike Skinner | 1 |
| Jimmy Spencer | 1 |

# 2000 season

| Pos. | | Driver | Points | Starts | Poles | Wins | Top 5 | Top 10 | Winnings |
|------|---|--------|--------|--------|-------|------|-------|--------|----------|
| 1. | | Jeff Green | 5005 | 32 | 7 | 6 | 25 | 27 | $1,929,937 |
| 2. | | Jason Keller | 4389 | 32 | 0 | 1 | 13 | 19 | 1,174,448 |
| 3. | # | Kevin Harvick | 4113 | 31 | 2 | 3 | 8 | 16 | 995,274 |
| 4. | | Todd Bodine | 4075 | 32 | 1 | 1 | 14 | 19 | 935,269 |
| 5. | # | Ron Hornaday | 3870 | 32 | 0 | 2 | 6 | 13 | 958,836 |
| 6. | | Elton Sawyer | 3776 | 32 | 0 | 0 | 5 | 14 | 925,919 |
| 7. | | Randy LaJoie | 3670 | 32 | 0 | 1 | 4 | 9 | 873,179 |
| 8. | | Casey Atwood | 3404 | 32 | 2 | 0 | 0 | 8 | 775,615 |
| 9. | | David A Green | 3316 | 32 | 0 | 0 | 2 | 11 | 759,269 |
| 10. | # | Jimmie Johnson | 3264 | 31 | 0 | 0 | 0 | 6 | 549,271 |

# Raybestos Rookie of the Year candidate

## Race winners • 14

| | |
|---|---|
| Jeff Green | 6 |
| Mark Martin | 5 |
| Jeff Burton | 4 |
| Matt Kenseth | 4 |
| Kevin Harvick | 3 |
| Ron Hornaday | 2 |
| Todd Bodine | 1 |
| Tim Fedewa | 1 |
| Ron Fellows | 1 |
| Jeff Gordon | 1 |
| Jason Keller | 1 |
| Randy LaJoie | 1 |
| Sterling Marlin | 1 |
| Joe Nemechek | 1 |

## Money won

| | |
|---|---|
| Jeff Green | $1,929,937 |
| Jason Keller | 1,174,448 |
| Kevin Harvick | 995,274 |
| Ron Hornaday | 958,836 |
| Todd Bodine | 935,269 |
| Elton Sawyer | 925,919 |
| Randy LaJoie | 873,179 |
| Matt Kenseth | 839,305 |
| Casey Atwood | 775,615 |
| David Green | 759,269 |

## Pole winners • 16

| | |
|---|---|
| Jeff Green | 7 |
| Mark Martin | 4 |
| Jason Leffler | 3 |
| Casey Atwood | 2 |
| Kevin Harvick | 2 |
| Matt Kenseth | 2 |
| Dave Blaney | 1 |
| Todd Bodine | 1 |
| Tim Fedewa | 1 |
| Ron Fellows | 1 |
| Bobby Hamilton Jr. | 1 |
| Buckshot Jones | 1 |
| Hank Parker Jr. | 1 |
| Jeff Purvis | 1 |
| Hut Stricklin | 1 |
| Mike Skinner | 1 |

# 1999 season

| Pos. | Driver    • | Points | Starts | Poles | Wins | Top 5 | Top 10 | Winnings |
|------|-------------|--------|--------|-------|------|-------|--------|----------|
| 1. | Dale Earnhardt Jr. | 4647 | 32 | 3 | 6 | 18 | 22 | $985,195 |
| 2. | Jeff Green | 4367 | 31 | 3 | 3 | 15 | 19 | 735,040 |
| 3. | Matt Kenseth | 4327 | 32 | 2 | 4 | 14 | 20 | 859,660 |
| 4. | Todd Bodine | 4029 | 32 | 0 | 0 | 10 | 21 | 541,860 |
| 5. | Elton Sawyer | 3891 | 32 | 0 | 1 | 4 | 14 | 599,105 |
| 6. | Jeff Purvis | 3658 | 32 | 0 | 0 | 4 | 12 | 631,416 |
| 7. | Dave Blaney | 3582 | 31 | 4 | 0 | 5 | 12 | 499,660 |
| 8. | Jason Keller | 3537 | 32 | 3 | 2 | 5 | 12 | 631,850 |
| 9. | Mike McLaughlin | 3478 | 32 | 0 | 0 | 3 | 8 | 631,950 |
| 10. | Randy LaJoie | 3379 | 32 | 0 | 1 | 6 | 7 | 695,210 |

## Race winners • 15

| | |
|---|---|
| Dale Earnhardt Jr. | 6 |
| Mark Martin | 6 |
| Matt Kenseth | 4 |
| Jeff Green | 3 |
| Casey Atwood | 2 |
| Jason Keller | 2 |
| Jeff Burton | 1 |
| Jeff Gordon | 1 |
| Terry Labonte | 1 |
| Randy LaJoie | 1 |
| Joe Nemechek | 1 |
| Andy Santerre | 1 |
| Elton Sawyer | 1 |
| Mike Skinner | 1 |
| Michael Waltrip | 1 |

## Money won

| | |
|---|---|
| Dale Earnhardt Jr. | $985,195 |
| Matt Kenseth | 859,660 |
| Jeff Green | 735,040 |
| Randy LaJoie | 695,210 |
| Mike McLaughlin | 631,950 |
| Jason Keller | 631,850 |
| Jeff Purvis | 631,416 |
| Elton Sawyer | 599,105 |
| Tony Raines | 555,820 |
| Todd Bodine | 541,860 |

## Pole winners • 14

| | |
|---|---|
| Dave Blaney | 4 |
| Dale Earnhardt Jr. | 3 |
| Jeff Green | 3 |
| Jason Keller | 3 |
| Mark Martin | 3 |
| Ken Schrader | 3 |
| Casey Atwood | 2 |
| David Green | 2 |
| Matt Kenseth | 2 |
| Jeff Burton | 1 |
| Ward Burton | 1 |
| Ron Fellows | 1 |
| Hut Stricklin | 1 |
| Dick Trickle | 1 |

# 1998 season

| Pos. | Driver | Points | Starts | Poles | Wins* | Top 5 | Top 10 | Winnings |
|------|--------|--------|--------|-------|-------|-------|--------|----------|
| 1. | Dale Earnhardt Jr. | 4469 | 31 | 3 | 7 | 16 | 22 | $1,332,701 |
| 2. | Matt Kenseth | 4421 | 31 | 1 | 3 | 17 | 23 | 991,965 |
| 3. | Mike McLaughlin | 4045 | 31 | 1 | 2 | 11 | 16 | 828,313 |
| 4. | Randy LaJoie | 3543 | 31 | 0 | 1 | 7 | 12 | 783,703 |
| 5. | Elton Sawyer | 3533 | 31 | 0 | 0 | 4 | 10 | 576,089 |
| 6. | Phil Parsons | 3525 | 31 | 0 | 0 | 5 | 9 | 550,352 |
| 7. | Tim Fedewa | 3515 | 31 | 1 | 2 | 4 | 10 | 526,520 |
| 8. | Elliott Sadler | 3470 | 31 | 1 | 2 | 5 | 10 | 635,058 |
| 9. | Buckshot Jones | 3453 | 31 | 1 | 1 | 6 | 9 | 484,932 |
| 10. | Hermie Sadler | 3340 | 31 | 0 | 0 | 2 | 5 | 405,691 |

## Race winners • 16

D. Earnhardt Jr. .............................7
J. Burton ......................................3
M. Kenseth ....................................3
T. Fedewa ......................................2
M. Martin ......................................2
M. McLaughlin .................................2
J. Nemechek ...................................2
E. Sadler ......................................2
E. Berrier .....................................1
R. Fellows .....................................1
B. Jones .......................................1
B. Labonte .....................................1
R. LaJoie ......................................1
K. Lepage ......................................1
J. Spencer .....................................1
D. Trickle .....................................1

## Money won

D. Earnhardt Jr. ...................$1,332,701
M. Kenseth ...........................991,965
M. McLaughlin ........................828,313
R. LaJoie ............................783,703
E. Sadler ............................635,058
E. Sawyer ............................576,089
P. Parsons ...........................550,352
J. Purvis ............................536,415
T. Fedewa ............................526,520
B. Jones .............................484,932

## Pole winners • 24

D. Earnhardt Jr. ...............................3
C. Atwood ......................................2
J. Burton ......................................2
R. Pressley ....................................2
J. Nemechek ....................................2
T. Stewart .....................................2
J. Bessey ......................................1
D. Blaney ......................................1
T. Fedewa ......................................1
S. Grissom .....................................1
K. Grubb .......................................1
W. Grubb .......................................1
S. Hall ........................................1
B. Jones .......................................1
M. Kenseth .....................................1
B. Labonte .....................................1
K. Lepage ......................................1
M. Martin ......................................1
M. McLaughlin ..................................1
J. Purvis ......................................1
E. Sadler ......................................1
B. Said ........................................1
A. Santerre ....................................1
D. Trickle .....................................1

# 1997 season

| Pos. | | Driver | Points | Starts | Poles | Wins | Top 5 | Top 10 | Winnings |
|------|---|--------|--------|--------|-------|------|-------|--------|----------|
| 1. | | Randy LaJoie | 4,381 | 30 | 2 | 5 | 15 | 21 | $1,105,201 |
| 2. | | Todd Bodine | 4,115 | 30 | 0 | 1 | 9 | 22 | 658,295 |
| 3. | # | Steve Park | 4,080 | 30 | 1 | 3 | 12 | 20 | 677,921 |
| 4. | | Mike McLaughlin | 3,614 | 30 | 2 | 2 | 7 | 14 | 585,173 |
| 5. | | Elliott Sadler | 3,534 | 30 | 4 | 3 | 6 | 10 | 556,372 |
| 6. | | Phil Parsons | 3,523 | 30 | 0 | 0 | 5 | 12 | 411,026 |
| 7. | | Buckshot Jones | 3,437 | 30 | 0 | 0 | 5 | 14 | 446,637 |
| 8. | | Elton Sawyer | 3,419 | 30 | 0 | 0 | 6 | 9 | 349,229 |
| 9. | | Tim Fedewa | 3,398 | 30 | 1 | 0 | 4 | 11 | 346,424 |
| 10. | | Hermie Sadler | 3,340 | 30 | 2 | 0 | 2 | 7 | 328,154 |

**# Raybestos Rookie of the Year candidate**

## Race winners • 13

M. Martin ......................................6
R. LaJoie ......................................5
S. Park ........................................3
E. Sadler ......................................3
J. Burton ......................................2
M. McLaughlin .................................2
J. Nemechek ...................................2
J. Spencer .....................................2
J. Bessey ......................................1
T. Bodine ......................................1
J. Green .......................................1
B. Labonte .....................................1
D. Trickle .....................................1

## Money won

R. Lajoie ..........................$1,105,201
S. Park ..............................677,921
T. Bodine ............................658,295
M. McLaughlin ........................585,173
E. Sadler ............................556,372
B. Jones .............................446,637
P. Parsons ...........................411,026
K. Lepage ............................396,937
M. Martin ............................373,469
J. Keller ............................372,681

## Pole winners • 15

E. Sadler ......................................4
M. Martin ......................................3
J. Nemechek ....................................3
J. Green .......................................2
R. LaJoie ......................................2
M. McLaughlin ..................................2
H. Sadler ......................................2
D. Trickle .....................................2
T. Bender ......................................1
J. Bessey ......................................1
J. Burton ......................................1
T. Fedewa ......................................1
S. Hall ........................................1
S. Park ........................................1
M. Waltrip .....................................1

# 1996 season

| Pos. | Driver | Points | Starts | Poles | Wins | Top 5 | Top 10 | Winnings |
|------|--------|--------|--------|-------|------|-------|--------|----------|
| 1. | Randy LaJoie | 3,714 | 26 | 2 | 5 | 11 | 20 | $532,823 |
| 2. | David Green | 3,685 | 26 | 4 | 2 | 13 | 18 | 469,118 |
| 3. | Todd Bodine | 3,064 | 26 | 0 | 1 | 3 | 9 | 281,616 |
| 4. | Jeff Green | 3,059 | 26 | 1 | 0 | 5 | 13 | 369,285 |
| 5. | Chad Little | 2,984 | 26 | 1 | 0 | 2 | 7 | 317,394 |
| 6. | Jason Keller | 2,900 | 26 | 0 | 0 | 3 | 10 | 281,902 |
| 7. | Jeff Purvis | 2,894 | 26 | 2 | 2 | 4 | 7 | 266,026 |
| 8. | Kevin Lepage | 2,870 | 26 | 0 | 1 | 3 | 10 | 254,925 |
| 9. | Phil Parsons | 2,854 | 26 | 0 | 0 | 5 | 6 | 215,023 |
| 10. | Mike McLaughlin | 2,853 | 26 | 0 | 0 | 7 | 10 | 290,701 |

## Race winners • 13

M. Martin.................6
R. LaJoie.................5
T. Labonte................3
D. Green..................2
J. Purvis.................2
T. Bodine.................1
J. Fuller.................1
S. Grissom................1
B. Jones..................1
B. Labonte................1
K. Lepage.................1
G. Sacks..................1
K. Wallace................1

## Money won

R. Lajoie ............$532,823
D. Green .............. 469,118
C. Little ............. 317,394
M. McLaughlin ......... 290,701
J. Keller ............. 281,902
T. Bodine ............. 281,616
J. Green .............. 269,285
J. Purvis ............. 266,026
K. Lepage ............. 254,925
H. Sadler ............. 238,511

## Pole winners • 16

D. Green .................4
B. Labonte ...............3
R. Craven ................2
R. LaJoie ................2
M. Martin ................2
J. Purvis ................2
J. Fuller ................1
J. Green .................1
D. Jarrett ...............1
B. Jones .................1
C. Little ................1
S. Marlin ................1
J. Nemechek ..............1
H. Sadler ................1
D. Trickle ...............1
M. Waltrip ...............1

# 1995 season

| Pos. | Driver | Points | Starts | Poles | Wins | Top 5 | Top 10 | Winnings |
|------|--------|--------|--------|-------|------|-------|--------|----------|
| 1. | Johnny Benson | 3,688 | 26 | 0 | 2 | 12 | 19 | $469,129 |
| 2. | Chad Little | 3,284 | 26 | 0 | 6 | 11 | 13 | 529,056 |
| 3. | Mike McLaughlin | 3,273 | 26 | 1 | 1 | 9 | 14 | 317,075 |
| 4. | Jason Keller | 3,211 | 26 | 1 | 1 | 6 | 12 | 257,880 |
| 5. | Jeff Green | 3,182 | 26 | 1 | 0 | 6 | 12 | 241,187 |
| 6. | Larry Pearson | 3,029 | 26 | 1 | 2 | 5 | 8 | 276,057 |
| 7. | Tim Fedewa | 3,022 | 26 | 1 | 1 | 4 | 4 | 253,907 |
| 8. | Phil Parsons | 2,985 | 26 | 0 | 0 | 3 | 9 | 177,358 |
| 9. | Elton Sawyer | 2,952 | 26 | 1 | 0 | 2 | 9 | 250,833 |
| 10. | # Jeff Fuller | 2,845 | 26 | 0 | 0 | 1 | 6 | 174,950 |

# Raybestos Rookie of the Year candidate

## Race winners • 14

C. Little..................6
D. Jarrett.................3
M. Martin..................3
J. Benson..................2
S. Grissom.................2
L. Pearson.................2
T. Bodine..................1
T. Fedewa..................1
D. Green...................1
J. Keller..................1
T. Labonte.................1
M. McLaughlin..............1
J. Rumley..................1
K. Wallace.................1

## Money won

C. Little.............$529,056
J. Benson ............. 469,129
M. McLaughlin..........317,075
L. Pearson ............ 276,057
D. Green .............. 274,628
J. Keller ............. 257,880
T. Fedewa ............. 253,907
E. Sawyer .............250,833
J. Green .............. 241,187
M. Martin .............210,475

## Pole winners • 21

D. Green .................4
R. Bickle ................1
B. Dotter ................1
T. Fedewa ................1
J. Green..................1
D. Jarrett................1
J. Keller.................1
T. Labonte................1
R. LaJoie.................1
T. Leslie.................1
C. Markham................1
M. Martin.................1
M. McLaughlin.............1
J. Nemechek...............1
L. Pearson................1
J. Purvis.................1
S. Reeves.................1
E. Sawyer.................1
D. Setzer.................1
D. Waltrip................1
M. Waltrip................1

318

# 1994 season

| Pos. | Driver | Points | Starts | Poles | Wins | Top 5 | Top 10 | Winnings |
|------|--------|--------|--------|-------|------|-------|--------|----------|
| 1. | David Green | 3,725 | 28 | 9 | 1 | 10 | 14 | $391,670 |
| 2. | Ricky Craven | 3,679 | 28 | 1 | 2 | 8 | 16 | 273,000 |
| 3. | Chad Little | 3,662 | 28 | 0 | 0 | 10 | 14 | 234,022 |
| 4. | Kenny Wallace | 3,554 | 28 | 1 | 3 | 11 | 15 | 307,017 |
| 5. | Hermie Sadler | 3,466 | 28 | 0 | 1 | 6 | 11 | 238,204 |
| 6. # | Johnny Benson | 3,303 | 28 | 0 | 1 | 6 | 9 | 190,011 |
| 7. | Bobby Dotter | 3,299 | 28 | 0 | 0 | 2 | 8 | 176,093 |
| 8. | Larry Pearson | 3,277 | 27 | 0 | 0 | 3 | 12 | 161,859 |
| 9. # | Dennis Setzer | 3,273 | 28 | 0 | 2 | 4 | 11 | 214,246 |
| 10. | Tim Fedewa | 3,125 | 28 | 0 | 0 | 1 | 8 | 142,034 |

**# Raybestos Rookie of the Year candidate**

## Race winners • 17

| | |
|---|---|
| T. Labonte | 4 |
| M. Martin | 3 |
| K. Wallace | 3 |
| M. Wallace | 3 |
| R. Craven | 2 |
| D. Setzer | 2 |
| J. Benson | 1 |
| D. Cope | 1 |
| D. Earnhardt | 1 |
| H. Gant | 1 |
| D. Green | 1 |
| B. Labonte | 1 |
| J. Nemechek | 1 |
| P. Parsons | 1 |
| H. Sadler | 1 |
| E. Sawyer | 1 |
| K. Schrader | 1 |

## Money won

| | |
|---|---|
| D. Green | $391,670 |
| K. Wallace | 307,017 |
| R. Craven | 273,000 |
| H. Sadler | 238,204 |
| C. Little | 234,022 |
| T. Labonte | 215,438 |
| D. Setzer | 214,246 |
| M. Martin | 200,608 |
| J. Benson | 190,011 |
| T. Leslie | 188,567 |

## Pole winners • 14

| | |
|---|---|
| D. Green | 9 |
| J. Keller | 3 |
| M. Martin | 3 |
| H. Gant | 2 |
| D. Cope | 1 |
| R. Craven | 1 |
| B. Labonte | 1 |
| R. LaJoie | 1 |
| R. Pressley | 1 |
| J. Purvis | 1 |
| S. Robinson | 1 |
| M. Skinner | 1 |
| K. Wallace | 1 |
| K. Wallace | 1 |

# 1993 season

| Pos. | Driver | Points | Starts | Poles | Wins | Top 5 | Top 10 | Winnings |
|------|--------|--------|--------|-------|------|-------|--------|----------|
| 1. | Steve Grissom | 3,846 | 28 | 0 | 2 | 11 | 18 | $336,432 |
| 2. | Ricky Craven | 3,593 | 28 | 1 | 0 | 6 | 17 | 197,829 |
| 3. | David Green | 3,584 | 28 | 0 | 0 | 6 | 16 | 225,747 |
| 4. | Chuck Bown | 3,532 | 28 | 1 | 1 | 5 | 13 | 195,961 |
| 5. | Joe Nemechek | 3,443 | 28 | 3 | 0 | 8 | 11 | 254,346 |
| 6. | Ward Burton | 3,413 | 28 | 4 | 3 | 9 | 10 | 293,622 |
| 7. | Bobby Dotter | 3,406 | 28 | 2 | 0 | 3 | 8 | 160,003 |
| 8. | Robert Pressley | 3,389 | 28 | 0 | 3 | 8 | 13 | 254,723 |
| 9. | Todd Bodine | 3,387 | 28 | 1 | 3 | 9 | 13 | 240,899 |
| 10. # | Hermie Sadler | 3,362 | 28 | 0 | 1 | 4 | 8 | 149,596 |

**# Raybestos Rookie of the Year candidate**

## Race winners • 13

| | |
|---|---|
| M. Martin | 7 |
| T. Bodine | 3 |
| W. Burton | 3 |
| R. Pressley | 3 |
| D. Earnhardt | 2 |
| S. Grissom | 2 |
| M. Waltrip | 2 |
| C. Bown | 1 |
| J. Burton | 1 |
| B. Elliott | 1 |
| T. Leslie | 1 |
| J. Rumley | 1 |
| H. Sadler | 1 |

## Money won

| | |
|---|---|
| S. Grissom | $336,432 |
| W. Burton | 293,622 |
| R. Pressley | 254,723 |
| J. Nemechek | 254,346 |
| T. Bodine | 240,899 |
| M. Martin | 230,703 |
| D. Green | 225,747 |
| J. Burton | 212,843 |
| R. Craven | 197,829 |
| C. Bown | 195,961 |

## Pole winners • 16

| | |
|---|---|
| W. Burton | 4 |
| E. Irvan | 3 |
| J. Nemechek | 3 |
| B. Dotter | 2 |
| B. Elliott | 2 |
| T. Bodine | 1 |
| C. Bown | 1 |
| R. Craven | 1 |
| J. Green | 1 |
| B. Labonte | 1 |
| T. Labonte | 1 |
| T. Leslie | 1 |
| M. Martin | 1 |
| R. Mast | 1 |
| B. Miller | 1 |
| K. Schrader | 1 |

# 1992 season

| Pos. | Driver | Points | Starts | Poles | Wins | Top 5 | Top 10 | Winnings |
|------|--------|--------|--------|-------|------|-------|--------|----------|
| 1. | Joe Nemechek | 4,275 | 31 | 1 | 2 | 13 | 18 | $285,008 |
| 2. | Bobby Labonte | 4,272 | 31 | 0 | 3 | 13 | 19 | 329,985 |
| 3. | Todd Bodine | 4,212 | 31 | 2 | 3 | 11 | 19 | 284,284 |
| 4. | Jeff Gordon | 4,053 | 31 | 11 | 3 | 10 | 15 | 412,293 |
| 5. | Robert Pressley | 3,988 | 31 | 2 | 5 | 11 | 16 | 299,303 |
| 6. | Kenny Wallace | 3,966 | 31 | 2 | 1 | 7 | 15 | 166,167 |
| 7. | Butch Miller | 3,725 | 31 | 2 | 0 | 4 | 10 | 131,991 |
| 8. | Ward Burton | 3,648 | 31 | 0 | 1 | 3 | 10 | 203,116 |
| 9. | Jeff Burton | 3,609 | 31 | 0 | 1 | 4 | 10 | 202,775 |
| 10. | Tommy Houston | 3,599 | 31 | 0 | 1 | 2 | 10 | 133,065 |

## Race winners • 17

| | |
|---|---|
| R. Pressley | 5 |
| T. Bodine | 3 |
| J. Gordon | 3 |
| B. Labonte | 3 |
| H. Gant | 2 |
| E. Irvan | 2 |
| J. Nemechek | 2 |
| J. Spencer | 2 |
| J. Burton | 1 |
| W. Burton | 1 |
| B. Dotter | 1 |
| D. Earnhardt | 1 |
| S. Grissom | 1 |
| T. Houston | 1 |
| M. Martin | 1 |
| K. Wallace | 1 |
| M. Waltrip | 1 |

## Money won

| | |
|---|---|
| J. Gordon | $412,293 |
| B. Labonte | 329,985 |
| R. Pressley | 299,303 |
| J. Nemechek | 285,008 |
| T. Bodine | 284,284 |
| W. Burton | 203,116 |
| J. Burton | 202,775 |
| S. Grissom | 170,716 |
| C. Bown | 169,513 |
| K. Wallace | 166,167 |

## Pole winners • 14

| | |
|---|---|
| J. Gordon | 11 |
| T. Bodine | 2 |
| M. Martin | 2 |
| B. Miller | 2 |
| R. Pressley | 2 |
| K. Wallace | 2 |
| J. Bown | 1 |
| R. Craven | 1 |
| D. Earnhardt | 1 |
| S. Grissom | 1 |
| E. Irvan | 1 |
| J. Nemechek | 1 |
| J. Rumley | 1 |
| M. Waltrip | 1 |

# 1991 season

| Pos. | Driver | Points | Starts | Poles | Wins | Top 5 | Top 10 | Winnings |
|------|--------|--------|--------|-------|------|-------|--------|----------|
| 1. | Bobby Labonte | 4,264 | 31 | 2 | 2 | 10 | 21 | $246,368 |
| 2. | Kenny Wallace | 4,190 | 31 | 1 | 2 | 11 | 17 | 274,506 |
| 3. | Robert Pressley | 3,929 | 31 | 1 | 1 | 8 | 15 | 171,256 |
| 4. | Chuck Bown | 3,922 | 31 | 5 | 3 | 9 | 14 | 244,739 |
| 5. | Jimmy Hensley | 3,916 | 31 | 4 | 3 | 9 | 17 | 227,739 |
| 6. | Joe Nemechek | 3,902 | 31 | 0 | 0 | 5 | 16 | 124,255 |
| 7. | Todd Bodine | 3,825 | 31 | 2 | 1 | 7 | 15 | 136,273 |
| 8. | Tommy Houston | 3,777 | 31 | 0 | 0 | 5 | 11 | 163,827 |
| 9. | Tom Peck | 3,746 | 31 | 0 | 0 | 2 | 13 | 163,189 |
| 10. | Steve Grissom | 3,689 | 31 | 1 | 1 | 7 | 13 | 152,206 |

## Race winners • 16

| | |
|---|---|
| H. Gant | 5 |
| C. Bown | 3 |
| D. Earnhardt | 3 |
| J. Hensley | 3 |
| D. Jarrett | 3 |
| R. Craven | 2 |
| B. Labonte | 2 |
| K. Wallace | 2 |
| T. Bodine | 1 |
| J. Burton | 1 |
| D. Green | 1 |
| S. Grissom | 1 |
| E. Irvan | 1 |
| T. Labonte | 1 |
| B. Miller | 1 |
| R. Pressley | 1 |

## Money won

| | |
|---|---|
| K. Wallace | $274,506 |
| B. Labonte | 246,368 |
| C. Bown | 244,739 |
| J. Hensley | 227,969 |
| R. Pressley | 171,256 |
| T. Houston | 163,827 |
| T. Peck | 163,189 |
| S. Grissom | 152,206 |
| J. Burton | 144,798 |
| T. Bodine | 136,273 |

## Pole winners • 20

| | |
|---|---|
| C. Bown | 5 |
| J. Hensley | 4 |
| T. Bodine | 2 |
| J. Burton | 2 |
| B. Labonte | 2 |
| W. Burton | 1 |
| R. Craven | 1 |
| D. Earnhardt | 1 |
| H. Gant | 1 |
| J. Gordon | 1 |
| D. Green | 1 |
| S. Grissom | 1 |
| E. Irvan | 1 |
| T. Labonte | 1 |
| D. Mader | 1 |
| B. Miller | 1 |
| R. Pressley | 1 |
| E. Sawyer | 1 |
| J. Sprague | 1 |
| K. Wallace | 1 |

# 1990 season

| Pos. | Driver | Points | Starts | Poles | Wins | Top 5 | Top 10 | Winnings |
|---|---|---|---|---|---|---|---|---|
| 1. | Chuck Bown | 4,372 | 31 | 4 | 6 | 13 | 18 | $323,399 |
| 2. | Jimmy Hensley | 4,172 | 31 | 4 | 1 | 9 | 17 | 201,877 |
| 3. | Steve Grissom | 3,982 | 31 | 1 | 4 | 11 | 15 | 166,842 |
| 4. | Bobby Labonte | 3,977 | 31 | 2 | 0 | 6 | 17 | 136,936 |
| 5. | Tom Peck | 3,868 | 31 | 0 | 0 | 2 | 12 | 109,821 |
| 6. | Tommy Ellis | 3,829 | 31 | 3 | 1 | 5 | 13 | 205,863 |
| 7. | Kenny Wallace | 3,829 | 31 | 1 | 0 | 4 | 14 | 112,781 |
| 8. | L.D. Ottinger | 3,693 | 31 | 0 | 1 | 5 | 7 | 156,674 |
| 9. | Tommy Houston | 3,667 | 31 | 0 | 4 | 9 | 14 | 200,350 |
| 10. | Rick Mast | 3,617 | 31 | 1 | 3 | 8 | 10 | 127,965 |

## Race winners • 13

C. Bown ......................................6
S. Grissom..................................4
T. Houston..................................4
R. Mast.......................................3
H. Gant.......................................2
D. Jarrett....................................2
M. Waltrip...................................2
J. Burton.....................................1
T. Ellis........................................1
J. Hensley...................................1
S. Marlin.....................................1
M. Martin....................................1
L. Ottinger..................................1

## Money won

C. Bown .....................$323,399
T. Ellis .......................... 205,863
J. Hensley .................... 201,877
T. Houston .................... 200,350
S. Grissom .................... 166,842
L. Ottinger .................... 156,674
B. Hamilton ................... 156,281
E. Sawyer ..................... 144,699
B. Labonte..................... 136,936
R. Mast ......................... 127,965

## Pole winners • 17

C. Bown ......................................4
J. Hensley ..................................4
T. Ellis........................................3
R. Craven ...................................2
B. Labonte .................................2
M. Waltrip ..................................2
D. Allison ...................................1
E. Berrier ...................................1
J. Burton ....................................1
H. Gant ......................................1
S. Grissom .................................1
D. Mader ....................................1
R. Mast ......................................1
G. Sacks ....................................1
D. Trickle ...................................1
K. Wallace ..................................1
D. Waltrip ...................................1

# 1989 season

| Pos. | | Driver | Points | Starts | Poles | Wins | Top 5 | Top 10 | Winnings |
|---|---|---|---|---|---|---|---|---|---|
| 1. | | Rob Moroso | 4,001 | 29 | 6 | 4 | 12 | 16 | $346,849 |
| 2. | | Tommy Houston | 3,946 | 29 | 1 | 3 | 12 | 17 | 184,734 |
| 3. | | Tommy Ellis | 3,945 | 29 | 1 | 3 | 11 | 19 | 202,141 |
| 4. | | L.D. Ottinger | 3,916 | 29 | 0 | 1 | 7 | 16 | 109,821 |
| 5. | | Jack Ingram | 3,802 | 29 | 0 | 0 | 7 | 14 | 144,436 |
| 6. | # | Kenny Wallace | 3,750 | 29 | 3 | 0 | 4 | 16 | 88,423 |
| 7. | | Rick Mast | 3,558 | 29 | 2 | 2 | 9 | 13 | 127,028 |
| 8. | | Ronald Cooper | 3,557 | 29 | 0 | 1 | 4 | 10 | 106,068 |
| 9. | | Chuck Bown | 3,349 | 29 | 2 | 0 | 5 | 12 | 103,294 |
| 10. | | Tom Peck | 3,171 | 28 | 0 | 0 | 2 | 7 | 58,441 |

# Raybestos Rookie of the Year candidate

## Race winners • 18

R. Moroso ...................................4
T. Ellis........................................3
T. Houston..................................3
J. Spencer..................................3
D. Earnhardt...............................2
H. Gant.......................................2
R. Mast.......................................2
R. Wilson....................................2
G. Bodine....................................1
R. Cooper....................................1
B. Hamilton.................................1
B. Hillin.......................................1
M. Martin....................................1
L. Ottinger...................................1
R. Pressley..................................1
K. Schrader.................................1
D. Waltrip....................................1
M. Waltrip....................................1

## Money won

R. Moroso ...................$346,849
T. Ellis .......................... 202,141
T. Houston .................... 184,735
J. Ingram ...................... 144,436
R. Mast ......................... 127,028
L. Ottinger .................... 109,821
R. Cooper ..................... 106,068
J. Spencer .................... 103,726
C. Bown ........................ 103,294
M. Waltrip ....................... 90,487

## Pole winners • 17

R. Moroso ...................................6
M. Waltrip ...................................4
K. Wallace ..................................3
C. Bown ......................................2
R. Mast ......................................2
G. Bodine ...................................1
T. Ellis........................................1
H. Gant ......................................1
J. Hensley ..................................1
T. Houston ..................................1
D. Jarrett ....................................1
M. Martin ....................................1
G. Sacks ....................................1
K. Schrader ................................1
J. Spencer ..................................1
M. Shepherd ...............................1
R. Wilson ....................................1

# 1988 season

| Pos. | Driver | Points | Starts | Poles | Wins | Top 5 | Top 10 | Winnings |
|------|--------|--------|--------|-------|------|-------|--------|----------|
| 1. | Tommy Ellis | 4,310 | 30 | 5 | 3 | 12 | 20 | $200,003 |
| 2. | Rob Moroso | 4,071 | 30 | 2 | 2 | 10 | 19 | 181,618 |
| 3. | Mike Alexander | 4,053 | 30 | 1 | 1 | 10 | 17 | 151,303 |
| 4. | Larry Pearson | 4,050 | 30 | 5 | 3 | 13 | 16 | 164,593 |
| 5. | Tommy Houston | 4,042 | 30 | 2 | 3 | 11 | 17 | 123,385 |
| 6. | Jimmy Hensley | 3,904 | 30 | 0 | 1 | 7 | 13 | 125,615 |
| 7. | Jimmy Spencer | 3,839 | 30 | 0 | 0 | 5 | 13 | 64,112 |
| 8. | Rick Mast | 3,809 | 30 | 0 | 2 | 5 | 13 | 116,557 |
| 9. | L.D. Ottinger | 3,732 | 30 | 1 | 0 | 5 | 11 | 66,640 |
| 10. | Jack Ingram | 3,610 | 30 | 0 | 0 | 10 | 12 | 100,497 |

## Race winners • 18

| | |
|---|---|
| H. Gant | 5 |
| T. Ellis | 3 |
| T. Houston | 3 |
| L. Pearson | 3 |
| R. Mast | 2 |
| R. Moroso | 2 |
| M. Alexander | 1 |
| B. Allison | 1 |
| G. Bodine | 1 |
| D. Earnhardt | 1 |
| J. Hensley | 1 |
| B. Hillin | 1 |
| D. Jarrett | 1 |
| M. Martin | 1 |
| D. McCabe | 1 |
| M. Shepherd | 1 |
| D. Waltrip | 1 |
| M. Waltrip | 1 |

## Money won

| | |
|---|---|
| T. Ellis | $200,003 |
| R. Moroso | 181,618 |
| L. Pearson | 164,593 |
| M. Alexander | 151,303 |
| J. Hensley | 125,615 |
| T. Houston | 123,385 |
| R. Mast | 116,557 |
| J. Ingram | 100,497 |
| H. Gant | 88,847 |
| L. Ottinger | 66,640 |

## Pole winners • 12

| | |
|---|---|
| T. Ellis | 5 |
| L. Pearson | 5 |
| H. Gant | 4 |
| G. Bodine | 3 |
| T. Houston | 2 |
| R. Moroso | 2 |
| M. Alexander | 1 |
| B. Dotter | 1 |
| D. Earnhardt | 1 |
| D. Jarrett | 1 |
| L. Ottinger | 1 |
| M. Swaim | 1 |

# 1987 season

| Pos. | Driver | Points | Starts | Poles | Wins | Top 5 | Top 10 | Winnings |
|------|--------|--------|--------|-------|------|-------|--------|----------|
| 1. | Larry Pearson | 3,999 | 27 | 3 | 6 | 16 | 20 | $185,124 |
| 2. | Jimmy Hensley | 3,617 | 27 | 2 | 1 | 8 | 14 | 66,505 |
| 3. | Brett Bodine | 3,611 | 27 | 5 | 0 | 8 | 17 | 115,889 |
| 4. | Jack Ingram | 3,598 | 27 | 0 | 1 | 6 | 14 | 105,530 |
| 5. | Mike Alexander | 3,497 | 27 | 1 | 1 | 8 | 13 | 51,598 |
| 6. | Dale Jarrett | 3,444 | 27 | 0 | 1 | 5 | 11 | 84,025 |
| 7. | Brad Teague | 3,391 | 27 | 0 | 1 | 1 | 9 | 94,960 |
| 8. | Mark Martin | 3,349 | 27 | 6 | 3 | 5 | 13 | 65,208 |
| 9. | Rick Mast | 3,319 | 27 | 1 | 2 | 4 | 9 | 69,704 |
| 10. | L.D. Ottinger | 3,318 | 27 | 0 | 0 | 6 | 10 | 95,440 |

## Race winners • 15

| | |
|---|---|
| L. Pearson | 6 |
| H. Gant | 3 |
| M. Martin | 3 |
| M. Shepherd | 3 |
| R. Mast | 2 |
| M. Alexander | 1 |
| J. Aube | 1 |
| G. Bodine | 1 |
| D. Earnhardt | 1 |
| T. Ellis | 1 |
| J. Hensley | 1 |
| J. Ingram | 1 |
| D. Jarrett | 1 |
| L. Pollard | 1 |
| B. Teague | 1 |

## Money won

| | |
|---|---|
| L. Pearson | $256,372 |
| B. Bodine | 138,551 |
| J. Ingram | 124,929 |
| B. Teague | 106,172 |
| L. Ottinger | 102,702 |
| D. Jarrett | 97,499 |
| J. Hensley | 94,504 |
| T. Houston | 90,340 |
| H. Gant | 85,722 |
| D. Waltrip | 77,684 |

## Pole winners • 13

| | |
|---|---|
| M. Martin | 6 |
| B. Bodine | 5 |
| L. Pearson | 3 |
| H. Gant | 2 |
| J. Hensley | 2 |
| T. Houston | 2 |
| M. Alexander | 1 |
| G. Bodine | 1 |
| D. Dion | 1 |
| D. Earnhardt | 1 |
| R. Ingram | 1 |
| R. Mast | 1 |
| R. Wallace | 1 |

# 1986 season

| Pos. | Driver | Points | Starts | Poles | Wins | Top 5 | Top 10 | Winnings |
|---|---|---|---|---|---|---|---|---|
| 1. | Larry Pearson | 4,551 | 31 | 1 | 1 | 17 | 24 | $127,488 |
| 2. | Brett Bodine | 4,531 | 31 | 8 | 2 | 16 | 24 | 146,233 |
| 3. | Jack Ingram | 4,301 | 29 | 1 | 5 | 16 | 22 | 152,229 |
| 4. | Dale Jarrett | 4,261 | 31 | 5 | 1 | 14 | 19 | 71,463 |
| 5. | L.D. Ottinger | 4,153 | 31 | 0 | 1 | 12 | 20 | 79,363 |
| 6. | Tommy Houston | 4,121 | 31 | 4 | 4 | 12 | 18 | 108,038 |
| 7. | Ronnie Silver | 3,967 | 31 | 0 | 1 | 9 | 12 | 85,584 |
| 8. | Jimmy Hensley | 3,950 | 31 | 0 | 0 | 3 | 9 | 86,019 |
| 9. | Charlie Luck | 3,847 | 31 | 0 | 0 | 1 | 14 | 51,518 |
| 10. | Larry Pollard | 3,726 | 30 | 0 | 0 | 1 | 11 | 45,029 |

### Race winners • 13

D. Earnhardt ................5
J. Ingram ................5
T. Houston ................4
M. Shepherd ................4
D. Waltrip ................4
B. Bodine ................2
C. Bown ................1
D. Jarrett ................1
B. Miller ................1
L. Ottinger ................1
L. Pearson ................1
T. Richmond ................1
R. Silver ................1

### Money won

L. Pearson ................$184,344
J. Ingram ................ 174,482
B. Bodine ................ 173,181
D. Earnhardt ................ 150,558
T. Houston ................ 121,706
L. Ottinger ................ 96,476
R. Silver ................ 96,262
J. Hensley ................ 95,148
D. Jarrett ................ 90,701
D. Waltrip ................ 87,873

### Pole winners • 14

B. Bodine ................8
D. Jarrett ................5
T. Houston ................4
T. Richmond ................3
D. Waltrip ................2
M. Alexander ................1
D. Allison ................1
G. Bodine ................1
D. Earnhardt ................1
J. Ingram ................1
T. Labonte ................1
T. Labonte ................1
R. Porter ................1
M. Shepherd ................1

# 1985 season

| Pos. | Driver | Points | Starts | Poles | Wins | Top 5 | Top 10 | Winnings |
|---|---|---|---|---|---|---|---|---|
| 1. | Jack Ingram | 4,106 | 27 | 2 | 5 | 17 | 22 | $115,798 |
| 2. | Jimmy Hensley | 4,077 | 27 | 4 | 3 | 15 | 23 | 92,808 |
| 3. | Larry Pearson | 3,951 | 27 | 0 | 2 | 15 | 19 | 101,438 |
| 4. | Tommy Houston | 3,936 | 27 | 4 | 1 | 17 | 21 | 81,258 |
| 5. | Dale Jarrett | 3,774 | 27 | 0 | 0 | 9 | 17 | 51,323 |
| 6. | L.D. Ottinger | 3,732 | 27 | 0 | 0 | 6 | 19 | 65,748 |
| 7. | Rick Mast | 3,589 | 27 | 0 | 0 | 5 | 15 | 52,380 |
| 8. | Ronnie Silver | 3,425 | 27 | 0 | 1 | 3 | 13 | 49,758 |
| 9. | Larry Pollard | 3,197 | 24 | 0 | 0 | 2 | 12 | 30,235 |
| 10. | Eddie Falk | 3,044 | 27 | 0 | 0 | 0 | 4 | 30,145 |

### Race winners • 12

T. Ellis ................5
J. Ingram ................5
B. Bodine ................3
J. Hensley ................3
D. Waltrip ................3
L. Pearson ................2
G. Bodine ................1
D. Earnhardt ................1
T. Houston ................1
T. Labonte ................1
T. Richmond ................1
R. Silver ................1

### Money won

J. Ingram ................$164,709
L. Pearson ................ 120,453
J. Hensley ................ 115,963
T. Houston ................ 97,932
L. Ottinger ................ 77,291
T. Ellis ................ 73,936
G. Bodine ................ 71,433
D. Jarrett ................ 65,566
R. Mast ................ 61,977
R. Silver ................ 57,470

### Pole winners • 13

J. Hensley ................4
T. Houston ................4
B. Bodine ................3
T. Ellis ................3
G. Bodine ................2
J. Ingram ................2
T. Richmond ................2
B. Teague ................2
R. Bouchard ................1
D. Earnhardt ................1
A. Kulwicki ................1
M. Porter ................1
R. Wallace ................1

# 1984 season

| Pos. | Driver | Points | Starts | Poles | Wins | Top 5 | Top 10 | Winnings |
|---|---|---|---|---|---|---|---|---|
| 1. | Sam Ard | 4,552 | 28 | 7 | 8 | 24 | 26 | $217,531 |
| 2. | Jack Ingram | 4,126 | 29 | 0 | 8 | 17 | 19 | 122,953 |
| 3. | Tommy Houston | 4,070 | 29 | 4 | 2 | 15 | 22 | 104,778 |
| 4. | Dale Jarrett | 4,014 | 29 | 1 | 0 | 9 | 19 | 72,503 |
| 5. | Ronnie Silver | 3,398 | 26 | 0 | 0 | 8 | 14 | 52,133 |
| 6. | Joe Thurman | 3,221 | 27 | 0 | 0 | 2 | 8 | 51,383 |
| 7. | Charlie Luck | 3,172 | 26 | 0 | 0 | 1 | 9 | 40,279 |
| 8. | L.D. Ottinger | 3,069 | 26 | 3 | 0 | 3 | 10 | 43,264 |
| 9. | Jeff Hensley | 3,032 | 26 | 0 | 0 | 1 | 7 | 29,629 |
| 10. | Bob Shreeves | 2,869 | 25 | 0 | 0 | 0 | 7 | 33,739 |

## Race winners • 10

S. Ard ....................8
J. Ingram ................8
M. Shepherd .............3
R. Bouchard .............2
T. Houston ..............2
D. Waltrip ..............2
B. Allison .............1
G. Bodine ..............1
T. Ellis ...............1
L. Pearson .............1

## Money won

S. Ard .....................$217,531
J. Ingram ...................122,953
T. Houston ..................104,778
D. Jarrett ...................72,503
R. Silver ....................52,133
J. Thurman ...................51,383
D. Waltrip ...................50,280
L. Ottinger ..................43,264
G. Bodine ....................42,950
C. Luck ......................40,279

## Pole winners • 11

S. Ard ..................7
T. Ellis ................4
T. Houston ..............4
G. Bodine ...............3
R. Bouchard .............3
L. Ottinger .............3
E. Falk .................1
D. Jarrett ..............1
T. Richmond .............1
M. Shepherd .............1
D. Trickle ..............1

# 1983 season

| Pos. | Driver | Points | Starts | Poles | Wins | Top 5 | Top 10 | Winnings |
|---|---|---|---|---|---|---|---|---|
| 1. | Sam Ard | 5,454 | 35 | 10 | 10 | 23 | 30 | $192,362 |
| 2. | Jack Ingram | 5,367 | 35 | 1 | 5 | 23 | 29 | 126,956 |
| 3. | Tommy Houston | 4,933 | 35 | 1 | 4 | 14 | 22 | 104,561 |
| 4. | Tommy Ellis | 4,929 | 35 | 7 | 7 | 16 | 21 | 97,251 |
| 5. | Dale Jarrett | 4,837 | 35 | 4 | 0 | 17 | 21 | 55,360 |
| 6. | Ronnie Silver | 4,058 | 32 | 0 | 0 | 6 | 16 | 35,705 |
| 7. | Pete Silva | 3,945 | 31 | 0 | 0 | 6 | 13 | 42,900 |
| 8. | Jimmy Hensley | 3,716 | 29 | 0 | 0 | 5 | 16 | 26,305 |
| 9. | Eddie Falk | 3,617 | 30 | 0 | 0 | 1 | 13 | 21,162 |
| 10. | Jeff Hensley | 3,444 | 28 | 0 | 0 | 1 | 9 | 18,875 |

## Race winners • 10

S. Ard .....................10
T. Ellis ....................7
J. Ingram ...................5
T. Houston ..................4
D. Earnhardt ................2
B. Lindley ..................2
M. Shepherd .................2
N. Bonnett ..................1
R. Rudd .....................1
D. Waltrip ..................1

## Money won

S. Ard .....................$192,362
J. Ingram ...................126,956
T. Houston ..................104,561
T. Ellis .....................97,251
D. Jarrett ...................55,360
B. Lindley ...................44,488
P. Silva .....................42,900
P. Parsons ...................40,976
M. Shepherd ..................36,570
R. Silver ....................35,705

## Pole winners • 11

S. Ard .....................10
T. Ellis ....................7
D. Jarrett ..................4
P. Parsons ..................4
B. Lindley ..................3
D. Earnhardt ................1
T. Houston ..................1
J. Ingram ...................1
D. Pearson ..................1
L. Pearson ..................1
M. Shepherd .................1

# 1982 season

| Pos. | Driver | Points | Starts | Poles | Wins | Top 5 | Top 10 | Winnings |
|---|---|---|---|---|---|---|---|---|
| 1. | Jack Ingram | 4,495 | 29 | 1 | 7 | 23 | 24 | $122,100 |
| 2. | Sam Ard | 4,446 | 29 | 7 | 4 | 20 | 23 | 122,099 |
| 3. | Tommy Ellis | 3,873 | 29 | 5 | 1 | 13 | 16 | 78,782 |
| 4. | Tommy Houston | 3,827 | 29 | 0 | 2 | 11 | 18 | 67,792 |
| 5. | Phil Parsons | 3,783 | 29 | 2 | 1 | 5 | 18 | 62,839 |
| 6. | Dale Jarrett | 3,332 | 29 | 0 | 0 | 1 | 15 | 27,260 |
| 7. | Pete Silva | 2,349 | 18 | 0 | 0 | 5 | 8 | 18,127 |
| 8. | Jimmy Lawson | 2,106 | 18 | 0 | 0 | 0 | 5 | 12,458 |
| 9. | Bob Shreeves | 1,928 | 15 | 1 | 0 | 5 | 8 | 13,785 |
| 10. | Butch Lindley | 1,581 | 14 | 2 | 4 | 9 | 10 | 38,170 |

## Race winners • 14

J. Ingram ...................7
S. Ard ......................4
B. Lindley ..................4
D. Earnhardt ................2
T. Houston ..................2
M. Shepherd .................2
G. Bodine ...................1
T. Ellis ....................1
H. Gant .....................1
P. Parsons ..................1
D. Pearsons .................1
J. Ruttman ..................1
J. Settlemyre ...............1
D. Waltrip ..................1

## Money won

J. Ingram ...................$122,100
S. Ard .......................122,099
T. Ellis ......................78,782
T. Houston ....................67,792
P. Parsons ....................62,839
B. Lindley ....................38,170
D. Earnhardt ..................29,980
G. Bodine .....................29,005
D. Jarrett ....................27,260
M. Shepherd ...................23,955

## Pole winners • 12

S. Ard ......................7
T. Ellis ....................5
H. Gant .....................3
G. Bodine ...................2
B. Lindley ..................2
P. Parsons ..................2
D. Pearson ..................2
M. Shepherd .................2
J. Ingram ...................1
G. Neice ....................1
M. Porter ...................1
B. Shreeves .................1

NASCAR Craftsman Truck Series

# Milestones

**1993** Four off-road racing enthusiasts—Dick Landfield, Jimmy Smith, Jim Venable and Frank "Scoop" Vessels—build prototype racing pickup truck.

**February 1994** Group seeks NASCAR sanction for truck racing.

**May 14, 1994** NASCAR President Bill France announces creation of NASCAR Craftsman Truck Series, then titled NASCAR SuperTruck Series, during news conference at Sears Point Raceway in Sonoma, Calif.

**July 30, 1994** First of four demonstration races is held at Mesa Marin Raceway in Bakersfield, Calif. P.J. Jones is first NASCAR Craftsman Truck Series winner in a Ford owned by Vessels.

**Late 1994** Craftsman agrees to present series. A 20-race schedule is released. Total posted awards of $1.6 million are announced, along with complete national television package.

**Nov. 20, 1994** Rick Carelli wins first of three preview races held at Tucson Raceway Park. Each is broadcast live by TNN as part of its Winter Heat package.

**Feb. 5, 1995** NASCAR Craftsman Truck Series begins at Phoenix International Raceway. Mike Skinner, driving the GM Goodwrench Service Chevrolet is the first winner of a championship race, beating former NASCAR Cup Series champion Terry Labonte by just 0.09 seconds.

**June 3, 1995** Skinner's Ford Credit 200 victory at the Louisville Motor Speedway makes him first in the series to win two consecutive races.

**June 23, 1995** Joe Ruttman and Irvan-Simo Racing give Ford its first series win, in the Pizza Plus 150 at the Bristol Motor Speedway.

**July 15, 1995** Butch Miller, Raybestos Ford, edges Skinner in closest finish to date—0.0001-seconds—at Colorado National Speedway.

**July 29, 1995** Ron Hornaday Jr. drives Teresa Earnhardt's Papa John's Pizza Chevrolet to victory in series' first road race, at Heartland Park Topeka.

**Aug. 17, 1995** Hornaday's win at Flemington Speedway clinches first series manufacturer championship for Chevrolet.

**Oct. 27, 1995** Skinner wins first NASCAR Craftsman Truck Series championship at Phoenix, by 126 points over Ruttman. Championship is worth $428,096.

**Nov. 18, 1995** Second season of 24 races announced during awards banquet at Fairmont Hotel in San Francisco. Total posted awards increase to $4 million.

**February 1996** Sears Craftsman agrees to become title sponsor of NASCAR Craftsman Truck Series under new, three-year agreement.

**March 17, 1996** Dave Rezendes wins then-record $44,550 with victory in Florida Dodge Dealers 400 at Homestead-Miami Speedway.

**May 3, 1996** Rich Bickle, qualifying for the Craftsman 200 at Portland Speedway, drives Richard Petty-owned Cummins Engine Company Dodge to company's first fast qualifying time since the late 1970s in a major NASCAR series.

**June 9, 1996** Skinner's road racing victory, at Heartland Park Topeka, completes first three-wins-in-a-row streak in series history.

**July 6, 1996** 17 lead changes in Sears Auto Center 200 at The Milwaukee Mile sets series record.

**Sept. 8, 1996** Hornaday's New Hampshire International Speedway victory makes him first in series to win on short track, road course and super-speedway in single season.

**Oct. 26, 1996** Crowd of 58,000 for GM Goodwrench/Delco Battery 300 at Phoenix International Raceway sets series attendance record.

**Nov. 1, 1996** Bryan Reffner becomes fastest driver in series history, winning the Busch Pole at the Las Vegas Motor Speedway with a lap of 157.909 mph in the 1-800-COLLECT Ford. Sixty-one teams which attempt to qualify for the Carquest Auto Parts 420K is a series record.

**Nov. 3, 1996** Jack Sprague, driving the Quaker State Chevrolet, wins fastest race in series history at 120.782 mph. His $79,825 sets a single-race money won mark. Reffner becomes first Rookie of the Year.

**Nov. 16, 1996** Hornaday, celebrating 1996 NASCAR Craftsman Truck Series championship at Fairmont Hotel, sets season winnings mark of $625,634. Skinner's third-place awards make him first series millionaire. A $6 million, 26-race schedule is announced for the 1997 season, including events at Walt Disney World Speedway, the California Speedway and Texas Motor Speedway.

**Jan. 19, 1997** Walt Disney World Speedway near Orlando, Fla. hosts opening race of third season.

**March 1, 1997** Hornaday's win at Tucson Raceway Park makes him first competitor to win in all three seasons of the NASCAR Craftsman Truck Series.

**March 16, 1997** Kenny Irwin becomes first Rookie-of-the-Year candidate to win a race, capturing the Florida Dodge Dealers 400 at Homestead-Miami Speedway.

**May 24, 1997** Dodge gets its first victory in the NASCAR Craftsman Truck Series as Tony Raines wins Western Auto/Parts America 200 at I-70 Speedway in Kansas City, Mo.

**June 6, 1997** Mike Bliss, who laps Texas Motor Speedway at 175.667 mph, heads fastest field in series history. Starting field for the Pronto Auto Parts 400 averages 171.209. Hornaday, despite failing to finish, becomes NASCAR Craftsman Truck Series leading money winner at $1,051,221.

**Aug. 9, 1997** Hornaday's fifth consecutive short track victory, at Flemington Speedway, gives the Palmdale, Calif. driver the all time series win record at 17.

**Oct. 18, 1997** Bliss wins fastest race in series history, averaging 137.195 mph in The No Fear Challenge at the California Speedway.

**Nov. 9, 1997** Sprague becomes third different NASCAR Craftsman Truck

Series champion by a record, 232 points over Bickle. Ruttman's victory in the Carquest Auto Parts 420K is worth a record $83,000.

**Dec. 13, 1997** Sprague boosts the single-season, money-won record to $880,835. He also becomes the tour's all-time leading money winner. Five different drivers—Sprague, Hornaday, Ruttman, Skinner and Bliss—now have won more than $1 million during their NCTS careers.

**Jan. 18, 1998** Hornaday becomes the first driver to win a race in all four years of the NASCAR Craftsman Truck Series.

**June 20, 1998** Sprague records 21st consecutive top-10 finish at Bristol Motor Speedway. The mark eventually reaches 23. Hornaday's victory is his 13th on a short track, most in series history.

**July 18, 1998** Sprague wins the fastest race in series history, capturing The No Fear Challenge at California Speedway with an average speed of 141.844 mph.

**July 25, 1998** Series adopts "live" pit stop format for most venues.

**Sept. 19, 1998** Sprague finishes fourth at Gateway International Raceway to become the tour's first $2 million career winner.

**Oct. 10, 1998** Tom Hubert wins Bud Pole for Kragen/Exide 151 at Sears Point Raceway. He's the record 15th different driver to record a fast time.

**Oct. 18, 1998** Dennis Setzer's victory at Mesa Marin Raceway establishes a single-season record for series winners—14.

**Oct. 24, 1998** Bliss wins GM Goodwrench Service Plus/AC Delco 300 at Phoenix International Raceway to become the series' 12th consecutive different winner.

**Nov. 8, 1998** Hornaday becomes first two-time NASCAR Craftsman Truck Series champion, beating Sprague by three points. The pair finishes one-two in the season-ending Sam's Town 250 at Las Vegas Motor Speedway, with Sprague winning a race record $84,725.

**Dec. 11, 1998** Hornaday collects nearly $400,000 in post-season awards to set career and single season money won records of $2,442,586 and $915,407, respectively.

**March 20, 1999** The CART FedEx Championship Series and NASCAR Craftsman Truck Series share a weekend for the first time.

**March 27, 1999** Hornaday becomes first driver to win in all five seasons of the series when he captures Chevy Trucks NASCAR 150 at Phoenix International Raceway.

**April 3, 1999** Hornaday wins the series' 100th race, at Evergreen Speedway near Seattle, and $100,000 Craftsman bonus award.

**June 11, 1999** Dodge scores first NASCAR Craftsman Truck Series superspeedway victory when Dennis Setzer captures Pronto Auto Parts 400 at Texas Motor Speedway.

**July 24, 1999** The NASCAR Craftsman Truck Series visits Michigan Speedway for the first time. Greg Biffle wins the goracing.com 200.

**Sept. 13, 1999** Chevrolet, Dodge and Ford drivers participate in NASCAR test at Daytona International Speedway to lay the groundwork for a Speedweeks visit to the historic venue in 2000.

**Sept. 24, 1999** Biffle's victory in The Orleans 250 at Las Vegas Motor Speedway hands Ford its first series manufacturer championship. Biffle's ninth win of the year sets a single-season record.

**Oct. 15, 1999** The fastest field in NASCAR Craftsman Truck Series history, qualifying at an average speed of 175.373 mph, takes the green flag at Texas Motor Speedway.

**Oct. 30, 1999** Three drivers – Biffle, Sprague and Setzer – enter the season finale just 25 points apart in the series' closest three-way showdown. Sprague wins NAPA Auto Parts 200 to clinch his second NCTS title and post his 100th lead lap finish. His eight-point cushion, over Biffle, was the tour's second-tightest.

**Dec. 10, 1999** Postseason awards distributed at the fifth Annual Champion's Banquet make Sprague and Hornaday the first drivers to win $3 million in the NASCAR Craftsman Truck Series.

**Feb. 18, 2000** The World Center of Racing, Daytona International Speedway, hosts its first NASCAR Craftsman Truck Series event. The lead changes a record, 31 times before Mike Wallace drafts past Andy Houston entering the final set of turns of the 100th and final lap.

**June 17, 2000** The NASCAR Craftsman Truck Series opens Kentucky Speedway to the delight of a sell-out crowd.

**July 8, 2000** Kurt Busch becomes the first rookie to win back-to-back races on the series.

**Oct. 13, 2000** Greg Biffle closes out the championship race for the first time prior to the final race of the season. He is the first champion to drive a Ford to the title. It is the first NASCAR championship for team owner Jack Roush.

**Nov. 2, 2000** Greg Biffle is the first one-season millionaire, winning $1,002,510. He is the youngest champion at 30 years nine months 22 days and the first who didn't compete on the tour in 1995.

**April 4, 2001** Series celebrates 150th race at Martinsville Speedway in Virginia. Scott Riggs scores first NCTS victory for Jim Smith, an owner who has fielded at least one entry in every event.

**June 2, 2001** Dodge's eighth consecutive victory, at Dover Downs International Speedway, matches series record set in 1995 by Chevrolet.

**June 8, 2001** In winning for the first time at Texas Motor Speedway, Jack Sprague becomes the only competitor to win in six consecutive seasons on the NASCAR Craftsman Truck Series.

**June 29, 2001** Jack Sprague records 16th career Bud Pole at The Milwaukee Mile to become the series' all-time qualifying leader. He extends the mark to 20 by season's end.

**July 7, 2001** Ricky Hendrick becomes youngest winner In NCTS history (21 years three months five days) with his victory at Kansas Speedway.

**July 14, 2001** Jack Sprague finishes third at Kentucky Speedway and becomes the first $4 million winner in NCTS history.

**Sept. 28, 2001** Ted Musgrave's victory at South Boston Speedway gives Dodge its first NCTS manufacturer title.

**Oct. 14, 2001** Ted Musgrave's sixth win of 2001 gives Ultra Motorsports 11 victories on the season, breaking Roush Racing's record set in 1999.

**Nov. 3, 2001** By starting the final race of the season at California Speedway, Jack Sprague wraps up an unprecedented third NASCAR Craftsman Truck Series championship.

**2002** The NASCAR Craftsman Truck Series, the NASCAR Cup Series and NASCAR Busch Series, Grand National Division, will begin and end the season on the same weekend at the same tracks – Daytona International Speedway and Homestead-Miami Speedway, respectively.

**Feb. 15, 2002** Robert Pressley becomes second competitor (and first since the series' inaugural race) to win in his first NASCAR Craftsman Truck Series appearance. Pressley wins the Florida Dodge Dealers 250 at Daytona International Speedway.

**April 15, 2002** Winning from the 33rd starting position at Martinsville Speedway, Dennis Setzer races to victory from deepest in the field for a series race. Setzer is only the second provisional starter to win on the series.

**Sept. 13, 2002** Brendan Gaughan, the Raybestos Rookie-of-the-Year, completes sweep of two series races held at Texas Motor Speedway. Gaughan is the first repeat winner of any NASCAR race at the 1.5-mile superspeedway.

**Oct. 13, 2002** David Starr's victory at Las Vegas Motor Speedway gives owner Wayne Spears first win in team's 187th series appearance. That's the longest any owner has waited for win No. 1.

**Nov. 15, 2002** Mike Bliss becomes fifth NASCAR Craftsman Truck Series champion with fifth-place finish at Homestead-Miami Speedway. Finish is closest among top-three in series history—51 points. Xpress Motorsports is first championship team without NASCAR Cup Series owner or driver affiliation.

**Feb. 12, 2003** NASCAR announces that Toyota will join the Craftsman Truck Series in 2004, marking the first time a NASCAR series will include a foreign automaker.

**March 25, 2003** Dennis Setzer wins the Lucas Oil 250 at Mesa Marin Raceway to match the NASCAR Craftsman Truck Series record for victories in consecutive seasons. Setzer wins for the sixth straight season, matching the mark set by Jack Sprague in 2001.

**Oct. 10, 2003** Brendan Gaughan makes NASCAR Craftsman Truck Series history, winning his fourth consecutive race at Texas Motor Speedway and completing his second straight season sweep at the track.

**Nov. 14, 2003** Travis Kvapil, 27 and a native of Janesville, Wis., is the youngest driver to win the NASCAR Craftsman Truck Series championship. His nine-point margin of victory is the closest in NASCAR Craftsman Truck Series history. Kvapil set another NASCAR Craftsman Truck Series record by completing all but a single lap in 2003 – and that on the half-mile Mesa Marin Raceway. Xpress Motorsports' Steve Coulter becomes the first owner to win consecutive championships in the NASCAR Craftsman Truck Series.

**July 31, 2004** Toyota earns its first Truck Series win when Travis Kvapil captures the checkered flag in his No. 24 Bang Racing Line-X Tundra in the Line-X Spray-on Bedliners 200 at Michigan International Speedway.

**Nov. 19, 2004** Bobby Hamilton, 47, clinches the 2004 Truck Series championship with a 16th-place finish at Homestead, becoming the oldest driver to win the title. Fellow Dodge driver Kasey Kahne wins the race to become the first driver in NASCAR Craftsman Truck Series history to win in each of his first two series starts.

**NASCAR Craftsman Truck Series champ Bobby Hamilton celebrates after his victory at Memphis Motorsports Park.**

CRAFTSMAN TRUCK SERIES

WINNER
Memphis Motorsports Park
June 19, 2004

CRAFTSMAN TRUCK SERIES

# Joe Aramendia

**Birth date:** 04/23/63
**Birth Place:** San Antonio

## CAREER STATISTICS

| Year | Rank | Starts | Wins | Poles | Top 5 | Top 10 | Races Led | Laps Led |
|---|---|---|---|---|---|---|---|---|
| 2004 | 60 | 3 | 0 | 0 | 0 | 0 | 0 | 0 |
| TOTALS | | 3 | 0 | 0 | 0 | 0 | 0 | 0 |

# Johnny Benson

**Birth date:** 06/27/63 • **Birth place:** Grand Rapids, Mich.
**Truck:** TOYOTA • **Truck owner:** Gail Davis

## CAREER STATISTICS

| Year | Rank | Starts | Wins | Poles | Top 5 | Top 10 | Races Led | Laps Led |
|---|---|---|---|---|---|---|---|---|
| 1995 | 26 | 7 | 0 | 0 | 2 | 5 | 0 | 0 |
| 1996 | 37 | 4 | 0 | 1 | 1 | 4 | 2 | 119 |
| 1997 | 121 | 1 | 0 | 0 | 0 | 0 | 0 | 0 |
| 2004 | 25 | 13 | 0 | 0 | 5 | 8 | 1 | 5 |
| TOTALS | | 25 | 0 | 1 | 8 | 17 | 3 | 124 |

# Geoffrey Bodine

**Birth date:** 04/18/49
**Birth place:** Chemung, N.Y.

## CAREER STATISTICS

| Year | Rank | Starts | Wins | Poles | Top 5 | Top 10 | Races Led | Laps Led |
|---|---|---|---|---|---|---|---|---|
| 1995 | 20 | 10 | 0 | 0 | 6 | 7 | 3 | 167 |
| 1996 | 49 | 4 | 0 | 1 | 0 | 1 | 1 | 9 |
| 2000 | 94 | 1 | 0 | 0 | 0 | 0 | 0 | 0 |
| 2003 | 116 | 1 | 0 | 0 | 0 | 0 | 0 | 0 |
| 2004 | 40 | 5 | 0 | 0 | 0 | 1 | 0 | 0 |
| TOTALS | | 21 | 0 | 1 | 6 | 9 | 4 | 176 |

# Todd Bodine

**Birth date:** 02/27/64 • **Birth place:** Chemung, N.Y.
**Truck:** TOYOTA • **Truck owner:** Don Arnold

## CAREER STATISTICS (Todd Bodine)

| Year | Rank | Starts | Wins | Poles | Top 5 | Top 10 | Races Led | Laps Led |
|---|---|---|---|---|---|---|---|---|
| 1995 | 31 | 5 | 0 | 0 | 1 | 5 | 1 | 1 |
| 2004 | 27 | 10 | 2 | 0 | 4 | 5 | 3 | 127 |
| TOTALS | | 15 | 2 | 0 | 5 | 10 | 4 | 128 |

# Phil Bonifield

**Birth date:** 06/23/63 • **Birth place:** Napa, Calif.
**Truck:** CHEVROLET • **Truck owner:** Phil Bonifield

## CAREER STATISTICS

| Year | Rank | Starts | Wins | Poles | Top 5 | Top 10 | Races Led | Laps Led |
|---|---|---|---|---|---|---|---|---|
| 1999 | 31 | 14 | 0 | 0 | 0 | 0 | 0 | 0 |
| 2000 | 39 | 8 | 0 | 0 | 0 | 0 | 0 | 0 |
| 2001 | 33 | 12 | 0 | 0 | 0 | 0 | 0 | 0 |
| 2002 | 31 | 11 | 0 | 0 | 0 | 0 | 0 | 0 |
| 2003 | 20 | 21 | 0 | 0 | 0 | 0 | 0 | 0 |
| 2004 | 108 | 4 | 0 | 0 | 0 | 0 | 0 | 0 |
| TOTALS | | 70 | 0 | 0 | 0 | 0 | 0 | 0 |

# Charlie Bradberry

**Birth date:** 06/28/82 • **Birth place:** Chelsea, Ala.
**Truck:** CHEVROLET • **Truck owner:** Charlie Bradberry

## CAREER STATISTICS

| Year | Rank | Starts | Wins | Poles | Top 5 | Top 10 | Races Led | Laps Led |
|---|---|---|---|---|---|---|---|---|
| 2003 | 53 | 5 | 0 | 0 | 0 | 0 | 0 | 0 |
| 2004 | 45 | 6 | 0 | 0 | 0 | 0 | 0 | 0 |
| TOTALS | | 11 | 0 | 0 | 0 | 0 | 0 | 0 |

# Jamey Caudill

**Birth date:** 01/08/70 • **Birth place:** Four Oaks, N.C.
**Truck:** FORD • **Truck owner:** Robert Long

## CAREER STATISTICS

| Year | Rank | Starts | Wins | Poles | Top 5 | Top 10 | Races Led | Laps Led |
|---|---|---|---|---|---|---|---|---|
| 2002 | 95 | 2 | 0 | 0 | 0 | 0 | 0 | 0 |
| 2004 | 66 | 2 | 0 | 0 | 0 | 0 | 0 | 0 |
| TOTALS | | 4 | 0 | 0 | 0 | 0 | 0 | 0 |

# Chad Chaffin

**Birth date:** 07/20/68
**Birth place:** Smyrna, Tenn.

### CAREER STATISTICS

| Year | Rank | Starts | Wins | Poles | Top 5 | Top 10 | Races Led | Laps Led |
|---|---|---|---|---|---|---|---|---|
| 2000 | 55 | 3 | 0 | 0 | 1 | 1 | 0 | 0 |
| 2001 | 60 | 2 | 0 | 0 | 1 | 1 | 0 | 0 |
| 2002 | 77 | 2 | 0 | 0 | 0 | 0 | 0 | 0 |
| 2003 | 10 | 25 | 0 | 2 | 2 | 9 | 5 | 115 |
| 2004 | 10 | 25 | 2 | 0 | 6 | 10 | 4 | 61 |
| TOTALS | | 57 | 2 | 2 | 10 | 21 | 9 | 176 |

# Johnny Chapman

**Birth date:** 12/14/67
**Birth place:** Stony Point, N.C.

### CAREER STATISTICS

| Year | Rank | Starts | Wins | Poles | Top 5 | Top 10 | Races Led | Laps Led |
|---|---|---|---|---|---|---|---|---|
| 1996 | 57 | 4 | 0 | 0 | 0 | 0 | 0 | 0 |
| 1998 | 62 | 2 | 0 | 0 | 0 | 0 | 0 | 0 |
| 2003 | 45 | 6 | 0 | 0 | 0 | 0 | 0 | 0 |
| 2004 | 57 | 4 | 0 | 0 | 0 | 0 | 1 | 2 |
| TOTALS | | 16 | 0 | 0 | 0 | 0 | 1 | 2 |

# Terry Cook

**Birth date:** 02/26/68 • **Birth place:** Sylvania, Ohio
**Truck:** FORD • **Truck owner:** Greg Pollex/Keith Barnwell

### CAREER STATISTICS

| Year | Rank | Starts | Wins | Poles | Top 5 | Top 10 | Races Led | Laps Led |
|---|---|---|---|---|---|---|---|---|
| 1996 | 60 | 3 | 0 | 0 | 0 | 0 | 0 | 0 |
| 1997 | 24 | 15 | 0 | 1 | 0 | 0 | 0 | 0 |
| 1998 | 20 | 27 | 1 | 1 | 3 | 6 | 2 | 42 |
| 1999 | 15 | 25 | 0 | 0 | 1 | 3 | 1 | 15 |
| 2000 | 14 | 24 | 0 | 0 | 1 | 8 | 5 | 25 |
| 2001 | 7 | 24 | 0 | 1 | 5 | 16 | 5 | 67 |
| 2002 | 8 | 22 | 4 | 2 | 9 | 17 | 9 | 490 |
| 2003 | 9 | 25 | 0 | 2 | 0 | 13 | 4 | 84 |
| 2004 | 16 | 25 | 0 | 1 | 2 | 7 | 4 | 56 |
| TOTALS | | 190 | 5 | 8 | 21 | 70 | 30 | 779 |

# Matt Crafton

**Birth date:** 06/11/76
**Birth place:** Tulare, Calif.

### CAREER STATISTICS (Matt Crafton)

| Year | Rank | Starts | Wins | Poles | Top 5 | Top 10 | Races Led | Laps Led |
|---|---|---|---|---|---|---|---|---|
| 2000 | 83 | 1 | 0 | 0 | 0 | 1 | 0 | 0 |
| 2001 | 12 | 24 | 0 | 0 | 0 | 11 | 3 | 29 |
| 2002 | 15 | 22 | 0 | 0 | 0 | 6 | 0 | 0 |
| 2003 | 11 | 25 | 0 | 0 | 0 | 11 | 2 | 11 |
| 2004 | 5 | 25 | 0 | 0 | 6 | 17 | 5 | 41 |
| TOTALS | | 97 | 0 | 0 | 6 | 46 | 10 | 81 |

# Ricky Craven

**Birth date:** 05/24/66 • **Birth place:** Newburgh, Maine
**Truck:** FORD • **Truck owner:** Jack Roush

### CAREER STATISTICS

| Year | Rank | Starts | Wins | Poles | Top 5 | Top 10 | Races Led | Laps Led |
|---|---|---|---|---|---|---|---|---|
| 2004 | 105 | 1 | 0 | 0 | 0 | 0 | 0 | 0 |
| TOTALS | | 1 | 0 | 0 | 0 | 0 | 0 | 0 |

# Rick Crawford

**Birth date:** 07/26/58 • **Birth place:** Mobile, Ala.
**Truck:** FORD • **Truck owner:** Tom Mitchell

### CAREER STATISTICS

| Year | Rank | Starts | Wins | Poles | Top 5 | Top 10 | Races Led | Laps Led |
|---|---|---|---|---|---|---|---|---|
| 1997 | 12 | 26 | 0 | 0 | 1 | 10 | 2 | 24 |
| 1998 | 18 | 27 | 1 | 0 | 4 | 5 | 1 | 31 |
| 1999 | 14 | 25 | 0 | 0 | 3 | 10 | 4 | 46 |
| 2000 | 11 | 24 | 0 | 0 | 2 | 12 | 2 | 20 |
| 2001 | 8 | 24 | 0 | 0 | 10 | 16 | 10 | 201 |
| 2002 | 2 | 22 | 0 | 2 | 12 | 17 | 12 | 476 |
| 2003 | 7 | 25 | 1 | 0 | 10 | 16 | 8 | 256 |
| 2004 | 12 | 25 | 1 | 0 | 4 | 9 | 2 | 92 |
| TOTALS | | 198 | 3 | 2 | 46 | 95 | 41 | 1146 |

# Bobby Dotter

**Birth date:** 07/11/60
**Birth place:** Chicago

### CAREER STATISTICS

| Year | Rank | Starts | Wins | Poles | Top 5 | Top 10 | Races Led | Laps Led |
|---|---|---|---|---|---|---|---|---|
| 1996 | 96 | 1 | 0 | 0 | 0 | 0 | 0 | 0 |
| 1997 | 36 | 7 | 0 | 0 | 0 | 0 | 0 | 0 |
| 1998 | 81 | 1 | 0 | 0 | 0 | 0 | 0 | 0 |
| 2000 | 72 | 2 | 0 | 0 | 0 | 0 | 0 | 0 |
| 2001 | 15 | 24 | 0 | 0 | 0 | 1 | 2 | 2 |
| 2002 | 14 | 22 | 0 | 0 | 1 | 4 | 0 | 0 |
| 2003 | 29 | 10 | 0 | 0 | 0 | 0 | 1 | 1 |
| 2004 | 75 | 3 | 0 | 0 | 0 | 0 | 0 | 0 |
| TOTALS | | 70 | 0 | 0 | 1 | 5 | 3 | 3 |

# Kerry Earnhardt

**Birth date:** 12/08/69 • **Birth place:** Kannapolis, N.C.
**Truck:** CHEVROLET • **Truck owner:** Bill Ballew
No career NASCAR Craftsman Truck Series statistics

# Carl Edwards

**Birth date:** 08/15/79
**Birth place:** Columbia, Mo.

| Year | Rank | Starts | Wins | Poles | Top 5 | Top 10 | Races Led | Laps Led |
|------|------|--------|------|-------|-------|--------|-----------|----------|
| 2002 | 33 | 7 | 0 | 0 | 0 | 1 | 0 | 0 |
| 2003 | 8 | 25 | 3 | 1 | 13 | 15 | 13 | 363 |
| 2004 | 4 | 25 | 3 | 2 | 9 | 17 | 10 | 222 |
| **TOTALS** | | 57 | 6 | 3 | 22 | 33 | 23 | 585 |

# Brendan Gaughan

**Birth date:** 7/10/75 • **Birth place:** Los Angeles
**Truck:** DODGE • **Truck owner:** Michael Gaughan

### CAREER STATISTICS

| Year | Rank | Starts | Wins | Poles | Top 5 | Top 10 | Races Led | Laps Led |
|------|------|--------|------|-------|-------|--------|-----------|----------|
| 1997 | 99 | 1 | 0 | 0 | 0 | 0 | 0 | 0 |
| 1998 | 75 | 2 | 0 | 0 | 0 | 0 | 0 | 0 |
| 1999 | 75 | 2 | 0 | 0 | 0 | 0 | 0 | 0 |
| 2000 | 40 | 5 | 0 | 0 | 0 | 0 | 0 | 0 |
| 2001 | 31 | 7 | 0 | 0 | 2 | 3 | 4 | 56 |
| 2002 | 11 | 22 | 2 | 0 | 5 | 9 | 4 | 87 |
| 2003 | 4 | 25 | 6 | 3 | 14 | 18 | 16 | 652 |
| **TOTALS** | | 64 | 8 | 3 | 21 | 30 | 24 | 795 |

# Tina Gordon

**Birth date:** 03/14/69
**Birth place:** Cedar Bluff, Ala.

### CAREER STATISTICS

| Year | Rank | Starts | Wins | Poles | Top 5 | Top 10 | Races Led | Laps Led |
|------|------|--------|------|-------|-------|--------|-----------|----------|
| 2003 | 25 | 11 | 0 | 0 | 0 | 0 | 0 | 0 |
| 2004 | 49 | 5 | 0 | 0 | 0 | 0 | 0 | 0 |
| **TOTALS** | | 16 | 0 | 0 | 0 | 0 | 0 | 0 |

# Bobby Hamilton

**Birth date:** 05/29/57 • **Birth place:** Nashville
**Truck:** DODGE • **Truck owner:** Debbie Hamilton

### CAREER STATISTICS (Bobby Hamilton)

| Year | Rank | Starts | Wins | Poles | Top 5 | Top 10 | Races Led | Laps Led |
|------|------|--------|------|-------|-------|--------|-----------|----------|
| 1996 | 82 | 2 | 0 | 1 | 0 | 0 | 1 | 116 |
| 1997 | 56 | 2 | 0 | 0 | 1 | 2 | 0 | 0 |
| 1998 | 59 | 3 | 0 | 0 | 0 | 0 | 0 | 0 |
| 1999 | 36 | 5 | 0 | 1 | 1 | 1 | 2 | 89 |
| 2000 | 42 | 5 | 1 | 1 | 1 | 2 | 4 | 278 |
| 2001 | 38 | 5 | 1 | 0 | 2 | 3 | 2 | 258 |
| 2002 | 66 | 2 | 0 | 0 | 0 | 0 | 0 | 0 |
| 2003 | 6 | 25 | 2 | 1 | 10 | 18 | 13 | 394 |
| 2004 | 1 | 25 | 4 | 0 | 12 | 16 | 14 | 416 |
| **TOTALS** | | 74 | 8 | 4 | 27 | 42 | 36 | 1551 |

# Denny Hamlin

**Birth date:** 11/18/80
**Birth place:** Chesterfield, Va.

### CAREER STATISTICS

| Year | Rank | Starts | Wins | Poles | Top 5 | Top 10 | Races Led | Laps Led |
|------|------|--------|------|-------|-------|--------|-----------|----------|
| 2004 | 37 | 5 | 0 | 0 | 0 | 1 | 0 | 0 |
| **TOTALS** | | 5 | 0 | 0 | 0 | 1 | 0 | 0 |

# Kevin Harvick

**Birth date:** 12/08/75 • **Birth place:** Bakersfield, Calif.
**Truck:** CHEVROLET

### CAREER STATISTICS

| Year | Rank | Starts | Wins | Poles | Top 5 | Top 10 | Races Led | Laps Led |
|------|------|--------|------|-------|-------|--------|-----------|----------|
| 1995 | 89 | 1 | 0 | 0 | 0 | 0 | 0 | 0 |
| 1996 | 55 | 4 | 0 | 0 | 0 | 0 | 0 | 0 |
| 1997 | 27 | 13 | 0 | 0 | 0 | 2 | 0 | 0 |
| 1998 | 17 | 26 | 0 | 0 | 3 | 5 | 5 | 19 |
| 1999 | 12 | 25 | 0 | 0 | 6 | 11 | 6 | 214 |
| 2001 | 122 | 1 | 0 | 0 | 1 | 1 | 1 | 1 |
| 2002 | 30 | 5 | 1 | 0 | 3 | 4 | 3 | 189 |
| 2003 | 30 | 6 | 1 | 0 | 3 | 4 | 4 | 300 |
| 2004 | 53 | 2 | 0 | 0 | 2 | 2 | 0 | 0 |
| **TOTALS** | | 83 | 2 | 0 | 18 | 29 | 19 | 723 |

# Jerry Hill

**Birth date:** 07/25/61
**Birth place:** Port Tobacco, Md.

### CAREER STATISTICS

| Year | Rank | Starts | Wins | Poles | Top 5 | Top 10 | Races Led | Laps Led |
|------|------|--------|------|-------|-------|--------|-----------|----------|
| 2001 | 25 | 13 | 0 | 0 | 0 | 0 | 0 | 0 |
| 2002 | 23 | 21 | 0 | 0 | 0 | 0 | 0 | 0 |
| 2003 | 18 | 22 | 0 | 0 | 0 | 0 | 0 | 0 |
| 2004 | 73 | 2 | 0 | 0 | 0 | 0 | 0 | 0 |
| **TOTALS** | | 58 | 0 | 0 | 0 | 0 | 0 | 0 |

# Tracy Hines

**Birth date:** 05/01/72 • **Birth place:** New Castle, Ind.
**Truck:** CHEVROLET • **Truck owner:** Rhonda Thorson

### CAREER STATISTICS

| Year | Rank | Starts | Wins | Poles | Top 5 | Top 10 | Races Led | Laps Led |
|------|------|--------|------|-------|-------|--------|-----------|----------|
| 2003 | 54 | 4 | 0 | 0 | 0 | 0 | 0 | 0 |
| 2004 | 18 | 25 | 0 | 0 | 1 | 2 | 1 | 2 |
| TOTALS | | 29 | 0 | 0 | 1 | 2 | 1 | 2 |

# Shane Hmiel

**Birth date:** 05/15/80
**Birth place:** Conover, N.C.

### CAREER STATISTICS

| Year | Rank | Starts | Wins | Poles | Top 5 | Top 10 | Races Led | Laps Led |
|------|------|--------|------|-------|-------|--------|-----------|----------|
| 2004 | 13 | 25 | 1 | 0 | 4 | 10 | 10 | 320 |
| TOTALS | | 25 | 1 | 0 | 4 | 10 | 10 | 320 |

# Lance Hooper

**Birth date:** 06/01/67
**Birth place:** Palmdale, Calif.

### CAREER STATISTICS

| Year | Rank | Starts | Wins | Poles | Top 5 | Top 10 | Races Led | Laps Led |
|------|------|--------|------|-------|-------|--------|-----------|----------|
| 2000 | 28 | 13 | 0 | 0 | 0 | 0 | 0 | 0 |
| 2001 | 19 | 18 | 0 | 0 | 0 | 1 | 0 | 0 |
| 2002 | 20 | 22 | 0 | 0 | 0 | 0 | 1 | 1 |
| 2003 | 24 | 17 | 0 | 0 | 0 | 0 | 1 | 4 |
| 2004 | 43 | 5 | 0 | 0 | 0 | 0 | 0 | 0 |
| TOTALS | | 75 | 0 | 0 | 0 | 1 | 2 | 5 |

# Ron Hornaday Jr.

**Birth date:** 06/20/58 • **Birth place:** Palmdale, Calif.
**Truck:** CHEVROLET • **Truck owner:** Kevin Harvick

### CAREER STATISTICS

| Year | Rank | Starts | Wins | Poles | Top 5 | Top 10 | Races Led | Laps Led |
|------|------|--------|------|-------|-------|--------|-----------|----------|
| 1995 | 3 | 20 | 6 | 4 | 10 | 14 | 12 | 944 |
| 1996 | 1 | 24 | 4 | 2 | 18 | 23 | 14 | 834 |
| 1997 | 5 | 26 | 7 | 3 | 13 | 17 | 15 | 1213 |
| 1998 | 1 | 27 | 6 | 2 | 16 | 22 | 18 | 882 |
| 1999 | 7 | 25 | 2 | 0 | 7 | 16 | 16 | 943 |
| 2002 | 53 | 2 | 1 | 0 | 1 | 1 | 1 | 21 |
| 2004 | 85 | 1 | 0 | 0 | 0 | 0 | 0 | 0 |
| TOTALS | | 125 | 26 | 11 | 65 | 93 | 76 | 4837 |

# Andy Houston

**Birth date:** 11/07/70 • **Birth place:** Hickory, N.C.
**Truck:** CHEVROLET • **Truck owner:** Ken Weaver

### CAREER STATISTICS

| Year | Rank | Starts | Wins | Poles | Top 5 | Top 10 | Races Led | Laps Led |
|------|------|--------|------|-------|-------|--------|-----------|----------|
| 1997 | 48 | 4 | 0 | 0 | 0 | 0 | 0 | 0 |
| 1998 | 12 | 27 | 1 | 1 | 6 | 9 | 6 | 103 |
| 1999 | 8 | 25 | 0 | 1 | 5 | 14 | 3 | 17 |
| 2000 | 3 | 24 | 2 | 1 | 13 | 18 | 14 | 222 |
| 2002 | 38 | 5 | 0 | 0 | 0 | 0 | 0 | 0 |
| 2003 | 21 | 11 | 0 | 1 | 3 | 7 | 3 | 75 |
| 2004 | 20 | 24 | 0 | 0 | 0 | 3 | 1 | 1 |
| TOTALS | | 120 | 3 | 4 | 27 | 51 | 27 | 418 |

# Shelby Howard

**Birth date:** 07/25/85
**Birth place:** Greenwood, Ind.

### CAREER STATISTICS

| Year | Rank | Starts | Wins | Poles | Top 5 | Top 10 | Races Led | Laps Led |
|------|------|--------|------|-------|-------|--------|-----------|----------|
| 2004 | 33 | 8 | 0 | 0 | 0 | 0 | 0 | 0 |
| TOTALS | | 8 | 0 | 0 | 0 | 0 | 0 | 0 |

# Robert Huffman

**Birth date:** 03/12/68
**Birth place:** Claremont, N.C,

### CAREER STATISTICS

| Year | Rank | Starts | Wins | Poles | Top 5 | Top 10 | Races Led | Laps Led |
|------|------|--------|------|-------|-------|--------|-----------|----------|
| 1997 | 83 | 2 | 0 | 0 | 0 | 0 | 0 | 0 |
| 2004 | 23 | 24 | 0 | 0 | 0 | 6 | 1 | 5 |
| TOTALS | | 26 | 0 | 0 | 0 | 6 | 1 | 5 |

# Eric Jones

**Birth date:** 07/12/77 • **Birth place:** Granger, Iowa
**Truck:** CHEVROLET • **Truck owner:** Steve Chick Jr.

### CAREER STATISTICS

| Year | Rank | Starts | Wins | Poles | Top 5 | Top 10 | Races Led | Laps Led |
|------|------|--------|------|-------|-------|--------|-----------|----------|
| 2001 | 54 | 4 | 0 | 0 | 0 | 0 | 0 | 0 |
| 2002 | 29 | 9 | 0 | 0 | 0 | 0 | 0 | 0 |

## CAREER STATISTICS (Eric Jones)

| Year | Rank | Starts | Wins | Poles | Top 5 | Top 10 | Races Led | Laps Led |
|------|------|--------|------|-------|-------|--------|-----------|----------|
| 2003 | 27 | 9 | 0 | 0 | 0 | 1 | 0 | 0 |
| 2004 | 42 | 5 | 0 | 0 | 0 | 0 | 0 | 0 |
| **TOTALS** | | 27 | 0 | 0 | 0 | 1 | 0 | 0 |

# Kasey Kahne

**Birth date:** 04/10/80 • **Birth place:** Enumclaw, WA
**Truck:** DODGE • **Truck owner:** James Smith

## CAREER STATISTICS

| Year | Rank | Starts | Wins | Poles | Top 5 | Top 10 | Races Led | Laps Led |
|------|------|--------|------|-------|-------|--------|-----------|----------|
| 2004 | 47 | 2 | 2 | 0 | 2 | 2 | 2 | 149 |
| **TOTALS** | | 2 | 2 | 0 | 2 | 2 | 2 | 149 |

# Brad Keselowski

**Birth date:** 02/12/84
**Birth place:** Rochester Hills, Mich.

## CAREER STATISTICS

| Year | Rank | Starts | Wins | Poles | Top 5 | Top 10 | Races Led | Laps Led |
|------|------|--------|------|-------|-------|--------|-----------|----------|
| 2004 | 34 | 8 | 0 | 0 | 0 | 0 | 0 | 0 |
| **TOTALS** | | 8 | 0 | 0 | 0 | 0 | 0 | 0 |

# Frank Kimmel

**Birth date:** 04/30/62
**Birth place:** Clarksville, Ind.

## CAREER STATISTICS

| Year | Rank | Starts | Wins | Poles | Top 5 | Top 10 | Races Led | Laps Led |
|------|------|--------|------|-------|-------|--------|-----------|----------|
| 1995 | 80 | 1 | 0 | 0 | 0 | 0 | 0 | 0 |
| 1996 | 45 | 4 | 0 | 0 | 0 | 1 | 0 | 0 |
| 1997 | 119 | 1 | 0 | 0 | 0 | 0 | 0 | 0 |
| 1998 | 79 | 1 | 0 | 0 | 0 | 0 | 0 | 0 |
| 2001 | 97 | 1 | 0 | 0 | 0 | 0 | 0 | 0 |
| 2003 | 117 | 1 | 0 | 0 | 0 | 0 | 0 | 0 |
| 2004 | 50 | 3 | 0 | 0 | 0 | 1 | 1 | 6 |
| **TOTALS** | | 12 | 0 | 0 | 0 | 2 | 1 | 6 |

# Todd Kluever

**Birth date:** 07/06/78 • **Birth place:** Sun Prairie, Wis.
**Truck:** FORD • **Truck owner:** Jack Roush

No career NASCAR Craftsman Truck Series statistics

# Travis Kvapil

**Birth date:** 03/01/76
**Birth place:** Janesville, Wis.

## CAREER STATISTICS

| Year | Rank | Starts | Wins | Poles | Top 5 | Top 10 | Races Led | Laps Led |
|------|------|--------|------|-------|-------|--------|-----------|----------|
| 2001 | 4 | 24 | 1 | 0 | 11 | 18 | 9 | 55 |
| 2002 | 9 | 22 | 1 | 0 | 10 | 14 | 7 | 170 |
| 2003 | 1 | 25 | 1 | 0 | 13 | 22 | 11 | 49 |
| 2004 | 8 | 25 | 2 | 1 | 6 | 10 | 7 | 176 |
| **TOTALS** | | 96 | 5 | 1 | 40 | 64 | 34 | 450 |

# Randy LaJoie

**Birth date:** 08/28/61
**Birth place:** Norwalk, Conn.

## CAREER STATISTICS

| Year | Rank | Starts | Wins | Poles | Top 5 | Top 10 | Races Led | Laps Led |
|------|------|--------|------|-------|-------|--------|-----------|----------|
| 2003 | 94 | 1 | 0 | 0 | 0 | 0 | 0 | 0 |
| 2004 | 38 | 6 | 0 | 0 | 0 | 1 | 0 | 0 |
| **TOTALS** | | 7 | 0 | 0 | 0 | 1 | 0 | 0 |

# Bill Lester

**Birth date:** 02/06/61 • **Birth place:** Oakland
**Truck:** TOYOTA • **Truck owner:** Bill Davis

## CAREER STATISTICS

| Year | Rank | Starts | Wins | Poles | Top 5 | Top 10 | Races Led | Laps Led |
|------|------|--------|------|-------|-------|--------|-----------|----------|
| 2000 | 86 | 1 | 0 | 0 | 0 | 0 | 0 | 0 |
| 2001 | 59 | 5 | 0 | 0 | 0 | 0 | 0 | 0 |
| 2002 | 17 | 22 | 0 | 0 | 0 | 0 | 0 | 0 |
| 2003 | 14 | 25 | 0 | 1 | 0 | 1 | 2 | 17 |
| 2004 | 22 | 25 | 0 | 0 | 0 | 1 | 2 | 32 |
| **TOTALS** | | 78 | 0 | 1 | 0 | 2 | 4 | 49 |

# Kevin Love

**Birth date:** 06/08/79
**Birth place:** Midland, N.C.

## CAREER STATISTICS

| Year | Rank | Starts | Wins | Poles | Top 5 | Top 10 | Races Led | Laps Led |
|------|------|--------|------|-------|-------|--------|-----------|----------|
| 2004 | 41 | 5 | 0 | 0 | 0 | 0 | 0 | 0 |
| **TOTALS** | | 5 | 0 | 0 | 0 | 0 | 0 | 0 |

# Scott Lynch

**Birth date:** 05/14/80
**Birth place:** Burley, Idaho

### CAREER STATISTICS

| Year | Rank | Starts | Wins | Poles | Top 5 | Top 10 | Races Led | Laps Led |
|------|------|--------|------|-------|-------|--------|-----------|----------|
| 2003 | 74 | 2 | 0 | 0 | 0 | 0 | 0 | 0 |
| 2004 | 65 | 2 | 0 | 0 | 0 | 0 | 0 | 0 |
| TOTALS | | 4 | 0 | 0 | 0 | 0 | 0 | 0 |

# Randy MacDonald

**Birth date:** 07/26/62
**Birth place:** Oshawa, Ontario

### CAREER STATISTICS

| Year | Rank | Starts | Wins | Poles | Top 5 | Top 10 | Races Led | Laps Led |
|------|------|--------|------|-------|-------|--------|-----------|----------|
| 1996 | 112 | 1 | 0 | 0 | 0 | 0 | 0 | 0 |
| 1997 | 52 | 4 | 0 | 0 | 0 | 0 | 0 | 0 |
| 1998 | 32 | 10 | 0 | 0 | 0 | 1 | 0 | 0 |
| 1999 | 40 | 5 | 0 | 0 | 0 | 0 | 0 | 0 |
| 2000 | 19 | 24 | 0 | 0 | 0 | 1 | 0 | 0 |
| 2001 | 107 | 1 | 0 | 0 | 0 | 0 | 0 | 0 |
| 2002 | 19 | 22 | 0 | 0 | 0 | 0 | 0 | 0 |
| 2003 | 15 | 25 | 0 | 0 | 0 | 0 | 0 | 0 |
| 2004 | 90 | 1 | 0 | 0 | 0 | 0 | 0 | 0 |
| TOTALS | | 93 | 0 | 0 | 0 | 2 | 0 | 0 |

# Steadman Marlin

**Birth date:** 10/29/80
**Birth place:** Columbia, Tenn.

### CAREER STATISTICS

| Year | Rank | Starts | Wins | Poles | Top 5 | Top 10 | Races Led | Laps Led |
|------|------|--------|------|-------|-------|--------|-----------|----------|
| 2003 | 133 | 1 | 0 | 0 | 0 | 0 | 0 | 0 |
| 2004 | 63 | 2 | 0 | 0 | 0 | 0 | 0 | 0 |
| TOTALS | | 3 | 0 | 0 | 0 | 0 | 0 | 0 |

# Mark McFarland

**Birth date:** 02/01/78.
**Birth place:** Winchester, Va.

### CAREER STATISTICS (Mark McFarland)

| Year | Rank | Starts | Wins | Poles | Top 5 | Top 10 | Races Led | Laps Led |
|------|------|--------|------|-------|-------|--------|-----------|----------|
| 2003 | 67 | 3 | 0 | 0 | 0 | 0 | 0 | 0 |
| 2004 | 36 | 7 | 0 | 0 | 0 | 1 | 0 | 0 |
| TOTALS | | 10 | 0 | 0 | 0 | 1 | 0 | 0 |

# Jamie McMurray

**Birth date:** 06/03/76
**Birth place:** Joplin, Mo.

### CAREER STATISTICS

| Year | Rank | Starts | Wins | Poles | Top 5 | Top 10 | Races Led | Laps Led |
|------|------|--------|------|-------|-------|--------|-----------|----------|
| 1999 | 41 | 5 | 0 | 0 | 0 | 0 | 0 | 0 |
| 2000 | 22 | 16 | 0 | 2 | 1 | 4 | 1 | 6 |
| 2004 | 44 | 3 | 1 | 1 | 2 | 2 | 3 | 78 |
| TOTALS | | 24 | 1 | 3 | 3 | 6 | 4 | 84 |

# Chase Montgomery

**Birth date:** 09/29/83 • **Birth place:** Lebanon, Tenn.
**Truck:** DODGE • **Truck owner:** Bobby Hamilton

### CAREER STATISTICS

| Year | Rank | Starts | Wins | Poles | Top 5 | Top 10 | Races Led | Laps Led |
|------|------|--------|------|-------|-------|--------|-----------|----------|
| 2003 | 106 | 1 | 0 | 0 | 0 | 0 | 0 | 0 |
| 2004 | 21 | 25 | 0 | 0 | 0 | 0 | 0 | 0 |
| TOTALS | | 26 | 0 | 0 | 0 | 0 | 0 | 0 |

# Sean Murphy

**Birth date:** 06/29/84 • **Birth Place** Fort Lauderdale, Fla.
**Truck:** CHEVROLET • **Truck owner:** Bobby Dotter

### CAREER STATISTICS

| Year | Rank | Starts | Wins | Poles | Top 5 | Top 10 | Races Led | Laps Led |
|------|------|--------|------|-------|-------|--------|-----------|----------|
| 2004 | 51 | 4 | 0 | 0 | 0 | 0 | 2 | 12 |
| TOTALS | | 4 | 0 | 0 | 0 | 0 | 2 | 12 |

# Ted Musgrave

**Birth date:** 12/18/55 • **Birth place:** Franklin, Wis.
**Truck:** DODGE • **Truck owner:** Jim Smith

## CAREER STATISTICS (Ted Musgrave)

| Year | Rank | Starts | Wins | Poles | Top 5 | Top 10 | Races Led | Laps Led |
|---|---|---|---|---|---|---|---|---|
| 1995 | 66 | 1 | 0 | 0 | 1 | 1 | 0 | 0 |
| 1996 | 69 | 2 | 0 | 0 | 1 | 1 | 0 | 0 |
| 2001 | 2 | 24 | 7 | 2 | 13 | 18 | 15 | 810 |
| 2002 | 3 | 22 | 3 | 3 | 12 | 16 | 15 | 757 |
| 2003 | 3 | 25 | 3 | 4 | 14 | 18 | 18 | 796 |
| 2004 | 3 | 25 | 2 | 2 | 11 | 16 | 13 | 757 |
| TOTALS | | 99 | 15 | 11 | 52 | 70 | 61 | 3120 |

# Eric Norris

**Birth date:** 05/20/65 • **Birth place:** Santa Monica, Calif.
**Truck:** CHEVROLET • **Truck owner:** John Conely

### CAREER STATISTICS

| Year | Rank | Starts | Wins | Poles | Top 5 | Top 10 | Races Led | Laps Led |
|---|---|---|---|---|---|---|---|---|
| 1997 | 43 | 5 | 0 | 0 | 0 | 0 | 0 | 0 |
| 1999 | 74 | 2 | 0 | 0 | 0 | 0 | 0 | 0 |
| 2000 | 110 | 1 | 0 | 0 | 0 | 0 | 0 | 0 |
| 2001 | 62 | 3 | 0 | 0 | 0 | 0 | 0 | 0 |
| 2004 | 67 | 2 | 0 | 0 | 0 | 0 | 0 | 0 |
| TOTALS | | 13 | 0 | 0 | 0 | 0 | 0 | 0 |

# Steve Park

**Birth date:** 08/23/67 • **Birth place:** East Northport, N.Y.
**Truck:** DODGE • **Truck owner:** Michael Gaughan

### CAREER STATISTICS

| Year | Rank | Starts | Wins | Poles | Top 5 | Top 10 | Races Led | Laps Led |
|---|---|---|---|---|---|---|---|---|
| 1996 | 48 | 3 | 0 | 0 | 1 | 1 | 1 | 10 |
| 1997 | 101 | 1 | 0 | 0 | 0 | 0 | 0 | 0 |
| 2004 | 9 | 25 | 0 | 0 | 5 | 10 | 5 | 99 |
| TOTALS | | 29 | 0 | 0 | 6 | 11 | 6 | 109 |

# Hank Parker Jr.

**Birth date:** 10/07/74
**Birth place:** Denver, N.C.

### CAREER STATISTICS

| Year | Rank | Starts | Wins | Poles | Top 5 | Top 10 | Races Led | Laps Led |
|---|---|---|---|---|---|---|---|---|
| 2003 | 44 | 4 | 0 | 0 | 0 | 2 | 0 | 0 |
| 2004 | 17 | 25 | 0 | 0 | 2 | 4 | 1 | 34 |
| TOTALS | | 29 | 0 | 0 | 2 | 6 | 1 | 34 |

# J.R. Patton

**Birth date:** 09/12/83 • **Birth place:** Las Cruces, N.M.
**Truck:** FORD • **Truck owner:** Tom Elridge

### CAREER STATISTICS

| Year | Rank | Starts | Wins | Poles | Top 5 | Top 10 | Races Led | Laps Led |
|---|---|---|---|---|---|---|---|---|
| 2004 | 35 | 7 | 0 | 0 | 0 | 0 | 0 | 0 |
| TOTALS | | 7 | 0 | 0 | 0 | 0 | 0 | 0 |

# Ryan Ragan

**Birth date:** 12/24/85
**Birth place:** Unadilla, Ga.

### CAREER STATISTICS

| Year | Rank | Starts | Wins | Poles | Top 5 | Top 10 | Races Led | Laps Led |
|---|---|---|---|---|---|---|---|---|
| 2004 | 32 | 10 | 0 | 0 | 0 | 0 | 0 | 0 |
| TOTALS | | 10 | 0 | 0 | 0 | 0 | 0 | 0 |

# Deborah Renshaw

**Birth date:** 10/28/77 • **Birth place:** Bowling Green, Ky.
**Truck:** DODGE • **Truck owner:** Bobby Hamilton

### CAREER STATISTICS

| Year | Rank | Starts | Wins | Poles | Top 5 | Top 10 | Races Led | Laps Led |
|---|---|---|---|---|---|---|---|---|
| 2004 | 30 | 14 | 0 | 0 | 0 | 0 | 1 | 1 |
| TOTALS | | 14 | 0 | 0 | 0 | 0 | 1 | 1 |

# David Reutimann

**Birth date:** 03/02/70 • **Birth place:** Zephyrhills, Fla.
**Truck:** TOYOTA • **Truck owner:** Darrell Waltrip

### CAREER STATISTICS

| Year | Rank | Starts | Wins | Poles | Top 5 | Top 10 | Races Led | Laps Led |
|---|---|---|---|---|---|---|---|---|
| 2004 | 14 | 25 | 0 | 2 | 4 | 10 | 4 | 37 |
| TOTALS | | 25 | 0 | 2 | 4 | 10 | 4 | 37 |

# Loni Richardson

**Birth date:** 11/11/70 • **Birth place:** Paris, Texas
**Truck:** CHEVROLET • **Truck owner:** Larry Richardson

## CAREER STATISTICS (Loni Richardson)

| Year | Rank | Starts | Wins | Poles | Top 5 | Top 10 | Races Led | Laps Led |
|------|------|--------|------|-------|-------|--------|-----------|----------|
| 2001 | 57 | 4 | 0 | 0 | 0 | 0 | 0 | 0 |
| 2002 | 42 | 7 | 0 | 0 | 0 | 0 | 0 | 0 |
| 2003 | 73 | 3 | 0 | 0 | 0 | 0 | 0 | 0 |
| 2004 | 56 | 5 | 0 | 0 | 0 | 0 | 0 | 0 |
| TOTALS | | 19 | 0 | 0 | 0 | 0 | 0 | 0 |

# Jay Sauter

**Birth date:** 06/22/62
**Birth place:** West Salem, Wis.

## CAREER STATISTICS

| Year | Rank | Starts | Wins | Poles | Top 5 | Top 10 | Races Led | Laps Led |
|------|------|--------|------|-------|-------|--------|-----------|----------|
| 1996 | 25 | 8 | 0 | 0 | 2 | 5 | 0 | 0 |
| 1997 | 6 | 26 | 1 | 0 | 10 | 15 | 4 | 54 |
| 1998 | 4 | 27 | 1 | 0 | 7 | 14 | 8 | 113 |
| 1999 | 5 | 25 | 2 | 2 | 8 | 16 | 12 | 102 |
| 2004 | 48 | 4 | 0 | 0 | 0 | 0 | 0 | 0 |
| TOTALS | | 90 | 4 | 2 | 27 | 50 | 24 | 269 |

# Johnny Sauter

**Birth date:** 05/01/78
**Birth place:** Necedah, Wis.

## CAREER STATISTICS

| Year | Rank | Starts | Wins | Poles | Top 5 | Top 10 | Races Led | Laps Led |
|------|------|--------|------|-------|-------|--------|-----------|----------|
| 2003 | 69 | 3 | 0 | 0 | 0 | 1 | 0 | 0 |
| 2004 | 54 | 2 | 0 | 0 | 1 | 1 | 1 | 139 |
| TOTALS | | 5 | 0 | 0 | 1 | 2 | 1 | 139 |

# Ken Schrader

**Birth date:** 05/29/55 • **Birth place:** Fenton, Mo.
**Truck:** CHEVROLET • **Truck owner:** Ken Schrader

## CAREER STATISTICS

| Year | Rank | Starts | Wins | Poles | Top 5 | Top 10 | Races Led | Laps Led |
|------|------|--------|------|-------|-------|--------|-----------|----------|
| 1995 | 29 | 7 | 1 | 0 | 3 | 3 | 1 | 54 |
| 1996 | 44 | 4 | 0 | 0 | 0 | 2 | 0 | 0 |
| 1997 | 61 | 2 | 0 | 0 | 0 | 1 | 1 | 48 |
| 1999 | 118 | 1 | 0 | 0 | 0 | 0 | 0 | 0 |
| 2000 | 35 | 5 | 0 | 0 | 1 | 3 | 1 | 59 |
| 2001 | 28 | 8 | 0 | 0 | 1 | 5 | 0 | 0 |
| 2002 | 27 | 8 | 0 | 0 | 0 | 3 | 0 | 0 |
| 2003 | 23 | 11 | 0 | 0 | 0 | 3 | 0 | 0 |
| 2004 | 28 | 12 | 0 | 1 | 1 | 4 | 0 | 0 |
| TOTALS | | 58 | 1 | 1 | 6 | 24 | 3 | 161 |

# Dennis Setzer

**Birth date:** 02/27/60 • **Birth place:** Newton, N.C.
**Truck:** CHEVROLET • **Truck owner:** David Dollar

## CAREER STATISTICS

| Year | Rank | Starts | Wins | Poles | Top 5 | Top 10 | Races Led | Laps Led |
|------|------|--------|------|-------|-------|--------|-----------|----------|
| 1995 | 28 | 8 | 0 | 0 | 1 | 2 | 1 | 27 |
| 1997 | 124 | 1 | 0 | 0 | 0 | 0 | 0 | 0 |
| 1998 | 28 | 13 | 1 | 0 | 1 | 5 | 2 | 31 |
| 1999 | 3 | 25 | 3 | 1 | 11 | 19 | 12 | 427 |
| 2000 | 7 | 24 | 1 | 0 | 8 | 16 | 4 | 73 |
| 2001 | 9 | 24 | 1 | 2 | 8 | 15 | 7 | 99 |
| 2002 | 6 | 22 | 1 | 0 | 8 | 14 | 6 | 142 |
| 2003 | 2 | 25 | 3 | 0 | 15 | 23 | 8 | 437 |
| 2004 | 2 | 25 | 2 | 0 | 8 | 16 | 8 | 93 |
| TOTALS | | 167 | 12 | 3 | 60 | 110 | 48 | 1329 |

# Shane Sieg

**Birth date:** 08/23/82
**Birth place:** Tucker, Ga.

## CAREER STATISTICS

| Year | Rank | Starts | Wins | Poles | Top 5 | Top 10 | Races Led | Laps Led |
|------|------|--------|------|-------|-------|--------|-----------|----------|
| 2003 | 52 | 4 | 0 | 0 | 0 | 0 | 0 | 0 |
| 2004 | 24 | 19 | 0 | 0 | 0 | 1 | 3 | 3 |
| TOTALS | | 23 | 0 | 0 | 0 | 1 | 3 | 3 |

# Mike Skinner

**Birth date:** 06/28/57 • **Birth place:** Susanville, Calif.
**Truck:** TOYOTA • **Truck owner:** Bill Davis

## CAREER STATISTICS

| Year | Rank | Starts | Wins | Poles | Top 5 | Top 10 | Races Led | Laps Led |
|------|------|--------|------|-------|-------|--------|-----------|----------|
| 1995 | 1 | 20 | 8 | 10 | 17 | 18 | 13 | 1053 |
| 1996 | 3 | 24 | 8 | 5 | 17 | 20 | 18 | 1533 |
| 1997 | 44 | 4 | 0 | 0 | 2 | 2 | 2 | 40 |
| 1998 | 49 | 2 | 0 | 0 | 1 | 1 | 1 | 4 |
| 2003 | 48 | 4 | 0 | 0 | 0 | 0 | 1 | 3 |
| 2004 | 11 | 25 | 0 | 2 | 4 | 9 | 11 | 448 |
| TOTALS | | 79 | 16 | 17 | 41 | 50 | 46 | 3081 |

# Jason Small

**Birth date:** 06/07/79 • **Birth place:** Bakersfield, Calif.
**Truck:** CHEVROLET • **Truck owner:** Duke Thorson

### CAREER STATISTICS

| Year | Rank | Starts | Wins | Poles | Top 5 | Top 10 | Races Led | Laps Led |
|------|------|--------|------|-------|-------|--------|-----------|----------|
| 2000 | 102 | 2 | 0 | 0 | 0 | 0 | 0 | 0 |
| 2001 | 53 | 5 | 0 | 0 | 0 | 0 | 0 | 0 |
| 2002 | 21 | 22 | 0 | 0 | 0 | 2 | 0 | 0 |
| 2003 | 64 | 3 | 0 | 0 | 0 | 1 | 0 | 0 |
| 2004 | 52 | 4 | 0 | 0 | 0 | 0 | 0 | 0 |
| TOTALS | | 36 | 0 | 0 | 0 | 3 | 0 | 0 |

# Regan Smith

**Birth date:** 09/23/83 • **Birth place:** Cato, N.Y.
**Truck:** CHEVROLET • **Truck owner:** Dave Malcolmson

### CAREER STATISTICS

| Year | Rank | Starts | Wins | Poles | Top 5 | Top 10 | Races Led | Laps Led |
|------|------|--------|------|-------|-------|--------|-----------|----------|
| 2002 | 76 | 2 | 0 | 0 | 0 | 0 | 0 | 0 |
| 2004 | 78 | 1 | 0 | 0 | 0 | 1 | 0 | 0 |
| TOTALS | | 3 | 0 | 0 | 0 | 1 | 0 | 0 |

# Jimmy Spencer

**Birth date:** 02/15/57
**Birth place:** Berwick, Pa.

### CAREER STATISTICS

| Year | Rank | Starts | Wins | Poles | Top 5 | Top 10 | Races Led | Laps Led |
|------|------|--------|------|-------|-------|--------|-----------|----------|
| 2003 | 55 | 3 | 1 | 1 | 1 | 2 | 2 | 125 |
| 2004 | 55 | 3 | 0 | 0 | 0 | 0 | 0 | 0 |
| TOTALS | | 6 | 1 | 1 | 1 | 2 | 2 | 125 |

# Jack Sprague

**Birth date:** 08/08/64 • **Birth place:** Spring Lake, Mich.
**Truck:** CHEVROLET • **Truck owner:** Steve Coulter

### CAREER STATISTICS

| Year | Rank | Starts | Wins | Poles | Top 5 | Top 10 | Races Led | Laps Led |
|------|------|--------|------|-------|-------|--------|-----------|----------|
| 1995 | 5 | 20 | 0 | 1 | 4 | 15 | 3 | 55 |
| 1996 | 2 | 24 | 5 | 2 | 18 | 21 | 10 | 733 |
| 1997 | 1 | 26 | 3 | 5 | 16 | 23 | 13 | 1004 |
| 1998 | 2 | 27 | 5 | 4 | 16 | 23 | 13 | 837 |
| 1999 | 1 | 25 | 3 | 1 | 16 | 19 | 15 | 581 |

### CAREER STATISTICS (Jack Sprague)

| Year | Rank | Starts | Wins | Poles | Top 5 | Top 10 | Races Led | Laps Led |
|------|------|--------|------|-------|-------|--------|-----------|----------|
| 2000 | 5 | 24 | 3 | 0 | 13 | 15 | 10 | 492 |
| 2001 | 1 | 24 | 4 | 7 | 15 | 17 | 19 | 1386 |
| 2003 | 66 | 2 | 0 | 0 | 2 | 2 | 0 | 0 |
| 2004 | 7 | 25 | 1 | 6 | 8 | 13 | 10 | 510 |
| TOTALS | | 197 | 24 | 26 | 108 | 148 | 93 | 5598 |

# David Starr

**Birth date:** 10/11/67 • **Birth place:** Houston
**Truck:** CHEVROLET • **Truck owner:** Wayne Spears

### CAREER STATISTICS

| Year | Rank | Starts | Wins | Poles | Top 5 | Top 10 | Races Led | Laps Led |
|------|------|--------|------|-------|-------|--------|-----------|----------|
| 1998 | 43 | 5 | 0 | 0 | 0 | 0 | 1 | 1 |
| 1999 | 22 | 24 | 0 | 0 | 0 | 0 | 1 | 8 |
| 2000 | 29 | 13 | 0 | 0 | 0 | 0 | 1 | 6 |
| 2001 | 47 | 5 | 0 | 0 | 3 | 4 | 0 | 0 |
| 2002 | 5 | 22 | 1 | 2 | 8 | 16 | 8 | 111 |
| 2003 | 13 | 21 | 0 | 0 | 5 | 13 | 3 | 16 |
| 2004 | 6 | 25 | 2 | 1 | 8 | 16 | 4 | 78 |
| TOTALS | | 115 | 3 | 3 | 24 | 49 | 18 | 220 |

# Kelly Sutton

**Birth date:** 09/24/71 • **Birth place:** Crownsville, Md.
**Truck:** CHEVROLET • **Truck owner:** Ed Sutton

### CAREER STATISTICS

| Year | Rank | Starts | Wins | Poles | Top 5 | Top 10 | Races Led | Laps Led |
|------|------|--------|------|-------|-------|--------|-----------|----------|
| 2003 | 63 | 4 | 0 | 0 | 0 | 0 | 0 | 0 |
| 2004 | 26 | 19 | 0 | 0 | 0 | 0 | 0 | 0 |
| TOTALS | | 23 | 0 | 0 | 0 | 0 | 0 | 0 |

# Mike Wallace

**Birth date:** 03/10/59
**Birth place:** St. Louis

### CAREER STATISTICS

| Year | Rank | Starts | Wins | Poles | Top 5 | Top 10 | Races Led | Laps Led |
|------|------|--------|------|-------|-------|--------|-----------|----------|
| 1995 | 92 | 1 | 0 | 0 | 0 | 0 | 0 | 0 |
| 1997 | 22 | 15 | 0 | 0 | 1 | 7 | 2 | 95 |
| 1998 | 13 | 27 | 0 | 1 | 3 | 11 | 5 | 64 |
| 1999 | 6 | 25 | 2 | 0 | 12 | 14 | 10 | 261 |
| 2000 | 4 | 24 | 2 | 2 | 13 | 16 | 9 | 416 |
| 2002 | 44 | 4 | 0 | 0 | 1 | 2 | 1 | 3 |
| 2003 | 46 | 4 | 0 | 0 | 0 | 1 | 1 | 2 |
| 2004 | 68 | 1 | 0 | 0 | 1 | 1 | 1 | 4 |
| TOTALS | | 101 | 4 | 3 | 31 | 52 | 29 | 845 |

# Darrell Waltrip

**Birth date:** 02/05/47 • **Birth place:** Owensboro, Ky.
**Truck:** TOYOTA • **Truck owner:** Darrell Waltrip

## CAREER STATISTICS

| Year | Rank | Starts | Wins | Poles | Top 5 | Top 10 | Races Led | Laps Led |
|------|------|--------|------|-------|-------|--------|-----------|----------|
| 1995 | 41 | 4 | 0 | 0 | 0 | 2 | 0 | 0 |
| 1996 | 34 | 5 | 0 | 0 | 1 | 3 | 0 | 0 |
| 2002 | 62 | 2 | 0 | 0 | 0 | 1 | 0 | 0 |
| 2003 | 59 | 3 | 0 | 0 | 0 | 2 | 0 | 0 |
| 2004 | 94 | 2 | 0 | 0 | 0 | 0 | 0 | 0 |
| **TOTALS** | | 16 | 0 | 0 | 1 | 8 | 0 | 0 |

# Ken Weaver

**Birth date:** 02/10/56
**Birth place:** Dallas

## CAREER STATISTICS

| Year | Rank | Starts | Wins | Poles | Top 5 | Top 10 | Races Led | Laps Led |
|------|------|--------|------|-------|-------|--------|-----------|----------|
| 2003 | 47 | 5 | 0 | 0 | 0 | 0 | 0 | 0 |
| 2004 | 29 | 15 | 0 | 0 | 0 | 0 | 0 | 0 |
| **TOTALS** | | 20 | 0 | 0 | 0 | 0 | 0 | 0 |

# Paul White

**Birth date:** 04/09/63
**Birth place:** Temple, Texas

## CAREER STATISTICS

| Year | Rank | Starts | Wins | Poles | Top 5 | Top 10 | Races Led | Laps Led |
|------|------|--------|------|-------|-------|--------|-----------|----------|
| 2004 | 39 | 6 | 0 | 0 | 0 | 0 | 0 | 0 |
| **TOTALS** | | 6 | 0 | 0 | 0 | 0 | 0 | 0 |

# Brandon Whitt

**Birth date:** 10/15/82 • **Birth place:** El Cajon, Calif.
**Truck:** TOYOTA • **Truck owner:** Clean Line Motorsports

## CAREER STATISTICS

| Year | Rank | Starts | Wins | Poles | Top 5 | Top 10 | Races Led | Laps Led |
|------|------|--------|------|-------|-------|--------|-----------|----------|
| 2003 | 40 | 7 | 0 | 0 | 0 | 0 | 0 | 0 |
| 2004 | 19 | 25 | 0 | 0 | 0 | 0 | 0 | 0 |
| **TOTALS** | | 32 | 0 | 0 | 0 | 0 | 0 | 0 |

# Chris Wimmer

**Birth date:** 06/23/79 • **Birth place:** Wausau, Wis.
**Truck:** Ford • **Truck owner:** Mike Mittler

## CAREER STATISTICS

| Year | Rank | Starts | Wins | Poles | Top 5 | Top 10 | Races Led | Laps Led |
|------|------|--------|------|-------|-------|--------|-----------|----------|
| 2004 | 31 | 12 | 0 | 0 | 0 | 0 | 0 | 0 |
| **TOTALS** | | 12 | 0 | 0 | 0 | 0 | 0 | 0 |

# Jon Wood

**Birth date:** 10/25/81
**Birth place:** Stuart, Va.

## CAREER STATISTICS

| Year | Rank | Starts | Wins | Poles | Top 5 | Top 10 | Races Led | Laps Led |
|------|------|--------|------|-------|-------|--------|-----------|----------|
| 2001 | 17 | 16 | 0 | 0 | 2 | 4 | 3 | 31 |
| 2002 | 12 | 22 | 0 | 0 | 0 | 10 | 1 | 13 |
| 2003 | 5 | 25 | 2 | 2 | 10 | 20 | 10 | 349 |
| 2004 | 15 | 25 | 0 | 0 | 2 | 7 | 2 | 39 |
| **TOTALS** | | 88 | 2 | 2 | 14 | 41 | 16 | 432 |

Dennis Setzer won twice in 2004, at Charlotte and Texas, and finished second in the points standings.

# 2004 race by race

| No. | Date | Race | Track | Pole winner | Race winner |
|---|---|---|---|---|---|
| 1 | February 13 | Florida Dodge Dealers 250 | Daytona International Speedway | Terry Cook | Carl Edwards |
| 2 | March 13 | EasyCare Vehicle Service 200 | Atlanta Motor Speedway | David Reutimann | Bobby Hamilton |
| 3 | April 17 | Kroger 250 | Martinsville Speedway | Jack Sprague | Rick Crawford |
| 4 | May 16 | UAW/GM Ohio 250 | Mansfield Motorsports Speedway | Jack Sprague | Jack Sprague |
| 5 | May 21 | Infineon 200 | Lowe's Motor Speedway | David Starr | Dennis Setzer |
| 6 | June 4 | MBNA America 200 | Dover International Speedway | Carl Edwards | Chad Chaffin |
| 7 | June 11 | O'Reilly 400K | Texas Motor Speedway | Ted Musgrave | Dennis Setzer |
| 8 | June 19 | O'Reilly 200 | Memphis Motorsports Park | Jack Sprague | Bobby Hamilton |
| 9 | June 25 | Black Cat Fireworks 200 | The Milwaukee Mile | Ted Musgrave | Ted Musgrave |
| 10 | July 3 | O'Reilly Auto Parts 250 | Kansas Speedway | Dennis Setzer | Carl Edwards |
| 11 | July 10 | Built Ford Tough 225 | Kentucky Speedway | Dennis Setzer | Bobby Hamilton |
| 12 | July 17 | Dodge Dealers Ram Tough 200 | Gateway International Raceway | Jack Sprague | David Starr |
| 13 | July 31 | Line-X Spray-on Bedliners 200 | Michigan International Speedway | Dennis Setzer | Travis Kvapil |
| 14 | August 6 | Power Stroke Diesel 200 | Indianapolis Raceway Park | Jack Sprague | Chad Chaffin |
| 15 | August 14 | Toyota Tundra 200 | Nashville Superspeedway | Bobby Hamilton Jr. | Bobby Hamilton |
| 16 | August 25 | O'Reilly 200 by Valvoline | Bristol Motor Speedway | Ken Schrader | Carl Edwards |
| 17 | September 9 | Kroger 200 | Richmond International Raceway | Jamie McMurray | Ted Musgrave |
| 18 | September 18 | Sylvania 200 | New Hampshire Int'l Speedway | Jack Sprague | Travis Kvapil |
| 19 | September 25 | Las Vegas 350 | Las Vegas Motor Speedway | Mike Skinner | Shane Hmiel |
| 20 | October 2 | American Racing Wheels 200 | California Speedway | Travis Kvapil | Todd Bodine |
| 21 | October 16 | Silverado 350K | Texas Motor Speedway | Mike Skinner | Todd Bodine |
| 22 | October 23 | Kroger 200 | Martinsville Speedway | Set by points | Jamie McMurray |
| 23 | November 5 | Chevy Silverado 150 | Phoenix International Raceway | Jack Sprague | David Starr |
| 24 | November 12 | Darlington 200 | Darlington Raceway | Carl Edwards | Kasey Kahne |
| 25 | November 19 | Ford 200 | Homestead-Miami Speedway | David Reutimann | Kasey Kahne |

# 2004 points standings

| Rk. | Driver | Points | Starts | Run at Fin. | Top Finish | Times Led | Laps Led | Laps Comp. | Miles Comp. | Money Won |
|---|---|---|---|---|---|---|---|---|---|---|
| 1. | Bobby Hamilton | 2,624 | 25 | 25 | 1 | 31 | 416 | 4,192 | 4,747.868 | $973,428 |
| 2. | Dennis Setzer | 3,578 | 25 | 25 | 1 | 13 | 93 | 4,198 | 4,485.320 | $707,011 |
| 3. | Ted Musgrave | 3,554 | 25 | 24 | 1 | 24 | 757 | 4,085 | 4,510.330 | $728,883 |
| 4. | Carl Edwards | 3,493 | 25 | 24 | 1 | 18 | 222 | 4,110 | 4,555.070 | $638,905 |
| 5. | Matt Crafton | 3,379 | 25 | 24 | 3 | 5 | 41 | 4,101 | 4,588.820 | $444,307 |
| 6. | David Starr | 3,298 | 25 | 22 | 1 | 6 | 78 | 3,869 | 4,247.610 | $542,108 |
| 7. | Jack Sprague | 3,167 | 25 | 19 | 1 | 19 | 510 | 3,877 | 4,130.510 | $532,741 |
| 8. | Travis Kvapil | 3,152 | 25 | 24 | 1 | 11 | 176 | 4,009 | 4,519.890 | $511,563 |
| 9. | Steve Park | 3,138 | 25 | 24 | 3 | 6 | 99 | 4,128 | 4,580.130 | $356,001 |
| 10. | Chad Chaffin | 3,122 | 25 | 23 | 1 | 4 | 61 | 4,081 | 4,642.620 | $445,514 |
| 11. | Mike Skinner | 3,037 | 25 | 22 | 2 | 22 | 448 | 3,982 | 4,372.950 | $357,795 |
| 12. | Rick Crawford | 3,030 | 25 | 21 | 1 | 4 | 92 | 4,020 | 4,384.500 | $402,161 |
| 13. | Shane Hmiel | 2,954 | 25 | 18 | 1 | 18 | 320 | 3,630 | 4,114.980 | $388,862 |
| 14. | David Reutimann | 2,904 | 25 | 18 | 3 | 5 | 37 | 3,928 | 4,358.800 | $356,582 |
| 15. | Jon Wood | 2,835 | 25 | 21 | 4 | 4 | 39 | 3,935 | 4,289.540 | $311,510 |
| 16. | Terry Cook | 2,821 | 25 | 21 | 3 | 5 | 56 | 3,905 | 4,324.590 | $309,604 |
| 17. | Hank Parker Jr. | 2,737 | 25 | 22 | 3 | 1 | 34 | 3,901 | 4,177.980 | $308,085 |
| 18. | Tracy Hines | 2,604 | 25 | 20 | 5 | 1 | 2 | 3,893 | 4,111.090 | $284,656 |
| 19. | Brandon Whitt | 2,569 | 25 | 19 | 12 | 0 | 0 | 3,792 | 4,184.590 | $262,468 |
| 20. | Andy Houston | 2,540 | 24 | 20 | 7 | 1 | 1 | 3,646 | 4,050.000 | $281,512 |
| 21. | Chase Montgomery | 2,404 | 25 | 21 | 12 | 0 | 0 | 3,872 | 4441.110 | $245,342 |
| 22. | Bill Lester | 2,400 | 25 | 19 | 10 | 3 | 32 | 3,881 | 4,324.360 | $238,845 |
| 23. | Robert Huffman | 2,314 | 24 | 13 | 6 | 1 | 1 | 3,161 | 3,516.840 | $236,913 |
| 24. | Shane Sieg | 2,020 | 19 | 17 | 8 | 3 | 3 | 3,299 | 3,561.740 | $206,830 |
| 25. | Johnny Benson | 1,818 | 13 | 13 | 2 | 1 | 5 | 2,083 | 2,308.590 | $196,082 |
| 26. | Kelly Sutton | 1,432 | 19 | 8 | 20 | 0 | 0 | 1,998 | 2,210.780 | $150,917 |
| 27. | Todd Bodine | 1,317 | 10 | 8 | 1 | 8 | 127 | 1,450 | 1,757.160 | $201,005 |
| 28. | Ken Schrader | 1,297 | 12 | 8 | 5 | 0 | 0 | 1,773 | 1,893.260 | $103,797 |

| Rk. | Driver | Points | Starts | Run at Fin. | Top Finish | Times Led | Laps Led | Laps Comp. | Miles Comp. | Money Won |
|-----|--------|--------|--------|-------------|------------|-----------|----------|------------|-------------|-----------|
| 29. | Ken Weaver | 1,212 | 15 | 8 | 18 | 0 | 0 | 2,131 | 2,151.020 | $132,860 |
| 30. | Deborah Renshaw | 1,150 | 14 | 11 | 15 | 1 | 1 | 1,750 | 2,085.060 | $114,697 |
| 31. | Chris Wimmer | 942 | 12 | 5 | 18 | 0 | 0 | 1,292 | 1,521.100 | $94,805 |
| 32. | David Ragan | 802 | 10 | 4 | 19 | 0 | 0 | 1,105 | 1,324.760 | $84,640 |
| 33. | Shelby Howard | 707 | 8 | 6 | 21 | 0 | 0 | 1,350 | 1,332.760 | $90,511 |
| 34. | Brad Keselowski | 692 | 8 | 4 | 16 | 0 | 0 | 1,283 | 714.750 | $72,315 |
| 35. | J.R. Patton | 637 | 7 | 6 | 15 | 0 | 0 | 970 | 1,219.540 | $59,370 |
| 36. | Mark McFarland | 603 | 7 | 5 | 6 | 0 | 0 | 1,177 | 802.680 | $57,265 |
| 37. | Denny Hamlin | 582 | 5 | 5 | 10 | 0 | 0 | 899 | 940.550 | $43,910 |
| 38. | Randy LaJoie | 570 | 6 | 3 | 8 | 0 | 0 | 589 | 782.570 | $64,475 |
| 39. | Paul White | 516 | 6 | 6 | 14 | 0 | 0 | 1,025 | 1,028.980 | $52,275 |
| 40. | Geoffrey Bodine | 495 | 5 | 4 | 10 | 0 | 0 | 754 | 987.240 | $52,310 |
| 41. | Kevin Love | 494 | 5 | 4 | 11 | 0 | 0 | 969 | 750.500 | $46,510 |
| 42. | Eric Jones | 461 | 5 | 4 | 17 | 0 | 0 | 627 | 954.000 | $48,180 |
| 43. | Lance Hooper | 458 | 5 | 4 | 19 | 0 | 0 | 648 | 852.500 | $50,925 |
| 44. | Jamie McMurray | 444 | 3 | 2 | 1 | 4 | 78 | 605 | 469.320 | $72,245 |
| 45. | Charlie Bradberry | 417 | 6 | 2 | 21 | 0 | 0 | 707 | 568.020 | $41,137 |
| 46. | Bobby Hamilton Jr. | 395 | 3 | 2 | 4 | 9 | 132 | 498 | 507.320 | $24,915 |
| 47. | Kasey Kahne | 380 | 2 | 2 | 1 | 6 | 149 | 284 | 405.900 | $91,113 |
| 48. | Jay Sauter | 373 | 4 | 3 | 15 | 0 | 0 | 625 | 693.280 | $31,510 |
| 49. | Tina Gordon | 371 | 5 | 2 | 24 | 0 | 0 | 563 | 617.510 | $44,545 |
| 50. | Frank Kimmel | 344 | 3 | 3 | 8 | 1 | 6 | 356 | 638.880 | $38,555 |
| 51. | Sean Murphy | 338 | 4 | 2 | 22 | 2 | 12 | 548 | 439.740 | $29,315 |
| 52. | Jason Small | 331 | 4 | 2 | 21 | 0 | 0 | 348 | 551.400 | $34,405 |
| 53. | Kevin Harvick | 315 | 2 | 2 | 4 | 0 | 0 | 340 | 310.800 | $22,150 |
| 54. | Johnny Sauter | 310 | 2 | 2 | 2 | 2 | 139 | 409 | 293.950 | $33,900 |
| 55. | Jimmy Spencer | 303 | 3 | 2 | 16 | 0 | 0 | 602 | 564.350 | $24,187 |
| 56. | Loni Richardson | 290 | 5 | 0 | 34 | 0 | 0 | 71 | 88.310 | $40,599 |
| 57. | Johnny Chapman | 284 | 4 | 2 | 19 | 1 | 2 | 225 | 438.210 | $41,875 |
| 58. | P.J. Jones | 263 | 2 | 2 | 8 | 0 | 0 | 250 | 350.000 | $25,728 |
| 59. | Bobby Labonte | 246 | 2 | 1 | 3 | 1 | 4 | 287 | 130.500 | $24,780 |
| 60. | Joe Aramendia | 231 | 3 | 1 | 25 | 0 | 0 | 532 | 114.500 | $31,195 |
| 61. | Michael Waltrip | 215 | 2 | 1 | 5 | 3 | 49 | 148 | 210.600 | $19,087 |
| 62. | Butch Miller | 209 | 2 | 2 | 15 | 0 | 0 | 407 | 292.580 | $16,555 |
| 63. | Steadman Marlin | 209 | 2 | 2 | 17 | 0 | 0 | 230 | 450.200 | $20,875 |
| 64. | Wayne Edwards | 198 | 4 | 2 | 15 | 0 | 0 | 260 | 702.120 | $42,210 |
| 65. | Scott Lynch | 188 | 2 | 2 | 19 | 0 | 0 | 291 | 363.500 | $14,705 |
| 66. | Jamey Caudill | 182 | 2 | 2 | 19 | 0 | 0 | 450 | 280.600 | $15,355 |
| 67. | Eric Norris | 176 | 2 | 1 | 14 | 0 | 0 | 135 | 202.500 | $20,120 |
| 68. | Mike Wallace | 170 | 1 | 1 | 3 | 1 | 4 | 100 | 250.000 | $38,740 |
| 69. | Tony Stewart | 165 | 1 | 1 | 3 | 0 | 0 | 209 | 156.750 | $16,875 |
| 70. | Tim Schendel | 164 | 2 | 1 | 22 | 0 | 0 | 246 | 267.500 | $15,955 |
| 71. | Robby Gordon | 160 | 1 | 1 | 4 | 0 | 0 | 206 | 109.799 | $11,450 |
| 72. | Teri MacDonald | 155 | 2 | 2 | 25 | 0 | 0 | 437 | 266.250 | $17,155 |
| 73. | Jerry Hill | 152 | 2 | 1 | 26 | 0 | 0 | 174 | 243.660 | $19,105 |
| 74. | Dave Blaney | 150 | 1 | 1 | 6 | 0 | 0 | 200 | 200.000 | $18,048 |
| 75. | Bobby Dotter | 146 | 3 | 0 | 26 | 0 | 0 | 221 | 252.870 | $26,410 |
| 76. | Brad Teague | 143 | 2 | 1 | 27 | 0 | 0 | 149 | 221.720 | $16,30 |
| 77. | Greg Biffle | 142 | 1 | 1 | 8 | 0 | 0 | 134 | 201.000 | $12,925 |
| 78. | Regan Smith | 138 | 1 | 1 | 9 | 0 | 0 | 134 | 219.000 | $13,775 |
| 79. | Joey Clanton | 137 | 2 | 0 | 31 | 0 | 0 | 134 | 129.360 | $19,155 |
| 80. | Ryck Sanders | 134 | 2 | 0 | 32 | 0 | 0 | 105 | 144.750 | $17,640 |
| 81. | Kyle Busch | 130 | 1 | 1 | 11 | 0 | 0 | 200 | 137.200 | $8,575 |
| 82. | Dana White | 125 | 2 | 1 | 32 | 0 | 0 | 313 | 237.690 | $13,530 |
| 83. | Jim Sauter | 124 | 1 | 1 | 13 | 0 | 0 | 205 | 205.000 | $8,065 |
| 84. | J.J. Yeley | 124 | 1 | 1 | 13 | 0 | 0 | 100 | 200.000 | $10,040 |
| 85. | Ron Hornaday Jr. | 124 | 1 | 1 | 13 | 0 | 0 | 150 | 150.000 | $7,915 |
| 86. | Tony Raines | 112 | 1 | 1 | 17 | 0 | 0 | 132 | 203.280 | $7,815 |
| 87. | Andy Petree | 109 | 1 | 1 | 18 | 0 | 0 | 254 | 133,699 | $9,540 |
| 88. | Brandon Miller | 103 | 1 | 1 | 20 | 0 | 0 | 145 | 217.500 | $11,022 |
| 89. | Nick Tucker | 103 | 1 | 1 | 20 | 0 | 0 | 193 | 101.500 | $7,315 |
| 90. | Randy MacDonald | 100 | 1 | 0 | 21 | 0 | 0 | 83 | 207.500 | $15,190 |
| 91. | Sammy Sanders | 97 | 1 | 1 | 22 | 0 | 0 | 146 | 219.000 | $8,735 |
| 92. | Derrike Cope | 97 | 1 | 1 | 22 | 0 | 0 | 148 | 148.000 | $7,440 |
| 93. | Darrell Waltrip | 91 | 2 | 2 | 24 | 0 | 0 | 451 | 268.740 | $14,355 |

| Rk. | Driver | Points | Starts | Run at Fin. | Top Finish | Times Led | Laps Led | Laps Comp. | Miles Comp. | Money Won |
|-----|--------|--------|--------|-------------|------------|-----------|----------|------------|-------------|-----------|
| 94. | Devin Dowler | 91 | 1 | 1 | 24 | 0 | 0 | 246 | 123.000 | $6,915 |
| 95. | Jason Leffler | 91 | 1 | 1 | 24 | 0 | 0 | 149 | 203.530 | $6,640 |
| 96. | Chad Blount | 88 | 1 | 0 | 25 | 0 | 0 | 128 | 192.000 | $8,392 |
| 97. | Josh Richeson | 88 | 1 | 1 | 25 | 0 | 0 | 149 | 203.530 | $6,540 |
| 98. | Rick Gonzalez | 85 | 1 | 1 | 26 | 0 | 0 | 243 | 121.500 | $9,090 |
| 99. | Derrick Kelley | 85 | 1 | 0 | 26 | 0 | 0 | 125 | 200.000 | $10,065 |
| 100. | Erik Darnell | 85 | 1 | 1 | 26 | 0 | 0 | 200 | 200.00 | $7,265 |
| 101. | David Froelich Jr. | 79 | 1 | 1 | 28 | 0 | 0 | 197 | 147.750 | $8,140 |
| 102. | Jeff Jefferson | 79 | 1 | 1 | 28 | 0 | 0 | 189 | 189.000 | $7,215 |
| 103. | J.C. Stout | 73 | 1 | 1 | 30 | 0 | 0 | 196 | 147.000 | $8,090 |
| 104. | Rick Bogart | 73 | 1 | 1 | 30 | 0 | 0 | 133 | 199.500 | $7,115 |
| 105. | Ricky Craven | 70 | 1 | 0 | 31 | 0 | 0 | 82 | 86.760 | $7,060 |

# 2004 Champion

## 4 Bobby Hamilton

**Truck:** DODGE • **Truck owner:** Debbie Hamilton
**Birth date:** 05/29/57 • **Hometown:** Nashville

### NASCAR CRAFTSMAN TRUCK SERIES STATISTICS

**Seasons competed:** 9 (1996-2004)

**Career starts:** 74    **Career wins:** 8    **Career poles:** 4

**Championship season recap:** Hamilton, 47, became the oldest champion in series history when he won the title by 46 points over two-time runner-up Dennis Setzer. Hamilton, who led the series in victories and top five finishes, captured his first championship and became the first driver/owner to win a NASCAR national touring series title since Alan Kulwicki in 1992. In the final race at Homestead, Hamilton finished 16th to lock up the championship and both the driver's and manufacturer's titles for Dodge. It was the first driver's championship for Dodge in 10 years of racing in the NASCAR Craftsman Truck Series.

# Bobby Hamilton 2004 race by race

| No. | Race | Start | Finish | Points | Total points | Rank | Laps/ completed | Money won | Status |
|-----|------|-------|--------|--------|--------------|------|-----------------|-----------|--------|
| 1. | Florida Dodge Dealers 250 | 10 | 11 | 135 | 135 | 10 | 100/100 | $17,400 | Running |
| 2. | EasyCare Vehicle Service Contracts 200 | 12 | 1 | 185 | 320 | 3 | 133/133 | $50,850 | Running |
| 3. | Kroger 250 | 5 | 31 | 75 | 395 | 9 | 241/254 | $8,665 | Running |
| 4. | UAW/GM Ohio 250 | 6 | 4 | 165 | 560 | 4 | 252/252 | $14,925 | Running |
| 5. | Infineon 200 | 5 | 10 | 134 | 694 | 4 | 134/134 | $12,000 | Running |
| 6. | MBNA America 200 | 7 | 19 | 106 | 800 | 5 | 198/200 | $13,015 | Running |
| 7. | O'Reilly 400K | 12 | 7 | 146 | 946 | 5 | 167/167 | $15,000 | Running |
| 8. | O'Reilly 200 | 3 | 1 | 185 | 1,131 | 3 | 200/200 | $49,125 | Running |
| 9. | Black Cat Fireworks 200 | 3 | 6 | 155 | 1,286 | 3 | 205/205 | $12,075 | Running |
| 10. | O'Reilly Auto Parts 250 | 3 | 2 | 180 | 1,466 | 3 | 167/167 | $36,975 | Running |
| 11. | Built Ford Tough 225 | 3 | 1 | 190 | 1,656 | 2 | 153/153 | $80,125 | Running |
| 12. | Missouri-Illinois Dodge Dealers Ram Tough 200 | 2 | 17 | 117 | 1,773 | 2 | 174/174 | $11,015 | Running |
| 13. | Line-X Spray-on Truck Bedliners 200 | 2 | 5 | 165 | 1,938 | 2 | 100/100 | $15,850 | Running |
| 14. | Power Stroke Diesel 200 | 2 | 3 | 165 | 2,103 | 1 | 200/200 | $21,640 | Running |
| 15. | Toyota Tundra 200 | 15 | 1 | 185 | 2,288 | 1 | 150/150 | $49,485 | Running |
| 16. | O'Reilly 200 presented by Valvoline Maxlife | 13 | 12 | 127 | 2,415 | 1 | 206/206 | $9,890 | Running |
| 17. | Kroger 200 | 24 | 26 | 85 | 2,500 | 1 | 204/209 | $6,640 | Running |
| 18. | Sylvania 200 presented by Lowe's | 23 | 15 | 123 | 2,623 | 1 | 200/200 | $10,640 | Running |
| 19. | Las Vegas 350 | 8 | 5 | 155 | 2,778 | 1 | 146/146 | $13,775 | Running |
| 20. | American Racing Wheels 200 | 33 | 5 | 155 | 2,933 | 1 | 100/100 | $18,200 | Running |
| 21. | Silverado 350K | 32 | 3 | 165 | 3,098 | 1 | 146/146 | $32,520 | Running |
| 22. | Kroger 200 | 1 | 26 | 90 | 3,188 | 2 | 182/200 | $6,790 | Running |
| 23. | Chevy Silverado 150 | 8 | 7 | 146 | 3,334 | 1 | 150/150 | $11,000 | Running |
| 24. | Darlington 200 | 5 | 2 | 175 | 3,509 | 1 | 150/150 | $28,150 | Running |
| 25. | Ford 200 | 9 | 16 | 115 | 3,624 | 1 | 134/134 | $13,865 | Running |

**2003 Champion**

## 16 Travis Kvapil

**Truck:** CHEVROLET • **Truck owner:** Steve Coulter
**Birth date:** 03/01/76 • **Hometown:** Janesville, Wis.

### NASCAR CRAFTSMAN TRUCK SERIES STATISTICS

**Seasons competed:** 3 (2001-2004)
**Career starts:** 96     **Career wins:** 5     **Career poles:** 1
**Career highlights:** Series champion in 2003 who came from third in the points standings entering the final race to win. … Set a record in 2003 for best miles completed percentage and fewest uncompleted miles. … 2001 season included Raybestos Rookie of the Year honors, his first NASCAR Craftsman Truck Series victory and a fourth-place finish in the points standings.

**2002 Champion**

## 16 Mike Bliss

**Truck:** CHEVROLET • **Truck owner:** Steve Coulter
**Birth date:** 04/05/65 • **Hometown:** Milwaukee, Ore.

### NASCAR CRAFTSMAN TRUCK SERIES STATISTICS

**Seasons competed:** 7 (1995-99, 2001-02)
**Career starts:** 144     **Career wins:** 12     **Career poles:** 18
**Career highlights:** Fourth series champion to have competed in first NASCAR Craftsman Truck Series event. … Ranks second all-time in poles with 18. … One of three series competitors with at least one victory in six different seasons.

**01, 99 & 97 Champion**

## 24 Jack Sprague

**Truck:** CHEVROLET • **Truck owner:** Rick Hendrick
**Birth date:** 08/08/64 • **Hometown:** Spring Lake, Mich.

### NASCAR CRAFTSMAN TRUCK SERIES STATISTICS

**Seasons competed:** 9 (1995-2001, 2003-04)
**Career starts:** 197     **Career wins:** 24     **Career poles:** 26
**Career highlights:** First three-time NASCAR Craftsman Truck Series champion. … Most poles (26) in series history. … The only competitor to win a race in seven different seasons … Leading money winner in NASCAR Craftsman Truck Series competition ($5,155,289).

## 54 Greg Biffle

**Truck:** FORD • **Truck owner:** Jack Roush
**Birth date:** 12/23/65 • **Hometown:** Vancouver, Wash.

### NASCAR CRAFTSMAN TRUCK SERIES STATISTICS

**Seasons competed:** 5 (1998-2001)
**Career Starts:** 81    **Career wins:** 16    **Career poles:** 12
**Career highlights:** 1998 Raybestos Rookie of the Year. ... Set season record for most victories—nine—in 1999 ... First series competitor to win $1 million in season (2000), ... 2001 NASCAR Busch Series Raybestos Rookie of the Year and 2002 NASCAR Busch Series champion.

## 16 Ron Hornaday Jr.

**Truck:** CHEVROLET • **Truck owner:** Teresa Earnhardt
**Birth date:** 06/20/58 • **Hometown:** Palmdale, Calif.

### NASCAR CRAFTSMAN TRUCK SERIES STATISTICS

**Seasons competed:** 6 (1995-99, 2002)
**Career starts:** 125    **Career wins:** 26    **Career poles:** 11
**Career highlights:** Won the pole for first NASCAR Craftsman Truck Series race at Phoenix International Raceway. ... First two-time series champion. ... Most victories in NASCAR Craftsman Truck Series history.

## 3 Mike Skinner

**Truck:** CHEVROLET • **Truck owner:** Richard Childress
**Birth date:** 12/23/65 • **Hometown:** Vancouver, Wash.

### NASCAR CRAFTSMAN TRUCK SERIES STATISTICS

**Seasons competed:** 6 (1995-98, 2003-04)
**Career Starts:** 79    **Career wins:** 16    **Career poles:** 17
**Career highlights:** Won first NASCAR Craftsman Truck Series race held on February 5, 1995 at Phoenix International Raceway. ... Holds record for most poles in a season, 10 in 1995 ... First NASCAR Craftsman Truck Series champion (1995). ... Daytona 500 pole winner (1997).

# Series champions

| Year | Truck No. | Driver | Owner | Truck | Wins | Poles | Winnings |
|------|-----------|--------|-------|-------|------|-------|----------|
| 1995 | 3 | Mike Skinner | Richard Childress | Chevrolet | 8 | 10 | $428,096 |
| 1996 | 16 | Ron Hornaday Jr. | Teresa Earnhardt | Chevrolet | 4 | 2 | $625,634 |
| 1997 | 24 | Jack Sprague | Rick Hendrick | Chevrolet | 3 | 5 | $880,835 |
| 1998 | 16 | Ron Hornaday Jr. | Teresa Earnhardt | Chevrolet | 6 | 2 | $915,407 |
| 1999 | 24 | Jack Sprague | Rick Hendrick | Chevrolet | 3 | 1 | $834,016 |
| 2000 | 50 | Greg Biffle | Jack Roush | Ford | 5 | 4 | $1,002,510 |
| 2001 | 24 | Jack Sprague | Rick Hendrick | Chevrolet | 4 | 7 | $967,493 |
| 2002 | 16 | Mike Bliss | Steve Coulter | Chevrolet | 5 | 4 | $894,388 |
| 2003 | 16 | Travis Kvapil | Steve Coulter | Chevrolet | 1 | 0 | $872,395 |
| 2004 | 4 | Bobby Hamilton | Debbie Hamilton | Dodge | 4 | 0 | $973,428 |

# 2004 Raybestos Rookie of the Year

## 17 David Reutimann

**Car:** TOYOTA • **Truck owner:** Darrell Waltrip
**Birth date:** 03/02/70 • **Hometown:** Zephyrhills, Fla.

### NASCAR CRAFTSMAN TRUCK SERIES STATISTICS

**Seasons Competed:** 1 (2004)
**Career starts:** 25   **Career wins:** 0   **Career poles:** 2
**Rookie of the Year season recap:** Reutimann clinched the Truck Series rookie of the year award at Homestead, where he won the pole and finished fourth in the race to beat Tracy Hines for top rookie honors by 67 points. Reutimann posted four top fives and 10 top 10s during the season and finished 14th in Truck Series points. Reutimann started his campaign for the rookie award early in the season; he captured the Bud pole at Atlanta in the second race of the season and finished third, behind veterans Bobby Hamilton and Mike Skinner.

# Rookie of the Year winners

| Year | Driver | Points | Rank | Races | Poles | Wins | Top 5 | Top 10 | Winnings | Hometown |
|------|--------|--------|------|-------|-------|------|-------|--------|----------|----------|
| 1996 | Bryan Reffner | 2,961 | 9 | 24 | 2 | 0 | 3 | 9 | $200,898 | Wisconsin Rapids, Wis. |
| 1997 | Kenny Irwin | 3,220 | 10 | 26 | 0 | 2 | 7 | 10 | $349,645 | Indianapolis, Ind. |
| 1998 | Greg Biffle | 3,276 | 8 | 27 | 4 | 0 | 8 | 12 | $459,782 | Vancouver, Wash. |
| 1999 | Mike Stefanik | 3,074 | 13 | 25 | 0 | 0 | 1 | 9 | $287,981 | Coventry, R.I. |
| 2000 | Kurt Busch | 3,596 | 2 | 24 | 4 | 4 | 13 | 16 | $745,632 | Las Vegas, Nev. |
| 2001 | Travis Kvapil | 3,547 | 4 | 24 | 0 | 1 | 11 | 18 | $560,661 | Janesville, Wis. |
| 2002 | Brendan Gaughan | 2,893 | 11 | 22 | 0 | 2 | 5 | 9 | $422,647 | Las Vegas, Nev. |
| 2003 | Carl Edwards | 3,416 | 8 | 25 | 1 | 3 | 13 | 15 | $608,080 | Columbia, Mo. |
| 2004 | David Reutimann | 2,904 | 14 | 25 | 2 | 0 | 4 | 10 | $356,582 | Zephyrhills, Fla. |

# Rookie records

**Most rookies (race):** 14—multiple times, most recent, Loudon, N.H., May 31, 1997
**Fewest rookies (race):** 2—multiple times, most recent, Homestead, Nov. 13, 2003
**Best finish, rookie:** 1st—Kenny Irwin (2 times, 1997); Tony Raines (1997); Randy Tolsma (1997); Andy Houston (1998); Kurt Busch (4 times, 2000); Ricky Hendrick (2001); Travis Kvapil (2001); Brendan Gaughan (2 times, 2002); Carl Edwards (3 times, 2003)
**Most wins by rookie:** 4—Kurt Busch, 2000

**Most rookie winners (season):** 3—1997
**Quickest win by rookie:** 5th start—Tony Raines, 1997
**Most top 5 finishes by rookie:** 13—Carl Edwards, 2003; Kurt Busch, 2000
**Most top-10 finishes by rookie:** 19—Ricky Hendrick, 2001
**Most poles by rookie:** 4—Greg Biffle, 1998; Kurt Busch, 2000
**Most consecutive poles by rookie:** 3—Greg Biffle, 1998
**Most starts:** 27—Greg Biffle, Andy Houston, Scot Walters, 1998
**Most money won:** $745,632—Kurt Busch, 2000
**Best championship finish:** 2nd—Kurt Busch, 2000

# Miscellaneous records

## Series Records, Season—Drivers

**Most wins:** 9—Greg Biffle, 1999

**Most wins on short track:** 7—Mike Skinner, 1996; Ron Hornaday Jr., 1997

**Most wins on road course:** 2—Ron Hornaday Jr., 1995; Joe Ruttman, 1997

**Most wins on superspeedway:** 6—Brendan Gaughan , 2003

**Most consecutive wins:** 3—Mike Skinner, 1996 (Tucson, Colorado, Topeka,); Ron Hornaday Jr., 1997 (Milwaukee, Louisville, Colorado); Greg Biffle, 2000 (Texas, Kentucky, Watkins Glen)

**Most consecutive wins on short track:** 5—Ron Hornaday Jr., 1997 (Bristol, Louisville, Colorado, Indianapolis, Flemington)

**Most wins leading all laps:** 2—Mike Skinner, 1995; Ron Hornaday Jr., 1997

**Most poles:** 10—Mike Skinner, 1995

**Most consecutive poles:** 10—Mike Skinner, 1995

**Most poles, rookie:** 4—Greg Biffle, 1998; Kurt Busch, 2000

**Most wins from pole:** 4—Mike Skinner, 1995 and 1996

**Most top 5 finishes:** 18 – Ron Hornaday Jr., Jack Sprague, 1996

**Most laps completed:** 4,939—Jay Sauter, 1998

**Most miles completed:** 4,710.7—Bobby Hamilton, 2004

**Best miles completed percentage:** 99.9676 percent—Ron Hornaday Jr., 1996

**Fewest uncompleted laps:** 2—Joe Ruttman, 1995, Ron Hornaday Jr., 1996

**Fewest uncompleted miles:** 0.666-mile—Joe Ruttman, 1995

**Best laps completed percentage:** 99.9995 percent—Ron Hornaday Jr., 1996

**Most laps led:** 1,533—Mike Skinner, 1996

**Most miles led:** 1,443.02—Jack Sprague, 2001

**Most times led:** 52—Jack Sprague, 2001

**Most races led:** 19—Greg Biffle, 2000, Jack Sprague, 2001

**Consecutive races led:** 11—Jack Sprague, 2001 (May 6, 2001—Aug. 3, 2001)

**Most races completed:** 27—Joe Ruttman, Jay Sauter, 1998

**Best races completed percentage:** 100 percent—Joe Ruttman, 1995; Ron Hornaday Jr., 1996; Mike Bliss, 1997; Jay Sauter, Joe Ruttman, 1998; Bobby Hamilton, 2004; Dennis Setzer, 2004.

**Most races completed/lead lap:** 24—Jack Sprague, 1997

**Most money won (race):** $86,760—Carl Edwards, Daytona, February 13, 2004

**Most money won (season):** $1,002,510—Greg Biffle, 2000

**Most money won (season, race winnings only):** $634,235—Greg Biffle, 2000

# Series Race Records-Wins

**Most wins:** 26—Ron Hornaday Jr.

**Most short track wins:** 15—Ron Hornaday Jr.

**Most road course wins:** 3—Ron Hornaday Jr., Joe Ruttman

**Most superspeedway wins:** 13—Jack Sprague

**Most wins (track):** 4—Brendan Gaughan: Texas, 2002-2003

**Most consecutive short track wins:** 5—Ron Hornaday Jr.: Bristol, Louisville, Denver, Indianapolis, Flemington, 1997

**Most consecutive road course wins:** 2—Ron Hornaday Jr.: Topeka, Sonoma, 1995

**Most consecutive superspeedway wins:** 3—Mike Skinner: Phoenix, Milwaukee, Phoenix, 1995

**Most consecutive wins (track):** 4—Brendan Gaughan: Texas, 2002-2003

**Win from farthest back:** 33rd—Dennis Setzer: Martinsville, April 13, 2002

**Most wins from pole:** 8—Mike Skinner

**Most wins leading all laps:** 3—Mike Skinner (Most recently, Ron Hornaday Jr., Louisville, July 12, 1997)

**Consecutive wins from pole:** 2—Rich Bickle: Portland, May 3, 1997 and Evergreen, Wash., May 10, 1997

**Most winners (season):** 14—1998

**Most consecutive different winners (same season):** 12—1998 (Aug. 1, New Hampshire, through Oct. 24, Phoenix)

**Most Races before first win:** 120—Rick Crawford (Win came at Daytona, February 14, 2003)

**Most races between wins:** 73—Randy Tolsma: Win No. 1, Bakersfield, Oct. 12, 1997; Win No. 2, Nashville, Aug. 12, 2000

**Most races without win:** 154—Lance Norick

# Poles/Speeds

**Most poles:** 26—Jack Sprague

**Most poles (superspeedway):** 17—Jack Sprague

**Most poles (road course):** 4—Ron Fellows

**Most poles (short track):** 11—Mike Skinner

**Most poles (track):** 3—Jack Sprague: Phoenix; Ron Fellows: Watkins Glen

**Most fast qualifiers/pole winners:** 15—1998

**Most consecutive different pole winners (same season):** 8—1997, 1998

**Most consecutive different pole winners (continuing):** 9—1995-96

**Consecutive poles (superspeedway):** 3—Jack Sprague, Jason Leffler

**Most wins (season) by pole winner:** 10—2000

**Fastest official lap:** 187.563 mph—Joe Ruttman, Daytona, Feb. 16, 2000

**Fastest official lap (superspeedway):** 187.563 mph—Joe Ruttman, Daytona, Feb. 16, 2000

**Fastest official sap (road course):** 117.366 mph—Ron Fellows, Watkins Glen, Aug. 24, 1997

**Fastest official lap (short track):** 126.922 mph—Ken Schrader, Bristol, August 25, 2004

# All-time race winners

| Driver | Total |
|--------|-------|
| Ron Hornaday Jr. | 26 |
| Jack Sprague | 24 |
| Mike Skinner | 16 |
| Greg Biffle | 16 |
| Ted Musgrave | 15 |
| Joe Ruttman | 13 |
| Mike Bliss | 12 |
| Dennis Setzer | 12 |
| Brendan Gaughan | 8 |
| Bobby Hamilton | 8 |
| Carl Edwards | 6 |
| Terry Cook | 5 |
| Scott Riggs | 5 |
| Travis Kvapil | 5 |
| Kurt Busch | 4 |
| Rick Carelli | 4 |
| Tony Raines | 4 |

| Driver | Total |
|--------|-------|
| Jay Sauter | 4 |
| Mike Wallace | 4 |
| Rick Crawford | 3 |
| Rich Bickle | 3 |
| Andy Houston | 3 |
| Dave Rezendes | 3 |
| David Starr | 3 |
| Todd Bodin | 2 |
| Chad Chaffin | 2 |
| Stacy Compton | 2 |
| Ron Fellows | 2 |
| Jimmy Hensley | 2 |
| Kenny Irwin | 2 |
| Kasey Kahne | 2 |
| Robert Pressley | 2 |
| Randy Tolsma | 2 |
| Kevin Harvick | 2 |

| Driver | Total |
|--------|-------|
| Tony Stewart | 2 |
| Jon Wood | 2 |
| Ricky Hendrick | 1 |
| Shane Hmiel | 1 |
| Bob Keselowski | 1 |
| Terry Labonte | 1 |
| Jason Leffler | 1 |
| Mark Martin | 1 |
| Jamie McMurray | 1 |
| Butch Miller | 1 |
| Bryan Reffner | 1 |
| Boris Said | 1 |
| Ken Schrader | 1 |
| Jimmy Spencer | 1 |
| **Different winners** | **48** |
| **Total races** | **242** |

# All-time pole winners

| Driver | Total |
|--------|-------|
| Jack Sprague | 26 |
| Mike Bliss | 18 |
| Joe Ruttman | 17 |
| Mike Skinner | 17 |
| Greg Biffle | 12 |
| Ron Hornaday Jr. | 11 |
| Ted Musgrave | 11 |
| Jason Leffler | 10 |
| Stacy Compton | 9 |
| Terry Cook | 8 |
| Rich Bickle | 6 |
| Bryan Reffner | 5 |
| Scott Riggs | 5 |
| Kurt Busch | 4 |
| Bobby Hamilton | 4 |
| Jimmy Hensley | 4 |
| Andy Houston | 4 |
| Carl Edwards | 3 |
| Ron Fellows | 3 |
| Brendan Gaughan | 3 |
| Jamie McMurray | 3 |
| Dennis Setzer | 3 |
| David Starr | 3 |
| Mike Wallace | 3 |
| Chad Chaffin | 2 |
| Rick Crawford | 2 |

| Driver | Total |
|--------|-------|
| David Reutimann | 2 |
| Boris Said | 2 |
| Jay Sauter | 2 |
| Randy Tolsma | 2 |
| Jon Wood | 2 |
| Johnny Benson | 1 |
| Geoffrey Bodine | 1 |
| Chuck Bown | 1 |
| Tobey Butler | 1 |
| Michael Dokken | 1 |
| Bobby Hamilton Jr. | 1 |
| Tom Hubert | 1 |
| Kenny Irwin | 1 |
| Travis Kvapil | 1 |
| Terry Labonte | 1 |
| Bill Lester | 1 |
| Butch Miller | 1 |
| Steve Park | 1 |
| Tony Raines | 1 |
| Dave Rezendes | 1 |
| Ken Schrader | 1 |
| Bill Sedgwick | 1 |
| Jimmy Spencer | 1 |
| Tim Steele | 1 |
| **Different winners** | **50** |

**\* Time trials held in 230 events.**

# Most starts 1995-2004

1. Rick Crawford ...............................198
2. Jack Sprague ...............................197
3. Terry Cook ...................................190
4. Joe Ruttman* ...............................168
5. Dennis Setzer ..............................167
6. Lance Norick* ..............................153
7. Jimmy Hensley* ...........................146
8. Mike Bliss* ..................................144
9. Rick Carelli* ................................134
10. Ron Hornaday Jr. .........................125

**\*Did not participate in 2004**

# 2003 season

| Pos. | Driver | Points | Starts | Poles | Wins | Top 5 | Top 10 | Winnings |
|------|--------|--------|--------|-------|------|-------|--------|----------|
| 1. | Travis Kvapil | 3,837 | 25 | 0 | 1 | 13 | 22 | $872,395 |
| 2. | Dennis Setzer | 3,828 | 25 | 0 | 3 | 15 | 23 | $654,455 |
| 3. | Ted Musgrave | 3,819 | 25 | 4 | 3 | 14 | 18 | $764,195 |
| 4. | Brendan Gaughan | 3,797 | 25 | 3 | 6 | 14 | 18 | $771,290 |
| 5. | Jon Wood | 3,659 | 25 | 2 | 2 | 10 | 20 | $545,965 |
| 6. | Bobby Hamilton | 3,627 | 25 | 1 | 2 | 10 | 18 | $521,915 |
| 7. | Rick Crawford | 3,578 | 25 | 0 | 1 | 10 | 16 | $505,240 |
| 8. | Carl Edwards # | 3,416 | 25 | 1 | 3 | 13 | 15 | $608,080 |
| 9. | Terry Cook | 3,212 | 25 | 2 | 0 | 0 | 13 | $337,160 |
| 10. | Chad Chaffin | 3.143 | 25 | 2 | 0 | 2 | 9 | $333,770 |

**# Raybestos Rookie of the Year contenders**

## Race winners • 12

| | |
|---|---|
| Brendan Gaughan | 6 |
| Carl Edwards | 3 |
| Ted Musgrave | 3 |
| Dennis Setzer | 3 |
| Bobby Hamilton | 2 |
| Jon Wood | 2 |
| Rick Crawford | 1 |
| Kevin Harvick | 1 |
| Travis Kvapil | 1 |
| Jason Leffler | 1 |
| Jimmy Spencer | 1 |
| Tony Stewart | 1 |

## Money won

| | |
|---|---|
| Travis Kvapil | $872,395 |
| Brendan Gaughan | $771,290 |
| Ted Musgrave | $764,195 |
| Dennis Setzer | $654,455 |
| Carl Edwards | $608,080 |
| Jon Wood | $545,965 |
| Bobby Hamilton | $521,915 |
| Rick Crawford | $505,240 |
| Terry Cook | $337,160 |
| Robert Pressley | $337,085 |

## Pole winners • 11

| | |
|---|---|
| Ted Musgrave | 4 |
| Brendan Gaughan | 3 |
| Chad Chaffin | 2 |
| Terry Cook | 2 |
| Jason Leffler | 2 |
| Jon Wood | 2 |
| Carl Edwards | 1 |
| Bobby Hamilton | 1 |
| Andy Houston | 1 |
| Bill Lester | 1 |
| Jimmy Spencer | 1 |

# 2002 season

| Pos. | Driver | Points | Starts | Poles | Wins | Top 5 | Top 10 | Winnings |
|------|--------|--------|--------|-------|------|-------|--------|----------|
| 1. | Mike Bliss | 3,259 | 22 | 4 | 5 | 13 | 18 | $894,388 |
| 2. | Rick Crawford | 3,313 | 22 | 2 | 0 | 12 | 17 | $544,359 |
| 3. | Ted Musgrave | 3,308 | 22 | 3 | 3 | 12 | 16 | $651,797 |
| 4. | Jason Leffler | 3,156 | 22 | 8 | 0 | 11 | 15 | $525,619 |
| 5. | David Starr | 3,144 | 22 | 2 | 1 | 8 | 16 | $473,712 |
| 6. | Dennis Setzer | 3,132 | 22 | 0 | 1 | 8 | 14 | $502,040 |
| 7. | Robert Pressley | 3,097 | 22 | 0 | 2 | 7 | 15 | $495,817 |
| 8. | Terry Cook | 3,070 | 22 | 2 | 4 | 9 | 17 | $521,465 |
| 9. | Travis Kvapil | 3,039 | 22 | 0 | 1 | 10 | 14 | $414,326 |
| 10. | Coy Gibbs | 3,010 | 22 | 0 | 0 | 4 | 14 | $364,907 |

## Race winners • 11

| | |
|---|---|
| Mike Bliss | 5 |
| Terry Cook | 4 |
| Ted Musgrave | 3 |
| Brendan Gaughan | 2 |
| Robert Pressley | 2 |
| Kevin Harvick | 1 |
| Ron Hornaday Jr. | 1 |
| Travis Kvapil | 1 |
| Dennis Setzer | 1 |
| David Starr | 1 |
| Tony Stewart | 1 |

## Money won

| | |
|---|---|
| Mike Bliss | $894,388 |
| Ted Musgrave | $651,797 |
| Rick Crawford | $544,359 |
| Jason Leffler | $525,619 |
| Terry Cook | $521,465 |
| Dennis Setzer | $502,040 |
| Robert Pressley | $495,817 |
| Brendan Gaughan | $414,326 |
| Travis Kvapil | $414,326 |

## Pole winners • 6

| | |
|---|---|
| Jason Leffler | 8 |
| Mike Bliss | 4 |
| Ted Musgrave | 3 |
| Terry Cook | 2 |
| Rick Crawford | 2 |
| David Starr | 2 |

# 2001 season

| Pos. | Driver | Points | Starts | Poles | Wins | Top 5 | Top 10 | Winnings |
|------|--------|--------|--------|-------|------|-------|--------|----------|
| 1. | Jack Sprague | 3,670 | 24 | 7 | 4 | 15 | 17 | $967,493 |
| 2. | Ted Musgrave | 3,597 | 24 | 2 | 7 | 13 | 18 | $726,406 |
| 3. | Joe Ruttman | 3,570 | 24 | 4 | 2 | 10 | 20 | $597,129 |
| 4. | Travis Kvapil # | 3,547 | 24 | 0 | 1 | 11 | 18 | $560,661 |
| 5. | Scott Riggs | 3,526 | 24 | 4 | 5 | 14 | 16 | $677,888 |
| 6. | Ricky Hendrick # | 3,412 | 24 | 0 | 1 | 8 | 19 | $442,031 |
| 7. | Terry Cook | 3,327 | 24 | 1 | 0 | 5 | 16 | $427,773 |
| 8. | Rick Crawford | 3,320 | 24 | 0 | 0 | 10 | 16 | $423,761 |
| 9. | Dennis Setzer | 3,306 | 24 | 2 | 1 | 8 | 15 | $416,492 |
| 10. | Coy Gibbs | 2,875 | 24 | 0 | 0 | 2 | 7 | $290,922 |

**# Raybestos Rookie of the Year contenders**

### Race winners • 9

| | |
|---|---|
| Ted Musgrave | 7 |
| Scott Riggs | 5 |
| Jack Sprague | 4 |
| Greg Biffle | 2 |
| Joe Ruttman | 2 |
| Bobby Hamilton | 1 |
| Travis Kvapil | 1 |
| Ricky Hendrick | 1 |
| Dennis Setzer | 1 |

### Money won

| | |
|---|---|
| Jack Sprague | $967,493 |
| Ted Musgrave | $726,406 |
| Scott Riggs | $677,888 |
| Joe Ruttman | $597,129 |
| Travis Kvapil | $560,661 |
| Ricky Hendrick | $442,031 |
| Terry Cook | $427,773 |
| Rick Crawford | $423,761 |
| Dennis Setzer | $416,492 |
| Lance Norick | $303,697 |

### Pole winners • 7

| | |
|---|---|
| Jack Sprague | 7 |
| Scott Riggs | 4 |
| Joe Ruttman | 4 |
| Ted Musgrave | 2 |
| Dennis Setzer | 2 |
| Stacy Compton | 1 |
| Terry Cook | 1 |

# 2000 season

| Pos. | Driver | Points | Starts | Poles | Wins | Top 5 | Top 10 | Winnings |
|------|--------|--------|--------|-------|------|-------|--------|----------|
| 1. | Greg Biffle | 3,826 | 24 | 4 | 5 | 18 | 18 | $1,002,510 |
| 2. | Kurt Busch # | 3,596 | 24 | 4 | 4 | 13 | 16 | $745,632 |
| 3. | Andy Houston | 3,566 | 24 | 1 | 2 | 13 | 18 | $614,539 |
| 4. | Mike Wallace | 3,450 | 24 | 2 | 2 | 13 | 16 | $624,505 |
| 5. | Jack Sprague | 3,316 | 24 | 0 | 3 | 13 | 15 | $567,536 |
| 6. | Joe Ruttman | 3,278 | 24 | 8 | 3 | 10 | 11 | $578,086 |
| 7. | Dennis Setzer | 3,214 | 24 | 0 | 1 | 8 | 16 | $431,711 |
| 8. | Randy Tolsma | 3,157 | 24 | 0 | 1 | 6 | 15 | $447,892 |
| 9. | Bryan Reffner | 3,153 | 24 | 2 | 1 | 3 | 16 | $375,542 |
| 10. | Steve Grissom | 3,113 | 24 | 0 | 0 | 6 | 11 | $310,529 |

**# Raybestos Rookie of the Year contenders**

### Race winners • 11

| | |
|---|---|
| Greg Biffle | 5 |
| Kurt Busch | 4 |
| Joe Ruttman | 3 |
| Jack Sprague | 3 |
| Andy Houston | 2 |
| Mike Wallace | 2 |
| Rick Carelli | 1 |
| Bobby Hamilton | 1 |
| Bryan Reffner | 1 |
| Dennis Setzer | 1 |
| Randy Tolsma | 1 |

### Money won

| | |
|---|---|
| Greg Biffle | $1,002,510 |
| Kurt Busch | 745,632 |
| Mike Wallace | 624,505 |
| Andy Houston | 614,539 |
| Joe Ruttman | 578,086 |
| Jack Sprague | 567,536 |
| Randy Tolsma | 447,892 |
| Dennis Setzer | 431,711 |
| Bryan Reffner | 375,542 |
| Jimmy Hensley | 317,936 |

### Pole winners • 8

| | |
|---|---|
| Joe Ruttman | 8 |
| Greg Biffle | 4 |
| Kurt Busch | 4 |
| Mike Wallace | 2 |
| Jamie McMurray | 2 |
| Bryan Reffner | 2 |
| Bobby Hamilton | 1 |
| Andy Houston | 1 |

# 1999 season

| Pos. | Driver | Points | Starts | Poles | Wins | Top 5 | Top 10 | Winnings |
|------|--------|--------|--------|-------|------|-------|--------|----------|
| 1. | Jack Sprague | 3,747 | 25 | 1 | 3 | 16 | 19 | $834,016 |
| 2. | Greg Biffle | 3,739 | 25 | 4 | 9 | 14 | 19 | $763,238 |
| 3. | Dennis Setzer | 3,639 | 25 | 1 | 3 | 11 | 19 | $628,835 |
| 4. | Stacy Compton | 3,623 | 25 | 6 | 0 | 12 | 17 | $481,922 |
| 5. | Jay Sauter | 3,543 | 25 | 2 | 2 | 8 | 16 | $482,118 |
| 6. | Mike Wallace | 3,494 | 25 | 0 | 2 | 12 | 14 | $478,900 |
| 7. | Ron Hornaday Jr. | 3,488 | 25 | 0 | 2 | 7 | 16 | $576,152 |
| 8. | Andy Houston | 3,359 | 25 | 1 | 0 | 5 | 14 | $312,323 |
| 9. | Mike Bliss | 3,294 | 25 | 3 | 1 | 6 | 13 | $349,284 |
| 10. | Jimmy Hensley | 3,280 | 25 | 0 | 1 | 7 | 14 | $332,170 |

## Race winners • 10

Greg Biffle ...................................................9
Dennis Setzer ...............................................3
Jack Sprague ...............................................3
Ron Hornaday Jr. ..........................................2
Jay Sauter ...................................................2
Mike Wallace ...............................................2
Mike Bliss ...................................................1
Rick Carelli .................................................1
Ron Fellows .................................................1
Jimmy Hensley .............................................1

## Money won

Jack Sprague ..................................$834,016
Greg Biffle .....................................$763,238
Dennis Setzer .................................$628,835
Ron Hornaday Jr. .............................$576,152
Jay Sauter .....................................$482,118
Stacy Compton ................................$481,922
Mike Wallace ..................................$478,900
Terry Cook ....................................$438,676
Mike Bliss .....................................$349,284
Jimmy Hensley ................................$332,170

## Pole winners • 12

Stacy Compton ...............................................6
Greg Biffle ...................................................4
Mike Bliss ...................................................3
Boris Said ...................................................2
Jay Sauter ...................................................2
Ron Fellows .................................................1
Bobby Hamilton .............................................1
Andy Houston ...............................................1
Dennis Setzer ...............................................1
Jack Sprague ...............................................1
Tim Steele ...................................................1
Randy Tolsma ...............................................1

# 1998 season

| Pos. | Driver | Points | Starts | Poles | Wins | Top 5 | Top 10 | Winnings |
|------|--------|--------|--------|-------|------|-------|--------|----------|
| 1. | Ron Hornaday Jr. | 4,072 | 27 | 2 | 6 | 16 | 22 | $915,407 |
| 2. | Jack Sprague | 4,069 | 27 | 4 | 5 | 16 | 23 | $745,171 |
| 3. | Joe Ruttman | 3,874 | 27 | 2 | 1 | 14 | 19 | $547,933 |
| 4. | Jay Sauter | 3,672 | 27 | 0 | 1 | 7 | 14 | $457,765 |
| 5. | Tony Raines | 3,596 | 27 | 1 | 3 | 9 | 15 | $453,846 |
| 6. | Jimmy Hensley | 3,570 | 27 | 0 | 1 | 9 | 15 | $430,328 |
| 7. | Stacy Compton | 3,542 | 27 | 2 | 2 | 9 | 14 | $433,855 |
| 8. | Greg Biffle # | 3,276 | 27 | 4 | 0 | 8 | 12 | $459,782 |
| 9. | Ron Barfield | 3,227 | 27 | 0 | 0 | 2 | 10 | $268,910 |
| 10. | Mike Bliss | 3,216 | 27 | 4 | 2 | 5 | 9 | $395,844 |

**# Raybestos Rookie of the Year contenders**

## Race winners • 14

Ron Hornaday Jr. ..........................................6
Jack Sprague ...............................................5
Tony Raines .................................................3
Mike Bliss ...................................................2
Stacy Compton ..............................................2
Rick Carelli .................................................1
Terry Cook ...................................................1
Rick Crawford ...............................................1
Jimmy Hensley .............................................1
Andy Houston ...............................................1
Joe Ruttman .................................................1
Boris Said ...................................................1
Jay Sauter ...................................................1
Dennis Setzer ...............................................1

## Money won

Ron Hornaday Jr. .............................$915,407
Jack Sprague ..................................$745,171
Joe Ruttman ...................................$547,933
Greg Biffle .....................................$459,782
Jay Sauter .....................................$457,765
Tony Raines ...................................$453,846
Stacy Compton ................................$433,855
Jimmy Hensley ................................$430,328
Mike Bliss .....................................$395,844
Andy Houston .................................$350,487

## Pole winners • 15

Greg Biffle ...................................................4
Mike Bliss ...................................................4
Jack Sprague ...............................................4
Stacy Compton ..............................................2
Ron Hornaday Jr. ..........................................2
Joe Ruttman .................................................2
Chuck Bown .................................................1
Terry Cook ...................................................1
Ron Fellows .................................................1
Andy Houston ...............................................1
Tom Hubert ...................................................1
Tony Raines .................................................1
Boris Said ...................................................1
Randy Tolsma ...............................................1
Mike Wallace ...............................................1

# 1997 season

| Pos. | Driver | Points | Starts | Poles | Wins | Top 5 | Top 10 | Winnings |
|------|--------|--------|--------|-------|------|-------|--------|----------|
| 1. | Jack Sprague | 3,969 | 26 | 5 | 3 | 16 | 23 | $880,835 |
| 2. | Rich Bickle | 3,737 | 26 | 4 | 3 | 15 | 17 | $485,180 |
| 3. | Joe Ruttman | 3,736 | 26 | 2 | 5 | 13 | 17 | $641,444 |
| 4. | Mike Bliss | 3,611 | 26 | 6 | 1 | 11 | 18 | $541,555 |
| 5. | Ron Hornaday Jr. | 3,574 | 26 | 3 | 7 | 13 | 17 | $604,830 |
| 6. | Jay Sauter | 3,467 | 26 | 0 | 1 | 10 | 15 | $412,264 |
| 7. | Rick Carelli | 3,461 | 26 | 0 | 0 | 6 | 17 | $331,325 |
| 8. | Jimmy Hensley | 3,385 | 26 | 2 | 0 | 4 | 13 | $312,820 |
| 9. | Chuck Bown | 3,320 | 26 | 0 | 0 | 4 | 13 | $290,921 |
| 10. | Kenny Irwin # | 3,220 | 26 | 0 | 2 | 7 | 10 | $349,645 |

# Raybestos Rookie of the Year contenders

## Race winners • 11

| | |
|---|---|
| Ron Hornaday Jr. | 7 |
| Joe Ruttman | 5 |
| Rich Bickle | 3 |
| Jack Sprague | 3 |
| Kenny Irwin | 2 |
| Mike Bliss | 1 |
| Ron Fellows | 1 |
| Bob Keselowski | 1 |
| Tony Raines | 1 |
| Jay Sauter | 1 |
| Tandy Tolsma | 1 |

## Money won

| | |
|---|---|
| Jack Sprague | $880,835 |
| Joe Ruttman | $641,444 |
| Ron Hornaday Jr. | $604,830 |
| Mike Bliss | $541,555 |
| Rich Bickle | $485,180 |
| Jay Sauter | $412,264 |
| Kenny Irwin | $349,645 |
| Rick Carelli | $331,325 |
| Jimmy Hensley | $312,820 |
| Butch Miller | $298,225 |

## Pole winners • 10

| | |
|---|---|
| Mike Bliss | 6 |
| Jack Sprague | 5 |
| Rich Bickle | 4 |
| Ron Hornaday Jr. | 3 |
| Jimmy Hensley | 2 |
| Joe Ruttman | 2 |
| Terry Cook | 1 |
| Michael Dokken | 1 |
| Ron Fellows | 1 |
| Dave Rezendes | 1 |

# 1996 season

| Pos. | Driver | Points | Starts | Poles | Wins | Top 5 | Top 10 | Winnings |
|------|--------|--------|--------|-------|------|-------|--------|----------|
| 1. | Ron Hornaday Jr. | 3,831 | 24 | 2 | 4 | 18 | 23 | $625,634 |
| 2. | Jack Sprague | 3,778 | 24 | 2 | 5 | 18 | 21 | $580,112 |
| 3. | Mike Skinner | 3,771 | 24 | 4 | 8 | 17 | 20 | $602,495 |
| 4. | Joe Ruttman | 3,275 | 24 | 0 | 0 | 7 | 16 | $276,013 |
| 5. | Mike Bliss | 3,190 | 24 | 2 | 2 | 9 | 11 | $345,322 |
| 6. | Dave Rezendes | 3,179 | 24 | 0 | 3 | 9 | 13 | $335,840 |
| 7. | Butch Miller | 3,126 | 24 | 1 | 0 | 7 | 11 | $258,333 |
| 8. | Jimmy Hensley | 3,029 | 24 | 1 | 0 | 5 | 14 | $228,936 |
| 9. | Bryan Reffner # | 2,961 | 24 | 3 | 0 | 3 | 9 | $200,898 |
| 10. | Rick Carelli | 2,953 | 24 | 0 | 1 | 2 | 9 | $227,575 |

# Raybestos Rookie of the Year contenders

## Race winners • 7

| | |
|---|---|
| Mike Skinner | 8 |
| Jack Sprague | 5 |
| Ron Hornaday Jr. | 4 |
| Dave Rezendes | 3 |
| Mike Bliss | 2 |
| Rick Carelli | 1 |
| Mark Martin | 1 |

## Season winnings

| | |
|---|---|
| Ron Hornaday Jr. | $625,634 |
| Mike Skinner | $602,495 |
| Jack Sprague | $580,112 |
| Mike Bliss | $345,322 |
| Dave Rezendes | $335,840 |
| Joe Ruttman | $276,013 |
| Butch Miller | $258,333 |
| Jimmy Hensley | $228,936 |
| Rick Carelli | $227,575 |
| Rich Bickle | $204,169 |

## Pole winners • 14

| | |
|---|---|
| Mike Skinner | 5 |
| Bryan Reffner | 3 |
| Rich Bickle | 2 |
| Mike Bliss | 2 |
| Ron Hornaday Jr. | 2 |
| Jack Sprague | 2 |
| Johnny Benson | 1 |
| Geoffrey Bodine | 1 |
| Tobey Butler | 1 |
| Bobby Hamilton | 1 |
| Jimmy Hensley | 1 |
| Kenny Irwin | 1 |
| Butch Miller | 1 |
| Steve Park | 1 |

# 1995 season

| Pos. | Driver | Points | Starts | Poles | Wins | Top 5 | Top 10 | Winnings |
|------|--------|--------|--------|-------|------|-------|--------|----------|
| 1. | Mike Skinner | 3,224 | 20 | 10 | 8 | 17 | 18 | $428,096 |
| 2. | Joe Ruttman | 3,098 | 20 | 1 | 2 | 9 | 18 | $264,798 |
| 3. | Ron Hornaday Jr. | 2,986 | 20 | 4 | 6 | 10 | 14 | $296,715 |
| 4. | Butch Miller | 2,812 | 20 | 0 | 1 | 9 | 14 | $182,633 |
| 5. | Jack Sprague | 2,740 | 20 | 1 | 0 | 4 | 15 | $116,501 |
| 6. | Rick Carelli | 2,683 | 20 | 0 | 0 | 5 | 10 | $132,013 |
| 7. | Bill Sedgwick | 2,681 | 20 | 1 | 0 | 6 | 13 | $119,918 |
| 8. | Mike Bliss | 2,626 | 19 | 0 | 1 | 5 | 12 | $144,354 |
| 9. | Scott Lagasse | 2,470 | 20 | 0 | 0 | 2 | 7 | $88,100 |
| 10. | Tobey Butler | 2,358 | 20 | 0 | 0 | 3 | 5 | $86,146 |

### Race winners • 7

| | |
|---|---|
| Mike Skinner | 8 |
| Ron Hornaday Jr. | 6 |
| Joe Ruttman | 2 |
| Mike Bliss | 1 |
| Terry Labonte | 1 |
| Butch Miller | 1 |
| Ken Schrader | 1 |

### Money won

| | |
|---|---|
| Mike Skinner | $428,096 |
| Ron Hornaday Jr. | $296,715 |
| Joe Ruttman | $264,798 |
| Butch Miller | $182,633 |
| Mike Bliss | $144,354 |
| Rick Carelli | $132,013 |
| Bill Sedgwick | $119,918 |
| Jack Sprague | $116,501 |
| Dave Rezendes | $90,814 |
| Scott Lagasse | $88,100 |

### Pole winners • 6

| | |
|---|---|
| Mike Skinner | 10 |
| Ron Hornaday Jr. | 4 |
| Terry Labonte | 1 |
| Joe Ruttman | 1 |
| Bill Sedgwick | 1 |
| Jack Sprague | 1 |

David Starr (75) had trouble in the opening race of the 2004 season at Daytona but rebounded to finish 12th. Steadman Marlin (67) finished 17th.

NASCAR tracks

# 2005 SCHEDULE

**NEXTEL CUP**

**Event:** Golden Corral 500
**Race:** No. 4 of 36
**Date:** March 20
**TV:** FOX. **Radio:** PRN

**Event:** Bass Pro Shops MBNA 500
**Race:** No. 33 of 36
**Date:** October 30
**TV:** NBC. **Radio:** PRN

**BUSCH SERIES**

**Event:** Aaron's 312
**Race:** No. 5 of 35
**Date:** March 19
**TV:** FX. **Radio:** PRN

**CRAFTSMAN TRUCK SERIES**

**Event:** EasyCare Vehicle Service 200
**Race:** No. 3 of 25
**Date:** March 18
**TV:** SPEED
**Radio:** MRN

**Event:** TBA (inaugural race)
**Race:** No. 22 of 25
**Date:** October 29
**TV:** SPEED
**Radio:** MRN

Race names subject to change

## TRACK FACTS

**Opened:** 1960
**Owner:** Speedway Motorsports, Inc.
**Location:** Hampton, Ga.
**Distance:** 1.54 miles
**Banking in turns:** 24 degrees
**Banking in straights:** 5 degrees
**Length of front stretch:** 2,332 feet
**Length of back stretch:** 1,800 feet
**Grandstand seating:** 124,000
**Tickets:** (770) 946-4211

**Back stretch:** 2,332 feet / 5°
24° Banking in Turns
**Front stretch:** 1,800 feet / 5°

# NEXTEL CUP

## TRACK RECORDS

**Most wins:** 8—Dale Earnhardt
**Oldest winner:** Morgan Shepherd, 51 years, 4 months, 27 days, March 20, 1993
**Youngest winner:** Jeff Gordon, 23 years, 7 months, 8 days, March 12, 1995
**Most lead changes:** 45—November 7, 1982
**Fewest lead changes:** 6—Three times, most recently, June 30, 1963
**Most leaders:** 17—March 12, 2000
**Fewest leaders:** 3—June 30, 1963
**Most laps led in a 400-mile race:** 167, Banjo Matthews, September 17, 1961
**Most laps led in a 500-mile race:** 308, Cale Yarborough, March 30, 1969
**Most cautions:** 11—Three times, most recently, November 14, 1993
**Fewest cautions:** 1—July 9, 1961
**Most caution laps:** 99—November 6, 1977
**Fewest caution laps:** 7—November 2, 1986
**Most on the lead lap:** 32—November 8, 1998
**Fewest on the lead lap:** 1—11 times, most recently, November 2, 1986
**Most running at the finish:** 39—October 27, 2002

**Fewest running at the finish:** 10—April 5, 1964
**Most laps led by a race winner:** 308—Cale Yarborough, March 30, 1969
**Fewest laps led by a race winner:** 1—David Pearson, September 17, 1961
**Closest margin of victory:** 0.006 seconds—Kevin Harvick defeated Jeff Gordon, March 11, 2001.
**Greatest margin of victory:** 1 lap, 3 seconds—Dale Earnhardt defeated Richard Petty, November 2, 1986.

## QUALIFYING AND RACE RECORDS

**QUALIFYING: Track:** Geoffrey Bodine, Ford; 197.478 mph, 28.074 seconds, November 15, 1997 (NAPA 500). **Spring race (Golden Corral 500):** Bobby Labonte, Pontiac;194.957 mph, 28.437 seconds, March 12, 1999. **Fall Race (Bass Pro Shops MBNA 500):** Geoffrey Bodine, Ford; 197.478 mph, 28.074 seconds, November 15, 1997.
**RACE: Track:** Dale Earnhardt, Chevrolet; 163.633 mph, November 12, 1995 (NAPA 500). **Spring race (Golden Corral 500):** Dale Earnhardt, Chevrolet; 161.298 mph, March 10, 1996. **Fall race (Bass Pro Shops MBNA 500):** Dale Earnhardt, Chevrolet; 163.633 mph, November 12, 1995. **Dixie 400:** Richard Petty, Plymouth; 130.244 mph, August 7, 1966. **Dixie 300:** Glenn "Fireball" Roberts, Pontiac; 112.653 mph, July 31, 1960. **Festival 250:** Fred Lorenzen, Ford; 118.098 mph, July 9, 1961.

## NEXTEL Cup YEAR BY YEAR WINNERS

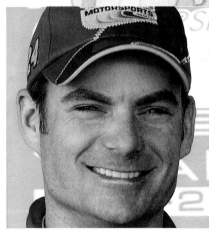

| Year | Event | Race Winner | Car Make | Avg. Speed | Start Pos. | Car Owner | Pole Winner | Pole Speed |
|------|-------|-------------|----------|-----------|-----------|-----------|-------------|-----------|
| 2004 | Bass/MBNA 500 | Ji. Johnson | Chevrolet | 145.847 | 8 | Rick Hendrick | R. Newman | 191.575 |
| | Golden Corral 500 | D.Earnhardt Jr. | Chevrolet | 158.679 | 7 | Teresa Earnhardt | R. Newman | 193.575 |
| j 2003 | Bass/MBNA 500 | J. Gordon | Chevrolet | 127.769 | 19 | Rick Hendrick | R. Newman | 194.295 |
| | Bass/MBNA 500 | B. Labonte | Chevrolet | 146.037 | 4 | Joe Gibbs | R. Newman | 191.417 |
| 2002 | NAPA 500 | K. Busch | Ford | 127.519 | 8 | Jack Roush | Trials Rained Out | |
| | MBNA America 500 | T. Stewart | Pontiac | 148..443 | 9 | Joe Gibbs | B. Elliott | 191.542 |
| 2001 | NAPA 500 | B. Labonte | Pontiac | 151.756 | 39 | Joe Gibbs | D. Earnhardt Jr. | 192.047 |
| | Cracker Barrel 500 | K. Harvick | Chevrolet | 143.273 | 5 | Richard Childress | D. Jarrett | 192.748 |
| 2000 | NAPA 500 | J. Nadeau | Chevrolet | 141.296 | 2 | Joe Hendrick | J. Gordon | 194.274 |
| | Cracker Barrel 500 | D. Earnhardt | Chevrolet | 131.759 | 35 | Richard Childress | D. Jarrett | 192.574 |
| 1999 | NAPA 500 | B. Labonte | Pontiac | 137.932 | 37 | Joe Gibbs | K. Lepage | 193.731 |
| | Cracker Barrel 500 | J. Gordon | Chevrolet | 143.296 | 8 | Rick Hendrick | B. Labonte | 194.957 |
| 1998 | NAPA 500 | J. Gordon | Chevrolet | 114.915 | 21 | Rick Hendrick | K. Irwin | 193.461 |
| i | Primestar 500 | B. Labonte | Pontiac | 139.501 | 14 | Joe Gibbs | J. Andretti | 192.841 |
| 1997 | NAPA 500 | B. Labonte | Chevrolet | 159.904 | 21 | Joe Gibbs | G. Bodine | 197.478 |
| | Primestar 500 | D. Jarrett | Ford | 132.731 | 9 | Robert Yates | R. Gordon | 186.507 |
| 1996 | NAPA 500 | B. Labonte | Chevrolet | 134.661 | 1 | Joe Gibbs | B. Labonte | 185.887 |
| | Purolator 500 | D. Earnhardt | Chevrolet | 161.298 | 18 | Richard Childress | J. Benson | 185.434 |
| 1995 | NAPA 500 | D. Earnhardt | Chevrolet | 163.633 | 11 | Richard Childress | D. Waltrip | 185.046 |
| | Purolator 500 | J. Gordon | Chevrolet | 150.115 | 3 | Rick Hendrick | D. Earnhardt | 185.077 |

## SPRING: GOLDEN CORRAL 500

**POLE WINNERS**

|  | |
|---|---|
| D. Earnhardt | 4 |
| Buddy Baker | 3 |
| R. Petty | 3 |
| C. Yarborough | 3 |
| D. Jarrett | 2 |
| G. Bodine | 2 |
| D. Pearson | 2 |
| M. Panch | 2 |
| A. Kulwicki | 2 |
| R. Newman | 2 |
| A. Foyt | 1 |
| L. Yarbrough | 1 |
| F. Lorenzen | 1 |
| D. Marcis | 1 |
| F. Roberts | 1 |
| Jr. Johnson | 1 |
| B. Matthews | 1 |
| T. Labonte | 1 |
| N. Bonnett | 1 |
| M. Martin | 1 |
| R. Wallace | 1 |
| L. Allen | 1 |
| J. Benson | 1 |
| R. Gordon | 1 |
| J. Andretti | 1 |
| B. Labonte | 1 |
| B. Elliott | 1 |

**RACE WINNERS**

|  | |
|---|---|
| C. Yarborough | 6 |
| D. Earnhardt | 5 |
| F. Lorenzen | 3 |
| B. Allison | 3 |
| J. Gordon | 2 |
| D. Pearson | 2 |
| R. Petty | 2 |
| D. Waltrip | 2 |
| B. Elliott | 2 |
| M. Shepherd | 2 |
| B. Labonte | 2 |
| A. Foyt | 1 |
| M. Panch | 1 |
| J. Hurtubise | 1 |
| B. Johns | 1 |
| B. Burdick | 1 |
| Buddy Baker | 1 |
| B. Parsons | 1 |
| R. Rudd | 1 |
| K. Schrader | 1 |
| E. Irvan | 1 |
| D. Jarrett | 1 |
| K. Harvick | 1 |
| T. Stewart | 1 |
| D. Earnhardt Jr. | 1 |

## FALL: BASS PRO SHOPS MBNA 500

**POLE WINNERS**

|  | |
|---|---|
| Buddy Baker | 4 |
| B. Elliott | 4 |
| H. Gant | 3 |
| C. Yarborough | 3 |
| R. Roberts | 3 |
| R. Wallace | 2 |
| F. Lorenzen | 2 |
| R. Newman | 2 |
| C. Pearson | 1 |
| R. Petty | 1 |
| D. Marcis | 1 |
| M. Panch | 1 |
| S. Sommers | 1 |
| C. Turner | 1 |
| Jr. Johnson | 1 |
| D. Dieringer | 1 |
| B. Allison | 1 |
| M. Shepherd | 1 |
| T. Richmond | 1 |
| A. Kulwicki | 1 |
| R. Mast | 1 |
| G. Sacks | 1 |
| D. Waltrip | 1 |
| B. Labonte | 1 |
| G. Bodine | 1 |
| K. Irwin | 1 |
| Lepage | 1 |
| J. Gordon | 1 |
| D. Earnhardt Jr. | 1 |

**RACE WINNERS**

|  | |
|---|---|
| B. Labonte | 4 |
| R. Petty | 4 |
| D. Earnhardt | 4 |
| N. Bonnett | 3 |
| B. Elliott | 3 |
| R. Wallace | 2 |
| M. Martin | 2 |
| D. Pearson | 2 |
| B. Allison | 2 |
| L. Yarbrough | 2 |
| J. Gordon | 2 |
| Buddy Baker | 1 |
| D. Waltrip | 1 |
| D. Marcis | 1 |
| M. Panch | 1 |
| F. Roberts | 1 |
| D. Hutcheson | 1 |
| Jr. Johnson | 1 |
| R. White | 1 |
| D. Jarrett | 1 |
| D. Allison | 1 |
| C. Yarborough | 1 |
| M. Shepherd | 1 |
| J. Nadeau | 1 |
| Ku. Busch | 1 |
| Ji. Johnson | 1 |

### FESTIVAL 250

**POLE WINNER**

| | |
|---|---|
| F. Roberts | 1 |

**RACE WINNER**

| | |
|---|---|
| F. Lorenzen | 1 |

## ALL ATLANTA RACES

**POLE WINNERS**

|  | |
|---|---|
| Buddy Baker | 7 |
| C. Yarborough | 6 |
| F. Roberts | 5 |
| B. Elliott | 5 |
| R. Petty | 4 |
| D. Earnhardt | 4 |
| R. Newman | 4 |
| R. Wallace | 3 |
| G. Bodine | 3 |
| D. Pearson | 3 |
| H. Gant | 3 |
| F. Lorenzen | 3 |
| M. Panch | 3 |
| A. Kulwicki | 3 |
| B. Labonte | 2 |
| D. Jarrett | 2 |
| Jr. Johnson | 2 |
| B. Allison | 2 |
| D. Marcis | 2 |
| A. Foyt | 1 |
| S. Sommers | 1 |
| L. Yarbrough | 1 |
| C. Turner | 1 |
| D. Dieringer | 1 |
| B. Matthews | 1 |
| T. Labonte | 1 |
| M. Shepherd | 1 |
| T. Richmond | 1 |
| M. Martin | 1 |
| N. Bonnett | 1 |
| R. Mast | 1 |
| L. Allen | 1 |
| G. Sacks | 1 |
| D. Waltrip | 1 |
| J. Benson | 1 |
| J. Gordon | 1 |
| R. Gordon | 1 |
| J. Andretti | 1 |
| K. Irwin | 1 |
| K. Lepage | 1 |
| D. Earnhardt Jr. | 1 |

**RACE WINNERS**

|  | |
|---|---|
| D. Earnhardt | 9 |
| C. Yarborough | 7 |
| R. Petty | 6 |
| B. Labonte | 6 |
| B. Allison | 5 |
| B. Elliott | 5 |
| F. Lorenzen | 4 |
| D. Pearson | 4 |
| J. Gordon | 4 |
| D. Waltrip | 3 |
| N. Bonnett | 3 |
| M. Shepherd | 3 |
| R. Wallace | 2 |
| M. Martin | 2 |
| L. Yarbrough | 2 |
| M. Panch | 2 |
| Buddy Baker | 2 |
| D. Marcis | 1 |
| A. Foyt | 1 |
| Jr. Johnson | 1 |
| R. White | 1 |
| J. Hurtubise | 1 |
| F. Roberts | 1 |
| N. Jarrett | 1 |
| D. Hutcherson | 1 |
| B. Johns | 1 |
| B. Burdick | 1 |
| D. Allison | 1 |
| B. Parsons | 1 |
| R. Rudd | 1 |
| K. Schrader | 1 |
| E. Irvan | 1 |
| D. Jarrett | 1 |
| J. Nadeau | 1 |
| K. Harvick | 1 |
| T. Stewart | 1 |
| K. Busch | 1 |
| D. Earnhardt Jr. | 1 |
| Ji. Johnson | 1 |

# NEXTEL Cup YEAR BY YEAR WINNERS (Atlanta, continued)

| Year | Event | Race Winner | Car Make | Avg. Speed | Start Pos. | Car Owner | Pole Winner | Pole Speed |
|---|---|---|---|---|---|---|---|---|
| 1994 | Hooters 500 | M. Martin | Ford | 148.982 | 5 | Jack Roush | G. Sacks | 185.830 |
| | Purolator 500 | E. Irvan | Ford | 146.136 | 7 | Robert Yates | L. Allen | 180.207 |
| 1993 | Hooters 500 | R. Wallace | Pontiac | 125.221 | 20 | Roger Penske | H. Gant | 176.902 |
| | Motorcraft 500 | M. Shepherd | Ford | 150.442 | 7 | Wood Brothers | R. Wallace | 178.749 |
| 1992 | Hooters 500 | B. Elliott | Ford | 133.322 | 11 | Junior Johnson | R. Mast | 180.183 |
| | Motorcraft 500 | B. Elliott | Ford | 147.746 | 4 | Junior Johnson | M. Martin | 179.923 |
| 1991 | Hardee's 500 | M. Martin | Ford | 137.968 | 4 | Jack Roush | B. Elliott | 177.937 |
| g | Motorcraft 500 | J. Schrader | Chevrolet | 140.470 | 5 | Rick Hendrick | A. Kulwicki | 174.413 |
| 1990 | Atl. Journal 500 | M. Shepherd | Ford | 140.911 | 20 | Bud Moore | R. Wallace | 175.222 |
| f | Motorcraft 500 | D. Earnhardt | Chevrolet | 156.849 | 1 | Richard Childress | Trials rained out | |
| 1989 | Atl. Journal 500 | D. Earnhardt | Chevrolet | 140.229 | 1 | Richard Childress | A. Kulwicki | 179.112 |
| | Motorcraft 500 | D. Waltrip | Chevrolet | 139.684 | 4 | Rick Hendrick | A. Kulwicki | 176.925 |
| 1988 | Atl. Journal 500 | R. Wallace | Pontiac | 129.024 | 1 | Blue Max | R. Wallace | 179.499 |
| | Motorcraft 500 | D. Earnhardt | Chevrolet | 137.588 | 2 | Richard Childress | G. Bodine | 176.623 |
| 1987 | Atl. Journal 500 | B. Elliott | Ford | 139.047 | 1 | Melling Racing | B. Elliott | 174.341 |
| | Motorcraft 500 | R. Rudd | Ford | 133.689 | 6 | Bud Moore | D. Earnhardt | 175.497 |
| 1986 | Atl. Journal 500 | D. Earnhardt | Chevrolet | 152.523 | 4 | Richard Childress | B. Elliott | 172.905 |
| | Motorcraft 500 | M. Shepherd | Buick | 132.126 | 3 | Jack Beebe | D. Earnhardt | 170.713 |
| 1985 | Atl. Journal 500 | B. Elliott | Ford | 139.597 | 3 | Harry Melling | H. Gant | 167.940 |
| | Coca-Cola 500 | B. Elliott | Ford | 140.273 | 3 | Harry Melling | N. Bonnett | 170.278 |
| 1984 | Atl. Journal 500 | D. Earnhardt | Chevrolet | 134.610 | 10 | Richard Childress | B. Elliott | 170.198 |
| | Coca-Cola 500 | B. Parsons | Chevrolet | 144.945 | 8 | Johnny Hayes | Buddy Baker | 166.642 |
| 1983 | Atl. Journal 500 | N. Bonnett | Chevrolet | 137.643 | 15 | Hodg./Rahmoc | T. Richmond | 168.151 |
| | Coca-Cola 500 | C. Yarborough | Chevrolet | 124.055 | 22 | Ranier Racing | G. Bodine | 167.703 |
| 1982 | Atl. Journal 500 | B. Allison | Buick | 130.884 | 9 | DiGard Rac. Co. | M. Shepherd | 166.779 |
| e | Coca-Cola 500 | D. Waltrip | Buick | 124.824 | 14 | Junior Johnson | D. Earnhardt | 163.774 |
| 1981 | Atl. Journal 500 | N. Bonnett | Ford | 130.391 | 5 | Wood Brothers | H. Gant | 163.266 |
| | Coca-Cola 500 | C. Yarborough | Buick | 133.619 | 17 | M.C. Anderson | T. Labonte | 162.940 |
| 1980 | Atl. Journal 500 | C. Yarborough | Chevrolet | 131.190 | 12 | Junior Johnson | B. Allison | 165.620 |
| | Atlanta 500 | D. Earnhardt | Chevrolet | 134.808 | 31 | Osterlund Rac. | Buddy Baker | 166.212 |
| 1979 | Dixie 500 | N. Bonnett | Mercury | 140.120 | 4 | Wood Brothers | Buddy Baker | 164.813 |
| | Atlanta 500 | Buddy Baker | Oldsmobile | 135.136 | 1 | Ranier Racing | Buddy Baker | 165.951 |
| 1978 | Dixie 500 | D. Allison | Chevrolet | 124.312 | 13 | Hoss Ellington | C. Yarborough | 168.425 |
| | Atlanta 500 | B. Allison | Ford | 142.520 | 4 | Bud Moore | C. Yarborough | 162.006 |
| d 1977 | Dixie 500 | D. Waltrip | Chevrolet | 110.052 | 8 | DiGard Rac. Co. | S. Sommers | 160.229 |
| | Atlanta 500 | R. Petty | Dodge | 144.093 | 1 | Petty Eng. | R. Petty | 162.501 |
| 1976 | Dixie 500 | D. Marcis | Dodge | 127.396 | 2 | Nord Krauskopf | Buddy Baker | 161.652 |
| | Atlanta 500 | D. Pearson | Mercury | 128.904 | 2 | Wood Brothers | D. Marcis | 160.709 |
| 1975 | Dixie 500 | Buddy Baker | Ford | 130.900 | 3 | Bud Moore | D. Marcis | 160.662 |
| | Atlanta 500 | R. Petty | Dodge | 133.496 | 1 | Petty Eng. | R. Petty | 159.029 |
| 1974 | Dixie 500 | R. Petty | Dodge | 131.651 | 2 | Petty Eng. | C. Yarborough | 156.750 |
| | Atlanta 500 | C. Yarborough | Chevrolet | 136.910 | 9 | Junior Johnson | D. Pearson | 159.242 |
| 1973 | Dixie 500 | D. Pearson | Mercury | 130.211 | 5 | Wood Brothers | R. Petty | 157.163 |
| * | Atlanta 500 | D. Pearson | Mercury | 139.351 | 9 | Wood Brothers | NONE | |
| 1972 | Dixie 500 | B. Allison | Chevrolet | 131.295 | 3 | Junior Johnson | D. Pearson | 158.353 |
| | Atlanta 500 | B. Allison | Chevrolet | 128.214 | 1 | Junior Johnson | B. Allison | 156.245 |
| 1971 | Dixie 500 | R. Petty | Plymouth | 129.061 | 3 | Petty Eng. | Buddy Baker | 155.796 |
| | Atlanta 500 | A. Foyt | Mercury | 131.375 | 1 | Wood Brothers | A. Foyt | 155.152 |
| 1970 | Dixie 500 | R. Petty | Plymouth | 142.712 | 6 | Petty Eng. | F. Lorenzen | 157.625 |
| c | Atlanta 500 | B. Allison | Dodge | 139.554 | 9 | Mario Rossi | C. Yarborough | 159.929 |
| 1969 | Dixie 500 | L. Yarbrough | Ford | 133.001 | 2 | Junior Johnson | C. Yarborough | 155.413 |
| † | Atlanta 500 | C. Yarborough | Mercury | 132.191 | 5 | Wood Brothers | D. Pearson | 156.794 |
| 1968 | Dixie 500 | L. Yarbrough | Mercury | 127.068 | 2 | Junior Johnson | Buddy Baker | 153.361 |
| | Atlanta 500 | C. Yarborough | Mercury | 125.564 | 4 | Wood Brothers | L. Yarbrough | 155.646 |
| 1967 | Dixie 500 | D. Hutcherson | Ford | 132.286 | 8 | Bondy Long | D. Dieringer | 150.669 |
| | Atlanta 500 | C. Yarborough | Ford | 131.238 | 5 | Wood Brothers | C. Yarborough | 148.996 |
| 1966 | Dixie 400 | R. Petty | Plymouth | 130.244 | 5 | Petty Eng. | C. Turner | 148.331 |
| | Atlanta 500 | J. Hurtubise | Plymouth | 131.266 | 5 | Norm Nelson | R. Petty | 147.742 |
| 1965 | Dixie 400 | M. Panch | Ford | 110.120 | 2 | Wood Brothers | F. Lorenzen | 143.407 |
| | Atlanta 500 | M. Panch | Ford | 129.410 | 1 | Wood Brothers | M. Panch | 145.581 |
| 1964 | Dixie 400 | N. Jarrett | Ford | 112.535 | 17 | Bondy Long | Ju. Johnson | 145.906 |
| | Atlanta 500 | F. Lorenzen | Ford | 132.959 | 1 | Holman-Moody | Ju. Johnson | 146.470 |
| 1963 | Dixie 400 | Ju. Johnson | Chevrolet | 121.134 | 2 | Ray Fox | M. Panch | 140.753 |
| | Atlanta 500 | F. Lorenzen | Ford | 130.582 | 2 | Holman-Moody | Ju. Johnson | 141.038 |
| 1962 | Dixie 400 | R. White | Chevrolet | 124.896 | 5 | Louis Clements | F. Roberts | 138.978 |
| b | Atlanta 500 | F. Lorenzen | Ford | 101.983 | 7 | Holman-Moody | Matthews | 137.640 |
| 1961 | Dixie 400 | D. Pearson | Pontiac | 125.384 | 5 | Ray Fox | F. Roberts | 136.294 |
| a | Festival 250 | F. Lorenzen | Ford | 118.007 | 5 | Holman-Moody | F. Roberts | 136.088 |
| | Atlanta 500 | B. Burdick | Ford | 124.172 | 7 | Bob Burdick | M. Panch | 135.755 |
| 1960 | Atlanta 500 | B. Johns | Pontiac | 134.596 | 5 | Cotton Owens | F. Roberts | 134.596 |
| | Dixie 300 | F. Roberts | Pontiac | 112.653 | 1 | Smokey Yunick | F. Roberts | 133.870 |

**KEY**

*  Qualifying was rained out; drivers drew for starting positions; Gordon Johncock started on the pole.
†  Pearson won the pole but chose to start 40th; Glotzbach started on the pole.
a  One-shot race.
b  Track remeasured, changed from 1.5 to 1.522 miles.
c  Cut to 407.89 miles by rain and darkness.
d  Cut to 436.814 miles by rain.
e  Name changed to Atlanta Motor Speedway.
f  First 47 laps run on Sunday, March 17, final 281 on March 18.
g  First race on the redesigned 1.54-mile track with backstretch now including the start-finish line.
h  Cut to 328.5 miles by rain.
i  Cut to 340.34 miles by rain.
j  Red-flagged after the second caution and completed on October 27.

# BUSCH SERIES

## Busch YEAR BY YEAR WINNERS (Atlanta)

| Year | Event | Race Winner | Car Make | Avg. Speed | Start Pos. | Pole Winner | Pole Speed | POLE WINNERS | | RACE WINNERS | |
|------|-------|-------------|----------|-----------|-----------|-------------|-----------|-----------|---|-----------|---|
| 2004 | Aaron's 312 | M. Kenseth | Ford | 133.343 | 28 | M. Bliss | 188.867 | M. Martin | 2 | M. Martin | 3 |
| 2003 | Aaron's 312 | G. Biffle | Chevrolet | 146.217 | 1 | G. Biffle | 192.300 | D. Trickle | 2 | J. Benson | 1 |
| 2002 | Aaron's 312 | J. McMurray | Chevrolet | 138.788 | 8 | Trials rained out | | T. Bender | 1 | W. Burton | 1 |
| 2001 | Aaron's 312 | J. Nemechek | Chevrolet | 143.954 | 3 | R. Newman | 191.661 | D. Blaney | 1 | H. Gant | 1 |
| 2000* | Aaron's 312 | M. Martin | Ford | 126.924 | 4 | M. Kenseth | 185.704 | J. Gordon | 1 | J. Gordon | 1 |
| 1999 | Yellow Freight 300 | M. Skinner | Chevrolet | 117.178 | 17 | D. Blaney | 186.775 | M. Kenseth | 1 | T. Labonte | 1 |
| 1998 | Stihl 300 | M. Martin | Ford | 138.193 | 10 | D. Trickle | 186.673 | R. Newman | 1 | J. McMurray | 1 |
| 1997 | Stihl 300 | M. Martin | Ford | 151.751 | 13 | T. Bender | 179.835 | S. Robinson | 1 | J. Nemechek | 1 |
| 1996 | Busch Light 300 | T. Labonte | Chevrolet | 139.656 | 11 | D. Trickle | 177.544 | G. Biffle | 1 | M. Skinner | 1 |
| 1995 | Busch Light 300 | J. Benson | Chevrolet | 145.767 | 10 | M. Martin | 176.623 | M. Bliss | 1 | G. Biffle | 1 |
| 1994 | Busch Light 300 | H. Gant | Chevrolet | 127.649 | 23 | S. Robinson | 174.330 | | | M. Kenseth | 1 |
| 1993 | Slick 50 300 | W. Burton | Chevrolet | 109.640 | 5 | M. Martin | 174.286 | | | | |
| 1992 | Atlanta 300 | J. Gordon | Chevrolet | 124.412 | 1 | J. Gordon | 173.821 | | | | |

*race changed to 203 laps

**QUALIFYING RECORD:** Greg Biffle, Chevrolet; 192.300 mph, October 24, 2003
**RACE RECORD:** Mark Martin, Ford; 151.751 mph, March 8, 1997

# CRAFTSMAN TRUCK SERIES

## Craftsman YEAR BY YEAR WINNERS (Atlanta)

| Year | Event | Race Winner | Car Make | Avg. Speed | Start Pos. | Pole Winner | Pole Speed | POLE WINNERS | | RACE WINNERS | |
|------|-------|-------------|----------|-----------|-----------|-------------|-----------|-----------|---|-----------|---|
| 2004 | EasyCare 200 | B. Hamilton | Dodge | 123.675 | 12 | D. Reutimann | 179.452 | D. Reutimann | 1 | B. Hamilton | 1 |

**QUALIFYING RECORD:** David Reutimann, Toyota; 179.452 mph, March 12, 2004
**RACE RECORD:** Bobby Hamilton, Dodge; 123.675 mph, March 13, 2004

# BRISTOL MOTOR SPEEDWAY

## 2005 SCHEDULE

### NEXTEL CUP
**Event:** Food City 500
**Race:** No. 5 of 36
**Date:** April 3
**TV:** FOX. **Radio:** PRN

**Event:** Sharpie 500
**Race:** No. 24 of 36
**Date:** August 27
**TV:** TNT. **Radio:** PRN

### BUSCH SERIES
**Event:** Sharpie Professional 250
**Race:** No. 7 of 35
**Date:** April 2
**TV:** FOX. **Radio:** PRN

**Event:** Food City 250
**Race:** No. 26 of 35
**Date:** August 26
**TV:** TNT. **Radio:** PRN

### CRAFTSMAN TRUCK SERIES
**Event:** O'Reilly 200
**Race:** No. 17 of 25
**Date:** August 24
**TV:** SPEED. **Radio:** MRN

Race names subject to change

## TRACK FACTS
**Opened:** 1961
**Owner:** Speedway Motorsports, Inc.
**Location:** Bristol, Tenn.
**Distance:** .533 miles
**Banking in turns:** 36 degrees
**Banking in straights:** 16 degrees
**Length of front stretch:** 650 feet
**Length of back stretch:** 650 feet
**Grandstand seating:** 160,000
**Tickets:** (423) 764-1161
**Website:** www.bristolmotorspeedway.com

Back stretch: 650 feet / 16°
Front stretch: 650 feet / 16°

# NEXTEL CUP

## TRACK RECORDS

**Most wins:** 12—Darrell Waltrip
**Oldest winner:** Dale Earnhardt, 48 years, 3 months, 30 days, August 28, 1999
**Youngest winner:** Kurt Busch, 23 years, 7 months, 20 days, March 24, 2002
**Most lead changes:** 40—April 14, 1991
**Fewest lead changes:** 0—March 25, 1973
**Most leaders:** 20—Twice, most recently, August 26, 1995
**Fewest leaders:** 1—March 25, 1973
**Most cautions:** 20—Three times, most recently, August 23, 2003
**Fewest cautions:** 0—Twice, most recently, April 2, 1995
**Most caution laps:** 167—July 25, 1965
**Fewest caution laps:** 0—Twice, most recently, April 2, 1995
**Most on the lead lap:** 25—March 25, 2001

**Fewest on the lead lap:** 1—22 times, most recently, August 22, 1981
**Most running at the finish:** 40—April 11, 1999
**Fewest running at the finish:** 7—March 20, 1966
**Most laps led by a race winner:** 500—Cale Yarborough, March 25, 1973
**Fewest laps led by a race winner:** 1—Fred Lorenzen, July 26, 1964
**Closest margin of victory:** 0.10 seconds—Terry Labonte defeated Dale Earnhardt, August 26, 1995.
**Greatest margin of victory:** 7 laps—Cale Yarborough defeated Dick Brooks, April 17, 1977.

## QUALIFYING AND RACE RECORDS

**QUALIFYING: Track:** Ryan Newman, Dodge; 128.709 mph, March 21, 2003. **Spring race (Food City 500):** Ryan Newman, Dodge; 128.709 mph, March 21, 2003.

**Fall race (Sharpie 500):** Jeff Gordon, Chevrolet; 127.597 mph, August 21, 2003.
**RACE: Track:** Charlie Glotzbach, Chevrolet; 101.074 mph, July 11, 1971.

(Volunteer 500). **Spring race (Food City 500):** Cale Yarborough, Chevrolet; 100.989 mph, April 17, 1977. **Fall race (Sharpie 500):** Charlie Glotzbach, Chevrolet; 101.074 mph, July 11, 1971.

## NEXTEL Cup YEAR BY YEAR WINNERS

| Year | Event | Race Winner | Car Make | Avg. Speed | Start Pos. | Car Owner | Pole Winner | Pole Speed |
|---|---|---|---|---|---|---|---|---|
| * 2004 | Sharpie 500 | D. Earnhardt Jr. | Chevrolet | 88.538 | 30 | Teresa Earnhardt | J. Gordon | 128.520 |
| | Food City 500 | K. Busch | Ford | 82.607 | 13 | Jack Roush | R. Newman | 128.313 |
| * 2003 | Sharpie 500 | K. Busch | Ford | 77.421 | 5 | Jack Roush | J. Gordon | 127.597 |
| | Food City 500 | K. Busch | Ford | 76.185 | 9 | Jack Roush | R. Newman | 128.709 |
| * 2002 | Sharpie 500 | J. Gordon | Chevrolet | 77.097 | 1 | Rick Hendrick | J. Gordon | 124.034 |
| | Food City 500 | K. Busch | Ford | 82.281 | 27 | Jack Roush | J. Gordon | 127.216 |
| * 2001 | Sharpie 500 | T. Stewart | Pontiac | 85.106 | 18 | Joe Gibbs | J. Green | 123.674 |
| | Food City 500 | E. Sadler | Ford | 86.949 | 38 | Wood Brothers | M. Martin | 126.303 |
| * 2000 | GoRacing.com 500 | R. Wallace | Ford | 85.394 | 1 | Roger Penske | R. Wallace | 125.477 |
| | Food City 500 | R. Wallace | Ford | 88.018 | 6 | Roger Penske | S. Park | 126.370 |
| * 1999 | Goody's 500 | D. Earnhardt | Chevrolet | 91.276 | 26 | Richard Childress | T. Stewart | 124.589 |
| | Food City 500 | R. Wallace | Ford | 93.363 | 1 | Roger Penske | R. Wallace | 125.142 |
| * 1998 | Goody's 500 | M. Martin | Ford | 86.918 | 4 | Jack Roush | R. Wallace | 125.554 |
| | Food City 500 | J. Gordon | Chevrolet | 82.850 | 2 | Rick Hendrick | R. Wallace | 124.275 |
| * 1997 | Goody's 500 | D. Jarrett | Ford | 80.013 | 3 | Robert Yates | K. Wallace | 123.039 |
| | Food City 500 | J. Gordon | Chevrolet | 75.035 | 5 | Rick Hendrick | R. Wallace | 123.586 |
| *h1996 | Goody's 500 | R. Wallace | Ford | 91.267 | 5 | Roger Penske | M. Martin | 124.857 |
| g | Food City 500 | J. Gordon | Chevrolet | 91.308 | 8 | Rick Hendrick | M. Martin | 123.578 |
| * 1995 | Goody's 500 | T. Labonte | Chevrolet | 81.979 | 2 | Rick Hendrick | M. Martin | 125.093 |
| | Food City 500 | J. Gordon | Chevrolet | 92.011 | 2 | Rick Hendrick | M. Martin | 124.605 |
| * 1994 | Goody's 500 | R. Wallace | Ford | 91.363 | 4 | Roger Penske | H. Gant | 124.186 |
| | Food City 500 | D. Earnhardt | Chevrolet | 89.647 | 24 | Richard Childress | C. Brown | 124.946 |
| * 1993 | Bud 500 | M. Martin | Ford | 88.172 | 1 | Jack Roush | M. Martin | 121.405 |
| | Food City 500 | R. Wallace | Pontiac | 84.730 | 1 | Roger Penske | R. Wallace | 120.938 |
| *f1992 | Bud 500 | D. Waltrip | Ford | 91.198 | 9 | Darrell Waltrip | E. Irvan | 120.535 |
| | Food City 500 | A. Kulwicki | Ford | 86.316 | 1 | Alan Kulwicki | A. Kulwicki | 122.474 |
| * 1991 | Bud 500 | A. Kulwicki | Ford | 82.028 | 5 | Alan Kulwicki | B. Elliott | 116.957 |
| | Valleydale 500 | R. Wallace | Pontiac | 72.809 | 1 | Roger Penske | R. Wallace | 118.051 |
| * 1990 | Busch 500 | E. Irvan | Chevrolet | 91.782 | 6 | Morgan-McClure | D. Earnhardt | 115.604 |
| | Valleydale 500 | Da. Allison | Ford | 87.258 | 19 | Robert Yates | E. Irvan | 116.157 |
| * 1989 | Busch 500 | D. Waltrip | Chevrolet | 78.775 | 9 | Rick Hendrick | A. Kulwicki | 117.043 |
| | Valleydale 500 | R. Wallace | Pontiac | 76.034 | 8 | Blue Max | M. Martin | 120.278 |
| * 1988 | Busch 500 | D. Earnhardt | Chevrolet | 78.775 | 5 | Richard Childress | A. Kulwicki | 116.893 |
| | Valleydale 500 | B. Elliott | Ford | 83.115 | 13 | Melling Racing | R. Wilson | 117.552 |
| * 1987 | Busch 500 | D. Earnhardt | Chevrolet | 90.373 | 6 | Richard Childress | T. Labonte | 115.758 |
| | Valleydale 500 | D. Earnhardt | Chevrolet | 75.621 | 3 | Richard Childress | H. Gant | 115.674 |
| * 1986 | Busch 500 | D. Waltrip | Chevrolet | 86.934 | 10 | Junior Johnson | G. Bodine | 114.665 |
| | Valleydale 500 | R. Wallace | Pontiac | 89.747 | 14 | Blue Max | G. Bodine | 114.850 |
| * 1985 | Busch 500 | D. Earnhardt | Chevrolet | 81.388 | 1 | Richard Childress | D. Earnhardt | 113.586 |
| | Valleydale 500 | D. Earnhardt | Chevrolet | 81.790 | 12 | Richard Childress | H. Gant | 112.778 |
| * 1984 | Busch 500 | T. Labonte | Chevrolet | 85.365 | 6 | Billy Hagan | G. Bodine | 111.734 |
| | Valleydale 500 | D. Waltrip | Chevrolet | 93.967 | 3 | Junior Johnson | R. Rudd | 111.390 |
| * 1983 | Busch 500 | D. Waltrip | Chevrolet | 89.430 | 2 | Junior Johnson | J. Rutman | 111.923 |
| | Valleydale 500 | D. Waltrip | Chevrolet | 93.445 | 13 | Junior Johnson | N. Bonnett | 110.409 |
| * 1982 | Busch 500 | D. Waltrip | Buick | 94.318 | 8 | Junior Johnson | T. Richmond | 112.507 |
| | Valleydale 500 | D. Waltrip | Buick | 94.025 | 1 | Junior Johnson | D. Waltrip | 111.068 |
| * 1981 | Busch 500 | D. Waltrip | Buick | 84.723 | 1 | Junior Johnson | D. Waltrip | 110.818 |
| | Valleydale 500 | D. Waltrip | Buick | 89.530 | 1 | Junior Johnson | D. Waltrip | 112.125 |
| * 1980 | Busch Vol. 500 | C. Yarborough | Chevrolet | 86.973 | 1 | Junior Johnson | C. Yarborough | 110.990 |
| e | Valleydale SE 500 | D. Earnhardt | Chevrolet | 96.977 | 4 | Osterlund Rac. | C. Yarborough | 111.688 |
| * 1979 | Volunteer 500 | D. Waltrip | Chevrolet | 91.493 | 5 | DiGard Rac. Co. | R. Petty | 110.524 |
| | Southeastern 500 | D. Earnhardt | Chevrolet | 91.033 | 9 | Osterlund Rac. | Buddy Baker | 111.668 |
| * 1978 | Volunteer 500 | C. Yarborough | Oldsmobile | 88.628 | 4 | Junior Johnson | L. Pond | 110.958 |
| d | Southeastern 500 | D. Waltrip | Chevrolet | 92.401 | 7 | DiGard Rac. Co. | N. Bonnett | 110.409 |
| 1977 | Volunteer 400 | C. Yarborough | Chevrolet | 79.726 | 1 | Junior Johnson | C. Yarborough | 109.746 |
| | Southeastern 500 | C. Yarborough | Chevrolet | 100.989 | 1 | Junior Johnson | C. Yarborough | 110.168 |
| 1976 | Volunteer 400 | C. Yarborough | Chevrolet | 99.175 | 2 | Junior Johnson | D. Waltrip | 110.300 |
| | Southeastern 400 | C. Yarborough | Chevrolet | 87.377 | 3 | Junior Johnson | Buddy Baker | 110.720 |
| 1975 | Volunteer 500 | R. Petty | Dodge | 97.016 | 4 | Petty Eng. | C. Yarborough | 110.162 |
| | Southeastern 500 | R. Petty | Dodge | 97.053 | 2 | Petty Eng. | Buddy Baker | 110.951 |
| 1974 | Volunteer 500 | C. Yarborough | Chevrolet | 75.430 | 3 | Junior Johnson | R. Petty | 107.351 |
| | Southeastern 500 | C. Yarborough | Chevrolet | 64.533 | 3 | Junior Johnson | D. Allison | 107.785 |
| 1973 | Volunteer 500 | B. Parsons | Chevrolet | 91.342 | 2 | L.G. DeWitt | C. Yarborough | 106.472 |
| c | Southeastern 500 | C. Yarborough | Chevrolet | 88.952 | 1 | Junior Johnson | C. Yarborough | 107.608 |
| 1972 | Volunteer 500 | B. Allison | Chevrolet | 92.735 | 1 | Junior Johnson | B. Allison | 107.279 |
| | Southeastern 500 | B. Allison | Chevrolet | 92.826 | 1 | Junior Johnson | B. Allison | 106.875 |
| b 1971 | Volunteer 500 | C. Glotzbach | Chevrolet | 101.074 | 2 | Junior Johnson | R. Petty | 104.589 |
| | Southeastern 500 | D. Pearson | Ford | 91.704 | 1 | Holman-Moody | D. Pearson | 105.525 |
| 1970 | Volunteer 500 | B. Allison | Dodge | 84.880 | 10 | Bobby Allison | C. Yarborough | 107.375 |
| | Southeastern 500 | Do. Allison | Ford | 87.543 | 2 | Banjo Matthews | D. Pearson | 107.079 |
| a 1969 | Volunteer 500 | D. Pearson | Ford | 79.737 | 3 | Holman-Moody | C. Yarborough | 103.432 |
| | Southeastern 500 | B. Allison | Dodge | 81.455 | 4 | Mario Rossi | B. Isaac | 107.785 |
| 1968 | Volunteer 500 | D. Pearson | Ford | 76.310 | 6 | Holman-Moody | L. Yarbrough | 87.421 |
| | Southeastern 500 | D. Pearson | Ford | 77.247 | 2 | Holman-Moody | R. Petty | 88.582 |
| 1967 | Volunteer 500 | R. Petty | Plymouth | 78.705 | 1 | Petty Eng. | R. Petty | 86.621 |
| | Southeastern 500 | D. Pearson | Dodge | 75.930 | 14 | Cotton Owens | D. Dieringer | 87.124 |

**POLE WINNERS — SPRING: FOOD CITY 500**

| | |
|---|---|
| R. Wallace | 5 |
| M. Martin | 4 |
| Buddy Baker | 3 |
| B. Pearson | 3 |
| C. Yarborough | 3 |
| D. Waltrip | 2 |
| N. Bonnett | 2 |
| H. Gant | 2 |
| G. Bodine | 2 |
| F. Lorenzen | 2 |
| R. Newman | 2 |
| M. Panch | 2 |
| D. Allison | 1 |
| B. Allison | 1 |
| B. Isaac | 1 |
| D. Dieringer | 1 |
| F. Roberts | 1 |
| R. Rudd | 1 |
| R. Wilson | 1 |
| E. Irvan | 1 |
| A. Kulwicki | 1 |
| C. Brown | 1 |
| S. Park | 1 |
| J. Gordon | 1 |

**RACE WINNERS**

| | |
|---|---|
| R. Wallace | 6 |
| D. Waltrip | 5 |
| D. Earnhardt | 5 |
| C. Yarborough | 4 |
| J. Gordon | 4 |
| K. Busch | 3 |
| D. Pearson | 3 |
| B. Allison | 2 |
| R. Petty | 1 |
| D. Allison | 1 |
| D. Hutcherson | 1 |
| Jr. Johnson | 1 |
| F. Lorenzen | 1 |
| F. Roberts | 1 |
| B. Johns | 1 |
| J. Smith | 1 |
| B. Elliott | 1 |
| Da. Allison | 1 |
| A. Kulwicki | 1 |
| E. Sadler | 1 |

**POLE WINNERS — FALL: SHARPIE 500**

| | |
|---|---|
| C. Yarborough | 6 |
| R. Petty | 5 |
| M. Martin | 3 |
| D. Waltrip | 2 |
| G. Bodine | 2 |
| A. Kulwicki | 2 |
| D. Earnhardt | 2 |
| R. Wallace | 2 |
| J. Gordon | 2 |
| B. Allison | 1 |
| F. Roberts | 1 |
| C. Turner | 1 |
| B. Johns | 1 |
| L. Pond | 1 |
| T. Richmond | 1 |
| J. Ruttman | 1 |
| T. Labonte | 1 |
| B. Elliott | 1 |
| E. Irvan | 1 |
| H. Gant | 1 |
| K. Wallace | 1 |
| T. Stewart | 1 |
| J. Green | 1 |
| J. Gordon | 1 |

**RACE WINNERS**

| | |
|---|---|
| D. Waltrip | 7 |
| C. Yarborough | 5 |
| D. Earnhardt | 4 |
| R. Wallace | 3 |
| R. Petty | 2 |
| B. Allison | 2 |
| D. Pearson | 2 |
| F. Lorenzen | 2 |
| T. Labonte | 2 |
| M. Martin | 2 |
| C. Glotzbach | 1 |
| P. Goldsmith | 1 |
| D. Jarrett | 1 |
| J. Paschal | 1 |
| J. Weatherly | 1 |
| E. Irvan | 1 |
| A. Kulwicki | 1 |
| B. Parsons | 1 |
| D. Jarrett | 1 |
| R. Petty | 1 |
| J. Gordon | 1 |
| Ku. Busch | 1 |
| D. Earnhardt Jr. | 1 |

**POLE WINNERS — ALL BRISTOL RACES**

| | |
|---|---|
| C. Yarborough | 9 |
| R. Wallace | 7 |
| M. Martin | 7 |
| R. Petty | 6 |
| F. Lorenzen | 4 |
| D. Waltrip | 4 |
| G. Bodine | 3 |
| A. Kulwicki | 3 |
| Buddy Baker | 3 |
| J. Gordon | 3 |
| D. Pearson | 3 |
| B. Allison | 2 |
| N. Bonnett | 2 |
| D. Earnhardt | 2 |
| E. Irvan | 2 |
| R. Newman | 2 |
| F. Roberts | 2 |
| M. Panch | 2 |
| L. Pond | 1 |
| D. Allison | 1 |
| B. Isaac | 1 |
| D. Dieringer | 1 |
| L. Yarbrough | 1 |
| C. Turner | 1 |
| B. Johns | 1 |
| T. Richmond | 1 |
| J. Ruttman | 1 |
| R. Rudd | 1 |
| T. Labonte | 1 |
| R. Wilson | 1 |
| B. Elliott | 1 |
| H. Gant | 1 |
| C. Bown | 1 |
| K. Wallace | 1 |
| T. Stewart | 1 |
| S. Park | 1 |
| J. Green | 1 |

**RACE WINNERS**

| | |
|---|---|
| D. Waltrip | 12 |
| C. Yarborough | 9 |
| D. Earnhardt | 9 |
| R. Wallace | 9 |
| D. Pearson | 5 |
| J. Gordon | 5 |
| B. Allison | 4 |
| K. Busch | 4 |
| R. Petty | 3 |
| F. Lorenzen | 3 |
| T. Labonte | 2 |
| M. Martin | 2 |
| A. Kulwicki | 1 |
| D. Allison | 1 |
| C. Glotzbach | 1 |
| D. Hutcherson | 1 |
| P. Goldsmith | 1 |
| Jr. Johnson | 1 |
| D. Jarrett | 1 |
| F. Roberts | 1 |
| B. Johns | 1 |
| J. Paschal | 1 |
| J. Smith | 1 |
| J. Weatherly | 1 |
| B. Elliott | 1 |
| Da. Allison | 1 |
| E. Irvan | 1 |
| B. Parsons | 1 |
| D. Jarrett | 1 |
| E. Sadler | 1 |
| T. Stewart | 1 |

## NEXTEL Cup YEAR BY YEAR WINNERS (Bristol, continued)

| Year | Event | Race Winner | Car Make | Avg. Speed | Start Pos. | Car Owner | Pole Winner | Pole Speed |
|------|-------|-------------|----------|------------|------------|-----------|-------------|------------|
| 1966 | Volunteer 500 | P. Goldsmith | Plymouth | 77.963 | 4 | Ray Nichels | C. Turner | 84.309 |
| | Southeastern 500 | D. Hutcherson | Ford | 69.952 | 6 | Bondy Long | D. Pearson | 86.248 |
| 1965 | Volunteer 500 | **N. Jarrett** | Ford | 61.826 | 6 | Bondy Long | F. Lorenzen | 84.348 |
| | Southeastern 500 | Ju. Johnson | Ford | 74.938 | 3 | Junior Johnson | M. Panch | 84.626 |
| 1964 | Volunteer 500 | F. Lorenzen | Ford | 78.044 | 8 | Holman-Moody | R. Petty | 82.910 |
| | Southeastern 500 | F. Lorenzen | Ford | 72.196 | 2 | Holman-Moody | M. Panch | 80.640 |
| 1963 | Volunteer 500 | F. Lorenzen | Ford | 74.844 | 1 | Holman-Moody | F. Lorenzen | 82.229 |
| | Southeastern 500 | F. Roberts | Ford | 76.910 | 3 | Holman-Moody | F. Lorenzen | 80.681 |
| 1962 | Southeastern 500 | J. Paschal | Plymouth | 75.280 | 12 | Petty Eng. | F. Roberts | 80.321 |
| | Volunteer 500 | B. Johns | Pontiac | 73.320 | 6 | Shorty Johns | F. Roberts | 81.374 |
| 1961 | Southeastern 500 | J. Weatherly | Pontiac | 72.450 | 2 | Bud Moore | B. Johns | 80.645 |
| | Volunteer 500 | J. Smith | Pontiac | 68.370 | 12 | Jack Smith | F. Lorenzen | 79.225 |

*Night races. **a** Track reshaped and remeasured; turns banked from 22 to 36 degrees and track measured at .533 of a mile; 500 laps now cover 266.5 miles; before the change it was a .5-mile track and the distance was 500 laps, 250 miles. **b** Race run without a caution. **c** Yarborough led all 500 laps, 266.5 miles (March 25, 1973). **d** Name changed from Bristol International Speedway to Bristol International Raceway. **e** Called after 419 laps, rain. **f** Track surface is concrete. **g** Called after 342 laps, rain. **h** Name of track changed from Bristol International Raceway to Bristol Motor Speedway.

# BUSCH SERIES

## Busch YEAR BY YEAR WINNERS (Bristol)

| Year | Event | Race Winner | Car Make | Avg. Speed | Start Pos. | Pole Winner | Pole Speed | POLE WINNERS | | RACE WINNERS | |
|------|-------|-------------|----------|------------|------------|-------------|------------|--------------|--|--------------|--|
| 2004 | Food City 250 | D. Earnhardt Jr. | Chevrolet | 64.872 | 1 | D. Earnhardt Jr. | 126.570 | J. Keller | 3 | M. Shepherd | 4 |
| | Sharpie Pro. 250 | M. Truex Jr. | Chevrolet | 78.114 | 2 | G. Biffle | 127.132 | M. Shepherd | 3 | K. Harvick | 3 |
| 2003 | Channellock 250 | **K. Harvick** | Chevrolet | 68.304 | 11 | D. Green | 126.495 | T. Ellis | 2 | B. Bodine | 2 |
| | Food City 250 | M. Waltrip | Chevrolet | 71.951 | 4 | J. Keller | 126.021 | J. Green | 2 | T. Bodine | 2 |
| 2002 | Channellock 250 | J. Green | Chevrolet | 66.093 | 2 | S. Riggs | 126.270 | K. Harvick | 2 | S. Grissom | 2 |
| | Food City 250 | J. Spencer | Chevrolet | 83.455 | 10 | J. Keller | 124.428 | M. Martin | 2 | M. Kenseth | 2 |
| 2001 | Cheez-It 250 | M. Kenseth | Chevrolet | 72.103 | 2 | K. Harvick | 125.264 | D. Green | 2 | M. Martin | 2 |
| | Food City 250 | K. Harvick | Chefrolet | 78.872 | 2 | M. Skinner | 124.460 | D. Earnhardt Jr. | 2 | L. Pearson | 2 |
| 2000 | Cheez-It 250 | S. Marlin | Chevrolet | 74.813 | 16 | J. Green | 124.428 | G. Biffle | 1 | J. Spencer | 2 |
| | Food City 250 | K. Harvick | Chevrolet | 88.164 | 1 | K. Harvick | 123.356 | B. Bodine | 1 | M. Waltrip | 2 |
| 1999 | Moore's Snacks 250 | J. Keller | Chevrolet | 73.014 | 1 | J. Keller | 123.024 | G. Bodine | 1 | S. Ard | 1 |
| | Food City 250 | M. Kenseth | Chevrolet | 83.761 | 3 | J. Green | 122.537 | R. Bouchard | 1 | J. Burton | 1 |
| 1998 | Moore's Snacks 250 | E. Sadler | Chevrolet | 75.484 | 3 | D. Earnhardt Jr. | 122.217 | J. Burton | 1 | D. Earnhardt | 1 |
| | Ford City 250 | K. Lepage | Chevrolet | 76.887 | 5 | S. Grissom | 121.512 | W. Burton | 1 | D. Earnhardt Jr. | 1 |
| 1997 | Moore's Snacks 250 | J. Burton | Ford | 74.743 | 3 | H. Sadler | 120.938 | C. Bown | 1 | J. Fuller | 1 |
| | Food City 250 | J. Spencer | Chevrolet | 65.515 | 16 | R. LaJoie | 121.267 | D. Earnhardt | 1 | H. Gant | 1 |
| 1996 | Goody's 250 | M. Martin | Ford | 85.783 | 10 | C. Little | 121.198 | J. Fuller | 1 | D. Green | 1 |
| | Food City 250 | J. Fuller | Chevrolet | 74.603 | 1 | J. Fuller | 121.029 | H. Gant | 1 | J. Green | 1 |
| 1995 | Goody's 250 | S. Grissom | Chevrolet | 89.664 | 18 | D. Green | 122.474 | S. Grissom | 1 | J. Ingram | 1 |
| | Food City 250 | S. Grissom | Chevrolet | 87.234 | 28 | S. Reeves | 122.560 | B. Labonte | 1 | D. Jarrett | 1 |
| 1994 | Goody's 250 | D. Green | Chevrolet | 81.085 | 3 | M. Martin | 123.746 | R. LaJoie | 1 | J. Keller | 1 |
| | Food City 250 | K. Wallace | Ford | 87.616 | 7 | H. Gant | 123.364 | C. Little | 1 | K. Lepage | 1 |
| 1993 | Budweiser 250 | M. Waltrip | Pontiac | 77.911 | 9 | W. Burton | 122.945 | B. Miller | 1 | B. Labonte | 1 |
| | Food City 250 | T. Bodine | Chevrolet | 73.014 | 12 | Qualifying rained out | | P. Parsons | 1 | Str. Marlin | 1 |
| 1992 | Budweiser 250 | H. Gant | Buick | 92.929 | 18 | B. Miller | 121.267 | D. Pearson | 1 | R. Mast | 1 |
| | Food City 250 | T. Bodine | Chevrolet | 73.014 | 11 | K. Wallace | 118.189 | L. Pearson | 1 | L. Ottinger | 1 |
| 1991 | Budweiser 250 | B. Labonte | Oldsmobile | 92.839 | 21 | J. Burton | 117.286 | S. Reeves | 1 | P. Parsons | 1 |
| | Jay Johnson 250 | D. Jarrett | Pontiac | 71.822 | 11 | C. Bown | 116.737 | S. Riggs | 1 | E. Sadler | 1 |
| 1990# | Budweiser 250 | L. Ottinger | Oldsmobile | 79.936 | 13 | Qualifying rained out | | H. Sadler | 1 | M. Truex | 1 |
| | Jay Johnson 250 | R. Mast | Buick | 85.447 | 12 | B. Labonte | 114.850 | M. Skinner | 1 | K. Wallace | 1 |
| 1989 | Budweiser 200 | R. Wilson | Oldsmobile | 85.776 | 1 | R. Wilson | 119.299 | K. Wallace | 1 | D. Waltrip | 1 |
| | Jay Johnson 200 | M. Martin | Ford | 76.309 | 8 | M. Shepherd | 116.368 | R. Wilson | 1 | R. Wilson | 1 |
| 1988 | Budweiser 200 | **D. Earnhardt** | Chevrolet | 76.162 | 4 | L. Pearson | 117.057 | | | | |
| | Tri-City Pont. 200 | L. Pearson | Chevrolet | 70.609 | 7 | T. Ellis | 113.761 | | | | |
| 1987 | Budweiser 200 | M. Shepherd | Buick | 75.032 | 11 | D. Earnhardt | 117.653 | | | | |
| | Tri-City Pont. 200 | L. Pearson | Chevroelt | 70.609 | 4 | M. Martin | 117.754 | | | | |
| 1986 | Budweiser 200 | M. Shepherd | Buick | 75.032 | 2 | G. Bodine | 117.293 | | | | |
| | Tri-City Pont. 200 | B. Bodine | Oldsmobile | 76.293 | 1 | B. Bodine | 116.171 | | | | |
| 1985 | Budweiser 200 | D. Waltrip | Chevrolet | 74.372 | 16 | T. Ellis | 116.829 | | | | |
| | Tri-City Pont. 200 | B. Bodine | Pontiac | 71.331 | 4 | R. Bouchard | 116.964 | | | | |
| 1984 | No Spring race held | | | | | | | | | | |
| * | Free Service 200 | M. Shepherd | Buick | 75.872 | 1 | M. Shepherd | 116.045 | | | | |
| 1983 | Southeastern 150 | M. Shepherd | Oldsmobile | 85.255 | 7 | Qualifying rained out | | | | | |
| | Free Service 150 | S. Ard | Oldsmobile | 85.255 | 2 | P. Parsons | 115.231 | | | | |
| 1982 | Southeastern 150 | P. Parsons | Pontiac | 80.848 | 7 | D. Pearson | 114.816 | | | | |
| | Pet Dairy 150 | J. Ingram | Pontiac | 79.923 | 6 | M. Shepherd | 115.132 | | | | |

# Race length changed to 250 laps  * Race length changed to 200 laps

**QUALIFYING RECORD:** Greg Biffle, Ford; 127.321 mph, March 26, 2004
**RACE RECORD:** Harry Gant, Buick; 92.929 mph, April 4, 1992

### Craftsman YEAR BY YEAR WINNERS (Bristol)

| Year | Event | Race Winner | Car Make | Avg. Speed | Start Pos. | Pole Winner | Pole Speed | POLE WINNERS | | RACE WINNERS | |
|------|-------|-------------|----------|------------|------------|-------------|------------|--------------|---|--------------|---|
| 2004 | O'Reilly 200 | C. Edwards | Ford | 74.495 | 5 | K. Schrader | 126.922 | R. Hornaday | 2 | R. Hornaday | 2 |
| 2003 | O'Reilly 200 | T. Kvapil | Chevrolet | 88.813 | 12 | T. Musgrave | 123.562 | M. Skinner | 2 | R. Carelli | 1 |
| 1999 | Coca-Cola 200 | J. Sprague | Chevrolet | 75.380 | 3 | G. Biffle | 120.831 | G. Biffle | 1 | J. Ruttman | 1 |
| 1998 | Loadhandler 200 | R. Hornaday Jr. | Chevrolet | 80.883 | 1 | R. Hornaday Jr. | 121.213 | J. Sprague | 1 | T. Kvapil | 1 |
| 1997 | Loadhandler 200 | R. Hornaday Jr. | Chevrolet | 70.583 | 1 | R. Hornaday Jr. | 119.910 | T. Musgrave | 1 | C. Edwards | 1 |
| 1996 | Coca-Cola 200 | R. Carelli | Chevrolet | 83.992 | 2 | M. Skinner | 117.805 | K. Schrader | 1 | | |
| 1995 | Pizza Plus 15 | J. Ruttman | Ford | 72.408 | 3 | M. Skinner | 118.738 | | | | |

**QUALIFYING RECORD:** Ken Schrader, Chevrolet; 126.922 mph, August 25, 2004
**RACE RECORD:** Travis Kvapil, Chevrolet; 88.813 mph, August 20, 2003

# CALIFORNIA SPEEDWAY

## 2005 SCHEDULE

### NEXTEL CUP
**Event:** Auto Club 500
**Race:** No. 2 of 36
**Date:** February 27
**TV:** FOX. **Radio:** MRN

**Event:** Pop Secret 500
**Race:** No. 25 of 36
**Date:** September 4
**TV:** NBC. **Radio:** MRN

### BUSCH SERIES
**Event:** Stater Brothers 300
**Race:** No. 2 of 35
**Date:** February 26
**TV:** FOX. **Radio:** MRN

**Event:** Target House 300
**Race:** No. 27 of 35
**Date:** September 3
**TV:** NBC. **Radio:** MRN

### CRAFTSMAN TRUCK SERIES
**Event:** American Racing Wheels 200
**Race:** No. 2 of 25
**Date:** February 25
**TV:** SPEED. **Radio:** MRN

Race names subject to change

### TRACK FACTS
**Opened:** June 20, 1997
**Owner:** International Speedway Corp.
**Location:** Fontana, Calif.
**Distance:** 2.0 miles
**Banking in turns 1-4:** 14 degrees
**Banking in trioval:** 11 degrees
**Banking in back stretch:** 3 degrees
**Length of front stretch:** 3,100 feet
**Length of back stretch:** 2,500 feet
**Grandstand seating:** 92,000
**Tickets:** (800) 944-7223
**Website:** www.californiaspeedway.com

Back stretch: 2,500 feet / 3°

Front stretch: 3,100 feet / 11°

## NEXTEL CUP

### TRACK RECORDS

**Most wins:** 3—Jeff Gordon
**Oldest winner:** Rusty Wallace, 44 years, 8 months, 15 days, April 29, 2001
**Youngest winner:** Kurt Busch, 24 years, 8 months, 23 days, April 27, 2003
**Most lead changes:** 29—September 5, 2004
**Fewest lead changes:** 18—May 3, 1998
**Most leaders:** 15—April 30, 2000
**Fewest leaders:** 8—Twice, most recently, April 28, 2002
**Most cautions:** 11—September 5, 2004
**Fewest cautions:** 4—May 22, 1997
**Most caution laps:** 51—September 5, 2004
**Fewest caution laps:** 22—Twice, most recently, April 30, 2000
**Most on the lead lap:** 28—September 5, 2004
**Fewest on the lead lap:** 9—Twice, most recently, May 2, 1999

**Most running at the finish:** 40—April 29, 2001
**Fewest running at the finish:** 32—May 22, 1997
**Most laps led by a race winner:** 165—Mark Martin, May 3, 1998
**Fewest laps led by a race winner:** 26—Jeremy Mayfield, April 30, 2000
**Closest margin of victory:** 0.263 seconds—Elliott Sadler defeated Kasey Kahne, September 5, 2004.
**Greatest margin of victory:** 12.871 seconds—Jeff Gordon defeated Jimmie Johnson, May 2, 2004.

### QUALIFYING AND RACE RECORDS

**QUALIFYING: Track:** Ryan Newman, Chevrolet; 187.432 mph, April 26, 2002.
**RACE: Track:** Jeff Gordon, Chevrolet; 155.012 mph, June 22, 1997.

### NEXTEL Cup YEAR BY YEAR WINNERS

| Year | Event | Race Winner | Car Make | Avg. Speed | Start Pos. | Car Owner | Pole Winner | Pole Speed | POLE WINNERS | | RACE WINNERS | |
|------|-------|-------------|----------|------------|------------|-----------|-------------|------------|--------------|---|--------------|---|
| 2004 | Pop Secret 500 | E. Sadler | Ford | 128.324 | 17 | Robert Yates | B. Vickers | 187.417 | J. Gordon | 1 | M. Martin | 1 |
| | Auto Club 500 | J. Gordon | Chevrolet | 137.268 | 16 | Rick Hendrick | K. Kahne | 186.940 | K. Kahne | 1 | J. Mayfield | 1 |
| 2003 | Auto Club 500 | K. Busch | Ford | 140.111 | 16 | Jack Roush | S. Park | 186.838 | B. Labonte | 1 | R. Wallace | 1 |
| 2002 | NAPA Auto Parts 500 | J. Johnson | Chevrolet | 150.088 | 4 | Rick Hendrick | R. Newman | 187.432 | J. Nemechek | 1 | J. Johnson | 1 |
| 2001 | NAPA Auto Parts 500 | R. Wallace | Ford | 143.118 | 19 | Roger Penske | B. Labonte | 182.635 | R. Newman | 1 | | |
| 2000 | NAPA Auto Parts 500 | J. Mayfield | Ford | 149.378 | 24 | Roger Penske | M. Skinner | 186.061 | M. Skinner | 1 | | |
| 1999 | California 500 | J. Gordon | Chevrolet | 150.276 | 5 | Rick Hendrick | Trials rained out | | J. Gordon | 3 | | |
| 1998 | California 500 | M. Martin | Ford | 140.220 | 3 | Jack Roush | J. Gordon | 181.772 | | | | |
| 1997 | California 500 | J. Gordon | Chevrolet | 155.012 | 3 | Rick Hendrick | J. Nemechek | 183.015 | | | | |

**ALL CALIFORNIA RACES**

# BUSCH SERIES

## Busch YEAR BY YEAR WINNERS (California)

| Year | Event | Race Winner | Car Make | Avg. Speed | Start Pos. | Pole Winner | Pole Speed | POLE WINNERS | | RACE WINNERS | |
|------|-------|-------------|----------|------------|------------|-------------|------------|--------------|---|--------------|---|
| 2004 | Target House 300 | G. Biffle | Ford | 147.844 | 14 | C. Mears | 182.890 | J. Green | 1 | M. Kenseth | 3 |
| | Stater Bros. 300 | G. Biffle | Ford | 138.978 | 15 | J. Leffler | 182.223 | B. Hamilton Jr. | 1 | G. Biffle | 2 |
| 2003 | 1-800-PIT-SHOP.COM 300 | M. Kenseth | Ford | 129.419 | 19 | K. Harvick | 183.941 | S. Park | 1 | T. Bodine | 1 |
| 2002 | Auto Club 300 | S. Riggs | Ford | 131.403 | 6 | Trials rained out | | K. Harvick | 1 | D. Earnhardt Jr. | 1 |
| 2001 | Auto Club 300 | H. Parker Jr. | Chevrolet | 155.957 | 26 | B. Hamilton Jr. | 179.198 | J. Leffler | 1 | H. Parker Jr. | 1 |
| 2000 | Auto Club 300 | M. Kenseth | Chevrolet | 126.375 | 8 | J. Green | 178.258 | R. Pressley | 1 | S. Riggs | 1 |
| 1999 | Auto Club 300 | M. Kenseth | Chevrolet | 119.960 | 2 | Trials rained out | | C. Mears | 1 | | |
| 1998 | Kenwood 300 | D. Earnhardt Jr. | Chevrolet | 148.576 | 2 | R. Pressley | 174.073 | | | | |
| 1997 | Kenwood 300 | T. Bodine | Pontiac | 145.083 | 28 | S. Park | 175.157 | | | | |

**QUALIFYING RECORD:** Kevin Harvick, Chevrolet; 183.941 mph, April 25, 2003
**RACE RECORD:** Hank Parker Jr., Chevrolet; 155.957 mph, April 28, 2001

# CRAFTSMAN TRUCK SERIES

## Craftsman YEAR BY YEAR WINNERS (California)

| Year | Event | Race Winner | Car Make | Avg. Speed | Start Pos. | Pole Winner | Pole Speed | POLE WINNERS | | RACE WINNERS | |
|------|-------|-------------|----------|------------|------------|-------------|------------|--------------|---|--------------|---|
| 2004 | Am. Racing Wheels 200 | T. Bodine | Toyota | 127.141 | 9 | T. Kvapil | 178.669 | A. Houston | 2 | T. Musgrave | 3 |
| 2003 | Am. Racing Wheels 200 | T. Musgrave | Dodge | 145.926 | 10 | B. Gaughan | 173.716 | D. Starr | 2 | J. Sprague | 2 |
| 2002 | Am. Racing Wheels 200 | T. Musgrave | Dodge | 140.296 | 11 | D. Starr | 175.850 | M. Bliss | 1 | M. Bliss | 1 |
| 2001 | Auto Club 200 | T. Musgrave | Dodge | 113.297 | 12 | S. Riggs | 173.678 | K. Busch | 1 | K. Busch | 1 |
| 2000 | Motorola 200 | K. Busch | Ford | 144.260 | 1 | K. Busch | 177.388 | S. Riggs | 1 | T. Bodine | 1 |
| 1999 | NAPA Auto Parts 200 | J. Sprague | Chevrolet | 128.091 | 3 | A. Houston | 173.561 | T. Kvapil | 1 | | |
| 1998 | The No Fear Challenge | J. Sprague | Chevrolet | 141.844 | 10 | A. Houston | 172.022 | | | | |
| 1997 | The No Fear Challenge | M. Bliss | Ford | 137.195 | 1 | M. Bliss | 173.198 | | | | |

**QUALIFYING RECORD:** Travis Kvapil, Dodge; 178.669 mph, October 1, 2004
**RACE RECORD:** Ted Musgrave, Dodge; 145.926 mph, September 20, 2003

# CHICAGOLAND SPEEDWAY

## 2005 SCHEDULE

**NEXTEL CUP**
**Event:** Tropicana 400
**Race:** No. 18 of 36
**Date:** Juiy 10
**TV:** NBC. **Radio:** MRN

**BUSCH SERIES**
**Event:** Tropicana Twister 300
**Race:** No. 19 of 35
**Date:** July 9
**TV:** NBC. **Radio:** MRN

Race names subject to change

## TRACK FACTS

**Opened:** 2001
**Owner:** Raceway Associates LLC
**Location:** Joliet, Ill.
**Distance:** 1.5 miles
**Banking in turns:** 18 degrees
**Banking in trioval:** 11 degrees
**Banking in back stretch:** 5 degrees
**Length of front stretch:** 2,400 feet
**Length of back stretch:** 1,700 feet
**Grandstand seating:** 75,000
**Tickets:** (815) 727-7223
**Website:** www.chicagolandspeedway.com

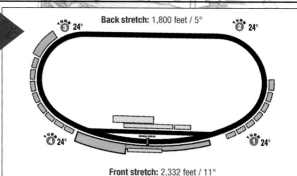

Back stretch: 1,800 feet / 5°
Front stretch: 2,332 feet / 11°

# NEXTEL CUP

## TRACK RECORDS

**Most wins:** 2—Kevin Harvick
**Oldest winner:** Kevin Harvick, 26 years, 7 months, 6 days, July 14, 2002
**Youngest winner:** Ryan Newman, 25 years, 7 months, 5 days, July 13, 2003
**Most lead changes:** 20—July 11, 2004
**Fewest lead changes:** 13—July 13, 2003
**Most leaders:** 13—July 11, 2004
**Fewest leaders:** 7—July 13, 2003
**Most cautions:** 10—July 15, 2001
**Fewest cautions:** 7—Twice, most recently, July 13, 2003
**Most caution laps:** 56—July 15, 2001
**Fewest caution laps:** 35—July 14, 2002
**Most on the lead lap:** 23—July 11, 2004

**Fewest on the lead lap:** 11—July 13, 2003
**Most at the finish:** 34—July 15, 2001
**Fewest running at the finish:** 33—July 14, 2002
**Most laps led by a race winner:** 160—Tony Stewart, July 11, 2004
**Fewest laps led by a race winner:** 29—Kevin Harvick, July 14, 2002
**Closest margin of victory:** 0.649 seconds—Kevin Harvick defeated Robert Pressley, July 15, 2001.
**Greatest margin of victory:** 2.925 seconds—Tony Stewart defeated Jimmie Johnson, July 11, 2004.

## QUALIFYING AND RACE RECORDS

**QUALIFYING: Track:** Jeff Gordon, Chevrolet, 186.942 mph, July 11, 2004.
**RACE: Track:** Kevin Harvick, Chevrolet, 136.832 mph, July 14, 2002.

## NEXTEL Cup YEAR BY YEAR WINNERS — ALL CHICAGOLAND RACES

| Year | Event | Race Winner | Car Make | Avg. Speed | Start Pos. | Car Owner | Pole Winner | Pole Speed |
|------|-------|-------------|----------|-----------|-----------|-----------|-------------|-----------|
| 2004 | Tropicana 400 | T. Stewart | Chevrolet | 129.507 | 10 | Joe Gibbs | J. Gordon | 186.942 |
| 2003 | Tropicana 400 | R. Newman | Dodge | 134.059 | 14 | Roger Penske | T. Stewart | 184.786 |
| 2002 | Tropicana 400 | K. Harvick | Chevrolet | 136.832 | 32 | Richard Childress | R. Newman | 183.051 |
| 2001 | Tropicana 400 | K. Harvick | Chevrolet | 131.759 | 6 | Richard Childress | T. Bodine | 183.717 |

| POLE WINNERS | | RACE WINNERS | |
|--------------|---|--------------|---|
| T. Bodine | 1 | K. Harvick | 2 |
| J. Gordon | 1 | R. Newman | 1 |
| R. Newman | 1 | T. Stewart | 1 |
| T. Stewart | 1 | | |

# BUSCH SERIES

## Busch YEAR BY YEAR WINNERS

| Year | Event | Race Winner | Car Make | Avg. Speed | Start Pos. | Pole Winner | Pole Speed |
|------|-------|-------------|----------|-----------|-----------|-------------|-----------|
| 2004 | Tropicana Twister 300 | J. Labonte | Dodge | 126.790 | 34 | B. Hamilton Jr. | 183.611 |
| 2003 | Tropicana Twister 300 | B. Hamilton Jr. | Ford | 129.730 | 3 | C. Mears | 181.757 |
| 2002 | Tropicana 300 | Jo. Sauter | Chevrolet | 128.008 | 20 | T. Bodine | 178.772 |
| 2001 | Sam's Club 300 | J. Johnson | Chevrolet | 119.469 | 6 | R. Newman | 181.886 |

| POLE WINNERS | | RACE WINNERS | |
|--------------|---|--------------|---|
| T. Bodine | 1 | J. Johnson | 1 |
| C. Mears | 1 | Jo. Sauter | 1 |
| R. Newman | 1 | B. Hamilton Jr. | 1 |
| B. Hamilton Jr. | 1 | J. Labonte | 1 |

**QUALIFYING RECORD:** Bobby Hamilton Jr., Ford; 183.611 mph, July 9, 2004
**RACE RECORD:** Bobby Hamilton Jr., Ford; 129.73 mph, July 12, 2003

# DARLINGTON RACEWAY

## 2005 SCHEDULE

**NEXTEL CUP**

**Event:** Carolina Dodge Dealers 500
**Race:** No. 10 of 36
**Date:** May 7
**TV:** FOX. **Radio:** MRN

**BUSCH SERIES**

**Event:** Diamond Hill Plywood 200
**Race:** No. 11 of 35
**Date:** May 6
**TV:** FX. **Radio:** MRN

*Race names subject to change*

## TRACK FACTS

**Opened:** 1950
**Owner:** International Speedway Corp.
**Location:** Darlington, S.C.
**Distance:** 1.366 miles
**Banking in Turns 1-2:** 25 degrees
**Banking in Turns 3-4:** 23 degrees
**Banking in straights:** 2 degrees
**Length of front stretch:** 1,229 feet
**Length of back stretch:** 1,229 feet
**Grandstand seating:** 60,000
**Tickets:** (843) 395-8499
**Website:** www.darlingtonraceway.com

**Back stretch:** 1,229 feet / 2°
23° Banking
**DARLINGTON** A NASCAR TRADITION
25° Banking
**Front stretch:** 1,229 feet / 2°

# NEXTEL CUP

## TRACK RECORDS

**Most wins:** 9—David Pearson and Dale Earnhardt
**Oldest winner:** Harry Gant, 51 years, 7 months, 22 days, September 1, 1991
**Youngest winner:** Terry Labonte, 23 years, 9 months, 16 days, September 1, 1980
**Most lead changes:** 41—September 6, 1982
**Fewest lead changes:** 4—September 4, 1950
**Most leaders:** 20—September 4, 1994
**Fewest leaders:** 2—May 9, 1964
**Most laps led in a 300-mile race:** 197—Junior Johnson, May 8, 1965
**Most laps led in a 400-mile race:** 281—Richard Petty, April 30, 1966
**Most laps led in a 500-mile race:** 351—Johnny Mantz, September 4, 1950
**Most cautions:** 15—March 26, 1995
**Fewest cautions:** 0—September 2, 1963
**Most caution laps:** 101—September 2, 1974
**Fewest caution laps:** 0—September 2, 1963
**Most on the lead lap:** 23—September 1, 2002
**Fewest on the lead lap:** 1—24 times, most recently, September 3, 1979
**Most running at the finish:** 41—March 21, 1999

**Fewest running at the finish:** 12—September 2, 1974
**Most laps led by a race winner:** 351—Johnny Mantz, September 4, 1950
**Fewest laps led by a race winner:** 1—Ricky Craven, March 16, 2003
**Closest margin of victory:** 0.002 seconds—Ricky Craven defeated Kurt Busch, March 16, 2003.
**Greatest margin of victory:** 2 laps—David Pearson defeated Bill Elliott, September 3, 1979.

## QUALIFYING AND RACE RECORDS

**QUALIFYING: Track:** Ward Burton, Pontiac; 173.797 mph, March 22, 1996 (TranSouth 400). **Spring race (Carolina Dodge Dealers 400):** Ward Burton, Pontiac; 173.797 mph, March 22, 1996. **Fall race (Southern 500):** Kenny Irwin, Ford; 170.970 mph, September 3, 1999. **RACE: Track:** Dale Earnhardt, Chevrolet; 139.958 mph, March 28, 1993 (TranSouth 500). **Spring race (Carolina Dodge Dealers 400):** Dale Earnhardt, Chevrolet; 139.958 mph, March 28, 1993. **Fall race (Southern 500):** Jeff Gordon, Chevrolet; 139.031 mph, September 6, 1998. **400 miles:** David Pearson, Ford; 132.699 mph, May 11, 1968 (Rebel 400). **300 miles:** Fred Lorenzen, Ford; 130.013 mph, May 9, 1964 (Rebel 300). **100 miles:** Dick Rathmann, Hudson; 83.818 mph, May 10, 1952 (Grand National 100).

## SPRING: CAROLINA DODGE DEALERS 400

### POLE WINNERS

| | |
|---|---|
| D. Pearson | 6 |
| F. Lorenzen | 5 |
| B. Elliott | 3 |
| D. Allison | 3 |
| G. Bodine | 3 |
| J. Gordon | 3 |
| K. Schrader | 2 |
| M. Martin | 2 |
| B. Parsons | 2 |
| F. Roberts | 2 |
| C. Glotzbach | 1 |
| R. Petty | 1 |
| C. Turner | 1 |
| C. Yarborough | 1 |
| B. Allison | 1 |
| L. Yarbrough | 1 |
| Buddy Baker | 1 |
| T. Richmond | 1 |
| S. Marlin | 1 |
| W. Burton | 1 |
| D. Jarrett | 1 |
| R. Craven | 1 |
| E. Sadler | 1 |
| K. Kahne | 1 |

### RACE WINNERS

| | |
|---|---|
| D. Pearson | 7 |
| D. Earnhardt | 6 |
| D. Waltrip | 4 |
| D. Jarrett | 3 |
| F. Lorenzen | 2 |
| F. Roberts | 2 |
| R. Petty | 2 |
| H. Gant | 2 |
| B. Elliott | 2 |
| J. Weatherly | 2 |
| S. Marlin | 2 |
| Buddy Baker | 1 |
| Jr. Johnson | 1 |
| N. Stacy | 1 |
| C. Turner | 1 |
| L. Yarbrough | 1 |
| B. Parsons | 1 |
| B. Allison | 1 |
| L. Speed | 1 |
| R. Rudd | 1 |
| J. Gordon | 1 |
| J. Burton | 1 |
| W. Burton | 1 |
| R. Craven | 1 |
| Ji. Johnson | 1 |

## FALL: SOUTHERN 500

### POLE WINNERS

| | |
|---|---|
| D. Pearson | 6 |
| F. Roberts | 5 |
| R. Petty | 3 |
| B. Allison | 3 |
| B. Elliott | 2 |
| D. Jarrett | 2 |
| D. Waltrip | 2 |
| H. Gant | 2 |
| F. Flock | 2 |
| Da. Allison | 2 |
| C. Glotzbach | 1 |
| Jr. Johnson | 1 |
| F. Lorenzen | 1 |
| F. Mundy | 1 |
| C. Owens | 1 |
| E. Pagan | 1 |
| S. Thompson | 1 |
| C. Turner | 1 |
| C. Yarborough | 1 |
| L. Yarbrough | 1 |
| N. Bonnett | 1 |
| T. Richmond | 1 |
| Buck Baker | 1 |
| A. Kulwicki | 1 |
| D. Earnhardt | 1 |
| S. Marlin | 1 |
| K. Schrader | 1 |
| G. Bodine | 1 |
| J. Andretti | 1 |
| B. Labonte | 1 |
| K. Irwin | 1 |
| J. Mayfield | 1 |
| Ku. Busch | 1 |
| T. Labonte | 1 |

### RACE WINNERS

| | |
|---|---|
| C. Yarborough | 5 |
| J. Gordon | 5 |
| B. Allison | 4 |
| D. Earnhardt | 3 |
| Buck Baker | 3 |
| H. Thomas | 3 |
| D. Pearson | 3 |
| B. Elliott | 3 |
| F. Roberts | 2 |
| H. Gant | 2 |
| D. Dieringer | 1 |
| L. Frank | 1 |
| N. Jarrett | 1 |
| R. Petty | 1 |
| J. Mantz | 1 |
| J. Reed | 1 |
| N. Stacy | 1 |
| S. Thompson | 1 |
| C. Turner | 1 |
| L. Yarbrough | 1 |
| T. Labonte | 1 |
| N. Bonnett | 1 |
| Buddy Baker | 1 |
| T. Richmond | 1 |
| D. Waltrip | 1 |
| M. Martin | 1 |
| F. Flock | 1 |
| J. Burton | 1 |
| B. Labonte | 1 |
| W. Burton | 1 |
| R. Newman | 1 |
| Ji. Johnson | 1 |

## ALL DARLINGTON RACES

### POLE WINNERS

| | |
|---|---|
| D. Pearson | 12 |
| F. Roberts | 7 |
| F. Lorenzen | 6 |
| B. Elliott | 5 |
| R. Petty | 4 |
| B. Allison | 4 |
| G. Bodine | 4 |
| K. Schrader | 3 |
| D. Jarrett | 3 |
| D. Allison | 3 |
| J. Gordon | 3 |
| F. Flock | 2 |
| C. Glotzbach | 2 |
| C. Turner | 2 |
| C. Yarborough | 2 |
| D. Waltrip | 2 |
| B. Parsons | 2 |
| H. Gant | 2 |
| T. Richmond | 2 |
| L. Yarbrough | 2 |
| Da. Allison | 2 |
| S. Marlin | 2 |
| M. Martin | 2 |
| B. Labonte | 1 |
| Jr. Johnson | 1 |
| F. Mundy | 1 |
| C. Owens | 1 |
| E. Pagan | 1 |
| S. Thompson | 1 |
| Buddy Baker | 1 |
| N. Bonnett | 1 |
| Buck Baker | 1 |
| A. Kulwicki | 1 |
| D. Earnhardt | 1 |
| J. Andretti | 1 |
| W. Burton | 1 |
| K. Irwin | 1 |
| J. Mayfield | 1 |
| Ku. Busch | 1 |
| R. Craven | 1 |
| R. Newman | 1 |
| E. Sadler | 1 |
| K. Kahne | 1 |

### RACE WINNERS

| | |
|---|---|
| D. Pearson | 10 |
| D. Earnhardt | 9 |
| J. Gordon | 6 |
| C. Yarborough | 5 |
| B. Allison | 5 |
| D. Waltrip | 5 |
| B. Elliott | 5 |
| F. Roberts | 4 |
| H. Gant | 4 |
| R. Petty | 3 |
| H. Thomas | 3 |
| Buck Baker | 3 |
| D. Jarrett | 3 |
| J. Burton | 2 |
| W. Burton | 2 |
| F. Lorenzen | 2 |
| J. Weatherly | 2 |
| N. Stacy | 2 |
| L. Yarbrough | 2 |
| C. Turner | 2 |
| Buddy Baker | 2 |
| S. Marlin | 2 |
| T. Labonte | 2 |
| Ji. Johnson | 2 |
| D. Dieringer | 1 |
| L. Frank | 1 |
| N. Jarrett | 1 |
| J. Mantz | 1 |
| J. Reed | 1 |
| S. Thompson | 1 |
| F. Flock | 1 |
| B. Parsons | 1 |
| N. Bonnett | 1 |
| T. Richmond | 1 |
| L. Speed | 1 |
| R. Rudd | 1 |
| M. Martin | 1 |
| Jr. Johnson | 1 |
| B. Labonte | 1 |
| R. Craven | 1 |

# NEXTEL Cup YEAR BY YEAR WINNERS (Darlington)

| Year | Event | Race Winner | Car Make | Avg. Speed | Start Pos. | Car Owner | Pole Winner | Pole Speed |
|---|---|---|---|---|---|---|---|---|
| 2004 | Southern 500 | Ji. Johnson | Chevrolet | 125.044 | 4 | Rick Hendrick | Trials rained out | |
| | Car. Dodge Dlrs. 400 | Ji. Johnson | Chevrolet | 114.001 | 11 | Rick Hendrick | K. Kahne | 171.716 |
| 2003 | Southern 500 | T. Labonte | Chevrolet | 120.744 | 3 | Rick Hendrick | R. Newman | 169.048 |
| | Car. Dodge Dlrs. 400 | R. Craven | Pontiac | 126.214 | 31 | Cal Wells | E. Sadler | 170.147 |
| 2002 | Southern 500 | J. Gordon | Chevrolet | 118.617 | 3 | Rick Hendrick | Trials rained out | |
| | Car. Dodge Dlrs. 400 | S. Marlin | Dodge | 126.070 | 11 | Chip Ganassi | R. Craven | 170.089 |
| 2001 | Southern 500 | W. Burton | Dodge | 122.773 | 37 | Bill Davis | K. Busch | 168.048 |
| | Car. Dodge Dlrs. 400 | D. Jarrett | Ford | 126.588 | 2 | Robert Yates | Trials rained out | |
| 2000 | Southern 500 | B. Labonte | Pontiac | 108.273 | 37 | Joe Gibbs | J. Mayfield | 169.444 |
| | Mall.com 400 | W. Burton | Pontiac | 128.076 | 3 | Bill Davis | J. Gordon | 172.662 |
| 1999 | Southern 500 | J. Burton | Ford | 107.816 | 15 | Jack Roush | K. Irwin | 170.970 |
| | TranSouth 400 | J. Burton | Ford | 121.294 | 9 | Jack Roush | J. Gordon | 173.167 |
| 1998 | Pepsi 500 | J. Gordon | Chevrolet | 139.031 | 5 | Rick Hendrick | D. Jarrett | 168.879 |
| | TranSouth 400 | D. Jarrett | Ford | 127.962 | 3 | Robert Yates | M. Martin | 168.665 |
| 1997 | Mtn. Dew 500 | J. Gordon | Chevrolet | 121.149 | 7 | Rick Hendrick | B. Labonte | 170.661 |
| | TranSouth 400 | D. Jarrett | Ford | 121.162 | 1 | Robert Yates | D. Jarrett | 171.095 |
| 1996 | Mtn. Dew 500 | J. Gordon | Chevrolet | 135.757 | 2 | Rick Hendrick | D. Jarrett | 170.934 |
| | TranSouth 400 | J. Gordon | Chevrolet | 124.792 | 2 | Rick Hendrick | W. Burton | 173.797 |
| 1995 | Mtn. Dew 500 | J. Gordon | Chevrolet | 121.231 | 5 | Rick Hendrick | J. Andretti | 167.379 |
| | TranSouth 400 | S. Marlin | Chevrolet | 111.392 | 5 | Morgan McClure | J. Gordon | 170.833 |
| 1994 | Mtn. Dew 500 | B. Elliott | Ford | 127.952 | 9 | Junior Johnson | G. Bodine | 166.998 |
| | TranSouth 400 | D. Earnhardt | Chevrolet | 132.432 | 9 | Richard Childress | B. Elliott | 165.553 |
| 1993 | Mtn. Dew 500 | M. Martin | Ford | 137.932 | 4 | Jack Roush | K. Schrader | 161.259 |
| | TranSouth 500 | D. Earnhardt | Chevrolet | 139.958 | 1 | Richard Childress | Trials rained out | |
| 1992 | Mtn. Dew 500 | D. Waltrip | Chevrolet | 129.114 | 5 | Darrell Waltrip | S. Marlin | 162.249 |
| | TranSouth 500 | B. Elliott | Ford | 139.364 | 2 | Junior Johnson | S. Marlin | 163.067 |
| 1991 | Heinz 500 | H. Gant | Oldsmobile | 133.508 | 5 | Leo Jackson | Da. Allison | 162.506 |
| | TranSouth 500 | R. Rudd | Chevrolet | 135.594 | 13 | Rick Hendrick | G. Bodine | 161.939 |
| 1990 | Heinz 500 | D. Earnhardt | Chevrolet | 123.141 | 1 | Richard Childress | D. Earnhardt | 158.448 |
| | TranSouth 500 | D. Earnhardt | Chevrolet | 124.073 | 15 | Richard Childress | G. Bodine | 162.996 |
| 1989 | Heinz 500 | D. Earnhardt | Chevrolet | 135.462 | 10 | Richard Childress | A. Kulwicki | 160.156 |
| | TranSouth 500 | H. Gant | Oldsmobile | 115.475 | 10 | Jackson Bros. | M. Martin | 161.111 |
| 1988 | Southern 500 | B. Elliott | Ford | 128.297 | 1 | Melling Racing | B. Elliott | 160.827 |
| | TranSouth 500 | L. Speed | Oldsmobile | 131.284 | 8 | Lake Speed | K. Schrader | 162.657 |
| 1987 | Southern 500 | D. Earnhardt | Chevrolet | 115.520 | 5 | Richard Childress | Da. Allison | 157.232 |
| | TranSouth 500 | D. Earnhardt | Chevrolet | 122.540 | 2 | Richard Childress | K. Schrader | 158.387 |
| 1986 | Southern 500 | T. Richmond | Chevrolet | 121.068 | 1 | Rick Hendrick | T. Richmond | 158.489 |
| | TranSouth 500 | D. Earnhardt | Chevrolet | 128.994 | 4 | Richard Childress | G. Bodine | 159.197 |
| 1985 | Southern 500 | B. Elliott | Ford | 121.254 | 1 | Melling Racing | B. Elliott | 156.641 |
| | TranSouth 500 | B. Elliott | Ford | 126.295 | 1 | Melling Racing | B. Elliott | 157.454 |
| 1984 | Southern 500 | H. Gant | Chevrolet | 128.270 | 1 | Mach 1 | H. Gant | 155.502 |
| | TranSouth 500 | D. Waltrip | Chevrolet | 119.925 | 9 | Junior Johnson | B. Parsons | 156.328 |
| 1983 | Southern 500 | B. Allison | Buick | 123.343 | 14 | DiGard Rac. Co. | Bonnett | 157.187 |
| | TranSouth 500 | H. Gant | Buick | 130.406 | 5 | Mach 1 | Richmond | 157.818 |
| 1982 | Southern 500 | C. Yarborough | Buick | 115.224 | 9 | M. C. Anderson | D. Pearson | 155.739 |
| | CRC Rebel 500 | D. Earnhardt | Ford | 123.554 | 5 | Bud Moore | Buddy Baker | 153.979 |
| 1981 | Southern 500 | N. Bonnett | Ford | 126.410 | 3 | Wood Brothers | H. Gant | 152.693 |
| | CRC Rebel 500 | D. Waltrip | Buick | 126.703 | 3 | Junior Johnson | B. Elliott | 153.896 |
| 1980 | Southern 500 | T. Labonte | Chevrolet | 115.210 | 10 | Stratagraph Rac. | D. Waltrip | 153.838 |
| | CRC Rebel 500 | D. Pearson | Chevrolet | 112.397 | 2 | Hoss Ellington | B. Parsons | 155.866 |
| 1979 | Southern 500 | D. Pearson | Chevrolet | 126.259 | 5 | Osterlund Rac. | B. Allison | 154.880 |
| | CRC Rebel 500 | D. Waltrip | Chevrolet | 121.721 | 2 | DiGard Rac. Co. | D. Allison | 154.797 |
| 1978 | Southern 500 | C. Yarborough | Oldsmobile | 116.828 | 6 | Junior Johnson | D. Pearson | 153.685 |
| | Rebel 500 | B. Parsons | Chevrolet | 127.544 | 8 | L. G. DeWitt | B. Allison | 151.862 |
| 1977 | Southern 500 | D. Pearson | Mercury | 106.797 | 5 | Wood Brothers | D. Waltrip | 153.493 |
| | Rebel 500 | D. Waltrip | Chevrolet | 128.817 | 4 | DiGard Rac. Co. | D. Pearson | 151.269 |
| 1976 | Southern 500 | D. Pearson | Mercury | 120.534 | 1 | Wood Brothers | D. Pearson | 154.699 |
| | Rebel 500 | D. Pearson | Mercury | 122.973 | 1 | Wood Brothers | D. Pearson | 154.171 |
| 1975 | Southern 500 | B. Allison | Matador | 116.825 | 3 | Roger Penske | D. Pearson | 153.401 |
| | Rebel 500 | B. Allison | Matador | 117.597 | 5 | Roger Penske | D. Pearson | 155.433 |
| 1974 | Southern 500 | C. Yarborough | Chevrolet | 111.075 | 4 | Junior Johnson | R. Petty | 150.132 |
| | Rebel 500 | D. Pearson | Mercury | 117.543 | 2 | Wood Brothers | D. Allison | 150.689 |
| 1973 | Southern 500 | C. Yarborough | Chevrolet | 134.033 | 8 | Junior Johnson | D. Pearson | 150.366 |
| | Rebel 500 | D. Pearson | Mercury | 122.655 | 1 | Wood Brothers | D. Pearson | 153.463 |
| 1972 | Southern 500 | B. Allison | Chevrolet | 128.124 | 1 | Junior Johnson | B. Allison | 152.228 |
| | Rebel 400 | D. Pearson | Mercury | 124.406 | 1 | Wood Brothers | D. Pearson | 148.209 |
| 1971 | Southern 500 | B. Allison | Mercury | 131.398 | 1 | Holman-Moody | B. Allison | 147.915 |
| | Rebel 400 | Buddy Baker | Dodge | 130.678 | 5 | Petty Eng. | D. Allison | 149.826 |
| 1970 | Southern 500 | Buddy Baker | Dodge | 128.817 | 2 | Cotton Owens | D. Pearson | 150.555 |
| | Rebel 400 | Pearson | Ford | 129.668 | 3 | Holman-Moody | C. Glotzbach | 153.822 |
| 1969 | Southern 500 | L. Yarbrough | Ford | 105.612 | 4 | Junior Johnson | C. Yarborough | 151.985 |
| | Rebel 400 | L. Yarbrough | Mercury | 131.572 | 4 | Junior Johnson | C. Yarborough | 152.293 |
| 1968 | Southern 500 | C. Yarborough | Mercury | 126.132 | 2 | Wood Brothers | Glotzbach | 144.830 |
| | Rebel 400 | D. Pearson | Ford | 132.699 | 2 | Holman-Moody | L. Yarbrough | 148.850 |
| 1967 | Southern 500 | R. Petty | Plymouth | 130.423 | 1 | Petty Eng. | R. Petty | 143.436 |
| | Rebel 400 | R. Petty | Plymouth | 125.738 | 2 | Petty Eng. | D. Pearson | 144.536 |
| 1966 | Southern 500 | D. Dieringer | Mercury | 114.830 | 3 | Bud Moore | L. Yarbrough | 140.058 |
| | Rebel 400 | R. Petty | Plymouth | 131.993 | 1 | Petty Eng. | R. Petty | 140.815 |
| 1965 | Southern 500 | N. Jarrett | Ford | 115.878 | 10 | Bondy Long | Ju. Johnson | 137.571 |
| | Rebel 300 | Ju. Johnson | Ford | 111.849 | 3 | Holly Farms | F. Lorenzen | 138.133 |
| 1964 | Southern 500 | Buck Baker | Dodge | 117.757 | 6 | Ray Fox | R. Petty | 136.815 |
| | Rebel 300 | F. Lorenzen | Ford | 130.013 | 1 | Holman-Moody | F. Lorenzen | 135.727 |

| Year | Event | Race Winner | Car Make | Avg. Speed | Start Pos. | Car Owner | Pole Winner | Pole Speed |
|---|---|---|---|---|---|---|---|---|
| 1963 | Southern 500 | F. Roberts | Ford | 129.784 | 9 | Holman-Moody | F. Lorenzen | 133.648 |
| e | Rebel 300 | **J. Weatherly** | Pontiac | 122.745 | 6 | Bud Moore | F. Lorenzen | 131.718 |
| 1962 | Southern 500 | L. Frank | Ford | 117.965 | 10 | Ratus Walters | F. Roberts | 130.246 |
| d | Rebel 300 | N. Stacy | Ford | 117.429 | 3 | Holman-Moody | F. Lorenzen | 129.810 |
| 1961 | Southern 500 | N. Stacy | Ford | 117.787 | 3 | Nelson Stacy | F. Roberts | 128.680 |
| | Rebel 300 | F. Lorenzen | Ford | 119.520 | 1 | Holman-Moody | F. Lorenzen | 128.965 |
| 1960 | Southern 500 | Buck Baker | Pontiac | 105.901 | 2 | Jack Smith | F. Roberts | 125.459 |
| c | Rebel 300 | J. Weatherly | Ford | 102.646 | 2 | Holman-Moody | F. Roberts | 127.750 |
| 1959 | Southern 500 | J. Reed | Chevrolet | 111.836 | 14 | Jim Reed | F. Roberts | 123.734 |
| 1958 | Southern 500 | F. Roberts | Chevrolet | 102.590 | 2 | Frank Strickland | E. Pagan | 116.952 |
| 1957 | Southern 500 | S. Thompson | Chevrolet | 100.100 | 7 | S. Thompson | C. Owens | 117.416 |
| 1956 | Southern 500 | C. Turner | Ford | 95.067 | 11 | Holman-Moody | S. Thompson | 119.659 |
| 1955 | Southern 500 | H. Thomas | Chevrolet | 92.789 | 8 | Smokey Yunick | F. Roberts | 110.682 |
| 1954 | Southern 500 | H. Thomas | Hudson | 95.027 | 23 | Herb Thomas | Buck Baker | 108.261 |
| b 1953 | Southern 500 | Buck Baker | Oldsmobile | 92.881 | 7 | Johnny Griffin | F. Flock | 107.983 |
| 1952 | Southern 500 | F. Flock | Oldsmobile | 74.513 | 1 | Frank Christian | F. Flock | 88.550 |
| | Grand National 100 | D. Rathmann | Hudson | 83.818 | 4 | Walt Chapman | None—Conditions | |
| 1951 | Southern 500 | H. Thomas | Hudson | 76.907 | 2 | Herb Thomas | F. Mundy | 84.173 |
| a 1950 | Southern 500 | J. Mantz | Plymouth | 75.251 | 43 | Bill France Sr. | C.Turner | 82.034 |

**KEY**

* The qualifying speeds of Charlie Glotzbach and Cale Yarborough were identical; Glotzbach won the pole because he qualified ahead of Yarborough, but each was credited with being the fastest qualifier.
t Shortened by 50 miles because of the energy shortage.
a Bill France Sr., Hubert Westmoreland, Curtis Turner and Alvin Hawkins were co-owners of the car.
b Changed from 1.25-mile to 1.375-mile track.
c The race was halted after 57 laps and completed the following Saturday.
d The last convertible race.
e A 300-mile race divided into two 150-milers.
f Shortened to 316.25 miles because of rain and darkness.
g Track remeasured at 1.386 miles (367 laps for 500-mile race).
h Shortened to 258.17 miles because of rain and darkness.
i Shortened to 275.932 miles because of rain.
j Shortened to 407.068 miles because of rain.
k Shortened to 479.466 miles because of rain and darkness.
l Front and back straightaway flip-flopped.
m Shortened to 224.024 miles because of rain.
n Shortened to 368.82 miles because of rain and darkness.
o Shortened to 448.048 miles because of rain.

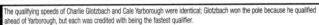

# BUSCH SERIES

## Busch YEAR BY YEAR WINNERS (Darlington)

| Year | Event | Race Winner | Car Make | Avg. Speed | Start Pos. | Pole Winner | Pole Speed | POLE WINNERS | | RACE WINNERS | |
|---|---|---|---|---|---|---|---|---|---|---|---|
| 2004 | BI-LO 200 | J. McMurray | Dodge | 109.711 | 34 | Trials rained out | | M. Martin | 8 | M. Martin | 8 |
| | Diamond Hill Plywood 200 | G. Biffle | Ford | 120.141 | 4 | Ky. Busch | 168.619 | G. Bodine | 4 | J. Burton | 4 |
| 2003 | Darlingtonraceway.com 200 | T. Bodine | Chevrolet | 124.550 | 13 | Trials rained out | | T. Richmond | 3 | H. Gant | 4 |
| | Winn-Dixie 200 | B. Vickers | Chevrolet | 114.744 | 4 | K. Harvick | 167.516 | R. Bouchard | 2 | G. Bodine | 3 |
| 2002 | Darlington.com 200 | J. Burton | Ford | 124.143 | 1 | J. Burton | 168.250 | J. Burton | 2 | D. Earnhardt | 3 |
| | Gatorade 200 | J. Burton | Ford | 92.525 | 33 | Trials rained out | | H. Gant | 2 | R. Bouchard | 2 |
| 2001 | SunCom 200 | **J. Green** | Ford | 128.742 | 13 | R. Newman | 170.301 | R. Newman | 2 | D. Jarrett | 2 |
| | South Carolina 200 | J. Burton | Ford | 102.479 | 24 | R. Newman | 169.246 | L. Pearson | 2 | R. Pressley | 2 |
| 2000 | SunCom 200 | M. Martin | Ford | 113.519 | 1 | M. Martin | 167.038 | W. Burton | 1 | D. Waltrip | 2 |
| | Bumper to Bumper 200 | M. Martin | Ford | 118.215 | 1 | M. Martin | 164.965 | R. Craven | 1 | N. Bonnett | 1 |
| 1999 | Diamond Hill 300 | M. Kenseth | Chevrolet | 121.945 | 9 | M. Martin | 166.568 | D. Earnhardt | 1 | J. Green | 1 |
| | Dura Lube 200 | M. Martin | Ford | 132.227 | 2 | W. Burton | 167.676 | T. Fedewa | 1 | J. Ingram | 1 |
| 1998 | Diamond Hill 300 | B. Labonte | Pontiac | 100.443 | 9 | J. Burton | 162.577 | J. Green | 1 | M. Kenseth | 1 |
| | Dura Lube 200 | D. Trickle | Chevrolet | 123.233 | 4 | M. McLaughlin | 164.661 | J. Hensley | 1 | B. Labonte | 1 |
| 1997 | Diamond Hill 200 | R. LaJoie | Chevrolet | 115.569 | 11 | E. Sadler | 166.051 | J. Ingram | 1 | T. Labonte | 1 |
| | Dura Lube 200 | J. Burton | Ford | 118.080 | 10 | M. Martin | 163.745 | R. LaJoie | 1 | R. LaJoie | 1 |
| 1996 | Dura Lube 200 | M. Martin | Ford | 120.763 | 2 | J. Green | 166.337 | M. McLaughlin | 1 | L. Pearson | 1 |
| | Dura Lube 200 | T. Labonte | Chevrolet | 128.468 | 2 | M. Martin | 165.799 | G. Sacks | 1 | D. Trickle | 1 |
| 1995 | Mark III Vans 200 | L. Pearson | Chevrolet | 108.087 | 36 | T. Fedewa | 162.905 | E. Sadler | 1 | M. Waltrip | 1 |
| | Gatorade 200 | M. Martin | Ford | 115.183 | 5 | L. Pearson | 161.429 | K. Schrader | 1 | B. Vickers | 1 |
| 1994 | Mark III Vans 200 | M. Martin | Ford | 117.965 | 1 | M. Martin | 161.011 | K. Wallace | 1 | T. Bodine | 1 |
| | Gatorade 200 | M. Martin | Ford | 124.824 | 2 | R. LaJoie | 161.022 | S. Barrett | 1 | G. Biffle | 1 |
| 1993 | Mark III Vans 200 | R. Pressley | Chevrolet | 109.197 | 7 | Trials rained out | | K. Harvick | 1 | J. McMurray | 1 |
| | Gatorade 200 | M. Martin | Ford | 117.638 | 3 | R. Craven | 157.909 | Ky. Busch | 1 | | |
| 1992 | Mark III Vans 200 | R. Pressley | Oldsmobile | 130.982 | 2 | M. Martin | 159.068 | | | | |
| | Gatorade 200 | **M. Waltrip** | Pontiac | 138.140 | 15 | M. Martin | 159.652 | | | | |
| 1991 | Pontiac 200 | D. Jarrett | Pontiac | 115.551 | 6 | J. Hensley | 158.894 | | | | |
| | Gatorade 200 | D. Earnhardt | Chevrolet | 134.141 | 16 | H. Gant | 158.899 | | | | |
| 1990 | Pontiac 200 | H. Gant | Buick | 129.689 | 3 | K. Wallace | 156.821 | | | | |
| | Gatorade 200 | D. Jarrett | Pontiac | 136.342 | 28 | G. Sacks | 155.056 | | | | |
| 1989 | Country Squire 200 | G. Bodine | Chevrolet | 118.681 | 1 | G. Bodine | 156.631 | | | | |
| | Gatorade 200 | H. Gant | Buick | 119.170 | 3 | K. Schrader | 156.597 | | | | |
| 1988 | Country Squire 200 | G. Bodine | Chevrolet | 115.514 | 1 | G. Bodine | 156.826 | | | | |
| | Gatorade 200 | H. Gant | Buick | 136.009 | 2 | G. Bodine | 156.422 | | | | |
| 1987 | Country Squire 200 | D. Earnhardt | Chevrolet | 137.850 | 2 | G. Bodine | 157.646 | | | | |
| | Gatorade 200 | H. Gant | Buick | 103.196 | 20 | L. Pearson | 154.978 | | | | |

## Busch YEAR BY YEAR WINNERS (Darlington, continued)

| Year | Event | Race Winner | Car Make | Avg. Speed | Start Pos. | Pole Winner | Pole Speed |
|------|-------|-------------|----------|------------|------------|-------------|------------|
| 1986 | Dixie Cup 200 | D. Waltrip | Pontiac | 123.423 | 5 | T. Richmond | 157.298 |
|      | Gatorade 200 | D. Earnhardt | Chevrolet | 138.746 | 2 | T. Richmond | 154.749 |
| 1985 | Dixie Cup 200 | J. Ingram | Oldsmobile | 108.460 | 11 | D. Earnhardt | 154.341 |
|      | Pontiac 200 | D. Waltrip | Chevrolet | 116.595 | 6 | T. Richmond | 155.704 |
| 1984 | Dixie Cup 200 | R. Bouchard | Pontiac | 97.992 | 1 | R. Bouchard | 151.815 |
|      | Darlington 200 | R. Bouchard | Pontiac | 109.115 | 1 | R. Bouchard | 153.392 |
| 1983 | No spring race | | | | | | |
|      | Darlington 250 | **N. Bonnett** | Pontiac | 131.299 | 2 | J. Ingram | 152.630 |
| 1982 | TranSouth 200 | G. Bodine | Pontiac | 129.018 | 3 | H. Gant | 154.259 |
|      | No fall race | | | | | | |

**QUALIFYING RECORD:** Ryan Newman, Ford; 170.301 mph, March 16, 2001
**RACE RECORD:** Michael Waltrip, Pontiac; 138.140 mph, September 5, 1992

# DAYTONA INTERNATIONAL SPEEDWAY

TRACKS

## 2005 SCHEDULE

### NEXTEL CUP
**Event:** Daytona 500
**Race:** No. 1 of 36
**Date:** February 20
**TV:** FOX. **Radio:** MRN

**Event:** Pepsi 400
**Race:** No. 17 of 36
**Date:** July 2
**TV:** NBC. **Radio:** MRN

### BUSCH SERIES
**Event:** Hershey's Kisses 300
**Race:** No. 1 of 35
**Date:** February 19
**TV:** FOX. **Radio:** MRN

**Event:** Winn-Dixie 250
**Race:** No. 18 of 34
**Date:** July 1
**TV:** TNT. **Radio:** MRN

### CRAFTSMAN TRUCK SERIES
**Event:** Florida Dodge Dealers 250
**Race:** No. 1 of 25
**Date:** February 18
**TV:** SPEED. **Radio:** MRN

Race names subject to change

## TRACK FACTS
**Opened:** 1959
**Owner:** International Speedway Corp.
**Location:** Daytona Beach, Fla.
**Distance:** 2.5 miles
**Banking in turns:** 31 degrees
**Banking in trioval:** 18 degrees
**Banking in back stretch:** 3 degrees
**Length of front stretch:** 3,800 feet
**Length of back stretch:** 3,400 feet
**Grandstand seating:** 168,000
**Tickets:** (386) 253-7223
**Website:** www.daytonausa.com

Back stretch: 3,400 feet / 3°

31° 31°

31° 31°

Front stretch: 3,800 feet / 18°

# NEXTEL CUP

## TRACK RECORDS

**Most wins:** 10—Richard Petty
**Oldest winner:** Bobby Allison, 50 years, 2 months, 11 days, February 14, 1988
**Youngest winner:** Jeff Gordon, 23 years, 10 months, 27 days, July 1, 1995
**Most lead changes:** 59—February 17, 1974
**Fewest lead changes:** 1—Twice, most recently, February 22, 1963
**Most leaders:** 15—Three times, most recently, February 18, 1996
**Fewest leaders:** 1—Twice, most recently, February 22, 1963
**Most laps led in a 400-mile race:** 142—Cale Yarborough, July 4, 1968
**Most laps led in a 500-mile race:** 184—Richard Petty, February 23, 1964
**Most cautions:** 12—July 1, 1989
**Fewest cautions:** 0—12 times, most recently, February 11, 1971
**Most caution laps:** 60—February 25, 1968
**Fewest caution laps:** 0—12 times, most recently February 11, 1971
**Most on the lead lap:** 33—February 16, 2003*
**Fewest on the lead lap:** 1—Eight times, most recently, February 15, 1976
**Most running at the finish:** 40—July 5, 2003

**Fewest running at the finish:** 7—February 12, 1965
**Most laps led by a race winner:** 184—Richard Petty, February 23, 1964
**Fewest laps led by a race winner:** 1—Jimmy Spencer, July 2, 1994
**Closest margin of victory:** 0.029 seconds—John Andretti defeated Terry Labonte, July 5, 1997.
**Greatest margin of victory:** 33.2 seconds—Bobby Allison defeated Cale Yarborough, February 19, 1978.
*Rain-shortened to 109 laps, 272.5 miles

## QUALIFYING AND RACE RECORDS

**QUALIFYING: Track:** Bill Elliott, Ford; 210.364 mph, February 9, 1987 (Daytona 500). **Winter race (Daytona 500):** Bill Elliott, Ford; 210.364 mph, February 9, 1987. **Summer race (Pepsi 400):** Sterling Marlin, Chevrolet; 203.666 mph, July 3, 1986. **Firecracker 250:** Edwin "Banjo" Matthews, Pontiac; 160.490 mph, July 1, 1962.
**RACE: Winter race (Daytona 500):** Buddy Baker, Oldsmobile; 177.602 mph, February 17, 1980.

## SUMMER: PEPSI 400/250 RACES

| POLE WINNERS | |
|---|---|
| C. Yarborough | 8 |
| S. Marlin | 3 |
| D. Allison | 2 |
| F. Roberts | 2 |
| D. Dieringer | 2 |
| D. Earnhardt | 2 |
| J. Gordon | 2 |
| L. Yarbrough | 1 |
| B. Allison | 1 |
| B. Isaac | 1 |
| A. Foyt | 1 |
| J. Smith | 1 |
| Jr. Johnson | 1 |
| M. Panch | 1 |
| B. Matthews | 1 |
| C. Glotzbach | 1 |
| N. Bonnett | 1 |
| Buddy Baker | 1 |
| G. Bodine | 1 |
| B. Elliott | 1 |
| Da. Allison | 1 |
| D. Waltrip | 1 |
| M. Martin | 1 |
| G. Sacks | 1 |
| E. Irvan | 1 |
| D. Pearson | 1 |
| M. Skinner | 1 |
| B. Labonte | 1 |
| J. Nemechek | 1 |
| D. Jarrett | 1 |
| K. Harvick | 1 |
| S. Park | 1 |

| RACE WINNERS | |
|---|---|
| D. Pearson | 5 |
| C. Yarborough | 4 |
| R. Petty | 3 |
| B. Allison | 3 |
| F. Roberts | 3 |
| J. Gordon | 3 |
| A. Foyt | 2 |
| B. Elliott | 2 |
| D. Earnhardt | 2 |
| D. Allison | 1 |
| B. Isaac | 1 |
| S. McQuagg | 1 |
| J. Smith | 1 |
| N. Bonnett | 1 |
| Buddy Baker | 1 |
| G. Sacks | 1 |
| T. Richmond | 1 |
| L. Yarbrough | 1 |
| Da. Allison | 1 |
| E. Irvan | 1 |
| J. Spencer | 1 |
| S. Marlin | 1 |
| J. Andretti | 1 |
| D. Jarrett | 1 |
| J. Burton | 1 |
| D. Earnhardt Jr. | 1 |
| M. Waltrip | 1 |
| G. Biffle | 1 |

## WINTER: DAYTONA 500

| POLE WINNERS | |
|---|---|
| Buddy Baker | 4 |
| C. Yarborough | 4 |
| B. Elliott | 4 |
| F. Roberts | 3 |
| K. Schrader | 3 |
| D. Allison | 2 |
| D. Jarrett | 2 |
| A. Foyt | 1 |
| D. Pearson | 1 |
| D. Dieringer | 1 |
| P. Goldsmith | 1 |
| B. Isaac | 1 |
| C. Owens | 1 |
| R. Petty | 1 |
| C. Turner | 1 |
| B. Welborn | 1 |
| R. Stott | 1 |
| B. Allison | 1 |
| B. Parsons | 1 |
| R. Rudd | 1 |
| Da. Allison | 1 |
| S. Marlin | 1 |
| K. Petty | 1 |
| L. Allen | 1 |
| D. Earnhardt | 1 |
| M. Skinner | 1 |
| B. Labonte | 1 |
| J. Gordon | 1 |
| Ji. Johnson | 1 |
| J. Green | 1 |
| G. Biffle | 1 |

| RACE WINNERS | |
|---|---|
| R. Petty | 7 |
| C. Yarborough | 4 |
| B. Allison | 3 |
| D. Jarrett | 3 |
| B. Elliott | 2 |
| S. Marlin | 2 |
| J. Gordon | 2 |
| M. Waltrip | 2 |
| A. Foyt | 1 |
| T. Lund | 1 |
| P. Hamilton | 1 |
| Jr. Johnson | 1 |
| F. Lorenzen | 1 |
| M. Panch | 1 |
| L. Petty | 1 |
| F. Roberts | 1 |
| L. Yarbrough | 1 |
| Buddy Baker | 1 |
| M. Andretti | 1 |
| G. Bodine | 1 |
| D. Waltrip | 1 |
| D. Cope | 1 |
| E. Irvan | 1 |
| Da. Allison | 1 |
| B. Parsons | 1 |
| D. Pearson | 1 |
| D. Earnhardt | 1 |
| W. Burton | 1 |
| D. Earnhardt Jr. | 1 |

## ALL DAYTONA RACES

| POLE WINNERS | |
|---|---|
| C. Yarborough | 12 |
| Buddy Baker | 5 |
| F. Roberts | 5 |
| B. Elliott | 5 |
| D. Allison | 4 |
| S. Marlin | 4 |
| K. Schrader | 4 |
| D. Dieringer | 3 |
| D. Earnhardt | 3 |
| D. Jarrett | 3 |
| J. Gordon | 3 |
| M. Skinner | 2 |
| B. Labonte | 2 |
| A. Foyt | 2 |
| B. Allison | 2 |
| Da. Allison | 2 |
| D. Pearson | 2 |
| P. Goldsmith | 1 |
| Jr. Johnson | 1 |
| B. Matthews | 1 |
| C. Owens | 1 |
| M. Panch | 1 |
| R. Petty | 1 |
| J. Smith | 1 |
| C. Turner | 1 |
| L. Yarbrough | 1 |
| B. Welborn | 1 |
| R. Stott | 1 |
| N. Bonnett | 1 |
| B. Parsons | 1 |
| G. Bodine | 1 |
| R. Rudd | 1 |
| M. Martin | 1 |
| G. Sacks | 1 |
| K. Petty | 1 |
| D. Waltrip | 1 |
| E. Irvan | 1 |
| L. Allen | 1 |
| C. Glotzbach | 1 |
| J. Nemechek | 1 |
| Ji. Johnson | 1 |
| K. Harvick | 1 |
| J. Green | 1 |
| S. Park | 1 |
| G. Biffle | 1 |

| RACE WINNERS | |
|---|---|
| R. Petty | 10 |
| C. Yarborough | 8 |
| D. Pearson | 6 |
| B. Allison | 6 |
| J. Gordon | 5 |
| F. Roberts | 4 |
| B. Elliott | 4 |
| D. Jarrett | 4 |
| D. Earnhardt | 3 |
| A. Foyt | 3 |
| S. Marlin | 3 |
| E. Irvan | 2 |
| Buddy Baker | 2 |
| L. Yarbrough | 2 |
| Da. Allison | 2 |
| M. Waltrip | 3 |
| D. Earnhardt Jr. | 2 |
| B. Parsons | 1 |
| P. Hamilton | 1 |
| B. Isaac | 1 |
| Jr. Johnson | 1 |
| F. Lorenzen | 1 |
| T. Lund | 1 |
| M. Panch | 1 |
| S. McQuagg | 1 |
| J. Smith | 1 |
| N. Bonnett | 1 |
| L. Petty | 1 |
| G. Sacks | 1 |
| G. Bodine | 1 |
| T. Richmond | 1 |
| D. Waltrip | 1 |
| D. Cope | 1 |
| M. Andretti | 1 |
| D. Allison | 1 |
| J. Andretti | 1 |
| J. Spencer | 1 |
| J. Burton | 1 |
| W. Burton | 1 |
| G. Biffle | 1 |

# QUALIFYING AND RACE RECORDS (Daytona, continued)

**Summer race (Pepsi 400):** Bobby Allison, Mercury; 173.473 mph, July 4, 1980
**Firecracker 250:** David Pearson, Pontiac; 154.194 mph, July 4, 1961
**Qualifying race, 125 miles:** Terry Labonte, Ford; 189.554 mph, February 16, 1989
**Qualifying race, 100 miles:** Fred Lorenzen, Ford; 174.583 mph, February 24, 1967

## NEXTEL Cup YEAR BY YEAR WINNERS (Daytona)

| Year | Event | Race Winner | Car Make | Avg. Speed | Start Pos. | Car Owner | Pole Winner | Pole Speed |
|---|---|---|---|---|---|---|---|---|
| 2004 | Pepsi 400 | J. Gordon | Chevrolet | 145.117 | 1 | Rick Hendrick | J. Gordon | 188.660 |
| | Daytona 500 | D. Earnhardt Jr. | Chevrolet | 156.345 | 3 | Teresa Earnhardt | G. Biffle | 188.387 |
| 2003 | Pepsi 400 | G. Biffle | Ford | 166.109 | 30 | Jack Roush | S. Park | 184.752 |
| f | Daytona 500 | M. Waltrip | Chevrolet | 133.870 | 4 | Teresa Earnhardt | J. Green | 186.606 |
| 2002 | Pepsi 400 | M. Waltrip | Chevrolet | 135.952 | 7 | Teresa Earnhardt | K. Harvick | 185.041 |
| | Daytona 500 | W. Burton | Dodge | 142.971 | 19 | Bill Davis | J. Johnson | 185.831 |
| #2001 | Pepsi 400 | D. Earnhardt Jr. | Chevrolet | 157.601 | 13 | Teresa Earnhardt | S. Marlin | 183.778 |
| | Daytona 500 | M. Waltrip | Chevrolet | 161.783 | 19 | Teresa Earnhardt | B. Elliott | 183.565 |
| 2000 | Pepsi 400 | J. Burton | Ford | 148.576 | 9 | Jack Roush | D. Jarrett | 187.547 |
| | Daytona 500 | D. Jarrett | Ford | 155.669 | 1 | Robert Yates | D. Jarrett | 191.091 |
| #1999 | Pepsi 400 | D. Jarrett | Ford | 169.213 | 12 | Robert Yates | J. Nemechek | 194.860 |
| | Daytona 500 | J. Gordon | Chevrolet | 161.551 | 1 | Rick Hendrick | J. Gordon | 195.067 |
| e1998 | Pepsi 400 | J. Gordon | Chevrolet | 144.549 | 8 | Rick Hendrick | B. Labonte | 193.611 |
| | Daytona 500 | D. Earnhardt | Chevrolet | 172.712 | 4 | Richard Childress | B. Labonte | 192.415 |
| 1997 | Pepsi 400 | J. Andretti | Ford | 167.791 | 3 | Cale Yarborough | M. Skinner | 189.777 |
| | Daytona 500 | J. Gordon | Chevrolet | 148.295 | 6 | Rick Hendrick | M. Skinner | 189.813 |
| d1996 | Pepsi 400 | S. Marlin | Chevrolet | 161.602 | 2 | Morgan-McClure | J. Gordon | 188.869 |
| | Daytona 500 | D. Jarrett | Ford | 154.308 | 7 | Robert Yates | D. Earnhardt | 189.510 |
| 1995 | Pepsi 400 | J. Gordon | Chevrolet | 166.976 | 3 | Rick Hendrick | D. Earnhardt | 191.355 |
| | Daytona 500 | S. Marlin | Chevrolet | 141.710 | 3 | Morgan-McClure | D. Jarrett | 193.498 |
| 1994 | Pepsi 400 | J. Spencer | Ford | 155.558 | 3 | Junior Johnson | D. Earnhardt | 191.339 |
| | Daytona 500 | S. Marlin | Chevrolet | 156.931 | 4 | Morgan-McClure | L. Allen | 190.158 |
| 1993 | Pepsi 400 | D. Earnhardt | Chevrolet | 151.755 | 5 | Richard Childress | E. Irvan | 190.327 |
| | Daytona 500 | D. Jarrett | Chevrolet | 154.972 | 2 | Joe Gibbs | K. Petty | 189.426 |
| 1992 | Pepsi 400 | E. Irvan | Chevrolet | 170.457 | 6 | Morgan-McClure | S. Marlin | 189.366 |
| | Daytona 500 | Da. Allison | Ford | 160.256 | 6 | Robert Yates | S. Marlin | 192.213 |
| 1991 | Pepsi 400 | B. Elliott | Ford | 159.116 | 10 | Melling Racing | S. Marlin | 190.331 |
| | Daytona 500 | E. Irvan | Chevrolet | 148.148 | 2 | Morgan-McClure | Da. Allison | 195.955 |
| 1990 | Pepsi 400 | D. Earnhardt | Chevrolet | 160.894 | 3 | Richard Childress | G. Sacks | 195.533 |
| | Daytona 500 | D. Cope | Chevrolet | 165.761 | 12 | Bob Whitcomb | K. Schrader | 196.515 |
| 1989 | Pepsi 400 | Da. Allison | Ford | 132.207 | 8 | Robert Yates | M. Martin | 191.861 |
| | Daytona 500 | D. Waltrip | Chevrolet | 148.466 | 2 | Rick Hendrick | K. Schrader | 196.996 |
| 1988 | Pepsi 400 | B. Elliott | Ford | 163.302 | 38 | Melling Racing | D. Waltrip | 193.819 |
| | Daytona 500 | B. Allison | Buick | 137.531 | 3 | Stavola Brothers | K. Schrader | 193.823 |
| 1987 | Pepsi 400 | B. Allison | Buick | 161.074 | 11 | Stavola Brothers | Da. Allison | 198.085 |
| | Daytona 500 | B. Elliott | Ford | 176.263 | 1 | Melling Racing | B. Elliott | 210.364 |
| 1986 | Pepsi 400 | T. Richmond | Chevrolet | 131.916 | 9 | Rick Hendrick | C. Yarborough | 203.519 |
| | Daytona 500 | G. Bodine | Chevrolet | 148.124 | 2 | Rick Hendrick | B. Elliott | 205.039 |
| 1985 | Pepsi 400 | G. Sacks | Chevrolet | 158.730 | 9 | Bill Gardner | B. Elliott | 201.523 |
| | Daytona 500 | B. Elliott | Ford | 172.265 | 1 | Melling Racing | B. Elliott | 205.114 |
| 1984 | Pepsi 400 | R. Petty | Pontiac | 171.204 | 6 | Curb Racing | C. Yarborough | 199.743 |
| | Daytona 500 | C. Yarborough | Chevrolet | 150.994 | 1 | Ranier Racing | C. Yarborough | 201.848 |
| 1983 | Firecracker 400 | Buddy Baker | Ford | 167.442 | 8 | Wood Brothers | C. Yarborough | 196.635 |
| | Daytona 500 | C. Yarborough | Pontiac | 155.979 | 8 | Ranier Racing | R. Rudd | 198.864 |
| 1982 | Firecracker 400 | B. Allison | Buick | 163.099 | 9 | DiGard Rac. Co. | G. Bodine | 194.721 |
| | Daytona 500 | B. Allison | Buick | 153.991 | 7 | DiGard Rac. Co. | B. Parsons | 196.317 |
| 1981 | Firecracker 400 | C. Yarborough | Buick | 142.588 | 1 | M.C. Anderson | C. Yarborough | 192.852 |
| | Daytona 500 | R. Petty | Buick | 169.651 | 8 | Petty Eng. | B. Allison | 194.624 |
| 1980 | Firecracker 400 | B. Allison | Mercury | 173.473 | 14 | Bud Moore | C. Yarborough | 194.670 |
| | Daytona 500 | Buddy Baker | Oldsmobile | 177.602 | 1 | Ranier Racing | Buddy Baker | 194.009 |
| 1979 | Firecracker 400 | N. Bonnett | Mercury | 172.890 | 2 | Wood Brothers | Buddy Baker | 193.196 |
| | Daytona 500 | R. Petty | Oldsmobile | 143.977 | 13 | Petty Eng. | Buddy Baker | 196.049 |
| 1978 | Firecracker 400 | D. Pearson | Mercury | 154.340 | 3 | Wood Brothers | C. Yarborough | 186.803 |
| | Daytona 500 | B. Allison | Ford | 159.730 | 33 | Bud Moore | C. Yarborough | 187.536 |
| 1977 | Firecracker 400 | R. Petty | Dodge | 142.716 | 5 | Petty Eng. | N. Bonnett | 187.191 |
| | Daytona 500 | C. Yarborough | Chevrolet | 153.218 | 4 | Junior Johnson | D. Allison | 188.048 |
| 1976 | Firecracker 400 | C. Yarborough | Chevrolet | 160.966 | 2 | Junior Johnson | A. Foyt | 183.090 |
| | Daytona 500 | D. Pearson | Mercury | 152.181 | 7 | Wood Brothers | R. Stott | 183.456 |
| 1975 | Firecracker 400 | R. Petty | Dodge | 158.381 | 13 | Petty Eng. | D. Allison | 186.737 |
| | Daytona 500 | B. Parsons | Chevrolet | 153.649 | 32 | L.G. DeWitt | D. Allison | 185.827 |
| 1974 | Firecracker 400 | D. Pearson | Mercury | 138.301 | 1 | Wood Brothers | D. Pearson | 180.759 |
| c | Daytona 500 | R. Petty | Dodge | 140.894 | 2 | Petty Eng. | D. Pearson | 185.817 |
| 1973 | Firecracker 400 | D. Pearson | Mercury | 158.468 | 6 | Wood Brothers | B. Allison | 179.619 |
| | Daytona 500 | R. Petty | Dodge | 157.205 | 7 | Petty Eng. | Buddy Baker | 185.662 |
| 1972 | Firecracker 400 | D. Pearson | Mercury | 160.821 | 2 | Wood Brothers | B. Isaac | 186.277 |
| | Daytona 500 | A. Foyt | Mercury | 161.550 | 2 | Wood Brothers | B. Isaac | 186.632 |
| 1971 | Firecracker 400 | B. Isaac | Dodge | 161.947 | 21 | Nord Krauskopf | D. Allison | 183.228 |
| | Daytona 500 | R. Petty | Plymouth | 144.462 | 5 | Petty Eng. | A. Foyt | 182.744 |
| 1970 | Firecracker 400 | D. Allison | Ford | 162.235 | 15 | Banjo Matthews | C. Yarborough | 191.640 |
| | Daytona 500 | P. Hamilton | Plymouth | 149.601 | 9 | Petty Eng. | C. Yarborough | 194.015 |
| 1969 | Firecracker 400 | L. Yarbrough | Ford | 160.875 | 9 | Junior Johnson | C. Yarborough | 190.706 |
| | Daytona 500 | L. Yarbrough | Ford | 157.950 | 19 | Junior Johnson | Buddy Baker | 188.901 |
| 1968 | Firecracker 400 | C. Yarborough | Mercury | 167.247 | 4 | Wood Brothers | C. Glotzbach | 188.901 |
| | Daytona 500 | C. Yarborough | Mercury | 143.251 | 1 | Wood Brothers | C. Yarborough | 189.222 |

TRACKS

## NEXTEL Cup YEAR BY YEAR WINNERS (Daytona, continued)

| Year | Event | Race Winner | Car Make | Avg. Speed | Start Pos. | Car Owner | Pole Winner | Pole Speed |
|---|---|---|---|---|---|---|---|---|
| 1967 | Firecracker 400 | C. Yarborough | Ford | 143.583 | 2 | Wood Brothers | D. Dieringer | 179.802 |
|  | Daytona 500 | M. Andretti | Ford | 146.926 | 12 | Holman-Moody | C. Turner | 180.831 |
| 1966 b | Firecracker 400 | S. McQuagg | Dodge | 153.813 | 4 | Ray Nichels | L. Yarbrough | 176.660 |
|  | Daytona 500 | R. Petty | Plymouth | 160.627 | 1 | Petty Eng. | R. Petty | 175.163 |
| 1965 a | Firecracker 400 | A. Foyt | Ford | 150.046 | 11 | Banjo Matthews | M. Panch | 171.510 |
|  | Daytona 500 | F. Lorenzen | Ford | 141.539 | 4 | Holman-Moody | D. Dieringer | 171.151 |
| 1964 | Firecracker 400 | A. Foyt | Dodge | 151.451 | 19 | Ray Nichels | D. Dieringer | 172.678 |
|  | Daytona 500 | R. Petty | Plymouth | 154.334 | 2 | Petty Eng. | P. Goldsmith | 174.910 |
| 1963 | Firecracker 400 | F. Roberts | Ford | 150.927 | 3 | Holman-Moody | Jr. Johnson | 166.005 |
|  | Daytona 500 | T. Lund | Ford | 151.566 | 12 | Wood Brothers | F. Roberts | 160.943 |
| 1962 | Firecracker 250 | F. Roberts | Pontiac | 153.688 | 4 | Smokey Yunick | B. Matthews | 160.499 |
| * | Daytona 500 | F. Roberts | Pontiac | 152.529 | 1 | Smokey Yunick | F. Roberts | 156.999 |
| *1961 | Firecracker 250 | D. Pearson | Pontiac | 154.294 | 2 | Ray Fox | F. Roberts | 157.150 |
| * | Daytona 500 | M. Panch | Pontiac | 149.601 | 4 | Smokey Yunick | F. Roberts | 155.709 |
| *1960 | Firecracker 250 | J. Smith | Pontiac | 146.842 | 1 | Jack Smith | J. Smith | 152.129 |
|  | Daytona 500 | Jr. Johnson | Chevrolet | 124.740 | 9 | John Masoni | C. Owens | 149.892 |
| *1959 | Firecracker 250 | F. Roberts | Pontiac | 140.581 | 1 | Smokey Yunick | F. Roberts | 144.997 |
| * | Daytona 500 | L. Petty | Oldsmobile | 135.521 | 15 | Petty Eng. | B. Welborn | 140.581 |

**KEY**
| | |
|---|---|
| * | Caution-free race. |
| # | Night race. |
| a | Reduced to 332.5 miles because of rain. |
| b | Reduced to 495 miles because of rain. |
| c | Reduced to 450 miles because of energy shortage. |
| d | Reduced to 293 miles because of rain. |
| e | Took place in October, rather than July. |
| f | Reduced to 272.500 miles because of rain. |

# BUSCH SERIES

## Busch YEAR BY YEAR WINNERS (Daytona)

| Year | Event | Race Winner | Car Make | Avg. Speed | Start Pos. | Pole Winner | Pole Speed | POLE WINNERS | | RACE WINNERS | |
|---|---|---|---|---|---|---|---|---|---|---|---|
| 2004 | Winn-Dixie 250 | M. Wallace | Ford | 135.014 | 16 | M. Bliss | 181.969 | J. Nemechek | 5 | D. Earnhardt | 7 |
|  | Hershey's Kisses 300 | D. Earnhardt Jr. | Chevrolet | 127.179 | 8 | M. Truex Jr. | 181.138 | M. Waltrip | 3 | D. Earnhardt Jr. | 4 |
| 2003 | Daytona 250 | D. Earnhardt Jr. | Chevrolet | 153.715 | 1 | D. Earnhardt Jr. | 186.308 | K. Schrader | 2 | R. LaJoie | 3 |
|  | Koolerz 300 | D. Earnhardt Jr. | Chevrolet | 143.770 | 2 | J. Nemechek | 186.050 | S. Ard | 1 | D. Waltrip | 3 |
| 2002 | EAS/GNC 300 | D. Earnhardt Jr. | Chevrolet | 147.662 | 4 | J. Nemechek | 186.254 | D. Green | 1 | G. Bodine | 2 |
|  | Stacker/GNC 250 | J. Nemechek | Pontiac | 125.892 | 1 | J. Nemechek | 185.793 | T. Houston | 1 | J. Nemechek | 2 |
| 2001 | NAPA Auto Parts 300 | R. LaJoie | Pontiac | 135.152 | 2 | J. Nemechek | 186.966 | L.D. Ottinger | 1 | B. Allison | 1 |
| 2000 | Napa Auto Parts 300 | M. Kenseth | Chevrolet | 140.735 | 8 | H. Stricklin | 187.336 | L. Pearson | 1 | S. Grissom | 1 |
| 1999 | Napa Auto Parts 300 | R. LaJoie | Chevrolet | 138.391 | 2 | K. Schrader | 189.865 | M. Porter | 1 | M. Kenseth | 1 |
| 1998 | Napa Auto Parts 300 | J. Nemechek | Chevrolet | 137.213 | 1 | M. McLaughlin | 190.134 | J. Purvis | 1 | C. Little | 1 |
| 1997 | Gargoyles 300 | R. LaJoie | Chevrolet | 149.688 | 14 | E. Sadler | 190.508 | E. Sadler | 1 | M. Wallace | 1 |
| 1996 | Goody's 300 | S. Grissom | Chevrolet | 140.772 | 4 | J. Purvis | 189.733 | H. Stricklin | 1 | | |
| 1995 | Goody's 300 | C. Little | Ford | 150.732 | 42 | M. Waltrip | 185.326 | M. Swaim | 1 | | |
| 1994 | Goody's 300 | D. Earnhardt | Chevrolet | 144.135 | 7 | M. Waltrip | 184.555 | K. Wallace | 1 | | |
| 1993 | Goody's 300 | D. Earnhardt | Chevrolet | 146.440 | 5 | K. Schrader | 186.513 | R. Wallace | 1 | | |
| 1992 | Goody's 300 | D. Earnhardt | Chevrolet | 132.434 | 4 | M. Waltrip | 186.556 | D. Waltrip | 1 | | |
| 1991 | Goody's 300 | D. Earnhardt | Chevrolet | 144.192 | 3 | D. Green | 188.675 | D. Earnhardt Jr. | 1 | | |
| 1990 | Goody's 300 | D. Earnhardt | Chevrolet | 149.357 | 2 | D. Waltrip | 188.945 | M. Truex Jr. | 1 | | |
| 1989 | Goody's 300 | D. Waltrip | Chevrolet | 131.211 | 9 | K. Wallace | 192.271 | M. Bliss | 1 | | |
| 1988 | Goody's 300 | B. Allison | Buick | 132.825 | 9 | M. Swaim | 189.825 | | | | |
| 1987 | Goody's 300 | G. Bodine | Chevrolet | 155.106 | 5 | T. Houston | 194.389 | | | | |
| 1986 | Goody's 300 | D. Earnhardt | Pontiac | 148.924 | 9 | L. Pearson | 191.310 | | | | |
| 1985 | Goody's 300 | G. Bodine | Pontiac | 157.137 | 2 | R. Wallace | 187.438 | | | | |
| 1984 | Goody's 300 | D. Waltrip | Pontiac | 156.613 | 12 | L. Ottinger | 187.682 | | | | |
| 1983 | Goody's 300 | D. Waltrip | Pontiac | 147.642 | 5 | S. Ard | 185.774 | | | | |
| 1982 | Goody's 300 | D. Earnhardt | Pontiac | 154.529 | 5 | M. Porter | 184.569 | | | | |

**QUALIFYING RECORD:** Tommy Houston, Buick; 194.389 mph, February 10, 1987
**RACE RECORD:** Geoffrey Bodine, Pontiac; 157.137 mph, February 16, 1985

# CRAFTSMAN TRUCK SERIES

## Craftsman YEAR BY YEAR WINNERS (Daytona)

| Year | Event | Race Winner | Car Make | Avg. Speed | Start Pos. | Pole Winner | Pole Speed | POLE WINNERS | | RACE WINNERS | |
|---|---|---|---|---|---|---|---|---|---|---|---|
| 2004 | Fla. Dodge Dealers 250 | C. Edwards | Ford | 112.570 | 6 | T. Cook | 183.643 | J. Ruttman | 2 | R. Pressley | 1 |
| 2003 | Fla. Dodge Dealers 250 | R. Crawford | Ford | 127.642 | 19 | J. Leffler | 182.994 | T. Musgrave | 1 | J. Ruttman | 1 |
| 2002 | Fla Dodge Dealers 250 | R. Pressley | Dodge | 140.121 | 2 | T. Musgrave | 187.215 | J. Leffler | 1 | R. Crawford | 1 |
| 2001 | Fla Dodge Dealers 250 | J. Ruttman | Dodge | 129.407 | 1 | J. Ruttman | 186.123 | T. Cook | 1 | C. Edwards | 1 |
| 2000 | Daytona 250 | M. Wallace | Ford | 130.152 | 2 | J. Ruttman | 187.563 | | | M. Wallace | 1 |

**QUALIFYING RECORD:** Joe Ruttman, Dodge; 187.563 mph, February 16, 2000
**RACE RECORD:** Robert Pressley, Dodge; 140.121 mph, February 15, 2002

## 2005 SCHEDULE

**NEXTEL CUP**

**Event:** MBNA 400
**Race:** No. 13 of 36
**Date:** June 5
**TV:** FX. **Radio:** MRN

**Event:** MBNA America 400
**Race:** No. 28 of 36
**Date:** September 25
**TV:** TNT. **Radio:** MRN

**BUSCH SERIES**

**Event:** MBNA America 200
**Race:** No. 14 of 35
**Date:** June 4
**TV:** FX. **Radio:** MRN

**Event:** Stacker 200
**Race:** No. 29 of 35
**Date:** September 24
**TV:** TNT. **Radio:** MRN

**CRAFTSMAN TRUCK SERIES**

**Event:** MBNA America 200
**Race:** No. 8 of 25
**Date:** June 10
**TV:** SPEED. **Radio:** MRN

Race names subject to change

### TRACK FACTS

**Opened:** 1969
**Owner:** Dover Downs Entertainment Inc.
**Location:** Dover, Del.
**Distance:** 1 mile
**Banking in turns:** 24 degrees
**Banking in straights:** 9 degrees
**Length of front stretch:** 1,076 feet
**Length of back stretch:** 1,076 feet
**Grandstand seating:** 140,000
**Tickets:** (800) 441-7223
**Website:** www.doverspeedway.com

Back stretch: 1,076 feet / 9°

24° Banking in Turns

Front stretch: 1,076 feet / 9°

## NEXTEL CUP

### TRACK RECORDS

**Most wins:** 7—Richard Petty and Bobby Allison
**Oldest winner:** Harry Gant, 52 years, 4 months, 21 days, May 31, 1992
**Youngest winner:** Jeff Gordon, 24 years, 1 month, 13 days, September 17, 1995
**Most lead changes:** 29—Twice, most recently, May 18, 1986
**Fewest lead changes:** 3—October 17, 1971
**Most leaders:** 13—Twice, most recently, September 24, 2000
**Fewest leaders:** 3—Five times, most recently, May 16, 1982
**Most laps led in a 300-mile race:** 186, Richard Petty, September 20, 1970
**Most laps led in a 400-mile race:** 381, Jeff Gordon, June 3, 2001
**Most laps led in a 500-mile race:** 491, Richard Petty, September 15, 1974
**Most cautions:** 16—September 19, 1993
**Fewest cautions:** 0—June 6, 1971
**Most caution laps:** 103—September 19, 1993
**Fewest caution laps:** 0—June 6, 1971
**Most on the lead lap:** 17—June 2, 2002
**Fewest on the lead lap:** 1—11 times, most recently, September 15, 1991
**Most running at the finish:** 39—June 2, 2002

**Fewest running at the finish:** 13—May 17, 1981
**Most laps led by a race winner:** 491—Richard Petty, September 15, 1974
**Fewest laps led by a race winner:** 8—Dale Jarrett, May 31, 1998
**Closest margin of victory:** 0.091 seconds—Ricky Rudd defeated Mark Martin, June 1, 1997.
**Greatest margin of victory:** 3 laps—Bobby Allison defeated Dave Marcis, May 16, 1982.

### QUALIFYING AND RACE RECORDS

**QUALIFYING:** Jeremy Mayfield, Dodge; 161.522 mph, June 4, 2004. **Spring race (MBNA America 400):** Jeremy Mayfield, Dodge; 161.522 mph, June 4, 2004. **Fall race (MBNA America 400):** Rusty Wallace, Ford; 159.964 mph, September 25, 1999.
**RACE: Track:** (400 miles): Mark Martin, Ford; 132.719 mph, September 21, 1997 (MBNA 400). **Spring race (MBNA America 400):** Mark Martin, Ford; 132.719 mph, September 21, 1997. **Fall race (MBNA America 400):** Bobby Labonte, Pontiac; 120.603 mph, June 6, 1999. **Track record (500 miles):** Bill Elliott, Ford; 125.945 mph, September 16, 1990 (MBNA 500). **Miller 500:** Derrike Cope, Chevrolet; 123.960 mph, June 3, 1990.

**TRACKS**

### NEXTEL Cup YEAR BY YEAR WINNERS

| Year | Event | Race Winner | Car Make | Avg. Speed | Start Pos. | Car Owner | Pole Winner | Pole Speed |
|------|-------|-------------|----------|-----------|-----------|-----------|-------------|-----------|
| 2004 | MBNA America 400 | R. Newman | Dodge | 119.067 | 2 | Roger Penske | J. Mayfield | 159.405 |
| | MBNA America 400 | M. Martin | Ford | 97.042 | 7 | Jack Roush | J. Mayfield | 161.522 |
| 2003 | MBNA America 400 | R. Newman | Dodge | 108.82 | 5 | Roger Penske | Trials rained out | |
| | MBNA Armed Forces 400 | R. Newman | Dodge | 106.896 | 1 | Roger Penske | R. Newman | 158.716 |
| 2002 | MBNA Am. Heroes 400 | J. Johnson | Chevrolet | 120.805 | 19 | Rick Hendrick | R. Wallace | 156.822 |
| | MBNA Platinum 400 | J. Johnson | Chevrolet | 117.551 | 10 | Rick Hendrick | M. Kenseth | 154.939 |
| 2001 | MBNA Cal Ripken 400 | D. Earnhardt Jr. | Chevrolet | 101.559 | 27 | Dale Earnhardt | D. Jarrett | 154.919 |
| | MBNA Platinum 400 | J. Gordon | Chevrolet | 120.361 | 2 | Rick Hendrick | Trials rained out | |
| 2000 | MBNA.com 400 | T. Stewart | Pontiac | 115.191 | 27 | Joe Gibbs | J. Mayfield | 159.872 |
| | MBNA Platinum 400 | T. Stewart | Pontiac | 109.514 | 16 | Joe Gibbs | R. Wallace | 157.411 |
| 1999 | MBNA Gold 400 | M. Martin | Ford | 127.434 | 8 | Jack Roush | R. Wallace | 159.964 |
| | MBNA Platinum 400 | B. Labonte | Pontiac | 120.603 | 1 | Joe Gibbs | B. Labonte | 159.320 |
| 1998 | MBNA Gold 400 | M. Martin | Ford | 113.834 | 1 | Jack Roush | M. Martin | 155.966 |
| | MBNA Platinum 400 | D. Jarrett | Ford | 119.522 | 4 | Robert Yates | R. Wallace | 155.898 |
| 1997 | MBNA 400 | M. Martin | Ford | 132.719 | 1 | Jack Roush | M. Martin | 152.033 |
| | Miller 500 | R. Rudd | Ford | 114.635 | 13 | Ricky Rudd | B. Labonte | 152.788 |
| 1996 | MBNA 500 | J. Gordon | Chevrolet | 105.646 | 3 | Rick Hendrick | B. Labonte | 155.086 |
| | Miller 500 | J. Gordon | Chevrolet | 122.741 | 1 | Rick Hendrick | J. Gordon | 154.785 |
| 1995 | MBNA 500 | J. Gordon | Chevrolet | 124.740 | 2 | Rick Hendrick | R. Mast | 153.446 |
| | Miller 500 | K. Petty | Pontiac | 119.880 | 37 | Felix Sabates | J. Gordon | 153.669 |

| FALL DOVER 400 POLE WINNERS | |
|---|---|
| M. Martin | 3 |
| A. Kulwicki | 3 |
| R. Wallace | 3 |
| B. Allison | 2 |
| C. Yarborough | 2 |
| E. Irvan | 2 |
| R. Rudd | 2 |
| B. Elliott | 2 |
| G. Bodine | 2 |
| Buddy Baker | 1 |
| N. Bonnett | 1 |
| D. Marcis | 1 |
| J.D. McDuffie | 1 |
| D. Earnhardt | 1 |
| T. Labonte | 1 |
| D. Pearson | 1 |
| Da. Allison | 1 |
| R. Mast | 1 |
| B. Labonte | 1 |
| J. Mayfield | 1 |
| D. Jarrett | 1 |

| RACE WINNERS | |
|---|---|
| R. Petty | 4 |
| H. Gant | 3 |
| R. Rudd | 3 |
| M. Martin | 3 |
| B. Allison | 2 |
| D. Pearson | 2 |
| D. Waltrip | 2 |
| B. Elliott | 2 |
| R. Wallace | 2 |
| J. Gordon | 2 |
| B. Parsons | 1 |
| N. Bonnett | 1 |
| D. Earnhardt | 1 |
| C. Yarborough | 1 |
| T. Stewart | 1 |
| D. Earnhardt Jr. | 1 |
| Ji. Johnson | 1 |
| R. Newman | 1 |

| SPRING MBNA AMERICA 400 POLE WINNERS | |
|---|---|
| D. Pearson | 5 |
| R. Petty | 2 |
| D. Waltrip | 2 |
| R. Rudd | 2 |
| E. Irvan | 2 |
| B. Isaac | 2 |
| J. Gordon | 2 |
| B. Labonte | 2 |
| R. Wallace | 2 |
| Buddy Baker | 1 |
| C. Yarborough | 1 |
| J. Ruttman | 1 |
| T. Labonte | 1 |
| A. Kulwicki | 1 |
| M. Martin | 1 |
| D. Trickle | 1 |
| M. Waltrip | 1 |
| B. Bodine | 1 |
| D. Marcis | 1 |
| M. Kenseth | 1 |
| R. Newman | 1 |
| J. Mayfield | 1 |

| RACE WINNERS | |
|---|---|
| B. Allison | 5 |
| R. Petty | 3 |
| D. Pearson | 3 |
| J. Gordon | 2 |
| B. Elliott | 2 |
| D. Earnhardt | 2 |
| C. Yarborough | 2 |
| B. Parsons | 1 |
| N. Bonnett | 1 |
| J. Ridley | 1 |
| G. Bodine | 1 |
| Da. Allison | 1 |
| D. Cope | 1 |
| K. Schrader | 1 |
| H. Gant | 1 |
| R. Wallace | 1 |
| R. Rudd | 1 |
| D. Jarrett | 1 |
| B. Labonte | 1 |
| T. Stewart | 1 |
| Ji. Johnson | 1 |
| R. Newman | 1 |
| M. Martin | 1 |

| ALL DOVER RACES POLE WINNERS | |
|---|---|
| D. Pearson | 6 |
| R. Wallace | 5 |
| R. Rudd | 4 |
| A. Kulwicki | 4 |
| M. Martin | 4 |
| C. Yarborough | 3 |
| B. Elliott | 3 |
| B. Labonte | 3 |
| J. Mayfield | 3 |
| Buddy Baker | 2 |
| D. Marcis | 2 |
| D. Waltrip | 2 |
| T. Labonte | 2 |
| R. Petty | 2 |
| G. Bodine | 2 |
| E. Irvan | 2 |
| B. Isaac | 2 |
| J. Gordon | 2 |
| N. Bonnett | 1 |
| D. Earnhardt | 1 |
| J. Ruttman | 1 |
| Da. Allison | 1 |
| D. Trickle | 1 |
| M. Waltrip | 1 |
| B. Bodine | 1 |
| J. McDuffie | 1 |
| R. Mast | 1 |
| D. Jarrett | 1 |
| M. Kenseth | 1 |
| R. Newman | 1 |

| RACE WINNERS | |
|---|---|
| B. Allison | 7 |
| R. Petty | 7 |
| D. Pearson | 5 |
| J. Gordon | 4 |
| B. Elliott | 4 |
| R. Rudd | 4 |
| H. Gant | 4 |
| M. Martin | 4 |
| D. Earnhardt | 3 |
| R. Wallace | 3 |
| C. Yarborough | 3 |
| M. Martin | 3 |
| R. Newman | 3 |
| D. Waltrip | 3 |
| B. Parsons | 2 |
| N. Bonnett | 2 |
| T. Stewart | 2 |
| J. Johnson | 2 |
| G. Bodine | 1 |
| D. Cope | 1 |
| K. Schrader | 1 |
| D. Allison | 1 |
| K. Petty | 1 |
| J. Ridley | 1 |
| B. Labonte | 1 |
| D. Earnhardt Jr. | 1 |
| D. Jarrett | 1 |

## NEXTEL Cup YEAR BY YEAR WINNERS (Dover, continued)

| | Year | Event | Race Winner | Car Make | Avg. Speed | Start Pos. | Car Owner | Pole Winner | Pole Speed |
|---|---|---|---|---|---|---|---|---|---|
| | 1994 | SpitFire 500 | R. Wallace | Ford | 112.556 | 10 | Roger Penske | G. Bodine | 152.840 |
| | | Budweiser 500 | R. Wallace | Ford | 102.529 | 6 | Roger Penske | E. Irvan | 151.956 |
| | 1993 | SpitFire 500 | R. Wallace | Pontiac | 100.334 | 1 | Roger Penske | R. Wallace | 151.564 |
| | | Budweiser 500 | D. Earnhardt | Chevrolet | 105.600 | 8 | Richard Childress | E. Irvan | 151.541 |
| | 1992 | Peak 500 | R. Rudd | Chevrolet | 115.289 | 6 | Rick Hendrick | A. Kulwicki | 145.267 |
| | | Budweiser 500 | H. Gant | Oldsmobile | 109.456 | 15 | Leo Jackson | B. Bodine | 147.408 |
| | 1991 | Peak 500 | H. Gant | Oldsmobile | 110.179 | 10 | Leo Jackson | A. Kulwicki | 146.825 |
| | | Budweiser 500 | K. Schrader | Chevrolet | 120.152 | 19 | Rick Hendrick | M. Waltrip | 143.392 |
| | 1990 | Peak 500 | B. Elliot | Ford | 125.945 | 1 | Melling Racing | B. Elliott | 144.928 |
| | | Budweiser 500 | D. Cope | Chevrolet | 123.960 | 15 | Bob Whitcomb | D. Trickle | 145.814 |
| | 1989 | Peak 500 | D. Earnhardt | Chevrolet | 122.909 | 15 | Richard Childress | Da. Allison | 146.169 |
| | | Budweiser 500 | D. Earnhardt | Chevrolet | 121.670 | 2 | Richard Childress | M. Martin | 144.387 |
| | 1988 | Delaware 500 | B. Elliott | Ford | 109.349 | 3 | Melling Racing | M. Martin | 148.075 |
| | | Budweiser 500 | B. Elliott | Ford | 118.726 | 17 | Melling Racing | A. Kulwicki | 146.681 |
| | 1987 | Delaware 500 | R. Rudd | Ford | 124.706 | 13 | Bud Moore | A. Kulwicki | 145.826 |
| | | Budweiser 500 | Da. Allison | Ford | 112.958 | 2 | Ranier Racing | B. Elliott | 145.056 |
| | 1986 | Delaware 500 | R. Rudd | Ford | 114.329 | 11 | Bud Moore | G. Bodine | 146.205 |
| | | Budweiser 500 | G. Bodine | Chevrolet | 115.009 | 3 | Rick Hendrick | R. Rudd | 138.217 |
| | 1985 | Delaware 500 | H. Gant | Chevrolet | 120.538 | 4 | Mach 1 | B. Elliott | 141.543 |
| | | Budweiser 500 | B. Elliott | Ford | 123.094 | 4 | Melling Racing | T. Labonte | 138.106 |
| d | 1984 | Delaware 500 | H. Gant | Chevrolet | 111.856 | 4 | Mach 1 | Trials rained out | |
| | | Budweiser 500 | R. Petty | Pontiac | 118.717 | 5 | Curb Racing | R. Rudd | 140.807 |
| | 1983 | Budweiser 500 | B. Allison | Buick | 116.077 | 7 | DiGard Rac. Co. | T. Labonte | 139.573 |
| | | Mason-Dixon 500 | B. Allison | Buick | 114.847 | 10 | DiGard Rac. Co. | J. Ruttman | 139.616 |
| | 1982 | CRC Chemicals 500 | D. Waltrip | Buick | 107.642 | 3 | Junior Johnson | R. Rudd | 139.384 |
| | | Mason-Dixon 500 | B. Allison | Chevrolet | 120.136 | 3 | DiGard Rac. Co. | D. Waltrip | 139.308 |
| | 1981 | CRC Chemicals 500 | N. Bonnett | Ford | 119.561 | 3 | Wood Brothers | R. Rudd | 136.757 |
| | | Mason-Dixon 500 | J. Ridley | Ford | 116.595 | 11 | Junie Donlavey | D. Pearson | 138.425 |
| | 1980 | CRC Chemicals 500 | D. Waltrip | Chevrolet | 116.024 | 2 | DiGard Rac. Co. | C. Yarborough | 137.583 |
| | | Mason-Dixon 500 | B. Allison | Ford | 113.866 | 8 | Bud Moore | C. Yarborough | 138.814 |
| | 1979 | CRC Chemicals 500 | R. Petty | Chevrolet | 114.366 | 4 | Petty Eng. | D. Earnhardt | 135.726 |
| | | Mason-Dixon 500 | N. Bonnett | Mercury | 111.269 | 5 | Wood Brothers | D. Waltrip | 136.103 |
| | 1978 | Delaware 500 | B. Allison | Ford | 119.323 | 2 | Bud Moore | J. McDuffie | 135.480 |
| | | Mason-Dixon 500 | D. Pearson | Mercury | 114.664 | 3 | Wood Brothers | Buddy Baker | 135.452 |
| | 1977 | Delaware 500 | B. Parsons | Chevrolet | 114.708 | 7 | L. G. DeWitt | N. Bonnett | 134.233 |
| | | Mason-Dixon 500 | C. Yarborough | Chevrolet | 123.327 | 6 | Junior Johnson | R. Petty | 136.033 |
| | 1976 | Delaware 500 | C. Yarborough | Chevrolet | 115.740 | 1 | Junior Johnson | C. Yarborough | 133.377 |
| | | Mason-Dixon 500 | B. Parsons | Chevrolet | 115.436 | 7 | L. G. DeWitt | D. Marcis | 136.013 |
| | 1975 | Delaware 500 | R. Petty | Dodge | 111.372 | 3 | Petty Eng. | D. Marcis | 133.953 |
| c | | Mason-Dixon 500 | D. Pearson | Mercury | 100.820 | 1 | Wood Brothers | D. Pearson | 136.612 |
| | 1974 | Delaware 500 | R. Petty | Dodge | 113.640 | 2 | Petty Eng. | Buddy Baker | 133.640 |
| b | | Mason-Dixon 500 | C. Yarborough | Chevrolet | 115.057 | 3 | Junior Johnson | D. Pearson | 134.403 |
| | 1973 | Delaware 500 | D. Pearson | Mercury | 112.852 | 1 | Wood Brothers | D. Pearson | 124.649 |
| | | Mason-Dixon 500 | D. Pearson | Mercury | 119.745 | 1 | Wood Brothers | D. Pearson | 133.111 |
| | 1972 | Delaware 500 | D. Pearson | Mercury | 120.506 | 2 | Wood Brothers | B. Allison | 133.323 |
| | | Mason-Dixon 500 | B. Allison | Chevrolet | 118.019 | 2 | Junior Johnson | B. Isaac | 130.809 |
| | 1971 | Delaware 500 | R. Petty | Plymouth | 123.254 | 4 | Petty Eng. | B. Allison | 132.811 |
| a | | Mason-Dixon 500 | B. Allison | Ford | 123.119 | 2 | Holman-Moody | R. Petty | 129.486 |
| | 1970 | Mason-Dixon 300 | R. Petty | Plymouth | 112.103 | 2 | Petty Eng. | B. Isaac | 129.538 |
| | 1969 | Mason-Dixon 300 | R. Petty | Ford | 115.772 | 3 | Petty Eng. | D. Pearson | 130.430 |

**KEY**
a Caution-free race.
b Reduced to 450 miles because of the energy shortage.
c First 140 miles run on Sunday, May 18; final 360 miles run on Monday.
d Starting lineup determined by car owner points standings.

## Busch YEAR BY YEAR WINNERS (Dover)

| Year | Event | Race Winner | Car Make | Avg. Speed | Start Pos. | Pole Winner | Pole Speed |
|------|-------|-------------|----------|------------|------------|-------------|------------|
| 2004 | MBNA America 200 | G. Biffle | Ford | 87.934 | 7 | D. Green | 157.916 |
|  | Stacker 2 Hundred | M. Truex Jr. | Chevrolet | 122.013 | 2 | K. Kahne | 157.350 |
| 2003 | MBNA Armed Forces 200 | J. Nemechek | Chevrolet | 104.651 | 1 | J. Nemechek | 156.747 |
|  | Stacker 200 by YJ Stinger | B. Vickers | Chevrolet | 133.154 | 3 | Trials rained out | |
| 2002 | MBNA Platinum 200 | G. Biffle | Ford | 107.591 | 3 | J. Green | 155.347 |
|  | MBNA All-American 200 | S. Wimmer | Pontiac | 118.265 | 26 | K. Lepage | 155.767 |
| 2001 | MBNA Platinum 200 | J. Spencer | Chevrolet | 91.394 | 21 | Trials rained out | |
|  | MBNA.COM 200 | J. Green | Ford | 107.591 | 2 | R. Newman | 155.635 |
| 2000 | MBNA Platinum 200 | J. Keller | Chevrolet | 99.709 | 22 | K. Harvick | 154.912 |
|  | MBNA.com 200 | M. Kenseth | Chevrolet | 109.041 | 14 | M. Skinner | 155.932 |
| 1999 | MBNA Platinum 200 | D. Earnhardt Jr. | Chevrolet | 91.324 | 15 | D. Trickle | 155.213 |
|  | MBNA Gold 200 | C. Atwood | Chevrolet | 91.382 | 5 | M. Kenseth | 155.293 |
| 1998 | MBNA Platinum 200 | D. Earnhardt Jr. | Chevrolet | 130.152 | 16 | K. Lepage | 151.688 |
|  | MBNA Gold 200 | M. Kenseth | Chevrolet | 106.023 | 4 | K. Grubb | 153.498 |
| 1997 | Goodw./Delco 200 | B. Labonte | Pontiac | 114.358 | 2 | D. Trickle | 148.926 |
|  | MBNA 200 | J. Bessey | Chevrolet | 94.912 | 6 | D. Trickle | 147.656 |
| 1996 | Goodw./Delco 200 | R. LaJoie | Chevrolet | 96.308 | 16 | B. Labonte | 149.963 |
|  | MBNA 200 | R. LaJoie | Chevrolet | 118.343 | 24 | R. Craven | 150.069 |
| 1995 | Goodw./Delco 200 | M. McLaughlin | Chevrolet | 102.887 | 5 | T. Leslie | 147.832 |
|  | MBNA 200 | J. Rumley | Chevrolet | 108.975 | 24 | J. Keller | 149.409 |
| 1994 | Goodw./Delco 200 | M. Wallace | Chevrolet | 96.013 | 19 | R. Craven | 146.425 |
|  | Splitfire 200 | J. Benson | Chevrolet | 102.477 | 20 | H. Gant | 149.638 |
| 1993 | Goodw./Delco 200 | T. Bodine | Chevrolet | 116.694 | 5 | W. Burton | 145.92 |
|  | Splitfire 200 | T. Bodine | Chevrolet | 104.545 | 22 | T. Labonte | 147.366 |
| 1992 | Goodwrench 200 | R. Pressley | Oldsmobile | 89.408 | 4 | T. Bodine | 143.604 |
|  | Splitfire 200 | R. Pressley | Oldsmobile | 108.271 | 4 | J. Gordon | 143.079 |
| 1991 | Budweiser 200 | T. Bodine | Buick | 118.323 | 9 | D. Mader | 142.510 |
|  | Splitfire 200 | H. Gant | Buick | 126.538 | 16 | B. Miller | 145.396 |
| 1990 | Budweiser 200 | M. Waltrip | Pontiac | 108.091 | 4 | B. Labonte | 143.885 |
|  | Ames/Splitfire 200 | H. Gant | Buick | 123.097 | 3 | T. Ellis | 144.289 |
| 1989 | Budweiser 200 | R. Wilson | Oldsmobile | 114.122 | 8 | H. Gant | 142.006 |
|  | Ames/Peak 200 | K. Schrader | Chevrolet | 111.300 | 14 | M. Waltrip | 143.209 |
| 1988 | Budweiser 200 | B. Hillin | Buick | 112.236 | 15 | M. Alexander | 143.192 |
|  | Grand National 200 | M. Waltrip | Chevrolet | 116.073 | 5 | H. Gant | 143.896 |
| 1987 | Budweiser 200 | M. Martin | Ford | 101.408 | 5 | R. Mast | 141.995 |
|  | Grand National 200 | R. Mast | Buick | 113.529 | 3 | H. Gant | 140.685 |
| 1986 | Budweiser 200 | D. Waltrip | Pontiac | 107.914 | 2 | B. Bodine | 137.546 |
|  | Grand National 200 | M. Shepherd | Buick | 113.798 | 1 | M. Shepherd | 141.093 |
| 1985 | Budweiser 200 | D. Waltrip | Chevrolet | 108.926 | 8 | J. Ingram | 135.941 |
| 1984 | Budweiser 200 | S. Ard | Oldsmobile | 111.888 | 2 | R. Bouchard | 139.184 |
| 1983 | Sportsman 200 | R. Rudd | Oldsmobile | 118.285 | 12 | D. Pearson | 137.504 |
| 1982 | Sportsman 200 | J. Ruttman | Pontiac | 111.679 | 9 | H. Gant | 138.021 |

**POLE WINNERS**

| | |
|---|---|
| H. Gant | 5 |
| D. Trickle | 3 |
| R. Craven | 2 |
| B. Labonte | 2 |
| K. LePage | 2 |
| M. Alexander | 1 |
| B. Bodine | 1 |
| T. Bodine | 1 |
| R. Bouchard | 1 |
| W. Burton | 1 |
| T. Ellis | 1 |
| J. Gordon | 1 |
| D. Green | 1 |
| J. Green | 1 |
| K. Grubb | 1 |
| K. Harvick | 1 |
| J. Ingram | 1 |
| J. Keller | 1 |
| M. Kenseth | 1 |
| T. Labonte | 1 |
| D. Mader III | 1 |
| R. Mast | 1 |
| B. Miller | 1 |
| R. Newman | 1 |
| D. Pearson | 1 |
| M. Shepherd | 1 |
| M. Skinner | 1 |
| M. Waltrip | 1 |
| J. Nemechek | 1 |
| K. Kahne | 1 |

**RACE WINNERS**

| | |
|---|---|
| T. Bodine | 3 |
| G. Biffle | 2 |
| D. Earnhardt Jr. | 2 |
| H. Gant | 2 |
| M. Kenseth | 2 |
| R. LaJoie | 2 |
| R. Pressley | 2 |
| D. Waltrip | 2 |
| M. Waltrip | 2 |
| S. Ard | 1 |
| C. Atwood | 1 |
| J. Benson | 1 |
| J. Bessey | 1 |
| J. Green | 1 |
| B. Hillin | 1 |
| J. Keller | 1 |
| B. Labonte | 1 |
| M. Martin | 1 |
| R. Mast | 1 |
| M. McLaughlin | 1 |
| R. Rudd | 1 |
| J. Rumley | 1 |
| J. Ruttman | 1 |
| K. Schrader | 1 |
| M. Shepherd | 1 |
| J. Spencer | 1 |
| M. Wallace | 1 |
| R. Wilson | 1 |
| S. Wimmer | 1 |
| J. Nemechek | 1 |
| B. Vickers | 1 |
| M. Truex Jr. | 1 |

**QUALIFYING RECORD:** David Green, Chevrolet; 157.916 mph, June 4, 2004
**RACE RECORD:** Dale Earnhardt Jr., Chevrolet; 130.152 mph, May 30, 1998

# CRAFTSMAN TRUCK SERIES

## Craftsman YEAR BY YEAR WINNERS (Dover)

| Year | Event | Race Winner | Car Make | Avg. Speed | Start Pos. | Pole Winner | Pole Speed |
|------|-------|-------------|----------|------------|------------|-------------|------------|
| 2004 | MBNA America 200 | C. Chaffin | Dodge | 98.996 | 9 | C. Edwards | 152.892 |
| 2003 | MBNA Armed Forces 200 | J. Leffler | Dodge | 97.232 | 26 | B. Hamilton | Rained out |
| 2002 | MBNA America 200 | T. Musgrave | Dodge | 104.545 | 2 | R. Crawford | 150.414 |
| 2001 | MBNA E-Commerce 200 | S. Riggs | Dodge | 99.256 | 1 | S. Riggs | 150.288 |
| 2000 | MBNA E-Commerce.com 200 | Ku. Busch | Ford | 97.168 | 1 | Ku. Busch | 151.764 |

**POLE WINNERS**

| | |
|---|---|
| Ku. Busch | 1 |
| R. Crawford | 1 |
| C. Edwards | 1 |
| S. Riggs | 1 |

**RACE WINNERS**

| | |
|---|---|
| Ku. Busch | 1 |
| C. Chaffin | 1 |
| T. Musgrave | 1 |
| S. Riggs | 1 |
| J. Leffler | 1 |

**QUALIFYING RECORD:** Carl Edwards, Ford; 152.892 mph, June 4, 2004
**RACE RECORD:** Ted Musgrave, Dodge; 104.545 mph, May 31, 2002

TRACKS

## 2005 SCHEDULE

**NEXTEL CUP**
Event: Ford 400
Race: No. 36 of 36
Date: November 20
TV: NBC. Radio: MRN

**BUSCH SERIES**
Event: Ford 300
Race: No. 35 of 35
Date: November 19
TV: NBC. Radio: MRN

**CRAFTSMAN TRUCK SERIES**
Event: Ford 200
Race: No. 25 of 25
Date: November 18
TV: SPEED. Radio: MRN

Race names subject to change

### TRACK FACTS
Opened: Fall 1995
Owner: International Speedway Corp.
Location: Homestead, Fla.
Distance: 1.5 miles
Banking in turns: Variable, 18 to 20 degrees
Banking in straights: 4 degrees
Length of front stretch: 1,760 feet
Length of back stretch: 1,760 feet
Grandstand seating: 65,000
Tickets: (305) 230-7223
Website: www.homesteadmiamispeedway.com

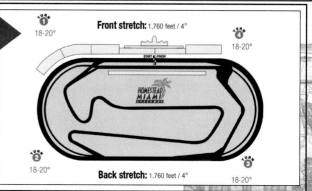

Front stretch: 1,760 feet / 4°
Back stretch: 1,760 feet / 4°

## NEXTEL CUP

### TRACK RECORDS

**Most wins:** 2—Tony Stewart
**Oldest winner:** Bill Elliott, 46 years, 1 month, 3 days, November 11, 2001
**Youngest winner:** Kurt Busch, 24 years, 3 months, 13 days, November 17, 2002
**Most lead changes:** 21—November 16, 2003
**Fewest lead changes:** 12—November 17, 2002
**Most leaders:** 12—November 14, 2003
**Fewest leaders:** 6—November 17, 2002
**Most cautions:** 14—November 21, 2004
**Fewest cautions:** 1—November 14, 1999
**Most caution laps:** 79—November 21, 2004
**Fewest caution laps:** 5—November 14, 1999
**Most on the lead lap:** 25—November 11, 2001
**Fewest on the lead lap:** 6—November 12, 2000

**Most running at the finish:** 42—November 11, 2001
**Fewest running at the finish:** 32—November 21, 2004
**Most laps led by a race winner:** 166—Tony Stewart, November 12, 2000
**Fewest laps led by a race winner:** 1—Bobby Labonte, November 16, 2003
**Closest margin of victory:** 0.342 seconds—Greg Biffle defeated Jimmie Johnson, November 21, 2004.
**Greatest margin of victory:** 5.289 seconds—Tony Stewart defeated Bobby Labonte, November 14, 1999.

### QUALIFYING AND RACE RECORDS

**QUALIFYING:** Jamie McMurray, Dodge; 181.111 mph, November 14, 2003.
**RACE:** Tony Stewart, Pontiac; 140.335 mph, November 14, 1999.

### NEXTEL Cup YEAR BY YEAR WINNERS — ALL HOMESTEAD RACES

| Year | Event | Race Winner | Car Make | Avg. Speed | Start Pos. | Car Owner | Pole Winner | Pole Speed | POLE WINNERS | | RACE WINNERS | |
|---|---|---|---|---|---|---|---|---|---|---|---|---|
| 2004 | Ford 400 | G. Biffle | Ford | 105.623 | 2 | Jack Roush | Ku. Busch | 179.319 | Ku. Busch | 2 | T. Stewart | 2 |
| 2003 | Ford 400 | B. Labonte | Chevrolet | 116.868 | 2 | Joe Gibbs | J. McMurray | 181.111 | D. Green | 2 | G. Biffle | 1 |
| 2002 | Ford 400 | Ku. Busch | Ford | 116.462 | 1 | Jack Roush | Ku. Busch | 154.365 | S. Park | 1 | B. Elliott | 1 |
| 2001 | Pennzoil Freedom 400 | B. Elliott | Dodge | 117.449 | 1 | Ray Evernham | B. Elliott | 155.226 | B. Elliott | 1 | Ku. Busch | 1 |
| 2000 | Pennzoil 400 | T. Stewart | Pontiac | 127.480 | 13 | Joe Gibbs | S. Park | 156.440 | J. McMurray | 1 | B. Labonte | 1 |
| 1999 | Pennzoil 400 | T. Stewart | Pontiac | 140.335 | 7 | Joe Gibbs | D. Green | 155.759 | | | | |

## BUSCH SERIES

### Busch YEAR BY YEAR WINNERS

| Year | Event | Race Winner | Car Make | Avg. Speed | Start Pos. | Pole Winner | Pole Speed | POLE WINNERS | | RACE WINNERS | |
|---|---|---|---|---|---|---|---|---|---|---|---|
| 2004 | Ford 300 | K. Harvick | Chevrolet | 110.482 | 12 | C. Mears | 177.936 | J. Green | 2 | J. Nemechek | 3 |
| 2003 | Ford 300 | K.Kahne | Ford | 121.376 | 3 | G. Biffle | 177.416 | C. Atwood | 1 | J. Burton | 1 |
| 2002 | Ford 300 | S. Wimmer | Pontiac | 123.542 | 26 | J. Green | 152.031 | B. Hamilton Jr. | 1 | J. Gordon | 1 |
| 2001 | GNC Live Well 300 | J. Nemechek | Chevrolet | 132.191 | 20 | J. Green | 150.939 | B. Labonte | 1 | K. Harvick | 1 |
| 2000 | Miami 300 | J. Gordon | Chevrolet | 125.450 | 6 | B. Hamilton Jr. | 151.490 | M. McLaughlin | 1 | D. Jarrett | 1 |
| 1999 | Hotwheels.com 300 | J. Nemechek | Chevrolet | 124.596 | 12 | H. Stricklin | 149.456 | C. Mears | 1 | K. Lepage | 1 |
| 1998 | Jiffy Lube 300 | J. Bruton | Ford | 129.605 | 23 | C. Atwood | 148.262 | J. Nemechek | 1 | S. Wimmer | 1 |
| 1997 | Jiffy Lube 300 | J. Nemechek | Chevrolet | 112.900 | 3 | M. McLaughlin | 147.771 | H. Stricklin | 1 | K. Kahne | 1 |
| 1996 | Jiffy Lube 300 | K. Lepage | Chevrolet | 119.158 | 10 | B. Labonte | 139.074 | G. Biffle | 1 | | |
| 1995 | Jiffy Lube 300 | D. Jarrett | Ford | 92.229 | 26 | J. Nemechek | 134.628 | | | | |

**QUALIFYING RECORD:** Casey Mears, Dodge, 177.936 mph, November 19, 2004
**RACE RECORD:** Joe Nemechek, Chevrolet; 132.191 mph, November 10, 2001

# CRAFTSMAN TRUCK SERIES

## Craftsman YEAR BY YEAR WINNERS (Homestead)

| Year | Event | Race Winner | Car Make | Avg. Speed | Start Pos. | Pole Winner | Pole Speed | POLE WINNERS | | RACE WINNERS | |
|------|-------|-------------|----------|------------|------------|-------------|------------|--------------|--|--------------|--|
| 2004 | Ford 200 | K. Kahne | Dodge | 114.930 | 13 | D. Reutimann | 171.255 | J. Ruttman | 2 | R. Hornaday Jr. | 1 |
| 2003 | Ford 200 | B. Hamilton | Dodge | 120.439 | 1 | B. Hamilton | 169.252 | M. Bliss | 1 | A. Houston | 1 |
| 2002 | Ford 200 | R. Hornaday Jr. | Chevrolet | 133.260 | 5 | M. Bliss | 147.111 | G. Bodine | 1 | K. Irwin | 1 |
| 2001 | Fla. Dodge Dealers 400 | T. Musgrave | Dodge | 118.176 | 3 | S. Riggs | 146.017 | D. Reutimann | 1 | K. Kahne | 1 |
| 2000 | Fla. Dodge Dealers 400 | A. Houston | Chevrolet | 129.755 | 3 | J. Ruttman | 146.727 | S. Riggs | 1 | T. Musgrave | 1 |
| 1999 | Fla. Dodge Dealers 400 | M. Wallace | Ford | 109.813 | 10 | R. Tolsma | 149.813 | J. Sprague | 1 | D. Rezendes | 1 |
| 1998 | Fla. Dodge Dealers 400 | R. Crawford | Ford | 114.475 | 12 | J. Sprague | 149.283 | R. Tolsma | 1 | B. Hamilton | 1 |
| 1997 | Fla. Dodge Dealers 400 | K. Irwin | Ford | 98.565 | 5 | J. Ruttman | 140.221 | R. Crawford | 1 | | |
| 1996 | Fla. Dodge Dealers 400 | D. Rezendes | Ford | 102.000 | 10 | G. Bodine | 135.598 | B. Hamilton | 1 | | |

**QUALIFYING RECORD:** David Reutimann, Toyota; 171.255 mph, November 18, 2004
**RACE RECORD:** Ron Hornaday Jr., Chevrolet; 133.260 mph, November 15, 2002

# INDIANAPOLIS MOTOR SPEEDWAY

## 2005 SCHEDULE

### NEXTEL CUP

**Event:** Brickyard 400
**Race:** No. 21 of 36
**Date:** August 7
**TV:** NBC. **Radio:** IMS

### TRACK FACTS

**Opened:** 1909
**Owner:** Hulman-George Family, Hulman & Co.
**Location:** Indianapolis
**Distance:** 2.5 miles
**Banking in turns:** 9 degrees, 12 minutes
**Banking in straights:** 0 degrees
**Length of font stretch:** 3,300 feet
**Length of back stretch:** 3,300 feet
**Length of short straightaways:** 660 feet
**Grandstand seating:** 250,000
**Tickets:** (317) 481-6700
**Website:** www.brickyard400.com

Back stretch: 3,300 feet / 0°

Front stretch: 3,330 feet / 0°

**TRACKS**

## NEXTEL CUP

### TRACK RECORDS

**Most wins:** 4—Jeff Gordon
**Oldest winner:** Bill Elliott, 46 years, 9 months, 27 days, August 4, 2002
**Youngest winner:** Jeff Gordon, 23 years, 2 days, August 6, 1994
**Most lead changes:** 21—August 6, 1994
**Fewest lead changes:** 9—Twice, most recently, August 8, 2004
**Most leaders:** 13—Twice, most recently, August 3, 1996
**Fewest leaders:** 5—August 5, 2000
**Most cautions:** 13—August 8, 2004
**Fewest cautions:** 1—August 5, 1995
**Most caution laps:** 47—August 8, 2004
**Fewest caution laps:** 4—August 5, 1995
**Most on the lead lap:** 30—August 4, 2002
**Fewest on the lead lap:** 14—August 5, 2000

**Most running at the finish:** 39—Twice, most recently, August 5, 2000
**Fewest running at the finish:** 27—August 8, 2004
**Most laps led by a race winner:** 124—Jeff Gordon, August 8, 2004
**Fewest laps led by a race winner:** 11—Dale Jarrett, August 3, 1996
**Closest margin of victory:** 0.183 seconds—Ricky Rudd defeated Bobby Labonte, August 2, 1997.
**Greatest margin of victory:** 4.229 seconds—Bobby Labonte defeated Rusty Wallace, August 5, 2000.

### QUALIFYING AND RACE RECORDS

**QUALIFYING:** Casey Mears, Dodge, 186.293 mph, August 6, 2004.
**RACE:** Bobby Labonte, Pontiac, 155.912 mph, August 5, 2000.

## NEXTEL Cup YEAR BY YEAR WINNERS

| Year | Event | Race Winner | Car Make | Avg. Speed | Start Pos. | Car Owner | Pole Winner | Pole Speed | POLE WINNERS | | RACE WINNERS | |
|------|-------|-------------|----------|------------|------------|-----------|-------------|------------|--------------|--|--------------|--|
| 2004 | Brickyard 400 | J. Gordon | Chevrolet | 115.037 | 11 | Rick Hendrick | C. Mears | 186.293 | J. Gordon | 3 | J. Gordon | 4 |
| 2003 | Brickyard 400 | K. Harvick | Chevrolet | 134.544 | 1 | Richard Childress | K. Harvick | 184.343 | E. Irvan | 2 | D. Jarrett | 2 |
| 2002 | Brickyard 400 | B. Elliott | Dodge | 125.033 | 2 | Ray Evernham | T. Stewart | 182.960 | R. Mast | 1 | D. Earnhardt | 1 |
| 2001 | Brickyard 400 | J. Gordon | Chevrolet | 130.790 | 27 | Rick Hendrick | J. Spencer | 179.666 | R. Rudd | 1 | R. Rudd | 1 |
| 2000 | Brickyard 400 | B. Labonte | Pontiac | 155.912 | 3 | Joe Gibbs | R. Rudd | 181.068 | J. Spencer | 1 | B. Labonte | 1 |
| 1999 | Brickyard 400 | D. Jarrett | Ford | 148.194 | 4 | Robert Yates | J. Gordon | 179.612 | T. Stewart | 1 | B. Elliott | 1 |
| 1998 | Brickyard 400 | J. Gordon | Chevrolet | 126.770 | 3 | Rick Hendrick | E Irvan | 179.394 | K. Harvick | 1 | K. Harvick | 1 |
| 1997 | Brickyard 400 | R. Rudd | Ford | 130.814 | 7 | Ricky Rudd | E. Irvan | 177.736 | C. Mears | 1 | | |
| 1996 | Brickyard 400 | D. Jarrett | Ford | 139.508 | 24 | Robert Yates | J. Gordon | 176.419 | | | | |
| 1995 | Brickyard 400 | D. Earnhardt | Chevrolet | 155.206 | 13 | Richard Childress | J. Gordon | 172.536 | | | | |
| 1994 | Brickyard 400 | J. Gordon | Chevrolet | 131.977 | 3 | Rick Hendrick | R. Mast | 172.414 | | | | |

### ALL INDIANAPOLIS RACES

# INFINEON RACEWAY

## 2005 SCHEDULE

**NEXTEL CUP**

Event: Dodge/Save Mart 300

**Race:** No. 16 of 36
**Date:** June 26
**TV:** FOX. **Radio:** PRN
Race name subject to change

### TRACK FACTS

**Opened:** 1968
**Owner:** Speedway Motorsports, Inc.
**Location:** Sonoma, Calif.
**Distance:** 1.99-mile road course
**Turns:** 11, with varying lengths and degrees of banking.
**The chute:** 890 feet, 2.8 degrees of banking
**Grandstand seating:** 30,000
**Tickets:** (800) 870-7223
**Website:** www.infineonraceway.com

## NEXTEL CUP

### TRACK RECORDS

**Most wins:** 4—Jeff Gordon
**Most top 5s:** 6—Ricky Rudd
**Most top 10s:** 7—Dale Earnhardt, Mark Martin and Ricky Rudd
**Oldest winner:** Ricky Rudd, 45 years, 9 months, 11 days, June 23, 2002
**Youngest winner:** Jeff Gordon, 26 years, 10 months, 24 days, June 28, 1998
**Most lead changes:** 10—four times, most recently, June 23, 2002
**Fewest lead changes:** 3—June 11, 1989
**Most Leaders:** 9—Twice, most recently, May 23, 2002
**Fewest leaders:** 3—June 11, 1989
**Most cautions:** 9—June 10, 1990
**Fewest cautions:** 3—four times, most recently, June 23, 2002
**Most caution laps:** 26—June 27, 1999
**Fewest caution laps:** 7—June 7, 1992

**Most on the lead Lap:** 29—four times, most recently, June 22, 2003
**Fewest on the lead lap:** 14—twice, most recently, May 16, 1993
**Most running at the finish:** 42—May 5, 1996
**Fewest running at the finish:** 32—May 16, 1993
**Most laps led by a race winner:** 93—Jeff Gordon, June 27, 2004
**Fewest laps led by a race winner:** 2—Davey Allison June 9, 1991
**Closest margin of victory:** .05 seconds—Ricky Rudd defeated Rusty Wallace, June 11, 1989.
**Greatest margin of victory:** 9.56 seconds—Ernie Irvan defeated Geoffrey Bodine, May 15, 1994.

### QUALIFYING AND RACE RECORDS

**QUALIFYING: Track record (1.99 miles):** Tony Stewart, Pontiac; 93.476 mph, June 23, 2002.
**RACE: Track record (1.99 miles):** Ricky Rudd, Ford; 81.007 mph, June 23, 2002.

## NEXTEL Cup YEAR BY YEAR WINNERS

| Year | Event | Race Winner | Car Make | Avg. Speed | Start Pos. | Car Owner | Pole Winner | Pole Speed |
|------|-------|-------------|----------|-----------|-----------|-----------|-------------|-----------|
| 2004 | Dodge/Save Mart 350 | J. Gordon | Chevrolet | 77.456 | 1 | Rick Hendrick | J. Gordon | 94.303 |
| 2003 | Dodge/Save Mart 350 | R. Gordon | Chevrolet | 73.821 | 2 | Richard Childress | B. Said | 93.620 |
| c2002 | Dodge/Save Mart 350 | R. Rudd | Ford | 81.007 | 7 | Robert Yates | T. Stewart | 93.476 |
| b2001 | Dodge/Save Mart 350 | T. Stewart | Pontiac | 75.889 | 3 | Joe Gibbs | J. Gordon | 93.699 |
| 2000 | Save Mart/Kragen 350 | J. Gordon | Chevrolet | 78.789 | 5 | Rick Hendrick | R. Wallace | 99.309 |
| a1999 | Save Mart 350 | J. Gordon | Chevrolet | 70.378 | 1 | Rick Hendrick | J. Gordon | 98.519 |
| 1998 | Save Mart 350 | J. Gordon | Chevrolet | 72.387 | 1 | Rick Hendrick | J. Gordon | 98.711 |
| 1997 | Save Mart 300 | M. Martin | Ford | 75.788 | 1 | Jack Roush | M. Martin | 92.807 |
| 1996 | Save Mart 300 | R. Wallace | Ford | 77.673 | 7 | Roger Penske | T. Labonte | 92.524 |
| 1995 | Save Mart 300 | Earnhardt | Chevrolet | 70.681 | 4 | Richard Childress | R. Rudd | 92.132 |
| 1994 | Save Mart 300 | E. Irvan | Ford | 77.458 | 1 | Robert Yates | E. Irvan | 91.514 |
| 1993 | Save Mart 300 | G. Bodine | Ford | 77.013 | 3 | Bud Moore | D. Earnhardt | 91.838 |
| 1992 | Save Mart 300 | E. Irvan | Chevrolet | 81.413 | 2 | Morgan-McClure | R. Rudd | 90.985 |
| 1991 | Banquet 300 | Da. Allison | Ford | 72.970 | 13 | Robert Yates | R. Rudd | 90.634 |
| 1990 | Banquet 300 | R. Wallace | Pontiac | 69.245 | 11 | Blue Max | R. Rudd | 99.743 |
| 1989 | Banquet 300 | R. Rudd | Buick | 76.088 | 4 | King Racing | R. Wallace | 90.041 |

### ALL INFINEON RACES

| POLE WINNERS | | RACE WINNERS | |
|--------------|---|--------------|---|
| R. Rudd | 4 | J. Gordon | 4 |
| J. Gordon | 4 | E. Irvan | 2 |
| R. Wallace | 2 | R. Wallace | 2 |
| D. Earnhardt | 1 | R. Rudd | 2 |
| E. Irvan | 1 | Da. Allison | 1 |
| T. Labonte | 1 | G. Bodine | 1 |
| M. Martin | 1 | D. Earnhardt | 1 |
| T. Stewarat | 1 | M. Martin | 1 |
| B. Said | 1 | T. Stewart | 1 |
| | | R. Gordon | 1 |

**KEY**
a Track reconfigured from 2.52 miles to 1.949 miles.
b Track reconfigured from 1.949 miles to 2 miles.
c Track reconfigured from 2 miles to 1.99 miles.

## 2005 SCHEDULE

**NEXTEL CUP**
Event: Banquet 400
Race: No. 30 of 36
Date: October 9
TV: NBC. Radio: MRN

**BUSCH SERIES**
Event: Mr. Goodcents 300
Race: No. 30 of 35
Date: October 8
TV: TNT. Radio: MRN

**CRAFTSMAN TRUCK SERIES**
Event: O'Reilly Auto Parts 250
Race: No. 12 of 25
Date: July 2
TV: SPEED. Radio: MRN

Race names subject to change

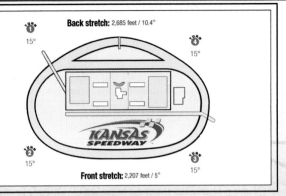

### TRACK FACTS
**Opened:** July 6, 2001
**Owner:** International Speedway Corp.
**Location:** Kansas City, Kan.
**Distance:** 1.5 miles
**Banking in turns:** 15 degrees
**Banking in front stretch:** 10.4 degrees
**Banking in back stretch:** 5 degrees
**Length of front stretch:** 2,685 feet
**Length of back stretch:** 2,207 feet
**Grandstand seating:** 80,187
**Tickets:** (913) 328-7223
**Website:** www.kansasspeedway.com

Back stretch: 2,685 feet / 10.4°
15°
15°
KANSAS SPEEDWAY
15°
15°
Front stretch: 2,207 feet / 5°

TRACKS

# NEXTEL CUP

## TRACK RECORDS

**Most wins:** 2—Jeff Gordon
**Oldest winner:** Joe Nemechek, 41 years, 13 days, October 10, 2004
**Youngest winner:** Ryan Newman, 26 years, 9 months, 27 days, October 5, 2003
**Most lead changes:** 24—October 10, 2004
**Fewest lead changes:** 13—September 29, 2002
**Most leaders:** 12—Twice, most recently, October 10, 2004
**Fewest leaders:** 10—September 29, 2002
**Most cautions:** 13—September 30, 2001
**Fewest cautions:** 9—Twice, most recently, October 10, 2004
**Most caution laps:** 70—September 30, 2001
**Fewest caution laps:** 39—October 10, 2004
**Most on the lead lap:** 24—October 5, 2003
**Fewest on the lead lap:** 9—September 29, 2002

**Most running at the finish:** 34—October 5, 2003
**Fewest running at the finish:** 27—September 29, 2002
**Most laps led by a race winner:** 116—Jeff Gordon, September 29, 2002
**Fewest laps led by a race winner:** 28—Ryan Newman, October 5, 2003
**Closest margin of victory:** 0.081 seconds—Joe Nemechek defeated Ricky Rudd, October 10, 2004.
**Greatest margin of victory:** 0.863 seconds—Ryan Newman defeated Bill Elliott, October 5, 2003.

## QUALIFYING AND RACE RECORDS

**QUALIFYING: Track:** Jimmie Johnson, Chevrolet; 180.373 mph, October 3, 2003.
**RACE: Track:** Joe Nemechek, Chevrolet; 128.058 mph, October 10, 2004.

### NEXTEL Cup YEAR BY YEAR WINNERS

| Year | Event | Race Winner | Car Make | Avg. Speed | Start Pos. | Car Owner | Pole Winner | Pole Speed |
|------|-------|-------------|----------|-----------|-----------|-----------|-------------|-----------|
| 2004 | Banquet 400 | J. Nemechek | Chevrolet | 128.058 | 1 | N. Bowers | J. Nemechek | 180.156 |
| 2003 | Banquet 400 | R. Newman | Dodge | 121.630 | 11 | R. Penske | J. Johnson | 180.373 |
| 2002 | Protection One 400 | J. Gordon | Chevrolet | 119.394 | 10 | R. Hendrick | D. Earnhardt Jr. | 177.924 |
| 2001 | Protection One 400 | J. Gordon | Chevrolet | 110.576 | 2 | R. Hendrick | J. Leffler | 176.499 |

**ALL KANSAS RACES**

| POLE WINNERS | | RACE WINNERS | |
|--------------|---|--------------|---|
| J. Leffler | 1 | J. Gordon | 2 |
| D. Earnhardt Jr. | 1 | R. Newman | 1 |
| Ji. Johnson | 1 | J. Nemechek | 1 |
| J. Nemechek | 1 | | |

# BUSCH SERIES

### Busch YEAR BY YEAR WINNERS

| Year | Event | Race Winner | Car Make | Avg. Speed | Start Pos. | Pole Winner | Pole Speed |
|------|-------|-------------|----------|-----------|-----------|-------------|-----------|
| 2004 | Mr. Goodcents 300 | J. Nemechek | Chevrolet | 117.504 | 19 | P. Menard | 176.062 |
| 2003 | Mr. Goodcents 300 | D. Green | Pontiac | 113.148 | 3 | M. Waltrip | 178.365 |
| 2002 | Mr. Goodcents 300 | J. Burton | Ford | 120.509 | 2 | M. Waltrip | 174.831 |
| 2001 | Mr. Goodcents 300 | J. Green | Ford | 129.125 | 12 | K. Lepage | 174.210 |

| POLE WINNERS | | RACE WINNERS | |
|--------------|---|--------------|---|
| M. Waltrip | 2 | J. Green | 1 |
| K. Lepage | 1 | J. Burton | 1 |
| P. Menard | 1 | D. Green | 1 |
| | | J. Nemechek | 1 |

**QUALIFYING RECORD:** Michael Waltrip, Chevrolet; 178.365 mph, October 3, 2003
**RACE RECORD:** Jeff Green, Ford; 129.125 mph, September 29, 2001

# CRAFTSMAN TRUCK SERIES

### Craftsman YEAR BY YEAR WINNERS

| Year | Event | Race Winner | Car Make | Avg. Speed | Start Pos. | Pole Winner | Pole Speed |
|------|-------|-------------|----------|-----------|-----------|-------------|-----------|
| 2004 | O'Reilly Auto Parts 250 | C. Edwards | Ford | 105.994 | 2 | D. Setzer | Rained out |
| 2003 | O'Reilly Auto Parts 250 | J. Wood | Ford | 114.253 | 3 | C. Chaffin | 166.323 |
| 2002 | O'Reilly Auto Parts 250 | M. Bliss | Chevrolet | 121.487 | 4 | J. Leffler | 165.812 |
| 2001 | O'Reilly Auto Parts 250 | Ricky Hendrick | Chevrolet | 125.094 | 2 | D. Setzer | 162.411 |

| POLE WINNERS | | RACE WINNERS | |
|--------------|---|--------------|---|
| D. Setzer | 2 | M. Bliss | 1 |
| J. Leffler | 1 | R. Hendrick | 1 |
| C. Chaffin | 1 | J. Wood | 1 |
| | | C. Edwards | 1 |

**QUALIFYING RECORD:** Chad Chaffin, Dodge; 166.323 mph, July 4, 2003
**RACE RECORD:** Ricky Hendrick, Chevrolet; 125.094 mph, July 7, 2001

# LAS VEGAS MOTOR SPEEDWAY

## 2005 SCHEDULE

**NEXTEL CUP**
**Event:** UAW-DaimlerChrysler 400
**Race:** No. 3 of 36
**Date:** March 13
**TV:** FOX. **Radio:** PRN

**BUSCH SERIES**
**Event:** Sam's Town 300
**Race:** No. 4 of 35
**Date:** March 12
**TV:** FX. **Radio:** PRN

**CRAFTSMAN TRUCK SERIES**
**Event:** Las Vegas 350
**Race:** No. 20 of 25
**Date:** September 24
**TV:** SPEED. **Radio:** MRN

Race names subject to change

### TRACK FACTS

**Opened:** June 25, 1996
**Owner:** Speedway Motorsports, Inc.
**Location:** Las Vegas
**Distance:** 1.5 miles
**Banking in turns:** 12 degrees
**Banking in front stretch:** 9 degrees
**Banking in back stretch:** 3 degrees
**Length of front stretch:** 2.275 feet
**Length of back stretch:** 1,572 feet
**Grandstand seating:** 137,000
**Tickets:** (702) 644-4444
**Website:** www.lvms.com

Back stretch: 1,572 feet / 3°
12° ③  12° ②
LAS VEGAS MOTOR SPEEDWAY
12° ④  12° ①
Front stretch: 2,275 feet / 9°

## NEXTEL CUP

### TRACK RECORDS

**Most wins:** 2—Jeff Burton, Matt Kenseth
**Oldest winner:** Sterling Marlin, 44 years, 8 months, 1 day, March 3, 2002
**Youngest winner:** Jeff Gordon, 29 years, 7 months, March 4, 2001
**Most lead changes:** 25—March 7, 1999
**Fewest lead changes:** 13—March 5, 2000
**Most Leaders:** 13—Twice, most recently, March 3, 2002
**Fewest leaders:** 7—March 5, 2000
**Most cautions:** 6—Three times, most recently, March 7, 2004
**Fewest cautions:** 2—Twice, most recently, March 5, 2000
**Most caution laps:** 37—March 7, 2004
**Fewest caution laps:** 9—March 1, 1998
**Most on the lead lap:** 20—March 3, 2002

**Fewest on the lead lap:** 10—Twice, most recently, March 7, 1999
**Most running at the finish:** 42—March 5, 2000
**Fewest running at the finish:** 33—March 7, 2004
**Most laps led by a race winner:** 123—Matt Kenseth, March 7, 2004
**Fewest laps led by a race winner:** 33—Jeff Gordon, March 4, 2001
**Closest margin of victory:** 1.065 seconds—Mark Martin defeated Jeff Burton, March 1, 1998.
**Greatest margin of victory:** 9.104 seconds—Matt Kenseth defeated Dale Earnhardt Jr., March 2, 2003.

### QUALIFYING AND RACE RECORDS

**QUALIFYING:** Kasey Kahne, Dodge, 174.904 mph, March 5, 2003.
**RACE:** Mark Martin, Ford, 146.554 mph, March 1, 1998.

### NEXTEL Cup YEAR BY YEAR WINNERS

| Year | Event | Race Winner | Car Make | Avg. Speed | Start Pos. | Car Owner | Pole Winner | Pole Speed |
|------|-------|-------------|----------|-----------|-----------|-----------|-------------|-----------|
| 2004 | UAW-DaimlerChrysler 400 | M. Kenseth | Ford | 128.790 | 25 | Jack Roush | K. Kahne | 174.904 |
| 2003 | UAW-DaimlerChrysler 400 | M. Kenseth | Ford | 132.934 | 17 | Jack Roush | B. Labonte | 173.016 |
| 2002 | UAW-DaimlerChrysler 400 | S. Marlin | Dodge | 136.754 | 24 | Chip Ganassi | T. Bodine | 172.850 |
| 2001 | UAW-DaimlerChrysler 400 | J. Gordon | Chevrolet | 135.546 | 24 | Rick Hendrick | D. Jarrett | 172.106 |
| a2000 | CarsDirect.com 400 | J. Burton | Ford | 119.982 | 11 | Jack Roush | R. Rudd | 172.563 |
| 1999 | Las Vegas 400 | J. Burton | Ford | 137.537 | 19 | Jack Roush | B. Labonte | 170.643 |
| 1998 | Las Vegas 400 | M. Martin | Ford | 146.554 | 7 | Jack Roush | D. Jarrett | 168.224 |
| a | 222.0 miles, rain | | | | | | | |

**ALL LAS VEGAS RACES**

| POLE WINNERS | | RACE WINNERS | |
|--------------|---|--------------|---|
| D. Jarrett | 2 | J. Burton | 2 |
| B. Labonte | 2 | M. Kenseth | 2 |
| R. Rudd | 1 | M. Martin | 1 |
| T. Bodine | 1 | J. Gordon | 1 |
| K. Kahne | 1 | S. Marlin | 1 |

## BUSCH SERIES

### Busch YEAR BY YEAR WINNERS

| Year | Event | Race Winner | Car Make | Avg. Speed | Start Pos. | Pole Winner | Pole Speed |
|------|-------|-------------|----------|-----------|-----------|-------------|-----------|
| 2004 | Sam's Town 300 | K. Harvick | Chevrolet | 122.172 | 11 | M. Bliss | 171.238 |
| 2003 | Sam's Town 300 | J. Nemechek | Chevrolet | 115.582 | 29 | Trials rained out | |
| 2002 | Sam's Town 300 | J. Burton | Ford | 123.796 | 1 | J. Burton | 169.168 |
| 2001 | Sam's Town 300 | T. Bodine | Chevrolet | 125.625 | 2 | M. Kenseth | 169.385 |
| 2000 | Sam's Town 300 | J. Burton | Ford | 135.118 | 7 | H. Parker Jr. | 166.328 |
| 1999 | Sam's Town 300 | M. Martin | Ford | 134.370 | 1 | M. Martin | 165.715 |
| 1998 | Sam's Town 300 | J. Spencer | Chevrolet | 114.129 | 7 | M. Martin | 162.577 |
| 1997 | Las Vegas 300 | J. Green | Chevrolet | 114.153 | 1 | J. Green | 159.311 |

| POLE WINNERS | | RACE WINNERS | |
|--------------|---|--------------|---|
| M. Martin | 2 | J. Burton | 2 |
| J. Burton | 1 | T. Bodine | 1 |
| J. Green | 1 | J. Green | 1 |
| M. Kenseth | 1 | M. Martin | 1 |
| H. Parker Jr. | 1 | J. Spencer | 1 |
| M. Bliss | 1 | J. Nemechek | 1 |
| | | K. Harvick | 1 |

**QUALIFYING RECORD:** Mike Bliss, Chevrolet; 171.238 mph, March 5, 2004
**RACE RECORD:** Jeff Burton, Ford; 135.118 mph, March 4, 2000

# CRAFTSMAN TRUCK SERIES

## Craftsman YEAR BY YEAR WINNERS (Las Vegas)

| Year | Event | Race Winner | Car Make | Avg. Speed | Start Pos. | Pole Winner | Pole Speed | POLE WINNERS | | RACE WINNERS | |
|------|-------|-------------|----------|------------|------------|-------------|------------|--------------|---|--------------|---|
| 2004 | Sam's Town 300 | K. Harvick | Chevrolet | 122.172 | 11 | M. Bliss | 171.238 | J. Sprague | 3 | J. Sprague | 2 |
| 2004 | Las Vegas 350 | S. Hmiel | Chevrolet | 123.865 | 21 | M. Skinner | 165.320 | S. Compton | 1 | G. Biffle | 1 |
| 2003 | Las Vegas 350 | B. Gaughan | Dodge | 123.826 | 1 | B. Gaughan | 162.152 | B. Reffner | 1 | T. Musgrave | 1 |
| 2002 | Las Vegas 350 | D. Starr | Chevrolet | 135.394 | 1 | D. Starr | 163.112 | D. Starr | 1 | J. Ruttman | 1 |
| 2001 | The Orleans 350 | T. Musgrave | Dodge | 128.091 | 10 | J. Sprague | 161.803 | B. Gaughan | 1 | B. Gaughan | 1 |
| 1999 | The Orleans 250 | G. Biffle | Ford | 127.229 | 5 | S. Compton | 161.796 | M. Bliss | 1 | K. Harvick | 1 |
| 1998 | Sam's Town 300 | J. Sprague | Chevrolet | 130.801 | 1 | J. Sprague | 161.749 | | | | |
| 1997 | Carquest Auto Parts 420K | J. Ruttman | Ford | 125.849 | 8 | J. Sprague | 161.310 | | | | |
| 1996 | Carquest Auto Parts 420K | J. Sprague | Chevrolet | 120.782 | 3 | B. Reffner | 157.909 | | | | |

**QUALIFYING RECORD:** Mike Skinner, Toyota; 165.320 mph, September 25, 2004
**RACE RECORD:** David Starr, Chevrolet; 135.394 mph, October 13, 2002

# LOWE'S MOTOR SPEEDWAY

## 2005 SCHEDULE

### NEXTEL CUP

**Event:** NASCAR NEXTEL All-Star Challenge*
**Date:** May 21
**TV:** FX. **Radio:** MRN

*Non-points race

**Event:** Coca-Cola 600
**Race:** No. 12 of 36
**Date:** May 29
**TV:** FOX. **Radio:** PRN

**Event:** UAW-GM Quality 500
**Race:** No. 31 of 36
**Date:** October 15
**TV:** NBC. **Radio:** PRN

### BUSCH SERIES

**Event:** CarQuest Auto Parts 350
**Race:** No. 13 of 35
**Date:** May 28
**TV:** FX. **Radio:** PRN

**Event:** SpongeBob SquarePants Movie 300
**Race:** No. 31 of 35
**Date:** October 14
**TV:** TNT. **Radio:** PRN

### CRAFTSMAN TRUCK SERIES

**Event:** Infineon 200
**Race:** No. 7 of 25
**Date:** May 20
**TV:** SPEED. **Radio:** MRN

Race names subject to change

## TRACK FACTS

**Opened:** June 1960
**Owner:** Speedway Motorsports, Inc.
**Location:** Concord, N.C.
**Distance:** 1.5-mile oval
**Banking in turns:** 24 degrees
**Banking in straights:** 5 degrees
**Length of front stretch:** 1,952 feet
**Length of back stretch:** 1,360 feet
**Grandstand seating:** 171,000
**Tickets:** (704) 455-3267
**Website:** www.lowesmotorspeedway.com

**Back stretch:** 1,360 feet / 5°
**Front stretch:** 1,952 feet / 5°
24° Banking in Turns

# NEXTEL CUP

## TRACK RECORDS

**Most wins:** 6—Darrell Waltrip and Bobby Allison
**Oldest winner:** Cale Yarborough, 46 years, 6 months, 9 days, October 6, 1985
**Youngest winner:** Jeff Gordon, 22 years, 9 months, 25 days, May 29, 1994
**Most lead changes:** 59—May 27, 1979
**Fewest lead changes:** 2—May 21, 1961
**Most leaders:** 18—May 29, 1988
**Fewest leaders:** 3—May 21, 1961
**Most laps led in a 400-mile race:** 209—Junior Johnson, October 13, 1968
**Most laps led in a 500-mile race:** 328—Ernie Irvan, October 10, 1993
**Most laps led in a 600-mile race:** 335—Jim Paschal, May 28, 1967
**Most cautions:** 14—May 25, 1980
**Fewest cautions:** 0—May 21, 1961
**Most caution laps:** 113—May 25, 1980
**Fewest caution laps:** 0— May 21, 1961
**Most on the lead lap:** 19— October 8, 2000
**Fewest on the lead lap:** 1—14 times, most recently, May 24, 1987
**Most running at the finish:** 39—October 11, 2003
**Fewest running at the finish:** 10—May 21, 1961

**Most laps led by a race winner:** 335—Jim Paschal, May 28, 1967
**Fewest laps led by a race winner:** 3—Joe Weatherly, May 21, 1961
**Closest margin of victory:** 0.24 seconds—Darrell Waltrip defeated Rusty Wallace, May 29, 1988
**Greatest margin of victory:** 1 lap, 5 seconds—Cale Yarborough defeated Bobby Allison, October 7, 1979.

## QUALIFYING AND RACE RECORDS

**QUALIFYING: Track:** Ryan Newman, Dodge; 188.877 mph October 14, 2004.
**Spring race (Coca-Cola 600):** Jimmie Johnson, Chevrolet; 187.052 mph, May 28, 2004.
**Fall race (UAW-GM Quality 500):** Ryan Newman, Dodge; 188.877 mph, October 14, 2004.
**RACE: Track:** Jeff Gordon, Chevrolet; 160.306 mph, October 11, 1999. (UAW-GM Quality 500).
**Spring race (Coca-Cola 600):** Bobby Labonte, Chevrolet; 151.952 mph, May 28, 1995.
**Fall race (UAW-GM Quality 500):** Jeff Gordon, Chevrolet; 160.306 mph, October 11, 1999.
**National 400:** Fred Lorenzen, Ford; 134.559 mph, October 18, 1964.
**100-mile qualifying race:** Richard Petty; Plymouth, 132.86 mph, May 21, 1961.

## SPRING COCA-COLA 600

**POLE WINNERS**

|  | |
|---|---|
| D. Pearson | 6 |
| J. Gordon | 5 |
| B. Elliott | 3 |
| D. Allison | 2 |
| R. Petty | 2 |
| C. Yarborough | 2 |
| N. Bonnett | 2 |
| Buddy Baker | 2 |
| K. Schrader | 2 |
| R. Newman | 2 |
| Ji. Johnson | 2 |
| B. Allison | 1 |
| C. Glotzbach | 1 |
| F. Lorenzen | 1 |
| Jr. Johnson | 1 |
| B. Isaac | 1 |
| J. Pardue | 1 |
| H. Gant | 1 |
| G. Bodine | 1 |
| Da. Allison | 1 |
| A. Kulwicki | 1 |
| M. Martin | 1 |
| F. Roberts | 1 |
| B. Labonte | 1 |
| D. Earnhardt Jr. | 1 |

**RACE WINNERS**

|  | |
|---|---|
| D. Waltrip | 5 |
| D. Pearson | 3 |
| Buddy Baker | 3 |
| B. Allison | 3 |
| D. Earnhardt | 3 |
| J. Gordon | 3 |
| J. Burton | 2 |
| R. Petty | 2 |
| F. Lorenzen | 2 |
| J. Paschal | 2 |
| N. Bonnett | 2 |
| Ji. Johnson | 2 |
| D. Allison | 1 |
| L. Yarbrough | 1 |
| M. Panch | 1 |
| N. Stacy | 1 |
| J. L. Johnson | 1 |
| B. Parsons | 1 |
| K. Petty | 1 |
| R. Wallace | 1 |
| Da. Allison | 1 |
| B. Labonte | 1 |
| D. Jarrett | 1 |
| M. Kenseth | 1 |
| M. Martin | 1 |

## FALL DOVER 400

**POLE WINNERS**

|  | |
|---|---|
| D. Pearson | 8 |
| C. Glotzbach | 3 |
| B. Labonte | 2 |
| C. Yarborough | 2 |
| H. Gant | 2 |
| A. Kulwicki | 2 |
| T. Richmond | 2 |
| F. Lorenzen | 2 |
| F. Roberts | 2 |
| J. Gordon | 2 |
| R. Newman | 2 |
| R. Petty | 1 |
| M. Panch | 1 |
| N. Bonnett | 1 |
| Buddy Baker | 1 |
| D. Waltrip | 1 |
| D. Parsons | 1 |
| B. Allison | 1 |
| B. Elliott | 1 |
| B. Bodine | 1 |
| M. Martin | 1 |
| W. Burton | 1 |
| R. Rudd | 1 |
| G. Bodine | 1 |
| D. Cope | 1 |
| J. Spencer | 1 |

**RACE WINNERS**

|  | |
|---|---|
| M. Martin | 3 |
| B. Allison | 3 |
| C. Yarborough | 3 |
| R. Petty | 2 |
| D. Earnhardt | 2 |
| B. Elliott | 2 |
| D. Allison | 2 |
| L. Yarbrough | 2 |
| Jr. Johnson | 2 |
| D. Jarrett | 2 |
| D. Pearson | 2 |
| Buddy Baker | 1 |
| B. Parsons | 1 |
| C. Glotzbach | 1 |
| J. Weatherly | 1 |
| S. Thompson | 1 |
| H. Gant | 1 |
| R. Wallace | 1 |
| K. Schrader | 1 |
| D. Waltrip | 1 |
| G. Bodine | 1 |
| Da. Allison | 1 |
| E. Irvan | 1 |
| T. Labonte | 1 |
| J. Gordon | 1 |
| B. Labonte | 1 |
| S. Marlin | 1 |
| J. McMurray | 1 |
| T. Stewart | 1 |
| Ji. Johnson | 1 |

## ALL CHARLOTTE RACES

**POLE WINNERS**

|  | |
|---|---|
| D. Pearson | 14 |
| J. Gordon | 7 |
| C. Yarborough | 4 |
| C. Glotzbach | 4 |
| B. Labonte | 3 |
| R. Petty | 3 |
| F. Lorenzen | 3 |
| N. Bonnett | 3 |
| Buddy Baker | 3 |
| H. Gant | 3 |
| A. Kulwicki | 3 |
| F. Roberts | 3 |
| D. Allison | 2 |
| B. Allison | 2 |
| M. Martin | 2 |
| K. Schrader | 2 |
| R. Richmond | 2 |
| G. Bodine | 2 |
| R. Newman | 2 |
| Ji. Johnson | 2 |
| M. Panch | 1 |
| B. Isaac | 1 |
| J. Pardue | 1 |
| B. Parsons | 1 |
| D. Waltrip | 1 |
| Da. Allison | 1 |
| B. Bodine | 1 |
| Jr. Johnson | 1 |
| W. Burton | 1 |
| R. Rudd | 1 |
| D. Cope | 1 |
| D. Earnhardt Jr. | 1 |
| J. Spencer | 1 |

**RACE WINNERS**

|  | |
|---|---|
| B. Allison | 6 |
| D. Waltrip | 6 |
| D. Earnhardt | 5 |
| J. Gordon | 4 |
| D. Pearson | 4 |
| Buddy Baker | 4 |
| F. Lorenzen | 4 |
| R. Petty | 4 |
| M. Martin | 4 |
| D. Jarrett | 3 |
| Do. Allison | 3 |
| L. Yarbrough | 3 |
| C. Yarborough | 3 |
| Ji. Johnson | 3 |
| N. Bonnett | 2 |
| B. Parsons | 2 |
| R. Wallace | 2 |
| B. Elliott | 2 |
| Jr. Johnson | 2 |
| J. Paschal | 2 |
| Da. Allison | 2 |
| B. Labonte | 2 |
| J. Burton | 2 |
| J. L. Johnson | 1 |
| J. Weatherly | 1 |
| S. Thompson | 1 |
| H. Gant | 1 |
| K. Petty | 1 |
| K. Schrader | 1 |
| C. Glotzbach | 1 |
| G. Bodine | 1 |
| M. Panch | 1 |
| E. Irvan | 1 |
| N. Stacy | 1 |
| T. Labonte | 1 |
| M. Kenseth | 1 |
| S. Marlin | 1 |
| J. McMurray | 1 |
| T. Stewart | 1 |

# NEXTEL Cup YEAR BY YEAR WINNERS (Lowe's)

| Year | Event | Race Winner | Car Make | Avg. Speed | Start Pos. | Car Owner | Pole Winner | Pole Speed |
|---|---|---|---|---|---|---|---|---|
| 2004 | UAW-GM Quality 500 | J. Johnson | Chevrolet | 130.214 | 9 | Rick Hendrick | R. Newman | 188.877 |
| | Coca-Cola 600 | J. Johnson | Chevrolet | 142.763 | 1 | Rick Hendrick | J. Johnson | 187.052 |
| 2003 | UAW-GM Quality 500 | T. Stewart | Chevrolet | 142.871 | 6 | Joe Gibbs | R. Newman | 186.657 |
| d | Coca-Cola 600 | J. Johnson | Chevrolet | 126.198 | 37 | Rick Hendrick | R. Newman | 185.312 |
| 2002 | UAW-GM Quality 500 | J. McMurray | Dodge | 141.481 | 5 | Chip Ganassi | Trials rained out | |
| | Coca-Cola 600 | M. Martin | Ford | 137.729 | 25 | Jack Roush | J. Johnson | 186.464 |
| 2001 | UAW-GM Quality 500 | S. Marlin | Dodge | 139.006 | 13 | Chip Ganassi | J. Spencer | 185.147 |
| * | Coca-Cola 600 | J. Burton | Dodge | 138.107 | 18 | Jack Roush | R. Newman | 185.217 |
| 2000 | UAW-GM Quality 500 | B. Labonte | Pontiac | 133.630 | 2 | Joe Gibbs | J. Gordon | 185.561 |
| | Coca-Cola 600 | M. Kenseth | Ford | 142.640 | 21 | Jack Roush | D. Earnhardt Jr. | 186.034 |
| 1999 | UAW-GM Quality 500 | J. Gordon | Chevrolet | 160.306 | 22 | Rick Hendrick | B. Labonte | 185.682 |
| * | Coca-Cola 600 | J. Burton | Ford | 151.367 | 2 | Jack Roush | B. Labonte | 185.230 |
| 1998 | UAW-GM Quality 500 | M. Martin | Ford | 123.188 | 2 | Jack Roush | D. Cope | 181.690 |
| * | Coca-Cola 600 | J. Gordon | Chevrolet | 136.424 | 1 | Rick Hendrick | J. Gordon | 182.976 |
| 1997 | UAW-GM Quality 500 | D. Jarrett | Ford | 144.323 | 5 | Robert Yates | G. Bodine | 184.256 |
| *c | Coca-Cola 600 | J. Gordon | Chevrolet | 136.745 | 1 | Rick Hendrick | J. Gordon | 184.300 |
| 1996 | UAW-GM Quality 500 | T. Labonte | Chevrolet | 143.143 | 16 | Rick Hendrick | B. Labonte | 184.068 |
| * | Coca-Cola 600 | D. Jarrett | Ford | 147.581 | 15 | Robert Yates | J. Gordon | 183.773 |
| 1995 | UAW-GM Quality 500 | M. Martin | Ford | 145.358 | 5 | Jack Roush | R. Rudd | 180.578 |
| * | Coca-Cola 600 | B. Labonte | Chevrolet | 151.952 | 2 | Joe Gibbs | J. Gordon | 183.861 |
| 1994 | Mello Yello 500 | D. Jarrett | Chevrolet | 145.922 | 22 | Joe Gibbs | W. Burton | 185.759 |
| * | Coca-Cola 600 | J. Gordon | Chevrolet | 139.445 | 1 | Rick Hendrick | J. Gordon | 181.439 |
| 1993 | Mello Yello 500 | E. Irvan | Ford | 154.537 | 2 | Robert Yates | A. Kulwicki | 177.684 |
| * | Coca-Cola 600 | D. Earnhardt | Chevrolet | 145.504 | 14 | Richard Childress | K. Schrader | 177.352 |
| 1992 | Mello Yello 500 | M. Martin | Ford | 153.537 | 4 | Jack Roush | A. Kulwicki | 179.027 |
| | Coca-Cola 600 | D. Earnhardt | Chevrolet | 132.980 | 13 | Richard Childress | B. Elliott | 175.479 |
| 1991 | Mello Yello 500 | G. Bodine | Ford | 138.984 | 6 | Junior Johnson | M. Martin | 176.499 |
| | Coca-Cola 600 | Da. Allison | Ford | 138.951 | 10 | Robert Yates | M. Martin | 174.820 |
| 1990 | Mello Yello 500 | Da. Allison | Ford | 137.428 | 5 | Robert Yates | B. Bodine | 174.385 |
| | Coca-Cola 600 | R. Wallace | Pontiac | 137.650 | 9 | Raymond Beadle | K. Schrader | 173.963 |
| 1989 | All Pro 500 | K. Schrader | Chevrolet | 149.863 | 2 | Rick Hendrick | B. Elliott | 174.081 |
| | Coca-Cola 600 | D. Waltrip | Chevrolet | 144.077 | 4 | Rick Hendrick | A. Kulwicki | 173.021 |
| 1988 | Oakwood 500 | R. Wallace | Pontiac | 130.677 | 3 | Raymond Beadle | A. Kulwicki | 175.896 |
| | Coca-Cola 600 | D. Waltrip | Chevrolet | 124.460 | 5 | Rick Hendrick | Da. Allison | 173.594 |
| 1987 | Oakwood 500 | B. Elliott | Ford | 128.443 | 7 | Melling Racing | B. Allison | 171.636 |
| | Coca-Cola 600 | K. Petty | Ford | 131.483 | 7 | Wood Brothers | B. Elliott | 170.901 |
| 1986 | Oakwood 500 | D. Earnhardt | Chevrolet | 132.403 | 3 | Richard Childress | T. Richmond | 167.078 |
| | Coca-Cola 600 | D. Earnhardt | Chevrolet | 140.406 | 3 | Richard Childress | G. Bodine | 164.511 |
| 1985 | Miller 500 | C. Yarborough | Ford | 136.761 | 4 | Ranier Racing | H. Gant | 166.139 |
| | World 600 | D. Waltrip | Chevrolet | 141.807 | 4 | Junior Johnson | B. Elliott | 164.703 |
| 1984 | Miller 500 | B. Elliott | Ford | 146.861 | 2 | Melling Racing | B. Parsons | 165.579 |
| | World 600 | B. Allison | Buick | 129.233 | 16 | DiGard Rac. Co. | H. Gant | 162.496 |
| 1983 | Miller 500 | R. Petty | Pontiac | 139.998 | 20 | Petty Eng. | T. Richmond | 163.073 |
| | World 600 | N. Bonnett | Chevrolet | 140.707 | 5 | Rahmoc | Buddy Baker | 162.841 |
| 1982 | National 500 | H. Gant | Buick | 137.208 | 7 | Mach 1 | H. Gant | 164.694 |
| | World 600 | N. Bonnett | Ford | 130.058 | 13 | Wood Brothers | D. Pearson | 162.511 |
| 1981 | National 500 | D. Waltrip | Buick | 117.483 | 1 | Junior Johnson | D. Pearson | 162.744 |
| | World 600 | B. Allison | Buick | 129.326 | 7 | Ranier Racing | N. Bonnett | 158.115 |
| 1980 | National 500 | D. Earnhardt | Chevrolet | 135.243 | 4 | Osterlund Rac. | Buddy Baker | 165.634 |
| | World 600 | B. Parsons | Chevrolet | 119.265 | 6 | M.C. Anderson | C. Yarborough | 165.194 |
| 1979 | NAPA 500 | C. Yarborough | Chevrolet | 134.266 | 4 | Junior Johnson | N. Bonnett | 164.304 |
| | World 600 | D. Waltrip | Chevrolet | 136.674 | 3 | DiGard Rac. Co. | N. Bonnett | 160.125 |
| 1978 | NAPA 500 | B. Allison | Ford | 141.826 | 8 | Bud Moore | D. Pearson | 161.355 |
| | World 600 | D. Waltrip | Chevrolet | 138.355 | 17 | DiGard Rac. Co. | D. Pearson | 160.551 |
| 1977 | NAPA 500 | B. Parsons | Chevrolet | 142.780 | 8 | L.G. DeWitt | D. Pearson | 160.892 |
| | World 600 | R. Petty | Dodge | 137.676 | 2 | Petty Eng. | D. Pearson | 161.435 |
| 1976 | National 500 | Do. Allison | Chevrolet | 141.226 | 15 | Hoss Ellington | D. Pearson | 161.223 |
| | World 600 | D. Pearson | Mercury | 137.352 | 1 | Wood Brothers | D. Pearson | 159.132 |
| 1975 | National 500 | R. Petty | Dodge | 132.209 | 9 | Petty Eng. | D. Pearson | 161.701 |
| | World 600 | R. Petty | Dodge | 145.327 | 3 | Petty Eng. | D. Pearson | 159.353 |
| 1974 | National 500 | D. Pearson | Mercury | 119.912 | 1 | Wood Brothers | D. Pearson | 158.749 |
| | World 600 | R. Petty | Mercury | 135.720 | 1 | Petty Eng. | D. Pearson | 157.498 |
| 1973 | National 500 | C. Yarborough | Chevrolet | 145.240 | 2 | Junior Johnson | D. Pearson | 158.315 |
| | World 600 | Buddy Baker | Dodge | 134.890 | 1 | Nord Krauskopf | Buddy Baker | 158.051 |
| 1972 | National 500 | B. Allison | Chevrolet | 133.234 | 4 | Junior Johnson | D. Pearson | 158.539 |
| | World 600 | Buddy Baker | Dodge | 142.255 | 6 | Petty Eng. | B. Allison | 158.162 |
| b 1971 | National 500 | B. Allison | Mercury | 126.140 | 3 | Holman-Moody | C. Glotzbach | 157.085 |
| | World 600 | B. Labonte | Mercury | 140.442 | 2 | Holman-Moody | C. Glotzbach | 157.788 |
| 1970 | National 500 | L. Yarbrough | Mercury | 123.246 | 5 | Junior Johnson | C. Glotzbach | 157.273 |
| | World 600 | D. Allison | Ford | 129.680 | 9 | Banjo Matthews | B. Isaac | 159.277 |
| 1969 | National 500 | D. Allison | Ford | 131.271 | 3 | Banjo Matthews | C. Yarborough | 162.162 |
| | World 600 | L. Yarbrough | Mercury | 134.361 | 2 | Junior Johnson | D. Allison | 159.296 |
| 1968 | National 500 | C. Glotzbach | Dodge | 135.324 | 1 | Cotton Owens | C. Glotzbach | 156.060 |
| a | World 600 | Buddy Baker | Dodge | 104.207 | 12 | Ray Fox | D. Allison | 159.223 |
| 1967 | National 500 | Buddy Baker | Dodge | 130.317 | 4 | Ray Fox | C. Yarborough | 154.872 |
| | World 600 | J. Paschal | Plymouth | 135.832 | 10 | Tom Friedkin | C. Yarborough | 154.385 |
| 1966 | National 400 | L. Yarbrough | Dodge | 130.576 | 17 | Jon Thorne | F. Lorenzen | 150.533 |
| | World 600 | M. Panch | Plymouth | 135.042 | 7 | Petty Eng. | R. Petty | 148.637 |
| 1965 | National 400 | F. Lorenzen | Ford | 119.117 | 1 | Holman-Moody | F. Lorenzen | 147.773 |
| | World 600 | F. Lorenzen | Ford | 121.772 | 1 | Holman-Moody | F. Lorenzen | 145.268 |

## Nextel YEAR BY YEAR WINNERS (Lowe's, continued)

| Year | Event | Race Winner | Car Make | Avg. Speed | Start Pos. | Car Owner | Pole Winner | Pole Speed |
|---|---|---|---|---|---|---|---|---|
| 1964 | National 400 | F. Lorenzen | Ford | 134.475 | 3 | Holman-Moody | R. Petty | 150.711 |
| | World 600 | J. Paschal | Plymouth | 125.772 | 12 | Petty Eng. | J. Pardue | 144.346 |
| 1963 | National 400 | Ju. Johnson | Chevrolet | 132.105 | 2 | Ray Fox | M. Panch | 143.017 |
| | World 600 | F. Lorenzen | Ford | 132.417 | 2 | Holman-Moody | Jr. Johnson | 141.148 |
| 1962 | National 400 | Ju. Johnson | Pontiac | 132.085 | 3 | Ray Fox | F. Roberts | 140.287 |
| | World 600 | N. Stacy | Ford | 125.552 | 18 | Holman-Moody | F. Roberts | 140.150 |
| 1961 | National 400 | J. Weatherly | Pontiac | 119.950 | 6 | Bud Moore | D. Pearson | 138.577 |
| | World 600 | D. Pearson | Pontiac | 111.633 | 3 | Ray Fox | F. R. Petty | 131.611 |
| 1960 | National 400 | S. Thompson | Ford | 112.905 | 3 | Wood Brothers | F. Roberts | 133.465 |
| | World 600 | J.L. Johnson | Chevrolet | 107.735 | 20 | Frank Strickland | F. Roberts | 133.904 |

**KEY**
* Twilight.
a 382.5 miles because of rain.
b 357 mile because of rain.
c 499.5 miles because of rain.
d 414.0 miles because of rain.

# BUSCH SERIES

## Busch YEAR BY YEAR WINNERS (Lowe's)

| Year | Event | Race Winner | Car Make | Avg. Speed | Start Pos. | Pole Winner | Pole Speed | POLE WINNERS | | RACE WINNERS | |
|---|---|---|---|---|---|---|---|---|---|---|---|
| 2004 | SpongeBob SquarePants 300 | M. Bliss | Chevrolet | 110.193 | 7 | C. Mears | 183.014 | H. Gant | 3 | M. Martin | 6 |
| | Carrquest Auto 300 | Ky. Busch | Chevrolet | 114.275 | 2 | G. Biffle | 183.542 | T. Richmond | 3 | H. Gant | 4 |
| 2003 | Carquest Auto 300 | M. Kenseth | Ford | 138.302 | 9 | K. Harvick | 184.445 | D. Blaney | 2 | D. Earnhardt | 3 |
| | Little Trees 300 | G. Biffle | Chevrolet | 148.576 | 4 | K. Harvick | 184.313 | G. Bodine | 2 | R. Moroso | 3 |
| 2002 | Carquest Auto 300 | J. Green | Chevrolet | 120.684 | 4 | R. Hornaday | 182.094 | B. Dotter | 2 | J. Burton | 2 |
| | Little Trees 300 | J. Burton | Ford | 142.443 | 2 | M. Waltrip | 180.343 | J. Gordon | 2 | J. Gordon | 2 |
| 2001 | Carquest Auto 300 | J. Green | Ford | 128.205 | 2 | Trials rained out | | M. Kenseth | 2 | J. Green | 2 |
| | Little Trees 300 | G. Biffle | Ford | 139.445 | 3 | J. Burton | 179.485 | M. Martin | 2 | D. Jarrett | 2 |
| 2000 | Carquest Auto 300 | J. Burton | Ford | 121.759 | 4 | D. Blaney | 177.608 | B. Labonte | 2 | T. Labonte | 2 |
| | All Pro 300 | M. Kenseth | Chevrolet | 145.064 | 1 | M. Kenseth | 178.956 | M. Waltrip | 2 | T. Richmond | 2 |
| 1999 | Carquest Auto 300 | M. Martin | Ford | 119.377 | 2 | D. Green | 176.569 | K. Harvick | 2 | D. Waltrip | 2 |
| | All Pro 300 | M. Waltrip | Chevrolet | 133.235 | 31 | M. Kenseth | 177.328 | R. Bickle | 1 | M. Waltrip | 2 |
| 1998 | Carquest Auto 300 | M. Martin | Ford | 133.449 | 6 | B. Labonte | 172.822 | B. Bodine | 1 | G. Biffle | 2 |
| | All Pro 300 | M. McLaughlin | Chevrolet | 145.376 | 3 | D. Blaney | 177.247 | J. Burton | 1 | M. Kenseth | 2 |
| 1997 | Carquest Auto 300 | J. Nemechek | Chevrolet | 126.954 | 2 | M. Martin | 175.012 | W. Burton | 1 | B. Allison | 1 |
| | All Pro 300 | J. Spencer | Chevrolet | 127.089 | 4 | J. Nemechek | 176.378 | D. Earnhardt | 1 | S. Ard | 1 |
| 1996 | Red Dog 300 | M. Martin | Ford | 155.799 | 17 | D. Jarrett | 171.996 | D. Green | 1 | C. Little | 1 |
| | All Pro 300 | M. Martin | Ford | 124.957 | 2 | B. Labonte | 174.272 | R. Hornaday | 1 | S. Marlin | 1 |
| 1995 | Red Dog 300 | C. Little | Ford | 131.707 | 7 | R. Bickle | 173.193 | D. Jarrett | 1 | M. McLaughlin | 1 |
| | All Pro 300 | M. Martin | Ford | 136.415 | 3 | B. Dotter | 172.051 | T. Leslie | 1 | J. Nemechek | 1 |
| 1994 | Champion 300 | P. Parsons | Chevrolet | 127.704 | 12 | M. Skinner | 172.480 | J. Nemechek | 1 | P. Parsons | 1 |
| | All Pro 300 | T. Labonte | Chevrolet | 134.831 | 16 | M. Martin | 176.696 | L.D. Ottinger | 1 | J. Spencer | 1 |
| 1993 | Champion 300 | M. Waltrip | Pontiac | 127.539 | 12 | T. Leslie | 172.574 | P. Parsons | 1 | Ky. Busch | 1 |
| | All Pro 300 | M. Martin | Ford | 113.960 | 5 | B. Dotter | 174.390 | L. Pearson | 1 | M. Bliss | 1 |
| 1992 | Champion 300 | J. Gordon | Ford | 127.207 | 1 | J. Gordon | 170.638 | G. Sacks | 1 | | |
| | All Pro 300 | J. Gordon | Ford | 120.954 | 1 | J. Gordon | 173.566 | M. Shepherd | 1 | | |
| 1991 | Champion 300 | D. Earnhardt | Chevrolet | 133.235 | 19 | J. Sprague | 167.167 | M. Skinner | 1 | | |
| | All Pro 300 | H. Gant | Buick | 121.937 | 33 | W. Burton | 172.574 | J. Sprague | 1 | | |
| 1990 | Champion 300 | J. Gordon | Pontiac | 132.337 | 3 | D. Trickle | 168.219 | D. Trickle | 1 | | |
| | All Pro 300 | S. Marlin | Oldsmobile | 132.272 | 32 | Trials rained out | | G. Biffle | 1 | | |
| 1989 | Champion 300 | R. Moroso | Oldsmobile | 136.450 | 4 | G. Sacks | 167.214 | C. Mears | 1 | | |
| | All Pro 300 | R. Moroso | Oldsmobile | 126.035 | 4 | M. Waltrip | 168.993 | | | | |
| 1988 | Winn-Dixie 300 | D. Jarrett | Oldsmobile | 139.969 | 6 | G. Bodine | 168.099 | | | | |
| | All Pro 300 | R. Moroso | Oldsmobile | 123.683 | 13 | H. Gant | 169.710 | | | | |
| 1987 | Winn-Dixie 300 | H. Gant | Buick | 139.643 | 16 | B. Bodine | 167.328 | | | | |
| | All Pro 300 | H. Gant | Buick | 131.868 | 1 | H. Gant | 168.940 | | | | |
| 1986 | Winn-Dixie 300 | T. Richmond | Pontiac | 139.715 | 1 | T. Richmond | 163.711 | | | | |
| | All Pro 300 | D. Earnhardt | Pontiac | 138.746 | 1 | D. Earnhardt | 161.599 | | | | |
| 1985 | Winn-Dixie 300 | T. Richmond | Pontiac | 119.284 | 1 | T. Richmond | 160.633 | | | | |
| | Miller 400* | T. Labonte | Pontiac | 140.485 | 14 | G. Bodine | 162.656 | | | | |
| 1984 | Mello Yello 300 | B. Allison | Oldsmobile | 126.198 | 8 | L. Ottinger | 162.421 | | | | |
| | Miller Time 300 | D. Waltrip | Pontiac | 123.499 | 6 | T. Richmond | 163.676 | | | | |
| 1983 | Mello Yello 300 | D. Earnhardt | Pontiac | 117.724 | 3 | M. Shepherd | 161.565 | | | | |
| | Miller Time 300 | S. Ard | Oldsmobile | 141.269 | 10 | L. Pearson | 162.235 | | | | |
| 1982 | Mello Yello 300 | H. Gant | Pontiac | 126.731 | 1 | H. Gant | 162.847 | | | | |
| | Miller 300 | D. Waltrip | Pontiac | 123.485 | 3 | P. Parsons | 162.191 | | | | |

* 400-mile race

**QUALIFYING RECORD:** Kevin Harvick, Chevrolet; 184.445 mph, May 23, 2003
**RACE RECORD:** Mark Martin, Ford; 155.996 mph, May 25, 1996

# CRAFTSMAN TRUCK SERIES

## Craftsman YEAR BY YEAR WINNERS (Lowe's)

| Year | Event | Race Winner | Car Make | Avg. Speed | Start Pos. | Pole Winner | Pole Speed | POLE WINNERS | | RACE WINNERS | |
|---|---|---|---|---|---|---|---|---|---|---|---|
| 2004 | Infineon 200 | D. Setzer | Chevrolet | 107.631 | 9 | D. Starr | 178.577 | B. Lester | 1 | T. Musgrave | 1 |
| 2003 | Hardee's 200 | T. Musgrave | Dodge | 114.768 | 8 | B. Lester | 175.593 | D. Starr | 1 | D. Setzer | 1 |

**QUALIFYING RECORD:** David Starr, Chevrolet; 178.577 mph, May 20, 2004
**RACE RECORD:** Ted Musgrave, Dodge; 114.768 mph, May 16, 2003

# MARTINSVILLE SPEEDWAY

## 2005 SCHEDULE

### NEXTEL CUP
**Event:** Advance Auto Parts 500
**Race:** No. 6 of 36
**Date:** April 10
**TV:** FOX. **Radio:** MRN

**Event:** Subway 500
**Race:** No. 32 of 36
**Date:** October 23
**TV:** NBC. **Radio:** MRN

### CRAFTSMAN TRUCK SERIES
**Event:** Kroger 250
**Race:** No. 4 of 25
**Date:** April 9
**TV:** SPEED. **Radio:** MRN

**Event:** Kroger 200
**Race:** No. 21 of 25
**Date:** October 22
**TV:** SPEED. **Radio:** MRN

Race names subject to change

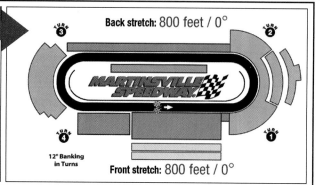

## TRACK FACTS
**Opened:** 1947
**Owner:** International Speedway Corp.
**Location:** Martinsville, Va.
**Distance:** .526 miles
**Banking in turns:** 12 degrees
**Banking in straights:** None
**Length of front stretch:** 800 feet
**Length of back stretch:** 800 feet
**Grandstand seating:** 91,000
**Tickets:** (276) 956-3151 or (877) 722-3849
**Website:** www.martinsvillespeedway.com

Back stretch: 800 feet / 0°
Front stretch: 800 feet / 0°
12° Banking in Turns

## NEXTEL CUP

### TRACK RECORDS

**Most wins:** 11—Darrell Waltrip
**Oldest winner:** Harry Gant, 51 years, 8 months, 12 days, September 22, 1991
**Youngest winner:** Richard Petty, 22 years, 9 months, 8 days, April 10, 1960
**Most lead changes:** 25—September 28, 1980
**Fewest lead changes:** 1—Three times, most recently, April 9, 1961
**Most leaders:** 14—October 15, 2001
**Fewest leaders:** 2—11 times, most recently, September 26, 1976
**Most laps led in a 200-lap race:** 193—Jim Paschal, May 16, 1954
**Most laps led in a 500-lap race:** 493—Fred Lorenzen, September 27, 1964
**Most cautions:** 18—October 1, 2000
**Fewest cautions:** 1—Three times, most recently, April 25, 1971
**Most caution laps:** 119—October 19, 2003
**Fewest caution laps:** 3—April 25, 1971
**Most on the lead lap:** 20—April 14, 2002
**Fewest on the lead lap:** 1—27 times, most recently, April 27, 1986
**Most running at the finish:** 42—April 18, 1999
**Fewest running at the finish:** 4—May 6, 1951
**Most laps led by a race winner:** 493—Fred Lorenzen, September 27, 1964
**Fewest laps led by a race winner:** 4—Richard Petty, April 25, 1971
**Closest margin of victory:** .19 seconds—Geoffrey Bodine defeated Rusty Wallace, September 28, 1992.
**Greatest margin of victory:** 1 lap, 1 second—Harry Gant defeated Butch Lindley, April 25, 1982.

### QUALIFYING AND RACE RECORDS

**QUALIFYING: Track:** Ryan Newman, Dodge; 97.043 mph, October 22, 2004 (Subway 500). **Spring race (Advance Auto Parts 500):** Tony Stewart, Pontiac; 95.275 mph, April 16, 1999. **Fall race (Subway 500):** Tony Stewart, Pontiac; 95.371 mph, September 29, 2000.
**RACE: Track:** Jeff Gordon, Chevrolet; 82.223 mph, September 22, 1996 (Hanes 500). **Spring race (Advance Auto Parts 500):** Rusty Wallace, Ford; 81.410 mph, April 21, 1996. **Fall race (Subway 500):** Ryan Newman, Dodge; 97.043 mph, October 22, 2004 (Subway 500).

## NEXTEL Cup YEAR BY YEAR WINNERS

| Year | Event | Race Winner | Car Make | Avg. Speed | Start Pos. | Car Owner | Pole Winner | Pole Speed |
|------|-------|-------------|----------|-----------|-----------|-----------|-------------|-----------|
| 2004 | Subway 500 | Ji. Johnson | Chevrolet | 66.103 | 18 | Rick Hendrick | R. Newman | 97.043 |
| | Advance Auto Prts. 500 | R. Wallace | Dodge | 68.169 | 17 | R. Penske | J. Gordon | 93.502 |
| 2003 | Subway 500 | J. Gordon | Chevrolet | 67.658 | 1 | Rick Hendrick | J. Gordon | 93.650 |
| | Virginia 500 | J. Gordon | Chevrolet | 75.557 | 1 | Rick Hendrick | J. Gordon | 94.307 |
| 2002 | Old Dominion 500 | K. Busch | Ford | 74.651 | 36 | Jack Roush | R. Newman | 92.837 |
| | Virginia 500 | B. Labonte | Pontiac | 73.951 | 15 | J. Gibbs | J. Gordon | 94.181 |
| 2001 | Old Dominion 500 | R. Craven | Ford | 75.750 | 6 | Cal Wells III | T. Bodine | 93.724 |
| m | Virginia 500 | D. Jarrett | Ford | 70.799 | 13 | Robert Yates | J. Gordon | 94.087 |
| 2000 | NAPA 500 | T. Stewart | Pontiac | 73.859 | 1 | Joe Gibbs | T. Stewart | 95.371 |
| | Goody's 500 | M. Martin | Ford | 71.161 | 21 | Jack Roush | R. Wallace | 94.827 |
| l 1999 | NAPA 500 | J. Gordon | Chevrolet | 72.347 | 5 | Rick Hendrick | J. Nemechek | 95.223 |
| | Goody's 500 | J. Andretti | Pontiac | 75.653 | 21 | Petty Eng. | T. Stewart | 95.275 |
| 1998 | NAPA 500 | R. Rudd | Ford | 73.350 | 2 | Ricky Rudd | E. Irvan | 93.600 |
| | Goody's 500 | B. Hamilton | Chevrolet | 70.709 | 1 | Morgan-McClure | B. Hamilton | 93.175 |
| 1997 | Hanes 500 | J. Burton | Ford | 73.078 | 10 | Jack Roush | W. Burton | 93.410 |
| | Goody's 500 | J. Gordon | Chevrolet | 70.347 | 4 | Rick Hendrick | K. Wallace | 93.961 |
| 1996 | Hanes 500 | J. Gordon | Chevrolet | 82.223 | 10 | Rick Hendrick | B. Hamilton | 94.120 |
| | Goody's 500 | R. Wallace | Ford | 81.410 | 5 | Roger Penske | R. Craven | 93.079 |
| 1995 | Goody's 500 | D. Earnhardt | Chevrolet | 73.946 | 2 | Richard Childress | Trials rained out | |
| k | Hanes 500 | R. Wallace | Ford | 72.145 | 15 | Roger Penske | B. Labonte | 93.308 |
| 1994 | Goody's 500 | R. Wallace | Ford | 77.139 | 7 | Roger Penske | T. Musgrave | 94.129 |
| | Hanes 500 | R. Wallace | Ford | 76.700 | 1 | Roger Penske | R. Wallace | 92.942 |
| 1993 | Goody's 500 | E. Irvan | Ford | 74.101 | 1 | Robert Yates | E. Irvan | 92.583 |
| | Hanes 500 | R. Wallace | Pontiac | 79.078 | 5 | Roger Penske | G. Bodine | 93.887 |
| 1992 | Goody's 500 | G. Bodine | Ford | 75.424 | 7 | Bud Moore | K. Petty | 92.497 |
| | Hanes 500 | M. Martin | Ford | 78.086 | 12 | Jack Roush | D. Waltrip | 92.956 |

## SPRING: ADVANCE AUTO PARTS 500

### POLE WINNERS

| | |
|---|---|
| D. Waltrip | 4 |
| J. Gordon | 4 |
| R. Rudd | 3 |
| G. Bodine | 3 |
| B. Allison | 2 |
| D. Pearson | 2 |
| F. Lorenzen | 2 |
| R. White | 2 |
| Buck Baker | 2 |
| R. Wallace | 2 |
| T. Labonte | 1 |
| L. Pond | 1 |
| N. Bonnett | 1 |
| D. Marcis | 1 |
| B. Parsons | 1 |
| C. Yarborough | 1 |
| D. Allison | 1 |
| L. Yarbrough | 1 |
| D. Dieringer | 1 |
| J. Paschal | 1 |
| Jr. Johnson | 1 |
| G. Wood | 1 |
| B. Johns | 1 |
| P. Goldsmith | 1 |
| J. Ruttman | 1 |
| T. Richmond | 1 |
| M. Shepherd | 1 |
| M. Martin | 1 |
| B. Labonte | 1 |
| R. Craven | 1 |
| K. Wallace | 1 |
| B. Hamilton | 1 |
| T. Stewart | 1 |

### RACE WINNERS

| | |
|---|---|
| R. Petty | 9 |
| D. Waltrip | 5 |
| R. Wallace | 5 |
| D. Earnhardt | 3 |
| C. Yarbrough | 3 |
| G. Bodine | 2 |
| F. Lorenzen | 2 |
| Buck Baker | 2 |
| H. Gant | 2 |
| M. Martin | 2 |
| J. Gordon | 2 |
| M. Shepherd | 1 |
| D. Pearson | 1 |
| B. Isaac | 1 |
| J. Paschal | 1 |
| Jr. Johnson | 1 |
| L. Petty | 1 |
| B. Welborn | 1 |
| R. Rudd | 1 |
| B. Hamilton | 1 |
| J. Andretti | 1 |
| D. Jarrett | 1 |
| B. Labonte | 1 |

## FALL: SUBWAY 500

### POLE WINNERS

| | |
|---|---|
| D. Waltrip | 4 |
| C. Yarborough | 4 |
| G. Bodine | 4 |
| G. Wood | 3 |
| R. Petty | 2 |
| B. Allison | 2 |
| Jr. Johnson | 2 |
| F. Lorenzen | 2 |
| M. Martin | 2 |
| E. Irvan | 2 |
| R. Newman | 2 |
| Buddy Baker | 1 |
| L. Pond | 1 |
| N. Bonnett | 1 |
| D. Pearson | 1 |
| B. Isaac | 1 |
| F. Roberts | 1 |
| E. Pagan | 1 |
| Buck Baker | 1 |
| R. Wallace | 1 |
| J. Hensley | 1 |
| R. Rudd | 1 |
| K. Petty | 1 |
| T. Musgrave | 1 |
| B. Hamilton | 1 |
| W. Burton | 1 |
| J. Nemechek | 1 |
| T. Stewart | 1 |
| T. Bodine | 1 |
| J. Gordon | 1 |

### RACE WINNERS

| | |
|---|---|
| R. Petty | 6 |
| D. Waltrip | 6 |
| D. Earnhardt | 4 |
| F. Lorenzen | 3 |
| C. Yarborough | 3 |
| J. Gordon | 3 |
| G. Bodine | 2 |
| R. Wallace | 2 |
| R. White | 2 |
| F. Roberts | 2 |
| R. Rudd | 2 |
| Buddy Baker | 1 |
| D. Marcis | 1 |
| E. Ross | 1 |
| B. Isaac | 1 |
| Jr. Johnson | 1 |
| N. Stacy | 1 |
| J. Weatherly | 1 |
| B. Welborn | 1 |
| J. Smith | 1 |
| H. Gant | 1 |
| E. Irvan | 1 |
| J. Burton | 1 |
| T. Stewart | 1 |
| R. Craven | 1 |
| Ku. Busch | 1 |
| Ji. Johnson | 1 |

## ALL MARTINSVILLE RACES

### POLE WINNERS

| | |
|---|---|
| D. Waltrip | 8 |
| G. Bodine | 7 |
| C. Yarborough | 5 |
| G. Wood | 5 |
| J. Gordon | 5 |
| B. Allison | 4 |
| F. Lorenzen | 4 |
| R. Rudd | 4 |
| D. Pearson | 3 |
| Jr. Johnson | 3 |
| Buck Baker | 3 |
| M. Martin | 3 |
| R. Wallace | 3 |
| R. White | 3 |
| R. Petty | 2 |
| B. Hamilton | 2 |
| E. Irvan | 2 |
| L. Pond | 2 |
| N. Bonnett | 2 |
| T. Stewart | 2 |
| R. Newman | 2 |
| Buddy Baker | 1 |
| D. Marcis | 1 |
| B. Parsons | 1 |
| D. Allison | 1 |
| L. Yarbrough | 1 |
| B. Isaac | 1 |
| D. Dieringer | 1 |
| J. Paschal | 1 |
| F. Roberts | 1 |
| B. Johns | 1 |
| P. Goldsmith | 1 |
| E. Pagan | 1 |
| J. Nemechek | 1 |
| C. Turner | 1 |
| J. Ruttman | 1 |
| T. Richmond | 1 |
| M. Shepherd | 1 |
| J. Hensley | 1 |
| T. Labonte | 1 |
| K. Petty | 1 |
| T. Musgrave | 1 |
| B. Labonte | 1 |
| R. Craven | 1 |
| K. Wallace | 1 |
| W. Burton | 1 |
| T. Bodine | 1 |

### RACE WINNERS

| | |
|---|---|
| R. Petty | 15 |
| D. Waltrip | 11 |
| R. Wallace | 7 |
| C. Yarborough | 6 |
| D.Earnhardt | 6 |
| J. Gordon | 5 |
| F. Lorenzen | 5 |
| G. Bodine | 4 |
| R. Rudd | 3 |
| H. Gant | 3 |
| J. Paschal | 3 |
| Jr. Johnson | 2 |
| R. White | 2 |
| Buck Baker | 2 |
| B. Welborn | 2 |
| B. Isaac | 2 |
| M. Martin | 2 |
| F. Roberts | 1 |
| M. Shepherd | 1 |
| Buddy Baker | 1 |
| D. Marcis | 1 |
| D. Pearson | 1 |
| N. Stacy | 1 |
| J. Weatherly | 1 |
| L. Petty | 1 |
| E. Ross | 1 |
| J. Smith | 1 |
| E. Irvan | 1 |
| J. Burton | 1 |
| B. Hamilton | 1 |
| J. Andretti | 1 |
| D. Jarrett | 1 |
| T. Stewart | 1 |
| R. Craven | 1 |
| Ku. Busch | 1 |
| B. Labonte | 1 |
| Ji. Johnson | 1 |

# NEXTEL Cup YEAR BY YEAR WINNERS (Martinsville, continued)

| Year | Event | Race Winner | Car Make | Avg. Speed | Start Pos. | Car Owner | Pole Winner | Pole Speed |
|---|---|---|---|---|---|---|---|---|
| 1991 | Goody's 500 | H. Gant | Oldsmobile | 74.535 | 12 | Leo Jackson | M. Martin | 93.171 |
| | Hanes 500 | D. Earnhardt | Chevrolet | 75.139 | 10 | Richard Childress | M. Martin | 91.949 |
| 1990 | Goody's 500 | G. Bodine | Ford | 76.386 | 14 | Junior Johnson | M. Martin | 91.571 |
| | Hanes 500 | G. Bodine | Ford | 77.423 | 1 | Junior Johnson | G. Bodine | 91.726 |
| 1989 | Goody's 500 | D. Waltrip | Chevrolet | 76.571 | 2 | Rick Hendrick | J. Hensley | 91.913 |
| | Pannill 500 | D. Waltrip | Chevrolet | 79.025 | 10 | Rick Hendrick | G. Bodine | 93.097 |
| 1988 | Goody's 500 | D. Waltrip | Chevrolet | 74.988 | 20 | Rick Hendrick | R. Wallace | 91.372 |
| | Pannill 500 | D. Earnhardt | Chevrolet | 74.740 | 14 | Richard Childress | R. Rudd | 91.328 |
| 1987 | Goody's 500 | D. Waltrip | Chevrolet | 76.410 | 14 | Rick Hendrick | G. Bodine | 91.218 |
| | Sovran Bank 500 | D. Earnhardt | Chevrolet | 72.808 | 4 | Richard Childress | M. Shepherd | 92.355 |
| 1986 | Goody's 500 | R. Wallace | Pontiac | 73.191 | 8 | Blue Max | G. Bodine | 90.599 |
| | Sovran Bank 500 | R. Rudd | Ford | 76.882 | 4 | Bud Moore | T. Richmond | 90.716 |
| 1985 | Goody's 500 | D. Earnhardt | Chevrolet | 70.694 | 11 | Richard Childress | G. Bodine | 90.521 |
| | Sovran Bank 500 | H. Gant | Chevrolet | 73.072 | 13 | Mach I | D. Waltrip | 90.279 |
| 1984 | Goody's 500 | D. Waltrip | Chevrolet | 75.532 | 3 | Junior Johnson | G. Bodine | 89.523 |
| | Sovran Bank 500 | G. Bodine | Chevrolet | 73.264 | 6 | Rick Hendrick | J. Ruttman | 89.426 |
| 1983 | Goody's 500 | R. Rudd | Chevrolet | 76.134 | 2 | Richard Childress | D. Waltrip | 89.342 |
| | Va. Nat'l Bank 500 | D. Waltrip | Chevrolet | 66.460 | 3 | Junior Johnson | R. Rudd | 89.910 |
| 1982 | Old Dominion 500 | D. Waltrip | Buick | 71.315 | 3 | Junior Johnson | R. Rudd | 89.132 |
| | Va. Nat'l Bank 500 | H. Gant | Buick | 75.073 | 3 | Mach I | T. Labonte | 89.988 |
| 1981 | Old Dominion 500 | D. Waltrip | Buick | 70.089 | 1 | Junior Johnson | D. Waltrip | 89.014 |
| | Virginia 500 | M. Shepherd | Pontiac | 75.019 | 12 | Cliff Stewart | R. Rudd | 89.056 |
| 1980 | Old Dominion 500 | D. Earnhardt | Chevrolet | 69.654 | 7 | Osterlund Racing | Buddy Baker | 88.500 |
| | Virginia 500 | D. Waltrip | Chevrolet | 69.049 | 1 | DiGard Rac. Co. | D. Waltrip | 88.566 |
| 1979 | Old Dominion 500 | Buddy Baker | Chevrolet | 75.119 | 7 | Ranier Racing | D. Waltrip | 82.650 |
| | Virginia 500 | R. Petty | Chevrolet | 76.562 | 2 | Petty Eng. | D. Waltrip | 87.383 |
| 1978 | Old Dominion 500 | C. Yarborough | Oldsmobile | 79.185 | 6 | Junior Johnson | L. Pond | 86.558 |
| | Virginia 500 | D. Waltrip | Chevrolet | 78.119 | 3 | DiGard Rac. Co. | L. Pond | 88.637 |
| 1977 | Old Dominion 500 | C. Yarborough | Chevrolet | 73.447 | 3 | Junior Johnson | N. Bonnett | 87.637 |
| j | Virginia 500 | C. Yarborough | Chevrolet | 77.405 | 5 | Junior Johnson | N. Bonnett | 88.923 |
| i 1976 | Old Dominion 500 | C. Yarborough | Chevrolet | 75.370 | 4 | Junior Johnson | D. Waltrip | 88.484 |
| | Virginia 500 | D. Waltrip | Chevrolet | 71.759 | 4 | DiGard Rac. Co. | D. Marcis | 86.286 |
| 1975 | Old Dominion 500 | D. Marcis | Dodge | 75.944 | 7 | Nord Krauskopf | C. Yarborough | 86.199 |
| | Virginia 500 | R. Petty | Dodge | 69.282 | 6 | Petty Eng. | B. Parsons | 85.789 |
| 1974 | Old Dominion 500 | E. Ross | Chevrolet | 66.232 | 11 | Allan Brooke | R. Petty | 84.119 |
| h | Virginia 500 | C. Yarborough | Chevrolet | 77.855 | 1 | Junior Johnson | C. Yarborough | 84.362 |
| g 1973 | Old Dominion 500 | R. Petty | Dodge | 68.631 | 6 | Petty Eng. | C. Yarborough | 85.922 |
| | Virginia 500 | D. Pearson | Mercury | 70.251 | 1 | Wood Brothers | D. Pearson | 86.369 |
| 1972 | Old Dominion 500 | R. Petty | Plymouth | 69.989 | 4 | Petty Eng. | B. Allison | 85.890 |
| | Virginia 500 | R. Petty | Plymouth | 72.657 | 3 | Petty Eng. | B. Allison | 84.163 |
| 1971 | Old Dominion 500 | B. Isaac | Dodge | 73.681 | 1 | Nord Krauskopf | B. Isaac | 83.635 |
| | Virginia 500 | R. Petty | Plymouth | 77.077 | 3 | Petty Eng. | D. Allison | 82.529 |
| 1970 | Old Dominion 500 | R. Petty | Plymouth | 72.159 | 4 | Petty Eng. | B. Allison | 82.167 |
| f | Virginia 500 | B. Isaac | Dodge | 68.512 | 2 | Nord Krauskopf | L. Yarbrough | 82.609 |
| e 1969 | Old Dominion 500 | R. Petty | Ford | 63.127 | 6 | Petty Eng. | D. Pearson | 83.197 |
| | Virginia 500 | R. Petty | Ford | 64.405 | 6 | Petty Eng. | B. Allison | 78.260 |
| 1968 | Old Dominion 500 | R. Petty | Plymouth | 72.159 | 6 | Petty Eng. | C. Yarborough | 77.279 |
| | Virginia 500 | C. Yarborough | Mercury | 66.686 | 3 | Wood Brothers | D. Pearson | 78.230 |
| 1967 | Old Dominion 500 | R. Petty | Plymouth | 69.605 | 5 | Petty Eng. | C. Yarborough | 77.386 |
| | Virginia 500 | R. Petty | Plymouth | 67.446 | 2 | Petty Eng. | D. Dieringer | 77.319 |
| 1966 | Old Dominion 500 | F. Lorenzen | Ford | 69.177 | 2 | Holman-Moody | Jr. Johnson | 75.598 |
| | Virginia 500 | J. Paschal | Plymouth | 69.156 | 1 | Tom Friedkin | J. Paschal | 76.345 |
| 1965 | Old Dominion 500 | Ju. Johnson | Ford | 67.056 | 3 | Junior Johnson | R. Petty | 74.503 |
| | Virginia 500 | F. Lorenzen | Ford | 66.765 | 2 | Holman-Moody | Jr. Johnson | 74.503 |
| 1964 | Old Dominion 500 | F. Lorenzen | Ford | 67.320 | 1 | Holman-Moody | F. Lorenzen | 74.196 |
| | Virginia 500 | F. Lorenzen | Ford | 70.098 | 1 | Holman-Moody | F. Lorenzen | 74.472 |
| 1963 | Old Dominion 500 | F. Lorenzen | Ford | 67.487 | 2 | Holman-Moody | Ju. Johnson | 73.379 |
| | Virginia 500 | R. Petty | Plymouth | 64.823 | 8 | Petty Eng. | R. White | 72.000 |
| 1962 | Old Dominion 500 | N. Stacy | Ford | 66.875 | 3 | Holman-Moody | F. Roberts | 71.513 |
| | Virginia 500 | R. Petty | Plymouth | 66.426 | 7 | Petty Eng. | F. Lorenzen | 71.287 |
| 1961 | Old Dominion 500 | J. Weatherly | Pontiac | 62.586 | 4 | Bud Moore | F. Lorenzen | 70.730 |
| | Virginia 500 | Ju. Johnson | Pontiac | 66.280 | 17 | Rex Lovette | R. White | 71.320 |
| cd | Grand Nat'l. 200 | F. Lorenzen | Ford | 68.370 | 2 | Holman-Moody | R. White | 70.280 |
| 1960 | Old Dominion 500 | R. White | Chevrolet | 60.440 | 2 | Louis Clements | G. Wood | 68.440 |
| | Virginia 500 | R. Petty | Plymouth | 63.940 | 4 | Petty Eng. | G. Wood | 69.150 |
| * 1959 | Old Dominion 500 | R. White | Chevrolet | 60.500 | 14 | Louis Clements | G. Wood | 69.471 |
| | Virginia 500 | L. Petty | Oldsmobile | 59.440 | 24 | Petty Eng. | B. Johns | 66.030 |
| *b 1958 | Old Dominion 500 | F. Roberts | Chevrolet | 64.340 | 4 | Frank Strickland | G. Wood(C) | 67.950 |
| | Virginia 500 | B. Welborn | Chevrolet | 61.160 | 20 | Bob Welborn | Buck Baker | 61.166 |
| * 1957 | Old Dominion 500 | B. Welborn(C) | Chevrolet(C) | 63.030 | 2 | Hugh Babb | E. Pagan | 65.837 |
| a | Virginia 500 | Buck Baker | Chevrolet | 57.138 | 6 | Buck Baker | P. Goldsmith | 65.693 |
| 1956 | Old Dominion 400 | J. Smith | Dodge | 61.140 | 23 | Carl Kiekhaefer | Buck Baker | 67.643 |
| | Virginia 500 | Buck Baker | Dodge | 60.950 | 1 | Carl Kiekhaefer | Buck Baker | |

### KEY

- (C) Convertible
- * Sweepstakes race, included Grand Nationals and convertibles (with regular points).
- a 220.5 miles (441 laps), accident.
- b 175 miles (350 laps), rain.
- c 74.5 miles (149 laps), rain; scheduled for 100 miles.
- d Special 100-mile points race.
- e Last year of 500-lap, 250-mile races; track remeasured at .525 of a mile and distance increased to 262.5 miles (500 laps) beginning with 1969 OD 500.
- f 197.925 miles (377 laps), rain.
- g 252 miles (480 laps), rain.
- h Race shortened by 26.25 miles, energy shortage.
- i 178.5 miles (340 laps), rain.
- j 201.6 miles (384 laps), rain.
- k 187.256 miles (356 laps), rain.
- l All pit stalls now on front straightaway.
- m Single pit road; garages added.

# CRAFTSMAN TRUCK SERIES

## Craftsman YEAR BY YEAR WINNERS (Martinsville)

| Year | Event | Race Winner | Car Make | Avg. Speed | Start Pos. | Pole Winner | Pole Speed |
|------|-------|-------------|----------|------------|------------|-------------|------------|
| 2004 | Martinsville 200 | J. McMurray | Chevrolet | 60.819 | 18 | Trials rained out | |
| | Kroger 250 | R. Crawford | Ford | 61.490 | 3 | J. Sprague | 92.375 |
| 2003 | Advance Auto Parts 200 | J. Wood | Ford | 72.069 | 2 | C. Edwards | 91.549 |
| 2003 | Advance Auto Parts 200 | D. Setzer | Chevrolet | 66.921 | 5 | T. Musgrave | 91.297 |
| 2002 | Advance Auto Parts 200 | D. Setzer | Chevrolet | 64.628 | 33 | T. Musgrave | 92.864 |
| 2001 | Advance Auto Parts 200 | S. Riggs | Dodge | 70.836 | 2 | J. Ruttman | 92.411 |
| 2000 | NAPA 250 | B. Hamilton | Dodge | 71.836 | 2 | M. Wallace | 93.070 |
| 1999 | NAPA 250 | J. Hensley | Dodge | 74.294 | 9 | M. Bliss | 94.275 |
| 1998 | NAPA 250 | J. Sauter | Chevrolet | 72.154 | 10 | G. Biffle | 91.891 |
| 1997 | Hanes 250 | R. Bickle | Chevrolet | 72.297 | 1 | R. Bickle | 92.796 |
| 1996 | Hanes 250 | M. Skinner | Chevrolet | 64.434 | 16 | B. Hamilton | 92.101 |
| 1995 | Goody's 150 | J. Ruttman | Ford | 65.072 | 2 | No trials held | |

| POLE WINNERS | | RACE WINNERS | |
|--------------|---|--------------|---|
| T. Musgrave | 2 | D. Setzer | 2 |
| R. Bickle | 1 | R. Bickle | 1 |
| G. Biffle | 1 | R. Crawford | 1 |
| M. Bliss | 1 | B. Hamilton | 1 |
| C. Edwards | 1 | J. Hensley | 1 |
| B. Hamilton | 1 | S. Riggs | 1 |
| J. Ruttman | 1 | J. Ruttman | 1 |
| M. Wallace | 1 | J. Sauter | 1 |
| J. Sprague | 1 | M. Skinner | 1 |
| | | J. Wood | 1 |
| | | J. McMurray | 1 |

**QUALIFYING RECORD:** Mike Bliss, Ford; 94.275 mph, April 16, 1999
**RACE RECORD:** Jimmy Hensley, Dodge; 74.294 mph, April 17, 1999

# MICHIGAN INTERNATIONAL SPEEDWAY

## 2005 SCHEDULE

**NEXTEL CUP**
**Event:** DHL 400
**Race:** No. 15 of 36
**Date:** June 19
**TV:** FOX. **Radio:** MRN

**Event:** GFS Marketplace 400
**Race:** No. 23 of 36
**Date:** August 21
**TV:** TNT. **Radio:** MRN

**BUSCH SERIES**
**Event:** Cabela's 250
**Race:** No. 25 of 35
**Date:** August 20
**TV:** TNT. **Radio:** MRN

**CRAFTSMAN TRUCK SERIES**
**Event:** Line-X Spray-On Bedliner 200
**Race:** No. 10 of 25
**Date:** June 18
**TV:** SPEED. **Radio:** MRN

Race names subject to change

TRACKS

## TRACK FACTS

**Opened:** 1968
**Owner:** International Speedway Corp.
**Location:** Brooklyn, Mich.
**Distance:** 2 miles
**Banking in turns:** 18 degrees
**Banking in front stretch:** 12 degrees
**Banking in back stretch:** 5 degrees
**Length of front stretch:** 3,600 feet
**Length of back stretch:** 2,242 feet
**Grandstand seating:** 136,373
**Tickets:** (800) 354-1010
**Website:** www.mispeedway.com

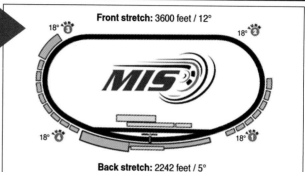

Front stretch: 3600 feet / 12°

Back stretch: 2242 feet / 5°

# NEXTEL CUP

## TRACK RECORDS

**Most wins:** 9—David Pearson
**Oldest winner:** Harry Gant, 52 years, 7 months, 6 days, August 16, 1992
**Youngest winner:** Kurt Busch, 24 years, 10 months, 11 days, June 15, 2003
**Most lead changes:** 65—August 16, 1981
**Fewest lead changes:** 7—August 12, 1984
**Most leaders:** 16—August 20, 1995
**Fewest leaders:** 5—Six times, most recently, August 12, 1984
**Most laps led in a 400-mile race:** 162—Rusty Wallace, August 20, 1989
**Most laps led in a 500-mile race:** 136—LeeRoy Yarbrough, June 15, 1969
**Most cautions:** 9—Twice, most recently, June 15, 2003
**Fewest cautions:** 0—Four times, most recently, June 11, 2000
**Most caution laps:** 63—August 24, 1975
**Fewest caution laps:** 0—Four times, most recently, June 11, 2000
**Most on the lead lap:** 32—August 18, 2002
**Fewest on the lead lap:** 2—Five times, most recently, June 15, 1975
**Most running at the finish:** 41—Three times, most recently, June 13, 1999

**Fewest running at the finish:** 14—June 16, 1974
**Most laps led by a race winner:** 162—Rusty Wallace, August 20, 1989
**Fewest laps led by a race winner:** 7—Dale Jarrett, August 18, 2002
**Closest margin of victory:** .085 seconds—Jeff Gordon defeated Ricky Rudd, June 10, 2001.
**Greatest margin of victory:** 15.71 seconds—Rusty Wallace defeated Morgan Shepherd, August 20, 1989.

## QUALIFYING AND RACE RECORDS

**QUALIFYING: Track:** Dale Earnhardt Jr., Chevrolet; 191.149 mph, August 18, 2000. **June race:** Jeff Gordon, Chevrolet; 190.865 mph, June 20, 2004. **August race:** Dale Earnhardt Jr., Chevrolet; 191.149 mph, August 18, 2000.
**RACE: Track:** Dale Jarrett, Ford; 173.997 mph, June 13, 1999. **June race:** Dale Jarrett, Ford; 173.997 mph, June 13, 1999. **August race:** Bobby Labonte, Chevrolet; 157.739 mph, August 20, 1995. **500 miles:** Cale Yarborough, Mercury; 139.254 mph, June 15, 1969. ***600 miles:** David Pearson, Ford; 115.508 mph, August 17, 1969.
*Cut to 330 miles, rain and darkness.

# NEXTEL Cup YEAR BY YEAR WINNERS (Michigan)

| Year | Event | Race Winner | Car Make | Avg. Speed | Start Pos. | Car Owner | Pole Winner | Pole Speed |
|------|-------|-------------|----------|-----------|-----------|-----------|-------------|-----------|
| 2004 | GFS Marketplace 400 | G. Biffle | Ford | 139.063 | 24 | Jack Roush | Trials rained out | |
| | DHL 400 | R. Newman | Dodge | 139.292 | 4 | Roger Penske | J. Gordon | 190.865 |
| 2003 | GFS Marketplace 400 | R. Newman | Dodge | 127.310 | 8 | Roger Penske | B. Labonte | 190.240 |
| | Sirius 400 | K. Busch | Ford | 131.219 | 4 | Jack Roush | B. Labonte | 190.365 |
| 2002 | Pepsi 400 | D. Jarrett | Ford | 140.566 | 8 | Robert Yates | D. Earnhardt Jr. | 189.668 |
| | Sirius 400 | M. Kenseth | Ford | 154.822 | 20 | Jack Roush | D. Jarrett | 189.071 |
| f 2001 | Pepsi 400 | S. Marlin | Dodge | 140.513 | 15 | Chip Ganassi | R. Craven | 188.127 |
| | Kmart 400 | J. Gordon | Chevrolet | 134.203 | 1 | Rick Hendrick | J. Gordon | 188.250 |
| 2000 | Pepsi 400 | R. Wallace | Ford | 132.597 | 10 | Roger Penske | D. Earnhardt Jr. | 191.149 |
| e | Kmart 400 | T. Stewart | Pontiac | 143.926 | 28 | Joe Gibbs | B. Labonte | 189.883 |
| 1999 | Pepsi 400 | B. Labonte | Pontiac | 144.332 | 19 | Joe Gibbs | W. Burton | 188.843 |
| b | Kmart 400 | D. Jarrett | Ford | 173.997 | 6 | Robert Yates | J. Gordon | 186.945 |
| 1998 | Pepsi 400 | J. Gordon | Chevrolet | 151.995 | 3 | Rick Hendrick | E. Irvan | 183.416 |
| | Miller 400 | M. Martin | Ford | 158.665 | 7 | Jack Roush | W. Burton | 181.561 |
| 1997 | DeVilbiss 400 | M. Martin | Ford | 126.880 | 2 | Jack Roush | J. Benson | 183.332 |
| | Miller 400 | E. Irvan | Ford | 153.338 | 20 | Robert Yates | D. Jarrett | 183.669 |
| 1996 | Goodwrench 400 | D. Jarrett | Ford | 139.792 | 11 | Robert Yates | J. Burton | 185.395 |
| | Miller 400 | R. Wallace | Ford | 166.033 | 18 | Roger Penske | B. Hamilton | 185.166 |
| 1995 | Goodwrench 400 | B. Labonte | Chevrolet | 157.739 | 1 | Joe Gibbs | B. Labonte | 184.403 |
| | Miller 400 | B. Labonte | Chevrolet | 134.141 | 19 | Joe Gibbs | J. Gordon | 186.611 |
| 1994 | Goodwrench 400 | G. Bodine | Ford | 139.914 | 5 | Geoff Bodine | G. Bodine | 181.082 |
| | Miller 400 | R. Wallace | Ford | 125.022 | 5 | Roger Penske | L. Allen | 180.641 |
| 1993 | Champion 400 | M. Martin | Ford | 144.564 | 12 | Jack Roush | K. Schrader | 180.750 |
| | Miller 400 | R. Rudd | Chevrolet | 148.484 | 2 | Rick Hendrick | B. Bodine | 175.456 |
| 1992 | Champion 400 | H. Gant | Oldsmobile | 146.056 | 24 | Leo Jackson | A. Kulwicki | 178.196 |
| | Miller 400 | Da. Allison | Ford | 152.672 | 1 | Robert Yates | Da. Allison | 176.258 |
| 1991 | Champion 400 | D. Jarrett | Ford | 142.972 | 11 | Wood Brothers | Kulwicki | 173.431 |
| | Miller 400 | Da. Allison | Ford | 160.912 | 4 | Robert Yates | M. Waltrip | 174.351 |
| 1990 | Champion 400 | M. Martin | Ford | 138.822 | 5 | Jack Roush | A. Kulwicki | 174.982 |
| | Miller 400 | D. Earnhardt | Chevrolet | 150.219 | 1 | Richard Childress | Trials rained out | |
| 1989 | Champion 400 | R. Wallace | Pontiac | 157.704 | 2 | Blue Max | G. Bodine | 175.962 |
| | Miller 400 | B. Elliott | Ford | 139.023 | 2 | Melling Racing | K. Schrader | 174.728 |
| 1988 | Champion 400 | Da. Allison | Ford | 156.863 | 4 | Ranier Racing | B. Elliott | 174.940 |
| | Miller 400 | R. Wallace | Pontiac | 153.551 | 5 | Blue Max | B. Elliott | 172.687 |
| 1987 | Champion 400 | B. Elliott | Ford | 138.648 | 3 | Melling Racing | Da. Allison | 170.705 |
| | Miller Am. 400 | D. Earnhardt | Chevrolet | 148.454 | 5 | Richard Childress | R. Wallace | 170.746 |
| 1986 | Champion 400 | B. Elliott | Ford | 135.376 | 3 | Melling Racing | B. Parsons | 171.924 |
| | Miller Am. 400 | B. Elliott | Ford | 138.851 | 8 | Melling Racing | Richmond | 172.031 |
| 1985 | Champion 400 | B. Elliott | Ford | 137.430 | 1 | Melling Racing | B. Elliott | 165.479 |
| d | Miller 400 | B. Elliott | Ford | 144.724 | 1 | Melling Racing | Trials rained out | |
| b 1984 | Champion 400 | D. Waltrip | Chevrolet | 153.863 | 7 | Junior Johnson | B. Elliott | 165.217 |
| | Miller 400 | B. Elliott | Ford | 134.705 | 1 | Melling Racing | B. Elliott | 164.339 |
| 1983 | Champion 400 | C. Yarborough | Chevrolet | 147.511 | 7 | Ranier Racing | Labonte | 162.437 |
| | Gabriel 400 | C. Yarborough | Chevrolet | 138.728 | 9 | Ranier Racing | Labonte | 161.965 |
| 1982 | Champion 400 | B. Allison | Buick | 136.454 | 10 | DiGard Rac. Co. | B. Elliott | 162.995 |
| | Gabriel 400 | C. Yarborough | Buick | 118.101 | 4 | M.C. Anderson | R. Bouchard | 162.404 |
| 1981 | Champion 400 | R. Petty | Buick | 123.457 | 7 | Petty Eng. | R. Bouchard | 161.501 |
| | Gabriel 400 | B. Allison | Buick | 130.589 | 4 | Ranier Racing | D. Waltrip | 160.471 |
| 1980 | Champion 400 | C. Yarborough | Chevrolet | 145.352 | 2 | Junior Johnson | Buddy Baker | 162.693 |
| | Gabriel 400 | B. Parsons | Chevrolet | 131.808 | 1 | M.C. Anderson | B. Parsons | 163.662 |
| 1979 | Champion 400 | R. Petty | Chevrolet | 130.376 | 5 | Petty Eng. | D. Pearson | 162.992 |
| | Gabriel 400 | Buddy Baker | Chevrolet | 135.798 | 3 | Ranier Racing | N. Bonnett | 162.371 |
| 1978 | Champion 400 | D.Pearson | Mercury | 129.566 | 1 | Wood Brothers | D.Pearson | 164.073 |
| | Gabriel 400 | C. Yarborough | Oldsmobile | 149.563 | 3 | Junior Johnson | D. Pearson | 163.936 |
| 1977 | Champion 400 | D. Waltrip | Chevrolet | 137.944 | 3 | DiGard Rac. Co. | D.Pearson | 160.346 |
| | CAM2 400 | C. Yarborough | Chevrolet | 135.033 | 4 | Junior Johnson | D.Pearson | 159.175 |
| 1976 | Champion 400 | D.Pearson | Mercury | 140.078 | 1 | Wood Brothers | D.Pearson | 160.875 |
| | CAM2 400 | D.Pearson | Mercury | 141.148 | 8 | Wood Brothers | R. Petty | 158.569 |
| 1975 | Champion 400 | R. Petty | Dodge | 107.583 | 4 | Petty Eng. | D.Pearson | 159.798 |
| | Motor State 400 | D.Pearson | Mercury | 131.398 | 3 | Wood Brothers | C. Yarborough | 158.541 |
| 1974 | Yankee 400 | D.Pearson | Mercury | 133.045 | 1 | Wood Brothers | D.Pearson | 157.946 |
| c | Motor State 400 | R. Petty | Dodge | 127.987 | 4 | Petty Eng. | D.Pearson | 156.426 |
| b 1973 | Motor State 400 | D.Pearson | Mercury | 153.485 | 2 | Wood Brothers | Buddy Baker | 158.273 |
| 1972 | Yankee 400 | D.Pearson | Mercury | 134.416 | 4 | Wood Brothers | R. Petty | 157.607 |
| | Motor State 400 | D.Pearson | Mercury | 146.639 | 3 | Wood Brothers | B. Isaac | 160.764 |
| 1971 | Yankee 400* | B. Allison | Mercury | 149.862 | 2 | Holman-Moody | P. Hamilton | 161.901 |
| | Motor State 400* | B. Allison | Mercury | 149.567 | 1 | Holman-Moody | B. Allison | 161.190 |
| 1970 | Yankee 400* | C. Glotzbach | Dodge | 147.571 | 1 | Ray Nichels | C. Glotzbach | 157.363 |
| | Motor State 400 | C. Yarborough | Mercury | 138.302 | 4 | Wood Brothers | P. Hamilton | 162.737 |
| a 1969 | Yankee 600 | D. Pearson | Ford | 115.508 | 1 | Holman-Moody | D. Pearson | 161.714 |
| | Motor State 500 | C. Yarborough | Mercury | 139.254 | 4 | Wood Brothers | D. Allison | 160.135 |

## AUGUST: GFS MARKETPLACE 400

### POLE WINNERS

| | |
|---|---|
| D. Pearson | 7 |
| B. Elliott | 4 |
| A. Kulwicki | 3 |
| G. Bodine | 2 |
| D. Earnhardt Jr. | 2 |
| B. Labonte | 2 |
| P. Hamilton | 1 |
| C. Glotzbach | 1 |
| Buddy Baker | 1 |
| R. Bouchard | 1 |
| T. Labonte | 1 |
| B. Parsons | 1 |
| Da. Allison | 1 |
| R. Petty | 1 |
| K. Schrader | 1 |
| J. Burton | 1 |
| J. Benson Jr. | 1 |
| E. Irvan | 1 |
| W. Burton | 1 |
| R. Craven | 1 |

### RACE WINNERS

| | |
|---|---|
| D. Pearson | 5 |
| M. Martin | 3 |
| R. Petty | 3 |
| B. Elliott | 3 |
| D. Jarrett | 3 |
| B. Allison | 2 |
| C. Yarborough | 2 |
| D. Waltrip | 2 |
| B. Labonte | 2 |
| R. Wallace | 2 |
| Da. Allison | 1 |
| C. Glotzbach | 1 |
| H. Gant | 1 |
| G. Bodine | 1 |
| J. Gordon | 1 |
| S. Marlin | 1 |
| Ku. Busch | 1 |
| G. Biffle | 1 |

## JUNE: SIRIUS 400

### POLE WINNERS

| | |
|---|---|
| J. Gordon | 4 |
| D. Pearson | 3 |
| B. Elliott | 2 |
| D. Jarrett | 2 |
| B. Labonte | 2 |
| C. Yarborough | 1 |
| R. Petty | 1 |
| B. Allison | 1 |
| D. Allison | 1 |
| Buddy Baker | 1 |
| B. Hamilton | 1 |
| B. Isaac | 1 |
| N. Bonnett | 1 |
| B. Parsons | 1 |
| D. Waltrip | 1 |
| R. Bouchard | 1 |
| T. Labonte | 1 |
| T. Richmond | 1 |
| R. Wallace | 1 |
| K. Schrader | 1 |
| M. Waltrip | 1 |
| Da. Allison | 1 |
| B. Bodine | 1 |
| L. Allen | 1 |
| B. Hamilton | 1 |
| W. Burton | 1 |

### RACE WINNERS

| | |
|---|---|
| C. Yarborough | 6 |
| D. Pearson | 4 |
| B. Elliott | 4 |
| R. Wallace | 2 |
| D. Earnhardt | 2 |
| Da. Allison | 2 |
| B. Allison | 2 |
| R. Newman | 2 |
| R. Petty | 1 |
| Buddy Baker | 1 |
| B. Parsons | 1 |
| R. Rudd | 1 |
| B. Labonte | 1 |
| E. Irvan | 1 |
| M. Martin | 1 |
| D. Jarrett | 1 |
| T. Stewart | 1 |
| J. Gordon | 1 |
| M. Kenseth | 1 |

## ALL MICHIGAN RACES

### POLE WINNERS

| | |
|---|---|
| D. Pearson | 10 |
| B. Elliott | 6 |
| J. Gordon | 4 |
| A. Kulwicki | 3 |
| R. Petty | 2 |
| Buddy Baker | 2 |
| R. Bouchard | 2 |
| T. Labonte | 2 |
| K. Schrader | 2 |
| G. Bodine | 2 |
| Da. Allison | 2 |
| B. Parsons | 2 |
| P. Hamilton | 2 |
| W. Burton | 2 |
| B. Labonte | 2 |
| D. Jarrett | 2 |
| D. Earnhardt Jr. | 2 |
| B. Labonte | 2 |
| C. Yarborough | 1 |
| C. Glotzbach | 1 |
| D. Allison | 1 |
| B. Isaac | 1 |
| N. Bonnett | 1 |
| D. Waltrip | 1 |
| T. Richmond | 1 |
| R. Wallace | 1 |
| B. Allison | 1 |
| M. Waltrip | 1 |
| B. Bodine | 1 |
| L. Allen | 1 |
| B. Hamilton | 1 |
| J. Burton | 1 |
| J. Benson Jr. | 1 |
| E. Irvan | 1 |
| R. Craven | 1 |

### RACE WINNERS

| | |
|---|---|
| D. Pearson | 9 |
| C. Yarborough | 8 |
| B. Elliott | 7 |
| R. Wallace | 5 |
| R. Petty | 4 |
| B. Allison | 4 |
| M. Martin | 4 |
| D. Jarrett | 4 |
| B. Labonte | 3 |
| Da. Allison | 3 |
| J. Gordon | 2 |
| D. Waltrip | 2 |
| D. Earnhardt | 2 |
| R. Newman | 2 |
| C. Glotzbach | 1 |
| Buddy Baker | 1 |
| H. Gant | 1 |
| R. Rudd | 1 |
| G. Bodine | 1 |
| B. Parsons | 1 |
| E. Irvan | 1 |
| T. Stewart | 1 |
| S. Marlin | 1 |
| M. Kenseth | 1 |
| Ku. Busch | 1 |
| G. Biffle | 1 |

## Busch YEAR BY YEAR WINNERS (Michigan)

| Year | Event | Race Winner | Car Make | Avg. Speed | Start Pos. | Pole Winner | Pole Speed | POLE WINNERS | | RACE WINNERS | |
|------|-------|-------------|----------|------------|------------|-------------|------------|--------------|---|--------------|---|
| 2004 | Cabela's 250 | Ky. Busch | Chevrolet | 122.166 | 2 | Trials rained out | | D. Blaney | 1 | T. Bodine | 2 |
| 2003 | Cabela's 250 | K. Harvick | Chevrolet | 140.850 | 5 | K. Kahne | 186.490 | J. Burton | 1 | M. Martin | 2 |
| 2002 | Cabela's 250 | M. Waltrip | Chevrolet | 135.644 | 2 | K. Lepage | 185.644 | D. Cope | 1 | J. Burton | 1 |
| 2001 | NAPAonline.com 250 | R. Newman | Ford | 139.557 | 2 | J. Spencer | 184.824 | R. Craven | 1 | D. Earnhardt Jr. | 1 |
| 2000 | NAPAonline.com 250 | T. Bodine. | Chevrolet | 162.749 | 16 | B. Jones | 184.786 | B. Elliott | 1 | B. Labonte | 1 |
| 1999 | NAPA 200 | Earnhardt Jr. | Chevrolet | 158.975 | 3 | D. Blaney | 180.054 | J. Gordon | 1 | R. Newman | 1 |
| 1998 | Pepsi 200 | J. Burton | Ford | 167.910 | 1 | J. Burton | 177.052 | D. Jarrett | 1 | J. Purvis | 1 |
| 1997 | Detroit Gasket 200 | S. Park | Chevrolet | 159.681 | 4 | H. Sadler | 175.511 | B. Jones | 1 | S. Park | 1 |
| 1996 | Detroit Gasket 200 | J. Purvis | Chevrolet | 161.038 | 27 | R. Craven | 174.965 | K. Lepage | 1 | M. Waltrip | 1 |
| 1995 | Detroit Gasket 200 | M. Martin | Ford | 169.571 | 2 | D. Jarrett | 174.199 | H. Sadler | 1 | K. Harvick | 1 |
| 1994 | Detroit Gasket 200 | B. Labonte | Chevrolet | 142.461 | 7 | D. Cope | 175.426 | J. Spencer | 1 | Ky. Busch | 1 |
| 1993 | Detroit Gasket 200 | M. Martin | Ford | 124.611 | 2 | B. Elliott | 175.447 | K. Kahne | 1 | | |
| 1992 | Detroit Gasket 200 | T. Bodine | Chevrolet | 125.414 | 12 | J. Gordon | 173.135 | | | | |

*Changed to 125 laps

**QUALIFYING RECORD:** Kasey Kahne, Ford; 186.490, August 15, 2003
**RACE RECORD:** Mark Martin, Ford; 169.571 mph, August 19, 1995

## Craftsman YEAR BY YEAR WINNERS (Michigan)

| Year | Event | Race Winner | Car Make | Avg. Speed | Start Pos. | Pole Winner | Pole Speed | POLE WINNERS | | RACE WINNERS | |
|------|-------|-------------|----------|------------|------------|-------------|------------|--------------|---|--------------|---|
| 2004 | Line-X S-O. Tr. Bed.. | T. Kvapil | Toyota | 125.479 | 8 | Trials rained out | | S. Compton | 1 | G. Biffle | 2 |
| 2003 | Sears 200 | B. Gaughan | Dodge | 154.044 | 6 | J. Leffler | 178.037 | J. McMurray | 1 | R. Pressley | 1 |
| 2002 | Michigan 200 | R. Pressley | Dodge | 142.208 | 8 | Trials rained out | | J. Leffler | 1 | B. Gaughan | 1 |
| 2000 | Michigan 200 | G. Biffle | Ford | 138.408 | 2 | J. McMurray | 177.144 | | | T. Kvapil | 1 |
| 1999 | goracing.com200 | G. Biffle | Ford | 121.889 | 11 | S. Compton | 175.717 | | | | |

**QUALIFYING RECORD:** Jason Leffler, Dodge; 178.037 mph, July 25, 2003
**RACE RECORD:** Brendan Gaughan, Dodge; 154.044 mph, July 26, 2003

# NEW HAMPSHIRE INTERNATIONAL SPEEDWAY

## 2005 SCHEDULE

**NEXTEL CUP**
**Event:** Siemens 300
**Race:** No. 19 of 36
**Date:** July 17
**TV:** TNT. **Radio:** MRN

**Event:** Sylvania 300
**Race:** No. 27 of 36
**Date:** September 18
**TV:** TNT. **Radio:** MRN

**BUSCH SERIES**
**Event:** Siemens 200
**Race:** No. 20 of 35
**Date:** July 16
**TV:** TNT. **Radio:** MRN

**CRAFTSMAN TRUCK SERIES**
**Event:** Sylvania 200
**Race:** No. 19 of 25
**Date:** September 17
**TV:** SPEED. **Radio:** MRN

Race names subject to change

### TRACK FACTS

**Opened:** June 5, 1990
**Owner:** Bob Bahre
**Location:** Loudon, N.H.
**Distance:** 1.058 miles
**Banking in turns:** 12 degrees
**Banking in straights:** 2 degrees
**Length of front stretch:** 1,500 feet
**Length of back stretch:** 1,500 feet
**Grandstand seating:** 91,000
**Tickets:** 603-783-4931
**Website:** www.nhis.com

Back stretch: 1,500 feet / 2°
12° Banking in Turns
Front stretch: 1,500 feet / 2°

## NEXTEL CUP

### TRACK RECORDS

**Most wins:** 4—Jeff Burton
**Oldest winner:** Dale Jarrett, 44 years, 7 months, 26 days, July 22, 2001
**Youngest winner:** Jeff Gordon, 23 years, 11 months, 5 days, July 9, 1995
**Most lead changes:** 23—July 14, 1996
**Fewest lead changes:** 1—July 17, 2000
**Most leaders:** 15—July 14, 1996
**Fewest leaders:** 1—July 17, 2000
**Most cautions:** 17—July 10, 1994
**Fewest cautions:** 2—July 13, 1997
**Most caution laps:** 78—July 10, 1994

**Fewest caution laps:** 10—July 13, 1997
**Most on the lead lap:** 30—July 21, 2002
**Fewest on the lead lap:** 7—July 11,19 93
**Most running at the finish:** 39—Three times, most recently, July 20, 2003
**Fewest running at the finish:** 30—Twice, most recently, September 17, 2000
**Most laps led by a race winner:** 300—Jeff Burton, September 17, 2000
**Fewest laps led by a race winner:** 2—Jeff Burton, July 11, 1999
**Closest margin of victory:** .607 seconds—Kurt Busch defeated Jeff Gordon, July 25, 2004.
**Greatest margin of victory:** 6.240 seconds—Jimmie Johnson defeated Ricky Rudd, September 14, 2003.

# QUALIFYING AND RACE RECORDS

**QUALIFYING: Track:** Ryan Newman, Ford; 133.357 mph, September 12, 2003 (Sylvania 300).
**Summer race (Siemens 300):** Ryan Newman, Ford; 132.360 mph, July 23, 2004.
**Fall race (Sylvania 300):** Ryan Newman, Ford; 133.357 mph, September 12, 2003.
**RACE: Track:** Jeff Burton, Ford; 117.134 mph, July 13, 1997 (Jiffy Lube 300).
**Summer race (Siemens 300):** Jeff Burton, Ford; 117.134 mph, July 13, 1997.
**Fall race (Sylvania 300):** Jeff Gordon, Chevrolet; 112.078 mph, August 30, 1998.

## NEXTEL Cup YEAR BY YEAR WINNERS (New Hampshire)

| Year | Event | Race Winner | Car Make | Avg. Speed | Start Pos. | Car Owner | Pole Winner | Pole Speed |
|---|---|---|---|---|---|---|---|---|
| 2004 | Sylvania 300 | Ku. Busch | Ford | 109.753 | 7 | Jack Roush | Trials rained out | |
| | Siemens 300 | Ku. Busch | Ford | 97.862 | 32 | Jack Roush | R. Newman | 132.360 |
| 2003 | Sylvania 500 | J. Johnson | Chevrolet | 106.580 | 8 | Rick Hendrick | R. Newman | 133.357 |
| | New England 300 | J. Johnson | Chevrolet | 96.924 | 6 | Rick Hendrick | Trials rained out | |
| 2002 | New Hampshire 300 | R. Newman | Ford | 105.081 | 1 | Roger Penske | R. Newman | 132.241 |
| | New England 300 | W. Burton | Dodge | 92.342 | 31 | Bill Davis | B. Elliott | 131.469 |
| b 2001 | New Hampshire 300 | R. Gordon | Chevrolet | 103.594 | 31 | Richard Childress | Canceled | |
| | New England 300 | D. Jarrett | Ford | 102.131 | 9 | Robert Yates | J. Gordon | 131.770 |
| 2000 | Dura-Lube/Kmart 300 | J. Burton | Ford | 102.003 | 2 | Jack Roush | B. Labonte | 127.632 |
| a | thatlook.com 300 | T. Stewart | Pontiac | 103.145 | 6 | Joe Gibbs | R. Wallace | 132.089 |
| 1999 | Dura-Lube/Kmart 300 | J. Nemechek | Chevrolet | 100.673 | 11 | Felix Sebates | R. Wallace | 129.820 |
| | Jiffy Lube 300 | J. Burton | Ford | 101.876 | 38 | Jack Roush | J. Gordon | 131.171 |
| 1998 | CMT 300 | J. Gordon | Chevrolet | 112.078 | 1 | Rick Hendrick | J. Gordon | 129.033 |
| | Jiffy Lube 300 | J. Burton | Ford | 102.996 | 5 | Jack Roush | R. Craven | 128.394 |
| 1997 | CMT 300 | J. Gordon | Chevrolet | 100.364 | 13 | Rick Hendrick | K. Schrader | 129.182 |
| | Jiffy Lube 300 | J. Burton | Ford | 117.134 | 15 | Jack Roush | K. Schrader | 129.423 |
| 1996 | Jiffy Lube 300 | E. Irvan | Ford | 98.930 | 6 | Robert Yates | R. Craven | 129.379 |
| 1995 | Slick 50 300 | J. Gordon | Chevrolet | 107.029 | 21 | Rick Hendrick | M. Martin | 128.815 |
| 1994 | Slick 50 300 | R. Rudd | Ford | 87.599 | 3 | Ricky Rudd | E. Irvan | 127.197 |
| 1993 | Slick 50 300 | R. Wallace | Pontiac | 105.947 | 33 | Roger Penske | M. Martin | 126.871 |

**KEY**
a — Race shortened to 273 laps, rain.
b — Qualifying was called off after the terrorist attacks, then the race was rescheduled for November 23, 2001.

### FALL: NEW HAMPSHIRE 300

**POLE WINNERS**
| | |
|---|---|
| R. Newman | 2 |
| K. Schrader | 1 |
| J. Gordon | 1 |
| R. Wallace | 1 |
| B. Labonte | 1 |

**RACE WINNERS**
| | |
|---|---|
| J. Gordon | 2 |
| J. Nemechek | 1 |
| J. Burton | 1 |
| R. Gordon | 1 |
| R. Newman | 1 |
| Ji. Johnson | 1 |
| Ku. Busch | 1 |

### SUMMER: NEW ENGLAND 300

**POLE WINNERS**
| | |
|---|---|
| M. Martin | 2 |
| R. Craven | 2 |
| J. Gordon | 2 |
| E. Irvan | 1 |
| K. Schrader | 1 |
| R. Wallace | 1 |
| B. Elliott | 1 |
| R. Newman | 1 |

**RACE WINNERS**
| | |
|---|---|
| J. Burton | 3 |
| R. Wallace | 1 |
| R. Rudd | 1 |
| J. Gordon | 1 |
| E. Irvan | 1 |
| T. Stewart | 1 |
| D. Jarrett | 1 |
| W. Burton | 1 |
| Ji. Johnson | 1 |
| Ku. Busch | 1 |

### ALL NEW HAMPSHIRE RACES

**POLE WINNERS**
| | |
|---|---|
| J. Gordon | 3 |
| R. Newman | 3 |
| M. Martin | 2 |
| K. Schrader | 2 |
| R. Craven | 2 |
| R. Wallace | 2 |
| B. Labonte | 1 |
| E. Irvan | 1 |
| B. Elliott | 1 |

**RACE WINNERS**
| | |
|---|---|
| J. Burton | 4 |
| J. Gordon | 3 |
| Ji. Johnson | 2 |
| Ku. Busch | 2 |
| R. Wallace | 1 |
| E. Irvan | 1 |
| J. Nemechek | 1 |
| T. Stewart | 1 |
| R. Rudd | 1 |
| D. Jarrett | 1 |
| R. Gordon | 1 |
| W. Burton | 1 |
| R. Newman | 1 |

---

# BUSCH SERIES

## Busch YEAR BY YEAR WINNERS (New Hampshire)

| Year | Event | Race Winner | Car Make | Avg. Speed | Start Pos. | Pole Winner | Pole Speed |
|---|---|---|---|---|---|---|---|
| 2004 | Siemens 200 | M. Kenseth | Ford | 93.709 | 21 | J. McMurray | 130.007 |
| 2003 | New England 200 | D. Green | Pontiac | 108.005 | 37 | Trials rained out | |
| 2002 | Busch 200 | B. Hamilton Jr. | Ford | 110.368 | 2 | S. Hmiel | 129.406 |
| 2001 | CVS Pharmacy 200 | J. Keller | Ford | 108.714 | 4 | K. Harvick | 130.716 |
| 2000 | Busch 200 | T. Fedewa | Chevrolet | 89.366 | 1 | T. Fedewa | 130.247 |
| 1999 | NASCAR Busch Series 200 | E. Sawyer | Ford | 103.324 | 2 | J. Green | 128.637 |
| 1998 | Gumout 200 | B. Jones | Pontiac | 100.829 | 26 | J. Bessey | 127.701 |
| 1997 | U.S. Cellular 200 | M. McLaughlin | Chevrolet | 76.752 | 12 | Trials rained out | |
| 1996* | Stanley 200 | R. LaJoie | Chevrolet | 96.953 | 2 | Trials rained out | |
| 1995 | NE Chevy 250 | C. Little | Ford | 104.972 | 9 | M. McLaughlin | 124.903 |
| 1994 | NE Chevy 250 | D. Cope | Ford | 88.527 | 14 | B. Labonte | 124.871 |
| 1993 | NE Chevy 250 | R. Pressley | Chevrolet | 89.560 | 3 | J. Nemechek | 124.875 |
| 1992 | Budweiser 300 | J. Burton | Oldsmobile | 95.907 | 23 | K. Wallace | 122.532 |
| | NE Chevy 250 | J. Nemechek | Chevrolet | 94.897 | 10 | E. Irvan | 122.422 |
| 1991 | Budweiser 300 | K. Wallace | Pontiac | 109.093 | 3 | J. Hensley | 128.470 |
| | NE Chevy 250 | R. Craven | Chevrolet | 90.832 | 1 | R. Craven | 121.800 |
| 1990 | Budweiser 300 | T. Ellis | Buick | 85.797 | 4 | J. Hensley | 123.410 |
| | NE Chevy 250 | R. Mast | Buick | 94.405 | 18 | R. Craven | 122.085 |

*Race shortened to 200 laps

**POLE WINNERS**
| | |
|---|---|
| R. Craven | 2 |
| J. Hensley | 2 |
| J.Bessey | 1 |
| T. Fedewa | 1 |
| J.Green | 1 |
| K. Harvick | 1 |
| S. Hmiel | 1 |
| E. Irvan | 1 |
| B. Labonte | 1 |
| M. McLaughlin | 1 |
| J. Nemechek | 1 |
| K. Wallace | 1 |
| J. McMurray | 1 |
| J. Burton | 1 |

**RACE WINNERS**
| | |
|---|---|
| D. Cope | 1 |
| R. Craven | 1 |
| T. Ellis | 1 |
| T. Fedewa | 1 |
| B. Hamilton Jr. | 1 |
| Buckshot Jones | 1 |
| J. Keller | 1 |
| R. LaJoie | 1 |
| C. Little | 1 |
| R. Mast | 1 |
| M. McLaughlin | 1 |
| J. Nemechek | 1 |
| R. Pressley | 1 |
| E. Sawyer | 1 |
| K. Wallace | 1 |
| D. Green | 1 |
| M. Kenseth | 1 |

**QUALIFYING RECORD:** Kevin Harvick, Chevrolet; 130.716 mph, May 11, 2001
**RACE RECORD:** Bobby Hamilton Jr., Ford; 110.368 mph, May 11, 2002

---

# CRAFTSMAN TRUCK SERIES

## Craftsman YEAR BY YEAR WINNERS (New Hampshire)

| Year | Event | Race Winner | Car Make | Avg. Speed | Start Pos. | Pole Winner | Pole Speed |
|---|---|---|---|---|---|---|---|
| 2004 | New Hampshire 200 | T. Kvapil | Toyota | 89.482 | 3 | J. Sprague | 128.515 |
| 2003 | New Hampshire 200 | J. Spencer | Dodge | 103.867 | 1 | J. Spencer | 127.346 |
| 2002 | New England 200 | T. Cook | Ford | 103.549 | 2 | J. Leffler | 128.424 |
| 2001 | New England 200 | J. Sprague | Chevrolet | 109.244 | 1 | J. Sprague | 128.091 |
| 2000 | thatlook.com 200 | K. Busch | Ford | 98.491 | 5 | J. Ruttman | 127.885 |
| 1999 | Pennzoil Tripleheader | D. Setzer | Dodge | 101.810 | 10 | S. Compton | 126.745 |
| 1998 | Pennzoil Tripleheader | A. Houston | Chevrolet | 104.222 | 7 | M. Wallace | 126.994 |
| 1997 | Pennzoil Tripleheader | J. Sauter | Chevrolet | 97.138 | 26 | J. Sprague | 126.985 |
| 1996 | Pennzoil Tripleheader | R. Hornaday Jr. | Chevrolet | 97.129 | 8 | M. Skinner | 124.891 |

**POLE WINNERS**
| | |
|---|---|
| J. Sprague | 3 |
| S. Compton | 1 |
| J. Leffler | 1 |
| J. Ruttman | 1 |
| M. Skinner | 1 |
| M. Wallace | 1 |
| J. Spencer | 1 |

**RACE WINNERS**
| | |
|---|---|
| K. Busch | 1 |
| T. Cook | 1 |
| R. Hornaday Jr. | 1 |
| A. Houston | 1 |
| J. Sauter | 1 |
| D. Setzer | 1 |
| J. Sprague | 1 |
| J. Spencer | 1 |
| T. Kvapil | 1 |

**QUALIFYING RECORD:** Jack Sprague, Chevrolet; 128.515 mph, September 17, 2004
**RACE RECORD:** Jack Sprague, Chevrolet; 109.244 mph, July 21, 2001

# PHOENIX INTERNATIONAL SPEEDWAY

## 2005 SCHEDULE

**NEXTEL CUP**
**Event:** Arizona 500*
**Race:** No. 8 of 36
**Date:** April 23
**TV:** FX. **Radio:** MRN
*Inaugural event

**Event:** Checker Auto Parts 500
**Race:** No. 35 of 36
**Date:** November 13
**TV:** NBC. **Radio:** MRN

**BUSCH SERIES**
**Event:** Arizona 200
Race No. 9 of 35
**Date:** Arpil 22
**TV:** FX. **Radio:** MRN

**Event:** Bashas' Supermarkets 200
Race No. 34 of 35
**Date:** November 12
**TV:** NBC. **Radio:** MRN

**CRAFTSMAN TRUCK SERIES**
**Event:** Chevy Silverado 150
**Race:** No. 24 of 25
**Date:** November 11
**TV:** SPEED. **Radio:** MRN

Race names subject to change

**TRACKS**

### TRACK FACTS
**Opened:** 1964
**Owner:** International Speeeedway Corp.
**Location:** Avondale, Ariz.
**Distance:** 1 mile
**Banking in Turns 1-2:** 11 degrees
**Banking in Turns 3-4:** 9 degrees
**Banking in straights:** None
**Length of front stretch:** 1,179 feet
**Length of back stretch:** 1,551 feet
**Grandstand seating:** 76,812
**Tickets:** (602) 252-2227
**Website:** www.phoenixintlraceway.com

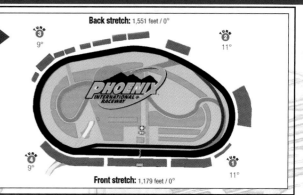

Back stretch: 1,551 feet / 0°
Turn 3 — 9°
Turn 2 — 11°
Turn 4 — 9°
Turn 1 — 11°
Front stretch: 1,179 feet / 0°

## NEXTEL CUP

### TRACK RECORDS

**Most wins:** 2—Jeff Burton and Davey Allison
**Oldest winner:** Rusty Wallace, 42 years, 2 months, 11 days, October 25, 1998
**Youngest winner:** Tony Stewart, 28 years, 5 months, 18 days, November 7, 1999
**Most lead changes:** 23—November 5, 2000
**Fewest lead changes:** 1—November 4, 1990
**Most leaders:** 16—October 29, 1995
**Fewest leaders:** 2—November 4, 1990
**Most cautions:** 10—Twice, most recently, November 2, 2003
**Fewest cautions:** 2—November 7, 1999
**Most caution laps:** 66—November 2, 2003
**Fewest caution laps:** 10—November 7, 1999
**Most on the lead lap:** 29—November 2, 2003
**Fewest on the lead lap:** 3—October 30, 1994

**Most running at the finish:** 41—Twice, most recently, November 7, 1999
**Fewest running at the finish:** 27—November 5, 1989
**Most laps led by a race winner:** 262—Dale Earnhardt, November 4, 1990
**Fewest laps led by a race winner:** 30—Davey Allison, November 1, 1992
**Closest margin of victory:** 0.17 seconds—Mark Martin defeated Ernie Irvan, October 31, 1993.
**Greatest margin of victory:** 11.44 seconds—Davey Allison defeated Darrell Waltrip, November 3, 1991.

### QUALIFYING AND RACE RECORDS

**QUALIFYING:** Ryan Newman, Dodge; 135.854 mph, November 5, 2004.
**RACE: (312 miles):** Tony Stewart, Pontiac; 118.132 mph, November 7, 1999.

### NEXTEL Cup YEAR BY YEAR WINNERS

| Year | Event | Race Winner | Car Make | Avg. Speed | Start Pos. | Car Owner | Pole Winner | Pole Speed |
|---|---|---|---|---|---|---|---|---|
| 2004 | Checker Auto Parts 500 | D. Earnhardt. Jr. | Chevrolet | 94.848 | 14 | Dale Earnhardt, Inc. | R. Newman | 135.854 |
| 2003 | Checker Auto Parts 500 | D. Earnhardt. Jr. | Chevrolet | 93.984 | 11 | Dale Earnhardt, Inc. | R. Newman | 133.675 |
| 2002 | Checker Auto Parts 500 | M. Kenseth | Ford | 113.857 | 28 | Jack Roush | R. Newman | 132.655 |
| 2001 | Checker Auto Parts 500 | J. Burton | Ford | 102.613 | 3 | Jack Roush | C. Atwood | 131.296 |
| 2000 | Checker/Dura-Lube 500 | J. Burton | Ford | 105.041 | 2 | Jack Roush | R. Wallace | 134.178 |
| 1999 | Dura-Lube 500 | T. Stewart | Pontiac | 118.132 | 11 | Joe Gibbs | J. Andretti | 132.670 |
| a1998 | Dura-Lube 500 | R. Wallace | Ford | 108.211 | 6 | Roger Penske | K. Schrader | 131.234 |
| 1997 | Dura-Lube 500 | D. Jarrett | Ford | 110.824 | 9 | Robert Yates | B. Hamilton | 130.933 |
| 1996 | Dura-Lube 500 | B. Hamilton | Pontiac | 109.709 | 17 | Petty Enterprises | B. Labonte | 131.076 |
| 1995 | Dura-Lube 500 | R. Rudd | Ford | 102.128 | 29 | Ricky Rudd | B. Elliott | 130.020 |
| 1994 | Slick 50 500 | T. Labonte | Chevrolet | 107.463 | 19 | Rick Hendrick | S. Marlin | 129.833 |
| 1993 | Slick 50 500 | M. Martin | Ford | 100.375 | 3 | Jack Roush | B. Elliott | 129.482 |
| 1992 | Pyroil 500 | Da. Allison | Ford | 103.885 | 12 | Robert Yates | R. Wallace | 128.141 |
| 1991 | Pyroil 500 | Da. Allison | Ford | 95.746 | 13 | Robert Yates | B. Bodine | 127.589 |
| 1990 | Checker 500 | D. Earnhardt | Chevrolet | 96.786 | 3 | Richard Childress | R. Wallace | 124.443 |
| 1989 | Autoworks 500 | B. Elliott | Ford | 105.683 | 13 | Melling Racing | K. Schrader | 124.645 |
| 1988 | Checker 500 | A. Kulwicki | Ford | 90.457 | 21 | Alan Kulwicki | G. Bodine | 123.203 |

a 257 miles, rain

**ALL PHOENIX RACES**

| POLE WINNERS | | RACE WINNERS | |
|---|---|---|---|
| R. Wallace | 3 | J. Burton | 2 |
| R. Newman | 3 | Da. Allison | 2 |
| G. Bodine | 2 | D. Earnhardt Jr. | 2 |
| B. Elliott | 2 | A. Kulwicki | 1 |
| K. Schrader | 2 | B. Elliott | 1 |
| S. Marlin | 1 | D. Earnhardt | 1 |
| B. Labonte | 1 | M. Martin | 1 |
| B. Hamilton | 1 | T. Labonte | 1 |
| J. Andretti | 1 | B. Hamilton | 1 |
| C. Atwood | 1 | R. Rudd | 1 |
| | | D. Jarrett | 1 |
| | | R. Wallace | 1 |
| | | T. Stewart | 1 |
| | | M. Kenseth | 1 |

## BUSCH SERIES

### Busch YEAR BY YEAR WINNERS

| Year | Event | Race Winner | Car Make | Avg. Speed | Start Pos. | Pole Winner | Pole Speed |
|---|---|---|---|---|---|---|---|
| 2004 | Bashas' Supermarkets 200 | J. McMurray | Dodge | 96.031 | 3 | Ky. Busch | 133.819 |
| 2003 | Bashas' Supermarkets 200 | B. Hamilton Jr. | Ford | 96.734 | 4 | K. Harvick | 132.930 |
| 2002 | Bashas' Supermarkets 200 | S. Wimmer | Pontiac | 96.709 | 18 | G. Biffle | 132.193 |
| 2001 | Outback Steakhouse 200 | G. Biffle | Ford | 99.834 | 4 | J. Spencer | 131.339 |
| 2000 | Outback Steakhouse 200 | J. Burton | Ford | 115.145 | 3 | J. Leffler | 130.957 |
| 1999 | Outback Steakhouse 200 | J. Gordon | Chevrolet | 115.053 | 3 | K. Schrader | 129.580 |

| POLE WINNERS | | RACE WINNERS | |
|---|---|---|---|
| H. Gant | 3 | G. Biffle | 1 |
| G. Biffle | 1 | J. Burton | 1 |
| J. Leffler | 1 | J. Gordon | 1 |
| K. Schrader | 1 | S. Wimmer | 1 |
| J. Spencer | 1 | B. Hamilton Jr. | 1 |
| K. Harvick | 1 | Ky. Busch | 1 |
| J. McMurray | 1 | | |

**QUALIFYING RECORD:** Kyle Busch, Chevrolet; 133.819 mph, November 4, 2004
**RACE RECORD:** Jeff Burton, Pontiac; 115.145 mph, November 4, 2000

# CRAFTSMAN TRUCK SERIES

## Craftsman YEAR BY YEAR WINNERS (Phoenix)

| Year | Event | Race Winner | Car Make | Avg. Speed | Start Pos. | Pole Winner | Pole Speed | POLE WINNERS | | RACE WINNERS | |
|------|-------|-------------|----------|-----------|-----------|-------------|-----------|--------------|---|--------------|---|
| 2004 | Chevy Silverado 150 | D. Starr | Chevrolet | 90.756 | 5 | J. Sprague | 131.186 | M. Bliss | 2 | J. Sprague | 3 |
| 2003 | Chevy Silverado 150 | K. Harvick | Chevrolet | 107.527 | 2 | T. Musgrave | 129.427 | S. Compton | 2 | R. Hornaday Jr. | 2 |
| 2002 | Chevy Silverado 150 | K. Harvick | Chevrolet | 108.014 | 3 | R. Crawford | 128.329 | R. Crawford | 1 | J. Ruttman | 2 |
| 2001 | Chevy Silverado 150 | G. Biffle | Ford | 92.726 | 11 | S. Compton | 127.700 | R. Hornaday Jr. | 1 | M. Skinner | 2 |
| 2000 | Chevy Trucks NASCAR 150 | J. Ruttman | Dodge | 99.797 | 1 | J. Ruttman | 129.204 | J. Ruttman | 1 | K. Harvick | 2 |
| 1999 | Chevy Trucks NASCAR 150 | R. Hornaday Jr. | Chevrolet | 95.137 | 5 | J. Sprague | 128.402 | M. Skinner | 1 | G. Biffle | 1 |
| 1998 | Chevy Trucks Desert Star | R. Hornaday Jr. | Chevrolet | 101.714 | 4 | S. Compton | 127.596 | T. Musgrave | 1 | M. Bliss | 1 |
| 1998 | GM Goodwrench 300 | M. Bliss | Ford | 103.669 | 1 | M. Bliss | 127.155 | J. Sprague | 1 | D. Starr | 1 |
| 1997 | Chevy Trucks Desert Star | J. Sprague | Chevrolet | 103.053 | 1 | J. Sprague | 121.236 | | | | |
| 1997 | GM Goodwrench 300 | J. Ruttman | Ford | 103.942 | 7 | M. Bliss | 127.741 | | | | |
| 1996 | Chevrolet Desert Star Cl. | J. Sprague | Chevrolet | 84.780 | 2 | M. Skinner | 125.257 | | | | |
| 1996 | GM Goodwrench 300 | J. Sprague | Chevrolet | 95.289 | 1 | J. Sprague | 126.957 | | | | |
| 1995 | Skoal Copper World | M. Skinner | Chevrolet | 87.565 | 16 | R. Hornaday Jr. | 123.665 | | | | |
| 1995 | GM Goodwrench 200 | M. Skinner | Chevrolet | 91.102 | 3 | J. Sprague | 124.378 | | | | |

**QUALIFYING RECORD:** Jack Sprague, Chevrolet; 131.186 mph, November 3, 2004
**RACE RECORD:** Kevin Harvick, Chevrolet; 108.014 mph, November 8, 2002

# POCONO RACEWAY

**TRACHS**

## 2005 SCHEDULE

### NEXTEL CUP

**Event:** Pocono 500
**Race:** No. 14 of 36
**Date:** June 12
**TV:** FOX. **Radio:** MRN

**Event:** Pennsylvania 500
**Race:** No. 20 of 36
**Date:** July 24
**TV:** TNT. **Radio:** MRN

Race names subject to change

## TRACK FACTS

**Date Opened:** October 20, 1968
**Owner:** Pocono Raceway, Inc.
**Location:** Long Pond, Pa.
**Distance:** 2.5 miles
**Banking in Turn 1:** 14 degrees
**Banking in Turn 2:** 8 degrees
**Banking in Turn 3:** 6 degrees
**Length of front stretch:** 3,740 feet
**Length of short stretch:** 1,780 feet
**Length of back stretch:** 3,055 feet
**Grandstand seating:** 70,000
**Tickets:** (800) 722-3939
**Website:** www.poconoraceway.com

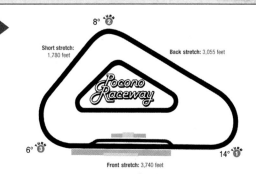

# NEXTEL CUP

## TRACK RECORDS

**Most wins:** 5—Bill Elliott
**Oldest winner:** Harry Gant, 50 years, 5 months, 7 days, June 17,1990
**Youngest winner:** Jeff Gordon, 24 years, 10 months, 12 days, June 16, 1996
**Most lead changes:** 56—July 30, 1979
**Fewest lead changes:** 9—July 26, 1998
**Most leaders:** 16—Twice, most recently, June 8, 2003
**Fewest leaders:** 4—Twice, most recently, June 9, 1985
**Most cautions:** 13—June 17, 1990
**Fewest cautions:** 1—July 30, 1978
**Most caution laps:** 53—June 8, 1986
**Fewest caution laps:** 3—July 30, 1978
**Most on the lead lap:** 26—July 28, 2002
**Fewest on the lead lap:** 2—Twice, most recently, June 6, 1982
**Most running at the finish:** 39—July 29, 2001
**Fewest running at the finish:** 18—July 25, 1982
**Most laps led by a race winner:** 164—Jeff Gordon, July 26, 1998

**Fewest laps led by a race winner:** 4—Bobby Labonte, July 29, 2001
**Closest margin of victory:** 0.02 seconds—Bill Elliott defeated Harry Gant June 09, 1985.
**Greatest margin of victory:** 24 seconds—Richard Petty defeated Buddy Baker, August 1, 1976.

## QUALIFYING AND RACE RECORDS

**QUALIFYING: Track:** Kasey Kahne, Dodge; 172.533 mph, June 11, 2004 (Pocono 500). **Spring race (Pocono 500):** Kasey Kahne, Dodge; 172.533 mph, June 11, 2004.
**Fall race (Pennsylvania 500):** Tony Stewart, Pontiac; 172.391 mph, July 21, 2000.
**RACE: Track:** Rusty Wallace, Ford; 144.892 mph, July 21, 1996 (Miller Genuine Draft 500). **Spring race (Pocono 500):** Alan Kulwicki, Ford; 144.023 mph, June 14, 1992. **Fall race (Pennsylvania 500):** Rusty Wallace, Ford; 144.892 mph, July 21, 1996.

## POLE WINNERS — SPRING POCONO 500

| Driver | Wins |
|---|---|
| K. Schrader | 3 |
| R. Wallace | 3 |
| J. Gordon | 2 |
| M. Martin | 1 |
| E. Irvan | 1 |
| H. Gant | 1 |
| T. Labonte | 1 |
| G. Bodine | 1 |
| B. Elliott | 1 |
| D. Waltrip | 1 |
| D. Pearson | 1 |
| A. Kulwicki | 1 |
| B. Hamilton | 1 |
| S. Marlin | 1 |
| R. Rudd | 1 |
| Ji. Johnson | 1 |
| K. Kahne | 1 |

## RACE WINNERS — SPRING POCONO 500

| Driver | Wins |
|---|---|
| J. Gordon | 2 |
| B. Allison | 2 |
| T. Richmond | 2 |
| T. Labonte | 2 |
| J. Mayfield | 2 |
| H. Gant | 1 |
| D. Waltrip | 1 |
| G. Bodine | 1 |
| B. Elliott | 1 |
| C. Yarborough | 1 |
| A. Kulwicki | 1 |
| R. Wallace | 1 |
| B. Labonte | 1 |
| K. Petty | 1 |
| R. Rudd | 1 |
| D. Jarrett | 1 |
| T. Stewart | 1 |
| Ji. Johnson | 1 |

## POLE WINNERS — FALL PENNSYLVANIA 500

| Driver | Wins |
|---|---|
| B. Elliott | 4 |
| C. Yarborough | 3 |
| D. Waltrip | 2 |
| K. Schrader | 2 |
| H. Gant | 2 |
| T. Richmond | 2 |
| M. Martin | 2 |
| M. Shepherd | 1 |
| B. Parsons | 1 |
| B. Allison | 1 |
| A. Kulwicki | 1 |
| Da. Allison | 1 |
| G. Bodine | 1 |
| W. Burton | 1 |
| M. Skinner | 1 |
| T. Stewart | 1 |
| J. Nemechek | 1 |
| T. Bodine | 1 |
| R. Newman | 1 |
| C. Mears | 1 |

## RACE WINNERS — FALL PENNSYLVANIA 500

| Driver | Wins |
|---|---|
| B. Elliott | 4 |
| D. Waltrip | 3 |
| R. Wallace | 3 |
| B. Labonte | 2 |
| D. Earnhardt | 2 |
| G. Bodine | 2 |
| R. Petty | 2 |
| T. Richmond | 2 |
| D. Jarrett | 2 |
| H. Gant | 1 |
| B. Parsons | 1 |
| D. Pearson | 1 |
| C. Yarborough | 1 |
| N. Bonnett | 1 |
| B. Allison | 1 |
| J. Gordon | 1 |
| R. Newman | 1 |
| Ji. Johnson | 1 |

## POLE WINNERS — ALL POCONO RACES

| Driver | Wins |
|---|---|
| K. Schrader | 5 |
| B. Elliott | 5 |
| D. Waltrip | 3 |
| C. Yarborough | 3 |
| M. Martin | 3 |
| R. Wallace | 3 |
| H. Gant | 2 |
| T. Richmond | 2 |
| A. Kulwicki | 2 |
| G. Bodine | 2 |
| J. Gordon | 2 |
| B. Parsons | 1 |
| D. Pearson | 1 |
| T. Labonte | 1 |
| M. Shepherd | 1 |
| B. Allison | 1 |
| E. Irvan | 1 |
| Buddy Baker | 1 |
| Da. Allison | 1 |
| B. Hamilton | 1 |
| J. Nemechek | 1 |
| W. Burton | 1 |
| S. Marlin | 1 |
| M. Skinner | 1 |
| T. Stewart | 1 |
| R. Rudd | 1 |
| T. Bodine | 1 |
| R. Newman | 1 |
| Ji. Johnson | 1 |
| K. Kahne | 1 |

## RACE WINNERS — ALL POCONO RACES

| Driver | Wins |
|---|---|
| C. Mears | 1 |
| B. Elliott | 5 |
| D. Waltrip | 4 |
| T. Richmond | 4 |
| R. Wallace | 4 |
| G. Bodine | 3 |
| J. Gordon | 3 |
| B. Labonte | 3 |
| B. Allison | 3 |
| D. Jarrett | 3 |
| H. Gant | 2 |
| D. Earnhardt | 2 |
| R. Petty | 2 |
| C. Yarborough | 2 |
| T. Labonte | 2 |
| J. Mayfield | 2 |
| B. Parsons | 1 |
| D. Pearson | 1 |
| A. Kulwicki | 1 |
| K. Petty | 1 |
| R. Rudd | 1 |
| R. Newman | 1 |
| T. Stewart | 1 |
| Ji. Johnson | 2 |

# NEXTEL Cup YEAR BY YEAR WINNERS (Pocono)

| Year | Event | Race Winner | Car Make | Avg. Speed | Start Pos. | Car Owner | Pole Winner | Pole Speed |
|---|---|---|---|---|---|---|---|---|
| 2004 | Pennsylvania 500 | J. Johnson | Chevrolet | 126.271 | 14 | Rick Hendrick | C. Mears | 171.720 |
| | Pocono 500 | J. Johnson | Chevrolet | 112.129 | 5 | Rick Hendrick | K. Kahne | 172.533 |
| 2003 | Pennsylvania 500 | R. Newman | Dodge | 127.705 | 1 | Roger Penske | R. Newman | 170.358 |
| | Pocono 500 | T. Stewart | Chevrolet | 134.892 | 4 | Joe Gibbs | J. Gibbs | 170.645 |
| g 2002 | Pennsylvania 500 | B. Elliott | Dodge | 125.809 | 1 | Ray Evernham | B. Elliott | 170.568 |
| | Pocono 500 | D. Jarrett | Ford | 143.426 | 13 | Robert Yates | Trials rained out | |
| 2001 | Pennsylvania 500 | B. Labonte | Pontiac | 134.590 | 11 | Joe Gibbs | T. Bodine | 170.326 |
| | Pocono 500 | R. Rudd | Ford | 134.389 | 1 | Robert Yates | R. Rudd | 170.503 |
| 2000 | Pennsylvania 500 | R. Wallace | Ford | 130.662 | 2 | Roger Penske | T. Stewart | 172.391 |
| * | Pocono 500 | J. Mayfield | Ford | 139.741 | 22 | Penske-Kranefuss | R. Wallace | 171.625 |
| 1999 | Pennsylvania 500 | B. Labonte | Pontiac | 116.982 | 4 | Joe Gibbs | M. Skinner | 170.451 |
| | Pocono 500 | B. Labonte | Pontiac | 118.898 | 3 | Joe Gibbs | S. Marlin | 170.506 |
| 1998 | Pennsylvania 500 | J. Gordon | Chevrolet | 134.660 | 2 | Rick Hendrick | W. Burton | 168.805 |
| | Pocono 500 | J. Mayfield | Ford | 117.809 | 3 | Penske-Kranefuss | J. Gordon | 168.042 |
| 1997 | Pennsylvania 500 | D. Jarrett | Ford | 142.068 | 4 | Robert Yates | J. Nemechek | 168.881 |
| | Pocono 500 | J. Gordon | Chevrolet | 139.828 | 11 | Rick Hendrick | B. Hamilton | 168.089 |
| 1996 | Miller 500 | R. Wallace | Ford | 144.892 | 13 | Roger Penske | M. Martin | 168.410 |
| | Teamwork 500 | J. Gordon | Chevrolet | 139.104 | 1 | Rick Hendrick | J. Gordon | 169.725 |
| 1995 | Miller 500 | D. Jarrett | Ford | 134.038 | 15 | Robert Yates | B. Elliott | 162.496 |
| | Teamwork 500 | T. Labonte | Chevrolet | 137.720 | 27 | Rick Hendrick | K. Schrader | 163.375 |
| 1994 | Miller 500 | G. Bodine | Ford | 136.075 | 1 | Geoff Bodine | G. Bodine | 163.689 |
| | Teamwork 500 | R. Wallace | Chevrolet | 128.801 | 1 | Roger Penske | R. Wallace | 164.558 |
| 1993 | Miller 500 | D. Earnhardt | Chevrolet | 133.343 | 11 | Richard Childress | K. Schrader | 162.934 |
| | Champion SP 500 | K. Petty | Pontiac | 138.005 | 8 | Felix Sabates | K. Schrader | 162.816 |
| 1992 | Miller 500 | D. Waltrip | Chevrolet | 134.058 | 8 | Darrell Waltrip | Da. Allison | 162.022 |
| | Champion SP 500 | A. Kulwicki | Ford | 144.023 | 6 | Alan Kulwicki | K. Schrader | 162.499 |
| f 1991 | Miller 500 | R. Wallace | Pontiac | 115.459 | 10 | Roger Penske | A. Kulwicki | 161.473 |
| | Champion SP 500 | D. Waltrip | Chevrolet | 122.666 | 13 | Darrell Waltrip | M. Martin | 161.996 |
| 1990 | AC S. Plug 500 | G. Bodine | Ford | 124.070 | 4 | Junior Johnson | M. Martin | 158.264 |
| | Miller Draft 500 | H. Gant | Oldsmobile | 120.600 | 16 | Jackson Bros. | E. Irvan | 158.750 |
| 1989 | AC S. Plug 500 | B. Elliott | Ford | 117.847 | 14 | Melling Racing | K. Schrader | 157.809 |
| | Miller HL 500 | T. Labonte | Ford | 131.320 | 23 | Junior Johnson | R. Wallace | 157.489 |
| 1988 | AC S. Plug 500 | B. Elliott | Ford | 122.866 | 2 | Melling Racing | M. Shepherd | 157.153 |
| | Miller HL 500 | B. Elliott | Chevrolet | 126.147 | 3 | Rick Hendrick | A. Kulwicki | 158.806 |
| 1987 | Summer 500 | D. Earnhardt | Chevrolet | 121.745 | 16 | Richard Childress | T. Richmond | 155.979 |
| | Miller HL 500 | T. Richmond | Chevrolet | 122.166 | 3 | Rick Hendrick | T. Labonte | 155.502 |
| e 1986 | Summer 500 | T. Richmond | Chevrolet | 124.218 | 5 | Rick Hendrick | H. Gant | 154.392 |
| | Miller HL 500 | T. Richmond | Chevrolet | 123.166 | 3 | Rick Hendrick | G. Bodine | 153.625 |
| d 1985 | Summer 500 | B. Elliott | Ford | 134.008 | 2 | Melling Racing | B. Elliott | 151.973 |
| | Van Scoy 500 | B. Elliott | Ford | 138.974 | 1 | Melling Racing | B. Elliott | 152.563 |
| 1984 | Like Cola 500 | H. Gant | Chevrolet | 121.351 | 3 | Mach 1 | B. Elliott | 152.184 |
| c | Van Scoy 500 | C. Yarborough | Chevrolet | 138.164 | 12 | Ranier Racing | D. Pearson | 150.921 |
| 1983 | Like Cola 500 | T. Richmond | Pontiac | 114.818 | 1 | Blue Max | B. Elliott | 151.981 |
| | Van Scoy 500 | B. Allison | Buick | 128.636 | 7 | DiGard Rac. Co. | D. Waltrip | 152.315 |
| 1982 | Mt. Dew 500 | B. Allison | Buick | 115.496 | 4 | DiGard Rac. Co. | C. Yarborough | 150.764 |
| b | Van Scoy 500 | B. Allison | Buick | 113.579 | 3 | DiGard Rac. Co. | Trials rained out | |
| 1981 | Mt. Dew 500 | D. Waltrip | Buick | 119.111 | 1 | Junior Johnson | D. Waltrip | 150.148 |
| 1980 | Coca-Cola 500 | N. Bonnett | Mercury | 124.395 | 2 | Wood Brothers | C. Yarborough | 151.469 |
| * 1979 | Coca-Cola 500 | C. Yarborough | Chevrolet | 115.207 | 2 | Junior Johnson | H. Gant | 148.711 |
| 1978 | Coca-Cola 500 | D. Waltrip | Chevrolet | 142.540 | 4 | DiGard Rac. Co. | B. Parsons | 149.235 |
| 1977 | Coca-Cola 500 | B. Parsons | Chevrolet | 128.379 | 4 | L.G. DeWitt | D. Waltrip | 147.591 |
| 1976 | Purolator 500 | R. Petty | Dodge | 115.875 | 5 | Petty Eng. | C. Yarborough | 147.865 |
| 1975 | Purolator 500 | Pearson | Mercury | 111.179 | 2 | Wood Brothers | B. Allison | 146.491 |
| a 1974 | Purolator 500 | R. Petty | Dodge | 115.593 | 3 | Petty Eng. | Buddy Baker | 144.122 |

## KEY

* Rain delayed event until Monday.
a Race shortened to 480 miles, rain.
b Starting lineup determined by NASCAR Winston Cup car owner point standings.
c Pearson qualified Neil Bonnett's car.
d Elliott awarded pole 2 1/2 weeks after race when test showed pole winner used illegal fuel.
e Race shortened to 375 miles, rain.
f Race shortened to 447.5 miles, rain.
g Race shortened to 437.5 miles, rain.

## 2005 SCHEDULE

### NEXTEL CUP

**Event:** Chevy American Revolution 400
**Race:** No. 11 of 36
**Date:** May 14
**TV:** FX. **Radio:** MRN

**Event:** Chevy Rock & Roll 400
**Race:** No. 26 of 36
**Date:** September 10
**TV:** TNT. **Radio:** MRN

### BUSCH SERIES

**Event:** Funai 250
**Race:** No. 13 of 35
**Date:** May 13
**TV:** FX. **Radio:** MRN

**Event:** Emerson Radio 250
**Race:** No. 28 of 35
**Date:** September 9
**TV:** TNT. **Radio:** MRN

### CRAFTSMAN TRUCK SERIES

**Event:** Kroger 200
**Race:** No. 18 of 25
**Date:** September 8
**TV:** SPEED. **Radio:** MRN

Race names subject to change

### TRACK FACTS

**Date opened:** October 12, 1946
**Owner:** International Speedway Corp.
**Location:** Richmond, Va.
**Distance:** .750 miles
**Banking in turns:** 14 degrees
**Banking on front stretch:** 8 degrees
**Banking on back stretch:** 2 degrees
**Length of front stretch:** 1,290 feet
**Length of back stretch:** 860 feet
**Grandstand seating:** 105,000
**Tickets:** (804) 345-7223
**Website:** www.rir.com

Backstretch: 860 feet / 2°
14° 3  14° 2
14° 4  14° 1
Frontstretch: 1,290 feet / 8°

## NEXTEL CUP

### TRACK RECORDS

**Most wins:** 9—Richard Petty
**Oldest winner:** Harry Gant, 51 Years, 7 months, 28 days, September 7, 1991
**Youngest winner:** Richard Petty, 23 years, 9 months, 21 days, April 23, 1961
**Most lead changes:** 25—Twice, most recently, March 3, 1996
**Fewest lead changes:** 2—Seven times, most recently, February 23, 1975
**Most leaders:** 16—September 10, 1994
**Fewest leaders:** 2—Eight times, most recently, March 11, 1979
**Most laps led in a 400 lap race:** 369, Bobby Allison, September 9, 1979
**Most cautions:** 15—May 3, 2003
**Fewest cautions:** 0—March 7, 1976
**Most caution laps:** 123—Twice, most recently, September 8, 1974
**Fewest caution laps:** 0—March 7, 1976
**Most on the lead lap:** 22—May 6, 2000
**Fewest on the lead lap:** 1—22 times, most recently, October 12, 1975
**Most running at the finish:** 39—Three times, most recently, September 11, 1999
**Fewest running at the finish:** 1—April 19, 1953
**Most laps led by a race winner:** 488—David Pearson, September 13, 1970
**Fewest laps led by a race winner:** 4—Kyle Petty, February 23, 1986

**Closest margin of victory:** 0.051 seconds—Jeff Burton defeated Jeff Gordon, September 12, 1998.
**Greatest margin of victory:** 6 laps— Richard Petty defeated Lennie Pond, February 23, 1975.

### QUALIFYING AND RACE RECORDS

**QUALIFYING: Track:** Dale Earnhardt Jr., Chevrolet; 129.983 mph, May 14, 2004 (Chevy American Revolution 400).
**Spring race (Chevy American Revolution 400):** Dale Earnhardt Jr., Chevrolet; 129.983 mph, May 14, 2004.
**Fall race (Chevy Rock & Roll 400):** Jimmie Johnson, Chevrolet; 126.145 mph, September 6, 2002. **Dirt:** Tom Pistone, Ford; 70.978 mph, May 15, 1966, .5-mile track (Richmond 250).
**RACE: Track record (300 miles):** Dale Jarrett, Ford; 109.047 mph, September 6, 1997 (Exide Batteries 400).
**Spring Race (Pontiac Excitement 400):** Rusty Wallace, Ford; 108.499 mph, March 2, 1997. **Fall race (Chevy Rock & Roll 400):** Dale Jarrett, Ford; 109.047 mph, September 6, 1997. **271 miles:** James Hylton, Ford; 82.044 mph, March 1, 1970, .542-mile track (Richmond 500). **250 miles:** Bobby Allison, Ford; 76.388 mph, September 7, 1969, .5625-mile track (Capital City 250). **216.8 miles:** Cale Yarborough, Oldsmobile; 83.608 mph, March 11, 1979, .542-mile track (Richmond 400). **187.5 miles:** Richard Petty, Plymouth; 85.659 mph, September 8, 1968, .625-mile track (Capital City 300). **150 miles:** Ned Jarrett, Ford; 66.339 mph, September 8, 1963, .5-mile dirt track (Capital City 300). **125 miles:** David Pearson, Dodge; 66.539 mph, May 15, 1966, .5-mile dirt track (Richmond 250).

TRACKS

### NEXTEL Cup YEAR BY YEAR WINNERS

| | Year | Event | Race Winner | Car Make | Avg. Speed | Start Pos. | Car Owner | Pole Winner | Pole Speed |
|---|---|---|---|---|---|---|---|---|---|
| * | 2004 | Chevy Rock & Roll 400 | J. Mayfield | Dodge | 98.946 | 7 | Ray Evernham | R. Newman | 128.700 |
| | | Chevy Am. Revolution 400 | D. Earnhardt Jr. | Chevrolet | 98.253 | 4 | Teresa Earnhardt | B. Vickers | 129.983 |
| * | 2003 | Chevy Rock & Roll 400 | R. Newman | Dodge | 94.945 | 11 | Roger Penske | M. Skinner | 125.792 |
| *p | | Pontiac Excitement 400 | J. Nemechek | Chevrolet | 126.511 | 2 | Joe Hendrick | T. Labonte | 126.511 |
| * | 2002 | Chevrolet 400 | M. Kenseth | Ford | 94.787 | 25 | Jack Roush | Ji. Johnson | 126.145 |
| | | Pontiac 400 | T. Stewart | Pontiac | 86.824 | 3 | Joe Gibbs | W. Burton | 127.389 |
| * | 2001 | Chevrolet 400 | R. Rudd | Ford | 95.146 | 9 | Robert Yates | J. Gordon | 124.902 |
| | | Pontiac 400 | T. Stewart | Pontiac | 95.872 | 7 | Joe Gibbs | M. Martin | 124.613 |
| * | 2000 | Chevrolet 400 | J. Gordon | Chevrolet | 99.871 | 13 | Rick Hendrick | J. Burton | 125.780 |
| | | Pontiac 400 | D. Earnhardt Jr. | Chevrolet | 99.374 | 5 | Dale Earnhardt | R. Wallace | 124.740 |
| * | 1999 | Exide Batteries 400 | T. Stewart | Pontiac | 104.006 | 2 | Joe Gibbs | M. Skinner | 125.465 |
| | | Pontiac 400 | D. Jarrett | Ford | 100.102 | 21 | Robert Yates | J. Gordon | 126.499 |
| * | 1998 | Exide Batteries 400 | J. Burton | Ford | 91.985 | 3 | Jack Roush | R. Wallace | 125.377 |
| | | Pontiac 400 | T. Labonte | Chevrolet | 97.044 | 16 | Rick Hendrick | J. Gordon | 125.558 |
| * | 1997 | Exide Batteries 400 | D. Jarrett | Ford | 109.047 | 23 | Robert Yates | B. Elliott | 124.723 |
| o | | Pontiac 400 | R. Wallace | Ford | 108.499 | 7 | Roger Penske | No trials held | |

387

## SPRING RICHMOND 400

**POLE WINNERS**

| | |
|---|---|
| B. Allison | 5 |
| R. Petty | 4 |
| D. Waltrip | 4 |
| J. Gordon | 3 |
| M. Shepherd | 2 |
| R. Rudd | 2 |
| N. Bonnett | 2 |
| T. Labonte | 2 |
| Jr. Johnson | 1 |
| D. Marcis | 1 |
| D. Pearson | 1 |
| B. Isaac | 1 |
| T. Pistone | 1 |
| D. Jarrett | 1 |
| R. White | 1 |
| A. Kulwicki | 1 |
| G. Bodine | 1 |
| Da. Allison | 1 |
| B. Elliott | 1 |
| K. Schrader | 1 |
| T. Musgrave | 1 |
| R. Wallace | 1 |
| M. Martin | 1 |
| W. Burton | 1 |
| B. Vickers | 1 |

**RACE WINNERS**

| | |
|---|---|
| R. Petty | 6 |
| D. Pearson | 4 |
| D. Earnhardt | 3 |
| R. Wallace | 2 |
| T. Labonte | 2 |
| D. Waltrip | 2 |
| C. Yarborough | 2 |
| D. Marcis | 2 |
| B. Allison | 2 |
| T. Stewart | 2 |
| D. Earnhardt Jr. | 2 |
| J. Weatherly | 1 |
| B. Parsons | 1 |
| J. Hylton | 1 |
| Jr. Johnson | 1 |
| R. White | 1 |
| R. Rudd | 1 |
| K. Petty | 1 |
| N. Bonnett | 1 |
| M. Martin | 1 |
| B. Elliott | 1 |
| Da. Allison | 1 |
| E. Irvan | 1 |
| J. Gordon | 1 |
| D. Jarrett | 1 |
| J. Nemechek | 1 |

## FALL CHEVROLET 400

**POLE WINNERS**

| | |
|---|---|
| R. Petty | 4 |
| *B, Allison | 4 |
| B. Parsons | 3 |
| D. Waltrip | 3 |
| E. Irvan | 2 |
| D. Earnhardt | 2 |
| M. Martin | 2 |
| B. Elliott | 2 |
| R. Wallace | 2 |
| N. Jarrett | 2 |
| *B. Dennis | 1 |
| D. Hutcherson | 1 |
| R. White | 1 |
| J. Weatherly | 1 |
| Jr. Johnson | 1 |
| C. Yarborough | 1 |
| D. Pearson | 1 |
| G. Bodine | 1 |
| H. Gant | 1 |
| A. Kulwicki | 1 |
| Da. Allison | 1 |
| B. Labonte | 1 |
| T. Musgrave | 1 |
| M. Skinner | 2 |
| J. Burton | 1 |
| J. Gordon | 1 |
| J. Johnson | 1 |
| R. Newman | 1 |

**RACE WINNERS**

| | |
|---|---|
| R. Petty | 7 |
| B. Allison | 5 |
| D. Waltrip | 4 |
| R. Wallace | 4 |
| D. Earnhardt | 2 |
| D. Pearson | 2 |
| C. Yarborough | 1 |
| N. Bonnett | 1 |
| C. Owens | 1 |
| N. Jarrett | 1 |
| B. Parsons | 1 |
| T. Richmond | 1 |
| Da. Allison | 1 |
| H. Gant | 1 |
| T. Labonte | 1 |
| E. Irvan | 1 |
| D. Jarrett | 1 |
| J. Burton | 1 |
| T. Stewart | 1 |
| J. Gordon | 1 |
| R. Rudd | 1 |
| M. Kenseth | 1 |
| R. Newman | 1 |
| J. Mayfield | 1 |

* The pole winner was the fastest qualifier in every race.

## ALL RICHMOND RACES

**POLE WINNERS**

| | |
|---|---|
| *B. Allison | 8 |
| R. Petty | 8 |
| D. Waltrip | 7 |
| B. Elliott | 3 |
| J. Gordon | 3 |
| B. Parsons | 3 |
| R. Wallace | 3 |
| M. Martin | 3 |
| D. Pearson | 2 |
| N. Bonnett | 2 |
| A. Kulwicki | 2 |
| M. Shepherd | 2 |
| G. Bodine | 2 |
| R. Rudd | 2 |
| N. Jarrett | 2 |
| Jr. Johnson | 2 |
| R. White | 2 |
| Da. Allison | 2 |
| E. Irvan | 2 |
| T. Musgrave | 2 |
| D. Earnhardt | 2 |
| M. Skinner | 2 |
| T. Labonte | 2 |
| J. Weatherly | 1 |
| D. Hutcherson | 1 |
| B. Isaac | 1 |
| *B. Dennis | 1 |
| C. Yarborough | 1 |
| T. Pistone | 1 |
| H. Gant | 1 |
| D. Marcis | 1 |
| K. Schrader | 1 |
| B. Labonte | 1 |
| J. Burton | 1 |
| J. Johnson | 1 |
| R. Newman | 1 |

**RACE WINNERS**

| | |
|---|---|
| R. Petty | 13 |
| B. Allison | 7 |
| R. Wallace | 6 |
| Pearson | 6 |
| D. Waltrip | 6 |
| D. Earnhardt | 5 |
| T. Labonte | 3 |
| C. Yarborough | 3 |
| J. Weatherly | 3 |
| T. Stewart | 3 |
| D. Jarrett | 2 |
| R. Rudd | 2 |
| B. Parsons | 2 |
| D. Marcis | 2 |
| Da. Allison | 2 |
| N. Bonnett | 2 |
| E. Irvan | 2 |
| J. Gordon | 2 |
| L. Petty | 2 |
| C. Owens | 2 |
| D. Jarrett | 1 |
| R. White | 1 |
| K. Petty | 1 |
| T. Richmond | 1 |
| M. Martin | 1 |
| H. Gant | 1 |
| B. Elliott | 1 |
| Jr. Johnson | 1 |
| J. Hylton | 1 |
| J. Burton | 1 |
| D. Earnhardt Jr. | 2 |
| J. Nemechek | 1 |
| R. Newman | 1 |
| J. Mayfield | 1 |

* The pole winner was the fastest qualifier in every race except the 1971 Capital City 500. Bill Dennis won the pole, but Bobby Allison was the fastest qualifier.

# NEXTEL Cup YEAR BY YEAR WINNERS (Richmond, continued)

| | Year | Event | Race Winner | Car Make | Avg. Speed | Start Pos. | Car Owner | Pole Winner | Pole Speed |
|---|---|---|---|---|---|---|---|---|---|
| * | 1996 | Miller 400 | E. Irvan | Ford | 105.469 | 16 | Robert Yates | M. Martin | 122.744 |
| | | Pontiac 400 | J. Gordon | Chevrolet | 102.750 | 2 | Rick Hendrick | T. Labonte | 123.728 |
| * | 1995 | Miller 400 | R. Wallace | Ford | 104.459 | 7 | Roger Penske | D. Earnhardt | 122.543 |
| | | Pontiac 400 | T. Labonte | Chevrolet | 106.425 | 24 | Rick Hendrick | J. Gordon | 124.757 |
| * | 1994 | Miller 400 | T. Labonte | Chevrolet | 104.156 | 3 | Rick Hendrick | T. Musgrave | 124.052 |
| | | Pontiac 400 | E. Irvan | Ford | 98.334 | 7 | Robert Yates | T. Musgrave | 123.474 |
| * | 1993 | Miller 400 | R. Wallace | Pontiac | 99.917 | 3 | Roger Penske | B. Labonte | 122.006 |
| | | Pontiac 400 | Da. Allison | Ford | 107.709 | 14 | Robert Yates | K. Schrader | 123.164 |
| * | 1992 | Miller 400 | R. Wallace | Pontiac | 104.661 | 3 | Roger Penske | E. Irvan | 120.784 |
| | | Pontiac 400 | B. Elliott | Ford | 104.378 | 1 | Junior Johnson | B. Elliott | 121.337 |
| * | 1991 | Miller 400 | H. Gant | Oldsmobile | 101.361 | 13 | Leo Jackson | R. Wallace | 120.590 |
| | | Pontiac 400 | D. Earnhardt | Chevrolet | 105.397 | 19 | Richard Childress | Da. Allison | 120.428 |
| | 1990 | Miller High Life 400 | D. Earnhardt | Chevrolet | 95.567 | 6 | Richard Childress | E. Irvan | 119.872 |
| | | Pontiac 400 | M. Martin | Ford | 92.158 | 6 | Jack Roush | R. Rudd | 119.617 |
| | 1989 | Miller High Life 400 | R. Wallace | Pontiac | 88.380 | 6 | Blue Max | B. Elliott | 121.136 |
| | | Pontiac 400 | R. Wallace | Pontiac | 89.619 | 2 | Blue Max | G. Bodine | 120.573 |
| m | 1988 | Miller High Life 400 | Da. Allison | Ford | 95.770 | 1 | Ranier Racing | Da. Allison | 122.850 |
| | | Pontiac 400 | N. Bonnett | Pontiac | 66.401 | 3 | Rahmoc | M. Shepherd | 94.645 |
| | 1987 | Wrangler Indigo 400 | D. Earnhardt | Chevrolet | 67.074 | 8 | Richard Childress | A. Kulwicki | 94.052 |
| | | Miller High Life 400 | D. Earnhardt | Chevrolet | 81.520 | 3 | Richard Childress | A. Kulwicki | 95.153 |
| | 1986 | Wrangler Indigo 400 | T. Richmond | Chevrolet | 70.161 | 4 | Rick Hendrick | H. Gant | 93.966 |
| l | | Miller High Life 400 | K. Petty | Ford | 71.078 | 12 | Wood Brothers | No time trials held | |
| | 1985 | Wrangler SanforSet 400 | D. Waltrip | Chevrolet | 72.508 | 22 | Junior Johnson | G. Bodine | 94.535 |
| | | Miller High Life 400 | D. Earnhardt | Chevrolet | 67.945 | 4 | Richard Childress | D. Waltrip | 95.218 |
| | 1984 | Wrangler SanforSet 400 | D. Waltrip | Chevrolet | 74.780 | 1 | Junior Johnson | D. Waltrip | 92.518 |
| | | Miller High Life 400 | R. Rudd | Ford | 76.736 | 4 | Bud Moore | D. Waltrip | 93.817 |
| | 1983 | Wrangler SanforSet 400 | B. Allison | Buick | 79.381 | 6 | DiGard Rac. Co. | D. Waltrip | 96.069 |
| | | Richmond 400 | B. Allison | Chevrolet | 79.584 | 6 | DiGard Rac. Co. | R. Rudd | 93.439 |
| | 1982 | Wrangler SanforSet 400 | B. Allison | Chevrolet | 82.800 | 1 | DiGard Rac. Co. | B. Allison | 93.435 |
| k | | Richmond 400 | D. Marcis | Chevrolet | 72.914 | 6 | Dave Marcis | D. Waltrip | 93.256 |
| | 1981 | Wrangler SanforSet 400 | B. Parsons | Ford | 69.998 | 4 | Bud Moore | M. Martin | 93.435 |
| | | Richmond 400 | D. Waltrip | Buick | 76.570 | 7 | Junior Johnson | M. Shepherd | 92.821 |
| | 1980 | Capital City 400 | B. Allison | Ford | 79.722 | 2 | Bud Moore | C. Yarborough | 93.466 |
| | | Richmond 400 | D. Waltrip | Chevrolet | 67.703 | 1 | DiGard Rac. Co. | D. Waltrip | 93.695 |
| | 1979 | Capital City 400 | B. Allison | Ford | 80.604 | 2 | Bud Moore | D. Earnhardt | 92.605 |
| | | Richmond 400 | C. Yarborough | Oldsmobile | 83.608 | 9 | Junior Johnson | B. Allison | 92.957 |
| | 1978 | Capital City 400 | D. Waltrip | Chevrolet | 79.568 | 1 | DiGard Rac. Co. | D. Waltrip | 91.964 |
| | | Richmond 400 | B. Parsons | Chevrolet | 80.304 | 3 | L.G. DeWitt | N. Bonnett | 93.382 |
| | 1977 | Capital City 400 | N. Bonnett | Dodge | 80.644 | 2 | Jim Stacy | B. Parsons | 92.281 |
| j | | Richmond 400 | C. Yarborough | Chevrolet | 73.084 | 7 | Junior Johnson | N. Bonnett | 93.632 |
| | 1976 | Capital City 400 | C. Yarborough | Chevrolet | 77.993 | 6 | Junior Johnson | B. Parsons | 92.460 |
| i | | Richmond 400 | D. Marcis | Dodge | 72.792 | 2 | Nord Krauskopf | B. Allison | 92.715 |
| | 1975 | Capital City 500 | D. Waltrip | Chevrolet | 81.886 | 2 | DiGard Rac. Co. | B. Parsons | 91.071 |
| | | Richmond 500 | R. Petty | Dodge | 74.913 | 1 | Petty Eng. | R. Petty | 93.340 |
| | 1974 | Capital City 500 | R. Petty | Dodge | 64.430 | 1 | Petty Eng. | R. Petty | 88.852 |
| | | Richmond 500 | B. Allison | Chevrolet | 80.095 | 1 | Bobby Allison | B. Allison | 90.353 |
| | 1973 | Capital City 500 | R. Petty | Dodge | 63.215 | 5 | Petty Eng. | B. Allison | 90.245 |
| | | Richmond 500 | R. Petty | Dodge | 74.764 | 8 | Petty Eng. | B. Allison | 90.952 |
| | 1972 | Capital City 500 | R. Petty | Plymouth | 75.899 | 3 | Petty Eng. | B. Allison | 89.669 |
| | | Richmond 500 | R. Petty | Plymouth | 76.258 | 3 | Petty Eng. | B. Allison | 90.573 |
| | 1971 | Capital City 500 | R. Petty | Plymouth | 80.025 | 11 | Petty Eng. | B. Allison | |
| | | Richmond 500 | R. Petty | Plymouth | 79.836 | 28 | Petty Eng. | D. Marcis | 87.178 |
| | 1970 | Capital City 500 | R. Petty | Plymouth | 81.476 | 1 | Petty Eng. | R. Petty | 87.014 |
| h | | Richmond 500 | J. Hylton | Ford | 82.044 | 1 | Hylton Eng. | R. Petty | 89.137 |
| g | 1969 | Capital City 500 | B. Allison | Dodge | 76.388 | 26 | Mario Rossi | R. Petty | 91.257 |
| f | | Richmond 250 | D. Pearson | Ford | 73.752 | 1 | Holman-Moody | D. Pearson | 82.538 |
| | 1968 | Capital City 300 | D. Pearson | Plymouth | 85.659 | 1 | Petty Eng. | R. Petty | 103.178 |
| d | | Richmond 250 | D. Pearson | Ford | 65.217 | 16 | Holman-Moody | B. Isaac | 67.822 |
| c | 1967 | Capital City 300 | R. Petty | Plymouth | 57.631 | 2 | Petty Eng. | Draw Position | |
| | | Richmond 250 | R. Petty | Plymouth | 65.982 | 1 | Petty Eng. | R. Petty | 70.038 |
| | 1966 | Capital City 300 | D. Pearson | Dodge | 62.886 | 1 | Cotton Owens | D. Pearson | 70.644 |
| | | Richmond 250 | D. Pearson | Dodge | 66.539 | 4 | Cotton Owens | T. Pistone | 70.978 |
| | 1965 | Capital City 300 | D. Pearson | Dodge | 60.983 | 2 | Cotton Owens | D. Hutcherson | 67.340 |
| | | Richmond 250 | Ju. Johnson | Ford | 61.416 | 1 | Junior Johnson | Ju. Johnson | 67.847 |
| | 1964 | Capital City 300 | C. Owens | Dodge | 61.955 | 3 | Cotton Owens | N. Jarrett | 66.890 |
| | | Richmond 250 | D. Pearson | Dodge | 58.660 | 10 | Cotton Owens | N. Jarrett | 69.070 |
| | 1963 | Capital City 300 | N. Jarrett | Ford | 66.339 | 7 | Bob Robinson | J. Weatherly | 68.104 |
| | | Richmond 250 | J. Weatherly | Pontiac | 58.624 | 3 | Bud Moore | R. White | 69.151 |
| | 1962 | Capital City 300 | J. Weatherly | Pontiac | 64.980 | 2 | Bud Moore | R. White | 66.127 |
| b | | Richmond 250 | R. White | Chevrolet | 51.360 | 20 | Louis Clements | Draw Position | |
| | 1961 | Capital City 250 | J. Weatherly | Pontiac | 61.677 | 7 | Bud Moore | Ju. Johnson | 65.010 |
| a | | Richmond 200 | R. Petty | Plymouth | 62.456 | 1 | Petty Eng. | R. Petty | 66.667 |
| | 1960 | Capital City 200 | S. Thompson | Ford | 63.739 | 3 | Wood Brothers | N. Jarrett | 64.410 |
| | | Richmond 300 | L. Petty | Plymouth | 62.251 | 10 | Petty Eng. | N. Jarrett | 64.560 |
| | 1959 | Capital City 200 | C. Owens | Ford | 60.362 | 1 | Cotton Owens | C. Owens | 62.674 |
| | | Richmond 200 | T. Pistone | Ford | 56.881 | 12 | Carl Rupert | Buck Baker | 66.420 |
| | 1958 | Capital City 200 | S. Thompson | Chevrolet | 57.878 | 1 | A. "Speedy" Thompson | S. Thompson | 62.915 |
| | 1957 | Richmond 200 | P. Goldsmith | Ford | 62.445 | 7 | Pete DePaolo | R. Hepler | 64.239 |
| | 1956 | Richmond 200 | Buck Baker | Dodge | 56.232 | 1 | Carl Kiekhafer | Buck Baker | 67.091 |
| | 1955 | Richmond 200 | Tim Flock | Chrysler | 54.299 | 22 | Carl Kiekhafer | No time trials held | |
| | 1953 | Richmond 200 | L. Petty | Dodge | 45.535 | | Petty Eng. | Buck Baker | 48.465 |

## RICHMOND KEY

| | |
|---|---|
| * | Night race. |
| a | Last 100-mile, 200-lap race. |
| b | Time trials called off, too wet; race called after 90 miles, 180 laps, darkness. |
| c | Time trials called off; too wet. |
| d | Last race on .5-mile dirt track; distance was 125 miles, 250 laps. |
| e | Track asphalted and remeasured at .625-mile; Distance changed to 187.5 miles, 300 laps. |
| f | Track remeasured at .5625-mile; distance was 250 miles, 462 laps. |
| g | Track remeasured at .5-mile; distance was 250 miles, 500 laps. |
| h | Track remeasured at .542-mile, 500 laps, 271 miles. |
| i | Distance changed from 500 laps, 271 miles, to 400 laps, 216.8 miles. |
| j | Race called after 132.79 miles, 245 laps; rain. |
| k | Race called after 135.5 miles, 250 laps; rain. |
| l | Time trials rained out. |
| m | Track rebuilt to .75 miles. |
| n | Postponed February 26 to March 26 because of snow. |
| o | Time trials rained out. |
| p | Race called after 294.75 miles, 393 laps, rain. |

# BUSCH SERIES

## Busch YEAR BY YEAR WINNERS (Richmond)

| Year | Event | Race Winner | Car Make | Avg. Speed | Start Pos. | Pole Winner | Pole Speed | POLE WINNERS | | RACE WINNERS | |
|---|---|---|---|---|---|---|---|---|---|---|---|
| 2004 | Funai 250 | Ky. Busch | Chevrolet | 85.023 | 1 | Ky. Busch | 129.348 | T. Ellis | 5 | M. Martin | 5 |
| | Emerson Radio 250 | R. Gordon | Chevrolet | 86.372 | 3 | K. Kahne | 127.678 | M. Waltrip | 5 | H. Gant | 4 |
| 2003 | Hardee's 250 | K. Harvick | Chevrolet | 74.652 | 15 | M. Waltrip | 125.523 | S. Ard | 2 | K. Wallace | 3 |
| | Funai 250 | Jo. Sauter | Chevrolet | 99.543 | 30 | Trials rained out | | T. Bodine | 2 | S. Ard | 2 |
| 2002 | Hardee's 250 | J. Keller | Ford | 80.138 | 2 | Trials rained out | | J. Burton | 2 | J. Burton | 2 |
| | Funai 250 | D. Earnhardt Jr. | Chevrolet | 78.089 | 1 | D. Earnhardt Jr. | 126.868 | J. Green | 2 | D. Earnhardt Jr. | 2 |
| 2001 | Hardee's 250 | J. Spencer | Chevrolet | 84.028 | 3 | M. Kenseth | 125.780 | J. Keller | 2 | T. Ellis | 2 |
| | Autolite/Fram 250 | J. Spencer | Chevrolet | 90.156 | 3 | J. Green | 125.122 | B. Bodine | 1 | B. Lindley | 2 |
| 2000 | Hardee's 250 | J. Green | Chevrolet | 81.023 | 1 | J. Green | 123.085 | G. Bodine | 1 | J. Spencer | 2 |
| | Autolite/Fram 250 | J. Burton | Ford | 89.203 | 2 | T. Bodine | 123.768 | C. Bown | 1 | D. Earnhardt | 1 |
| 1999 | Hardee's 250 | M. Martin | Ford | 90.060 | 2 | J. Keller | 124.907 | D. Earnhardt Jr. | 1 | J. Green | 1 |
| | Autolite 250 | D. Earnhardt Jr. | Chevrolet | 87.754 | 20 | J. Burton | 121.984 | H. Gant | 1 | B. Hamilton | 1 |
| 1998 | Hardee's 250 | J. Burton | Ford | 95.799 | 8 | W. Grubb | 123.212 | J. Gordon | 1 | T. Houston | 1 |
| | Autolite 250 | D. Earnhardt Jr. | Chevrolet | 82.067 | 2 | A. Santerre | 123.604 | D. Green | 1 | D. Jarrett | 1 |
| 1997 | Hardee's 250 | M. Martin | Ford | 86.450 | 18 | Trials rained out | | W. Grubb | 1 | J. Keller | 1 |
| | Autolite 250 | S. Park | Chevrolet | 77.747 | 2 | M. Waltrip | 122.227 | J. Hensley | 1 | R. Mast | 1 |
| 1996 | Hardee's 250 | J. Purvis | Chevrolet | 98.168 | 1 | J. Purvis | 121.114 | M. Kenseth | 1 | J. Nemechek | 1 |
| | Autolite 250 | K. Wallace | Ford | 100.987 | 3 | M. Waltrip | 120.444 | B. Labonte | 1 | S. Park | 1 |
| 1995 | Hardee's 250 | K. Wallace | Ford | 96.291 | 21 | Trials rained out | | R. LaJoie | 1 | R. Pressley | 1 |
| | Autolite 250 | D. Jarrett | Ford | 104.928 | 6 | R. LaJoie | 119.846 | R. Mast | 1 | J. Purvis | 1 |
| 1994 | Hardee's 250 | J. Nemechek | Chevrolet | 91.253 | 3 | D. Green | 121.841 | L. Pearson | 1 | M. Shepherd | 1 |
| | Autolite 250 | K. Wallace | Ford | 97.487 | 6 | J. Keller | 121.968 | J. Purvis | 1 | K. Wallace | 1 |
| 1993 | Hardee's 200 | M. Martin | Ford | 103.766 | 2 | R. Mast | 120.876 | A. Santerre | 1 | M. Waltrip | 1 |
| **** | Autolite 250 | M. Martin | Ford | 98.511 | 4 | C. Bown | 120.903 | Ky. Busch | 1 | K. Harvick | 1 |
| 1992 | Hardee's 200 | H. Gant | Buick | 97.561 | 28 | J. Gordon | 120.466 | K. Kahne | 1 | J. Sauter | 1 |
| | Autolite 200 | R. Pressley | Oldsmobile | 95.373 | 14 | T. Bodine | 118.561 | | | Ky. Busch | 1 |
| 1991 | Pontiac 200 | H. Gant | Buick | 92.156 | 11 | J. Burton | 118.848 | | | R. Gordon | 1 |
| | Autolite 200 | H. Gant | Buick | 86.719 | 29 | B. Labonte | 119.617 | | | | |
| 1990 | Pontiac 200 | M. Waltrip | Pontiac | 88.091 | 1 | M. Waltrip | 118.561 | | | | |
| | Autolite 200 | R. Mast | Buick | 99.759 | 22 | M. Waltrip | 118.974 | | | | |
| 1989 | No Spring race held (snow) | | | | | | | | | | |
| | Commonwealth 200 | B. Hamilton | Oldsmobile | 92.071 | 29 | T. Ellis | 118.953 | | | | |
| 1988 | No Spring race | | | | | | | | | | |
| *** | Commonwealth 200 | H. Gant | Buick | 89.434 | 1 | H. Gant | 121.218 | | | | |
| 1987 | No Spring race | | | | | | | | | | |
| | Freedlander 200 | M. Martin | Ford | 66.180 | 16 | L. Pearson | 98.312 | | | | |
| 1986 | No Spring race | | | | | | | | | | |
| ** | Freedlander 200 | D. Earnhardt | Chevrolet | 76.174 | 4 | B. Bodine | 98.218 | | | | |
| 1985 | No Spring race | | | | | | | | | | |
| | 7-Eleven 150 | T. Ellis | Pontiac | 80.539 | 3 | J. Hensley | 97.638 | | | | |
| 1984 | Wrangler 150 | S. Ard | Oldsmobile | 75.084 | 3 | T. Ellis | 97.814 | | | | |
| | Miller Time 150 | T. Ellis | Oldsmobile | 65.199 | 1 | T. Ellis | 97.702 | | | | |
| 1983 | Eastern 150 | S. Ard | Oldsmobile | 73.639 | 1 | S. Ard | 96.800 | | | | |
| | Miller Time 150 | M. Shepherd | Oldsmobile | 63.848 | 3 | T. Ellis | 96.204 | | | | |
| 1982 | Eastern 150 | T. Houston | Chevrolet | 57.667 | 15 | G. Bodine | 96.207 | | | | |
| * | Spring 220 | B. Lindley | Pontiac | 59.894 | 3 | S. Ard | 96.671 | | | | |
| | Harvest 150 | B. Lindley | Pontiac | 76.839 | 7 | T. Ellis | 97.046 | | | | |

## KEY

| | |
|---|---|
| * | Special, one-time race. |
| ** | Race length increased to 200 laps. |
| *** | Track enlarged to .750 mile. |
| **** | Race length increased to 250 laps. |

**QUALIFYING RECORD:** Kyle Busch, Chevrolet; 129.348 mph, May 14, 2004
**RACE RECORD:** Dale Jarrett, Ford; 104.928 mph, September 8, 1995

TRACKS

## Craftsman YEAR BY YEAR WINNERS (Richmond)

| Year | Event | Race Winner | Car Make | Avg. Speed | Start Pos. | Pole Winner | Pole Speed | POLE WINNERS | | RACE WINNERS | |
|------|-------|-------------|----------|------------|------------|-------------|------------|--------------|---|--------------|---|
| 2004 | Kroger 200 | T. Musgrave | Dodge | 84.186 | 2 | J. McMurray | 125.436 | Ku. Busch | 1 | J. Sprague | 2 |
| 2003 | Virginia is for Lovers 200 | T. Stewart | Chevrolet | 91.062 | 27 | Trials rained out | | B. Hamilton | 1 | T. Stewart | 2 |
| 2002 | Virginia is for Lovers 200 | T. Stewart | Chevrolet | 91.340 | 25 | J. Leffler | 123.378 | R. Hornaday Jr. | 1 | G. Biffle | 1 |
| 2001 | Kroger 200 | J. Sprague | Chevrolet | 95.677 | 2 | D. Setzer | 121.359 | K. Irwin | 1 | R. Carelli | 1 |
| 2000 | Kroger 200 | R. Carelli | Ford | 98.684 | 10 | Ku. Busch | 121.457 | T. Labonte | 1 | B. Keselowski | 1 |
| 1999 | Virginia is for Lovers 200 | G. Biffle | Ford | 86.007 | 4 | B. Hamilton | 121.408 | J. Leffler | 1 | T. Labonte | 1 |
| 1998 | Virginia is for Lovers 200 | **J.Sprague** | Chevrolet | 85.878 | 2 | J. Ruttman | 121.633 | J. Ruttman | 1 | J. Sprague | 1 |
| 1997 | Virginia is for Lovers 200 | B. Keselowski | Dodge | 104.227 | 10 | R.Hornaday Jr. | 121.726 | D. Setzer | 1 | T. Musgrave | 1 |
| 1996 | Fas Mart Shootout | M. Skinner | Chevrolet | 78.665 | 2 | K. Irwin | 119.888 | J. McMurray | 1 | | |
| 1995 | Fas Mart Shootout | T. Labonte | Chevrolet | 78.595 | 1 | T. Labonte | 116.797 | | | | |

**QUALIFYING RECORD:** Jamie McMurray, Dodge; 125.436 mph, September 9, 2004
**RACE RECORD:** Bob Keselowski, Dodge; 104.167 mph, September 4, 1997

# TALLADEGA SUPERSPEEDWAY

## 2005 SCHEDULE

### NEXTEL CUP
**Event:** Aaron's 499
**Race:** No. 9 of 36
**Date:** May 1
**TV:** FOX. **Radio:** MRN

**Event:** EA Sports 500
**Race:** No. 29 of 36
**Date:** October 2
**TV:** NBC. **Radio:** MRN

### BUSCH SERIES
**Event:** Aaron's 312
**Race:** No. 10 of 35
**Date:** April 30
**TV:** FOX. **Radio:** MRN

Race names subject to change

### TRACK FACTS
**Opened:** September 1969
**Owner:** International Speedway Corp.
**Location:** Talladega, Ala.
**Distance:** 2.66 miles
**Banking in turns:** 33 degrees
**Banking in trioval:** 18 degrees
**Banking on back stretch:** 2 degrees
**Length of front stretch:** 4,300 feet
**Length of backstretch:** 4,000 feet
**Grandstand seating:** 143,000
**Tickets:** (256) 362-7223
**Website:** www.talladegasuperspeedway.com

Back stretch: 4,000 feet / 2°
33° Banking in Turns
Front stretch: 4,300 feet / 18°

# NEXTEL CUP

## TRACK RECORDS

**Most wins:** 10—Dale Earnhardt
**Oldest winner:** Harry Gant, 51 years, 3 months, 26 days, May 6, 1991
**Youngest winner:** Bobby Hillin, 22 years, 1 month, 22 days, July 27, 1986
**Most lead changes:** 75—May 6, 1984
**Fewest lead changes:** 13—May 6, 1973
**Most leaders:** 26—Twice, most recently, April 22, 2001
**Fewest leaders:** 4—May 16, 1971
**Most cautions:** 40—August 23, 1970
**Fewest cautions:** 0—Three times, most recently, October 6, 2002
**Most caution laps:** 62—May 7, 1972
**Fewest caution laps:** 0—Three times, most recently, October 6, 2002
**Most on the lead lap:** 29—April 22, 2001
**Fewest on the lead lap:** 1—Twice, most recently, May 6, 1979
**Most running at the finish:** 40—April 22, 2001

**Fewest running at the finish:** 14—July 27, 1986
**Most laps led by a race winner:** 153—Pete Hamilton, August 23, 1970
**Fewest laps led by a race winner:** 3—Twice, most recently, Bobby Hamilton, April 22, 2001
**Closest margin of victory:** 0.005 seconds—Dale Earnhardt defeated Ernie Irvan, July 25, 1993.
**Greatest margin of victory:** 1 lap, 50 seconds—Bobby Allison defeated Darrell Waltrip, May 6, 1979.

## QUALIFYING AND RACE RECORDS

**QUALIFYING: Track:** Bill Elliott, Ford; 212.809 mph, April 30, 1987. **Winston 500:** Bill Elliott, Ford; 212.809 mph, April 30, 1987. **Diehard 500:** Bill Elliott, Ford; 209.005 mph, July 24, 1986.
**RACE: Track:** Mark Martin, Ford; 188.354 mph, May 10, 1997. **Winston 500:** Mark Martin, Ford; 188.354 mph, May 10, 1997. **EA Sports 500:** Dale Earnhardt Jr., Chevrolet; 183.665 mph, October 6, 2002.

## NEXTEL Cup YEAR BY YEAR WINNERS

| | Year | Event | Race Winner | Car Make | Avg. Speed | Start Pos. | Car Owner | Pole Winner | Pole Speed |
|---|------|-------|-------------|----------|------------|------------|-----------|-------------|------------|
| | 2004 | EA Sports 500 | D. Earnhardt Jr. | Chevrolet | 156.929 | 10 | Teresa Earnhardt | J. Nemechek | 190.749 |
| | | Aaron's 499 | J. Gordon | Chevrolet | 129.396 | 11 | Rick Hendrick | R. Rudd | 191.180 |
| | 2003 | EA Sports 500 | **M. Waltrip** | Chevrolet | 156.045 | 18 | Dale Earnhardt Inc. | E. Sadler | 189.943 |
| | | Aaron's 499 | D. Earnhardt Jr. | Chevrolet | 144.625 | 2 | Dale Earnhardt Inc. | J. Mayfield | 186.489 |
| c | 2002 | EA Sports 500 | D. Earnhardt Jr. | Chevrolet | 183.665 | 13 | Dale Earnhardt | Trials rained out | |
| | | Aaron's 499 | D. Earnhardt Jr. | Chevrolet | 159.022 | 4 | Dale Earnhardt | J. Johnson | 186.532 |

## FALL: EA SPORTS 500

**POLE WINNERS**

| | |
|---|---|
| B. Elliott | 4 |
| E. Irvan | 4 |
| C. Yarborough | 3 |
| J. Nemechek | 3 |
| Buddy Baker | 2 |
| D. Pearson | 2 |
| B. Isaac | 2 |
| D. Allison | 1 |
| D. Marcis | 1 |
| A. Foyt | 1 |
| D. Waltrip | 1 |
| B. Allison | 1 |
| B. Parsons | 1 |
| Da. Allison | 1 |
| M. Martin | 1 |
| D. Earnhardt | 1 |
| T. Labonte | 1 |
| J. Andretti | 1 |
| B. Labonte | 1 |
| S. Compton | 1 |
| E. Sadler | 1 |

**RACE WINNERS**

| | |
|---|---|
| D. Earnhardt | 4 |
| Da. Allison | 3 |
| D. Pearson | 3 |
| Buddy Baker | 3 |
| B. Allison | 3 |
| D. Earnhardt Jr. | 3 |
| M. Martin | 2 |
| C. Yarborough | 2 |
| D. Waltrip | 2 |
| D. Allison | 1 |
| B. Hamilton | 1 |
| R. Petty | 1 |
| B. Elliott | 1 |
| B. Parsons | 1 |
| H. Gant | 1 |
| E. Irvan | 1 |
| S. Marlin | 1 |
| J. Gordon | 1 |
| D. Jarrett | 1 |
| M. Waltrip | 1 |

## SPRING: AARON'S 499

**POLE WINNERS**

| | |
|---|---|
| B. Elliott | 4 |
| C. Yarborough | 3 |
| B. Isaac | 3 |
| S. Marlin | 3 |
| J. Mayfield | 3 |
| D. Earnhardt | 3 |
| K. Schrader | 2 |
| D. Marcis | 2 |
| B. Allison | 1 |
| D. Allison | 1 |
| D. Pearson | 1 |
| B. Parsons | 1 |
| N. Bonnett | 1 |
| Buddy Baker | 1 |
| H. Gant | 1 |
| G. Bodine | 1 |
| D. Waltrip | 1 |
| M. Martin | 1 |
| E. Irvan | 1 |
| S. Compton | 1 |
| J. Johnson | 1 |
| R. Rudd | 1 |

**RACE WINNERS**

| | |
|---|---|
| D. Earnhardt | 6 |
| J. Gordon | 3 |
| T. Labonte | 2 |
| D. Waltrip | 2 |
| D. Earnhardt Jr. | 2 |
| R. Petty | 1 |
| D. Marcis | 1 |
| B. Allison | 1 |
| D. Allison | 1 |
| Buddy Baker | 1 |
| D. Brooks | 1 |
| J. Hylton | 1 |
| B. Hamilton | 1 |
| R. Brickhouse | 1 |
| L. Pond | 1 |
| N. Bonnett | 1 |
| R. Bouchard | 1 |
| C. Yarborough | 1 |
| B. Hillin | 1 |
| B. Elliott | 1 |
| K. Schrader | 1 |
| E. Irvan | 1 |
| J. Spencer | 1 |
| S. Marlin | 1 |
| B. Labonte | 1 |
| B. Hamilton | 1 |

## ALL TALLADEGA RACES

**POLE WINNERS**

| | |
|---|---|
| B. Elliott | 8 |
| C. Yarborough | 6 |
| B. Isaac | 5 |
| E. Irvan | 5 |
| D. Earnhardt | 3 |
| S. Marlin | 3 |
| D. Marcis | 3 |
| D. Pearson | 3 |
| Buddy Baker | 3 |
| J. Mayfield | 3 |
| J. Nemechek | 3 |
| M. Martin | 2 |
| K. Schrader | 2 |
| D. Waltrip | 2 |
| D. Allison | 2 |
| B. Allison | 2 |
| B. Parsons | 2 |
| S. Compton | 2 |
| A. Foyt | 1 |
| N. Bonnett | 1 |
| H. Gant | 1 |
| G. Bodine | 1 |
| Da. Allison | 1 |
| T. Labonte | 1 |
| J. Andretti | 1 |
| B. Labonte | 1 |
| Ji. Johnson | 1 |
| E. Sadler | 1 |
| R. Rudd | 1 |
| D. Earnhardt | 10 |

**RACE WINNERS**

| | |
|---|---|
| D. Earnhardt Jr. | 5 |
| D. Waltrip | 4 |
| Buddy Baker | 4 |
| B. Allison | 4 |
| Da. Allison | 3 |
| D. Pearson | 3 |
| C. Yarborough | 3 |
| J. Gordon | 3 |
| D. Allison | 2 |
| B. Hamilton | 2 |
| R. Petty | 2 |
| B. Elliott | 2 |
| E. Irvan | 2 |
| S. Marlin | 2 |
| T. Labonte | 2 |
| M. Martin | 2 |
| D. Brooks | 1 |
| J. Hylton | 1 |
| R. Brickhouse | 1 |
| L. Pond | 1 |
| N. Bonnett | 1 |
| R. Bouchard | 1 |
| B. Hillin | 1 |
| P. Parsons | 1 |
| K. Schrader | 1 |
| H. Gant | 1 |
| J. Spencer | 1 |
| D. Marcis | 1 |
| B. Labonte | 1 |
| D. Jarrett | 1 |
| B. Hamilton | 1 |
| M. Waltrip | 1 |

## NEXTEL Cup YEAR BY YEAR WINNERS (Talladega, continued)

| Year | Event | Race Winner | Car Make | Avg. Speed | Start Pos. | Car Owner | Pole Winner | Pole Speed |
|---|---|---|---|---|---|---|---|---|
| 2001 | EA Sports 500 | D. Earnhardt Jr. | Chevrolet | 164.185 | 6 | Dale Earnhardt | S. Compton | 185.240 |
| c | Talladega 500 | B. Hamilton | Chevrolet | 184.003 | 14 | Andy Petree | S. Compton | 184.861 |
| 2000 | Winston 500 | D. Earnhardt | Chevrolet | 165.681 | 20 | Richard Childress | J. Nemechek | 190.279 |
| | DieHard 500 | J. Gordon | Chevrolet | 161.157 | 36 | Rick Hendrick | J. Mayfield | 186.969 |
| 1999 | Winston 500 | D. Earnhardt | Chevrolet | 166.632 | 27 | Richard Childress | J. Nemechek | 198.331 |
| | DieHard 500 | D. Earnhardt | Chevrolet | 163.395 | 17 | Richard Childress | K. Schrader | 197.765 |
| 1998 | Winston 500 | D. Jarrett | Ford | 159.318 | 3 | Robert Yates | K. Schrader | 196.153 |
| | DieHard 500 | B. Labonte | Pontiac | 144.428 | 1 | Joe Gibbs | B. Labonte | 195.728 |
| 1997 | DieHard 500 | T. Labonte | Chevrolet | 156.601 | 6 | Rick Hendrick | E. Irvan | 193.271 |
| c | Winston 500 | M. Martin | Ford | 188.354 | 18 | Jack Roush | J. Andretti | 193.627 |
| b 1996 | DieHard 500 | J. Gordon | Chevrolet | 133.387 | 2 | Rick Hendrick | J. Mayfield | 192.370 |
| | Winston Select 500 | S. Marlin | Chevrolet | 149.999 | 4 | Morgan-McClure | E. Irvan | 192.855 |
| 1995 | Winston 500 | S. Marlin | Chevrolet | 173.188 | 1 | Morgan-McClure | S. Marlin | 194.212 |
| | Winston Select 500 | M. Martin | Ford | 178.902 | 3 | Jack Roush | T. Labonte | 196.532 |
| 1994 | Winston 500 | J. Spencer | Ford | 163.217 | 2 | Junior Johnson | D. Earnhardt | 193.470 |
| | Winston Select 500 | D. Earnhardt | Chevrolet | 157.478 | 4 | Richard Childress | E. Irvan | 193.298 |
| 1993 | DieHard 500 | D. Earnhardt | Chevrolet | 153.858 | 11 | Richard Childress | B. Elliott | 192.397 |
| | Winston 500 | E. Irvan | Chevrolet | 155.412 | 16 | Morgan-McClure | D. Earnhardt | 192.355 |
| 1992 | Winston 500 | E. Irvan | Chevrolet | 176.309 | 7 | Morgan-McClure | S. Marlin | 190.586 |
| | DieHard 500 | Da. Allison | Ford | 167.609 | 2 | Robert Yates | E. Irvan | 192.831 |
| 1991 | DieHard 500 | D. Earnhardt | Chevrolet | 147.383 | 4 | Richard Childress | S. Marlin | 192.085 |
| | Winston 500 | H. Gant | Oldsmobile | 165.620 | 2 | Leo Jackson | E. Irvan | 195.186 |
| 1990 | DieHard 500 | D. Earnhardt | Chevrolet | 174.430 | 1 | Richard Childress | D. Earnhardt | 192.513 |
| | Winston 500 | D. Earnhardt | Chevrolet | 159.571 | 5 | Richard Childress | B. Elliott | 199.388 |
| 1989 | DieHard 500 | T. Labonte | Ford | 157.354 | 5 | Junior Johnson | M. Martin | 194.800 |
| | Winston 500 | Da. Allison | Ford | 155.869 | 2 | Robert Yates | M. Martin | 193.061 |
| 1988 | Talladega DieHard 500 | K. Schrader | Chevrolet | 154.505 | 7 | Rick Hendrick | D. Waltrip | 196.274 |
| | Winston 500 | P. Parsons | Oldsmobile | 156.547 | 3 | Jackson Bros. | Da. Allison | 198.969 |
| 1987 | Talladega 500 | B. Elliott | Ford | 171.293 | 1 | Melling Racing | B. Elliott | 203.827 |
| a | Winston 500 | Da. Allison | Ford | 154.228 | 3 | Ranier Racing | B. Elliott | 212.809 |
| 1986 | Talladega 500 | B. Hillin | Buick | 151.552 | 13 | Stavola Bros. | B. Elliott | 209.005 |
| | Winston 500 | B. Allison | Buick | 157.698 | 2 | Stavola Bros. | B. Elliott | 212.229 |
| 1985 | Talladega 500 | C. Yarborough | Ford | 148.772 | 2 | Ranier Racing | B. Elliott | 207.578 |
| | Winston 500 | B. Elliott | Ford | 186.288 | 1 | Melling Racing | B. Elliott | 209.398 |
| 1984 | Talladega 500 | D. Earnhardt | Chevrolet | 155.485 | 3 | Richard Childress | C. Yarborough | 202.474 |
| | Winston 500 | C. Yarborough | Chevrolet | 172.988 | 1 | Ranier Racing | C. Yarborough | 202.692 |
| 1983 | Talladega 500 | D. Earnhardt | Ford | 170.611 | 4 | Bud Moore | C. Yarborough | 201.744 |
| | Winston 500 | R. Petty | Pontiac | 153.936 | 15 | Petty Eng. | C. Yarborough | 202.650 |
| 1982 | Talladega 500 | D. Waltrip | Buick | 168.157 | 2 | Junior Johnson | G. Bodine | 199.400 |
| | Winston 500 | D. Waltrip | Buick | 156.597 | 2 | Junior Johnson | B. Parsons | 200.176 |
| 1981 | Talladega 500 | R. Bouchard | Buick | 156.737 | 10 | Race Hill Farm | H. Gant | 195.897 |
| | Winston 500 | B. Allison | Buick | 149.376 | 1 | Ranier Racing | B. Allison | 195.864 |
| 1980 | Talladega 500 | N. Bonnett | Mercury | 166.894 | 2 | Wood Brothers | Buddy Baker | 198.545 |
| | Winston 500 | Buddy Baker | Oldsmobile | 170.481 | 2 | Ranier Racing | D. Pearson | 197.704 |
| 1979 | Talladega 500 | D. Waltrip | Oldsmobile | 161.229 | 8 | DiGard Rac. Co. | N. Bonnett | 193.600 |
| | Winston 500 | B. Allison | Ford | 154.770 | 12 | Bud Moore | D. Waltrip | 195.644 |
| 1978 | Talladega 500 | L. Pond | Oldsmobile | 174.700 | 5 | Ranier Racing | C. Yarborough | 192.917 |
| | Winston 500 | C. Yarborough | Oldsmobile | 159.699 | 1 | Junior Johnson | C. Yarborough | 191.904 |
| 1977 | Talladega 500 | Do. Allison | Chevrolet | 162.524 | 2 | Hoss Ellington | B. Parsons | 192.684 |
| | Winston 500 | D. Waltrip | Chevrolet | 164.877 | 11 | DiGard Rac. Co. | A. Foyt | 192.424 |
| 1976 | Talladega 500 | D. Marcis | Dodge | 157.547 | 1 | Nord Krauskopf | D. Marcis | 190.651 |
| | Winston 500 | Buddy Baker | Ford | 169.887 | 12 | Bud Moore | D. Marcis | 189.197 |
| 1975 | Talladega 500 | Buddy Baker | Ford | 130.892 | 1 | Bud Moore | D. Marcis | 191.340 |
| | Winston 500 | Buddy Baker | Ford | 144.948 | 1 | Bud Moore | Buddy Baker | 189.947 |
| 1974 | Talladega 500 | R. Petty | Dodge | 148.637 | 3 | Petty Eng. | D. Pearson | 184.926 |
| | Winston 500 | D. Pearson | Mercury | 130.220 | 1 | Wood Brothers | D. Pearson | 186.086 |
| 1973 | Talladega 500 | R. Brooks | Plymouth | 145.454 | 24 | Crawford Bros. | B. Allison | 187.064 |
| | Winston 500 | D. Pearson | Mercury | 131.956 | 2 | Wood Brothers | Buddy Baker | 193.435 |
| 1972 | Talladega 500 | J. Hylton | Mercury | 148.728 | 22 | James Hylton | B. Isaac | 190.677 |
| | Winston 500 | D. Pearson | Mercury | 134.400 | 2 | Wood Brothers | B. Isaac | 192.428 |
| 1971 | Talladega 500 | B. Allison | Mercury | 145.945 | 2 | Holman-Moody | Do. Allison | 187.323 |
| | Winston 500 | Do. Allison | Mercury | 147.419 | 1 | Wood Brothers | Do. Allison | 185.869 |
| 1970 | Talladega 500 | P. Hamilton | Plymouth | 158.517 | 4 | Petty Eng. | D. Isaac | 186.834 |
| | Alabama 500 | P. Hamilton | Plymouth | 152.321 | 6 | Petty Eng. | D. Isaac | 199.658 |
| 1969 | Talladega 500 | R. Brickhouse | Dodge | 153.778 | 9 | Ray Nichels | D. Isaac | 196.386 |

**KEY**
a 473.48 miles (178 laps), darkness.
b 343.14 miles (129 laps), darkness.
c Rescheduled to May 10; rain. Caution-free race.

# BUSCH SERIES

## Busch YEAR BY YEAR WINNERS (Talladega)

| Year | Event | Race Winner | Car Make | Avg. Speed | Start Pos. | Pole Winner | Pole Speed |
|---|---|---|---|---|---|---|---|
| 2004 | Aaron's 312 | M. Truex Jr. | Chevrolet | 136.783 | 3 | C. Bowyer | 184.253 |
| 2003 | Aaron's 312 | D. Earnhardt Jr. | Chevrolet | 114.768 | 3 | J. Nemechek | 188.649 |
| 2002 | Aaron's 312 | J. Keller | Ford | 157.691 | 12 | Jo. Sauter | 188.764 |
| 2001 | Subway 300 | M. McLaughlin | Pontiac | 131.258 | 14 | J. Nemechek | 189.729 |
| 2000 | Touchstone Energy 300 | J. Nemechek | Chevrolet | 153.859 | 35 | Trials rained out | |
| 1999 | Touchstone Energy 300 | T. Labonte | Chevrolet | 150.793 | 16 | K. Schrader | 192.455 |
| 1998* | Touchstone Energy 300 | J. Nemechek | Chevrolet | 118.196 | 1 | J. Nemechek | 189.628 |
| 1997 | Easy Care 500K | M. Martin | Ford | 168.937 | 23 | J. Nemechek | 193.517 |
| 1996 | Humminbird 500K | G. Sacks | Chevrolet | 139.438 | 7 | J. Nemechek | 192.878 |
| 1995 | Humminbird 500K | C. Little | Ford | 122.904 | 7 | J. Purvis | 189.921 |
| 1994 | Fram Filter 500K | K. Schrader | Chevrolet | 167.473 | 17 | J. Purvis | 186.703 |

**POLE WINNERS**

| | |
|---|---|
| J. Nemechek | 5 |
| J. Purvis | 2 |
| D. Earnhardt | 1 |
| B. Elliott | 1 |
| Jo. Sauter | 1 |
| K. Schrader | 1 |
| C. Bowyer | 1 |

**RACE WINNERS**

| | |
|---|---|
| J. Nemechek | 2 |
| D. Earnhardt | 1 |
| E. Irvan | 1 |
| J. Keller | 1 |
| T. Labonte | 1 |
| C. Little | 1 |
| M. Martin | 1 |
| M. McLaughlin | 1 |
| G. Sacks | 1 |
| K. Schrader | 1 |
| D. Earnhardt Jr. | 1 |
| M. Truex Jr. | 1 |

## Busch YEAR BY YEAR WINNERS (Talladega, continued)

| Year | Event | Race Winner | Car Make | Avg. Speed | Start Pos. | Pole Winner | Pole Speed |
|------|-------|-------------|----------|-----------|-----------|-------------|-----------|
| 1993 | Fram Filter 500K | D. Earnhardt | Chevrolet | 146.801 | 22 | B. Elliott | 188.404 |
| 1992 | Fram Filter 500K | E. Irvan | Chevrolet | 158.359 | 2 | D. Earnhardt | 184.733 |

*changed to 300 miles

**QUALIFYING RECORD:** Joe Nemechek, Chevrolet; 193.517 mph, April 24, 1997
**RACE RECORD:** Mark Martin, Ford; 168.937 mph, April 26, 1997

# TEXAS MOTOR SPEEDWAY

## 2005 SCHEDULE

### NEXTEL CUP

**Event:** Samsung/RadioShack 500
**Race:** No. 7 of 36
**Date:** April 17
**TV:** FOX. **Radio:** PRN

**Event:** Dickies 500*
**Race:** No. 34 of 36
**Date:** November 6
**TV:** NBC. **Radio:** PRN
*Inaugural event

### BUSCH SERIES

**Event:** O'Reilly 300
**Race:** No. 8 of 35
**Date:** April 16
**TV:** FOX. **Radio:** PRN

**Event:** O'Reilly Challenge*
**Race:** No. 33 of 35
**Date:** November 5
**TV:** NBC. **Radio:** PRN
*Inaugural event

### CRAFTSMAN TRUCK SERIES

**Event:** O'Reilly 400K
**Race:** No. 9 of 25
**Date:** June 10
**TV:** SPEED. **Radio:** MRN

**Event:** Silverado 350K
**Race:** No. 23 of 25
**Date:** November 4
**TV:** SPEED. **Radio:** MRN
Race names subject to change

## TRACK FACTS

**Date Opened:** February 5, 1996
**Owner:** Speedway Motorsports, Inc.
**Location:** Fort Worth, Texas
**Distance:** 1.5 miles
**Banking in turns:** 24 degrees
**Banking in straights:** 5 degrees
**Length of front stretch:** 2,250 feet
**Length of back stretch:** 1,330 feet
**Grandstand seating:** 154,861
**Tickets:** (817) 215-8500
**Website:** www.texasmotorspeedway.com

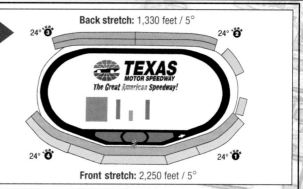

Back stretch: 1,330 feet / 5°
Front stretch: 2,250 feet / 5°

## NEXTEL CUP

### TRACK RECORDS

**Most wins:** 1—Jeff Burton, Dale Earnhardt Jr., Dale Jarrett, Matt Kenseth, Terry Labonte, Mark Martin, Ryan Newman
**Oldest winner:** Dale Jarrett, 44 years, 4 months, 6 days, April 1, 2001
**Youngest winner:** Ryan Newman, 25 years, 3 months, 22 days, March 30, 2003
**Most lead changes:** 29—April 2, 2000
**Fewest lead changes:** 18—April 1, 2001
**Most leaders:** 17—April 2, 2000
**Fewest leaders:** 7—April 1, 2001
**Most cautions:** 12—April 2, 2000
**Fewest cautions:** 7—Twice, most recently, April 8, 2002
**Most caution Laps:** 73—April 6, 1997
**Fewest caution Laps:** 39—March 28, 1999
**Most on the lead lap:** 14—April 2, 2000
**Fewest on the lead lap:** 8—April 6, 1997

**Most running at the finish:** 38—April 8, 2002
**Fewest running at the finish:** 29—Twice, most recently, April 5, 1998
**Most laps led by a race winner:** 124—Terry Labonte, March 28, 1999
**Fewest laps led by a race winner:** 37—Mark Martin, April 5, 1998
**Closest margin of victory:** 0.573 seconds—Mark Martin defeated Chad Little, April 5, 1998.
**Greatest margin of victory:** 5.920 seconds—Dale Earnhardt Jr. defeated Jeff Burton, April 2, 2000.

### QUALIFYING AND RACE RECORDS

**QUALIFYING:** Bill Elliott, Dodge; 194.224 mph, April 8, 2002.
**RACE:** Terry Labonte, Chevrolet; 144.276 mph, March 28, 1999.

## NEXTEL Cup YEAR BY YEAR WINNERS

| Year | Event | Race Winner | Car Make | Avg. Speed | Start Pos. | Car Owner | Pole Winner | Pole Speed |
|------|-------|-------------|----------|-----------|-----------|-----------|-------------|-----------|
| 2004 | Samsung/RadioShack 500 | E. Sadler | Ford | 138.845 | 19 | Robert Yates | B. Labonte | 193.903 |
| 2003 | Samsung/RadioShack 500 | R. Newman | Dodge | 134.517 | 3 | Roger Penske | B. Labonte | 193.514 |
| 2002 | Samsung/RadioShack 500 | M. Kenseth | Ford | 142.453 | 31 | Jack Roush | B. Elliott | 194.224 |
| 2001 | Harrah's 500 | D. Jarrett | Ford | 141.804 | 3 | Robert Yates | D. Earnhardt Jr. | 190.678 |
| 2000 | DirecTV 500 | D. Earnhardt Jr. | Chevrolet | 131.152 | 4 | Dale Earnhardt | T. Labonte | 192.137 |
| 1999 | Primestar 500 | T. Labonte | Chevrolet | 144.276 | 4 | Rick Hendrick | K. Irwin | 190.154 |
| 1998 | Texas 500 | M. Martin | Ford | 136.771 | 7 | Jack Roush | J. Mayfield | 185.906 |
| 1997 | Interstate Batteries 500 | J. Burton | Ford | 125.111 | 5 | Jack Roush | Trials rained out | |

### ALL TEXAS RACES

| POLE WINNERS | | RACE WINNERS | |
|--------------|---|--------------|---|
| B. Labonte | 2 | J. Burton | 1 |
| J. Mayfield | 1 | M. Martin | 1 |
| K. Irwin | 1 | T. Labonte | 1 |
| T. Labonte | 1 | D. Earnhardt Jr. | 1 |
| D. Earnhardt Jr. | 1 | D. Jarrett | 1 |
| B. Elliott | 1 | M. Kenseth | 1 |
| | | R. Newman | 1 |
| | | E. Sadler | 1 |

# BUSCH SERIES

## Busch YEAR BY YEAR WINNERS (Texas)

| Year | Event | Race Winner | Car Make | Avg. Speed | Start Pos. | Pole Winner | Pole Speed | POLE WINNERS | | RACE WINNERS | |
|------|-------|-------------|----------|-----------|-----------|-------------|-----------|--------------|---|--------------|---|
| 2004 | O'Reilly 300 | M. Kenseth | Ford | 115.482 | 15 | Ky. Busch | 189.847 | J. Green | 2 | M. Martin | 3 |
| 2003 | O'Reilly 300 | J. Nemechek | Chevrolet | 117.891 | 7 | J. Keller | 187.474 | D. Blaney | 1 | D. Earnhardt Jr. | 1 |
| 2002 | O'Reilly 300 | J. Purvis | Chevrolet | 102.136 | 13 | J. Green | 193.483 | M. Kenseth | 1 | K. Harvick | 1 |
| 2001 | Jani-King 300 | K. Harvick | Chevrolet | 126.212 | 7 | M. Kenseth | 189.880 | J. Leffler | 1 | J. Purvis | 1 |
| 2000 | Albertson's 300 | M. Martin | Ford | 108.130 | 2 | J. Leffler | 184.451 | E. Sadler | 1 | J. Nemechek | 1 |
| 1999 | Coca-Cola 300 | M. Martin | Ford | 127.417 | 2 | D. Blaney | 183.082 | J. Keller | 1 | | |
| 1998 | Coca-Cola 300 | D. Earnhardt Jr. | Chevrolet | 120.174 | 16 | E. Sadler | 179.229 | | | | |
| 1997 | Coca-Cola 300 | M. Martin | Ford | 122.993 | 20 | J. Green | 180.054 | | | | |

**QUALIFYING RECORD:** Jeff Green, Chevrolet; 193.483 mph, April 5, 2002
**RACE RECORD:** Mark Martin, Ford; 127.417 mph, March 27, 1999

# CRAFTSMAN TRUCK SERIES

## Craftsman YEAR BY YEAR WINNERS (Texas)

| Year | Event | Race Winner | Car Make | Avg. Speed | Start Pos. | Pole Winner | Pole Speed | POLE WINNERS | | RACE WINNERS | |
|------|-------|-------------|----------|-----------|-----------|-------------|-----------|--------------|---|--------------|---|
| 2004 | O'Reilly 400K | D. Setzer | Chevrolet | 148.959 | 4 | T. Musgrave | 180.971 | Ja. Sauter | 2 | B. Gaughan | 4 |
| | Silverado 350K | T. Bodine | Toyota | 115.169 | 22 | M. Skinner | 182.174 | M. Bliss | 2 | G. Biffle | 1 |
| 2003 | O'Reilly 400K | B. Gaughan | Dodge | 140.621 | 5 | Trials rained out | | G. Biffle | 1 | K. Irwin | 1 |
| | Silverado 350 | B. Gaughan | Dodge | 122.727 | 7 | A. Houston | 181.531 | J. Leffler | 1 | T. Kvapil | 1 |
| 2002 | O'Reilly 400K | B. Gaughan | Dodge | 129.569 | 10 | J. Leffler | 180.355 | B. Reffner | 1 | T. Raines | 1 |
| 2002 | Silverado 350 | B. Gaughan | Dodge | 137.736 | 5 | M. Bliss | 179.695 | S. Riggs | 1 | B. Reffner | 1 |
| 2001 | O'Reilly 400K | J. Sprague | Chevrolet | 133.620 | 3 | S. Riggs | Rained out | J.Sprague | 1 | Ja. Sauter | 1 |
| 2001 | Silverado 350 | T. Kvapil | Chevrolet | 112.020 | 7 | S. Riggs | 181.953 | A. Houston | 1 | D. Setzer | 1 |
| 2000 | Pronto Auto Parts 400 | G. Biffle | Ford | 126.932 | 1 | G. Biffle | 178.130 | | | J. Sprague | 1 |
| 2000 | O'Reilly 400 | B. Reffner | Chevrolet | 112.933 | 1 | B. Reffner | 180.373 | | | | |
| 1999 | Pronto Auto Parts 400 | D. Setzer | Dodge | 122.805 | 3 | J. Sauter | 179.718 | | | | |
| 1999 | O'Reilly 400 | J. Sauter | Chevrolet | 132.430 | 1 | J. Sauter | 179.152 | | | | |
| 1998 | Pronto Auto Parts 400 | T. Raines | Ford | 111.018 | 12 | J. Sprague | 178.642 | | | | |
| 1997 | Pronto Auto Parts 400 | K. Irwin | Ford | 131.823 | 5 | M. Bliss | 175.667 | | | | |

**QUALIFYING RECORD:** Scott Riggs, Dodge; 181.953 mph, October 4, 2001
**RACE RECORD:** Brendan Gaughan, Dodge; 140.621 mph, June 6, 2003

# WATKINS GLEN INTERNATIONAL

## 2005 SCHEDULE

**NEXTEL CUP**
**Event:** Sirius at the Glen
**Race:** No. 22 of 36
**Date:** August 14
**TV:** TNT. **Radio:** MRN

**BUSCH SERIES**
**Event:** TBA
**Race:** No. 24 of 35
**Date:** August 13
**TV:** NBC. **Radio:** MRN

Race names subject to change

### TRACK FACTS

**Date Opened:** September 15, 1956
**Owner:** International Speedway Corp.
**Location:** Watkins Glen, N.Y.
**Distance:** 2.45-mile road course
**Turns:** 11
**Banking:** Ranging from 6 to 10 degrees
**Pit road stretch:** 2,141 feet
**Length of back stretch:** 1,839 feet
**Tickets:** (607) 535-2481
**Website:** www.theglen.com

# NEXTEL CUP

## TRACK RECORDS

**Most wins:** 4—Jeff Gordon
**Oldest winner:** Geoffrey Bodine, 47 years, 3 months, 24 days, August 11, 1996
**Youngest winner:** Jeff Gordon, 26 years, 6 days, August 10, 1997
**Most lead changes:** 14—August 11, 1991
**Fewest lead changes:** 3—July 18, 1965
**Most leaders:** 12—August 13, 1995
**Fewest leaders:** 1—August 4, 1957
**Most cautions:** 8—August 14, 1988

**Fewest cautions:** 0—July 18, 1965
**Most caution Laps:** 36—August 14, 1988
**Fewest caution Laps:** 0—July 18, 1965
**Most on the lead lap:** 33—August 13, 2000
**Fewest on the lead lap:** 2—Twice, most recently, July 18, 1965
**Most running at the finish:** 39—Three times, most recently, August 10, 2003
**Fewest running at the finish:** 11—July 18, 1965
**Most laps led by a race winner:** 75—Mark Martin, August 14, 1994

## TRACK RECORDS (Watkins Glen, continued)

**Fewest laps led by a race winner:** 4—Ricky Rudd, August 14, 1988
**Closest margin of victory:** 0.172 seconds—Jeff Gordon defeated Jeff Burton, August 12, 2001.
**Greatest margin of victory:** 12 seconds—Rusty Wallace defeated Terry Labonte, August 10, 1987.

## QUALIFYING AND RACE RECORDS

**QUALIFYING: Track record (2.45 mile course):** Jeff Gordon, Chevrolet; 124.580 mph, August 8, 2003. **Track record (2.428 mile course):** Terry Labonte, Oldsmobile; 121.652 mph, August 9, 1991. **Track record (2.3 mile course):** Billy Wade, Mercury; 102.222 mph, July 18, 1964.
**RACE: Track record (220.5 miles):** Mark Martin, Ford; 100.303 mph, August 13, 1995.
**Track record (218.52 miles):** Ernie Irvan, Chevrolet; 98.77 mph, August 11, 1991. **Track record (151.8 miles):** Marvin Panch, Ford; 98.182 mph, July 18, 1965. **Track record (101.2 miles):** Buck Baker, Chevrolet; 82.08 mph, August 4, 1957.

### NEXTEL Cup YEAR BY YEAR WINNERS

| Year | Event | Race Winner | Car Make | Avg. Speed | Start Pos. | Car Owner | Pole Winner | Pole Speed |
|------|-------|-------------|----------|-----------|-----------|-----------|-------------|-----------|
| 2004 | Sirius at the Glen | T. Stewart | Chevrolet | 92.249 | 4 | Joe Gibbs | Trials rained out | |
| 2003 | Sirius at the Glen | R. Gordon | Chevrolet | 90.441 | 14 | Richard Childress | J. Gordon | 124.580 |
| 2002 | Sirius at The Glen | T. Stewart | Pontiac | 82.208 | 3 | Joe Gibbs | R. Rudd | 122.696 |
| 2001 | G. Crossing at The Glen | J. Gordon | Chevrolet | 89.081 | 13 | Rick Hendrick | D. Jarrett | 122.698 |
| d2000 | G. Crossing at The Glen | S. Park | Chevrolet | 91.336 | 18 | Dale Earnhardt | Trials rained out | |
| 1999 | Frontier at The Glen | J. Gordon | Chevrolet | 87.722 | 3 | Rick Hendrick | R. Wallace | 121.234 |
| 1998 | Bud at Glen | J. Gordon | Chevrolet | 94.466 | 1 | Rick Hendrick | J. Gordon | 120.331 |
| 1997 | Bud at Glen | J. Gordon | Chevrolet | 91.294 | 11 | Rick Hendrick | T. Bodine | 120.505 |
| 1996 | Bud at Glen | G. Bodine | Ford | 92.334 | 13 | Geoff Bodine | D. Earnhardt | 120.733 |
| 1995 | Bud at Glen | M. Martin | Ford | 103.030 | 1 | Jack Roush | M. Martin | 120.411 |
| 1994 | Bud at Glen | M. Martin | Ford | 93.752 | 1 | Jack Roush | M. Martin | 118.326 |
| 1993 | Bud at Glen | M. Martin | Ford | 84.771 | 1 | Jack Roush | M. Martin | 119.118 |
| c1992 | Bud at Glen | K. Petty | Pontiac | 88.980 | 2 | Felix Sabates | D. Earnhardt | 116.882 |
| b1991 | Bud at Glen | E. Irvan | Chevrolet | 98.977 | 3 | Morgan-McClure | T. Labonte | 121.652 |
| 1990 | Bud at Glen | R. Rudd | Chevrolet | 92.452 | 12 | Rick Hendrick | D. Earnhardt | 121.190 |
| 1989 | Bud at Glen | R. Wallace | Pontiac | 87.242 | 13 | Blue Max | M. Shepherd | 120.456 |
| 1988 | Bud at Glen | R. Rudd | Buick | 74.096 | 6 | King Racing | G. Bodine | 120.541 |
| 1987 | Bud at Glen | R. Wallace | Pontiac | 90.682 | 2 | Blue Max | T. Labonte | 117.956 |
| 1986 | Bud at Glen | T. Richmond | Chevrolet | 90.463 | 1 | Rick Hendrick | T. Richmond | 117.563 |
| *a1965 | The Glen 151.8 | M. Panch | Ford | 98.182 | 3 | Wood Brothers | Trials rained out | |
| *1964 | The Glen 151.8 | B. Wade | Mercury | 97.988 | 1 | Bud Moore | B. Wade | 102.222 |
| *1957 | The Glen 101.2 | Buck Baker | Chevrolet | 83.064 | 1 | Buck Baker | Buck Baker | 87.071 |

### ALL WATKINS GLEN RACES

| POLE WINNERS | | RACE WINNERS | |
|--------------|---|--------------|---|
| M. Martin | 3 | J. Gordon | 4 |
| D. Earnhardt | 3 | M. Martin | 3 |
| T. Labonte | 2 | R. Wallace | 2 |
| J. Gordon | 2 | R. Rudd | 2 |
| T. Richmond | 1 | T. Stewart | 2 |
| Buck Baker | 1 | T. Richmond | 1 |
| B. Wade | 1 | Buck Baker | 1 |
| G. Bodine | 1 | B. Wade | 1 |
| M. Shepherd | 1 | M. Panch | 1 |
| T. Bodine | 1 | E. Irvan | 1 |
| R. Wallace | 1 | K. Petty | 1 |
| D. Jarrett | 1 | G. Bodine | 1 |
| R. Rudd | 1 | S. Park | 1 |
| | | R. Gordon | 1 |

**KEY**
* Miles of event.
a Time trials rained out; drew for starting positions.
b Last race on 2.428-mile course; it was restructured and is now 2.45 miles.
c Race cut to 124.95 miles by rain.
d Drivers started via car owner points.

## BUSCH SERIES

### Busch YEAR BY YEAR WINNERS (Watkins Glen)

| Year | Event | Race Winner | Car Make | Avg. Speed | Start Pos. | Pole Winner | Pole Speed |
|------|-------|-------------|----------|-----------|-----------|-------------|-----------|
| 2001 | GNC Live Well 200 | R. Fellows | Chevrolet | 89.754 | 2 | S. Pruett | 121.052 |
| 2000 | Lysol 200 | R. Fellows | Chevrolet | 90.586 | 1 | R. Fellows | 119.504 |
| 1999 | Lysol 200 | D. Earnhardt Jr. | Chevrolet | 76.034 | 3 | R. Fellows | 117.060 |
| 1998 | Lysol 200 | R. Fellows | Chevrolet | 70.183 | 2 | B. Said | 117.675 |
| 1997 | Lysol 200 | M. McLaughlin | Chevrolet | 90.225 | 6 | J. Nemechek | 116.128 |
| 1996 | Lysol 200 | T. Labonte | Chevrolet | 91.468 | 9 | D. Green | 115.995 |
| 1995 | Lysol 200 | T. Labonte | Chevrolet | 84.186 | 1 | T. Labonte | 115.309 |
| 1994 | Fay's 150 | T. Labonte | Chevrolet | 93.717 | 21 | Trials rained out | |
| 1993 | Fay's 150 | B. Elliott | Ford | 89.970 | 2 | E. Irvan | 114.632 |
| 1992 | Fay's 150 | E. Irvan | Chevrolet | 93.991 | 22 | Trials rained out | |
| 1991 | Fay's 150 | T. Labonte | Oldsmobile | 94.003 | 1 | T. Labonte | 117.163 |

| POLE WINNERS | | RACE WINNERS | |
|--------------|---|--------------|---|
| T. Labonte | 2 | T. Labonte | 4 |
| R. Fellows | 2 | R. Fellows | 3 |
| E. Irvan | 1 | E. Irvan | 1 |
| D. Green | 1 | B. Elliott | 1 |
| J. Nemechek | 1 | M. McLaughlin | 1 |
| B. Said | 1 | D. Earnhardt Jr. | 1 |
| S. Pruett | 1 | | |

**QUALIFYING RECORD:** Scott Pruett, Ford; 121.052 mph, July 7, 2001
**RACE RECORD:** Terry Labonte, Oldsmobile; 94.003 mph, June 29, 1991

# AUTODROMO HERMANOS RODRIGUEZ

## 2005 SCHEDULE

**BUSCH SERIES**
Race name: TBA*
Race: No. 3 of 36
Date: March 6
TV: FOX. Radio: MRN
*Inaugural event

**TRACK FACTS**
Location: Mexico City, Mexico
Length: 2.48 miles
Road course

# GATEWAY INTERNATIONAL SPEEDWAY

## 2005 SCHEDULE

**BUSCH SERIES**
Event: Charter 250
Race: No. 22 of 35
Date: August 30
TV: FX. Radio: MRN

Race names subject to change

**CRAFTSMAN TRUCK SERIES**
Event: Missouri/Illinois Dodge Dealers Ram Tough 200
Race: No. 5 of 25
Date: April 30
TV: SPEED. Radio: MRN

**TRACK FACTS**
Location: Madison, Ill.
Distance: 1.25 miles
Banking in Turns 1-2: 11 degrees
Banking in Turns 3-4: 9 degrees
Length of front stretch: 1,922 feet
Length of back stretch: 1,976 feet
Website: www.gatewayraceway.com

## BUSCH SERIES

### Busch YEAR BY YEAR WINNERS

| Year | Event | Race Winner | Car Make | Avg. Speed | Start Pos. | Pole Winner | Pole Speed | POLE WINNERS | | RACE WINNERS | |
|---|---|---|---|---|---|---|---|---|---|---|---|
| 2004 | Charter Pipeline 250 | M. Truex | Chevrolet | 101.466 | 1 | M. Truex | 134.112 | C. Atwood | 1 | D. Earnhardt Jr. | 2 |
| 2003 | Charter Pipeline 250 | S. Riggs | Ford | 92.870 | 8 | A. Lewis | 131.903 | J. Bessey | 1 | K. Harvick | 2 |
| 2002 | Charter Pipeline 250 | G. Biffle | Ford | 106.926 | 7 | R. LaJoie | 131.911 | G. Biffle | 1 | G. Biffle | 1 |
| 2001 | Carquest Auto Parts 250 | K. Harvick | Chevrolet | 103.448 | 2 | G. Biffle | 132.357 | S. Hall | 1 | E. Sadler | 1 |
| 2000 | Carquest Auto Parts 250 | K. Harvick | Chevrolet | 116.595 | 4 | Trials rained out | | R. LaJoie | 1 | S. Riggs | 1 |
| 1999 | Carquest Auto Parts 250 | D. Earnhardt Jr. | Chevrolet | 104.227 | 18 | C. Atwood | 132.423 | A. Lewis | 1 | M. Truex | 1 |
| 1998 | Carquest Auto Parts 250 | D. Earnhardt Jr. | Chevrolet | 104.566 | 13 | S. Hall | 132.361 | M. Truex | 1 | | |
| 1997 | Gateway 300 | E. Sadler | Chevrolet | 78.803 | 12 | J. Bessey | 130.993 | | | | |

**QUALIFYING RECORD: Track:** Martin Truex Jr., Chevrolet, 134.112 mph, May 8, 2004
**RACE RECORD: Track:** Kevin Harvick, Chevrolet; 116.595 mph, July 29, 2000

## CRAFTSMAN TRUCK SERIES

### Craftsman YEAR BY YEAR WINNERS

| Year | Event | Race Winner | Car Make | Avg. Speed | Start Pos. | Pole Winner | Pole Speed | POLE WINNERS | | RACE WINNERS | |
|---|---|---|---|---|---|---|---|---|---|---|---|
| 2004 | Ram Tough 200 | D. Starr | Chevrolet | 93.694 | 14 | J. Sprague | 133.227 | G. Biffle | 2 | G. Biffle | 1 |
| 2003 | Ram Tough 200 | B. Gaughan | Dodge | 99.489 | 4 | Trials rained out | | C. Atwood | 1 | R. Carelli | 1 |
| 2002 | Ram Tough 200 | T. Cook | Ford | 109.323 | 8 | M. Bliss | 129.549 | M. Bliss | 1 | T. Cook | 1 |
| 2001 | Ram Tough 200 | T. Musgrave | Dodge | 112.237 | 1 | T. Musgrave | 129.971 | S. Compton | 1 | T. Musgrave | 1 |
| 2000 | Ram Tough 200 | J. Sprague | Chevrolet | 113.726 | 2 | G. Biffle | 132.279 | T. Musgrave | 1 | J. Sprague | 1 |
| 1999 | Ram Tough 200 | G. Biffle | Ford | 111.853 | 5 | S. Compton | 133.093 | J. Sprague | 1 | B. Gaughan | 1 |
| 1998 | Ram Tough 200 | R. Carelli | Chevrolet | 99.764 | 4 | G. Biffle | 131.218 | | | D. Starr | 1 |

**QUALIFYING RECORD: Track:** Jack Sprague, Chevrolet; 133.227 mph, July 16, 2004
**RACE RECORD: Track:** Jack Sprague, Chevrolet; 113.726 mph, May 7, 2000

# INDIANAPOLIS RACEWAY PARK

## 2005 SCHEDULE

**BUSCH SERIES**
Event: Kroger 200
Race: No. 23 of 35
Date: August 6
TV: TNT. Radio: MRN

Race names subject to change

**CRAFTSMAN TRUCK SERIES**
Event: Power Stroke Diesel 200
Race: No. 15 of 25
Date: August 5
TV: SPEED. Radio: MRN

**TRACK FACTS**
Location: Clermont, Ind.
Distance: .686 miles
Banking in turns: 7.5 degrees
Banking in straights: 2 degrees
Length of front stretch: 699 feet
Length of back stretch: 699 feet
Website: www.irponline.com

## Busch YEAR BY YEAR WINNERS (Indianapolis Raceway Park)

| Year | Event | Race Winner | Car Make | Avg. Speed | Start Pos. | Pole Winner | Pole Speed | POLE WINNERS | | RACE WINNERS | |
|------|-------|-------------|----------|-----------|-----------|-------------|-----------|--------------|---|--------------|---|
| 2004 | Kroger 200 | Ky. Busch | Chevrolet | 81.250 | 8 | Jo. Sauter | 111.248 | R. LaJoie | 2 | M. Shepherd | 3 |
| 2003 | Kroger 200 | B. Vickers | Chevrolet | 90.049 | 3 | S. Hmiel | 110.690 | M. Alexander | 1 | J. Keller | 2 |
| 2002 | Kroger 200 | G. Biffle | Ford | 81.788 | 1 | G. Biffle | 109.521 | S. Ard | 1 | R. LaJoie | 2 |
| 2001 | Kroger 200 | K. Harvick | Chevrolet | 72.785 | 12 | K. Wallace | 110.635 | G. Biffle | 1 | G. Biffle | 1 |
| 2000 | Kroger 200 | R. Hornaday | Chevrolet | 79.626 | 16 | J. Leffler | 112.597 | B. Bodine | 1 | D. Earnhardt Jr. | 1 |
| 1999 | Kroger 200 | J. Keller | Chevrolet | 73.293 | 1 | J. Keller | 112.352 | W. Burton | 1 | S. Grissom | 1 |
| 1998 | Kroger 200 | D. Earnhardt Jr. | Chevrolet | 78.883 | 16 | B. Jones | 111.409 | D. Green | 1 | K. Harvick | 1 |
| 1997 | Kroger 200 | R. LaJoie | Chevrolet | 59.652 | 1 | R. LaJoie | 111.193 | J. Hensley | 1 | J. Hensley | 1 |
| 1996 | Kroger 200 | R. LaJoie | Chevrolet | 77.551 | 1 | R. LaJoie | 109.270 | E. Irvan | 1 | R. Hornaday | 1 |
| 1995 | Kroger 200 | J. Keller | Chevrolet | 80.335 | 3 | E. Sawyer | 109.570 | B. Jones | 1 | T. Houston | 1 |
| 1994 | Kroger 200 | M. Wallace | Chevrolet | 82.156 | 5 | D. Green | 113.461 | J. Keller | 1 | B. Labonte | 1 |
| 1993 | Kroger 200 | T. Leslie | Chevrolet | 69.792 | 10 | E. Irvan | 109.828 | J. Leffler | 1 | T. Leslie | 1 |
| 1992 | Kroger 200 | J. Nemechek | Chevrolet | 83.943 | 3 | R. Pressley | 109.265 | K. Moore | 1 | B. Miller | 1 |
| 1991 | Kroger 200 | B. Labonte | Oldsmobile | 76.034 | 3 | W. Burton | 110.516 | L.D. Ottinger | 1 | J. Nemechek | 1 |
| 1990 | Kroger 200 | S. Grissom | Oldsmobile | 75.719 | 17 | J. Hensley | 110.260 | P. Parsons | 1 | L. Pearson | 1 |
| 1989 | Kroger 200 | M. Waltrip | Pontiac | 84.633 | 1 | M. Waltrip | 108.807 | R. Pressley | 1 | M. Wallace | 1 |
| 1988 | Kroger 200 | M. Shepherd | Buick | 76.553 | 2 | K. Moore | 105.895 | E. Sawyer | 1 | M. Waltrip | 1 |
| 1987 | Kroger 200 | L. Pearson | Pontiac | 73.402 | 11 | M. Alexander | 104.387 | D. Waltrip | 1 | B. Vickers | 1 |
| 1986 | Kroger 200 | B. Miller | Pontiac | 75.431 | 18 | D. Waltrip | 104.910 | M. Waltrip | 1 | Ky. Busch | 1 |
| 1985 | Kroger 200 | J. Hensley | Oldsmobile | 96.923 | 2 | B. Bodine | 105.121 | S. Hmiel | 1 | | |
| 1984 | Kroger 200 | M. Shepherd | Pontiac | 88.579 | 3 | L. Ottinger | 104.246 | Jo. Sauter | 1 | | |
| 1983 | Kroger 200 | T. Houston | Chevrolet | 79.600 | 7 | P. Parsons | 105.201 | | | | |
| 1982 | Kroger 200 | M. Shepherd | Oldsmobile | 67.234 | 5 | S. Ard | 104.436 | | | | |

**QUALIFYING RECORD: Track:** David Green, Chevrolet; 113.461 mph, August 4, 1994
**RACE RECORD: Track:** Jimmy Hensley, Oldsmobile; 96.923 mph, June 22, 1985

# CRAFTSMAN TRUCK SERIES

## Craftsman YEAR BY YEAR WINNERS (Indianapolis Raceway Park)

| Year | Event | Race Winner | Car Make | Avg. Speed | Start Pos. | Pole Winner | Pole Speed | POLE WINNERS | | RACE WINNERS | |
|------|-------|-------------|----------|-----------|-----------|-------------|-----------|--------------|---|--------------|---|
| 2004 | Power Stroke 200 | C. Chaffin | Dodge | 77.007 | 5 | J. Sprague | 110.275 | J. Ruttman | 2 | M. Skinner | 2 |
| 2003 | Power Stroke 200 | C. Edwards | Ford | 88.121 | 5 | T. Cook | 107.777 | M. Skinner | 2 | J. Sprague | 2 |
| 2002 | Power Stroke 200 | T. Cook | Ford | 74.018 | 1 | T. Cook | 108.549 | T. Cook | 2 | G. Biffle | 1 |
| 2001 | Power Stroke 200 | J. Sprague | Chevrolet | 80.745 | 2 | J. Ruttman | 109.043 | J. Hensley | 1 | T. Cook | 1 |
| 2000 | Power Stroke 200 | J. Ruttman | Dodge | 75.064 | 1 | J. Ruttman | 111.843 | D. Setzer | 1 | R. Hornaday Jr. | 1 |
| 1999 | Power Stroke 200 | G. Biffle | Ford | 88.704 | 3 | D. Setzer | 111.133 | R. Tolsma | 1 | J. Ruttman | 1 |
| 1998 | Cummins 200 | J. Sprague | Chevrolet | 77.235 | 3 | R. Tolsma | 110.829 | J. Sprague | 1 | C. Edwards | 1 |
| 1997 | Cummins 200 | R. Hornaday Jr. | Chevrolet | 81.753 | 2 | J. Hensley | 109.750 | | | C. Chaffin | 1 |
| 1996 | Cummins 200 | M. Skinner | Chevrolet | 85.720 | 1 | M. Skinner | 108.855 | | | | |
| 1995 | Action Packed 150 | M. Skinner | Chevrolet | 78.767 | 1 | M. Skinner | 108.387 | | | | |

**QUALIFYING RECORD:** Joe Ruttman, Dodge; 111.843 mph, August 2, 2000
**RACE RECORD:** Greg Biffle, Ford; 88.704 mph, August 5, 1999

# KENTUCKY SPEEDWAY

## 2005 SCHEDULE

**BUSCH SERIES**
Event: Meijer 300
Race: No. 16 of 35
Date: June 18
TV: FX. Radio: MRN
Race names subject to change

**CRAFTSMAN TRUCK SERIES**
Event: Built Ford Tough 225
Race: No. 9 of 25
Date: July 9
TV: SPEED. Radio: MRN

### TRACK FACTS
Location: Sparta, Ky.
Distance: 1.5 miles
Banking in turns: 14 degrees
Banking in straights: 8 degrees
Length of front stretch: 1,662 feet
Length of back stretch: 1,600 feet
Website: www.kentuckyspeedway.com

# BUSCH SERIES

## Busch YEAR BY YEAR WINNERS

| Year | Event | Race Winner | Car Make | Avg. Speed | Start Pos. | Pole Winner | Pole Speed | POLE WINNERS | | RACE WINNERS | |
|------|-------|-------------|----------|-----------|-----------|-------------|-----------|--------------|---|--------------|---|
| 2004 | Meijer 300 | Ky. Busch | Chevrolet | 126.642 | 2 | M. Truex | 180.102 | Ja. Sauter | 1 | K. Harvick | 1 |
| 2003 | Meijer 300 | B. Hamilton Jr. | Ford | 136.123 | 2 | S. Compton | 176.384 | S. Riggs | 1 | T. Bodine | 1 |
| 2002 | Kroger 300 | T. Bodine | Chevrolet | 127.164 | 6 | S. Riggs | 174.831 | S. Compton | 1 | B. Hamilton Jr. | 1 |
| 2001 | Outback Steakhouse 300 | K. Harvick | Chevrolet | 118.590 | 11 | Ja. Sauter | 171.860 | M. Truex | 1 | Ky. Busch | 1 |

**QUALIFYING RECORD: Track:** Stacy Compton, Chevrolet; 176.384 mph; June 13, 2003
**RACE RECORD: Track:** Bobby Hamilton Jr., Ford; 136.123 mph, June 14, 2003

## CRAFTSMAN TRUCK SERIES

### Craftsman YEAR BY YEAR WINNERS (Kentucky)

| Year | Event | Race Winner | Car Make | Avg. Speed | Start Pos. | Pole Winner | Pole Speed | POLE WINNERS | | RACE WINNERS | |
|------|-------|-------------|----------|------------|------------|-------------|------------|--------------|--|--------------|--|
| 2004 | Built Ford Tough 225 | B. Hamilton | Dodge | 122.600 | 3 | Trials rained out | | B. Reffner | 1 | G. Biffle | 1 |
| 2003 | Built Ford Tough 225 | C. Edwards | Ford | 122.393 | 5 | J. Wood | 169.641 | J. Sprague | 1 | S. Riggs | 1 |
| 2002 | Kroger 225 | M. Bliss | Chevrolet | 143.515 | 2 | J. Leffler | 168.303 | J. Leffler | 1 | M. Bliss | 1 |
| 2001 | Kroger 225 | S. Riggs | Dodge | 113.525 | 3 | J. Sprague | 167.115 | J. Wood | 1 | C. Edwards | 1 |
| 2000 | Kroger 225 | G. Biffle | Ford | 98.385 | 2 | B. Reffner | 168.460 | | | B. Hamilton | 1 |

**QUALIFYING RECORD: Track:** Jon Wood, Ford; 169.641 mph, July 11, 2003
**RACE RECORD: Track:** Mike Bliss, Chevrolet; 143.515 mph, July 13, 2002

# MEMPHIS MOTORSPORTS PARK

## 2005 SCHEDULE

**BUSCH SERIES**
**Event:** Sam's Town 250
**Race:** No. 30 of 34
**Date:** October 23
**TV:** TNT. **Radio:** MRN
Race names subject to change

**CRAFTSMAN TRUCK SERIES**
**Event:** O'Reilly 200
**Race:** No. 14 of 25
**Date:** July 23
**TV:** SPEED. **Radio:** MRN

### TRACK FACTS
**Location:** Millington, Tenn.
**Distance:** .75 miles
**Banking in turns:** 11 degrees
**Banking in straights:** 4 degrees
**Length of front stretch:** 1,100 feet
**Length of back stretch:** 1,100 feet
**Website:** www.memphismotorsportspark.com

## BUSCH SERIES

### Busch YEAR BY YEAR WINNERS

| Year | Event | Race Winner | Car Make | Avg. Speed | Start Pos. | Pole Winner | Pole Speed | POLE WINNERS | | RACE WINNERS | |
|------|-------|-------------|----------|------------|------------|-------------|------------|--------------|--|--------------|--|
| 2004 | Sam's Town 250 | M. Truex | Chevrolet | 78.561 | 1 | C. Bowyer | 120.198 | J. Green | 2 | J. Green | 1 |
| 2003 | Sam's Town 250 | B. Hamilton Jr. | Ford | 87.674 | 4 | D. Reutimann | 119.766 | G. Biffle | 1 | K. Harvick | 1 |
| 2002 | Sam's Town 250 | S. Wimmer | Pontiac | 79.337 | 6 | G. Biffle | 116.817 | D. Reutimann | 1 | R. LaJoie | 1 |
| 2001 | Sam's Town 250 | R. LaJoie | Chevrolet | 75.050 | 16 | Trials rained out | | C. Bowyer | 1 | S. Wimmer | 1 |
| 2000 | Sam's Town 250 | K. Harvick | Chevrolet | 92.352 | 2 | J. Green | 120.267 | | | B. Hamilton Jr. | 1 |
| 1999 | Sam's Town 250 | J. Green | Chevrolet | 76.583 | 1 | J. Green | 119.311 | | | M. Truex | 1 |

**QUALIFYING RECORD: Track:** Jeff Green, Chevrolet; 120.267 mph, October 28, 2000
**RACE RECORD: Track:** Kevin Harvick, Chevrolet; 92.352 mph, October 29, 2000

## CRAFTSMAN TRUCK SERIES

### Craftsman YEAR BY YEAR WINNERS

| Year | Event | Race Winner | Car Make | Avg. Speed | Start Pos. | Pole Winner | Pole Speed | POLE WINNERS | | RACE WINNERS | |
|------|-------|-------------|----------|------------|------------|-------------|------------|--------------|--|--------------|--|
| 2004 | O'Reilly 200 | B. Hamilton | Dodge | 77.821 | 3 | J. Sprague | 118.917 | G. Biffle | 2 | G. Biffle | 1 |
| 2003 | O'Reilly 200 | T. Musgrave | Dodge | 86.097 | 3 | J. Wood | 117.407 | J. Sprague | 2 | R. Hornaday Jr. | 1 |
| 2002 | Memphis 200 | T. Kvapil | Chevrolet | 89.065 | 3 | J. Leffler | 117.971 | B. Hamilton | 1 | T. Kvapil | 1 |
| 2001 | Memphis 200 | D. Setzer | Chevrolet | 82.279 | 4 | J. Sprague | 116.863 | J. Leffler | 1 | D. Setzer | 1 |
| 2000 | Quaker State 200 | J. Sprague | Chevrolet | 85.565 | 5 | B. Hamilton | 118.043 | J. Wood | 1 | J. Sprague | 1 |
| 1999 | Memphis 200 | G. Biffle | Ford | 75.303 | 1 | G. Biffle | 120.139 | | | T. Musgrave | 1 |
| 1998 | Memphis 200 | R. Hornaday Jr. | Chevrolet | 84.204 | 3 | G. Biffle | 118.901 | | | B. Hamilton | 1 |

**QUALIFYING RECORD: Track:** Greg Biffle, Ford; 120.139 mph, May 7, 1999
**RACE RECORD: Track:** Travis Kvapil, Chevrolet; 89.065 mph, June 22, 2002

# THE MILWAUKEE MILE

## 2005 SCHEDULE

**BUSCH SERIES**
**Event:** Alan Kulwicki 250
**Race:** No. 17 of 35
**Date:** June 25
**TV:** xx. **Radio:** MRN

Race names subject to change

**CRAFTSMAN TRUCK SERIES**
**Event:** GNC 200
**Race:** No. 11 of 25
**Date:** June 24
**TV:** SPEED. **Radio:** MRN

### TRACK FACTS
**Location:** West Allis, Wis.
**Distance:** 1 mile
**Banking in turns:** 9.25 degrees
**Banking in straights:** 2.5 degrees
**Length of front stretch:** 1,265 feet
**Length of back stretch:** 1,265 feet
**Website:** www.milwaukeemile.com

# BUSCH SERIES

## Busch YEAR BY YEAR WINNERS (Milwaukee)

| Year | Event | Race Winner | Car Make | Avg. Speed | Start Pos. | Pole Winner | Pole Speed | POLE WINNERS | | RACE WINNERS | |
|------|-------|-------------|----------|-----------|-----------|-------------|-----------|--------------|---|--------------|---|
| 2004 | Alan Kulwicki 250 | R. Hornaday | Chevrolet | 102.038 | 10 | D. Stremme | 122.553 | G. Biffle | 2 | G. Biffle | 2 |
| 2003 | GNC 250 | J. Keller | Ford | 103.093 | 7 | Trials rained out | | D. Trickle | 1 | S. Ard | 1 |
| 2002 | GNC Live Well 250 | G. Biffle | Ford | 94.182 | 1 | G. Biffle | 121.770 | A. Kulwicki | 1 | J. Ingram | 1 |
| 2001 | GNC Live Well 250 | G. Biffle | Ford | 102.389 | 2 | K. Harvick | 122.474 | B. Dotter | 1 | S. Grissom | 1 |
| 2000 | Sears Diehard 250 | J. Green | Chevrolet | 89.206 | 1 | J. Green | 121.572 | D. Green | 1 | M. Wallace | 1 |
| 1999 | Diehard 250 | C. Atwood | Chevrolet | 97.858 | 1 | C. Atwood | 121.421 | D. Setzer | 1 | D. Jarrett | 1 |
| 1998 | Diehard 250 | D. Earnhardt Jr. | Chevrolet | 97.890 | 2 | J. Purvis | 119.904 | H. Sadler | 1 | B. Jones | 1 |
| 1997 | Sears Auto Center 250 | R. LaJoie | Chevrolet | 99.141 | 10 | T. Fedewa | 118.468 | T. Fedewa | 1 | R. LaJoie | 1 |
| 1996 | Sears Auto Center 250 | B. Jones | Ford | 82.237 | 32 | H. Sadler | 118.320 | J. Purvis | 1 | D. Earnhardt Jr. | 1 |
| 1995 | Sears Auto Center 250 | D. Jarrett | Ford | 95.379 | 12 | D. Setzer | 114.650 | C. Atwood | 1 | C. Atwood | 1 |
| 1994 | Havoilne 250 | M. Wallace | Chevrolet | 100.999 | 25 | D. Green | 115.407 | J. Green | 1 | J. Green | 1 |
| *1993 | Havoline 250 | S. Grissom | Chevrolet | 89.003 | 14 | B. Dotter | 113.845 | K. Harvick | 1 | J. Keller | 1 |
| 1985 | Mil. Sentinel 200 | J. Ingram | Pontiac | 104.121 | 8 | A. Kulwicki | 112.711 | D. Stremme | 1 | R. Hornaday | 1 |
| 1984 | Red Carpet 200 | S. Ard | Oldsmobile | 97.206 | 3 | D. Trickle | 112.984 | | | | |

*Race distance increased to 250 miles.

**QUALIFYING RECORD: Track:** Kevin Harvick, Chevrolet; 122.474 mph, June 29, 2001
**RACE RECORD: Track:** Jason Keller, Ford; 103.093 mph, June 29, 2003

# CRAFTSMAN TRUCK SERIES

## Craftsman YEAR BY YEAR WINNERS (Milwaukee)

| Year | Event | Race Winner | Car Make | Avg. Speed | Start Pos. | Pole Winner | Pole Speed | POLE WINNERS | | RACE WINNERS | |
|------|-------|-------------|----------|-----------|-----------|-------------|-----------|--------------|---|--------------|---|
| 2004 | Black Cat 200 | T. Musgrave | Dodge | 83.230 | 1 | T. Musgrave | 121.980 | J. Sprague | 3 | T. Musgrave | 2 |
| 2003 | GNC 200 | B. Gaughan | Dodge | 109.689 | 2 | T. Cook | 119.996 | T. Cook | 2 | M. Skinner | 1 |
| 2002 | GNC Live Well 200 | T. Cook | Ford | 104.490 | 1 | T. Cook | 119.784 | M. Sinner | 1 | J. Sprague | 1 |
| 2001 | GNC Live Well 200 | T. Musgrave | Dodge | 92.929 | 3 | J. Sprague | 120.692 | M. Bliss | 1 | R. Hornaday Jr. | 1 |
| 2000 | DieHard 200 | K. Busch | Ford | 89.264 | 1 | K. Busch | 120.518 | G. Biffle | 1 | M. Bliss | 1 |
| 1999 | DieHard 200 | G. Biffle | Ford | 106.714 | 1 | G. Biffle | 121.102 | K. Busch | 1 | G. Biffle | 1 |
| 1998 | DieHard 200 | M. Bliss | Ford | 104.347 | 2 | J. Sprague | 120.530 | T. Musgrave | 1 | K. Busch | 1 |
| 1997 | DieHard 200 | R. Hornaday Jr. | Chevrolet | 105.665 | 5 | J. Sprague | 119.178 | | | T. Cook | 1 |
| 1996 | Sears Auto 200 | J. Sprague | Chevrolet | 87.816 | 8 | M. Bills | 118.265 | | | | |
| 1995 | Sears Auto 125 | M. Skinner | Chevrolet | 87.413 | 1 | M. Skinner | 112.535 | | | | |

**QUALIFYING RECORD: Track:** Greg Biffle, Ford; 121.102 mph, July 2, 1999
**RACE RECORD: Track:** Brendan Gaughan, Dodge; 109.689 mph, June 28, 2003

# NASHVILLE SUPERSPEEDWAY

# 2005 SCHEDULE

**BUSCH SERIES**
Event: Pepsi 300 by Mapco
Race: No. 6 of 35
Date: March 26
TV: FX. Radio: MRN

Event: Fed. Auto Parts 300
Race: No. 15 of 35
Date: June 11
TV: FX. Radio: MRN

**CRAFTSMAN TRUCK SERIES**
Event: Toyota Tundra 200
Race: No. 16 of 25
Date: August 13
TV: SPEED. Radio: MRN

Race names subject to change

## TRACK FACTS

**Location:** Nashville
**Length:** 1.333 miles
**Banking in turns:** 14 degrees
**Banking in front stretch:** 9 degrees
**Banking in back stretch:** 6 degrees
**Length of front stretch:** 2,494 feet
**Length of back stretch:** 2,203 feet
**Website:**
www.nashvillesuperspeedway.com

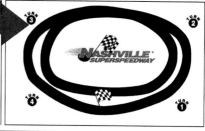

# BUSCH SERIES

## Busch YEAR BY YEAR WINNERS

| Year | Event | Race Winner | Car Make | Avg. Speed | Start Pos. | Pole Winner | Pole Speed | POLE WINNERS | | RACE WINNERS | |
|------|-------|-------------|----------|-----------|-----------|-------------|-----------|--------------|---|--------------|---|
| 2004 | Pepsi 300 | M. Waltrip | Chevrolet | 122.211 | 22 | M. Truex | 166.515 | M. Truex | 2 | S. Riggs | 2 |
| | Federated Auto Parts 300 | J. Leffler | Chevrolet | 114.708 | 2 | M. Truex | 163.569 | G. Biffle | 1 | G. Biffle | 1 |
| 2003 | Pepsi 300 | D. Green | Pontiac | 122.724 | 7 | R. LaJoie | 163.324 | K. Harvick | 1 | J. Sprague | 1 |
| | Trace Adkins Chr. 300 | S. Riggs | Ford | 118.547 | 3 | Trials rained out | | S. Hmiel | 1 | D. Green | 1 |
| 2002 | Pepsi 300 | S. Riggs | Ford | 111.038 | 3 | S. Hmiel | 161.440 | R. LaJoie | 1 | M. Waltrip | 1 |
| | Inside Traxx 300 | J. Sprague | Chevrolet | 125.244 | 5 | G. Biffle | 161.288 | | | J. Leffler | 1 |
| 2001 | Pepsi 300 | G. Biffle | Ford | 105.773 | 4 | K. Harvick | 159.678 | | | | |

**QUALIFYING RECORD: Track:** Randy LaJoie, Chevrolet; 163.324 mph, April 11, 2003
**RACE RECORD: Track:** David Green, Pontiac; 122.724 mph, April 12, 2003

TRACKS

# CRAFTSMAN TRUCK SERIES

## Craftsman YEAR BY YEAR WINNERS (Nashville)

| Year | Event | Race Winner | Car Make | Avg. Speed | Start Pos. | Pole Winner | Pole Speed | POLE WINNERS | | RACE WINNERS | |
|------|-------|-------------|----------|------------|------------|-------------|------------|--------------|---|--------------|---|
| 2004 | Toyota Tundra 200 | B. Hamilton | Dodge | 124.068 | 15 | B. Hamilton Jr. | 160.990 | M. Bliss | 1 | M. Bliss | 1 |
| 2003 | Federated Auto 200 | C. Edwards | Ford | 129.557 | 6 | C. Chaffin | 156.844 | S. Riggs | 1 | S. Riggs | 1 |
| 2002 | Federated Auto 200 | M. Bliss | Chevrolet | 129.442 | 1 | M. Bliss | 157.322 | C. Chaffin | 1 | C. Edwards | 1 |
| 2001 | Federated Auto 200 | S. Riggs | Dodge | 132.466 | 1 | S. Riggs | 155.477 | B. Hamilton Jr. | 1 | B. Hamilton | 1 |

QUALIFYING RECORD: **Track:** Bobby Hamilton Jr., Dodge; 160.990 mph, August 13, 2004
RACE RECORD: **Track:** Scott Riggs, Dodge; 132.466 mph, August 10, 2001

# PIKES PEAK INTERNATIONAL RACEWAY

## 2005 SCHEDULE

### BUSCH SERIES

**Event:** Goulds Pumps 250
**Race:** No. 21 of 35
**Date:** July 23
**TV:** TNT. **Radio:** MRN

Race name subject to change

### TRACK FACTS

**Location:** Fountain, Colo.
**Distance:** 1 mile
**Banking in turns:** 10 degrees
**Banking in front stretch:** 7 degrees
**Banking in back stretch:** 3 degrees
**Length of front stretch:** 1,510 feet
**Length of back stretch:** 1,350 feet
**Website:** www.ppir.com

# BUSCH SERIES

## Busch YEAR BY YEAR WINNERS

| Year | Event | Race Winner | Car Make | Avg. Speed | Start Pos. | Pole Winner | Pole Speed | POLE WINNERS | | RACE WINNERS | |
|------|-------|-------------|----------|------------|------------|-------------|------------|--------------|---|--------------|---|
| 2004 | Goulds/ITT Indus. 250 | G. Biffle | Ford | 107.181 | 25 | M. Truex | 137.478 | D. Blaney | 1 | J. Green | 1 |
| 2003 | TrimSpa 250 | S. Wimmer | Chevrolet | 108.919 | 16 | B. Hamilton Jr. | 133.318 | J. Keller | 1 | M. Kenseth | 1 |
| 2002 | Net Zero 250 | H. Parker Jr. | Dodge | 113.350 | 23 | J. Keller | 131.801 | M. Kenseth | 1 | H. Parker Jr. | 1 |
| 2001 | NAPA Autocare 250 | J. Purvis | Chevrolet | 120.160 | 7 | K. Wallace | 131.062 | J. Purvis | 1 | J. Purvis | 1 |
| 2000 | NAPA Autocare 250 | J. Green | Chevrolet | 118.421 | 2 | J. Purvis | 135.629 | K. Wallace | 1 | A. Santerre | 1 |
| 1999 | NAPA Autocare 250 | A. Santerre | Chevrolet | 104.663 | 20 | D. Blaney | 135.318 | B. Hamilton Jr. | 1 | S. Wimmer | 1 |
| 1998 | Lycos.com 250 | M. Kenseth | Chevrolet | 102.834 | 1 | M. Kenseth | 134.193 | M. Truex | 1 | G. Biffle | 1 |

QUALIFYING RECORD: **Track:** Martin Truex Jr., Chevrolet, July 30, 2004
RACE RECORD: **Track:** Jeff Purvis, Chevrolet; 120.160 mph, July 28, 2001

# MANSFIELD MOTORSPORTS SPEEDWAY

## 2005 SCHEDULE

### CRAFTSMAN TRUCK SERIES

**Event:** UAW-GM Ohio 250
**Race:** No. 6 of 25
**Date:** May 15
**TV:** SPEED. **Radio:** MRN

Race name subject to change

### TRACK FACTS

**Location:** Mansfield, Ohio
**Distance:** .44 miles
**Banking in turns:** compound banking from 12 to 16 degrees
**Banking in straights:** 6 degrees
**Length of straights:** 545 feet
**Website:** www.mansfield-speedway.com.

# CRAFTSMAN TRUCK SERIES

## Craftsman YEAR BY YEAR WINNERS

| Year | Event | Race Winner | Car Make | Avg. Speed | Start Pos. | Pole Winner | Pole Speed | RACE WINNER | |
|------|-------|-------------|----------|------------|------------|-------------|------------|-------------|---|
| 2004 | UAW/GM Ohio 250 | J. Sprague | Chevrolet | 54.706 | 1 | Trials rained out | | J. Sprague | 1 |

RACE RECORD: **Track:** Jack Sprague, Chevrolet; 54.706 mph, May 16, 2004

# NASCAR on television

For the fourth consecutive year, NASCAR and its broadcast partners provided programming that solidified the premier series as the No. 2 regular-season sport on television, falling behind only the NFL in terms of viewership numbers. NASCAR also has expanded its global reach to include television broadcasts in more than 100 countries in 21 languages each week, including the formation of a partnership with Craig Media Group to broadcast NEXTEL Cup races in Canada.

In 2004, NASCAR abandoned the points system it had used for decades and adopted the new Chase for the NASCAR NEXTEL Cup to increase end-of-season excitement, and it paid off for fans and with a boost in TV ratings.

The 2004 NASCAR NEXTEL Cup championship culminated with the closest points race in history, and coverage of the final race, the Ford 400 at Homestead, earned a 5.6 overnight rating in a measure of the nation's 55 largest markets. The rating was the best in the race's six-year history and the best ever for a NASCAR race going against NFL games. The final race's rating was 47 percent higher than 2003's 3.8 and 24 percent better than the previous high of 4.5 in 2002. The 2004 season's next-to-last race, held at Darlington, had a rating 50 percent higher than the previous year's, held at Rockingham. For the final 10 Chase races overall, NBC reported a 10 percent ratings boost over 2003.

In its fifth season as the home of NASCAR, **NASCAR on FOX** will broadcast the first half of the season in 2005, beginning with the 70-lap Budweiser Shootout from Daytona on February 12.

In 2003, NASCAR on FOX won an Emmy award for Outstanding Live Event Audio/Studio.

This year, FOX will broadcast NACAR's most prestigious event, the Daytona 500. FOX's cable partner, **FX**, will televise five events, including the NASCAR NEXTEL All-Star Challenge on May 21 from Charlotte. FX also will broadcast the Twin 125s, a nonpoints race, from Daytona, the Chevy American Revolution 400 from Richmond, the NEXTEL Open from Charlotte and the MBNA America 400 from Dover. FOX will wind up its 2004 NASCAR NEXTEL Cup schedule with the Dodge Save Mart 350 on June 26 in Sonoma.

In 2005, FOX will begin to broadcast all of its NASCAR races in high definition, and the network's coverage once again will be anchored by veteran race announcer Mike Joy. Three-time series champion Darrell Waltrip and former Daytona 500-winning crew chief Larry McReynolds return to provide race analysis. Pre-race coverage from the "Hollywood Hotel" will again be hosted by Chris Myers along with analyst Jeff Hammond, Waltrip's former crew chief.

**NBC** and **TNT** will again combine to provide coverage of the second half of the 2005 NASCAR NEXTEL Cup schedule, and both networks will broadcast all races in high definition. NBC's coverage begins with the Pepsi 400 on July 2 from Daytona and will include eight of the 10 races in the second annual Chase for the NASCAR NEXTEL Cup, culminating with the season finale from Homestead.

TNT's coverage begins with the Siemens 300 on July 17 from New Hampshire and includes the first two races in the Chase for the NASCAR NEXTEL Cup—the Sylvania 300 from New Hampshire and the MBNA America 400 from Dover. THE NBC broadcast team includes Allen Bestwick and Bill Weber, 1973 NASCAR Cup champion Benny Parsons and former NASCAR Cup driver Wally Dallenbach, who continues to run some races in the NASCAR Busch Series.

**NASCAR TV on SPEED Channel** continues to grow and deliver exclusive NASCAR coverage to a growing audience. Anchored by live NASCAR Craftsman Truck Series race coverage, SPEED's NASCAR block is built by programming such as "Trackside," "NASCAR Victory Lane" and "Inside NEXTEL Cup" along with shows that feature the history of the sport and its day-to-day happenings on the track and in the shop.

NASCAR TV provides viewers comprehensive behind-the-scenes coverage of the sport, including enhanced race replays and highlights. Qualifying for NASCAR NEXTEL Cup and NASCAR Busch Series events can also be seen on SPEED along with re-broadcasts of classic races, special event coverage such as SpeedWeeks and season previews and reviews.

**NASCAR IN CAR** is an Emmy® award winning viewing concept designed to give NASCAR fans the ultimate in-car access at any point during the race. NASCAR IN CAR features seven drivers on seven in-car camera channels, live team audio communications and real-time on-screen race data. NASCAR IN CAR uses cutting-edge technology to enhance the way fans watch NASCAR NEXTEL Cup Series races.

NASCAR IN CAR was developed in 2002 in conjunction with NASCAR's broadcast partners to complement NASCAR's live event coverage on FOX, FX, NBC and TNT. Visit www.goincar.com for more details.

## NASCAR on radio

**Motor Racing Network** (MRN) will broadcast 29 NASCAR NEXTEL Cup events in 2005, including the season-opening Daytona 500 and the season-ending Ford 400 at Homestead. MRN, a division of the International Speedway Corporation, also broadcasts most Busch Series and Craftsman Truck Series races. MRN has affiliates in 48 states and Canada and reaches 150 countries.

**Performance Racing Network** (PRN), owned and operated by Speedway Motorsports Inc., will air 10 NEXTEL Cup events in 2005, including three Chase for NASCAR NEXTEL Cup races.

Fans also can get coverage of all NEXTEL Cup races on **XM Satellite Radio**.